Attack on Titan Omnibus 8 is a work o̶̶
incidents are the products of the autho̶
Any resemblance to actual events, loca̶
coincidental.

A Kodansha Trade Paperback Original

Published in the United States by
Kodansha USA Publishing, LLC, New York.

Publication rights for this English edition arranged through
Kodansha Ltd., Tokyo.

First published in Japan in 2017 by Kodansha Ltd., Tokyo
as *Shingeki no kyojin*, volumes 22, 23, and 24.

ISBN 978-1-64651-489-2

Original cover design by Takashi Shimoyama/Manami Fukunaga (Red Rooster)

Printed in the United States of America.

9 8 7 6 5 4 3 2 1

Translation: Ko Ransom
Lettering: Steve Wands
Additional Lettering: Evan Hayden
Editing: Tiff Joshua TJ Ferentini
Kodansha USA Publishing edition cover design by Adam Del Re
Kodansha USA Publishing edition logo design by Phil Balsman

Publisher: Kiichiro Sugawara

Director of Publishing Services: Ben Applegate
Director of Publishing Operations: Dave Barrett
Associate Director of Publishing Operations: Stephen Pakula
Publishing Services Managing Editors: Alanna Ruse, Madison Salters
Senior Production Manager: Angela Zurlo

KODANSHA.US

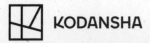

ATTACK on TITAN

ATTACK on TITAN

ATTACK on TITAN

ATTACK on TITAN

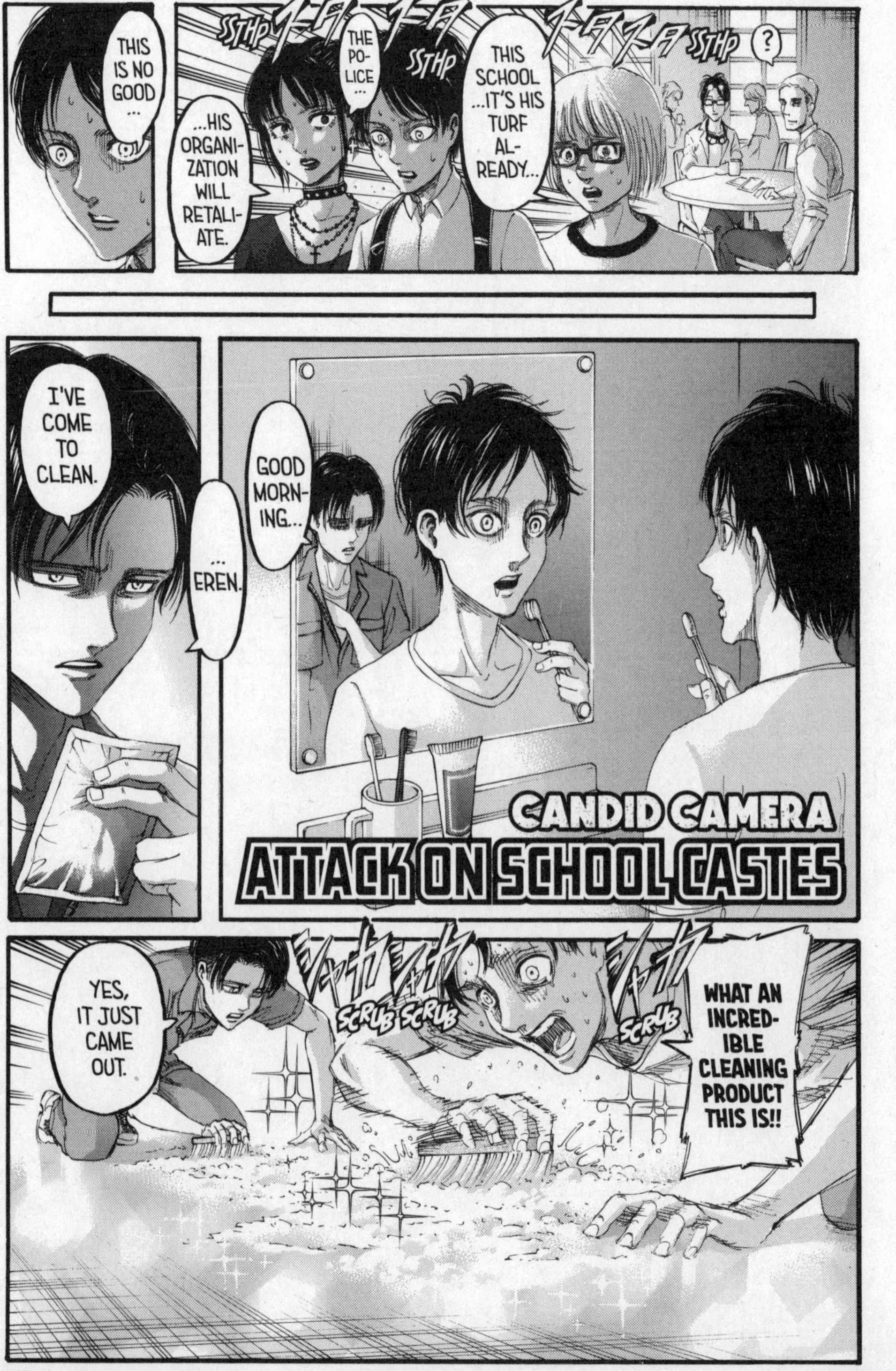
?
SSTHP
THIS SCHOOL ...IT'S HIS TURF AL-READY...
SSTHP
THE PO-LICE ...
SSTHP
...HIS ORGANI-ZATION WILL RETALI-ATE.
THIS IS NO GOOD ...
GOOD MORN-ING...
CANDID CAMERA
ATTACK ON SCHOOL CASTES
I'VE COME TO CLEAN.
... EREN.
WHAT AN INCRED-IBLE CLEANING PRODUCT THIS IS!!
SCRUB
SCRUB SCRUB
YES, IT JUST CAME OUT.

*Not a real preview.

MR. SMITH.
DR. ZOË.
THP THP
THERE'S A LITTLE SOME-THING WE WANTED TO ASK...
WE HEARD THAT YOU'RE GOOD FRIENDS WITH MISTER LEVI, THE JANITOR...
...!
THAT ...
WHAT ABOUT LEVI?
GO AHEAD, ASK US ANY-THING.

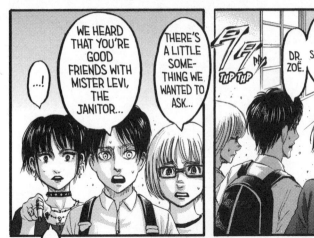

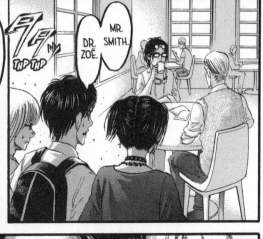

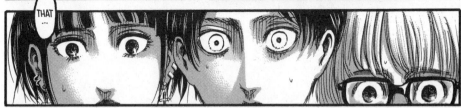

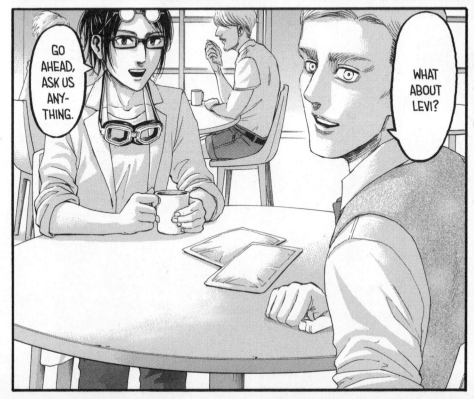

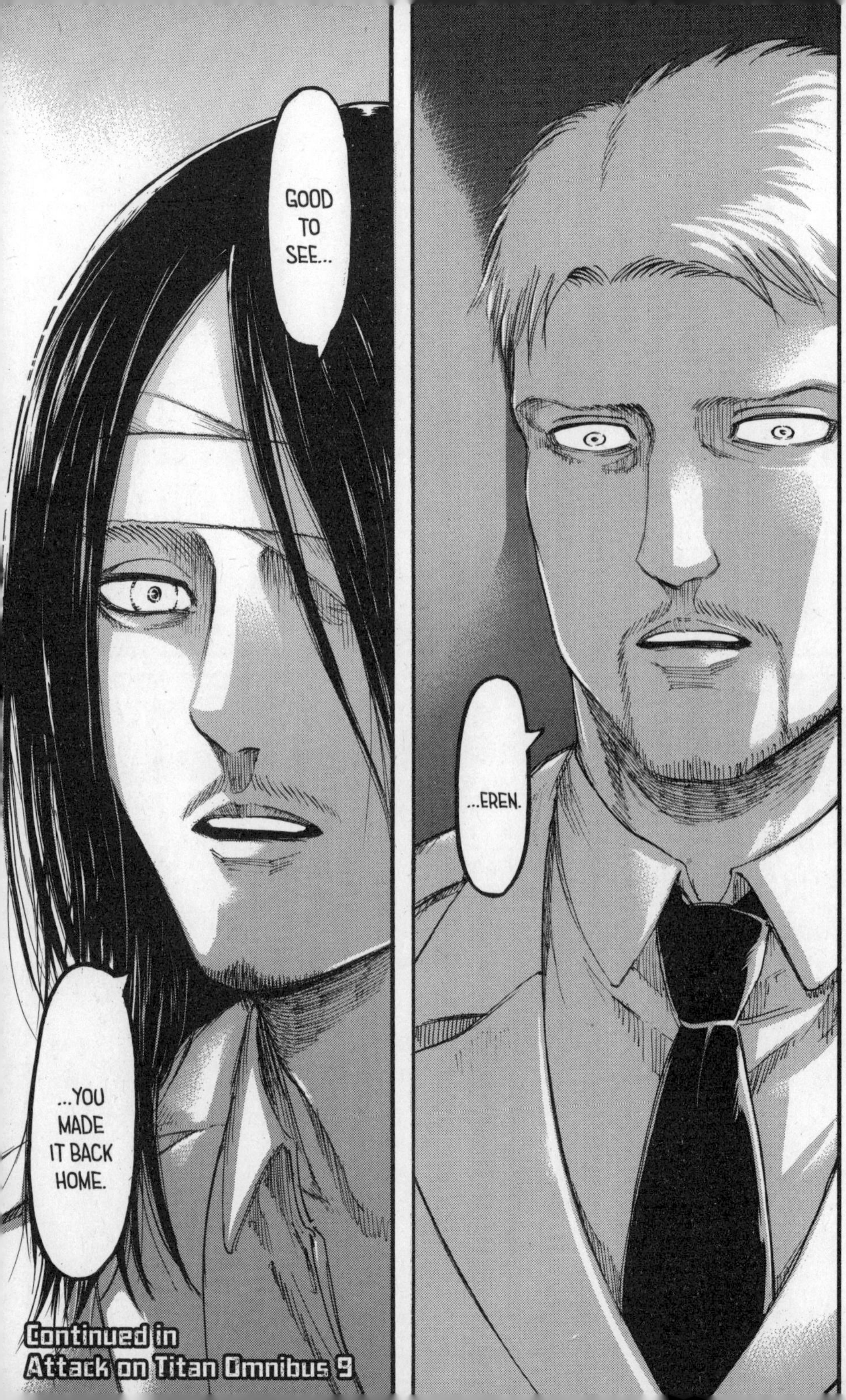
...EREN.
GOOD TO SEE...
...YOU MADE IT BACK HOME.

Continued in Attack on Titan Omnibus 9

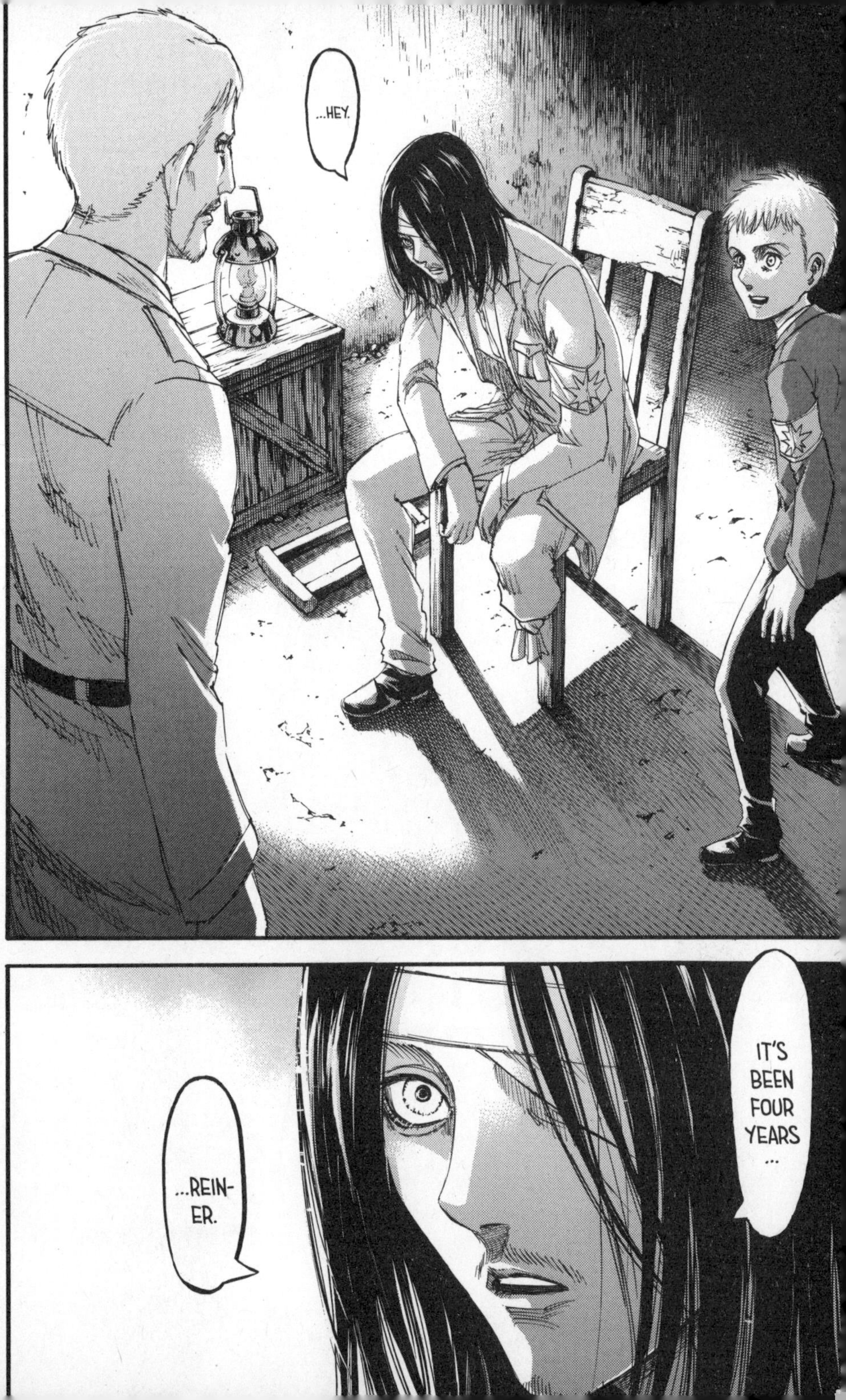
...HEY.
IT'S BEEN FOUR YEARS...
...REIN-ER.

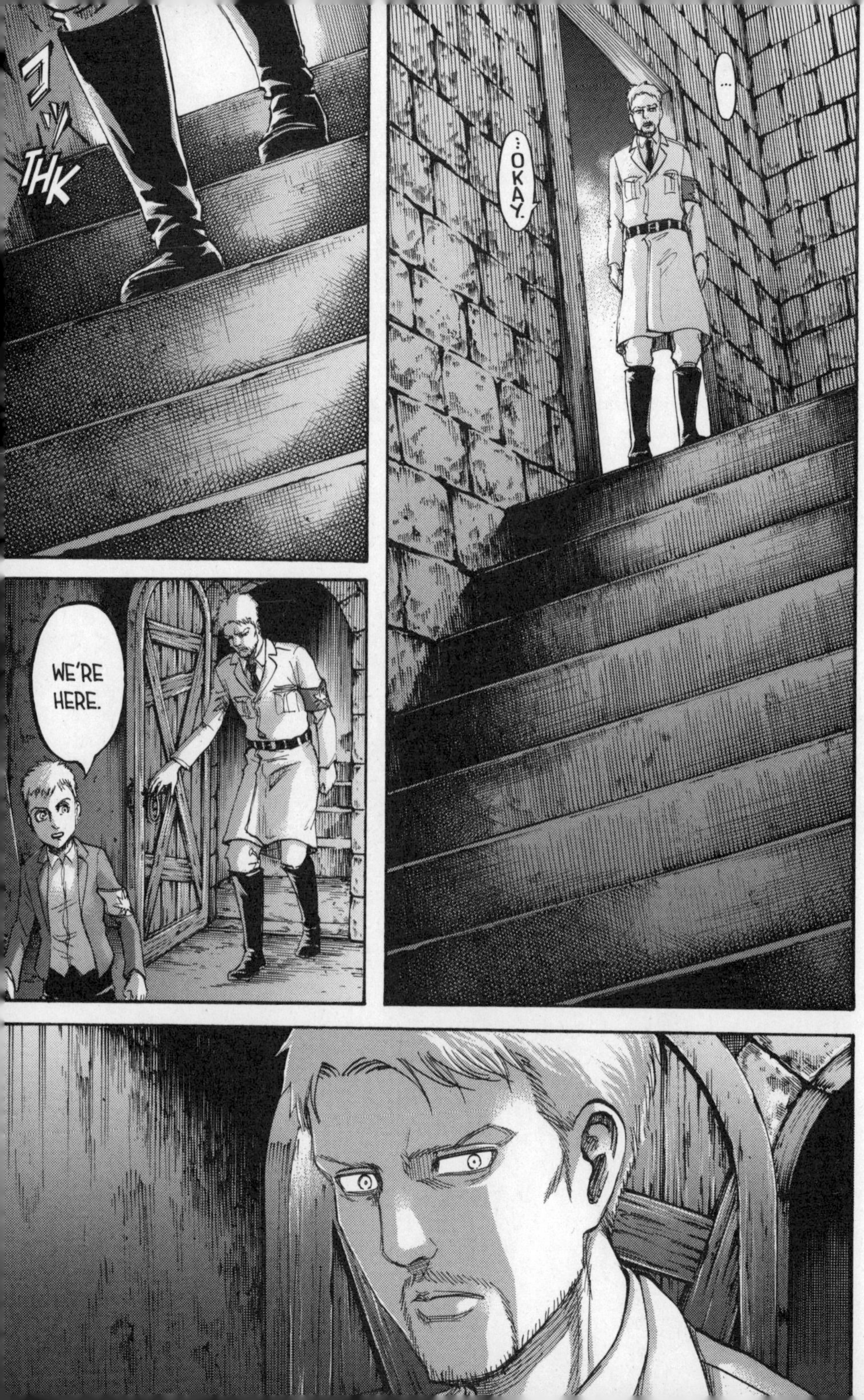

...
...OKAY.
コッ
THK
WE'RE HERE.

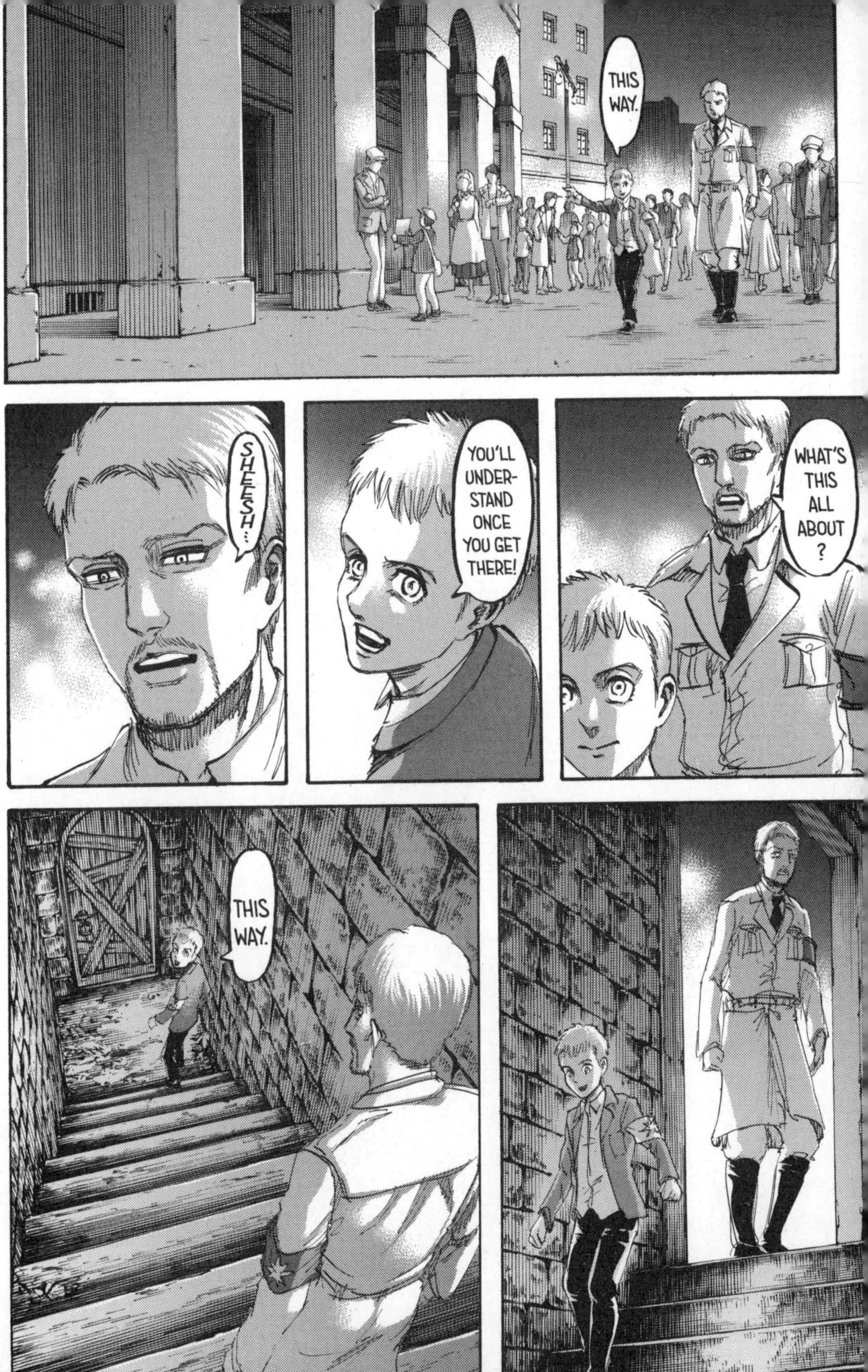
THIS WAY.
WHAT'S THIS ALL ABOUT?
YOU'LL UNDER-STAND ONCE YOU GET THERE!
SHEESH...
THIS WAY.

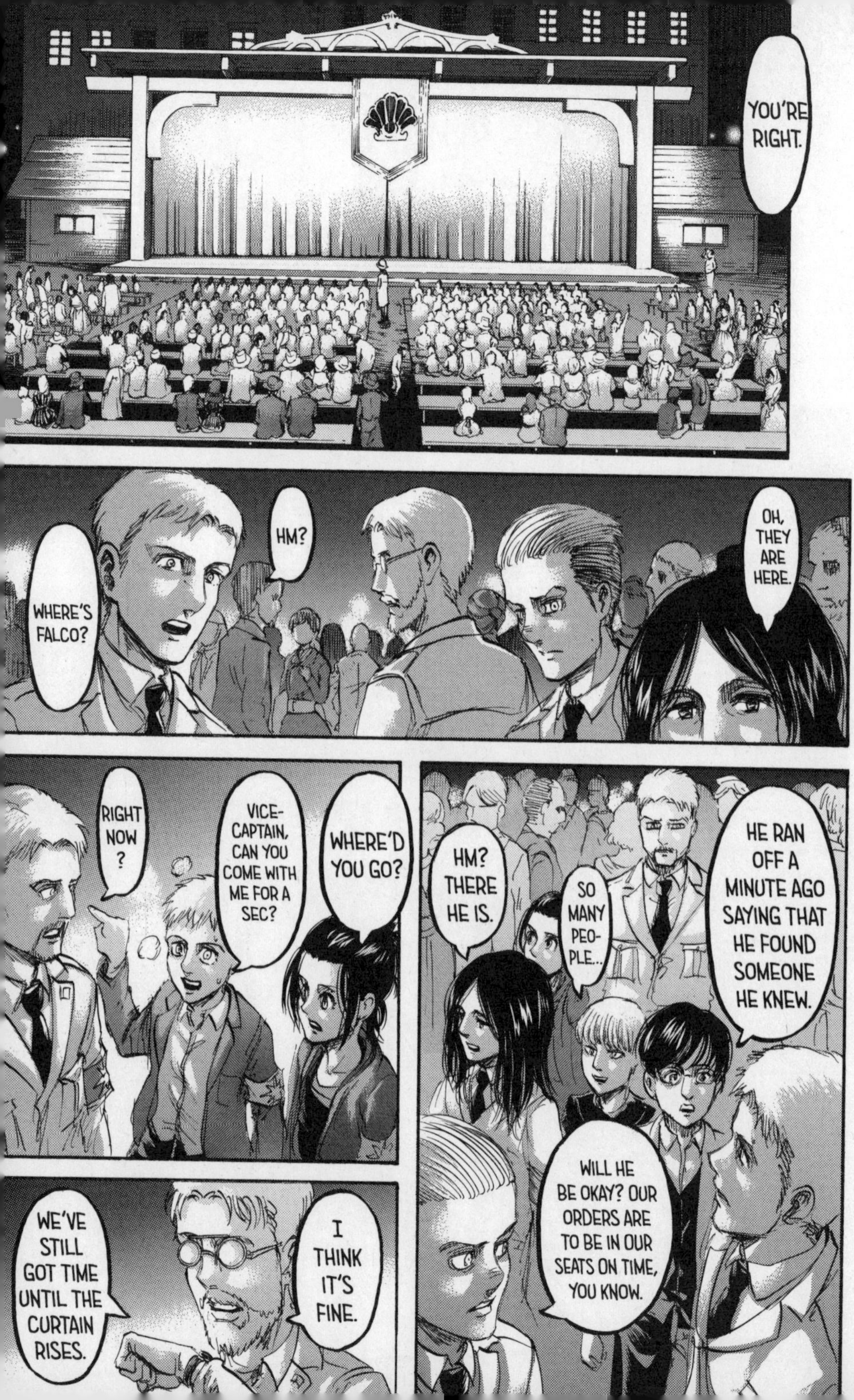
YOU'RE RIGHT.
OH, THEY ARE HERE.
HM?
WHERE'S FALCO?
HE RAN OFF A MINUTE AGO SAYING THAT HE FOUND SOMEONE HE KNEW.
SO MANY PEO-PLE...
HM? THERE HE IS.
WILL HE BE OKAY? OUR ORDERS ARE TO BE IN OUR SEATS ON TIME, YOU KNOW.
WHERE'D YOU GO?
VICE-CAPTAIN, CAN YOU COME WITH ME FOR A SEC?
RIGHT NOW?
I THINK IT'S FINE.
WE'VE STILL GOT TIME UNTIL THE CURTAIN RISES.

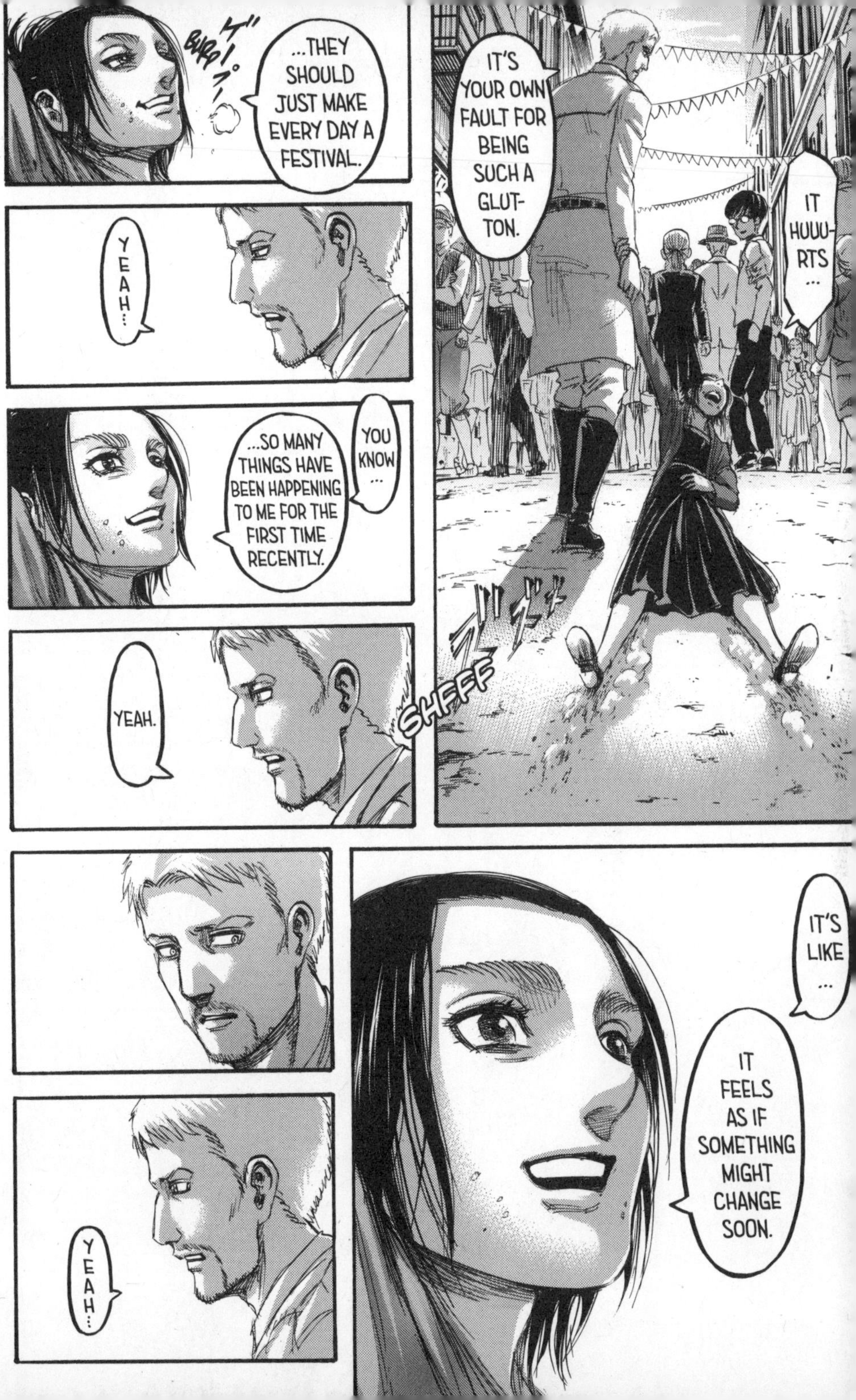
IT HUUURTS...
IT'S YOUR OWN FAULT FOR BEING SUCH A GLUTTON.
SHFFF
BURP
...THEY SHOULD JUST MAKE EVERY DAY A FESTIVAL.
YEAH...
YOU KNOW...
...SO MANY THINGS HAVE BEEN HAPPENING TO ME FOR THE FIRST TIME RECENTLY.
YEAH.
IT'S LIKE...
IT FEELS AS IF SOMETHING MIGHT CHANGE SOON.
YEAH...

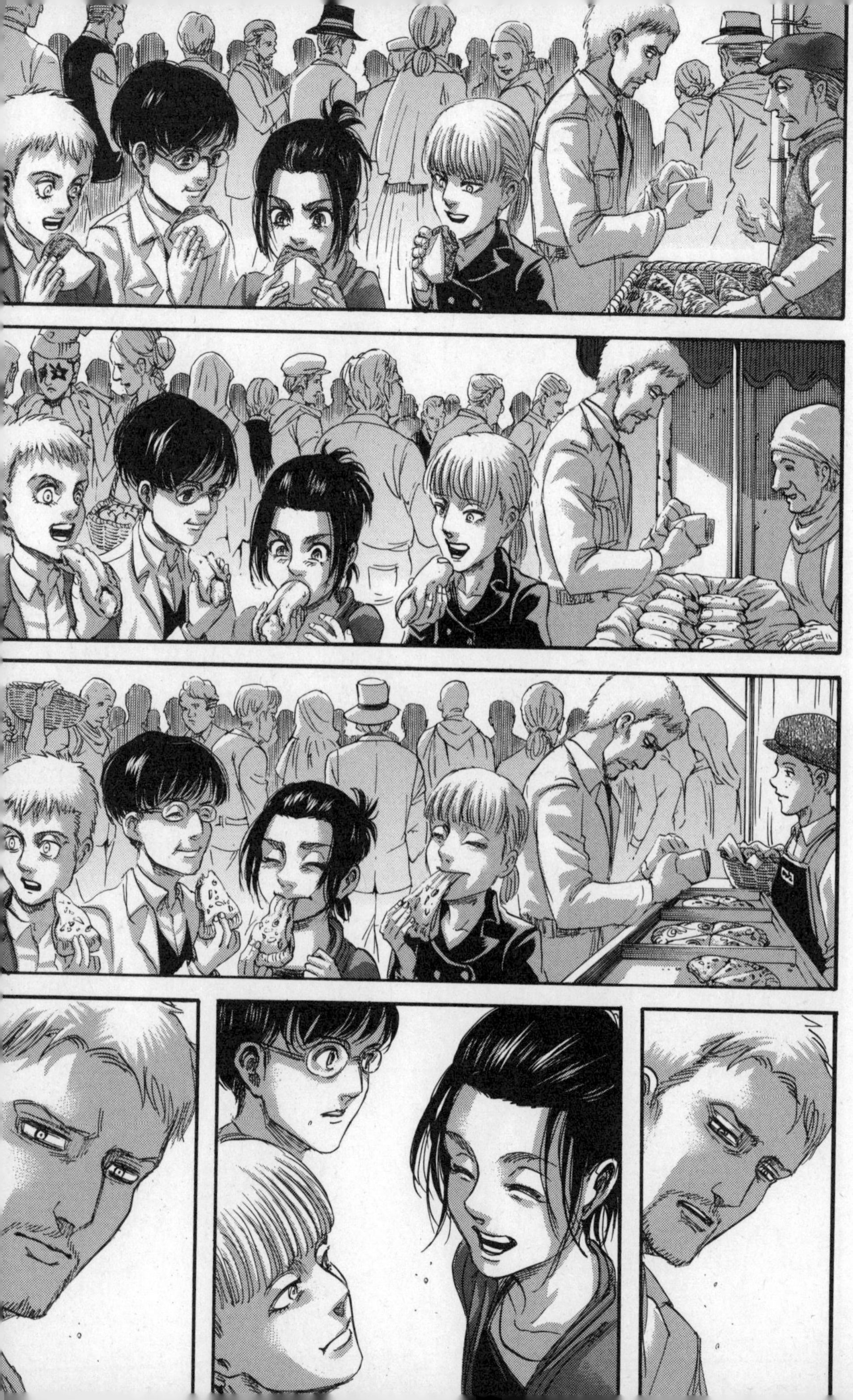

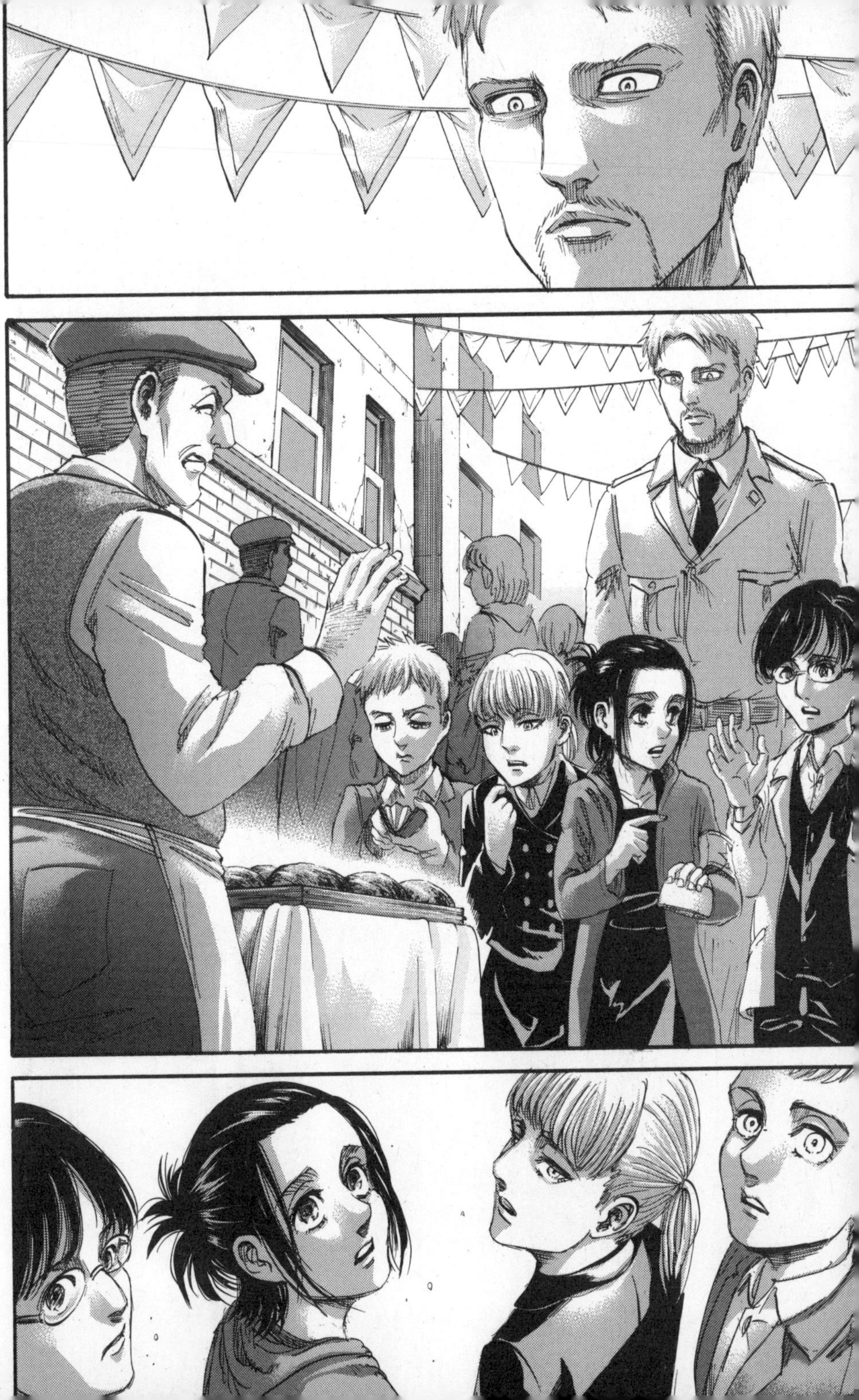

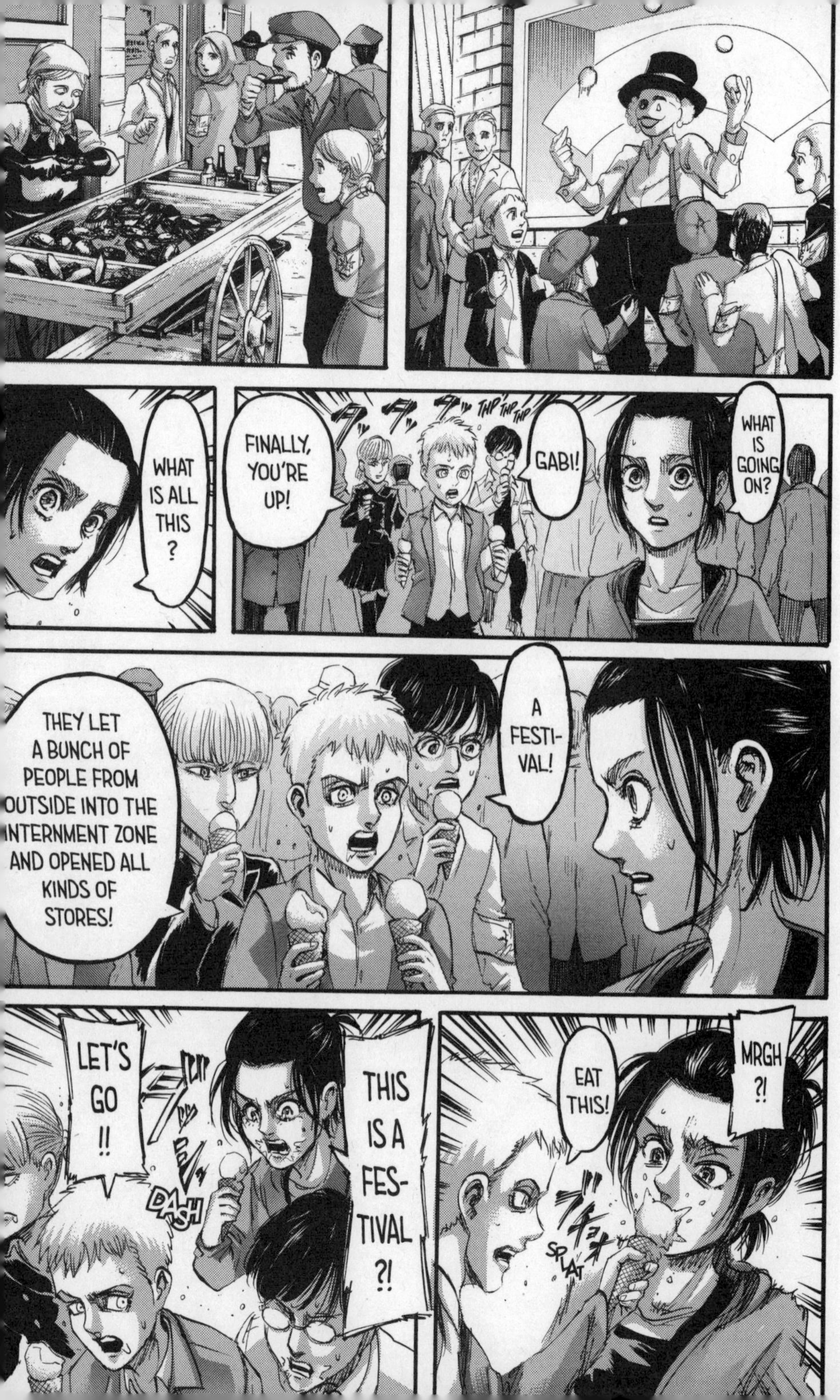
WHAT IS GOING ON?
GABI!
THP THP THP
FINALLY, YOU'RE UP!
WHAT IS ALL THIS ?
A FESTI-VAL!
THEY LET A BUNCH OF PEOPLE FROM OUTSIDE INTO THE INTERNMENT ZONE AND OPENED ALL KINDS OF STORES!
MRGH ?!
EAT THIS!
SPLAT
THIS IS A FES-TIVAL ?!
LET'S GO !!
DASH

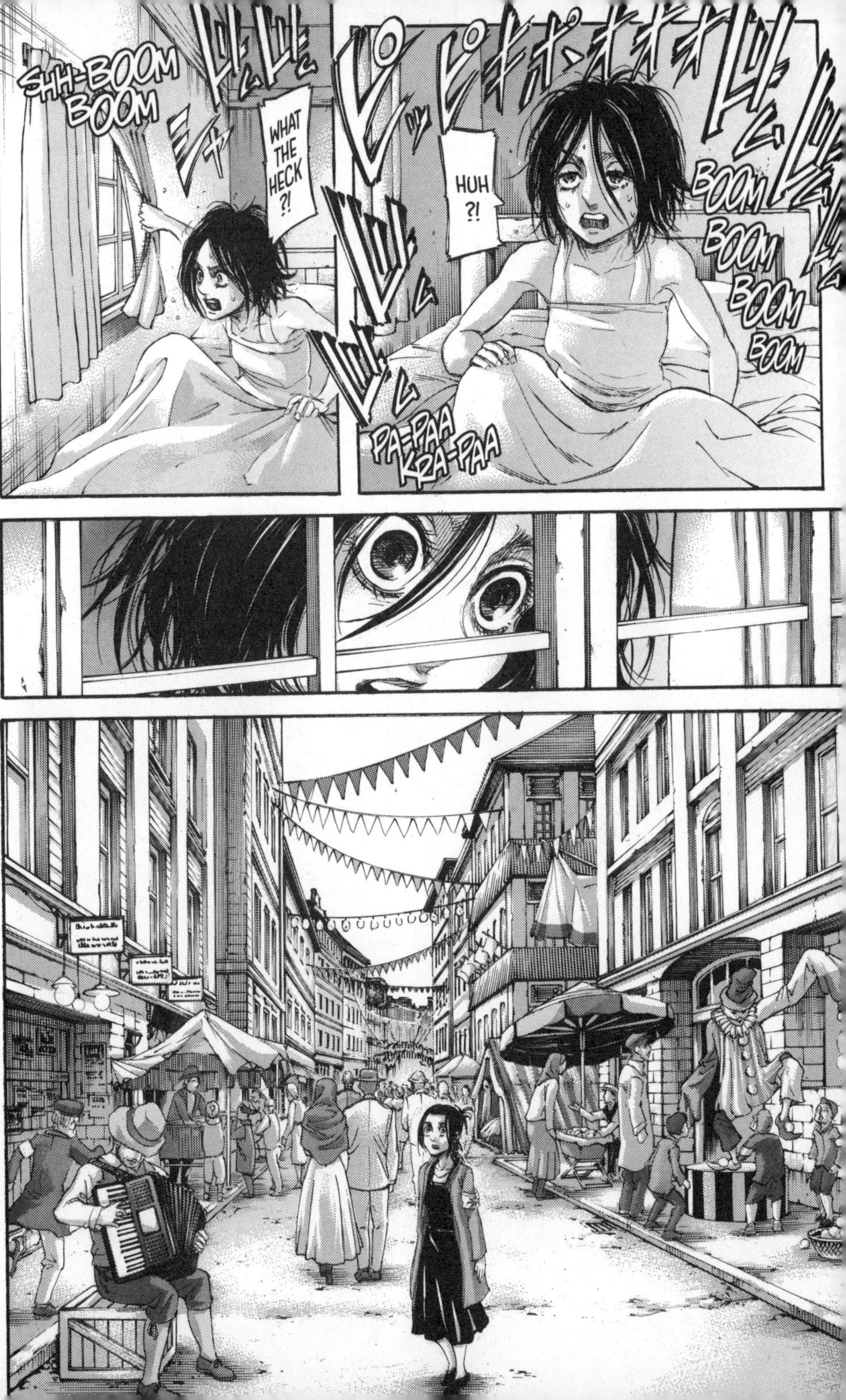
HUH ?!
BOOM BOOM BOOM BOOM BOOM
PA-PAA KRA-PAA
WHAT THE HECK ?!
SHH-BOOM BOOM

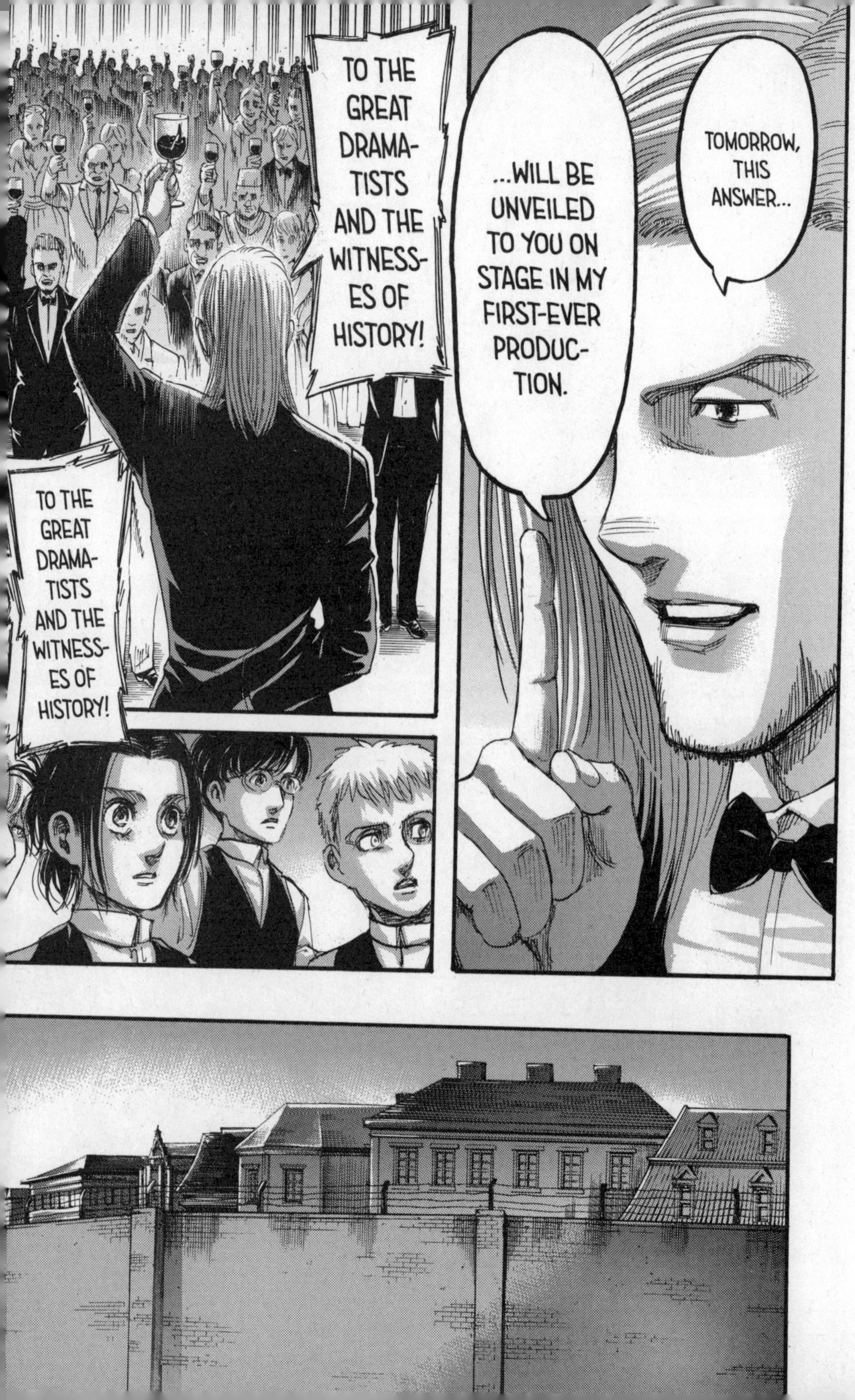
TOMORROW, THIS ANSWER...
...WILL BE UNVEILED TO YOU ON STAGE IN MY FIRST-EVER PRODUCTION.
TO THE GREAT DRAMATISTS AND THE WITNESSES OF HISTORY!
TO THE GREAT DRAMATISTS AND THE WITNESSES OF HISTORY!

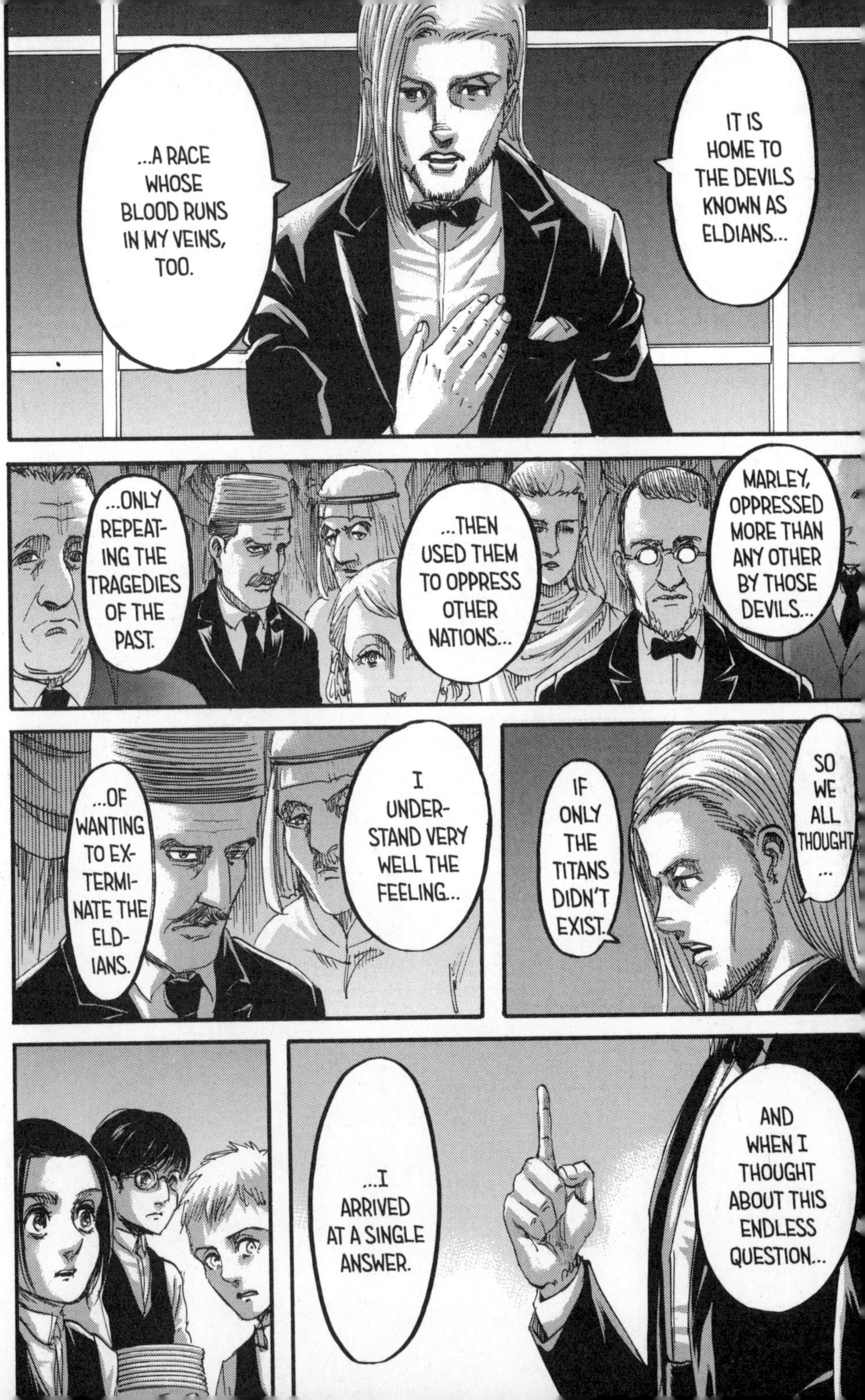
IT IS HOME TO THE DEVILS KNOWN AS ELDIANS...
...A RACE WHOSE BLOOD RUNS IN MY VEINS, TOO.
MARLEY, OPPRESSED MORE THAN ANY OTHER BY THOSE DEVILS...
...THEN USED THEM TO OPPRESS OTHER NATIONS...
...ONLY REPEATING THE TRAGEDIES OF THE PAST.
SO WE ALL THOUGHT...
IF ONLY THE TITANS DIDN'T EXIST.
I UNDERSTAND VERY WELL THE FEELING...
...OF WANTING TO EXTERMINATE THE ELDIANS.
AND WHEN I THOUGHT ABOUT THIS ENDLESS QUESTION...
...I ARRIVED AT A SINGLE ANSWER.

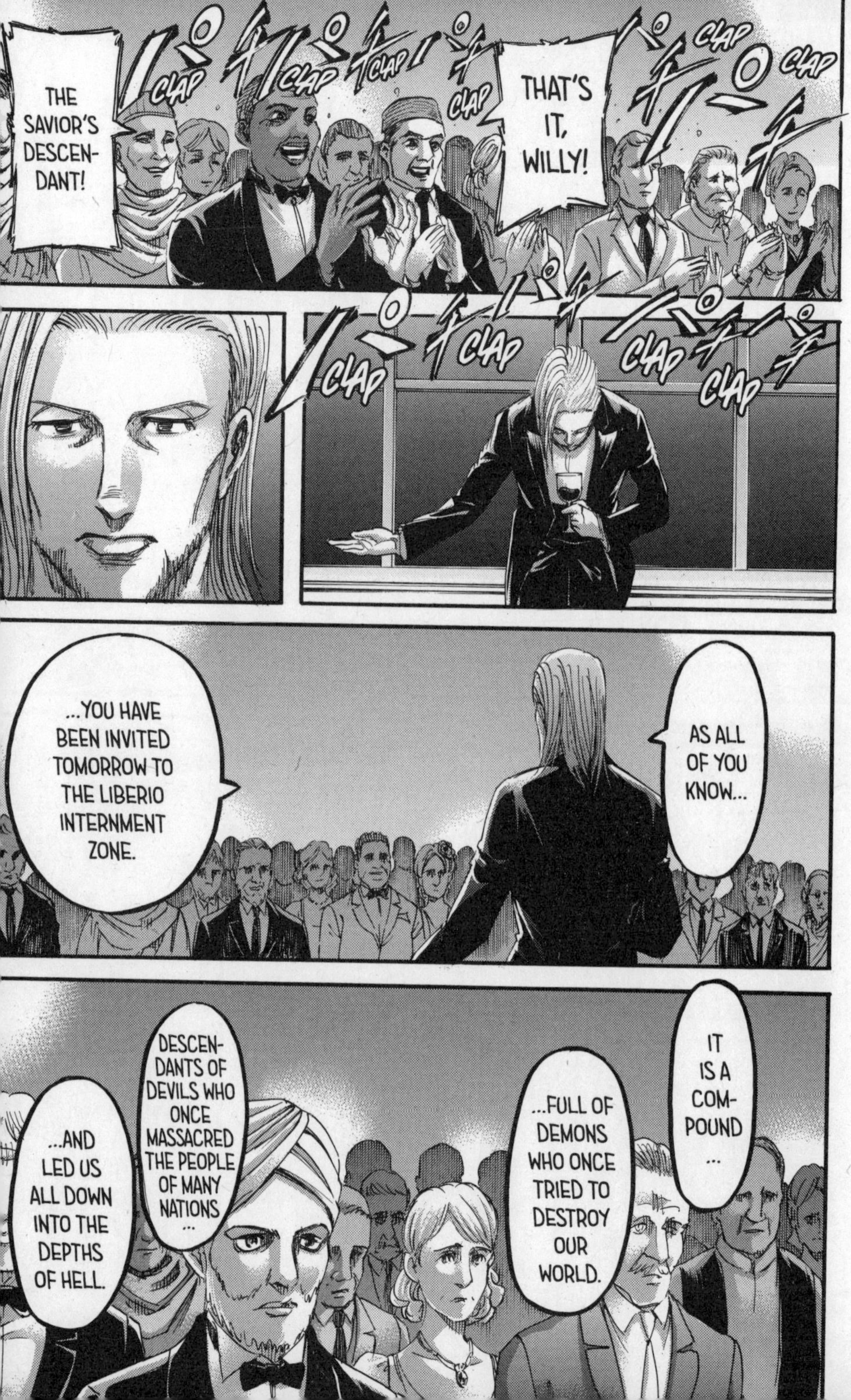
CLAP CLAP
THAT'S IT, WILLY!
CLAP CLAP CLAP CLAP
THE SAVIOR'S DESCENDANT!
CLAP CLAP CLAP
CLAP CLAP
AS ALL OF YOU KNOW...
...YOU HAVE BEEN INVITED TOMORROW TO THE LIBERIO INTERNMENT ZONE.
IT IS A COMPOUND...
...FULL OF DEMONS WHO ONCE TRIED TO DESTROY OUR WORLD.
DESCENDANTS OF DEVILS WHO ONCE MASSACRED THE PEOPLE OF MANY NATIONS...
...AND LED US ALL DOWN INTO THE DEPTHS OF HELL.

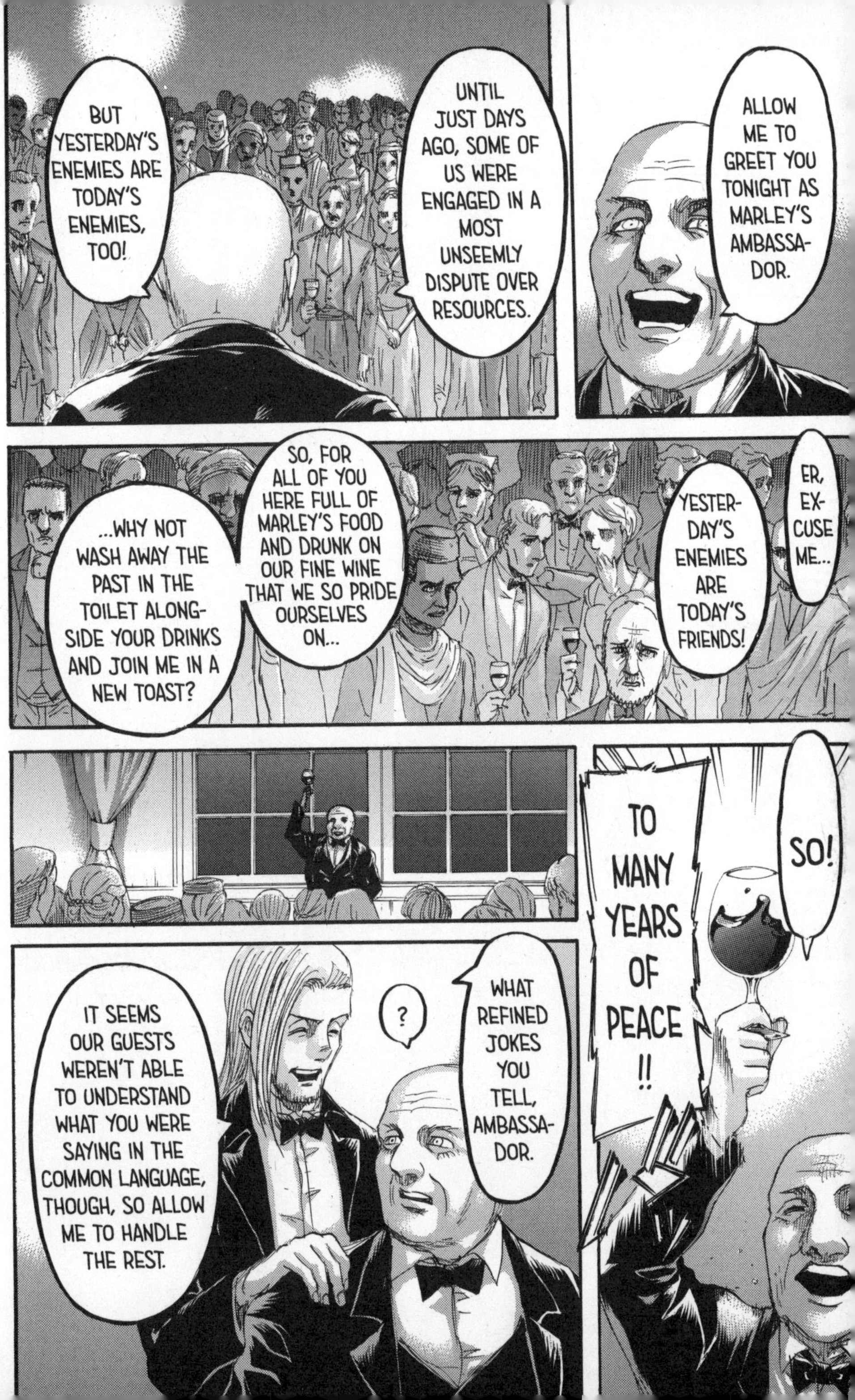
ALLOW ME TO GREET YOU TONIGHT AS MARLEY'S AMBASSADOR.
UNTIL JUST DAYS AGO, SOME OF US WERE ENGAGED IN A MOST UNSEEMLY DISPUTE OVER RESOURCES.
BUT YESTERDAY'S ENEMIES ARE TODAY'S ENEMIES, TOO!
ER, EXCUSE ME...
YESTERDAY'S ENEMIES ARE TODAY'S FRIENDS!
SO, FOR ALL OF YOU HERE FULL OF MARLEY'S FOOD AND DRUNK ON OUR FINE WINE THAT WE SO PRIDE OURSELVES ON...
...WHY NOT WASH AWAY THE PAST IN THE TOILET ALONGSIDE YOUR DRINKS AND JOIN ME IN A NEW TOAST?
SO!
TO MANY YEARS OF PEACE !!
WHAT REFINED JOKES YOU TELL, AMBASSADOR.
?
IT SEEMS OUR GUESTS WEREN'T ABLE TO UNDERSTAND WHAT YOU WERE SAYING IN THE COMMON LANGUAGE, THOUGH, SO ALLOW ME TO HANDLE THE REST.

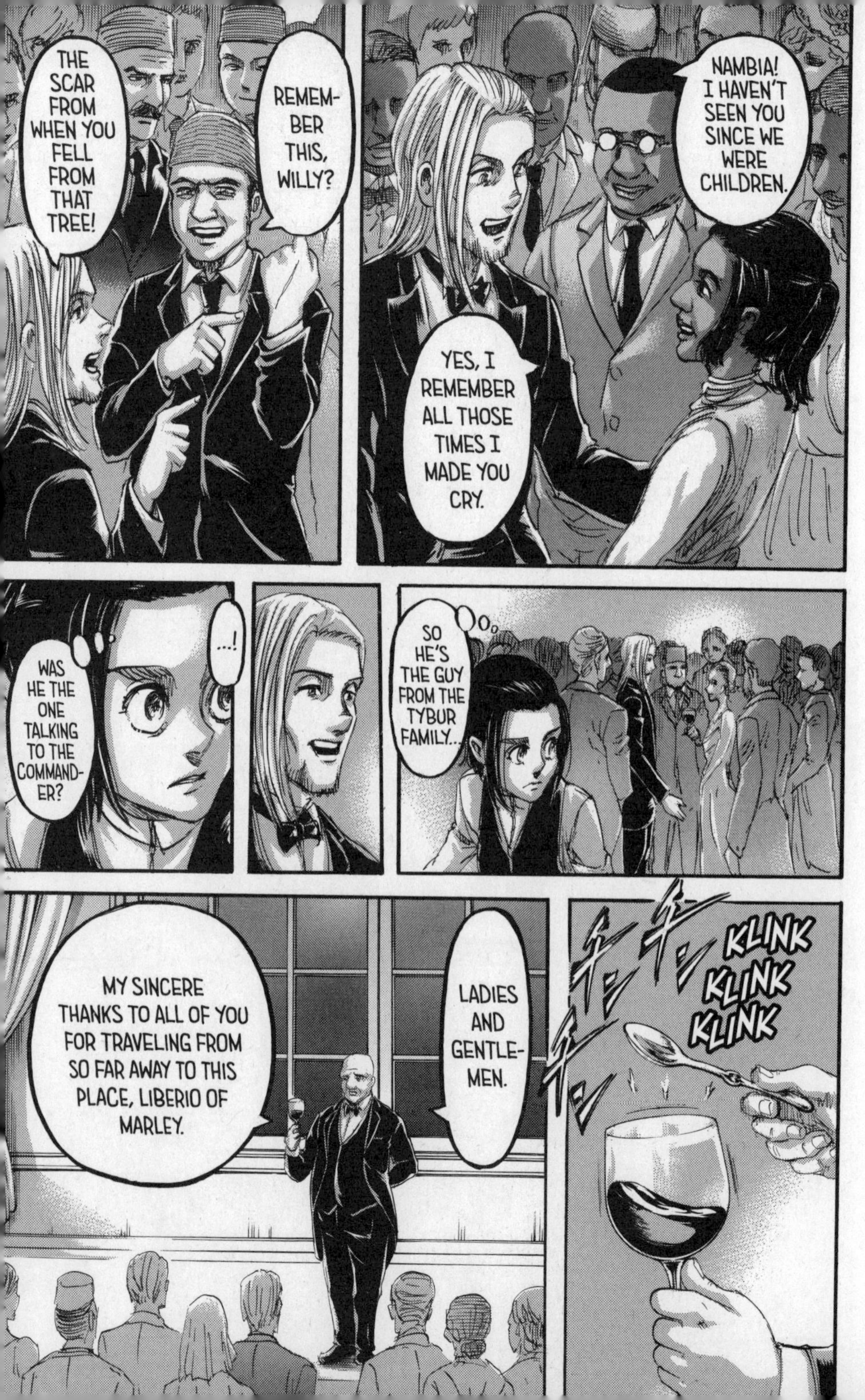
NAMBIA! I HAVEN'T SEEN YOU SINCE WE WERE CHILDREN.
YES, I REMEMBER ALL THOSE TIMES I MADE YOU CRY.
REMEM-BER THIS, WILLY?
THE SCAR FROM WHEN YOU FELL FROM THAT TREE!
SO HE'S THE GUY FROM THE TYBUR FAMILY...
...!
WAS HE THE ONE TALKING TO THE COMMAND-ER?
KLINK
KLINK
KLINK
LADIES AND GENTLE-MEN.
MY SINCERE THANKS TO ALL OF YOU FOR TRAVELING FROM SO FAR AWAY TO THIS PLACE, LIBERIO OF MARLEY.

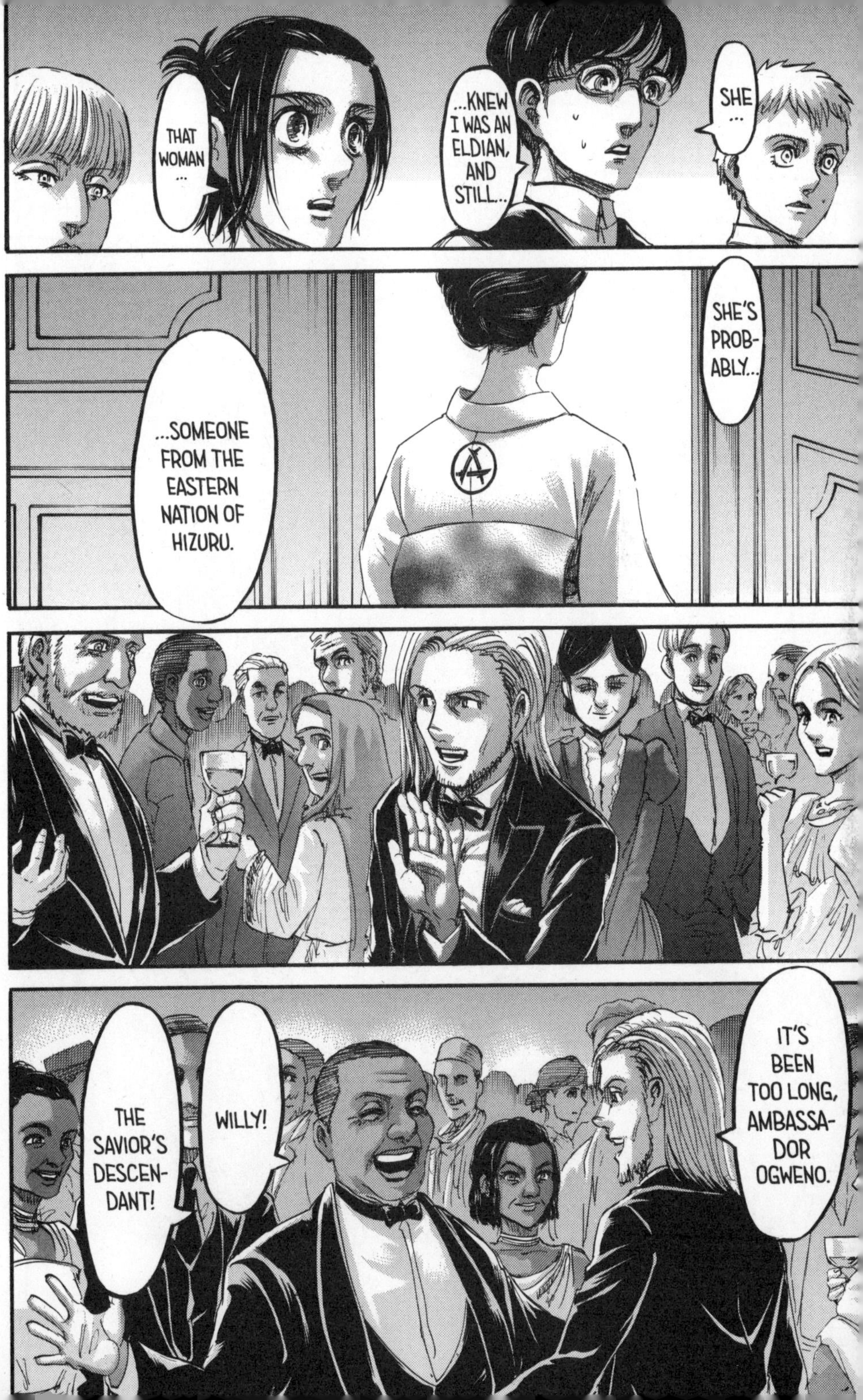
SHE ...
...KNEW I WAS AN ELDIAN, AND STILL...
THAT WOMAN ...
SHE'S PROBABLY...
...SOMEONE FROM THE EASTERN NATION OF HIZURU.
IT'S BEEN TOO LONG, AMBASSADOR OGWENO.
WILLY!
THE SAVIOR'S DESCENDANT!

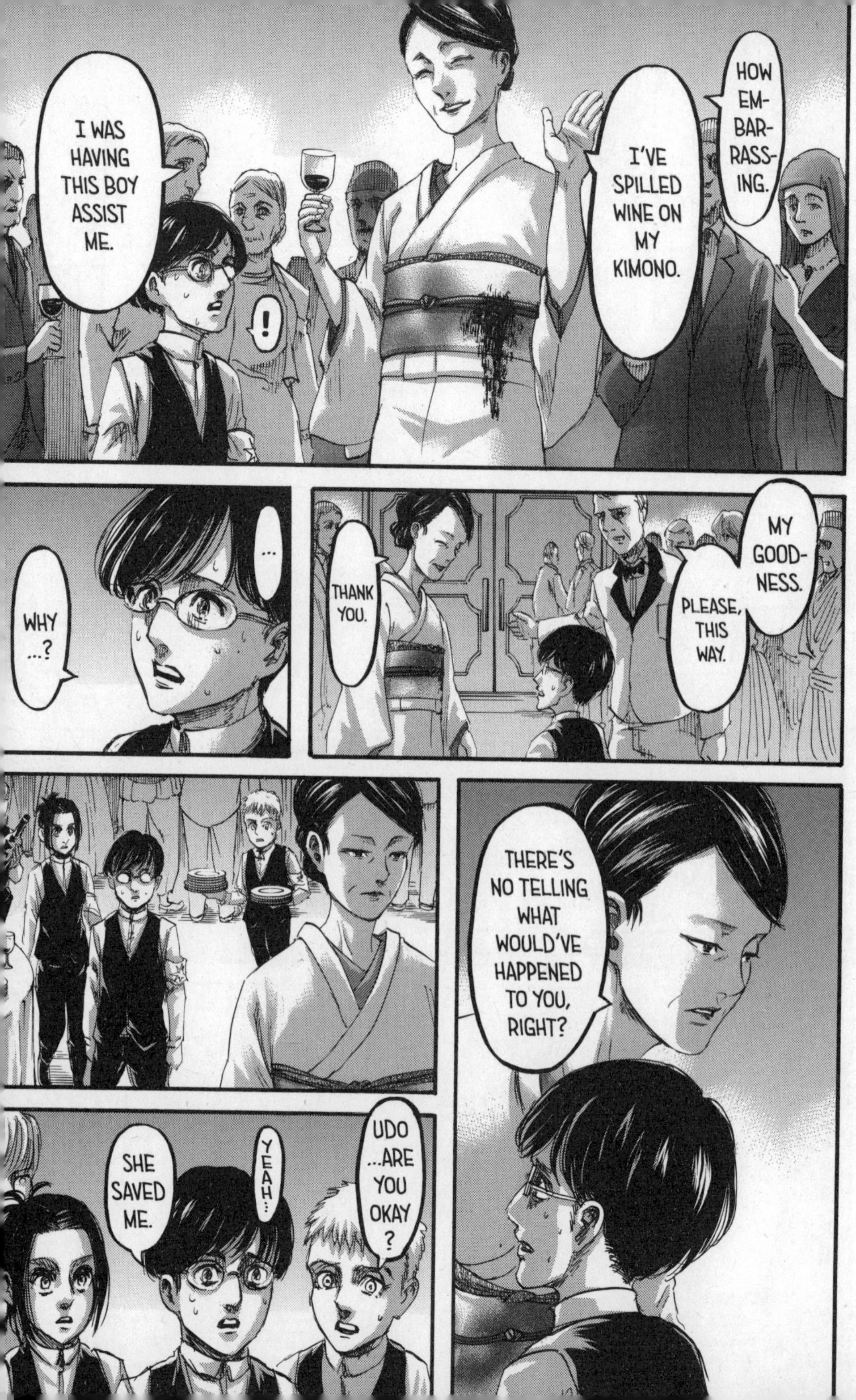
HOW EM-BAR-RASS-ING.
I'VE SPILLED WINE ON MY KIMONO.
!
I WAS HAVING THIS BOY ASSIST ME.
MY GOOD-NESS.
PLEASE, THIS WAY.
THANK YOU.
...
WHY ...?
THERE'S NO TELLING WHAT WOULD'VE HAPPENED TO YOU, RIGHT?
UDO ...ARE YOU OKAY?
YEAH...
SHE SAVED ME.

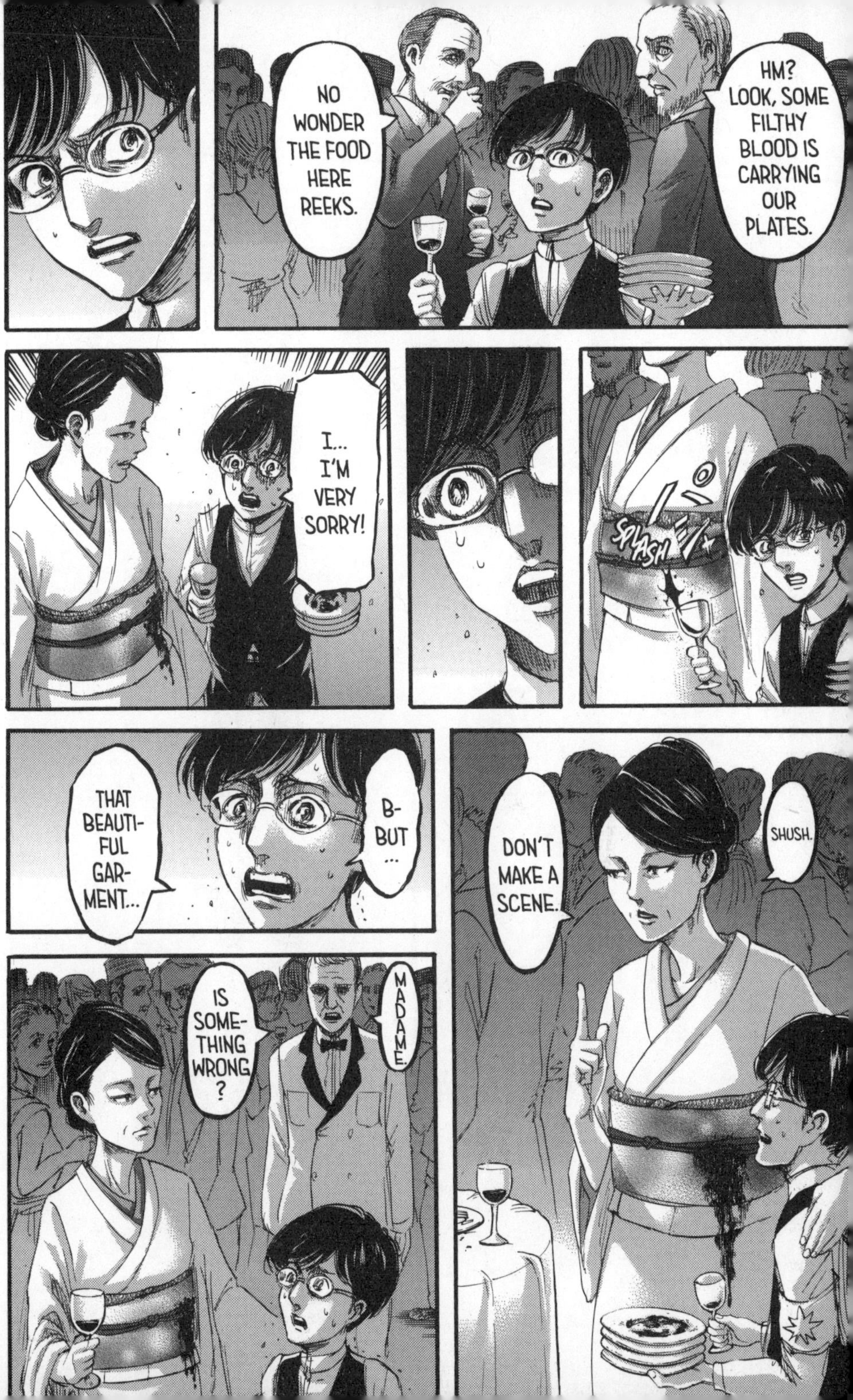
HM? LOOK, SOME FILTHY BLOOD IS CARRYING OUR PLATES.
NO WONDER THE FOOD HERE REEKS.
SPLASH
I... I'M VERY SORRY!
SHUSH.
DON'T MAKE A SCENE.
B-BUT...
THAT BEAUTI-FUL GAR-MENT...
MADAME.
IS SOME-THING WRONG?

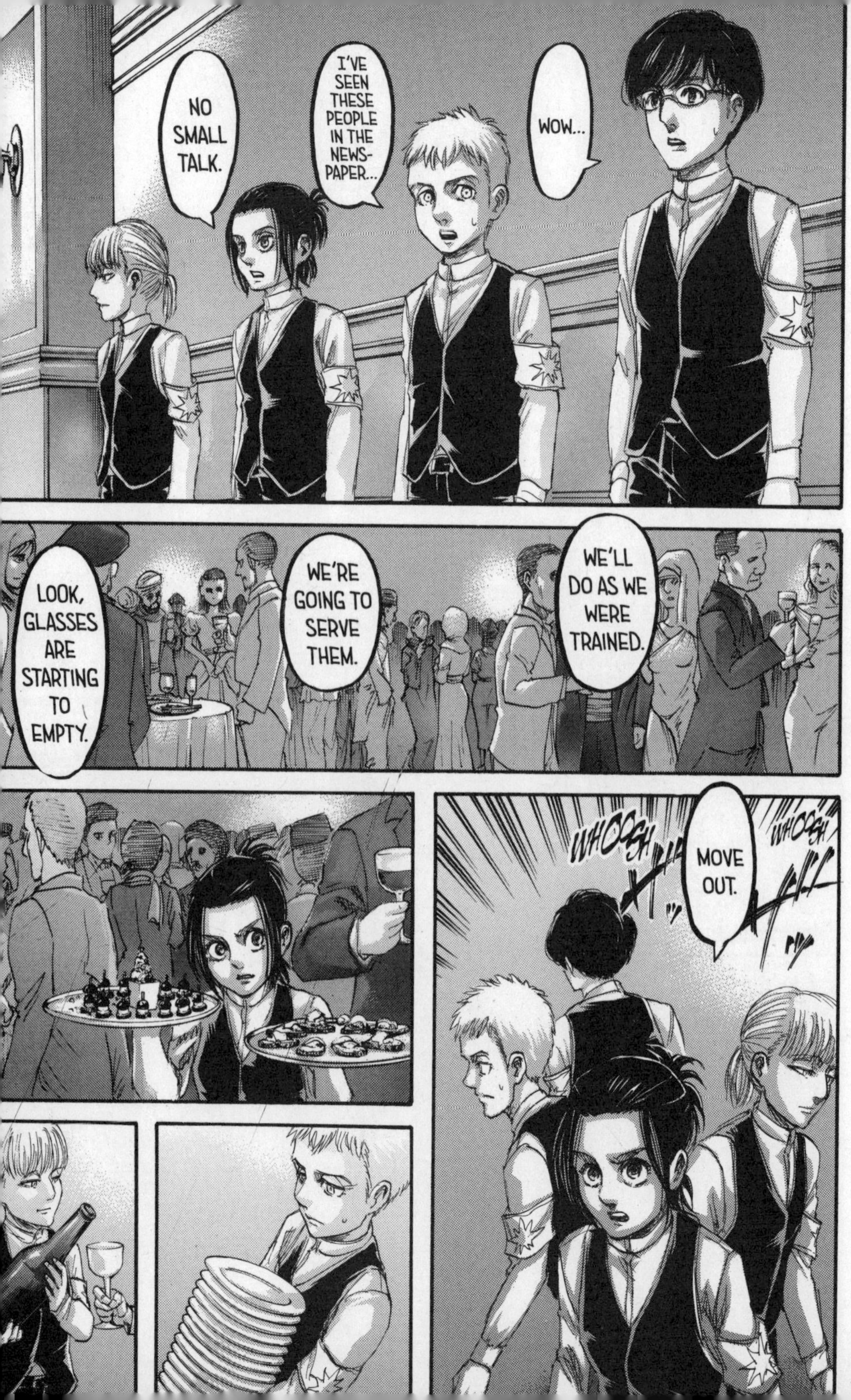
WOW...
I'VE SEEN THESE PEOPLE IN THE NEWS-PAPER...
NO SMALL TALK.
WE'LL DO AS WE WERE TRAINED.
WE'RE GOING TO SERVE THEM.
LOOK, GLASSES ARE STARTING TO EMPTY.
WHOOSH
MOVE OUT.
WHOOSH

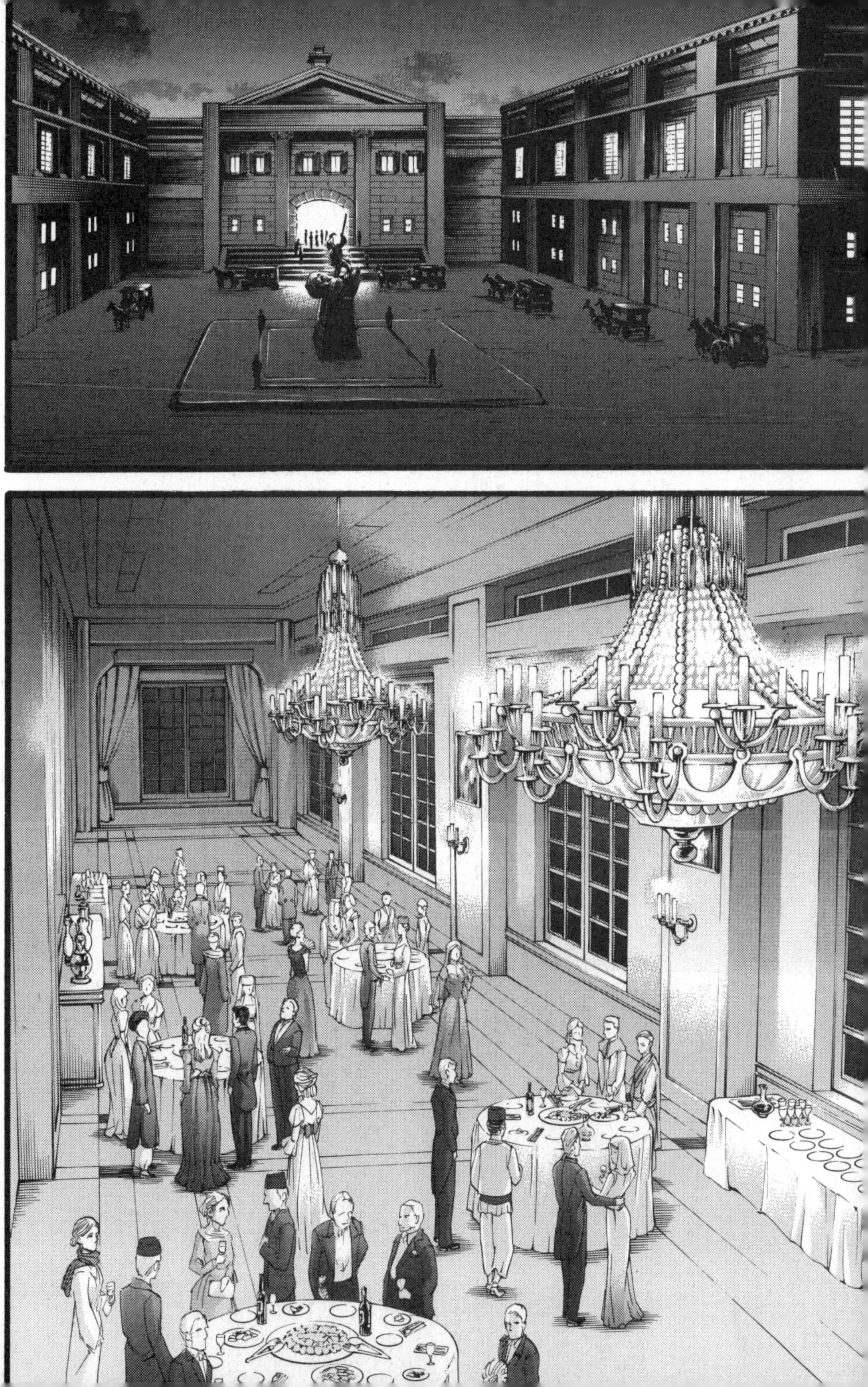

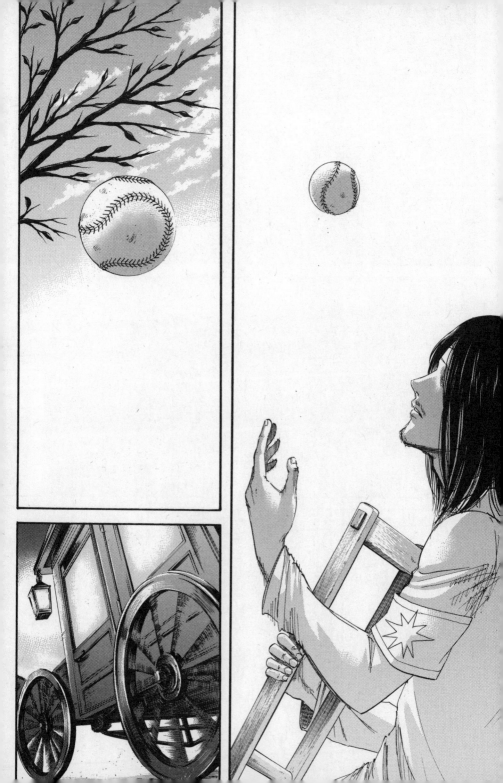

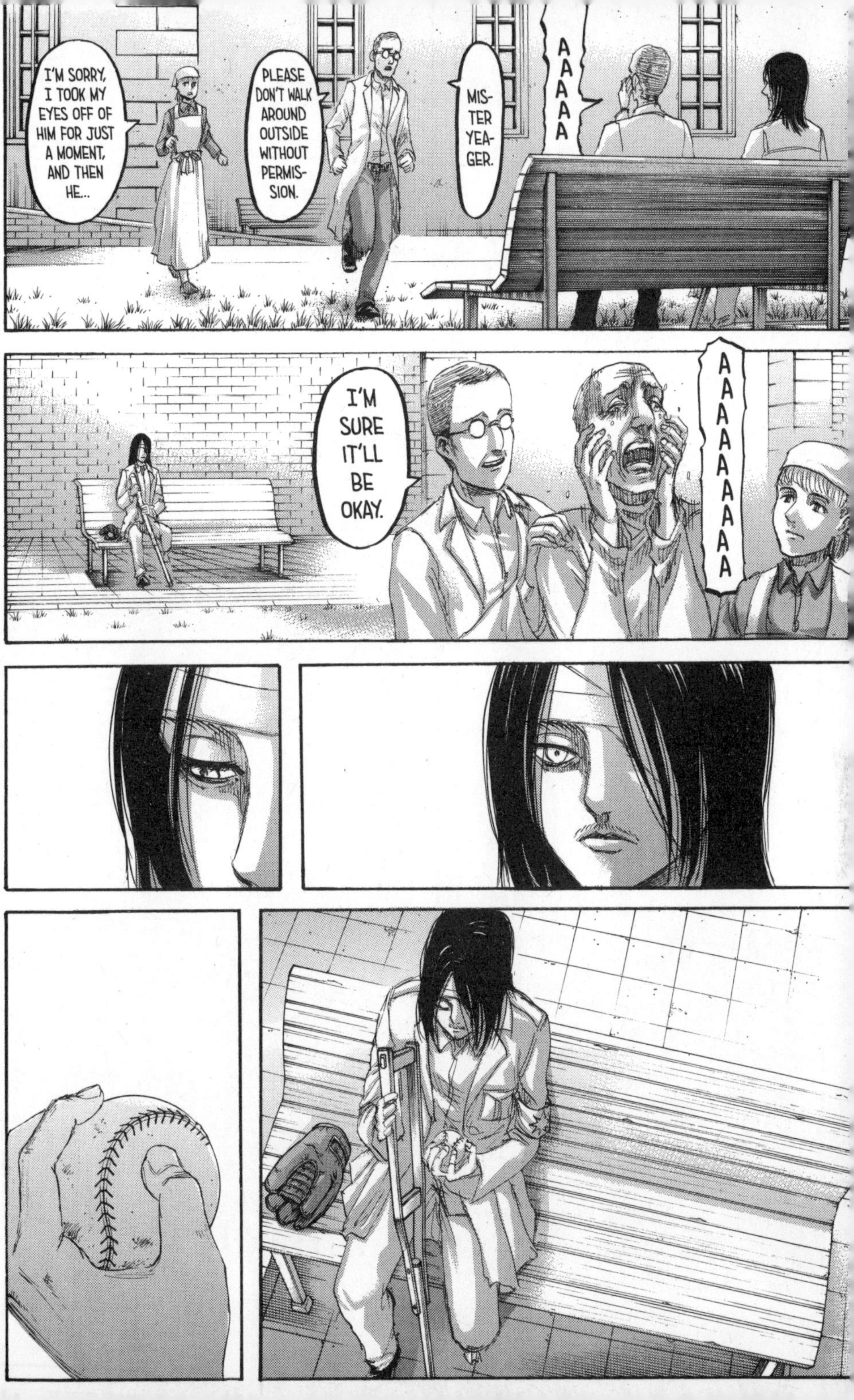
AAAAA
MISTER YEAGER.
PLEASE DON'T WALK AROUND OUTSIDE WITHOUT PERMISSION.
I'M SORRY, I TOOK MY EYES OFF OF HIM FOR JUST A MOMENT, AND THEN HE...
AAAAAAAAAA
I'M SURE IT'LL BE OKAY.

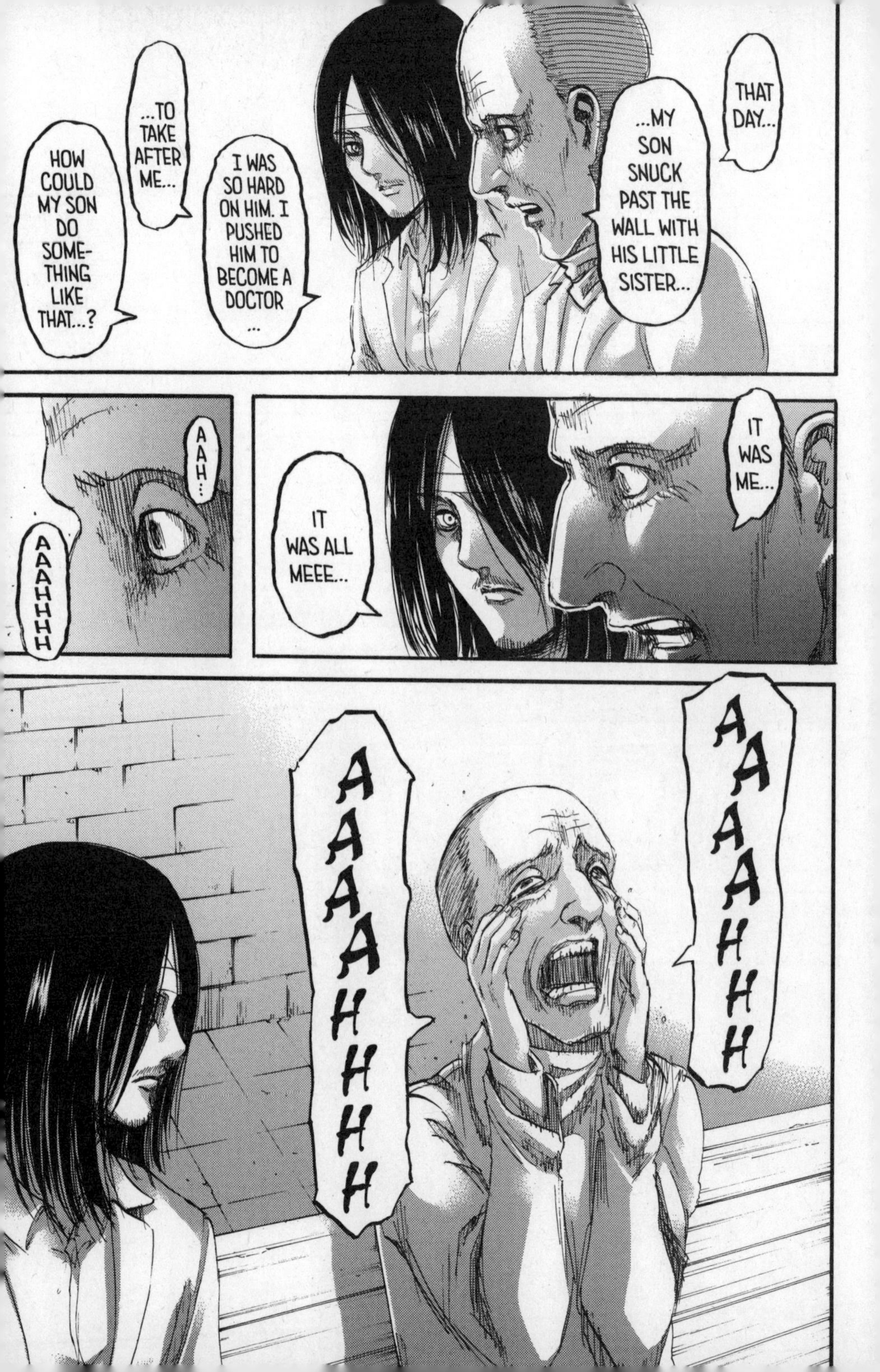
THAT DAY...
...MY SON SNUCK PAST THE WALL WITH HIS LITTLE SISTER...
I WAS SO HARD ON HIM. I PUSHED HIM TO BECOME A DOCTOR ...
...TO TAKE AFTER ME...
HOW COULD MY SON DO SOME-THING LIKE THAT...?
IT WAS ME...
IT WAS ALL MEEE...
AAH...
AAAHHHH
AAAAHHH
AAAAHHHH

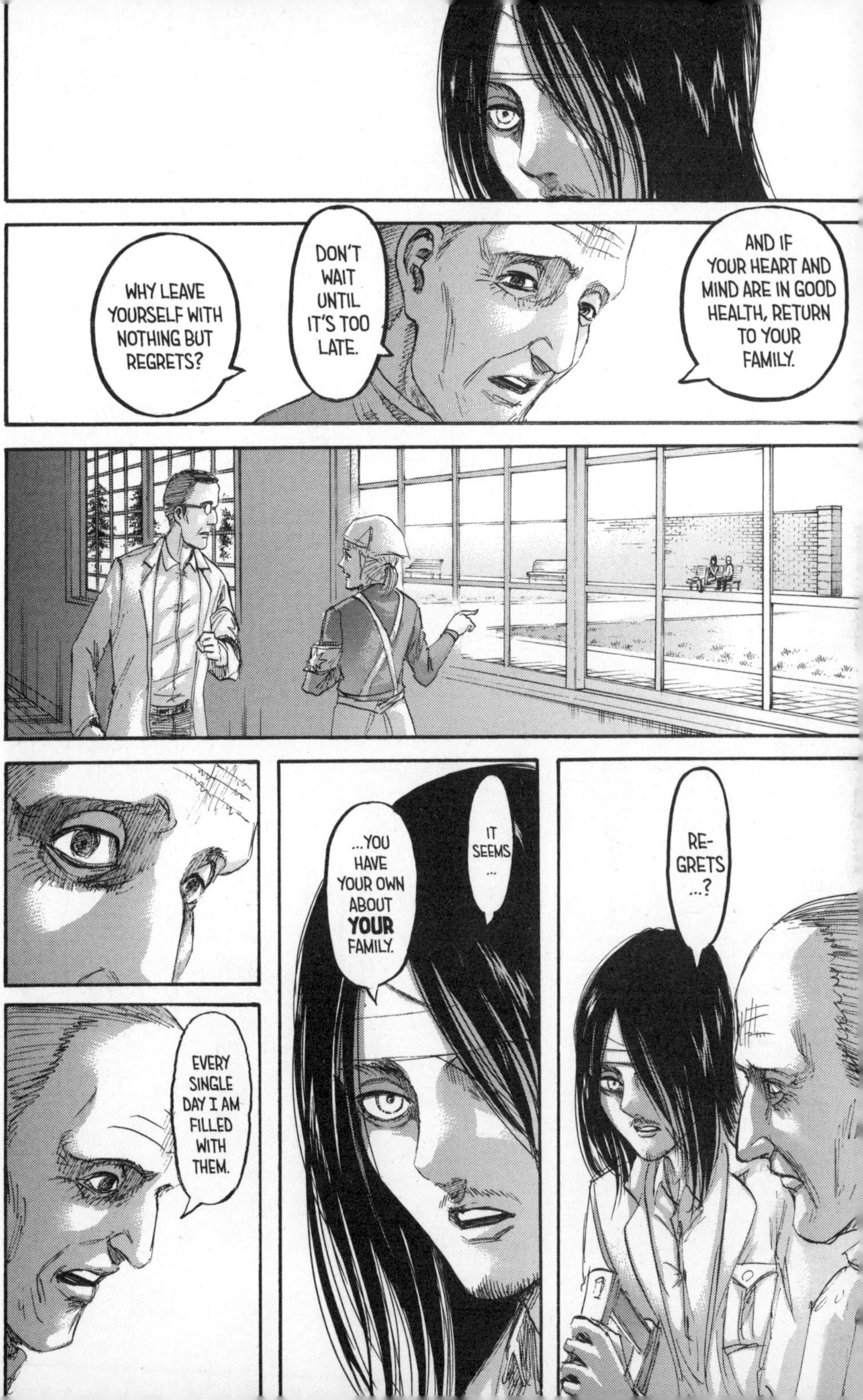
AND IF YOUR HEART AND MIND ARE IN GOOD HEALTH, RETURN TO YOUR FAMILY.
DON'T WAIT UNTIL IT'S TOO LATE.
WHY LEAVE YOURSELF WITH NOTHING BUT REGRETS?
RE-GRETS ...?
IT SEEMS ...
...YOU HAVE YOUR OWN ABOUT **YOUR** FAMILY.
EVERY SINGLE DAY I AM FILLED WITH THEM.

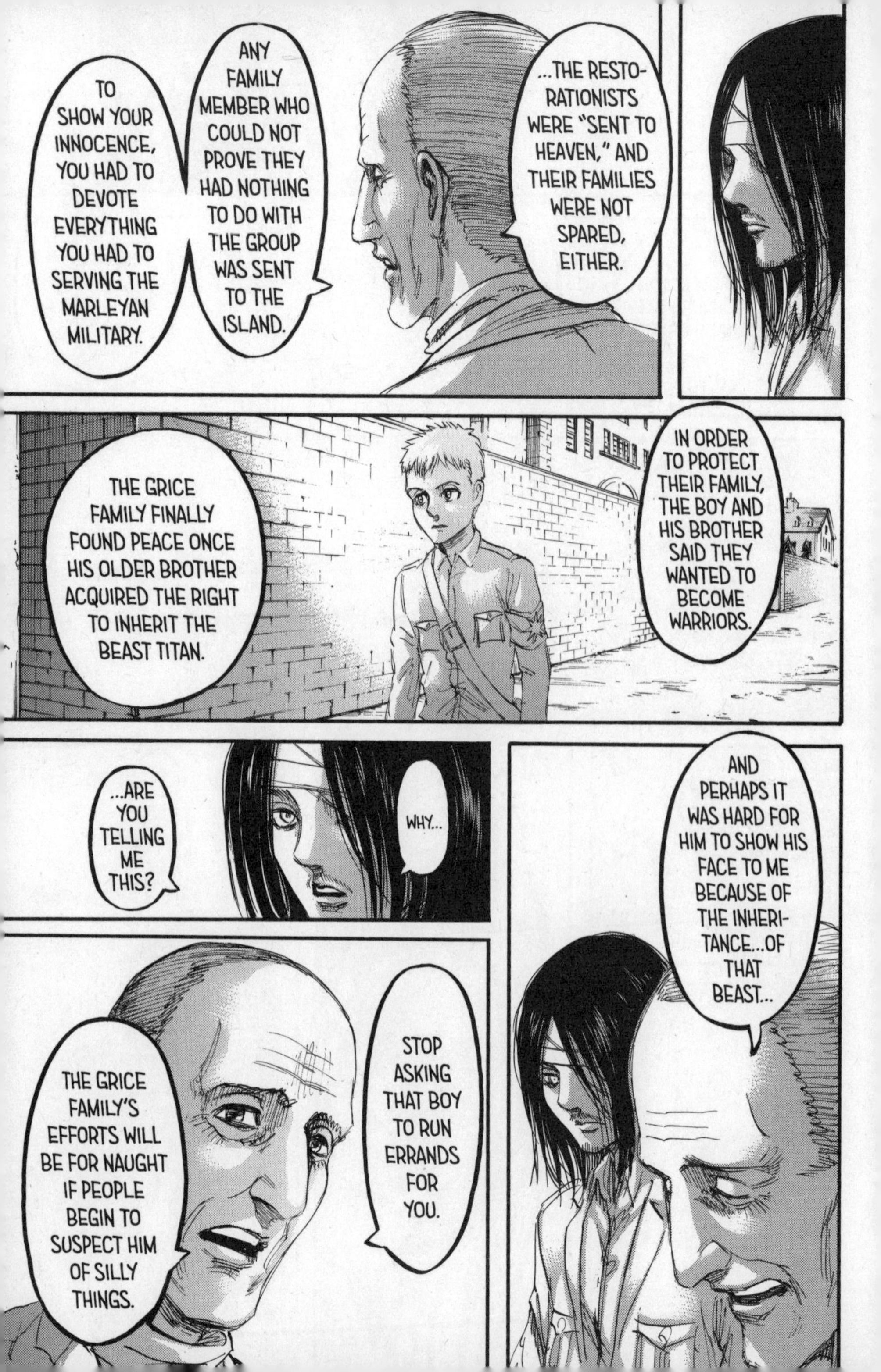
...THE RESTORATIONISTS WERE "SENT TO HEAVEN," AND THEIR FAMILIES WERE NOT SPARED, EITHER.
ANY FAMILY MEMBER WHO COULD NOT PROVE THEY HAD NOTHING TO DO WITH THE GROUP WAS SENT TO THE ISLAND.
TO SHOW YOUR INNOCENCE, YOU HAD TO DEVOTE EVERYTHING YOU HAD TO SERVING THE MARLEYAN MILITARY.
IN ORDER TO PROTECT THEIR FAMILY, THE BOY AND HIS BROTHER SAID THEY WANTED TO BECOME WARRIORS.
THE GRICE FAMILY FINALLY FOUND PEACE ONCE HIS OLDER BROTHER ACQUIRED THE RIGHT TO INHERIT THE BEAST TITAN.
AND PERHAPS IT WAS HARD FOR HIM TO SHOW HIS FACE TO ME BECAUSE OF THE INHERITANCE...OF THAT BEAST...
WHY...
...ARE YOU TELLING ME THIS?
STOP ASKING THAT BOY TO RUN ERRANDS FOR YOU.
THE GRICE FAMILY'S EFFORTS WILL BE FOR NAUGHT IF PEOPLE BEGIN TO SUSPECT HIM OF SILLY THINGS.

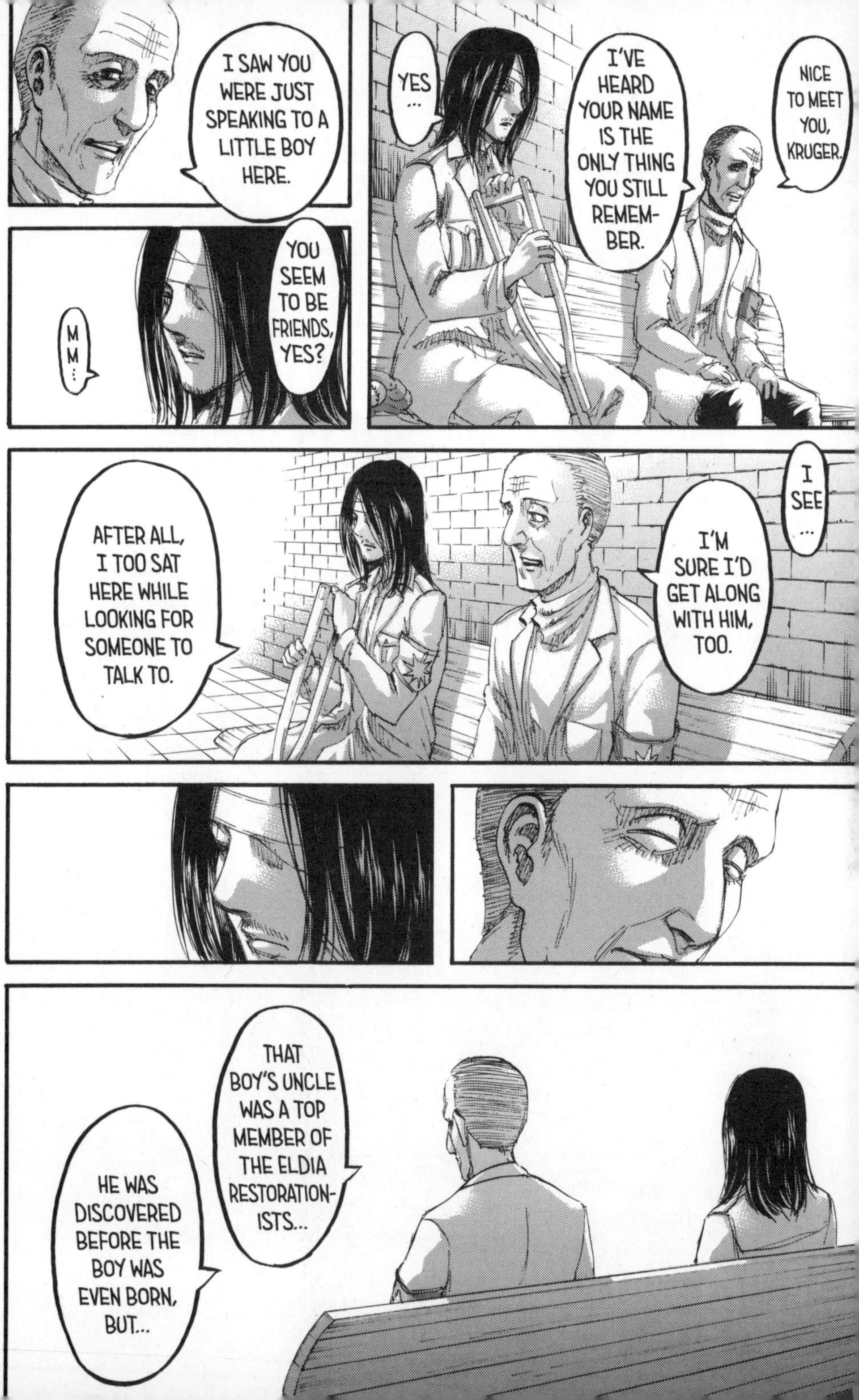
NICE TO MEET YOU, KRUGER.
I'VE HEARD YOUR NAME IS THE ONLY THING YOU STILL REMEMBER.
YES...
I SAW YOU WERE JUST SPEAKING TO A LITTLE BOY HERE.
YOU SEEM TO BE FRIENDS, YES?
MM...
I SEE...
I'M SURE I'D GET ALONG WITH HIM, TOO.
AFTER ALL, I TOO SAT HERE WHILE LOOKING FOR SOMEONE TO TALK TO.
THAT BOY'S UNCLE WAS A TOP MEMBER OF THE ELDIA RESTORATIONISTS...
HE WAS DISCOVERED BEFORE THE BOY WAS EVEN BORN, BUT...

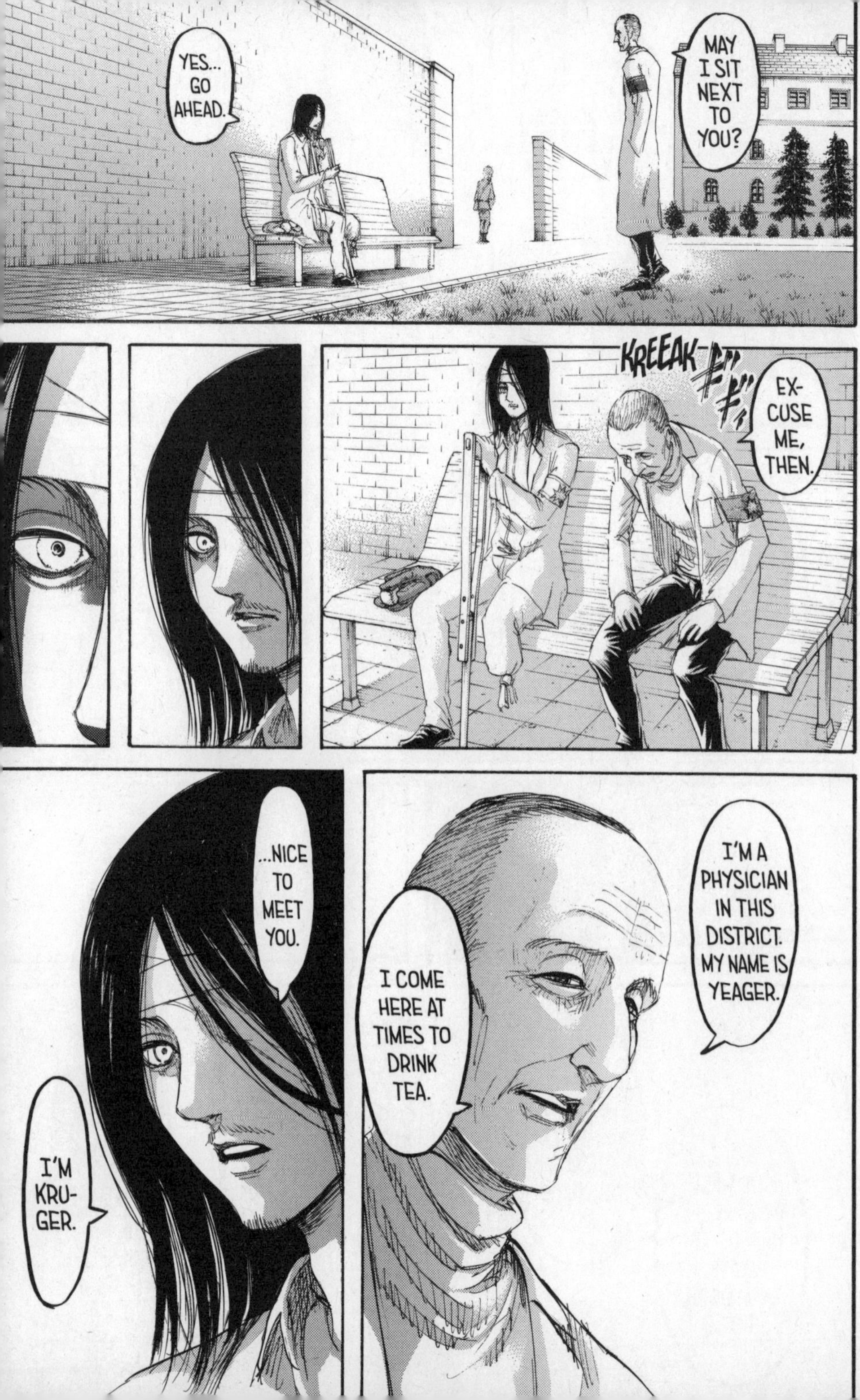
MAY I SIT NEXT TO YOU?
YES... GO AHEAD.
KREEAK
EX-CUSE ME, THEN.
I'M A PHYSICIAN IN THIS DISTRICT. MY NAME IS YEAGER.
I COME HERE AT TIMES TO DRINK TEA.
...NICE TO MEET YOU.
I'M KRU-GER.

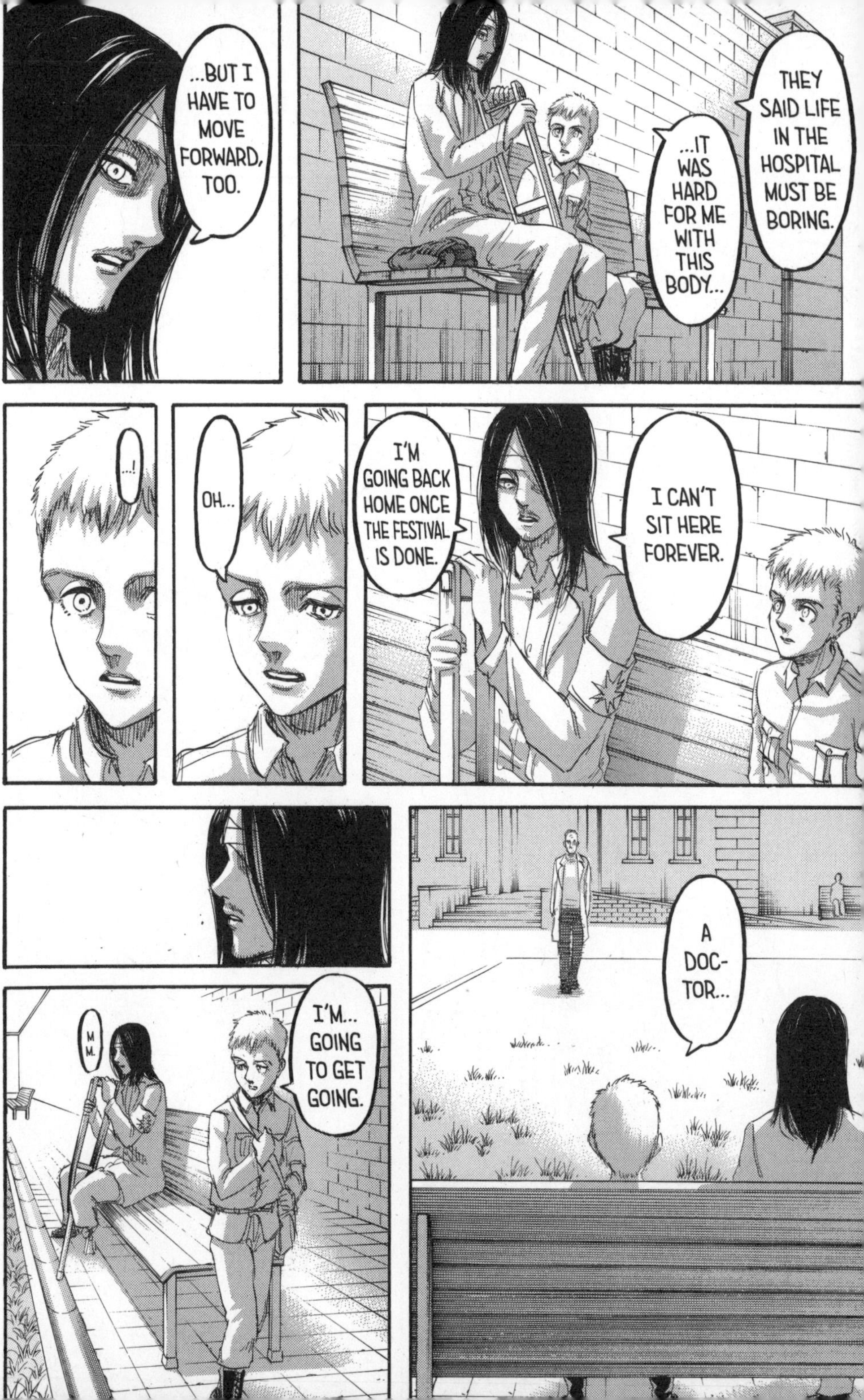
THEY SAID LIFE IN THE HOSPITAL MUST BE BORING.
...IT WAS HARD FOR ME WITH THIS BODY...
...BUT I HAVE TO MOVE FORWARD, TOO.
I CAN'T SIT HERE FOREVER.
I'M GOING BACK HOME ONCE THE FESTIVAL IS DONE.
OH...
...!
A DOC-TOR...
I'M... GOING TO GET GOING.
MM.

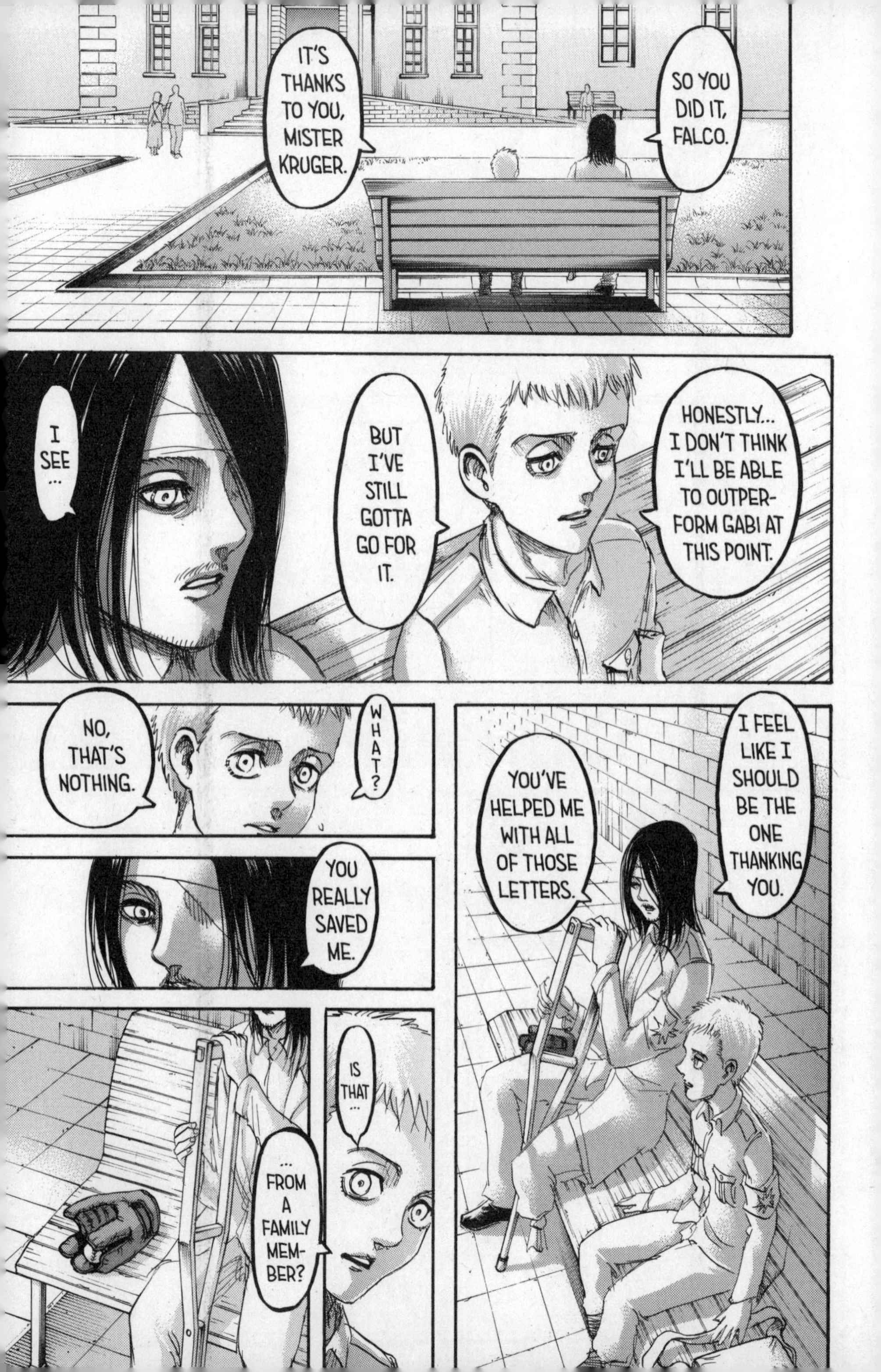
SO YOU DID IT, FALCO.
IT'S THANKS TO YOU, MISTER KRUGER.
HONESTLY... I DON'T THINK I'LL BE ABLE TO OUTPERFORM GABI AT THIS POINT.
BUT I'VE STILL GOTTA GO FOR IT.
I SEE...
I FEEL LIKE I SHOULD BE THE ONE THANKING YOU.
YOU'VE HELPED ME WITH ALL OF THOSE LETTERS.
WHAT?
NO, THAT'S NOTHING.
YOU REALLY SAVED ME.
IS THAT...
...FROM A FAMILY MEMBER?

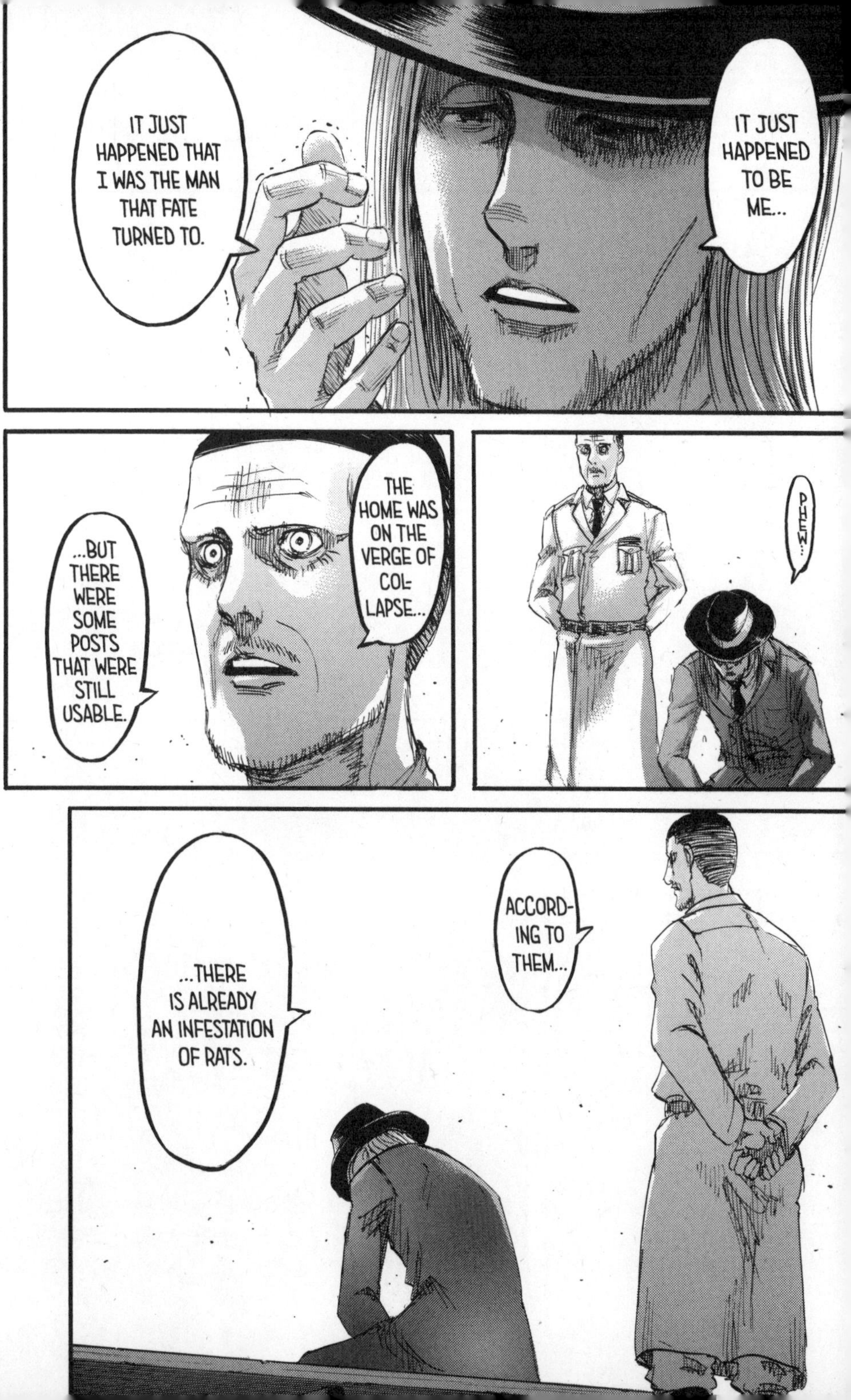
IT JUST HAPPENED TO BE ME...
IT JUST HAPPENED THAT I WAS THE MAN THAT FATE TURNED TO.
PHEW...
THE HOME WAS ON THE VERGE OF COLLAPSE...
...BUT THERE WERE SOME POSTS THAT WERE STILL USABLE.
ACCORDING TO THEM...
...THERE IS ALREADY AN INFESTATION OF RATS.

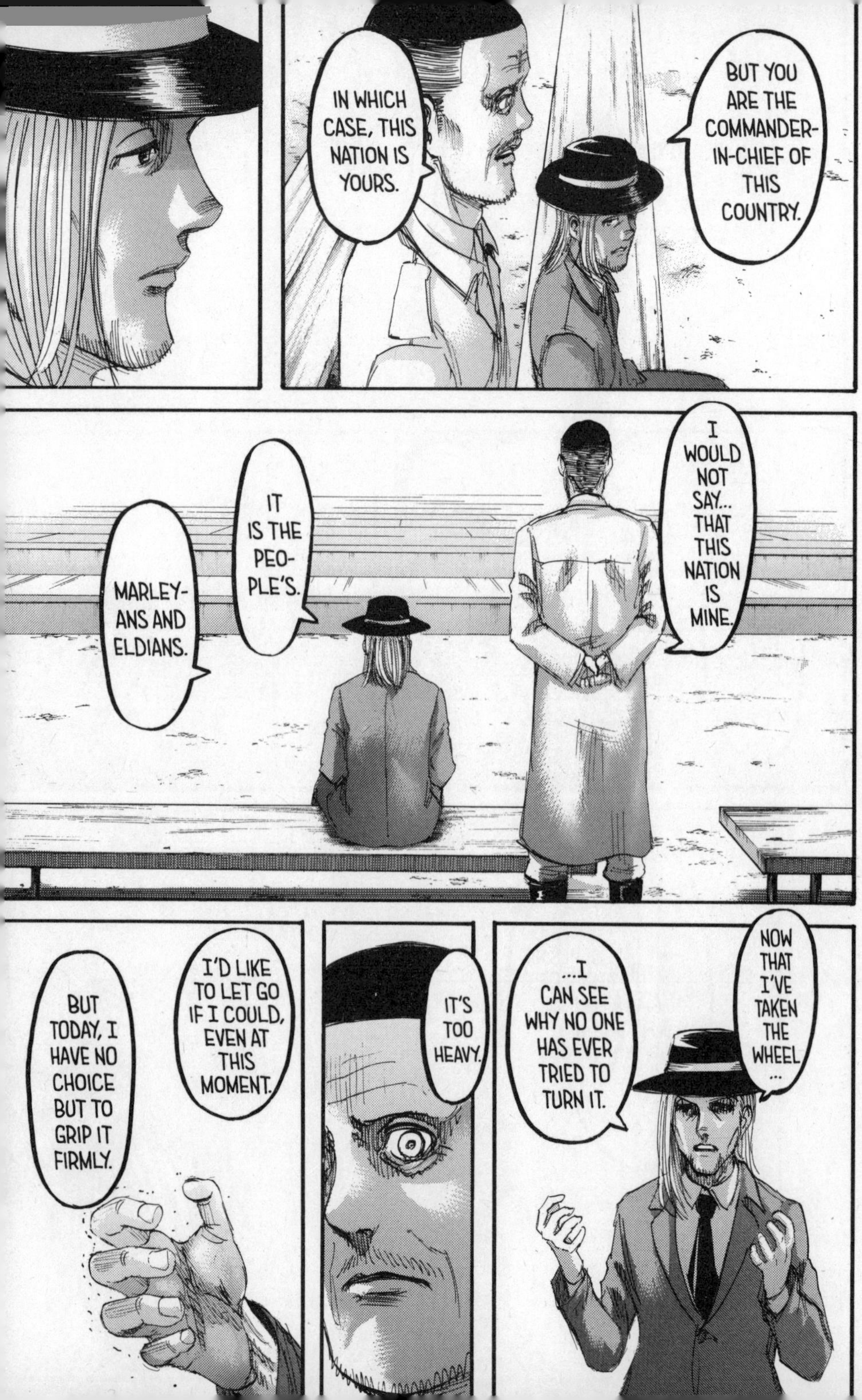
BUT YOU ARE THE COMMANDER-IN-CHIEF OF THIS COUNTRY.
IN WHICH CASE, THIS NATION IS YOURS.
I WOULD NOT SAY... THAT THIS NATION IS MINE.
IT IS THE PEOPLE'S.
MARLEYANS AND ELDIANS.
NOW THAT I'VE TAKEN THE WHEEL...
...I CAN SEE WHY NO ONE HAS EVER TRIED TO TURN IT.
IT'S TOO HEAVY.
I'D LIKE TO LET GO IF I COULD, EVEN AT THIS MOMENT.
BUT TODAY, I HAVE NO CHOICE BUT TO GRIP IT FIRMLY.

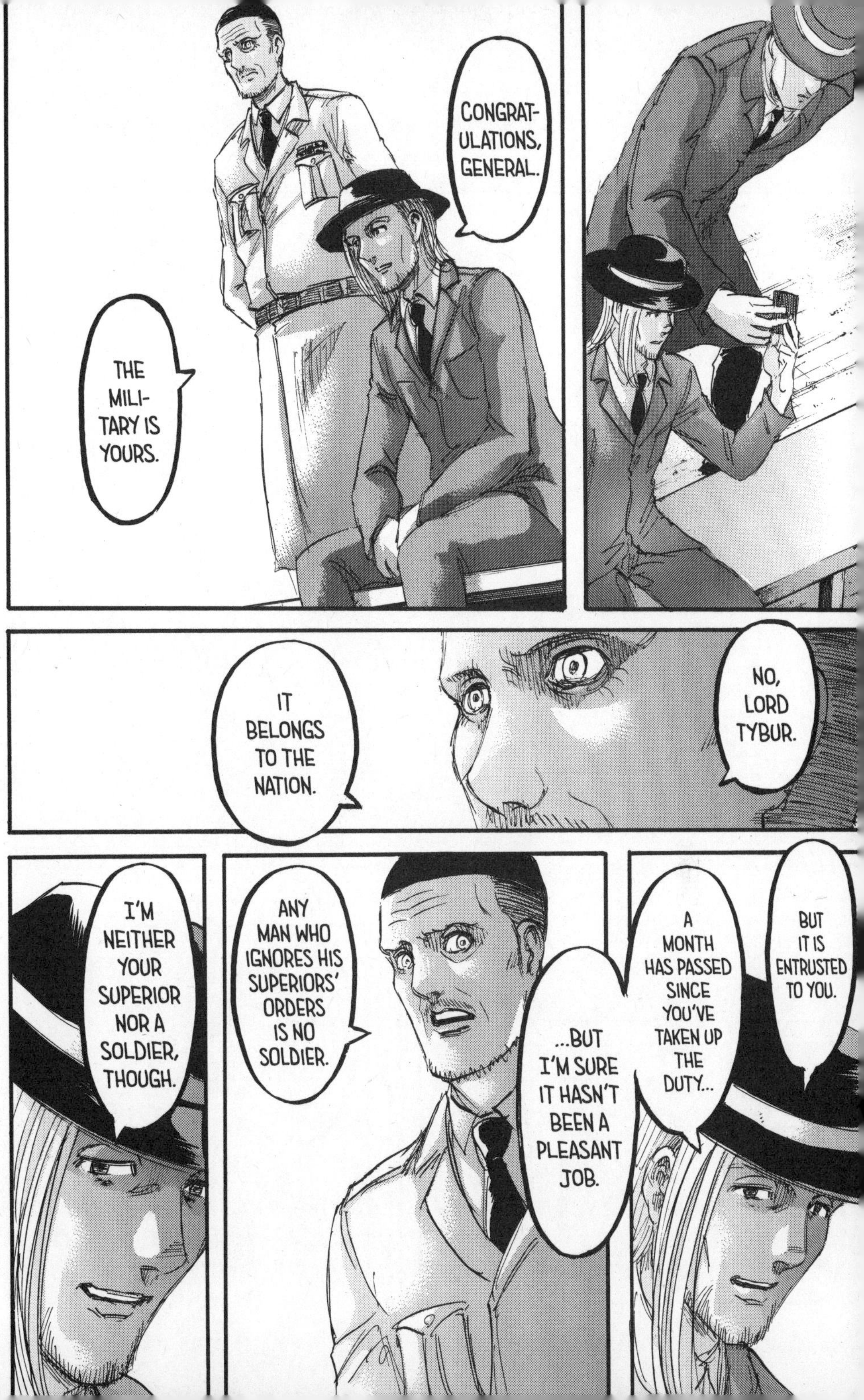
CONGRAT-ULATIONS, GENERAL.
THE MILI-TARY IS YOURS.
NO, LORD TYBUR.
IT BELONGS TO THE NATION.
BUT IT IS ENTRUSTED TO YOU.
A MONTH HAS PASSED SINCE YOU'VE TAKEN UP THE DUTY...
...BUT I'M SURE IT HASN'T BEEN A PLEASANT JOB.
ANY MAN WHO IGNORES HIS SUPERIORS' ORDERS IS NO SOLDIER.
I'M NEITHER YOUR SUPERIOR NOR A SOLDIER, THOUGH.

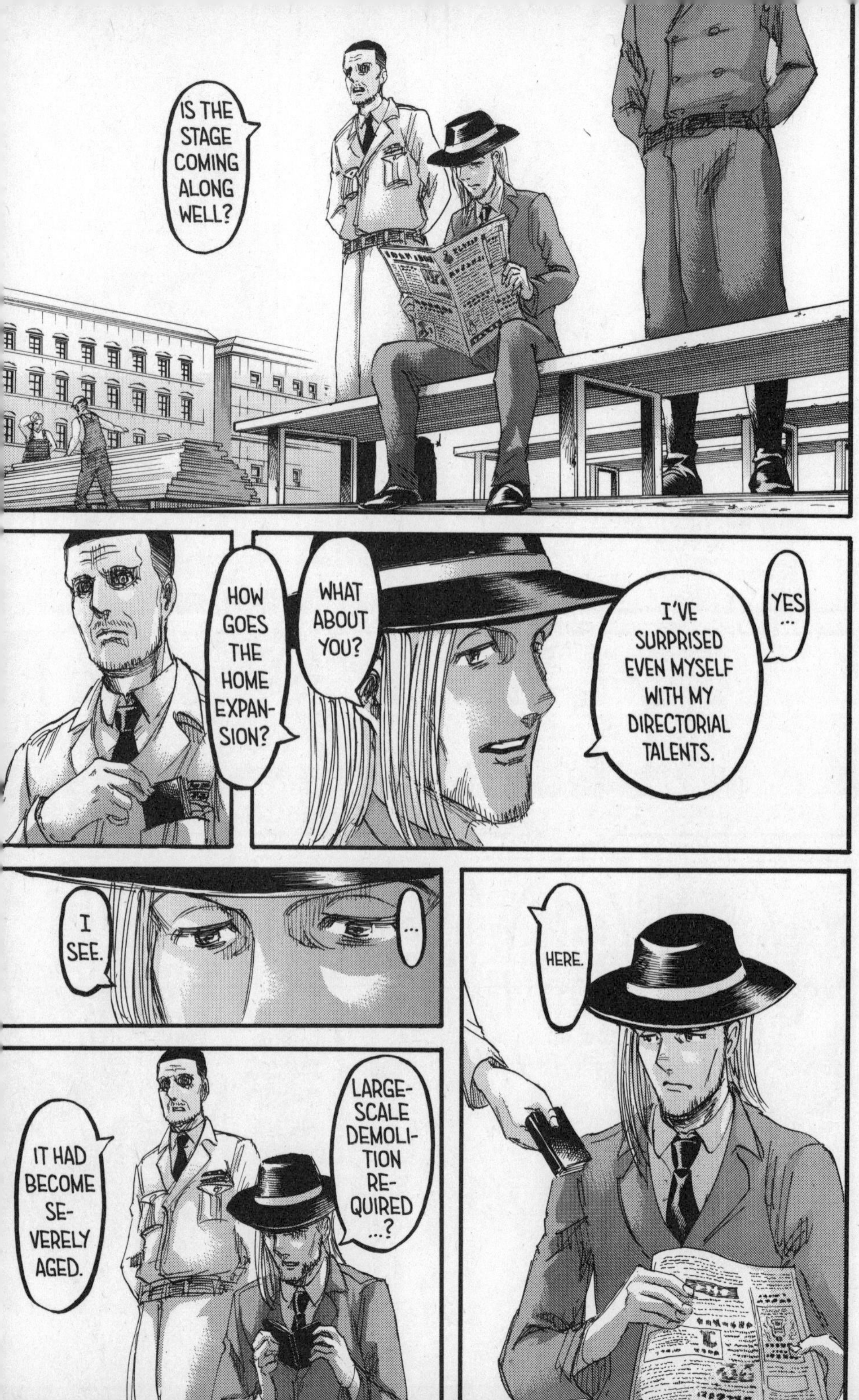
IS THE STAGE COMING ALONG WELL?
YES ...
I'VE SURPRISED EVEN MYSELF WITH MY DIRECTORIAL TALENTS.
WHAT ABOUT YOU?
HOW GOES THE HOME EXPANSION?
HERE.
...
I SEE.
LARGE-SCALE DEMOLITION REQUIRED ...?
IT HAD BECOME SEVERELY AGED.

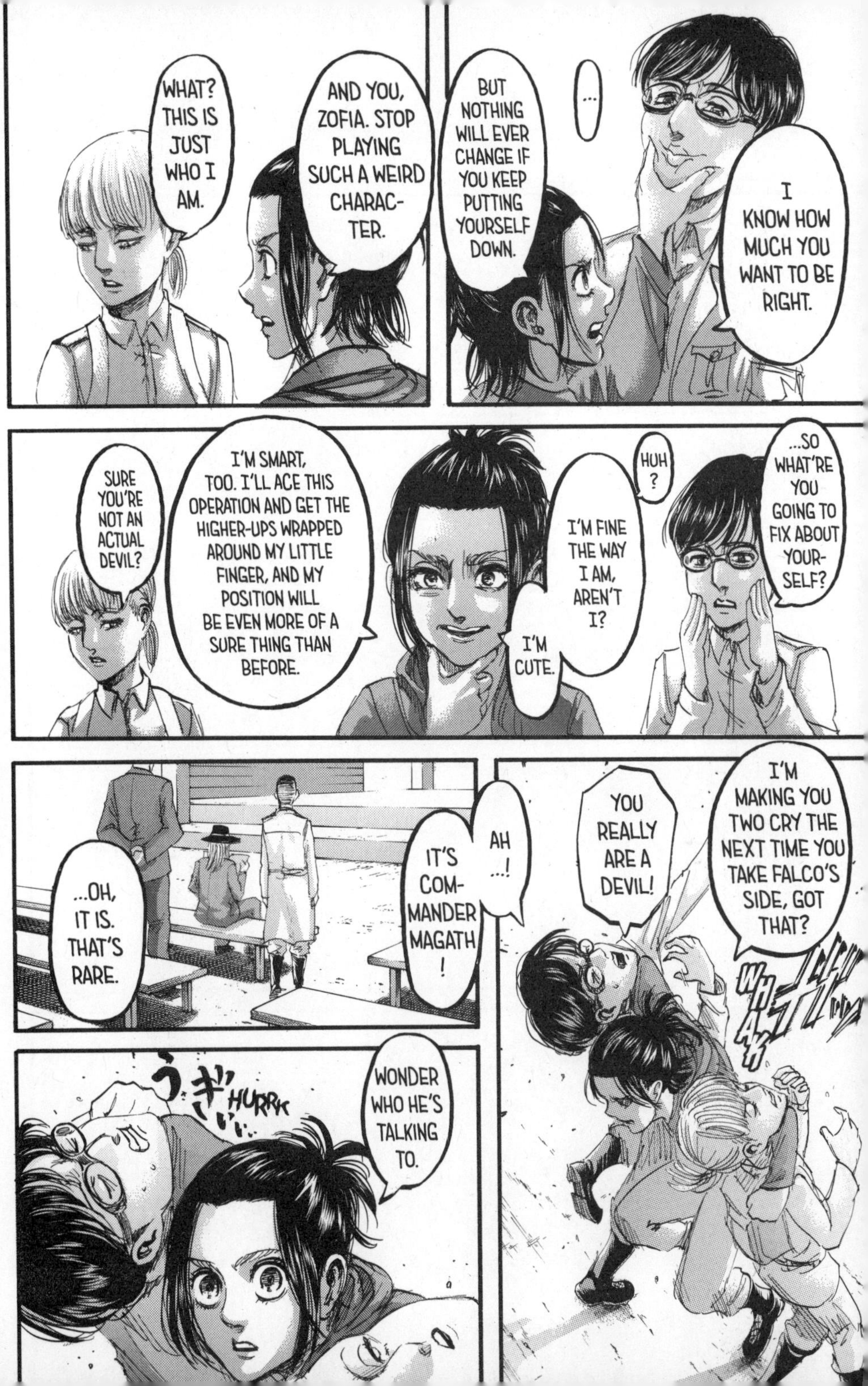
I KNOW HOW MUCH YOU WANT TO BE RIGHT.
...
BUT NOTHING WILL EVER CHANGE IF YOU KEEP PUTTING YOURSELF DOWN.
AND YOU, ZOFIA. STOP PLAYING SUCH A WEIRD CHARAC-TER.
WHAT? THIS IS JUST WHO I AM.
...SO WHAT'RE YOU GOING TO FIX ABOUT YOUR-SELF?
HUH?
I'M FINE THE WAY I AM, AREN'T I?
I'M CUTE.
I'M SMART, TOO. I'LL ACE THIS OPERATION AND GET THE HIGHER-UPS WRAPPED AROUND MY LITTLE FINGER, AND MY POSITION WILL BE EVEN MORE OF A SURE THING THAN BEFORE.
SURE YOU'RE NOT AN ACTUAL DEVIL?
I'M MAKING YOU TWO CRY THE NEXT TIME YOU TAKE FALCO'S SIDE, GOT THAT?
YOU REALLY ARE A DEVIL!
WHAM
AH...!
IT'S COM-MANDER MAGATH!
...OH, IT IS. THAT'S RARE.
WONDER WHO HE'S TALKING TO.
うぎぃぃ
HURRK

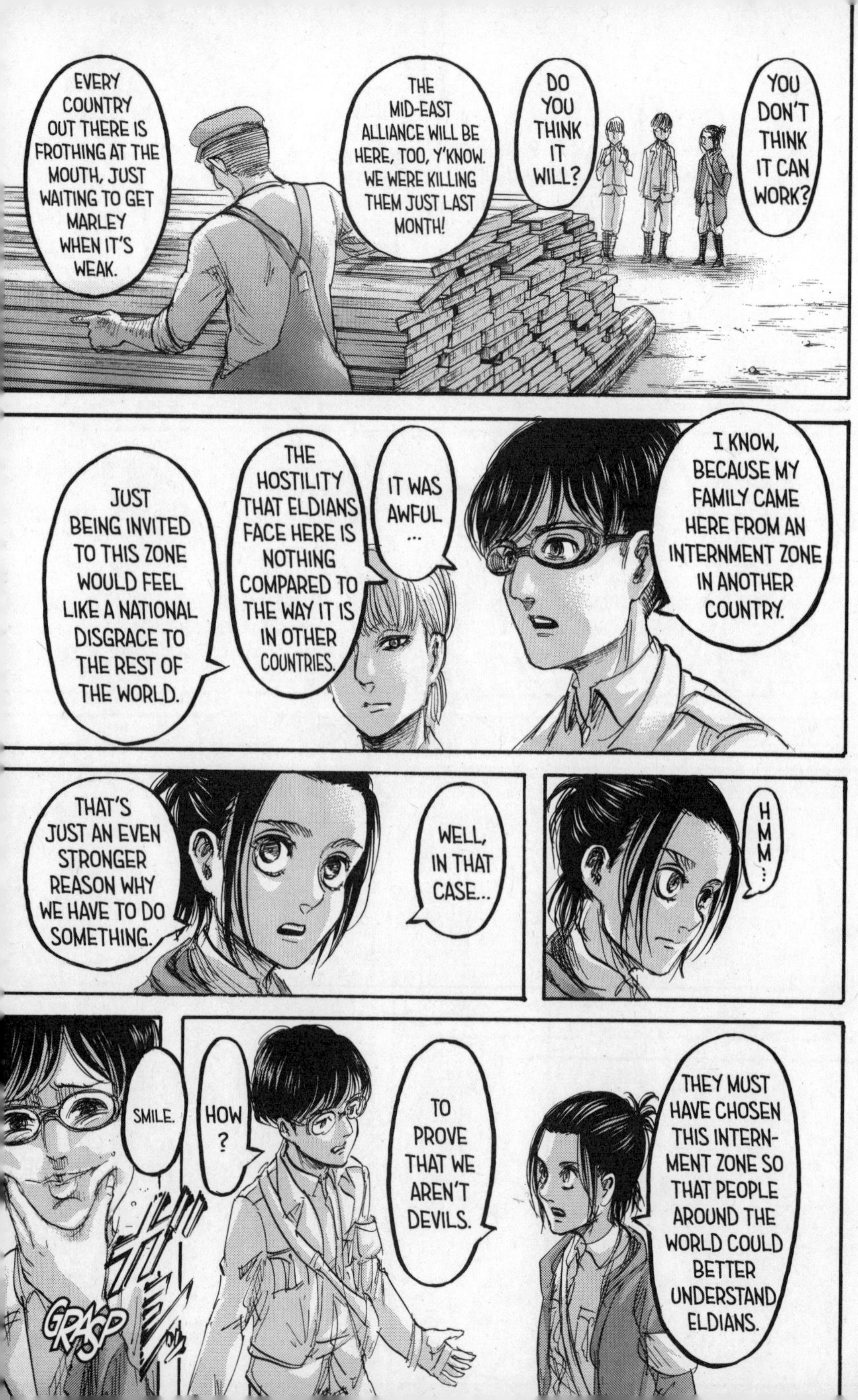
YOU DON'T THINK IT CAN WORK?
DO YOU THINK IT WILL?
THE MID-EAST ALLIANCE WILL BE HERE, TOO, Y'KNOW. WE WERE KILLING THEM JUST LAST MONTH!
EVERY COUNTRY OUT THERE IS FROTHING AT THE MOUTH, JUST WAITING TO GET MARLEY WHEN IT'S WEAK.
I KNOW, BECAUSE MY FAMILY CAME HERE FROM AN INTERNMENT ZONE IN ANOTHER COUNTRY.
IT WAS AWFUL...
THE HOSTILITY THAT ELDIANS FACE HERE IS NOTHING COMPARED TO THE WAY IT IS IN OTHER COUNTRIES.
JUST BEING INVITED TO THIS ZONE WOULD FEEL LIKE A NATIONAL DISGRACE TO THE REST OF THE WORLD.
HMM...
WELL, IN THAT CASE...
THAT'S JUST AN EVEN STRONGER REASON WHY WE HAVE TO DO SOMETHING.
THEY MUST HAVE CHOSEN THIS INTERN-MENT ZONE SO THAT PEOPLE AROUND THE WORLD COULD BETTER UNDERSTAND ELDIANS.
TO PROVE THAT WE AREN'T DEVILS.
HOW?
SMILE.
GRASP

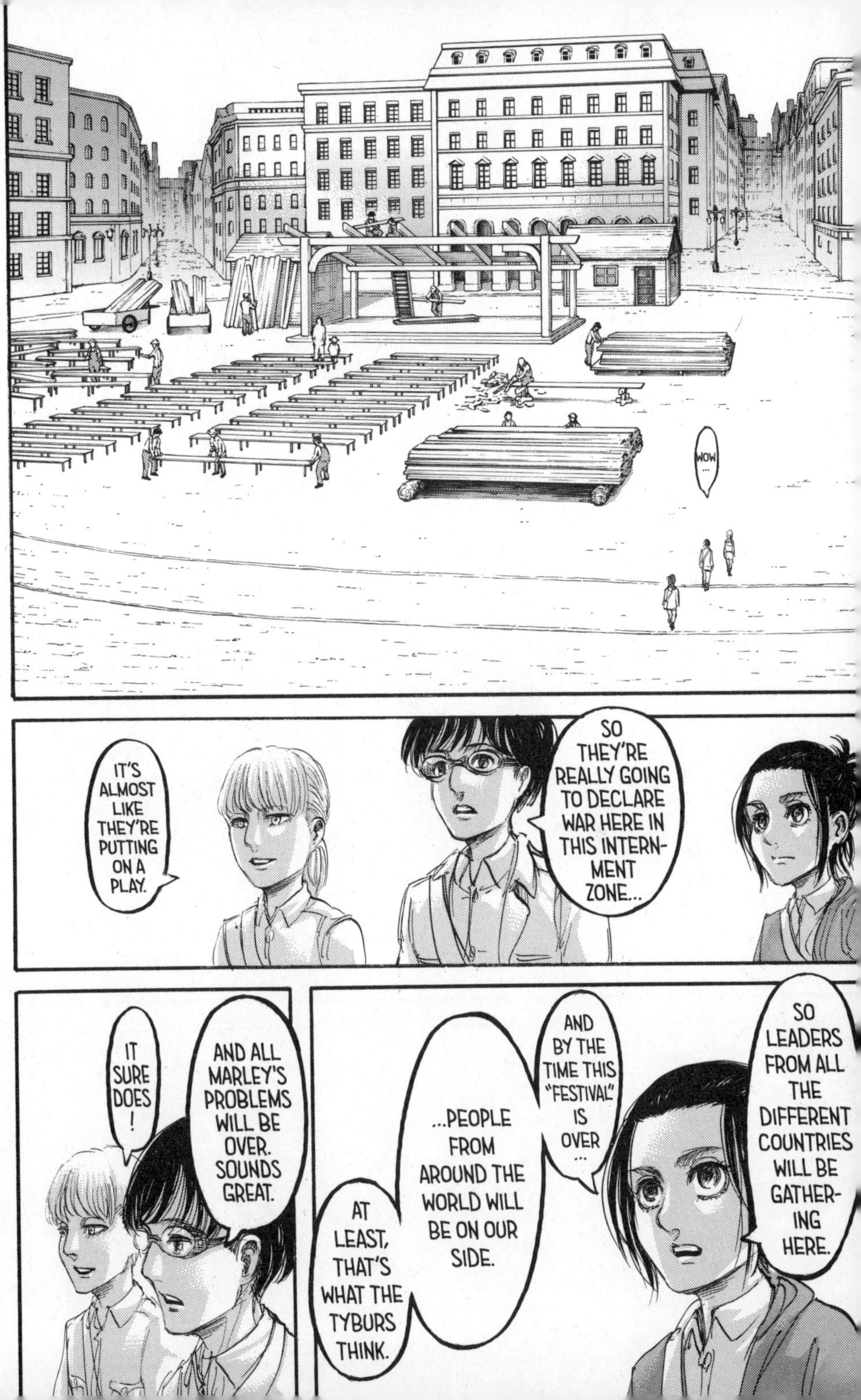
WOW ...
SO THEY'RE REALLY GOING TO DECLARE WAR HERE IN THIS INTERN-MENT ZONE...
IT'S ALMOST LIKE THEY'RE PUTTING ON A PLAY.
SO LEADERS FROM ALL THE DIFFERENT COUNTRIES WILL BE GATHER-ING HERE.
AND BY THE TIME THIS "FESTIVAL" IS OVER ...
...PEOPLE FROM AROUND THE WORLD WILL BE ON OUR SIDE.
AT LEAST, THAT'S WHAT THE TYBURS THINK.
AND ALL MARLEY'S PROBLEMS WILL BE OVER. SOUNDS GREAT.
IT SURE DOES!

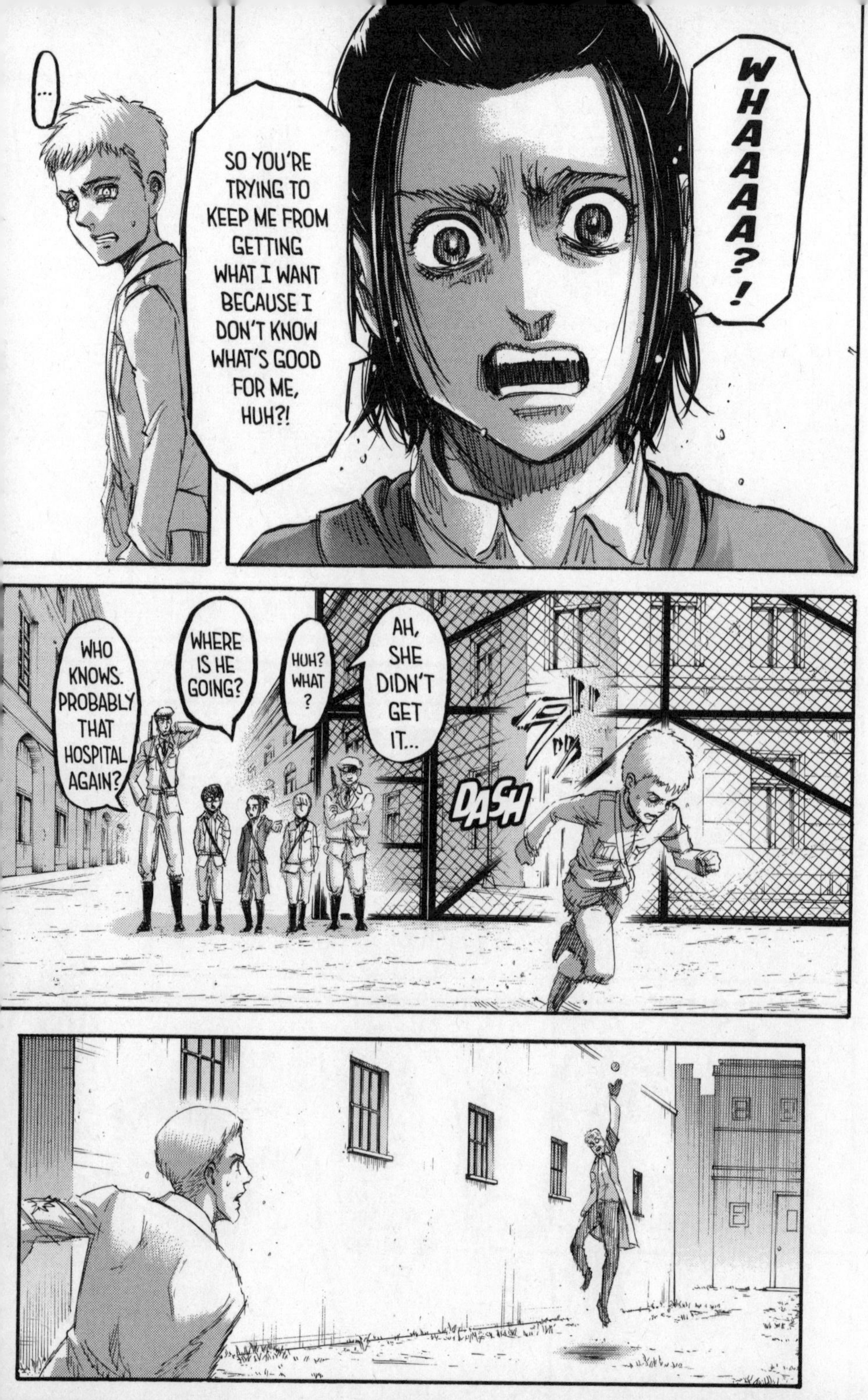
WHAAAAA?!
SO YOU'RE TRYING TO KEEP ME FROM GETTING WHAT I WANT BECAUSE I DON'T KNOW WHAT'S GOOD FOR ME, HUH?!
...
DASH
AH, SHE DIDN'T GET IT...
HUH? WHAT?
WHERE IS HE GOING?
WHO KNOWS. PROBABLY THAT HOSPITAL AGAIN?

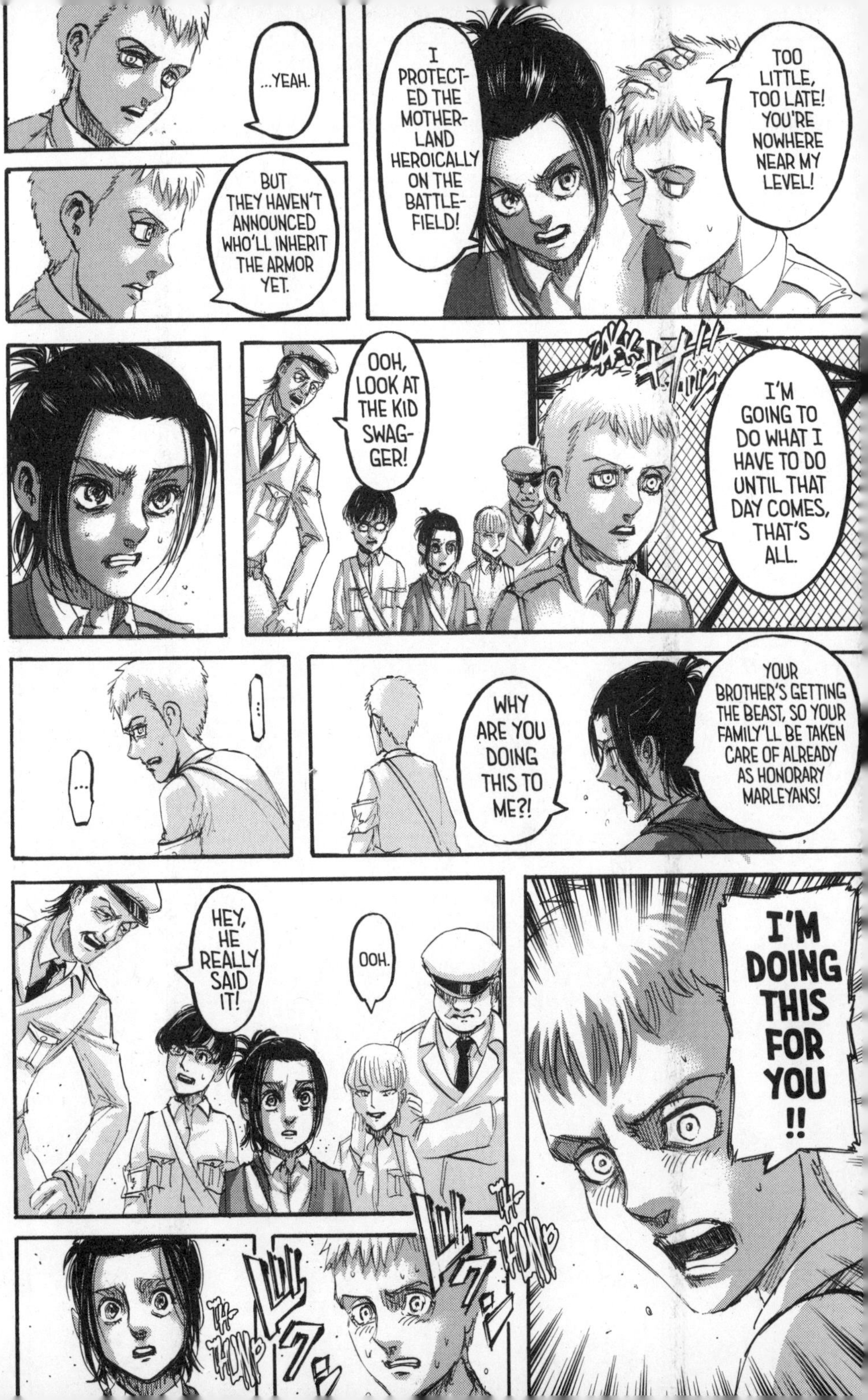
TOO LITTLE, TOO LATE! YOU'RE NOWHERE NEAR MY LEVEL!
I PROTECTED THE MOTHERLAND HEROICALLY ON THE BATTLEFIELD!
...YEAH.
BUT THEY HAVEN'T ANNOUNCED WHO'LL INHERIT THE ARMOR YET.
I'M GOING TO DO WHAT I HAVE TO DO UNTIL THAT DAY COMES, THAT'S ALL.
OOH, LOOK AT THE KID SWAGGER!
YOUR BROTHER'S GETTING THE BEAST, SO YOUR FAMILY'LL BE TAKEN CARE OF ALREADY AS HONORARY MARLEYANS!
WHY ARE YOU DOING THIS TO ME?!
...
...
I'M DOING THIS FOR YOU!!
HEY, HE REALLY SAID IT!
OOH.

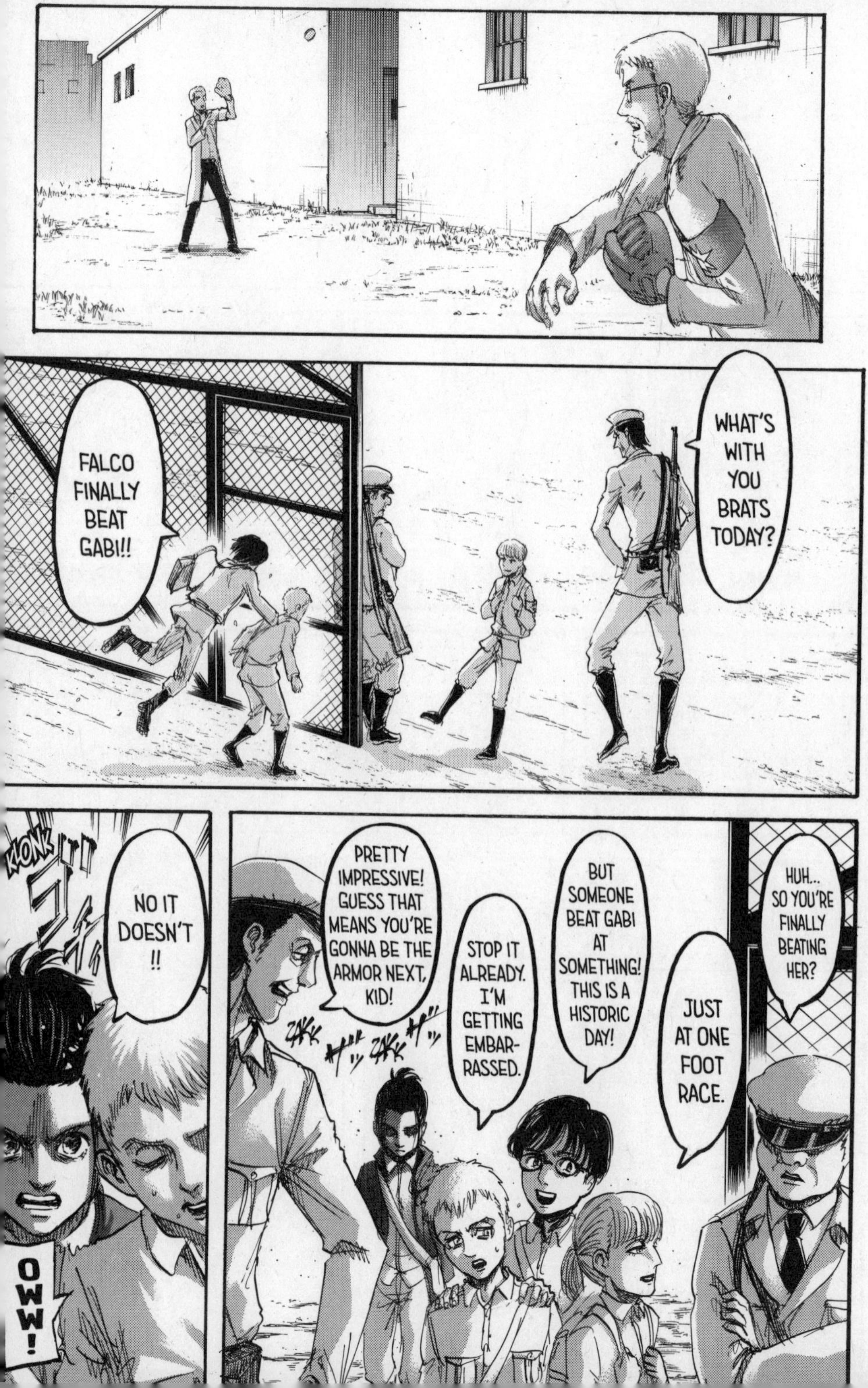
WHAT'S WITH YOU BRATS TODAY?
FALCO FINALLY BEAT GABI!!
HUH... SO YOU'RE FINALLY BEATING HER?
JUST AT ONE FOOT RACE.
BUT SOMEONE BEAT GABI AT SOMETHING! THIS IS A HISTORIC DAY!
STOP IT ALREADY. I'M GETTING EMBARRASSED.
PRETTY IMPRESSIVE! GUESS THAT MEANS YOU'RE GONNA BE THE ARMOR NEXT, KID!
ZAK ZAK
NO IT DOESN'T !!
KONK
OWW!

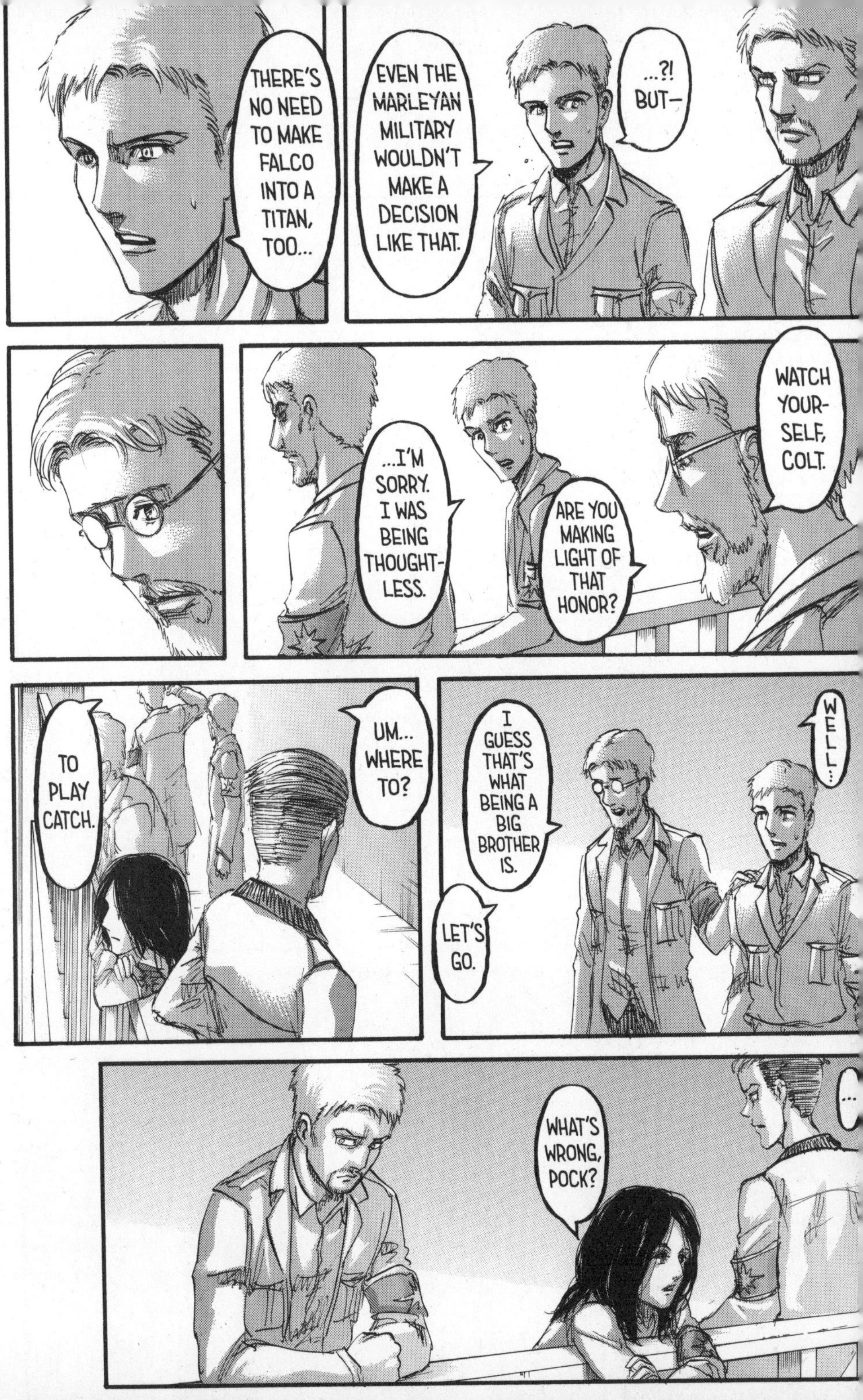
...?! BUT—
EVEN THE MARLEYAN MILITARY WOULDN'T MAKE A DECISION LIKE THAT.
THERE'S NO NEED TO MAKE FALCO INTO A TITAN, TOO...
WATCH YOURSELF, COLT.
ARE YOU MAKING LIGHT OF THAT HONOR?
...I'M SORRY. I WAS BEING THOUGHTLESS.
WELL...
I GUESS THAT'S WHAT BEING A BIG BROTHER IS.
LET'S GO.
UM... WHERE TO?
TO PLAY CATCH.
...
WHAT'S WRONG, POCK?

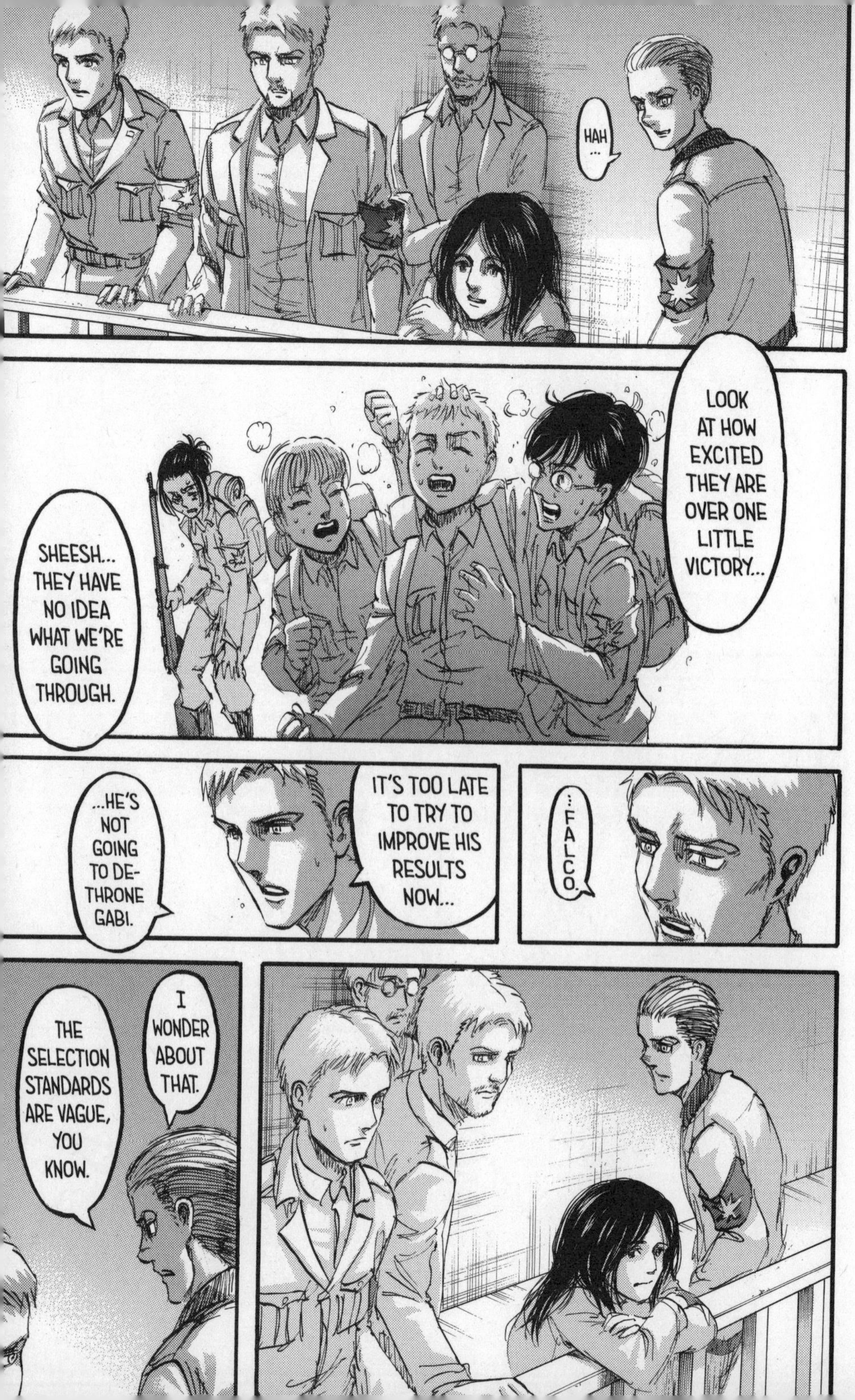
HAH...
LOOK AT HOW EXCITED THEY ARE OVER ONE LITTLE VICTORY...
SHEESH... THEY HAVE NO IDEA WHAT WE'RE GOING THROUGH.
...FALCO.
IT'S TOO LATE TO TRY TO IMPROVE HIS RESULTS NOW...
...HE'S NOT GOING TO DE-THRONE GABI.
I WONDER ABOUT THAT.
THE SELECTION STANDARDS ARE VAGUE, YOU KNOW.

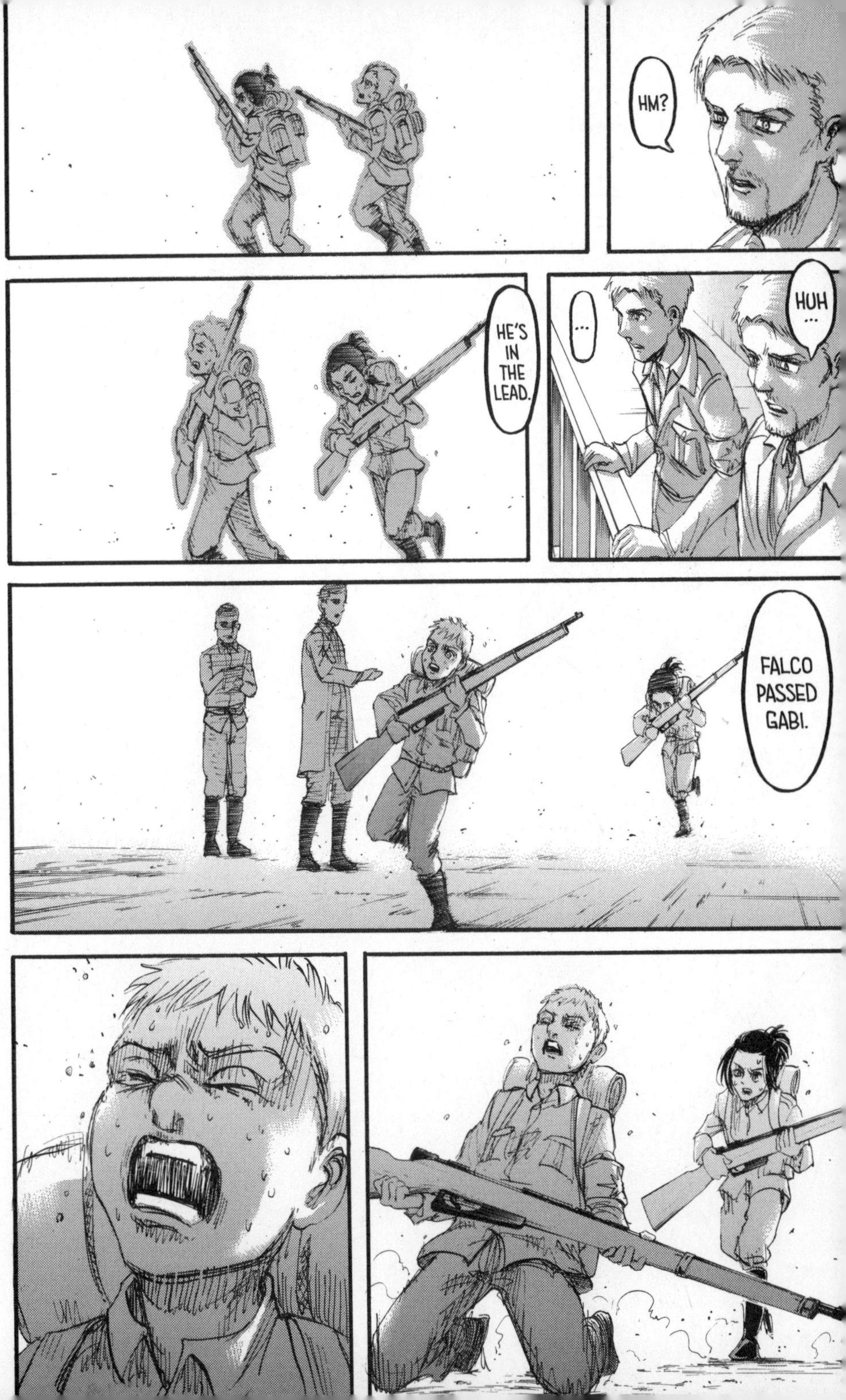
HM?
HUH…
…
HE'S IN THE LEAD.
FALCO PASSED GABI.

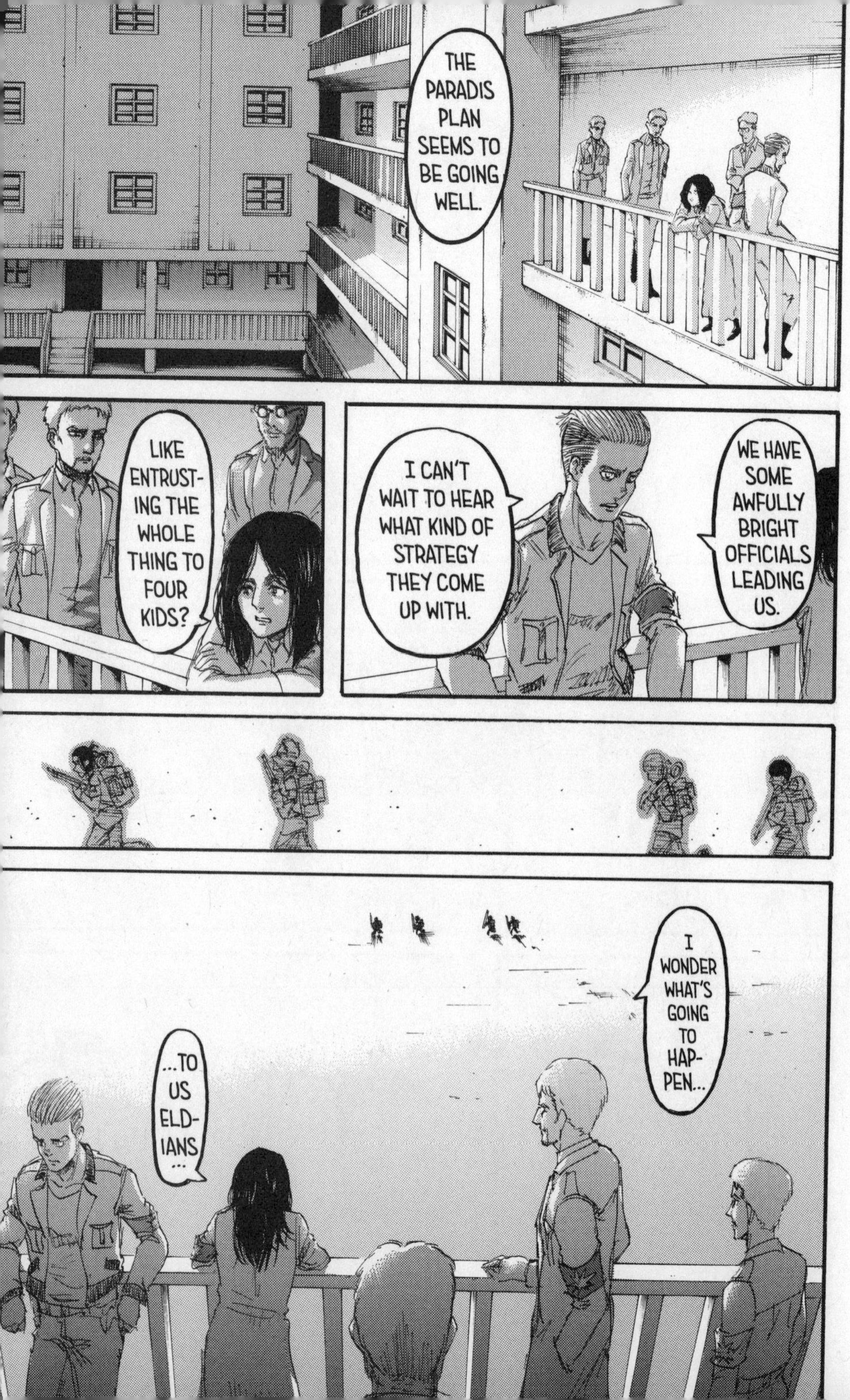
THE PARADIS PLAN SEEMS TO BE GOING WELL.
WE HAVE SOME AWFULLY BRIGHT OFFICIALS LEADING US.
I CAN'T WAIT TO HEAR WHAT KIND OF STRATEGY THEY COME UP WITH.
LIKE ENTRUSTING THE WHOLE THING TO FOUR KIDS?
I WONDER WHAT'S GOING TO HAPPEN...
...TO US ELDIANS...

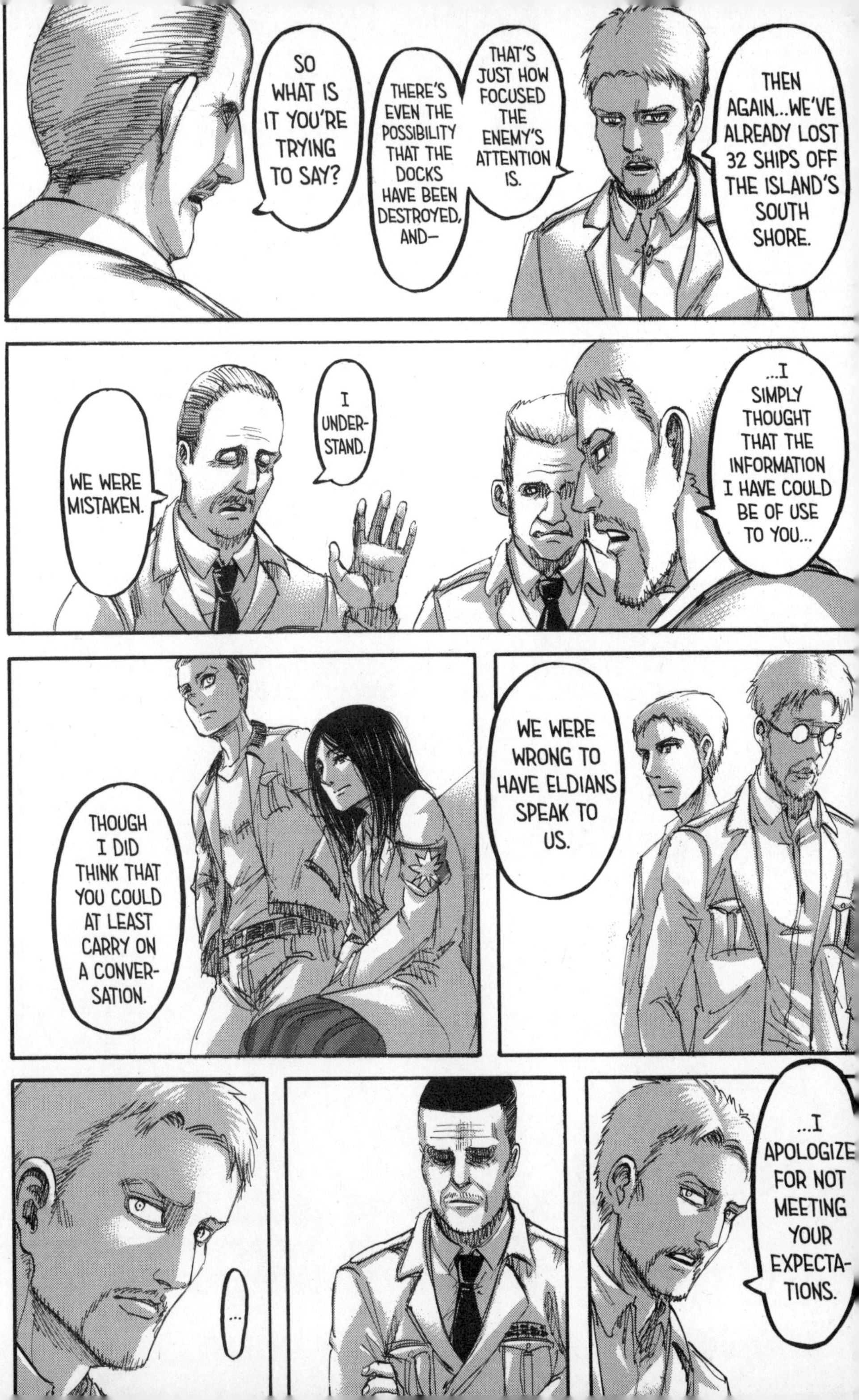
THEN AGAIN...WE'VE ALREADY LOST 32 SHIPS OFF THE ISLAND'S SOUTH SHORE.
THAT'S JUST HOW FOCUSED THE ENEMY'S ATTENTION IS.
THERE'S EVEN THE POSSIBILITY THAT THE DOCKS HAVE BEEN DESTROYED, AND—
SO WHAT IS IT YOU'RE TRYING TO SAY?
...I SIMPLY THOUGHT THAT THE INFORMATION I HAVE COULD BE OF USE TO YOU...
I UNDERSTAND.
WE WERE MISTAKEN.
WE WERE WRONG TO HAVE ELDIANS SPEAK TO US.
THOUGH I DID THINK THAT YOU COULD AT LEAST CARRY ON A CONVERSATION.
...I APOLOGIZE FOR NOT MEETING YOUR EXPECTATIONS.
...

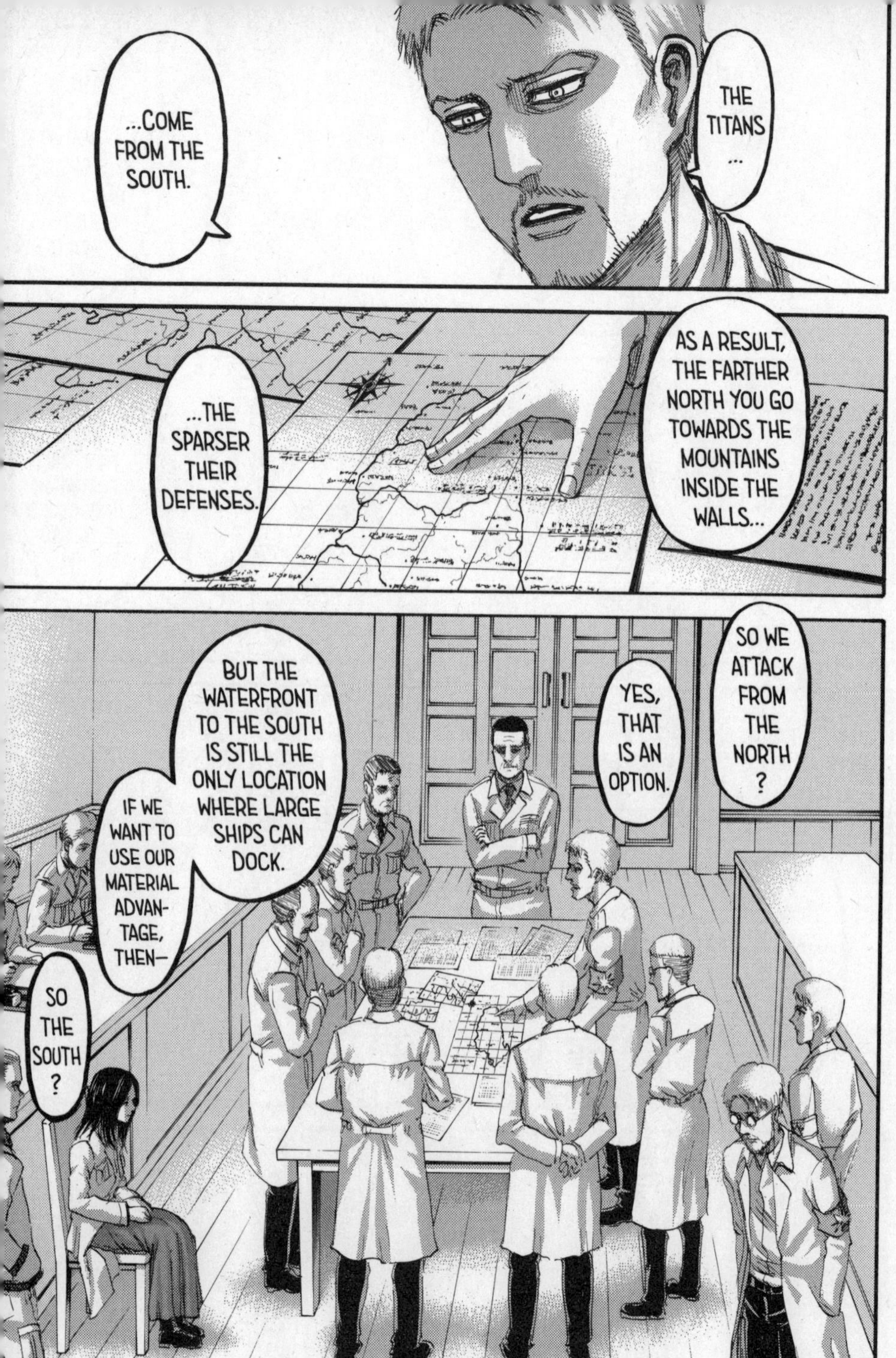
THE TITANS ...
...COME FROM THE SOUTH.
AS A RESULT, THE FARTHER NORTH YOU GO TOWARDS THE MOUNTAINS INSIDE THE WALLS...
...THE SPARSER THEIR DEFENSES.
SO WE ATTACK FROM THE NORTH ?
YES, THAT IS AN OPTION.
BUT THE WATERFRONT TO THE SOUTH IS STILL THE ONLY LOCATION WHERE LARGE SHIPS CAN DOCK.
IF WE WANT TO USE OUR MATERIAL ADVAN-TAGE, THEN—
SO THE SOUTH ?

Episode 98: Good to See

ATTACK on TITAN

パサァ
FSST

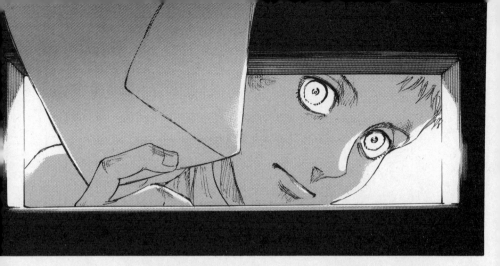

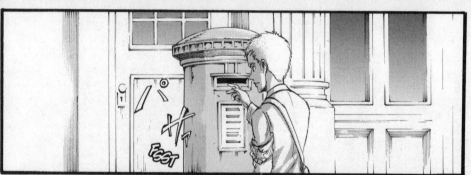

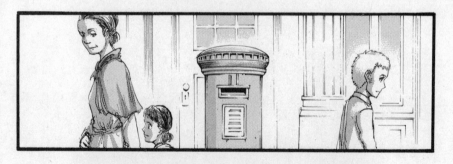

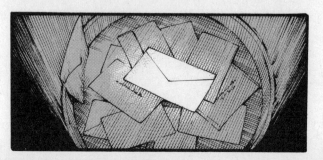

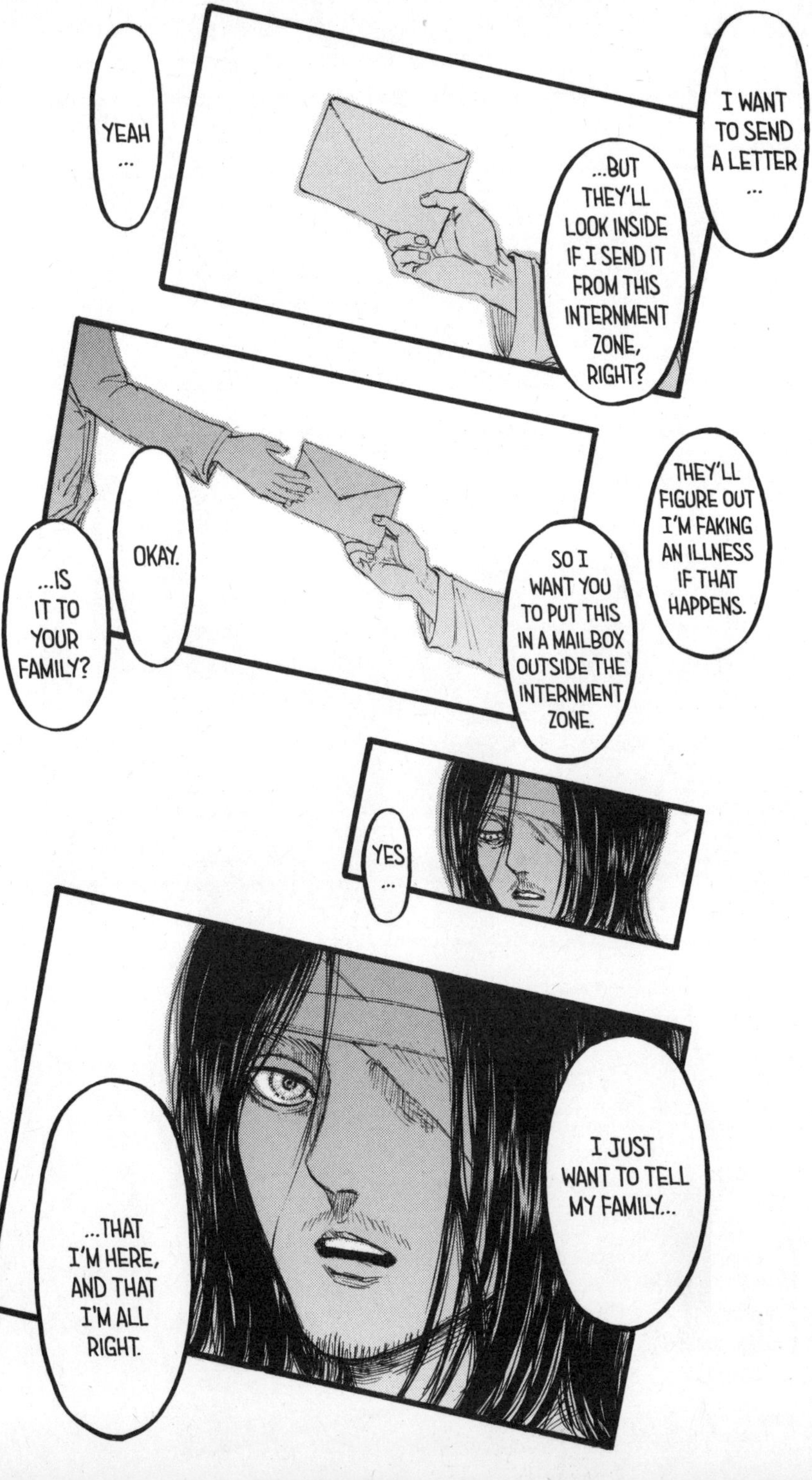
I WANT TO SEND A LETTER ...
...BUT THEY'LL LOOK INSIDE IF I SEND IT FROM THIS INTERNMENT ZONE, RIGHT?
YEAH ...
THEY'LL FIGURE OUT I'M FAKING AN ILLNESS IF THAT HAPPENS.
SO I WANT YOU TO PUT THIS IN A MAILBOX OUTSIDE THE INTERNMENT ZONE.
OKAY.
...IS IT TO YOUR FAMILY?
YES ...
I JUST WANT TO TELL MY FAMILY...
...THAT I'M HERE, AND THAT I'M ALL RIGHT.

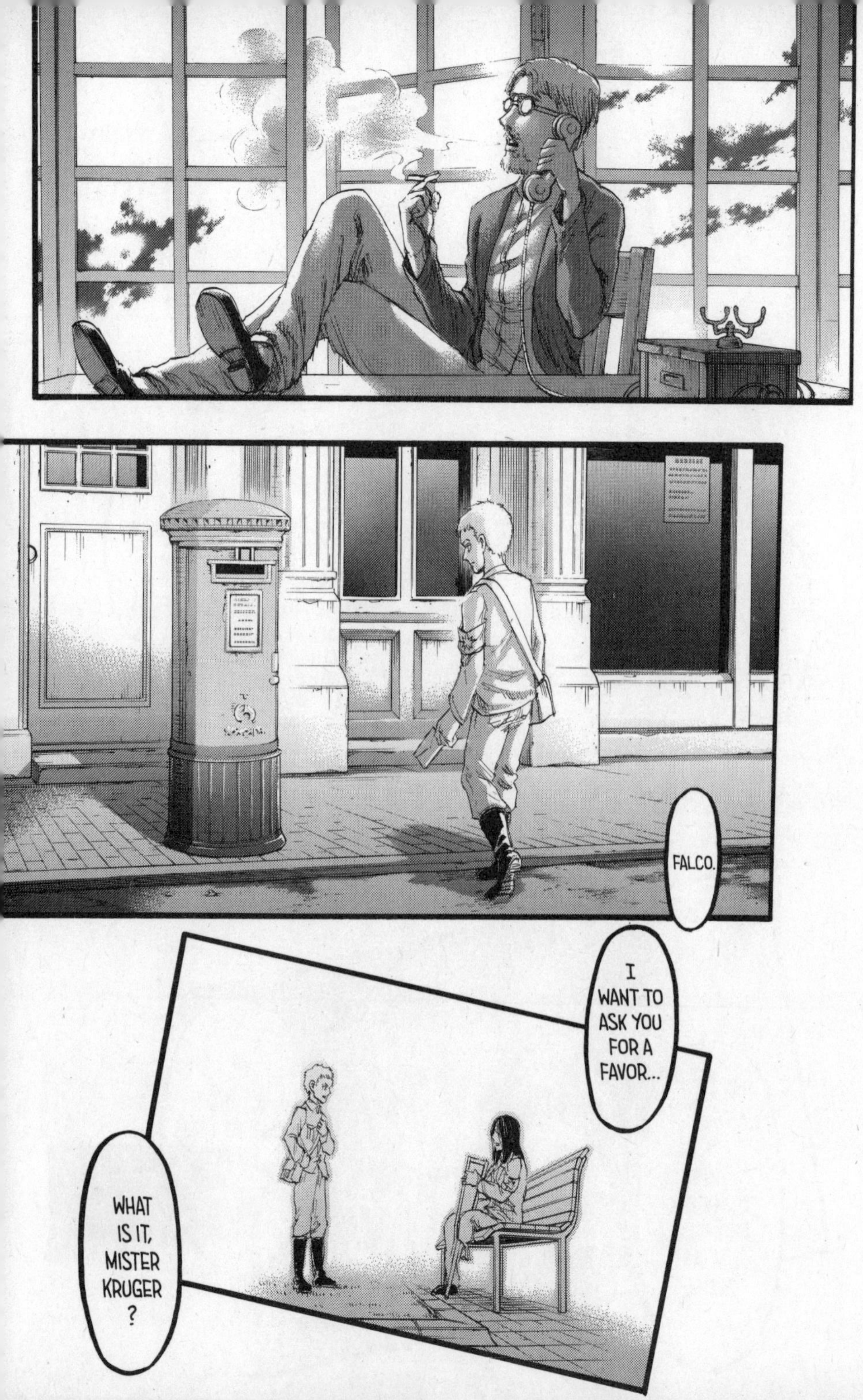
FALCO.
I WANT TO ASK YOU FOR A FAVOR...
WHAT IS IT, MISTER KRUGER?

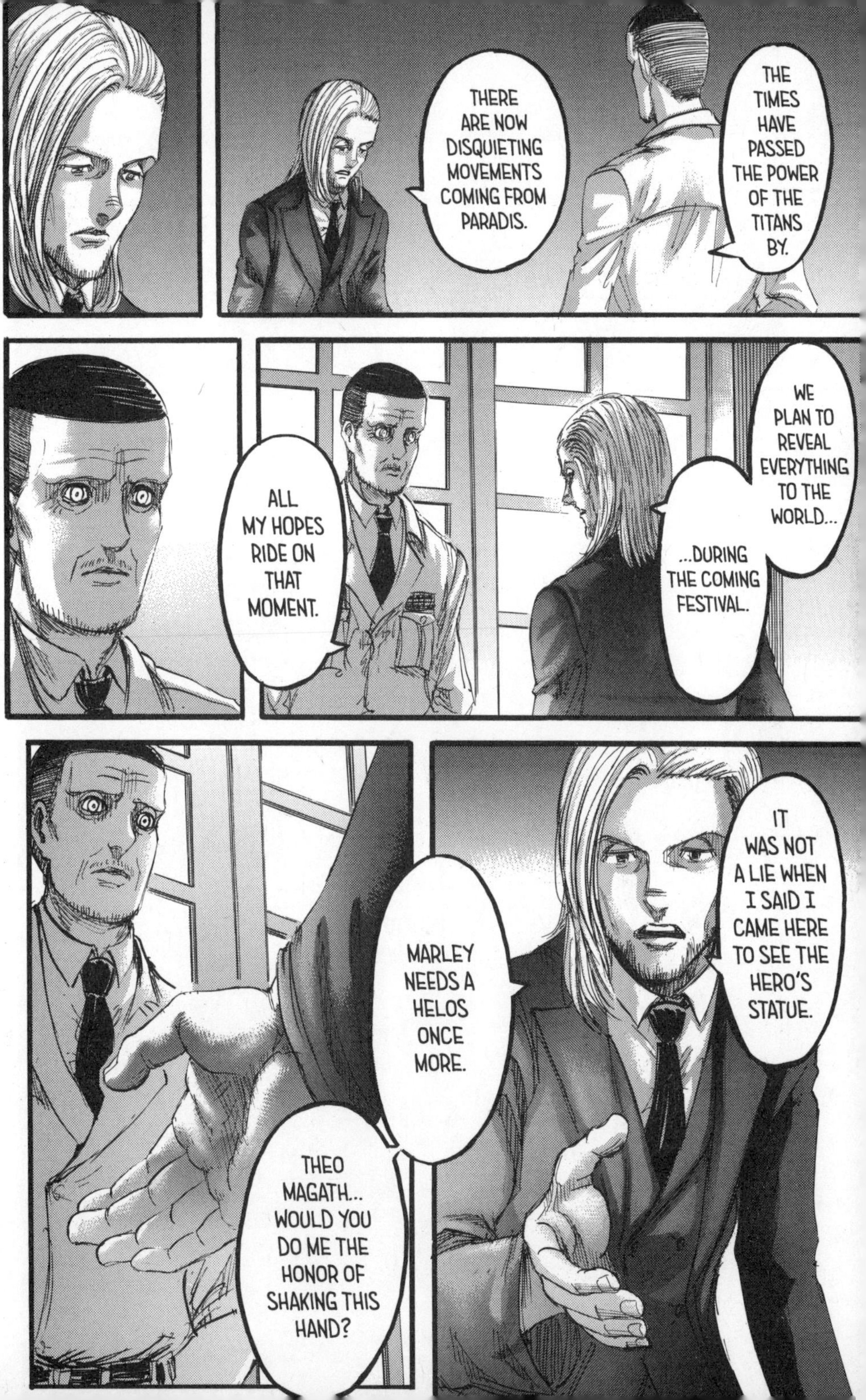
THE TIMES HAVE PASSED THE POWER OF THE TITANS BY.
THERE ARE NOW DISQUIETING MOVEMENTS COMING FROM PARADIS.
WE PLAN TO REVEAL EVERYTHING TO THE WORLD...
...DURING THE COMING FESTIVAL.
ALL MY HOPES RIDE ON THAT MOMENT.
IT WAS NOT A LIE WHEN I SAID I CAME HERE TO SEE THE HERO'S STATUE.
MARLEY NEEDS A HELOS ONCE MORE.
THEO MAGATH... WOULD YOU DO ME THE HONOR OF SHAKING THIS HAND?

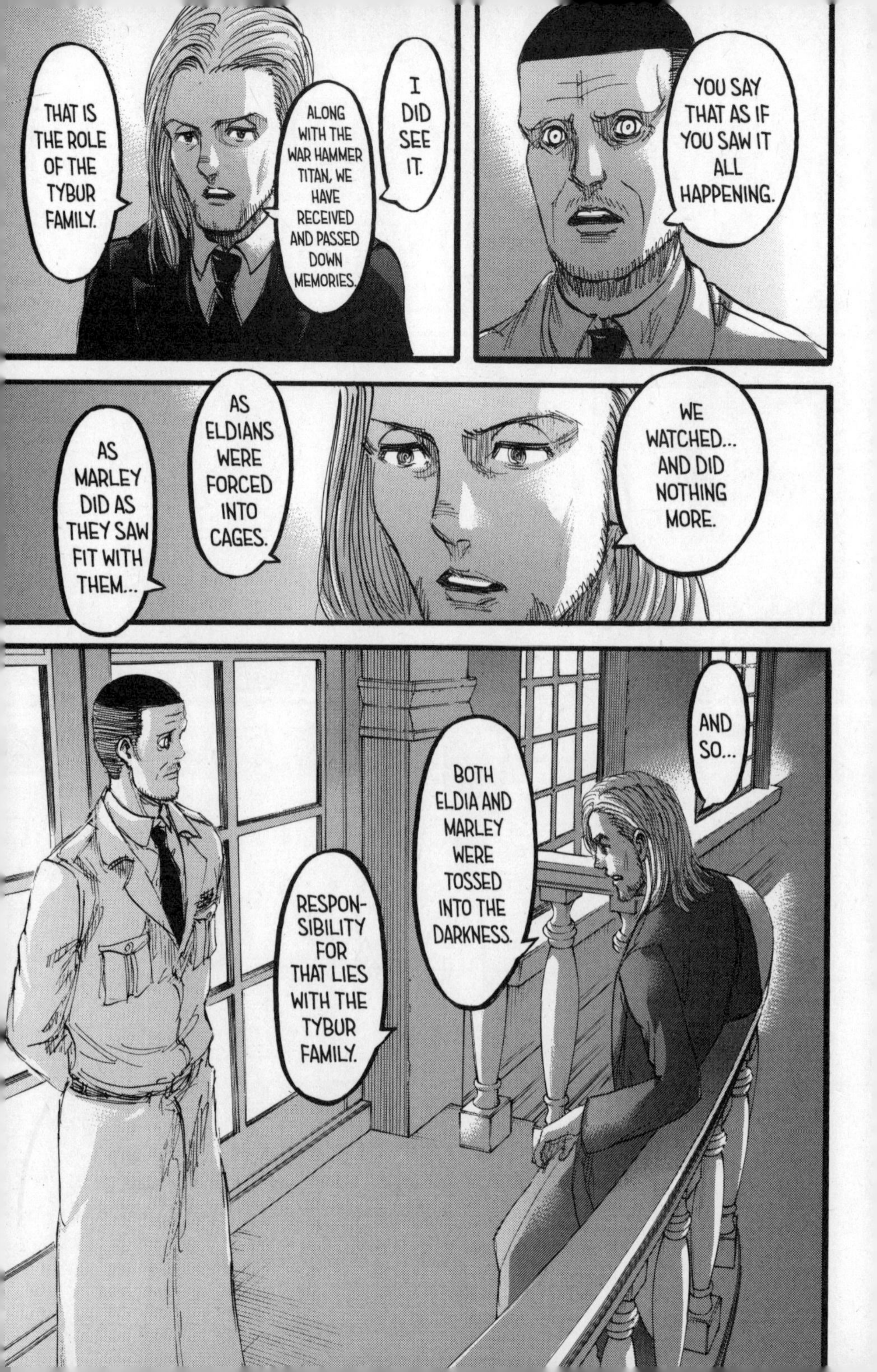
YOU SAY THAT AS IF YOU SAW IT ALL HAPPENING.
I DID SEE IT.
ALONG WITH THE WAR HAMMER TITAN, WE HAVE RECEIVED AND PASSED DOWN MEMORIES.
THAT IS THE ROLE OF THE TYBUR FAMILY.
WE WATCHED... AND DID NOTHING MORE.
AS ELDIANS WERE FORCED INTO CAGES.
AS MARLEY DID AS THEY SAW FIT WITH THEM...
AND SO...
BOTH ELDIA AND MARLEY WERE TOSSED INTO THE DARKNESS.
RESPON-SIBILITY FOR THAT LIES WITH THE TYBUR FAMILY.

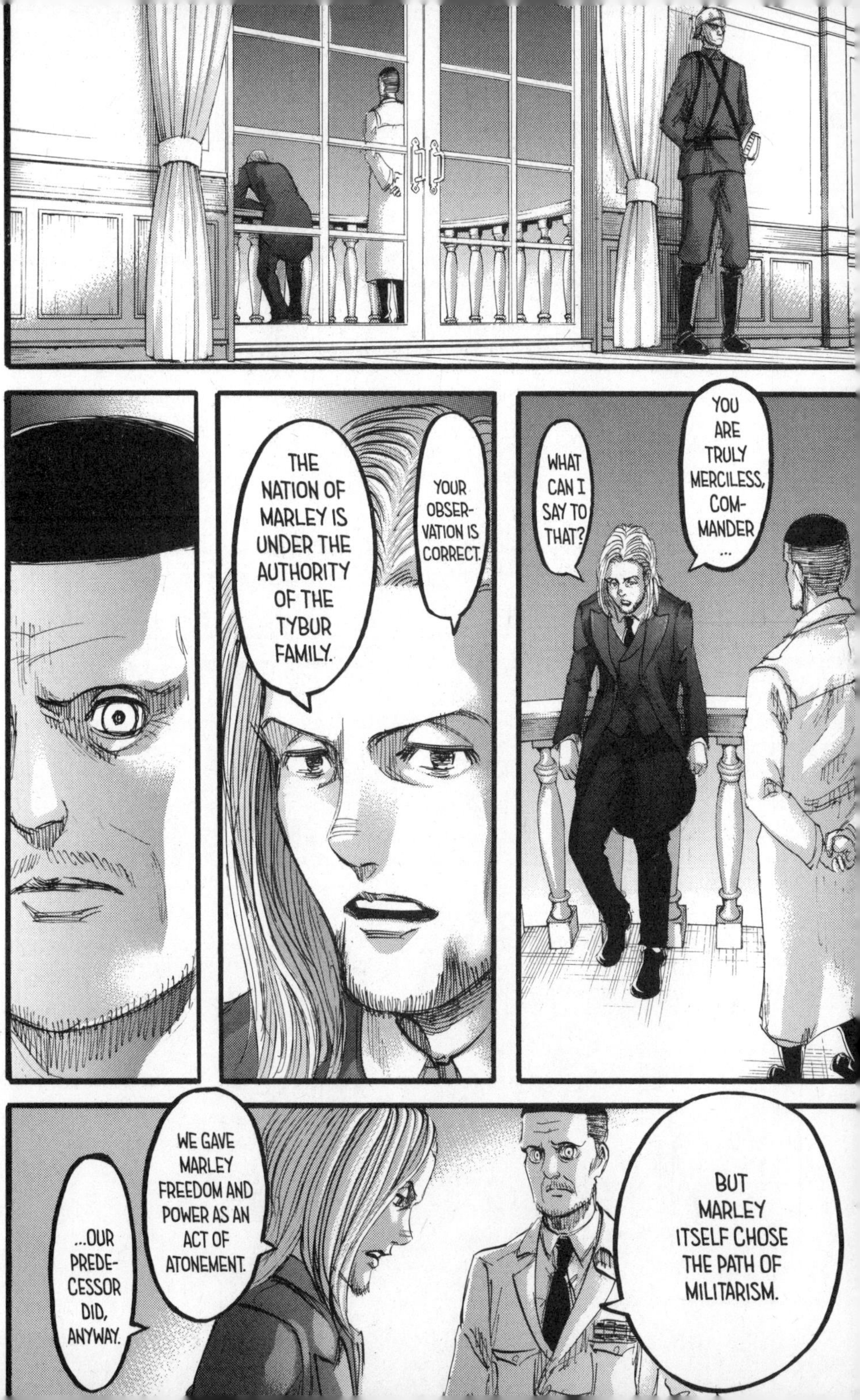
YOU ARE TRULY MERCILESS, COMMANDER...
WHAT CAN I SAY TO THAT?
YOUR OBSERVATION IS CORRECT.
THE NATION OF MARLEY IS UNDER THE AUTHORITY OF THE TYBUR FAMILY.
BUT MARLEY ITSELF CHOSE THE PATH OF MILITARISM.
WE GAVE MARLEY FREEDOM AND POWER AS AN ACT OF ATONEMENT.
...OUR PREDECESSOR DID, ANYWAY.

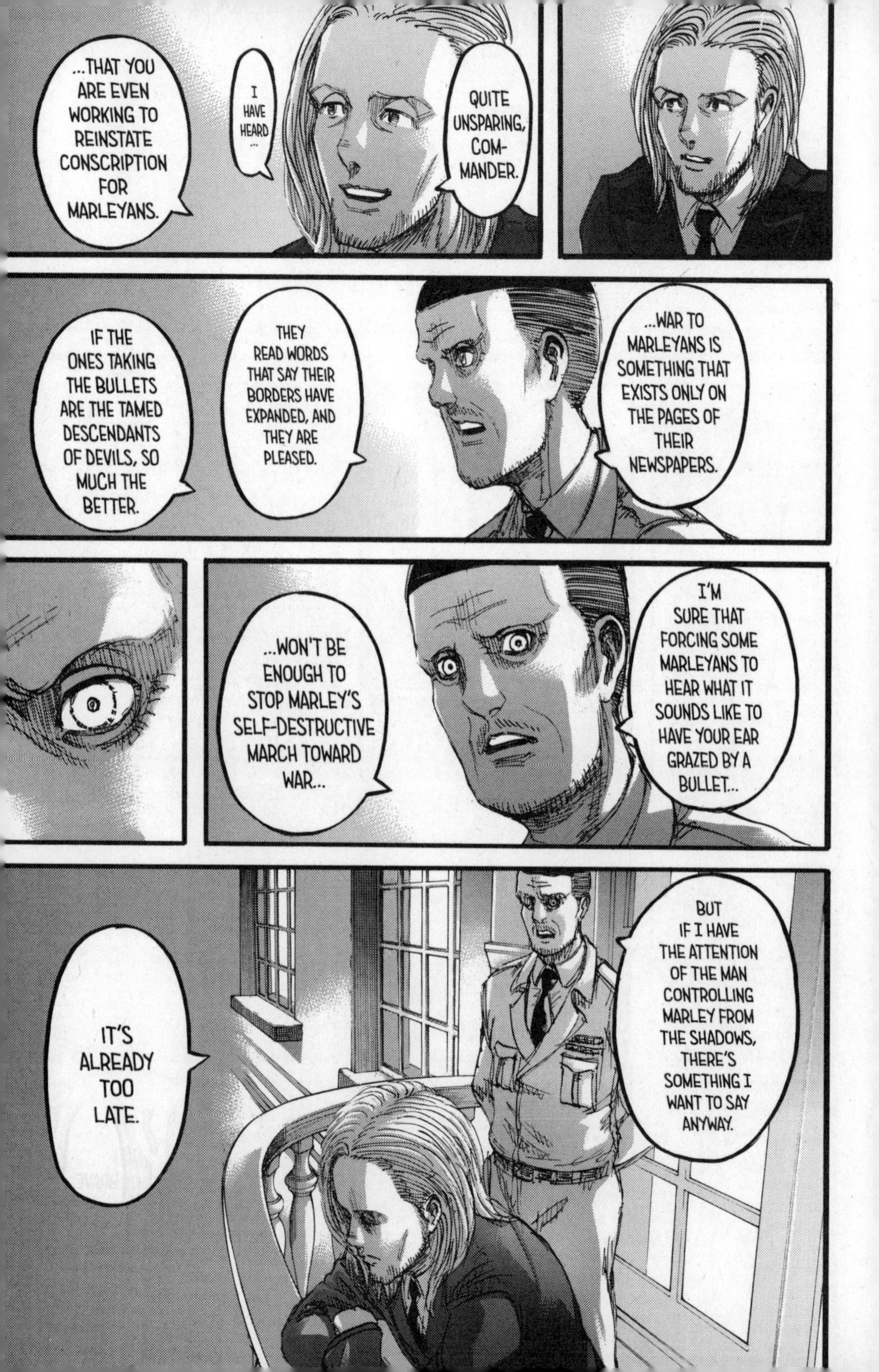
QUITE UNSPARING, COM-MANDER.
I HAVE HEARD...
...THAT YOU ARE EVEN WORKING TO REINSTATE CONSCRIPTION FOR MARLEYANS.
...WAR TO MARLEYANS IS SOMETHING THAT EXISTS ONLY ON THE PAGES OF THEIR NEWSPAPERS.
THEY READ WORDS THAT SAY THEIR BORDERS HAVE EXPANDED, AND THEY ARE PLEASED.
IF THE ONES TAKING THE BULLETS ARE THE TAMED DESCENDANTS OF DEVILS, SO MUCH THE BETTER.
I'M SURE THAT FORCING SOME MARLEYANS TO HEAR WHAT IT SOUNDS LIKE TO HAVE YOUR EAR GRAZED BY A BULLET...
...WON'T BE ENOUGH TO STOP MARLEY'S SELF-DESTRUCTIVE MARCH TOWARD WAR...
BUT IF I HAVE THE ATTENTION OF THE MAN CONTROLLING MARLEY FROM THE SHADOWS, THERE'S SOMETHING I WANT TO SAY ANYWAY.
IT'S ALREADY TOO LATE.

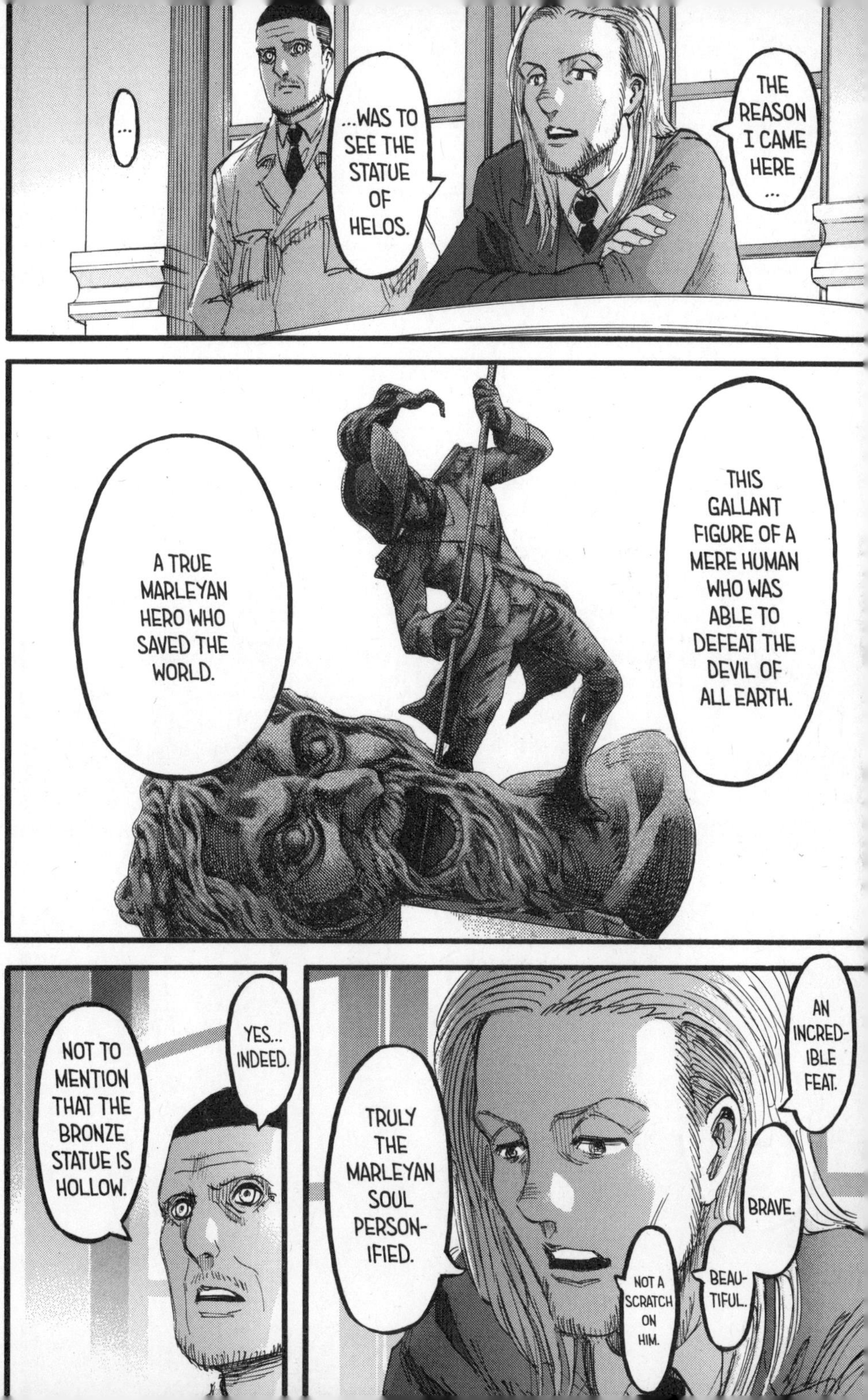
THE REASON I CAME HERE ...
...WAS TO SEE THE STATUE OF HELOS.
...
THIS GALLANT FIGURE OF A MERE HUMAN WHO WAS ABLE TO DEFEAT THE DEVIL OF ALL EARTH.
A TRUE MARLEYAN HERO WHO SAVED THE WORLD.
AN INCREDIBLE FEAT.
BRAVE.
BEAUTIFUL.
NOT A SCRATCH ON HIM.
TRULY THE MARLEYAN SOUL PERSONIFIED.
YES... INDEED.
NOT TO MENTION THAT THE BRONZE STATUE IS HOLLOW.

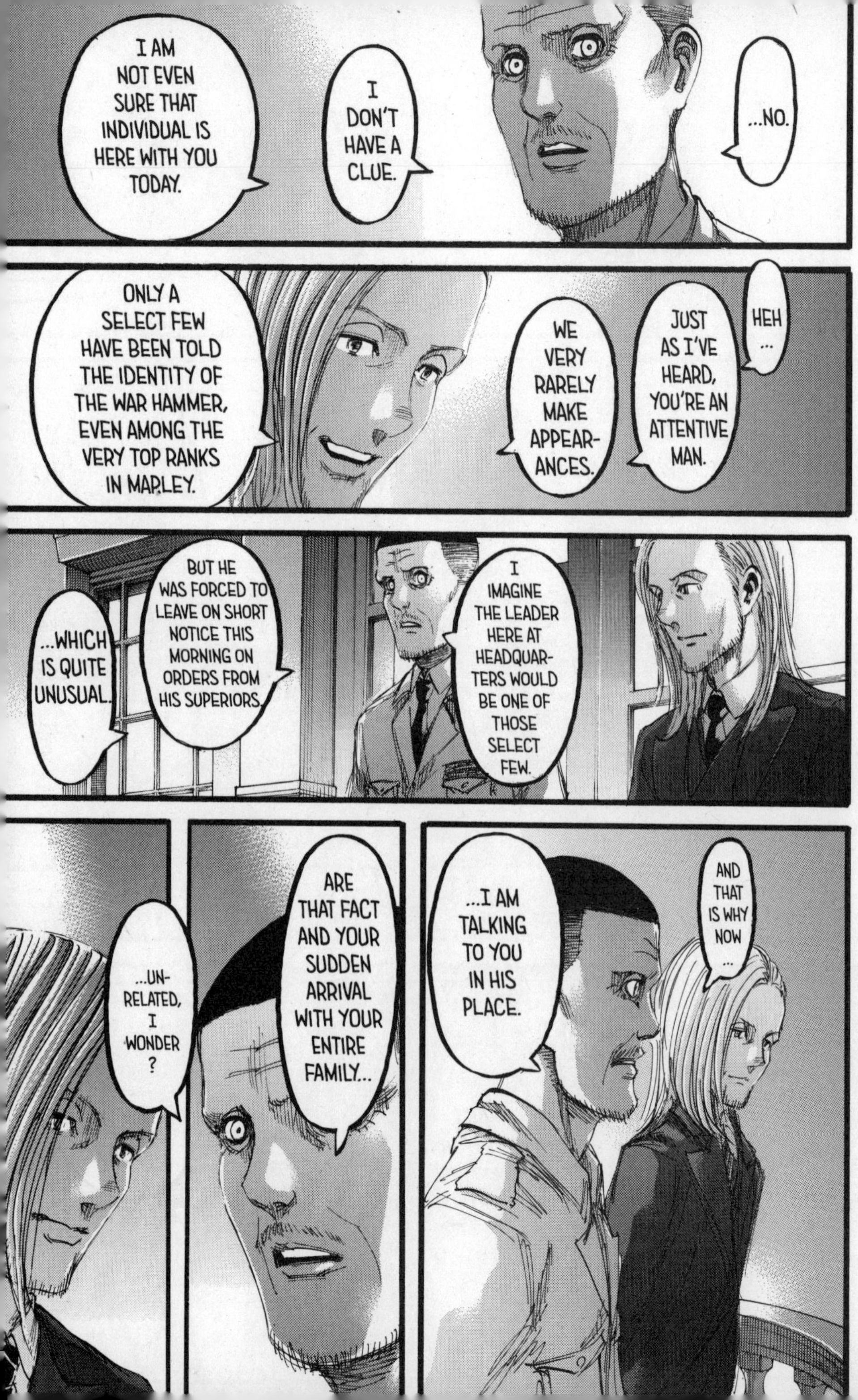
...NO.
I DON'T HAVE A CLUE.
I AM NOT EVEN SURE THAT INDIVIDUAL IS HERE WITH YOU TODAY.
HEH ...
JUST AS I'VE HEARD, YOU'RE AN ATTENTIVE MAN.
WE VERY RARELY MAKE APPEARANCES.
ONLY A SELECT FEW HAVE BEEN TOLD THE IDENTITY OF THE WAR HAMMER, EVEN AMONG THE VERY TOP RANKS IN MARLEY.
I IMAGINE THE LEADER HERE AT HEADQUARTERS WOULD BE ONE OF THOSE SELECT FEW.
BUT HE WAS FORCED TO LEAVE ON SHORT NOTICE THIS MORNING ON ORDERS FROM HIS SUPERIORS.
...WHICH IS QUITE UNUSUAL.
AND THAT IS WHY NOW ...
...I AM TALKING TO YOU IN HIS PLACE.
ARE THAT FACT AND YOUR SUDDEN ARRIVAL WITH YOUR ENTIRE FAMILY...
...UNRELATED, I WONDER?

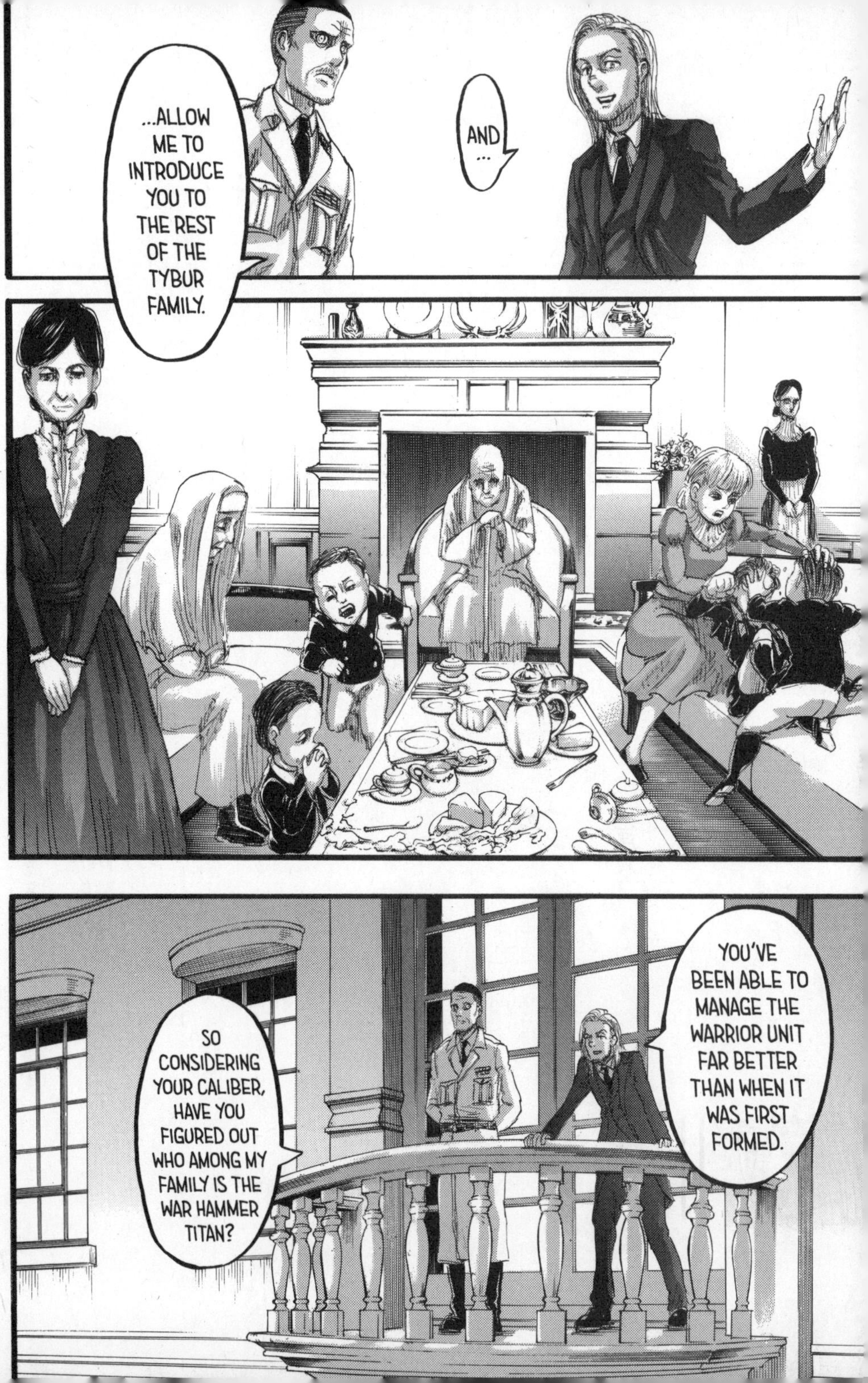
AND ...
...ALLOW ME TO INTRODUCE YOU TO THE REST OF THE TYBUR FAMILY.
YOU'VE BEEN ABLE TO MANAGE THE WARRIOR UNIT FAR BETTER THAN WHEN IT WAS FIRST FORMED.
SO CONSIDERING YOUR CALIBER, HAVE YOU FIGURED OUT WHO AMONG MY FAMILY IS THE WAR HAMMER TITAN?

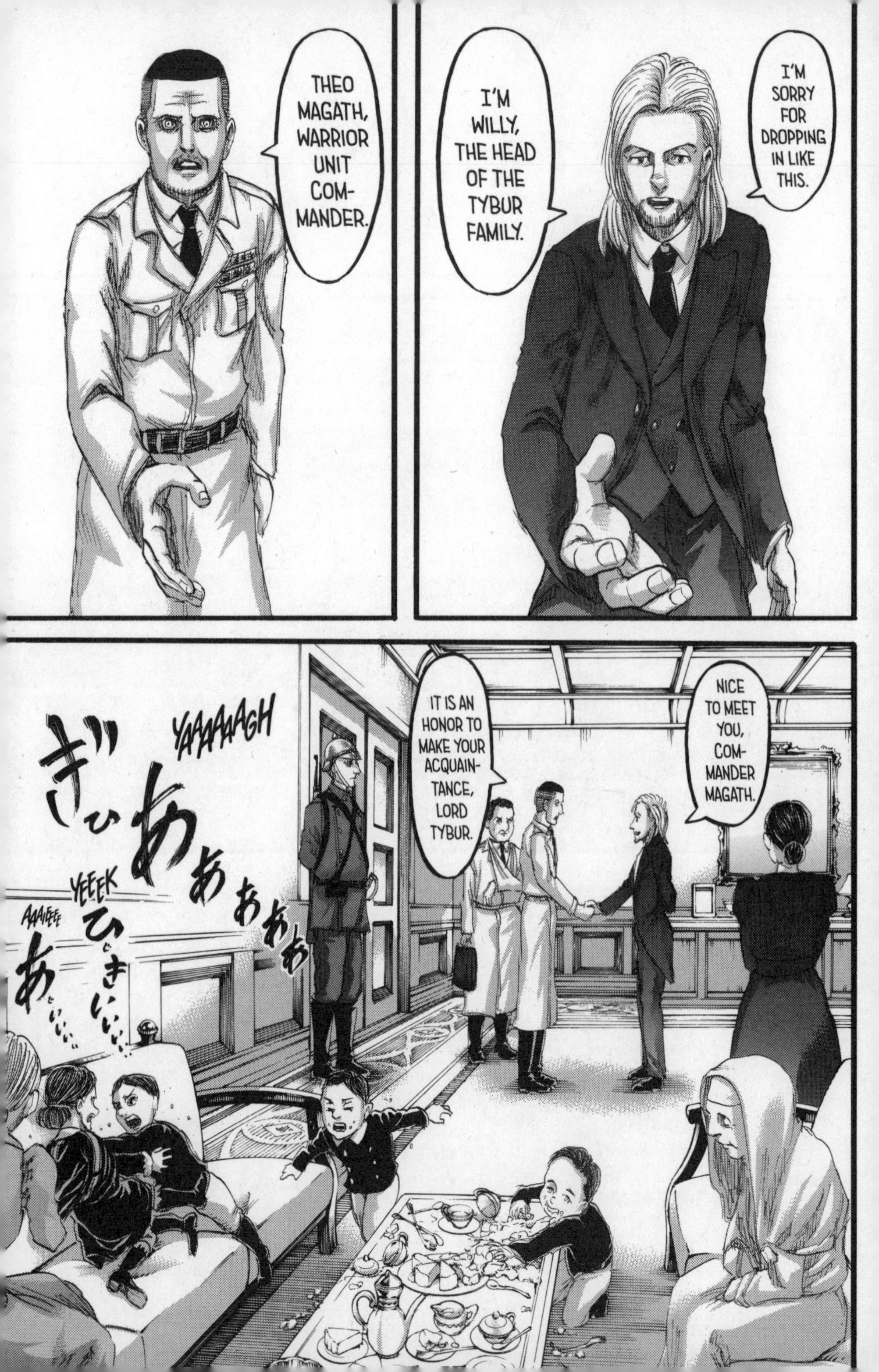
I'M SORRY FOR DROPPING IN LIKE THIS.
I'M WILLY, THE HEAD OF THE TYBUR FAMILY.
THEO MAGATH, WARRIOR UNIT COM-MANDER.
NICE TO MEET YOU, COM-MANDER MAGATH.
IT IS AN HONOR TO MAKE YOUR ACQUAIN-TANCE, LORD TYBUR.
YAAAAAAGH
YEEEK
AAAIEEEE

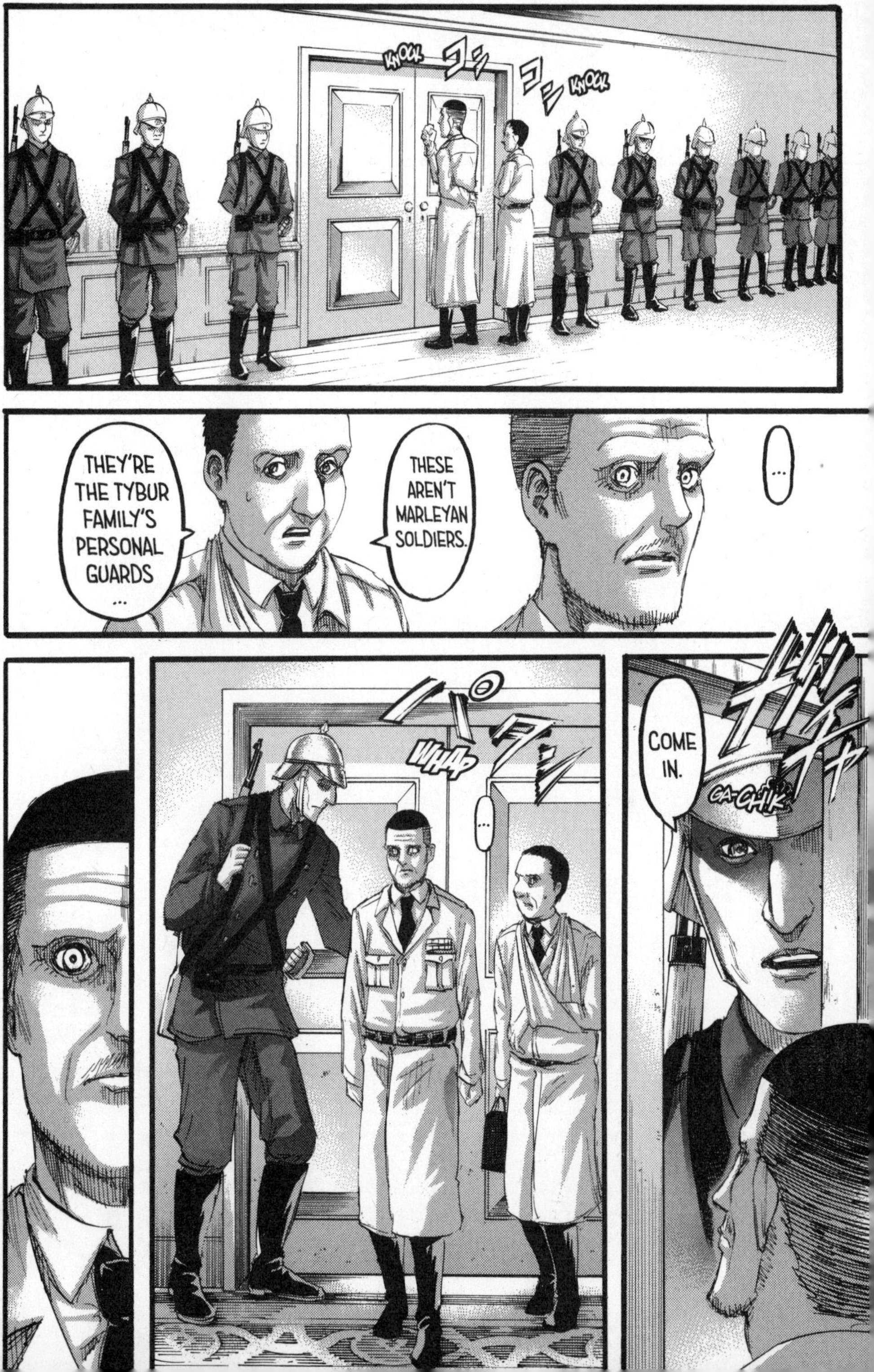
KNOCK
KNOCK
...
THESE AREN'T MARLEYAN SOLDIERS.
THEY'RE THE TYBUR FAMILY'S PERSONAL GUARDS ...
COME IN.
CA-CHIK
WHAP
...

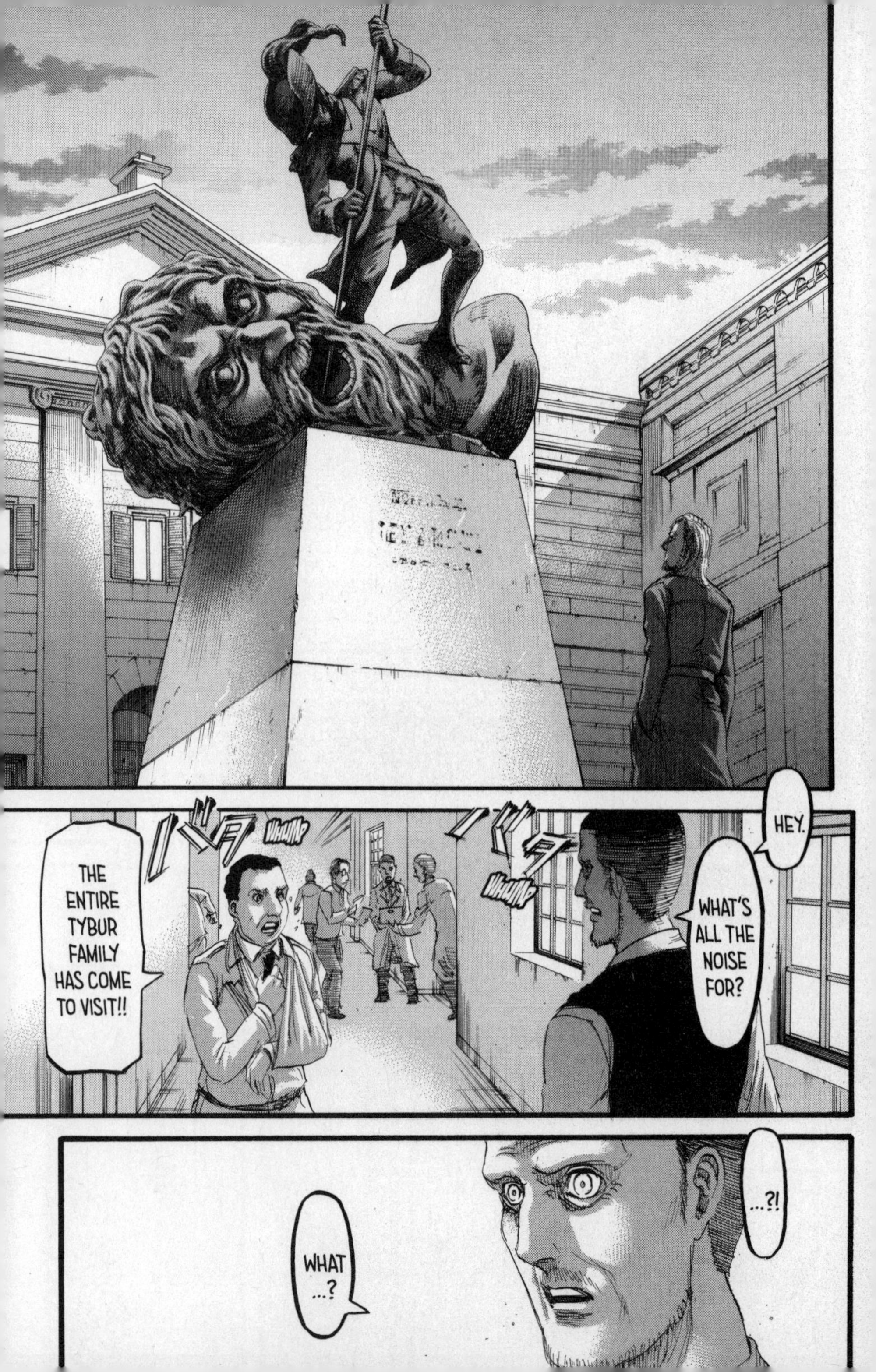
HEY.
WHAT'S ALL THE NOISE FOR?
WHUMP
WHUMP
THE ENTIRE TYBUR FAMILY HAS COME TO VISIT!!
...?!
WHAT ...?

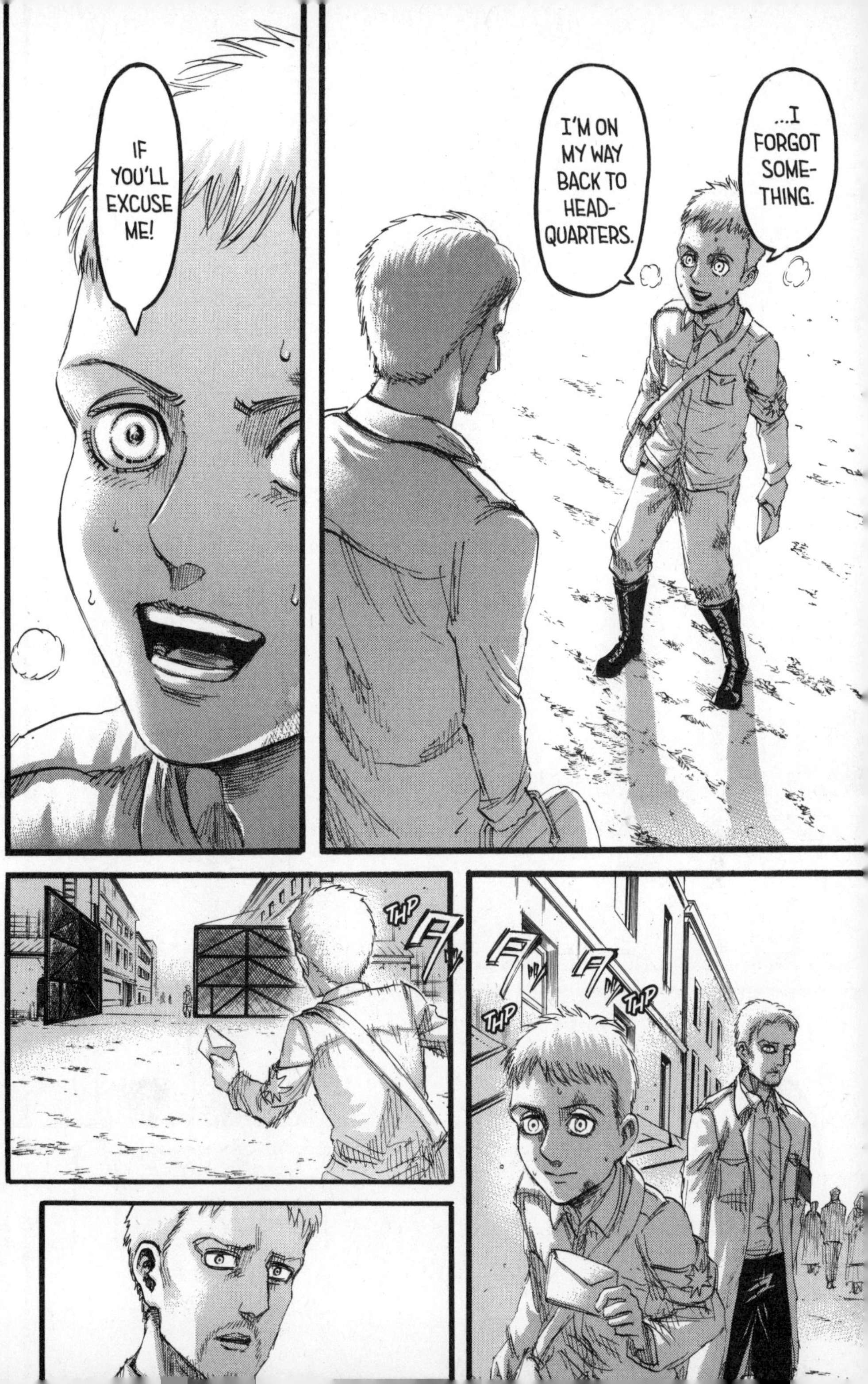
...I FORGOT SOME-THING.
I'M ON MY WAY BACK TO HEAD-QUARTERS.
IF YOU'LL EXCUSE ME!
THP
THP
THP

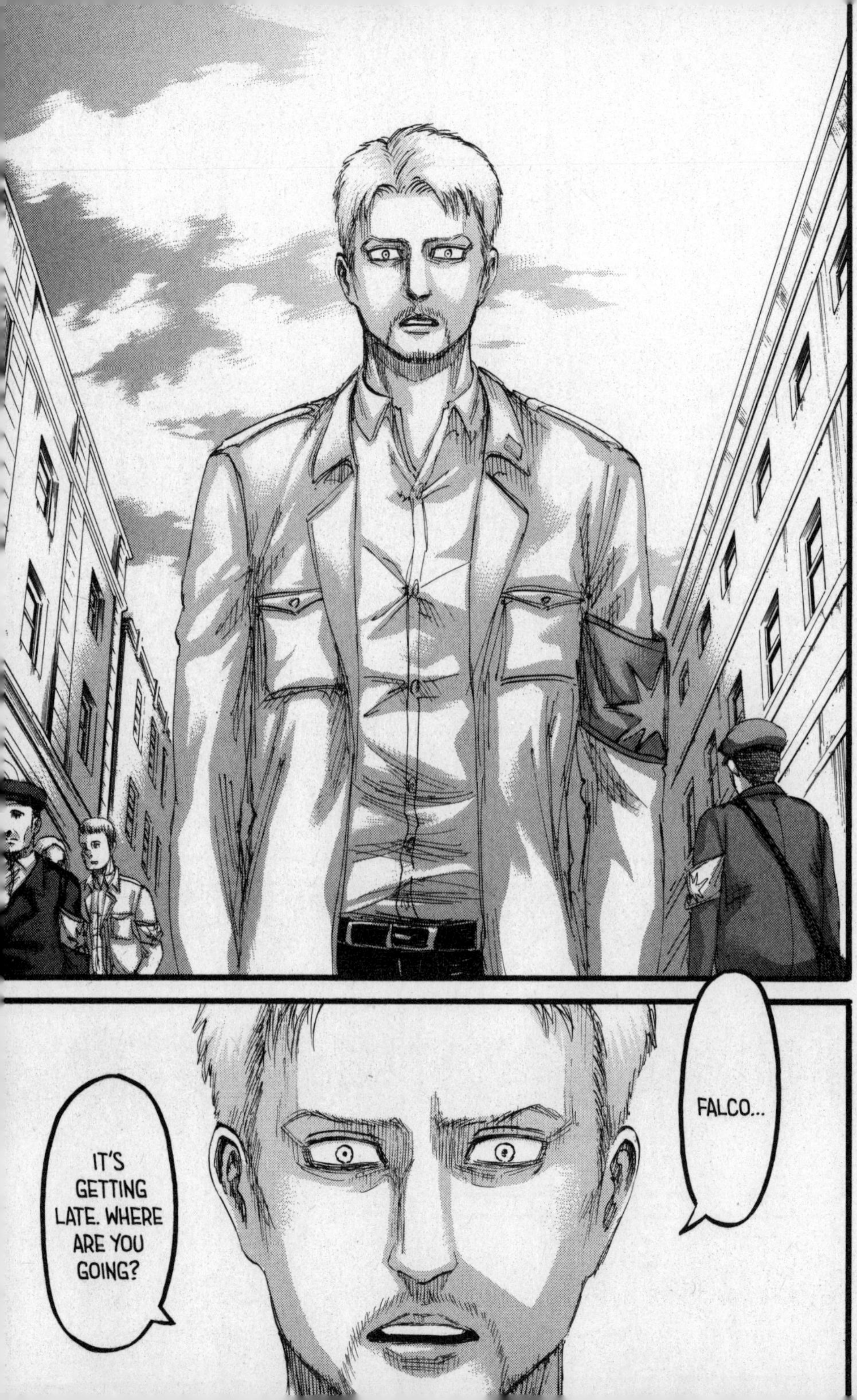
FALCO...
IT'S GETTING LATE. WHERE ARE YOU GOING?

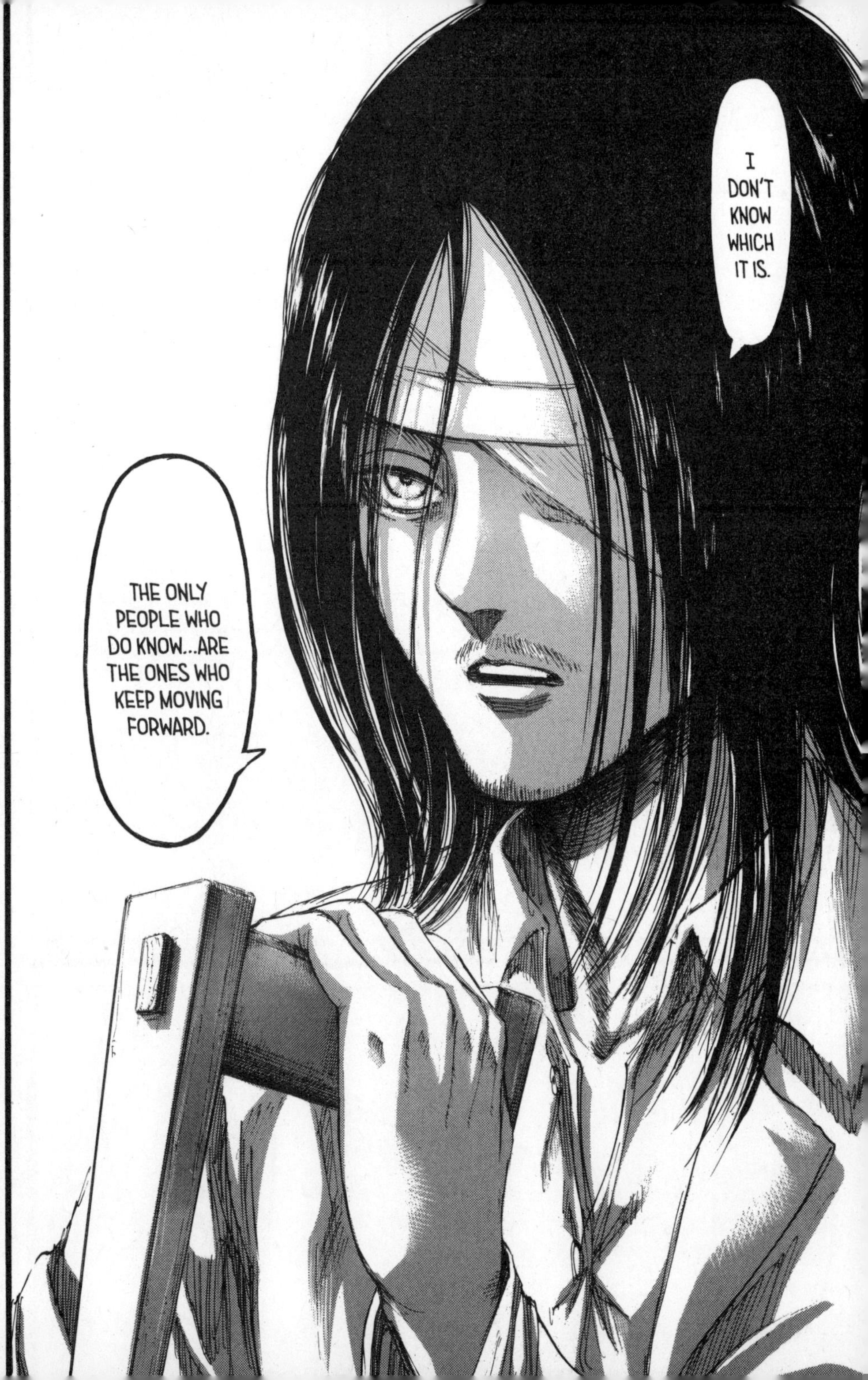
I DON'T KNOW WHICH IT IS.
THE ONLY PEOPLE WHO DO KNOW...ARE THE ONES WHO KEEP MOVING FORWARD.

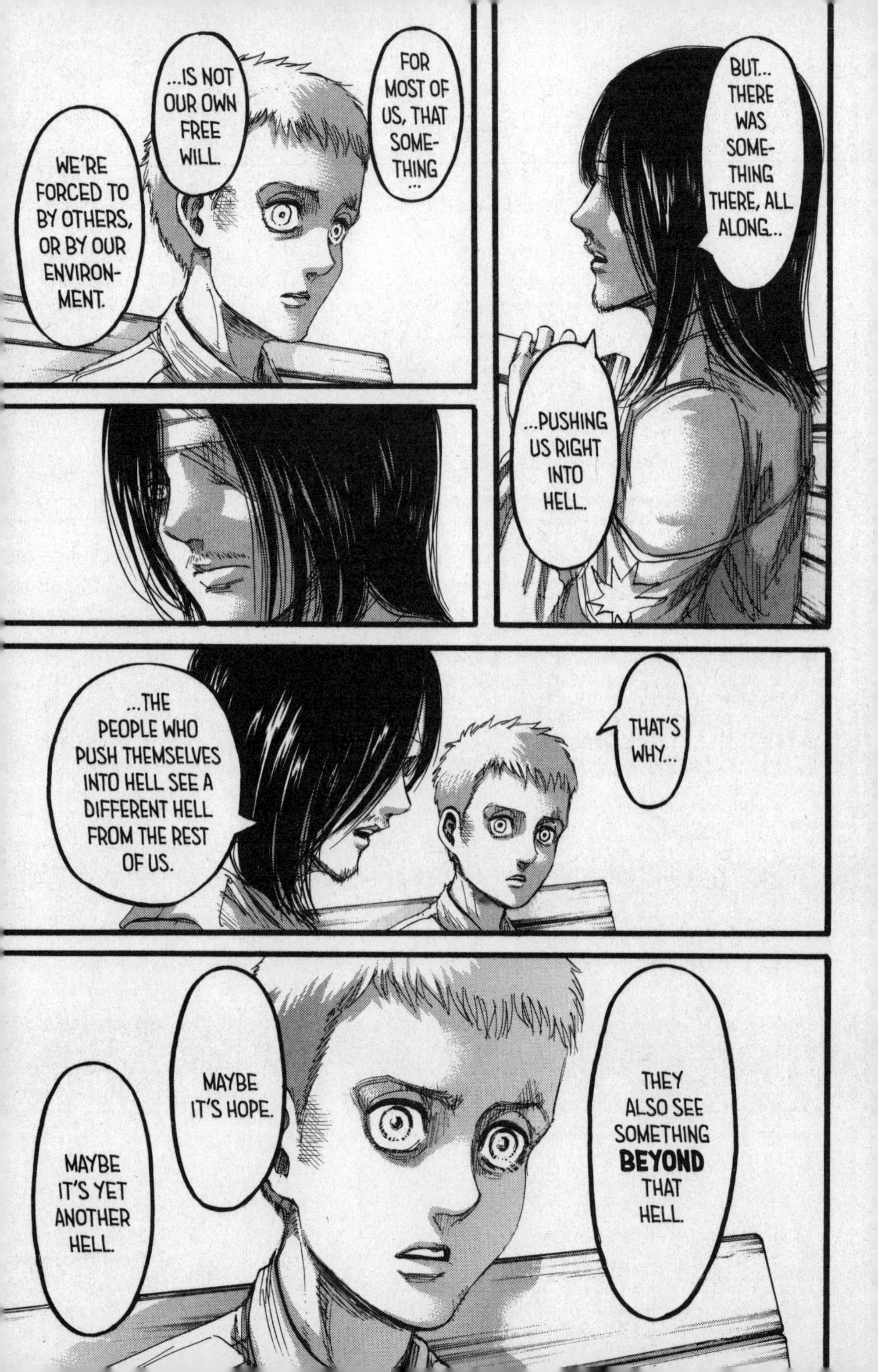
BUT... THERE WAS SOMETHING THERE, ALL ALONG...
...PUSHING US RIGHT INTO HELL.
FOR MOST OF US, THAT SOMETHING...
...IS NOT OUR OWN FREE WILL.
WE'RE FORCED TO BY OTHERS, OR BY OUR ENVIRONMENT.
THAT'S WHY...
...THE PEOPLE WHO PUSH THEMSELVES INTO HELL SEE A DIFFERENT HELL FROM THE REST OF US.
THEY ALSO SEE SOMETHING **BEYOND** THAT HELL.
MAYBE IT'S HOPE.
MAYBE IT'S YET ANOTHER HELL.

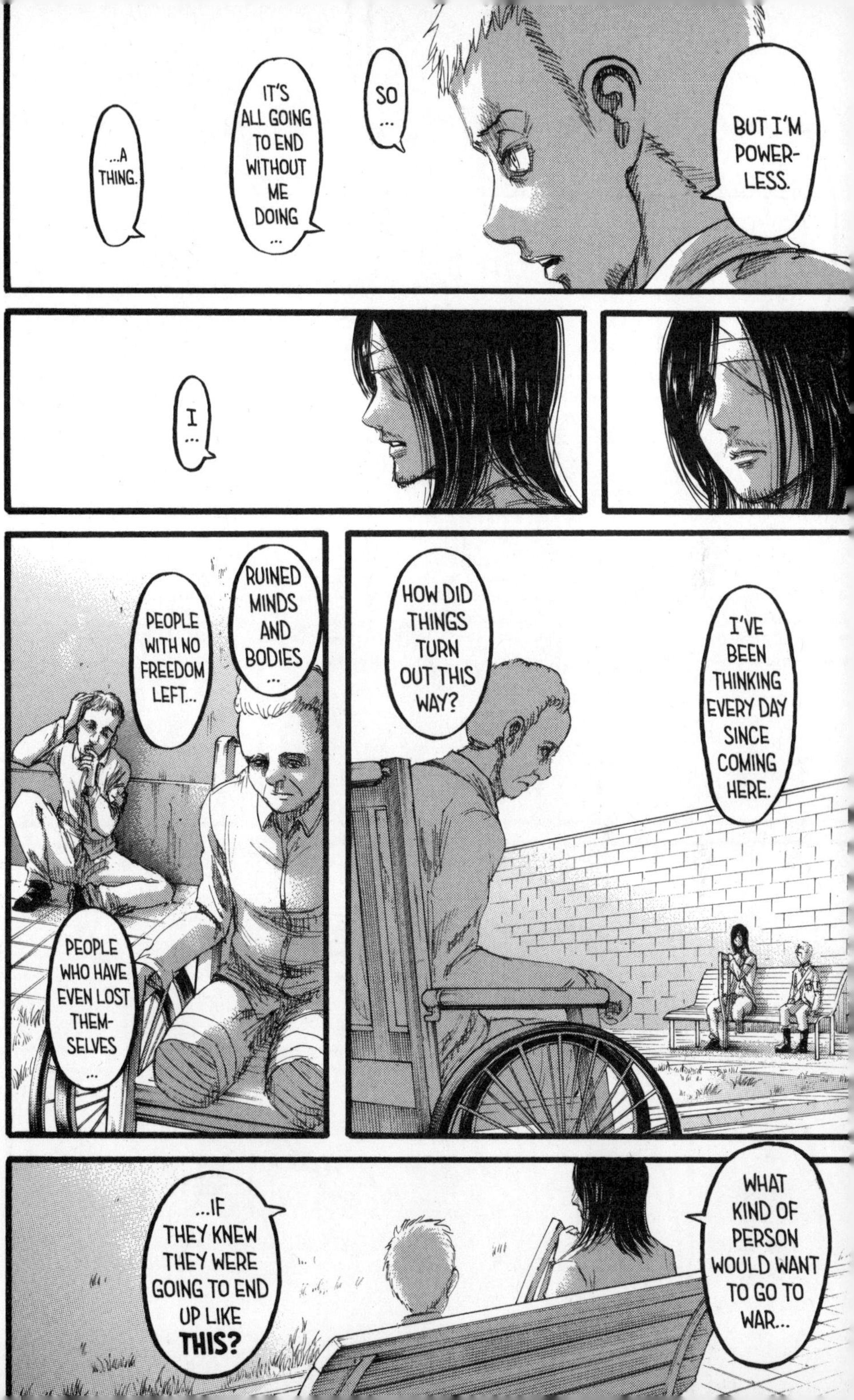
BUT I'M POWER-LESS.
SO ...
IT'S ALL GOING TO END WITHOUT ME DOING ...
...A THING.
I ...
I'VE BEEN THINKING EVERY DAY SINCE COMING HERE.
HOW DID THINGS TURN OUT THIS WAY?
RUINED MINDS AND BODIES ...
PEOPLE WITH NO FREEDOM LEFT...
PEOPLE WHO HAVE EVEN LOST THEM-SELVES ...
WHAT KIND OF PERSON WOULD WANT TO GO TO WAR...
...IF THEY KNEW THEY WERE GOING TO END UP LIKE **THIS?**

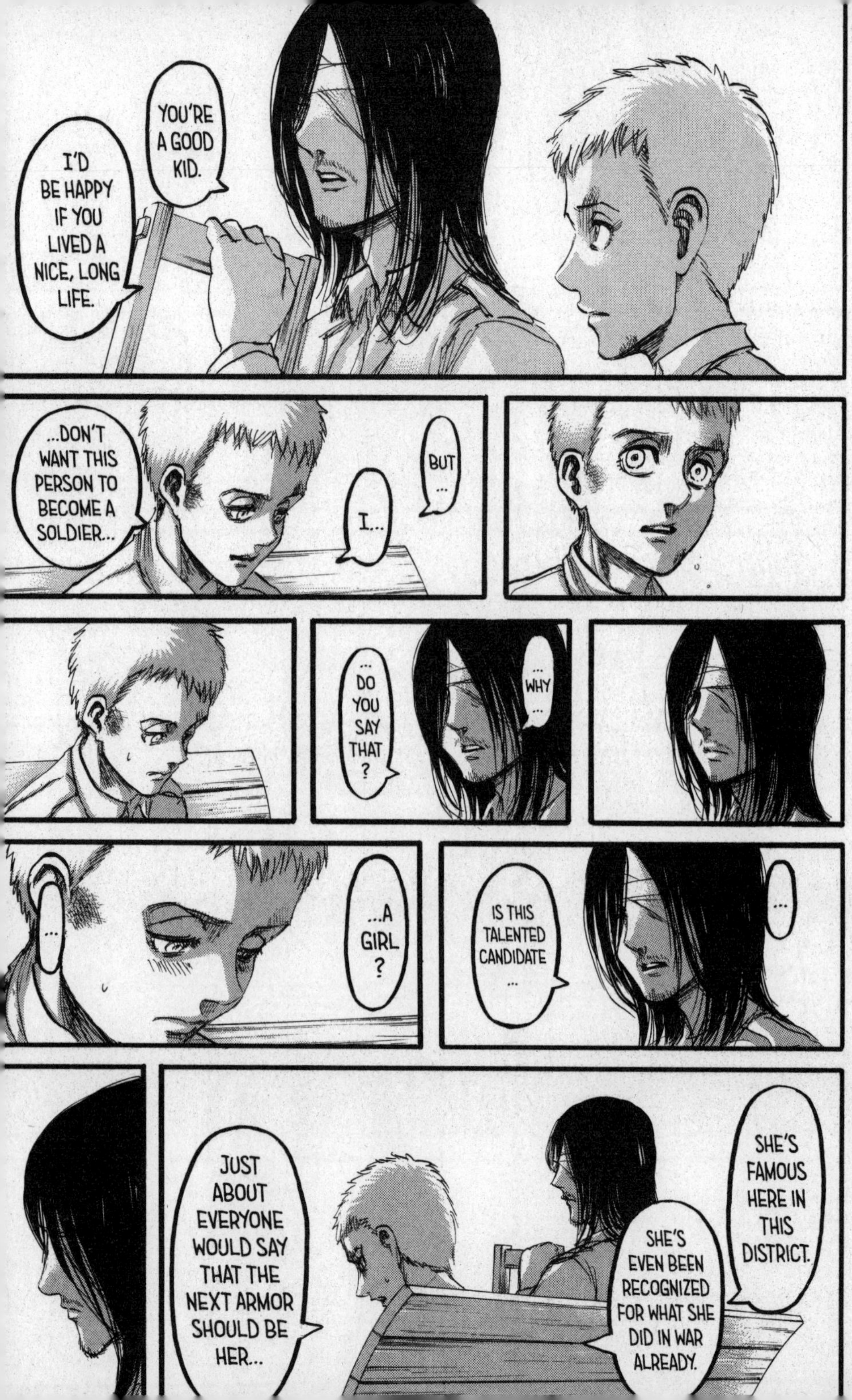
YOU'RE A GOOD KID.
I'D BE HAPPY IF YOU LIVED A NICE, LONG LIFE.
BUT...
I...
...DON'T WANT THIS PERSON TO BECOME A SOLDIER...
...WHY...
...DO YOU SAY THAT?
...
IS THIS TALENTED CANDIDATE...
...A GIRL?
...
SHE'S FAMOUS HERE IN THIS DISTRICT.
SHE'S EVEN BEEN RECOGNIZED FOR WHAT SHE DID IN WAR ALREADY.
JUST ABOUT EVERYONE WOULD SAY THAT THE NEXT ARMOR SHOULD BE HER...

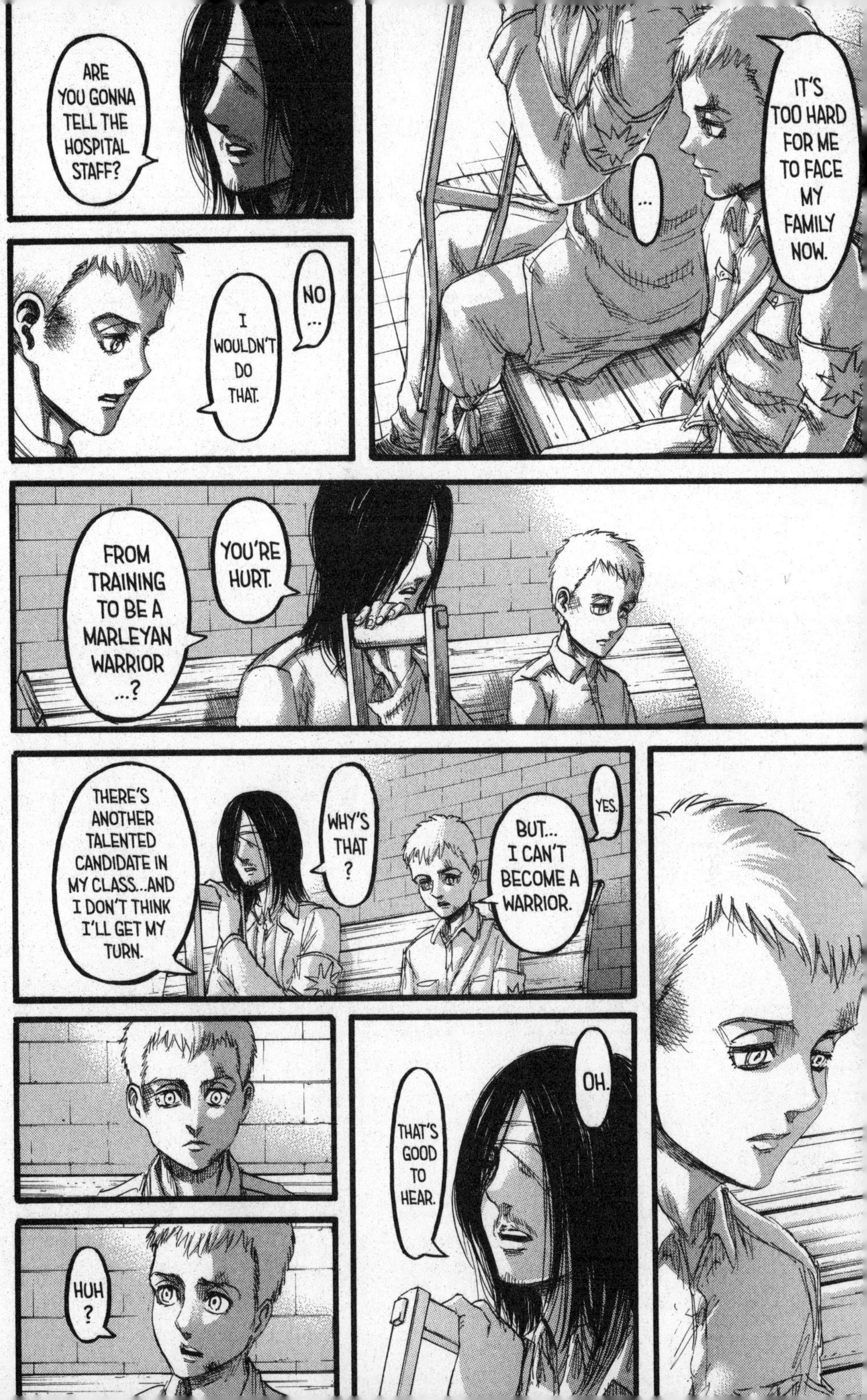
IT'S TOO HARD FOR ME TO FACE MY FAMILY NOW.
...
ARE YOU GONNA TELL THE HOSPITAL STAFF?
NO...
I WOULDN'T DO THAT.
YOU'RE HURT.
FROM TRAINING TO BE A MARLEYAN WARRIOR...?
YES.
BUT... I CAN'T BECOME A WARRIOR.
WHY'S THAT?
THERE'S ANOTHER TALENTED CANDIDATE IN MY CLASS...AND I DON'T THINK I'LL GET MY TURN.
OH.
THAT'S GOOD TO HEAR.
HUH?

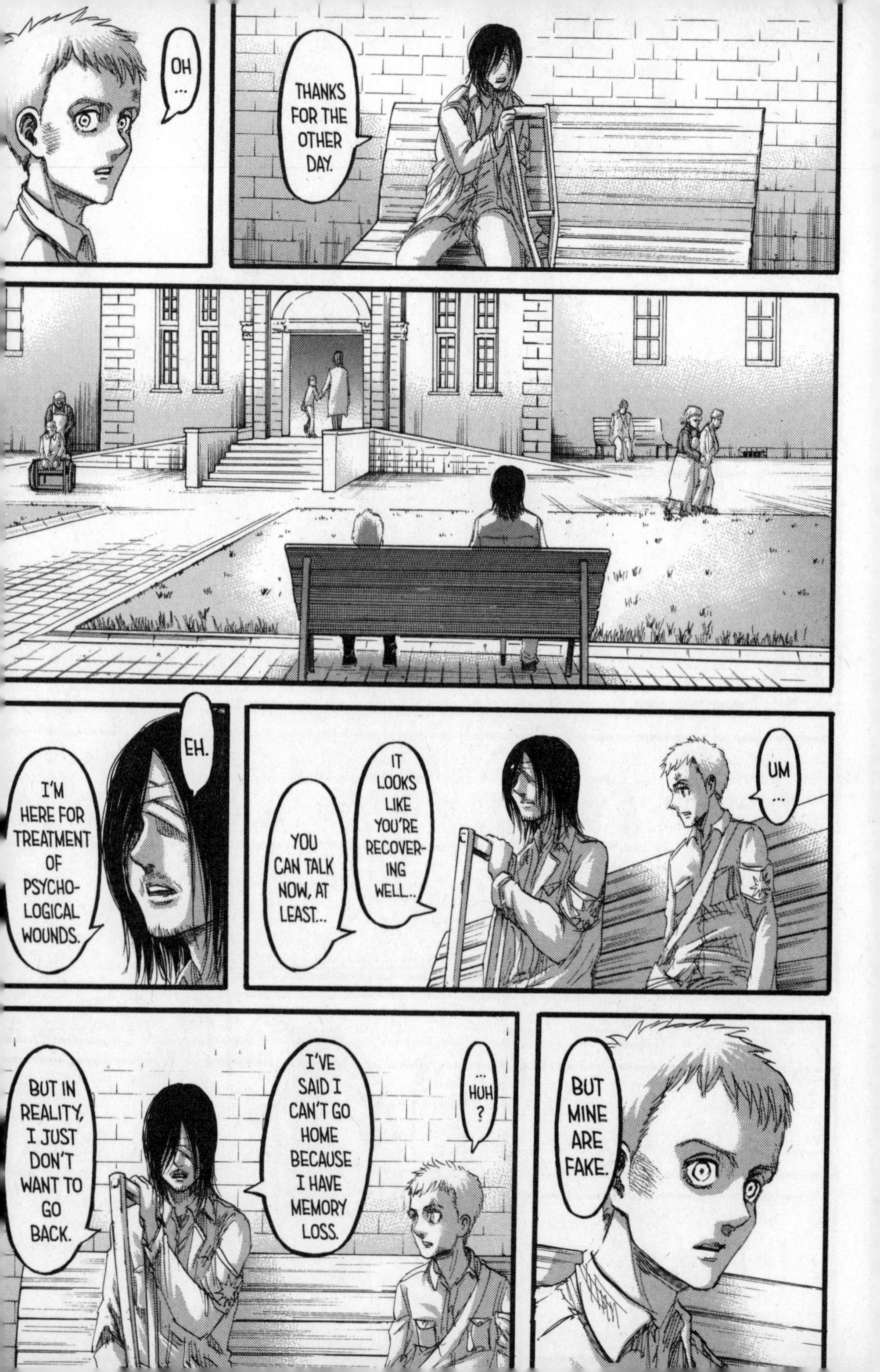
THANKS FOR THE OTHER DAY.
OH ...
UM ...
IT LOOKS LIKE YOU'RE RECOVER-ING WELL...
YOU CAN TALK NOW, AT LEAST...
EH.
I'M HERE FOR TREATMENT OF PSYCHO-LOGICAL WOUNDS.
BUT MINE ARE FAKE.
... HUH ?
I'VE SAID I CAN'T GO HOME BECAUSE I HAVE MEMORY LOSS.
BUT IN REALITY, I JUST DON'T WANT TO GO BACK.

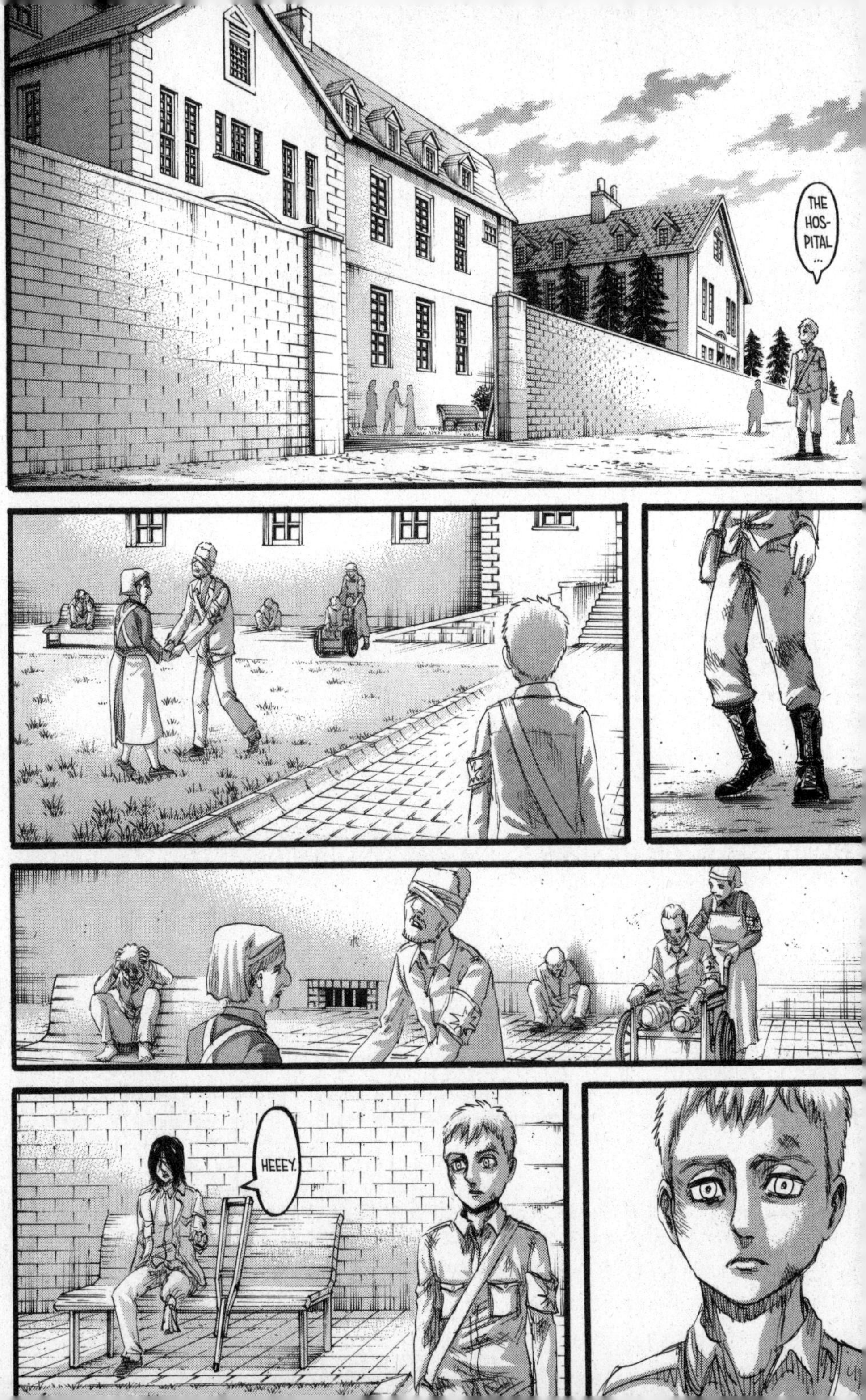
THE HOS-PITAL ...
HEEEY.

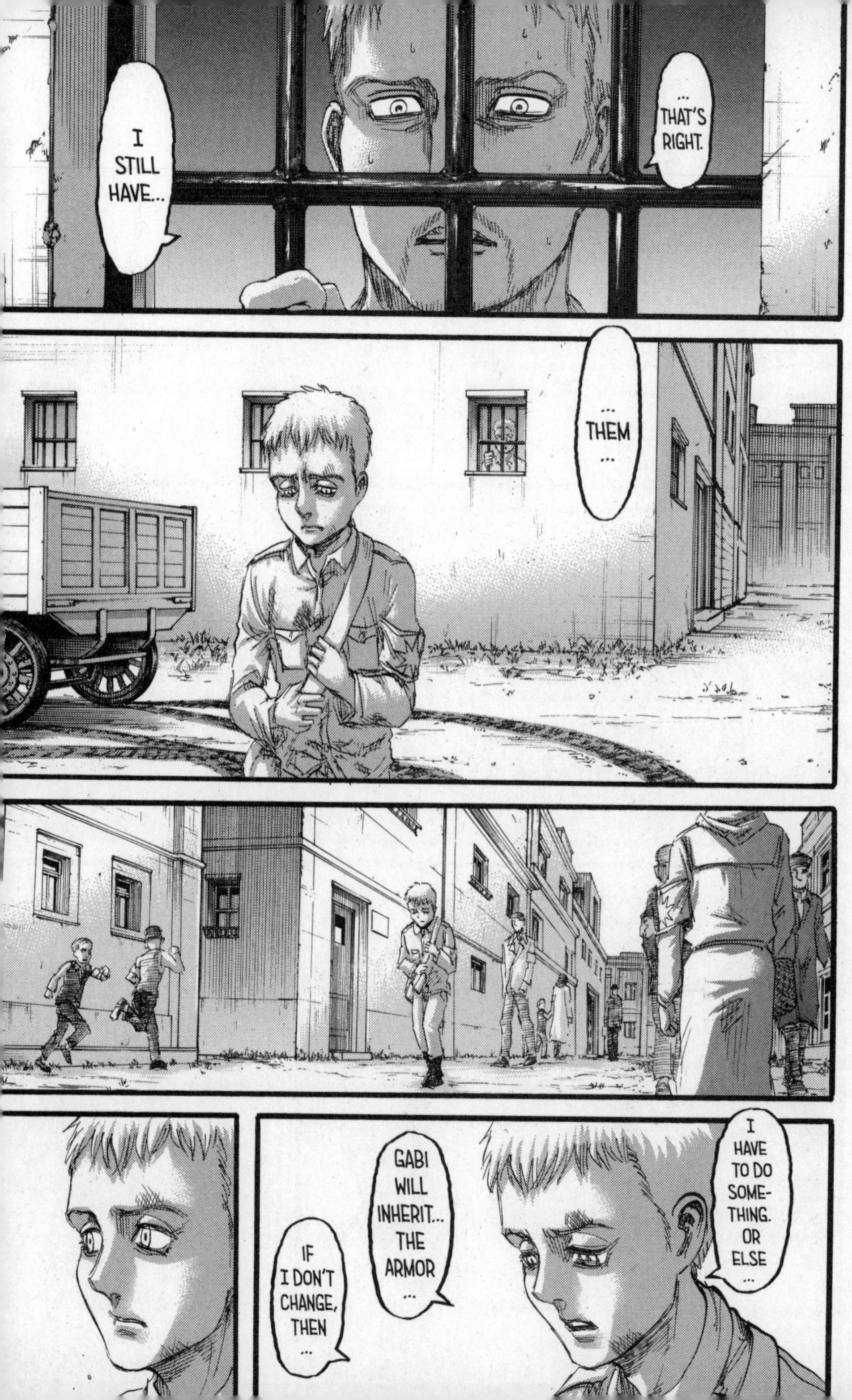
... THAT'S RIGHT.
I STILL HAVE...
... THEM ...
I HAVE TO DO SOME-THING. OR ELSE ...
GABI WILL INHERIT... THE ARMOR ...
IF I DON'T CHANGE, THEN ...

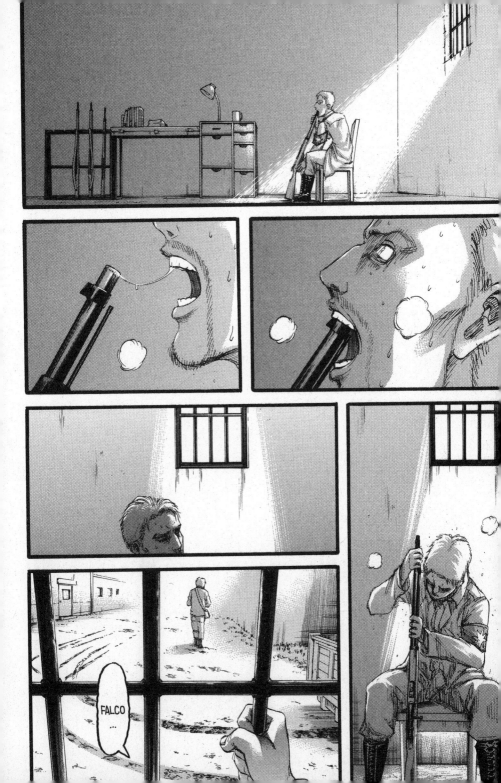

FALCO
...

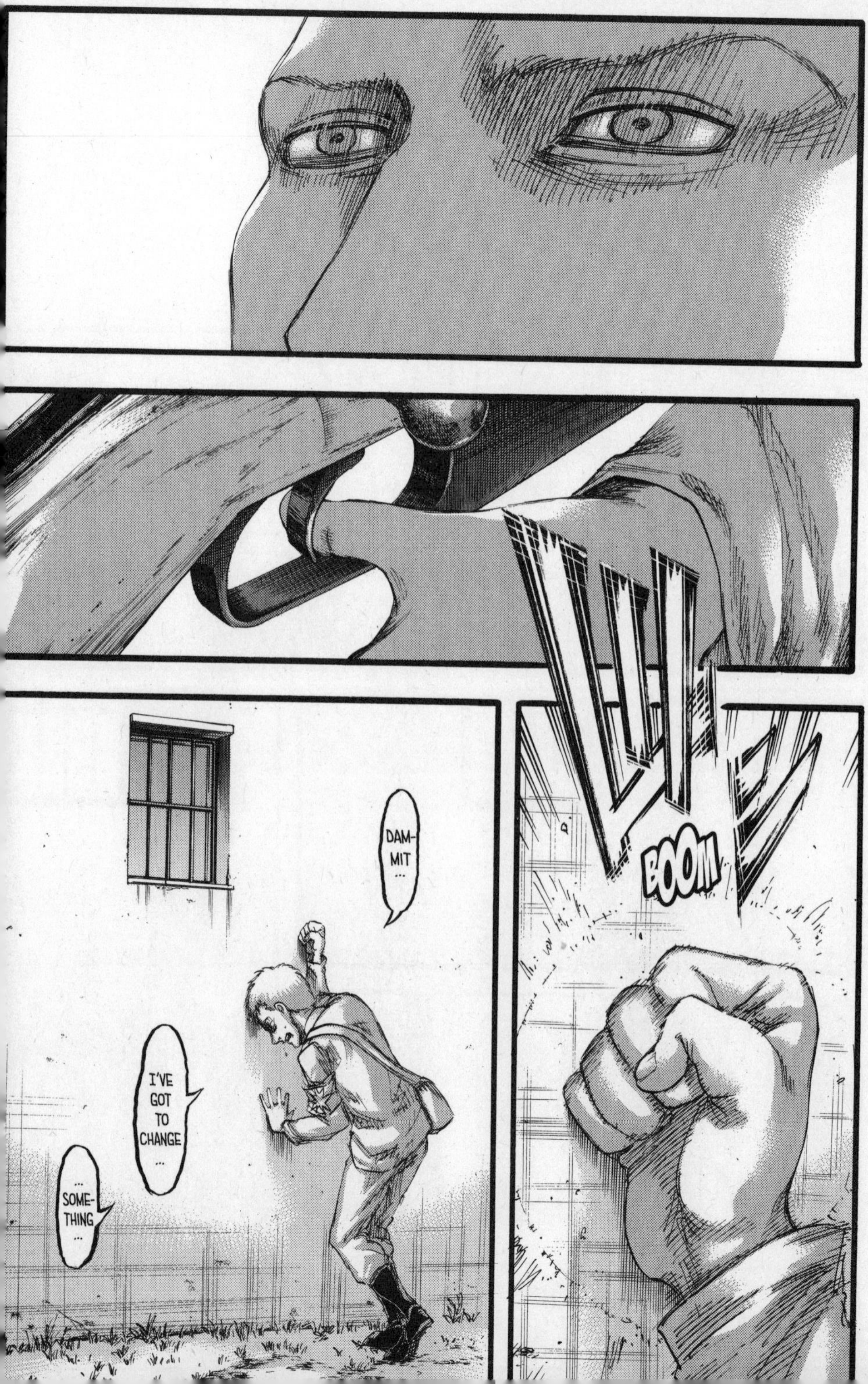
BOOM
DAM-MIT ...
I'VE GOT TO CHANGE ...
... SOMETHING ...

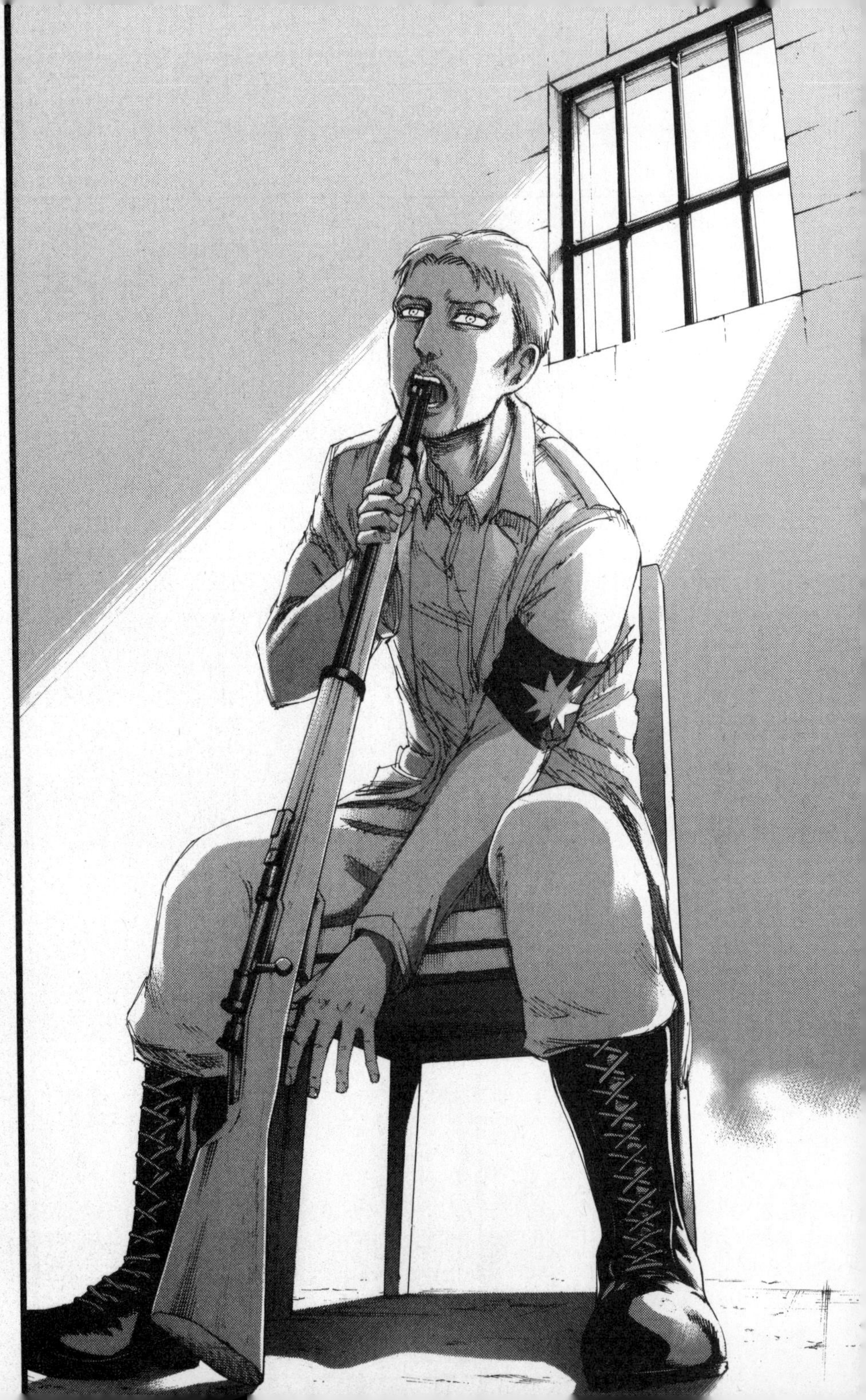

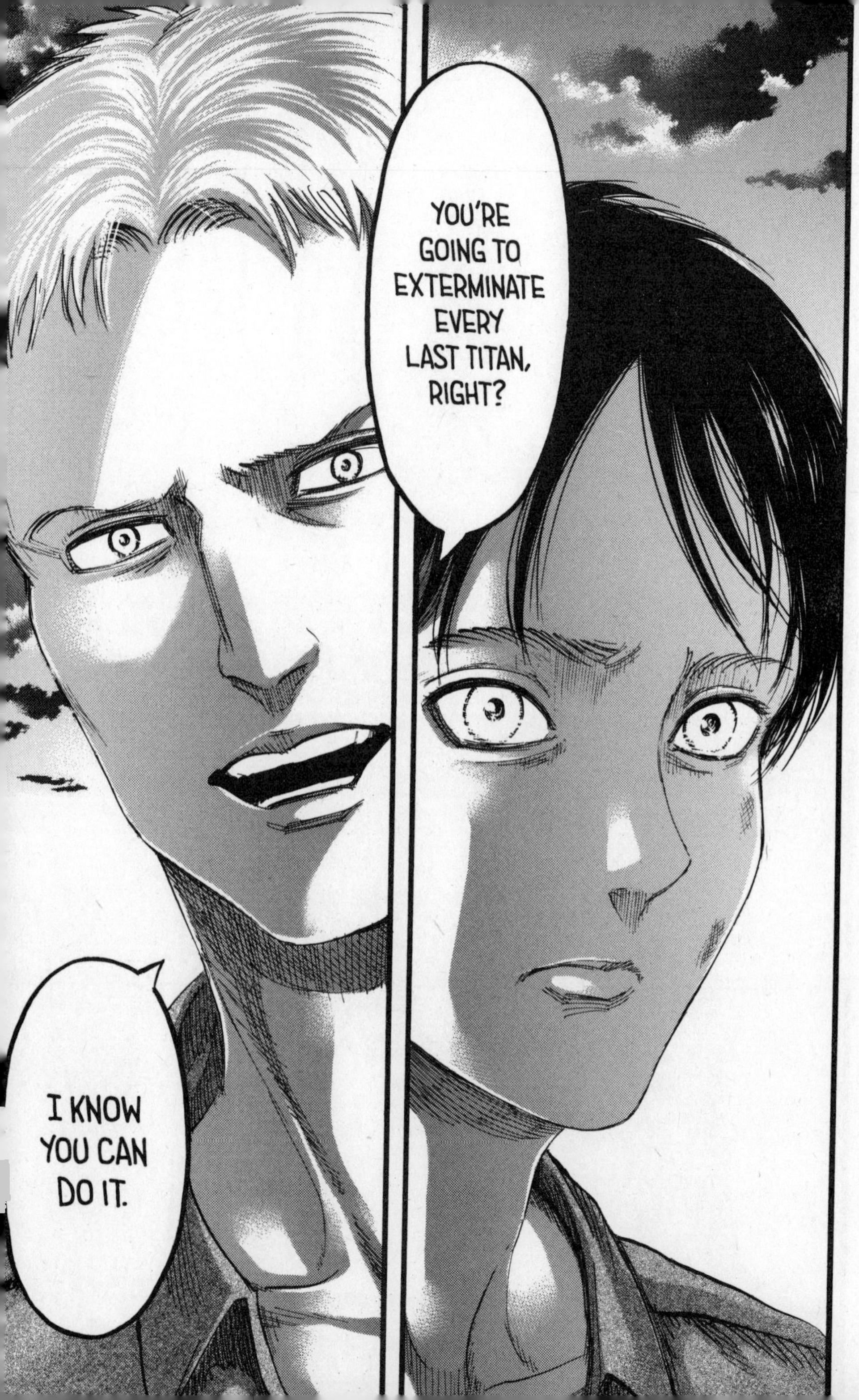
YOU'RE GOING TO EXTERMINATE EVERY LAST TITAN, RIGHT?
I KNOW YOU CAN DO IT.

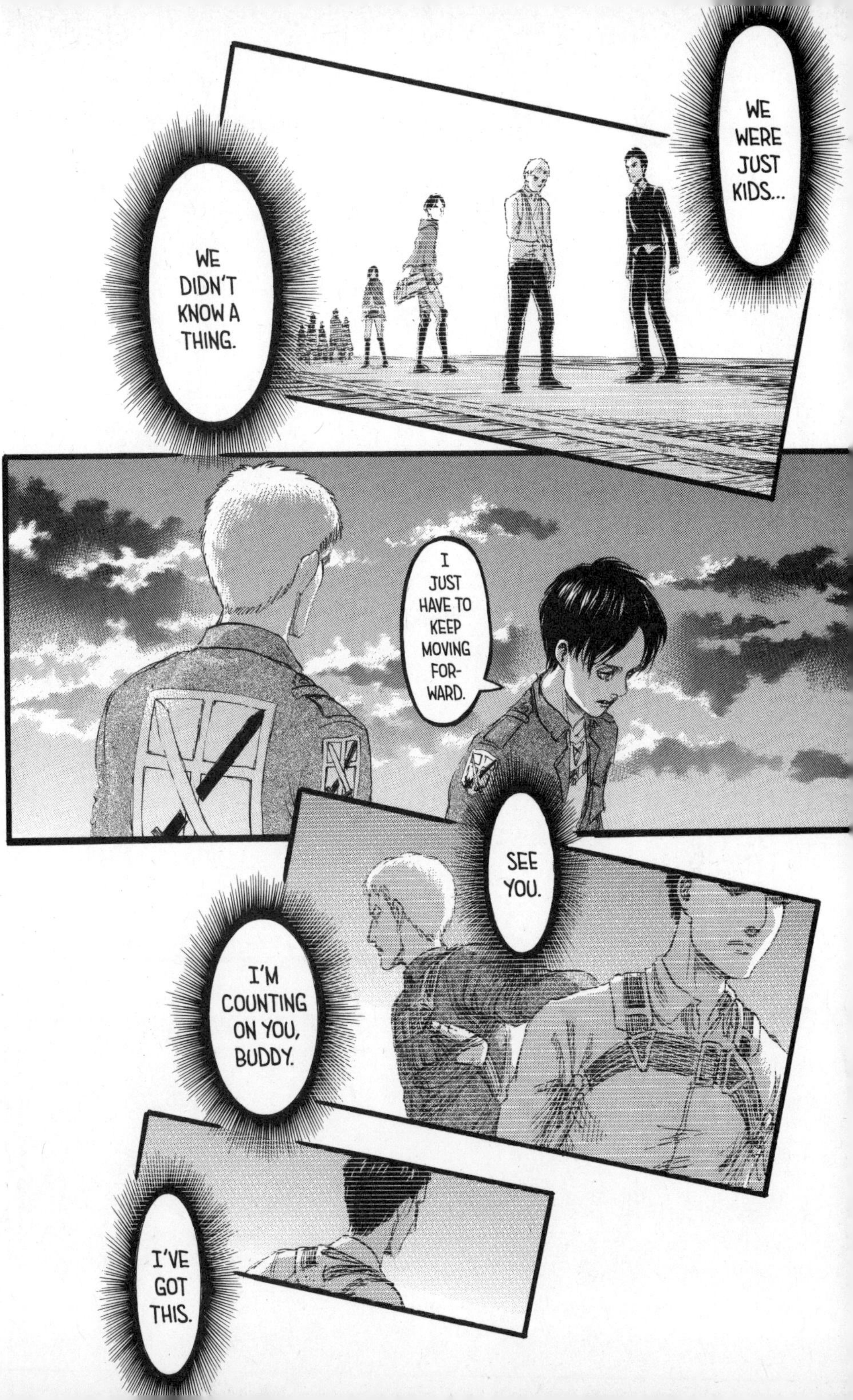
WE WERE JUST KIDS...
WE DIDN'T KNOW A THING.
I JUST HAVE TO KEEP MOVING FOR-WARD.
SEE YOU.
I'M COUNTING ON YOU, BUDDY.
I'VE GOT THIS.

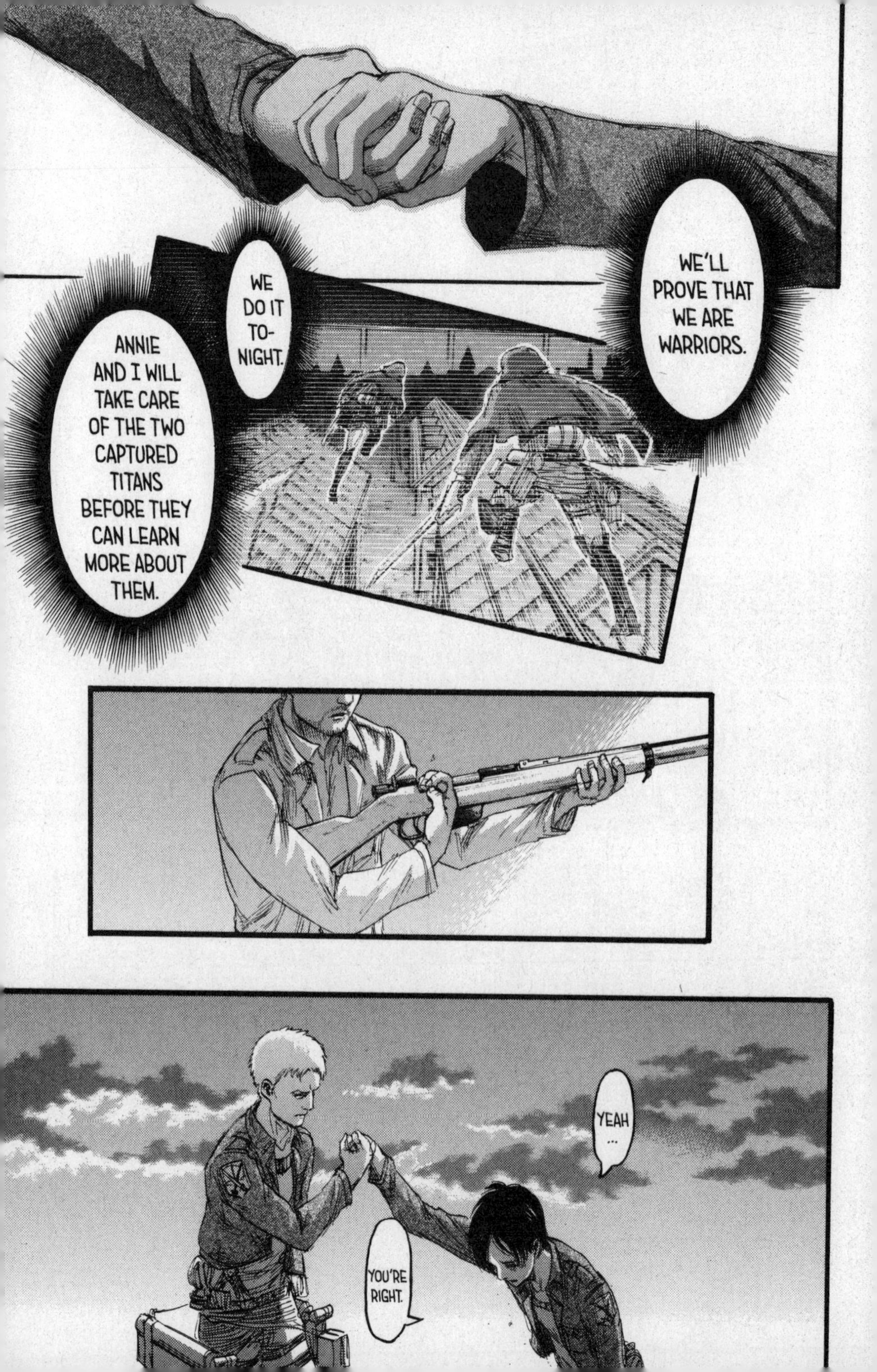
WE'LL PROVE THAT WE ARE WARRIORS.
WE DO IT TO-NIGHT.
ANNIE AND I WILL TAKE CARE OF THE TWO CAPTURED TITANS BEFORE THEY CAN LEARN MORE ABOUT THEM.
YEAH ...
YOU'RE RIGHT.

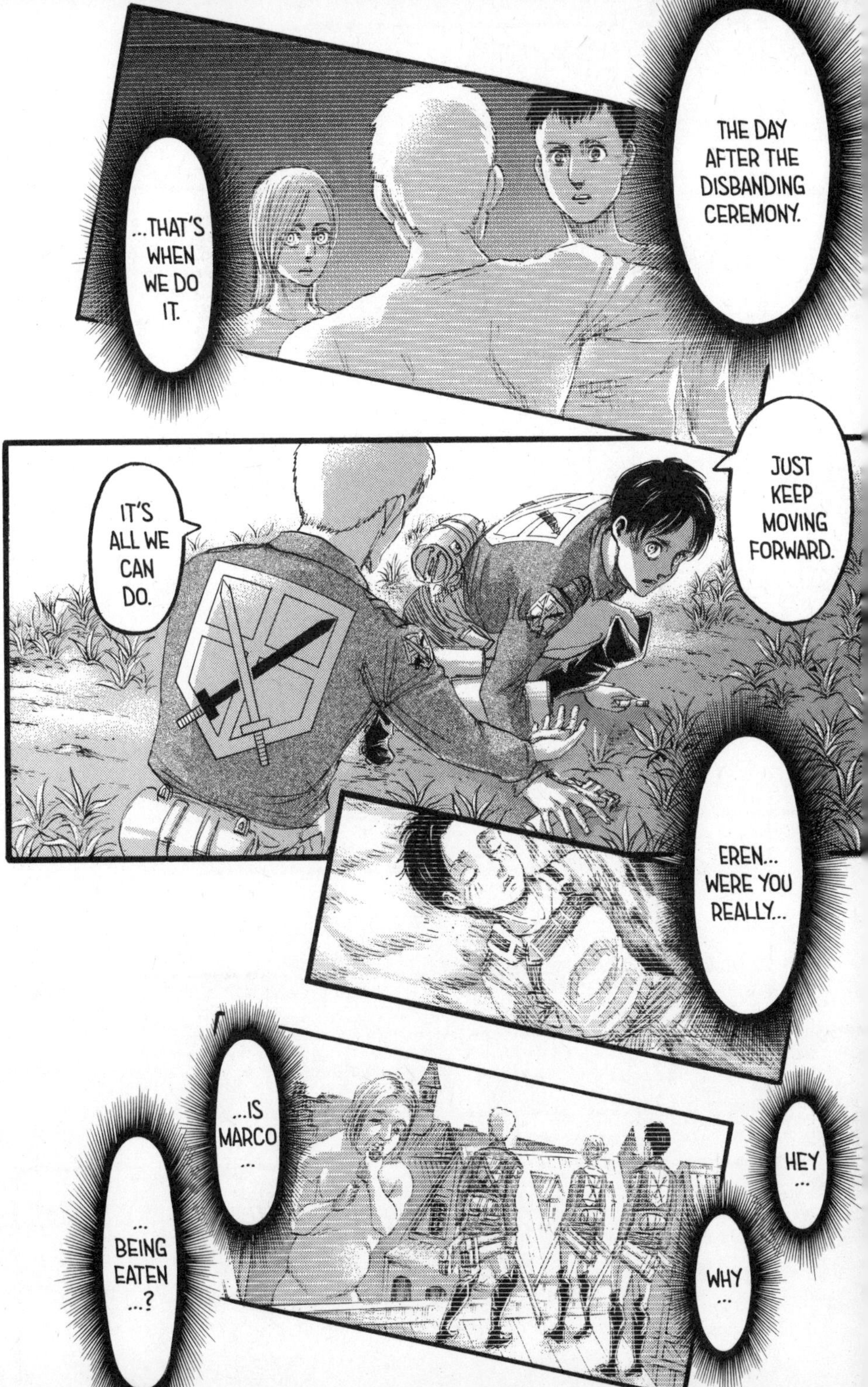
THE DAY AFTER THE DISBANDING CEREMONY.
...THAT'S WHEN WE DO IT.
JUST KEEP MOVING FORWARD.
IT'S ALL WE CAN DO.
EREN... WERE YOU REALLY...
HEY ...
WHY ...
...IS MARCO ...
... BEING EATEN ...?

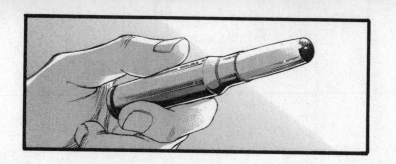

JUST
...

...DO
WHAT YOU
HAVE TO
DO.

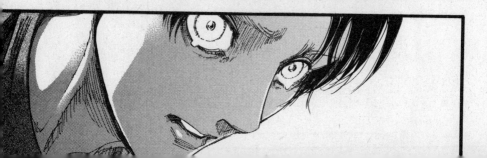

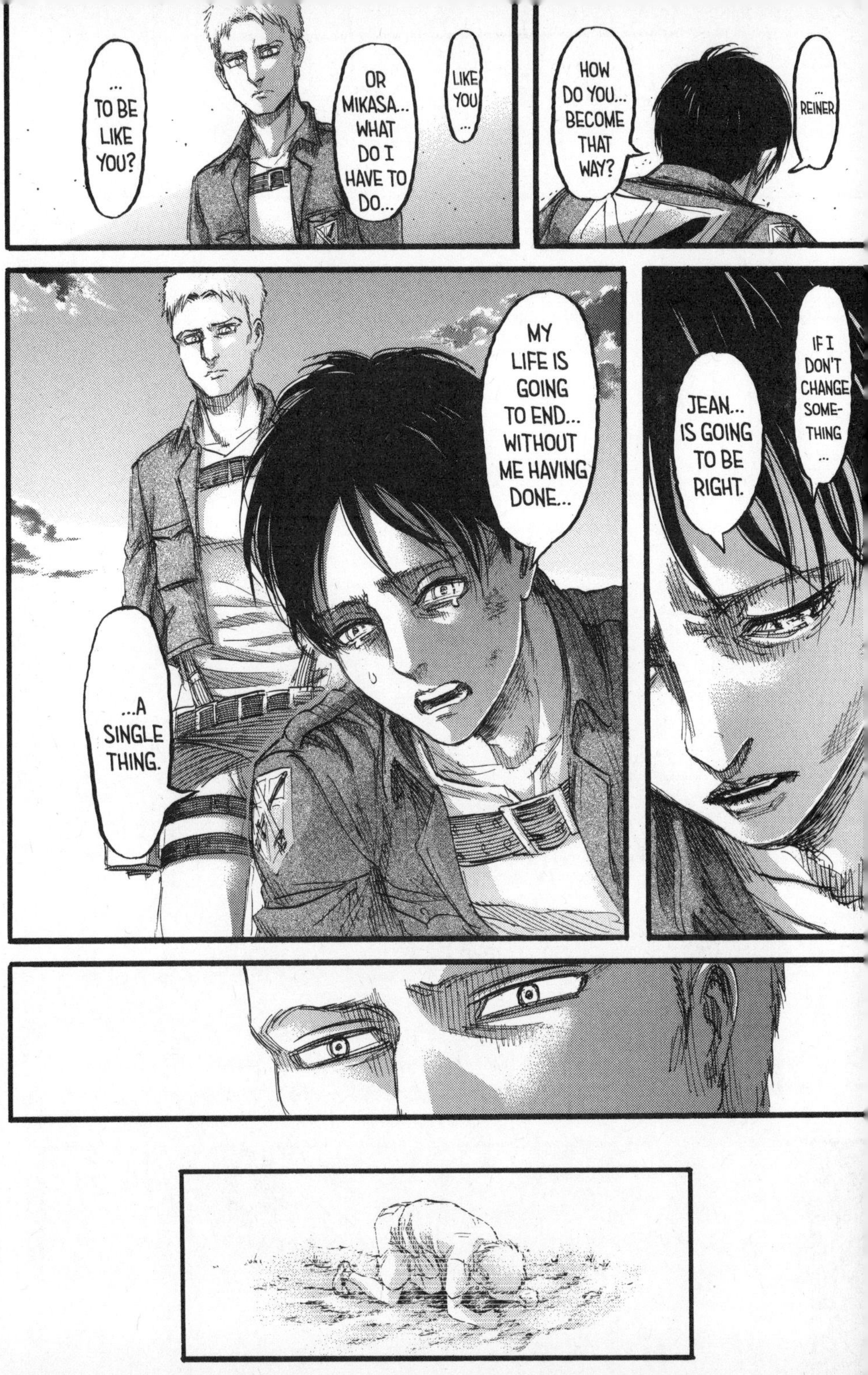
...REINER
HOW DO YOU... BECOME THAT WAY?
LIKE YOU...
OR MIKASA... WHAT DO I HAVE TO DO...
...TO BE LIKE YOU?
IF I DON'T CHANGE SOME-THING...
JEAN... IS GOING TO BE RIGHT.
MY LIFE IS GOING TO END... WITHOUT ME HAVING DONE...
...A SINGLE THING.

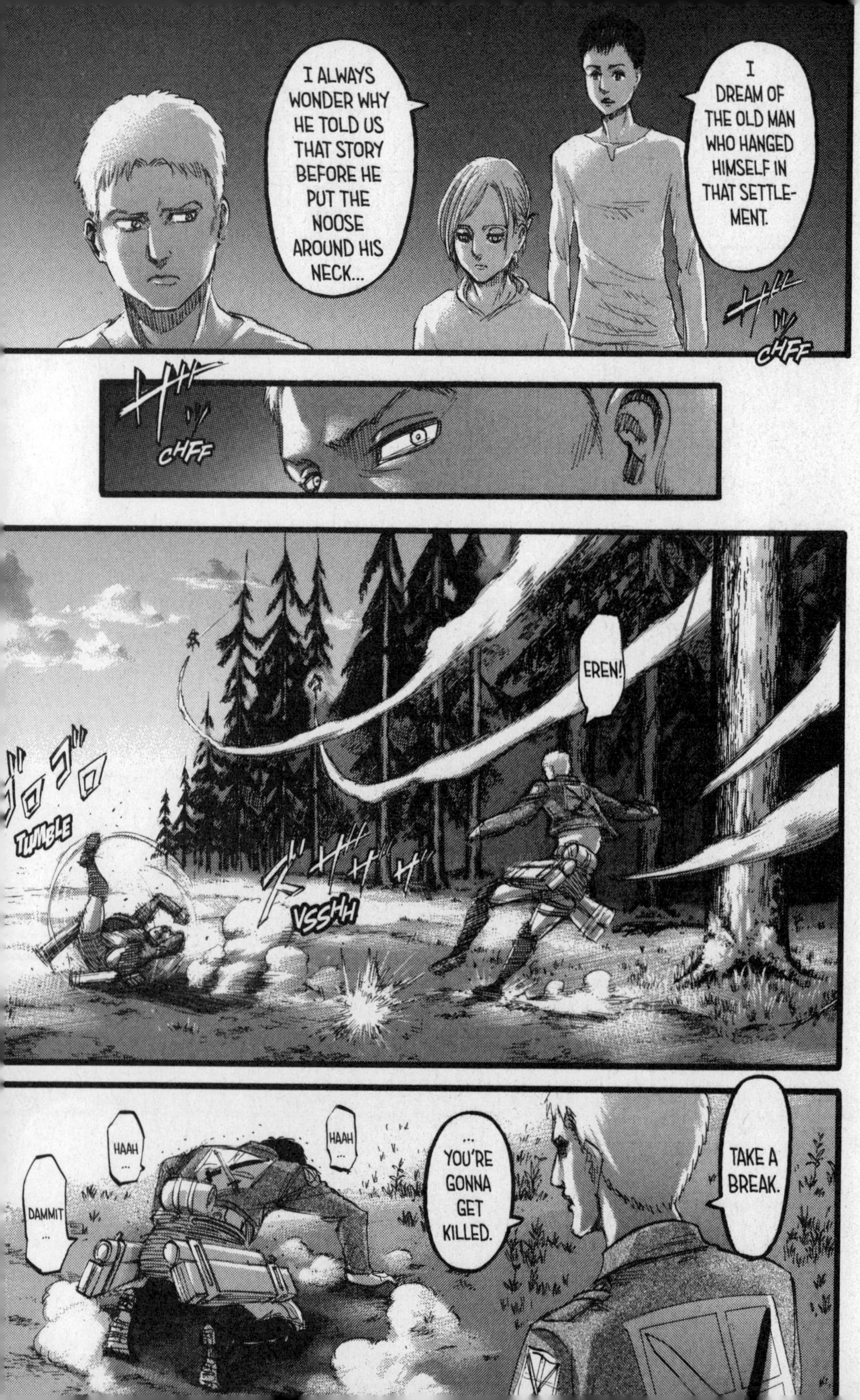
I DREAM OF THE OLD MAN WHO HANGED HIMSELF IN THAT SETTLEMENT.
I ALWAYS WONDER WHY HE TOLD US THAT STORY BEFORE HE PUT THE NOOSE AROUND HIS NECK...
CHFF
CHFF
EREN!
VSSHH
TUMBLE
TAKE A BREAK.
... YOU'RE GONNA GET KILLED.
HAAH ...
HAAH ...
DAMMIT ...

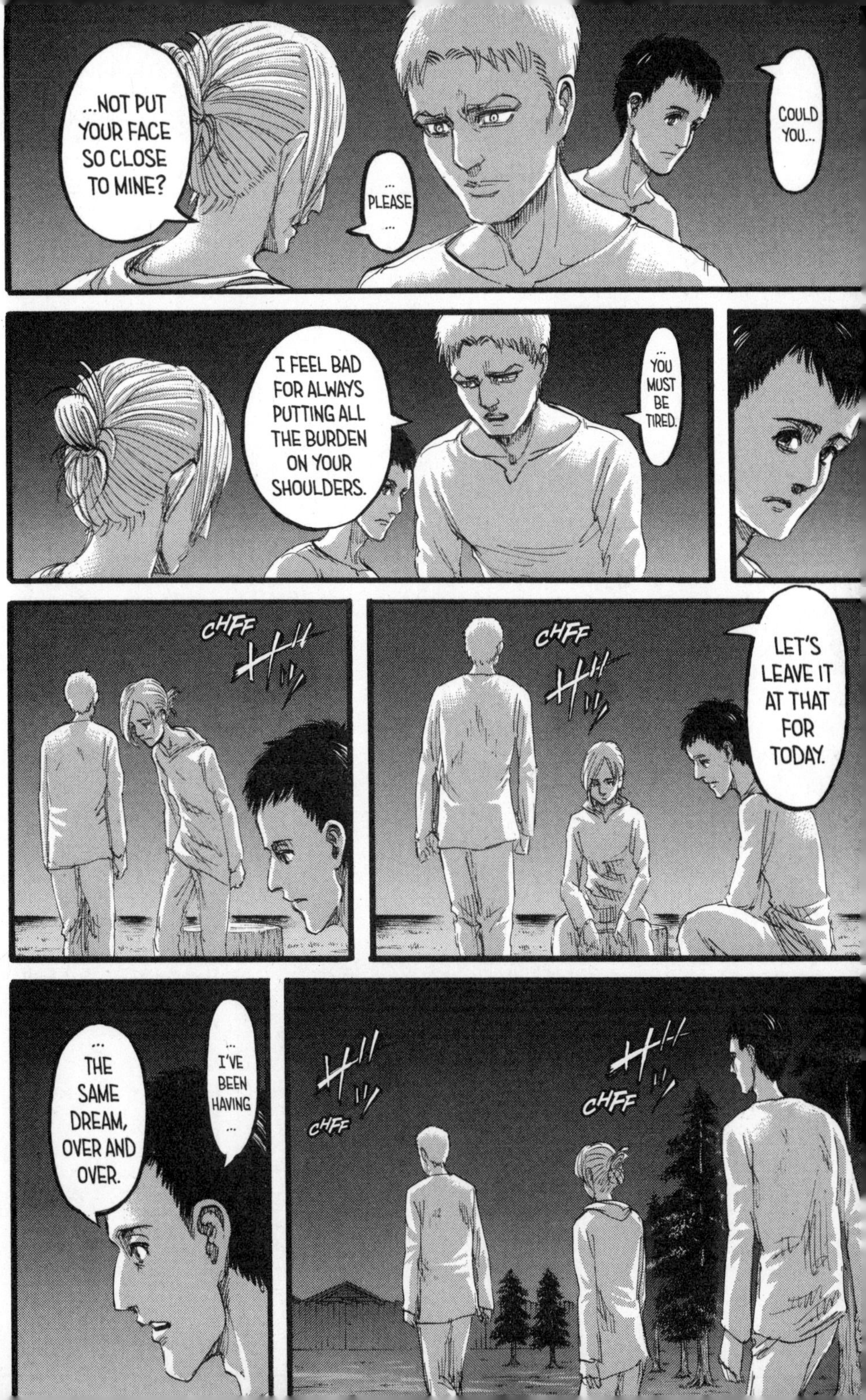
COULD YOU...
... PLEASE ...
...NOT PUT YOUR FACE SO CLOSE TO MINE?
... YOU MUST BE TIRED.
I FEEL BAD FOR ALWAYS PUTTING ALL THE BURDEN ON YOUR SHOULDERS.
LET'S LEAVE IT AT THAT FOR TODAY.
CHFF
CHFF
CHFF
... I'VE BEEN HAVING ...
... THE SAME DREAM, OVER AND OVER.
CHFF

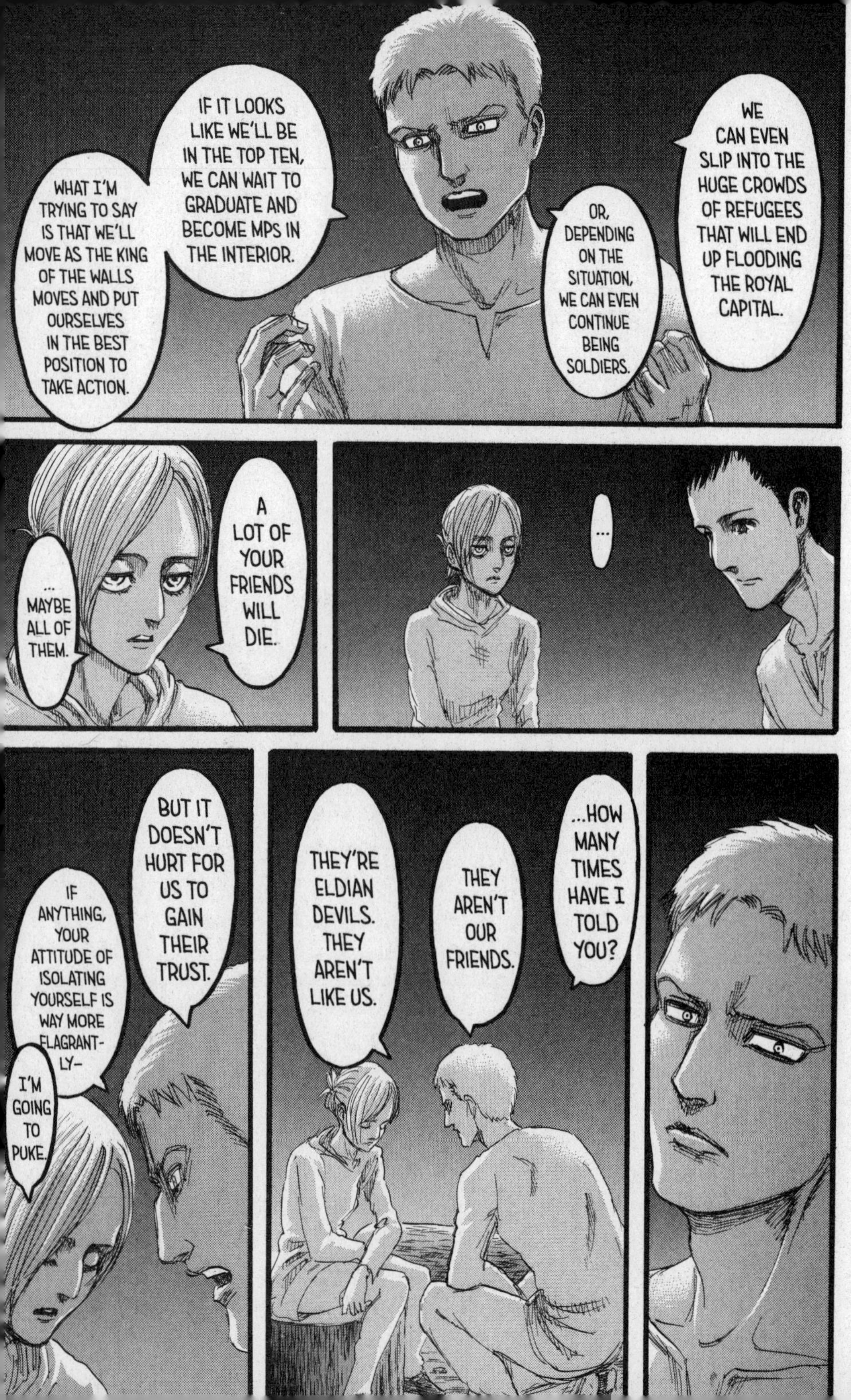
WE CAN EVEN SLIP INTO THE HUGE CROWDS OF REFUGEES THAT WILL END UP FLOODING THE ROYAL CAPITAL.
OR, DEPENDING ON THE SITUATION, WE CAN EVEN CONTINUE BEING SOLDIERS.
IF IT LOOKS LIKE WE'LL BE IN THE TOP TEN, WE CAN WAIT TO GRADUATE AND BECOME MPS IN THE INTERIOR.
WHAT I'M TRYING TO SAY IS THAT WE'LL MOVE AS THE KING OF THE WALLS MOVES AND PUT OURSELVES IN THE BEST POSITION TO TAKE ACTION.
...
A LOT OF YOUR FRIENDS WILL DIE.
... MAYBE ALL OF THEM.
...HOW MANY TIMES HAVE I TOLD YOU?
THEY AREN'T OUR FRIENDS.
THEY'RE ELDIAN DEVILS. THEY AREN'T LIKE US.
BUT IT DOESN'T HURT FOR US TO GAIN THEIR TRUST.
IF ANYTHING, YOUR ATTITUDE OF ISOLATING YOURSELF IS WAY MORE FLAGRANT-LY—
I'M GOING TO PUKE.

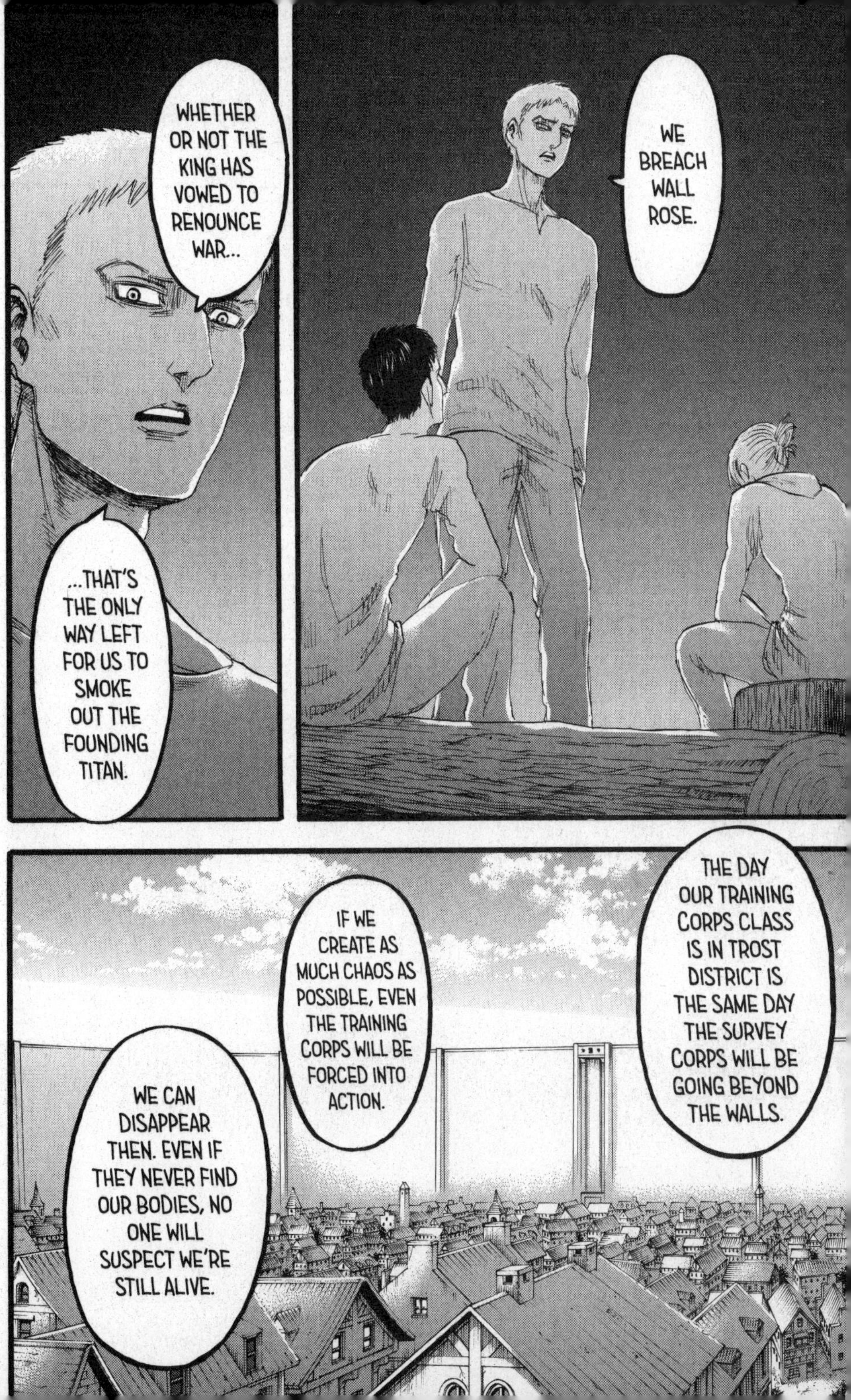
WE BREACH WALL ROSE.
WHETHER OR NOT THE KING HAS VOWED TO RENOUNCE WAR...
...THAT'S THE ONLY WAY LEFT FOR US TO SMOKE OUT THE FOUNDING TITAN.
THE DAY OUR TRAINING CORPS CLASS IS IN TROST DISTRICT IS THE SAME DAY THE SURVEY CORPS WILL BE GOING BEYOND THE WALLS.
IF WE CREATE AS MUCH CHAOS AS POSSIBLE, EVEN THE TRAINING CORPS WILL BE FORCED INTO ACTION.
WE CAN DISAPPEAR THEN. EVEN IF THEY NEVER FIND OUR BODIES, NO ONE WILL SUSPECT WE'RE STILL ALIVE.

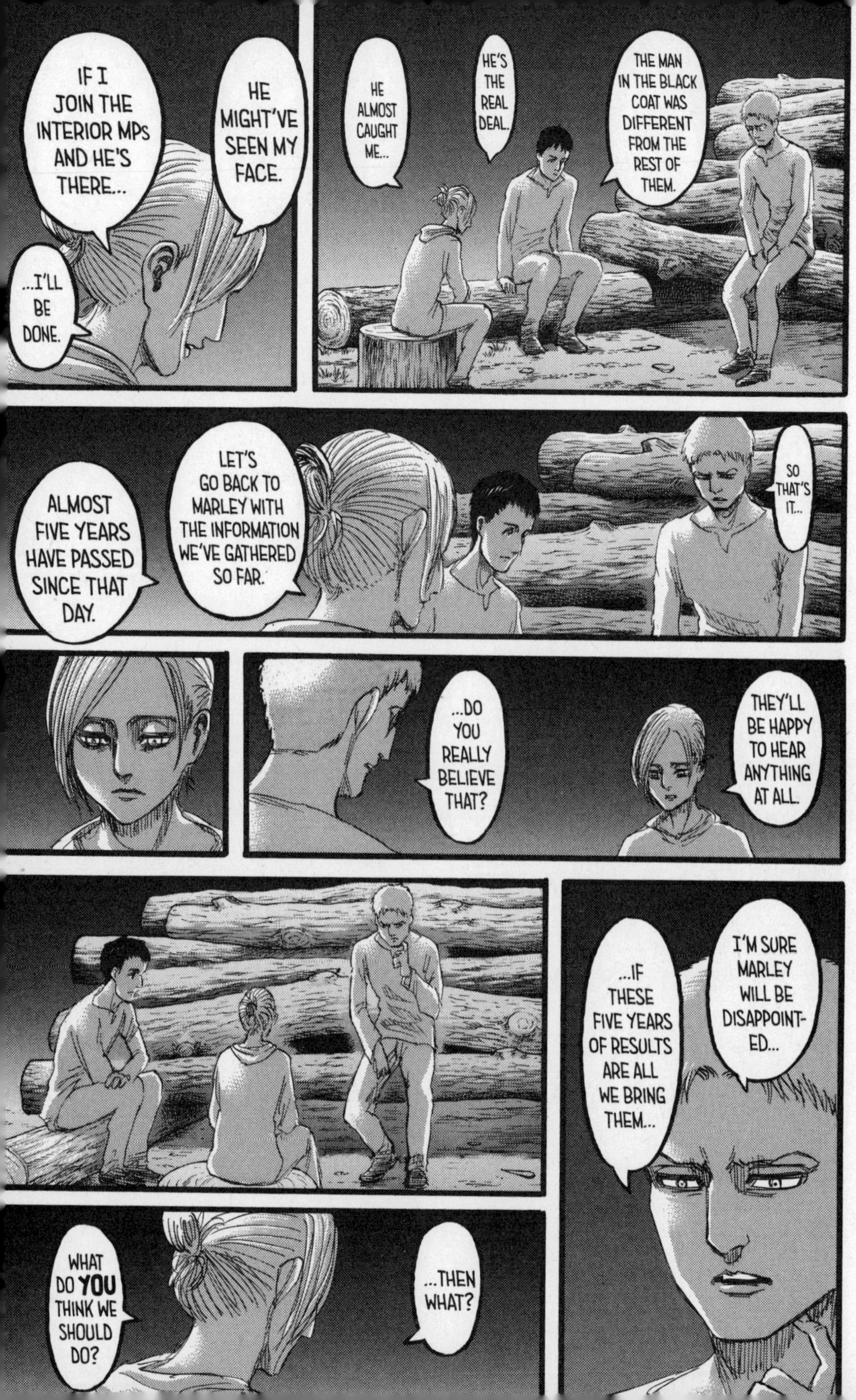
THE MAN IN THE BLACK COAT WAS DIFFERENT FROM THE REST OF THEM.
HE'S THE REAL DEAL.
HE ALMOST CAUGHT ME...
HE MIGHT'VE SEEN MY FACE.
IF I JOIN THE INTERIOR MPs AND HE'S THERE...
...I'LL BE DONE.
SO THAT'S IT...
LET'S GO BACK TO MARLEY WITH THE INFORMATION WE'VE GATHERED SO FAR.
ALMOST FIVE YEARS HAVE PASSED SINCE THAT DAY.
THEY'LL BE HAPPY TO HEAR ANYTHING AT ALL.
...DO YOU REALLY BELIEVE THAT?
I'M SURE MARLEY WILL BE DISAPPOINT-ED...
...IF THESE FIVE YEARS OF RESULTS ARE ALL WE BRING THEM...
...THEN WHAT?
WHAT DO **YOU** THINK WE SHOULD DO?

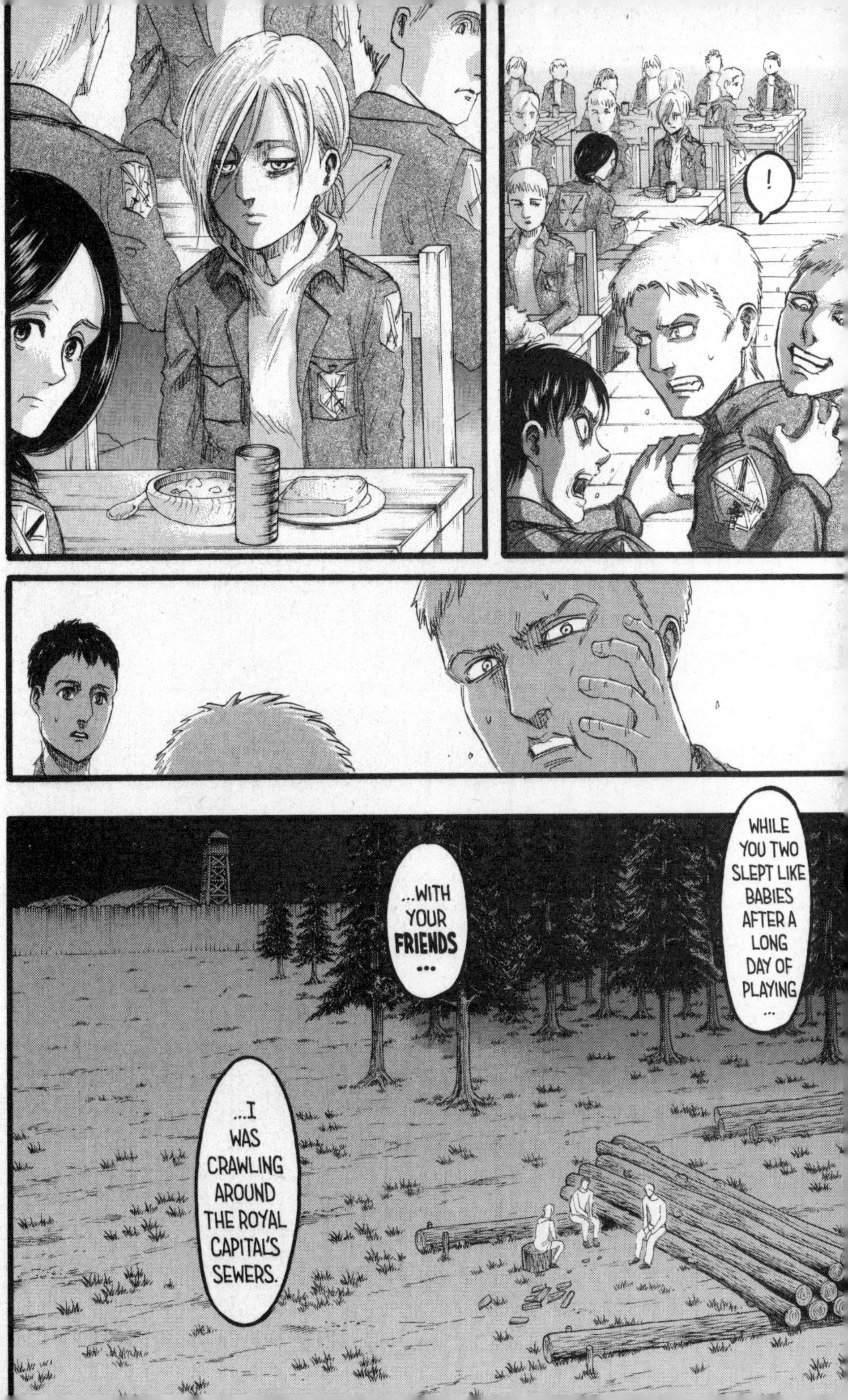
!
WHILE YOU TWO SLEPT LIKE BABIES AFTER A LONG DAY OF PLAYING ...
...WITH YOUR **FRIENDS** ...
...I WAS CRAWLING AROUND THE ROYAL CAPITAL'S SEWERS.

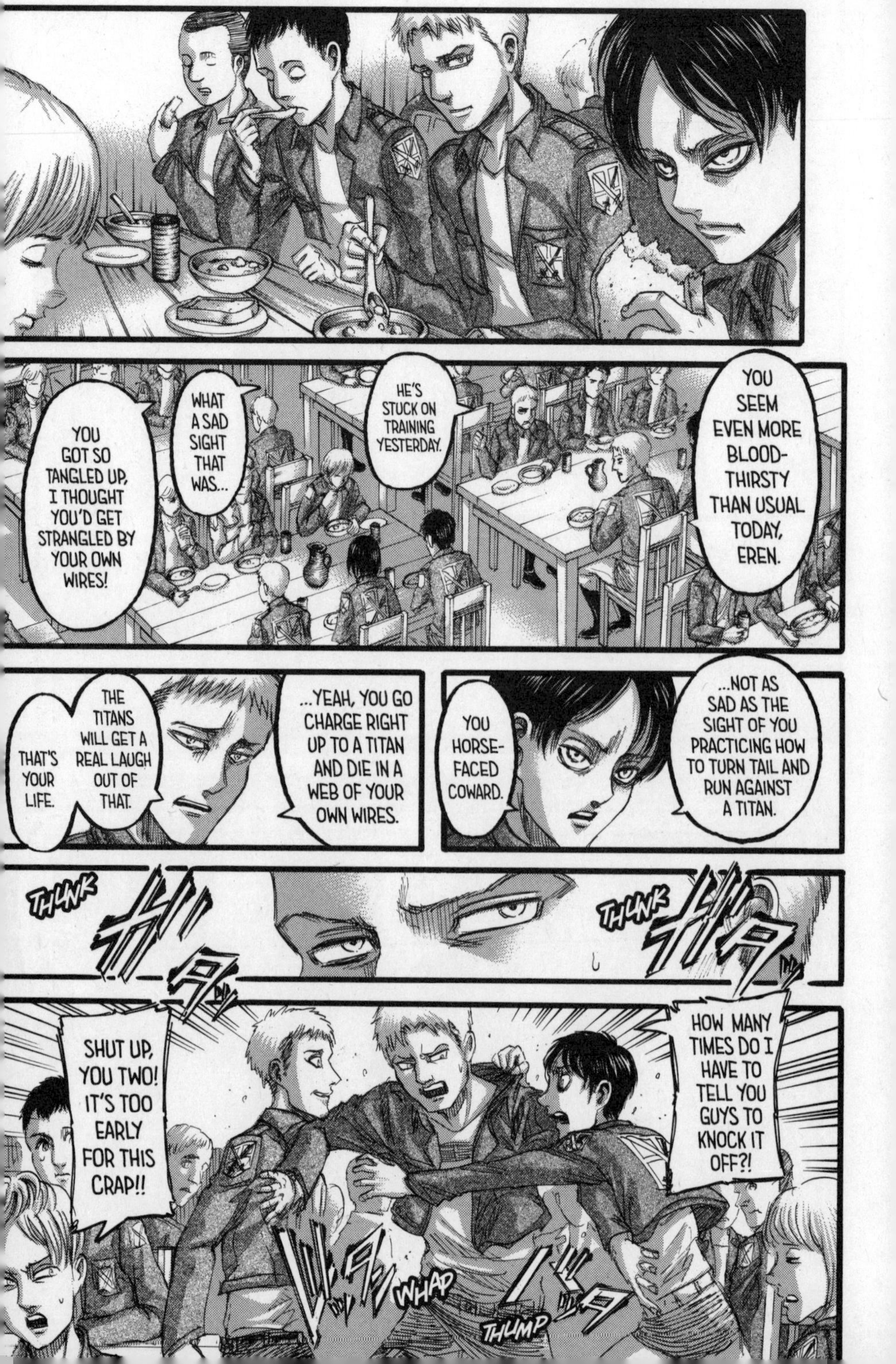
YOU SEEM EVEN MORE BLOOD-THIRSTY THAN USUAL TODAY, EREN.
HE'S STUCK ON TRAINING YESTERDAY.
WHAT A SAD SIGHT THAT WAS...
YOU GOT SO TANGLED UP, I THOUGHT YOU'D GET STRANGLED BY YOUR OWN WIRES!
...NOT AS SAD AS THE SIGHT OF YOU PRACTICING HOW TO TURN TAIL AND RUN AGAINST A TITAN.
YOU HORSE-FACED COWARD.
...YEAH, YOU GO CHARGE RIGHT UP TO A TITAN AND DIE IN A WEB OF YOUR OWN WIRES.
THE TITANS WILL GET A REAL LAUGH OUT OF THAT.
THAT'S YOUR LIFE.
THUNK
THUNK
HOW MANY TIMES DO I HAVE TO TELL YOU GUYS TO KNOCK IT OFF?!
SHUT UP, YOU TWO! IT'S TOO EARLY FOR THIS CRAP!!
THUMP
WHAP

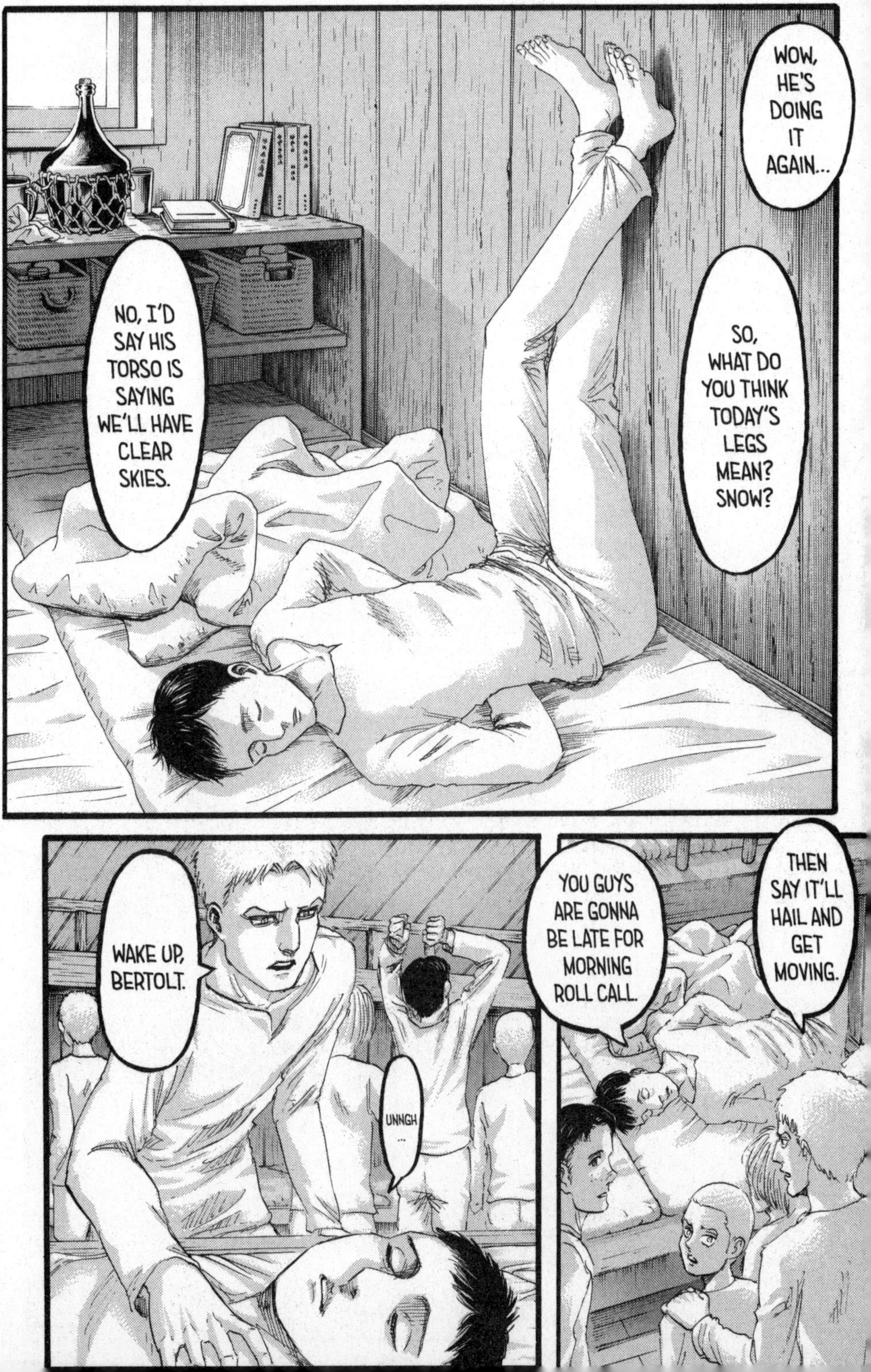
WOW, HE'S DOING IT AGAIN...
SO, WHAT DO YOU THINK TODAY'S LEGS MEAN? SNOW?
NO, I'D SAY HIS TORSO IS SAYING WE'LL HAVE CLEAR SKIES.
THEN SAY IT'LL HAIL AND GET MOVING.
YOU GUYS ARE GONNA BE LATE FOR MORNING ROLL CALL.
WAKE UP, BERTOLT.
UNNGH...

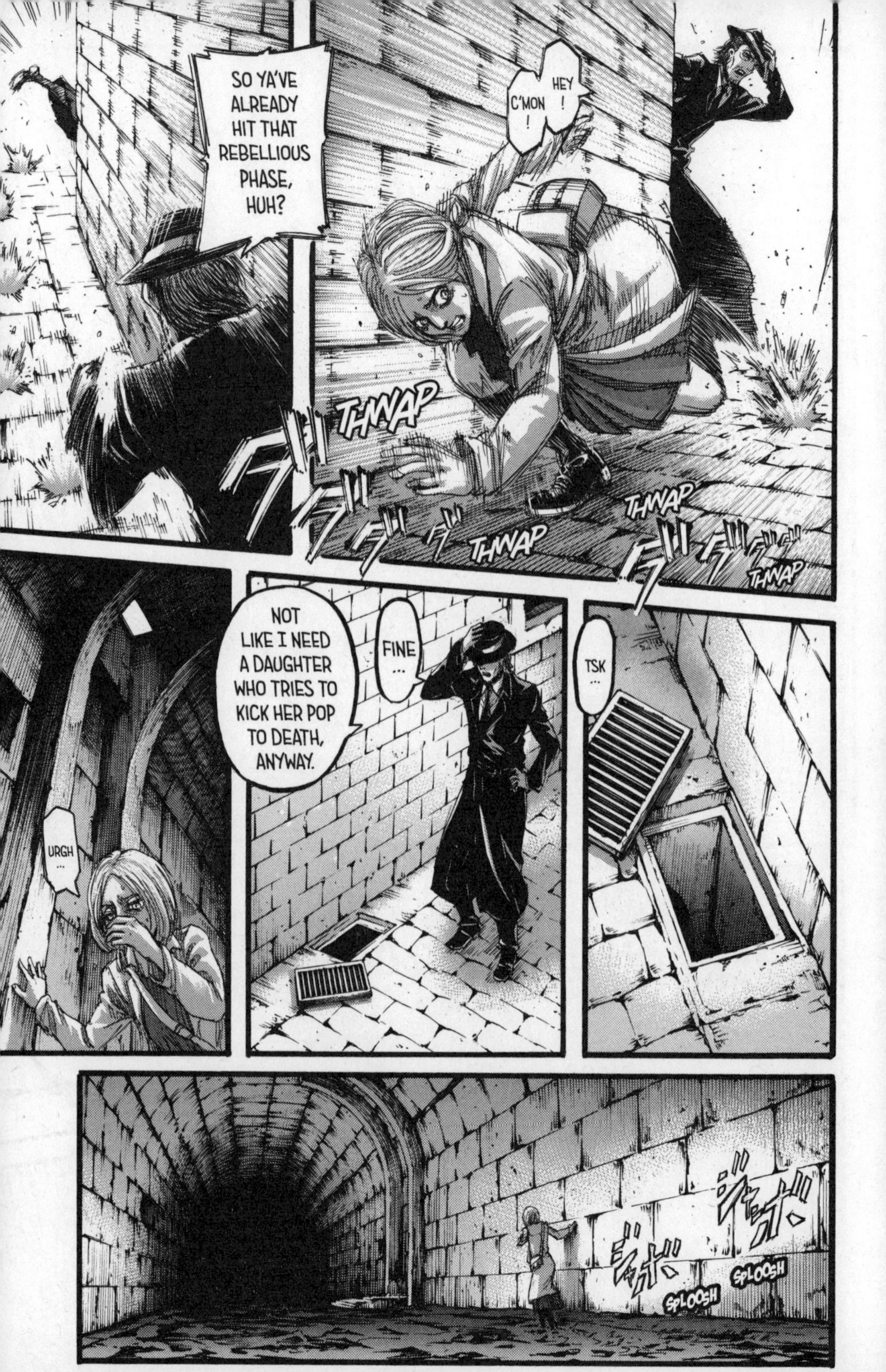
HEY! C'MON!
THWAP
THWAP
THWAP
THWAP
SO YA'VE ALREADY HIT THAT REBELLIOUS PHASE, HUH?
TSK…
FINE…
NOT LIKE I NEED A DAUGHTER WHO TRIES TO KICK HER POP TO DEATH, ANYWAY.
URGH…
SPLOOSH
SPLOOSH

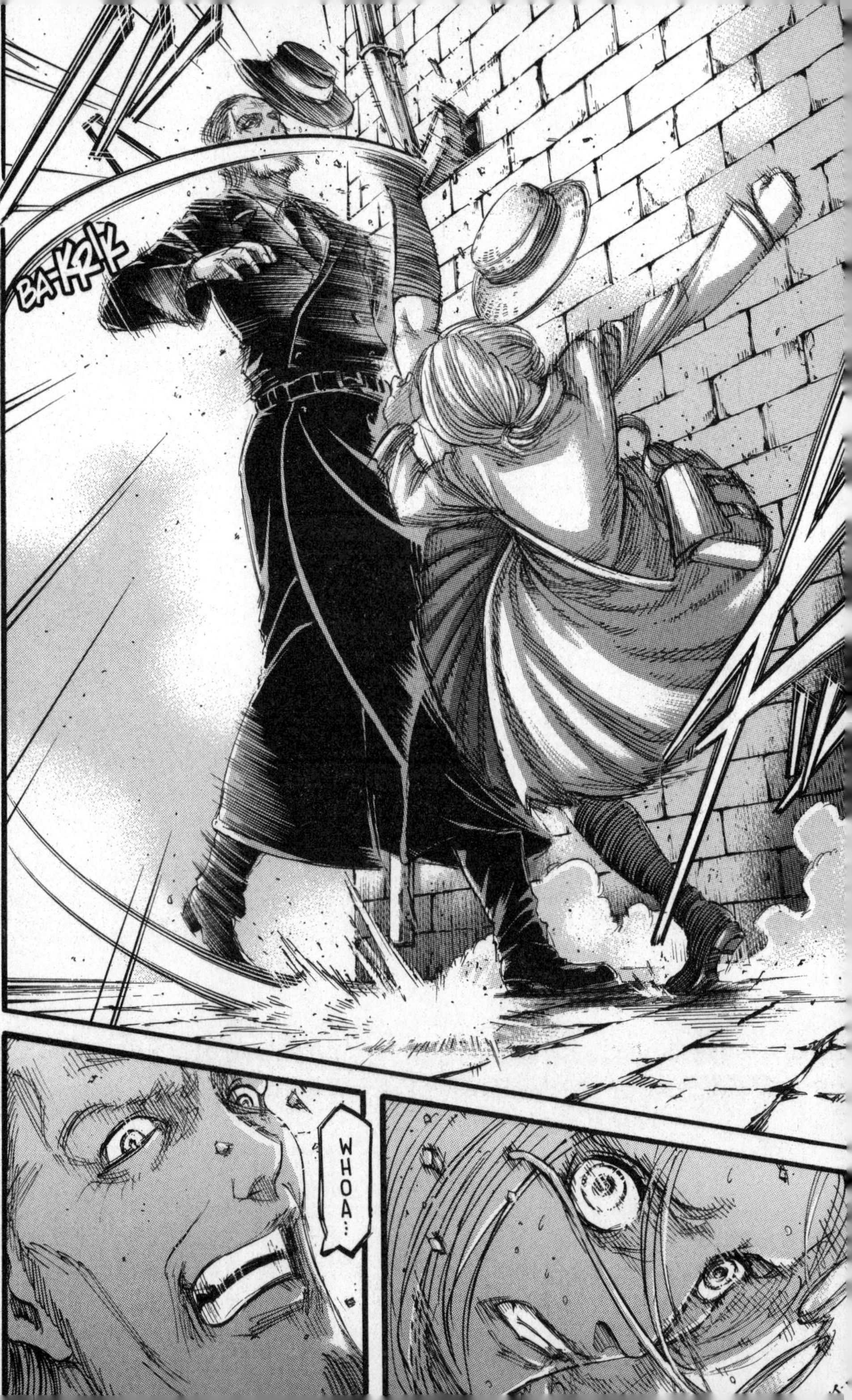
BA-KRIK
WHOA...

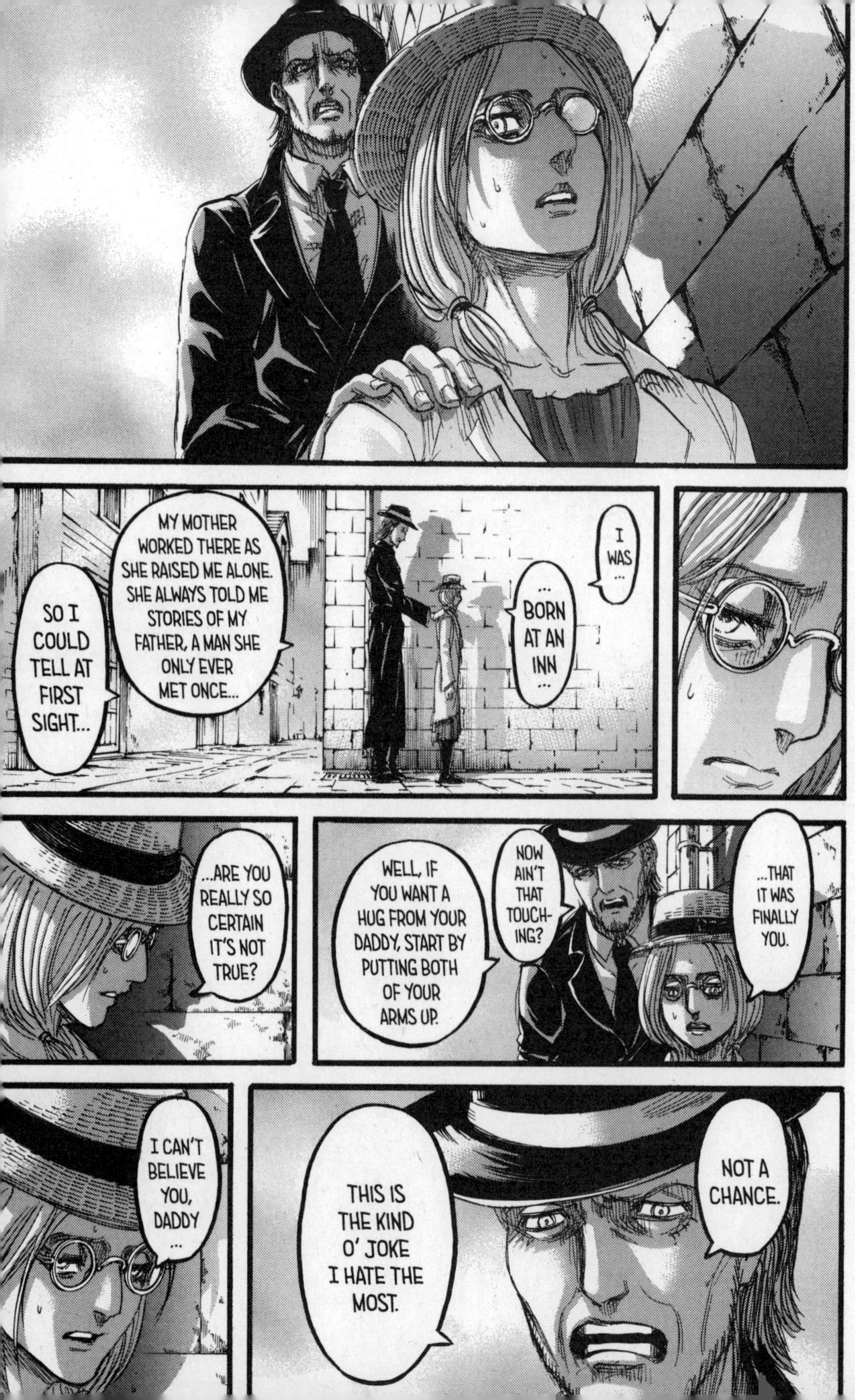
I WAS...
...BORN AT AN INN...
MY MOTHER WORKED THERE AS SHE RAISED ME ALONE. SHE ALWAYS TOLD ME STORIES OF MY FATHER, A MAN SHE ONLY EVER MET ONCE...
SO I COULD TELL AT FIRST SIGHT...
...THAT IT WAS FINALLY YOU.
NOW AIN'T THAT TOUCHING?
WELL, IF YOU WANT A HUG FROM YOUR DADDY, START BY PUTTING BOTH OF YOUR ARMS UP.
...ARE YOU REALLY SO CERTAIN IT'S NOT TRUE?
NOT A CHANCE.
THIS IS THE KIND O' JOKE I HATE THE MOST.
I CAN'T BELIEVE YOU, DADDY...

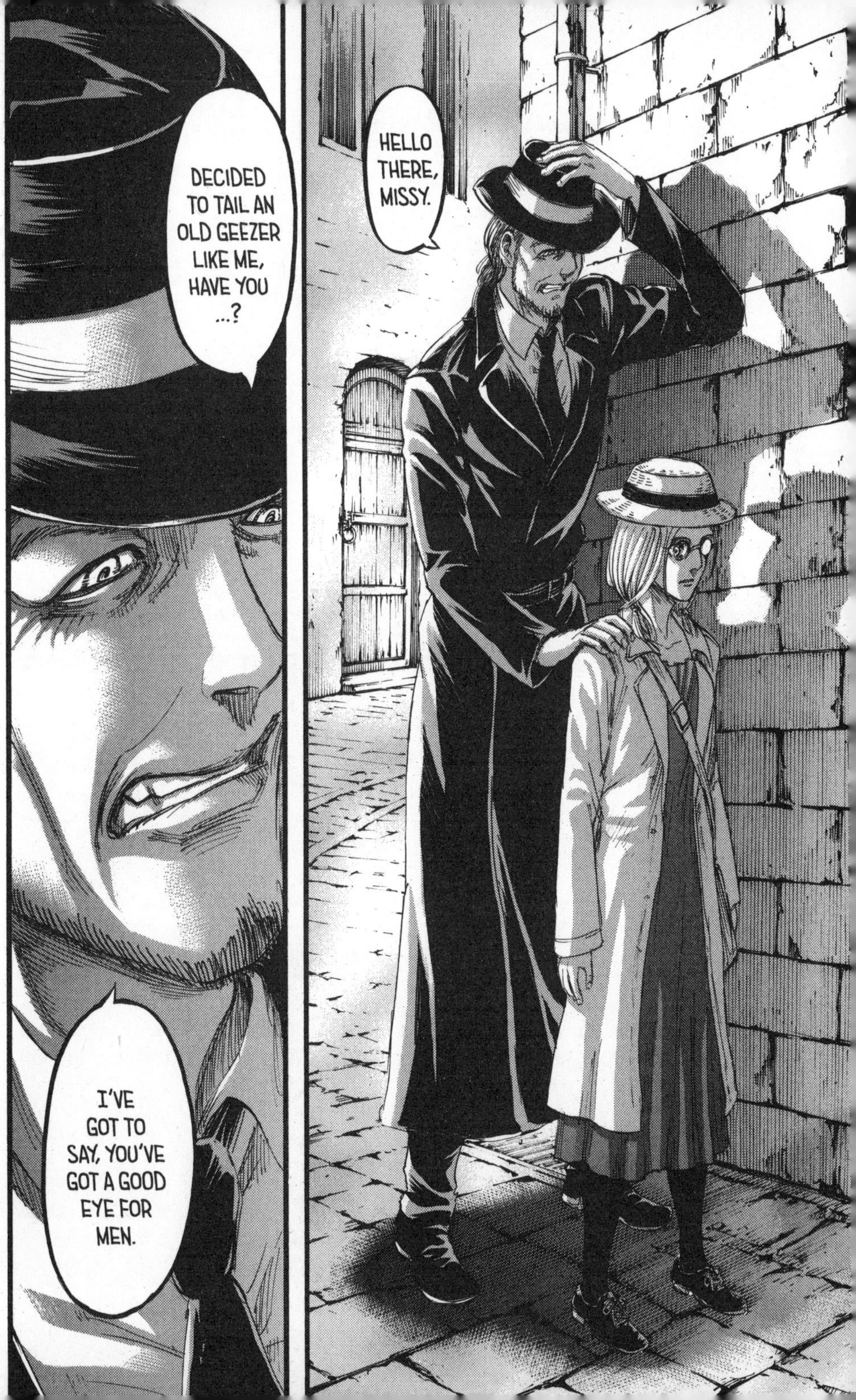
HELLO THERE, MISSY.
DECIDED TO TAIL AN OLD GEEZER LIKE ME, HAVE YOU ...?
I'VE GOT TO SAY, YOU'VE GOT A GOOD EYE FOR MEN.

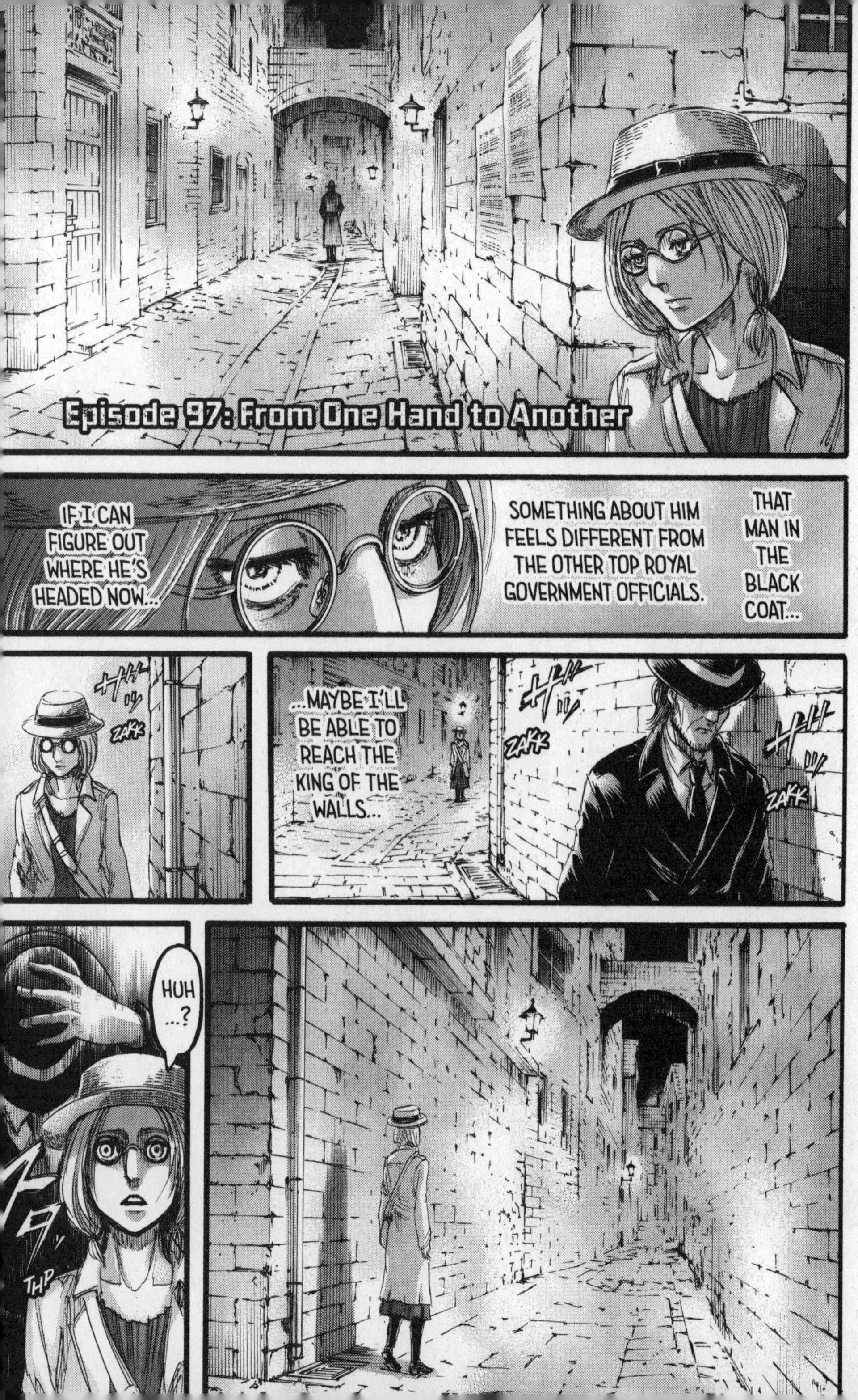
Episode 97: From One Hand to Another
THAT MAN IN THE BLACK COAT...
SOMETHING ABOUT HIM FEELS DIFFERENT FROM THE OTHER TOP ROYAL GOVERNMENT OFFICIALS.
IF I CAN FIGURE OUT WHERE HE'S HEADED NOW...
ZAKK
...MAYBE I'LL BE ABLE TO REACH THE KING OF THE WALLS...
ZAKK
ZAKK
HUH ...?
THP

ATTACK on TITAN

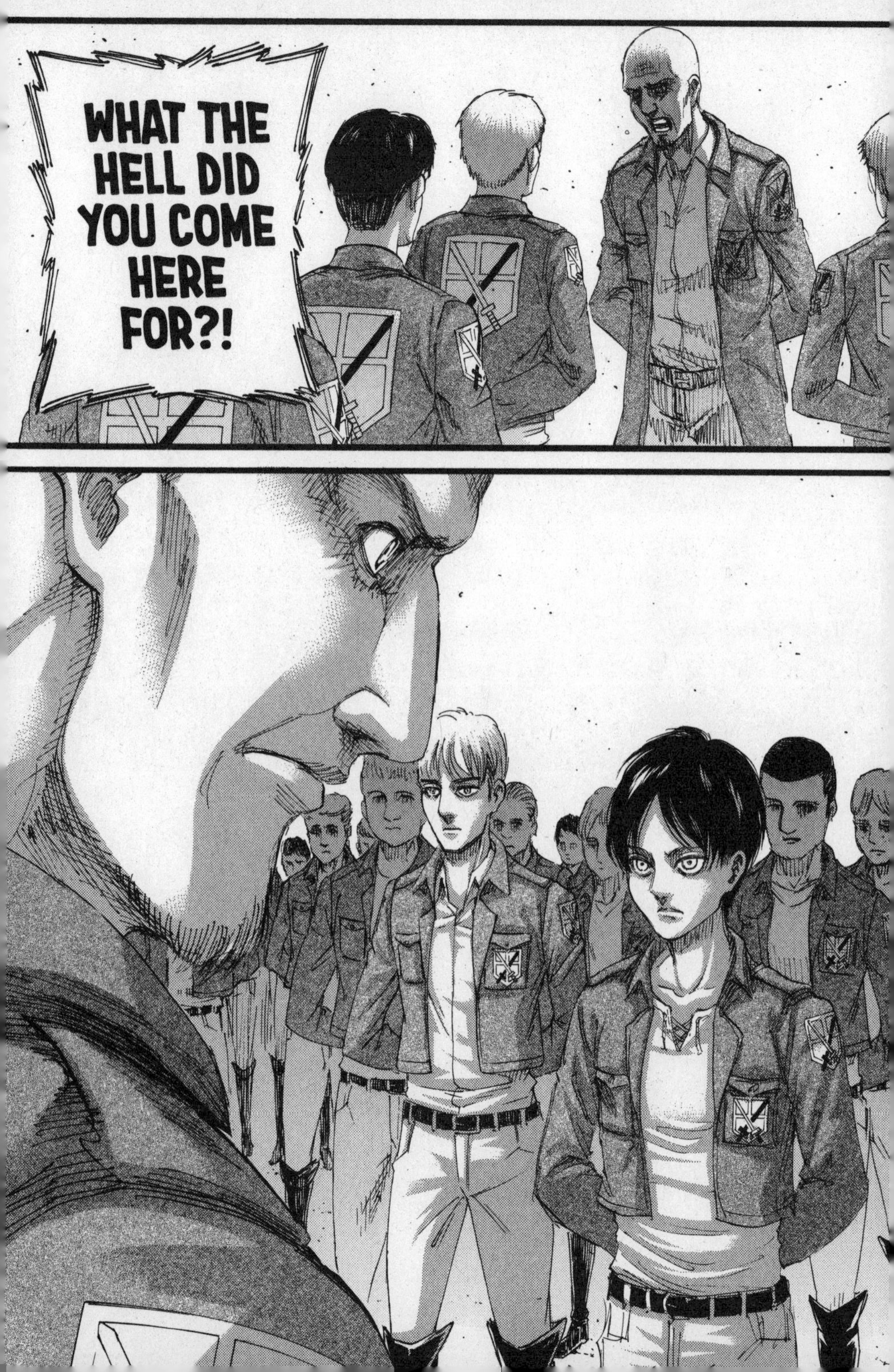
WHAT THE HELL DID YOU COME HERE FOR?!

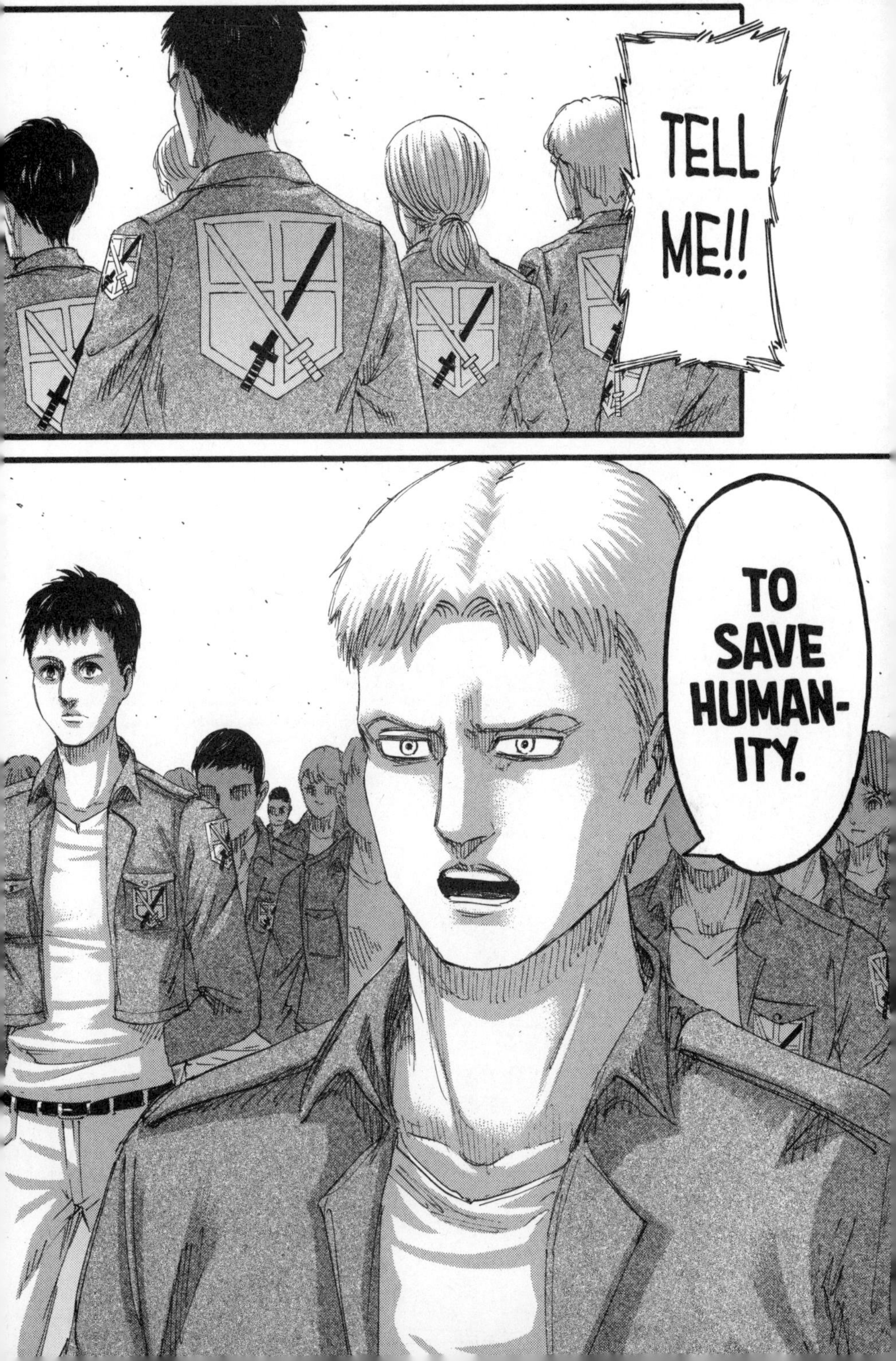
TELL ME!!
TO SAVE HUMAN-ITY.

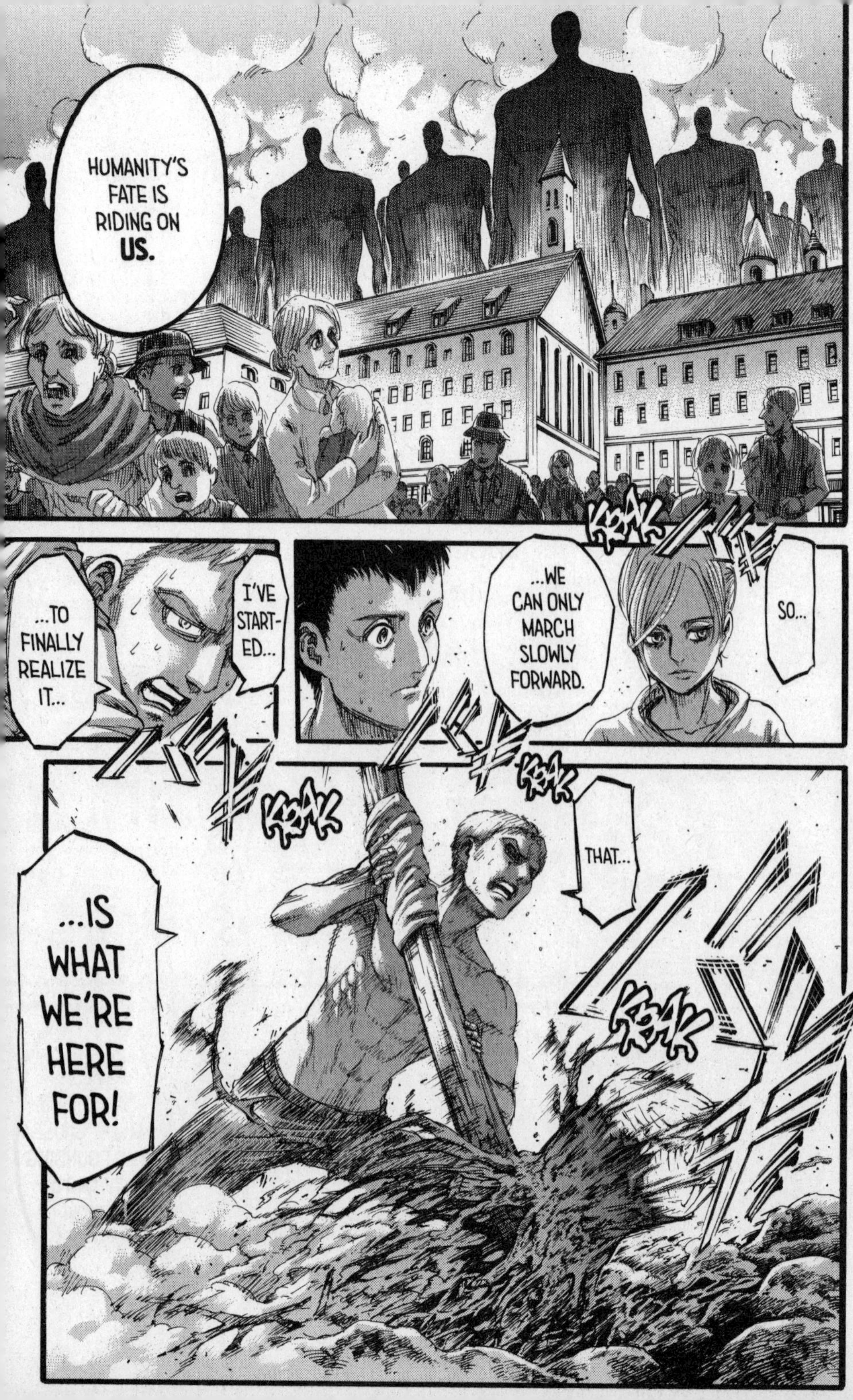
HUMANITY'S FATE IS RIDING ON US.
KRAK
SO...
...WE CAN ONLY MARCH SLOWLY FORWARD.
I'VE START-ED...
...TO FINALLY REALIZE IT...
KRAK
KRAK
THAT...
KRAK
...IS WHAT WE'RE HERE FOR!

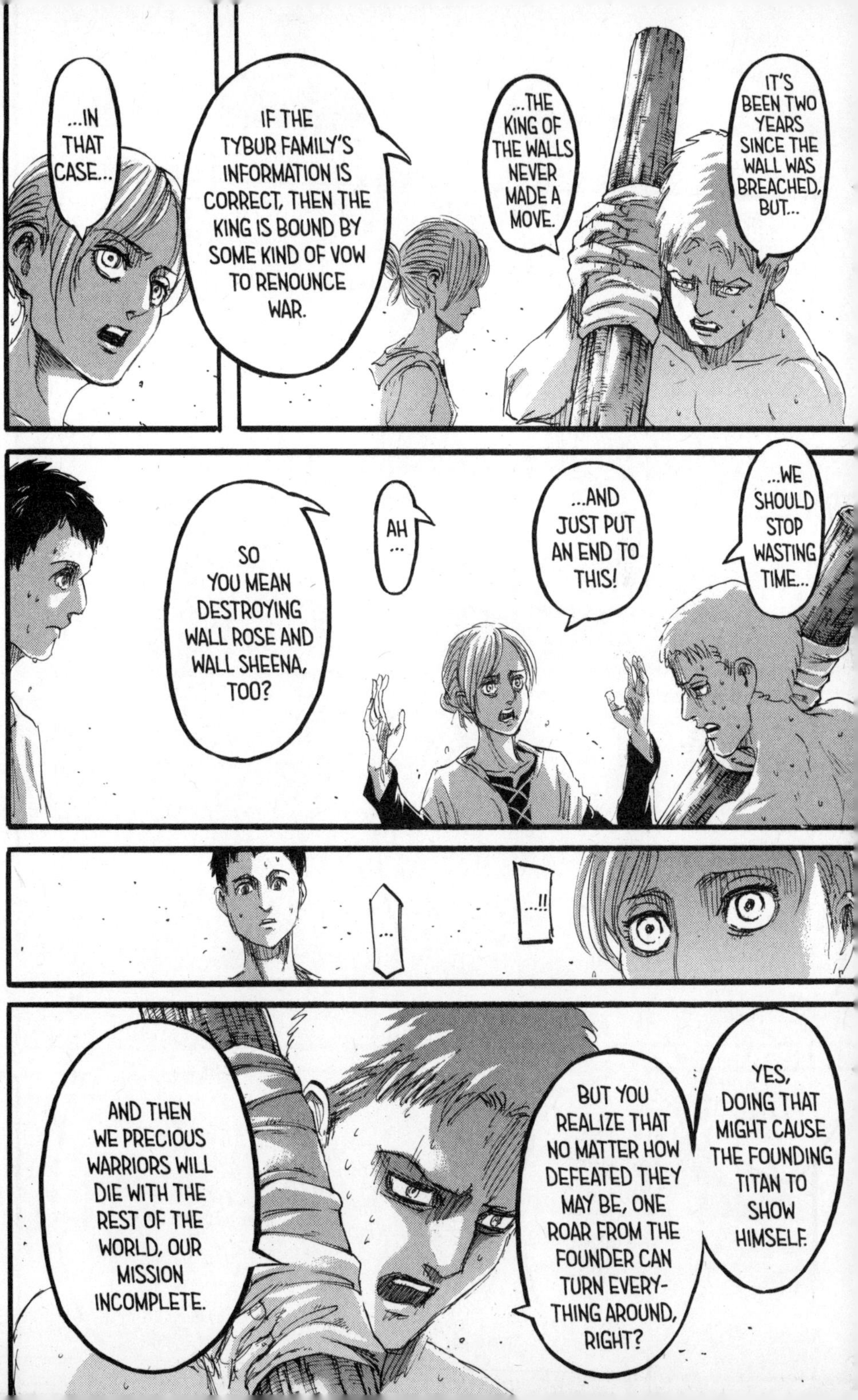
IT'S BEEN TWO YEARS SINCE THE WALL WAS BREACHED, BUT...
...THE KING OF THE WALLS NEVER MADE A MOVE.
IF THE TYBUR FAMILY'S INFORMATION IS CORRECT, THEN THE KING IS BOUND BY SOME KIND OF VOW TO RENOUNCE WAR.
...IN THAT CASE...
...WE SHOULD STOP WASTING TIME...
...AND JUST PUT AN END TO THIS!
AH ...
SO YOU MEAN DESTROYING WALL ROSE AND WALL SHEENA, TOO?
...!!
...
YES, DOING THAT MIGHT CAUSE THE FOUNDING TITAN TO SHOW HIMSELF.
BUT YOU REALIZE THAT NO MATTER HOW DEFEATED THEY MAY BE, ONE ROAR FROM THE FOUNDER CAN TURN EVERY-THING AROUND, RIGHT?
AND THEN WE PRECIOUS WARRIORS WILL DIE WITH THE REST OF THE WORLD, OUR MISSION INCOMPLETE.

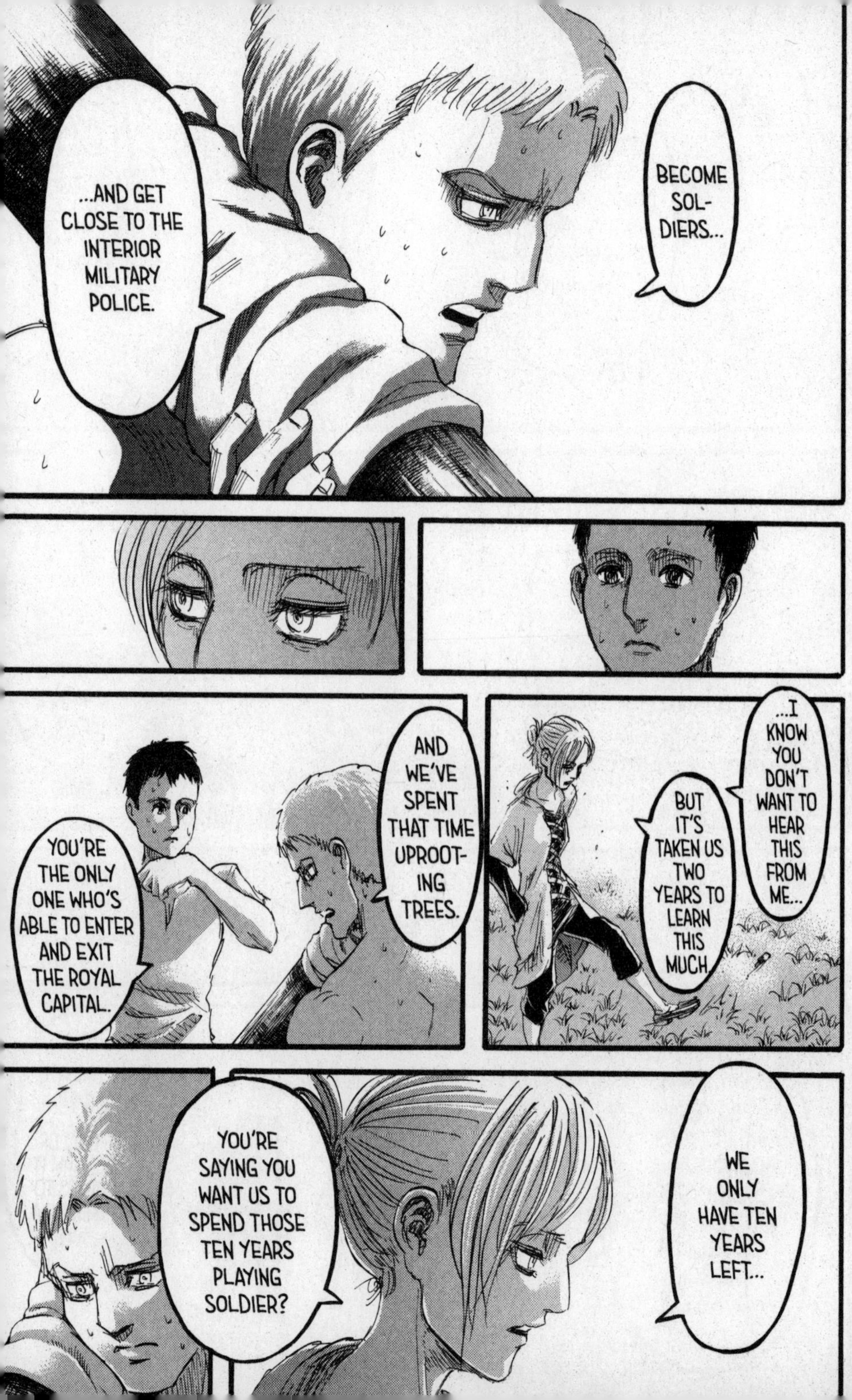
BECOME SOLDIERS...
...AND GET CLOSE TO THE INTERIOR MILITARY POLICE.
...I KNOW YOU DON'T WANT TO HEAR THIS FROM ME...
BUT IT'S TAKEN US TWO YEARS TO LEARN THIS MUCH.
AND WE'VE SPENT THAT TIME UPROOTING TREES.
YOU'RE THE ONLY ONE WHO'S ABLE TO ENTER AND EXIT THE ROYAL CAPITAL.
WE ONLY HAVE TEN YEARS LEFT...
YOU'RE SAYING YOU WANT US TO SPEND THOSE TEN YEARS PLAYING SOLDIER?

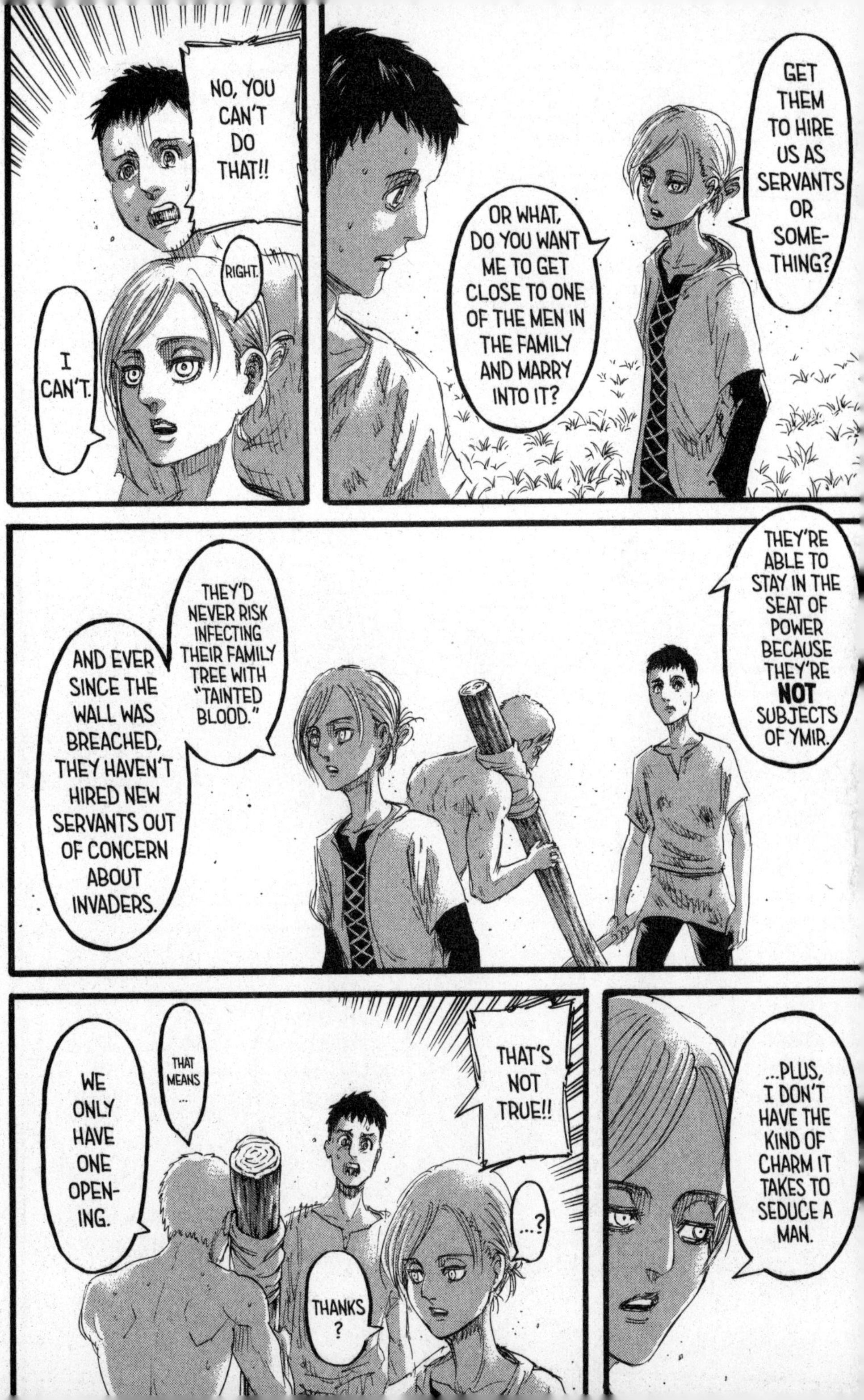
GET THEM TO HIRE US AS SERVANTS OR SOME-THING?
OR WHAT, DO YOU WANT ME TO GET CLOSE TO ONE OF THE MEN IN THE FAMILY AND MARRY INTO IT?
NO, YOU CAN'T DO THAT!!
RIGHT.
I CAN'T.
THEY'RE ABLE TO STAY IN THE SEAT OF POWER BECAUSE THEY'RE **NOT** SUBJECTS OF YMIR.
THEY'D NEVER RISK INFECTING THEIR FAMILY TREE WITH "TAINTED BLOOD."
AND EVER SINCE THE WALL WAS BREACHED, THEY HAVEN'T HIRED NEW SERVANTS OUT OF CONCERN ABOUT INVADERS.
...PLUS, I DON'T HAVE THE KIND OF CHARM IT TAKES TO SEDUCE A MAN.
THAT'S NOT TRUE!!
...?
THANKS?
THAT MEANS ...
WE ONLY HAVE ONE OPEN-ING.

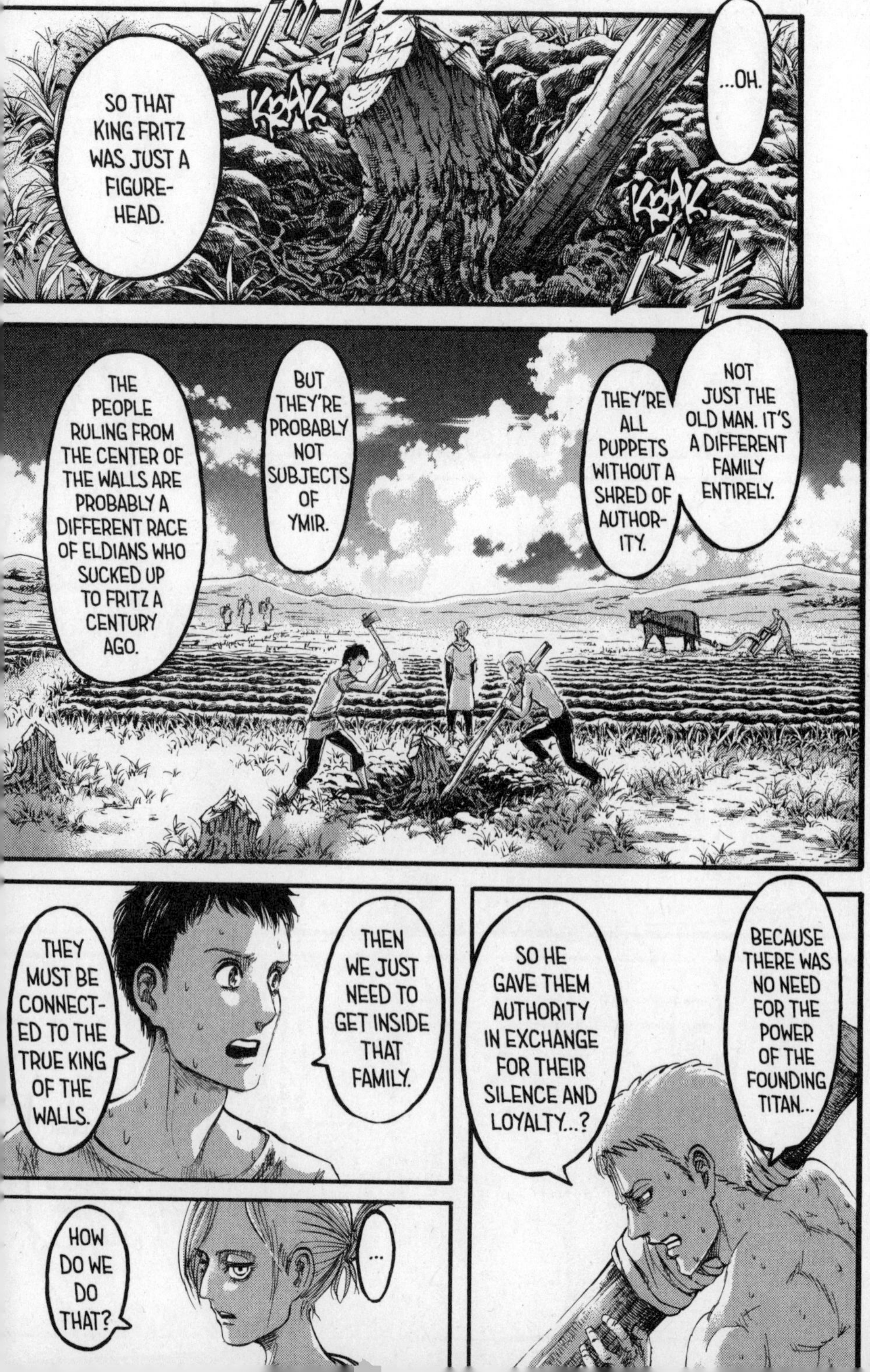
...OH.
KRAK
KRAK
SO THAT KING FRITZ WAS JUST A FIGURE-HEAD.
NOT JUST THE OLD MAN. IT'S A DIFFERENT FAMILY ENTIRELY.
THEY'RE ALL PUPPETS WITHOUT A SHRED OF AUTHOR-ITY.
BUT THEY'RE PROBABLY NOT SUBJECTS OF YMIR.
THE PEOPLE RULING FROM THE CENTER OF THE WALLS ARE PROBABLY A DIFFERENT RACE OF ELDIANS WHO SUCKED UP TO FRITZ A CENTURY AGO.
BECAUSE THERE WAS NO NEED FOR THE POWER OF THE FOUNDING TITAN...
SO HE GAVE THEM AUTHORITY IN EXCHANGE FOR THEIR SILENCE AND LOYALTY...?
THEN WE JUST NEED TO GET INSIDE THAT FAMILY.
THEY MUST BE CONNECT-ED TO THE TRUE KING OF THE WALLS.
...
HOW DO WE DO THAT?

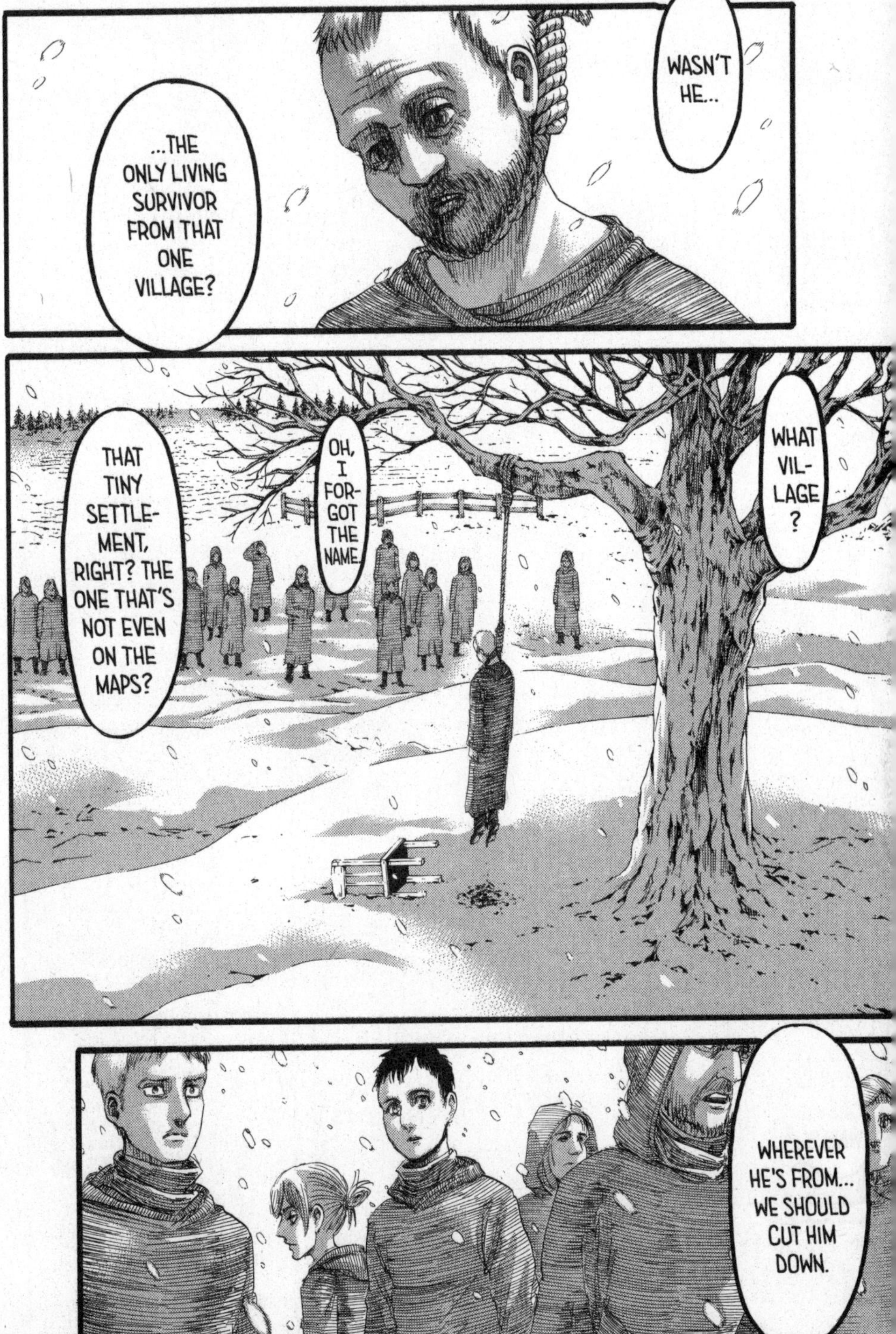
WASN'T HE...
...THE ONLY LIVING SURVIVOR FROM THAT ONE VILLAGE?
WHAT VIL-LAGE?
OH, I FOR-GOT THE NAME.
THAT TINY SETTLE-MENT, RIGHT? THE ONE THAT'S NOT EVEN ON THE MAPS?
WHEREVER HE'S FROM... WE SHOULD CUT HIM DOWN.

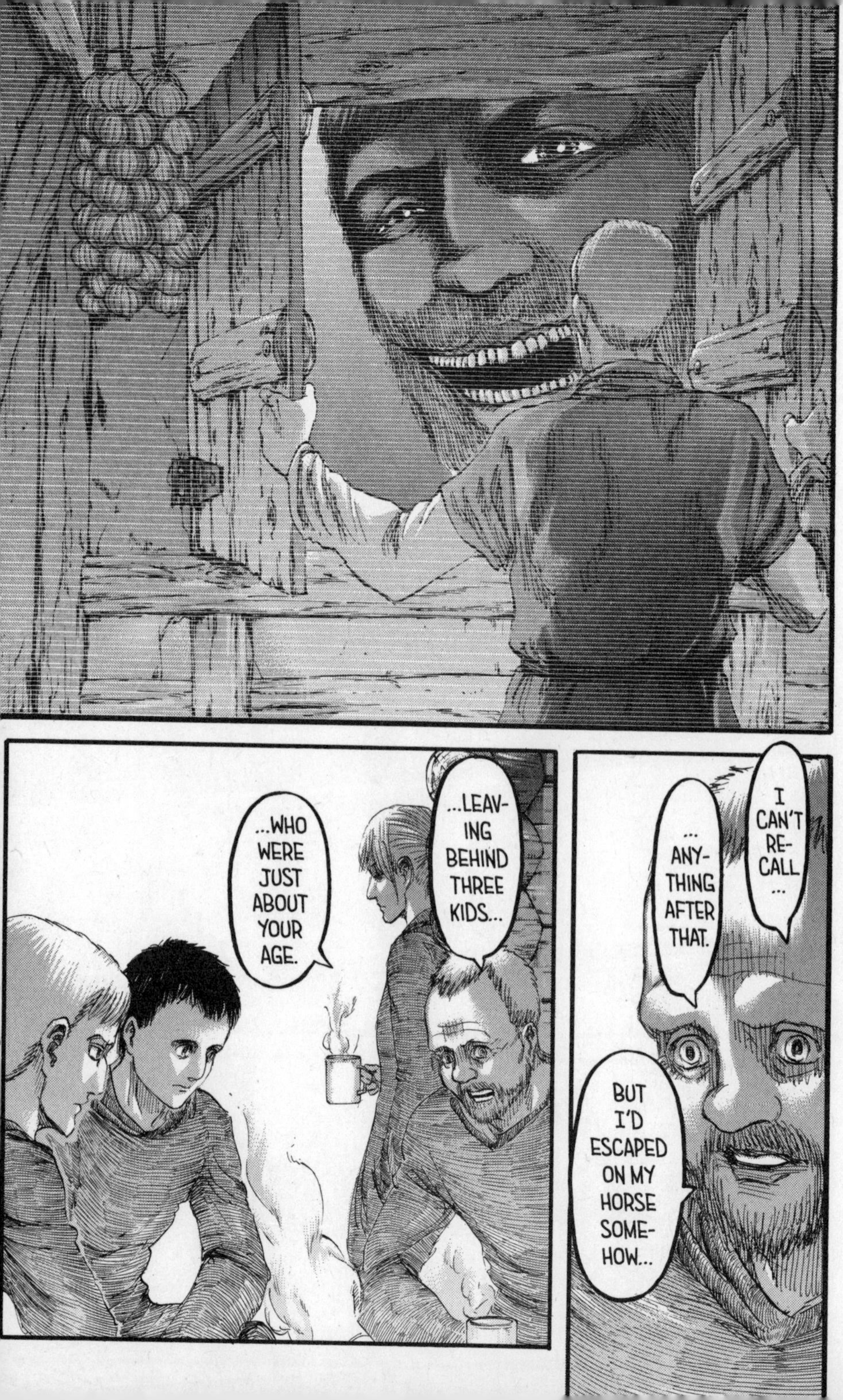
I CAN'T RECALL...
...ANYTHING AFTER THAT.
BUT I'D ESCAPED ON MY HORSE SOMEHOW...
...LEAVING BEHIND THREE KIDS...
...WHO WERE JUST ABOUT YOUR AGE.

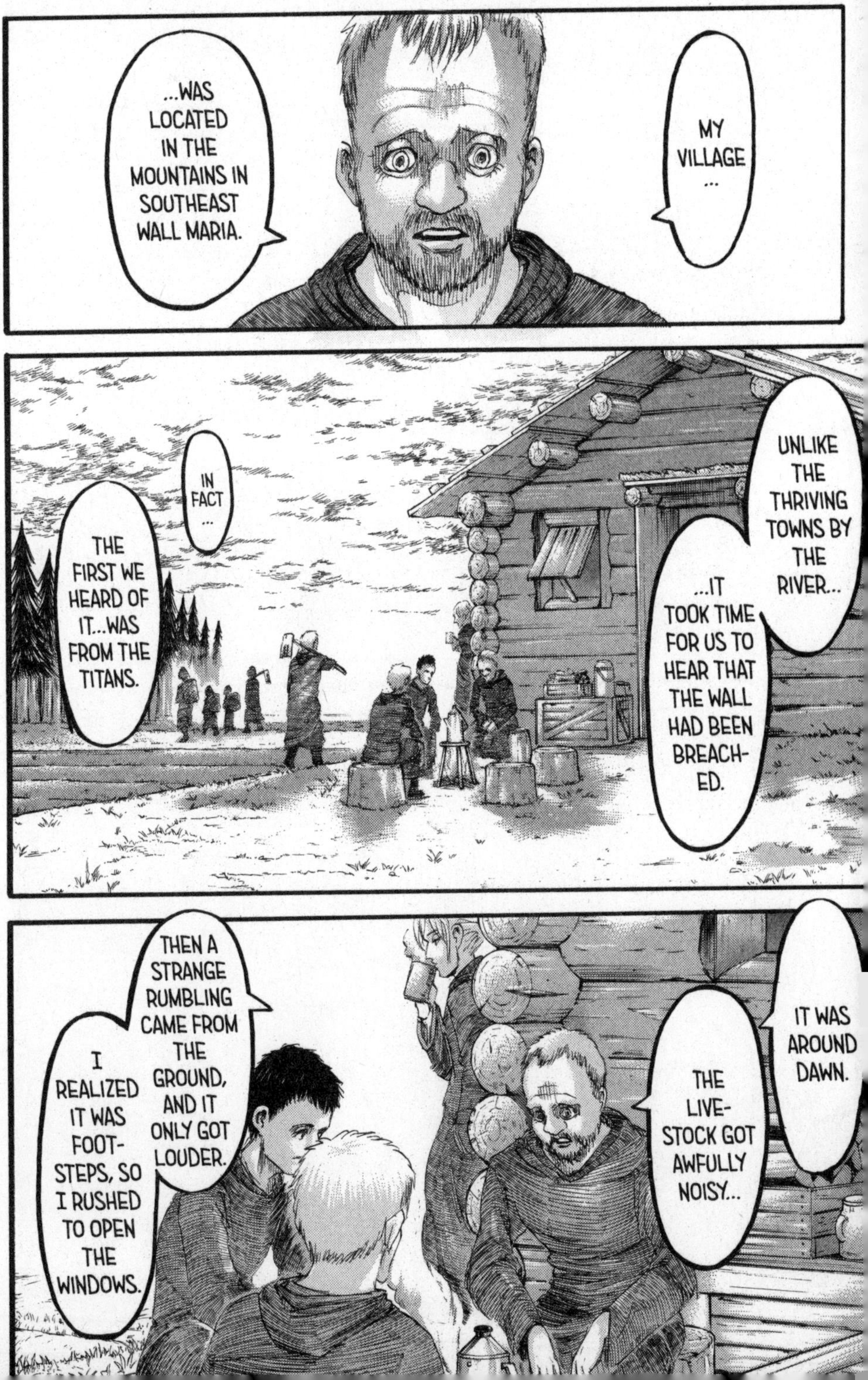
MY VILLAGE ...
...WAS LOCATED IN THE MOUNTAINS IN SOUTHEAST WALL MARIA.
UNLIKE THE THRIVING TOWNS BY THE RIVER...
...IT TOOK TIME FOR US TO HEAR THAT THE WALL HAD BEEN BREACHED.
IN FACT ...
THE FIRST WE HEARD OF IT...WAS FROM THE TITANS.
IT WAS AROUND DAWN.
THE LIVESTOCK GOT AWFULLY NOISY...
THEN A STRANGE RUMBLING CAME FROM THE GROUND, AND IT ONLY GOT LOUDER.
I REALIZED IT WAS FOOTSTEPS, SO I RUSHED TO OPEN THE WINDOWS.

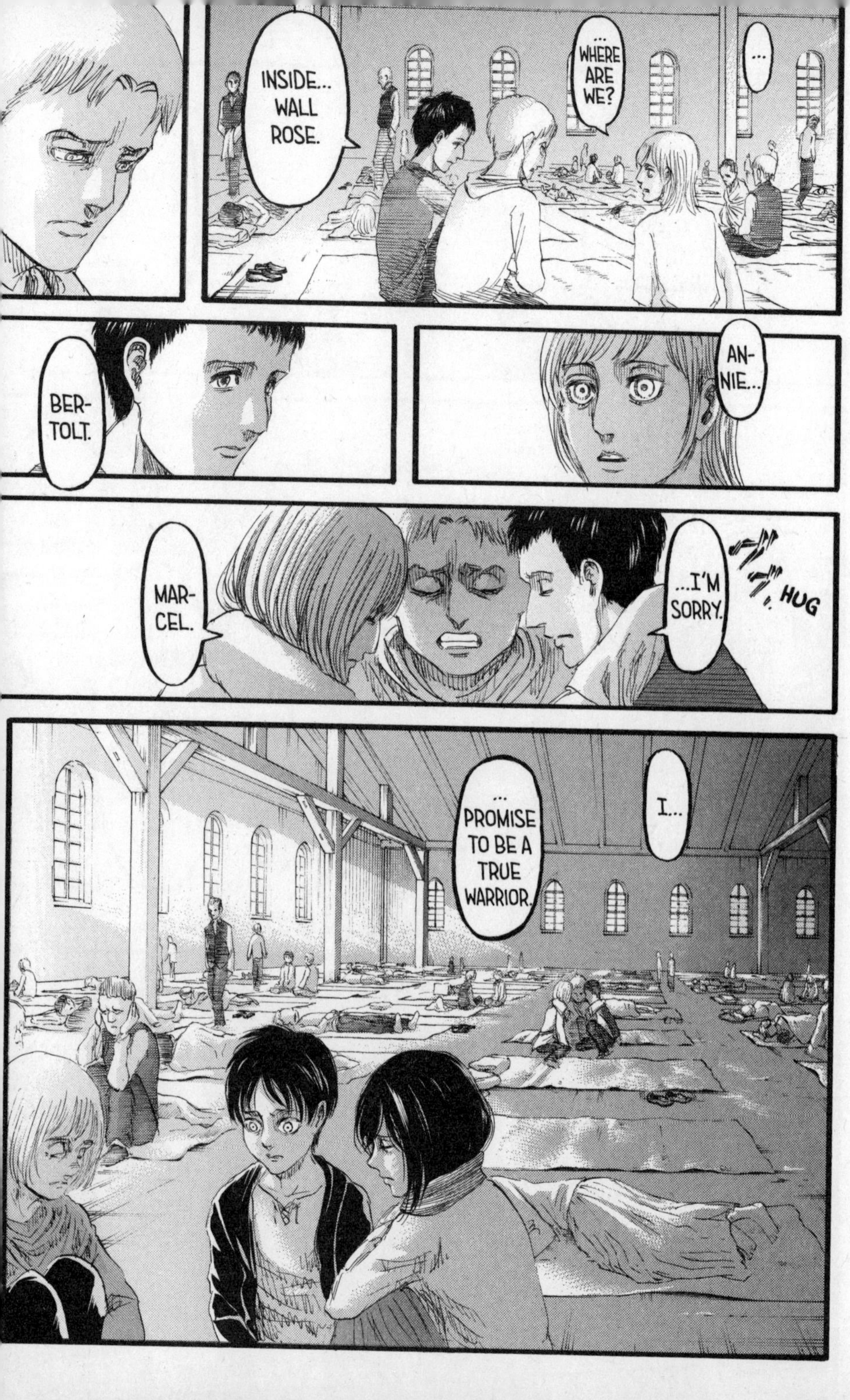
...
...WHERE ARE WE?
INSIDE... WALL ROSE.
AN-NIE...
BER-TOLT.
HUG
...I'M SORRY.
MAR-CEL.
I...
...PROMISE TO BE A TRUE WARRIOR.

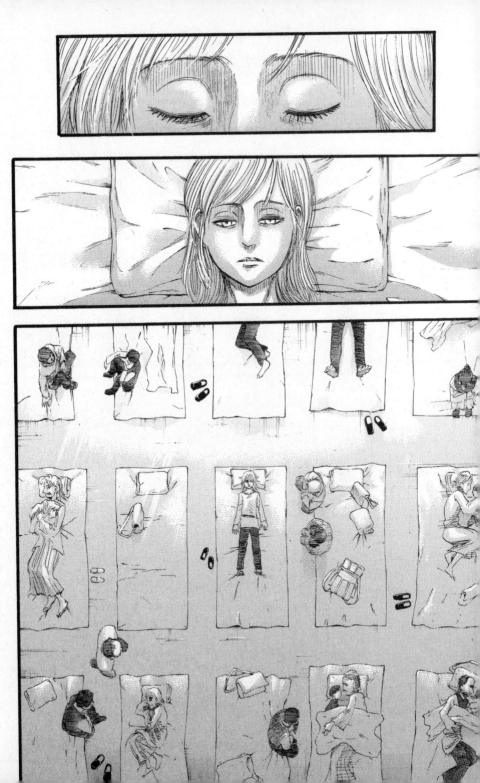

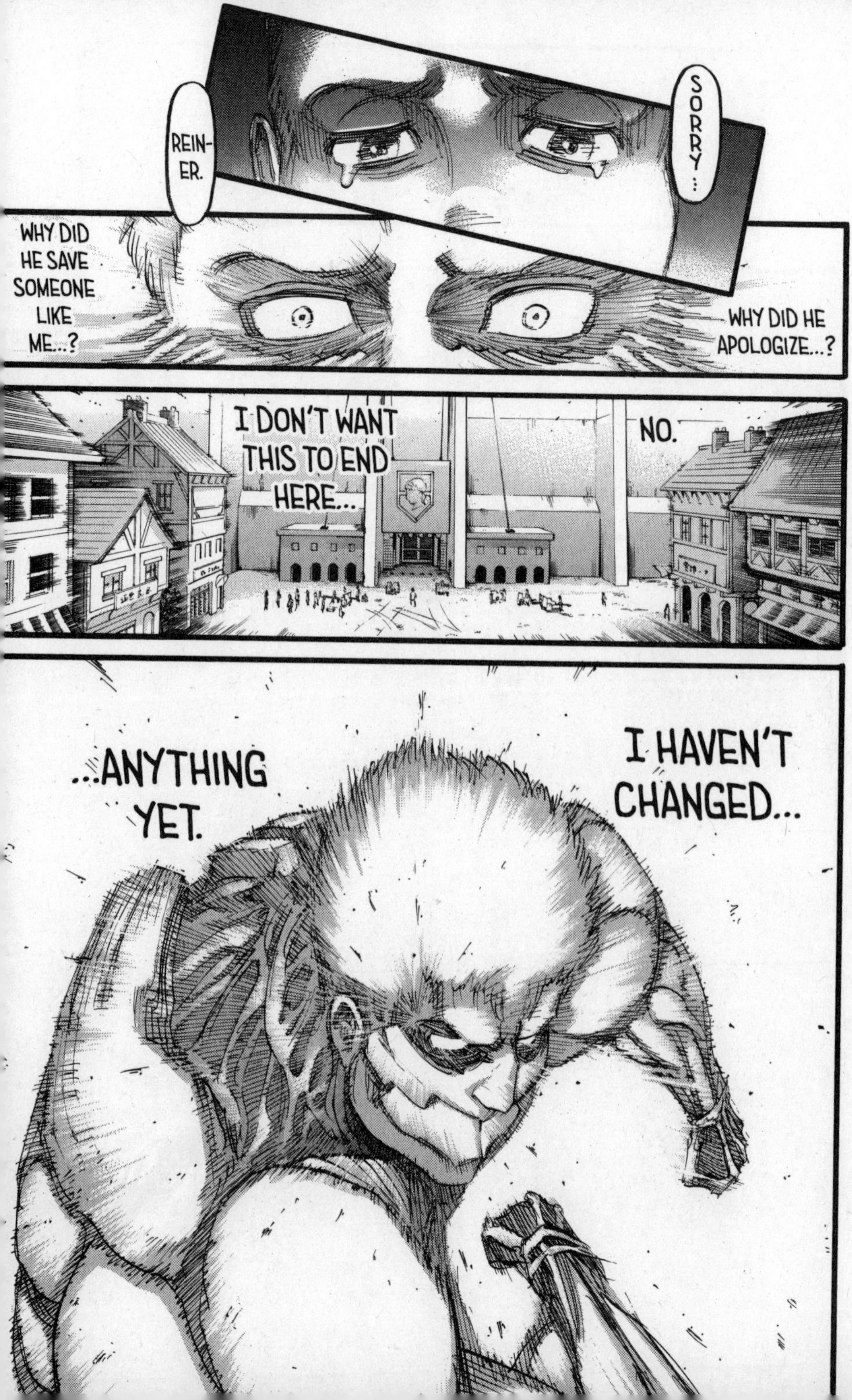
SORRY...
REIN-ER.
WHY DID HE APOLOGIZE...?
WHY DID HE SAVE SOMEONE LIKE ME...?
NO.
I DON'T WANT THIS TO END HERE...
I HAVEN'T CHANGED...
...ANYTHING YET.

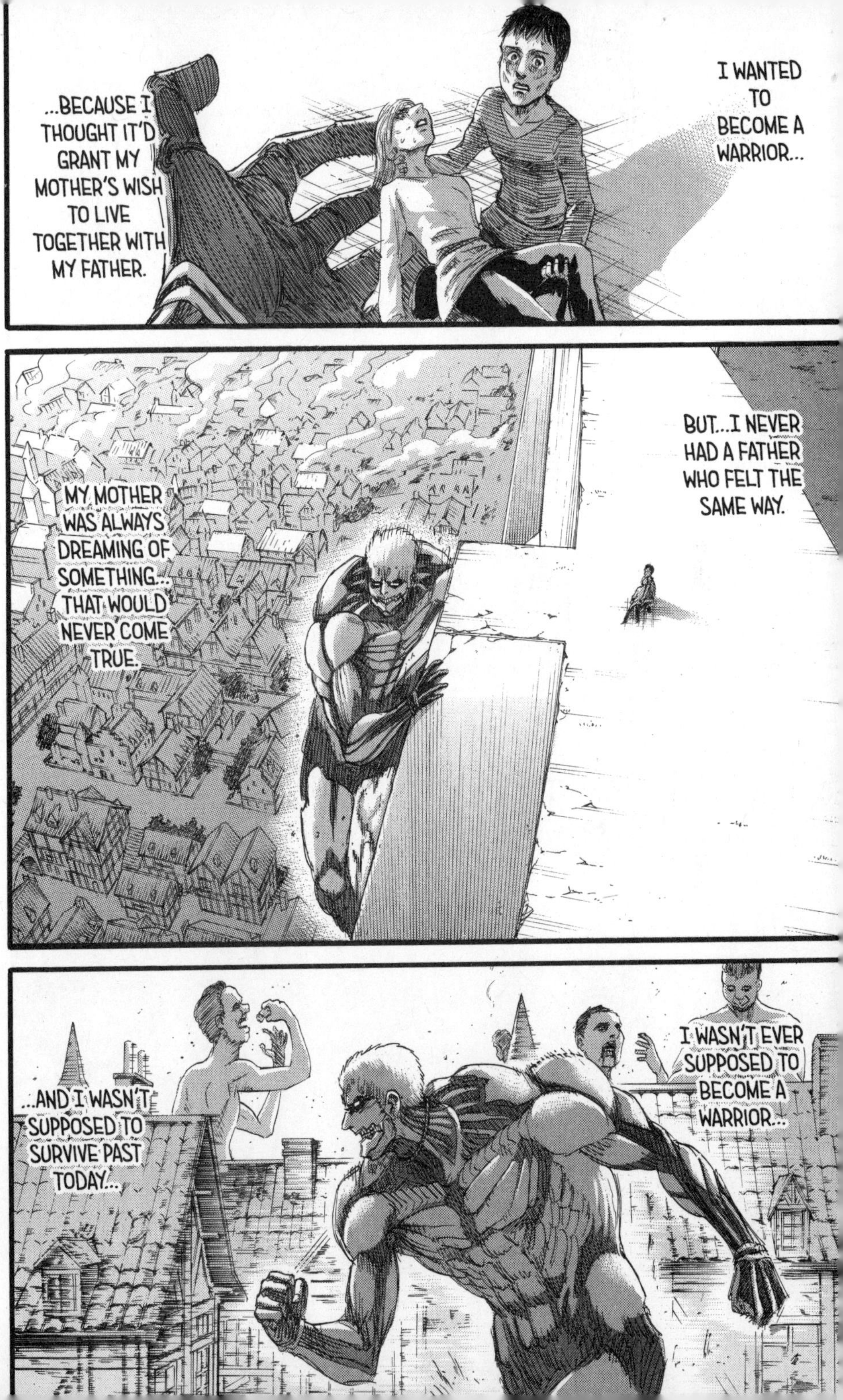
I WANTED TO BECOME A WARRIOR...
...BECAUSE I THOUGHT IT'D GRANT MY MOTHER'S WISH TO LIVE TOGETHER WITH MY FATHER.
BUT...I NEVER HAD A FATHER WHO FELT THE SAME WAY.
MY MOTHER WAS ALWAYS DREAMING OF SOMETHING... THAT WOULD NEVER COME TRUE.
I WASN'T EVER SUPPOSED TO BECOME A WARRIOR...
...AND I WASN'T SUPPOSED TO SURVIVE PAST TODAY...

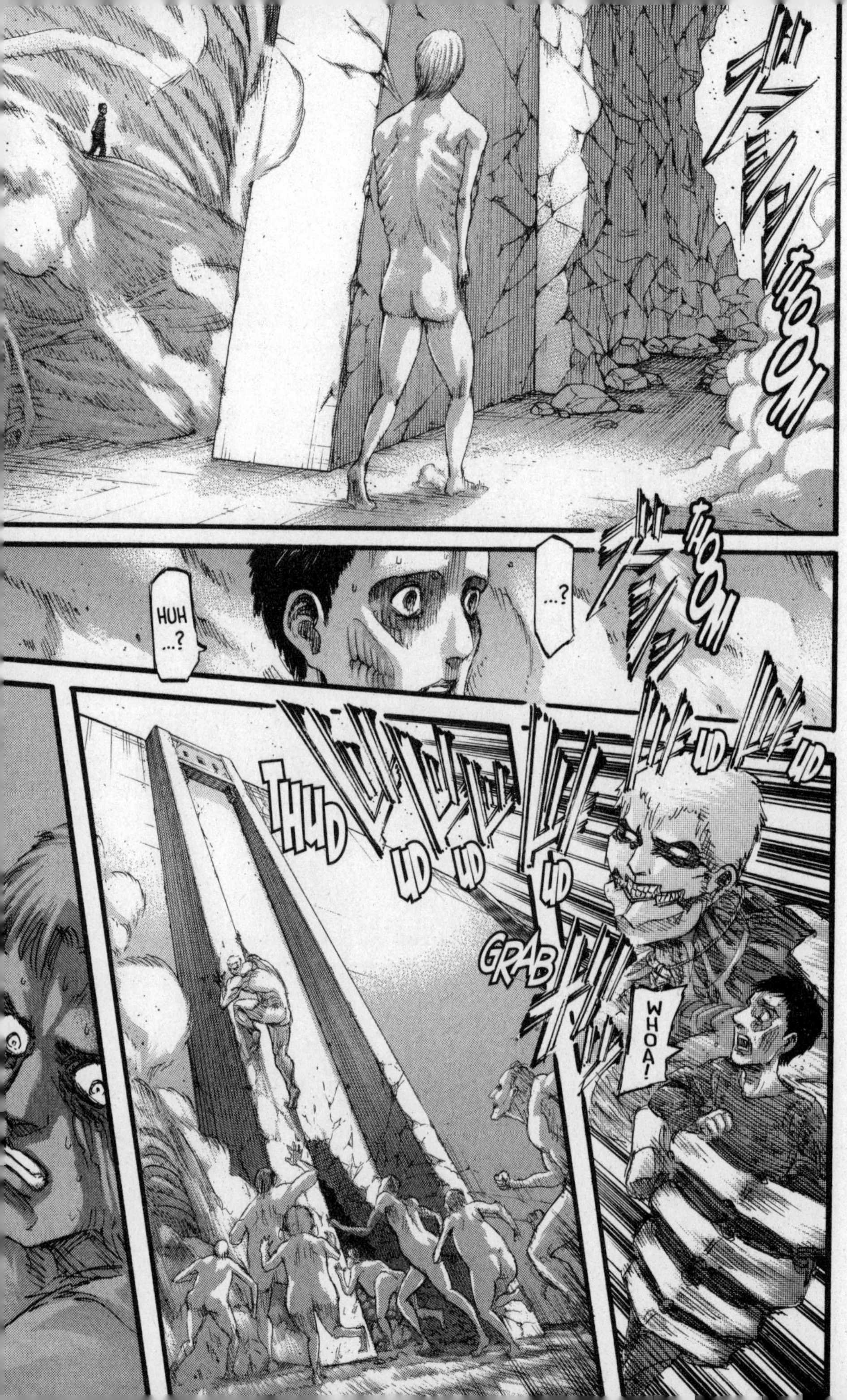
THOOOM
THOOOM
...?
HUH ...?
THUD
UD UD UD UD UD
GRAB
WHOA!

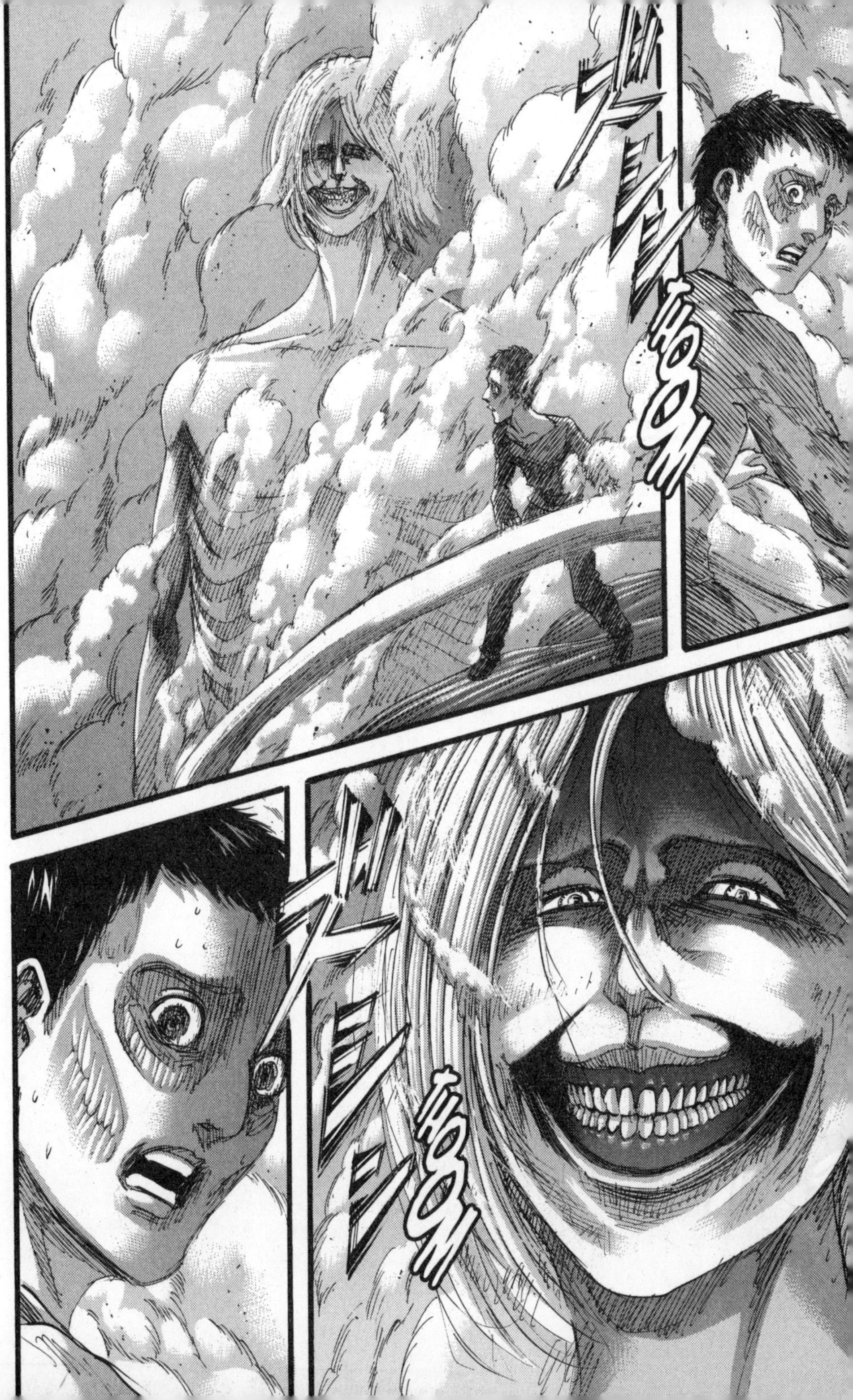
THOOM!
THOOM!

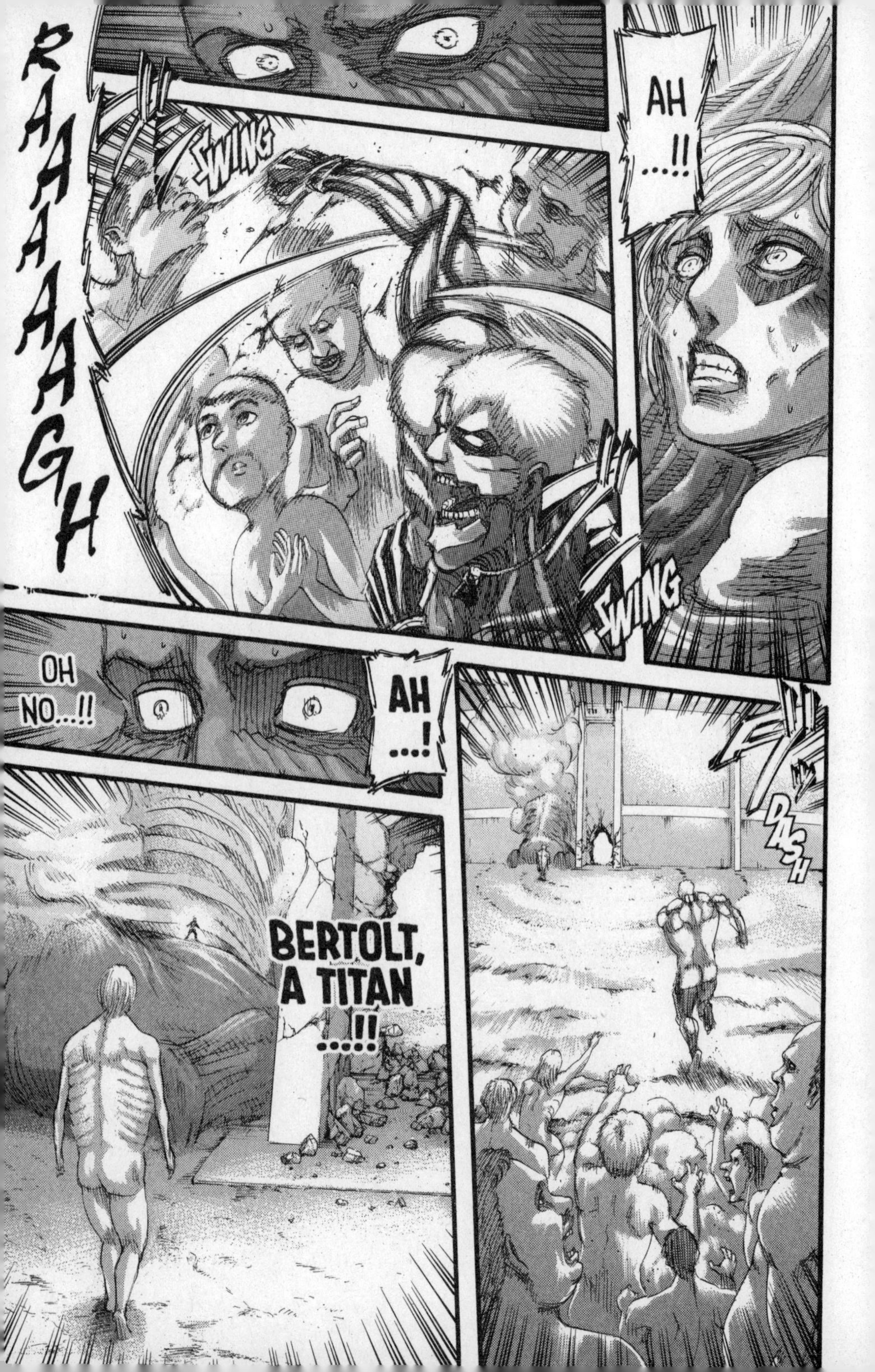

AH ...!!
SWING
RAAAAAGH
SWING
DASH
AH ...!
OH NO...!!
BERTOLT, A TITAN ...!!

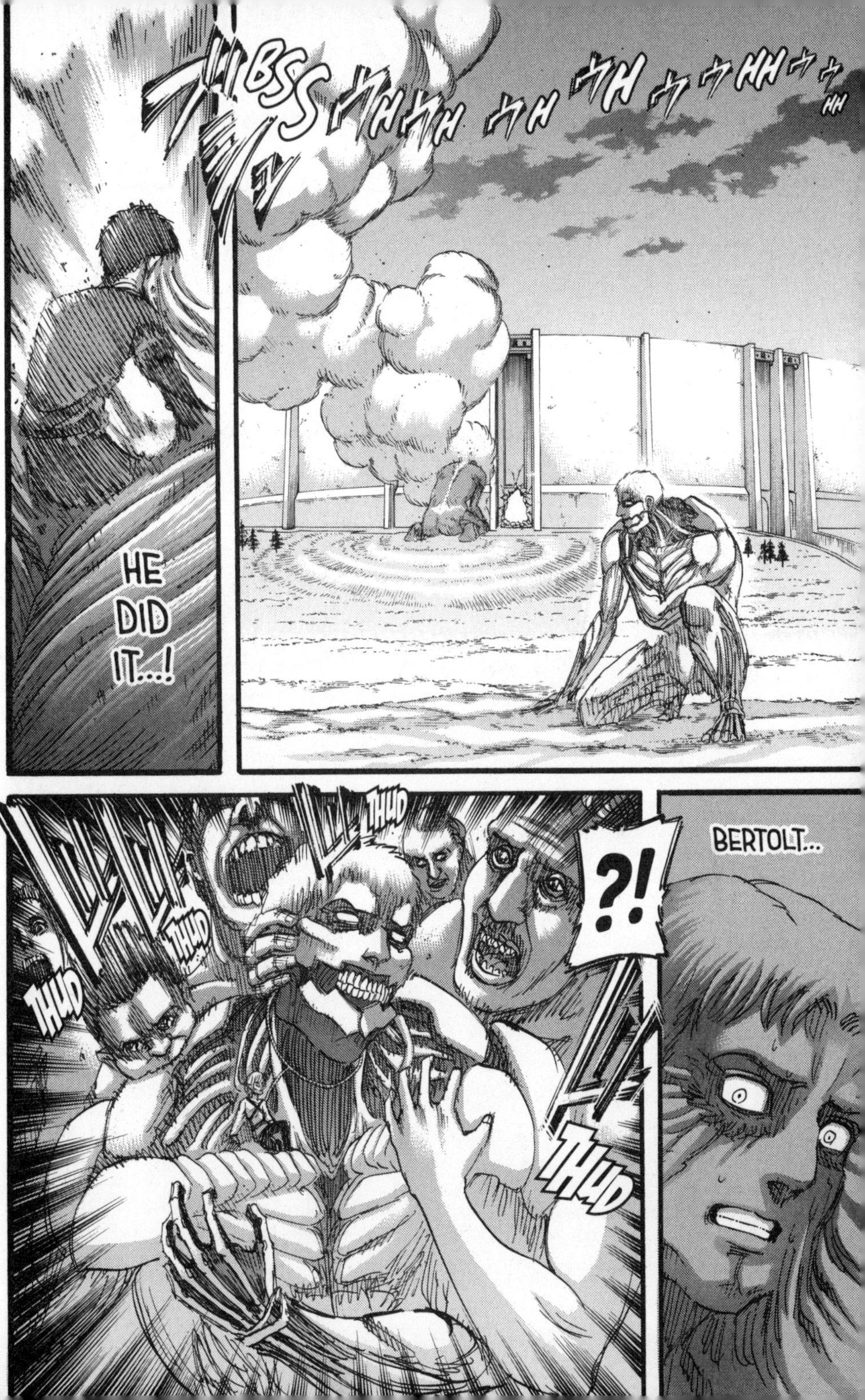
HE DID IT...!
BERTOLT...
?!
THUD
THUD
THUD
THUD

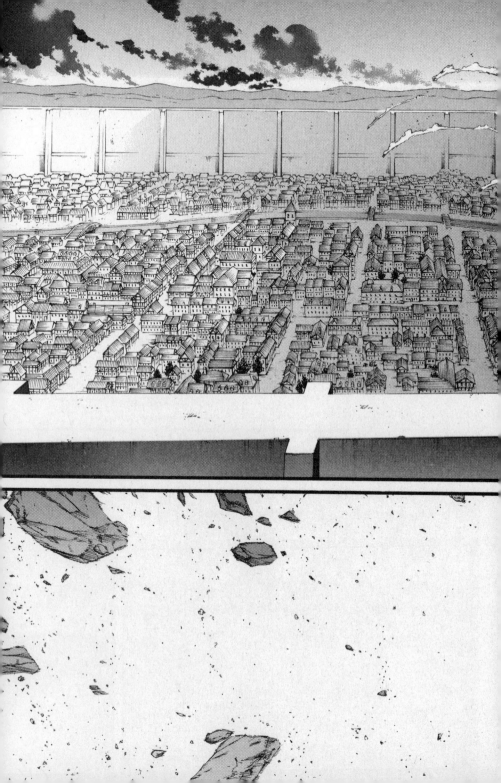

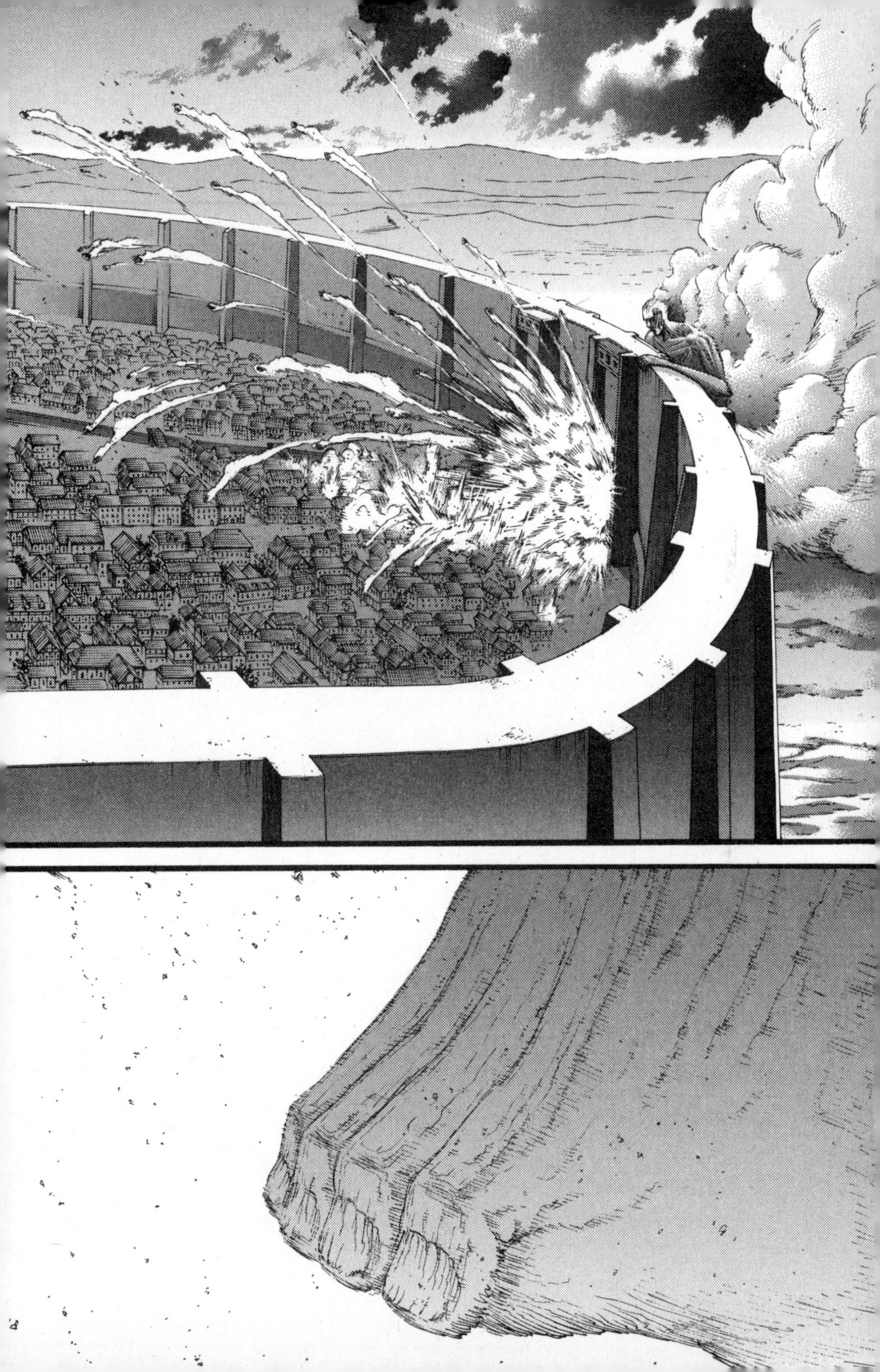

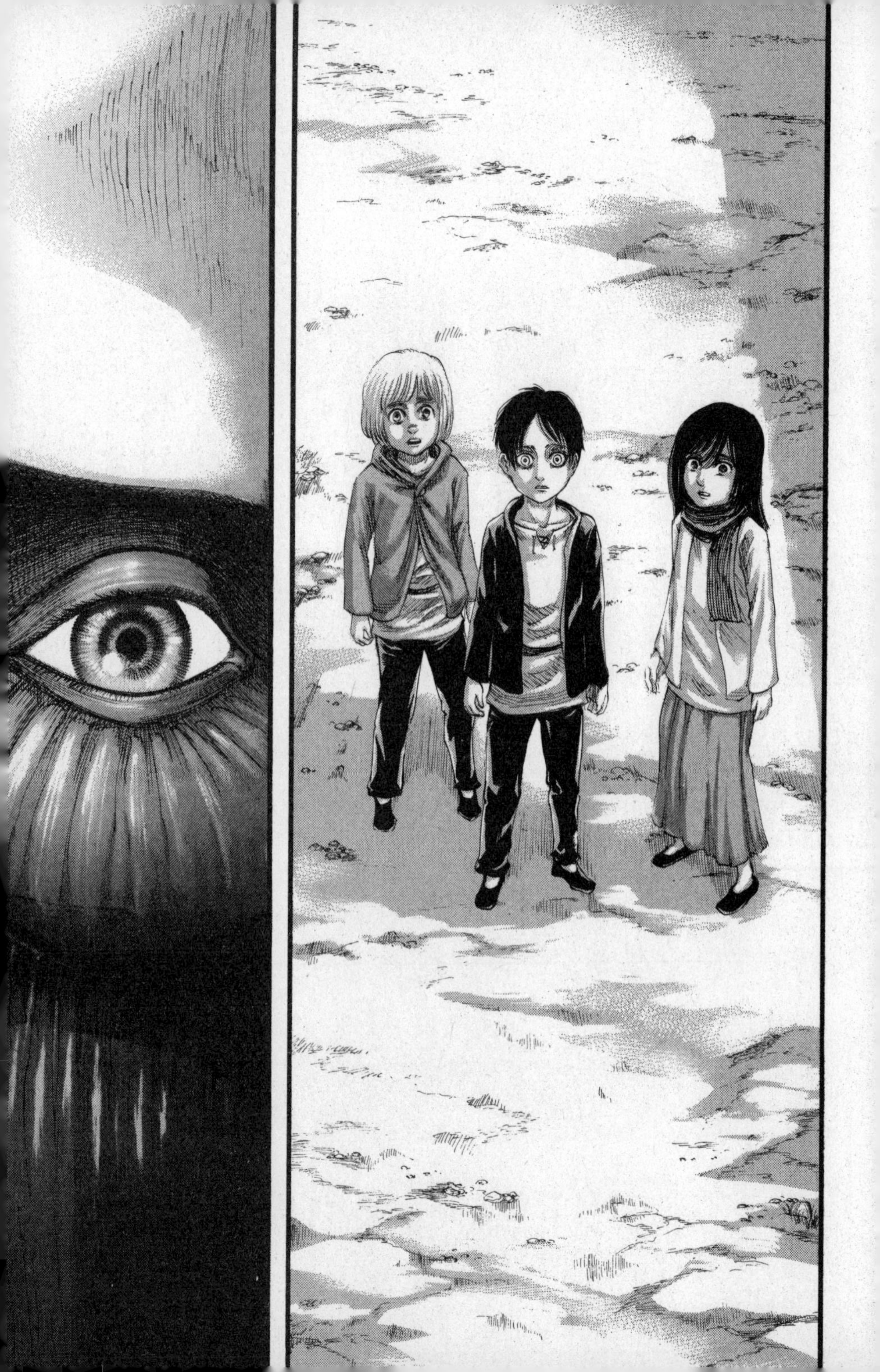

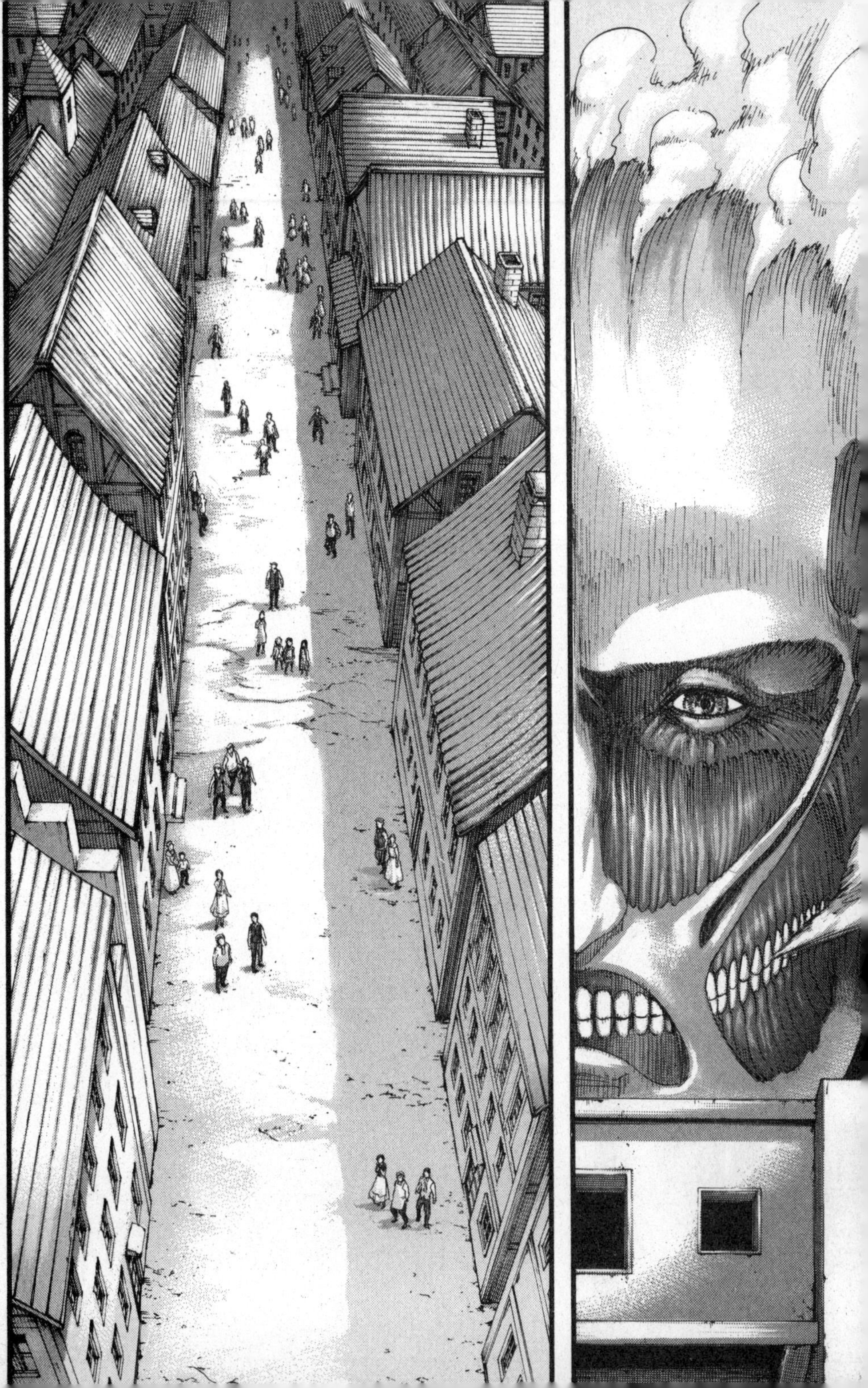

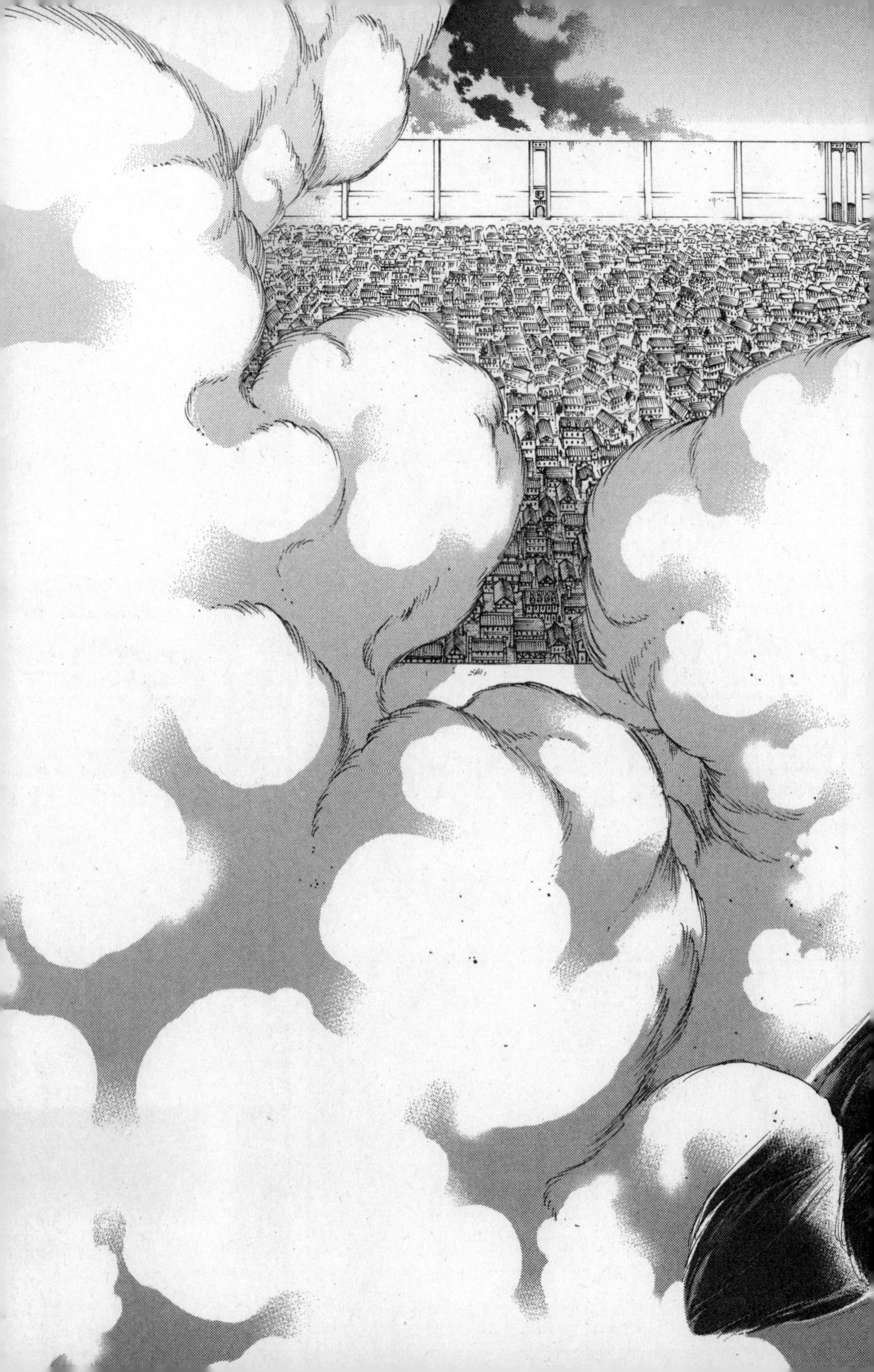

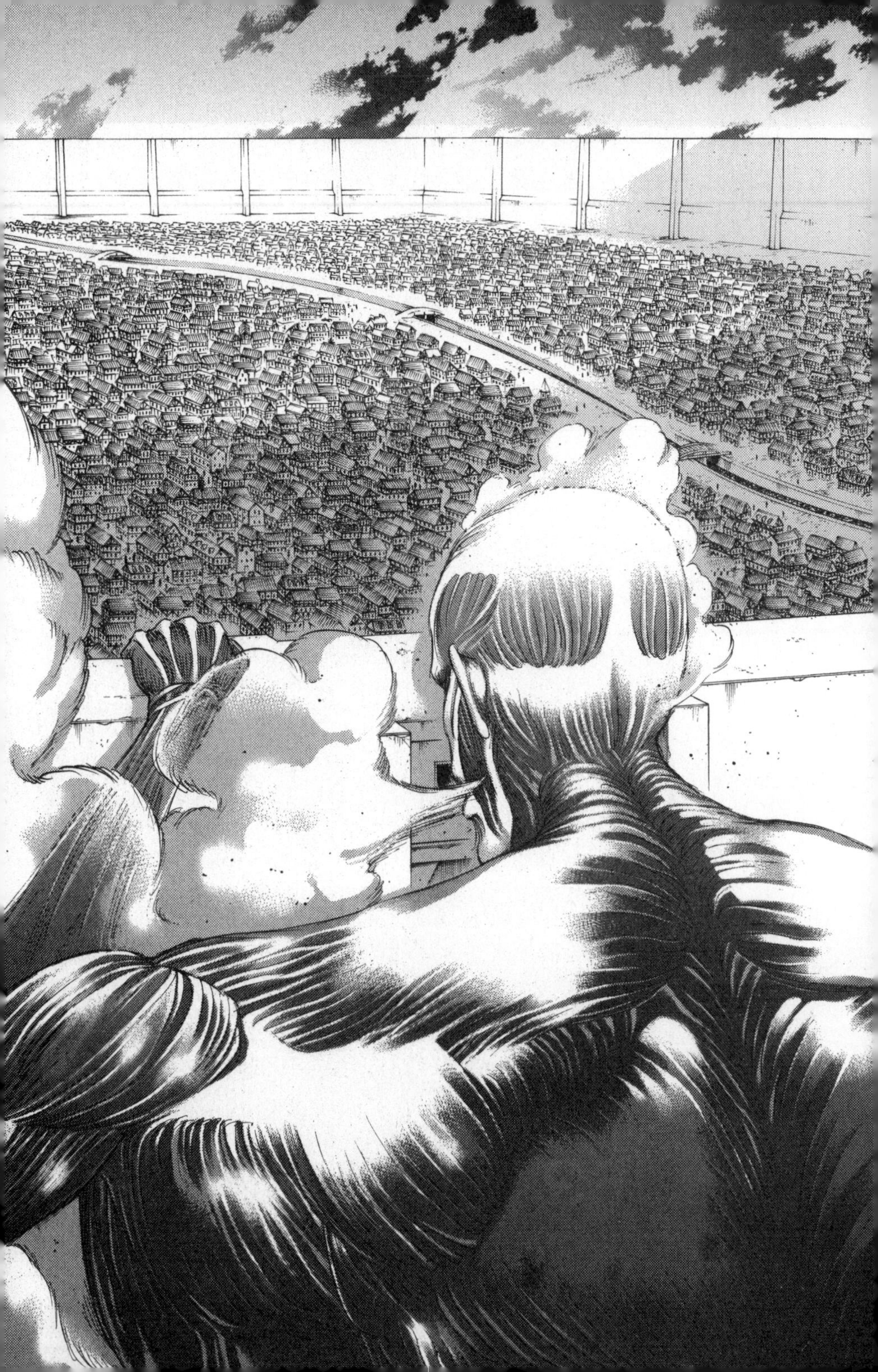

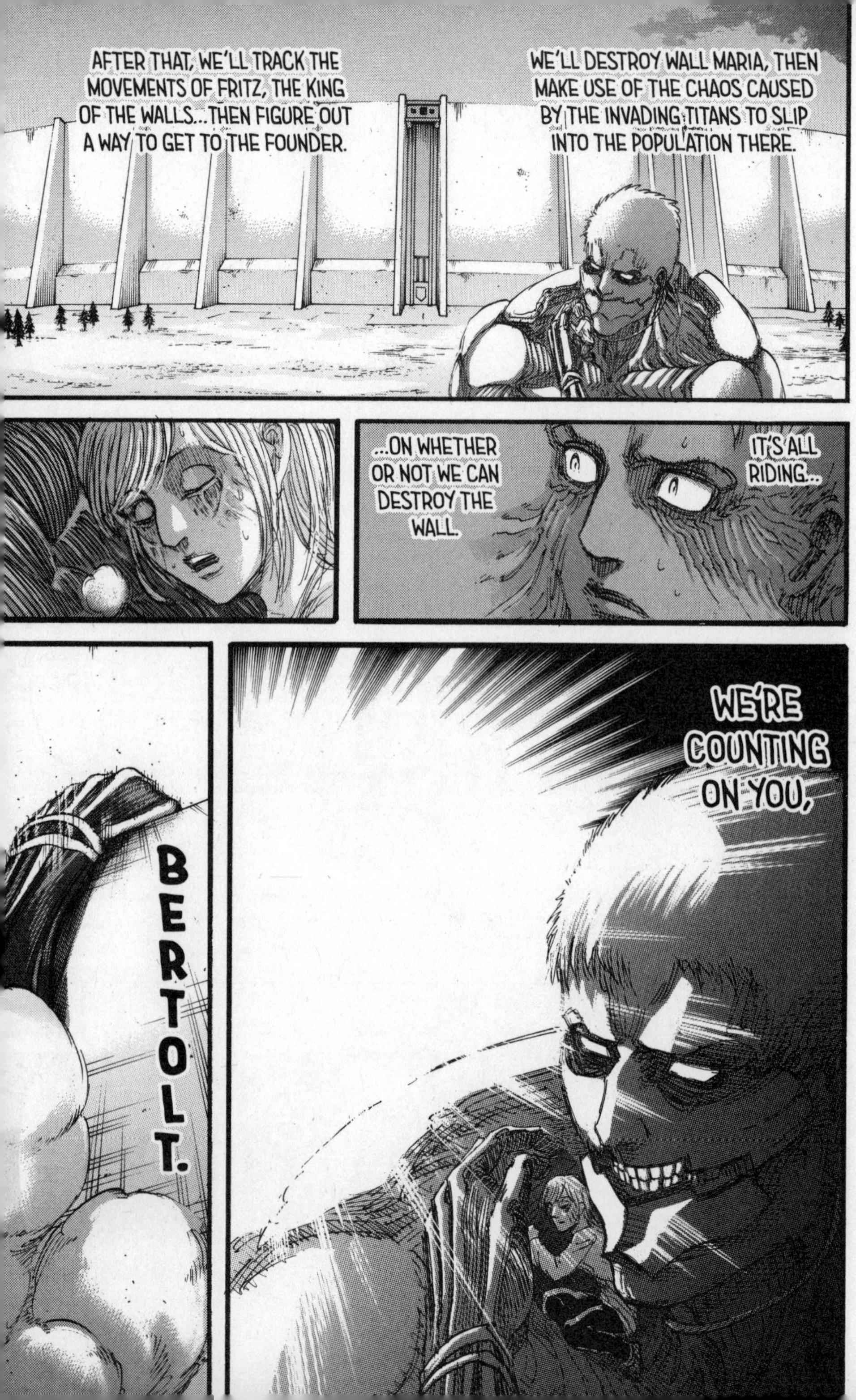
WE'LL DESTROY WALL MARIA, THEN MAKE USE OF THE CHAOS CAUSED BY THE INVADING TITANS TO SLIP INTO THE POPULATION THERE.
AFTER THAT, WE'LL TRACK THE MOVEMENTS OF FRITZ, THE KING OF THE WALLS...THEN FIGURE OUT A WAY TO GET TO THE FOUNDER.
IT'S ALL RIDING...
...ON WHETHER OR NOT WE CAN DESTROY THE WALL.
WE'RE COUNTING ON YOU,
BERTOLT.

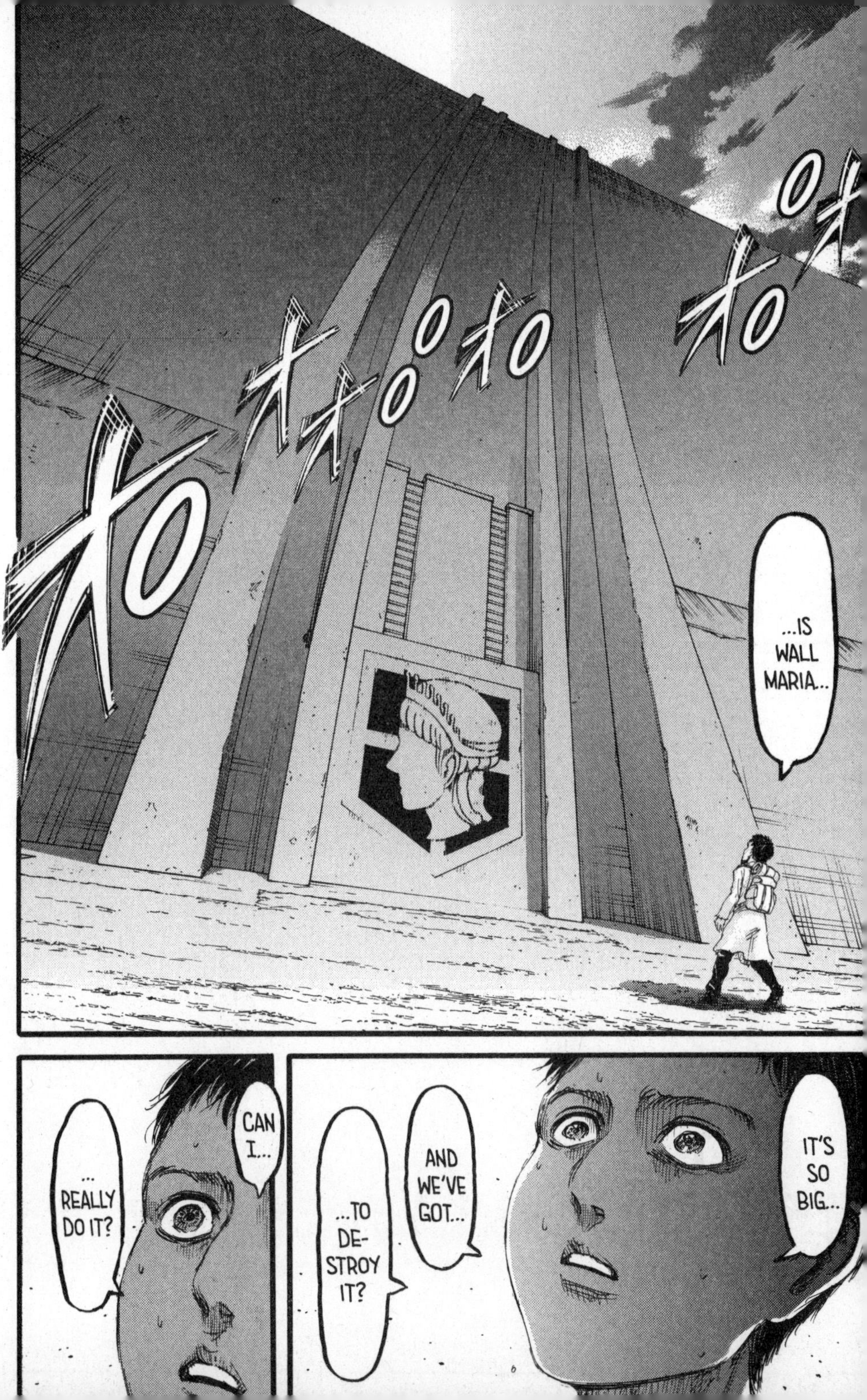
...IS WALL MARIA...
IT'S SO BIG...
AND WE'VE GOT...
...TO DE-STROY IT?
CAN I...
... REALLY DO IT?

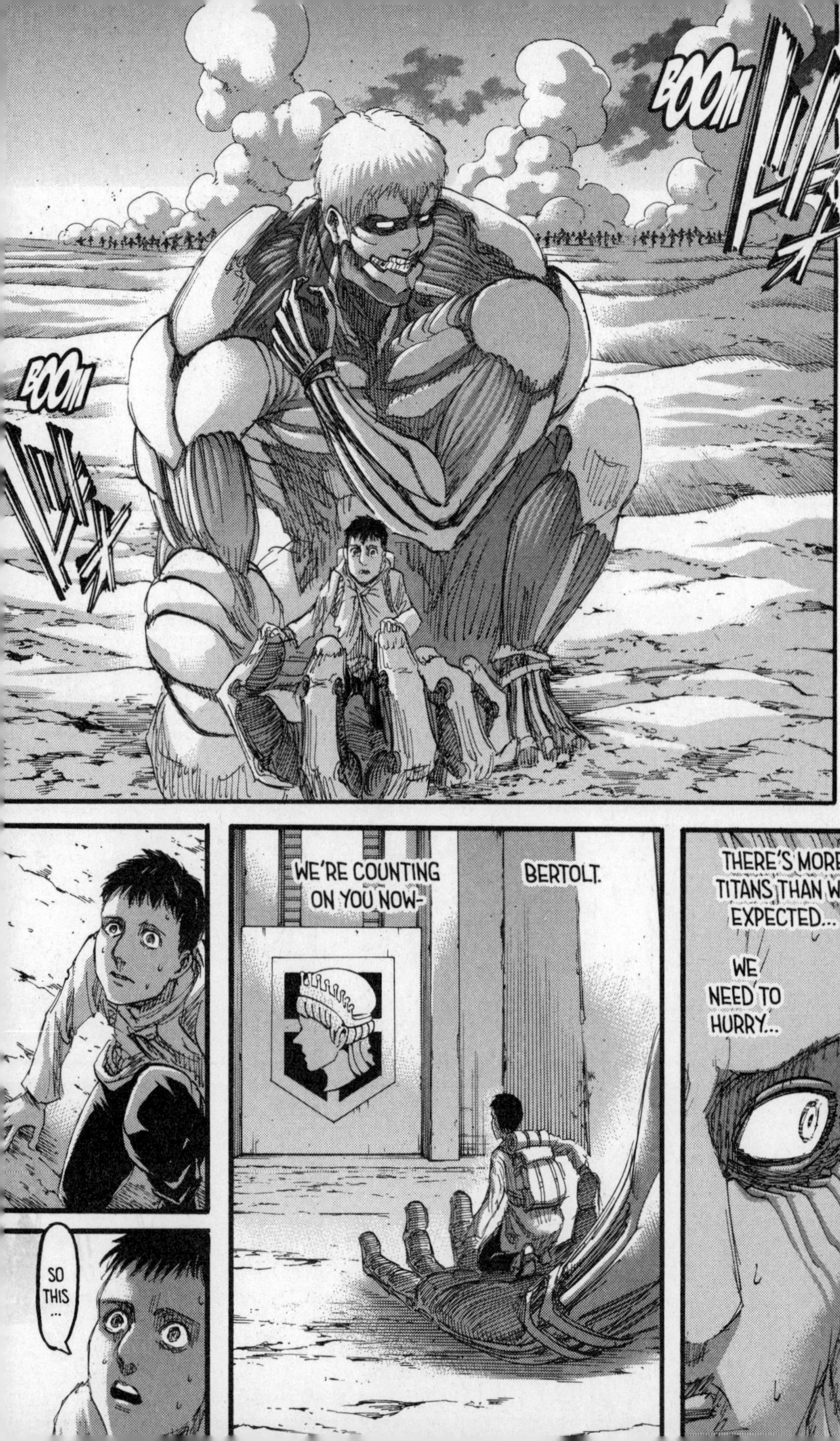
BOOM
BOOM
THERE'S MORE TITANS THAN WE EXPECTED...
WE NEED TO HURRY...
WE'RE COUNTING ON YOU NOW-
BERTOLT.
SO THIS ...

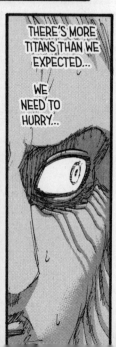

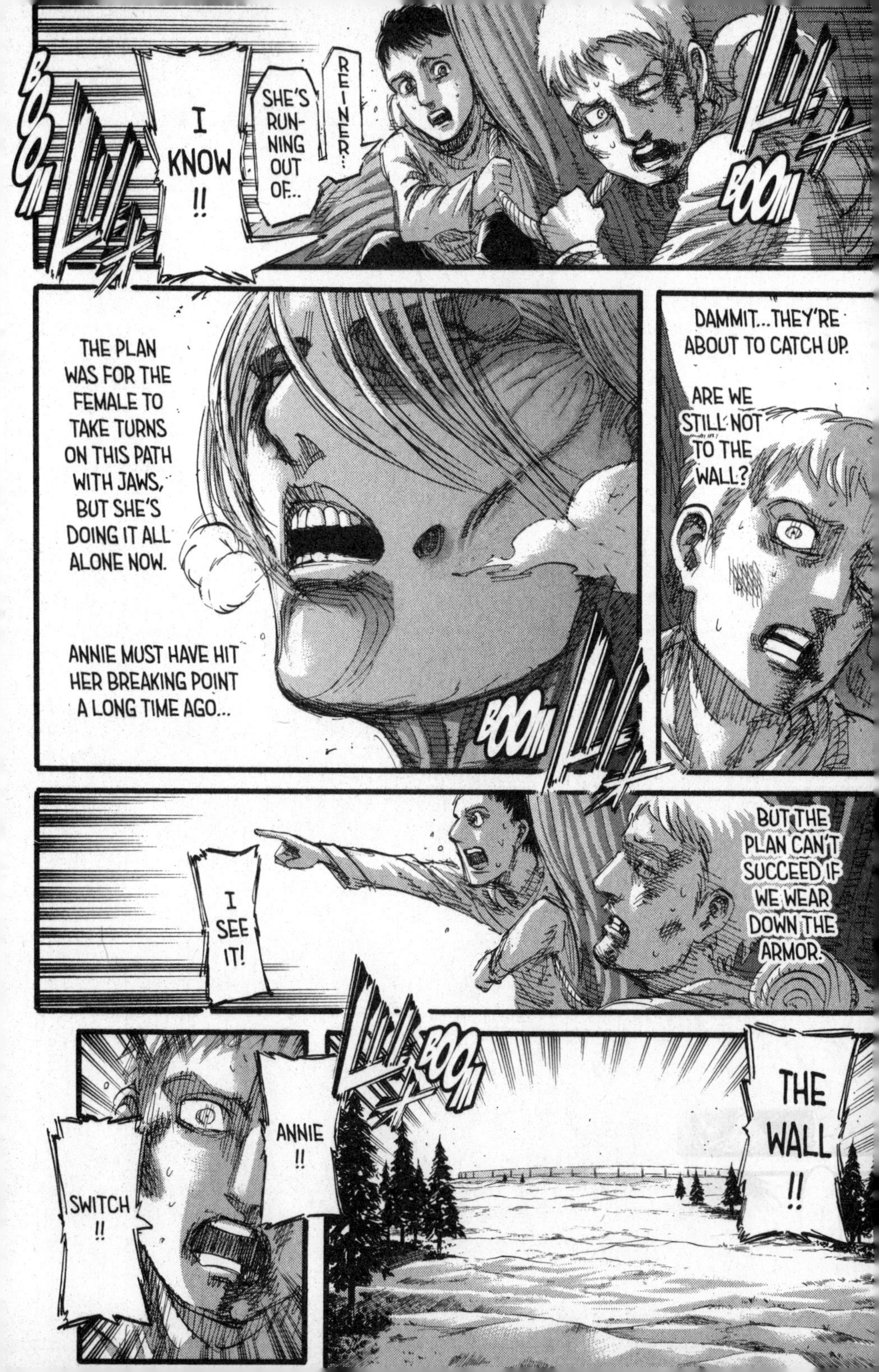
BOOM
REINER...
SHE'S RUNNING OUT OF...
I KNOW!!
BOOM
DAMMIT... THEY'RE ABOUT TO CATCH UP.
ARE WE STILL NOT TO THE WALL?
THE PLAN WAS FOR THE FEMALE TO TAKE TURNS ON THIS PATH WITH JAWS, BUT SHE'S DOING IT ALL ALONE NOW.
ANNIE MUST HAVE HIT HER BREAKING POINT A LONG TIME AGO...
BOOM
BUT THE PLAN CAN'T SUCCEED IF WE WEAR DOWN THE ARMOR.
I SEE IT!
THE WALL!!
BOOM
ANNIE!!
SWITCH!!

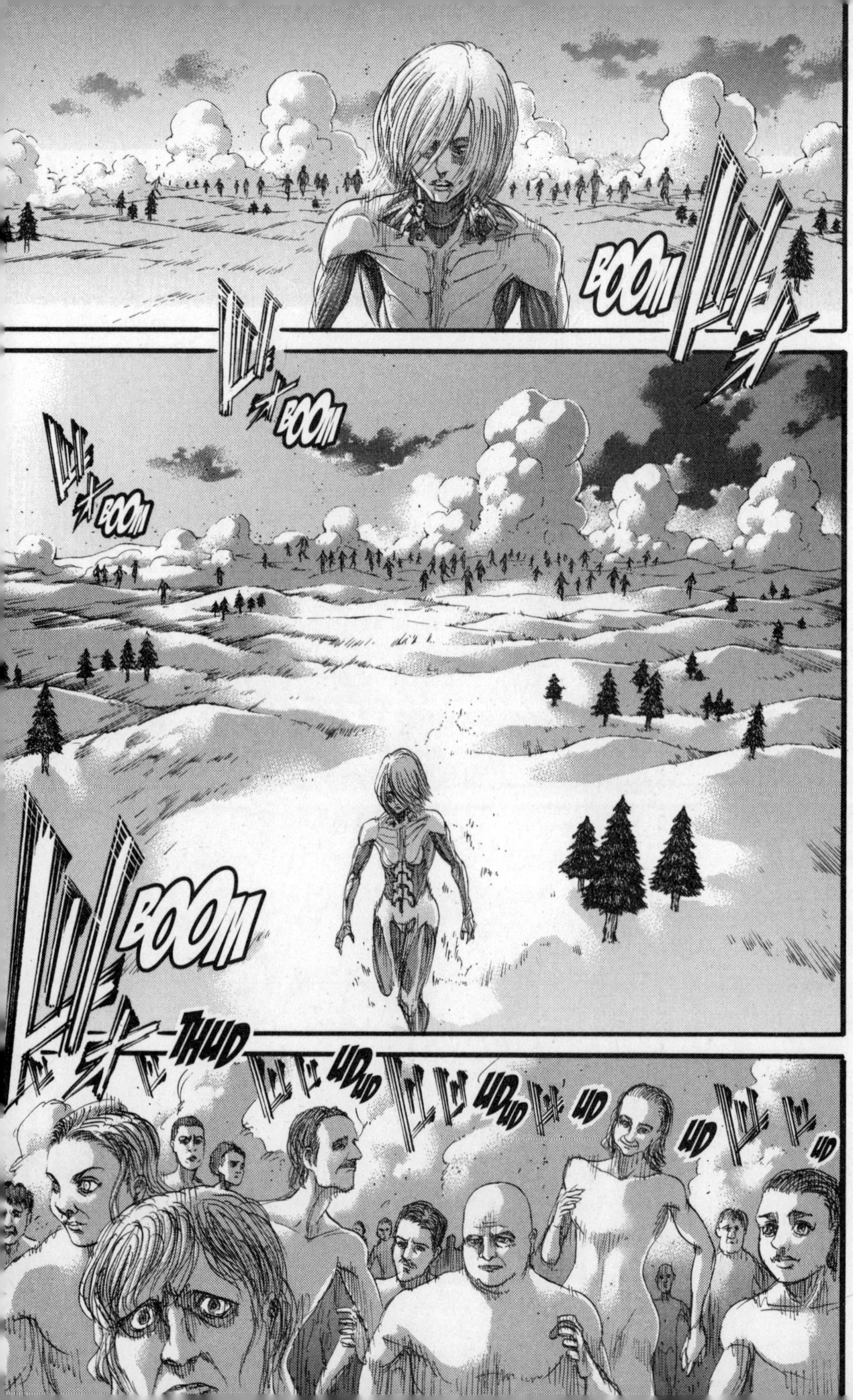
BOOM
BOOM
BOOM
BOOM
THUD
UD
UD
UD
UDUD
UDUD

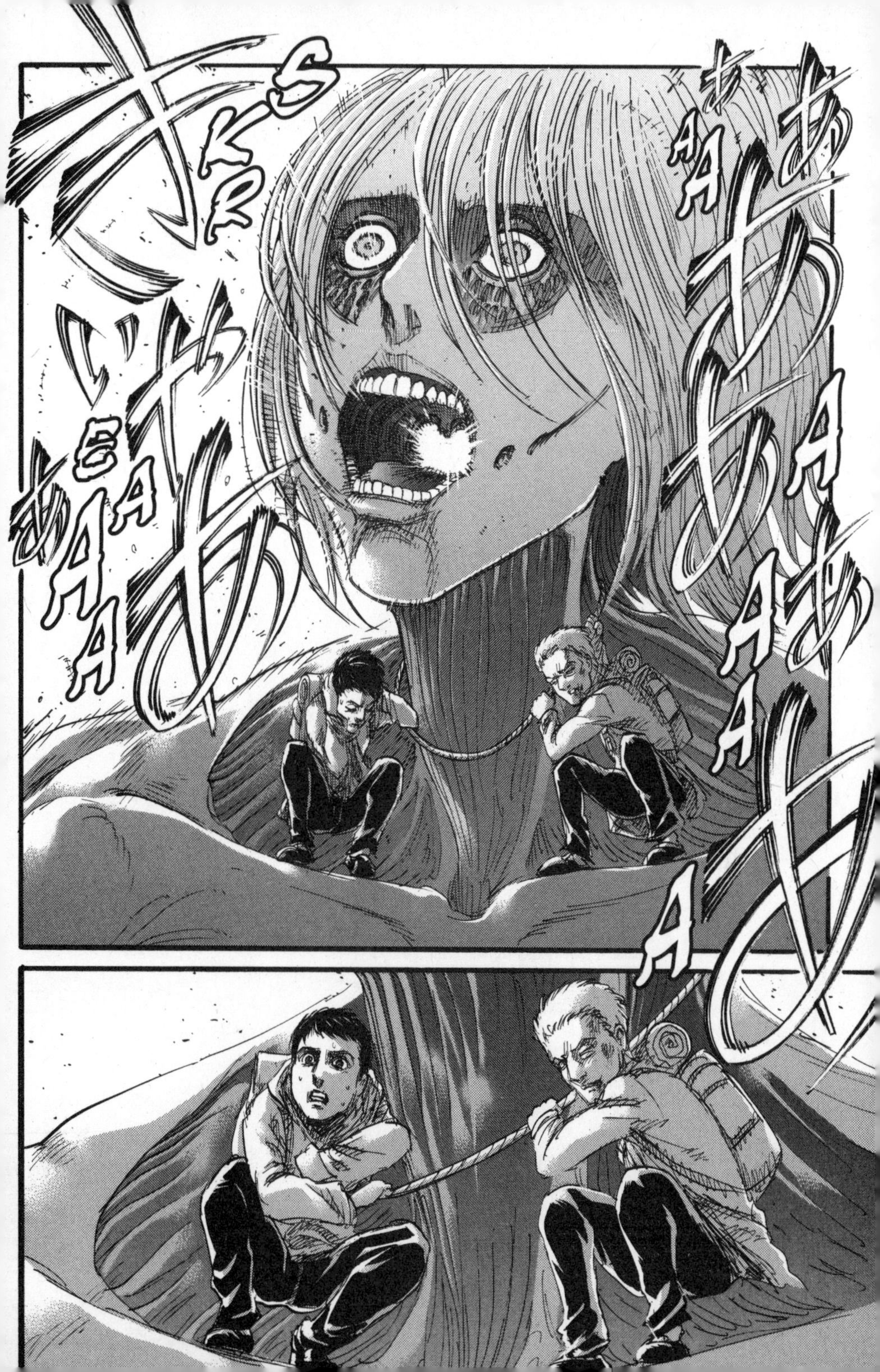
AAAAAAAA
SKREEAAAA

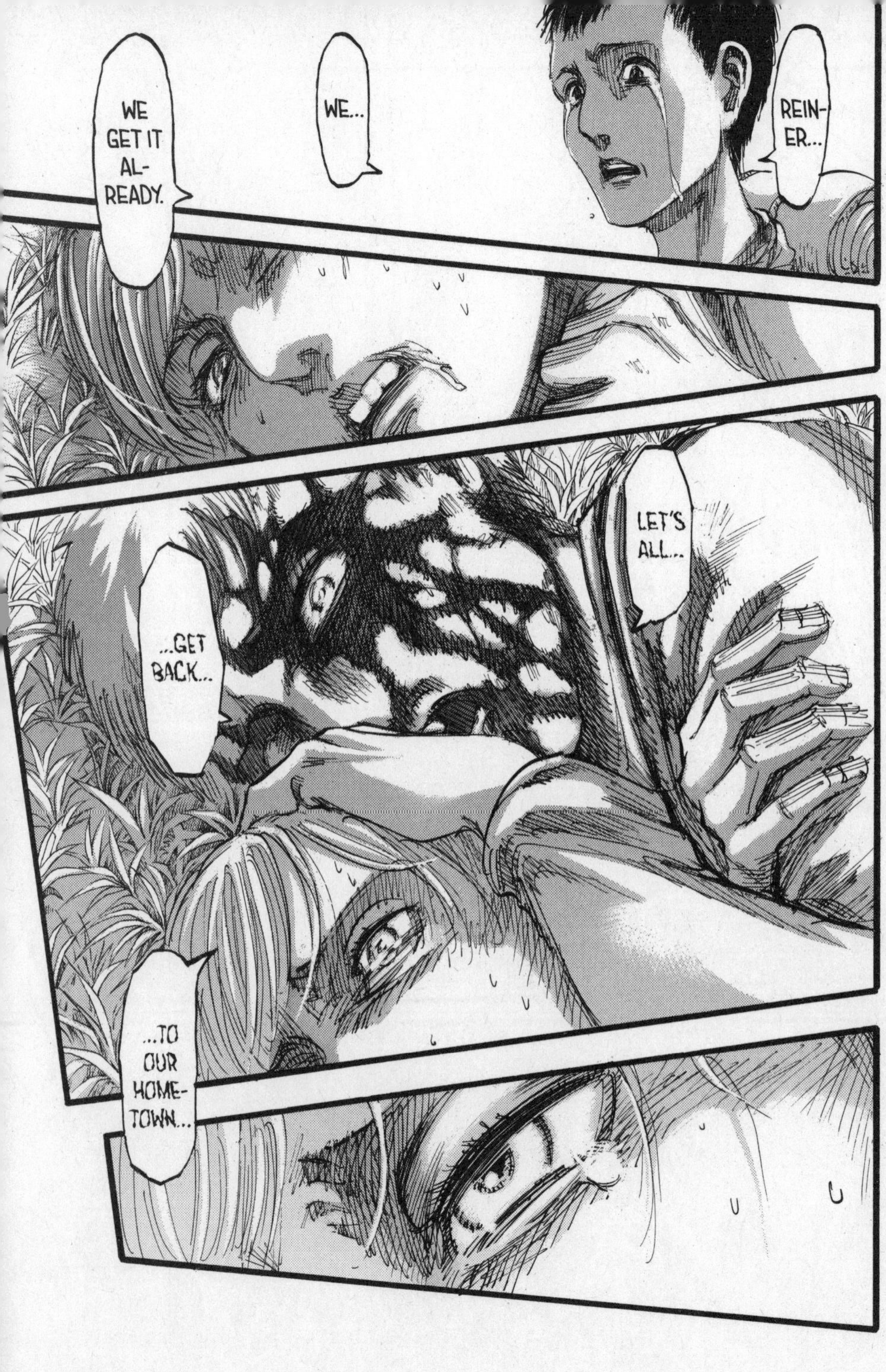
REIN-ER...
WE...
WE GET IT AL-READY.
LET'S ALL...
...GET BACK...
...TO OUR HOME-TOWN...

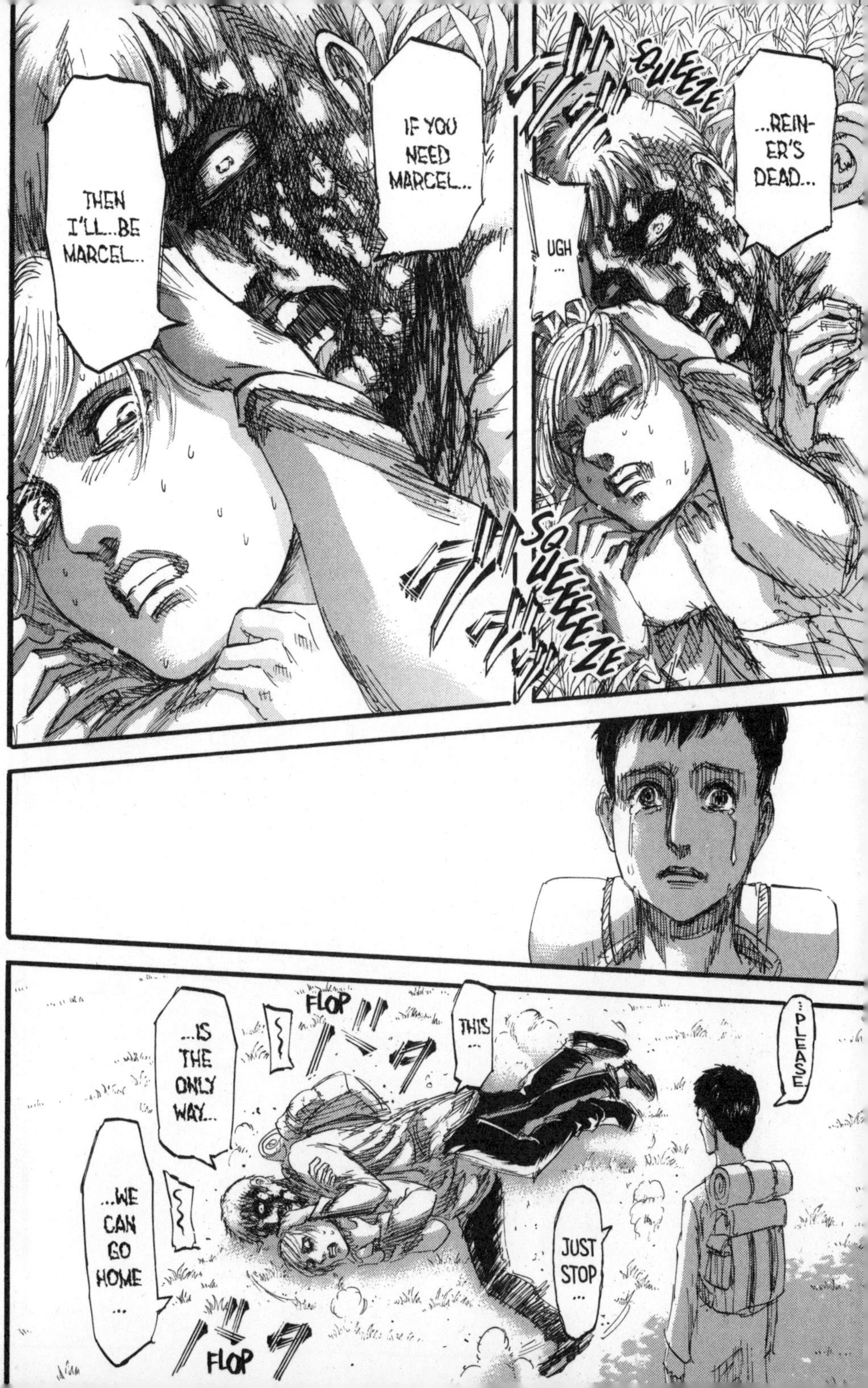
...REIN-ER'S DEAD...
SQUEEZE
UGH ...
IF YOU NEED MARCEL...
THEN I'LL...BE MARCEL...
SQUEEEEZE
...PLEASE
THIS ...
FLOP
...IS THE ONLY WAY...
...WE CAN GO HOME ...
JUST STOP ...
FLOP

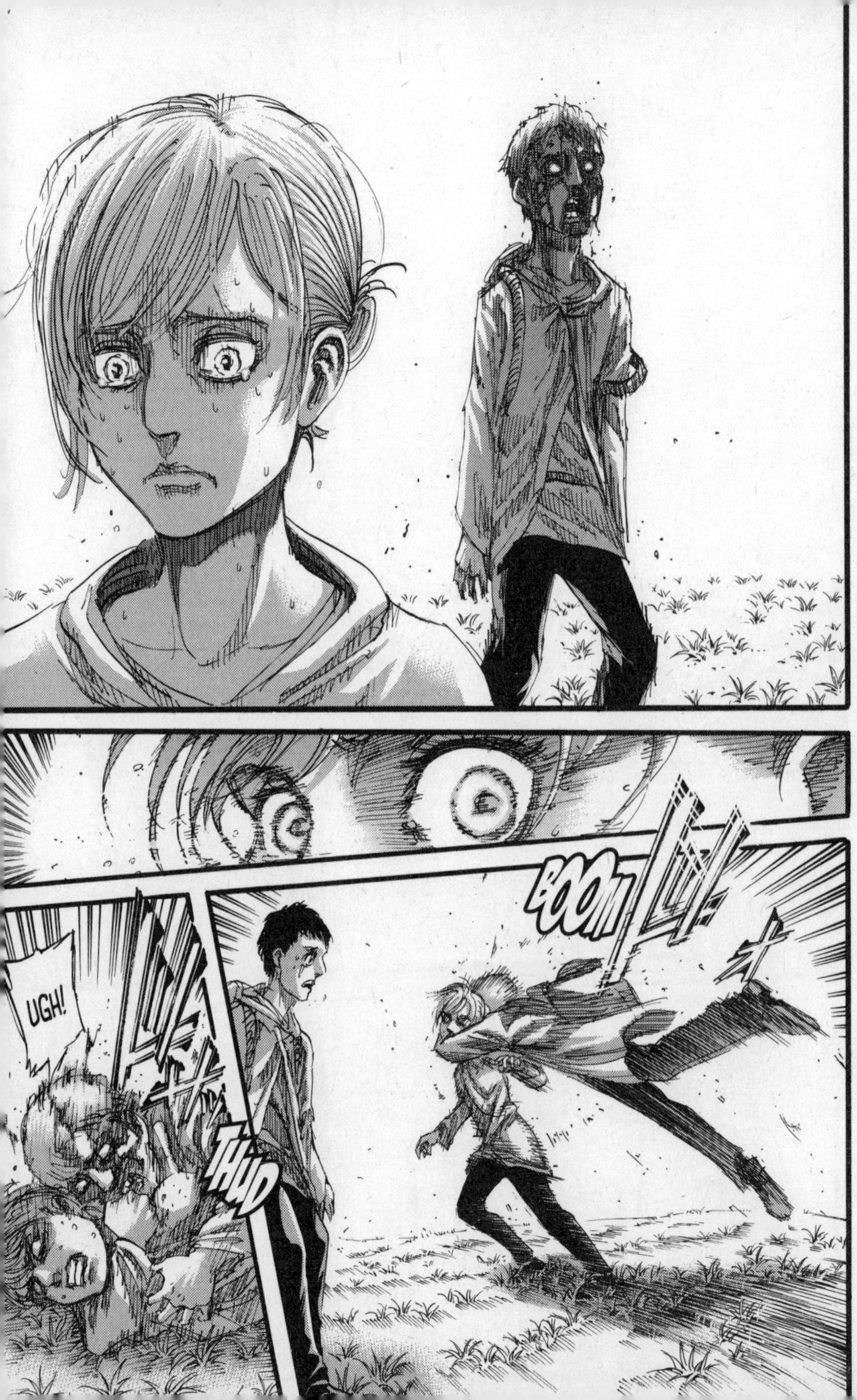
BOOM
UGH!
THUD

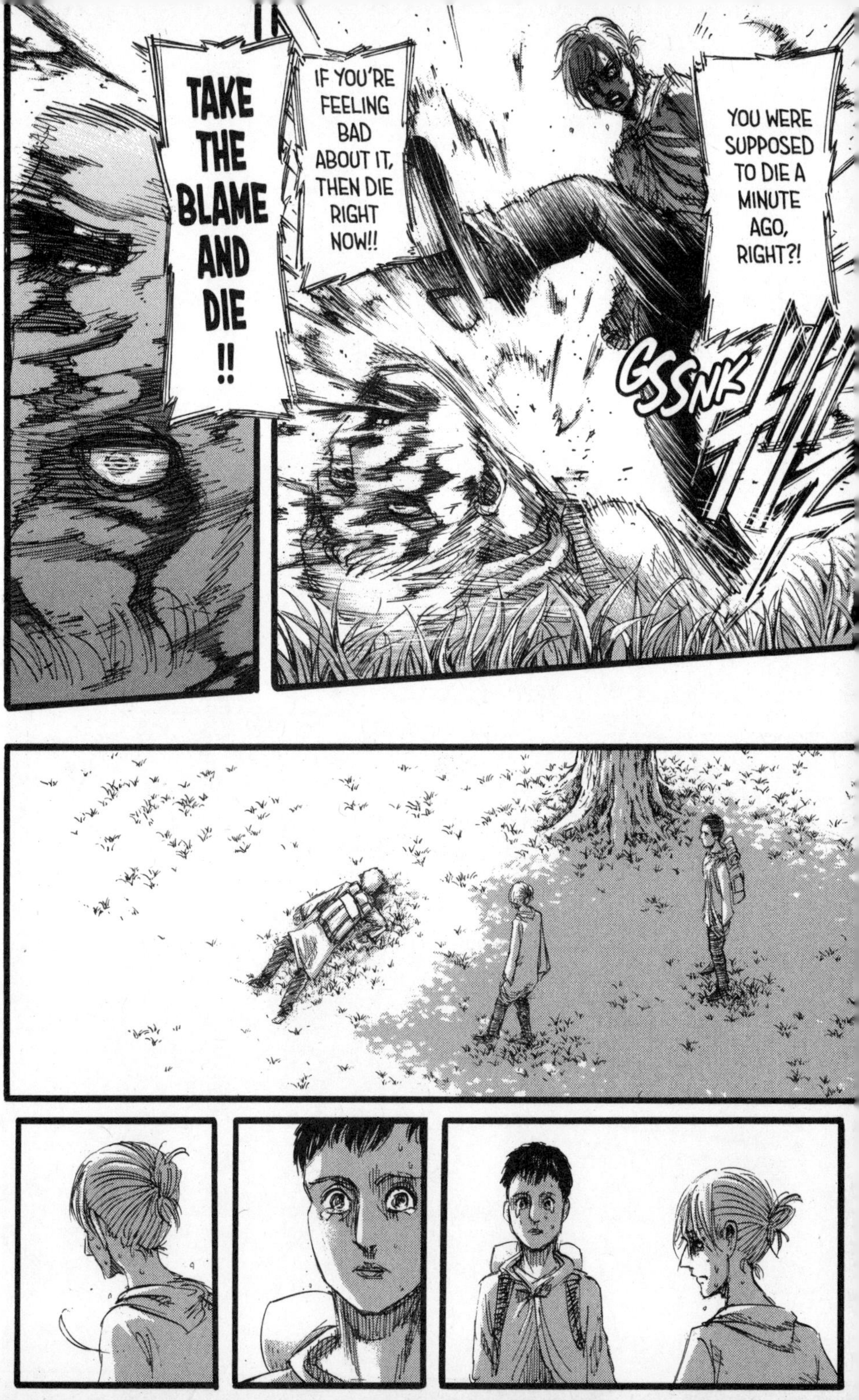
YOU WERE SUPPOSED TO DIE A MINUTE AGO, RIGHT?!
IF YOU'RE FEELING BAD ABOUT IT, THEN DIE RIGHT NOW!!
GSSNK
TAKE THE BLAME AND DIE !!

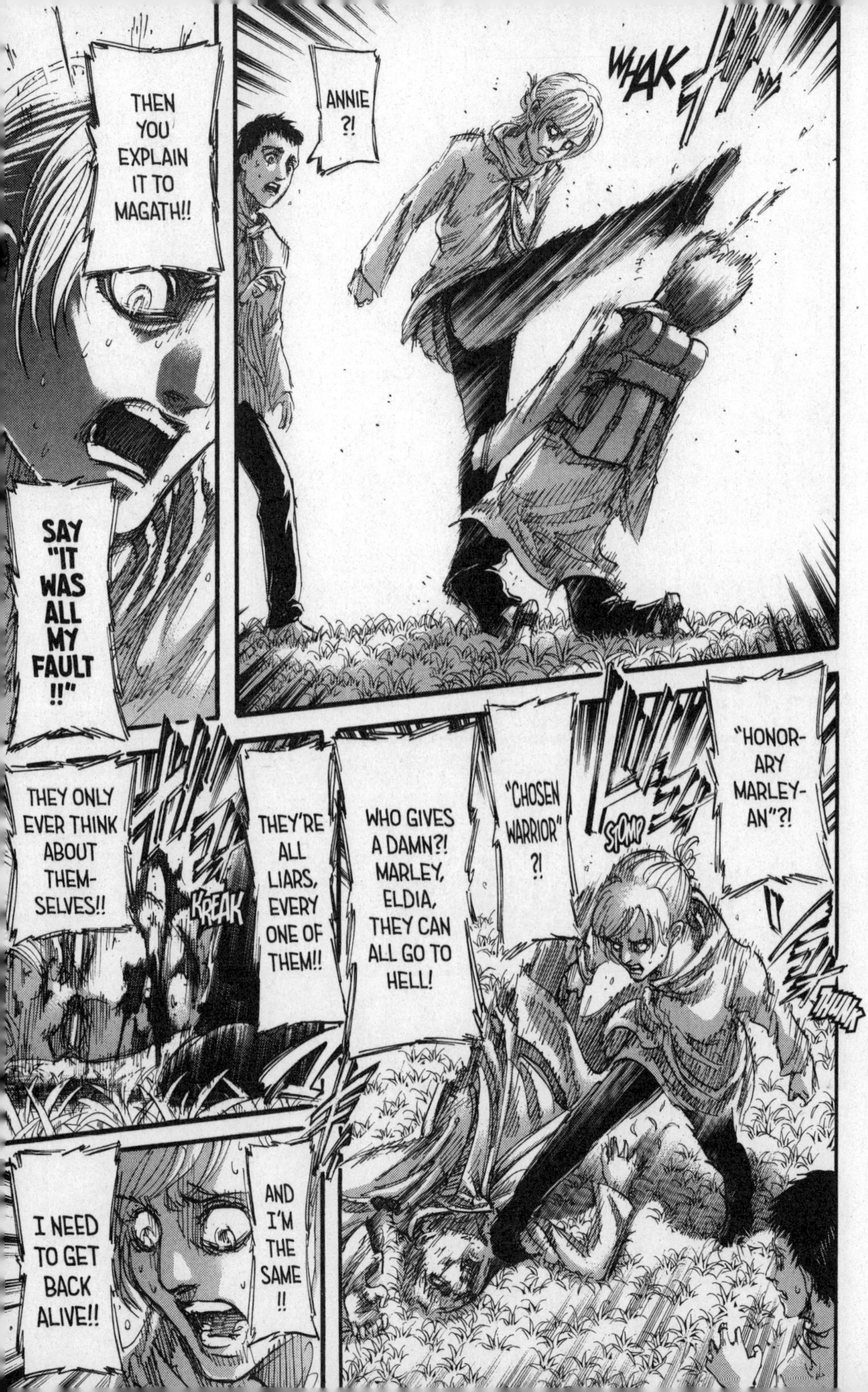
WHAK
ANNIE ?!
THEN YOU EXPLAIN IT TO MAGATH!!
SAY "IT WAS ALL MY FAULT!!"
"HONORARY MARLEY-AN"?!
STOMP
THUNK
"CHOSEN WARRIOR"?!
WHO GIVES A DAMN?! MARLEY, ELDIA, THEY CAN ALL GO TO HELL!
THEY'RE ALL LIARS, EVERY ONE OF THEM!!
KREAK
THEY ONLY EVER THINK ABOUT THEM-SELVES!!
AND I'M THE SAME!!
I NEED TO GET BACK ALIVE!!

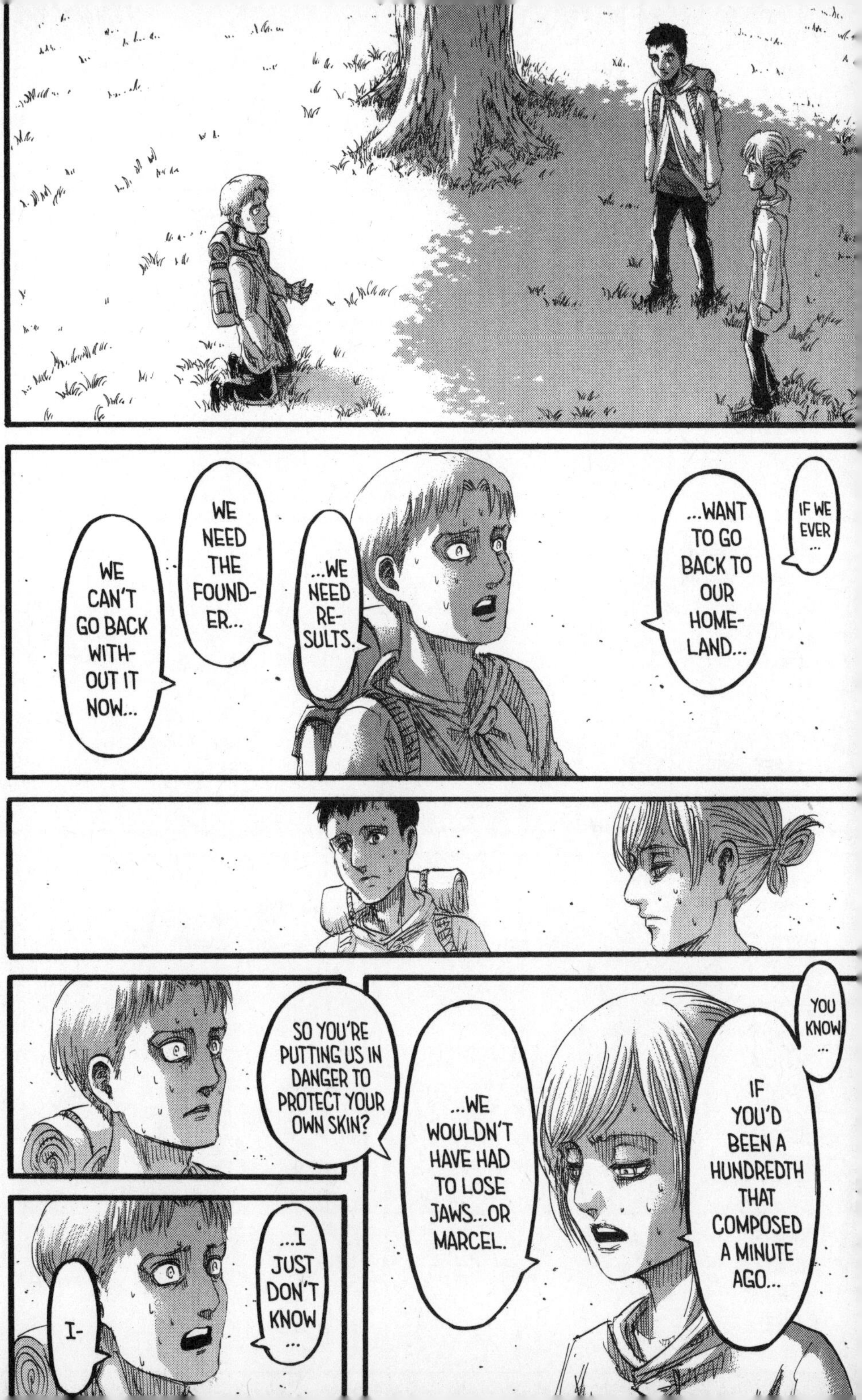
IF WE EVER...
...WANT TO GO BACK TO OUR HOMELAND...
...WE NEED RESULTS.
WE NEED THE FOUNDER...
WE CAN'T GO BACK WITHOUT IT NOW...
YOU KNOW...
IF YOU'D BEEN A HUNDREDTH THAT COMPOSED A MINUTE AGO...
...WE WOULDN'T HAVE HAD TO LOSE JAWS...OR MARCEL.
SO YOU'RE PUTTING US IN DANGER TO PROTECT YOUR OWN SKIN?
...I JUST DON'T KNOW...
I-

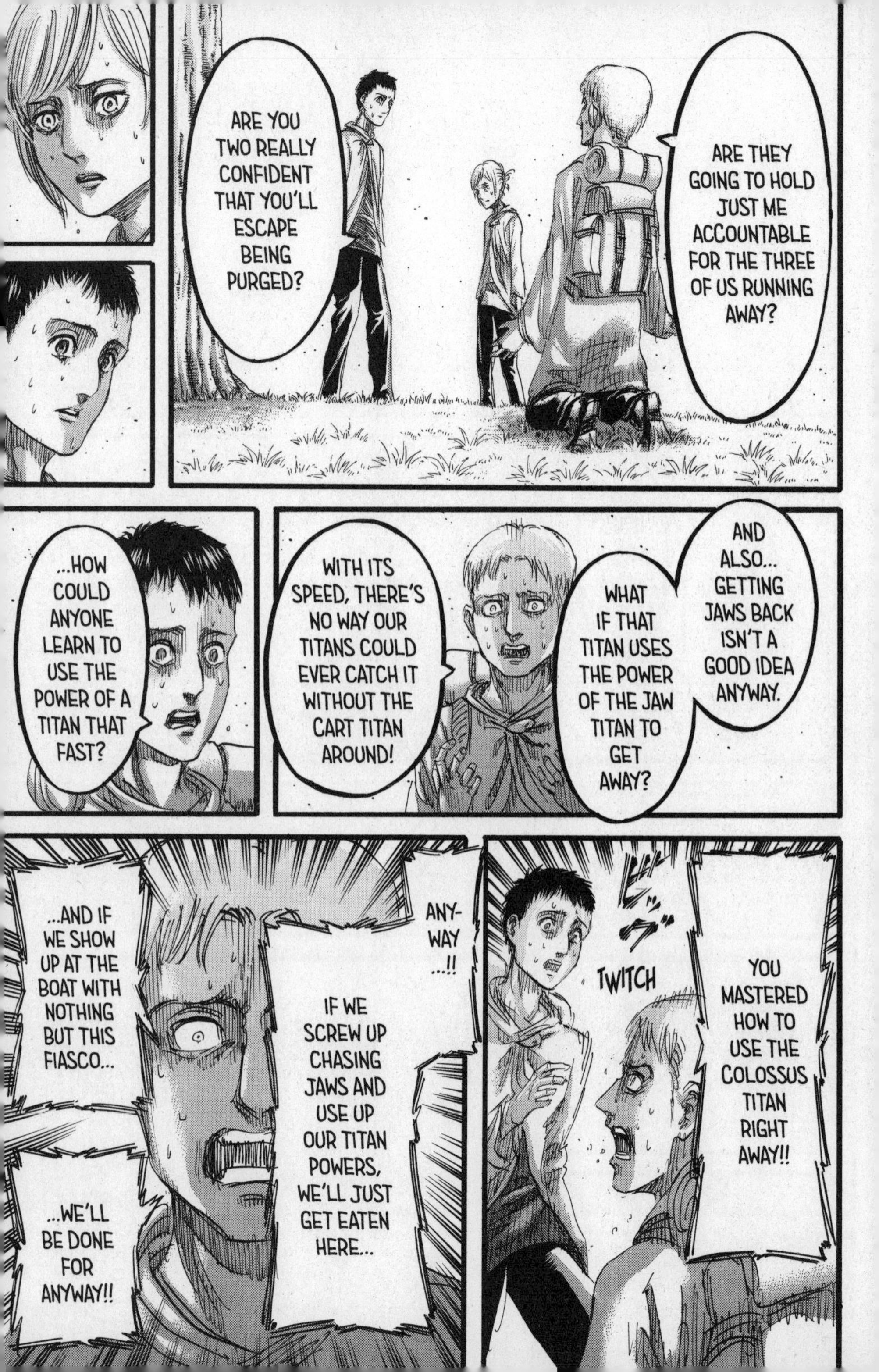
ARE THEY GOING TO HOLD JUST ME ACCOUNTABLE FOR THE THREE OF US RUNNING AWAY?
ARE YOU TWO REALLY CONFIDENT THAT YOU'LL ESCAPE BEING PURGED?
AND ALSO... GETTING JAWS BACK ISN'T A GOOD IDEA ANYWAY.
WHAT IF THAT TITAN USES THE POWER OF THE JAW TITAN TO GET AWAY?
WITH ITS SPEED, THERE'S NO WAY OUR TITANS COULD EVER CATCH IT WITHOUT THE CART TITAN AROUND!
...HOW COULD ANYONE LEARN TO USE THE POWER OF A TITAN THAT FAST?
YOU MASTERED HOW TO USE THE COLOSSUS TITAN RIGHT AWAY!!
TWITCH
ANY-WAY...!!
IF WE SCREW UP CHASING JAWS AND USE UP OUR TITAN POWERS, WE'LL JUST GET EATEN HERE...
...AND IF WE SHOW UP AT THE BOAT WITH NOTHING BUT THIS FIASCO...
...WE'LL BE DONE FOR ANYWAY!!

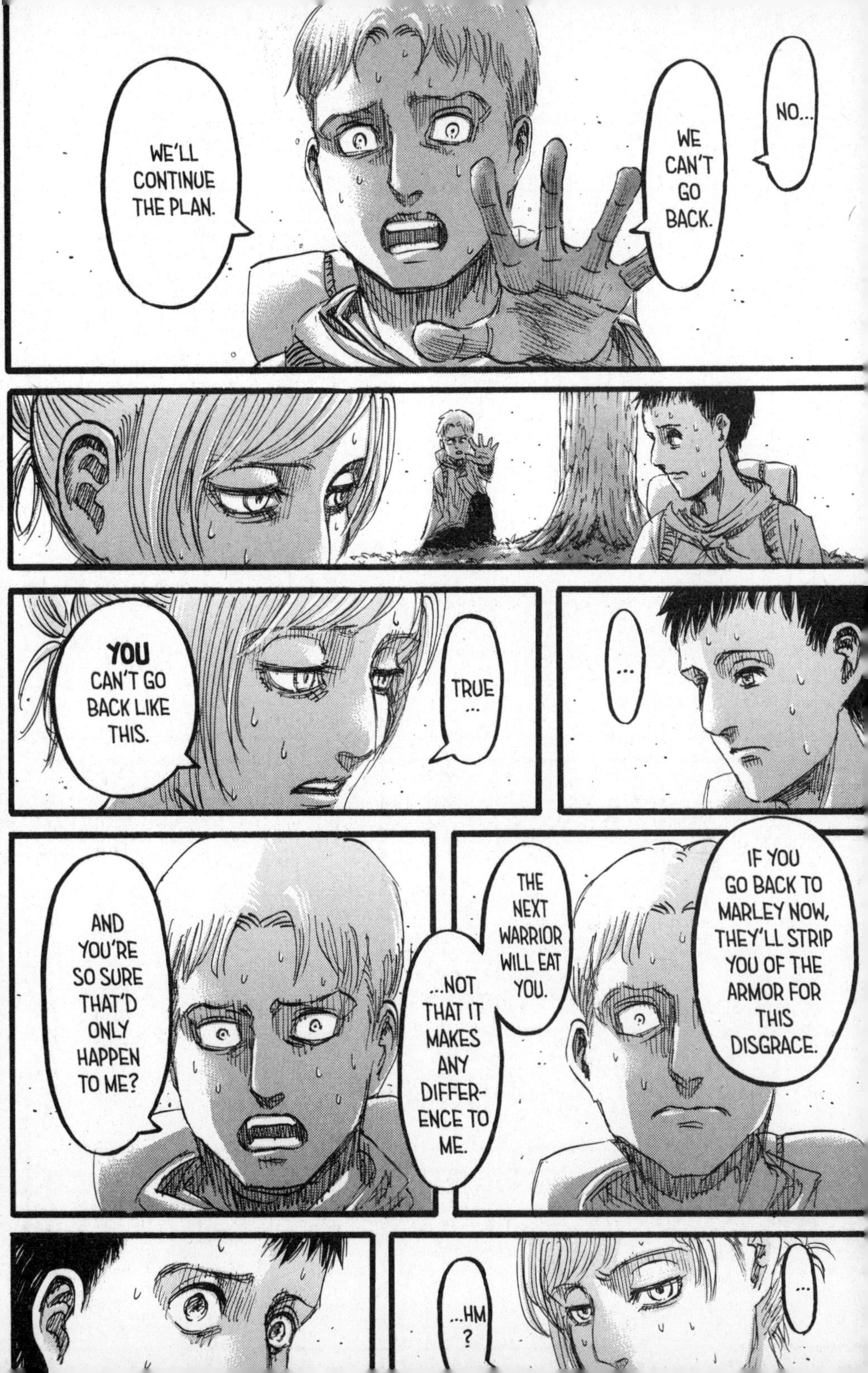
NO...
WE CAN'T GO BACK.
WE'LL CONTINUE THE PLAN.
...
TRUE ...
YOU CAN'T GO BACK LIKE THIS.
IF YOU GO BACK TO MARLEY NOW, THEY'LL STRIP YOU OF THE ARMOR FOR THIS DISGRACE.
THE NEXT WARRIOR WILL EAT YOU.
...NOT THAT IT MAKES ANY DIFFER-ENCE TO ME.
AND YOU'RE SO SURE THAT'D ONLY HAPPEN TO ME?
...
...HM ?

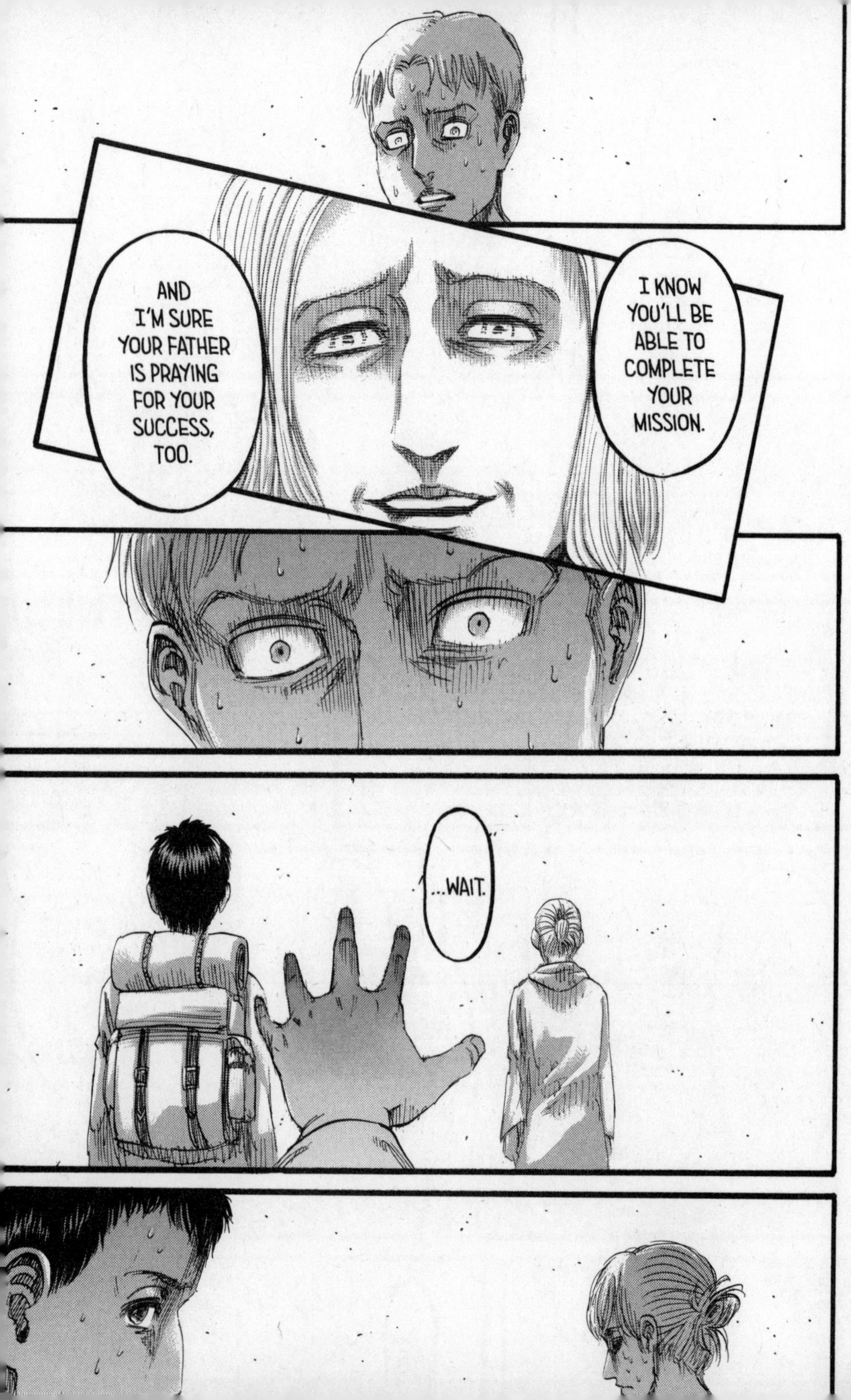
I KNOW YOU'LL BE ABLE TO COMPLETE YOUR MISSION.
AND I'M SURE YOUR FATHER IS PRAYING FOR YOUR SUCCESS, TOO.
...WAIT.

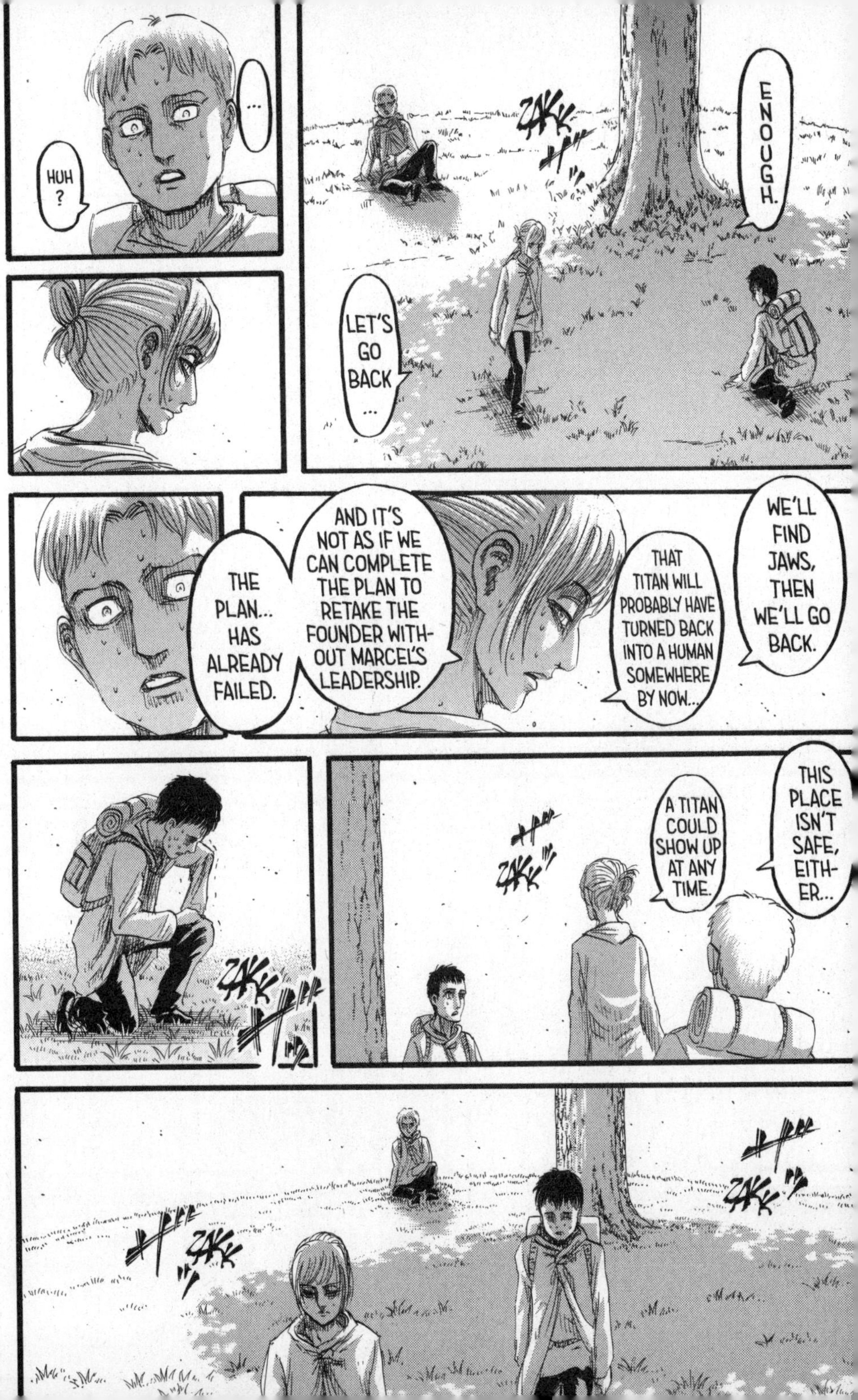
ENOUGH.
ZAKK
LET'S GO BACK...
...
HUH?
WE'LL FIND JAWS, THEN WE'LL GO BACK.
THAT TITAN WILL PROBABLY HAVE TURNED BACK INTO A HUMAN SOMEWHERE BY NOW...
AND IT'S NOT AS IF WE CAN COMPLETE THE PLAN TO RETAKE THE FOUNDER WITH-OUT MARCEL'S LEADERSHIP.
THE PLAN... HAS ALREADY FAILED.
THIS PLACE ISN'T SAFE, EITH-ER...
A TITAN COULD SHOW UP AT ANY TIME.
ZAKK
ZAKK
ZAKK
ZAKK

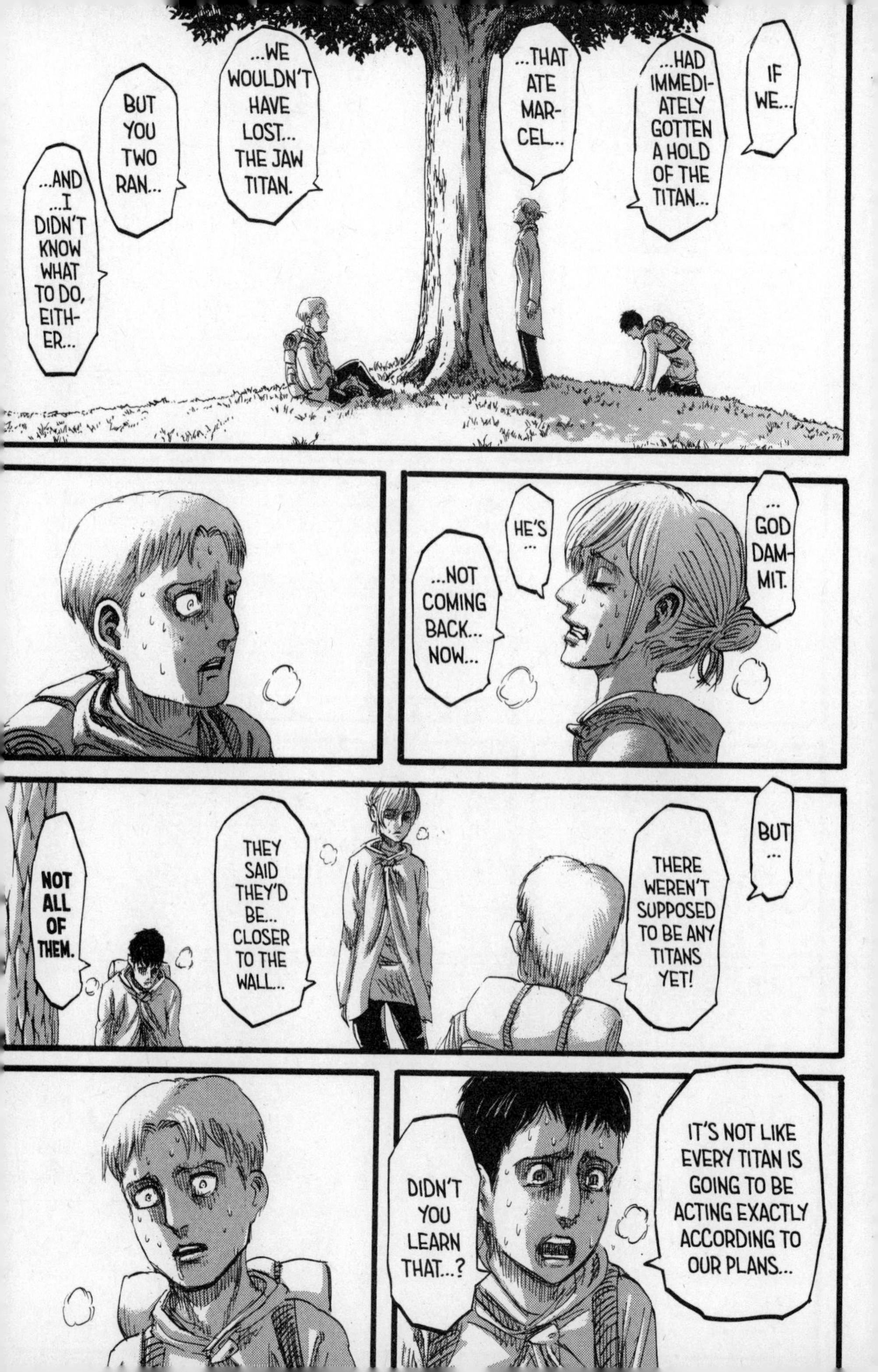
IF WE...
...HAD IMMEDIATELY GOTTEN A HOLD OF THE TITAN...
...THAT ATE MARCEL...
...WE WOULDN'T HAVE LOST... THE JAW TITAN.
BUT YOU TWO RAN...
...AND ...I DIDN'T KNOW WHAT TO DO, EITHER...
...GOD DAMMIT.
HE'S...
...NOT COMING BACK... NOW...
BUT...
THERE WEREN'T SUPPOSED TO BE ANY TITANS YET!
THEY SAID THEY'D BE... CLOSER TO THE WALL...
NOT ALL OF THEM.
IT'S NOT LIKE EVERY TITAN IS GOING TO BE ACTING EXACTLY ACCORDING TO OUR PLANS...
DIDN'T YOU LEARN THAT...?

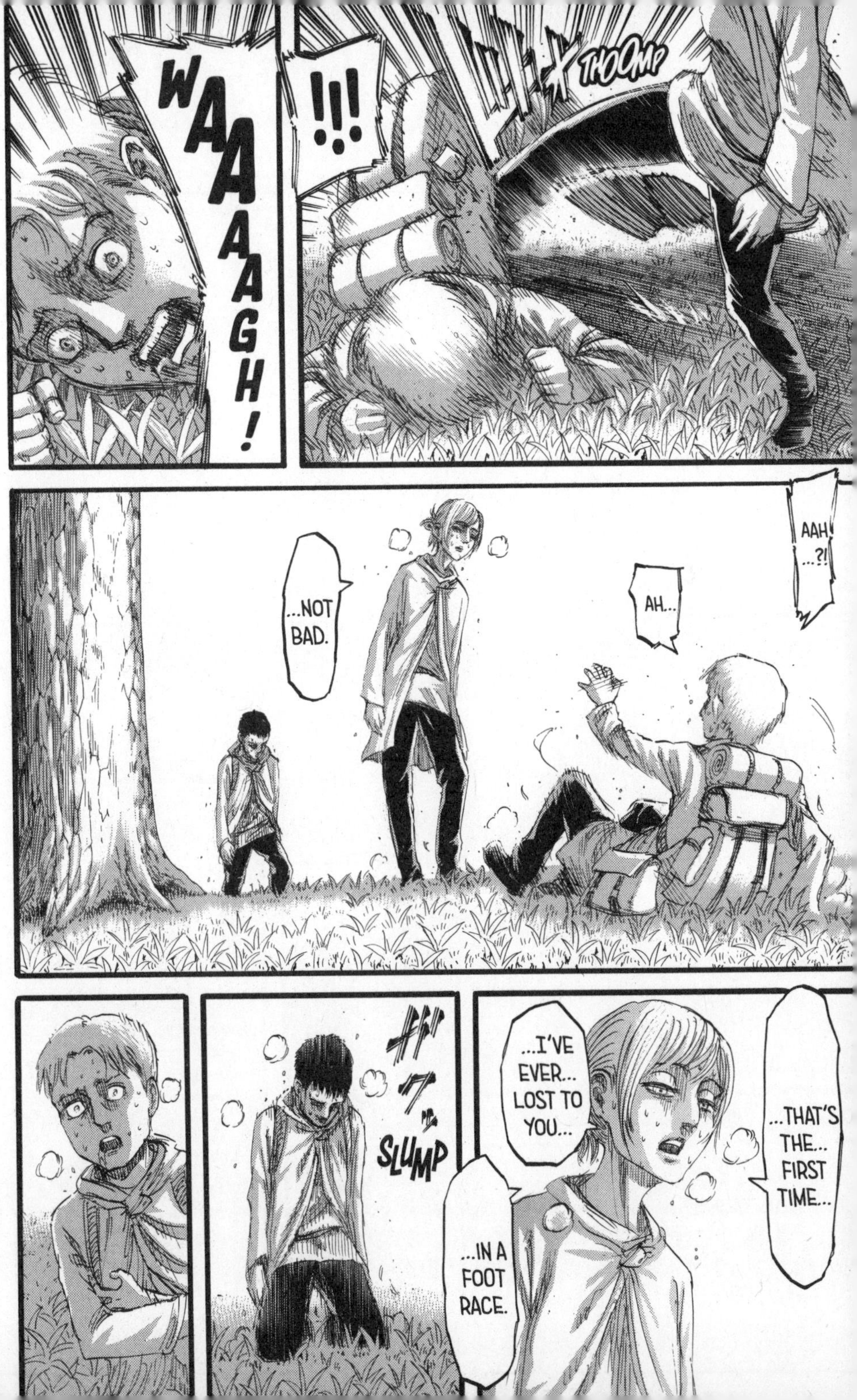
THOOMP
!!!
WAAAAAGH!
AAH ...?!
AH...
...NOT BAD.
...THAT'S THE... FIRST TIME...
...I'VE EVER... LOST TO YOU...
...IN A FOOT RACE.
SLUMP

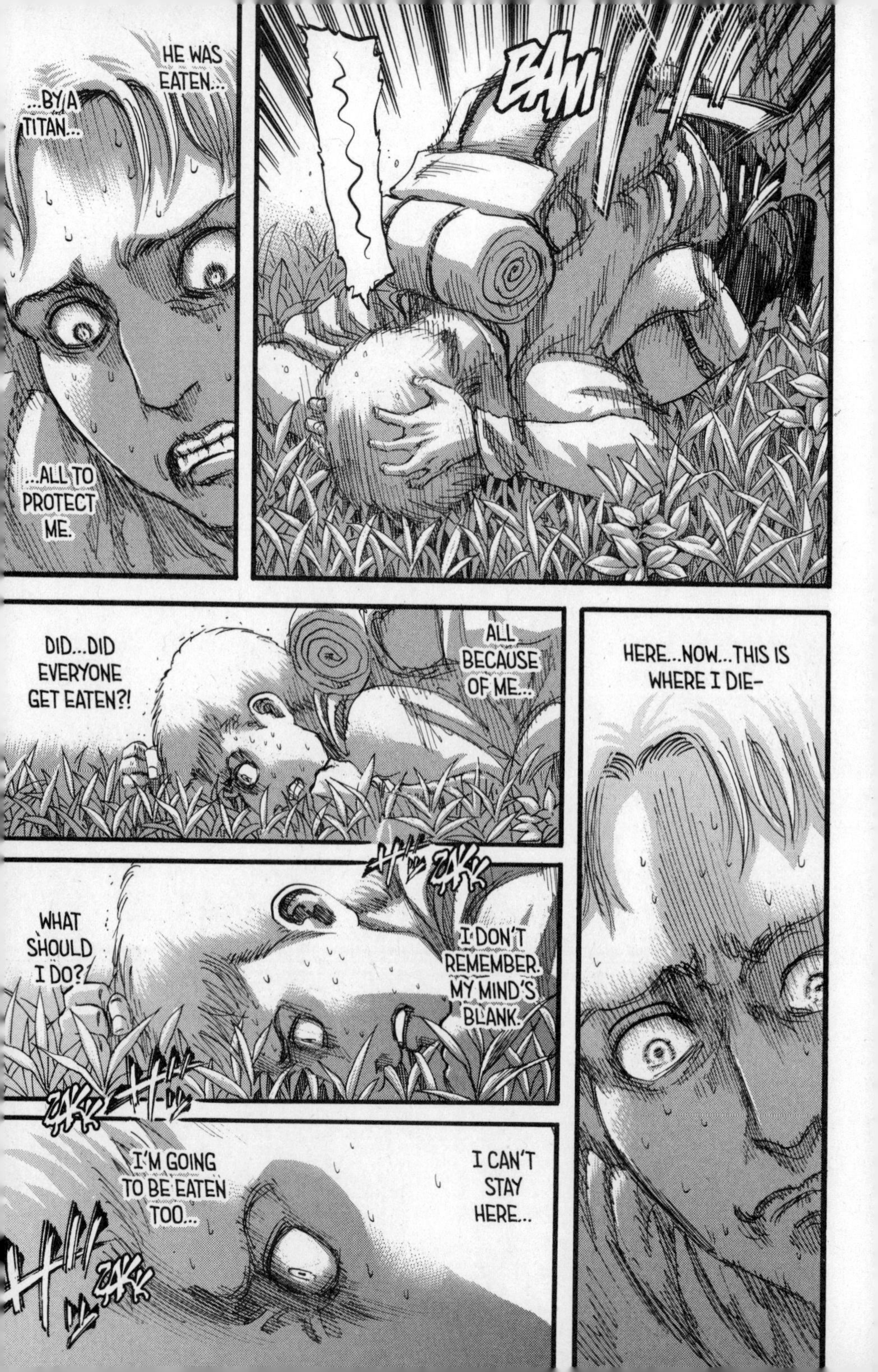

BAM
HE WAS EATEN...
...BY A TITAN...
...ALL TO PROTECT ME.
HERE...NOW...THIS IS WHERE I DIE-
ALL BECAUSE OF ME...
DID...DID EVERYONE GET EATEN?!
I DON'T REMEMBER. MY MIND'S BLANK.
WHAT SHOULD I DO?
I CAN'T STAY HERE...
I'M GOING TO BE EATEN TOO...

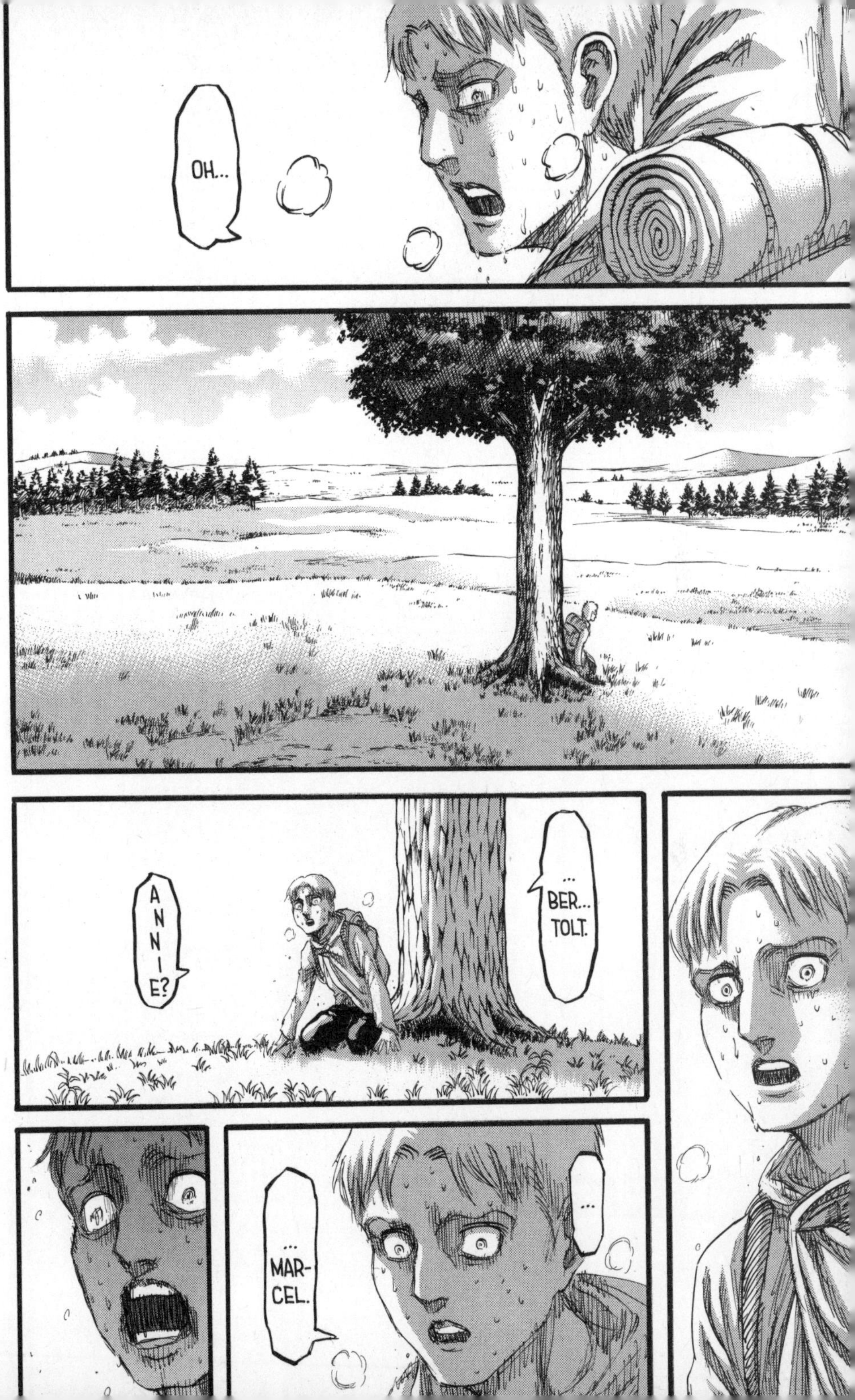
OH...
... BER... TOLT.
ANNIE?
...
... MAR-CEL.

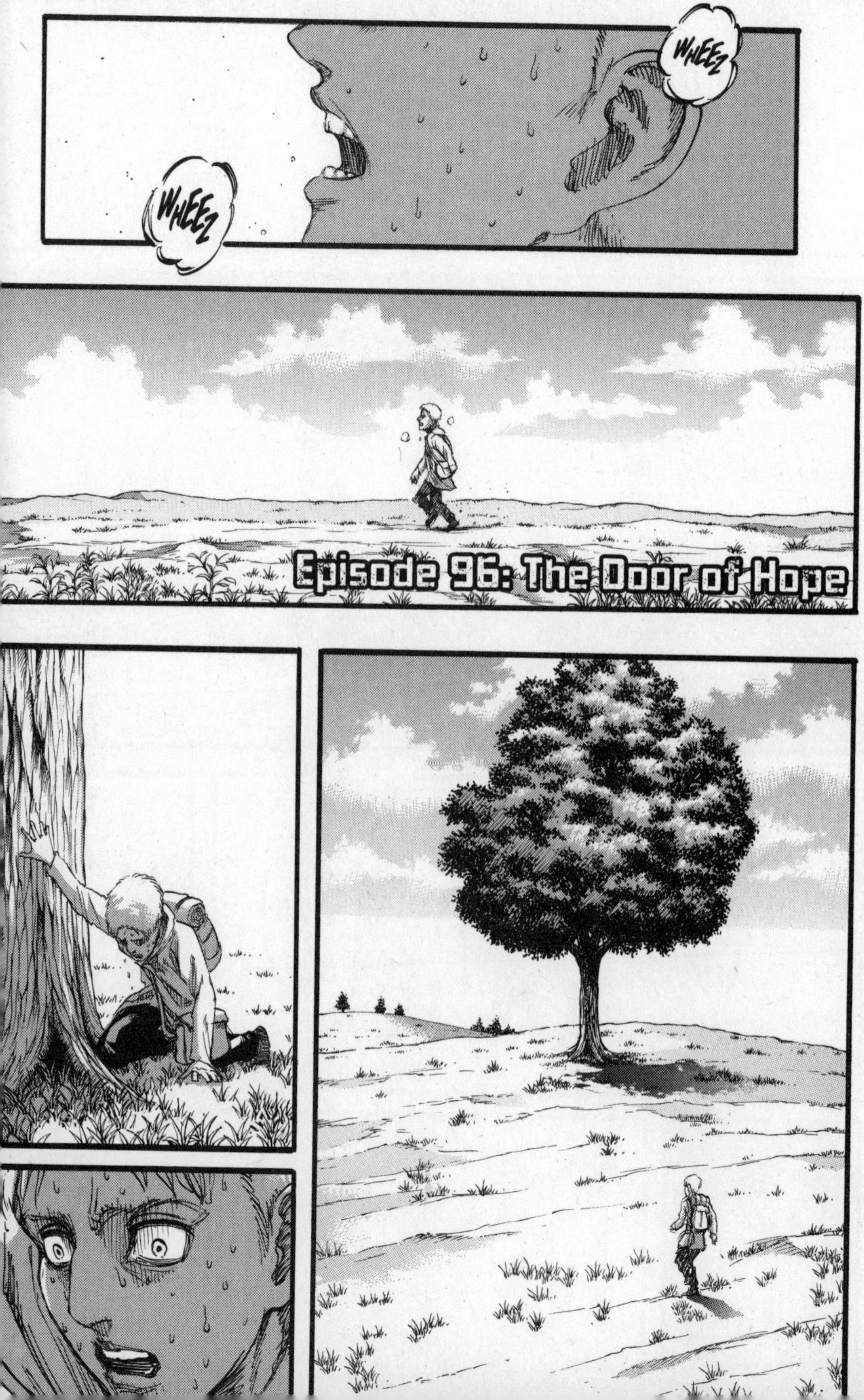
WHEEZ
WHEEZ
Episode 96: The Door of Hope

ATTACK on TITAN

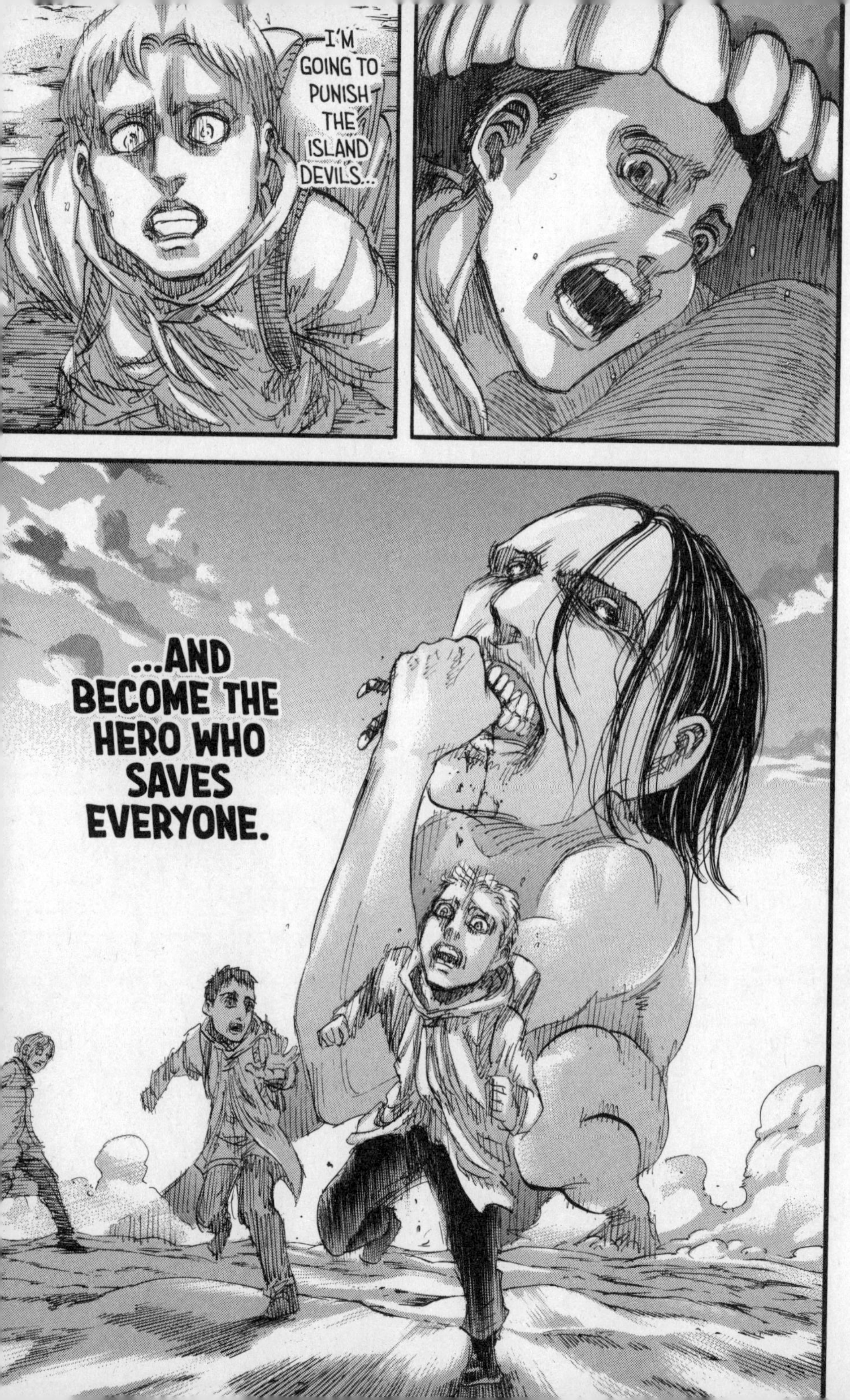
I'M GOING TO PUNISH THE ISLAND DEVILS...
...AND BECOME THE HERO WHO SAVES EVERYONE.

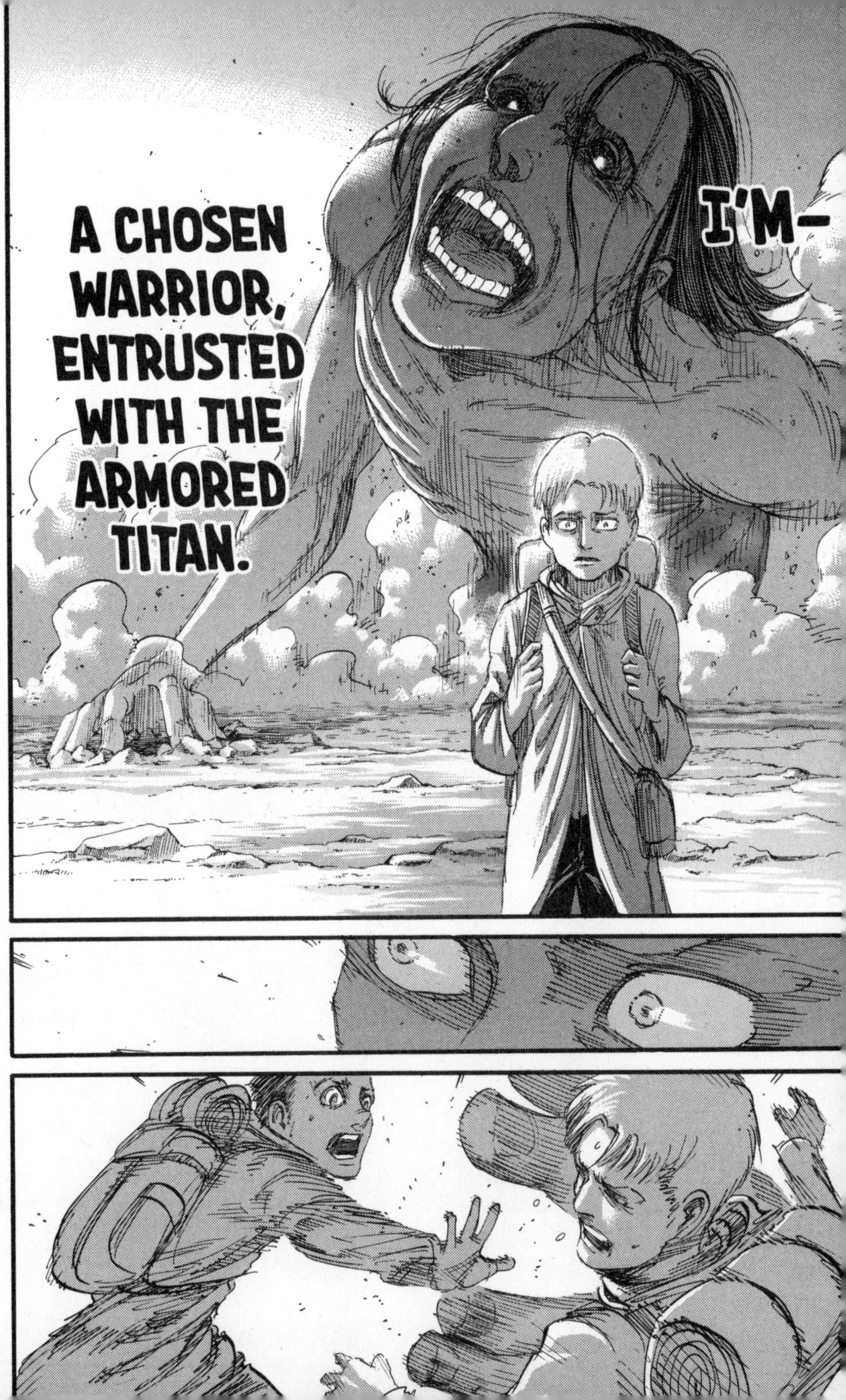
I'M-
A CHOSEN WARRIOR, ENTRUSTED WITH THE ARMORED TITAN.

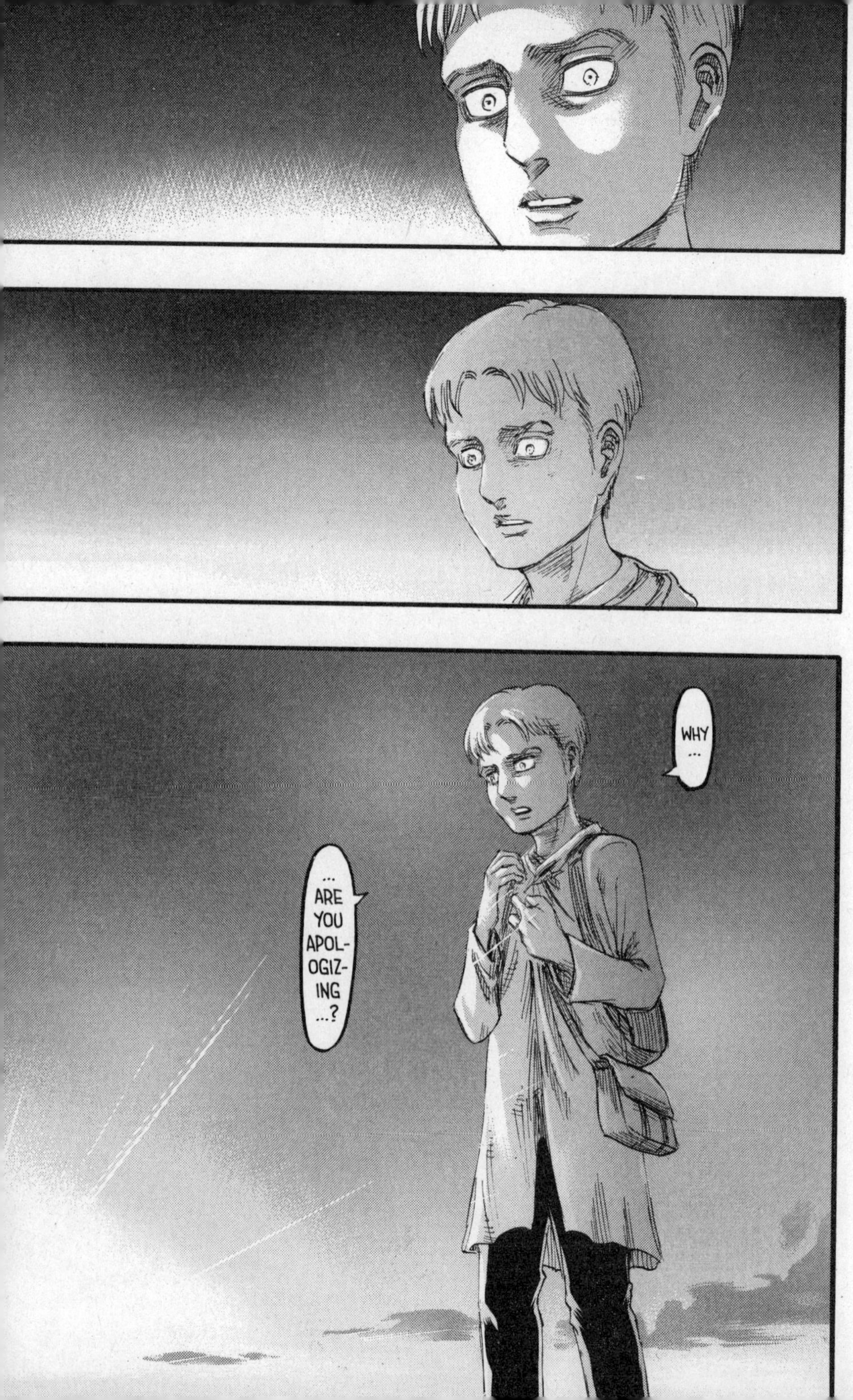
WHY ...
... ARE YOU APOLOGIZING ...?

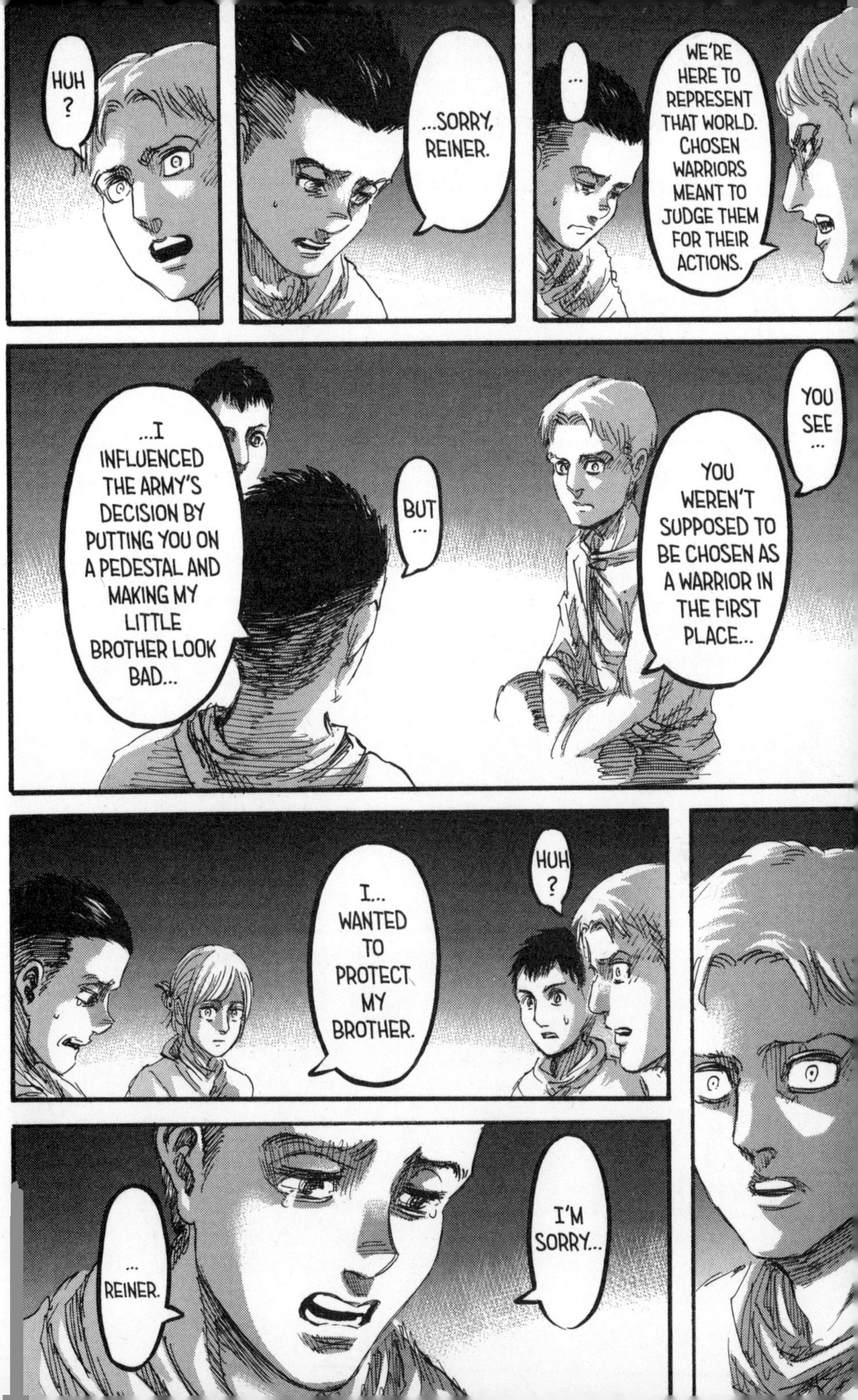
WE'RE HERE TO REPRESENT THAT WORLD. CHOSEN WARRIORS MEANT TO JUDGE THEM FOR THEIR ACTIONS.
...
...SORRY, REINER.
HUH ?
YOU SEE ...
YOU WEREN'T SUPPOSED TO BE CHOSEN AS A WARRIOR IN THE FIRST PLACE...
BUT ...
...I INFLUENCED THE ARMY'S DECISION BY PUTTING YOU ON A PEDESTAL AND MAKING MY LITTLE BROTHER LOOK BAD...
HUH ?
I... WANTED TO PROTECT MY BROTHER.
I'M SORRY...
... REINER.

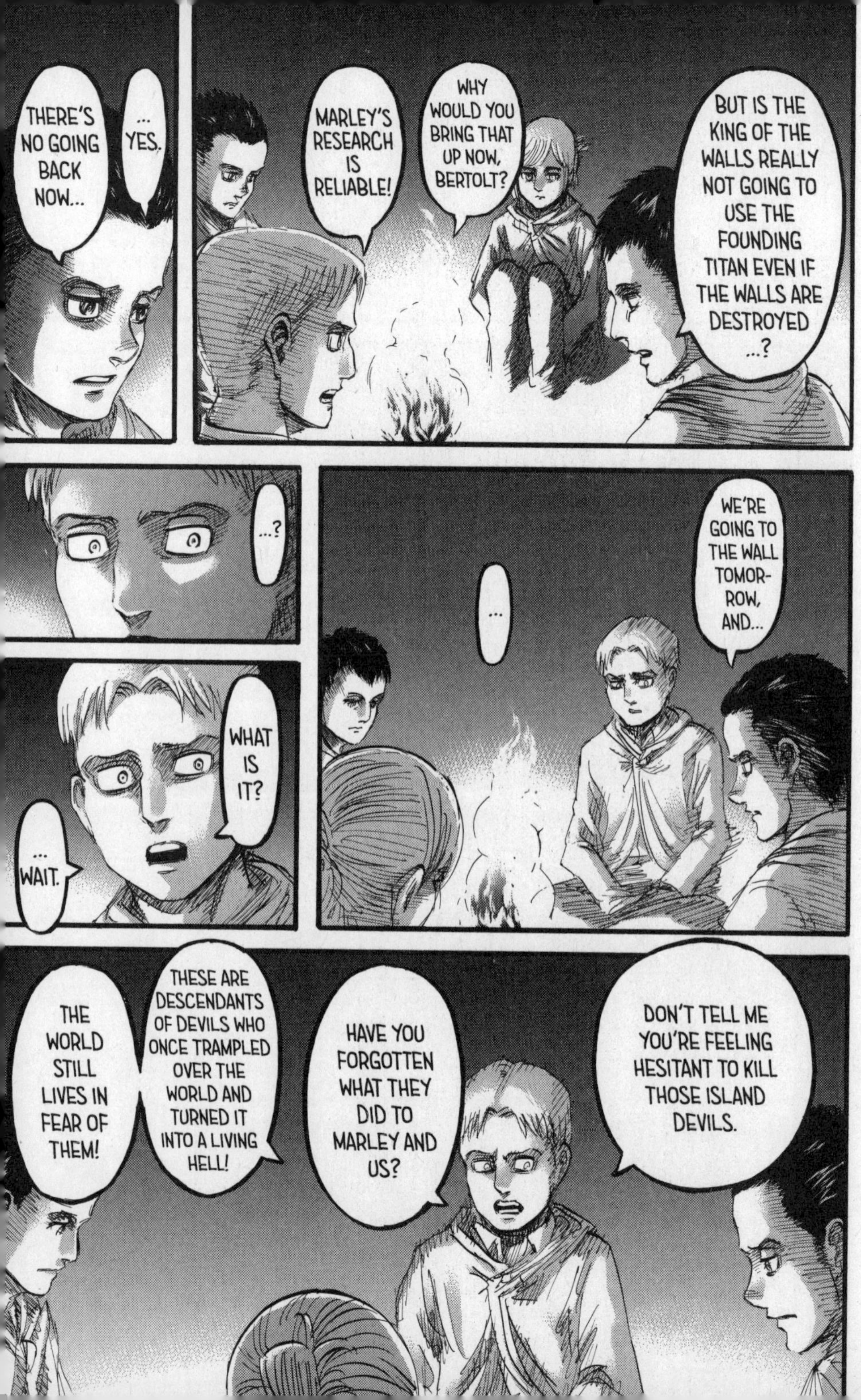
BUT IS THE KING OF THE WALLS REALLY NOT GOING TO USE THE FOUNDING TITAN EVEN IF THE WALLS ARE DESTROYED ...?
WHY WOULD YOU BRING THAT UP NOW, BERTOLT?
MARLEY'S RESEARCH IS RELIABLE!
... YES.
THERE'S NO GOING BACK NOW...
WE'RE GOING TO THE WALL TOMOR-ROW, AND...
...
...?
WHAT IS IT?
... WAIT.
DON'T TELL ME YOU'RE FEELING HESITANT TO KILL THOSE ISLAND DEVILS.
HAVE YOU FORGOTTEN WHAT THEY DID TO MARLEY AND US?
THESE ARE DESCENDANTS OF DEVILS WHO ONCE TRAMPLED OVER THE WORLD AND TURNED IT INTO A LIVING HELL!
THE WORLD STILL LIVES IN FEAR OF THEM!

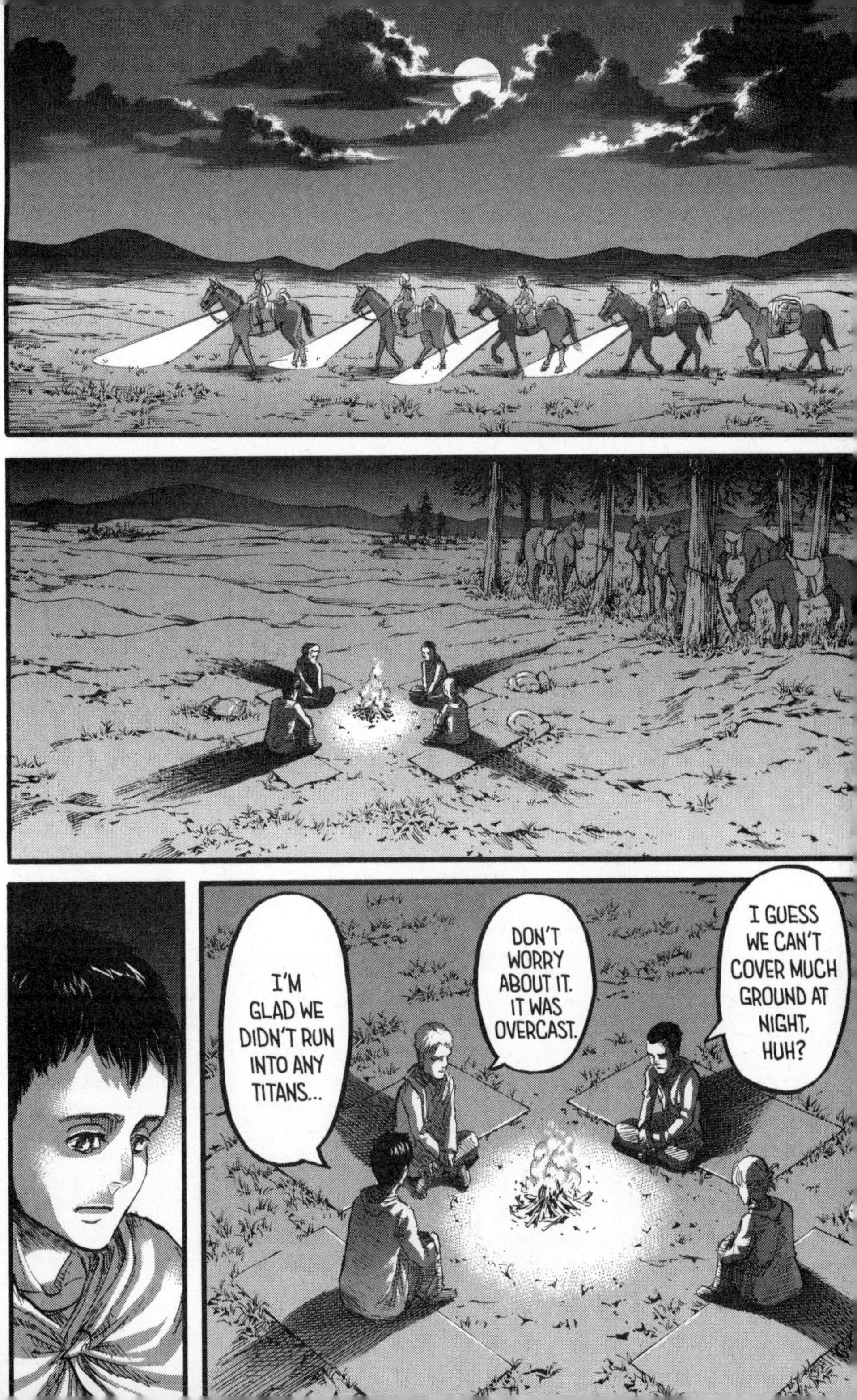
I GUESS WE CAN'T COVER MUCH GROUND AT NIGHT, HUH?
DON'T WORRY ABOUT IT. IT WAS OVERCAST.
I'M GLAD WE DIDN'T RUN INTO ANY TITANS...

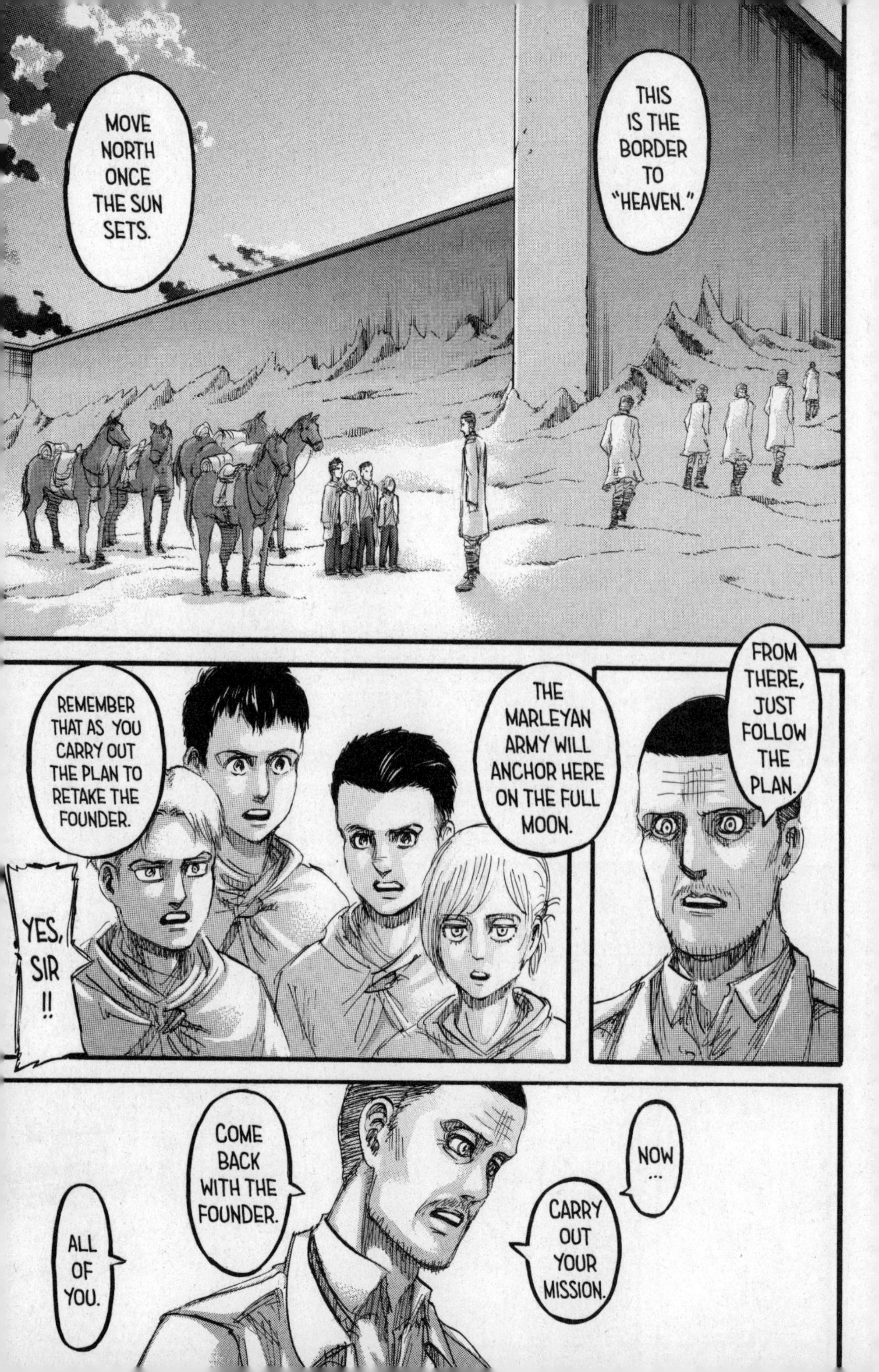
THIS IS THE BORDER TO "HEAVEN."
MOVE NORTH ONCE THE SUN SETS.
FROM THERE, JUST FOLLOW THE PLAN.
THE MARLEYAN ARMY WILL ANCHOR HERE ON THE FULL MOON.
REMEMBER THAT AS YOU CARRY OUT THE PLAN TO RETAKE THE FOUNDER.
YES, SIR!!
NOW...
CARRY OUT YOUR MISSION.
COME BACK WITH THE FOUNDER.
ALL OF YOU.

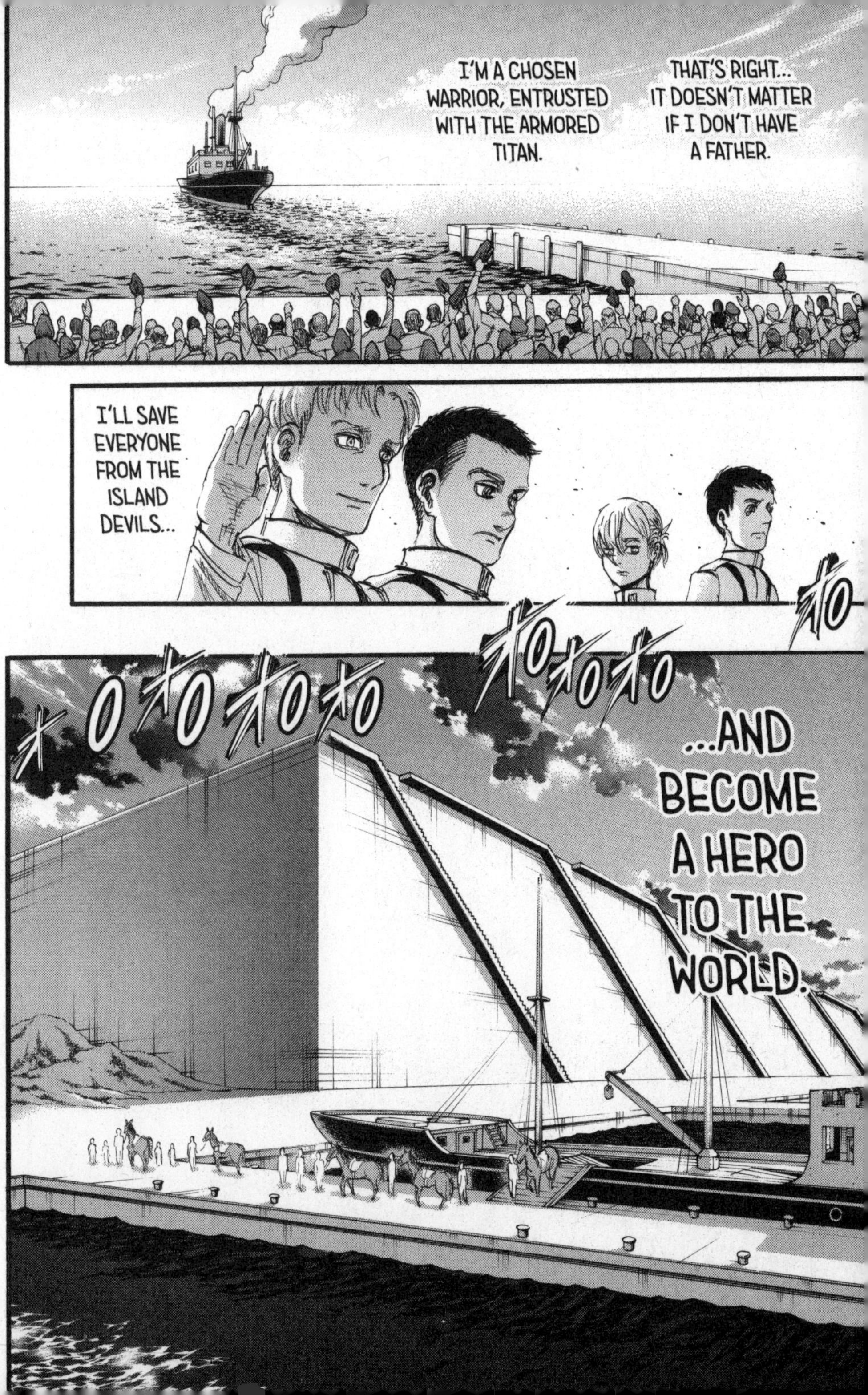
THAT'S RIGHT... IT DOESN'T MATTER IF I DON'T HAVE A FATHER.
I'M A CHOSEN WARRIOR, ENTRUSTED WITH THE ARMORED TITAN.
I'LL SAVE EVERYONE FROM THE ISLAND DEVILS...
...AND BECOME A HERO TO THE WORLD.

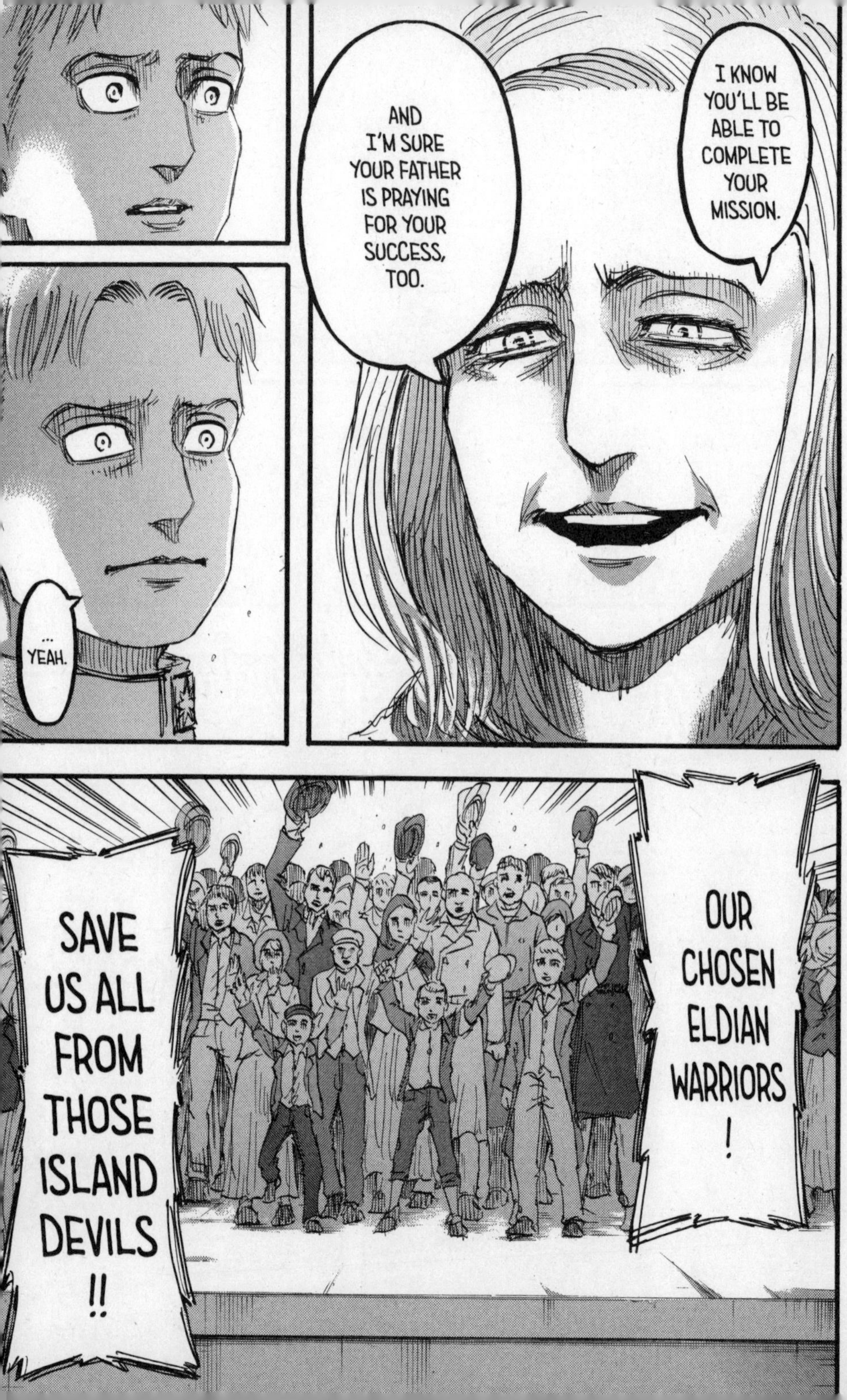
I KNOW YOU'LL BE ABLE TO COMPLETE YOUR MISSION.
AND I'M SURE YOUR FATHER IS PRAYING FOR YOUR SUCCESS, TOO.
... YEAH.
OUR CHOSEN ELDIAN WARRIORS!
SAVE US ALL FROM THOSE ISLAND DEVILS!!

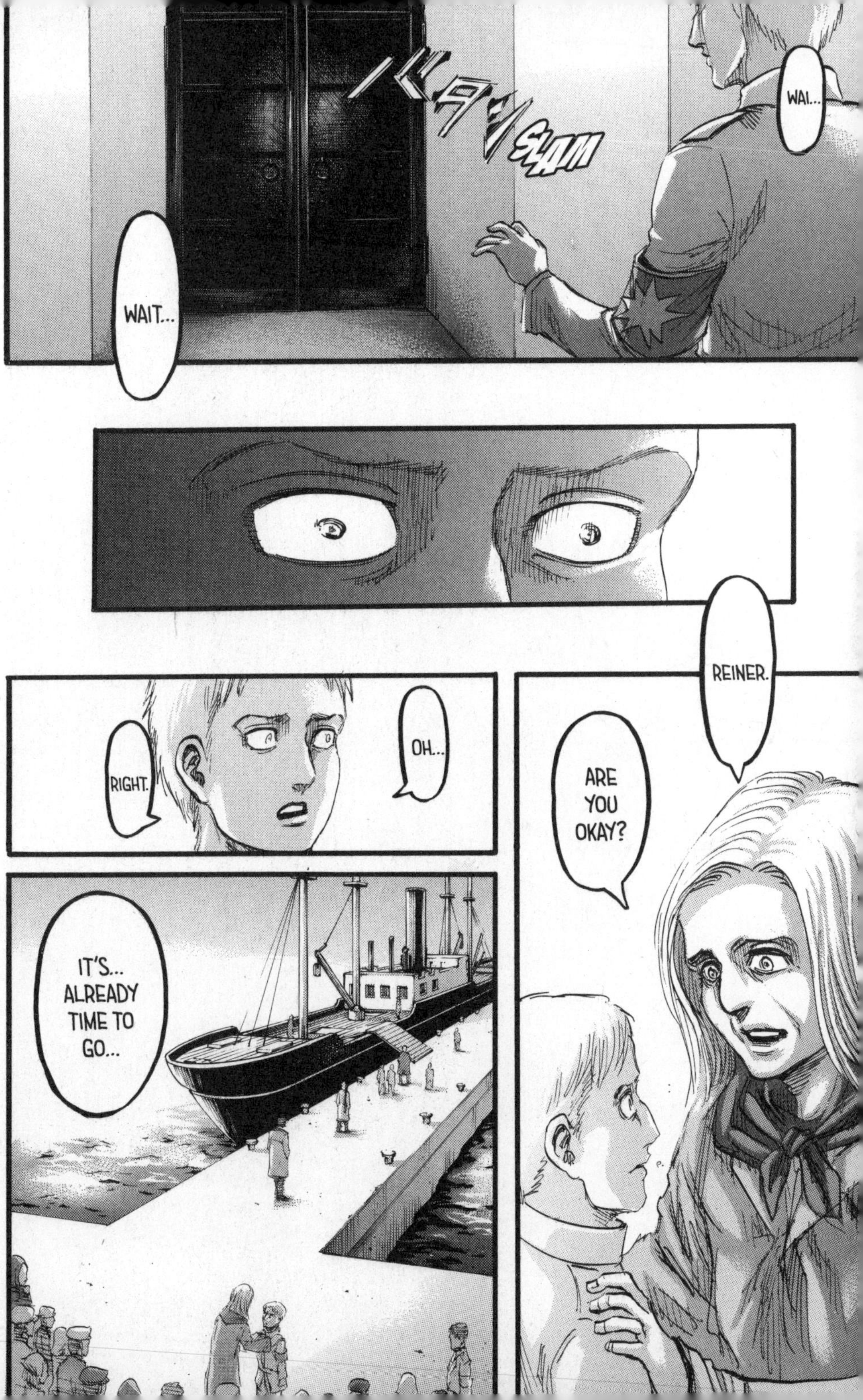
WAI...
バタン SLAM
WAIT...
REINER.
ARE YOU OKAY?
OH...
RIGHT.
IT'S... ALREADY TIME TO GO...

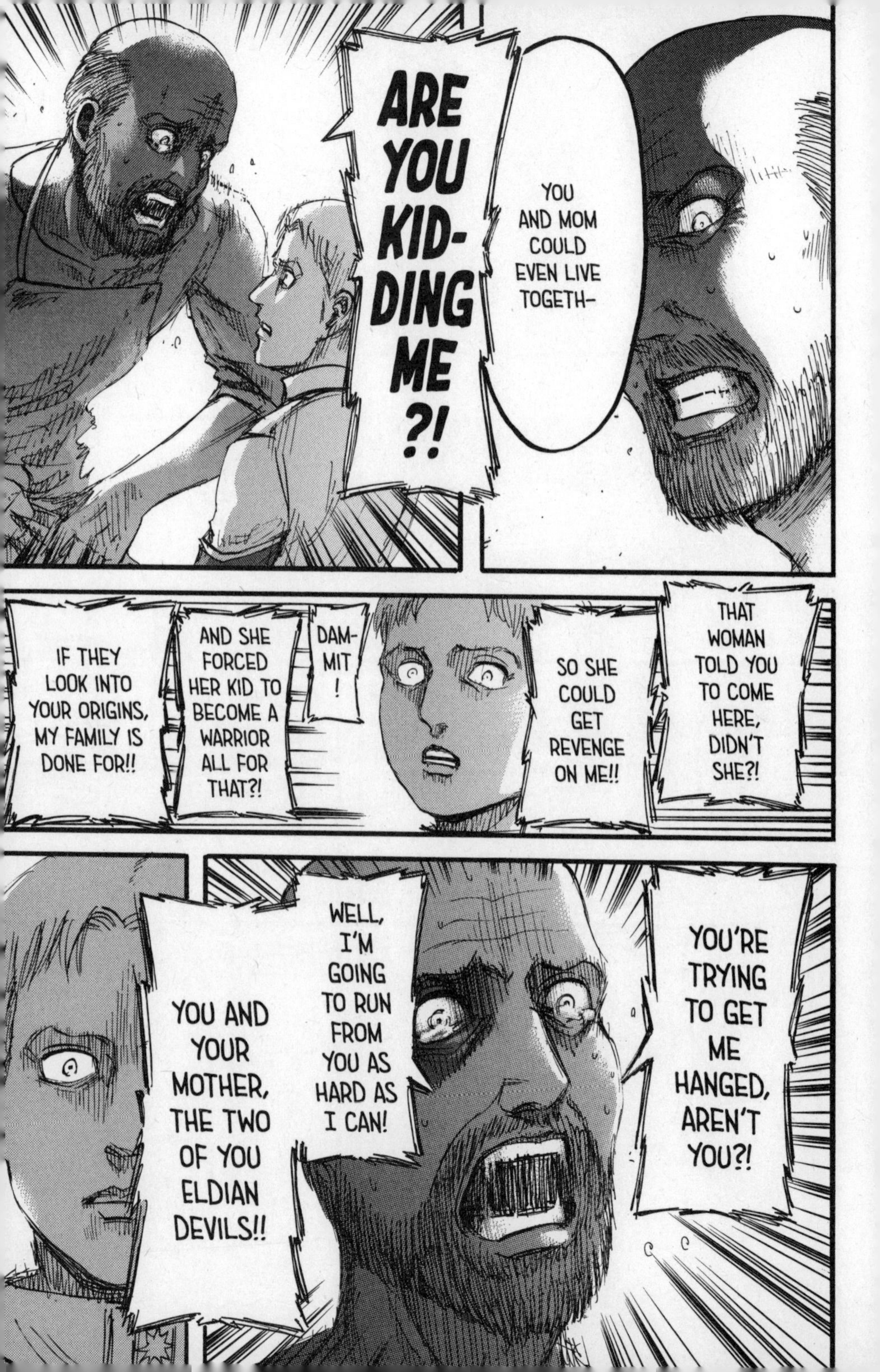
YOU AND MOM COULD EVEN LIVE TOGETH-
ARE YOU KID-DING ME?!
THAT WOMAN TOLD YOU TO COME HERE, DIDN'T SHE?!
SO SHE COULD GET REVENGE ON ME!!
DAM-MIT!
AND SHE FORCED HER KID TO BECOME A WARRIOR ALL FOR THAT?!
IF THEY LOOK INTO YOUR ORIGINS, MY FAMILY IS DONE FOR!!
YOU'RE TRYING TO GET ME HANGED, AREN'T YOU?!
WELL, I'M GOING TO RUN FROM YOU AS HARD AS I CAN!
YOU AND YOUR MOTHER, THE TWO OF YOU ELDIAN DEVILS!!

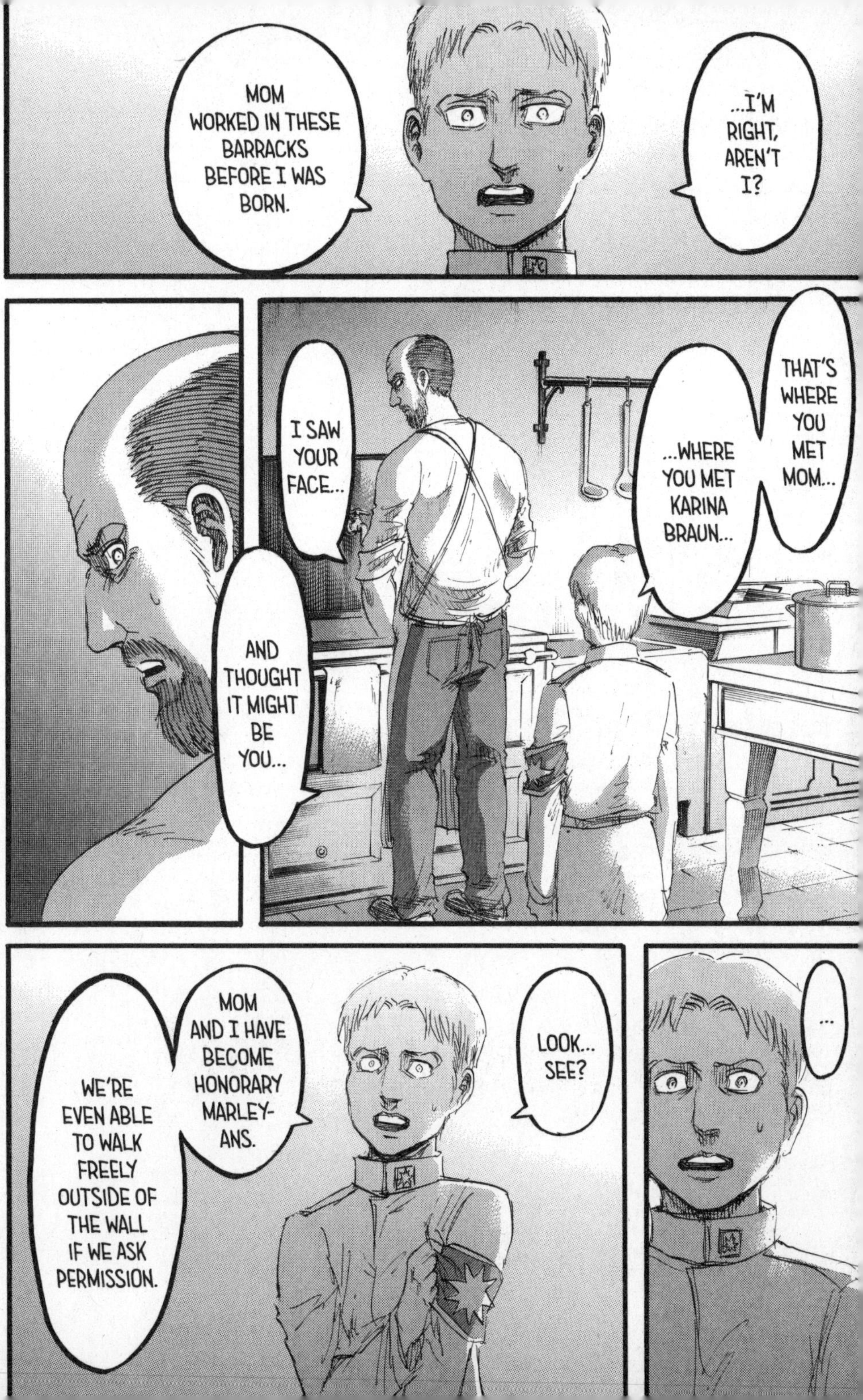
...I'M RIGHT, AREN'T I?
MOM WORKED IN THESE BARRACKS BEFORE I WAS BORN.
THAT'S WHERE YOU MET MOM...
...WHERE YOU MET KARINA BRAUN...
I SAW YOUR FACE...
AND THOUGHT IT MIGHT BE YOU...
...
LOOK... SEE?
MOM AND I HAVE BECOME HONORARY MARLEY-ANS.
WE'RE EVEN ABLE TO WALK FREELY OUTSIDE OF THE WALL IF WE ASK PERMISSION.

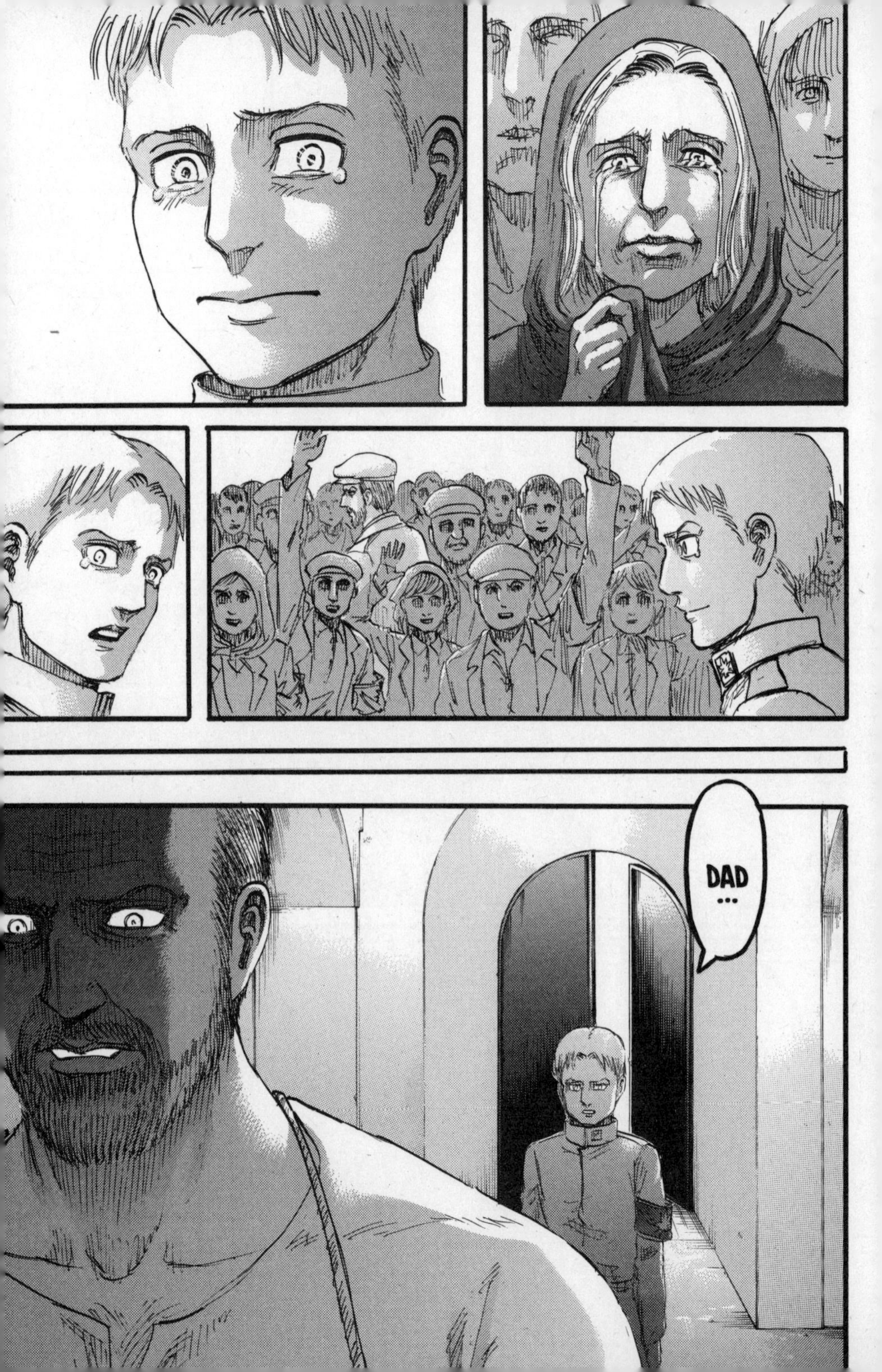
DAD
...

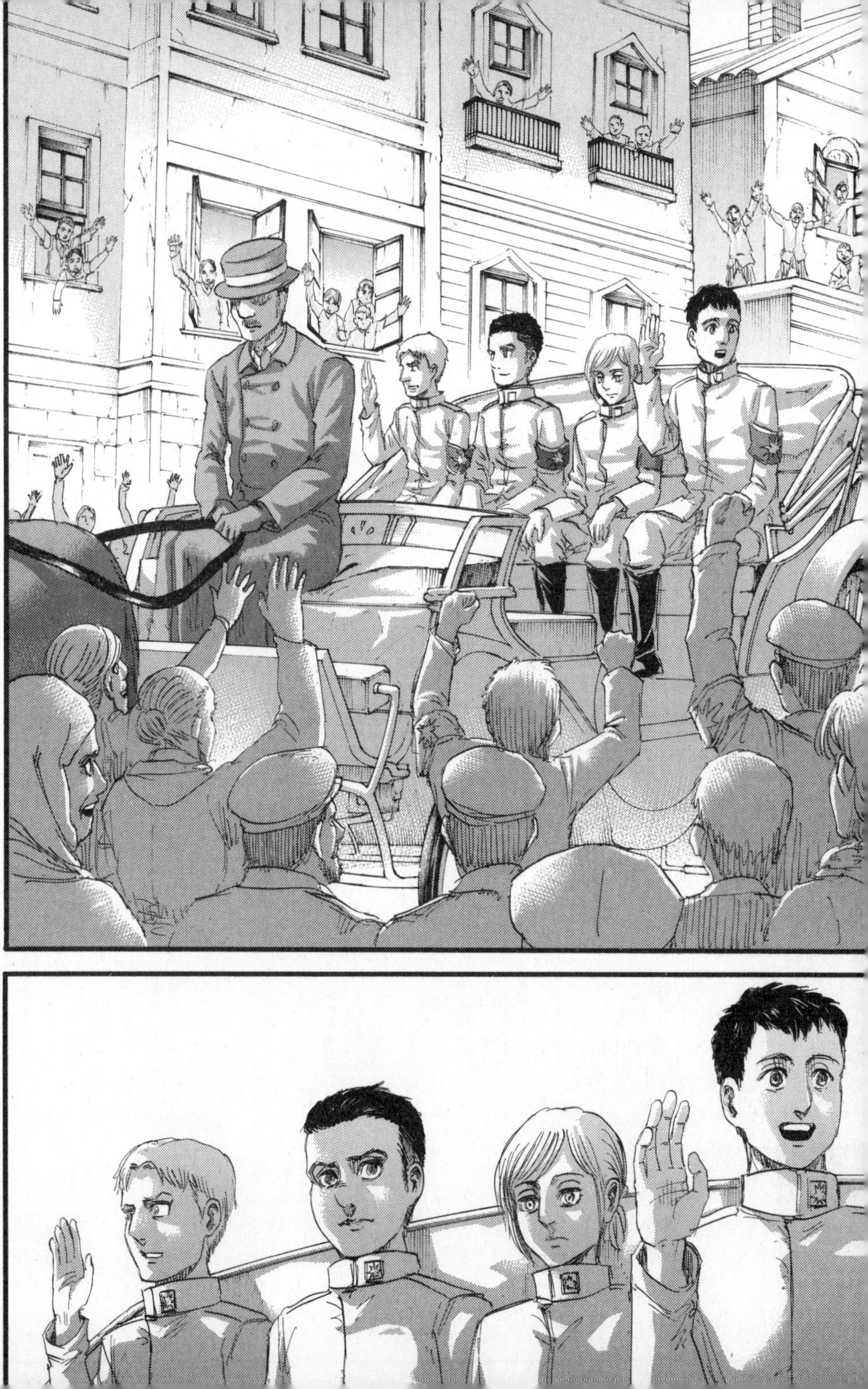

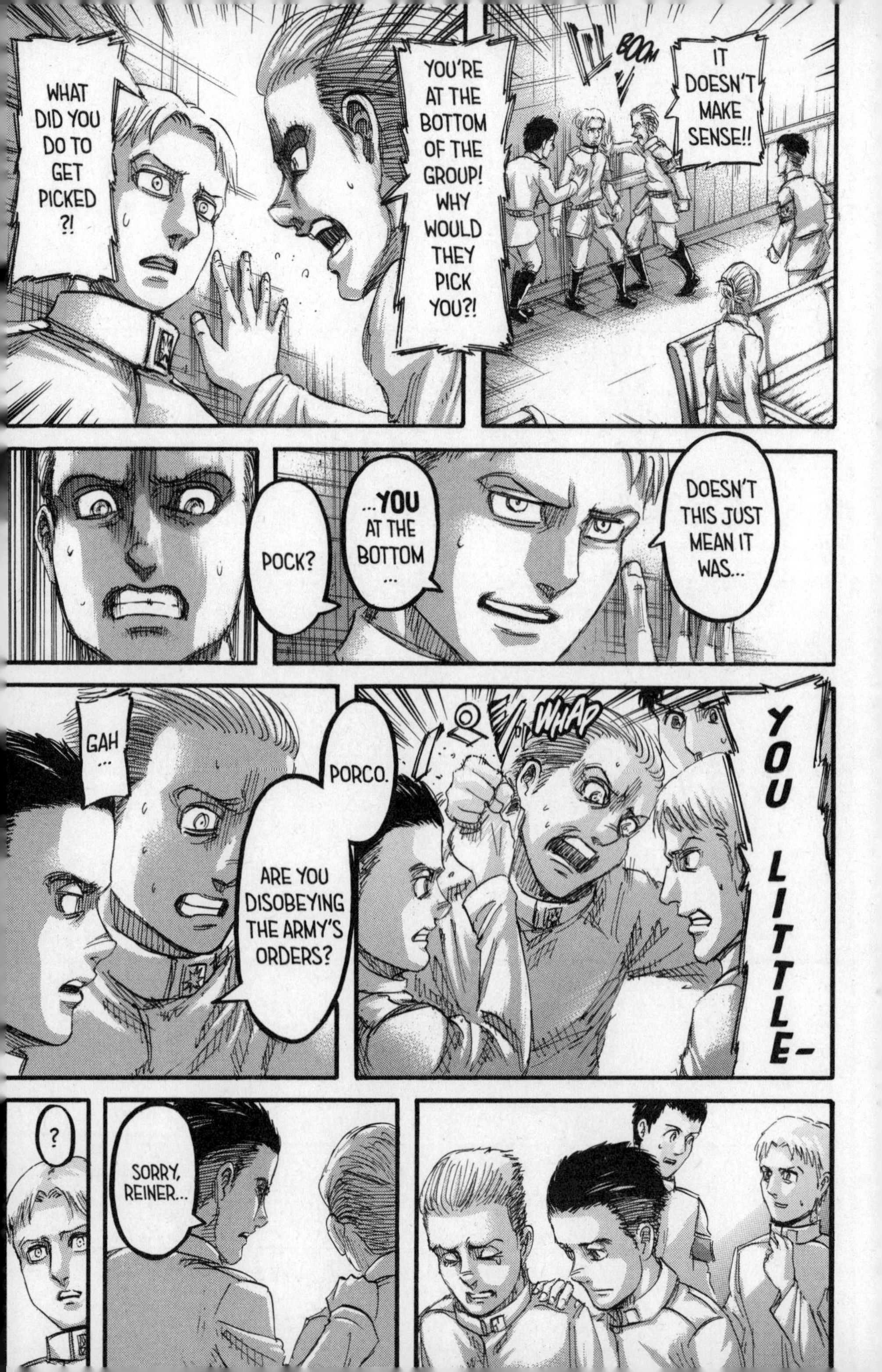
BOOM
IT DOESN'T MAKE SENSE!!
YOU'RE AT THE BOTTOM OF THE GROUP! WHY WOULD THEY PICK YOU?!
WHAT DID YOU DO TO GET PICKED?!
DOESN'T THIS JUST MEAN IT WAS...
...YOU AT THE BOTTOM...
POCK?
YOU LITTLE-
WHAP
PORCO.
ARE YOU DISOBEYING THE ARMY'S ORDERS?
GAH...
SORRY, REINER...
?

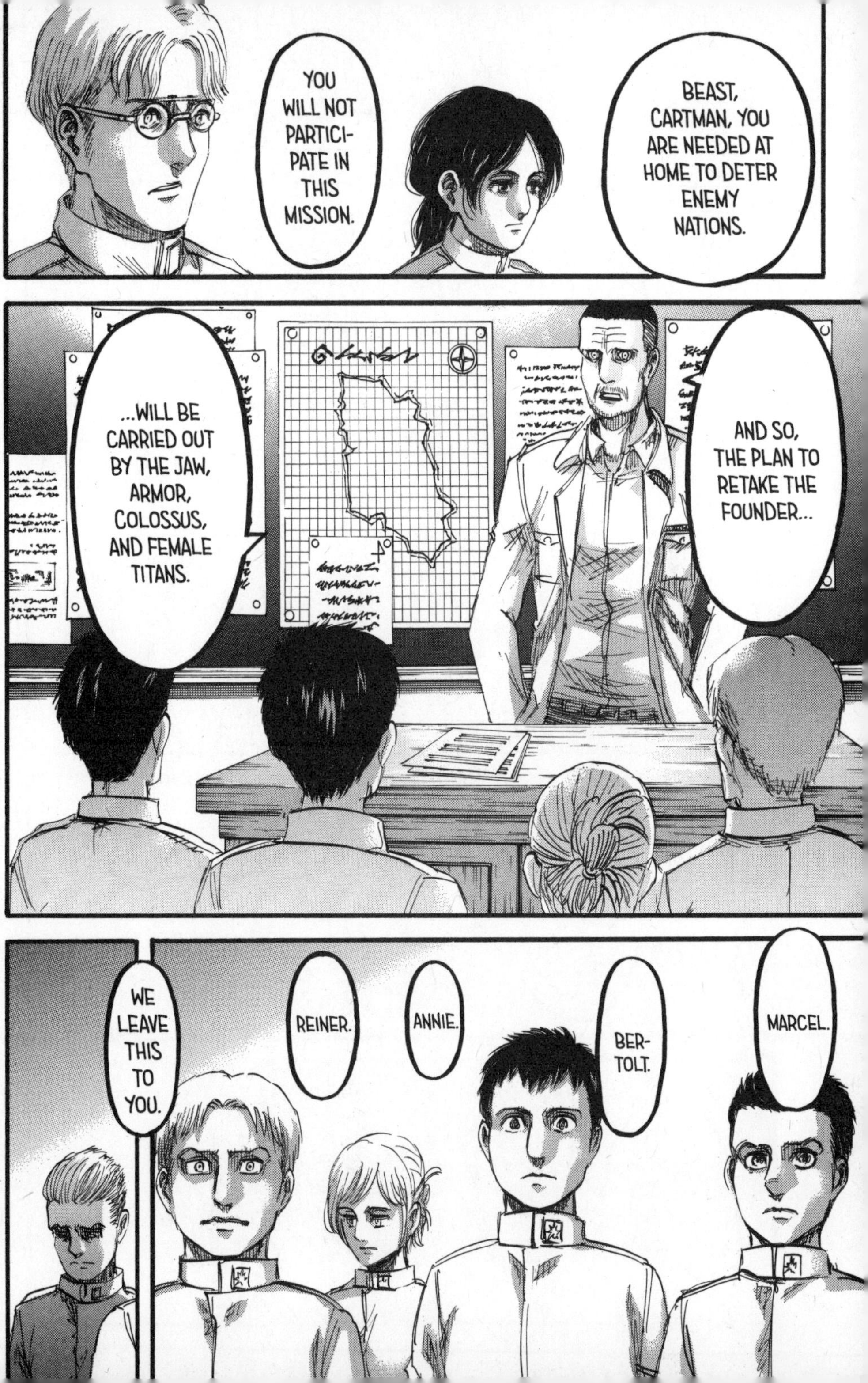
BEAST, CARTMAN, YOU ARE NEEDED AT HOME TO DETER ENEMY NATIONS.
YOU WILL NOT PARTICI-PATE IN THIS MISSION.
AND SO, THE PLAN TO RETAKE THE FOUNDER...
...WILL BE CARRIED OUT BY THE JAW, ARMOR, COLOSSUS, AND FEMALE TITANS.
MARCEL.
BER-TOLT.
ANNIE.
REINER.
WE LEAVE THIS TO YOU.

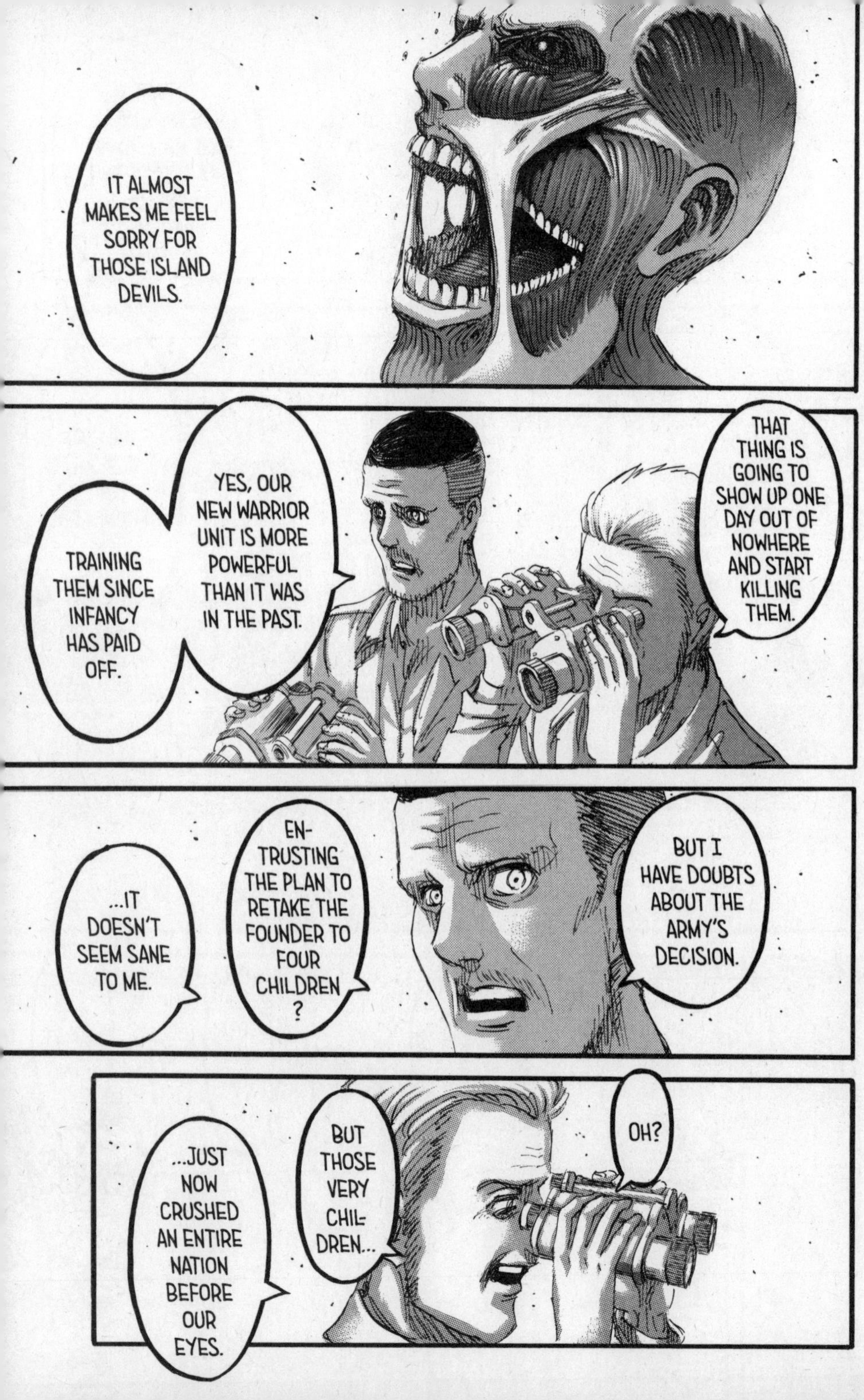
IT ALMOST MAKES ME FEEL SORRY FOR THOSE ISLAND DEVILS.
THAT THING IS GOING TO SHOW UP ONE DAY OUT OF NOWHERE AND START KILLING THEM.
YES, OUR NEW WARRIOR UNIT IS MORE POWERFUL THAN IT WAS IN THE PAST.
TRAINING THEM SINCE INFANCY HAS PAID OFF.
BUT I HAVE DOUBTS ABOUT THE ARMY'S DECISION.
ENTRUSTING THE PLAN TO RETAKE THE FOUNDER TO FOUR CHILDREN?
...IT DOESN'T SEEM SANE TO ME.
OH?
BUT THOSE VERY CHILDREN...
...JUST NOW CRUSHED AN ENTIRE NATION BEFORE OUR EYES.

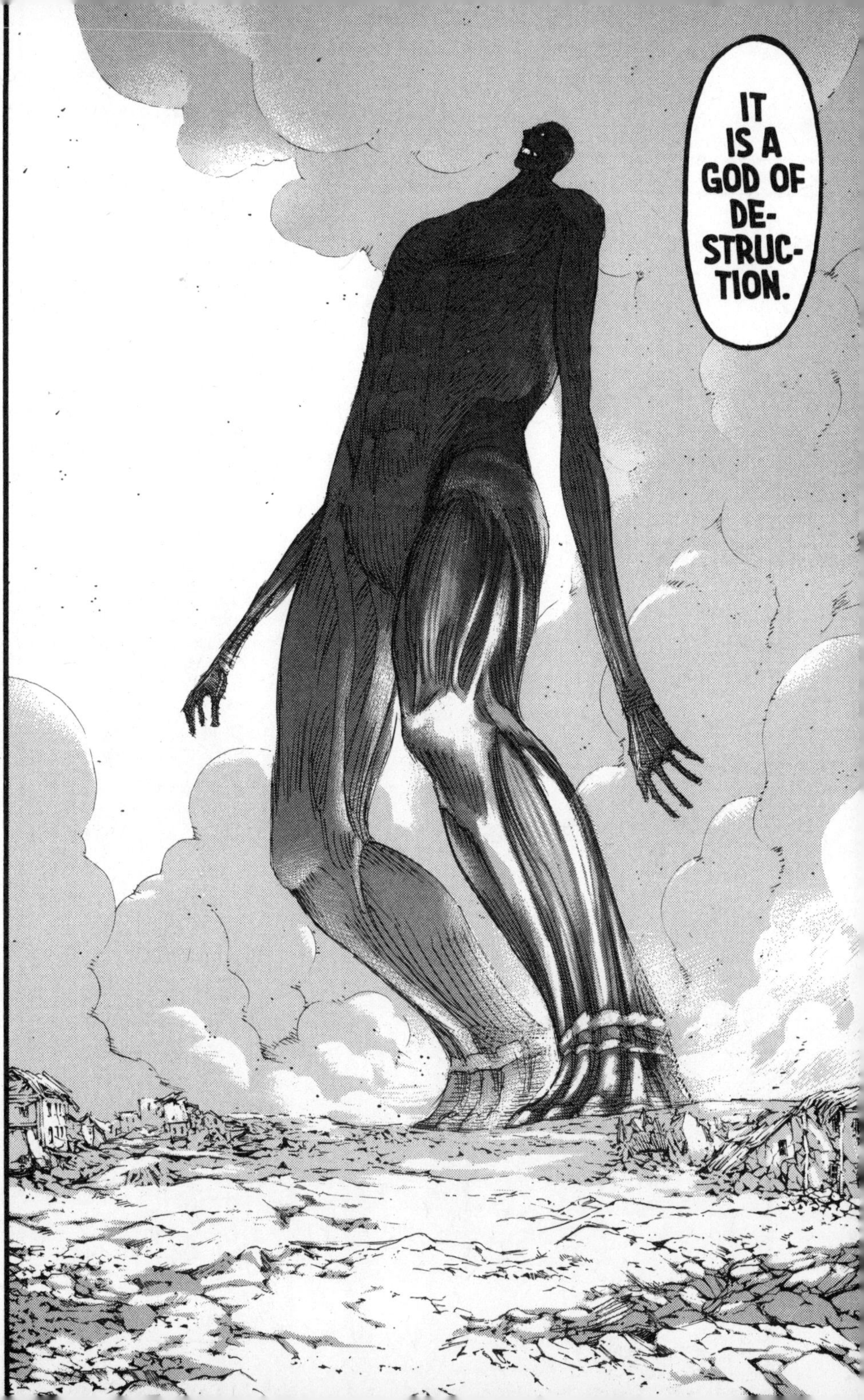
IT IS A GOD OF DESTRUCTION.

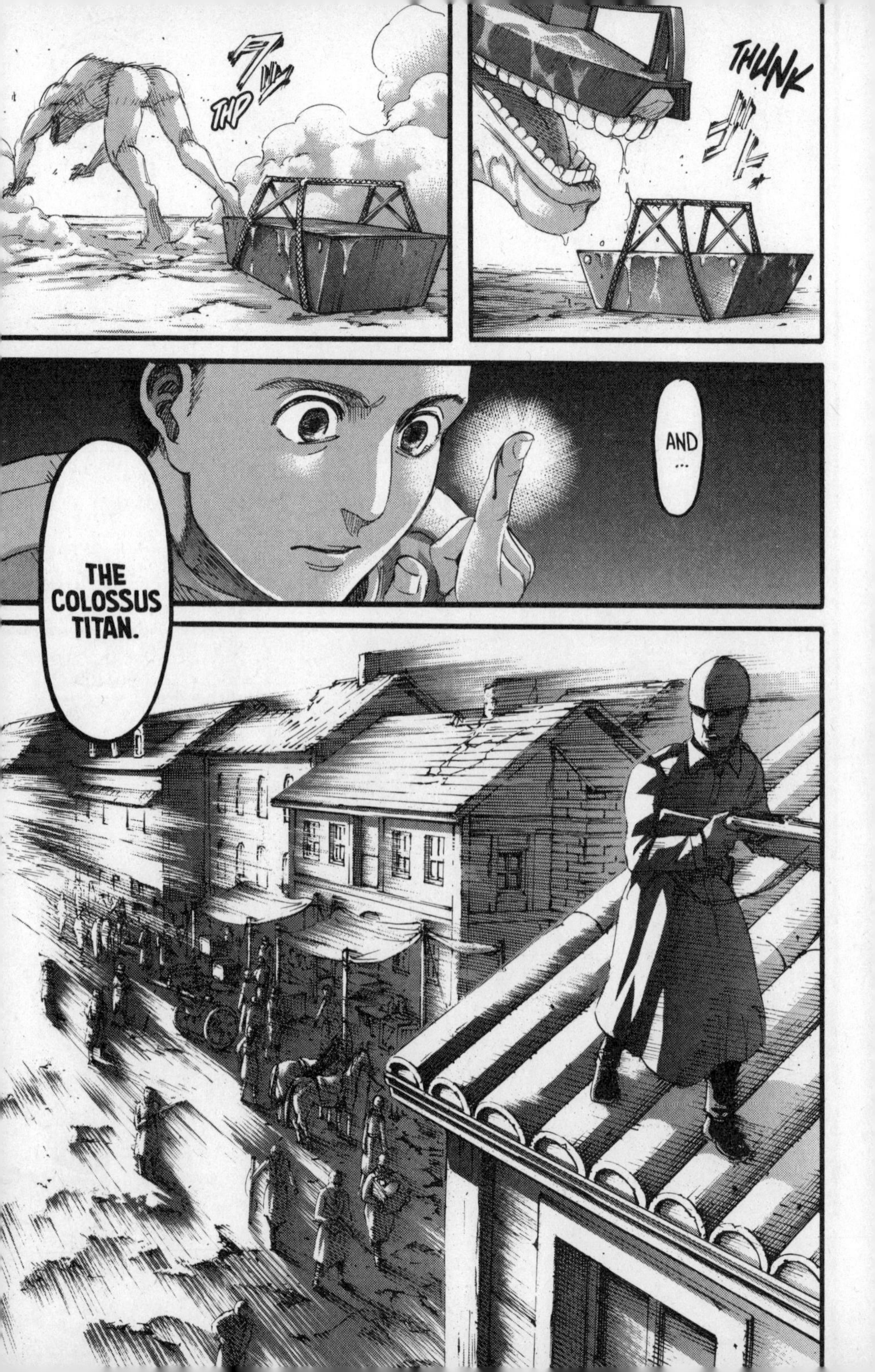
THUNK
THP
AND ...
THE COLOSSUS TITAN.

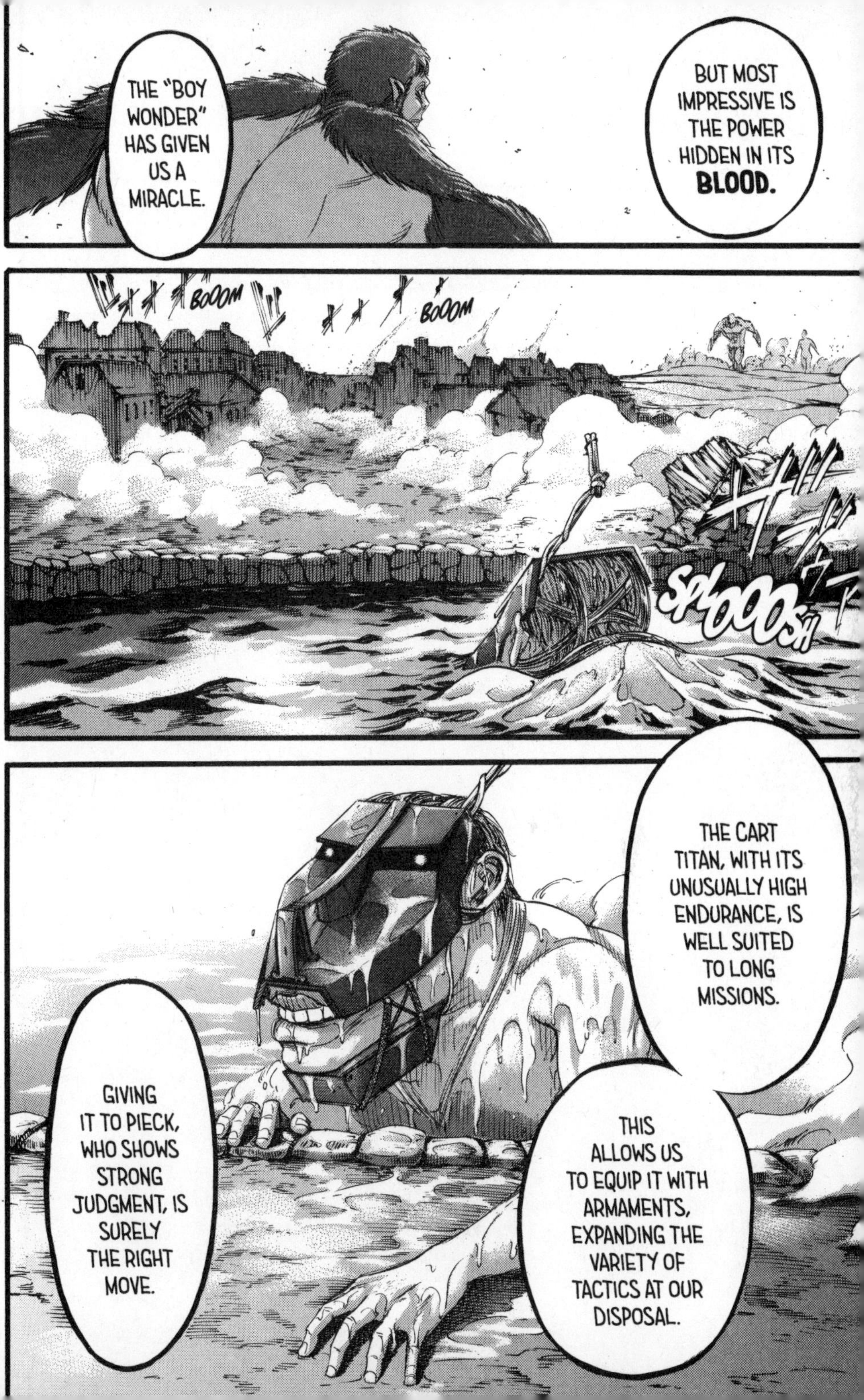
BUT MOST IMPRESSIVE IS THE POWER HIDDEN IN ITS **BLOOD.**
THE "BOY WONDER" HAS GIVEN US A MIRACLE.
BOOOM
BOOOM
SPLOOOSH
THE CART TITAN, WITH ITS UNUSUALLY HIGH ENDURANCE, IS WELL SUITED TO LONG MISSIONS.
THIS ALLOWS US TO EQUIP IT WITH ARMAMENTS, EXPANDING THE VARIETY OF TACTICS AT OUR DISPOSAL.
GIVING IT TO PIECK, WHO SHOWS STRONG JUDGMENT, IS SURELY THE RIGHT MOVE.

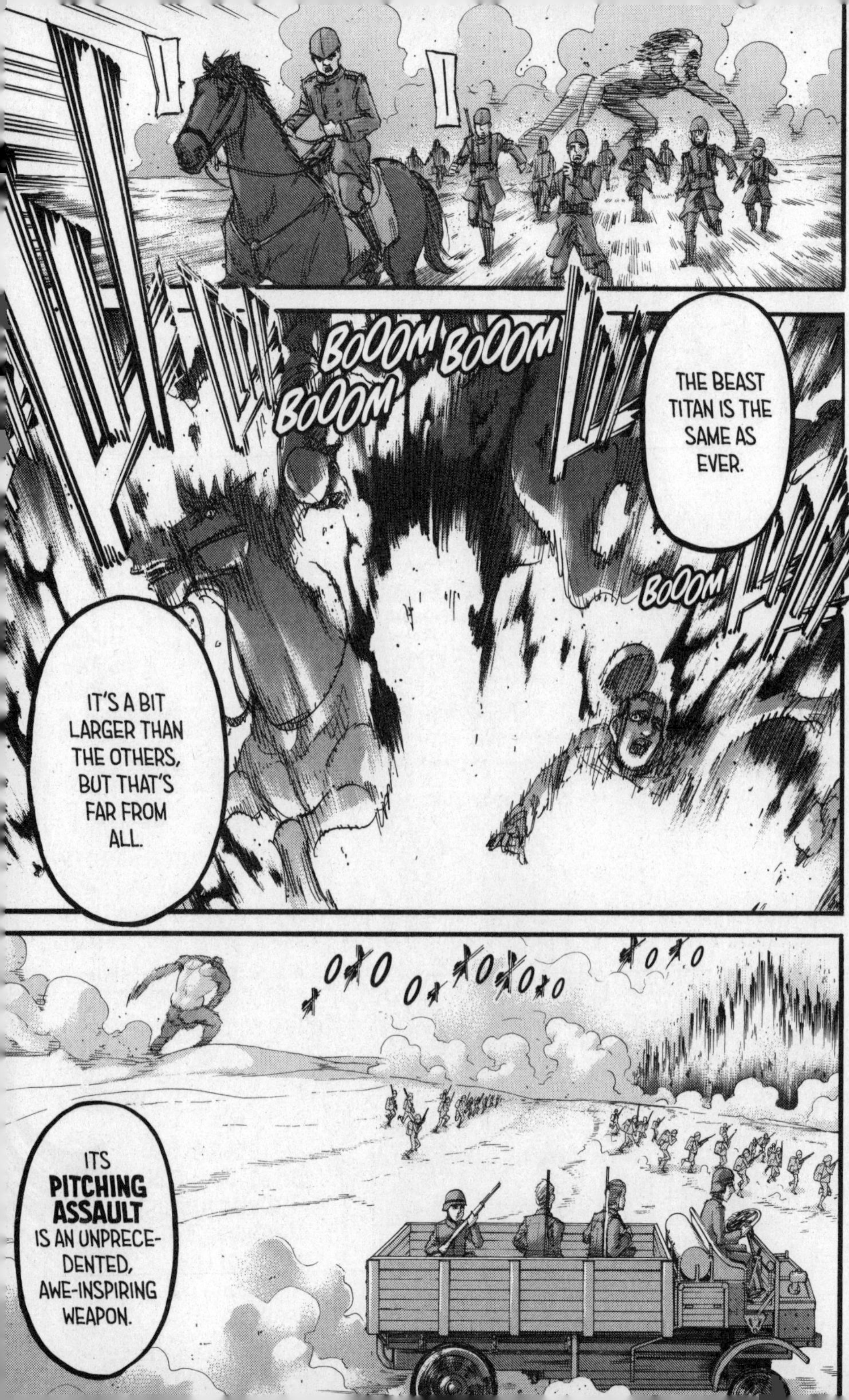
THE BEAST TITAN IS THE SAME AS EVER.
BOOOM BOOOM
BOOOM
BOOOM
IT'S A BIT LARGER THAN THE OTHERS, BUT THAT'S FAR FROM ALL.
ITS **PITCHING ASSAULT** IS AN UNPRECEDENTED, AWE-INSPIRING WEAPON.

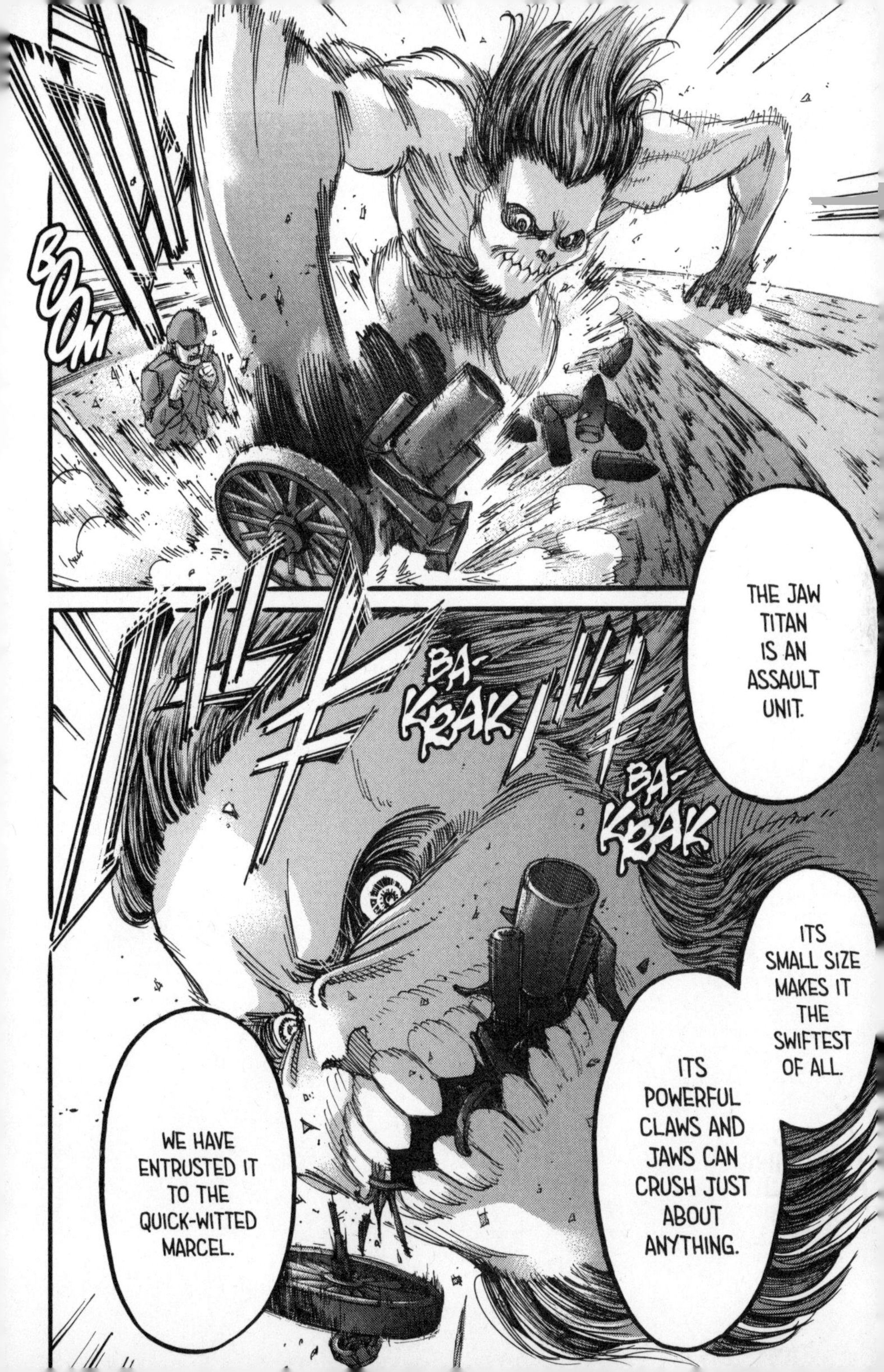
BOOM
THE JAW TITAN IS AN ASSAULT UNIT.
BA-KRAK
BA-KRAK
ITS SMALL SIZE MAKES IT THE SWIFTEST OF ALL.
ITS POWERFUL CLAWS AND JAWS CAN CRUSH JUST ABOUT ANYTHING.
WE HAVE ENTRUSTED IT TO THE QUICK-WITTED MARCEL.

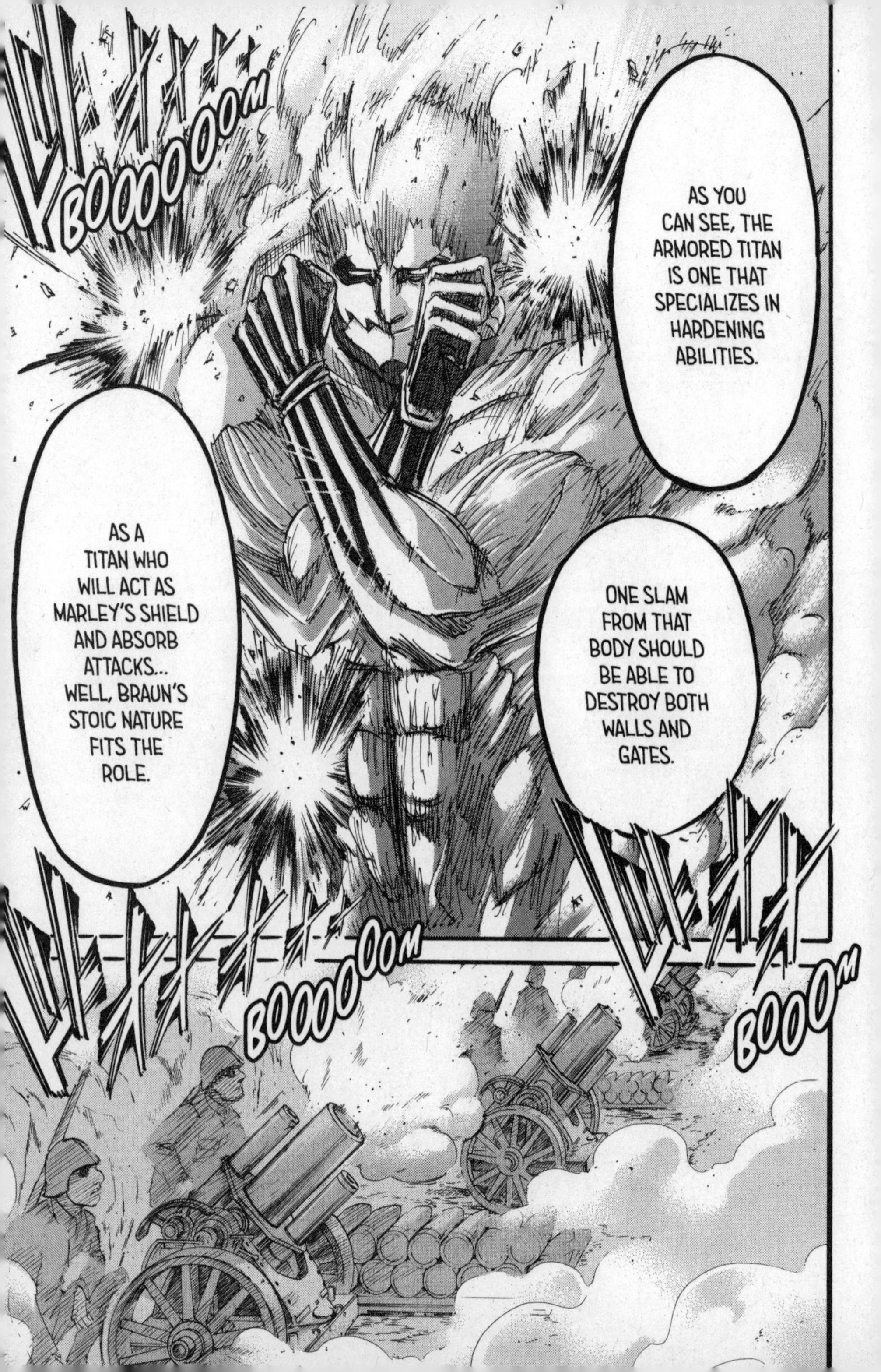

BOOOOOOM
AS YOU CAN SEE, THE ARMORED TITAN IS ONE THAT SPECIALIZES IN HARDENING ABILITIES.
ONE SLAM FROM THAT BODY SHOULD BE ABLE TO DESTROY BOTH WALLS AND GATES.
AS A TITAN WHO WILL ACT AS MARLEY'S SHIELD AND ABSORB ATTACKS... WELL, BRAUN'S STOIC NATURE FITS THE ROLE.
BOOOM
BOOOOOOM

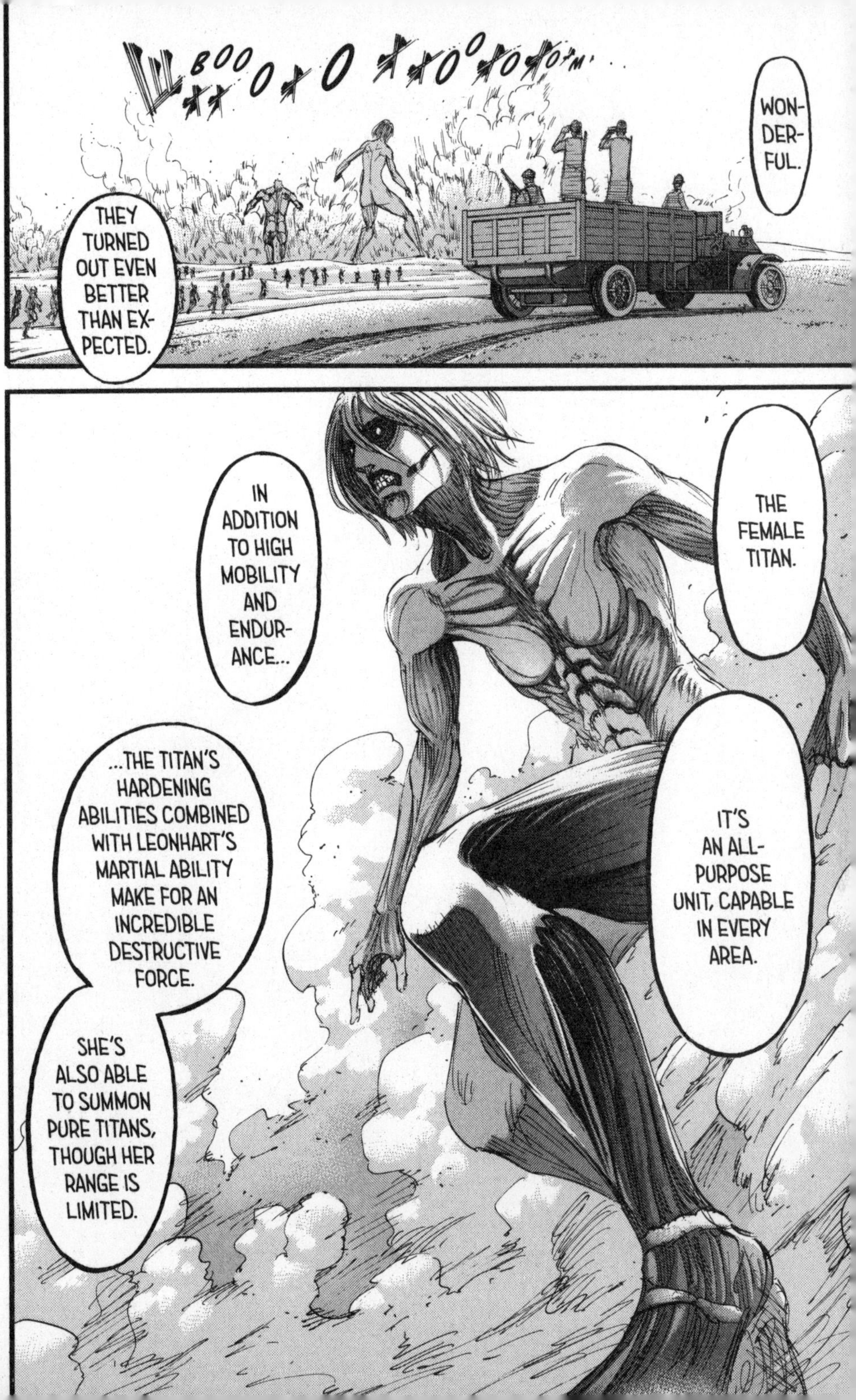
BOOOOOOOOOOM...
WONDERFUL.
THEY TURNED OUT EVEN BETTER THAN EXPECTED.
THE FEMALE TITAN.
IT'S AN ALL-PURPOSE UNIT, CAPABLE IN EVERY AREA.
IN ADDITION TO HIGH MOBILITY AND ENDURANCE...
...THE TITAN'S HARDENING ABILITIES COMBINED WITH LEONHART'S MARTIAL ABILITY MAKE FOR AN INCREDIBLE DESTRUCTIVE FORCE.
SHE'S ALSO ABLE TO SUMMON PURE TITANS, THOUGH HER RANGE IS LIMITED.

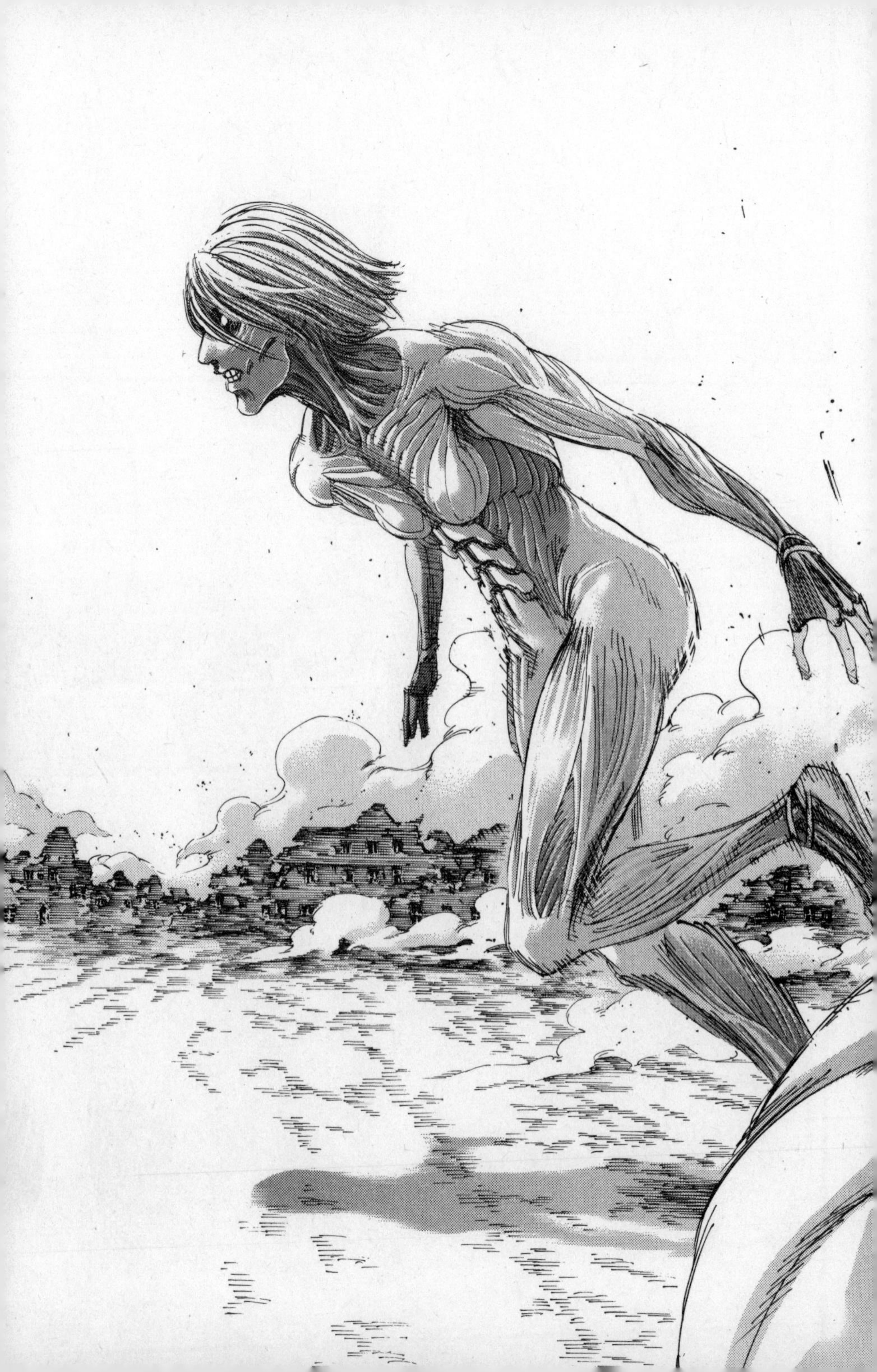

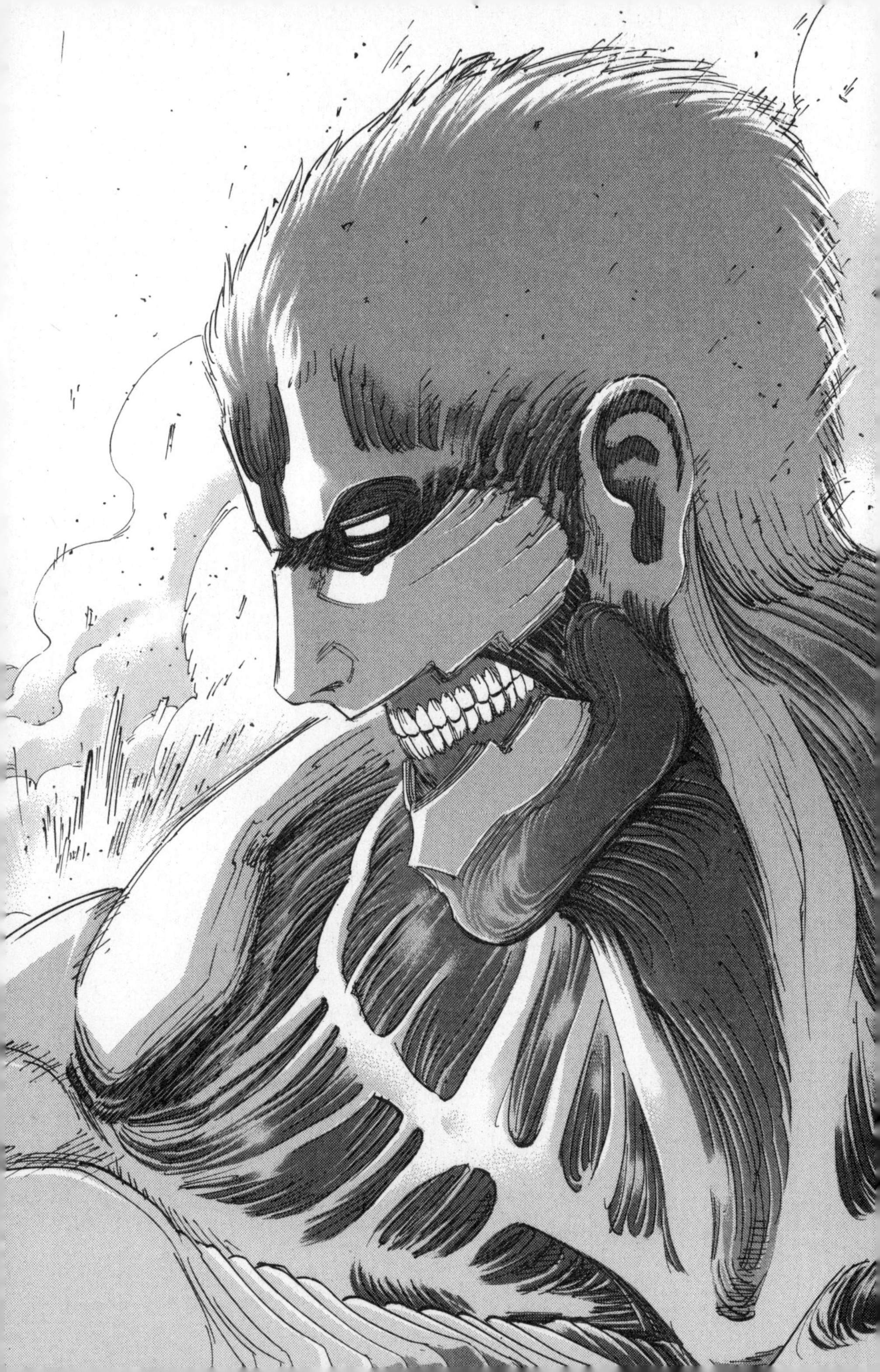

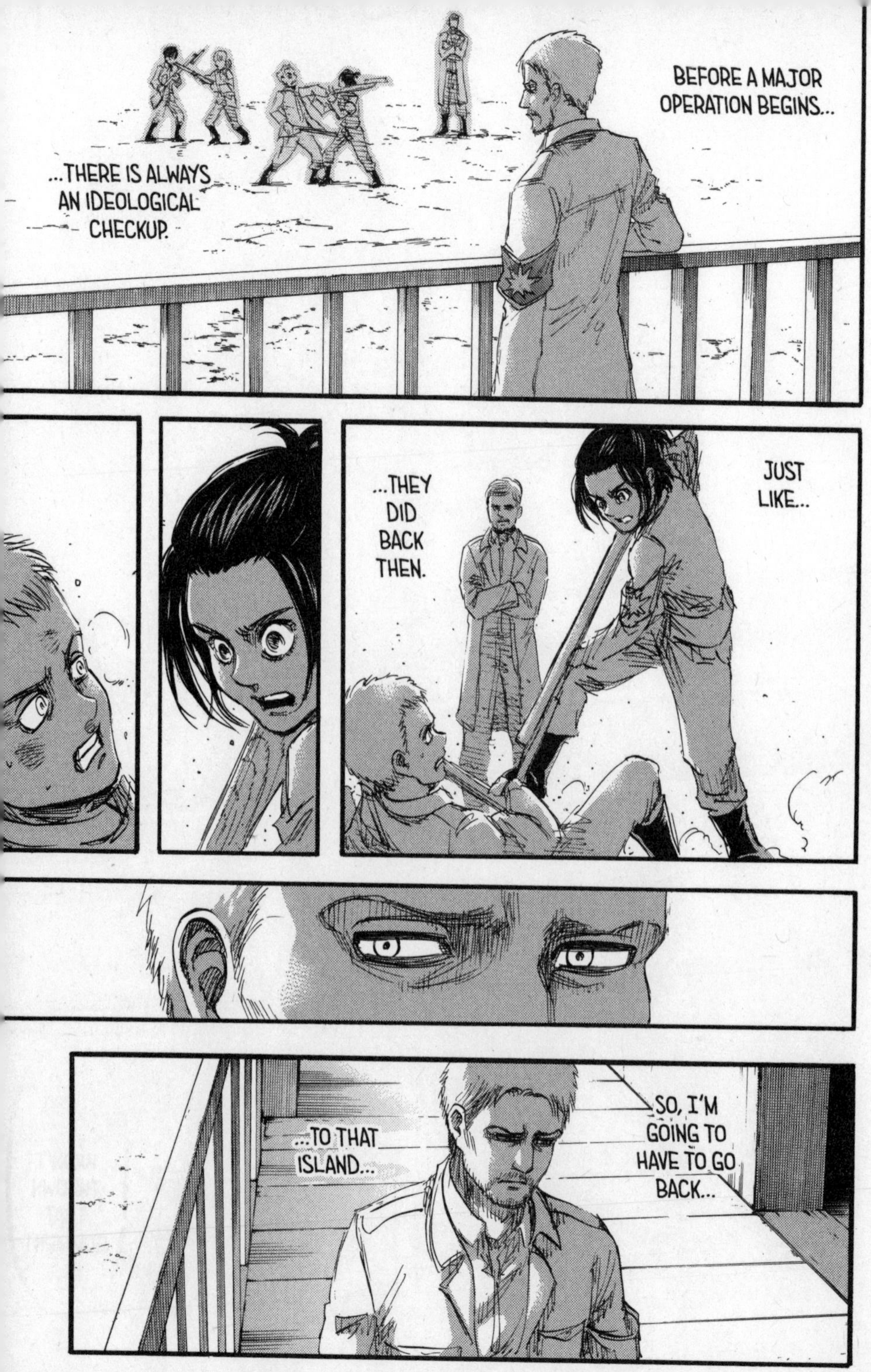
BEFORE A MAJOR OPERATION BEGINS...
...THERE IS ALWAYS AN IDEOLOGICAL CHECKUP.
JUST LIKE...
...THEY DID BACK THEN.
SO, I'M GOING TO HAVE TO GO BACK...
...TO THAT ISLAND...

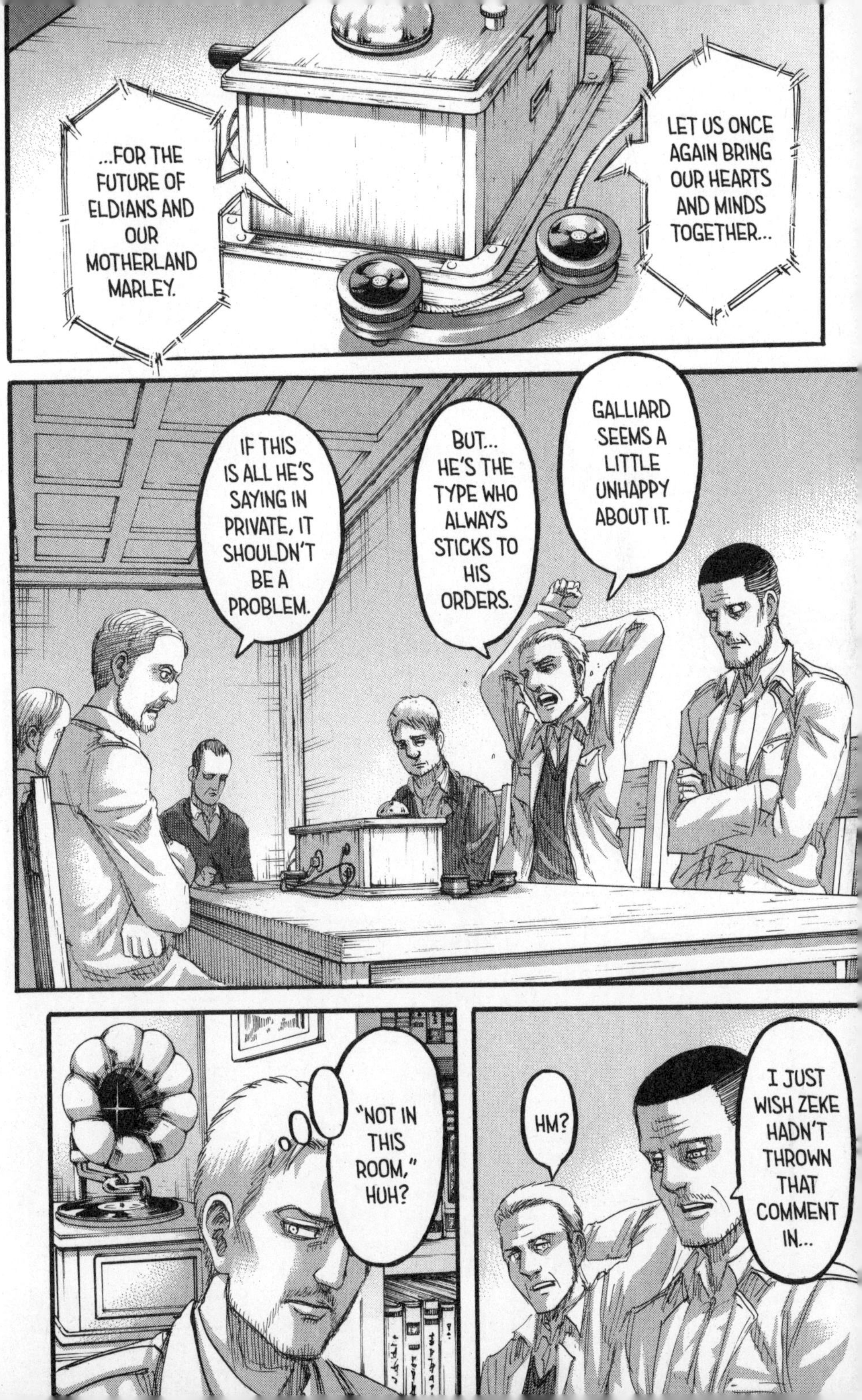
LET US ONCE AGAIN BRING OUR HEARTS AND MINDS TOGETHER...
...FOR THE FUTURE OF ELDIANS AND OUR MOTHERLAND MARLEY.
GALLIARD SEEMS A LITTLE UNHAPPY ABOUT IT.
BUT... HE'S THE TYPE WHO ALWAYS STICKS TO HIS ORDERS.
IF THIS IS ALL HE'S SAYING IN PRIVATE, IT SHOULDN'T BE A PROBLEM.
I JUST WISH ZEKE HADN'T THROWN THAT COMMENT IN...
HM?
"NOT IN THIS ROOM," HUH?

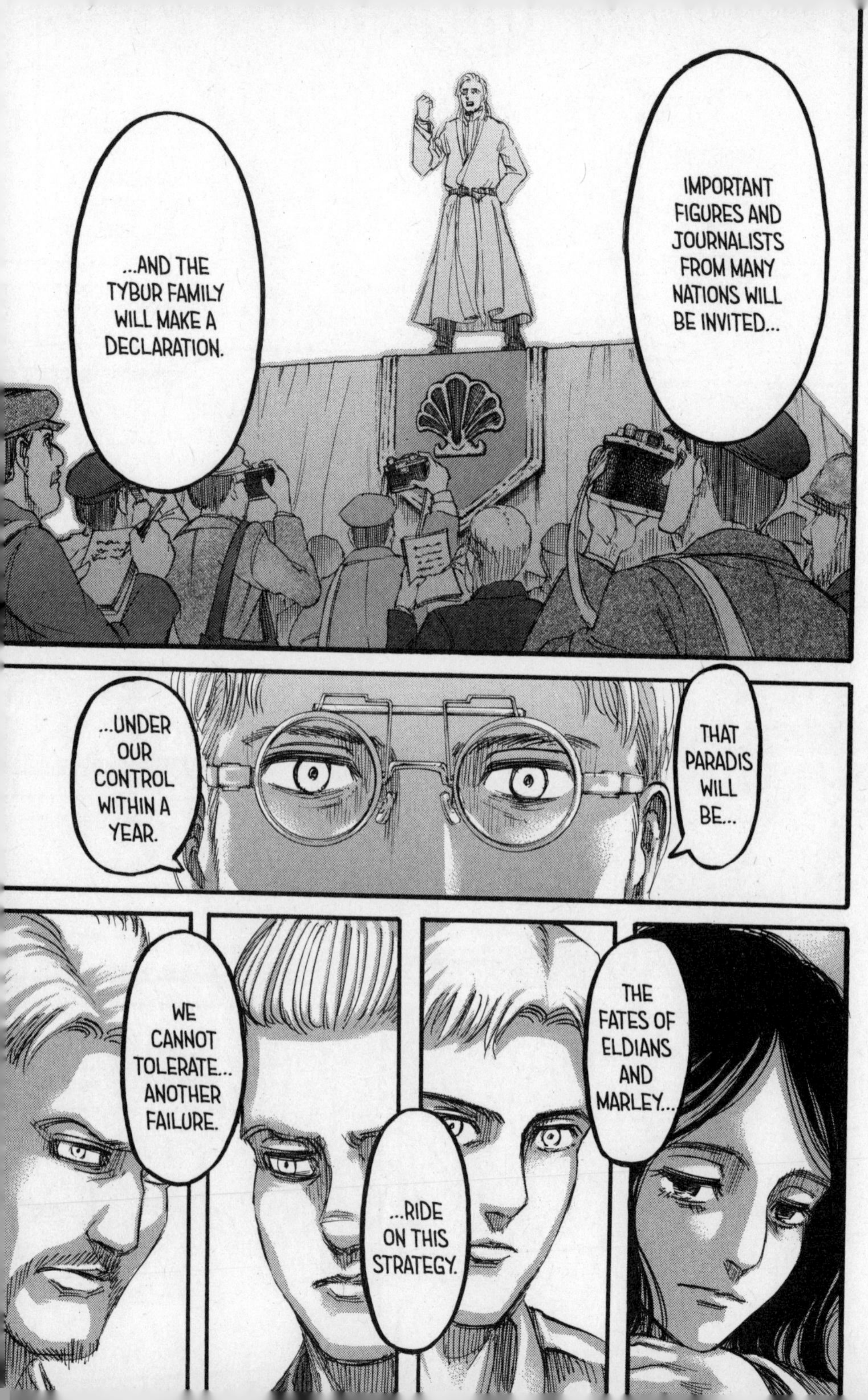
IMPORTANT FIGURES AND JOURNALISTS FROM MANY NATIONS WILL BE INVITED...
...AND THE TYBUR FAMILY WILL MAKE A DECLARATION.
THAT PARADIS WILL BE...
...UNDER OUR CONTROL WITHIN A YEAR.
THE FATES OF ELDIANS AND MARLEY...
...RIDE ON THIS STRATEGY.
WE CANNOT TOLERATE... ANOTHER FAILURE.

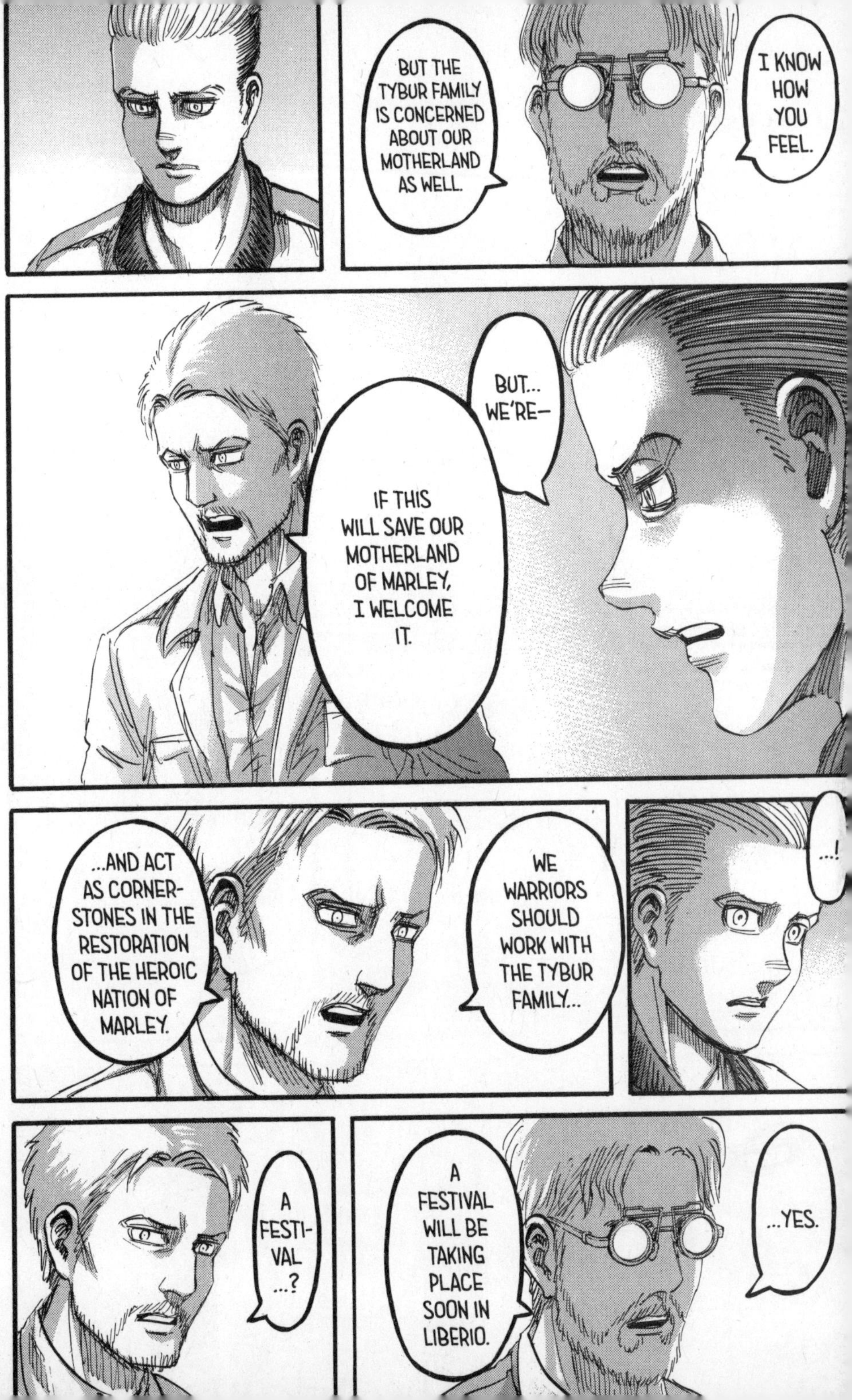
I KNOW HOW YOU FEEL.
BUT THE TYBUR FAMILY IS CONCERNED ABOUT OUR MOTHERLAND AS WELL.
BUT... WE'RE—
IF THIS WILL SAVE OUR MOTHERLAND OF MARLEY, I WELCOME IT.
...!
WE WARRIORS SHOULD WORK WITH THE TYBUR FAMILY...
...AND ACT AS CORNER-STONES IN THE RESTORATION OF THE HEROIC NATION OF MARLEY.
...YES.
A FESTIVAL WILL BE TAKING PLACE SOON IN LIBERIO.
A FESTI-VAL...?

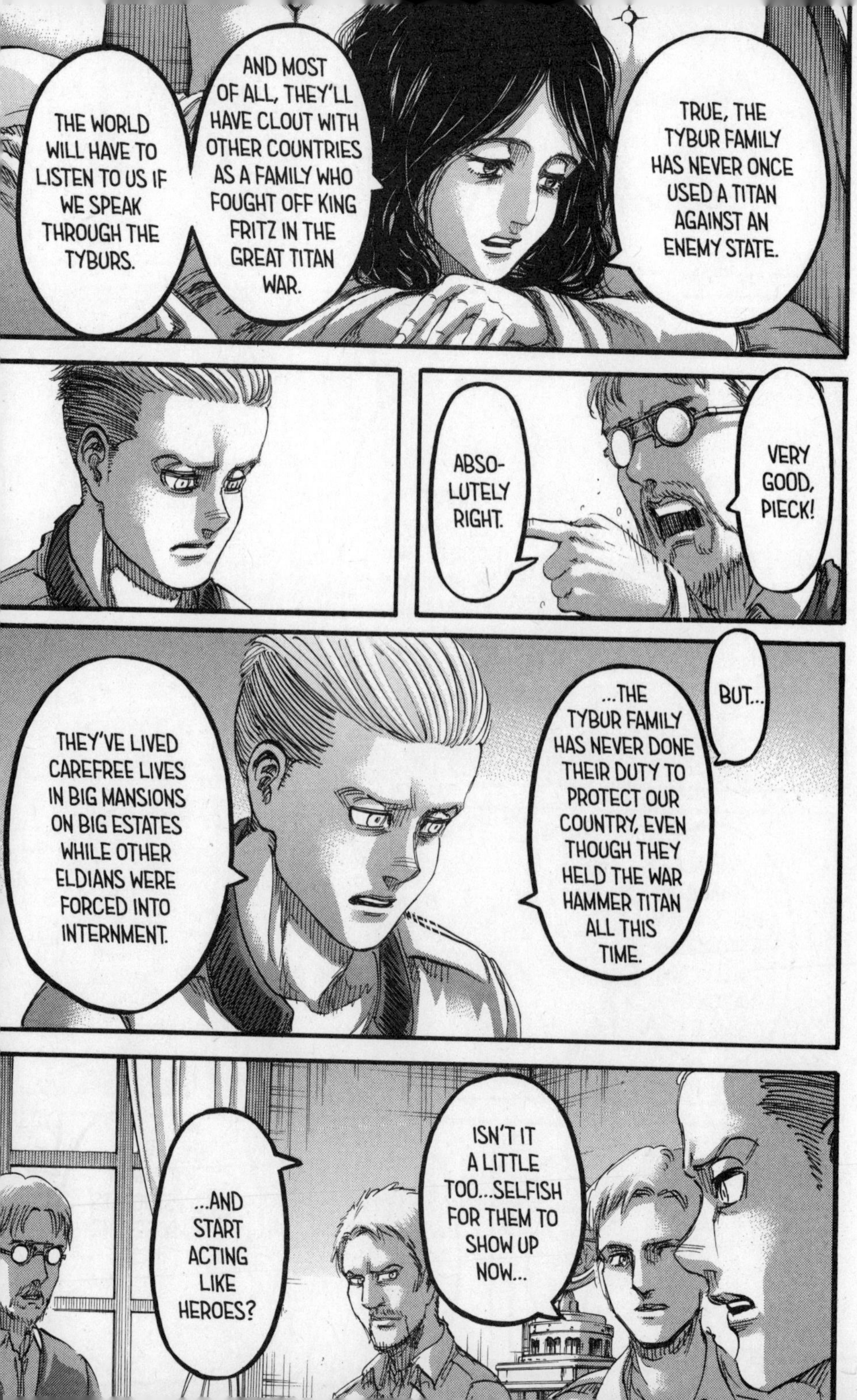
TRUE, THE TYBUR FAMILY HAS NEVER ONCE USED A TITAN AGAINST AN ENEMY STATE.
AND MOST OF ALL, THEY'LL HAVE CLOUT WITH OTHER COUNTRIES AS A FAMILY WHO FOUGHT OFF KING FRITZ IN THE GREAT TITAN WAR.
THE WORLD WILL HAVE TO LISTEN TO US IF WE SPEAK THROUGH THE TYBURS.
VERY GOOD, PIECK!
ABSO-LUTELY RIGHT.
BUT...
...THE TYBUR FAMILY HAS NEVER DONE THEIR DUTY TO PROTECT OUR COUNTRY, EVEN THOUGH THEY HELD THE WAR HAMMER TITAN ALL THIS TIME.
THEY'VE LIVED CAREFREE LIVES IN BIG MANSIONS ON BIG ESTATES WHILE OTHER ELDIANS WERE FORCED INTO INTERNMENT.
ISN'T IT A LITTLE TOO...SELFISH FOR THEM TO SHOW UP NOW...
...AND START ACTING LIKE HEROES?

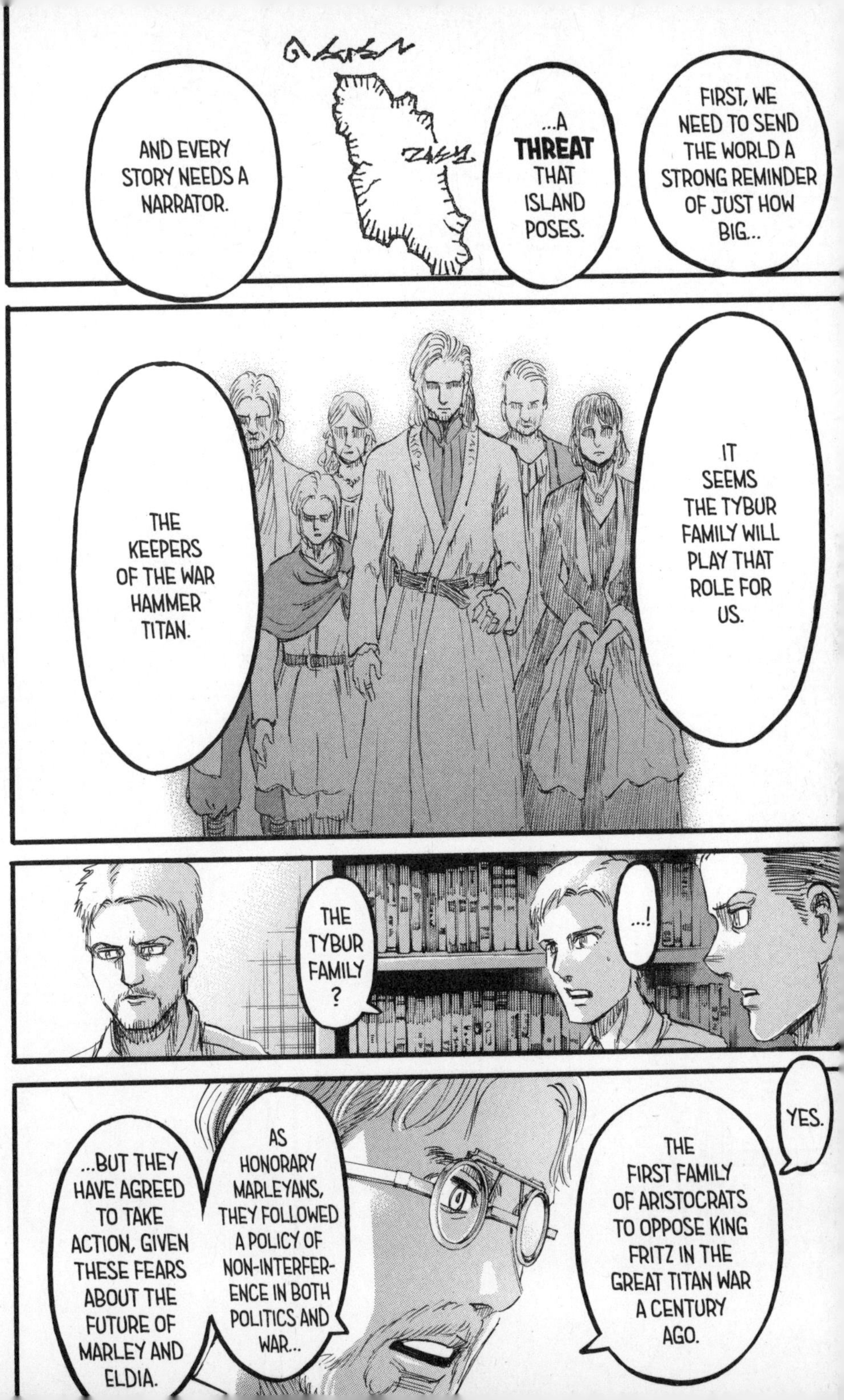
FIRST, WE NEED TO SEND THE WORLD A STRONG REMINDER OF JUST HOW BIG...
...A **THREAT** THAT ISLAND POSES.
AND EVERY STORY NEEDS A NARRATOR.
IT SEEMS THE TYBUR FAMILY WILL PLAY THAT ROLE FOR US.
THE KEEPERS OF THE WAR HAMMER TITAN.
...!
THE TYBUR FAMILY?
YES.
THE FIRST FAMILY OF ARISTOCRATS TO OPPOSE KING FRITZ IN THE GREAT TITAN WAR A CENTURY AGO.
AS HONORARY MARLEYANS, THEY FOLLOWED A POLICY OF NON-INTERFERENCE IN BOTH POLITICS AND WAR...
...BUT THEY HAVE AGREED TO TAKE ACTION, GIVEN THESE FEARS ABOUT THE FUTURE OF MARLEY AND ELDIA.

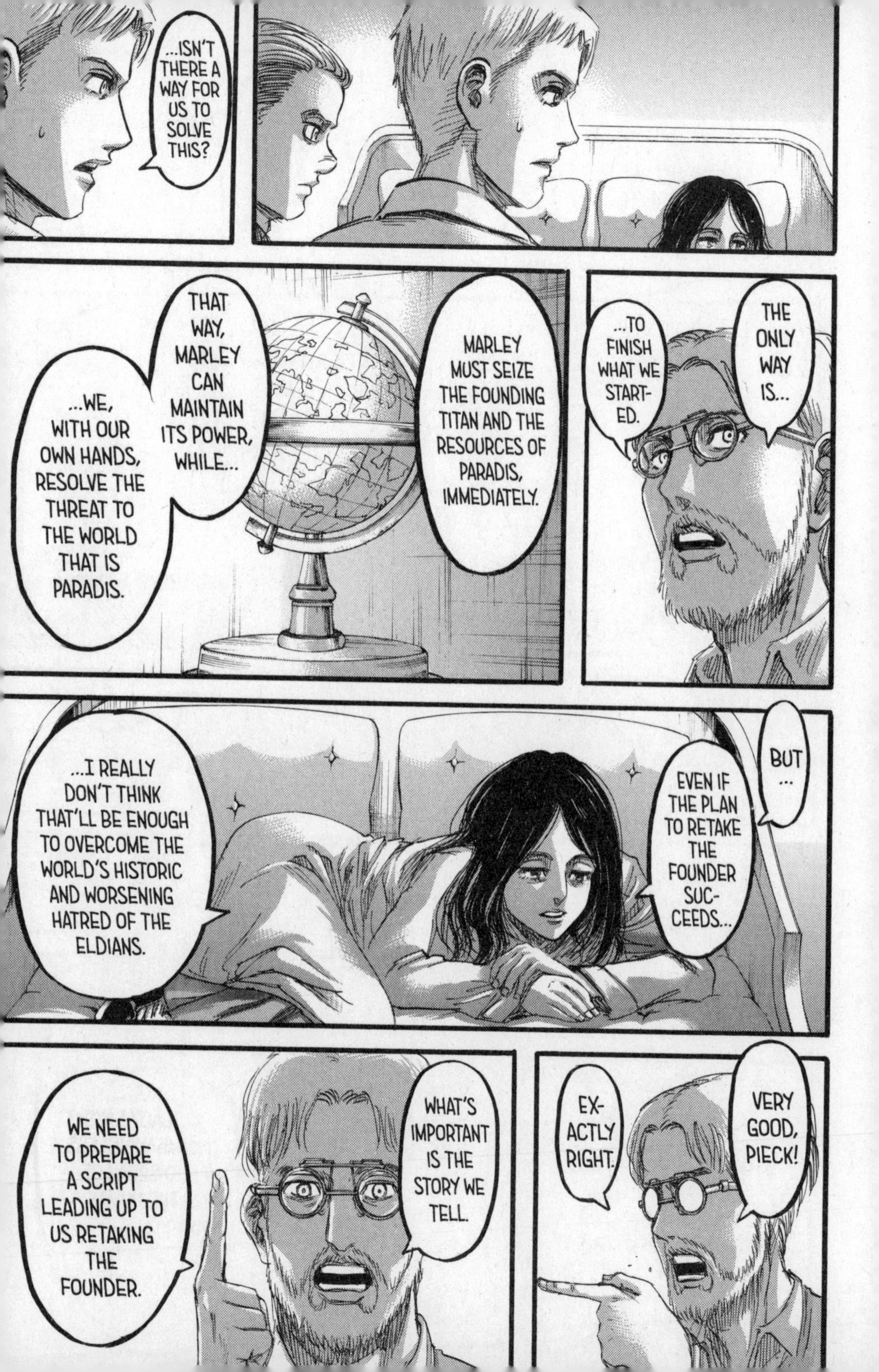
...ISN'T THERE A WAY FOR US TO SOLVE THIS?
THE ONLY WAY IS...
...TO FINISH WHAT WE START-ED.
MARLEY MUST SEIZE THE FOUNDING TITAN AND THE RESOURCES OF PARADIS, IMMEDIATELY.
THAT WAY, MARLEY CAN MAINTAIN ITS POWER, WHILE...
...WE, WITH OUR OWN HANDS, RESOLVE THE THREAT TO THE WORLD THAT IS PARADIS.
BUT...
EVEN IF THE PLAN TO RETAKE THE FOUNDER SUC-CEEDS...
...I REALLY DON'T THINK THAT'LL BE ENOUGH TO OVERCOME THE WORLD'S HISTORIC AND WORSENING HATRED OF THE ELDIANS.
VERY GOOD, PIECK!
EX-ACTLY RIGHT.
WHAT'S IMPORTANT IS THE STORY WE TELL.
WE NEED TO PREPARE A SCRIPT LEADING UP TO US RETAKING THE FOUNDER.

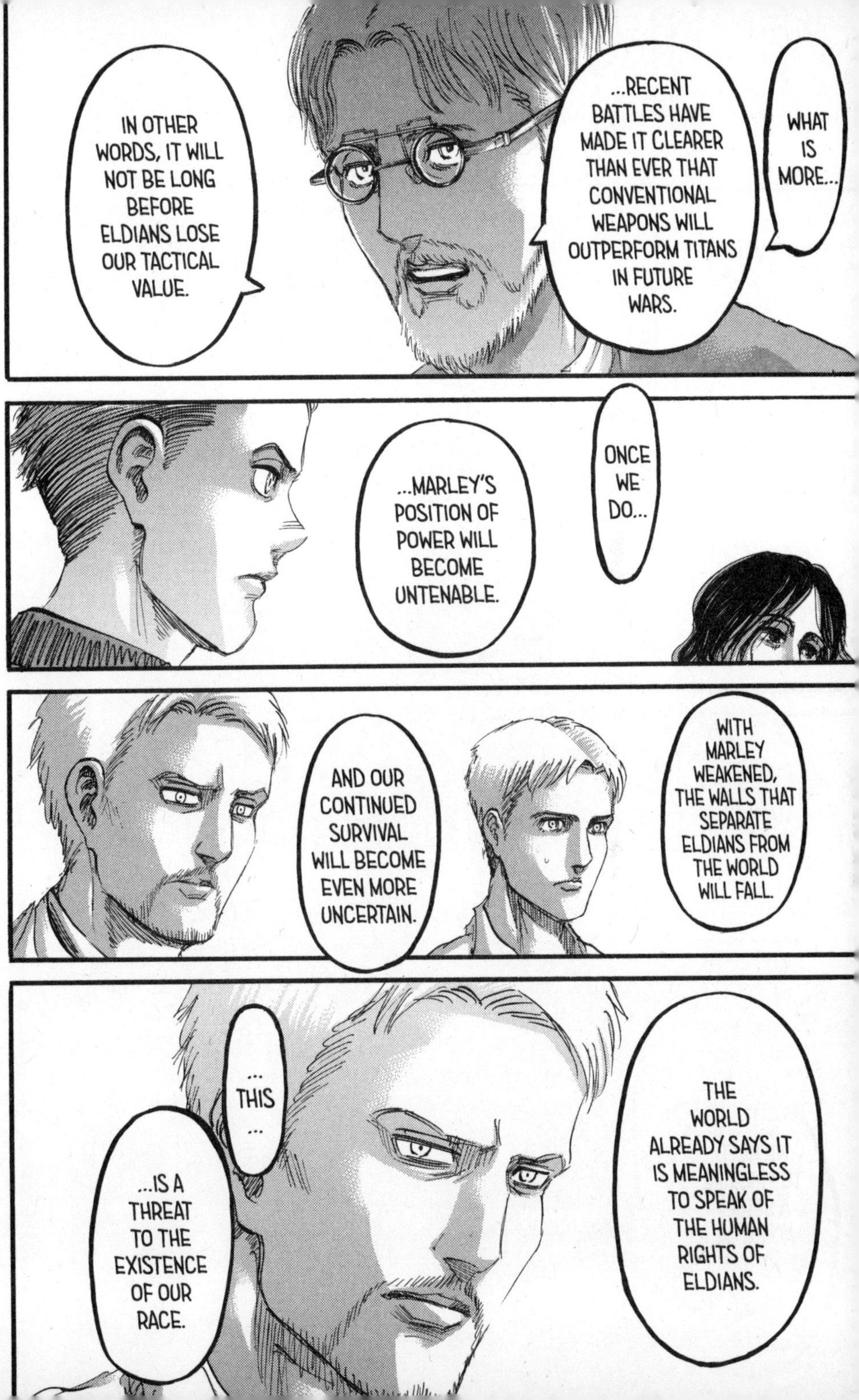
WHAT IS MORE...
...RECENT BATTLES HAVE MADE IT CLEARER THAN EVER THAT CONVENTIONAL WEAPONS WILL OUTPERFORM TITANS IN FUTURE WARS.
IN OTHER WORDS, IT WILL NOT BE LONG BEFORE ELDIANS LOSE OUR TACTICAL VALUE.
ONCE WE DO...
...MARLEY'S POSITION OF POWER WILL BECOME UNTENABLE.
WITH MARLEY WEAKENED, THE WALLS THAT SEPARATE ELDIANS FROM THE WORLD WILL FALL.
AND OUR CONTINUED SURVIVAL WILL BECOME EVEN MORE UNCERTAIN.
THE WORLD ALREADY SAYS IT IS MEANINGLESS TO SPEAK OF THE HUMAN RIGHTS OF ELDIANS.
... THIS ...
...IS A THREAT TO THE EXISTENCE OF OUR RACE.

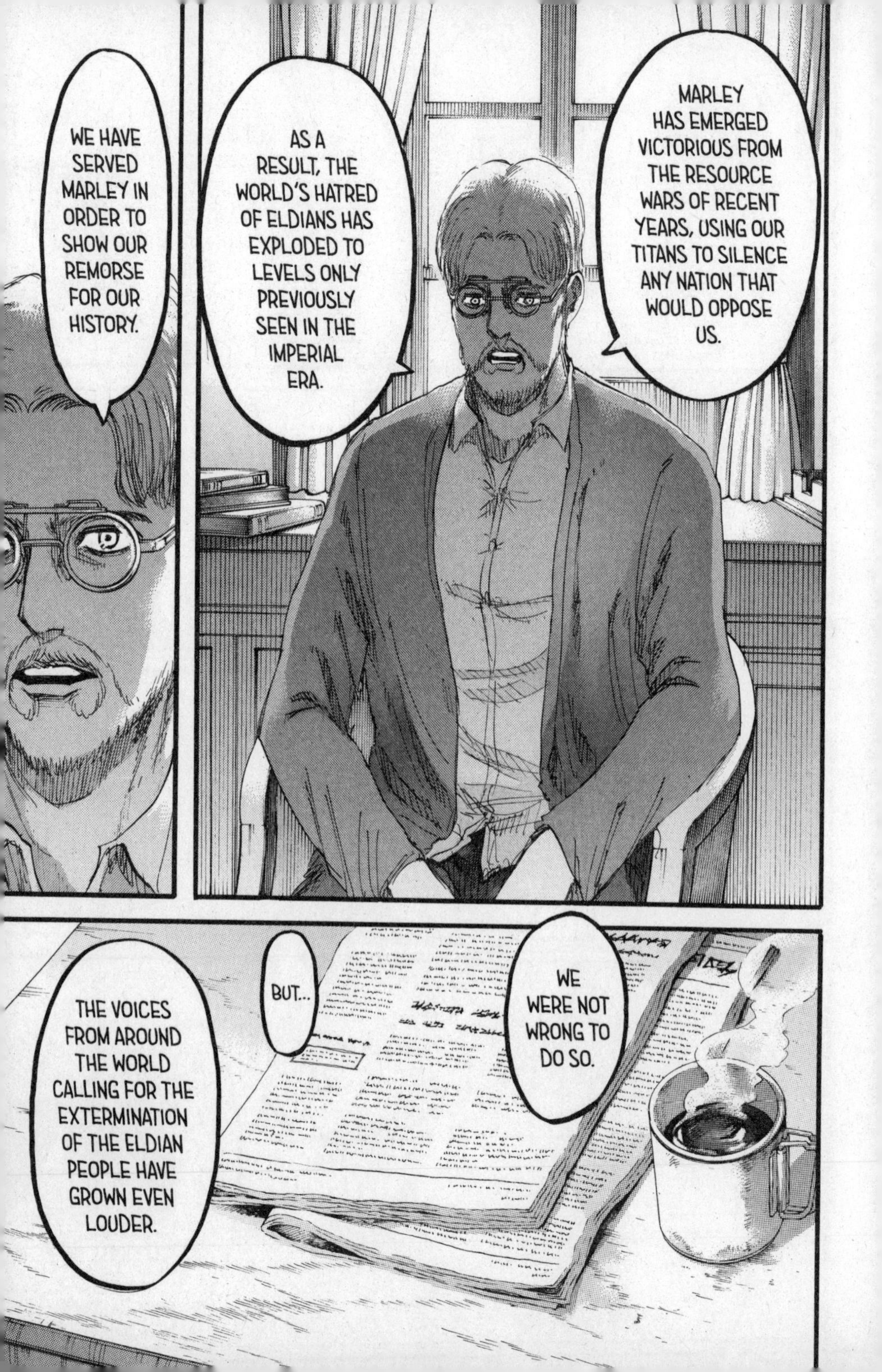
MARLEY HAS EMERGED VICTORIOUS FROM THE RESOURCE WARS OF RECENT YEARS, USING OUR TITANS TO SILENCE ANY NATION THAT WOULD OPPOSE US.
AS A RESULT, THE WORLD'S HATRED OF ELDIANS HAS EXPLODED TO LEVELS ONLY PREVIOUSLY SEEN IN THE IMPERIAL ERA.
WE HAVE SERVED MARLEY IN ORDER TO SHOW OUR REMORSE FOR OUR HISTORY.
WE WERE NOT WRONG TO DO SO.
BUT...
THE VOICES FROM AROUND THE WORLD CALLING FOR THE EXTERMINATION OF THE ELDIAN PEOPLE HAVE GROWN EVEN LOUDER.

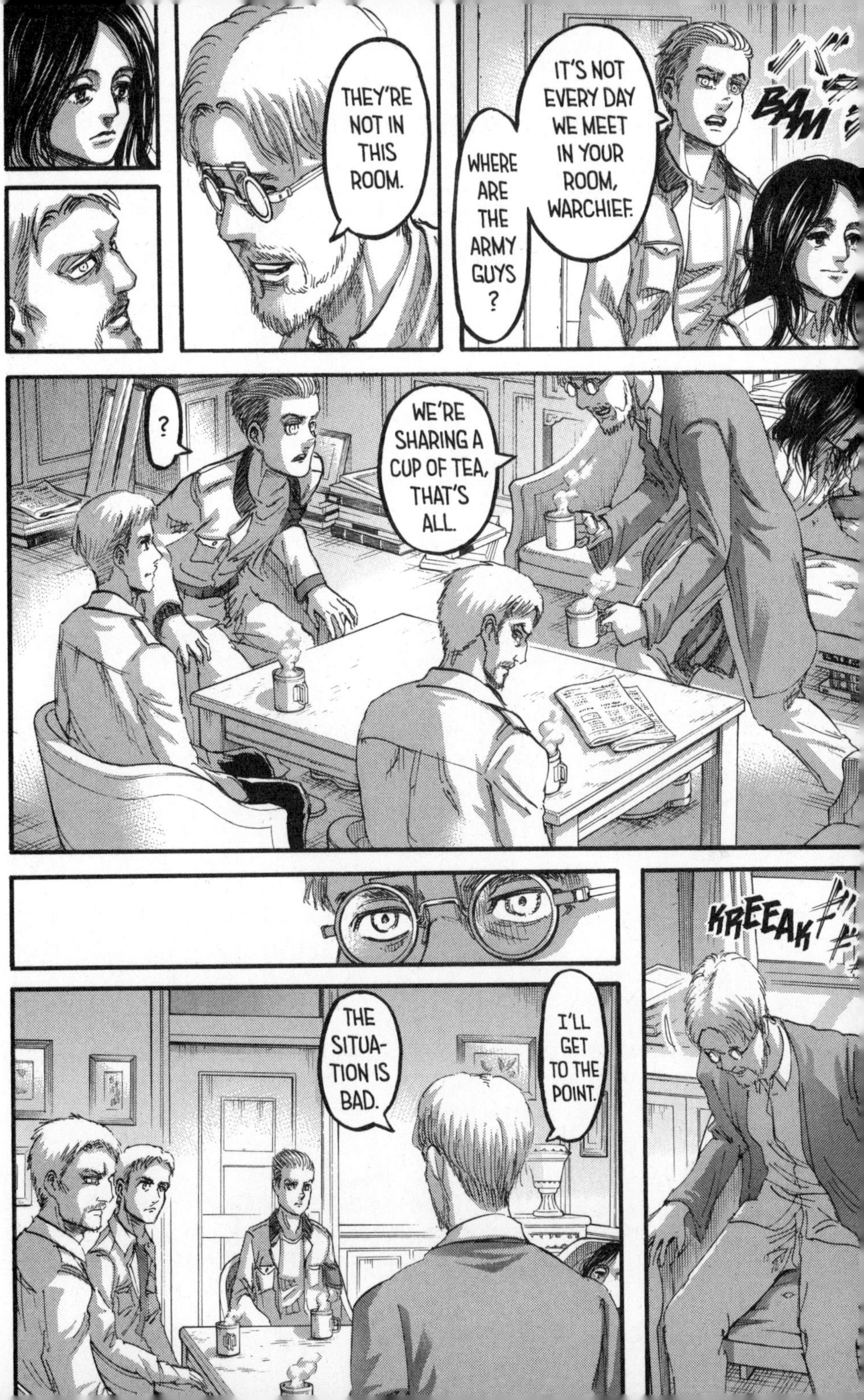
BAM
IT'S NOT EVERY DAY WE MEET IN YOUR ROOM, WARCHIEF.
WHERE ARE THE ARMY GUYS?
THEY'RE NOT IN THIS ROOM.
WE'RE SHARING A CUP OF TEA, THAT'S ALL.
?
KREEAK
I'LL GET TO THE POINT.
THE SITUA-TION IS BAD.

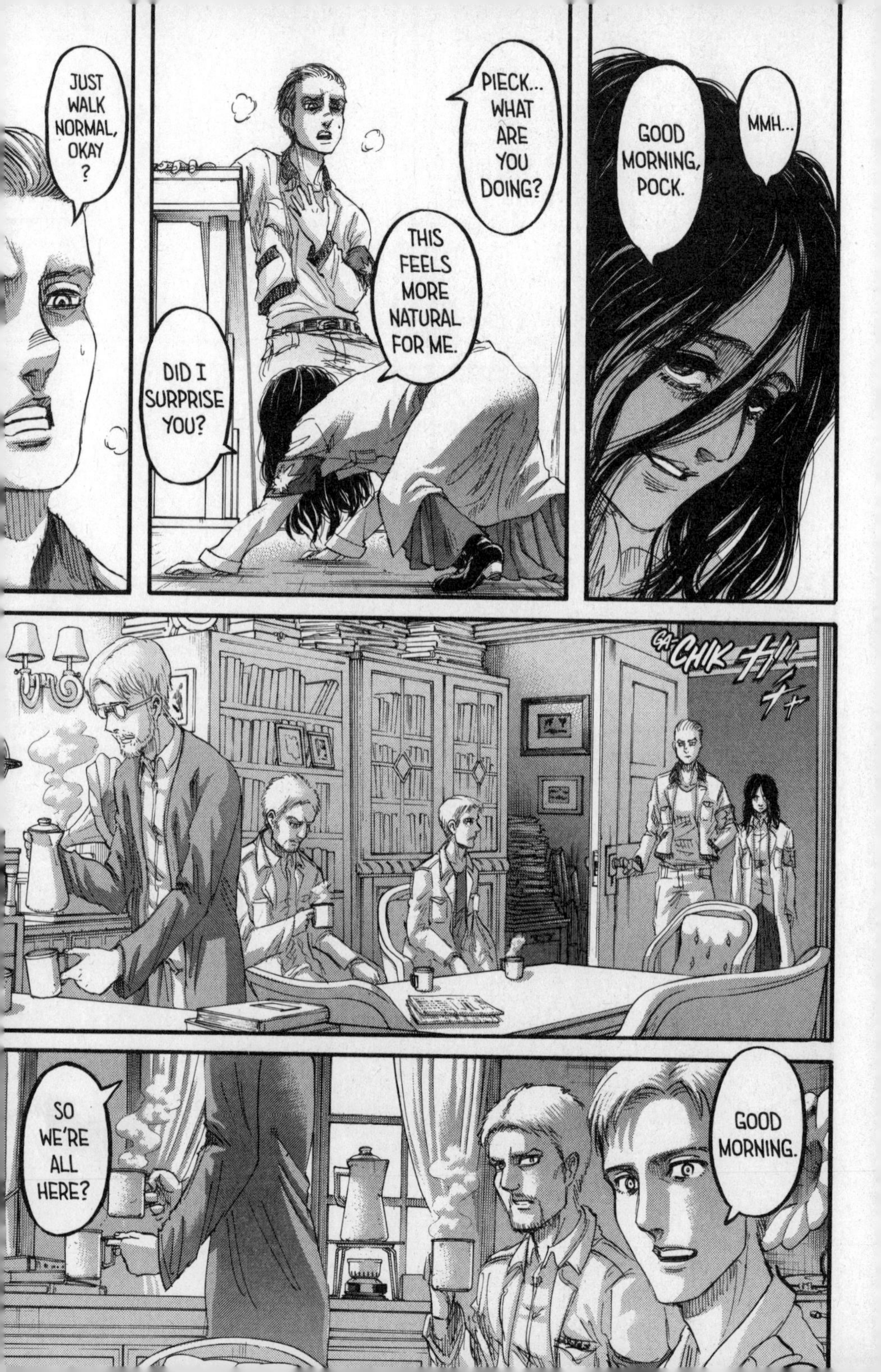
MMH...
GOOD MORNING, POCK.
PIECK... WHAT ARE YOU DOING?
THIS FEELS MORE NATURAL FOR ME.
DID I SURPRISE YOU?
JUST WALK NORMAL, OKAY ?
GA-CHIK
ガチャ
GOOD MORNING.
SO WE'RE ALL HERE?

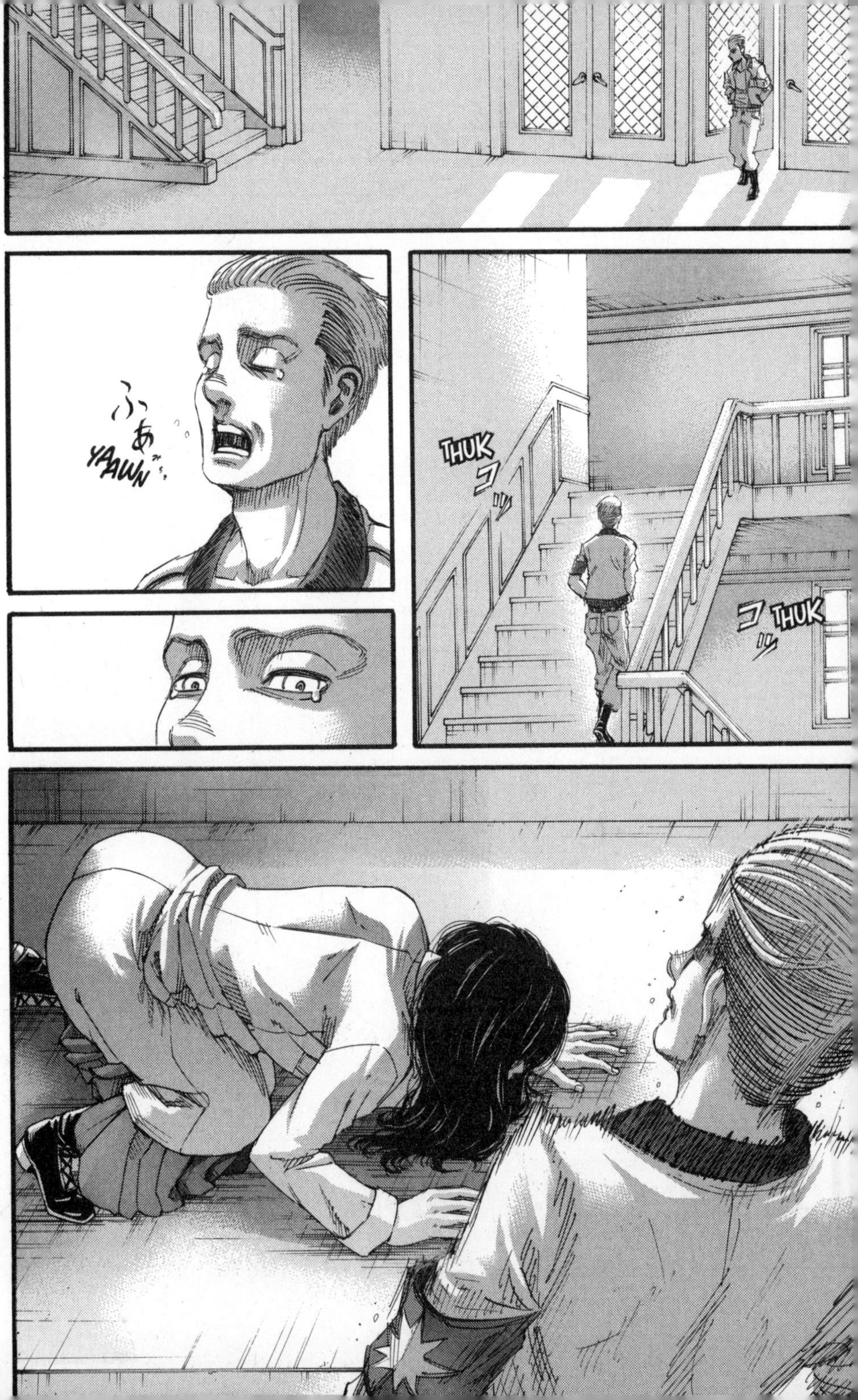
THUK
コッ
コッ
THUK
ふあ
YAAWN

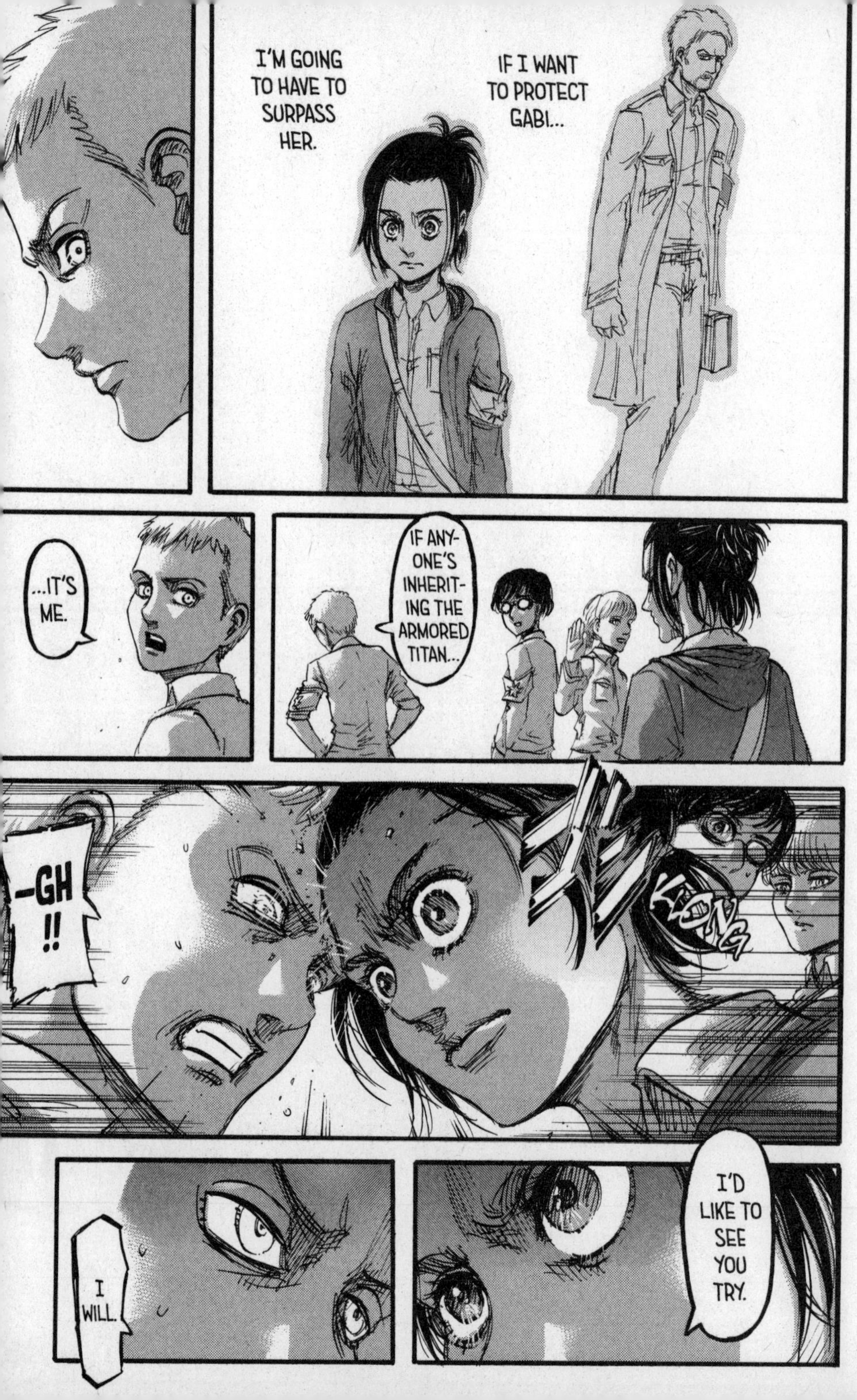
IF I WANT TO PROTECT GABI...
I'M GOING TO HAVE TO SURPASS HER.
IF ANY-ONE'S INHERIT-ING THE ARMORED TITAN...
...IT'S ME.
KONG
–GH!!
I'D LIKE TO SEE YOU TRY.
I WILL.

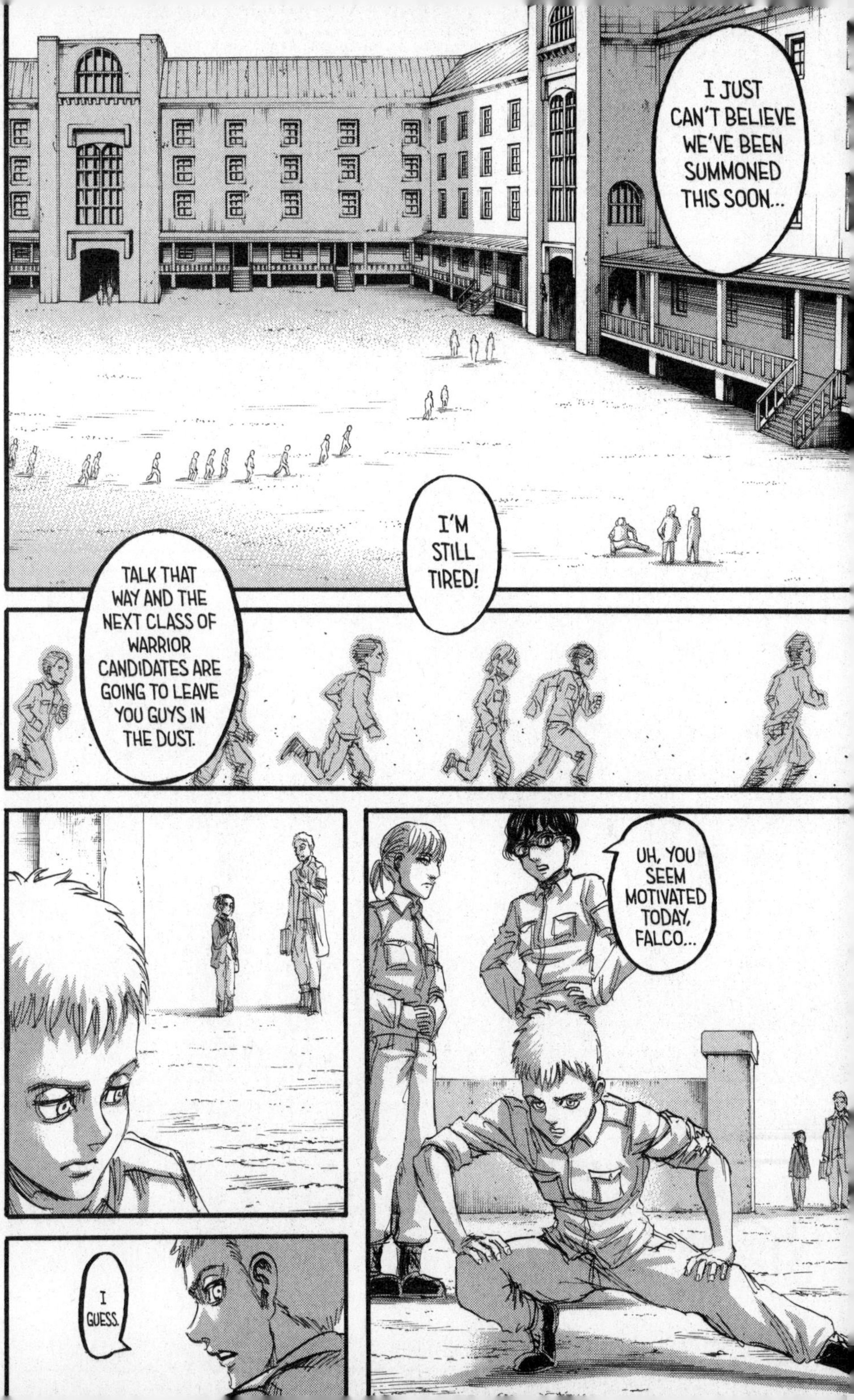
I JUST CAN'T BELIEVE WE'VE BEEN SUMMONED THIS SOON...
I'M STILL TIRED!
TALK THAT WAY AND THE NEXT CLASS OF WARRIOR CANDIDATES ARE GOING TO LEAVE YOU GUYS IN THE DUST.
UH, YOU SEEM MOTIVATED TODAY, FALCO...
I GUESS.

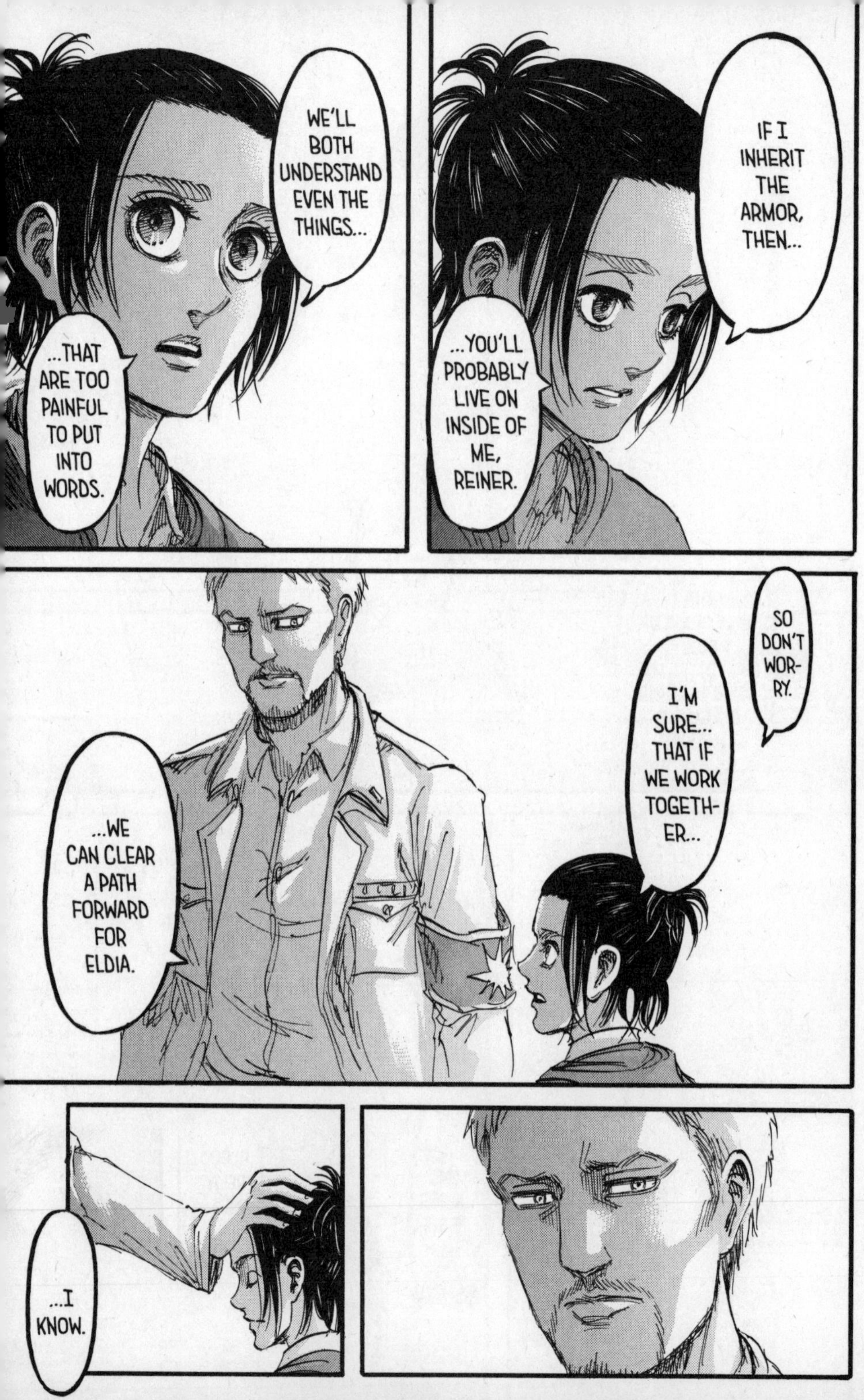
IF I INHERIT THE ARMOR, THEN...
...YOU'LL PROBABLY LIVE ON INSIDE OF ME, REINER.
WE'LL BOTH UNDERSTAND EVEN THE THINGS...
...THAT ARE TOO PAINFUL TO PUT INTO WORDS.
SO DON'T WOR-RY.
I'M SURE... THAT IF WE WORK TOGETH-ER...
...WE CAN CLEAR A PATH FORWARD FOR ELDIA.
...I KNOW.

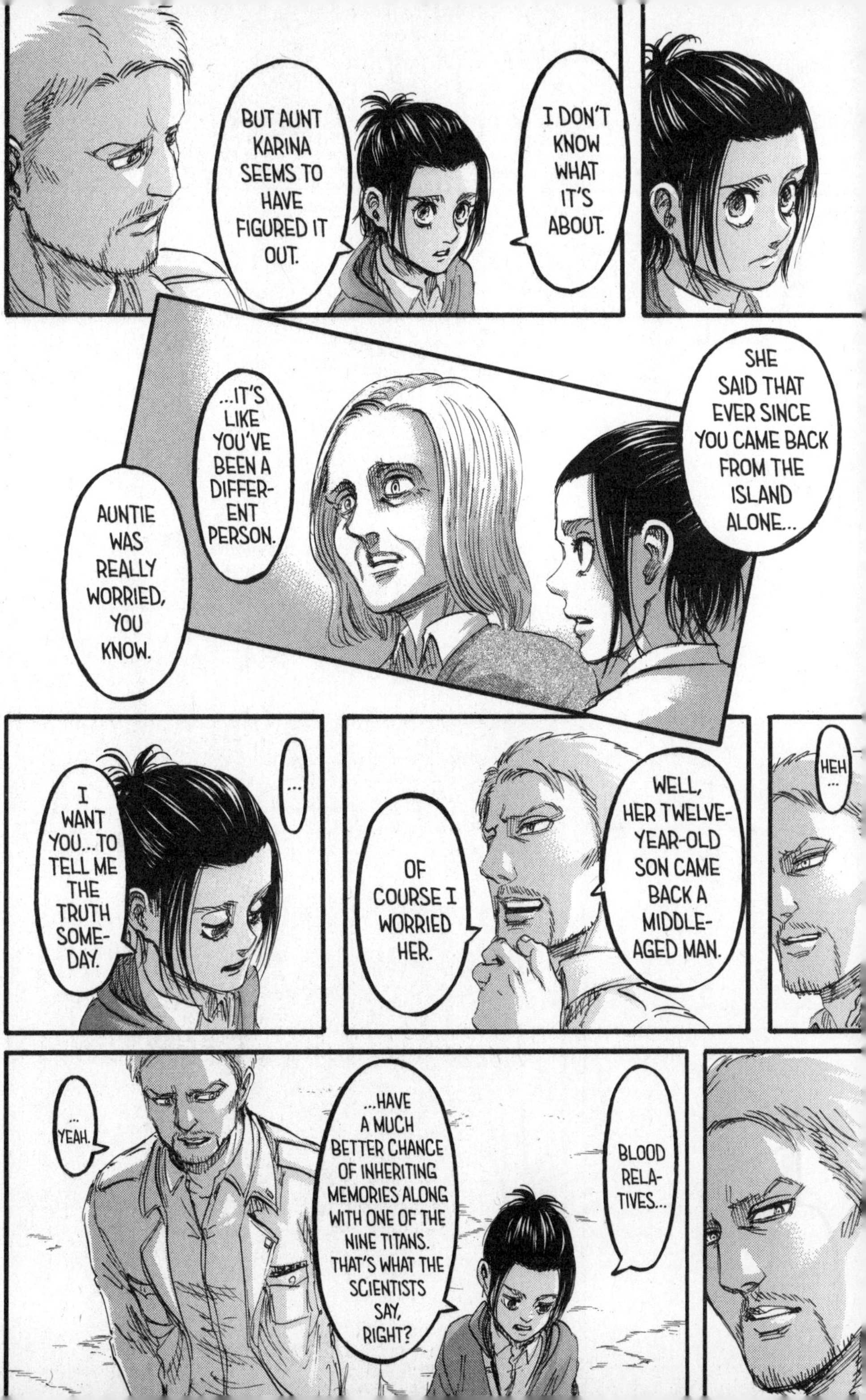
I DON'T KNOW WHAT IT'S ABOUT.
BUT AUNT KARINA SEEMS TO HAVE FIGURED IT OUT.
SHE SAID THAT EVER SINCE YOU CAME BACK FROM THE ISLAND ALONE...
...IT'S LIKE YOU'VE BEEN A DIFFERENT PERSON.
AUNTIE WAS REALLY WORRIED, YOU KNOW.
HEH...
WELL, HER TWELVE-YEAR-OLD SON CAME BACK A MIDDLE-AGED MAN.
OF COURSE I WORRIED HER.
...
I WANT YOU...TO TELL ME THE TRUTH SOMEDAY.
BLOOD RELATIVES...
...HAVE A MUCH BETTER CHANCE OF INHERITING MEMORIES ALONG WITH ONE OF THE NINE TITANS. THAT'S WHAT THE SCIENTISTS SAY, RIGHT?
...YEAH.

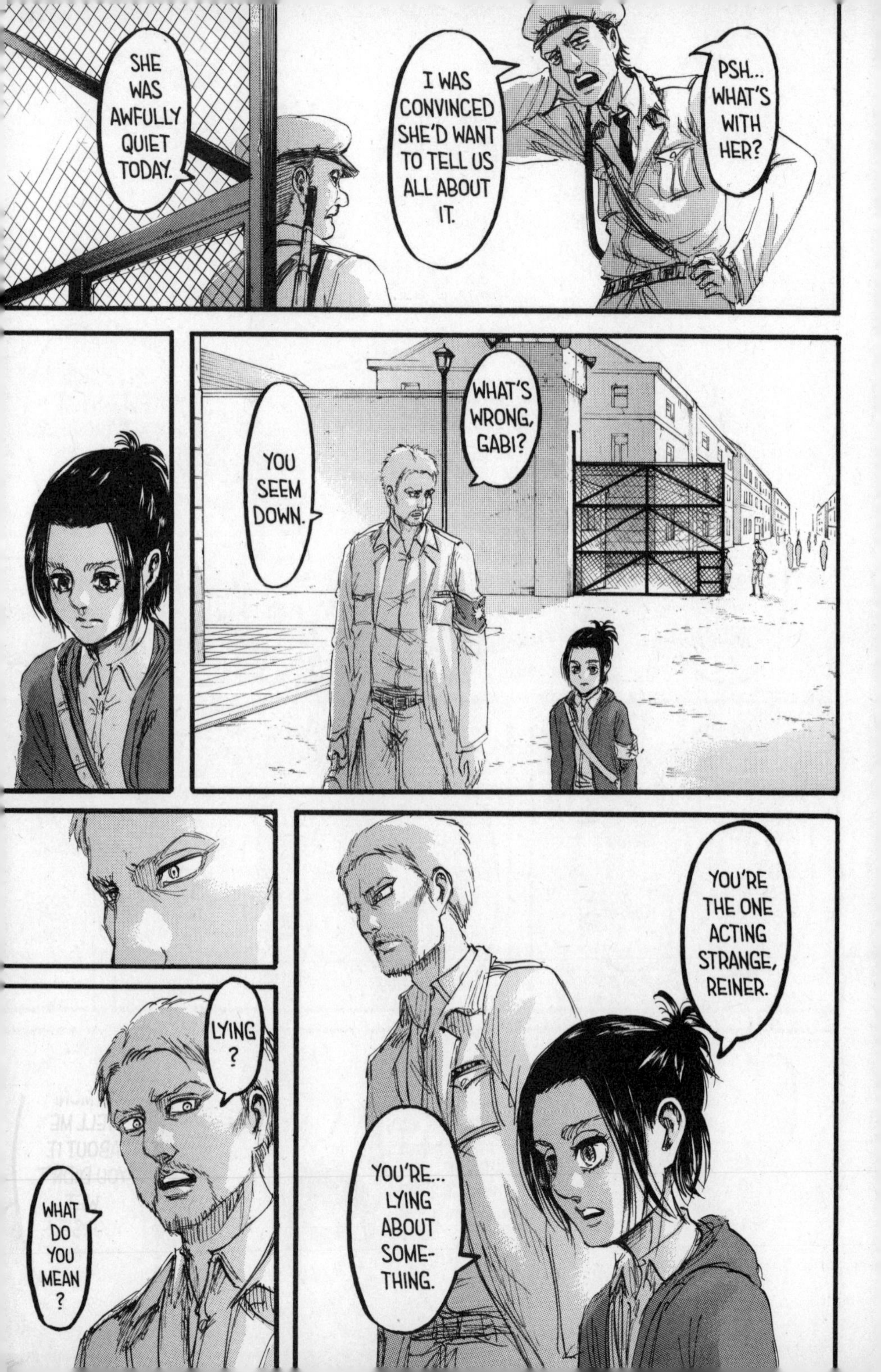
PSH... WHAT'S WITH HER?
I WAS CONVINCED SHE'D WANT TO TELL US ALL ABOUT IT.
SHE WAS AWFULLY QUIET TODAY.
WHAT'S WRONG, GABI?
YOU SEEM DOWN.
YOU'RE THE ONE ACTING STRANGE, REINER.
YOU'RE... LYING ABOUT SOMETHING.
LYING?
WHAT DO YOU MEAN?

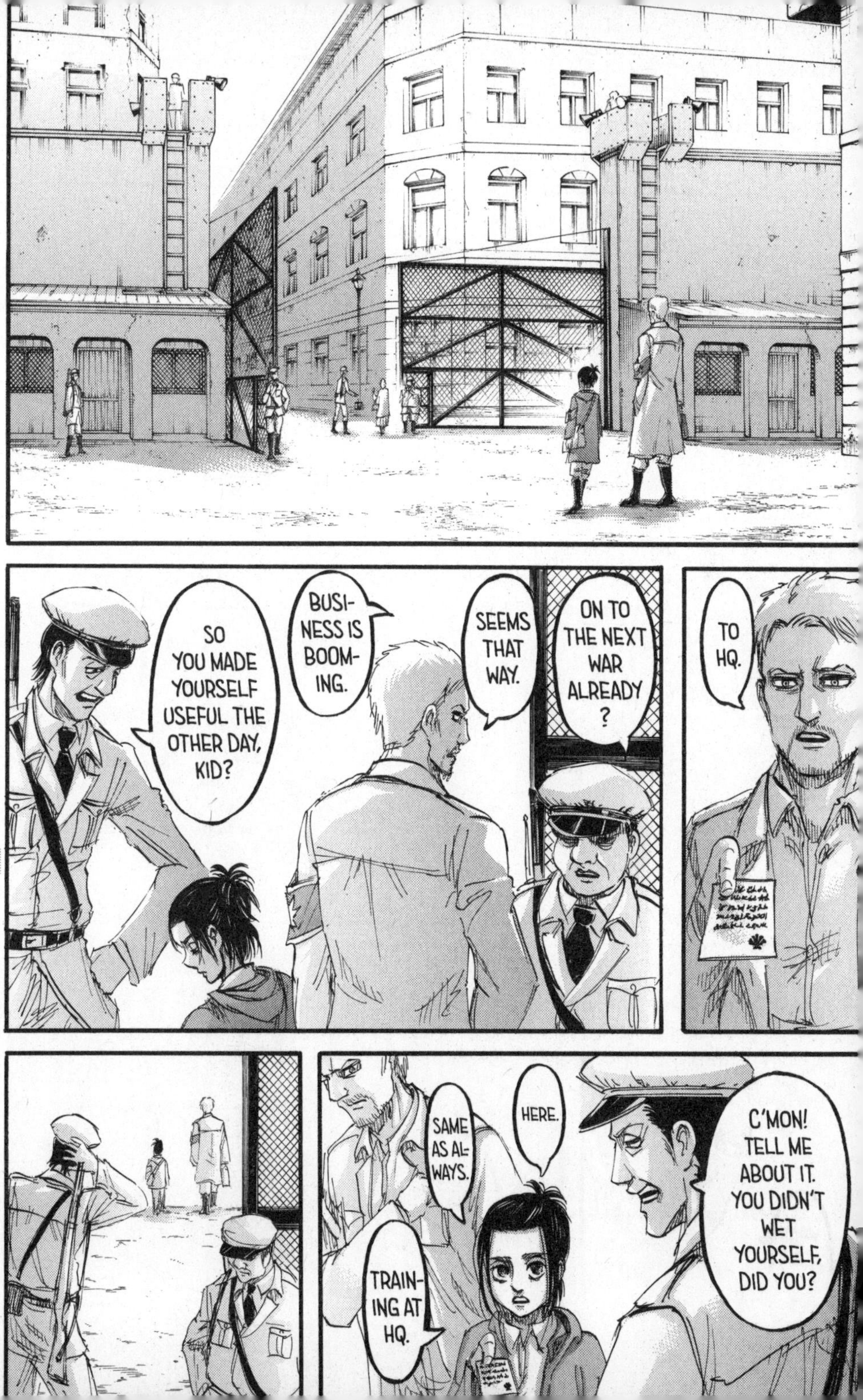
TO HQ.
ON TO THE NEXT WAR ALREADY?
SEEMS THAT WAY.
BUSINESS IS BOOMING.
SO YOU MADE YOURSELF USEFUL THE OTHER DAY, KID?
C'MON! TELL ME ABOUT IT. YOU DIDN'T WET YOURSELF, DID YOU?
HERE.
SAME AS ALWAYS.
TRAINING AT HQ.

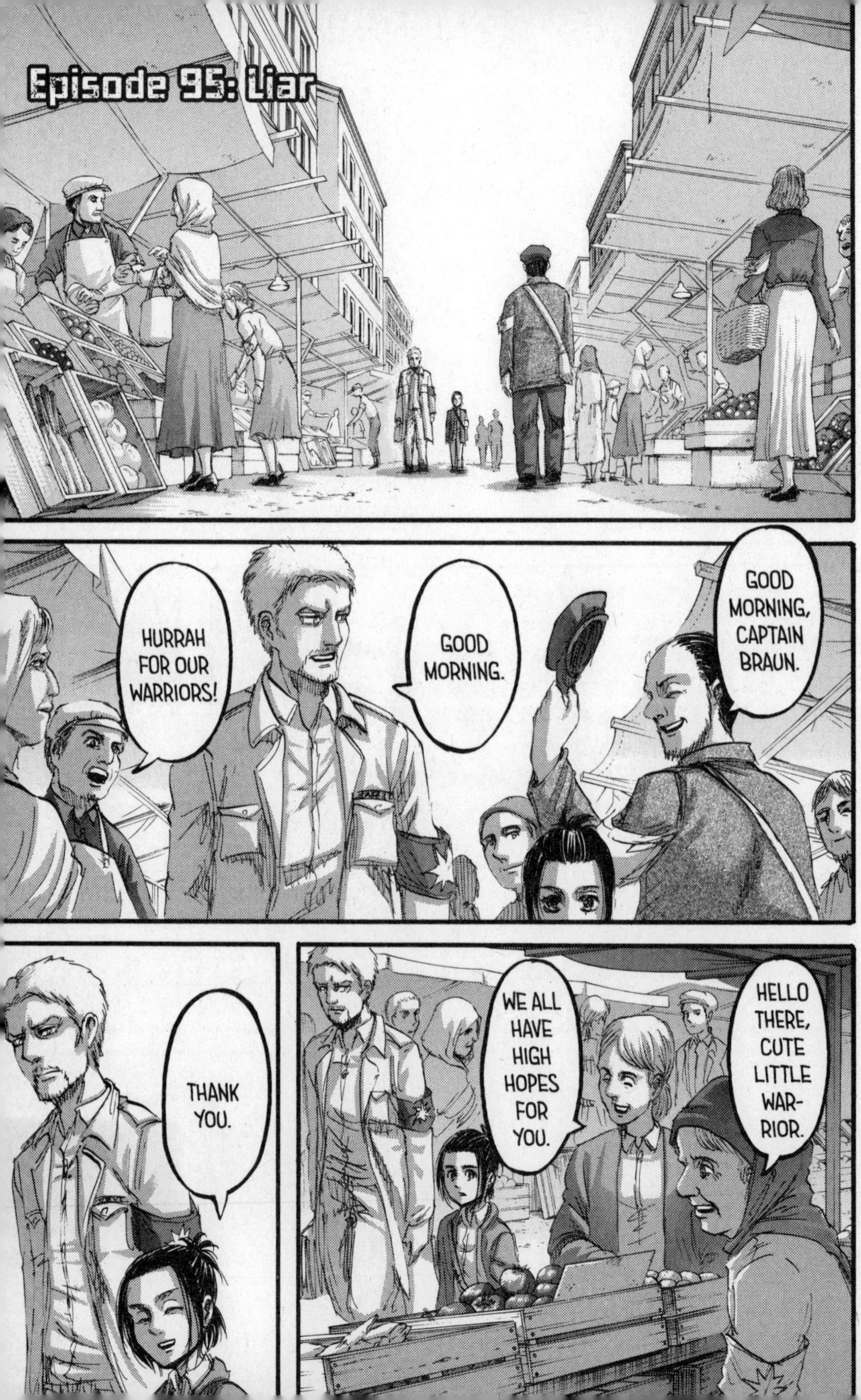
Episode 95: Liar
GOOD MORNING, CAPTAIN BRAUN.
GOOD MORNING.
HURRAH FOR OUR WARRIORS!
HELLO THERE, CUTE LITTLE WAR-RIOR.
WE ALL HAVE HIGH HOPES FOR YOU.
THANK YOU.

ATTACK on TITAN

ATTACK ON TITAN CHARACTERS: MARLEY ARC

THE ELDIAN WARRIORS IN THE MARLEYAN ARMY

WARRIOR CANDIDATES

IN CONTRAST TO GABI, ZOFIA GIVES OFF A COOL AND MATURE IMPRESSION, BUT SHE WILL OCCASIONALLY SAY AMUSINGLY ABSENTMINDED THINGS.

ZOFIA

THOUGH HE APPEARS TO BE A MILD-MANNERED, GLASSES-WEARING BOY, HE DEVELOPS A FOUL MOUTH WHENEVER HE GETS EXCITED. UNDERSTANDS FOREIGN LANGUAGES.

UDO

THE JAW TITAN

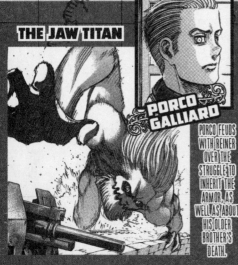

PORCO GALLIARD

PORCO FEUDS WITH REINER OVER THE STRUGGLE TO INHERIT THE ARMOR, AS WELL AS ABOUT HIS OLDER BROTHER'S DEATH.

THE CART TITAN

PIECK

WHILE SHE MAY SEEM LAZY, PERHAPS DUE TO THE EFFECTS OF WALKING ON ALL FOURS FOR EXTENDED PERIODS OF TIME, SHE IS RECOGNIZED FOR HER JUDGMENT.

THE FOUR WARRIORS WHO

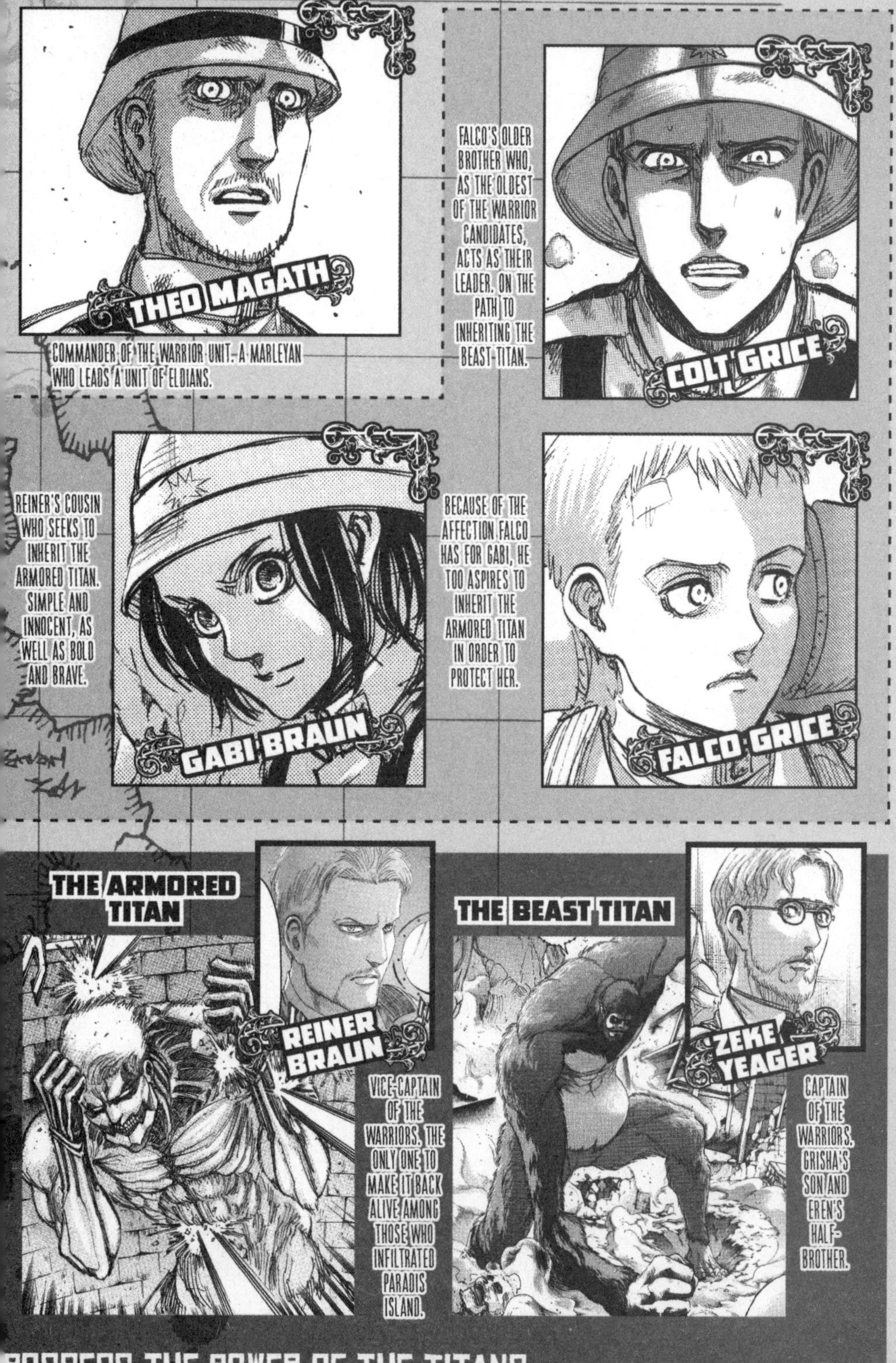
COLT GRICE
FALCO'S OLDER BROTHER WHO, AS THE OLDEST OF THE WARRIOR CANDIDATES, ACTS AS THEIR LEADER. ON THE PATH TO INHERITING THE BEAST TITAN.
THEO MAGATH
COMMANDER OF THE WARRIOR UNIT. A MARLEYAN WHO LEADS A UNIT OF ELDIANS.
FALCO GRICE
BECAUSE OF THE AFFECTION FALCO HAS FOR GABI, HE TOO ASPIRES TO INHERIT THE ARMORED TITAN IN ORDER TO PROTECT HER.
GABI BRAUN
REINER'S COUSIN WHO SEEKS TO INHERIT THE ARMORED TITAN. SIMPLE AND INNOCENT, AS WELL AS BOLD AND BRAVE.
THE BEAST TITAN
ZEKE YEAGER
CAPTAIN OF THE WARRIORS. GRISHA'S SON AND EREN'S HALF-BROTHER.
THE ARMORED TITAN
REINER BRAUN
VICE-CAPTAIN OF THE WARRIORS, THE ONLY ONE TO MAKE IT BACK ALIVE AMONG THOSE WHO INFILTRATED PARADIS ISLAND.

POSSESS THE POWER OF THE TITANS.

ATTACK ON TITAN 24

HAJIME ISAYAMA

ATTACK on TITAN

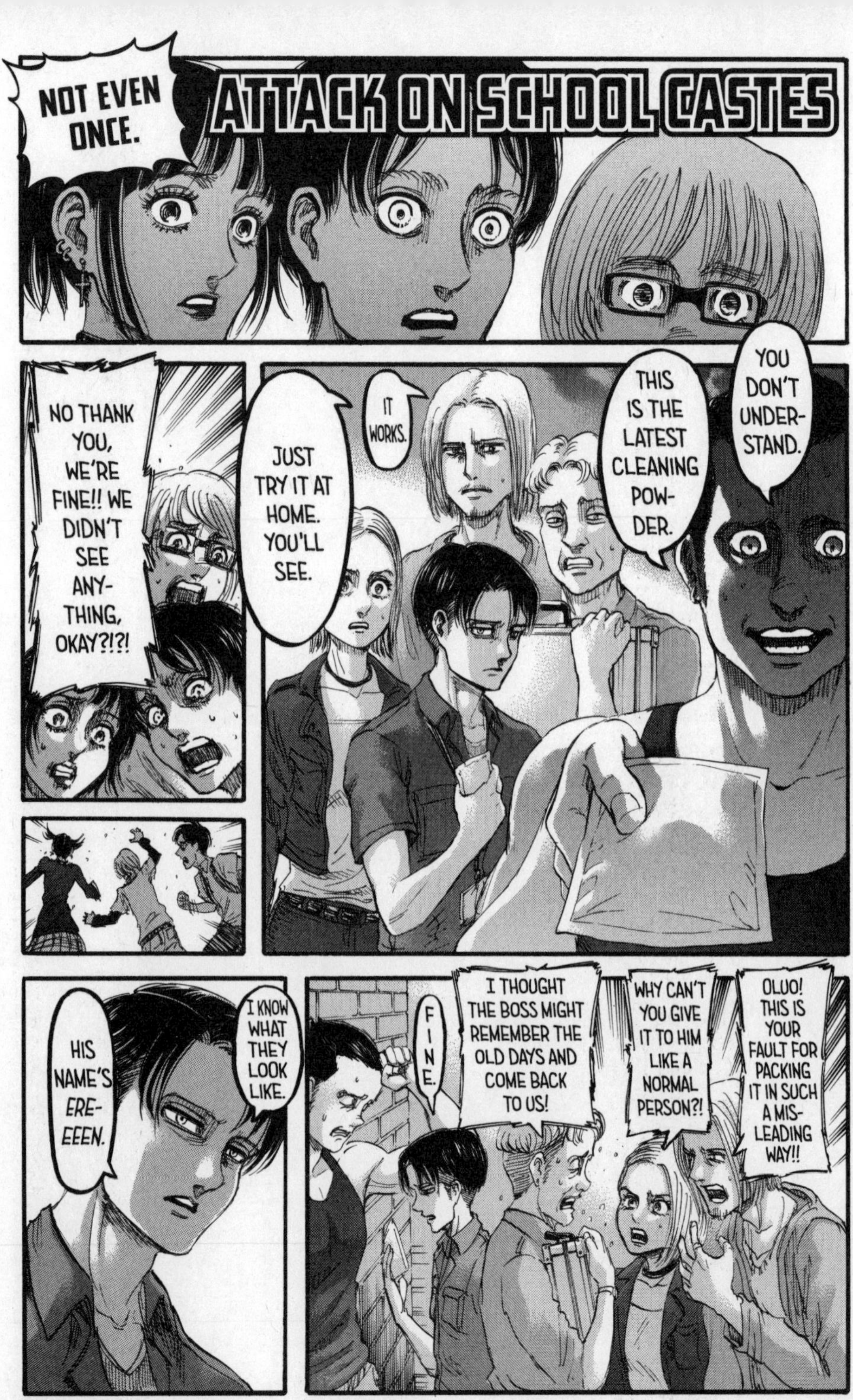
ATTACK ON SCHOOL CASTES
NOT EVEN ONCE.
YOU DON'T UNDER-STAND.
THIS IS THE LATEST CLEANING POW-DER.
IT WORKS.
JUST TRY IT AT HOME. YOU'LL SEE.
NO THANK YOU, WE'RE FINE!! WE DIDN'T SEE ANY-THING, OKAY?!?!
OLUO! THIS IS YOUR FAULT FOR PACKING IT IN SUCH A MIS-LEADING WAY!!
WHY CAN'T YOU GIVE IT TO HIM LIKE A NORMAL PERSON?!
I THOUGHT THE BOSS MIGHT REMEMBER THE OLD DAYS AND COME BACK TO US!
FINE.
I KNOW WHAT THEY LOOK LIKE.
HIS NAME'S *ERE-EEEN.*

*Not a real preview.

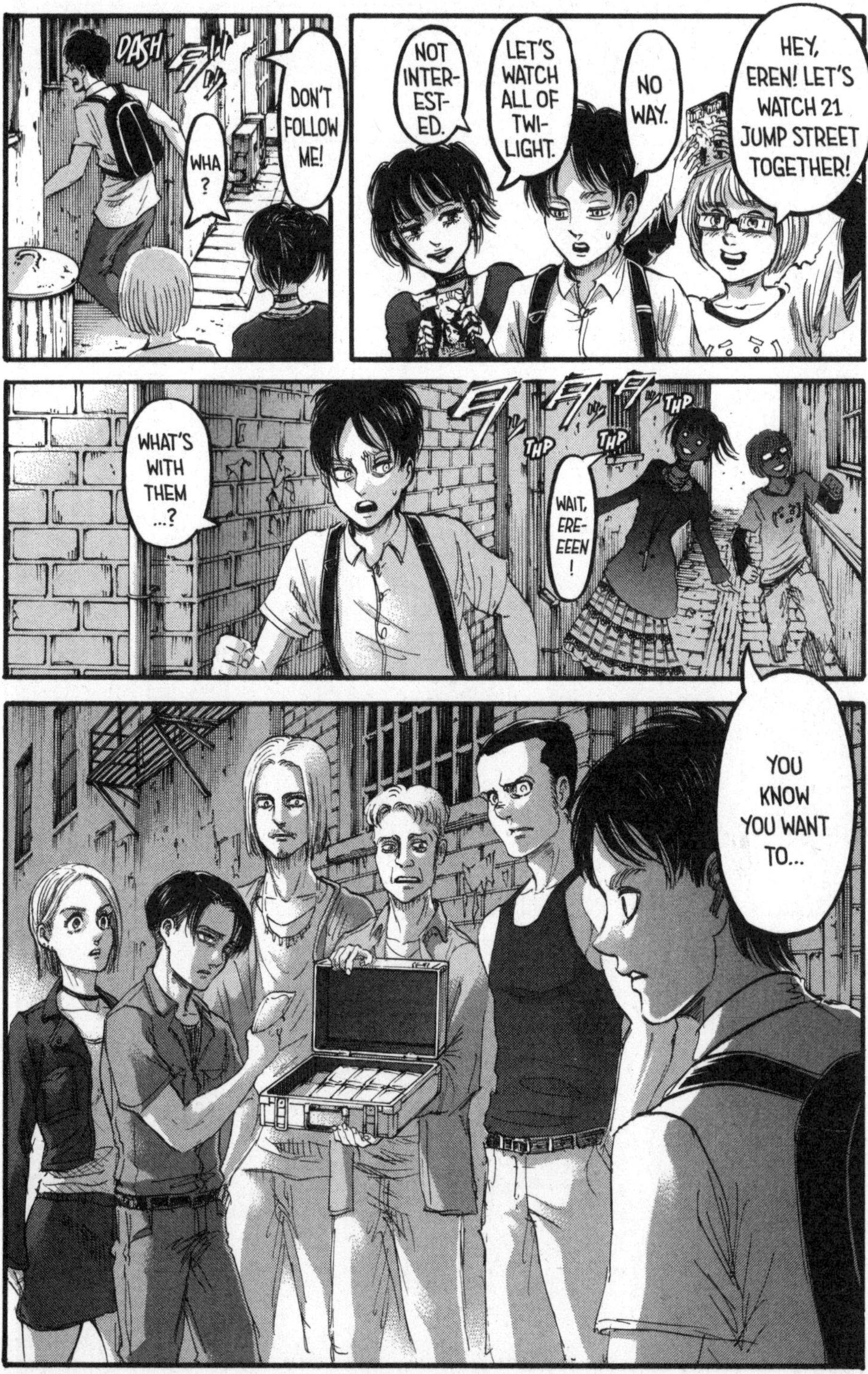
HEY, EREN! LET'S WATCH 21 JUMP STREET TOGETHER!
NO WAY.
LET'S WATCH ALL OF TWI-LIGHT.
NOT INTER-EST-ED.
DON'T FOLLOW ME!
DASH
WHA?
THP
THP
WAIT, ERE-EEEN!
THP
WHAT'S WITH THEM ...?
YOU KNOW YOU WANT TO...

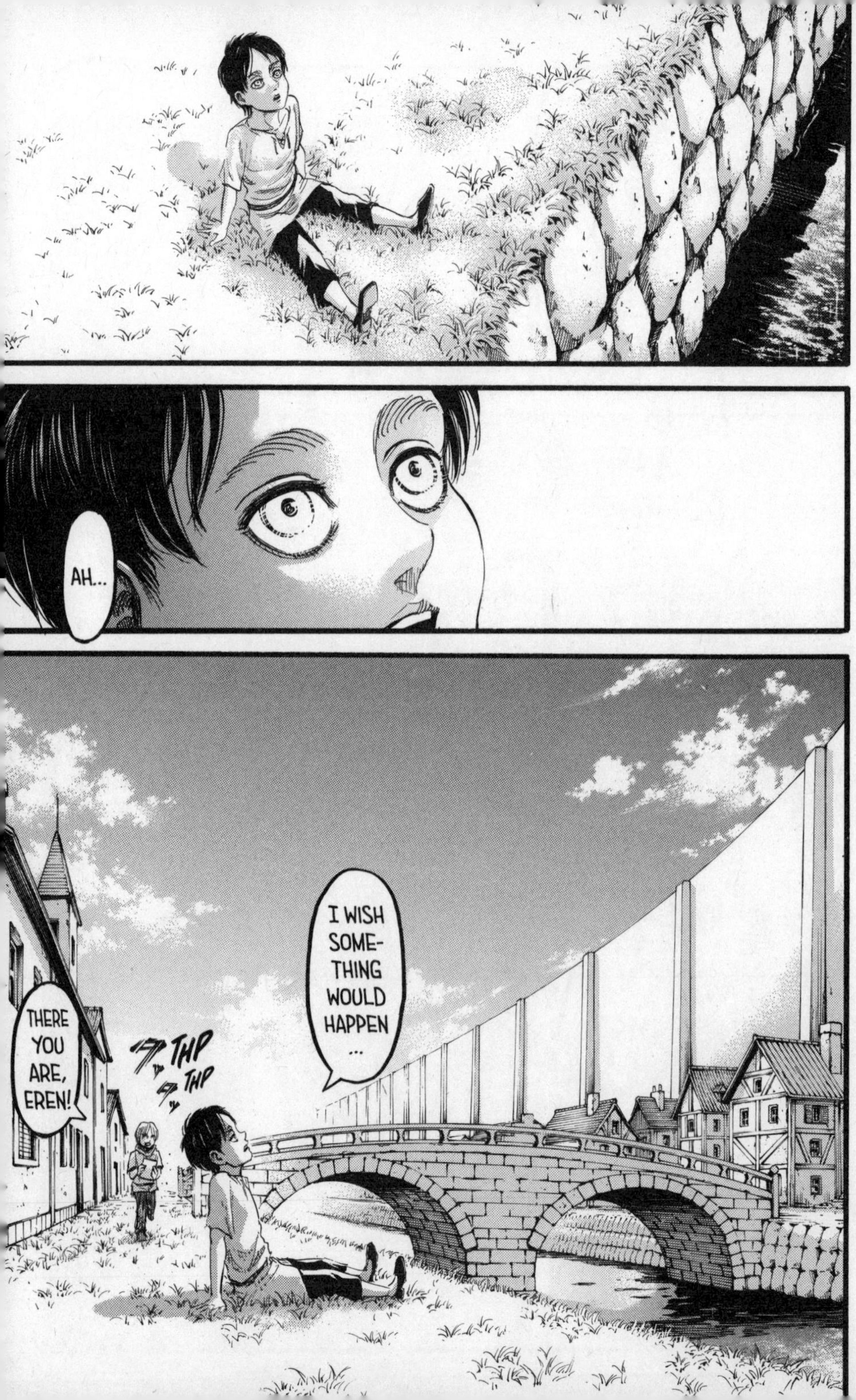
AH...
I WISH SOMETHING WOULD HAPPEN...
THP THP
THERE YOU ARE, EREN!

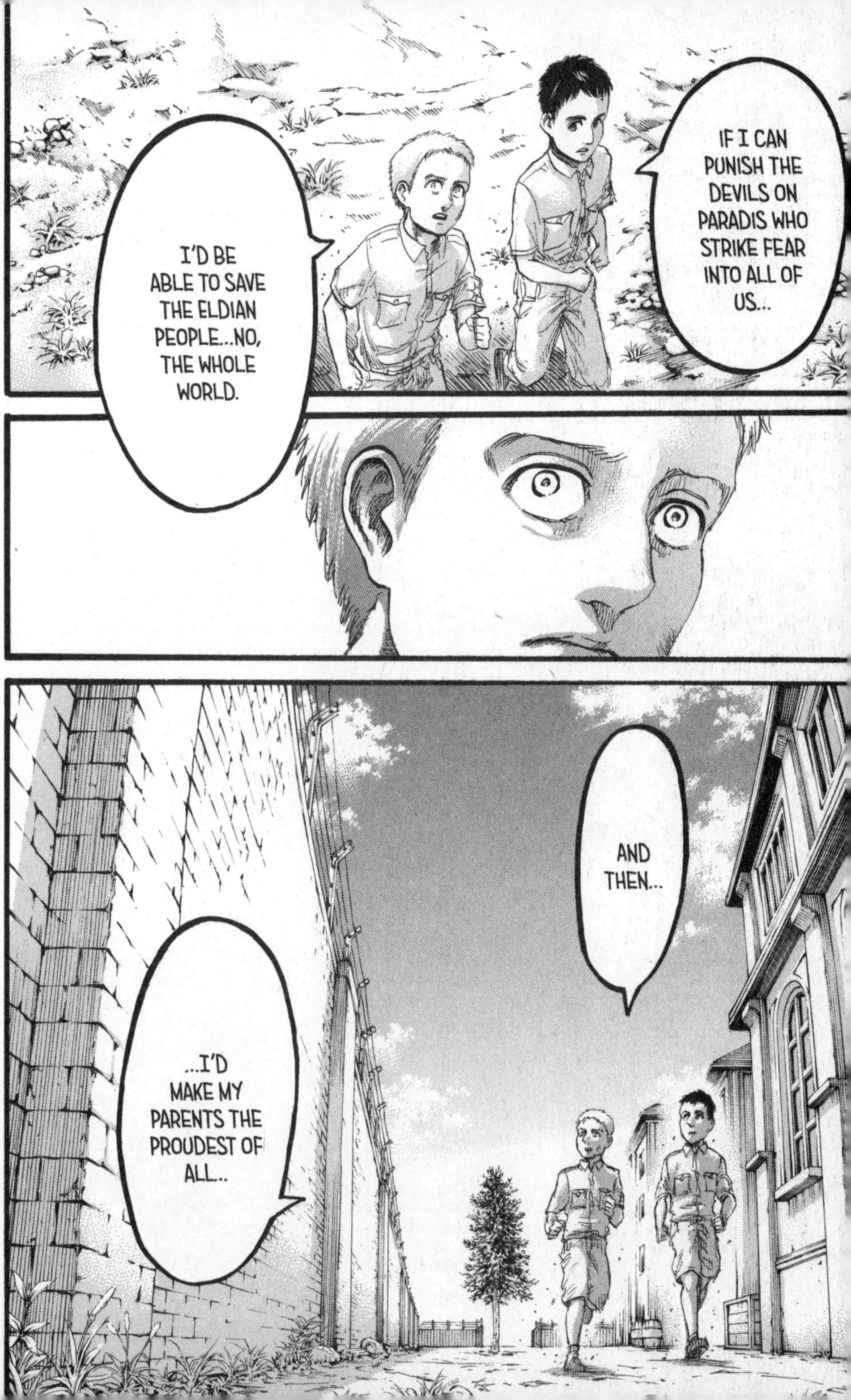
IF I CAN PUNISH THE DEVILS ON PARADIS WHO STRIKE FEAR INTO ALL OF US...
I'D BE ABLE TO SAVE THE ELDIAN PEOPLE...NO, THE WHOLE WORLD.
AND THEN...
...I'D MAKE MY PARENTS THE PROUDEST OF ALL...

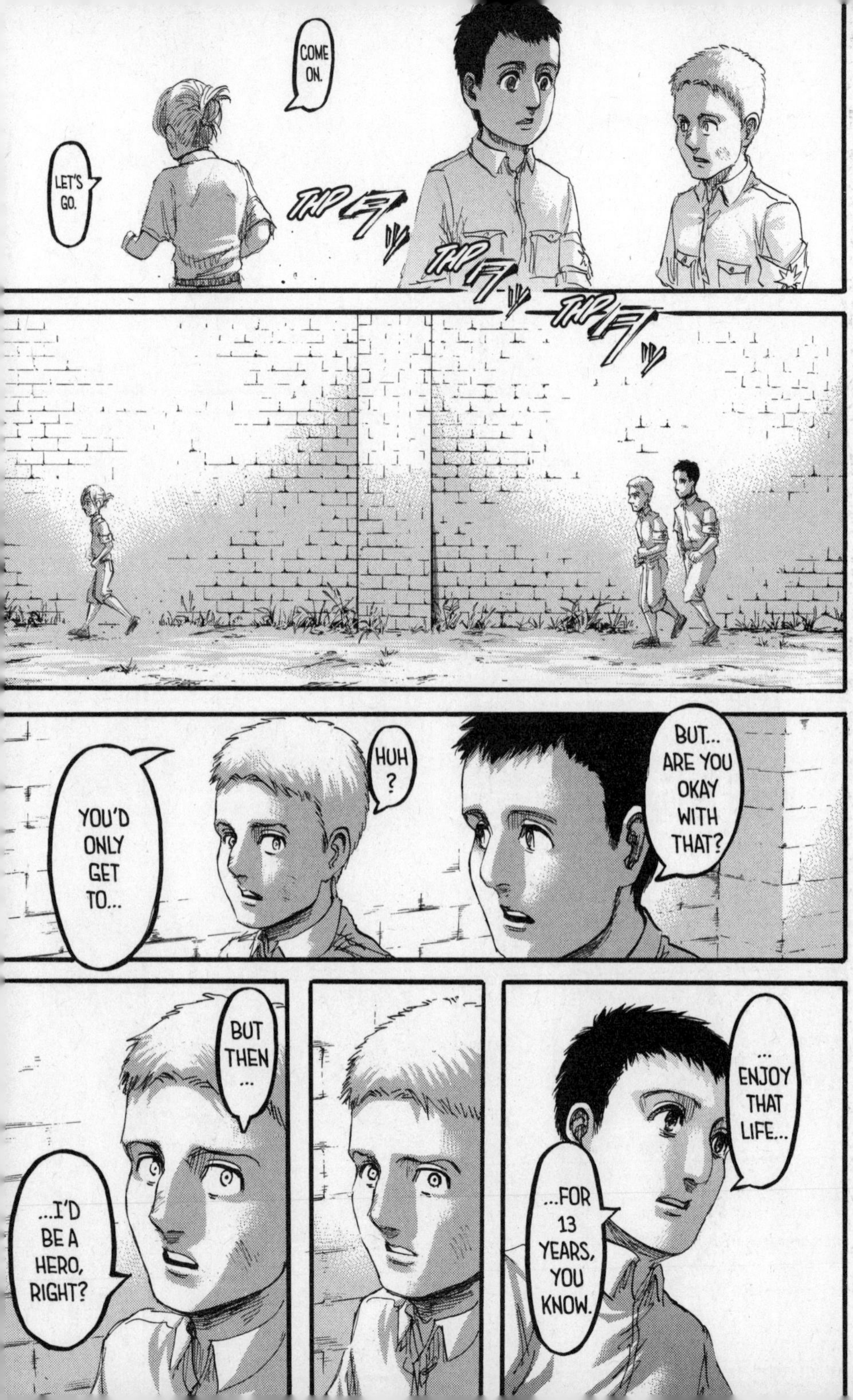
COME ON.
LET'S GO.
THP
THP
THP
BUT... ARE YOU OKAY WITH THAT?
HUH?
YOU'D ONLY GET TO...
...ENJOY THAT LIFE...
...FOR 13 YEARS, YOU KNOW.
BUT THEN...
...I'D BE A HERO, RIGHT?

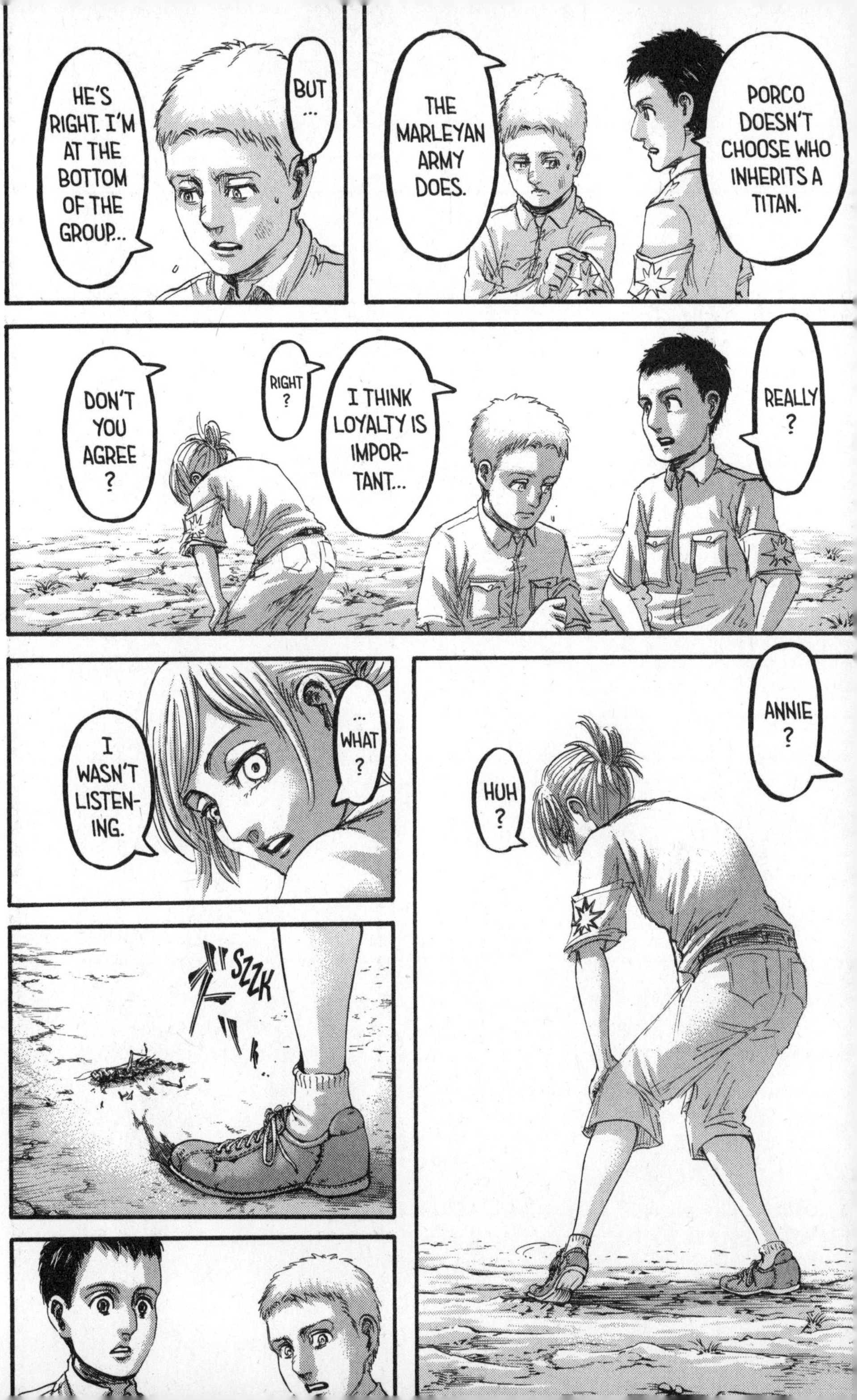
PORCO DOESN'T CHOOSE WHO INHERITS A TITAN.
THE MARLEYAN ARMY DOES.
BUT ...
HE'S RIGHT. I'M AT THE BOTTOM OF THE GROUP...
REALLY?
I THINK LOYALTY IS IMPOR-TANT...
RIGHT?
DON'T YOU AGREE?
ANNIE?
HUH?
...WHAT?
I WASN'T LISTEN-ING.
SZZK

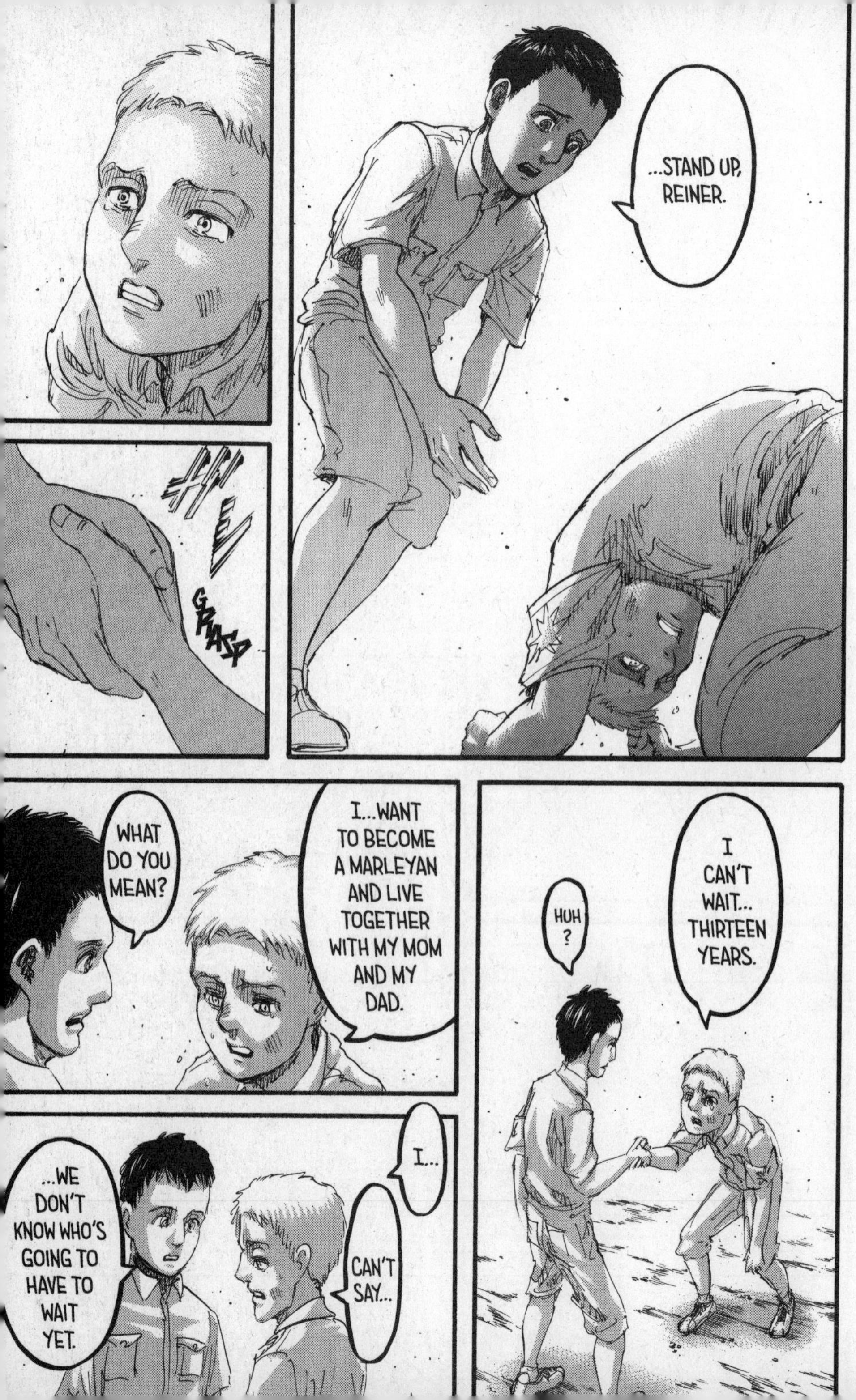
...STAND UP, REINER.
GRASP
I CAN'T WAIT... THIRTEEN YEARS.
HUH?
I...WANT TO BECOME A MARLEYAN AND LIVE TOGETHER WITH MY MOM AND MY DAD.
WHAT DO YOU MEAN?
I...
CAN'T SAY...
...WE DON'T KNOW WHO'S GOING TO HAVE TO WAIT YET.

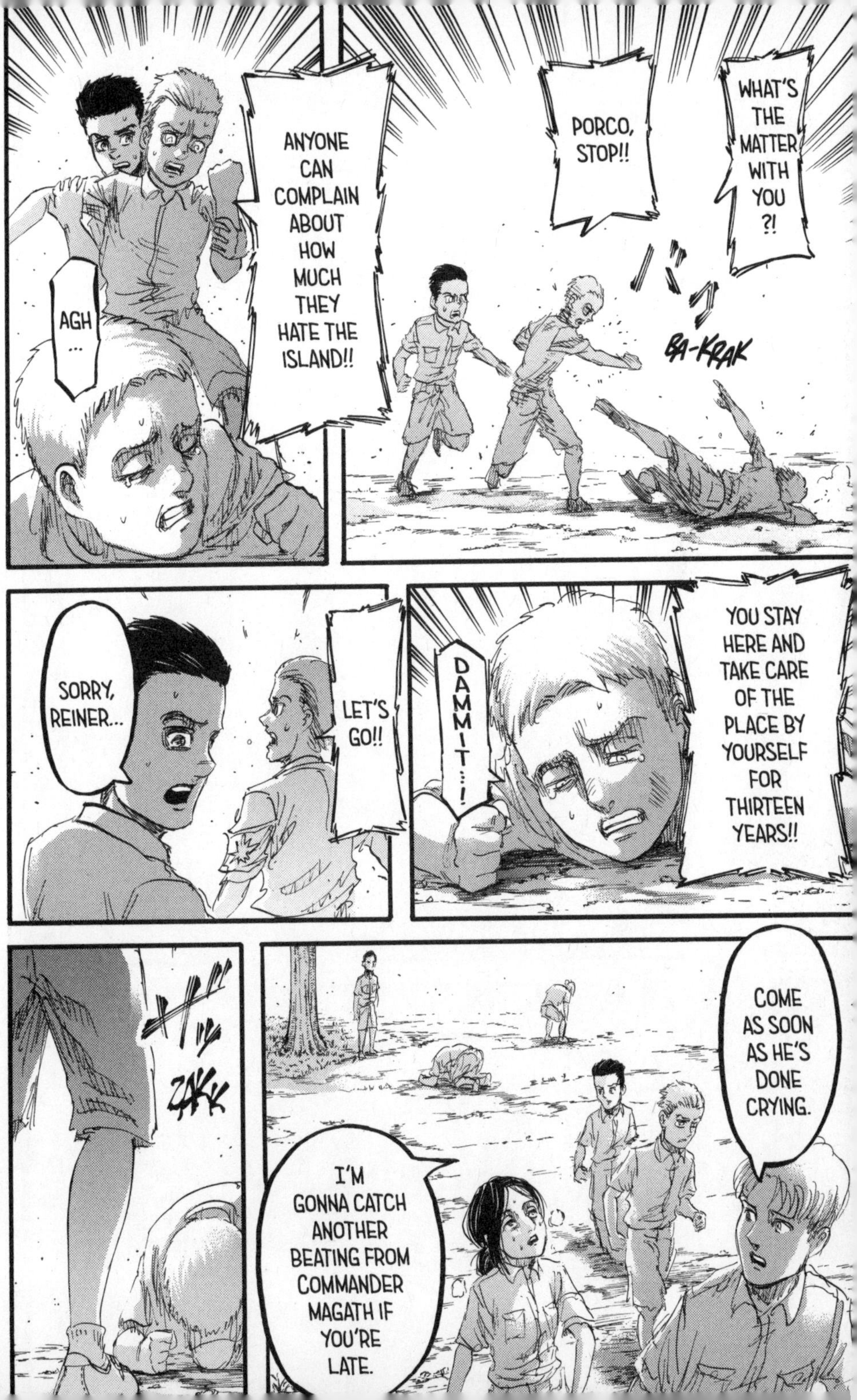
WHAT'S THE MATTER WITH YOU ?!
PORCO, STOP!!
BA-KRAK
ANYONE CAN COMPLAIN ABOUT HOW MUCH THEY HATE THE ISLAND!!
AGH ...
YOU STAY HERE AND TAKE CARE OF THE PLACE BY YOURSELF FOR THIRTEEN YEARS!!
DAMMIT...!
LET'S GO!!
SORRY, REINER...
COME AS SOON AS HE'S DONE CRYING.
I'M GONNA CATCH ANOTHER BEATING FROM COMMANDER MAGATH IF YOU'RE LATE.
ZAKK

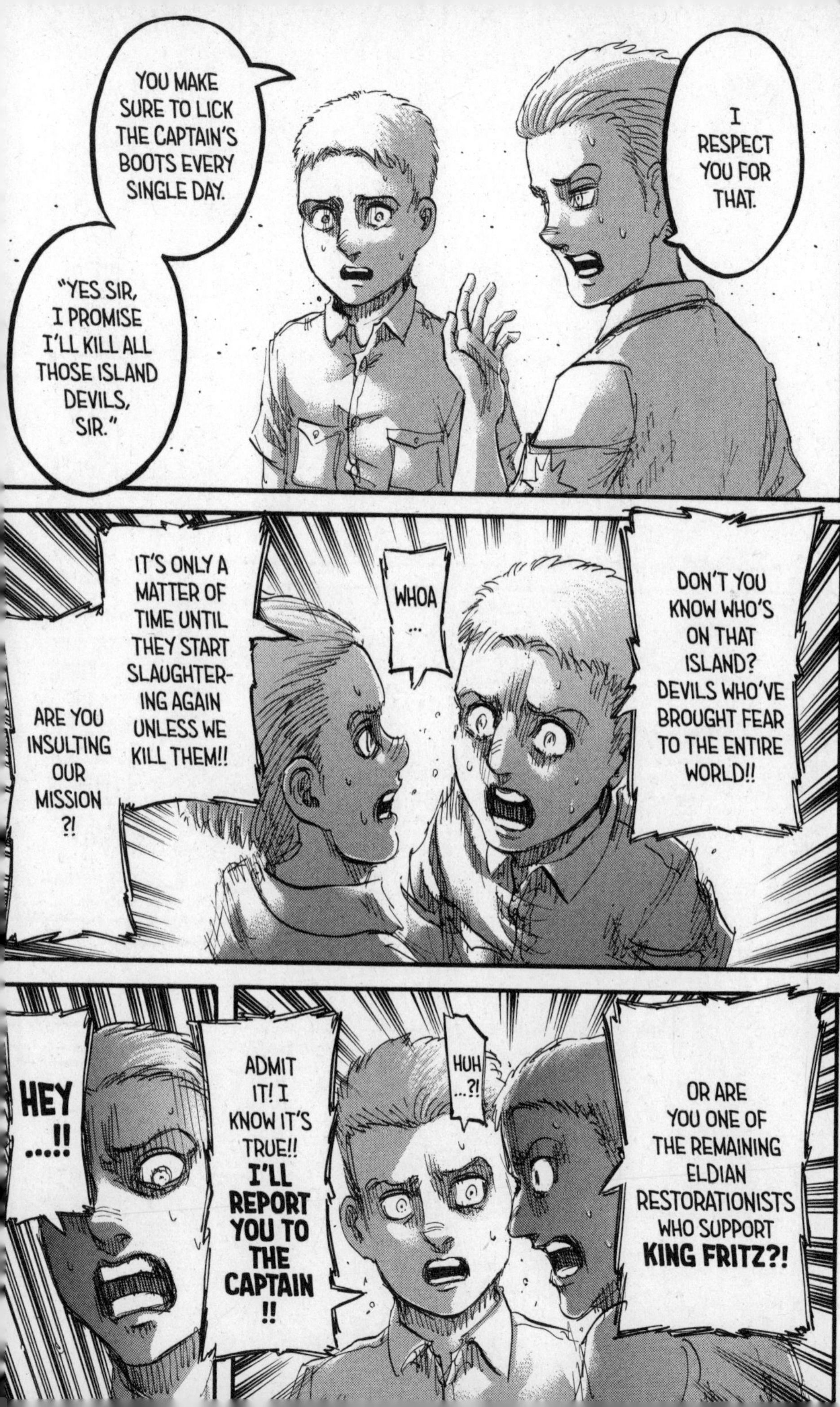
I RESPECT YOU FOR THAT.
YOU MAKE SURE TO LICK THE CAPTAIN'S BOOTS EVERY SINGLE DAY.
"YES SIR, I PROMISE I'LL KILL ALL THOSE ISLAND DEVILS, SIR."
DON'T YOU KNOW WHO'S ON THAT ISLAND? DEVILS WHO'VE BROUGHT FEAR TO THE ENTIRE WORLD!!
WHOA ...
IT'S ONLY A MATTER OF TIME UNTIL THEY START SLAUGHTERING AGAIN UNLESS WE KILL THEM!!
ARE YOU INSULTING OUR MISSION?!
OR ARE YOU ONE OF THE REMAINING ELDIAN RESTORATIONISTS WHO SUPPORT **KING FRITZ?!**
HUH ...?!
ADMIT IT! I KNOW IT'S TRUE!! **I'LL REPORT YOU TO THE CAPTAIN!!**
HEY ...!!

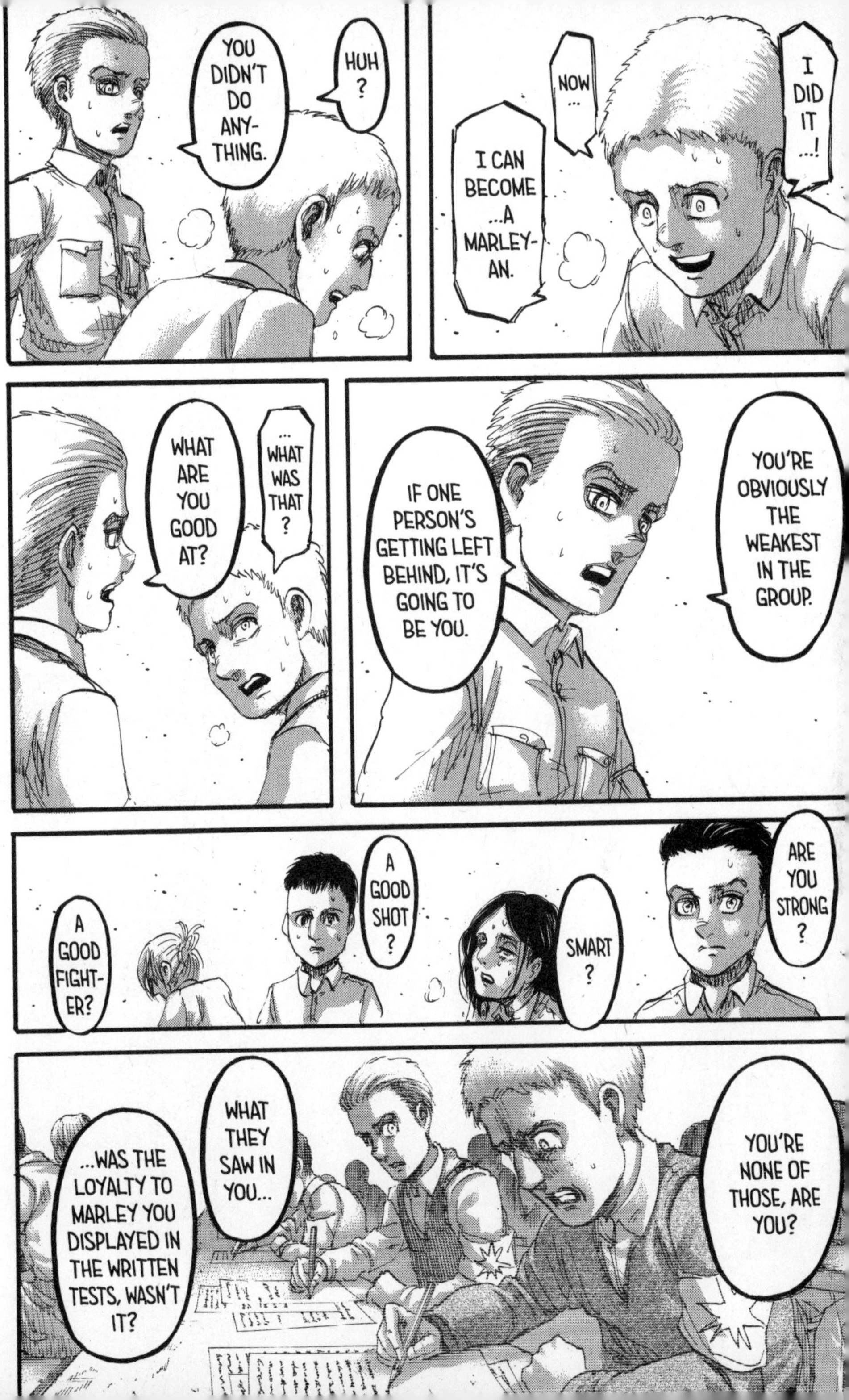
I DID IT ...!
NOW ...
I CAN BECOME ...A MARLEYAN.
HUH ?
YOU DIDN'T DO ANYTHING.
YOU'RE OBVIOUSLY THE WEAKEST IN THE GROUP.
IF ONE PERSON'S GETTING LEFT BEHIND, IT'S GOING TO BE YOU.
...WHAT WAS THAT ?
WHAT ARE YOU GOOD AT?
ARE YOU STRONG ?
SMART ?
A GOOD SHOT ?
A GOOD FIGHTER?
YOU'RE NONE OF THOSE, ARE YOU?
WHAT THEY SAW IN YOU...
...WAS THE LOYALTY TO MARLEY YOU DISPLAYED IN THE WRITTEN TESTS, WASN'T IT?

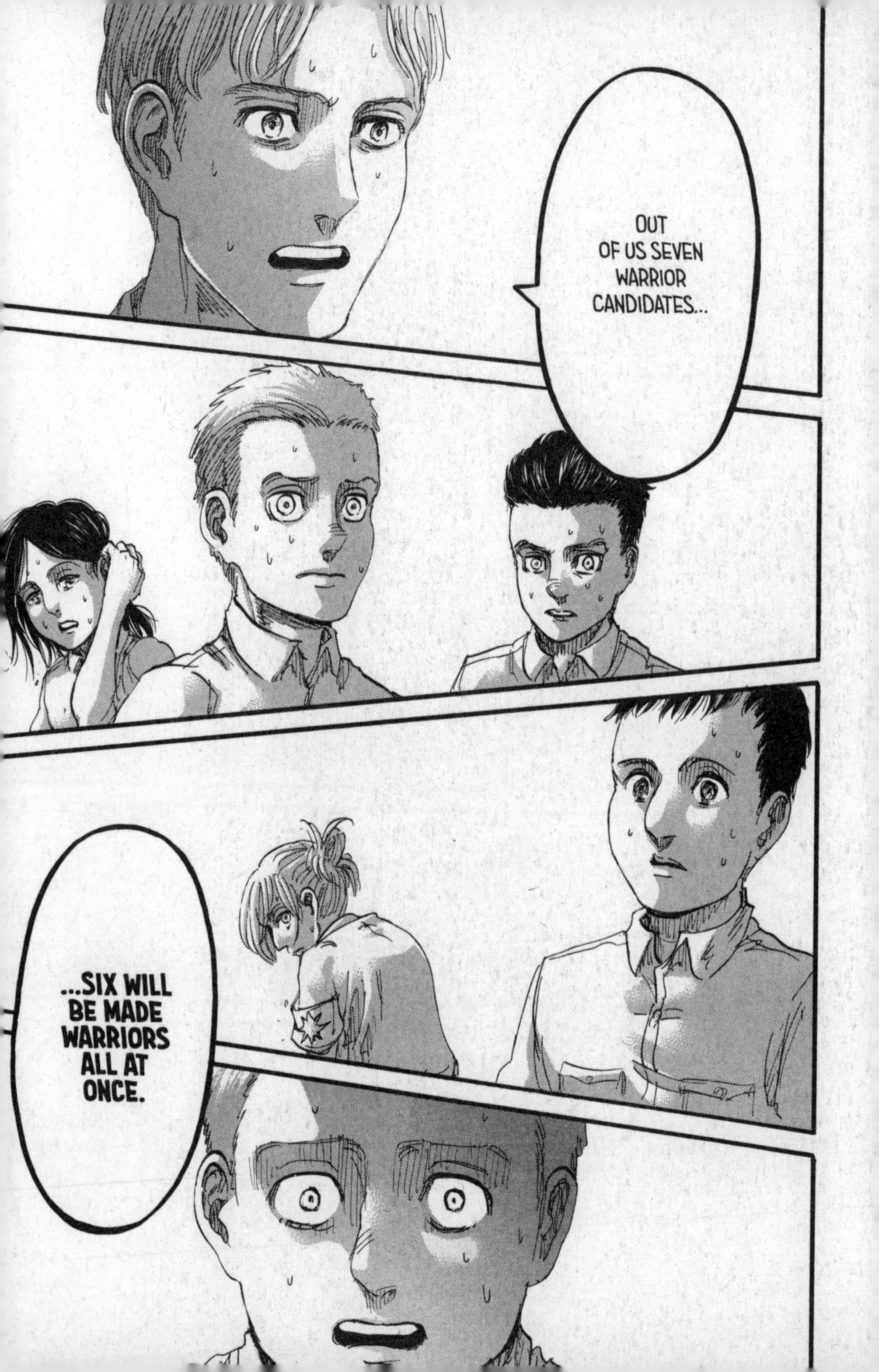

OUT OF US SEVEN WARRIOR CANDIDATES...
...SIX WILL BE MADE WARRIORS ALL AT ONCE.

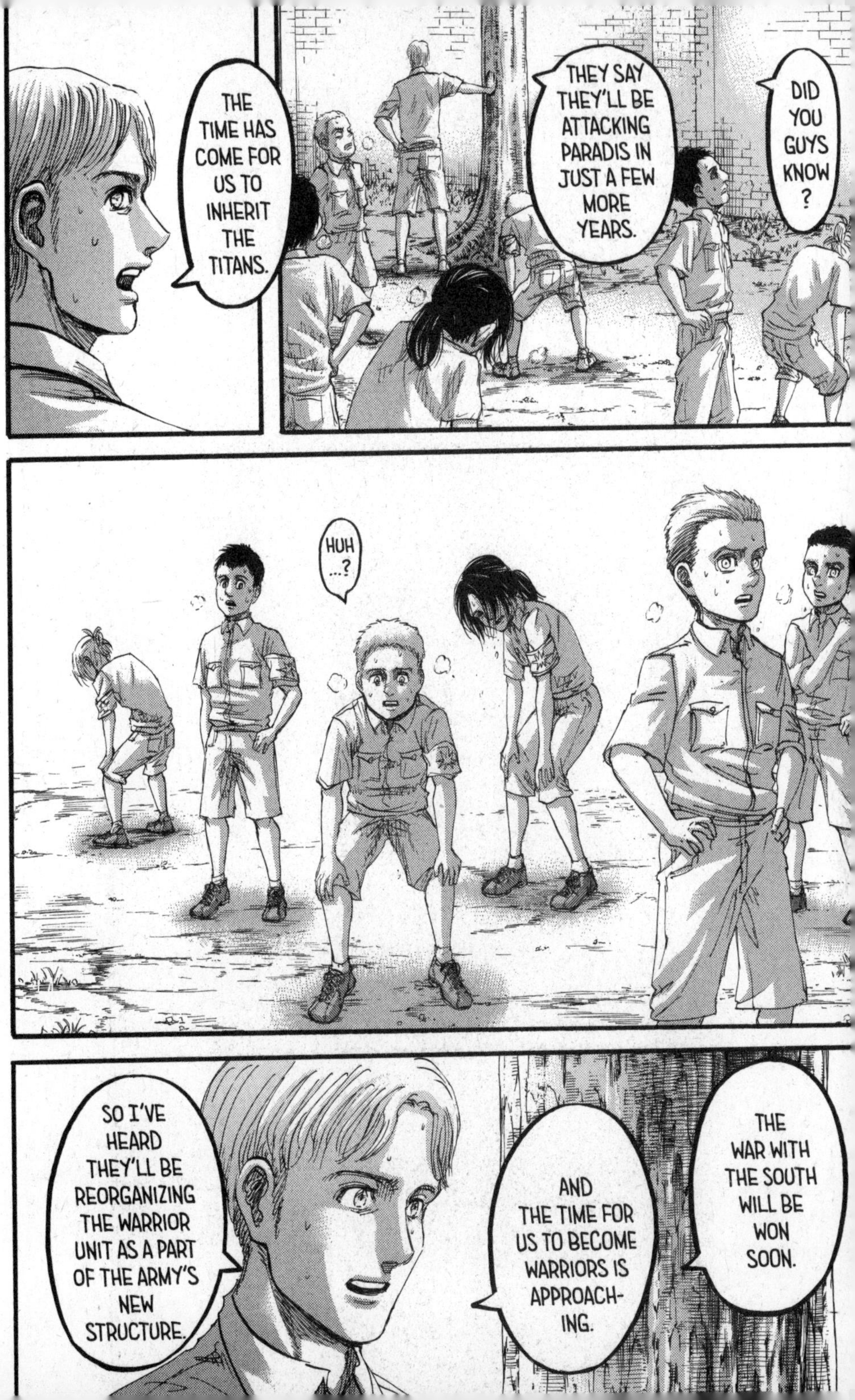
DID YOU GUYS KNOW?
THEY SAY THEY'LL BE ATTACKING PARADIS IN JUST A FEW MORE YEARS.
THE TIME HAS COME FOR US TO INHERIT THE TITANS.
HUH...?
THE WAR WITH THE SOUTH WILL BE WON SOON.
AND THE TIME FOR US TO BECOME WARRIORS IS APPROACH-ING.
SO I'VE HEARD THEY'LL BE REORGANIZING THE WARRIOR UNIT AS A PART OF THE ARMY'S NEW STRUCTURE.

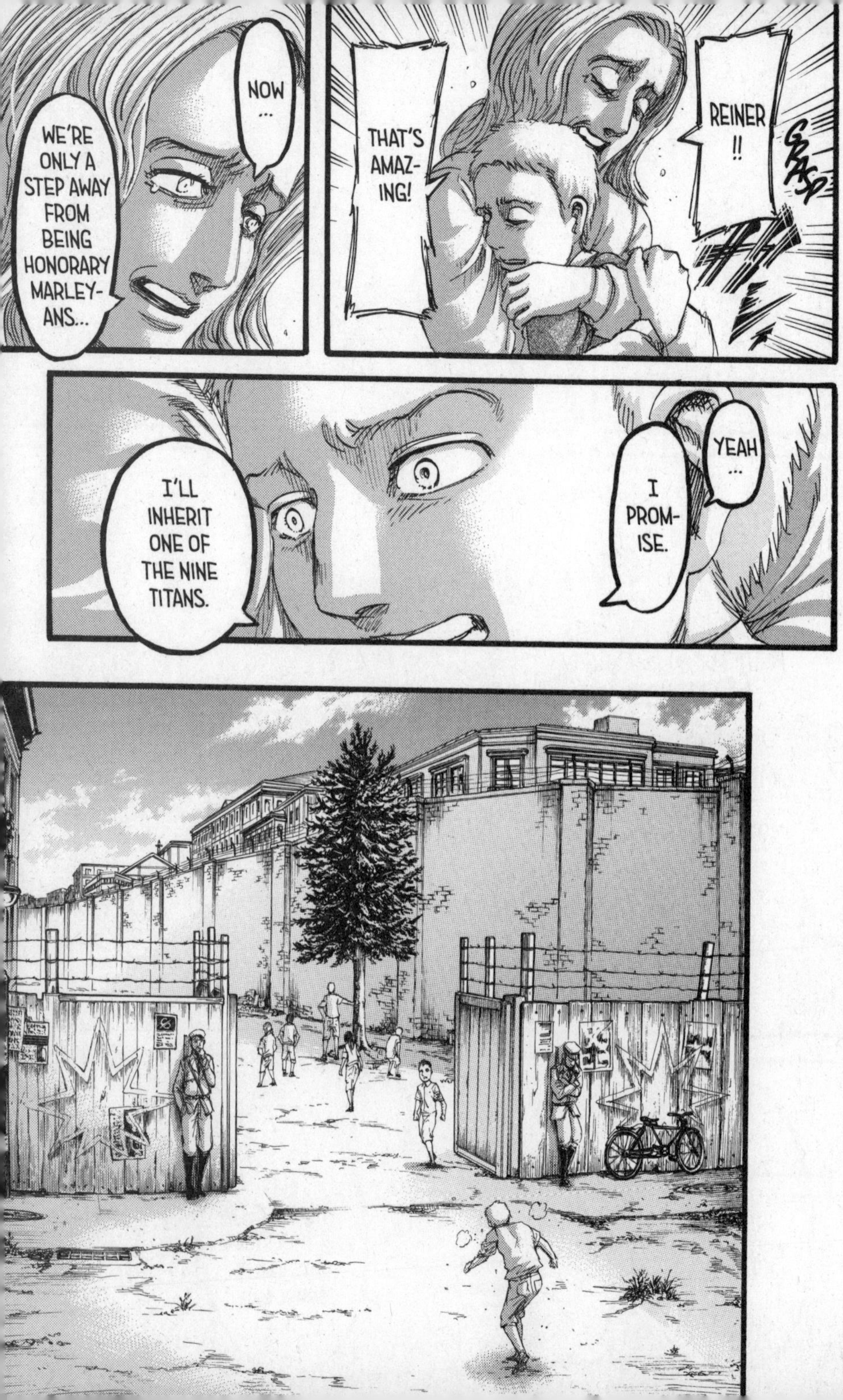
REINER !!
GRASP
THAT'S AMAZ-ING!
NOW ...
WE'RE ONLY A STEP AWAY FROM BEING HONORARY MARLEY-ANS...
YEAH ...
I PROM-ISE.
I'LL INHERIT ONE OF THE NINE TITANS.

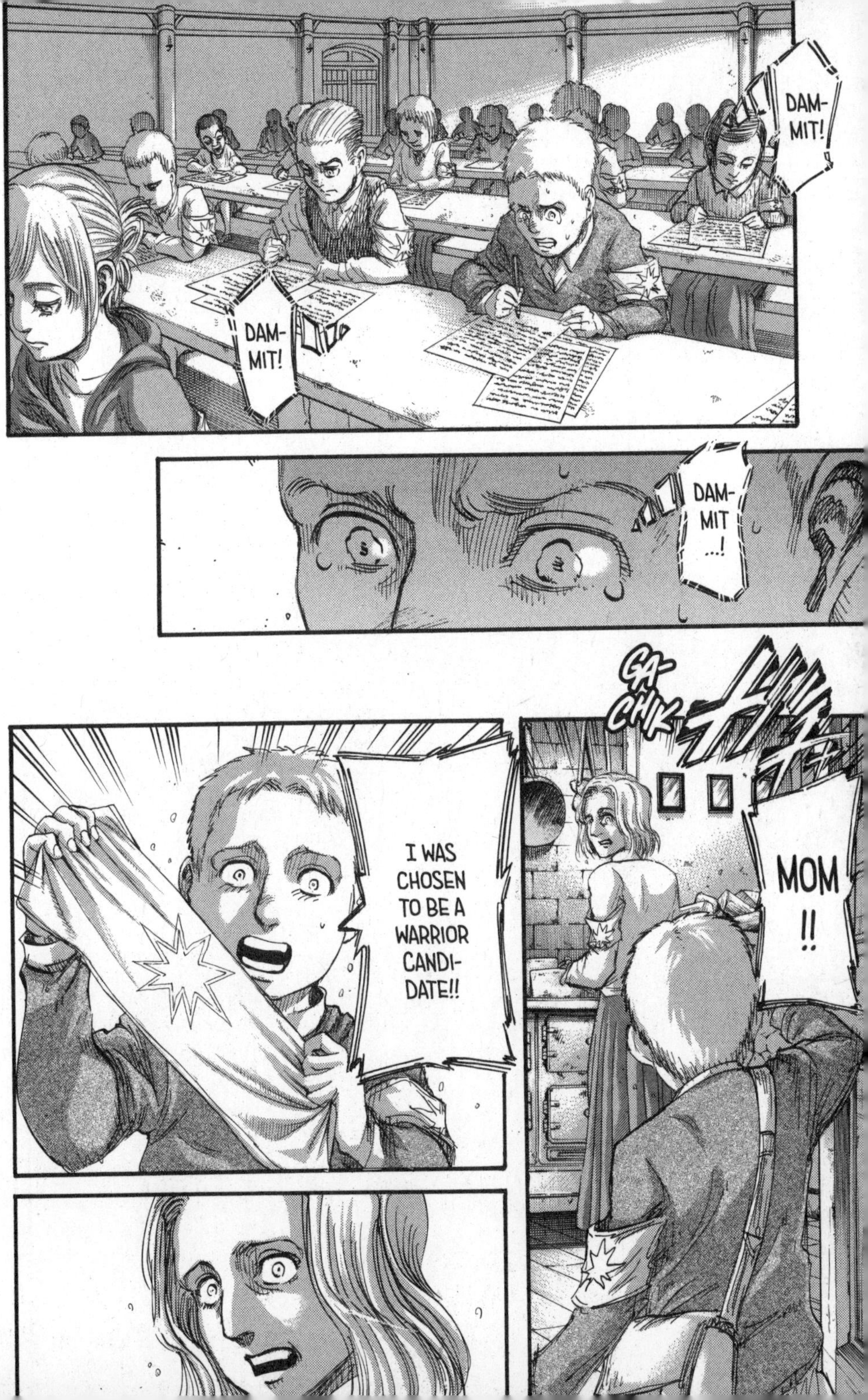
DAM-MIT!
DAM-MIT!
DAM-MIT ...!
GA-CHIK
MOM !!
I WAS CHOSEN TO BE A WARRIOR CANDI-DATE!!

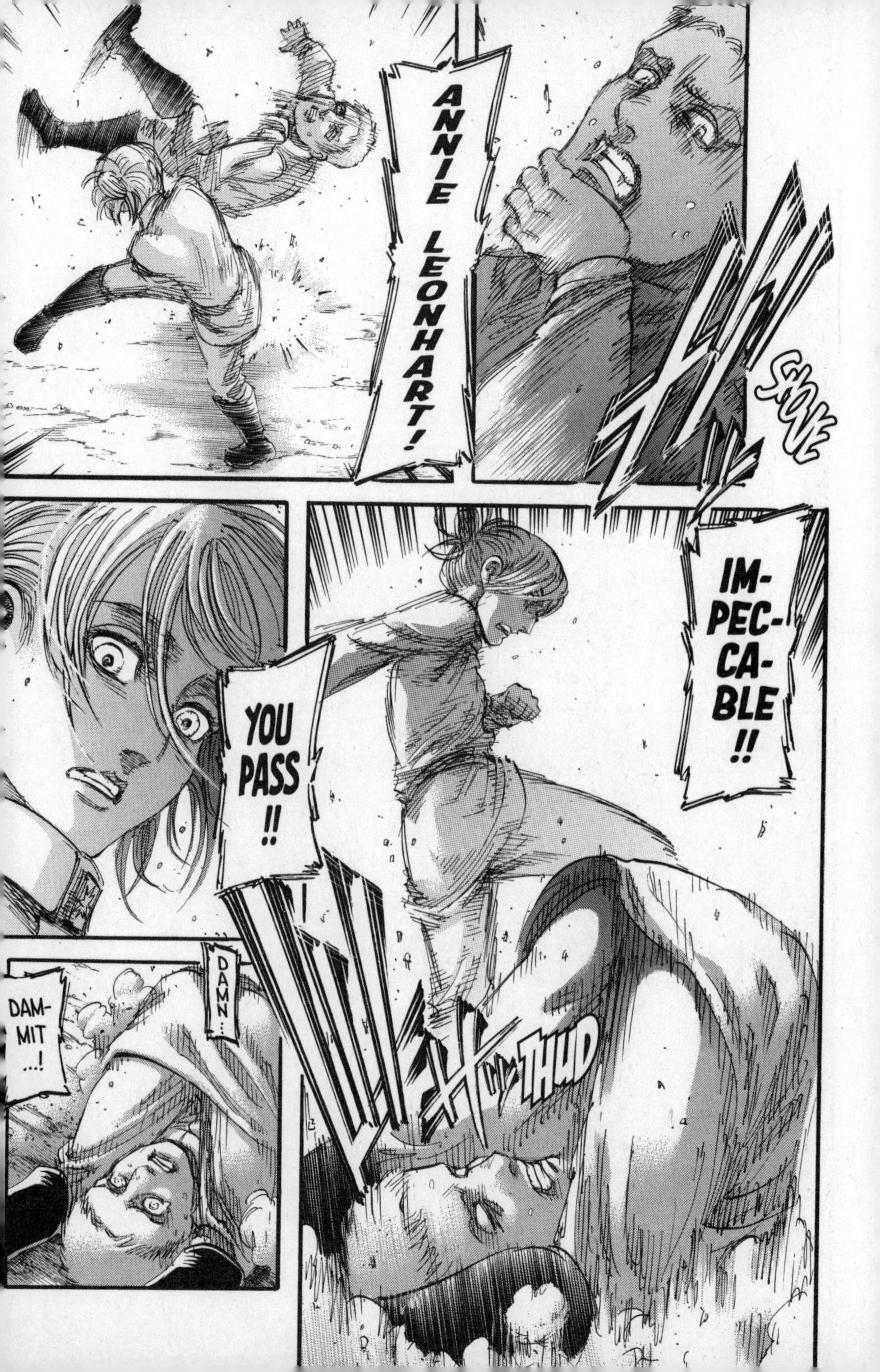
ANNIE LEONHART!
IM-PEC-CA-BLE!!
YOU PASS!!
THUD
DAMN...
DAM-MIT ...!

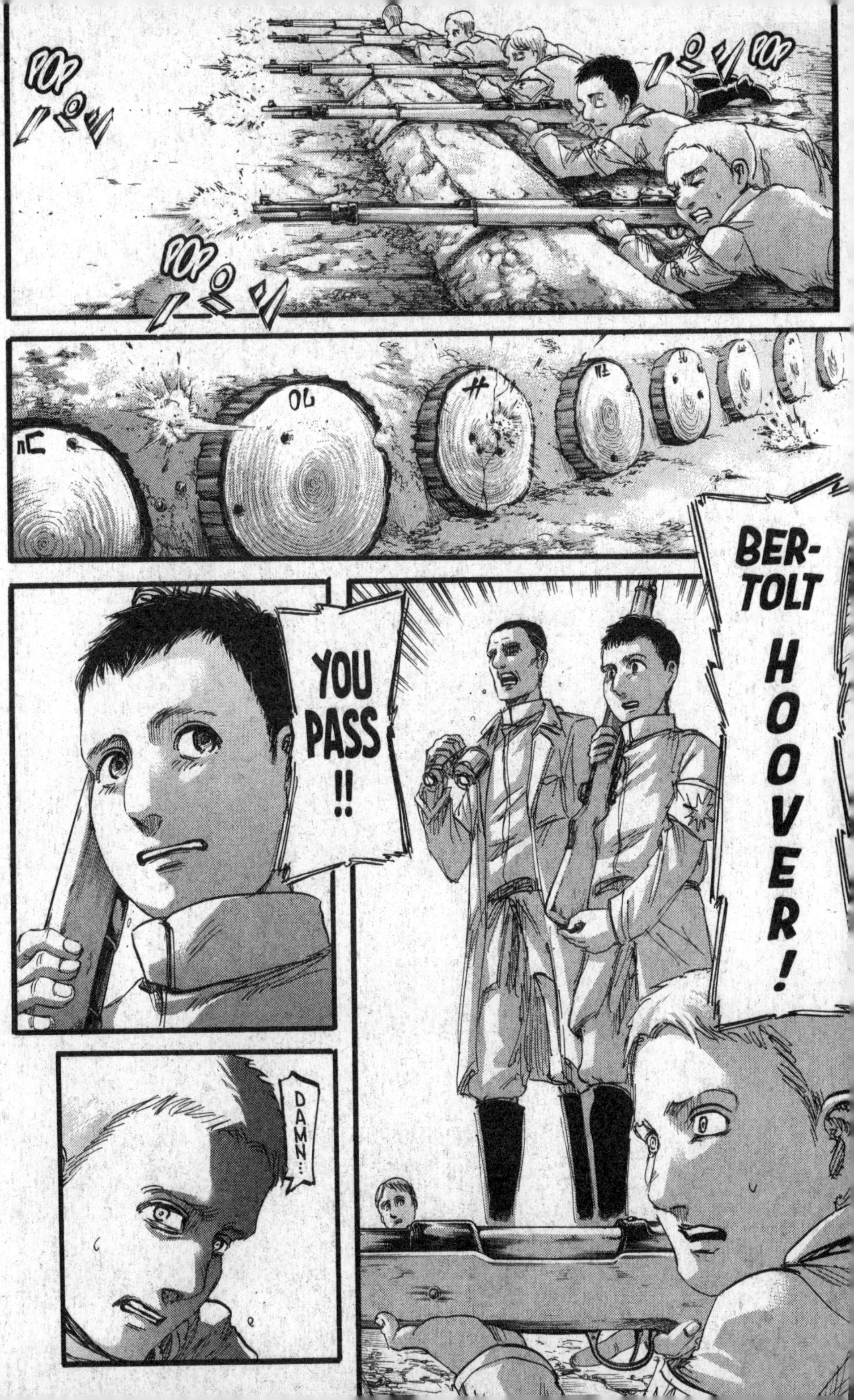
POP
POP
POP
BER-TOLT HOOVER!
YOU PASS!!
DAMN...

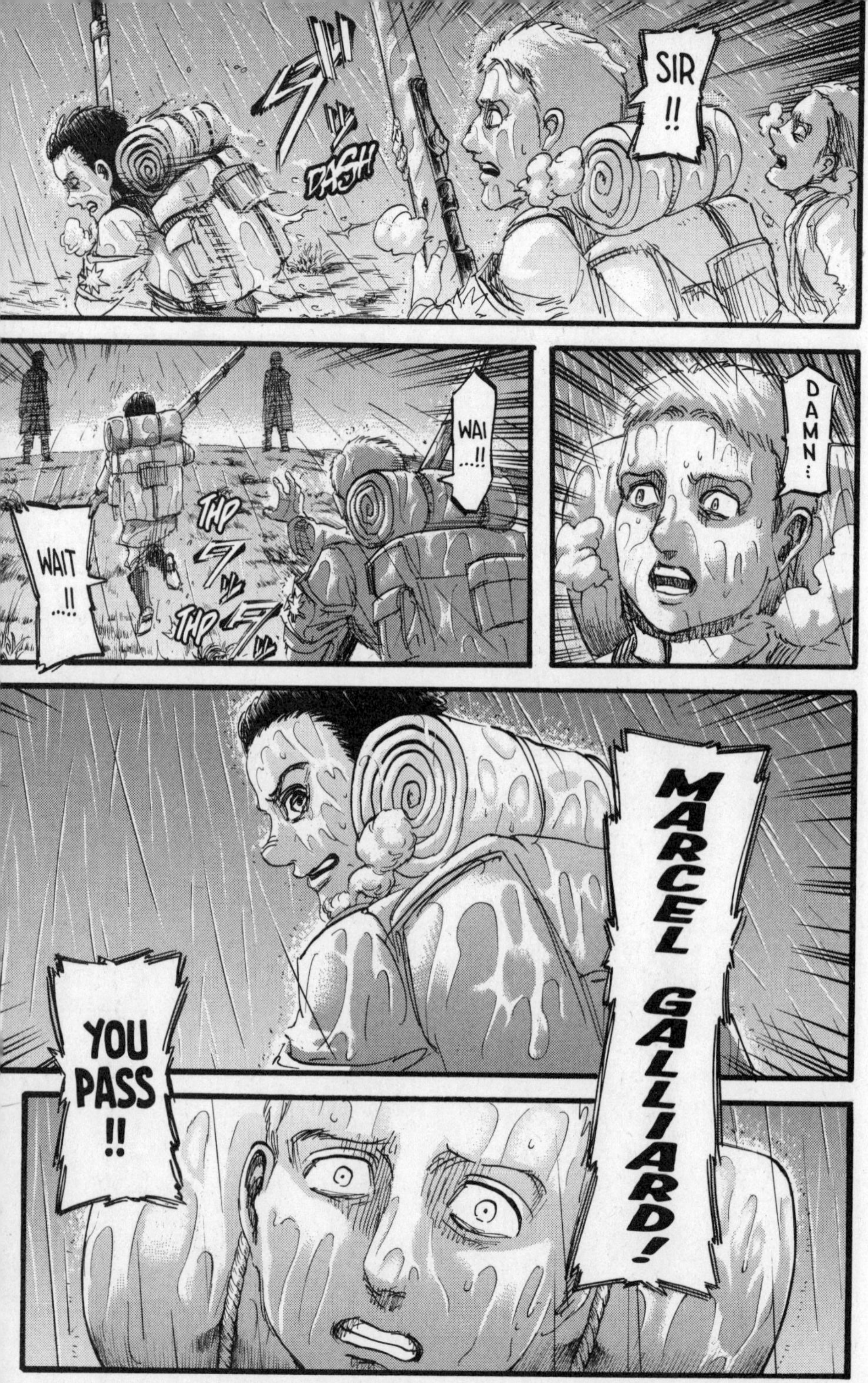
SIR !!
DASH
DAMN...
WAI ...!!
THP
THP
WAIT ...!!
MARCEL GALLIARD!
YOU PASS !!

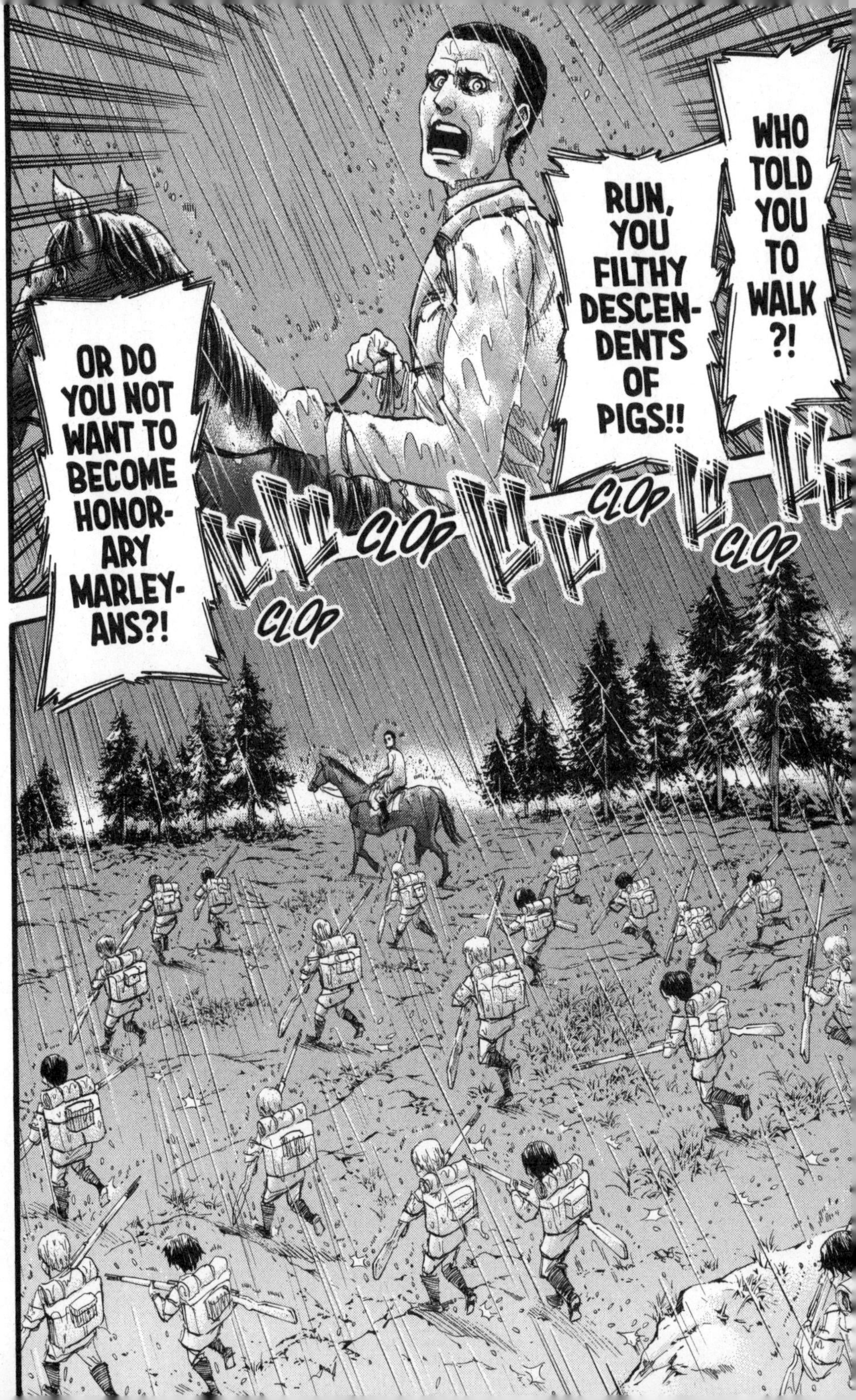
WHO TOLD YOU TO WALK?!
RUN, YOU FILTHY DESCENDENTS OF PIGS!!
OR DO YOU NOT WANT TO BECOME HONORARY MARLEYANS?!
CLOP
CLOP
CLOP
CLOP

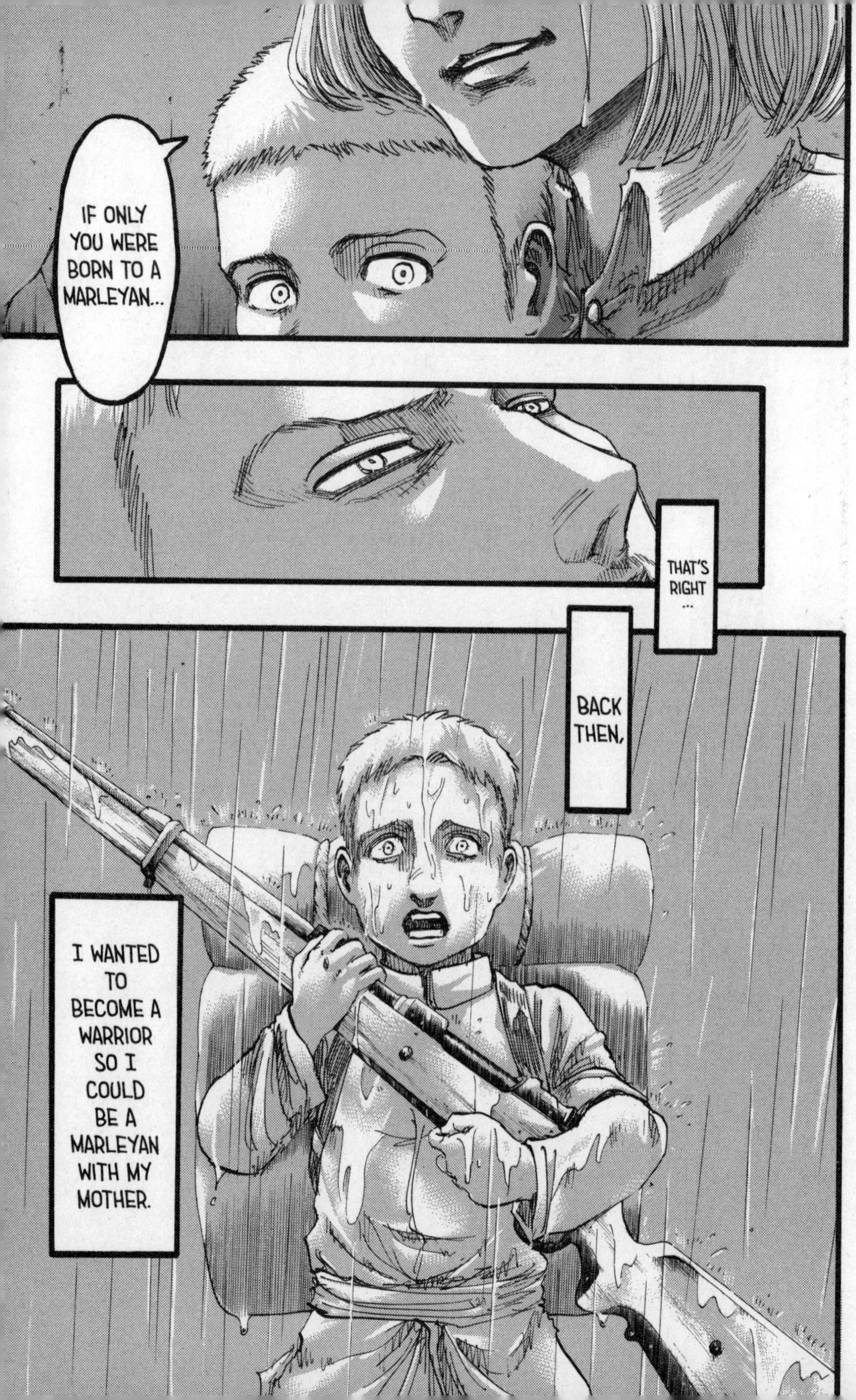
IF ONLY YOU WERE BORN TO A MARLEYAN...
THAT'S RIGHT ...
BACK THEN,
I WANTED TO BECOME A WARRIOR SO I COULD BE A MARLEYAN WITH MY MOTHER.

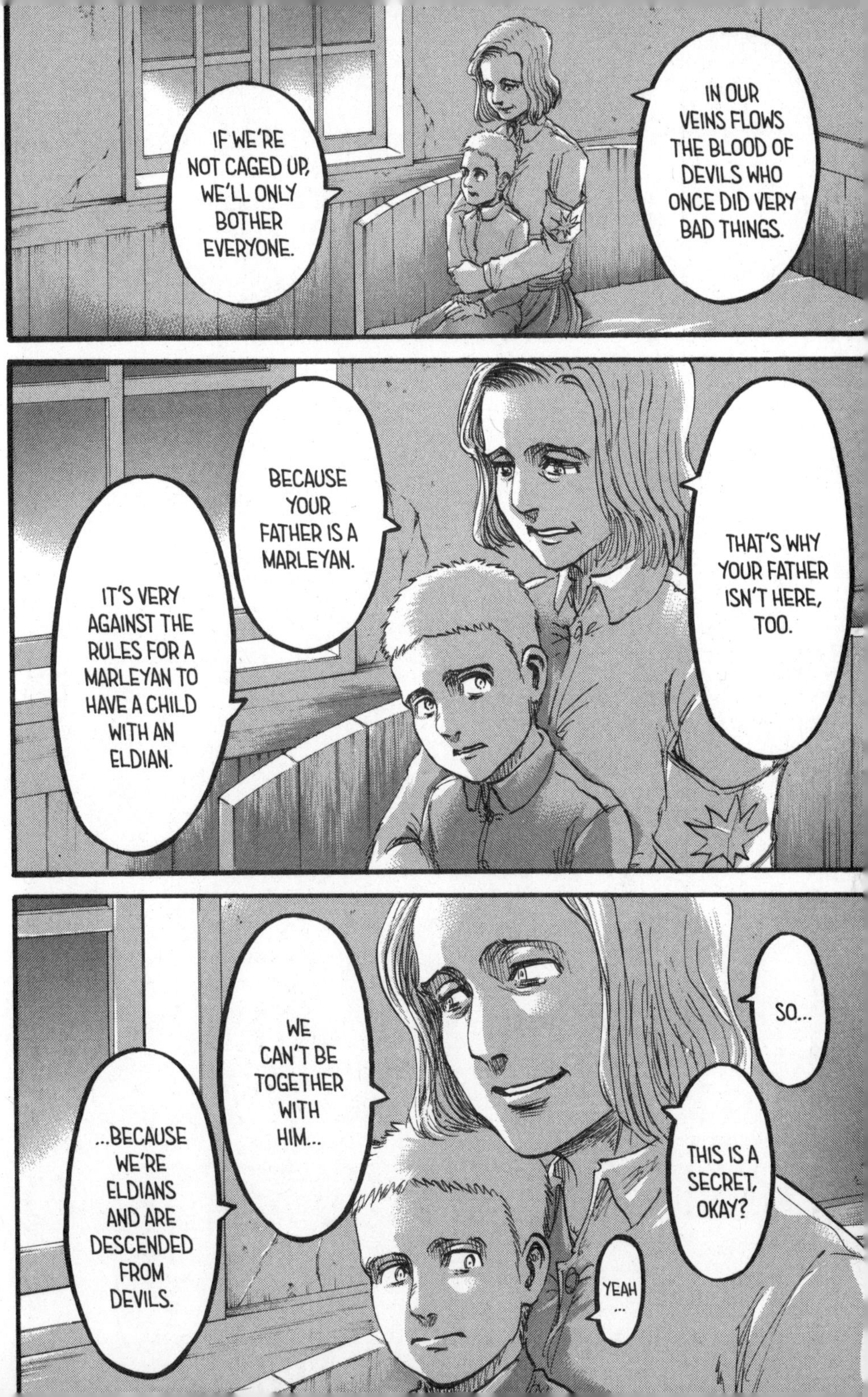
IN OUR VEINS FLOWS THE BLOOD OF DEVILS WHO ONCE DID VERY BAD THINGS.
IF WE'RE NOT CAGED UP, WE'LL ONLY BOTHER EVERYONE.
THAT'S WHY YOUR FATHER ISN'T HERE, TOO.
BECAUSE YOUR FATHER IS A MARLEYAN.
IT'S VERY AGAINST THE RULES FOR A MARLEYAN TO HAVE A CHILD WITH AN ELDIAN.
SO...
WE CAN'T BE TOGETHER WITH HIM...
...BECAUSE WE'RE ELDIANS AND ARE DESCENDED FROM DEVILS.
THIS IS A SECRET, OKAY?
YEAH ...

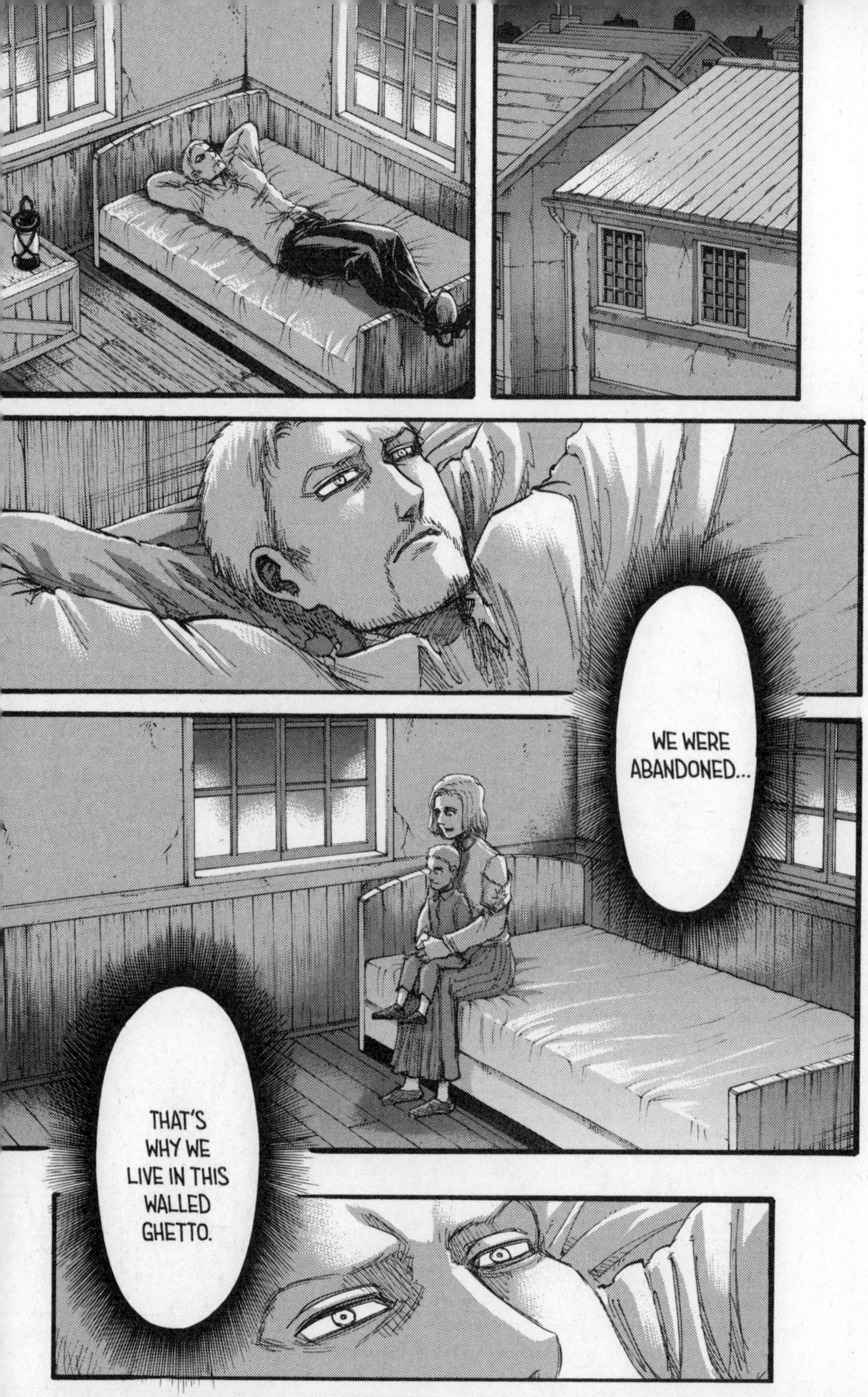
WE WERE ABANDONED...
THAT'S WHY WE LIVE IN THIS WALLED GHETTO.

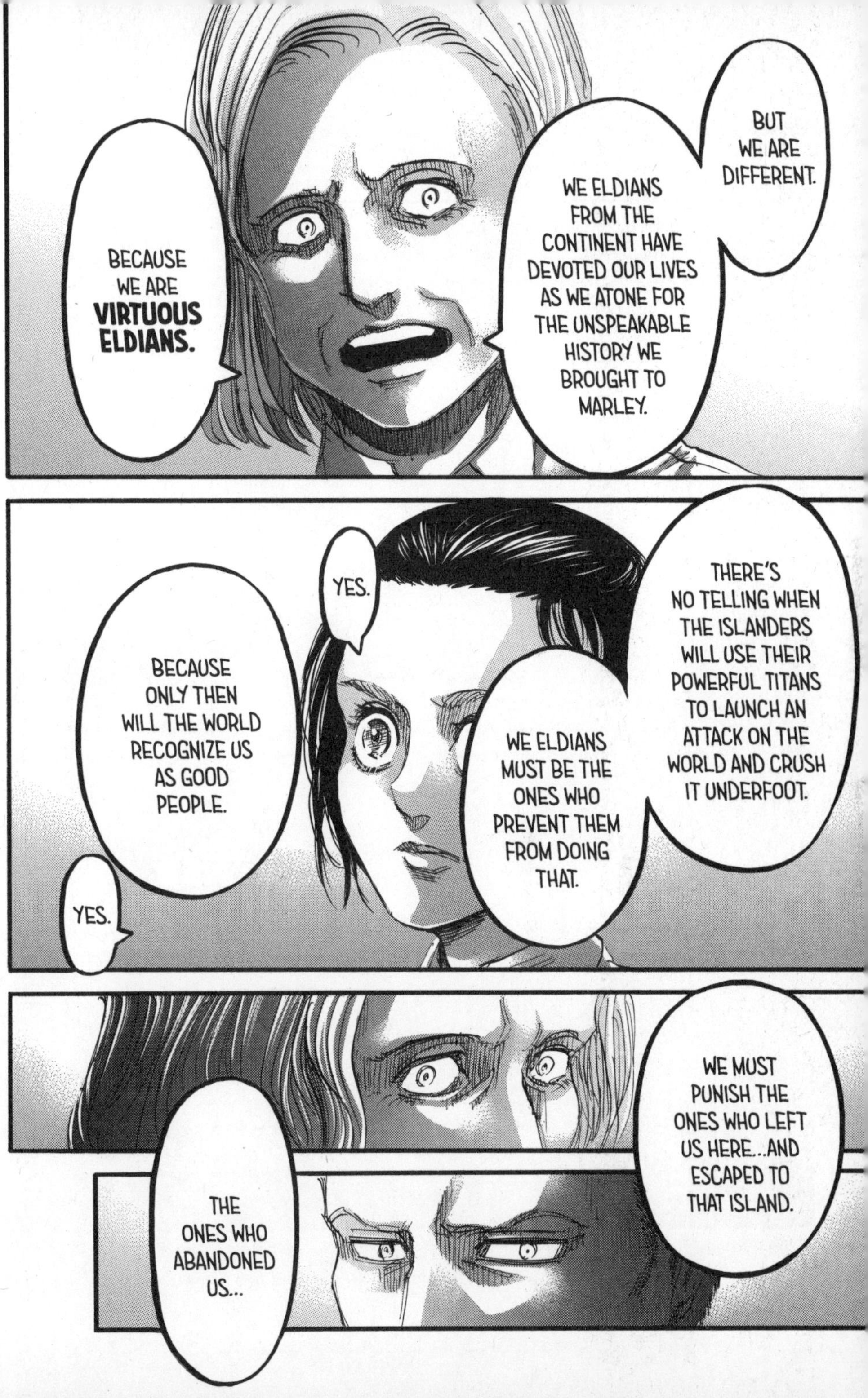
BUT WE ARE DIFFERENT.
WE ELDIANS FROM THE CONTINENT HAVE DEVOTED OUR LIVES AS WE ATONE FOR THE UNSPEAKABLE HISTORY WE BROUGHT TO MARLEY.
BECAUSE WE ARE **VIRTUOUS ELDIANS.**
THERE'S NO TELLING WHEN THE ISLANDERS WILL USE THEIR POWERFUL TITANS TO LAUNCH AN ATTACK ON THE WORLD AND CRUSH IT UNDERFOOT.
WE ELDIANS MUST BE THE ONES WHO PREVENT THEM FROM DOING THAT.
YES.
BECAUSE ONLY THEN WILL THE WORLD RECOGNIZE US AS GOOD PEOPLE.
YES.
WE MUST PUNISH THE ONES WHO LEFT US HERE...AND ESCAPED TO THAT ISLAND.
THE ONES WHO ABANDONED US...

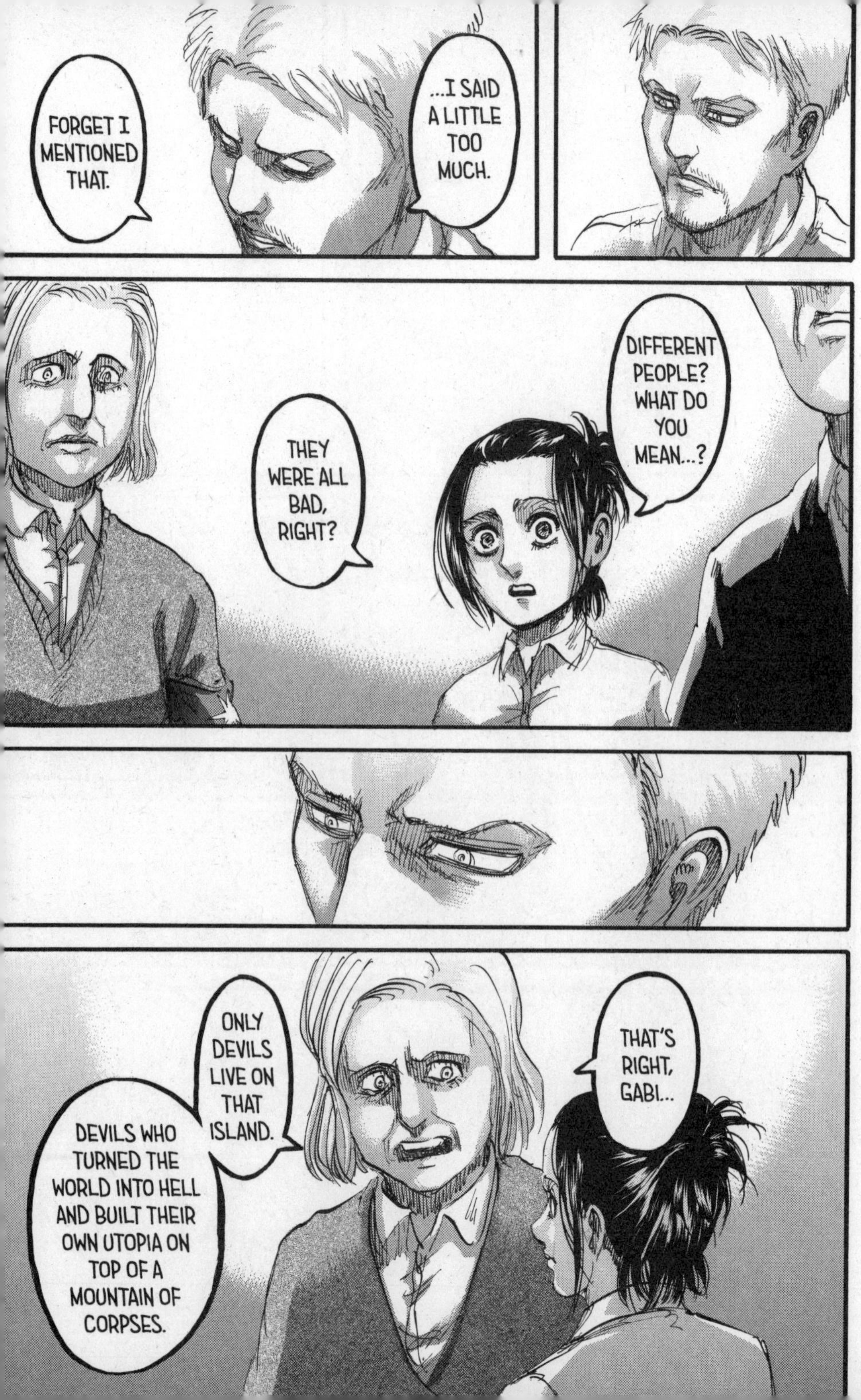
...I SAID A LITTLE TOO MUCH.
FORGET I MENTIONED THAT.
DIFFERENT PEOPLE? WHAT DO YOU MEAN...?
THEY WERE ALL BAD, RIGHT?
THAT'S RIGHT, GABI...
ONLY DEVILS LIVE ON THAT ISLAND.
DEVILS WHO TURNED THE WORLD INTO HELL AND BUILT THEIR OWN UTOPIA ON TOP OF A MOUNTAIN OF CORPSES.

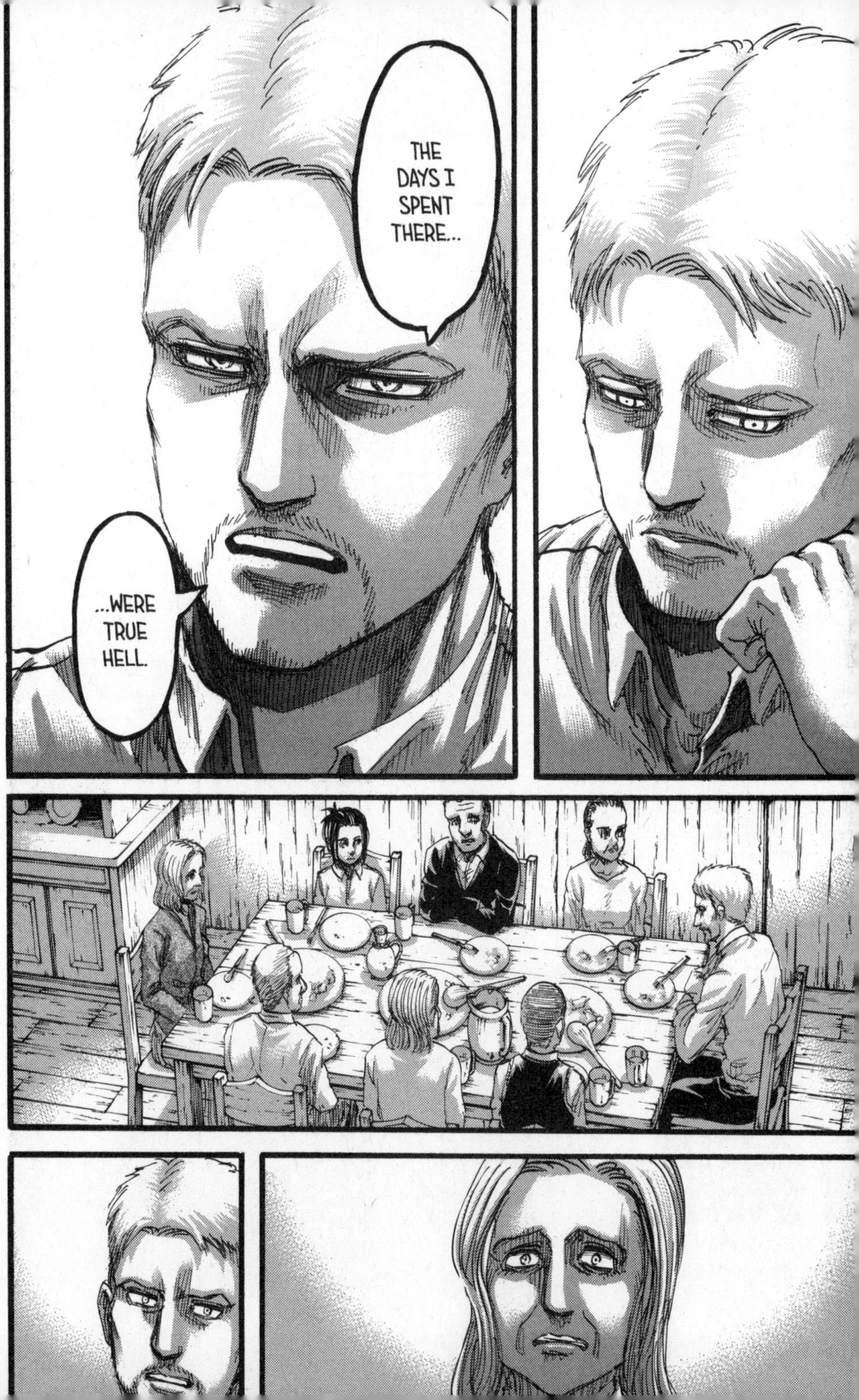
THE DAYS I SPENT THERE...
...WERE TRUE HELL.

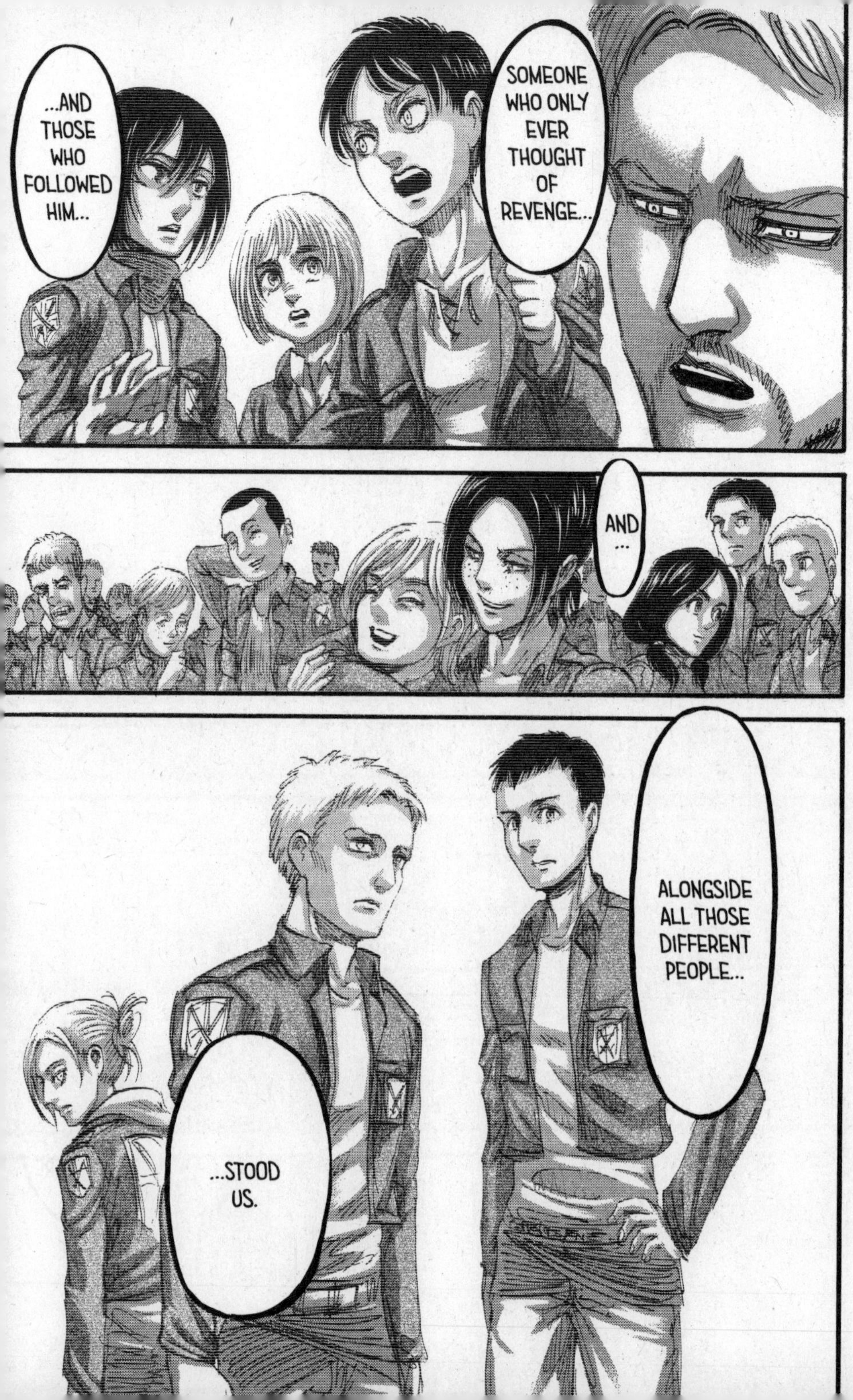
SOMEONE WHO ONLY EVER THOUGHT OF REVENGE...
...AND THOSE WHO FOLLOWED HIM...
AND ...
ALONGSIDE ALL THOSE DIFFERENT PEOPLE...
...STOOD US.

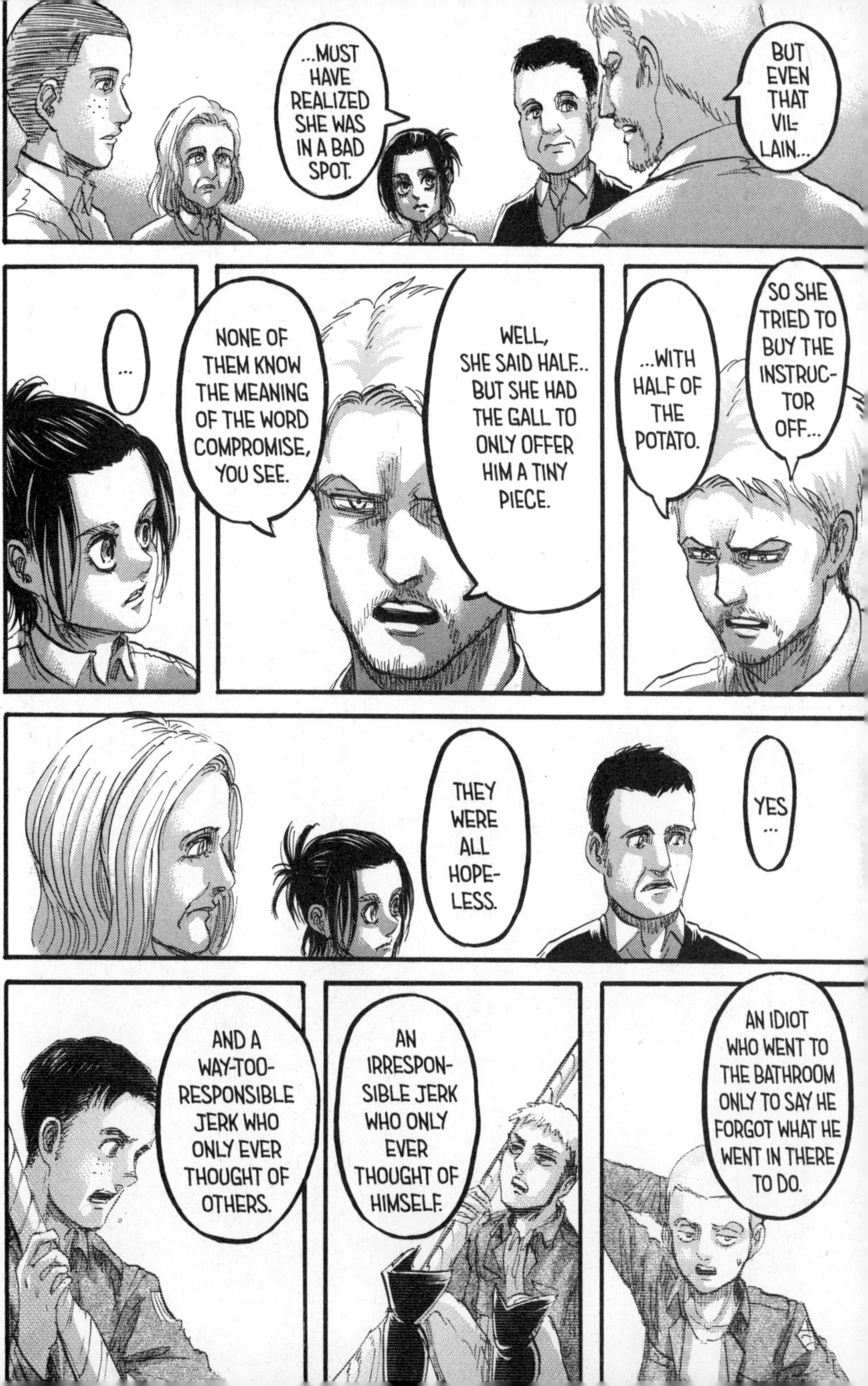
BUT EVEN THAT VILLAIN...
...MUST HAVE REALIZED SHE WAS IN A BAD SPOT.
SO SHE TRIED TO BUY THE INSTRUCTOR OFF...
...WITH HALF OF THE POTATO.
WELL, SHE SAID HALF... BUT SHE HAD THE GALL TO ONLY OFFER HIM A TINY PIECE.
NONE OF THEM KNOW THE MEANING OF THE WORD COMPROMISE, YOU SEE.
...
YES...
THEY WERE ALL HOPELESS.
AN IDIOT WHO WENT TO THE BATHROOM ONLY TO SAY HE FORGOT WHAT HE WENT IN THERE TO DO.
AN IRRESPONSIBLE JERK WHO ONLY EVER THOUGHT OF HIMSELF.
AND A WAY-TOO-RESPONSIBLE JERK WHO ONLY EVER THOUGHT OF OTHERS.

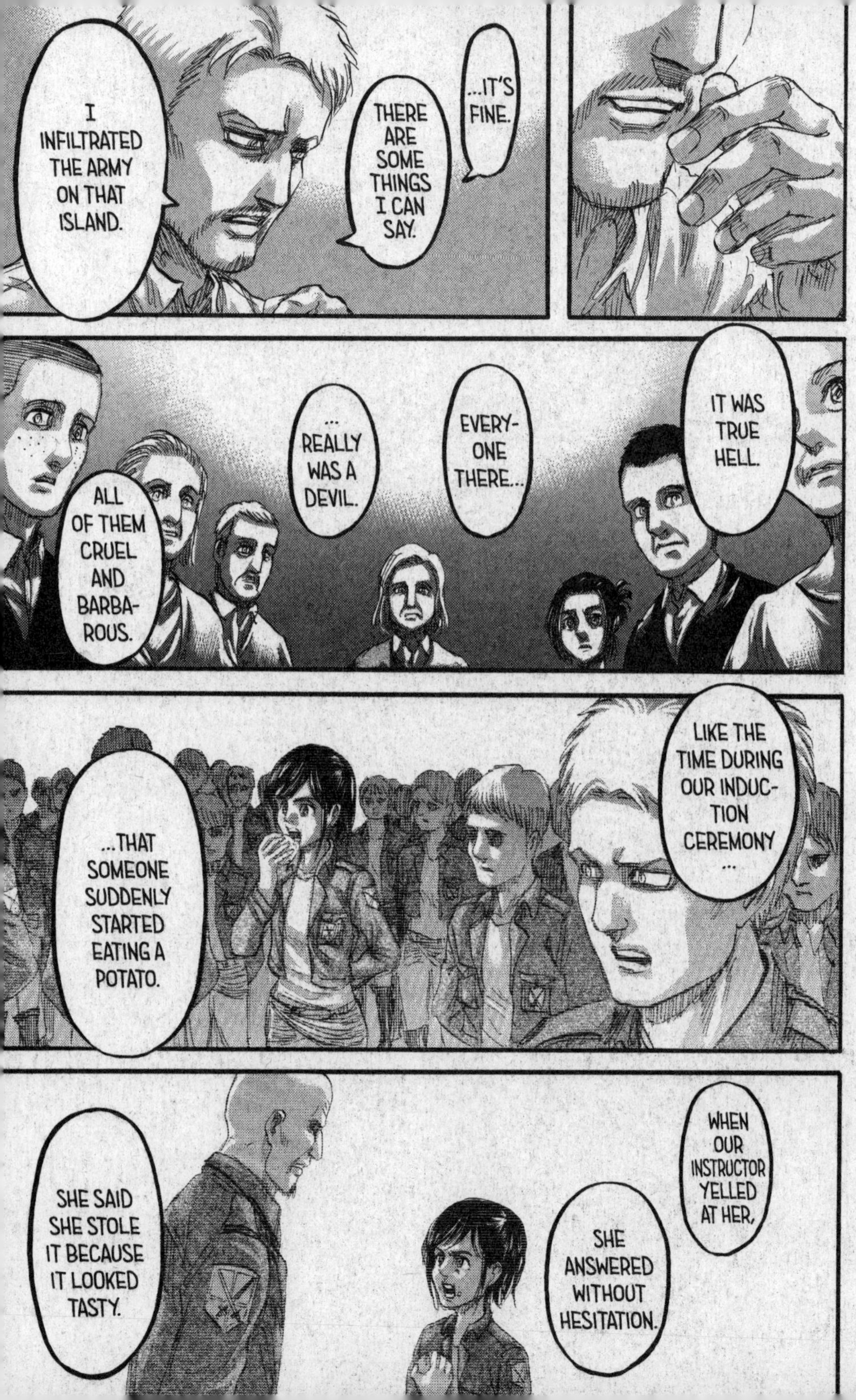
...IT'S FINE.
THERE ARE SOME THINGS I CAN SAY.
I INFILTRATED THE ARMY ON THAT ISLAND.
IT WAS TRUE HELL.
EVERYONE THERE...
... REALLY WAS A DEVIL.
ALL OF THEM CRUEL AND BARBAROUS.
LIKE THE TIME DURING OUR INDUCTION CEREMONY ...
...THAT SOMEONE SUDDENLY STARTED EATING A POTATO.
WHEN OUR INSTRUCTOR YELLED AT HER,
SHE ANSWERED WITHOUT HESITATION.
SHE SAID SHE STOLE IT BECAUSE IT LOOKED TASTY.

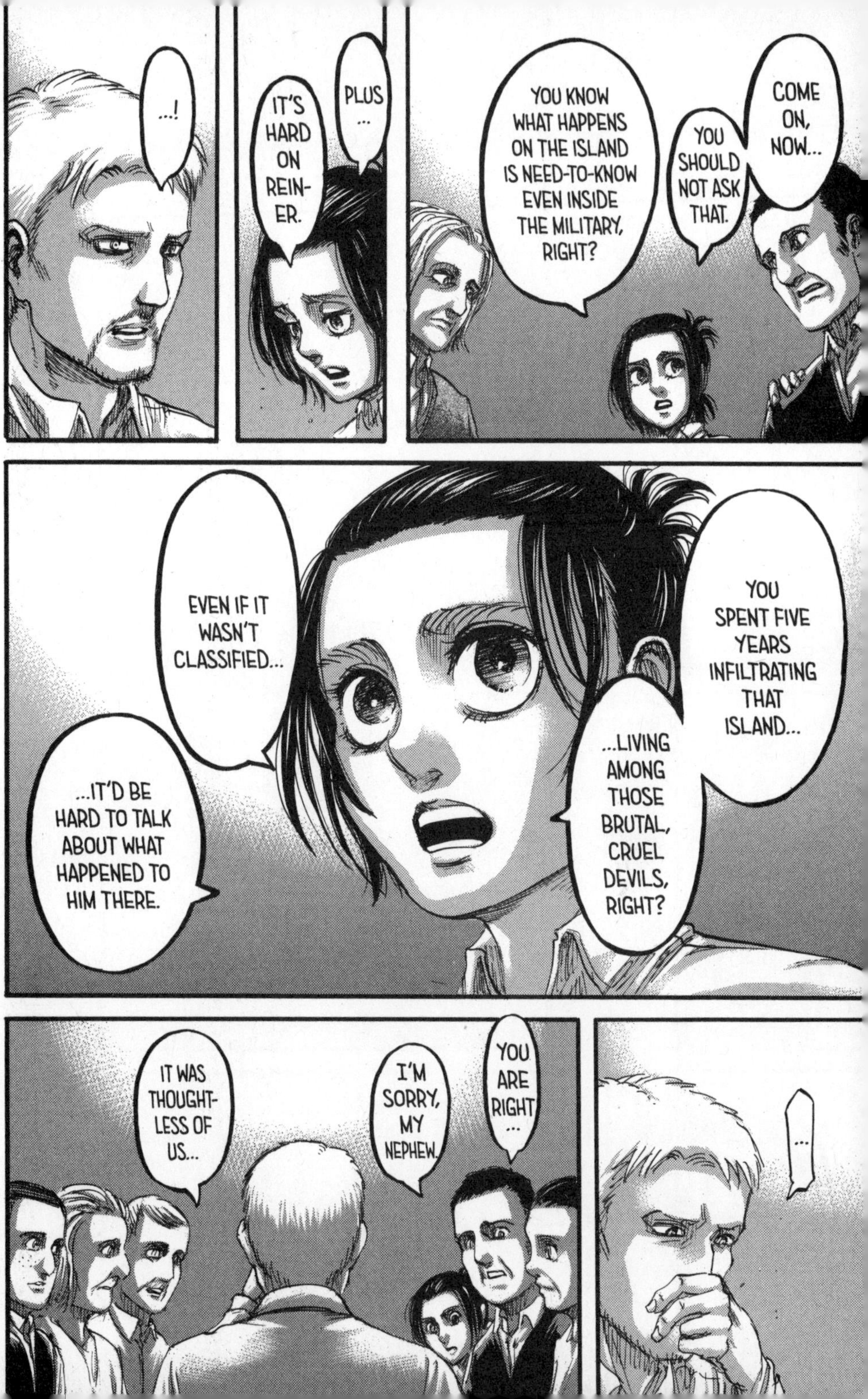
COME ON, NOW...
YOU SHOULD NOT ASK THAT.
YOU KNOW WHAT HAPPENS ON THE ISLAND IS NEED-TO-KNOW EVEN INSIDE THE MILITARY, RIGHT?
PLUS...
IT'S HARD ON REIN-ER.
...!
YOU SPENT FIVE YEARS INFILTRATING THAT ISLAND...
...LIVING AMONG THOSE BRUTAL, CRUEL DEVILS, RIGHT?
EVEN IF IT WASN'T CLASSIFIED...
...IT'D BE HARD TO TALK ABOUT WHAT HAPPENED TO HIM THERE.
...
YOU ARE RIGHT...
I'M SORRY, MY NEPHEW.
IT WAS THOUGHT-LESS OF US...

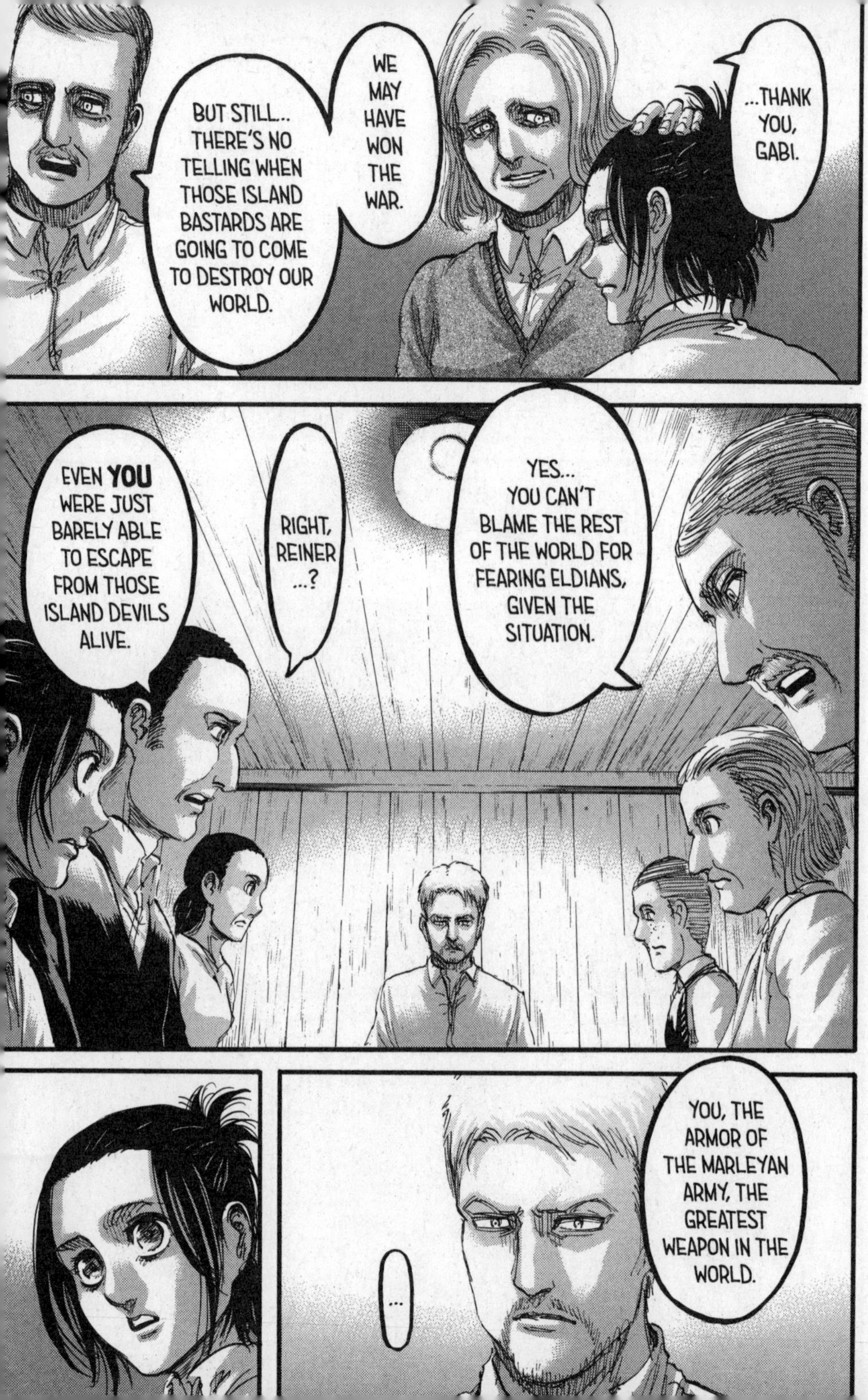
...THANK YOU, GABI.
WE MAY HAVE WON THE WAR.
BUT STILL... THERE'S NO TELLING WHEN THOSE ISLAND BASTARDS ARE GOING TO COME TO DESTROY OUR WORLD.
YES... YOU CAN'T BLAME THE REST OF THE WORLD FOR FEARING ELDIANS, GIVEN THE SITUATION.
RIGHT, REINER ...?
EVEN **YOU** WERE JUST BARELY ABLE TO ESCAPE FROM THOSE ISLAND DEVILS ALIVE.
YOU, THE ARMOR OF THE MARLEYAN ARMY, THE GREATEST WEAPON IN THE WORLD.
...

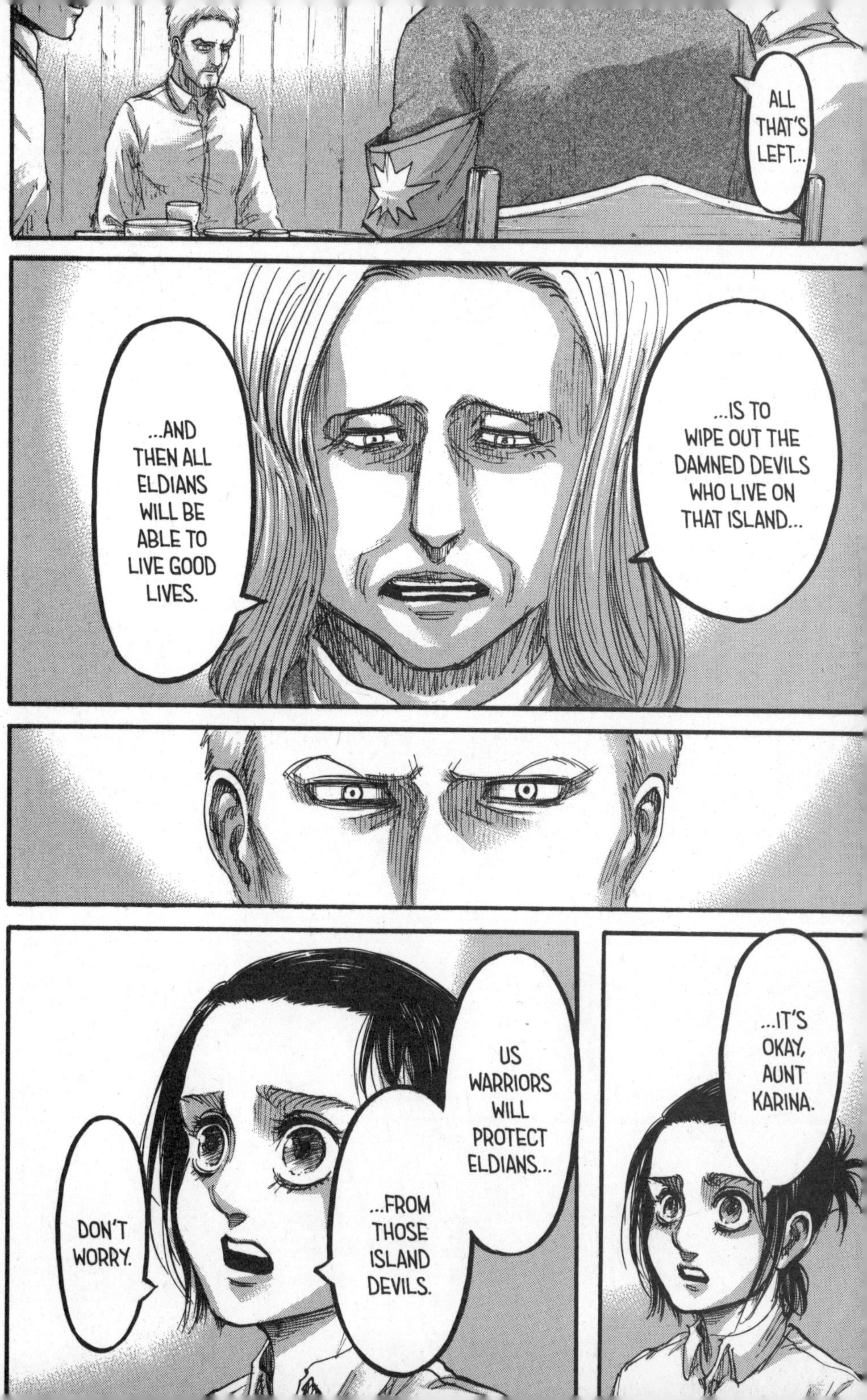
ALL THAT'S LEFT...
...IS TO WIPE OUT THE DAMNED DEVILS WHO LIVE ON THAT ISLAND...
...AND THEN ALL ELDIANS WILL BE ABLE TO LIVE GOOD LIVES.
...IT'S OKAY, AUNT KARINA.
US WARRIORS WILL PROTECT ELDIANS...
...FROM THOSE ISLAND DEVILS.
DON'T WORRY.

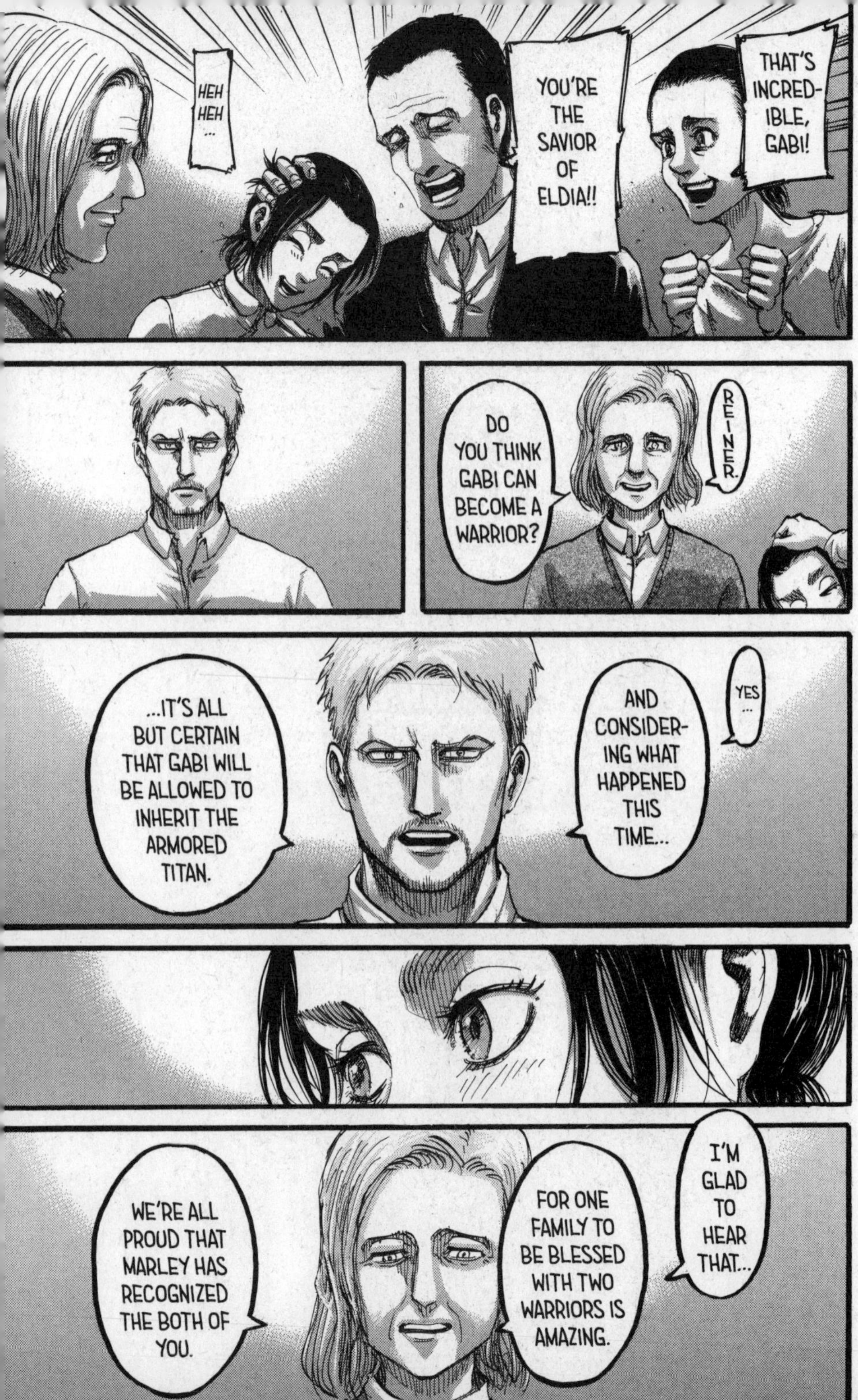
THAT'S INCRED-IBLE, GABI!
YOU'RE THE SAVIOR OF ELDIA!!
HEH HEH ...
REINER.
DO YOU THINK GABI CAN BECOME A WARRIOR?
YES ...
AND CONSIDER-ING WHAT HAPPENED THIS TIME...
...IT'S ALL BUT CERTAIN THAT GABI WILL BE ALLOWED TO INHERIT THE ARMORED TITAN.
I'M GLAD TO HEAR THAT...
FOR ONE FAMILY TO BE BLESSED WITH TWO WARRIORS IS AMAZING.
WE'RE ALL PROUD THAT MARLEY HAS RECOGNIZED THE BOTH OF YOU.

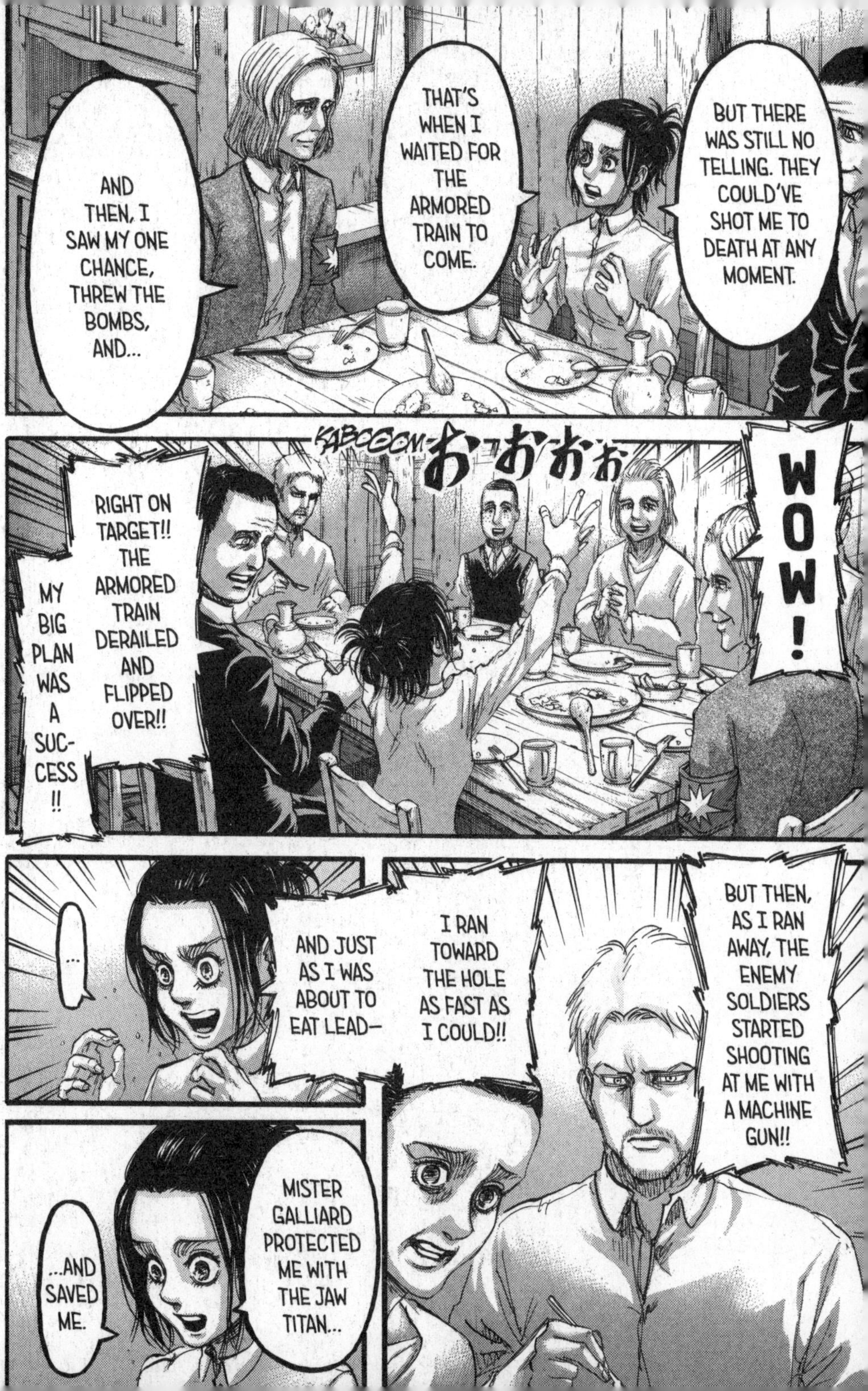
BUT THERE WAS STILL NO TELLING. THEY COULD'VE SHOT ME TO DEATH AT ANY MOMENT.
THAT'S WHEN I WAITED FOR THE ARMORED TRAIN TO COME.
AND THEN, I SAW MY ONE CHANCE, THREW THE BOMBS, AND...
WOW!
KABOOOM- おおおぉ
RIGHT ON TARGET!! THE ARMORED TRAIN DERAILED AND FLIPPED OVER!!
MY BIG PLAN WAS A SUC-CESS!!
BUT THEN, AS I RAN AWAY, THE ENEMY SOLDIERS STARTED SHOOTING AT ME WITH A MACHINE GUN!!
I RAN TOWARD THE HOLE AS FAST AS I COULD!!
AND JUST AS I WAS ABOUT TO EAT LEAD—
...
MISTER GALLIARD PROTECTED ME WITH THE JAW TITAN...
...AND SAVED ME.

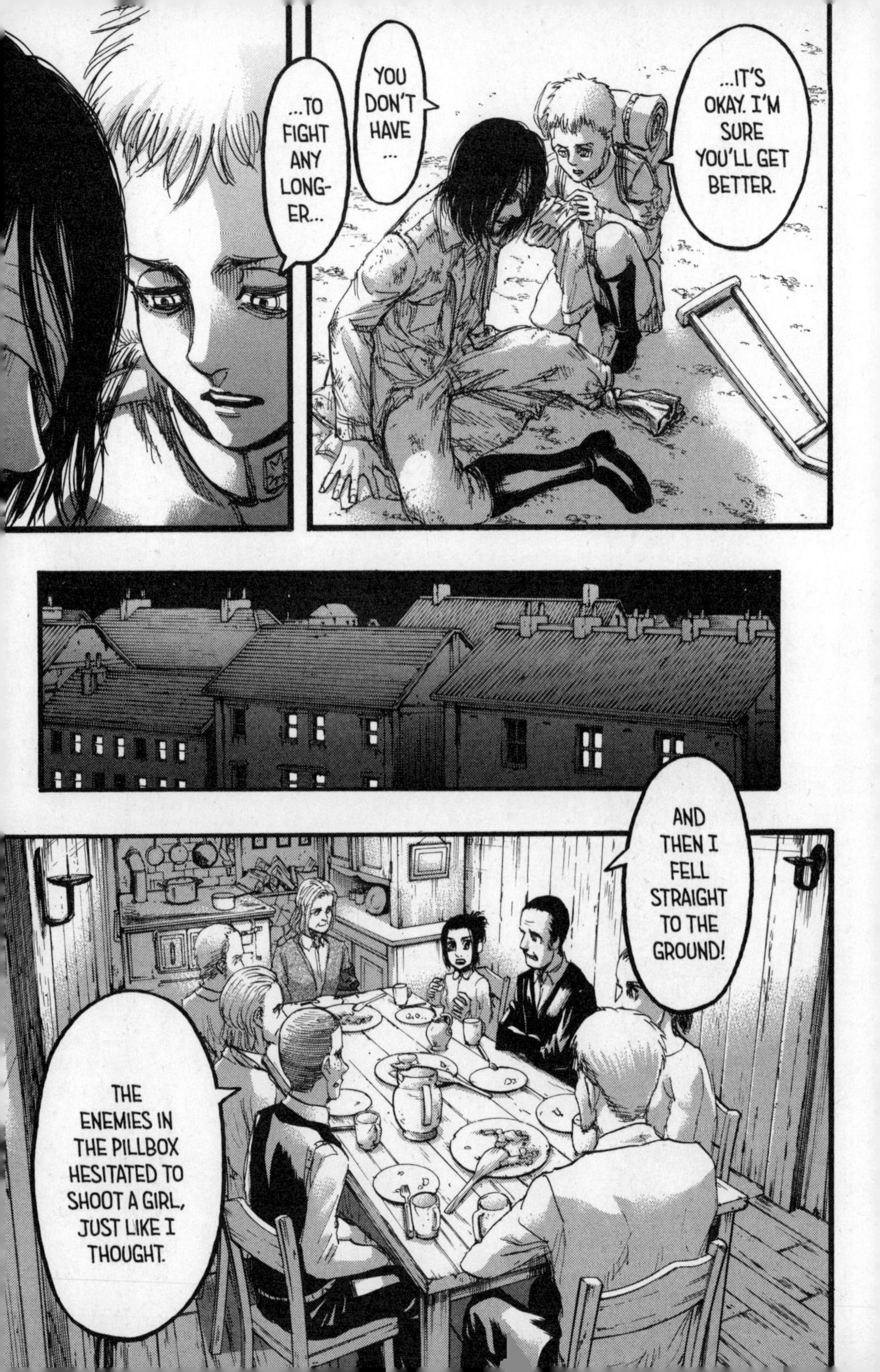

...IT'S OKAY. I'M SURE YOU'LL GET BETTER.
YOU DON'T HAVE ...
...TO FIGHT ANY LONG-ER...
AND THEN I FELL STRAIGHT TO THE GROUND!
THE ENEMIES IN THE PILLBOX HESITATED TO SHOOT A GIRL, JUST LIKE I THOUGHT.

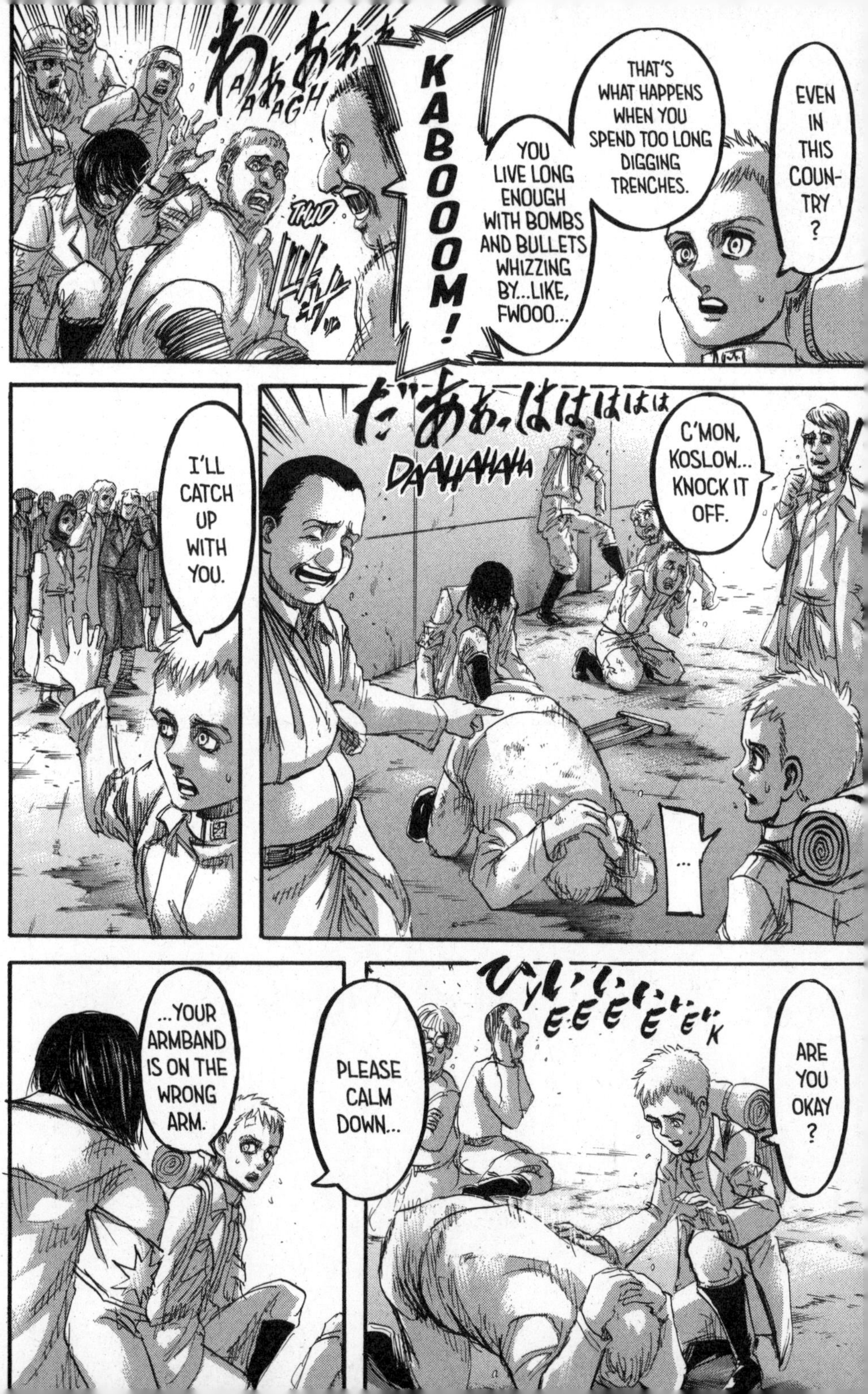
EVEN IN THIS COUNTRY?
THAT'S WHAT HAPPENS WHEN YOU SPEND TOO LONG DIGGING TRENCHES.
YOU LIVE LONG ENOUGH WITH BOMBS AND BULLETS WHIZZING BY...LIKE, FWOOO...
KABOOOOM!
わぁあぁぁ
AAAGH
THUD
C'MON, KOSLOW... KNOCK IT OFF.
だぁあっはははははは
DAAHAHAHA
...
I'LL CATCH UP WITH YOU.
ARE YOU OKAY?
ひぃいいいい
EEEEEEK
PLEASE CALM DOWN...
...YOUR ARMBAND IS ON THE WRONG ARM.

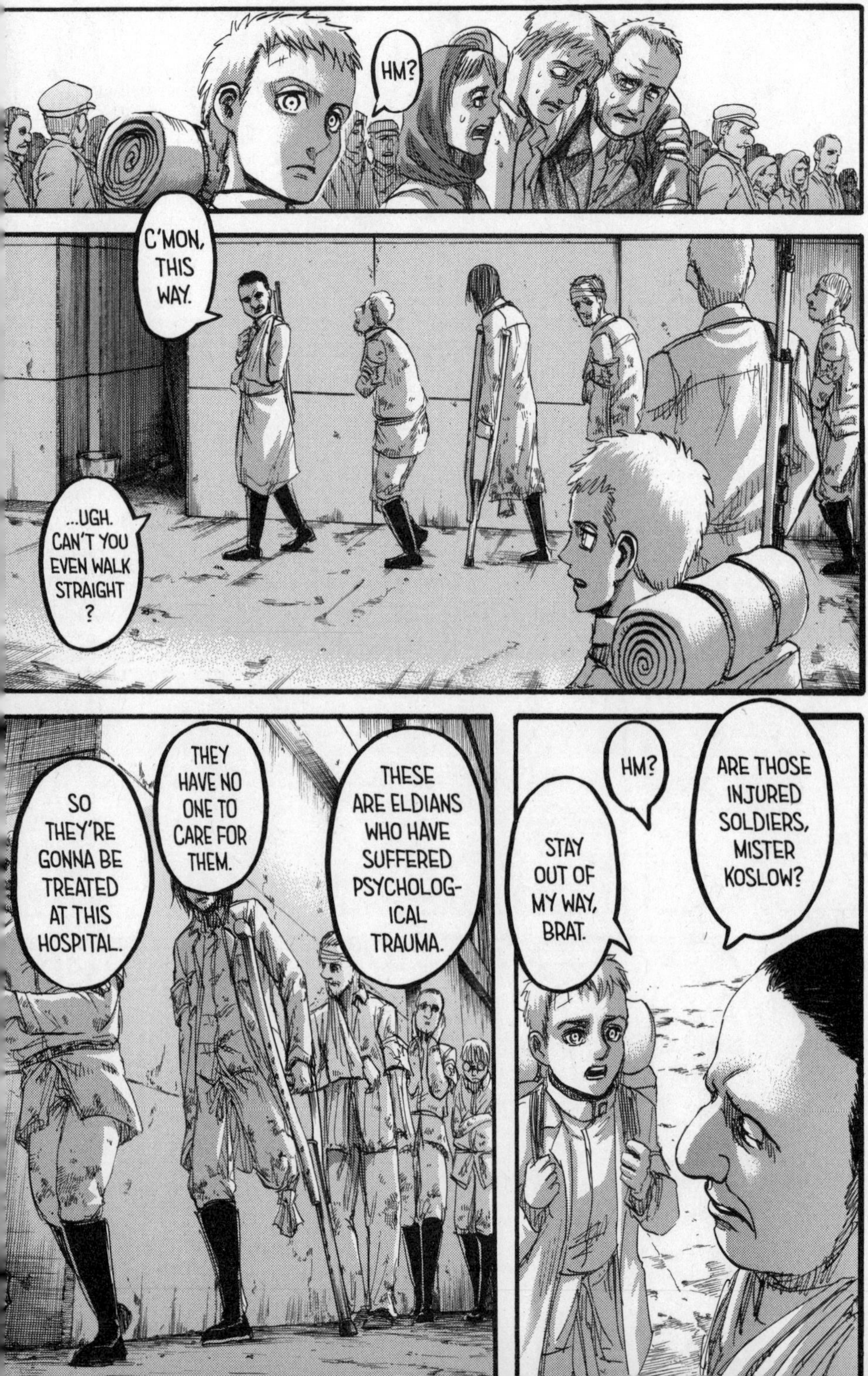
HM?
C'MON, THIS WAY.
...UGH. CAN'T YOU EVEN WALK STRAIGHT?
ARE THOSE INJURED SOLDIERS, MISTER KOSLOW?
HM?
STAY OUT OF MY WAY, BRAT.
THESE ARE ELDIANS WHO HAVE SUFFERED PSYCHOLOG-ICAL TRAUMA.
THEY HAVE NO ONE TO CARE FOR THEM.
SO THEY'RE GONNA BE TREATED AT THIS HOSPITAL.

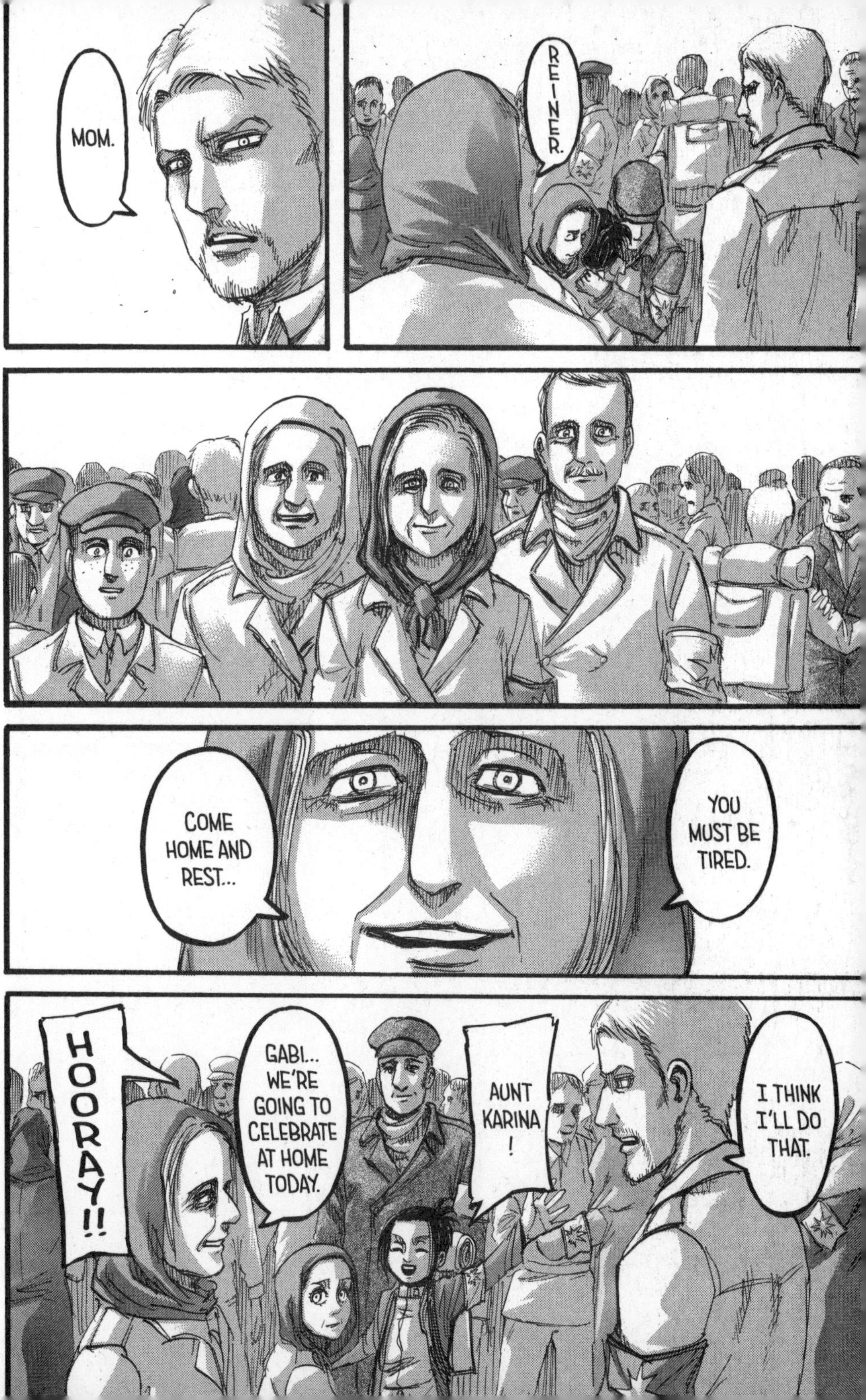
REINER.
MOM.
YOU MUST BE TIRED.
COME HOME AND REST...
I THINK I'LL DO THAT.
AUNT KARINA!
GABI... WE'RE GOING TO CELEBRATE AT HOME TODAY.
HOORAY!!

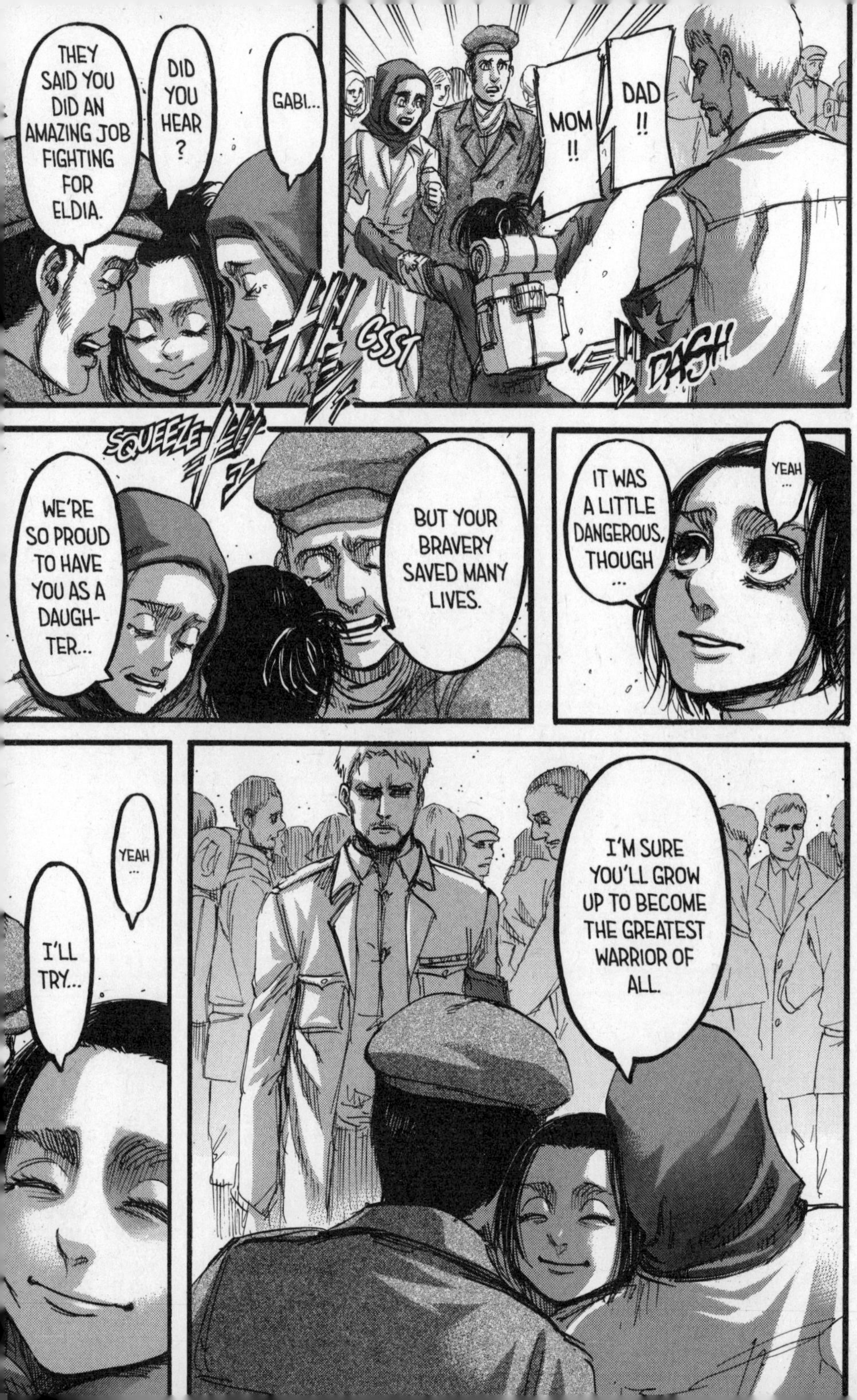
DAD !!
MOM !!
DASH
GSST
GABI...
DID YOU HEAR ?
THEY SAID YOU DID AN AMAZING JOB FIGHTING FOR ELDIA.
YEAH ...
IT WAS A LITTLE DANGEROUS, THOUGH ...
SQUEEZE
BUT YOUR BRAVERY SAVED MANY LIVES.
WE'RE SO PROUD TO HAVE YOU AS A DAUGH-TER...
I'M SURE YOU'LL GROW UP TO BECOME THE GREATEST WARRIOR OF ALL.
YEAH ...
I'LL TRY...

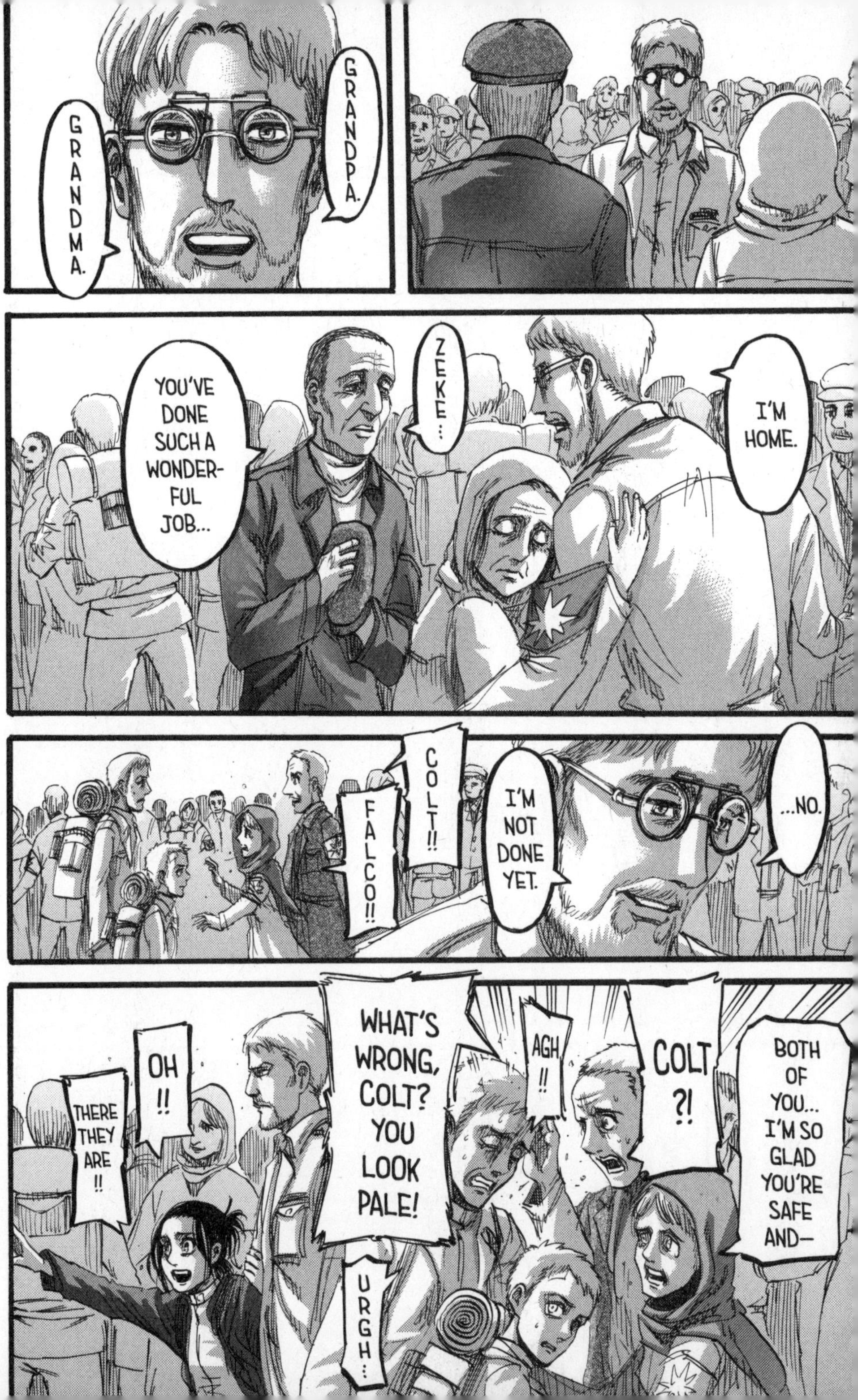
GRANDPA.
GRANDMA.
I'M HOME.
ZEKE...
YOU'VE DONE SUCH A WONDERFUL JOB...
...NO.
I'M NOT DONE YET.
COLT!!
FALCO!!
BOTH OF YOU... I'M SO GLAD YOU'RE SAFE AND—
COLT ?!
AGH !!
WHAT'S WRONG, COLT? YOU LOOK PALE!
URGH...
OH !!
THERE THEY ARE !!

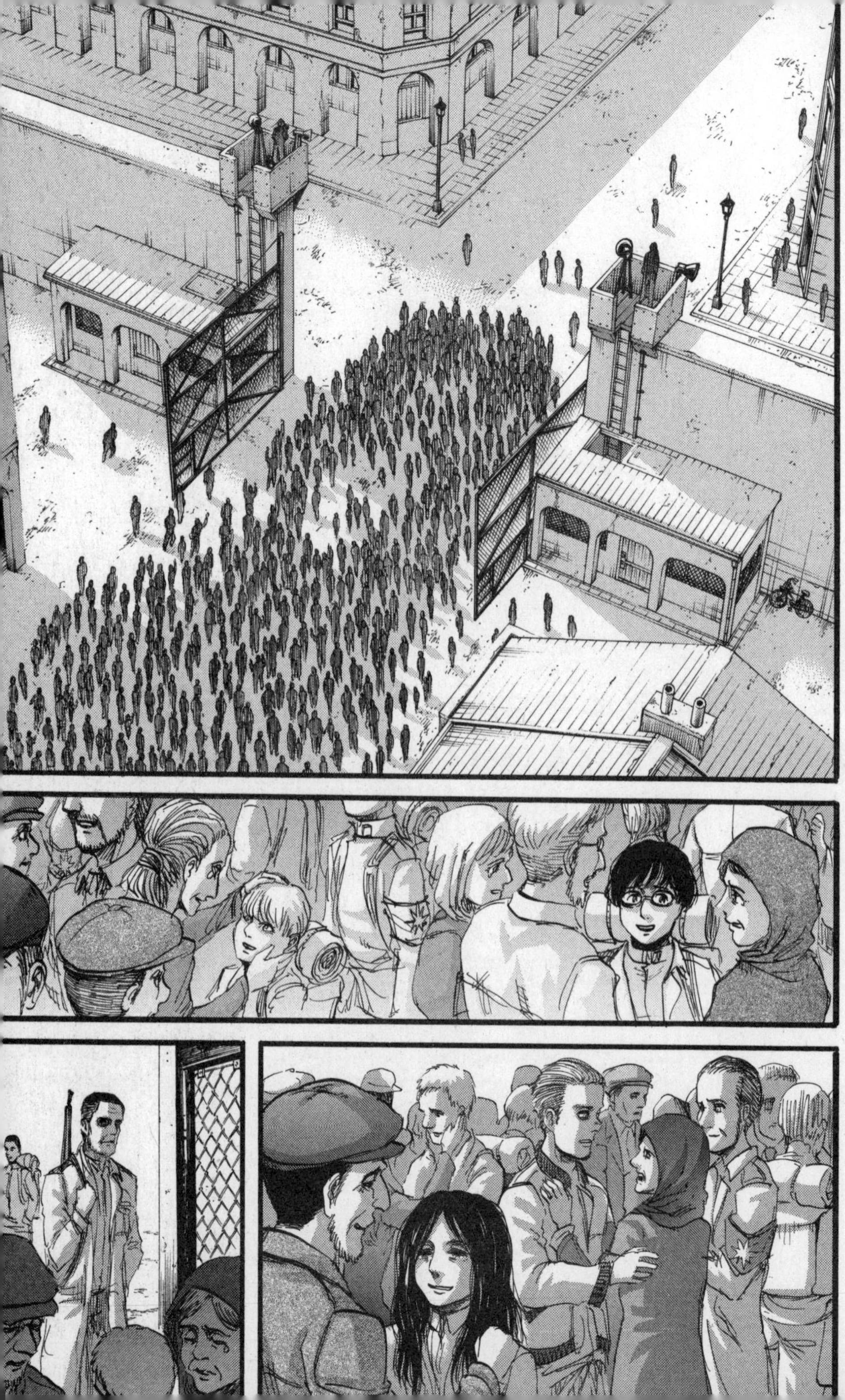

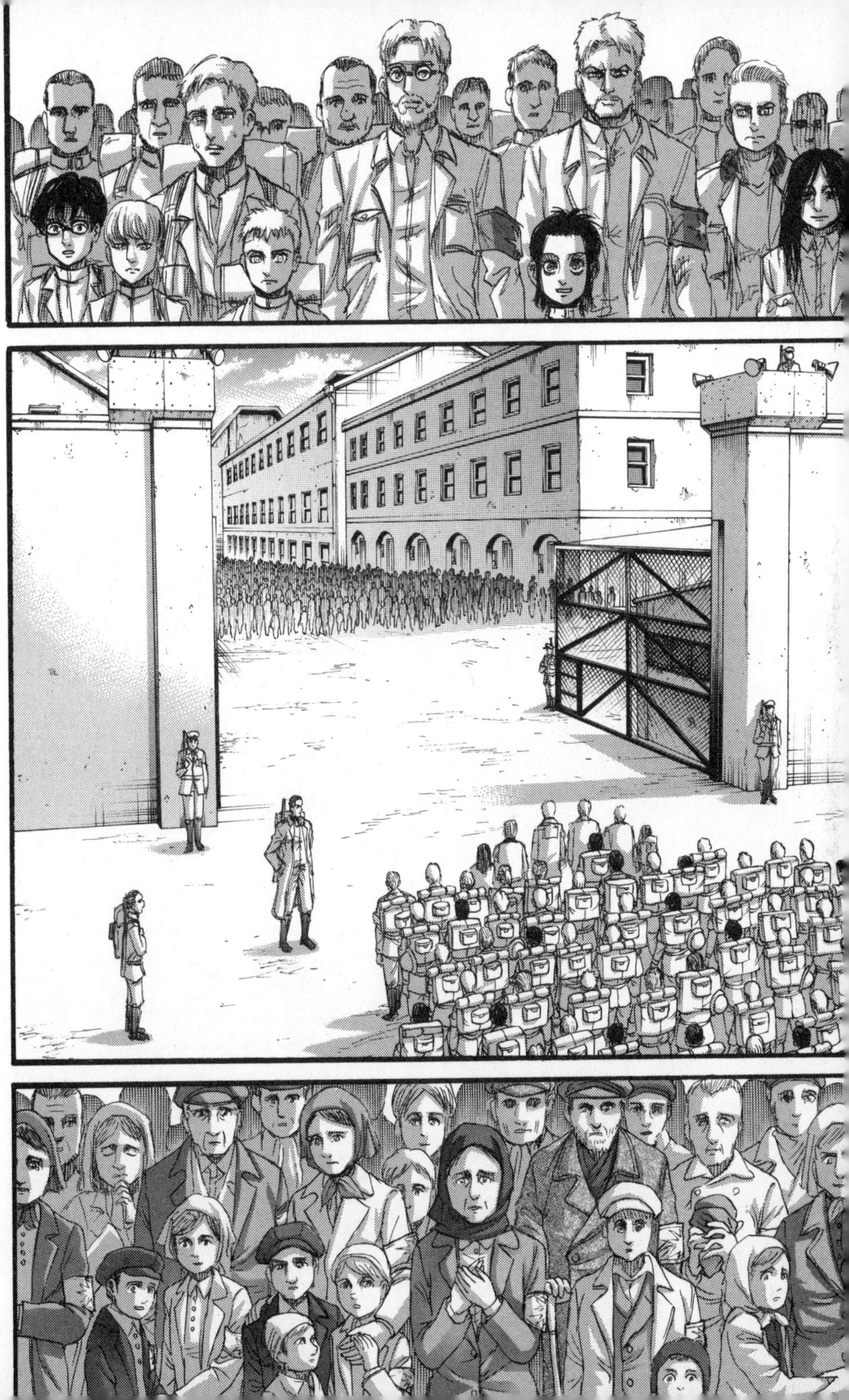

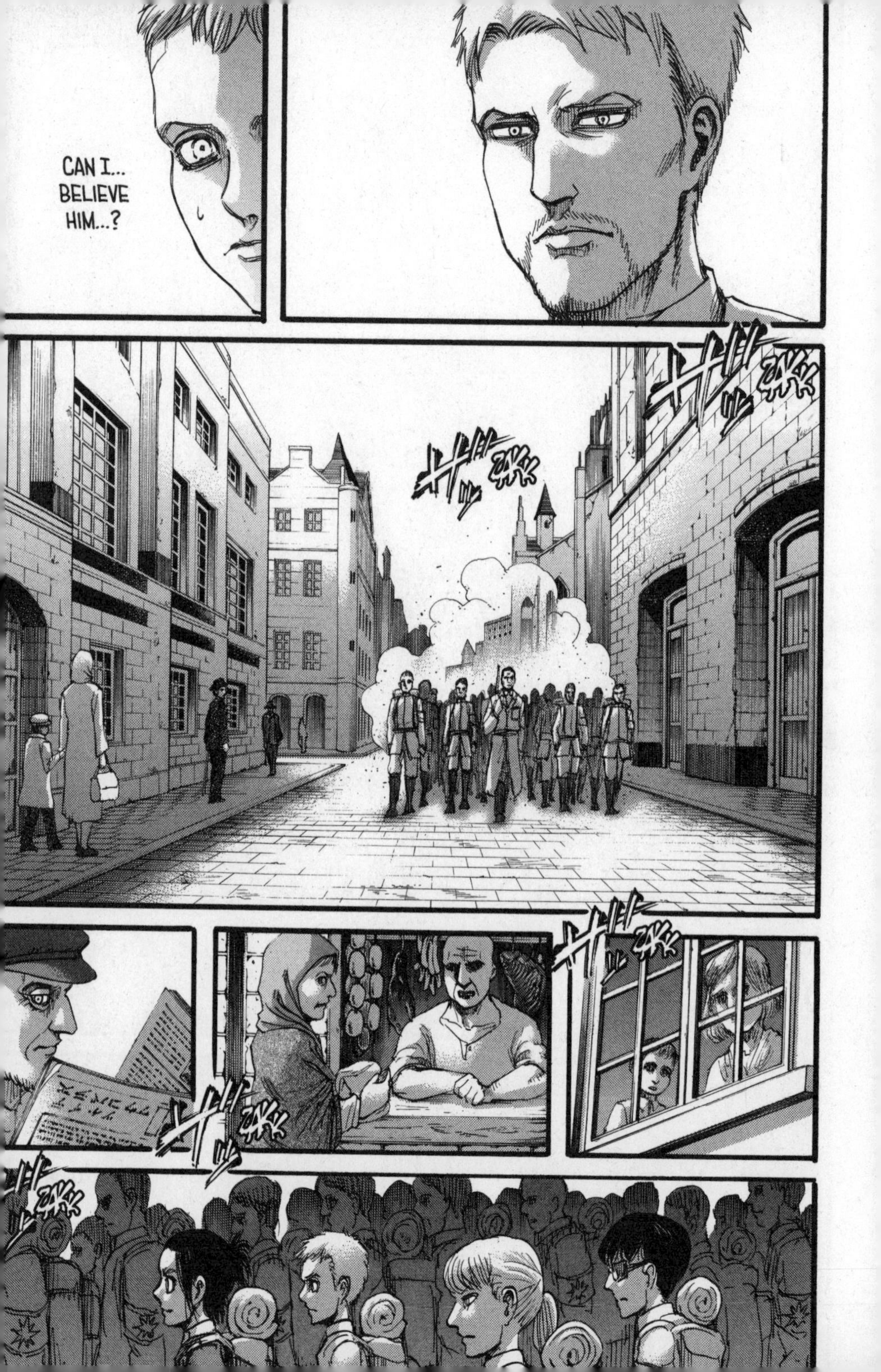
CAN I... BELIEVE HIM...?
STOMP ZAK
STOMP ZAK
STOMP ZAK
STOMP ZAK
STOMP ZAK

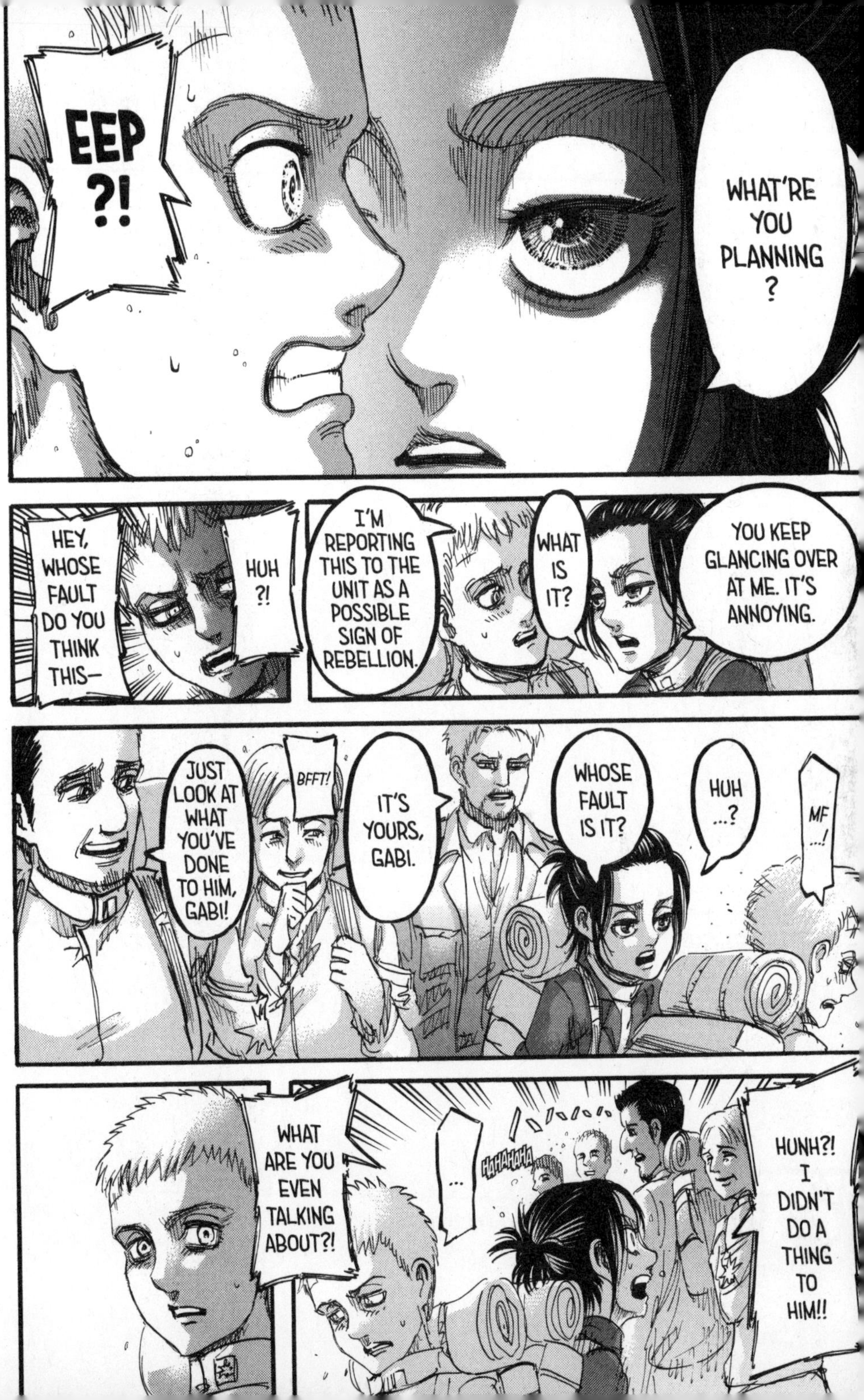
WHAT'RE YOU PLANNING?
EEP?!
YOU KEEP GLANCING OVER AT ME. IT'S ANNOYING.
WHAT IS IT?
I'M REPORTING THIS TO THE UNIT AS A POSSIBLE SIGN OF REBELLION.
HUH?!
HEY, WHOSE FAULT DO YOU THINK THIS—
MF...!
HUH...?
WHOSE FAULT IS IT?
IT'S YOURS, GABI.
BFFT!
JUST LOOK AT WHAT YOU'VE DONE TO HIM, GABI!
HUNH?! I DIDN'T DO A THING TO HIM!!
HAHAHAHA
...
WHAT ARE YOU EVEN TALKING ABOUT?!

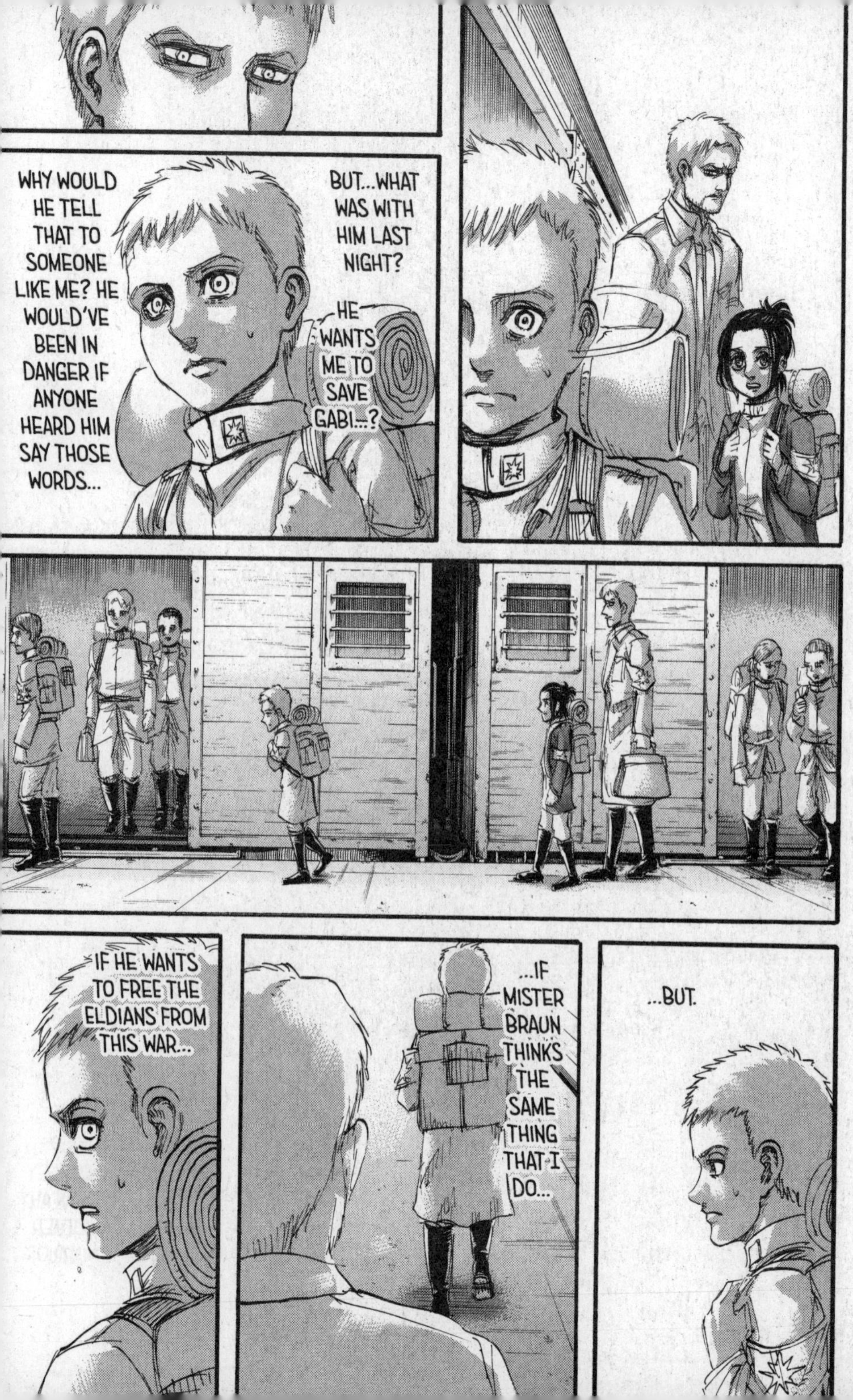
BUT...WHAT WAS WITH HIM LAST NIGHT?
WHY WOULD HE TELL THAT TO SOMEONE LIKE ME? HE WOULD'VE BEEN IN DANGER IF ANYONE HEARD HIM SAY THOSE WORDS...
HE WANTS ME TO SAVE GABI...?
...BUT.
...IF MISTER BRAUN THINKS THE SAME THING THAT I DO...
IF HE WANTS TO FREE THE ELDIANS FROM THIS WAR...

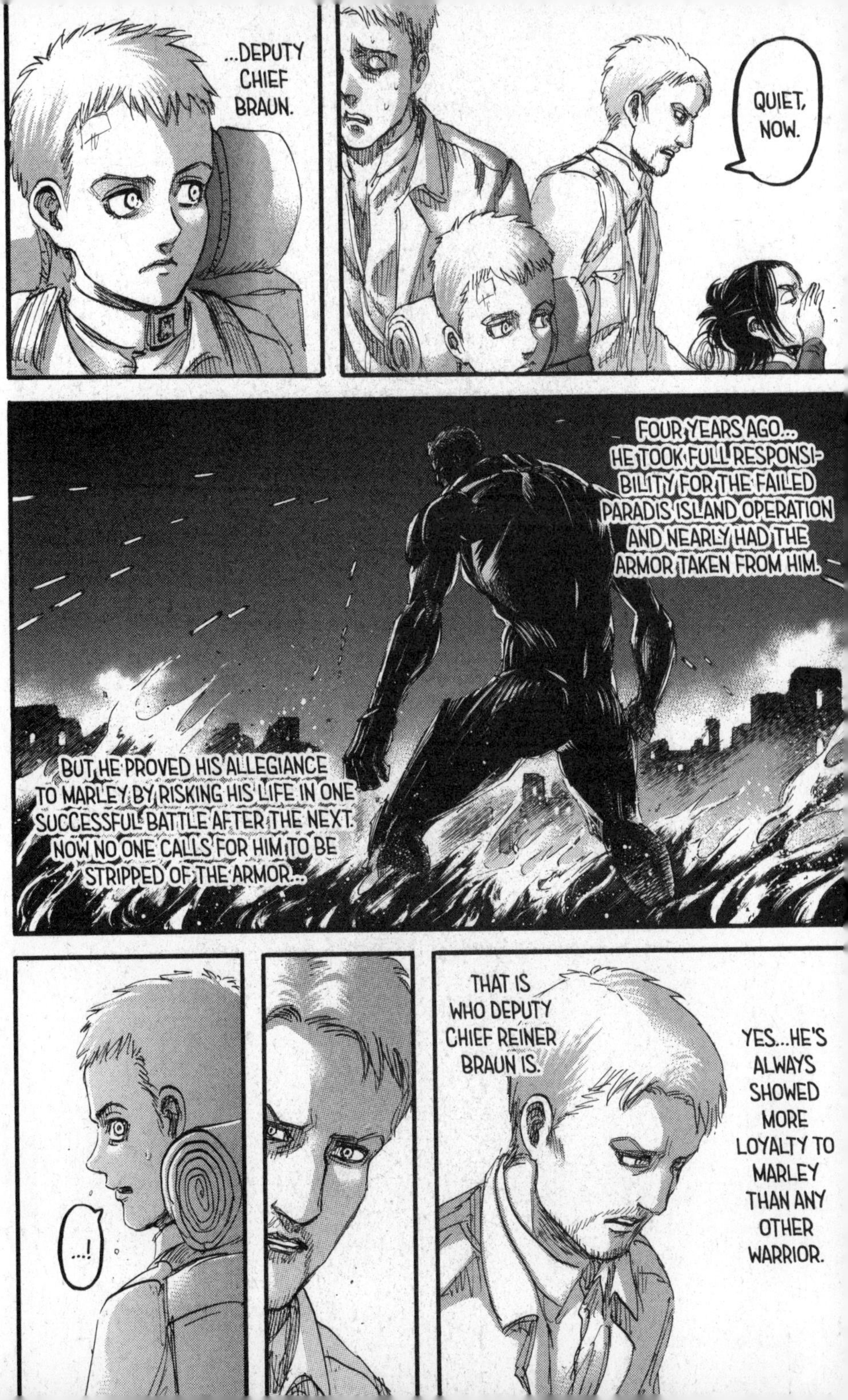
QUIET, NOW.
...DEPUTY CHIEF BRAUN.
FOUR YEARS AGO... HE TOOK FULL RESPONSIBILITY FOR THE FAILED PARADIS ISLAND OPERATION AND NEARLY HAD THE ARMOR TAKEN FROM HIM.
BUT HE PROVED HIS ALLEGIANCE TO MARLEY BY RISKING HIS LIFE IN ONE SUCCESSFUL BATTLE AFTER THE NEXT. NOW NO ONE CALLS FOR HIM TO BE STRIPPED OF THE ARMOR...
YES...HE'S ALWAYS SHOWED MORE LOYALTY TO MARLEY THAN ANY OTHER WARRIOR.
THAT IS WHO DEPUTY CHIEF REINER BRAUN IS.
...!

Episode 94: The Boy Inside the Walls

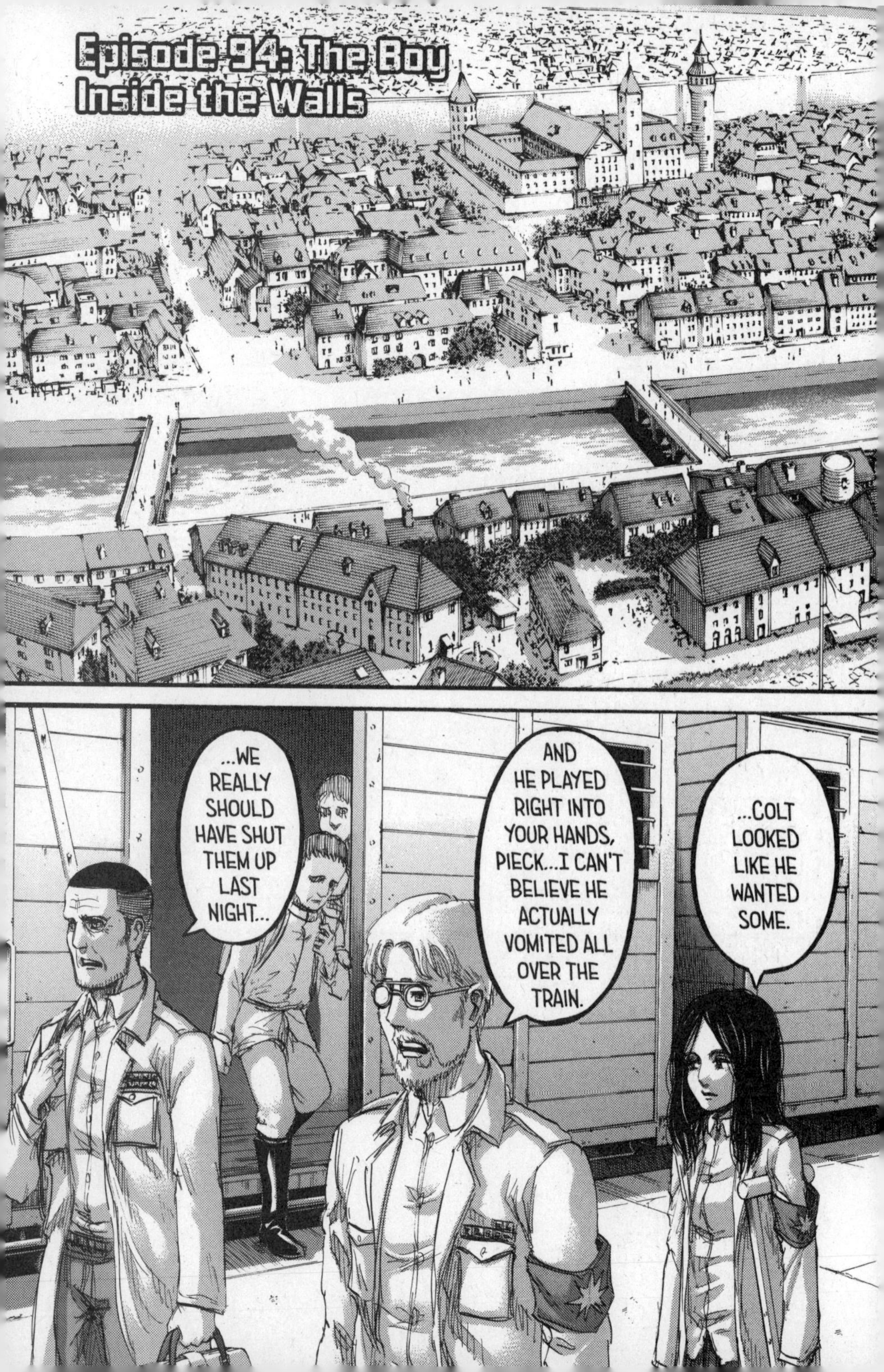
...COLT LOOKED LIKE HE WANTED SOME.
AND HE PLAYED RIGHT INTO YOUR HANDS, PIECK...I CAN'T BELIEVE HE ACTUALLY VOMITED ALL OVER THE TRAIN.
...WE REALLY SHOULD HAVE SHUT THEM UP LAST NIGHT...

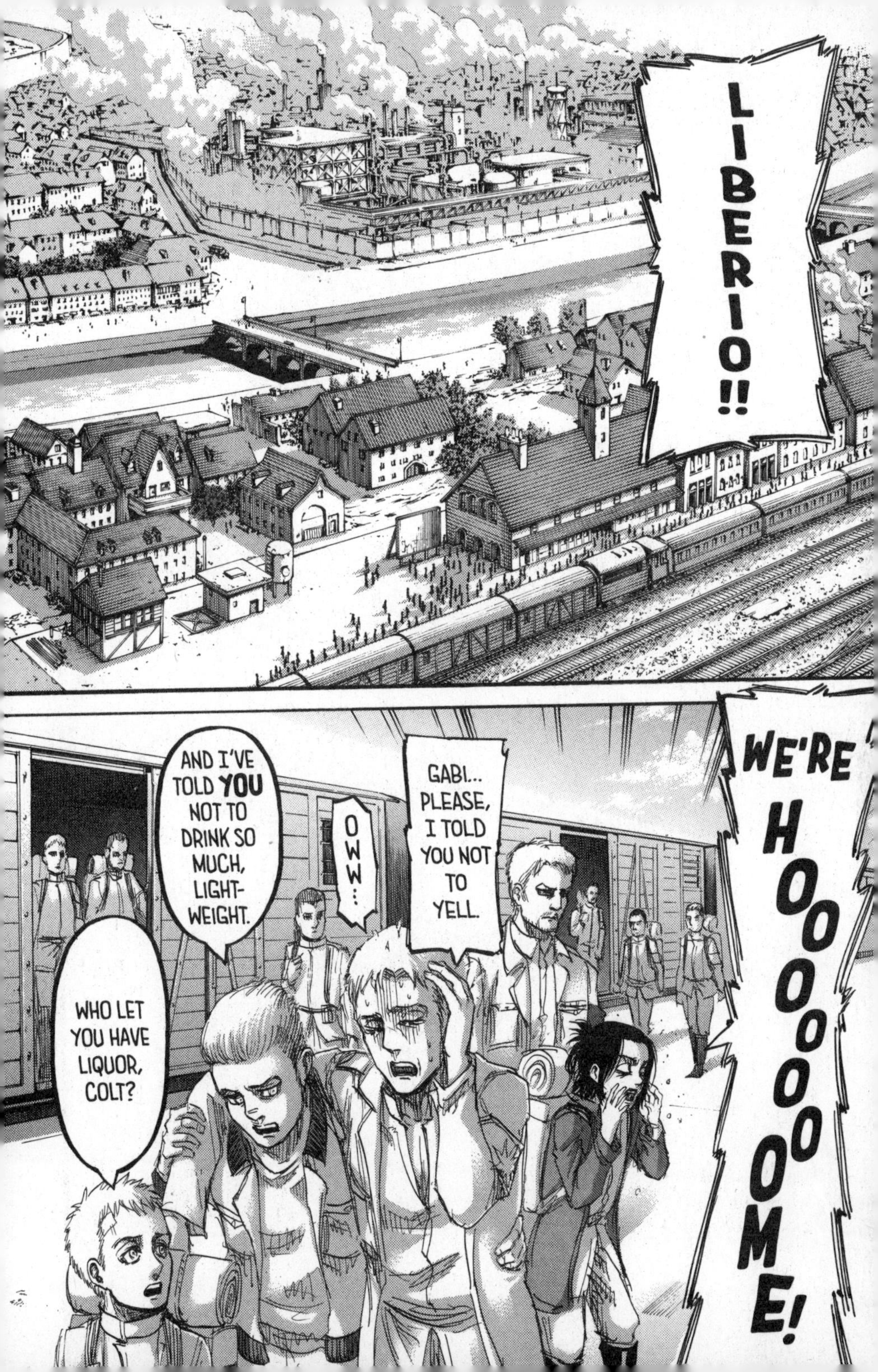
LIBERIO!!
WE'RE HOOOOOOOOME!
GABI... PLEASE, I TOLD YOU NOT TO YELL.
OWW...
AND I'VE TOLD YOU NOT TO DRINK SO MUCH, LIGHTWEIGHT.
WHO LET YOU HAVE LIQUOR, COLT?

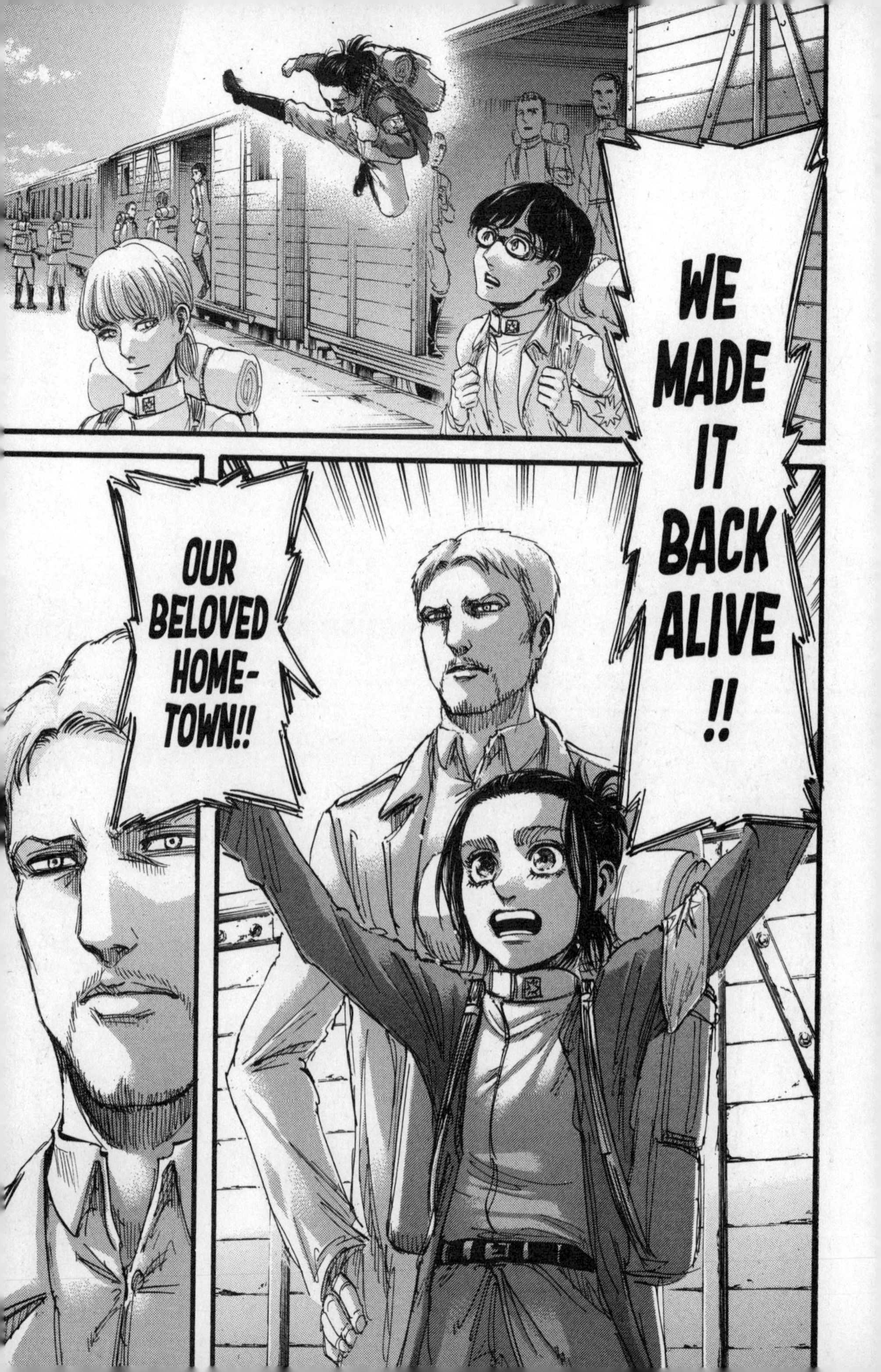
WE MADE IT BACK ALIVE!!
OUR BELOVED HOME-TOWN!!

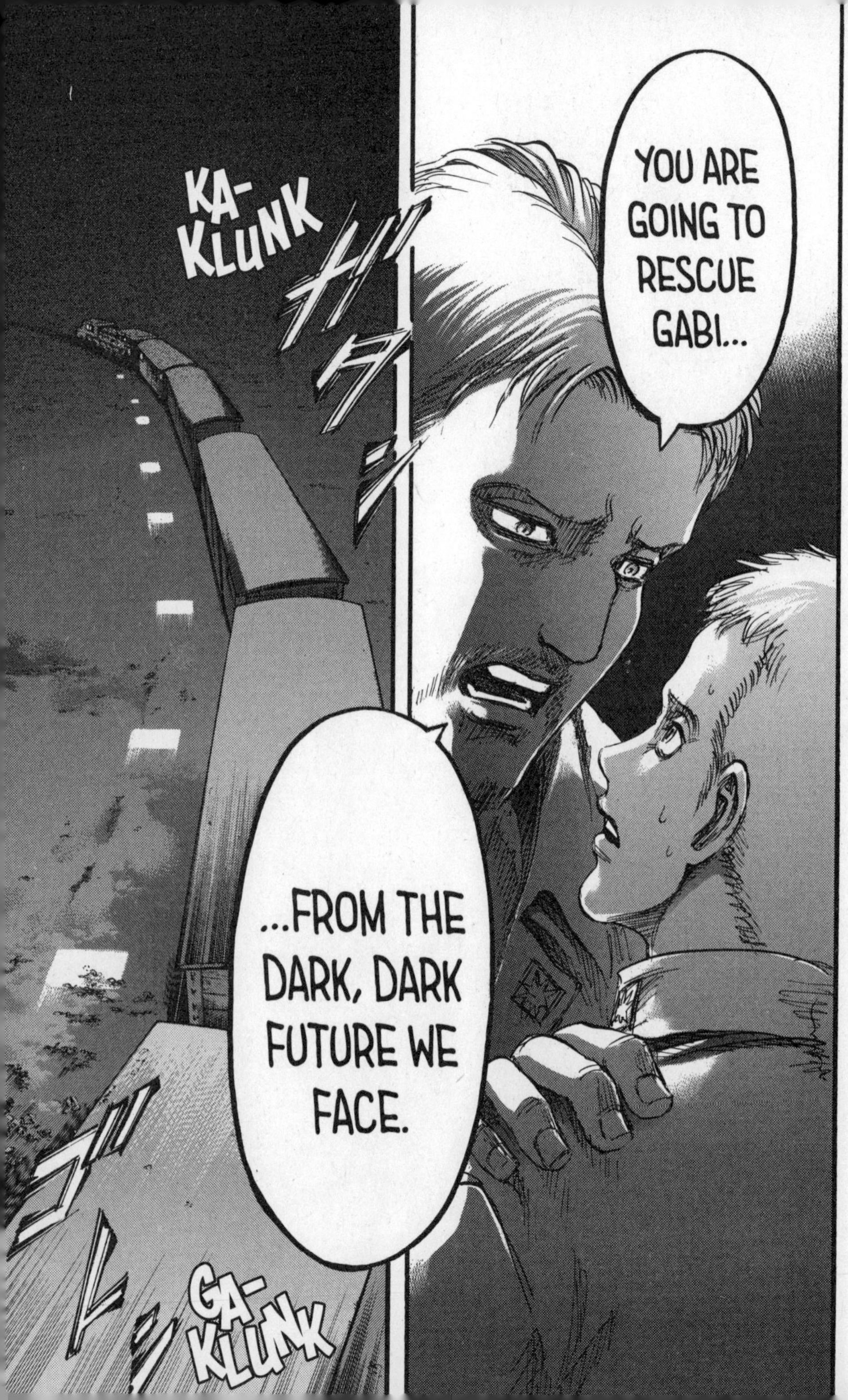
YOU ARE GOING TO RESCUE GABI...
KA-KLUNK
...FROM THE DARK, DARK FUTURE WE FACE.
GA-KLUNK

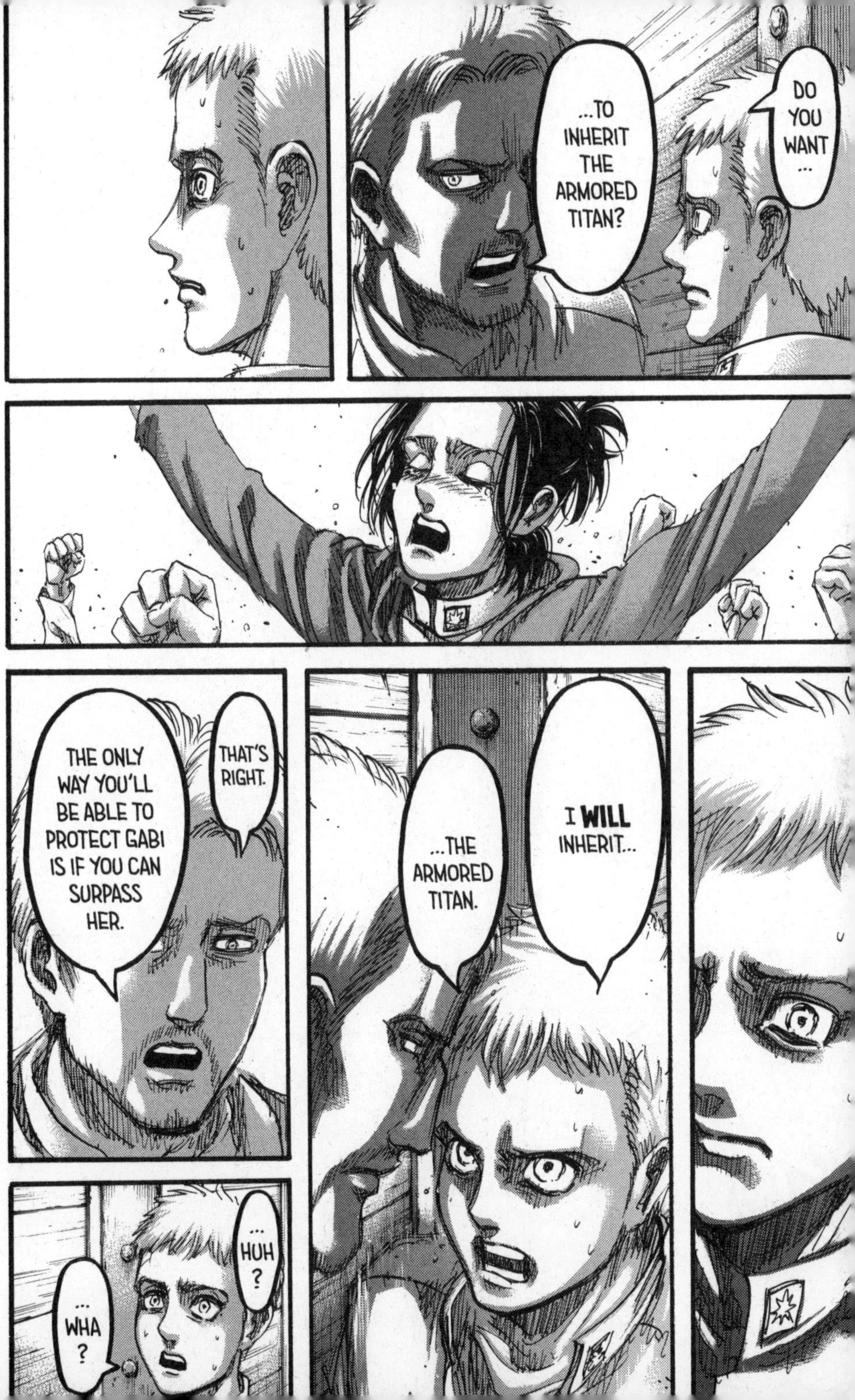
DO YOU WANT...
...TO INHERIT THE ARMORED TITAN?
I **WILL** INHERIT...
...THE ARMORED TITAN.
THAT'S RIGHT.
THE ONLY WAY YOU'LL BE ABLE TO PROTECT GABI IS IF YOU CAN SURPASS HER.
...HUH?
...WHA?

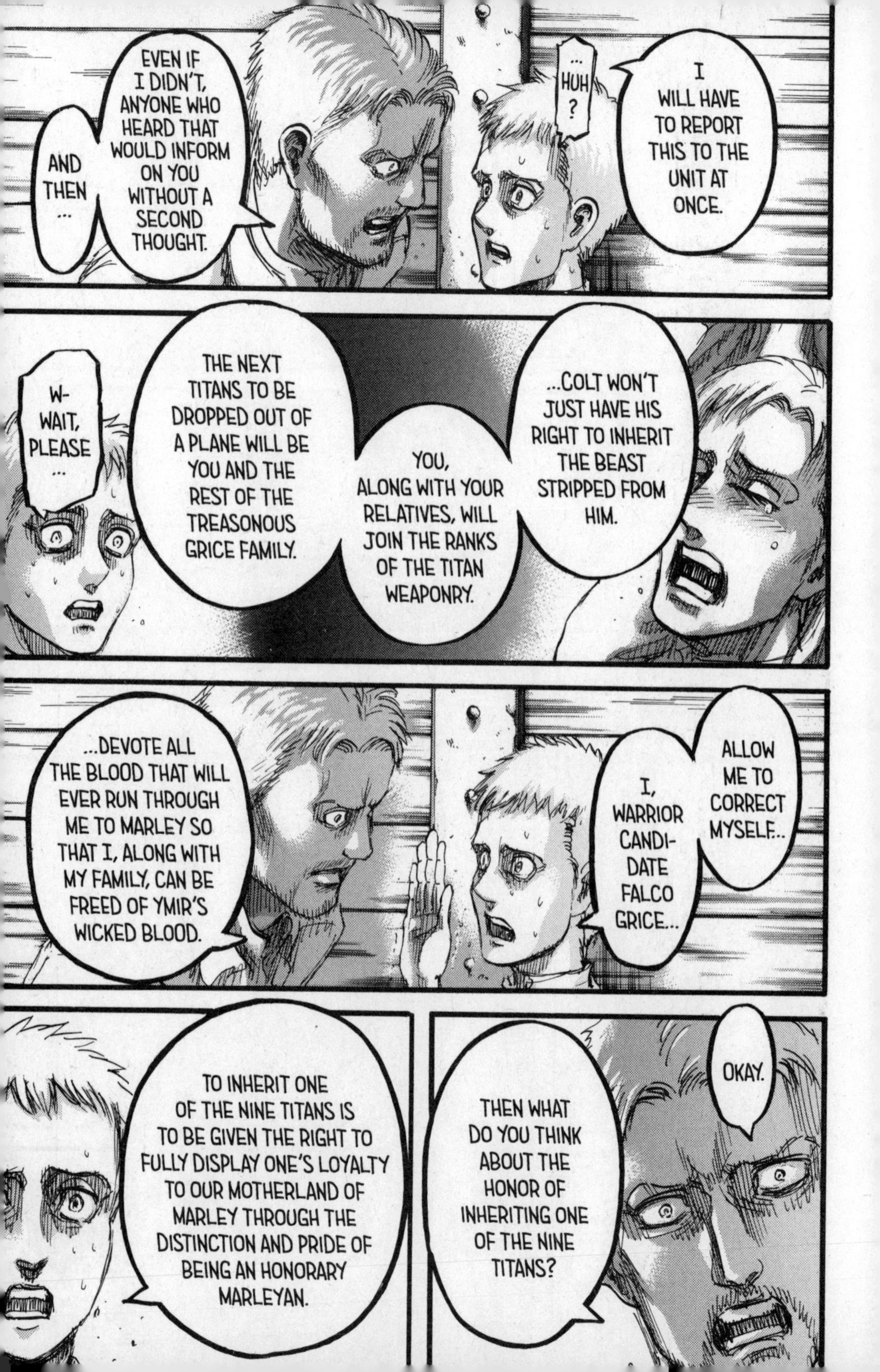
I WILL HAVE TO REPORT THIS TO THE UNIT AT ONCE.
...HUH?
EVEN IF I DIDN'T, ANYONE WHO HEARD THAT WOULD INFORM ON YOU WITHOUT A SECOND THOUGHT.
AND THEN...
...COLT WON'T JUST HAVE HIS RIGHT TO INHERIT THE BEAST STRIPPED FROM HIM.
YOU, ALONG WITH YOUR RELATIVES, WILL JOIN THE RANKS OF THE TITAN WEAPONRY.
THE NEXT TITANS TO BE DROPPED OUT OF A PLANE WILL BE YOU AND THE REST OF THE TREASONOUS GRICE FAMILY.
W-WAIT, PLEASE...
ALLOW ME TO CORRECT MYSELF...
I, WARRIOR CANDIDATE FALCO GRICE...
...DEVOTE ALL THE BLOOD THAT WILL EVER RUN THROUGH ME TO MARLEY SO THAT I, ALONG WITH MY FAMILY, CAN BE FREED OF YMIR'S WICKED BLOOD.
OKAY.
THEN WHAT DO YOU THINK ABOUT THE HONOR OF INHERITING ONE OF THE NINE TITANS?
TO INHERIT ONE OF THE NINE TITANS IS TO BE GIVEN THE RIGHT TO FULLY DISPLAY ONE'S LOYALTY TO OUR MOTHERLAND OF MARLEY THROUGH THE DISTINCTION AND PRIDE OF BEING AN HONORARY MARLEYAN.

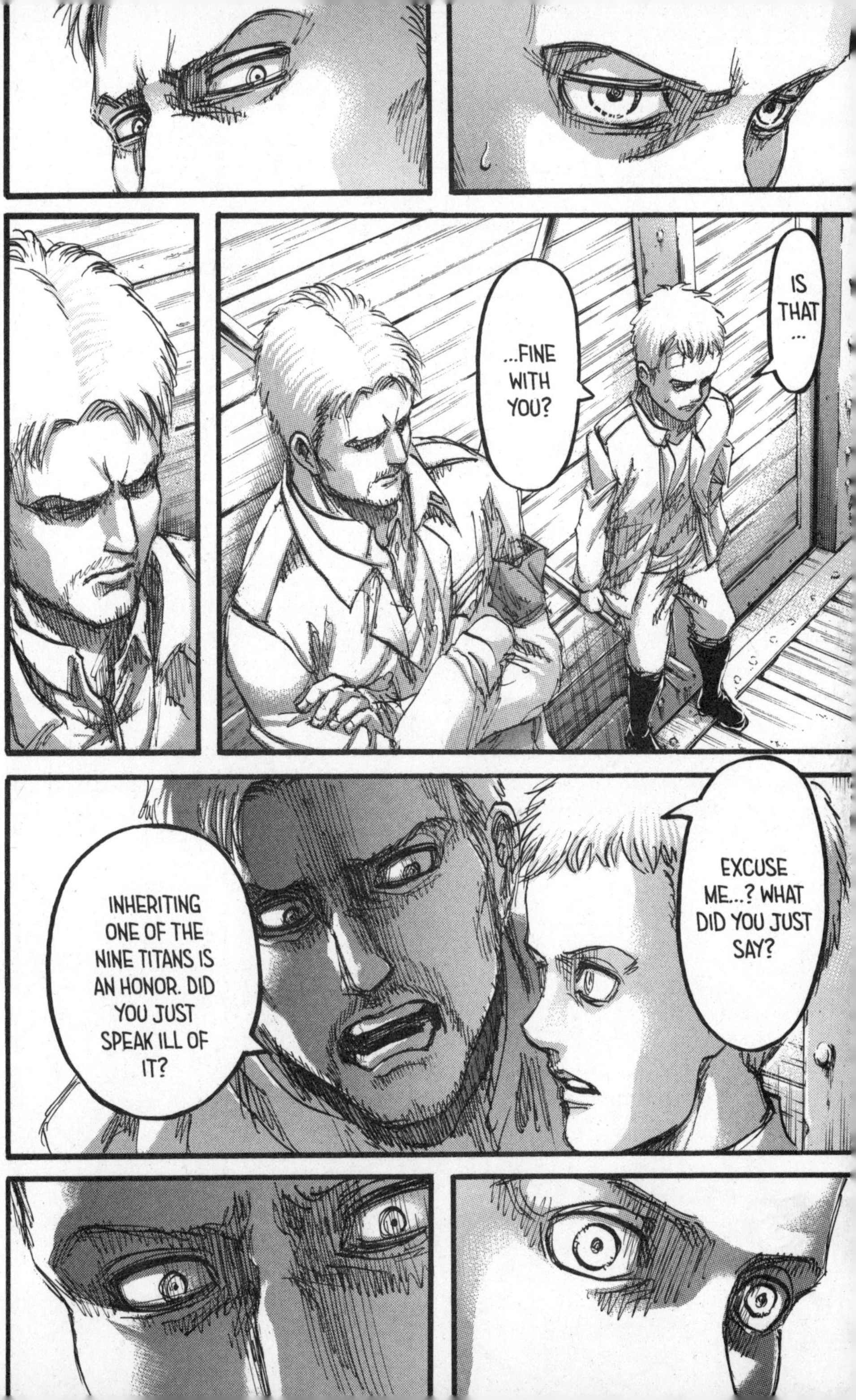
IS THAT ...
...FINE WITH YOU?
EXCUSE ME...? WHAT DID YOU JUST SAY?
INHERITING ONE OF THE NINE TITANS IS AN HONOR. DID YOU JUST SPEAK ILL OF IT?

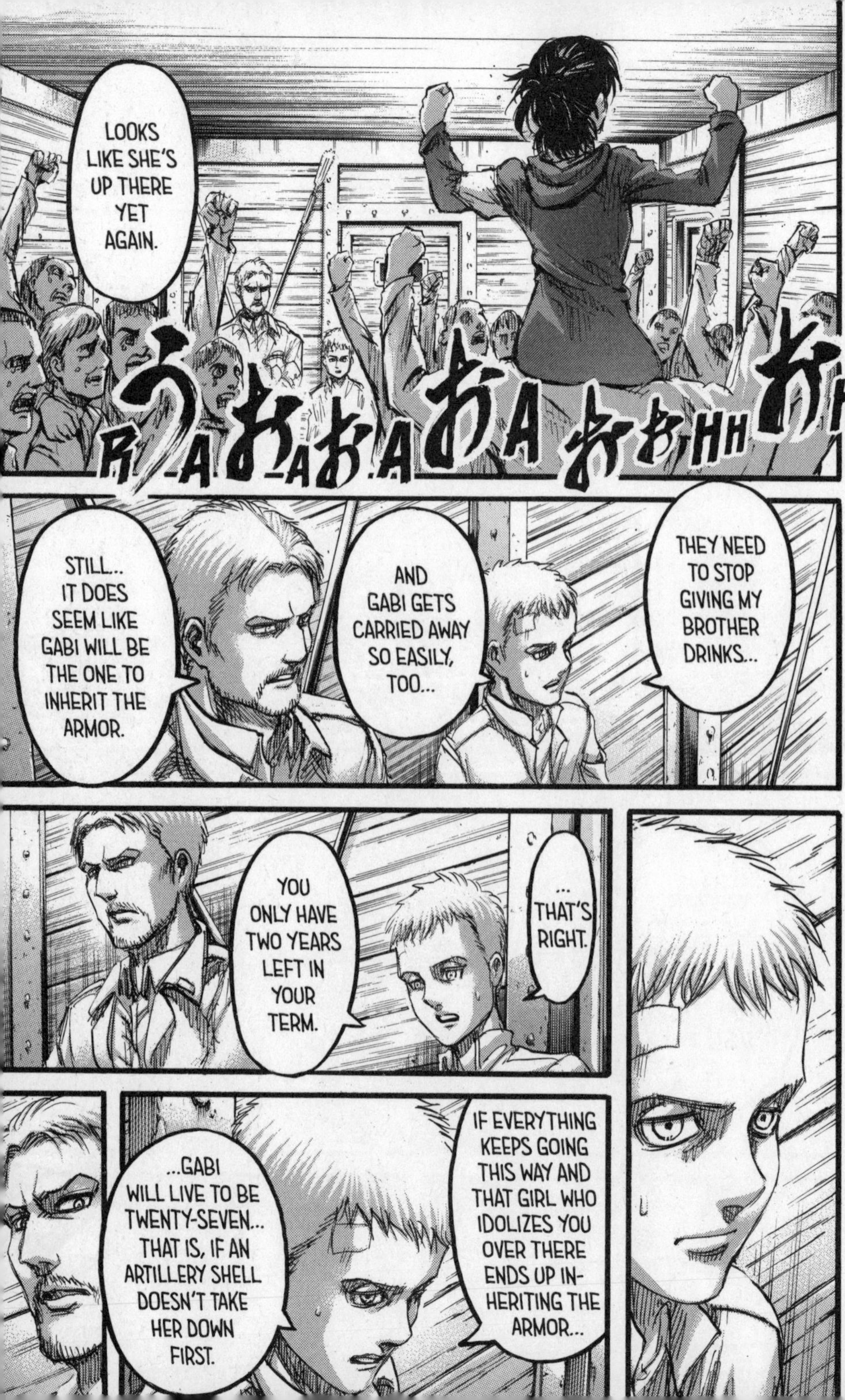
LOOKS LIKE SHE'S UP THERE YET AGAIN.
RうAおAおAあAおおHHおH
THEY NEED TO STOP GIVING MY BROTHER DRINKS...
AND GABI GETS CARRIED AWAY SO EASILY, TOO...
STILL... IT DOES SEEM LIKE GABI WILL BE THE ONE TO INHERIT THE ARMOR.
YOU ONLY HAVE TWO YEARS LEFT IN YOUR TERM.
... THAT'S RIGHT.
IF EVERYTHING KEEPS GOING THIS WAY AND THAT GIRL WHO IDOLIZES YOU OVER THERE ENDS UP IN-HERITING THE ARMOR...
...GABI WILL LIVE TO BE TWENTY-SEVEN... THAT IS, IF AN ARTILLERY SHELL DOESN'T TAKE HER DOWN FIRST.

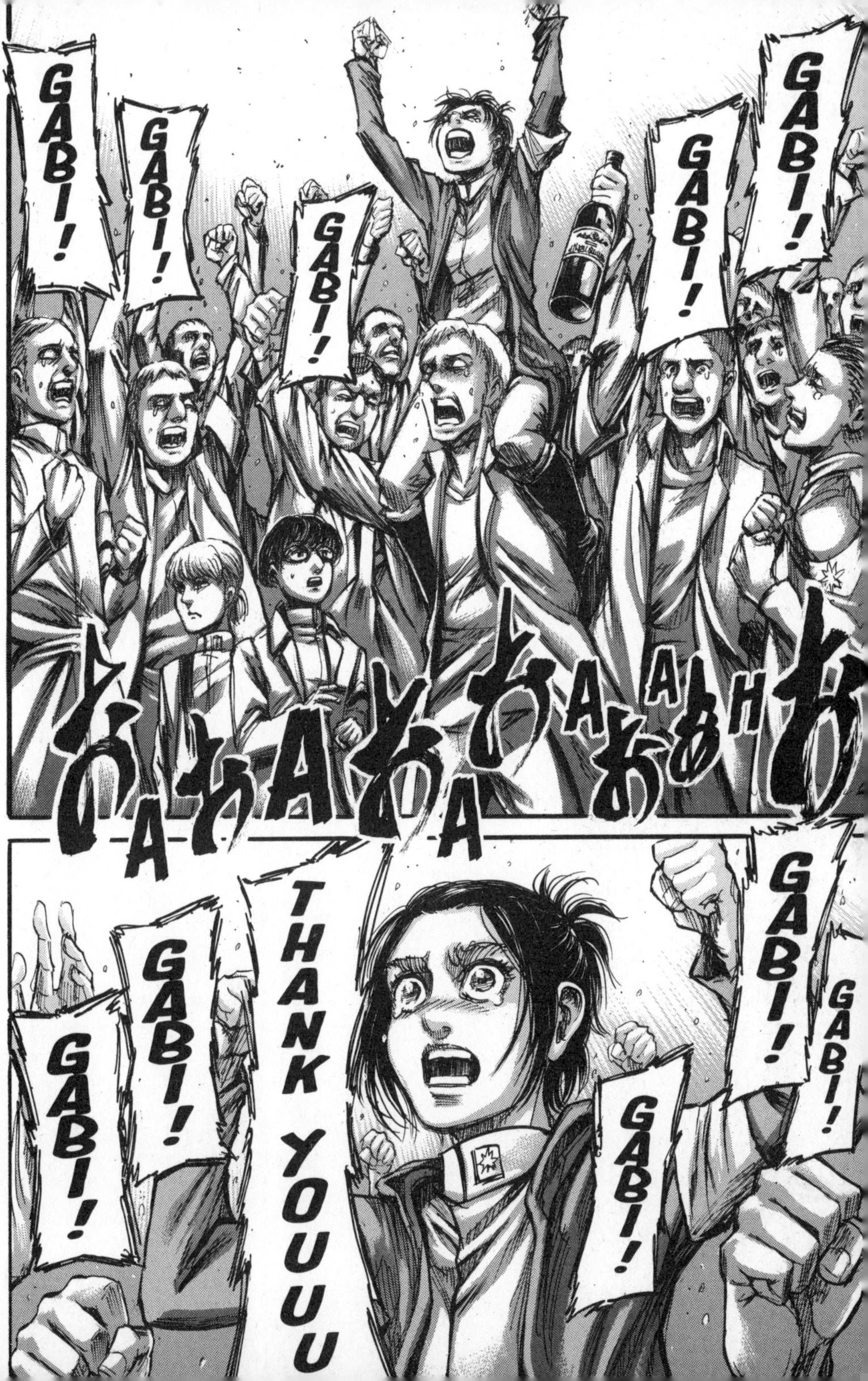
GABI!
GABI!
GABI!
GABI!
GABI!
AAAAAAH
GABI!
GABI!
GABI!
THANK YOUUU
GABI!
GABI!

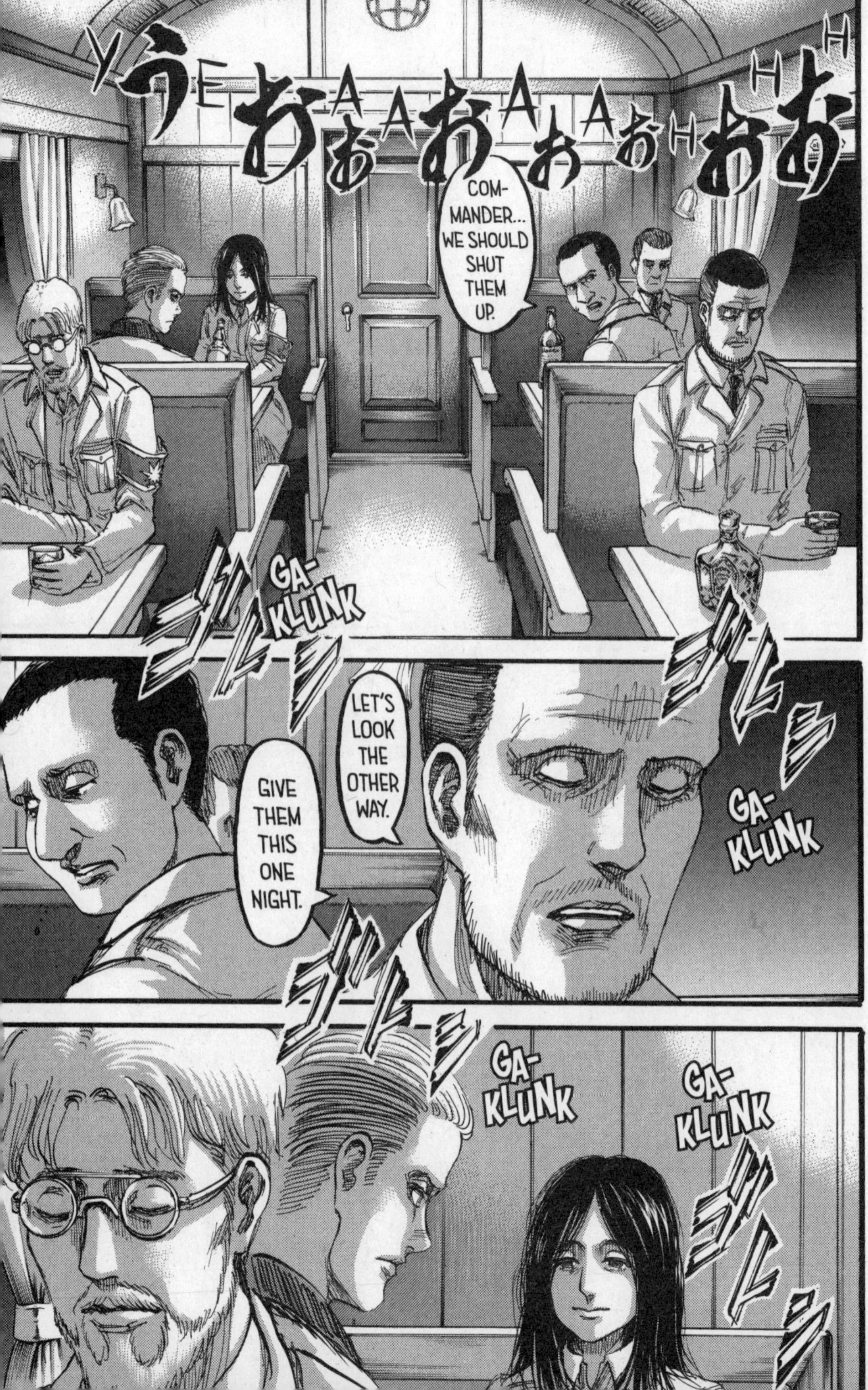
YEAAAAHHHHH
COM-MANDER... WE SHOULD SHUT THEM UP.
GA-KLUNK
GA-KLUNK
LET'S LOOK THE OTHER WAY.
GIVE THEM THIS ONE NIGHT.
GA-KLUNK
GA-KLUNK

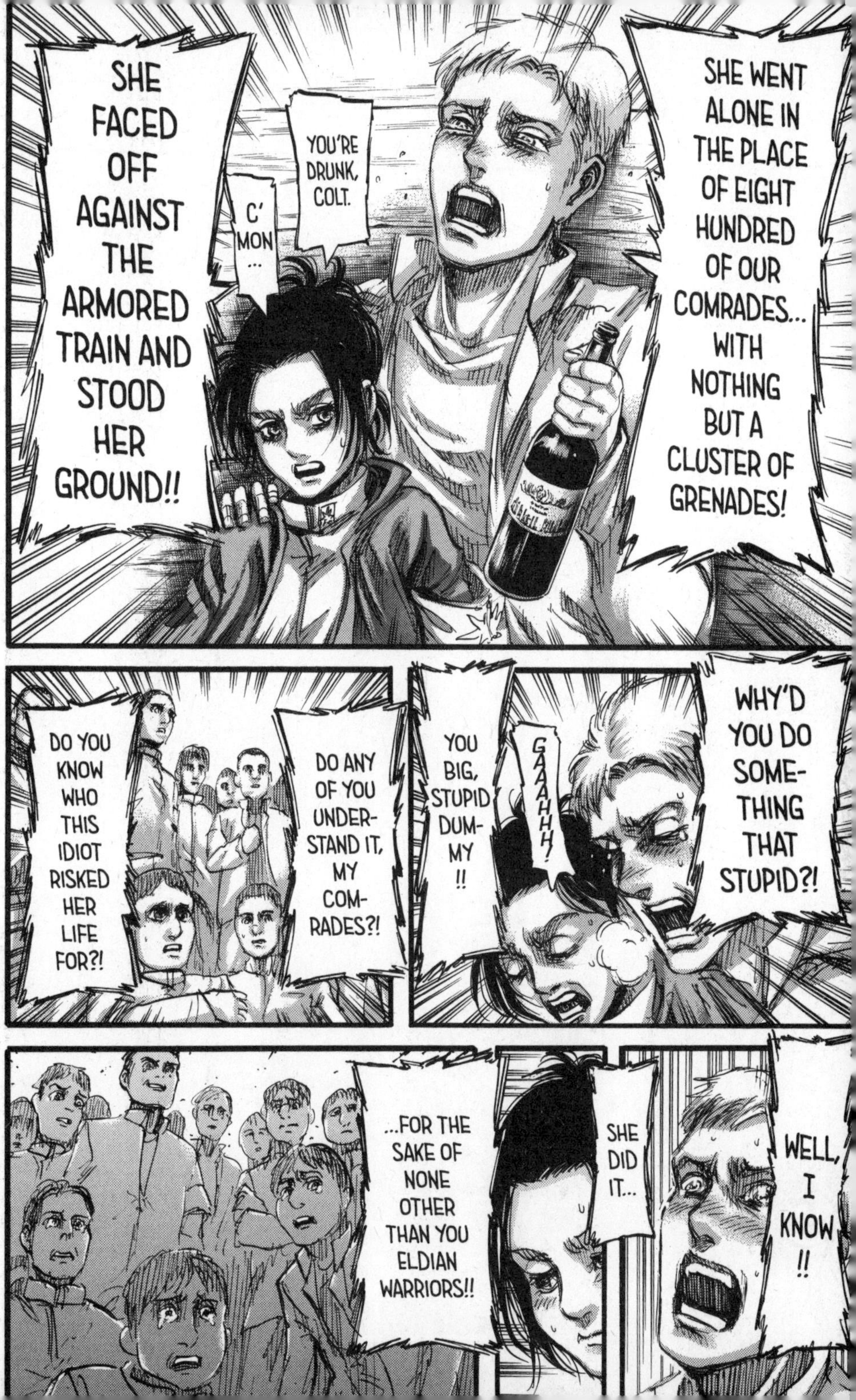
SHE WENT ALONE IN THE PLACE OF EIGHT HUNDRED OF OUR COMRADES... WITH NOTHING BUT A CLUSTER OF GRENADES!
YOU'RE DRUNK, COLT.
C'MON...
SHE FACED OFF AGAINST THE ARMORED TRAIN AND STOOD HER GROUND!!
WHY'D YOU DO SOMETHING THAT STUPID?!
GAAAAHHH!
YOU BIG, STUPID DUMMY!!
DO ANY OF YOU UNDERSTAND IT, MY COMRADES?!
DO YOU KNOW WHO THIS IDIOT RISKED HER LIFE FOR?!
WELL, I KNOW!!
SHE DID IT...
...FOR THE SAKE OF NONE OTHER THAN YOU ELDIAN WARRIORS!!

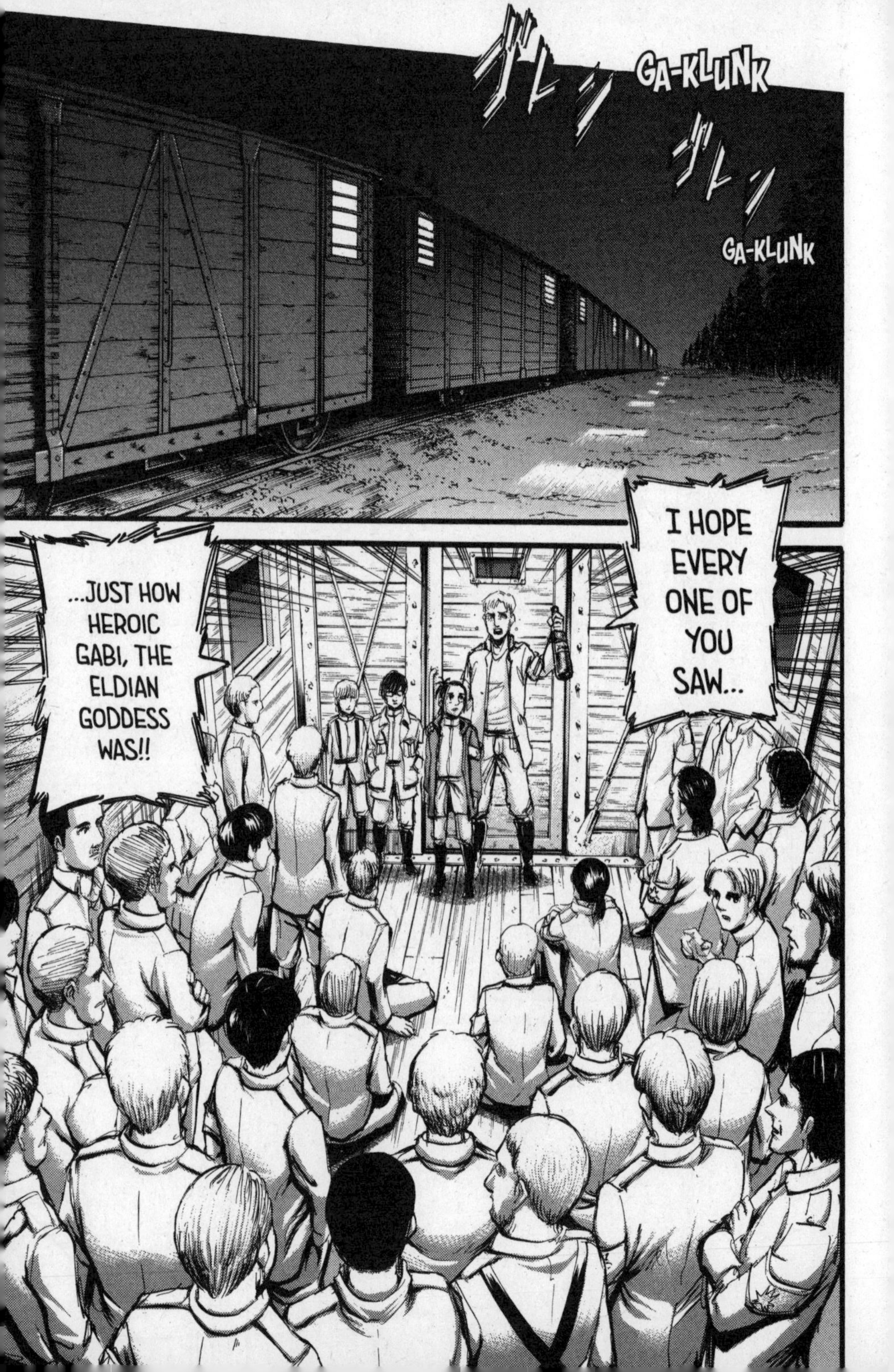
GA-KLUNK
GA-KLUNK
I HOPE EVERY ONE OF YOU SAW...
...JUST HOW HEROIC GABI, THE ELDIAN GODDESS WAS!!

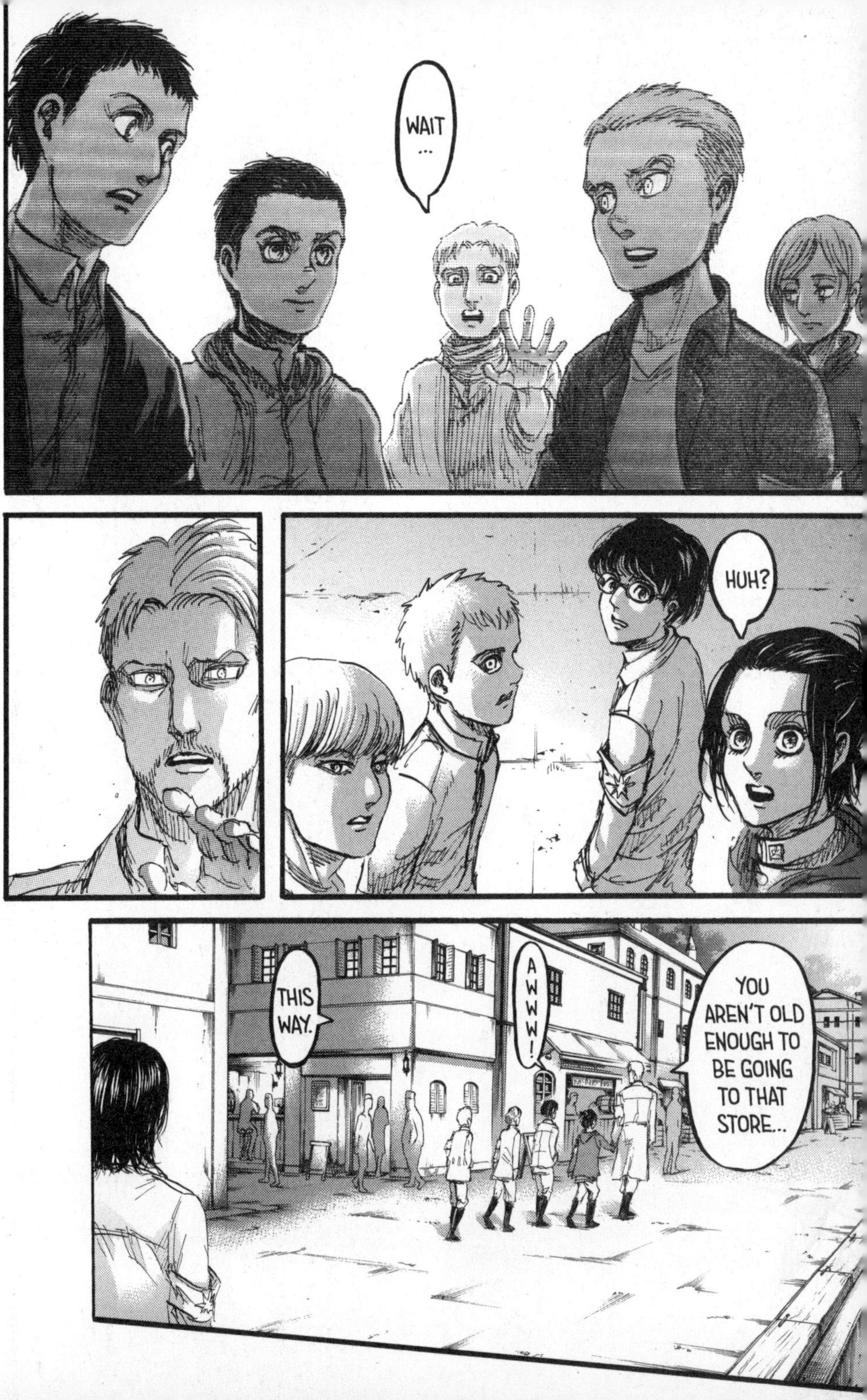
WAIT ...
HUH?
YOU AREN'T OLD ENOUGH TO BE GOING TO THAT STORE...
AWWW!
THIS WAY.

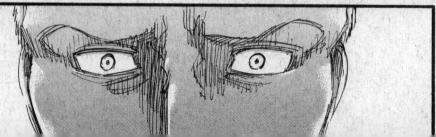

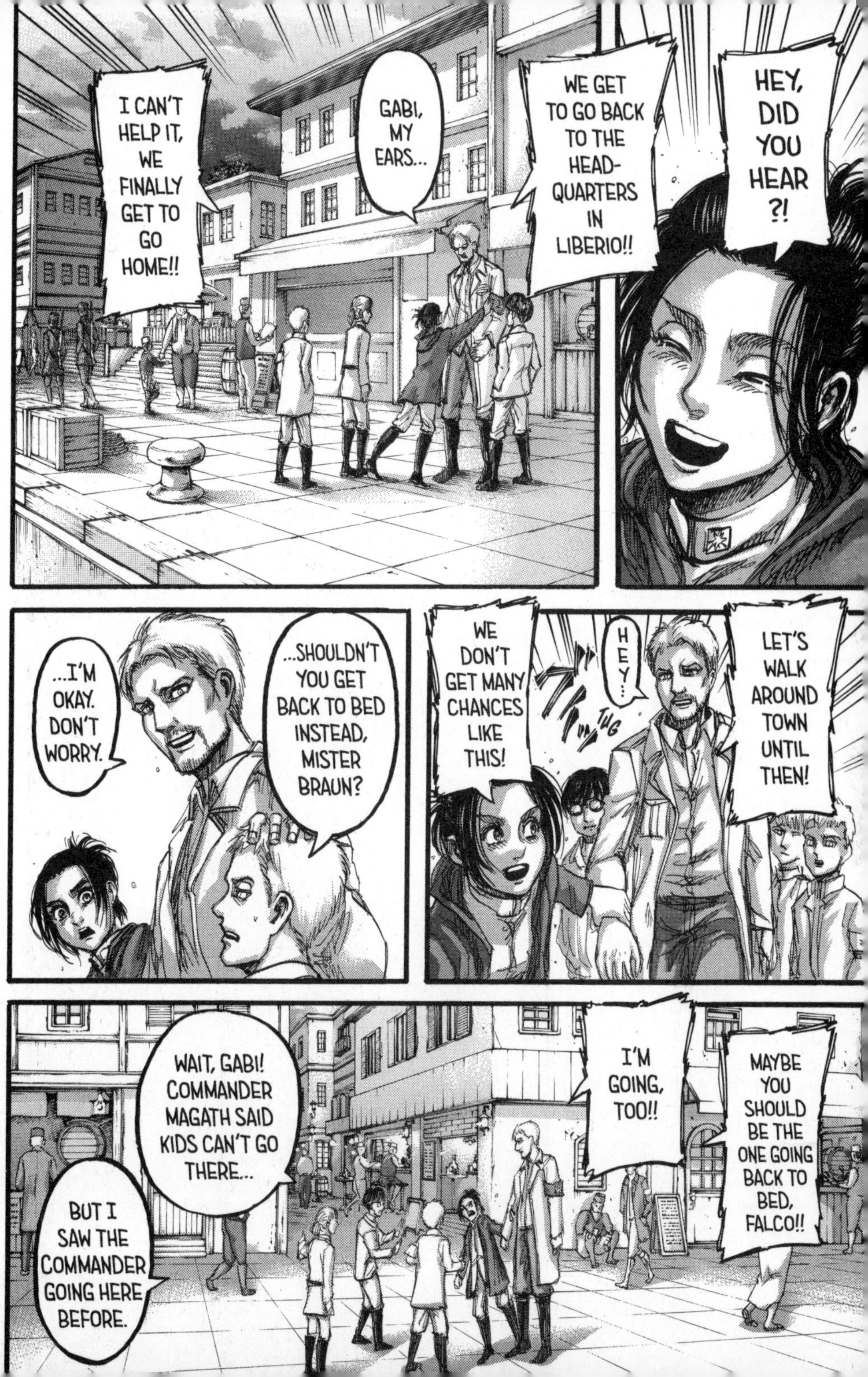
HEY, DID YOU HEAR?!
WE GET TO GO BACK TO THE HEADQUARTERS IN LIBERIO!!
GABI, MY EARS...
I CAN'T HELP IT, WE FINALLY GET TO GO HOME!!
LET'S WALK AROUND TOWN UNTIL THEN!
HEY...
TUG
WE DON'T GET MANY CHANCES LIKE THIS!
...SHOULDN'T YOU GET BACK TO BED INSTEAD, MISTER BRAUN?
...I'M OKAY. DON'T WORRY.
MAYBE YOU SHOULD BE THE ONE GOING BACK TO BED, FALCO!!
I'M GOING, TOO!!
WAIT, GABI! COMMANDER MAGATH SAID KIDS CAN'T GO THERE...
BUT I SAW THE COMMANDER GOING HERE BEFORE.

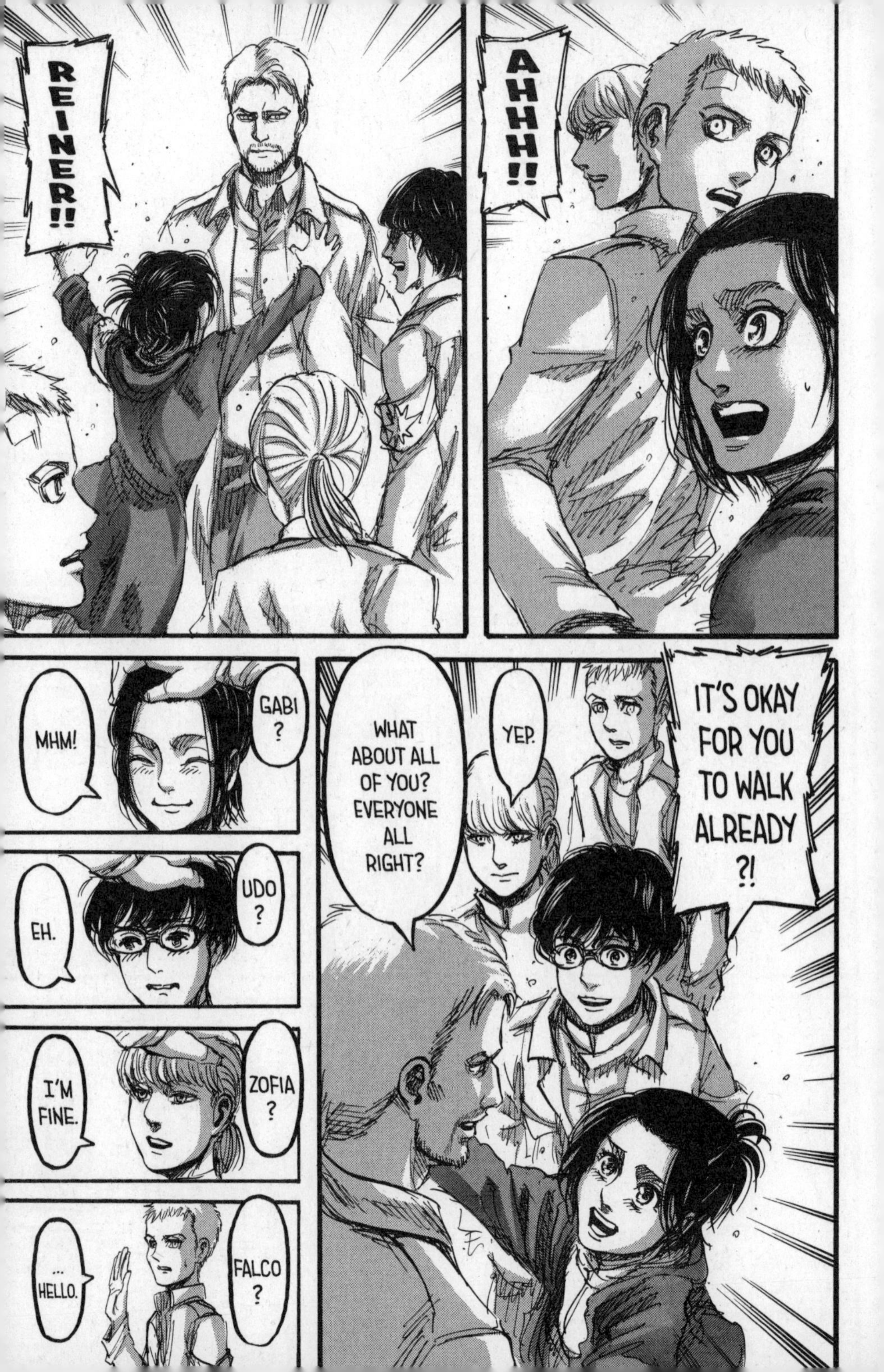
AHHH!!
REINER!!
IT'S OKAY FOR YOU TO WALK ALREADY ?!
WHAT ABOUT ALL OF YOU? EVERYONE ALL RIGHT?
YEP.
GABI ?
MHM!
UDO ?
EH.
ZOFIA ?
I'M FINE.
FALCO ?
... HELLO.

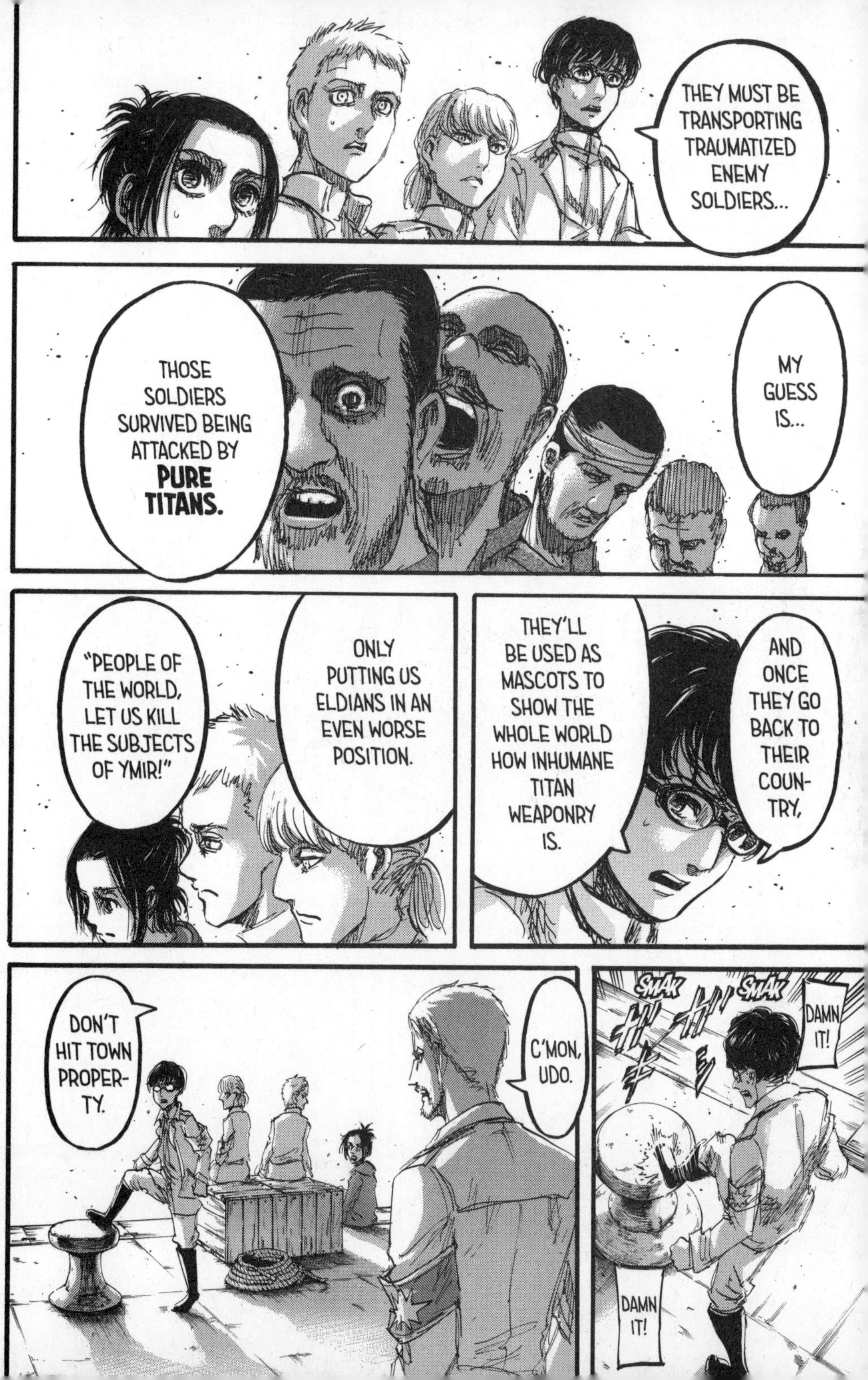

THEY MUST BE TRANSPORTING TRAUMATIZED ENEMY SOLDIERS...
MY GUESS IS...
THOSE SOLDIERS SURVIVED BEING ATTACKED BY **PURE TITANS.**
AND ONCE THEY GO BACK TO THEIR COUN-TRY,
THEY'LL BE USED AS MASCOTS TO SHOW THE WHOLE WORLD HOW INHUMANE TITAN WEAPONRY IS.
ONLY PUTTING US ELDIANS IN AN EVEN WORSE POSITION.
"PEOPLE OF THE WORLD, LET US KILL THE SUBJECTS OF YMIR!"
SMAK
SMAK
DAMN IT!
DAMN IT!
C'MON, UDO.
DON'T HIT TOWN PROPER-TY.

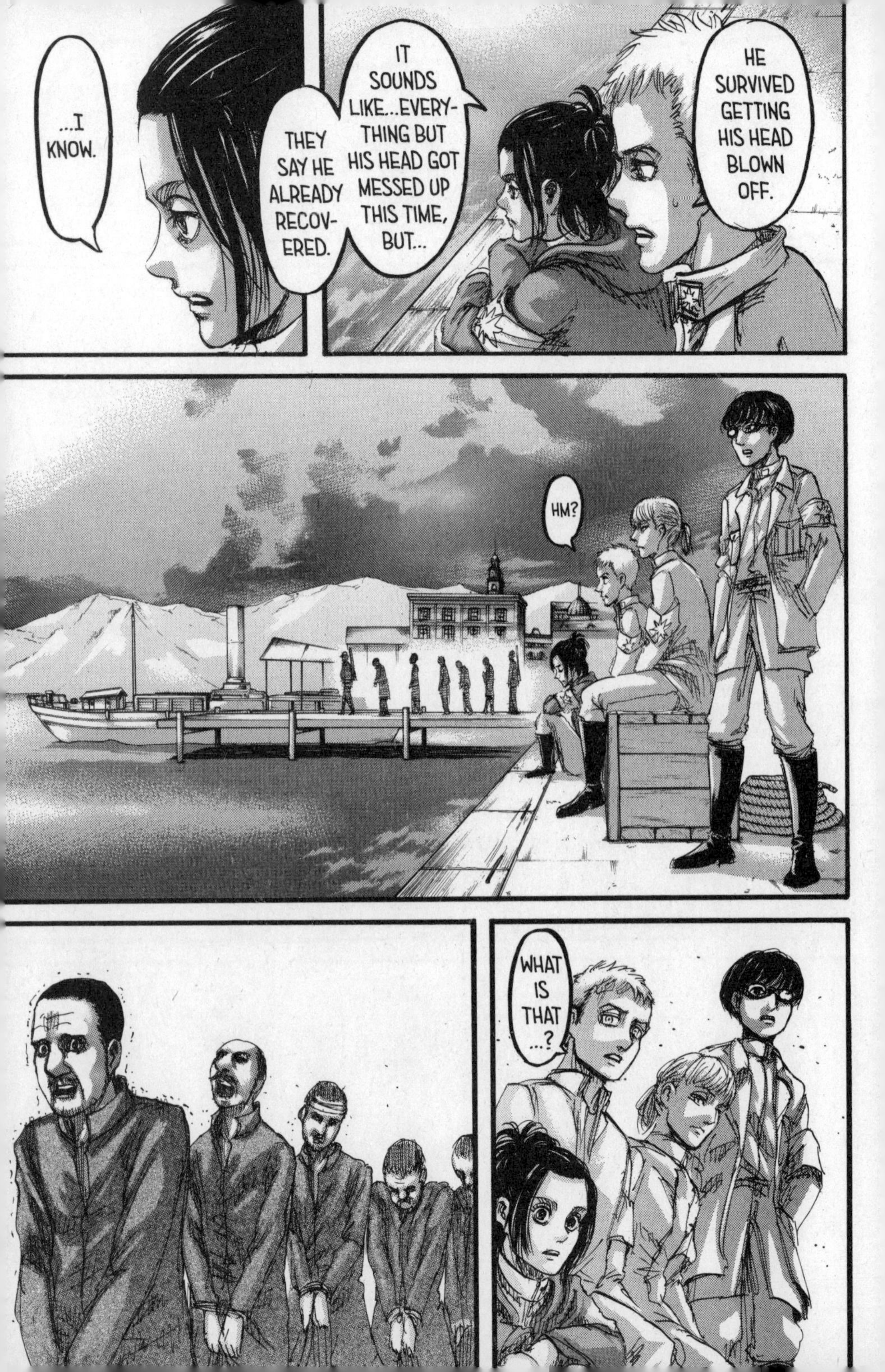
HE SURVIVED GETTING HIS HEAD BLOWN OFF.
IT SOUNDS LIKE...EVERYTHING BUT HIS HEAD GOT MESSED UP THIS TIME, BUT...
THEY SAY HE ALREADY RECOVERED.
...I KNOW.
HM?
WHAT IS THAT ...?

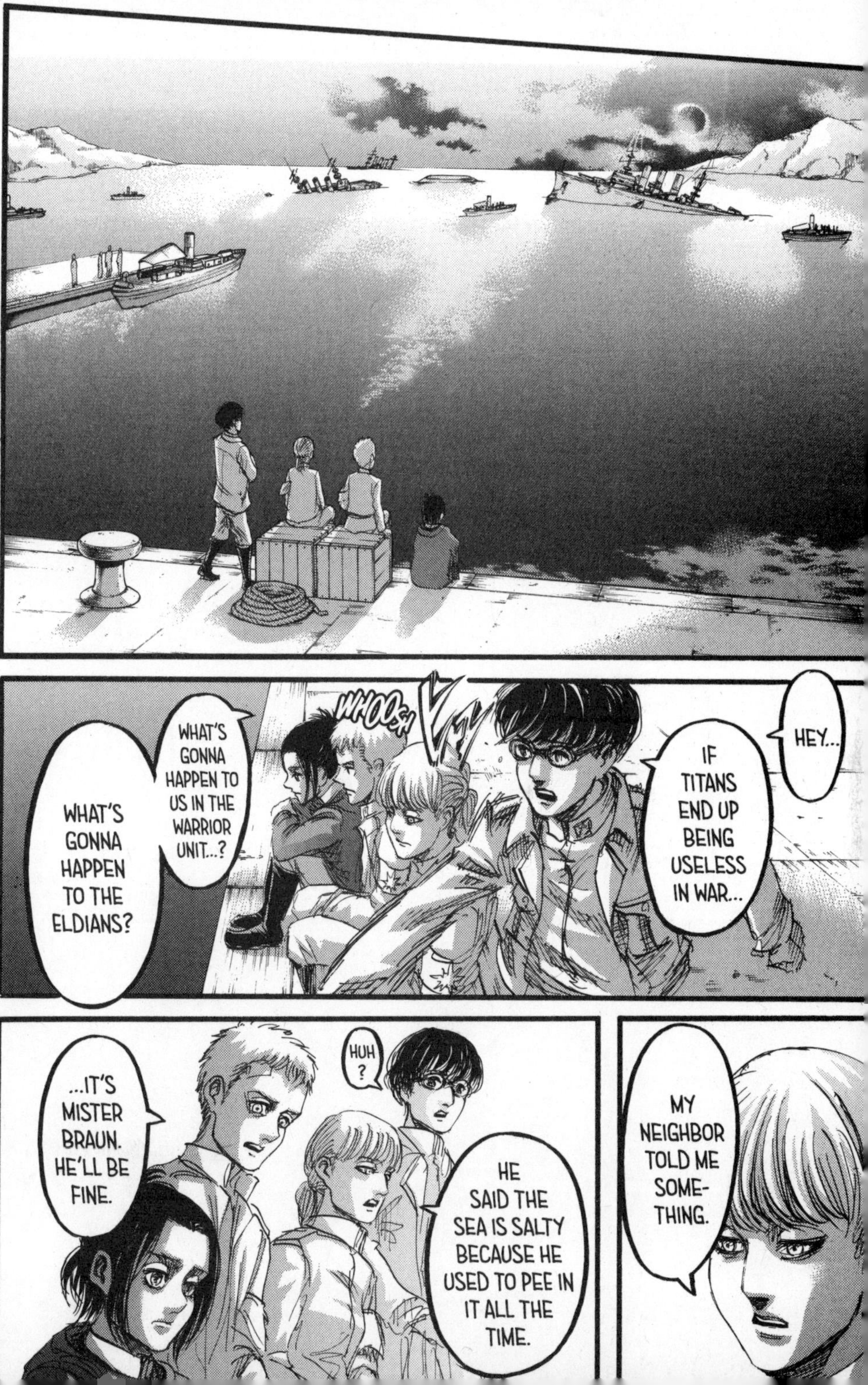
HEY...
IF TITANS END UP BEING USELESS IN WAR...
WHOOSH
WHAT'S GONNA HAPPEN TO US IN THE WARRIOR UNIT...?
WHAT'S GONNA HAPPEN TO THE ELDIANS?
MY NEIGHBOR TOLD ME SOME-THING.
HUH?
HE SAID THE SEA IS SALTY BECAUSE HE USED TO PEE IN IT ALL THE TIME.
...IT'S MISTER BRAUN. HE'LL BE FINE.

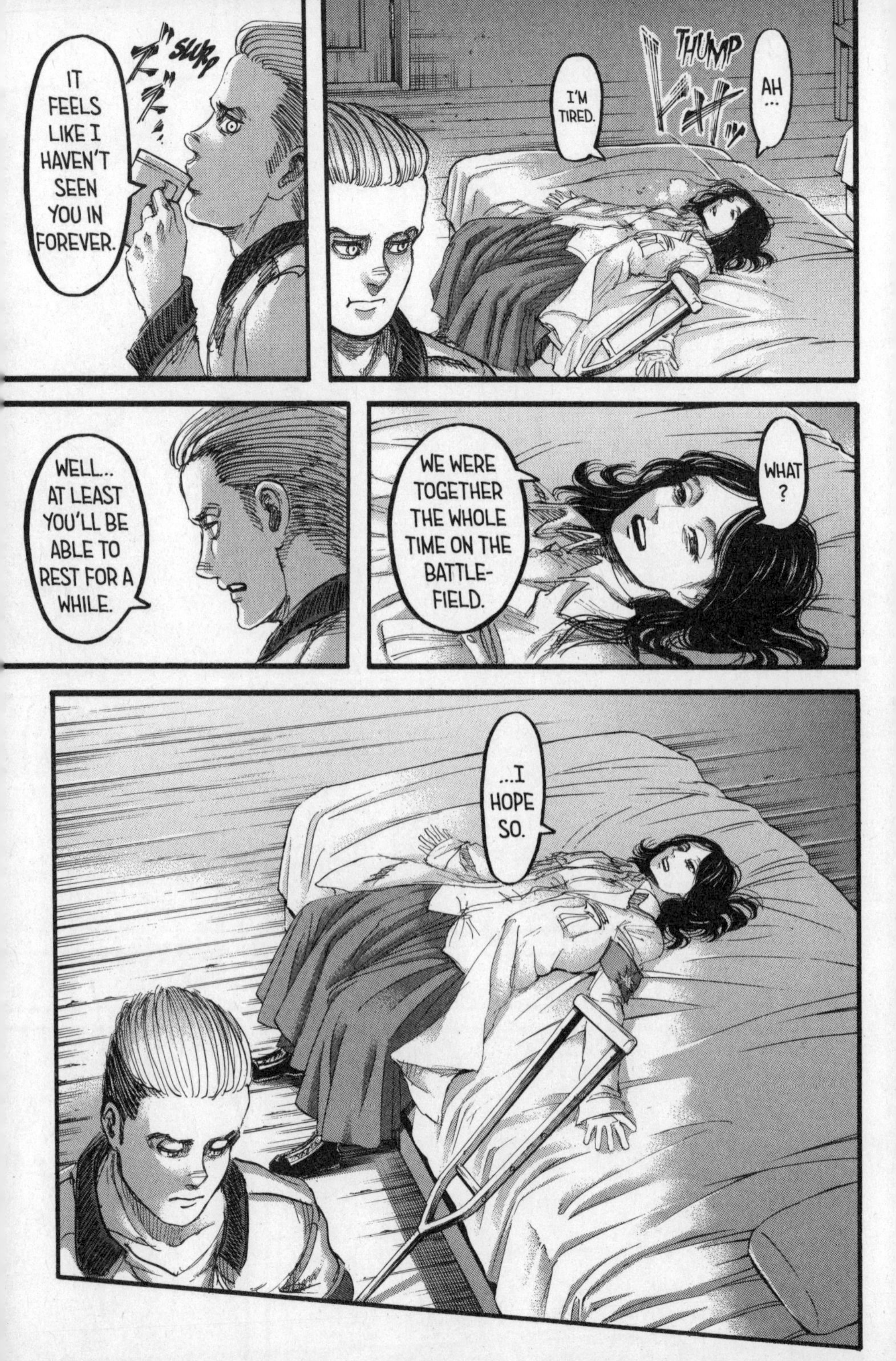
AH...
THUMP
I'M TIRED.
SLURP
IT FEELS LIKE I HAVEN'T SEEN YOU IN FOREVER.
WHAT?
WE WERE TOGETHER THE WHOLE TIME ON THE BATTLE-FIELD.
WELL... AT LEAST YOU'LL BE ABLE TO REST FOR A WHILE.
...I HOPE SO.

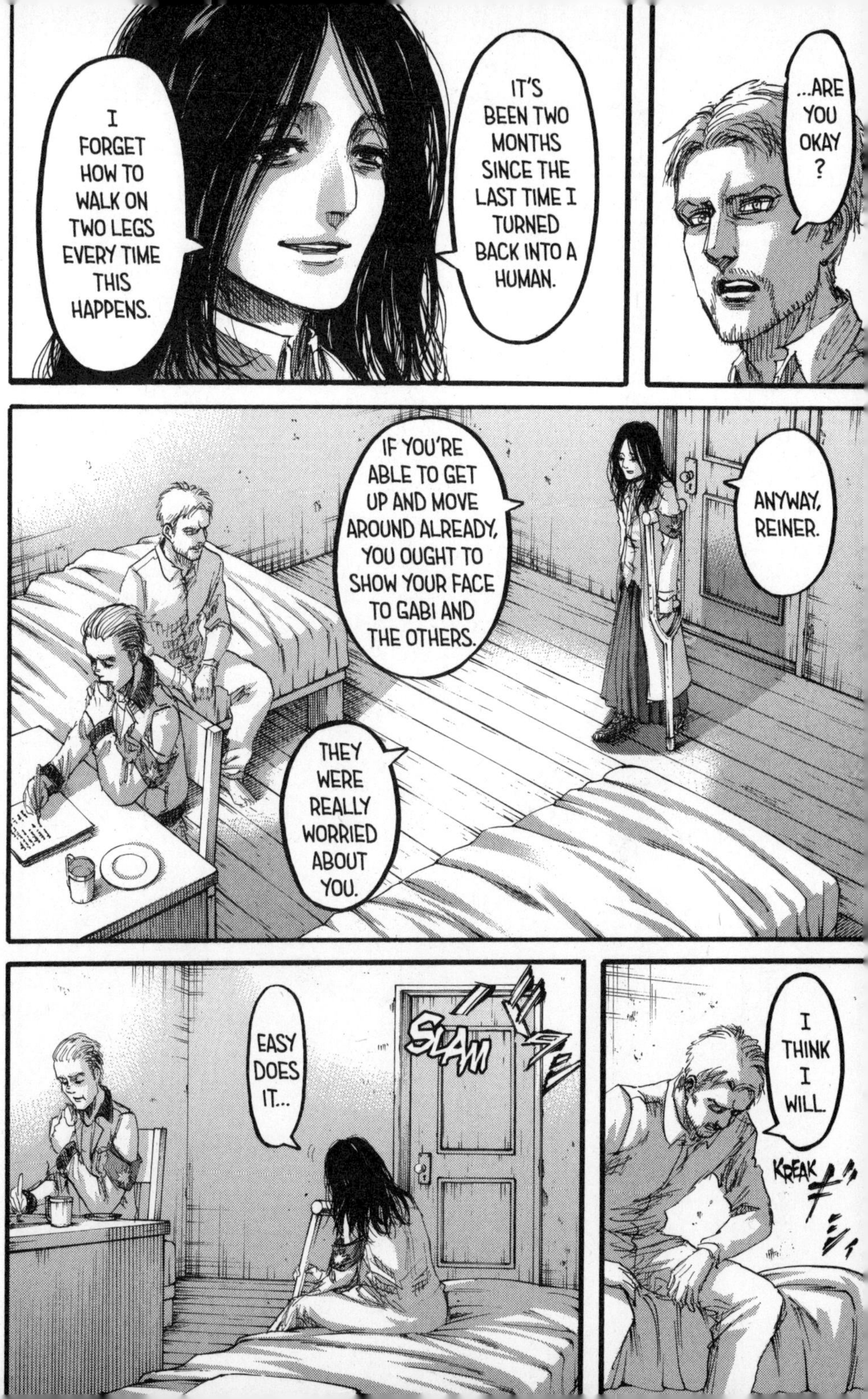
...ARE YOU OKAY?
IT'S BEEN TWO MONTHS SINCE THE LAST TIME I TURNED BACK INTO A HUMAN.
I FORGET HOW TO WALK ON TWO LEGS EVERY TIME THIS HAPPENS.
ANYWAY, REINER.
IF YOU'RE ABLE TO GET UP AND MOVE AROUND ALREADY, YOU OUGHT TO SHOW YOUR FACE TO GABI AND THE OTHERS.
THEY WERE REALLY WORRIED ABOUT YOU.
I THINK I WILL.
KREAK
SLAM
EASY DOES IT...

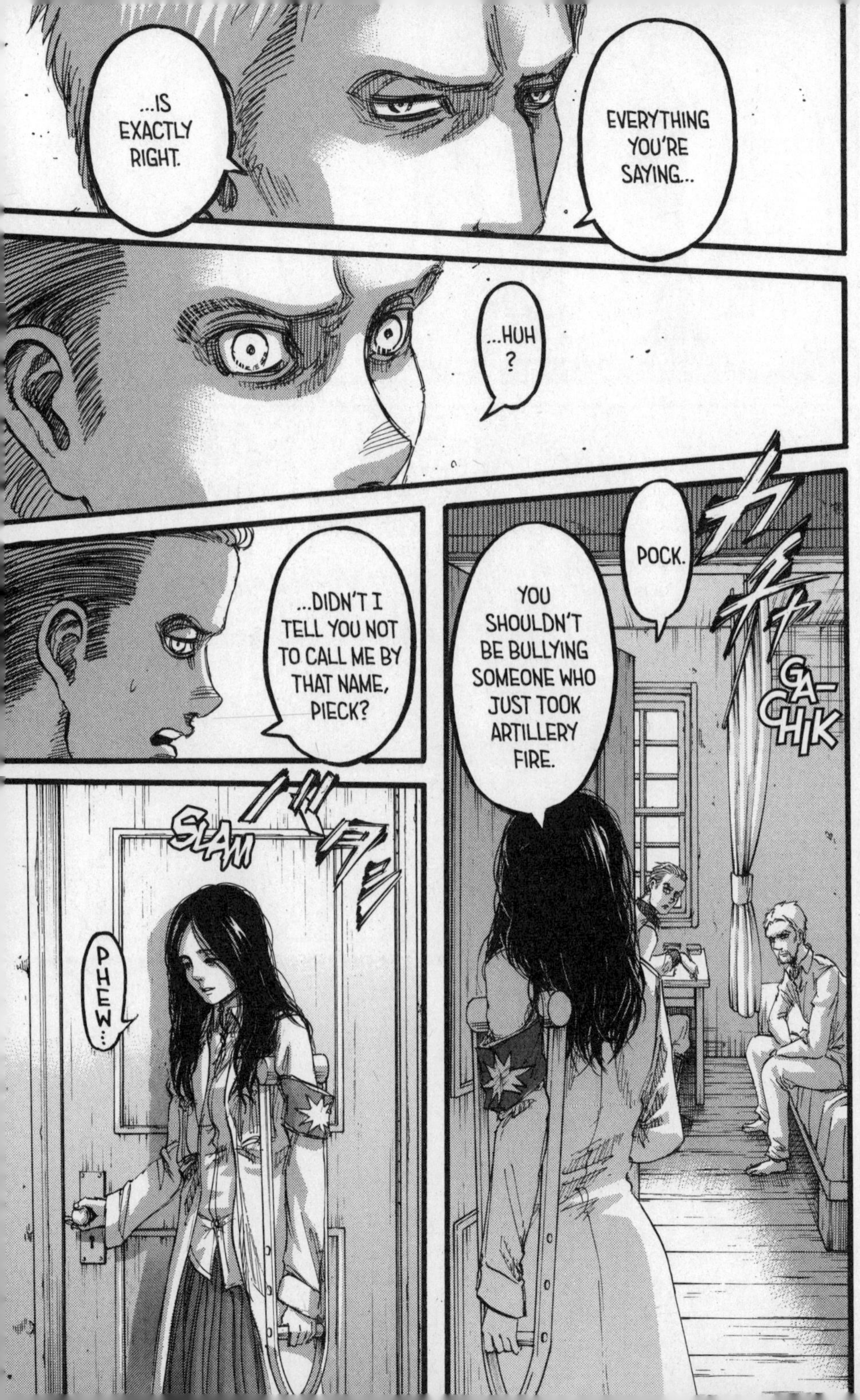
EVERYTHING YOU'RE SAYING...
...IS EXACTLY RIGHT.
...HUH?
GA-CHIK
POCK.
YOU SHOULDN'T BE BULLYING SOMEONE WHO JUST TOOK ARTILLERY FIRE.
...DIDN'T I TELL YOU NOT TO CALL ME BY THAT NAME, PIECK?
SLAM
PHEW...

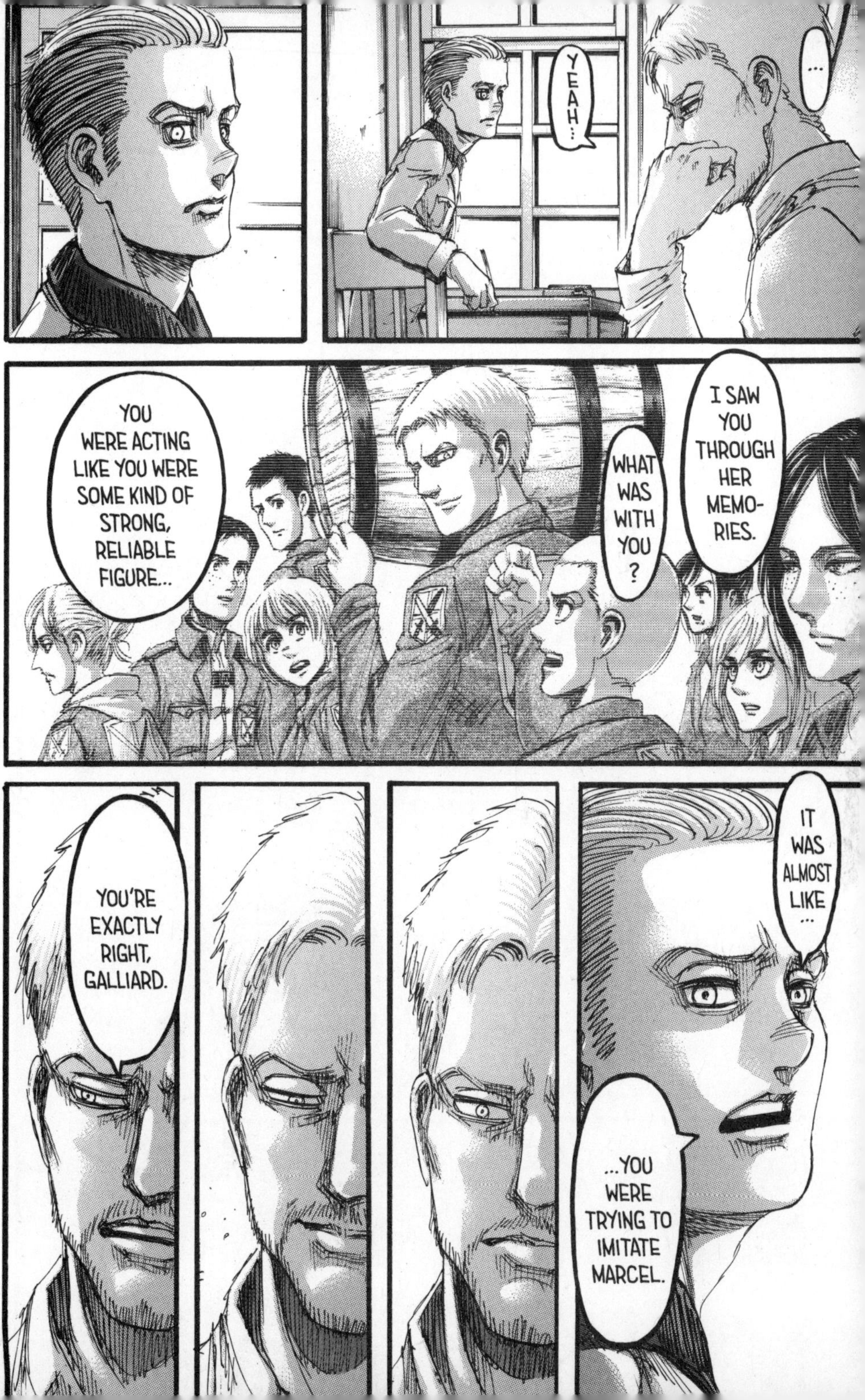
...
YEAH...
I SAW YOU THROUGH HER MEMORIES.
WHAT WAS WITH YOU?
YOU WERE ACTING LIKE YOU WERE SOME KIND OF STRONG, RELIABLE FIGURE...
IT WAS ALMOST LIKE...
...YOU WERE TRYING TO IMITATE MARCEL.
YOU'RE EXACTLY RIGHT, GALLIARD.

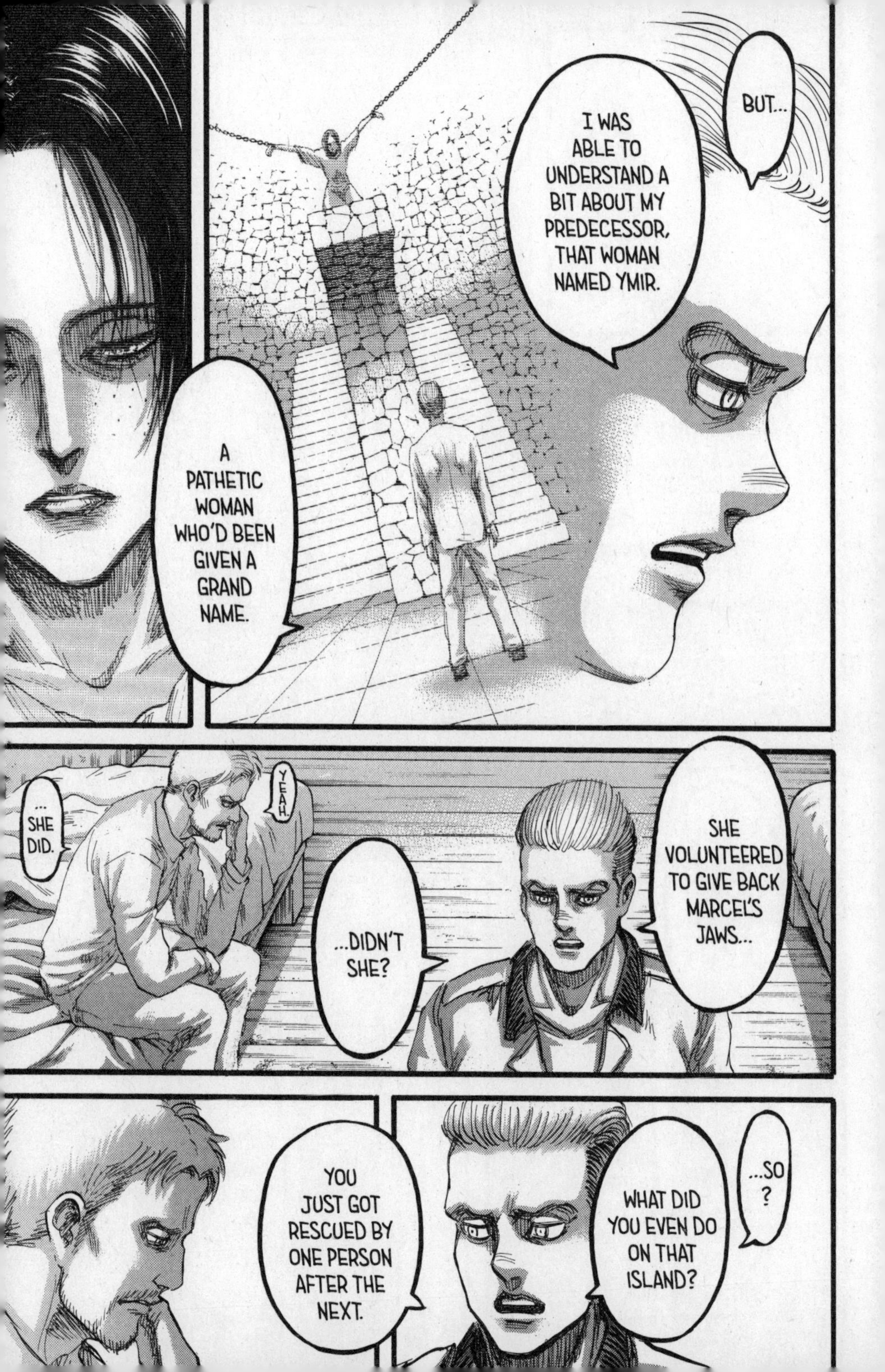
BUT...
I WAS ABLE TO UNDERSTAND A BIT ABOUT MY PREDECESSOR, THAT WOMAN NAMED YMIR.
A PATHETIC WOMAN WHO'D BEEN GIVEN A GRAND NAME.
SHE VOLUNTEERED TO GIVE BACK MARCEL'S JAWS...
...DIDN'T SHE?
YEAH.
...SHE DID.
...SO?
WHAT DID YOU EVEN DO ON THAT ISLAND?
YOU JUST GOT RESCUED BY ONE PERSON AFTER THE NEXT.

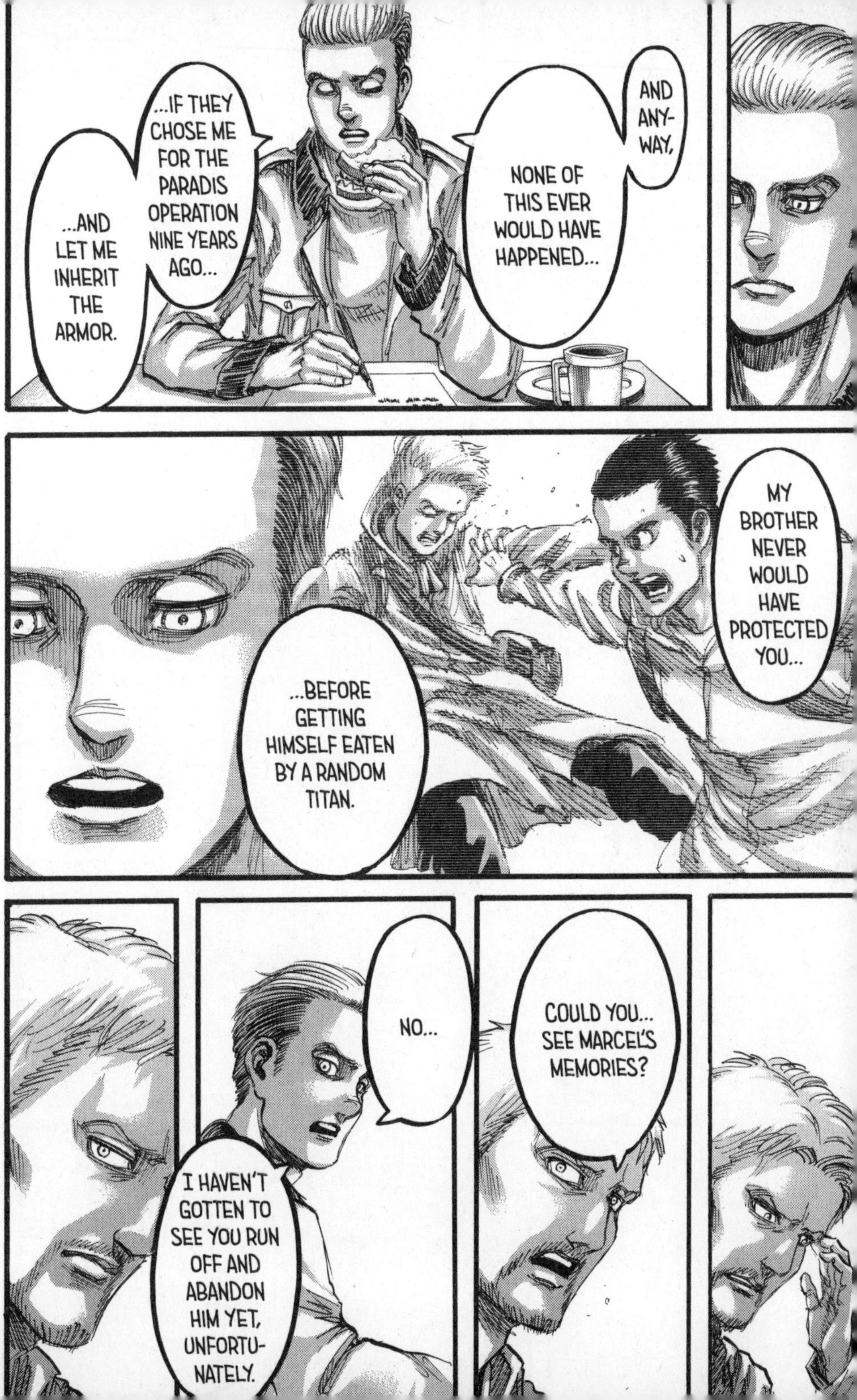
AND ANYWAY,
NONE OF THIS EVER WOULD HAVE HAPPENED...
...IF THEY CHOSE ME FOR THE PARADIS OPERATION NINE YEARS AGO...
...AND LET ME INHERIT THE ARMOR.
MY BROTHER NEVER WOULD HAVE PROTECTED YOU...
...BEFORE GETTING HIMSELF EATEN BY A RANDOM TITAN.
COULD YOU... SEE MARCEL'S MEMORIES?
NO...
I HAVEN'T GOTTEN TO SEE YOU RUN OFF AND ABANDON HIM YET, UNFORTUNATELY.

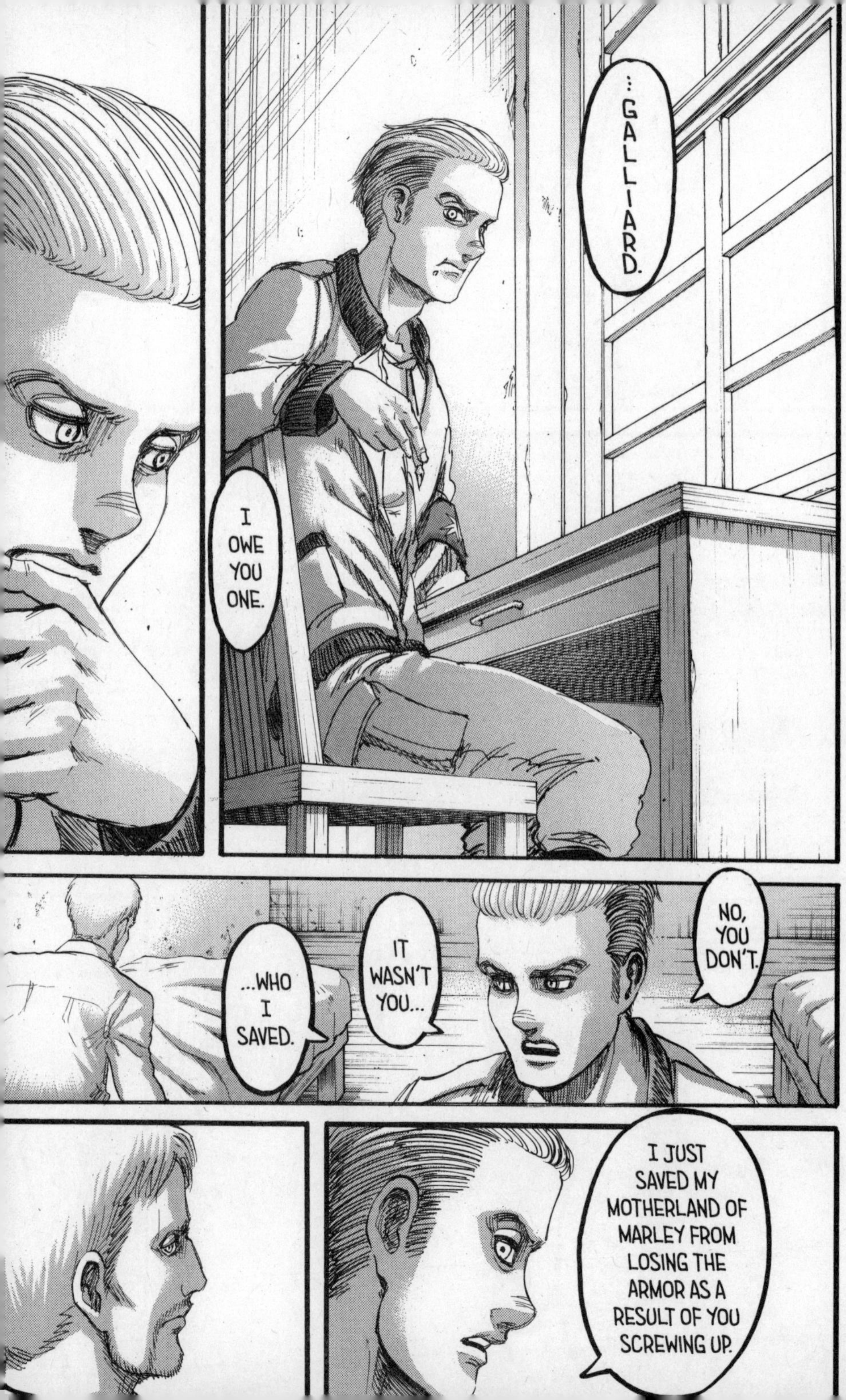
...GALLIARD.
I OWE YOU ONE.
NO, YOU DON'T.
IT WASN'T YOU...
...WHO I SAVED.
I JUST SAVED MY MOTHERLAND OF MARLEY FROM LOSING THE ARMOR AS A RESULT OF YOU SCREWING UP.

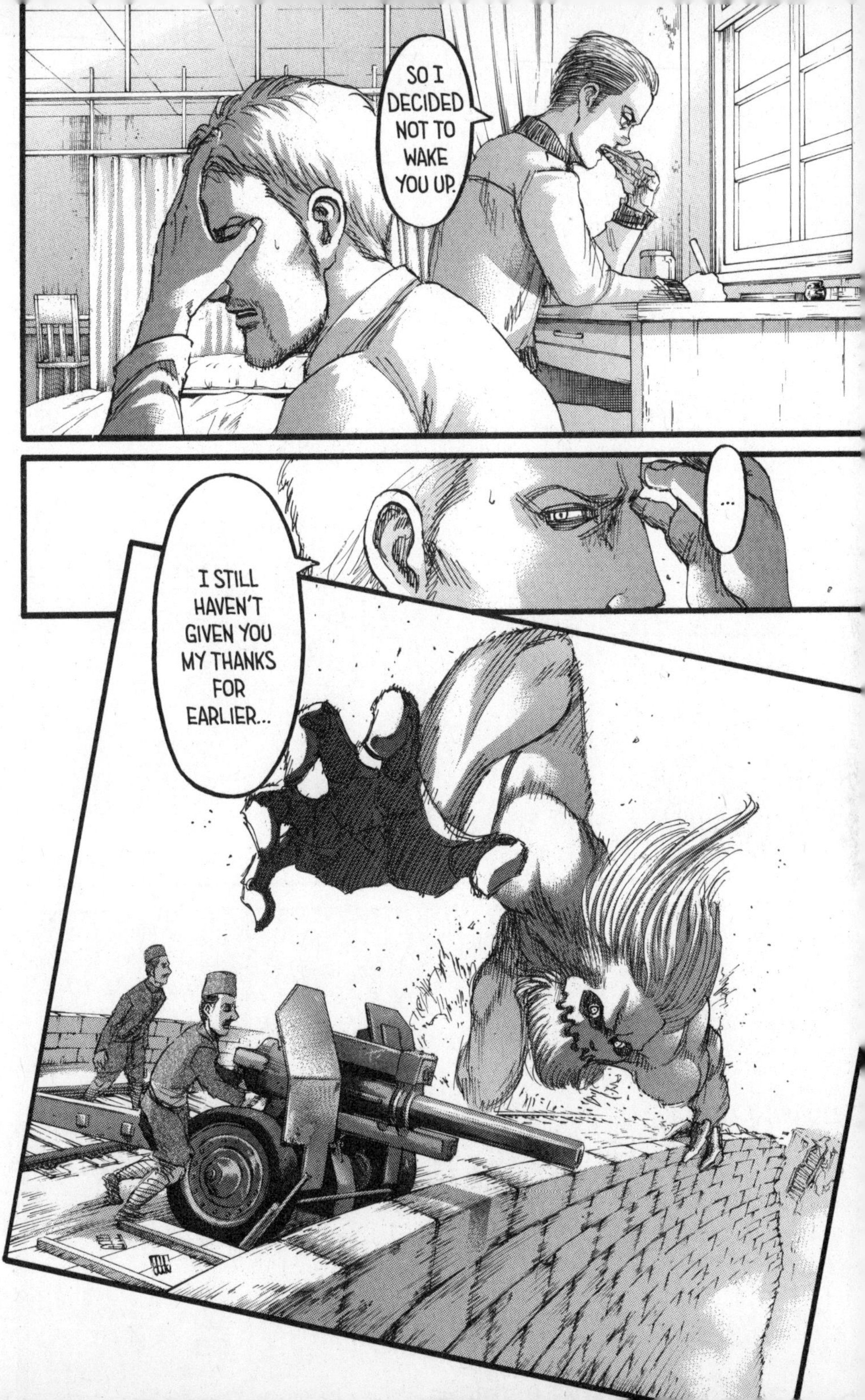
SO I DECIDED NOT TO WAKE YOU UP.
...
I STILL HAVEN'T GIVEN YOU MY THANKS FOR EARLIER...

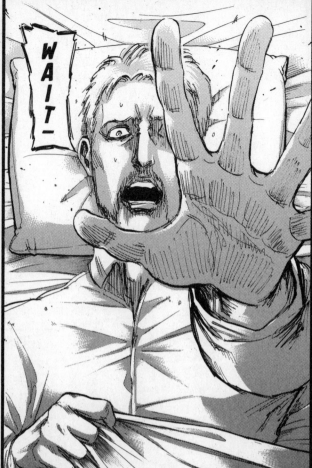

WAIT—

IT SOUNDED LIKE YOU WERE HAVING A NICE DREAM.

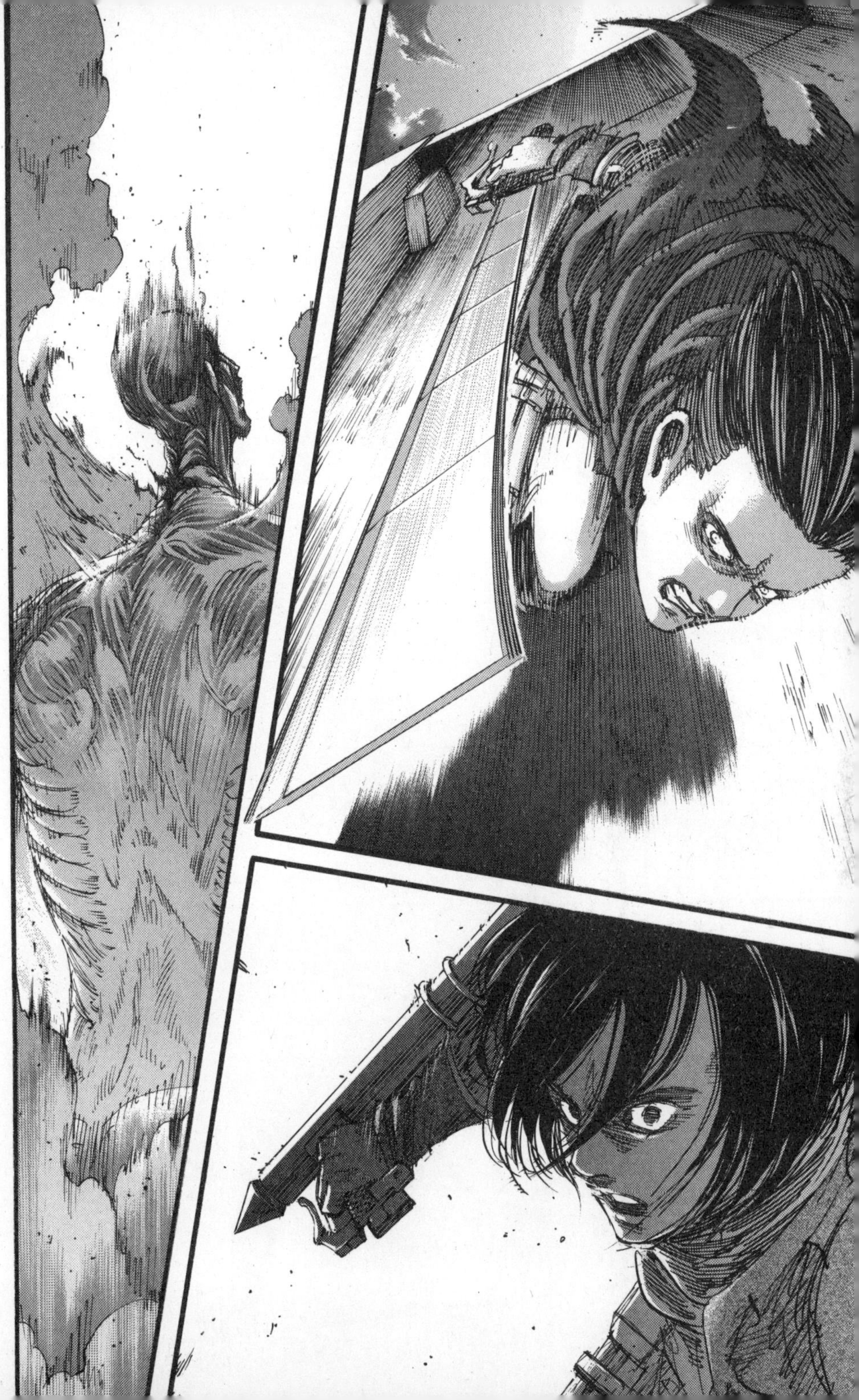

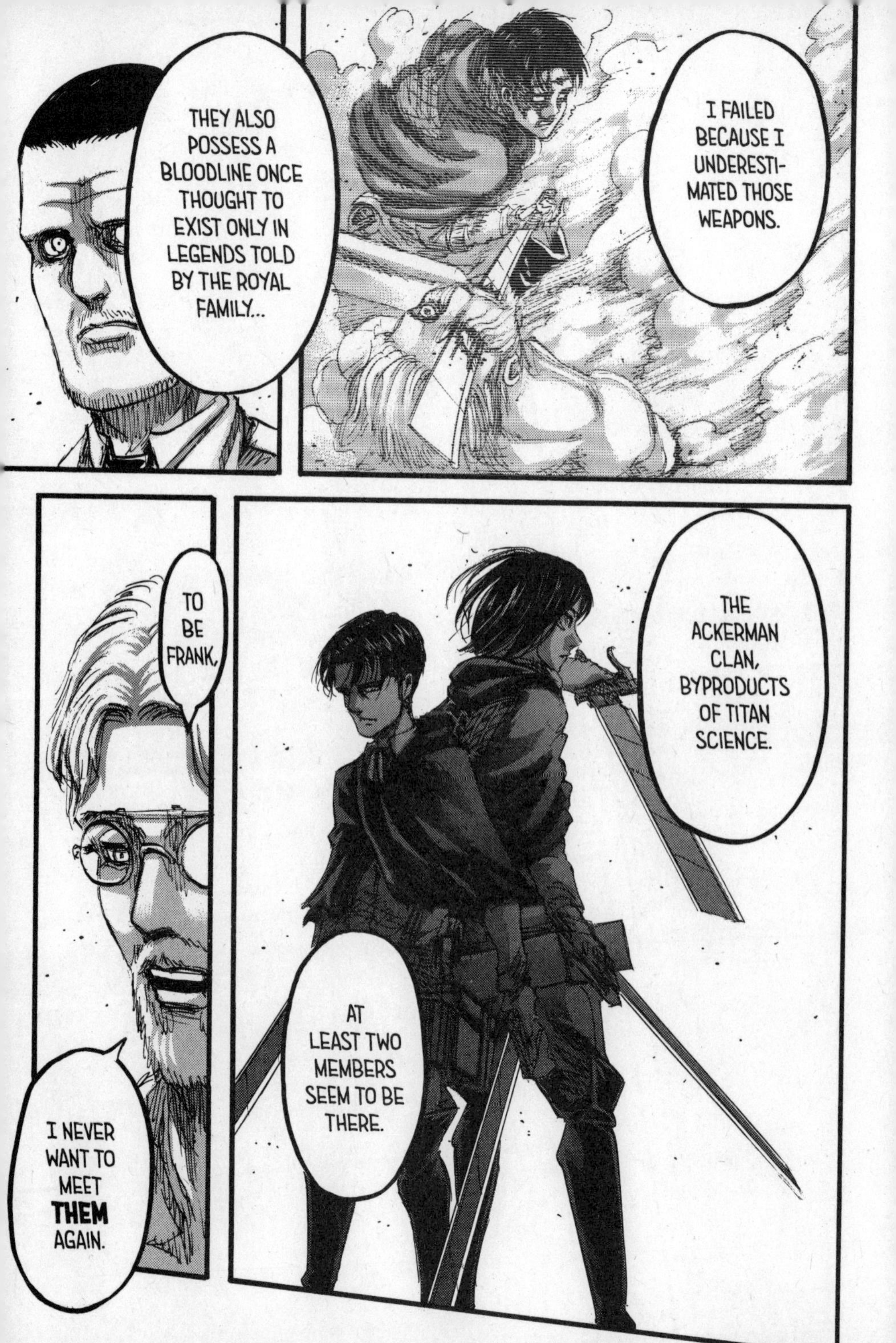
I FAILED BECAUSE I UNDERESTI- MATED THOSE WEAPONS.
THEY ALSO POSSESS A BLOODLINE ONCE THOUGHT TO EXIST ONLY IN LEGENDS TOLD BY THE ROYAL FAMILY...
THE ACKERMAN CLAN, BYPRODUCTS OF TITAN SCIENCE.
AT LEAST TWO MEMBERS SEEM TO BE THERE.
TO BE FRANK,
I NEVER WANT TO MEET **THEM** AGAIN.

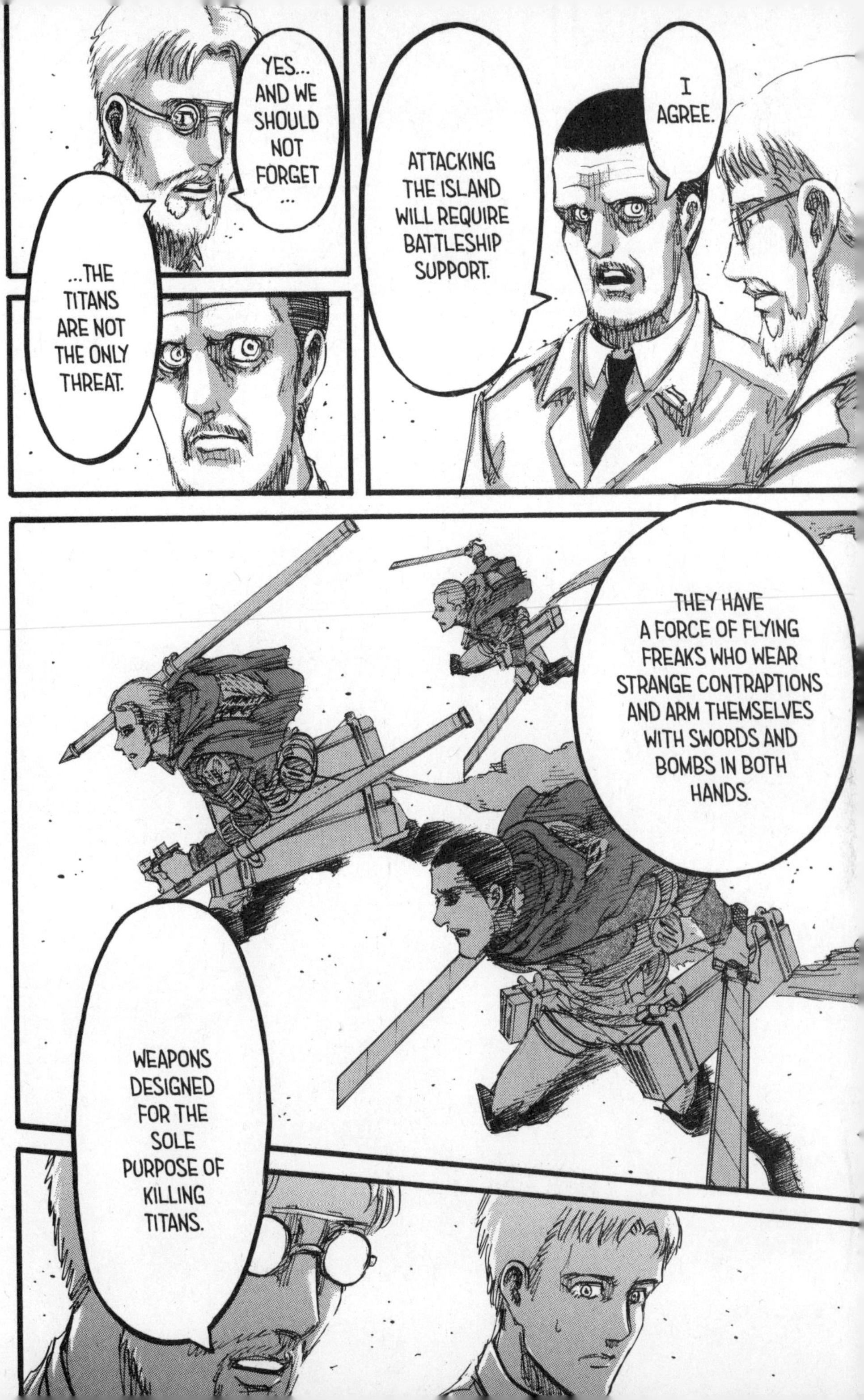
I AGREE.
ATTACKING THE ISLAND WILL REQUIRE BATTLESHIP SUPPORT.
YES... AND WE SHOULD NOT FORGET ...
...THE TITANS ARE NOT THE ONLY THREAT.
THEY HAVE A FORCE OF FLYING FREAKS WHO WEAR STRANGE CONTRAPTIONS AND ARM THEMSELVES WITH SWORDS AND BOMBS IN BOTH HANDS.
WEAPONS DESIGNED FOR THE SOLE PURPOSE OF KILLING TITANS.

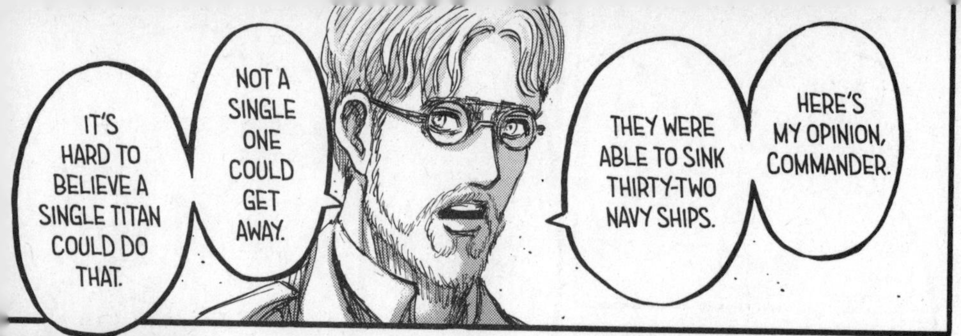
HERE'S MY OPINION, COMMANDER.
THEY WERE ABLE TO SINK THIRTY-TWO NAVY SHIPS.
NOT A SINGLE ONE COULD GET AWAY.
IT'S HARD TO BELIEVE A SINGLE TITAN COULD DO THAT.

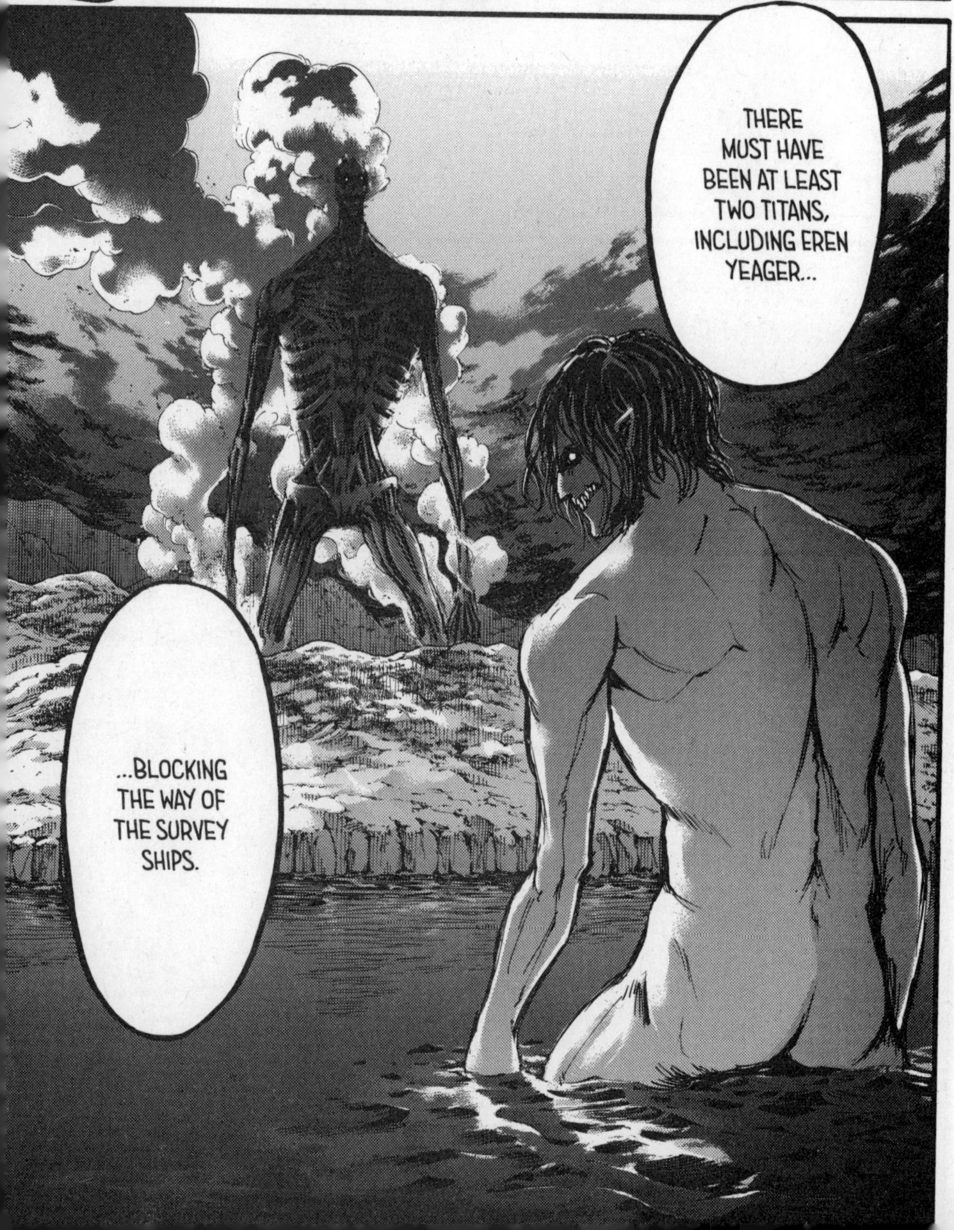
THERE MUST HAVE BEEN AT LEAST TWO TITANS, INCLUDING EREN YEAGER...
...BLOCKING THE WAY OF THE SURVEY SHIPS.

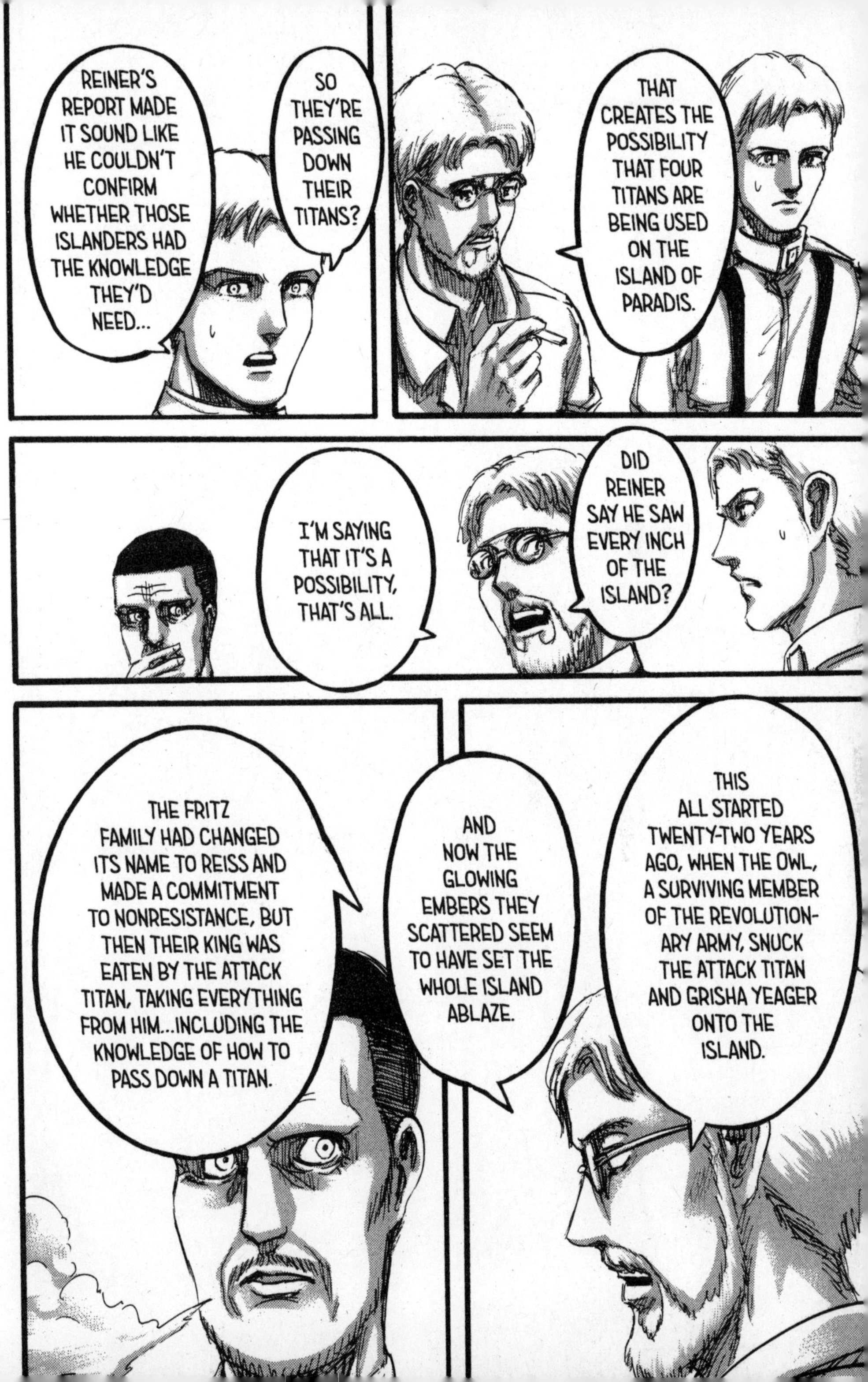
THAT CREATES THE POSSIBILITY THAT FOUR TITANS ARE BEING USED ON THE ISLAND OF PARADIS.
SO THEY'RE PASSING DOWN THEIR TITANS?
REINER'S REPORT MADE IT SOUND LIKE HE COULDN'T CONFIRM WHETHER THOSE ISLANDERS HAD THE KNOWLEDGE THEY'D NEED...
DID REINER SAY HE SAW EVERY INCH OF THE ISLAND?
I'M SAYING THAT IT'S A POSSIBILITY, THAT'S ALL.
THIS ALL STARTED TWENTY-TWO YEARS AGO, WHEN THE OWL, A SURVIVING MEMBER OF THE REVOLUTIONARY ARMY, SNUCK THE ATTACK TITAN AND GRISHA YEAGER ONTO THE ISLAND.
AND NOW THE GLOWING EMBERS THEY SCATTERED SEEM TO HAVE SET THE WHOLE ISLAND ABLAZE.
THE FRITZ FAMILY HAD CHANGED ITS NAME TO REISS AND MADE A COMMITMENT TO NONRESISTANCE, BUT THEN THEIR KING WAS EATEN BY THE ATTACK TITAN, TAKING EVERYTHING FROM HIM...INCLUDING THE KNOWLEDGE OF HOW TO PASS DOWN A TITAN.

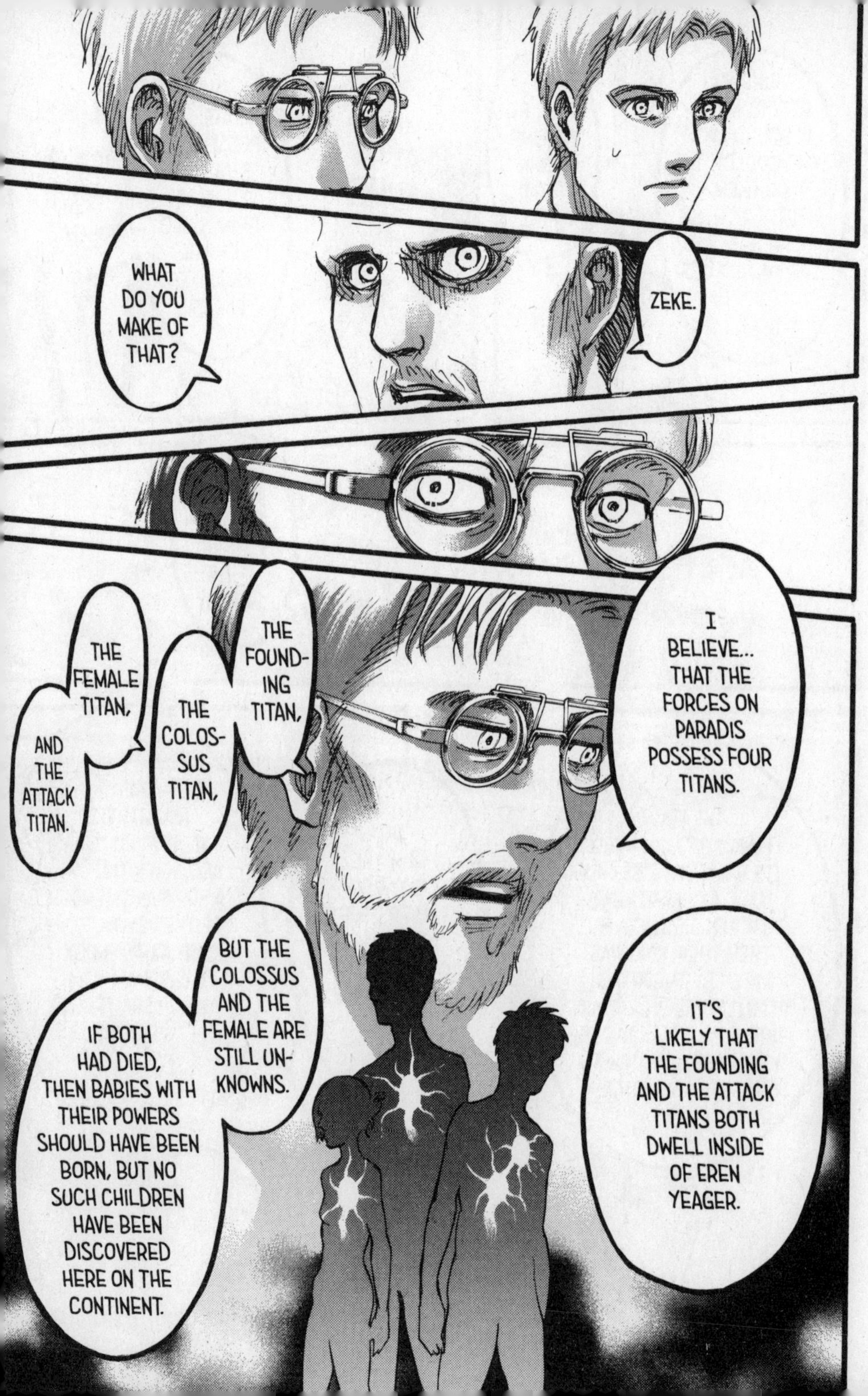
ZEKE.
WHAT DO YOU MAKE OF THAT?
I BELIEVE... THAT THE FORCES ON PARADIS POSSESS FOUR TITANS.
THE FOUNDING-ING TITAN,
THE COLOS-SUS TITAN,
THE FEMALE TITAN,
AND THE ATTACK TITAN.
IT'S LIKELY THAT THE FOUNDING AND THE ATTACK TITANS BOTH DWELL INSIDE OF EREN YEAGER.
BUT THE COLOSSUS AND THE FEMALE ARE STILL UN-KNOWNS.
IF BOTH HAD DIED, THEN BABIES WITH THEIR POWERS SHOULD HAVE BEEN BORN, BUT NO SUCH CHILDREN HAVE BEEN DISCOVERED HERE ON THE CONTINENT.

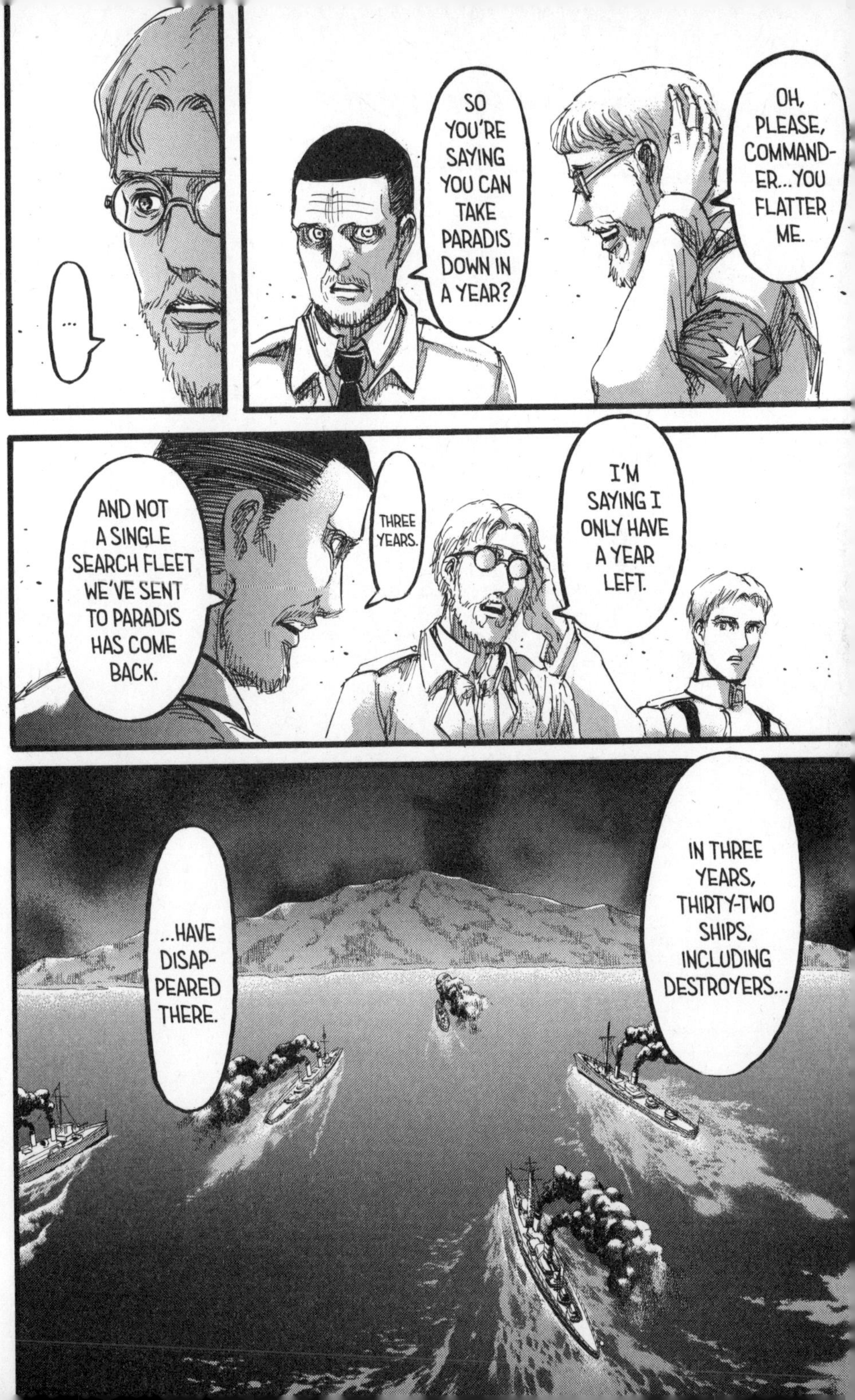
OH, PLEASE, COMMANDER...YOU FLATTER ME.
SO YOU'RE SAYING YOU CAN TAKE PARADIS DOWN IN A YEAR?
...
I'M SAYING I ONLY HAVE A YEAR LEFT.
THREE YEARS.
AND NOT A SINGLE SEARCH FLEET WE'VE SENT TO PARADIS HAS COME BACK.
IN THREE YEARS, THIRTY-TWO SHIPS, INCLUDING DESTROYERS...
...HAVE DISAPPEARED THERE.

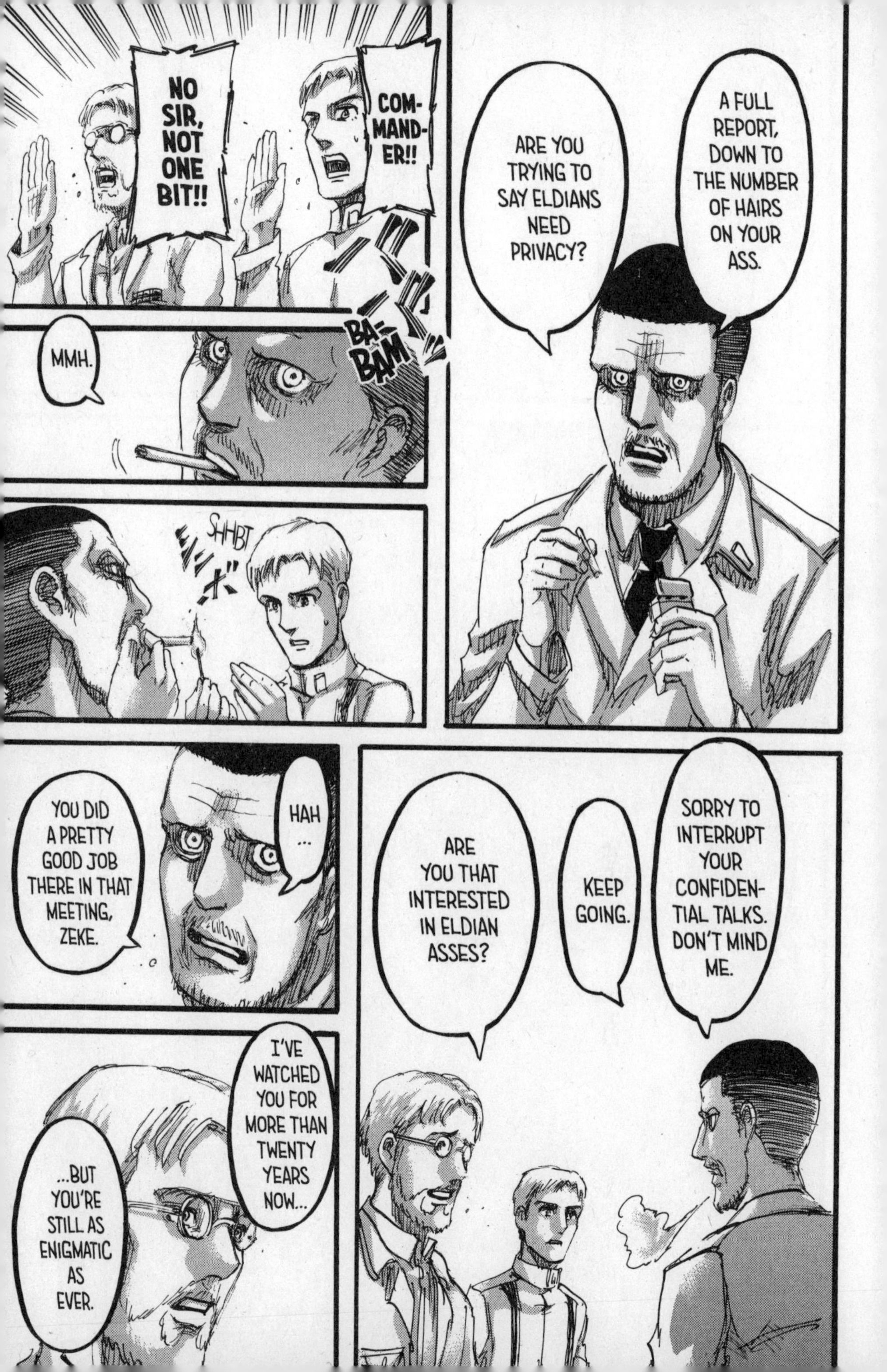
A FULL REPORT, DOWN TO THE NUMBER OF HAIRS ON YOUR ASS.
ARE YOU TRYING TO SAY ELDIANS NEED PRIVACY?
COM-MAND-ER!!
NO SIR, NOT ONE BIT!!
BA-BAM
MMH.
SHHBT
SORRY TO INTERRUPT YOUR CONFIDEN-TIAL TALKS. DON'T MIND ME.
KEEP GOING.
ARE YOU THAT INTERESTED IN ELDIAN ASSES?
HAH ...
YOU DID A PRETTY GOOD JOB THERE IN THAT MEETING, ZEKE.
I'VE WATCHED YOU FOR MORE THAN TWENTY YEARS NOW...
...BUT YOU'RE STILL AS ENIGMATIC AS EVER.

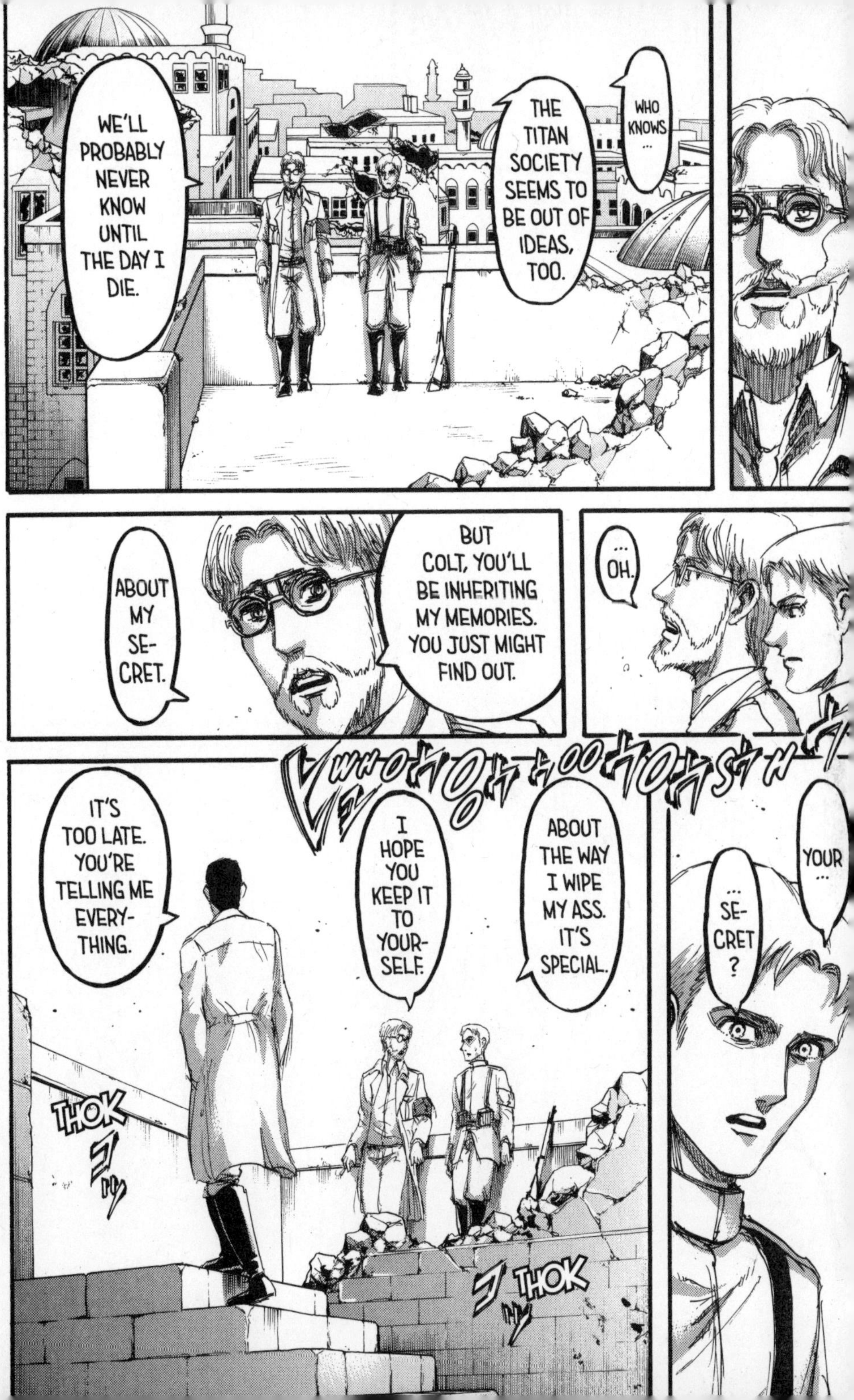
WHO KNOWS ...
THE TITAN SOCIETY SEEMS TO BE OUT OF IDEAS, TOO.
WE'LL PROBABLY NEVER KNOW UNTIL THE DAY I DIE.
... OH.
BUT COLT, YOU'LL BE INHERITING MY MEMORIES. YOU JUST MIGHT FIND OUT.
ABOUT MY SE-CRET.
YOUR ...
... SE-CRET ?
ABOUT THE WAY I WIPE MY ASS. IT'S SPECIAL.
I HOPE YOU KEEP IT TO YOUR-SELF.
IT'S TOO LATE. YOU'RE TELLING ME EVERY-THING.
THOK
THOK

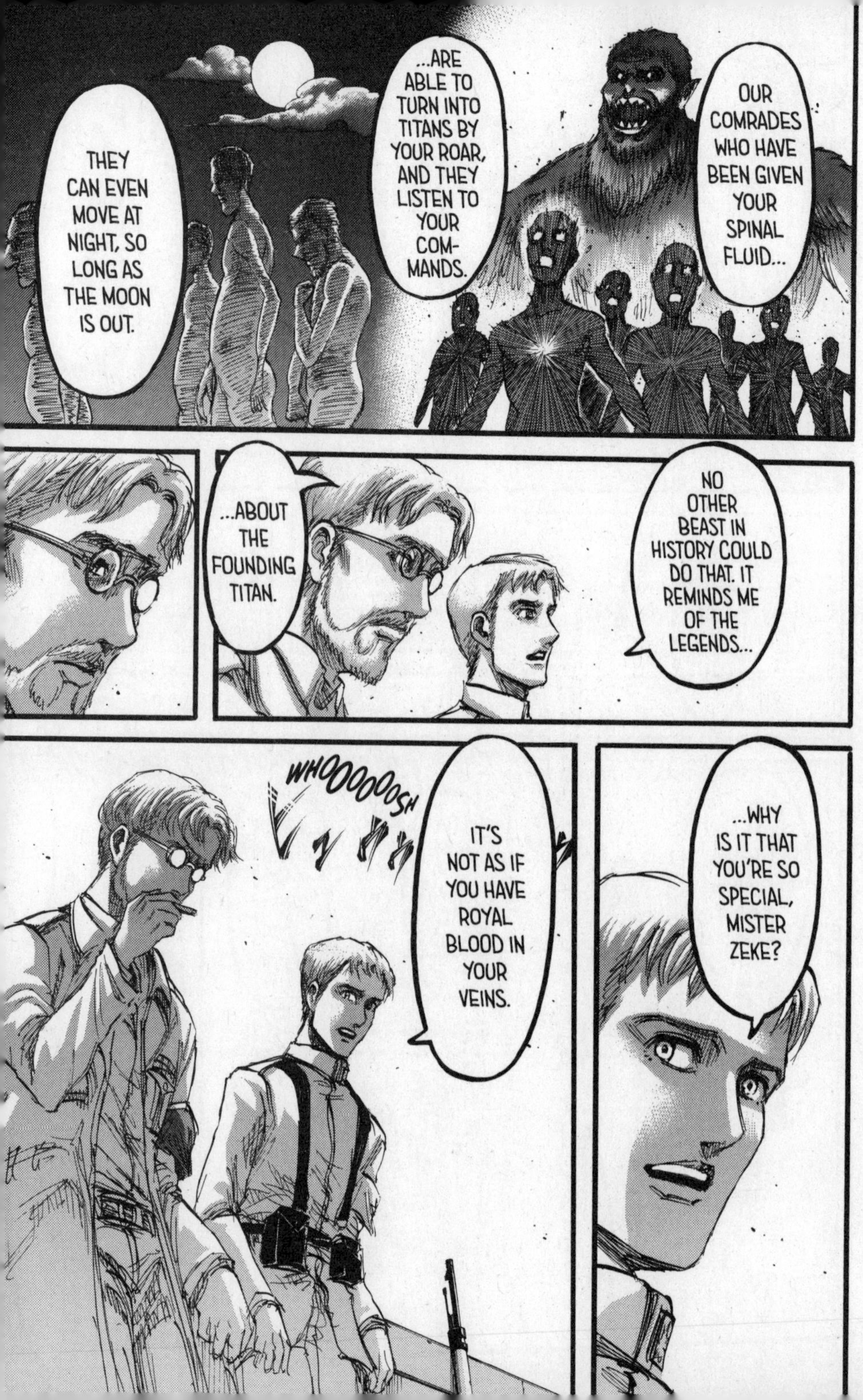
OUR COMRADES WHO HAVE BEEN GIVEN YOUR SPINAL FLUID...
...ARE ABLE TO TURN INTO TITANS BY YOUR ROAR, AND THEY LISTEN TO YOUR COMMANDS.
THEY CAN EVEN MOVE AT NIGHT, SO LONG AS THE MOON IS OUT.
NO OTHER BEAST IN HISTORY COULD DO THAT. IT REMINDS ME OF THE LEGENDS...
...ABOUT THE FOUNDING TITAN.
...WHY IS IT THAT YOU'RE SO SPECIAL, MISTER ZEKE?
IT'S NOT AS IF YOU HAVE ROYAL BLOOD IN YOUR VEINS.
WHOOOOOOOSH

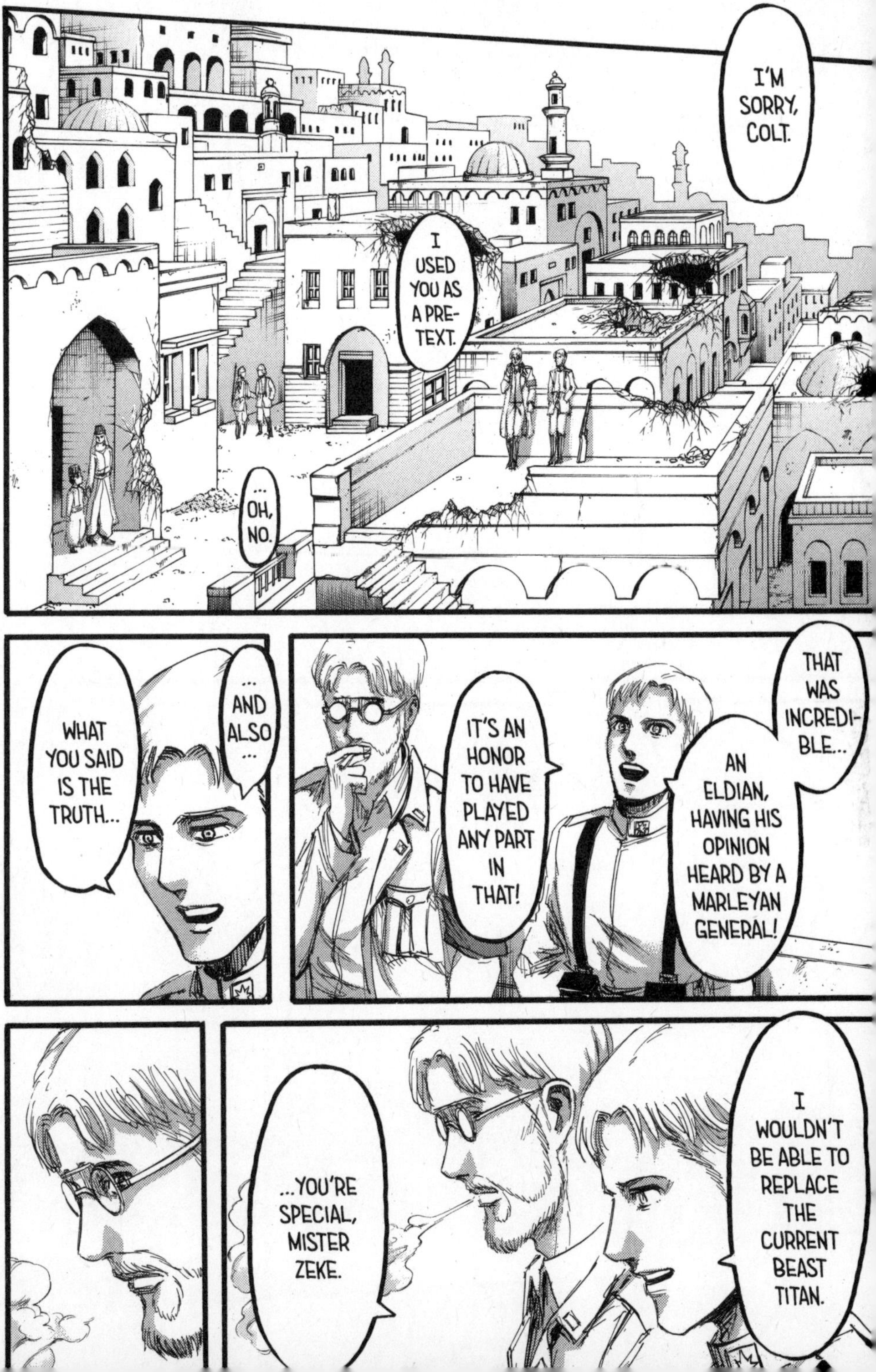
I'M SORRY, COLT.
I USED YOU AS A PRE-TEXT.
... OH, NO.
THAT WAS INCREDI-BLE...
AN ELDIAN, HAVING HIS OPINION HEARD BY A MARLEYAN GENERAL!
IT'S AN HONOR TO HAVE PLAYED ANY PART IN THAT!
... AND ALSO ...
WHAT YOU SAID IS THE TRUTH...
I WOULDN'T BE ABLE TO REPLACE THE CURRENT BEAST TITAN.
...YOU'RE SPECIAL, MISTER ZEKE.

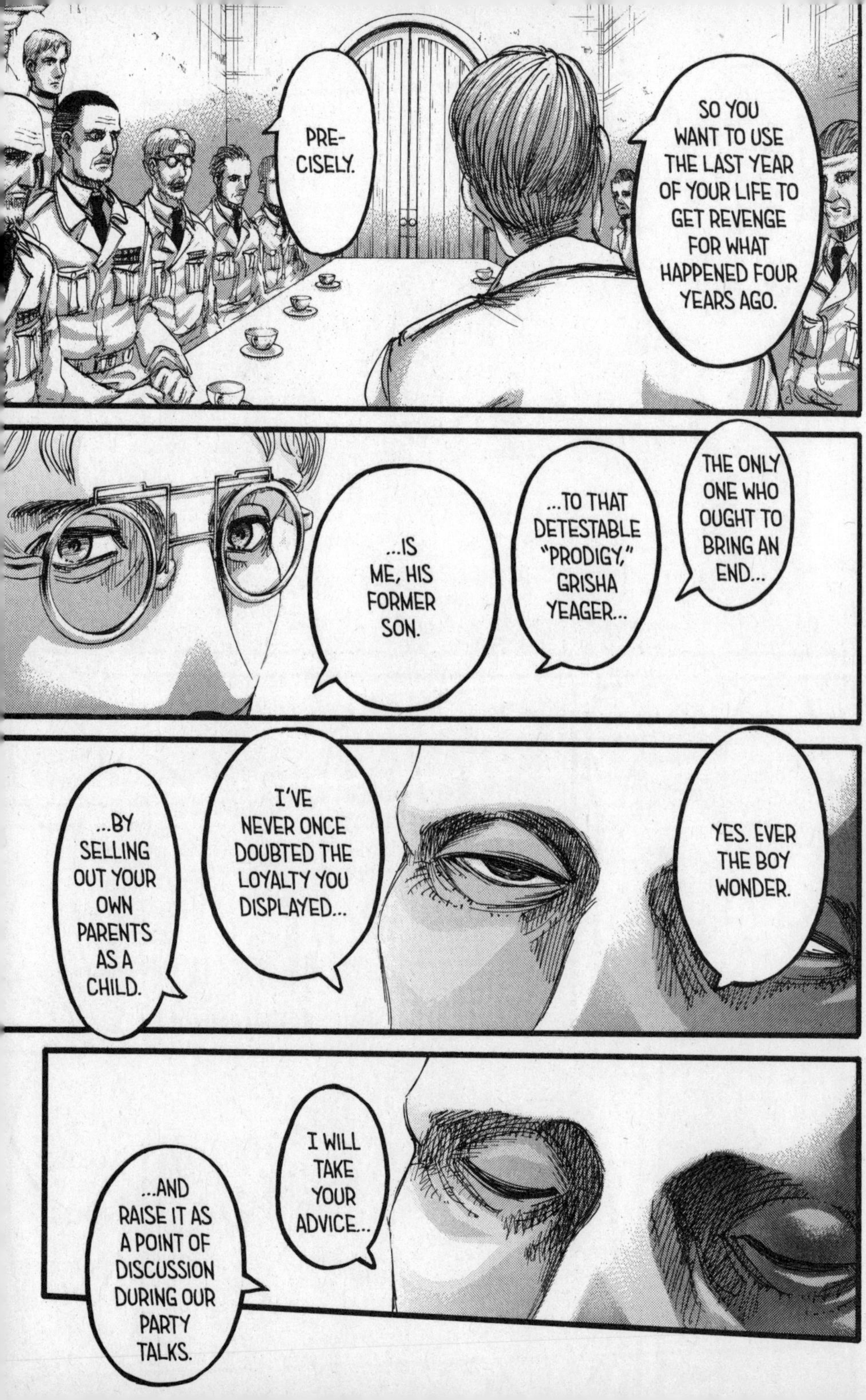
SO YOU WANT TO USE THE LAST YEAR OF YOUR LIFE TO GET REVENGE FOR WHAT HAPPENED FOUR YEARS AGO.
PRE-CISELY.
THE ONLY ONE WHO OUGHT TO BRING AN END...
...TO THAT DETESTABLE "PRODIGY," GRISHA YEAGER...
...IS ME, HIS FORMER SON.
YES. EVER THE BOY WONDER.
I'VE NEVER ONCE DOUBTED THE LOYALTY YOU DISPLAYED...
...BY SELLING OUT YOUR OWN PARENTS AS A CHILD.
I WILL TAKE YOUR ADVICE...
...AND RAISE IT AS A POINT OF DISCUSSION DURING OUR PARTY TALKS.

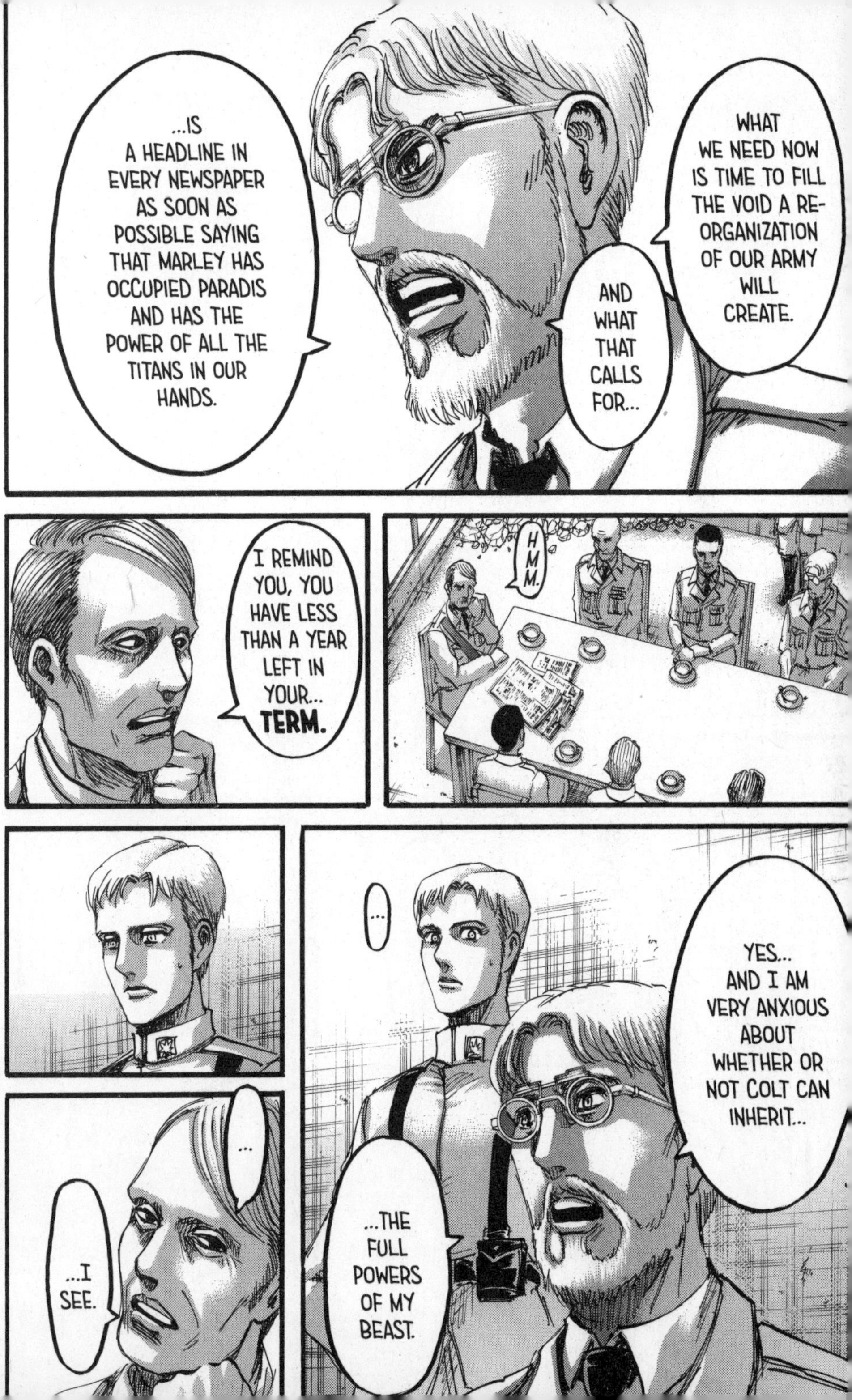
WHAT WE NEED NOW IS TIME TO FILL THE VOID A RE-ORGANIZATION OF OUR ARMY WILL CREATE.
AND WHAT THAT CALLS FOR...
...IS A HEADLINE IN EVERY NEWSPAPER AS SOON AS POSSIBLE SAYING THAT MARLEY HAS OCCUPIED PARADIS AND HAS THE POWER OF ALL THE TITANS IN OUR HANDS.
HMM.
I REMIND YOU, YOU HAVE LESS THAN A YEAR LEFT IN YOUR... **TERM.**
YES... AND I AM VERY ANXIOUS ABOUT WHETHER OR NOT COLT CAN INHERIT...
...
...THE FULL POWERS OF MY BEAST.
...
...I SEE.

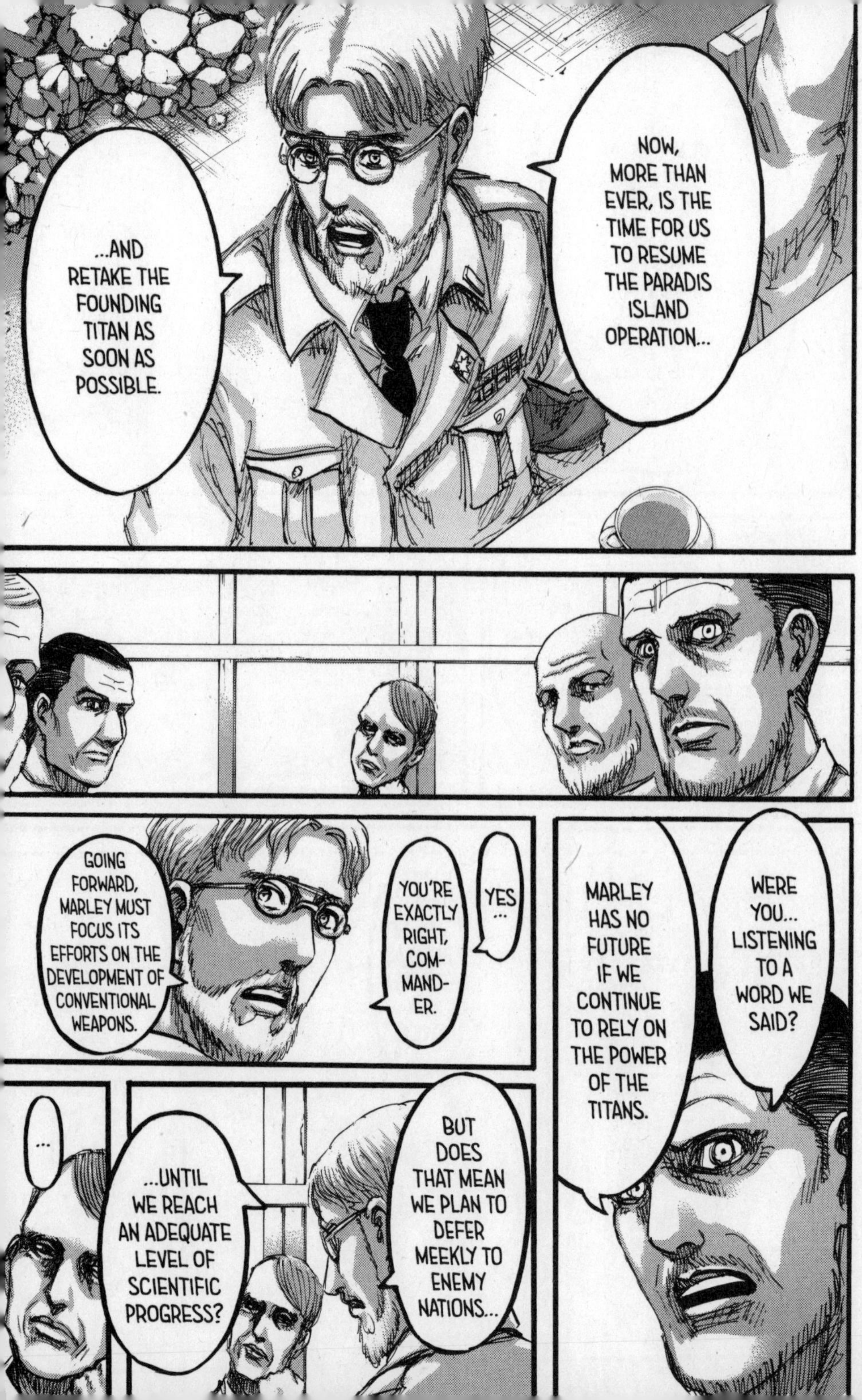
NOW, MORE THAN EVER, IS THE TIME FOR US TO RESUME THE PARADIS ISLAND OPERATION...
...AND RETAKE THE FOUNDING TITAN AS SOON AS POSSIBLE.
WERE YOU... LISTENING TO A WORD WE SAID?
MARLEY HAS NO FUTURE IF WE CONTINUE TO RELY ON THE POWER OF THE TITANS.
YES...
YOU'RE EXACTLY RIGHT, COM-MANDER.
GOING FORWARD, MARLEY MUST FOCUS ITS EFFORTS ON THE DEVELOPMENT OF CONVENTIONAL WEAPONS.
BUT DOES THAT MEAN WE PLAN TO DEFER MEEKLY TO ENEMY NATIONS...
...UNTIL WE REACH AN ADEQUATE LEVEL OF SCIENTIFIC PROGRESS?
...

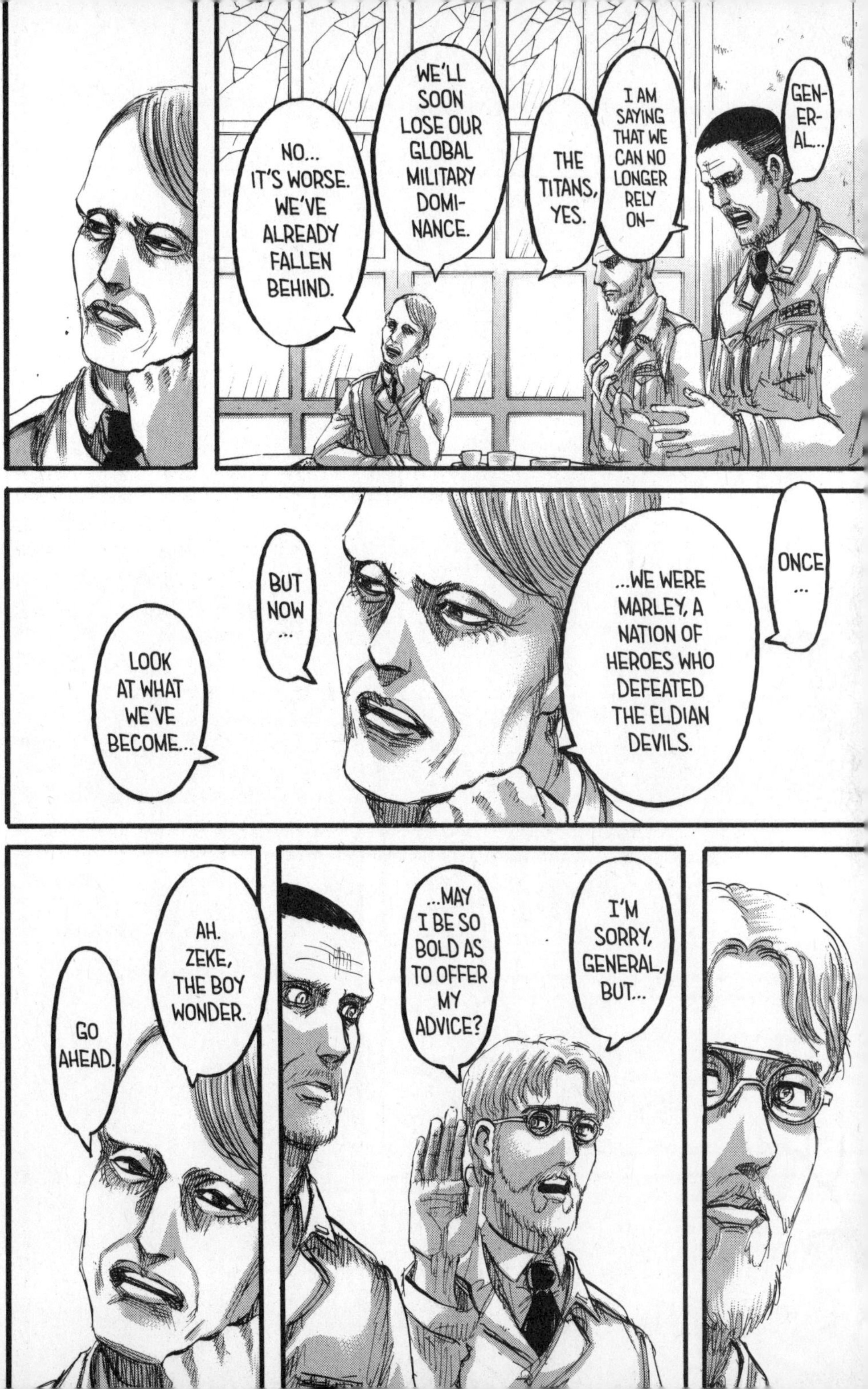
GEN-ER-AL...
I AM SAYING THAT WE CAN NO LONGER RELY ON-
THE TITANS, YES.
WE'LL SOON LOSE OUR GLOBAL MILITARY DOMI-NANCE.
NO... IT'S WORSE. WE'VE ALREADY FALLEN BEHIND.
ONCE...
...WE WERE MARLEY, A NATION OF HEROES WHO DEFEATED THE ELDIAN DEVILS.
BUT NOW...
LOOK AT WHAT WE'VE BECOME...
I'M SORRY, GENERAL, BUT...
...MAY I BE SO BOLD AS TO OFFER MY ADVICE?
AH. ZEKE, THE BOY WONDER.
GO AHEAD.

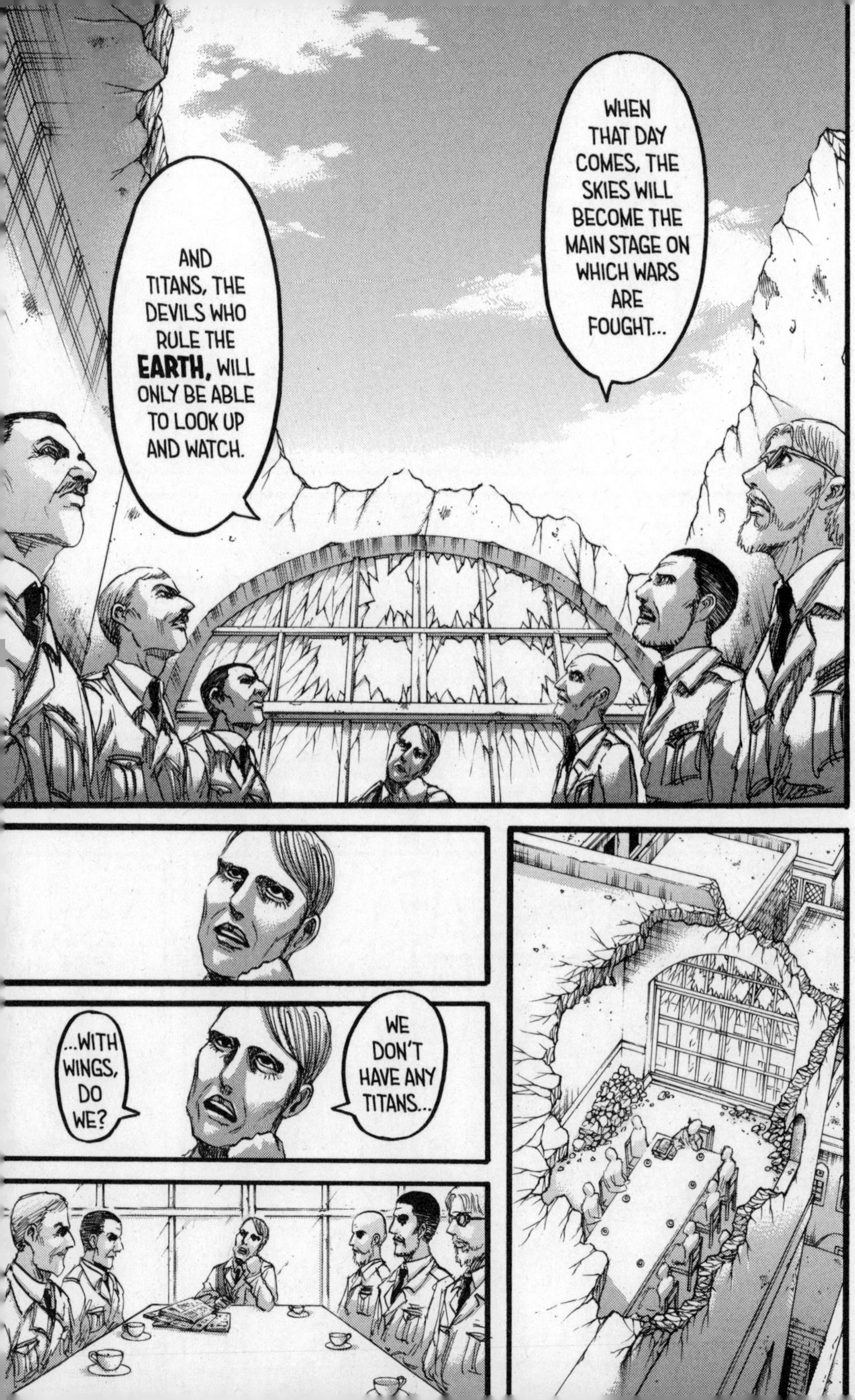
WHEN THAT DAY COMES, THE SKIES WILL BECOME THE MAIN STAGE ON WHICH WARS ARE FOUGHT...
AND TITANS, THE DEVILS WHO RULE THE **EARTH,** WILL ONLY BE ABLE TO LOOK UP AND WATCH.
WE DON'T HAVE ANY TITANS...
...WITH WINGS, DO WE?

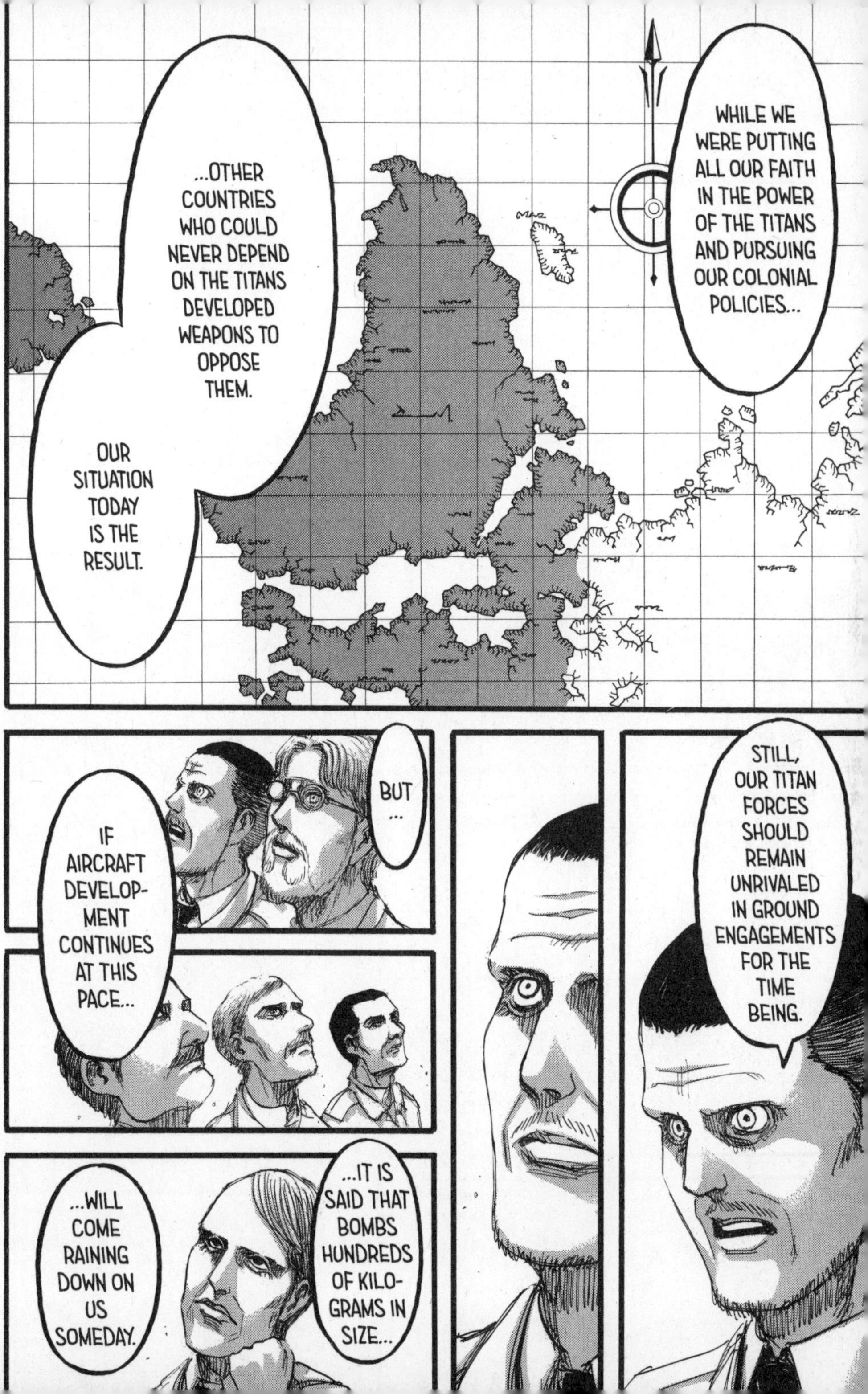
WHILE WE WERE PUTTING ALL OUR FAITH IN THE POWER OF THE TITANS AND PURSUING OUR COLONIAL POLICIES...
...OTHER COUNTRIES WHO COULD NEVER DEPEND ON THE TITANS DEVELOPED WEAPONS TO OPPOSE THEM.
OUR SITUATION TODAY IS THE RESULT.
STILL, OUR TITAN FORCES SHOULD REMAIN UNRIVALED IN GROUND ENGAGEMENTS FOR THE TIME BEING.
BUT ...
IF AIRCRAFT DEVELOP-MENT CONTINUES AT THIS PACE...
...IT IS SAID THAT BOMBS HUNDREDS OF KILO-GRAMS IN SIZE...
...WILL COME RAINING DOWN ON US SOMEDAY.

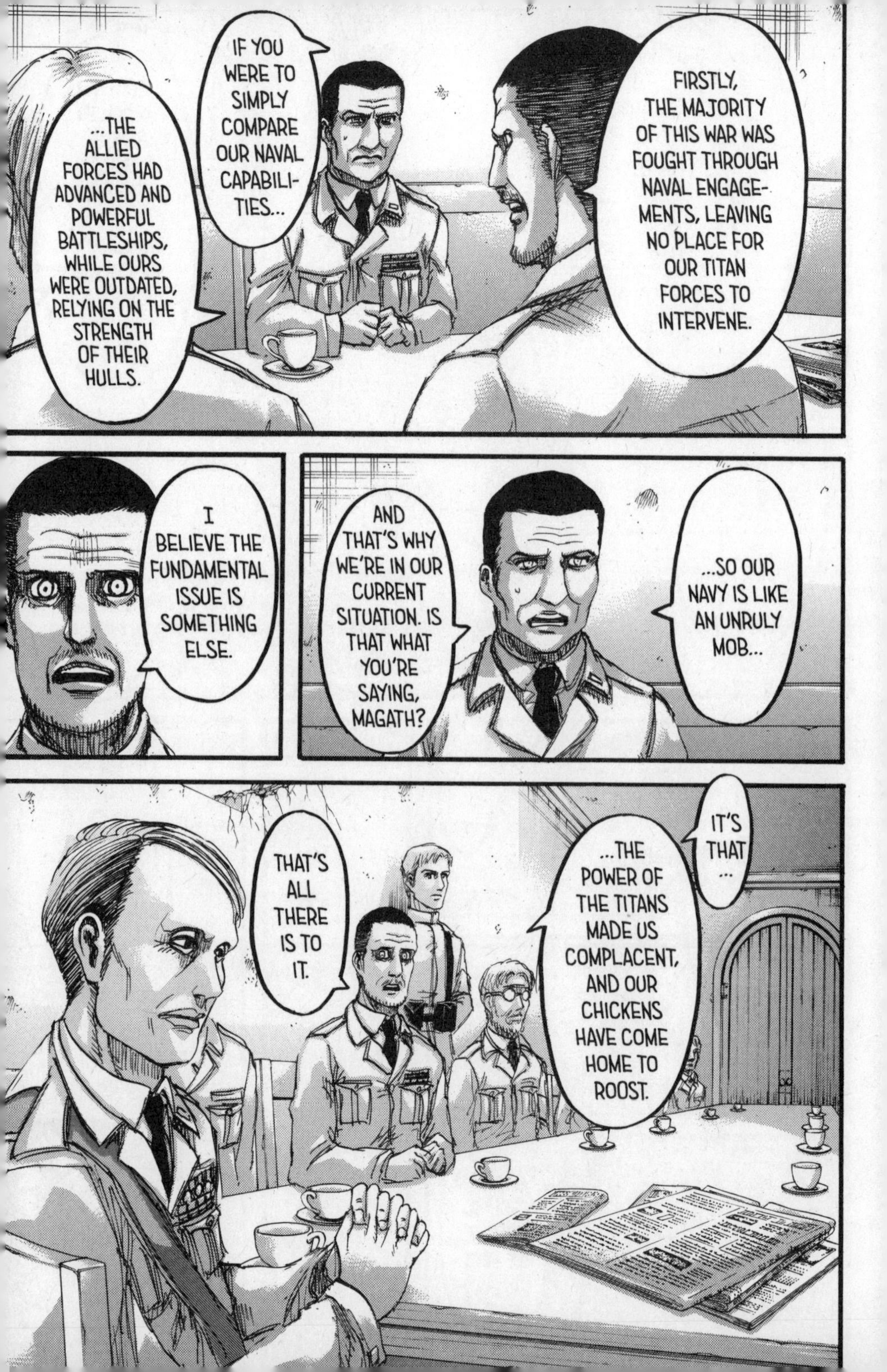
FIRSTLY, THE MAJORITY OF THIS WAR WAS FOUGHT THROUGH NAVAL ENGAGE-MENTS, LEAVING NO PLACE FOR OUR TITAN FORCES TO INTERVENE.
IF YOU WERE TO SIMPLY COMPARE OUR NAVAL CAPABILI-TIES...
...THE ALLIED FORCES HAD ADVANCED AND POWERFUL BATTLESHIPS, WHILE OURS WERE OUTDATED, RELYING ON THE STRENGTH OF THEIR HULLS.
...SO OUR NAVY IS LIKE AN UNRULY MOB...
AND THAT'S WHY WE'RE IN OUR CURRENT SITUATION. IS THAT WHAT YOU'RE SAYING, MAGATH?
I BELIEVE THE FUNDAMENTAL ISSUE IS SOMETHING ELSE.
IT'S THAT ...
...THE POWER OF THE TITANS MADE US COMPLACENT, AND OUR CHICKENS HAVE COME HOME TO ROOST.
THAT'S ALL THERE IS TO IT.

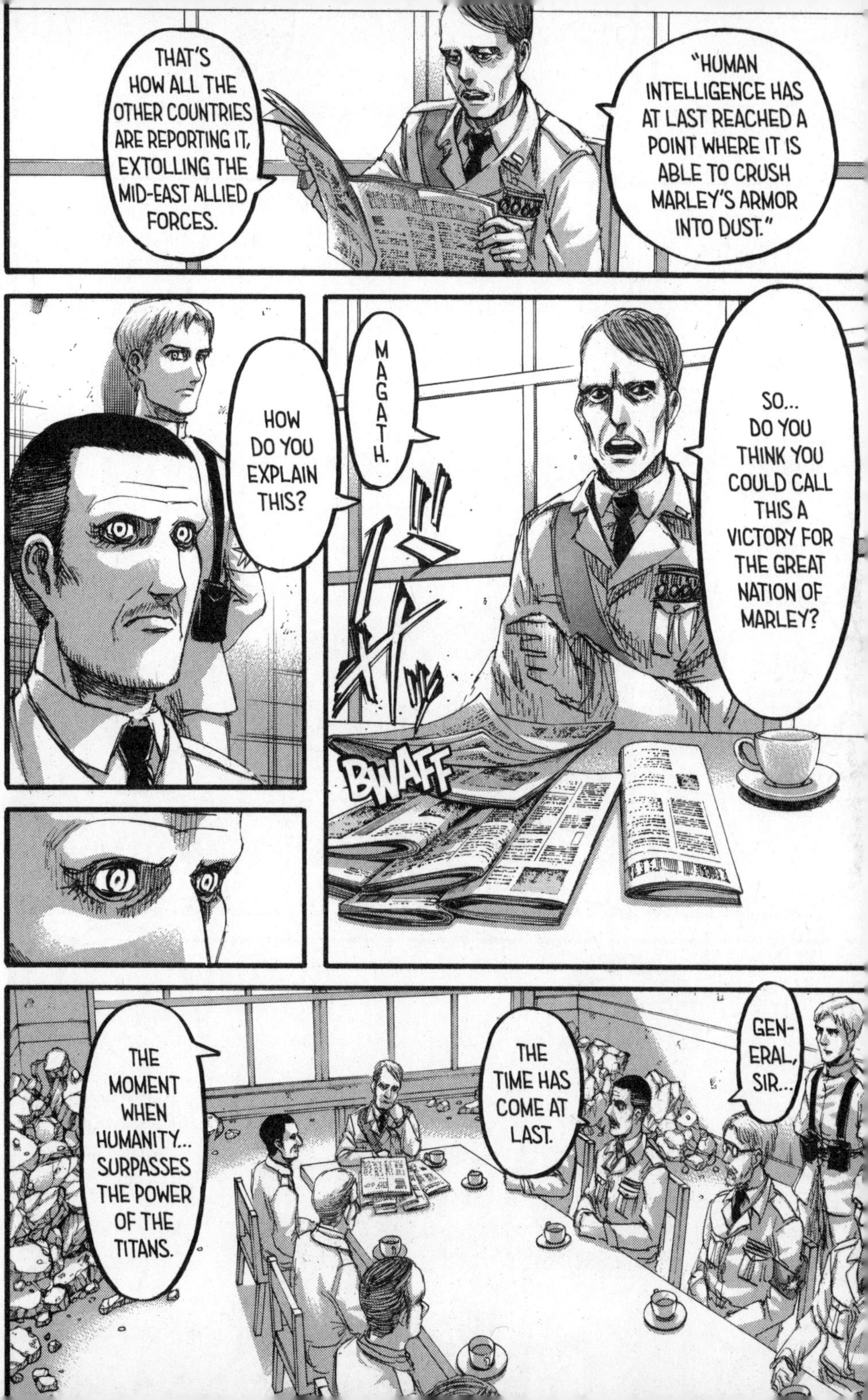
"HUMAN INTELLIGENCE HAS AT LAST REACHED A POINT WHERE IT IS ABLE TO CRUSH MARLEY'S ARMOR INTO DUST."
THAT'S HOW ALL THE OTHER COUNTRIES ARE REPORTING IT, EXTOLLING THE MID-EAST ALLIED FORCES.
SO... DO YOU THINK YOU COULD CALL THIS A VICTORY FOR THE GREAT NATION OF MARLEY?
MAGATH.
BWAFF
HOW DO YOU EXPLAIN THIS?
GEN-ERAL, SIR...
THE TIME HAS COME AT LAST.
THE MOMENT WHEN HUMANITY... SURPASSES THE POWER OF THE TITANS.

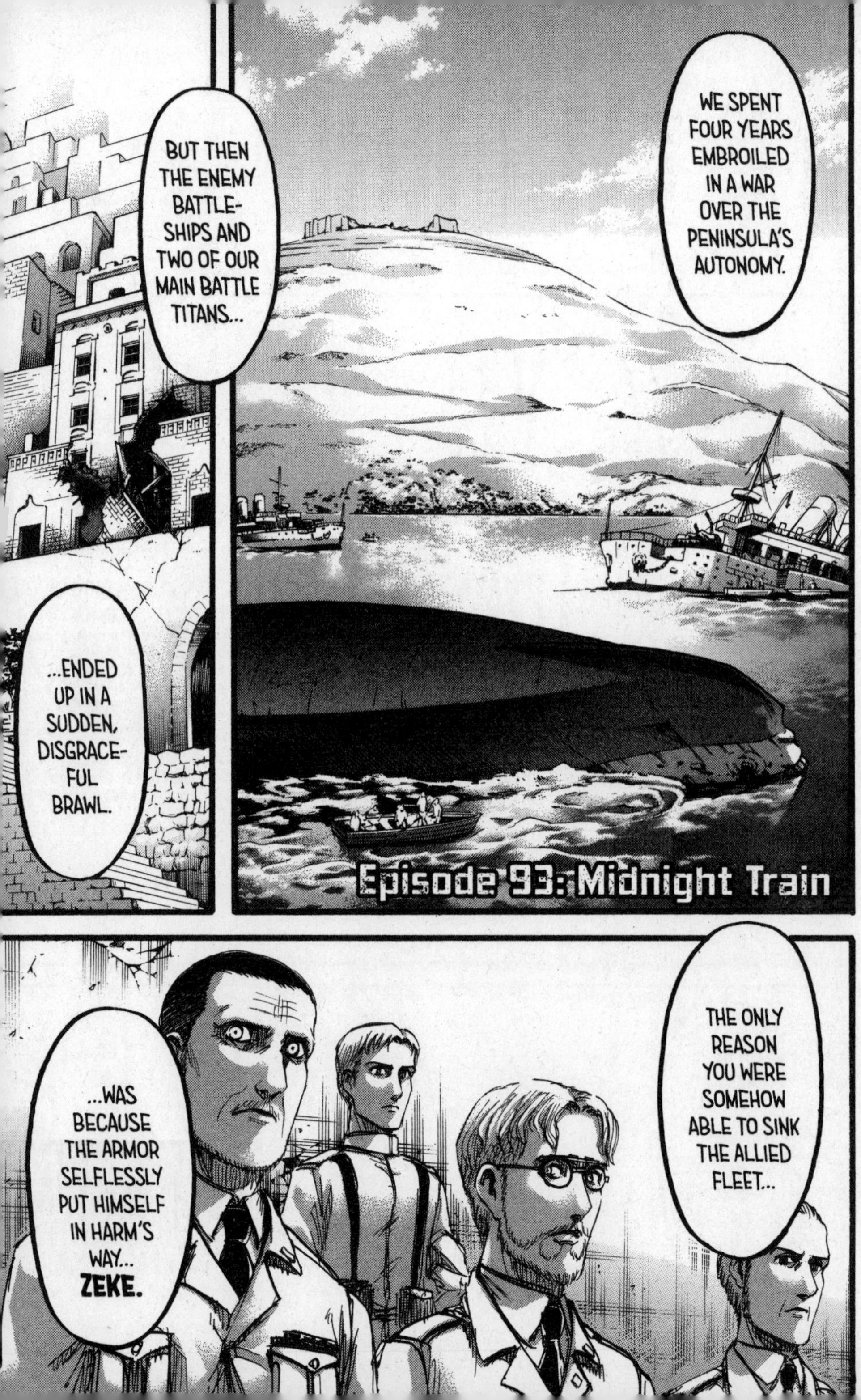
WE SPENT FOUR YEARS EMBROILED IN A WAR OVER THE PENINSULA'S AUTONOMY.
Episode 93: Midnight Train
BUT THEN THE ENEMY BATTLE-SHIPS AND TWO OF OUR MAIN BATTLE TITANS...
...ENDED UP IN A SUDDEN, DISGRACE-FUL BRAWL.
THE ONLY REASON YOU WERE SOMEHOW ABLE TO SINK THE ALLIED FLEET...
...WAS BECAUSE THE ARMOR SELFLESSLY PUT HIMSELF IN HARM'S WAY... **ZEKE.**

ATTACK on TITAN

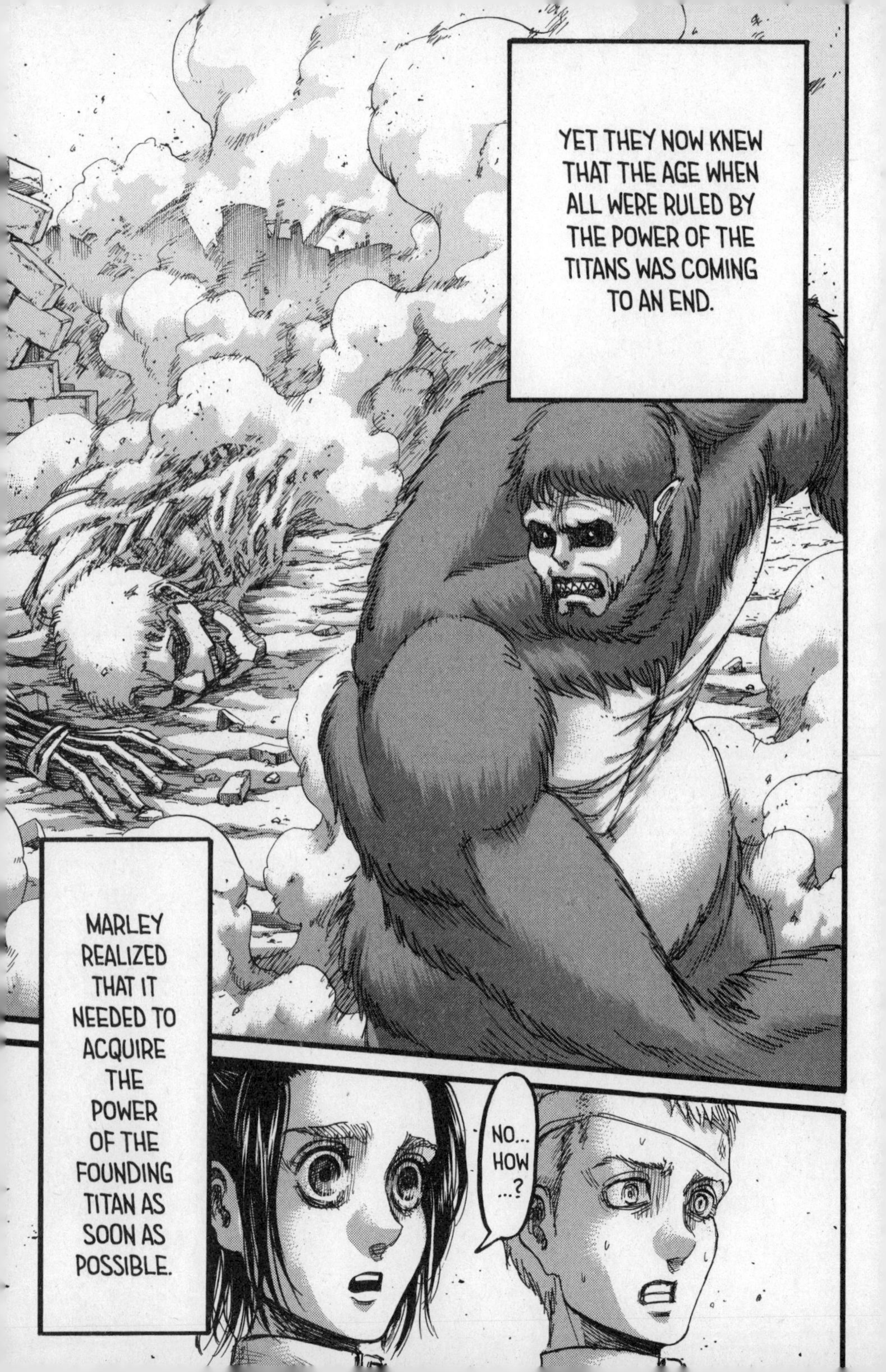
YET THEY NOW KNEW THAT THE AGE WHEN ALL WERE RULED BY THE POWER OF THE TITANS WAS COMING TO AN END.
NO... HOW ...?
MARLEY REALIZED THAT IT NEEDED TO ACQUIRE THE POWER OF THE FOUNDING TITAN AS SOON AS POSSIBLE.

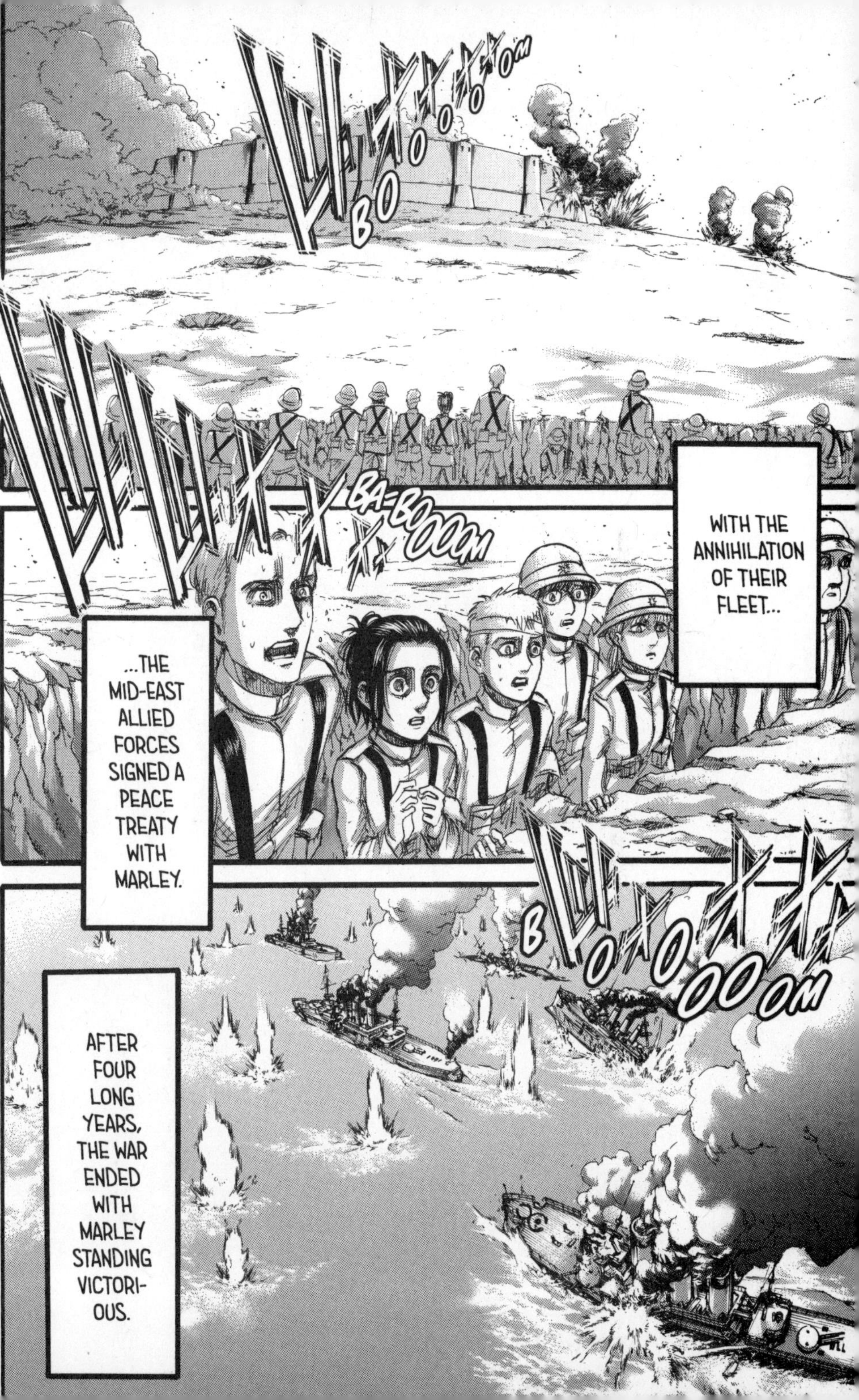
BOOOOOM
WITH THE ANNIHILATION OF THEIR FLEET...
BA-BOOOOM
...THE MID-EAST ALLIED FORCES SIGNED A PEACE TREATY WITH MARLEY.
BOOOOOOOM
AFTER FOUR LONG YEARS, THE WAR ENDED WITH MARLEY STANDING VICTORI-OUS.

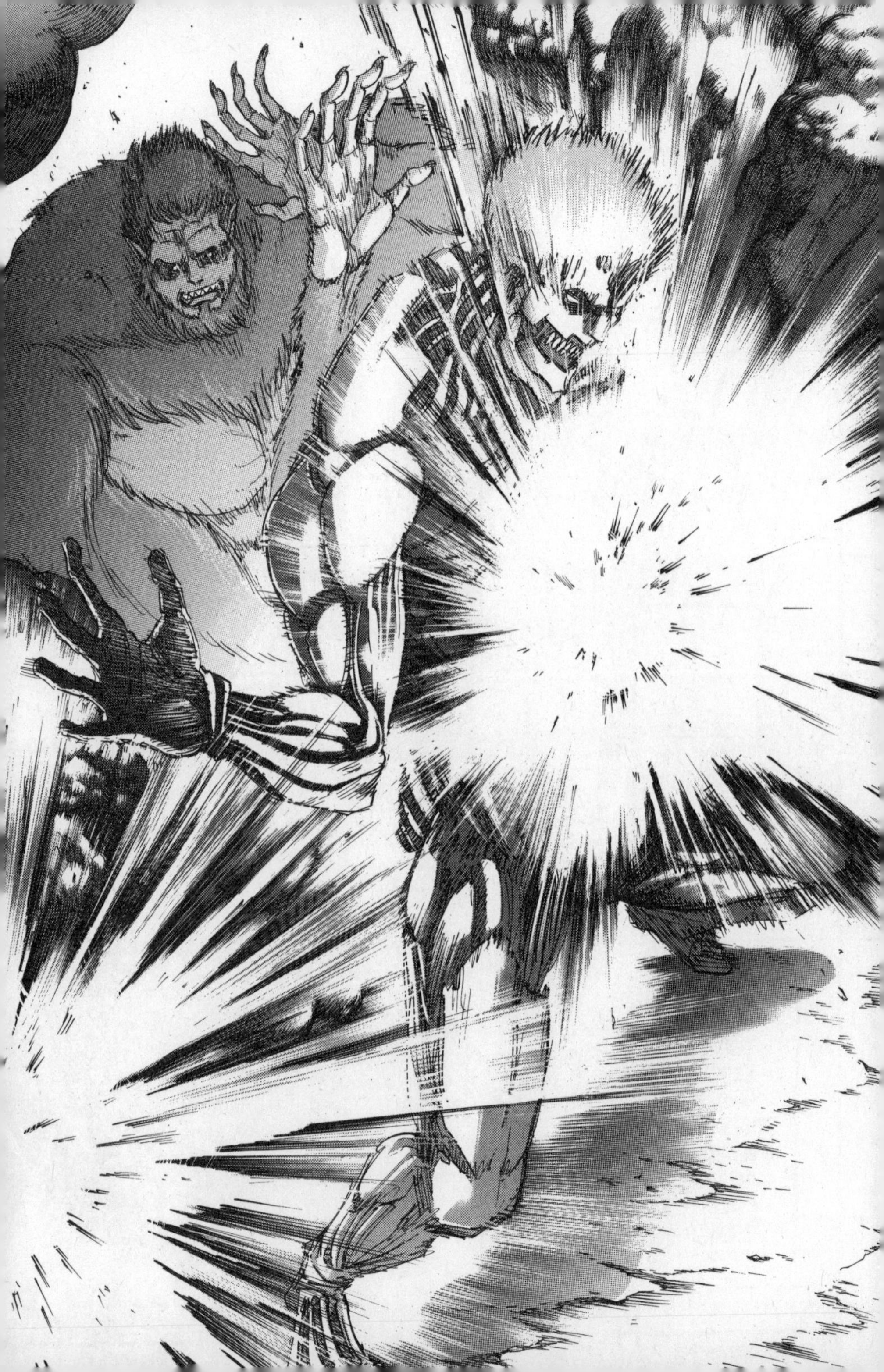

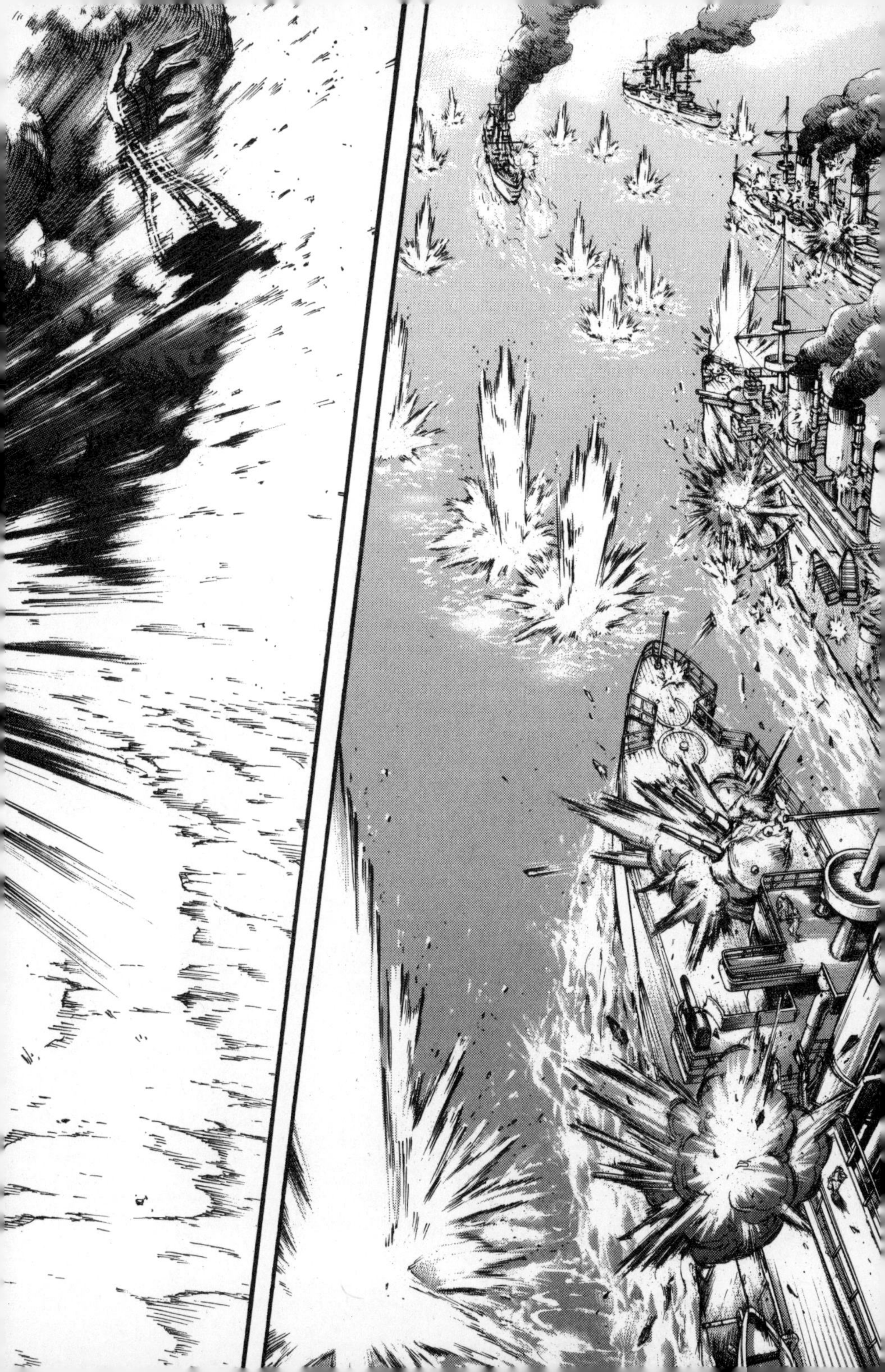

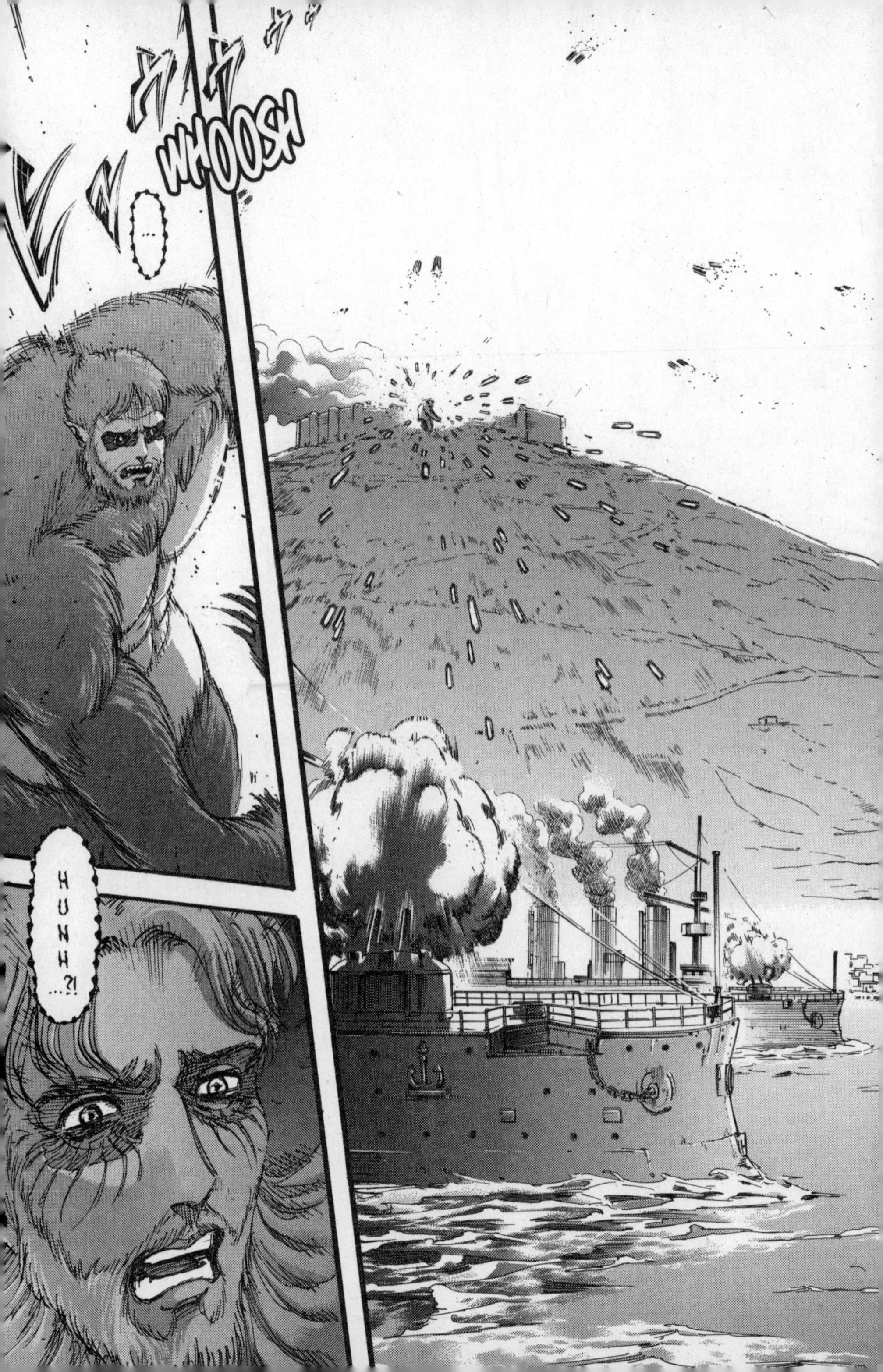
WHOOSH
...
HUNNH ...?!

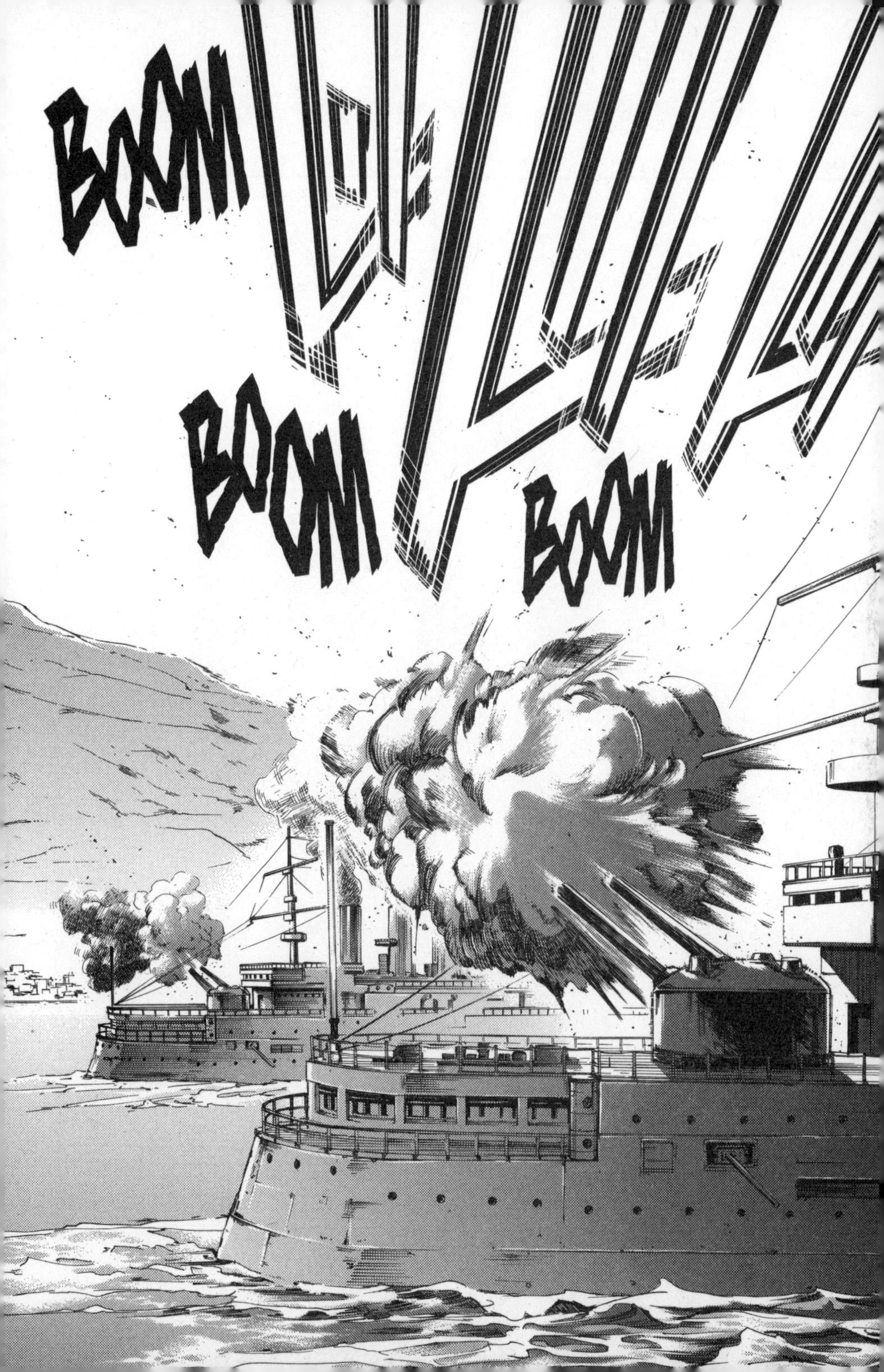
BOOM
BOOM
BOOM

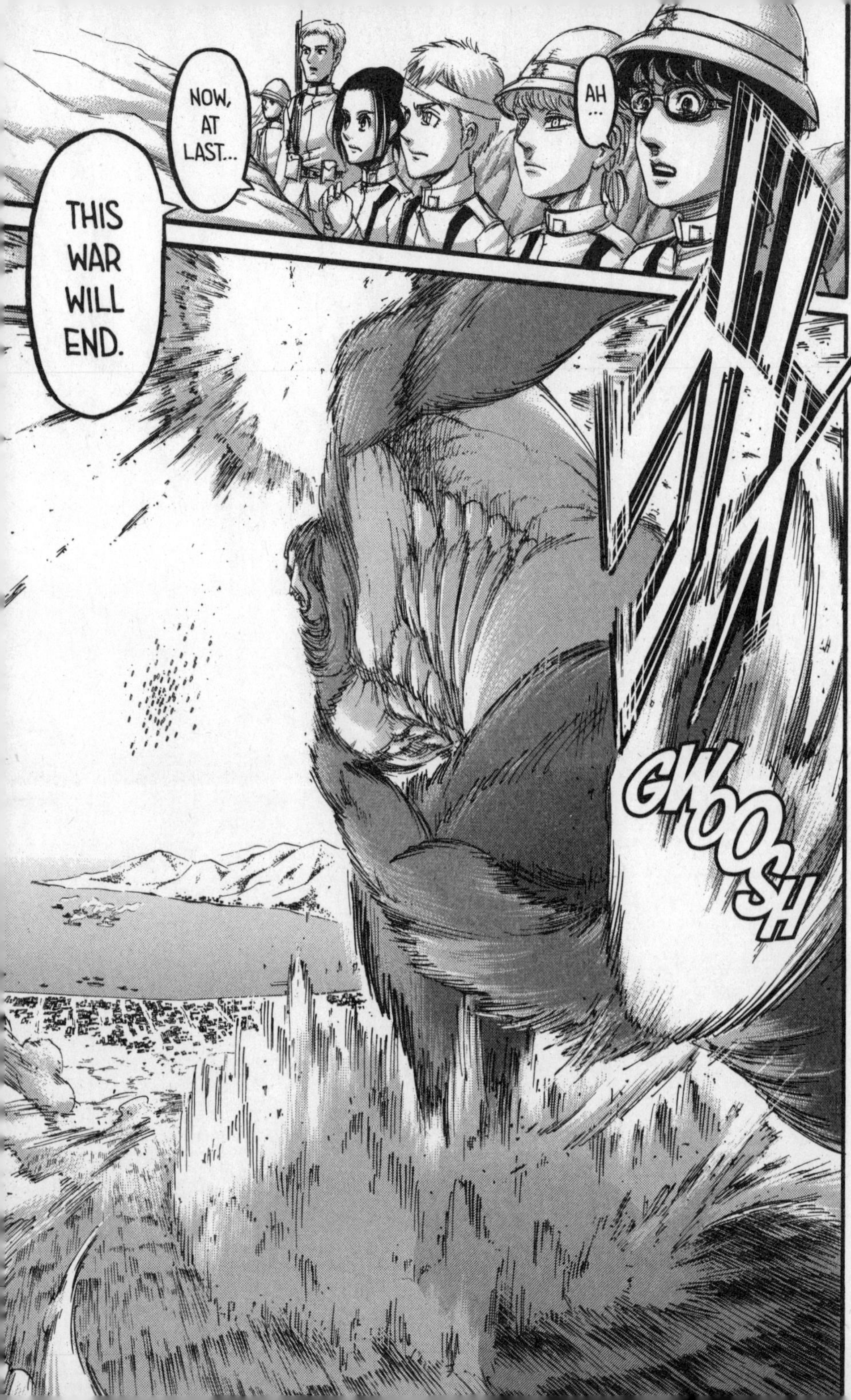
AH ...
NOW, AT LAST...
THIS WAR WILL END.
GWOOSH

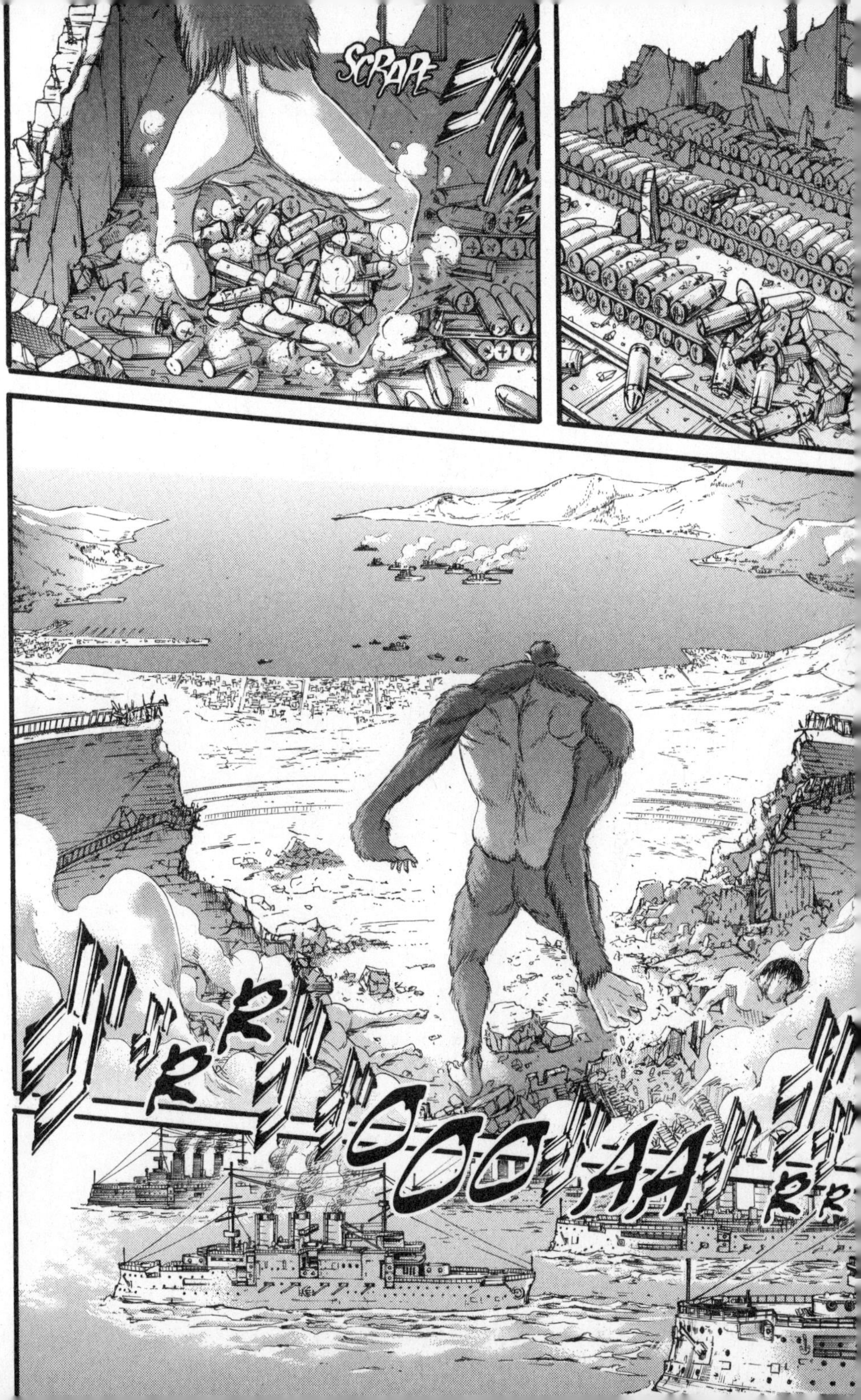
SCRAPE
RR
OOOAA
RR

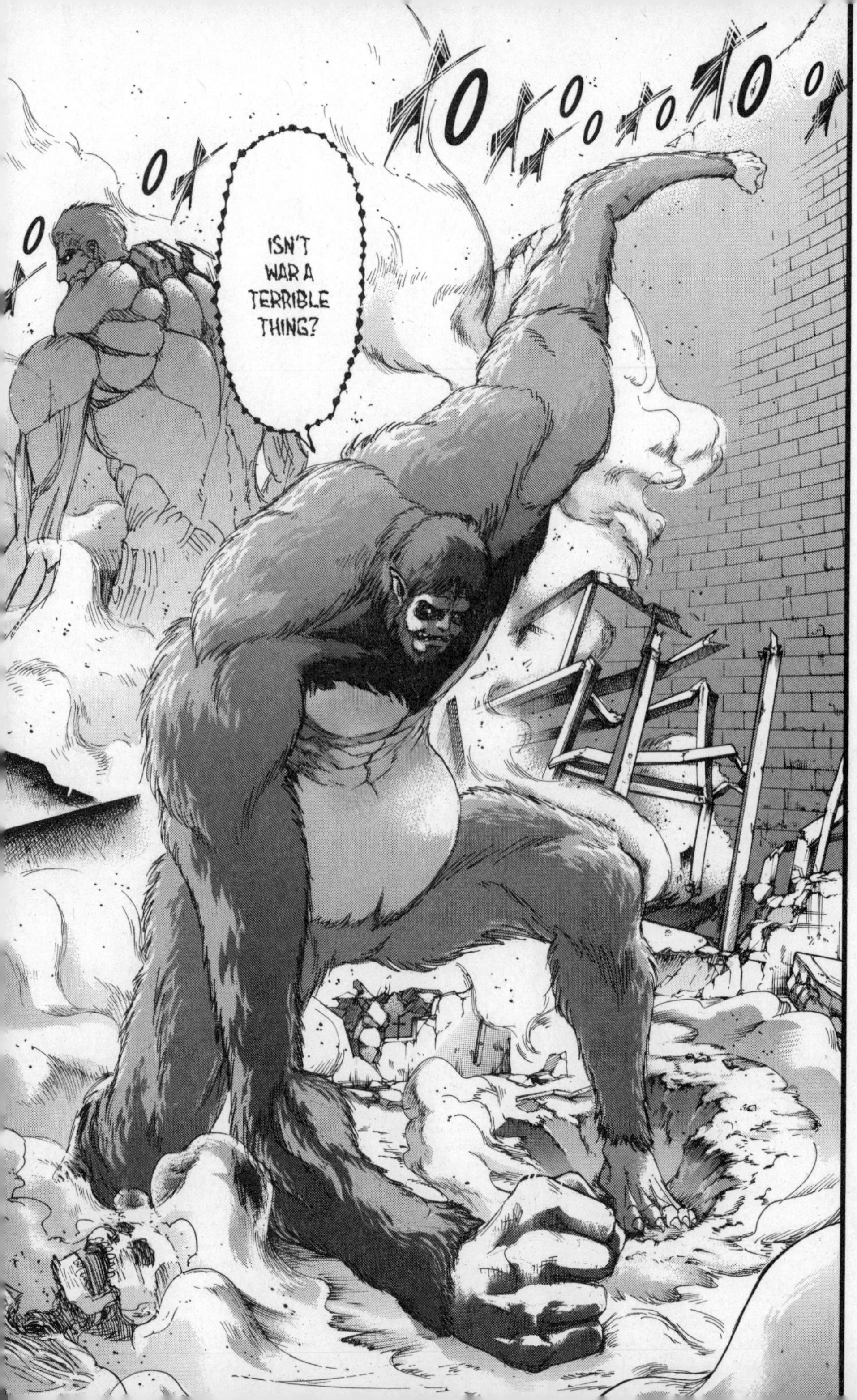
ISN'T WAR A TERRIBLE THING?

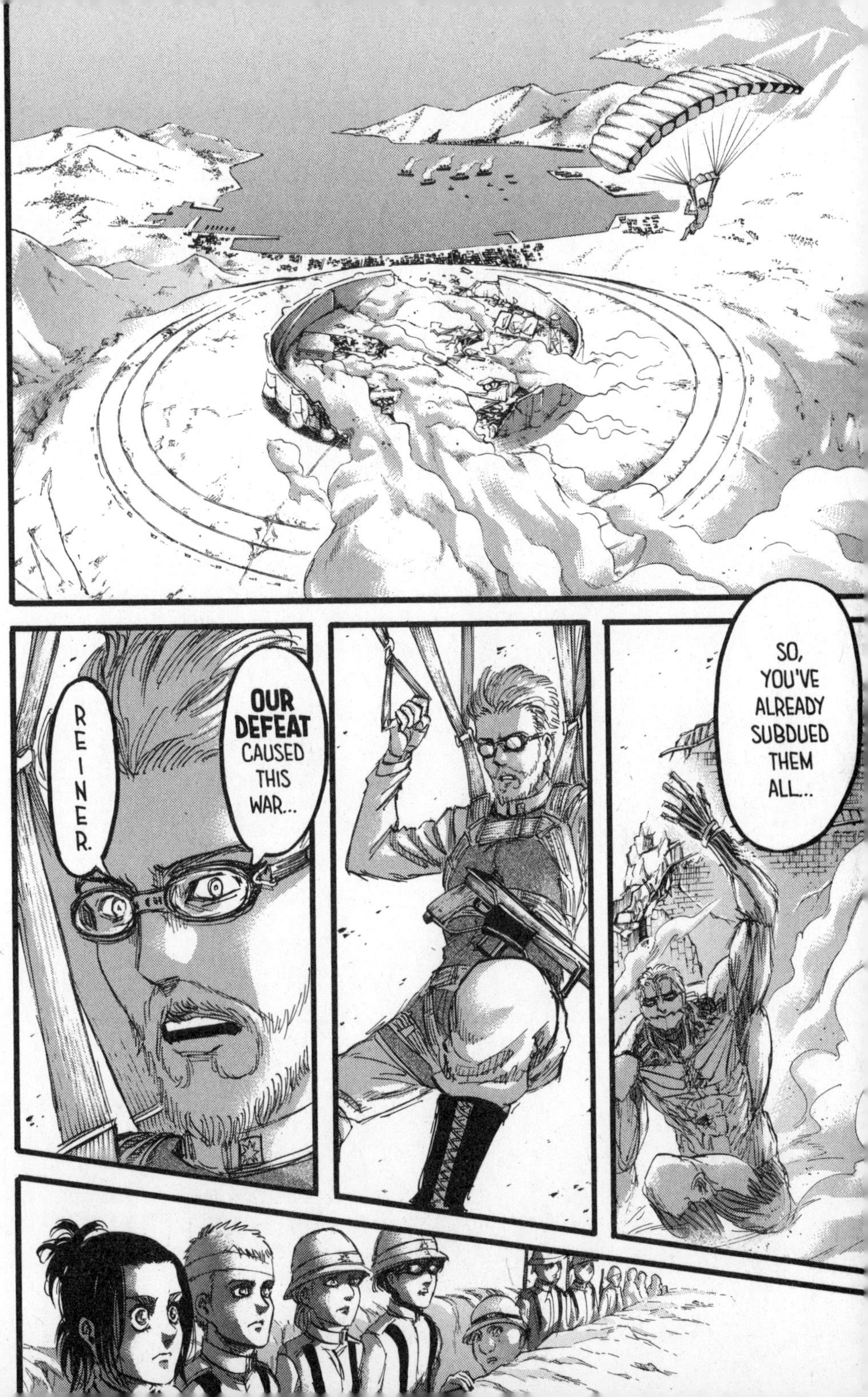
SO, YOU'VE ALREADY SUBDUED THEM ALL...
OUR DEFEAT CAUSED THIS WAR...
REINER.

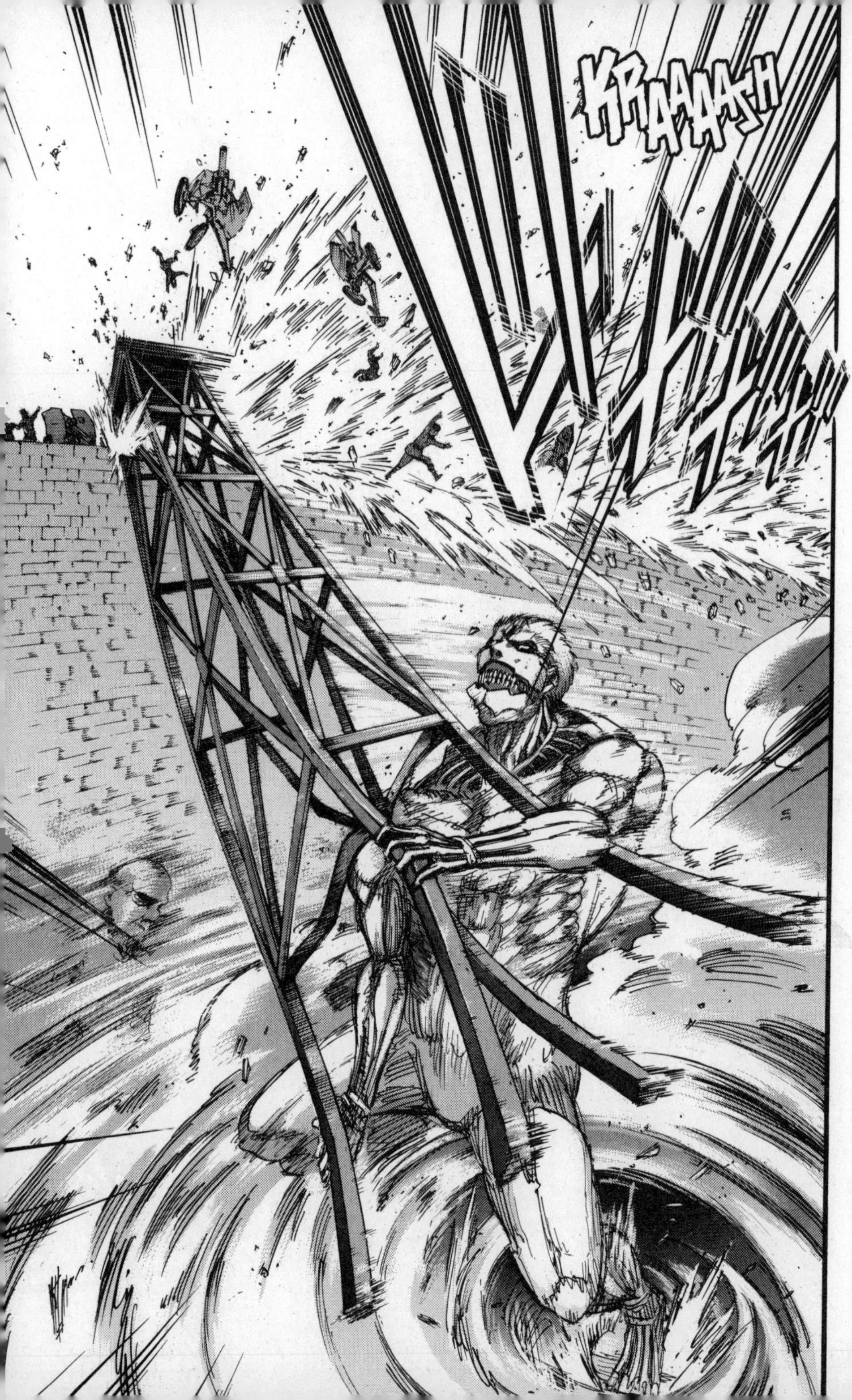
KRAAAASH

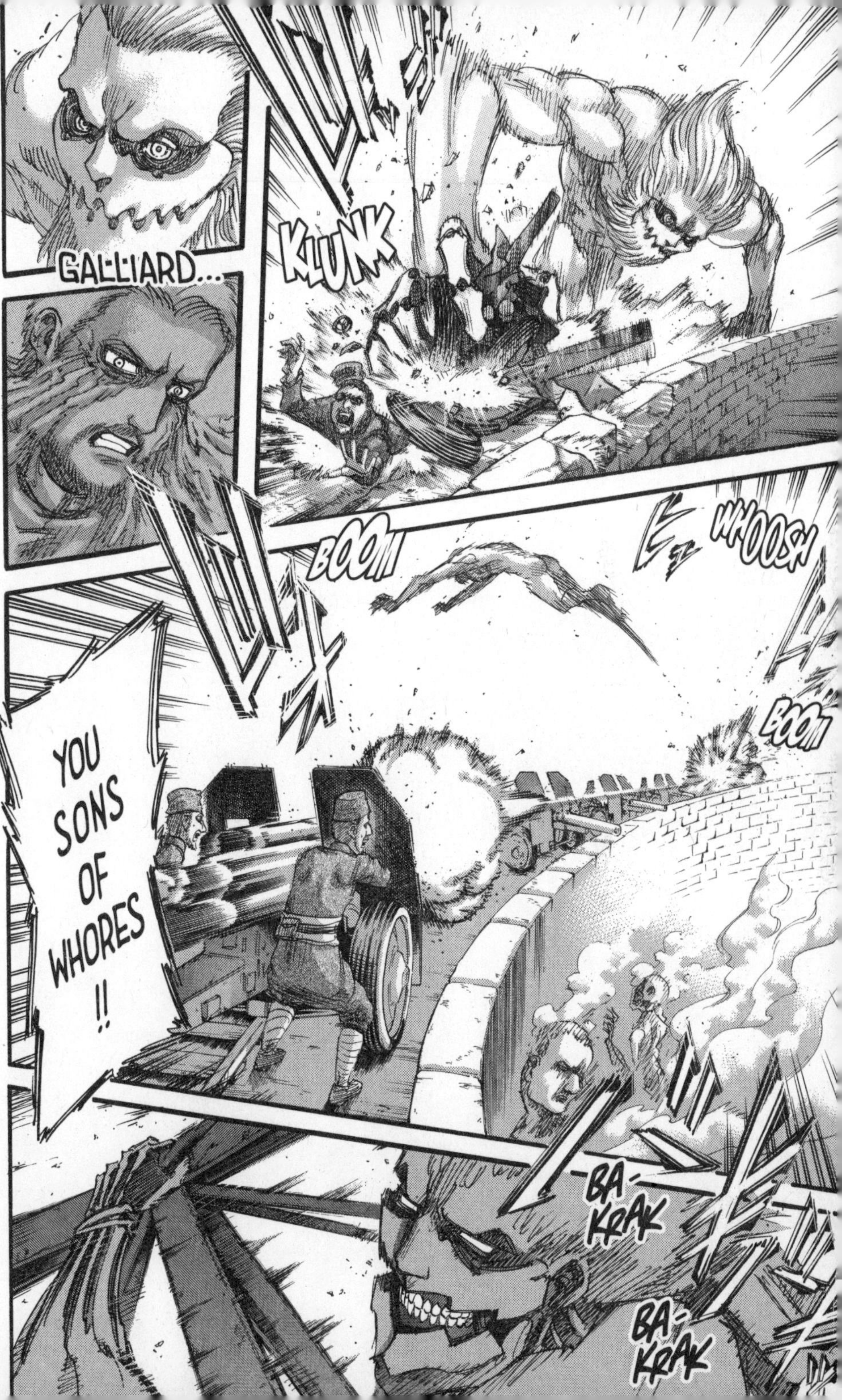
KLUNK
GALLIARD...
WHOOSH
BOOM
BOOM
YOU SONS OF WHORES!!
BA-KRAK
BA-KRAK

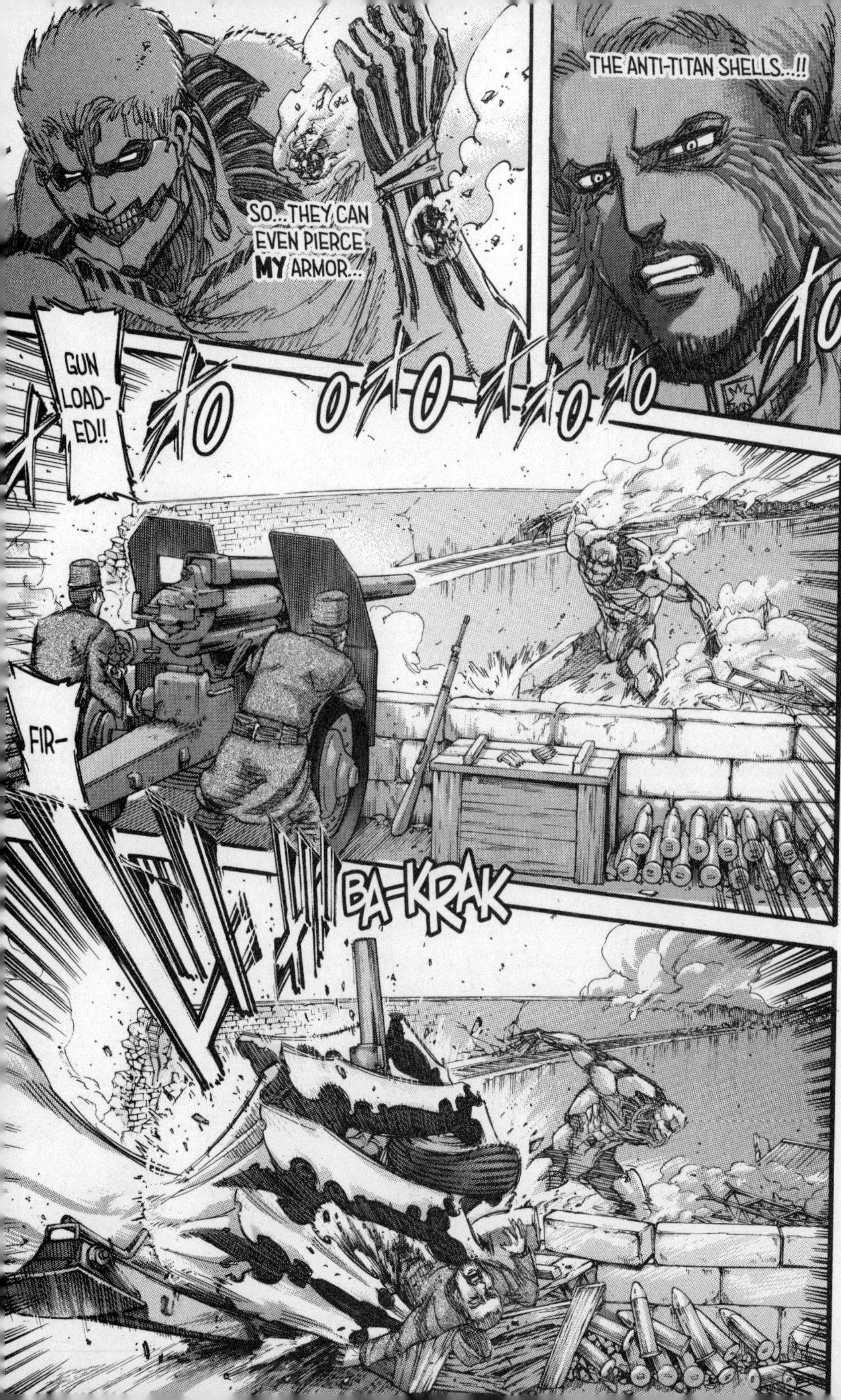
THE ANTI-TITAN SHELLS...!!
SO... THEY CAN EVEN PIERCE MY ARMOR...
GUN LOAD-ED!!
FIR-
BA-KRAK

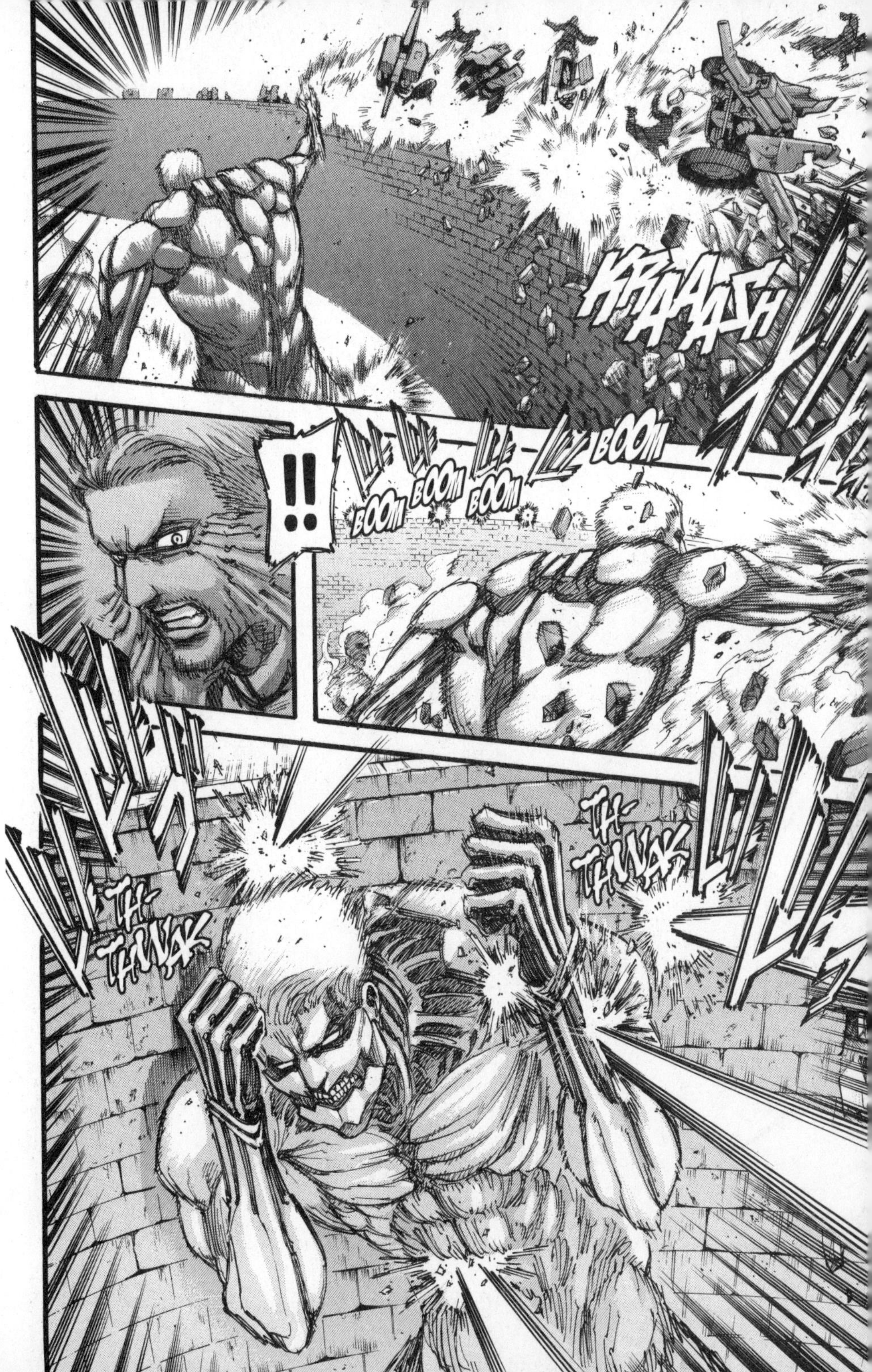
KRAAAASH
!!
BOOM BOOM BOOM BOOM
TH-THUNK
TH-THUNK

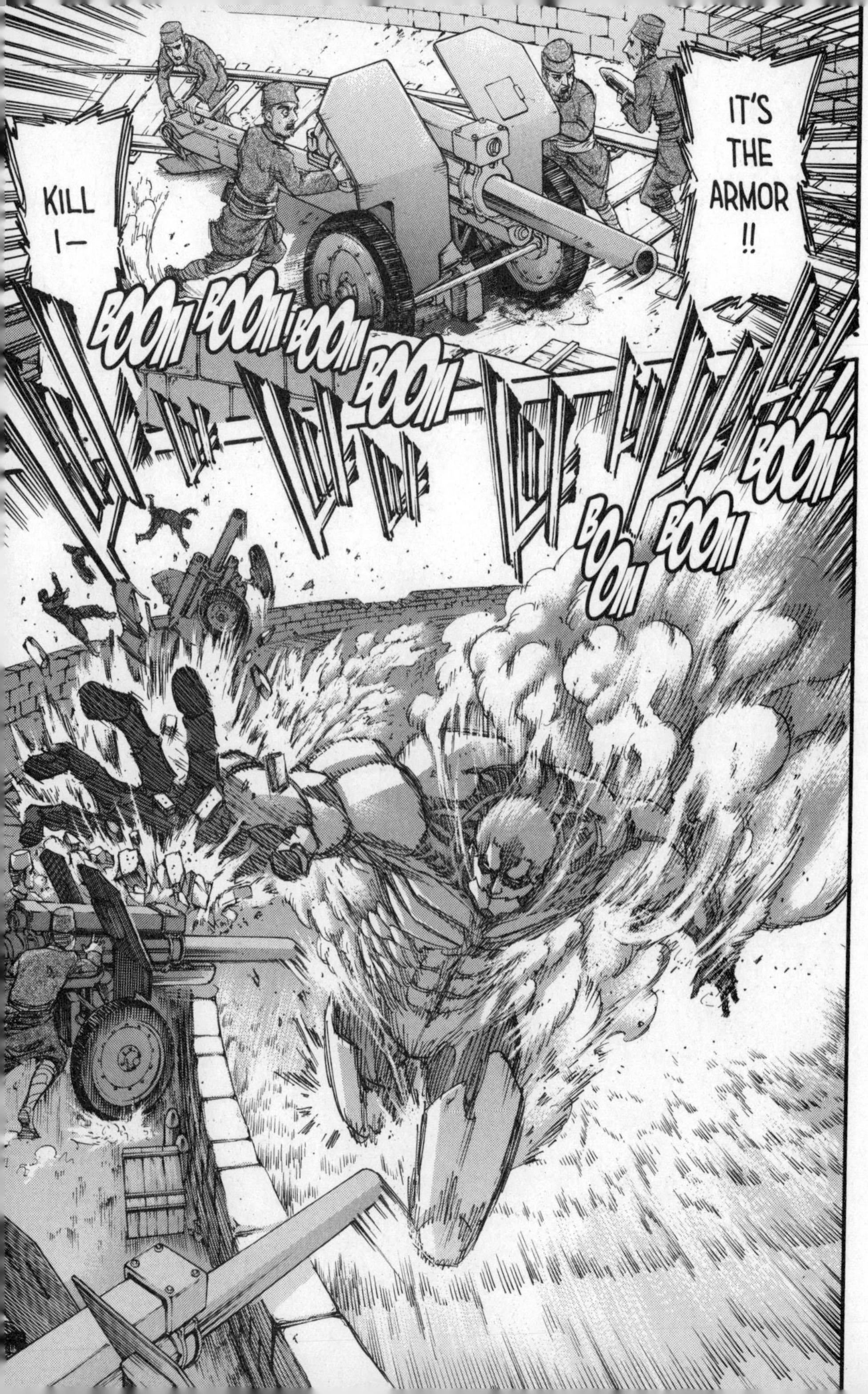
IT'S THE ARMOR !!
KILL I—
BOOM
BOOM
BOOM
BOOM
BOOM
BOOM
BOOM
BOOM

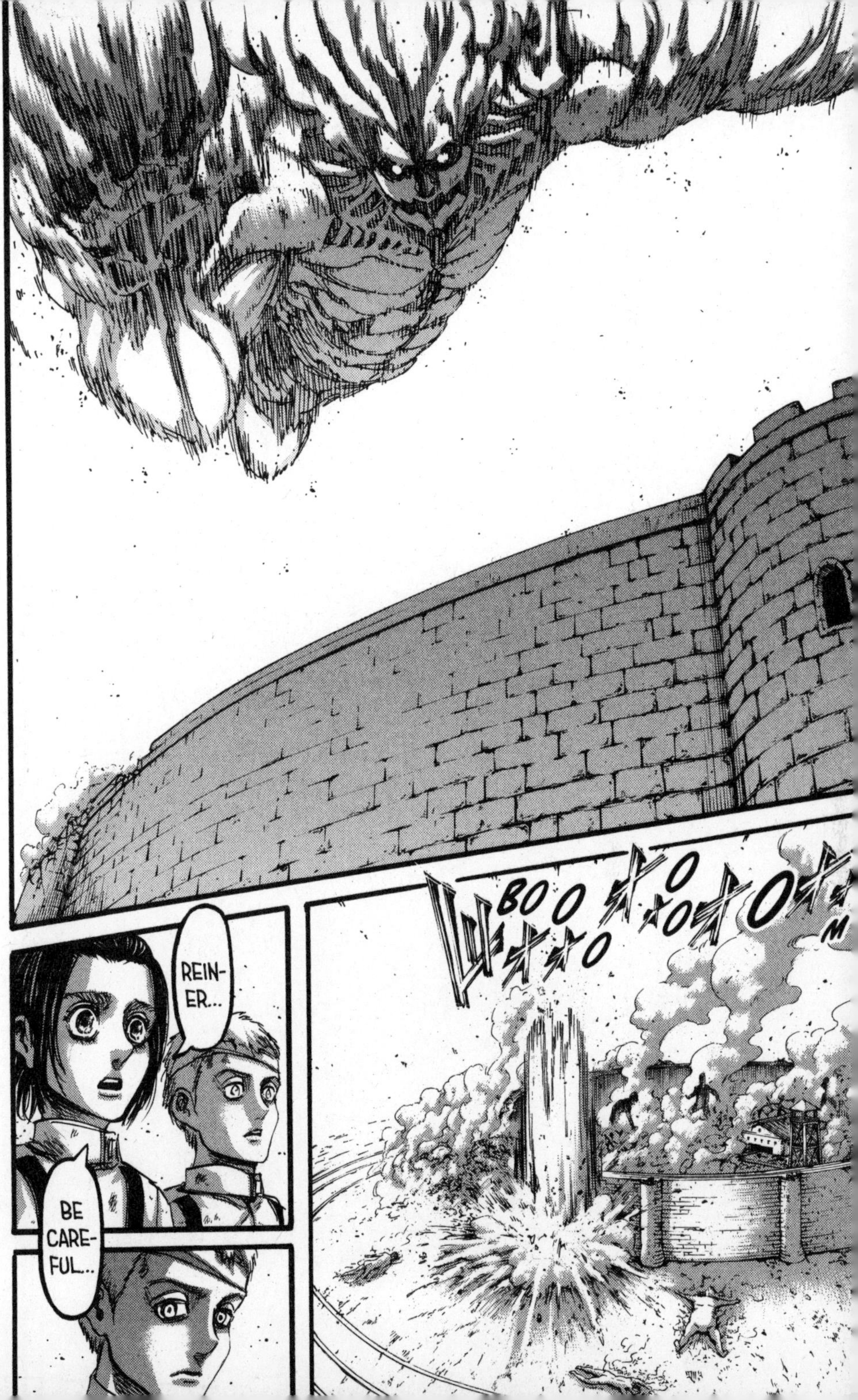
BOOOOOOM
REIN-ER...
BE CARE-FUL...

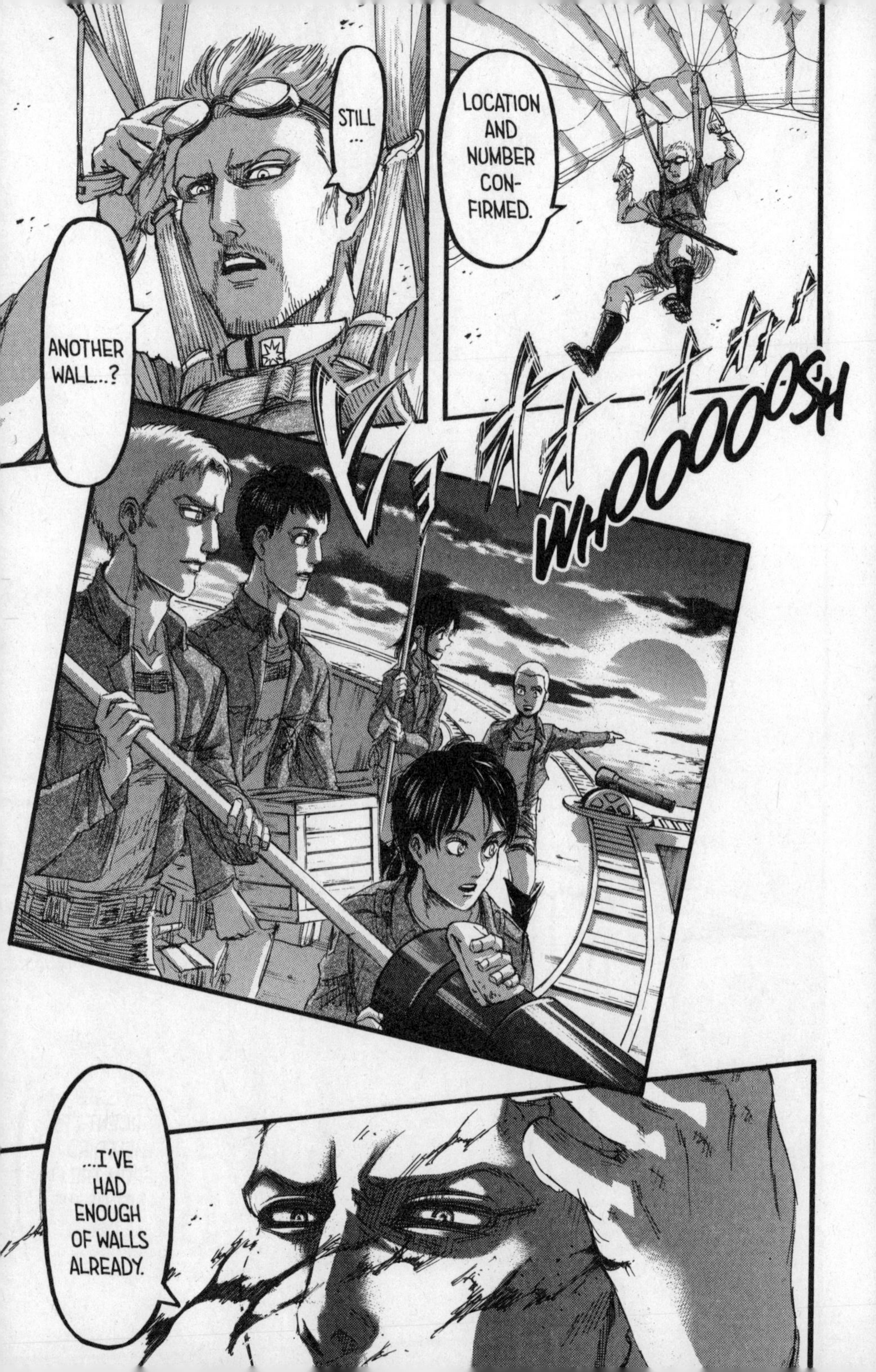
LOCATION AND NUMBER CON- FIRMED.
STILL ...
ANOTHER WALL...?
WHOOOOOOSH
...I'VE HAD ENOUGH OF WALLS ALREADY.

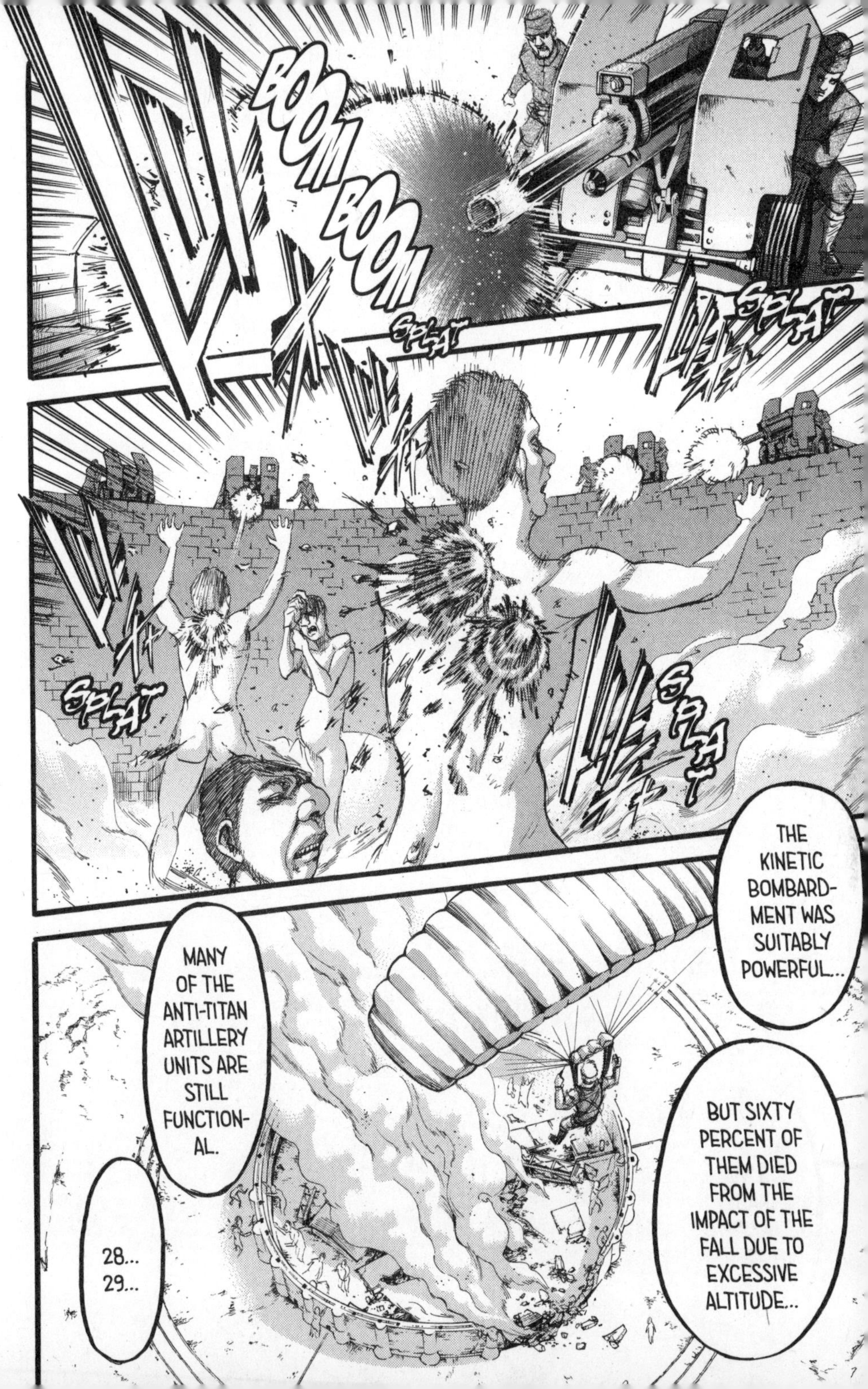
BOOM
BOOM
BOOM
SPLAT
SPLAT
SPLAT
SPLAT
THE KINETIC BOMBARD-MENT WAS SUITABLY POWERFUL...
BUT SIXTY PERCENT OF THEM DIED FROM THE IMPACT OF THE FALL DUE TO EXCESSIVE ALTITUDE...
MANY OF THE ANTI-TITAN ARTILLERY UNITS ARE STILL FUNCTION-AL.
28... 29...

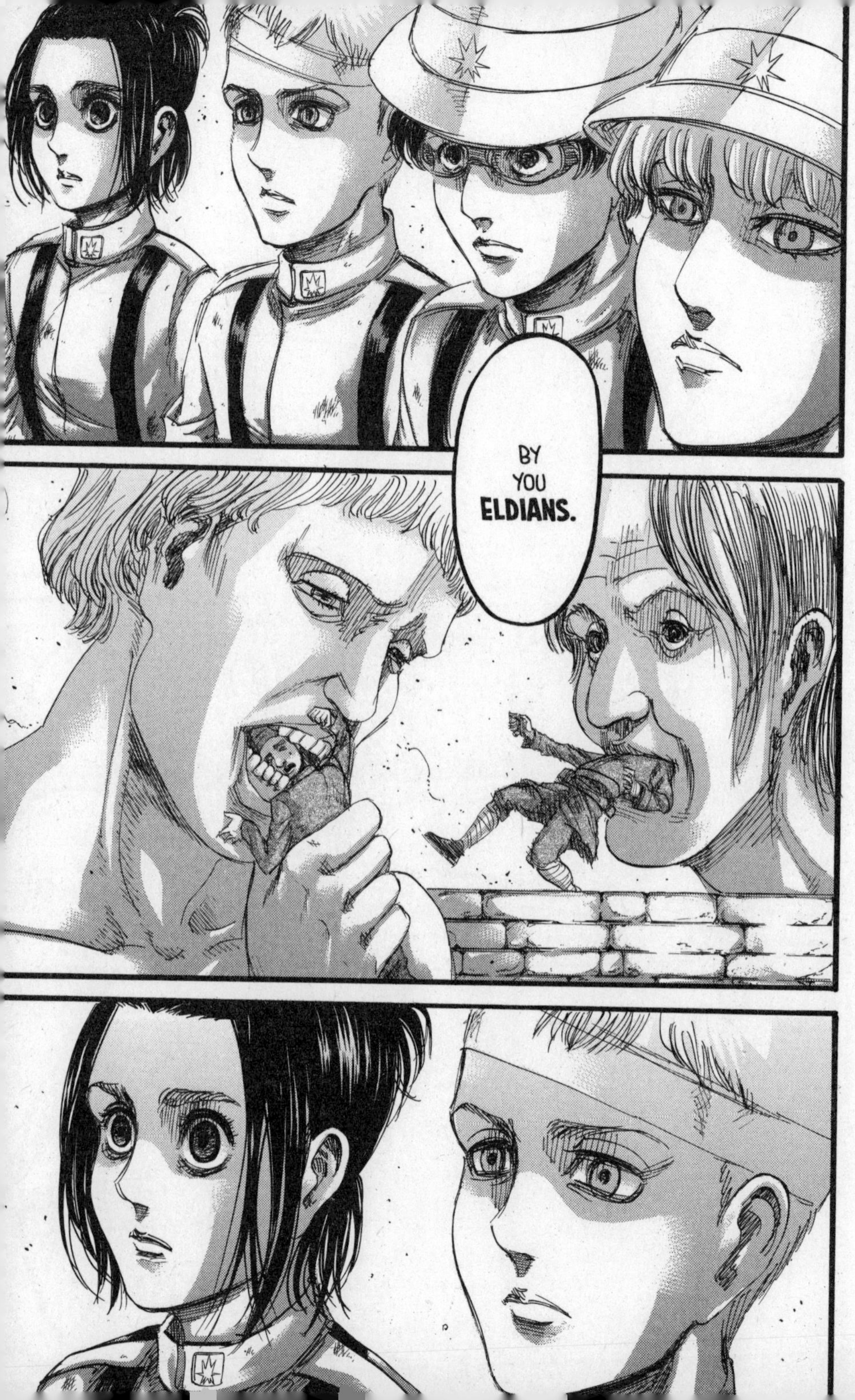
BY YOU ELDIANS.

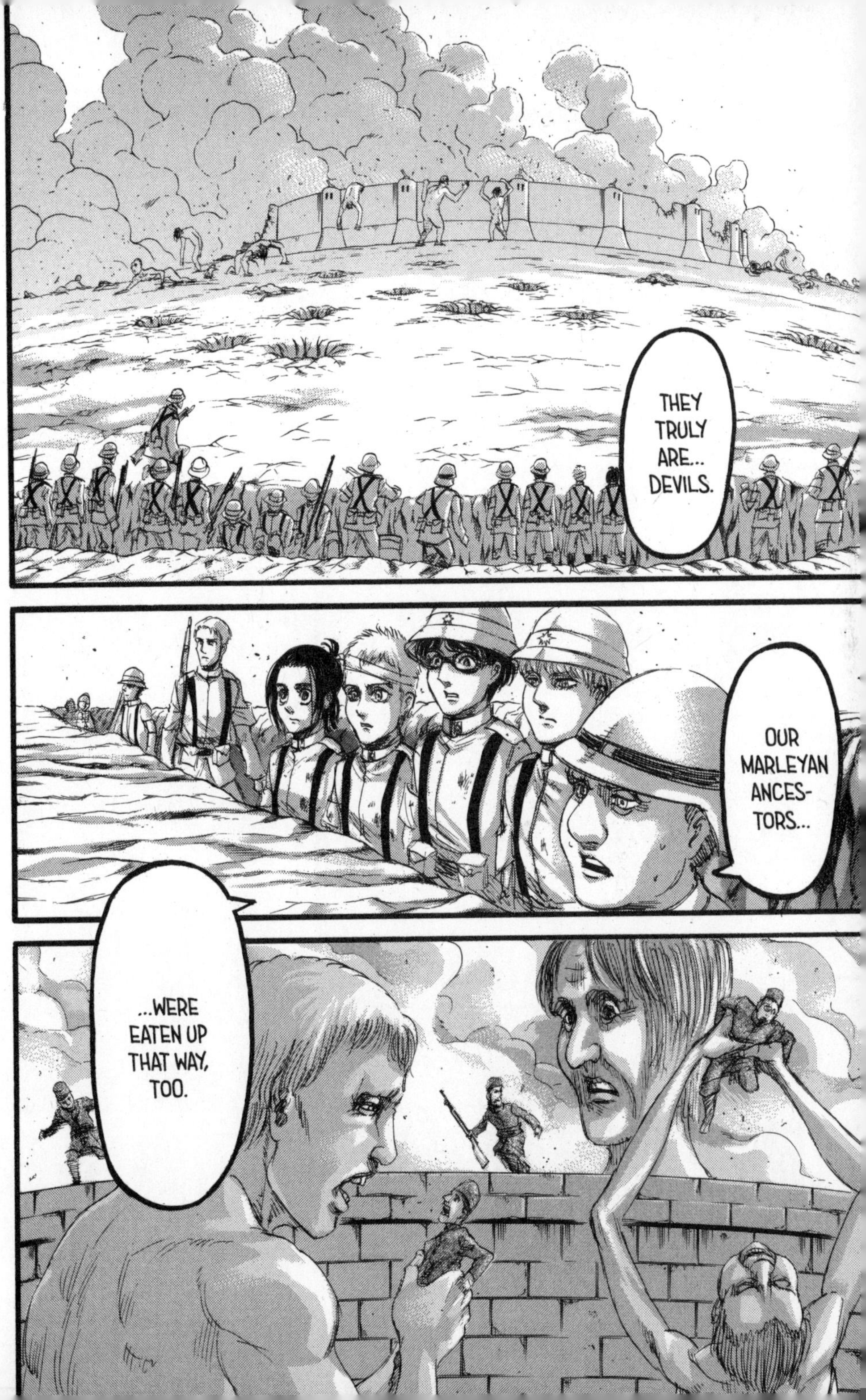
THEY TRULY ARE... DEVILS.
OUR MARLEYAN ANCESTORS...
...WERE EATEN UP THAT WAY, TOO.

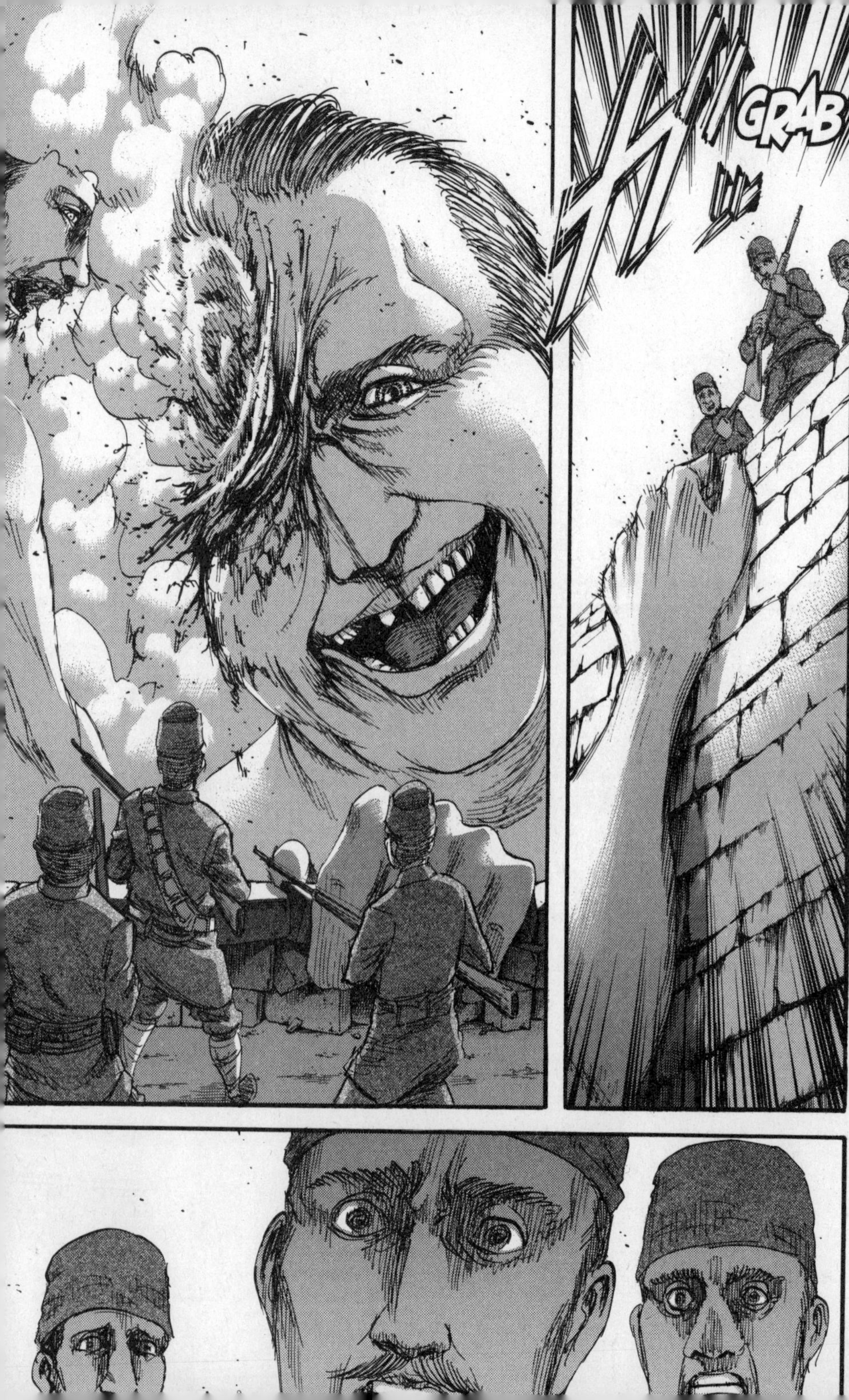
GRAB

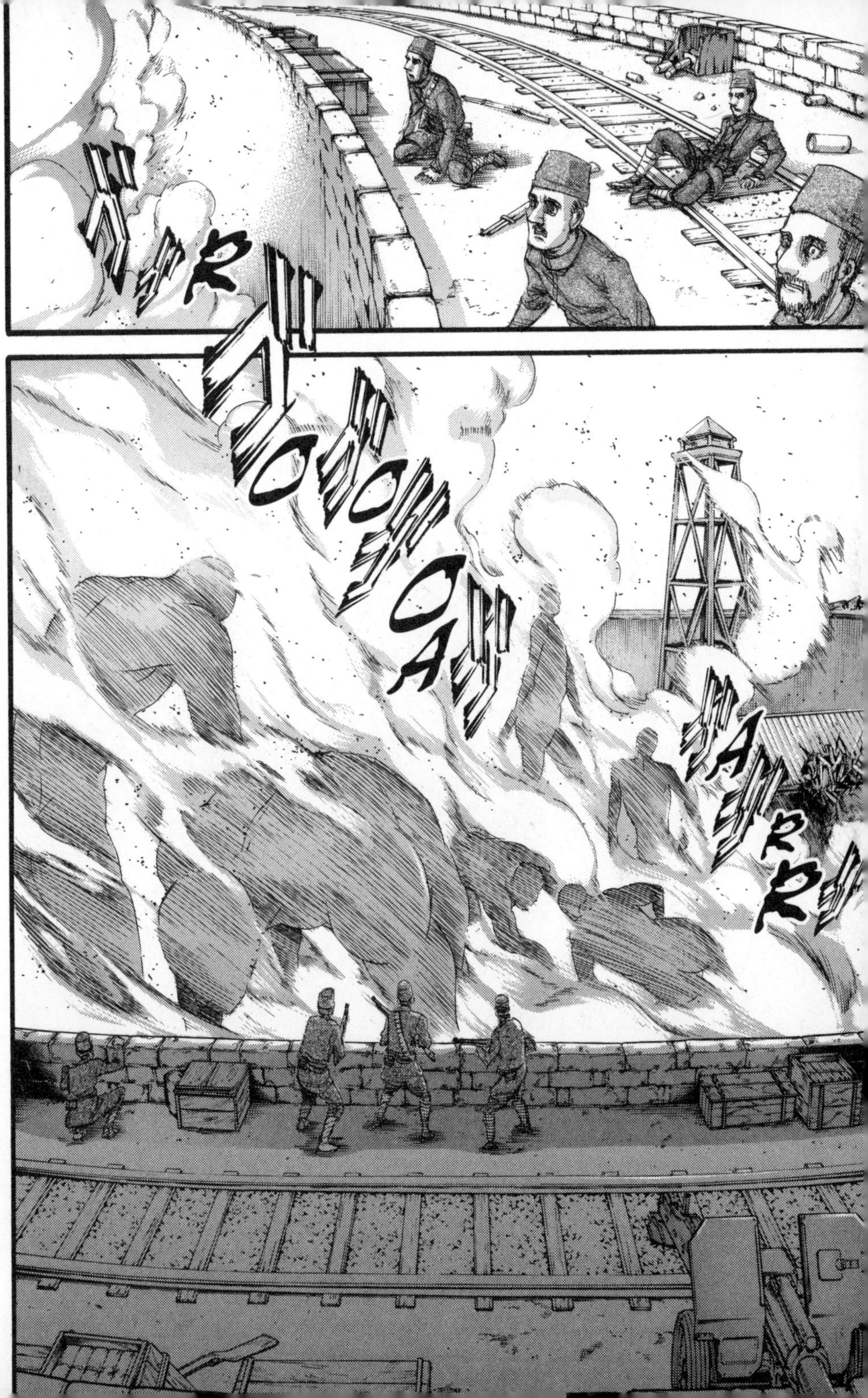

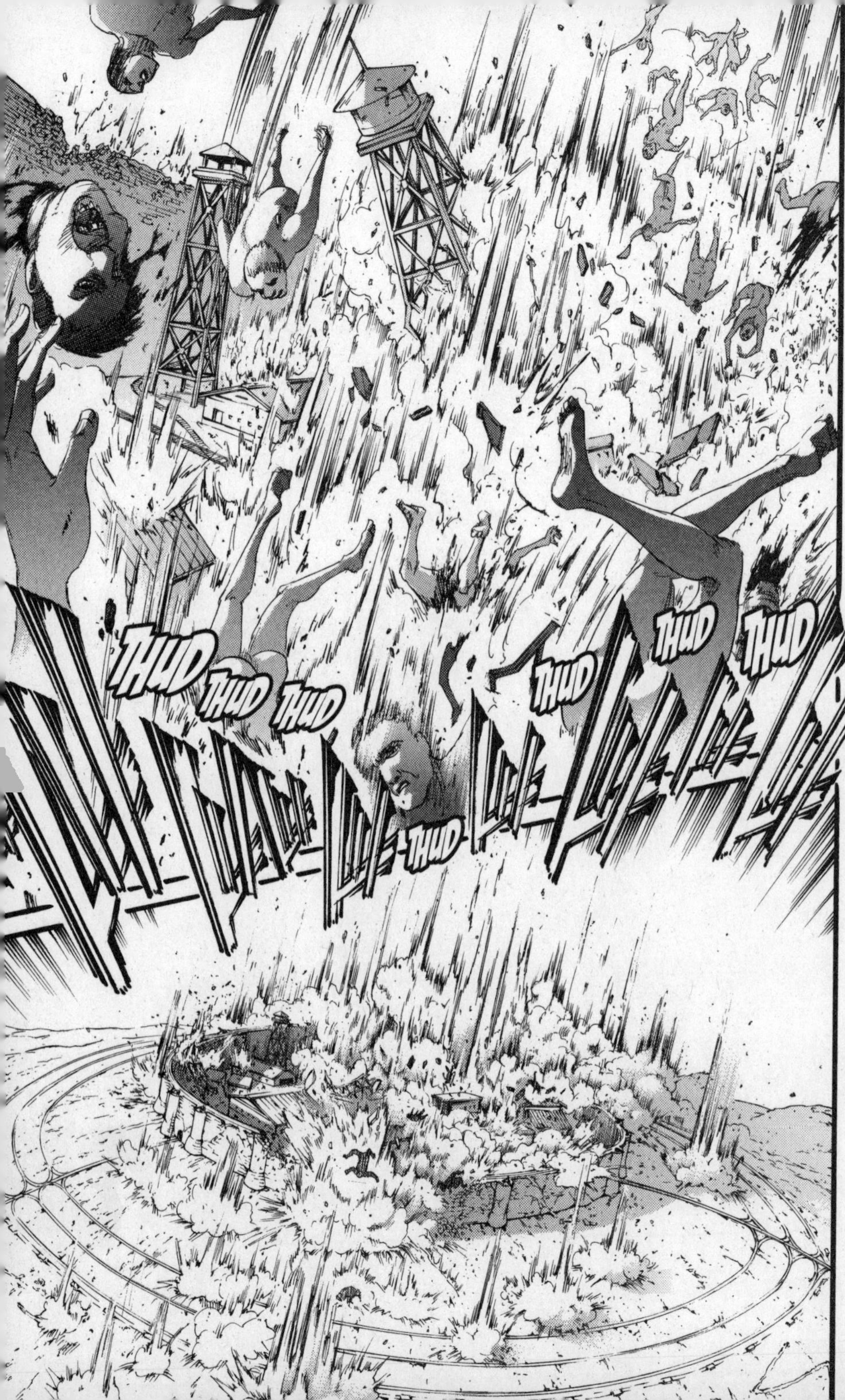
THUD
THUD
THUD
THUD
THUD
THUD
THUD

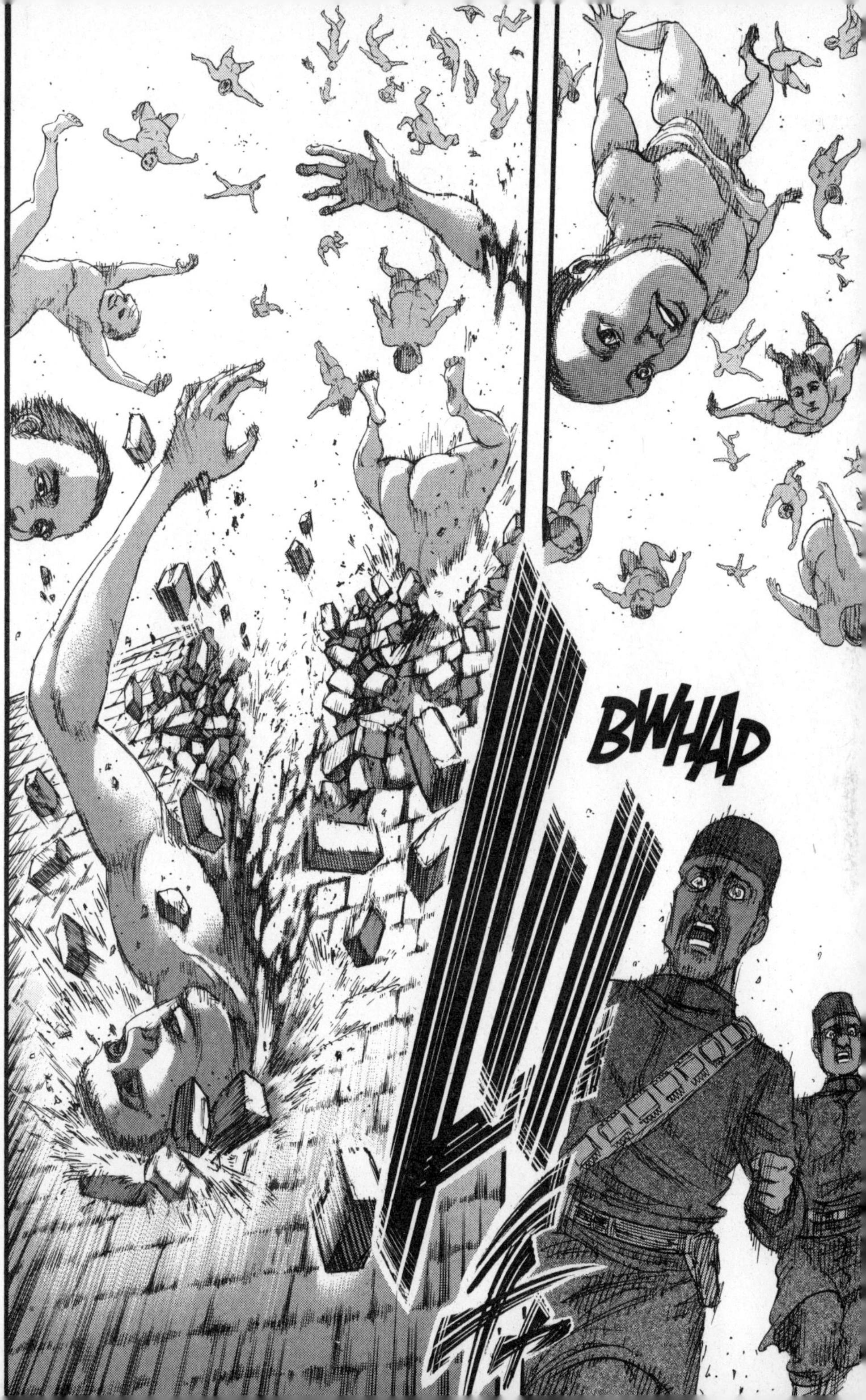
BWHAP

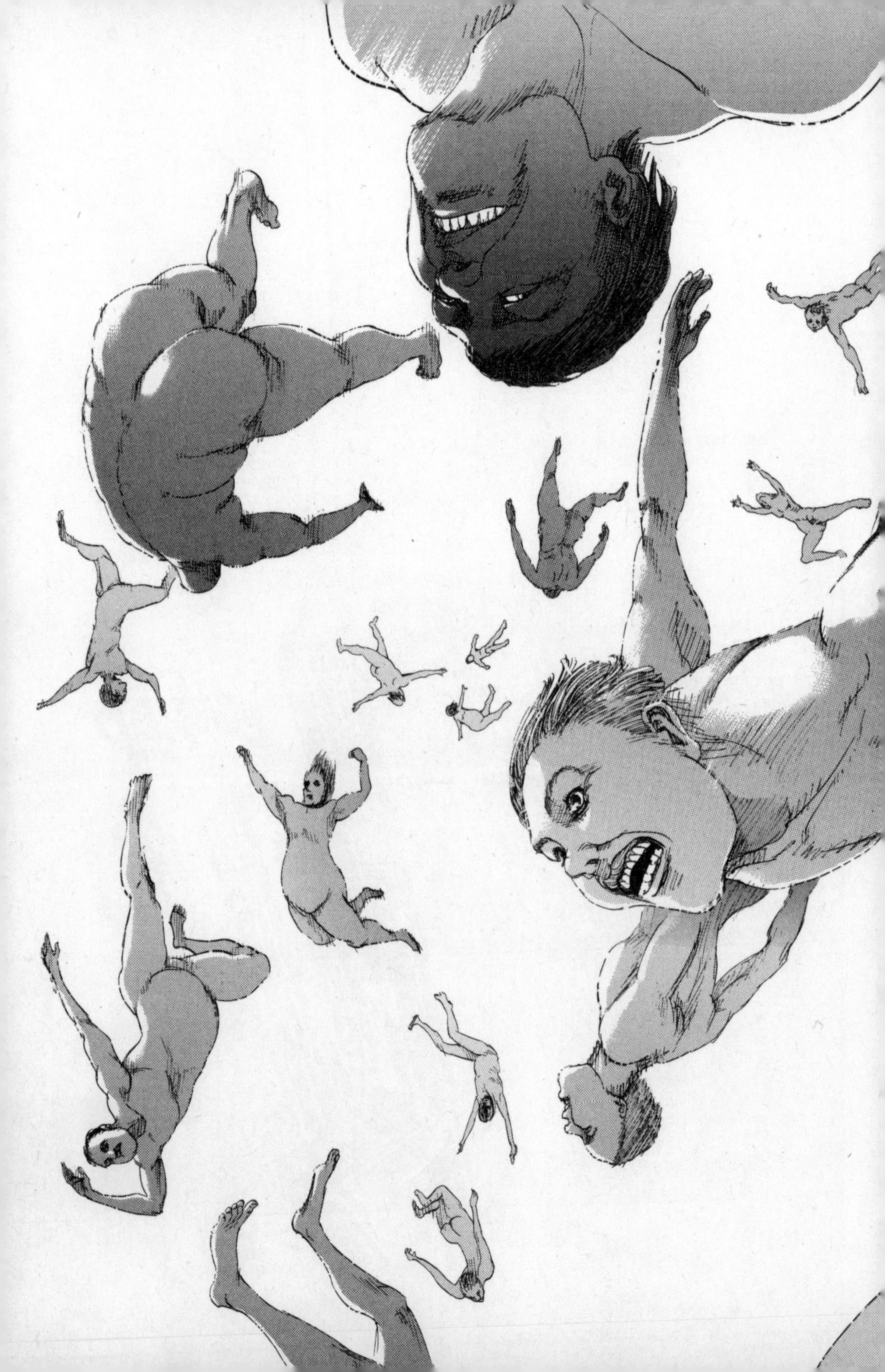

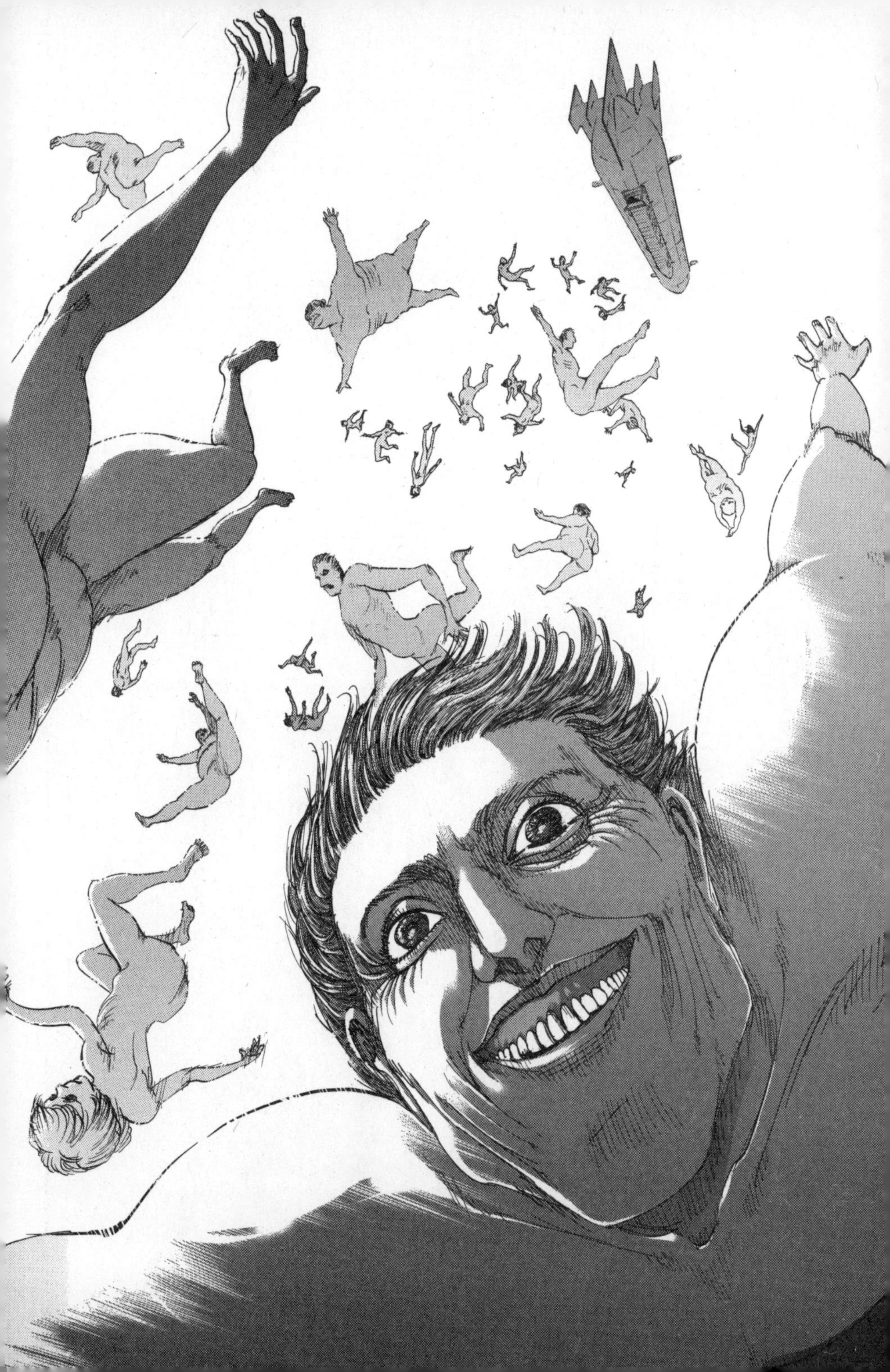

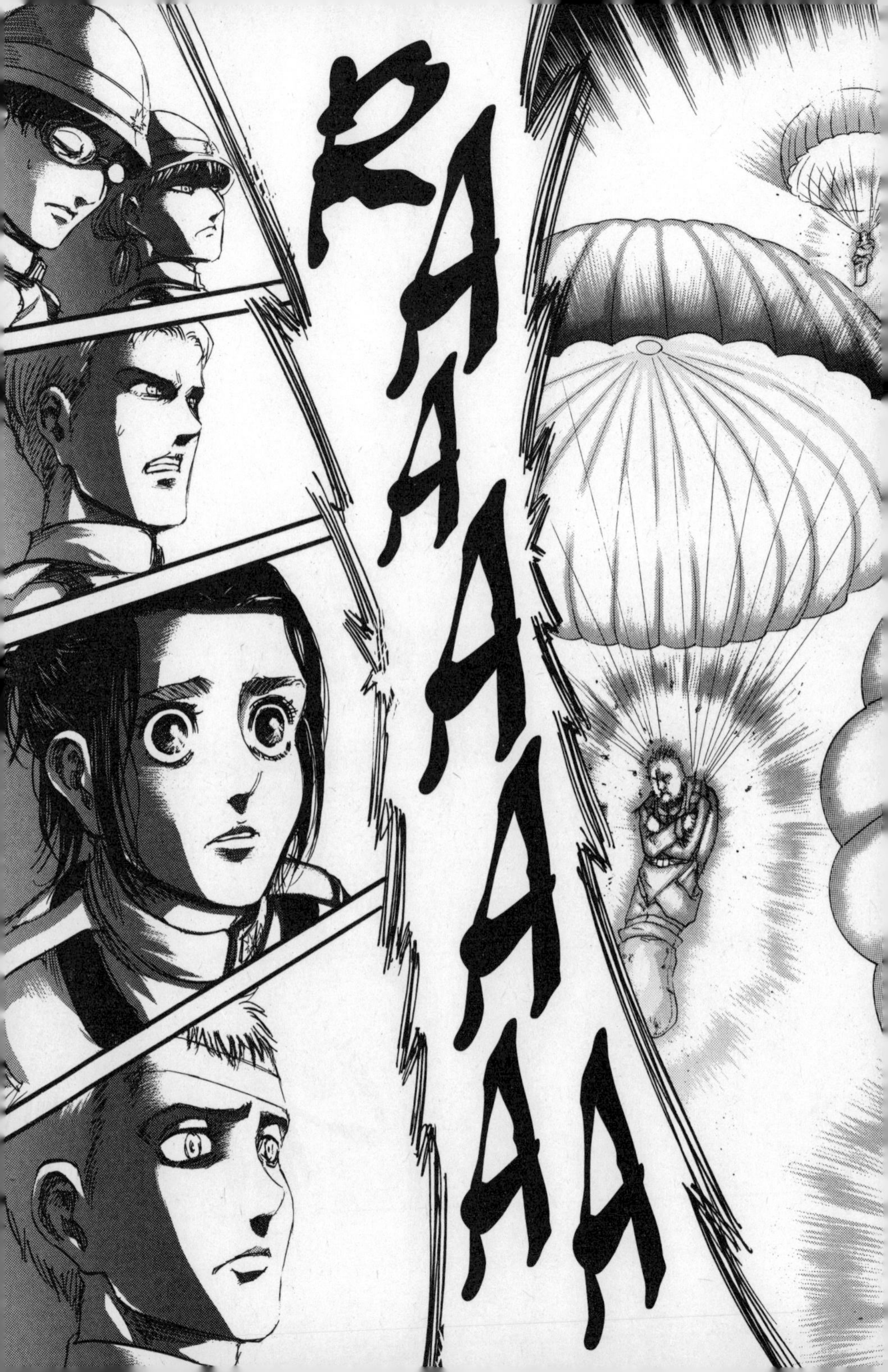
RAAAAAAAAA

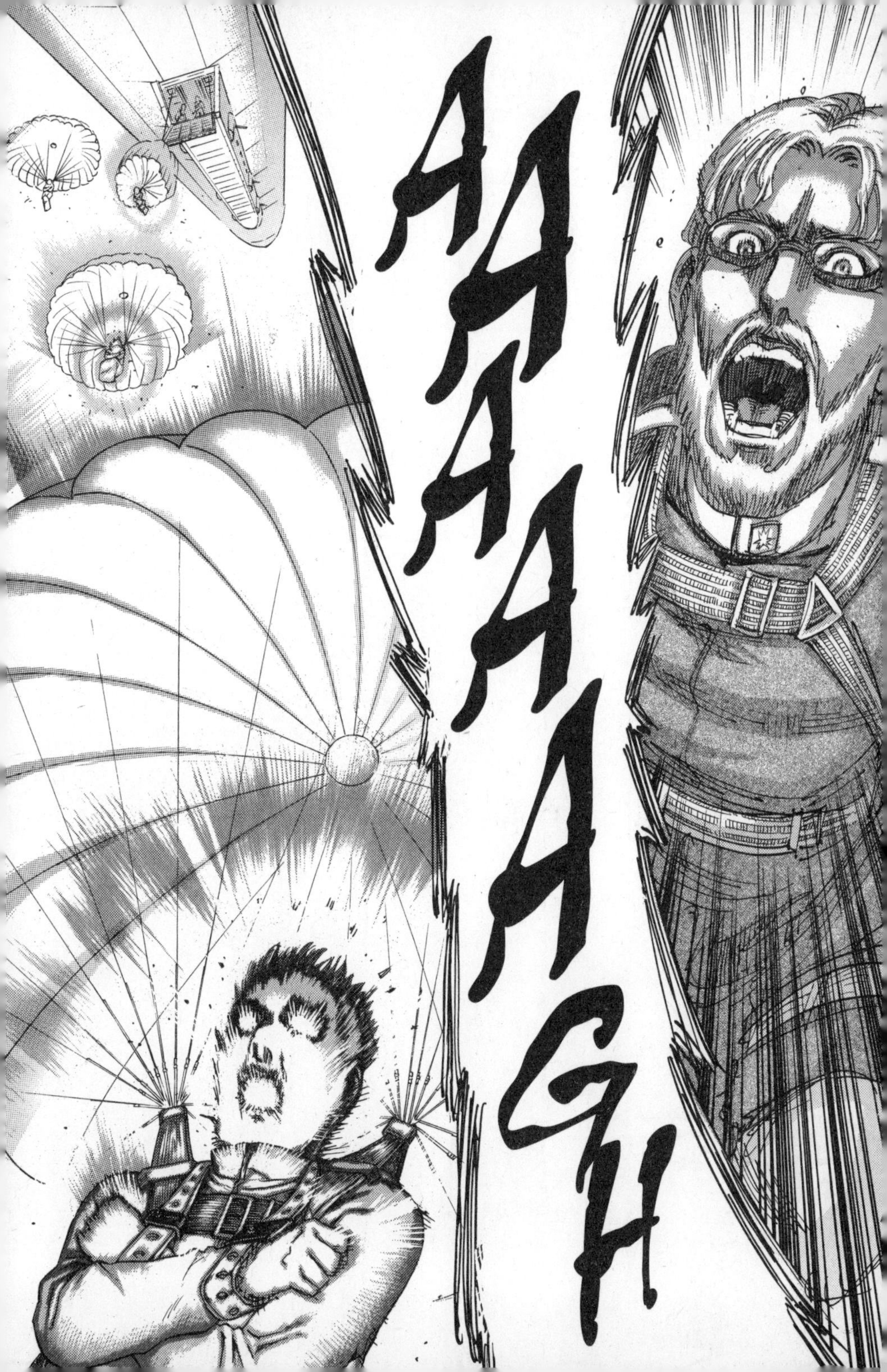
AAAAAAGH

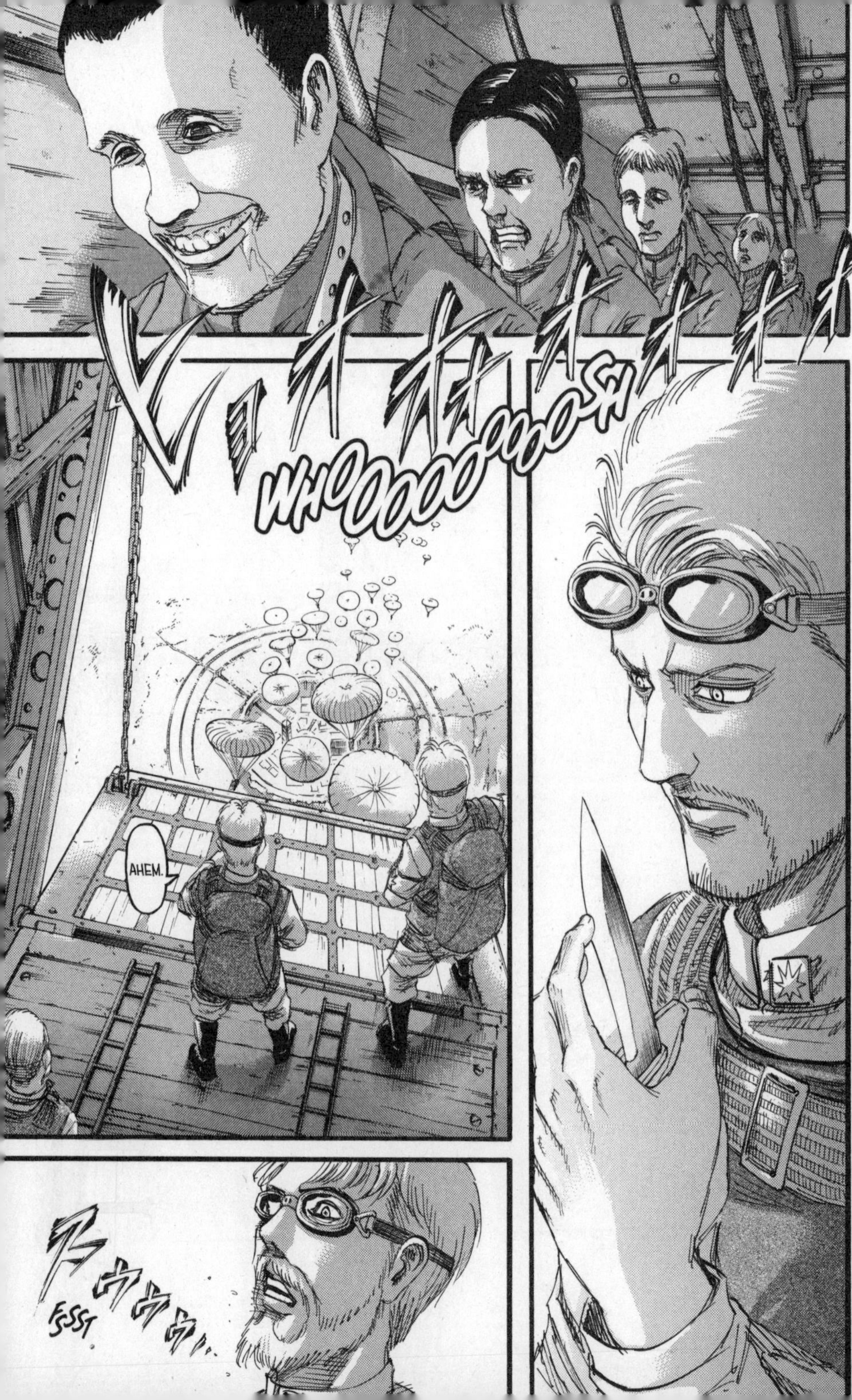

WHOOOOOOOOOOOSH
AHEM.
FSSST

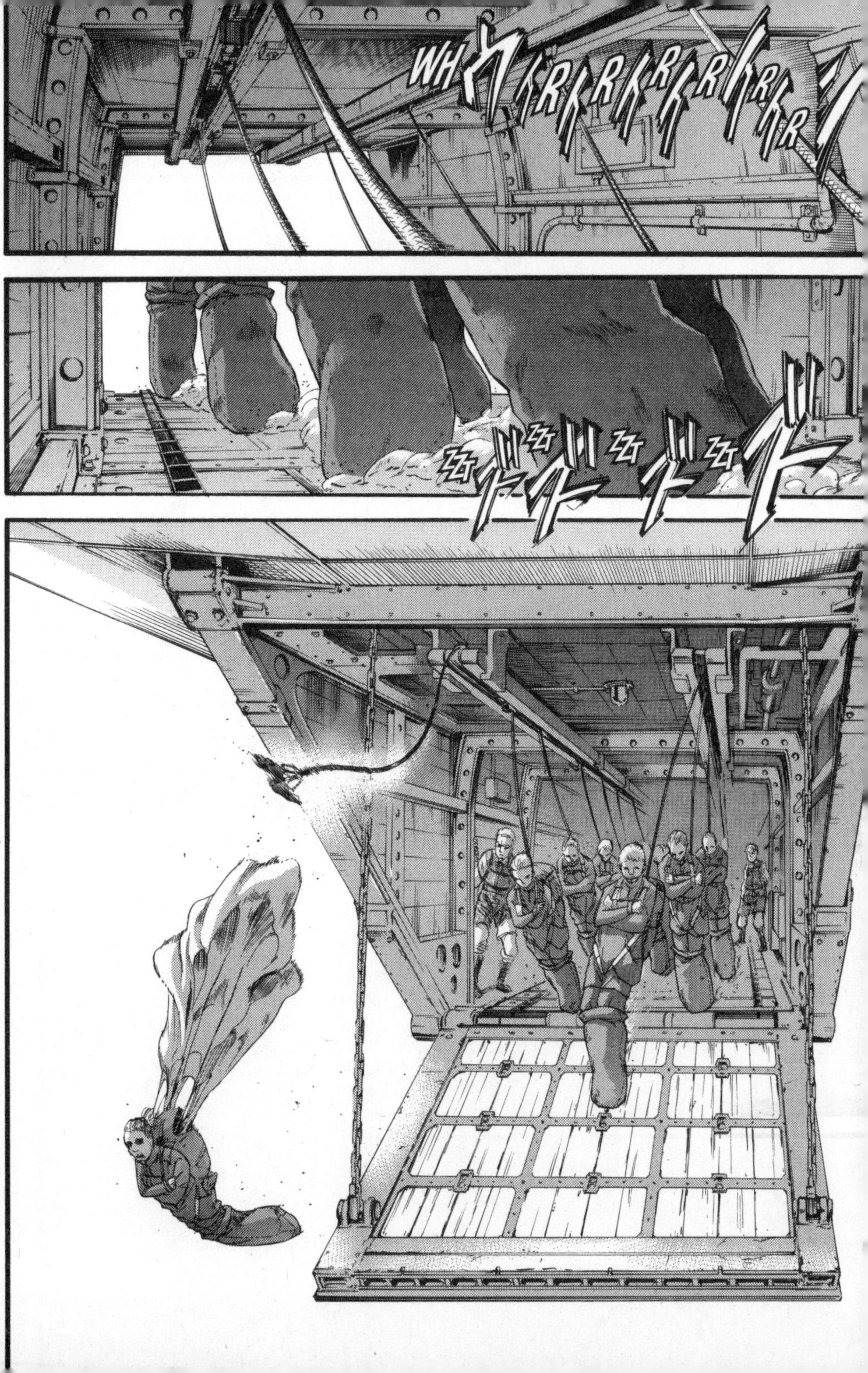
WHRRRRRRR
ZZT
ZZT
ZZT
ZZT

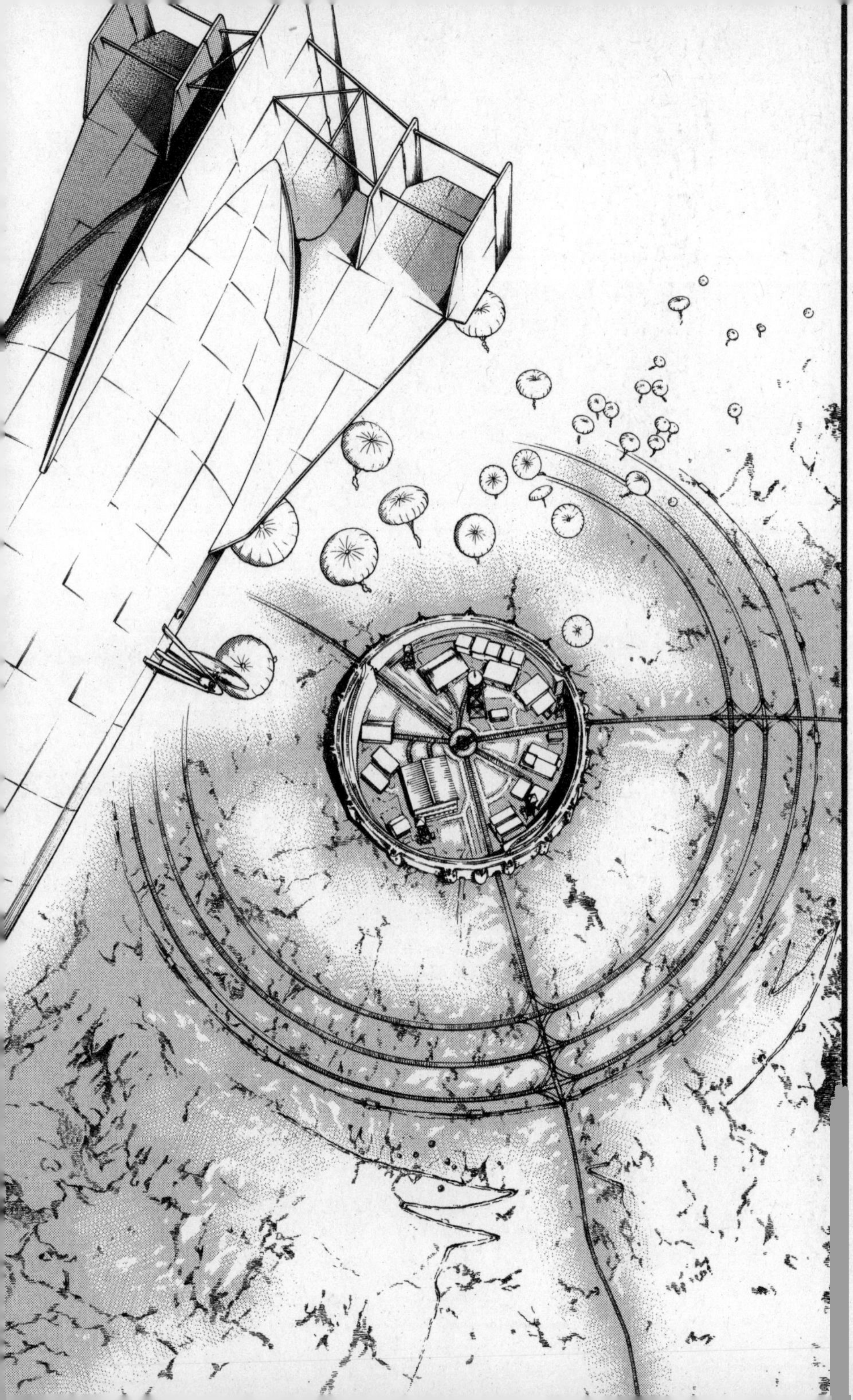

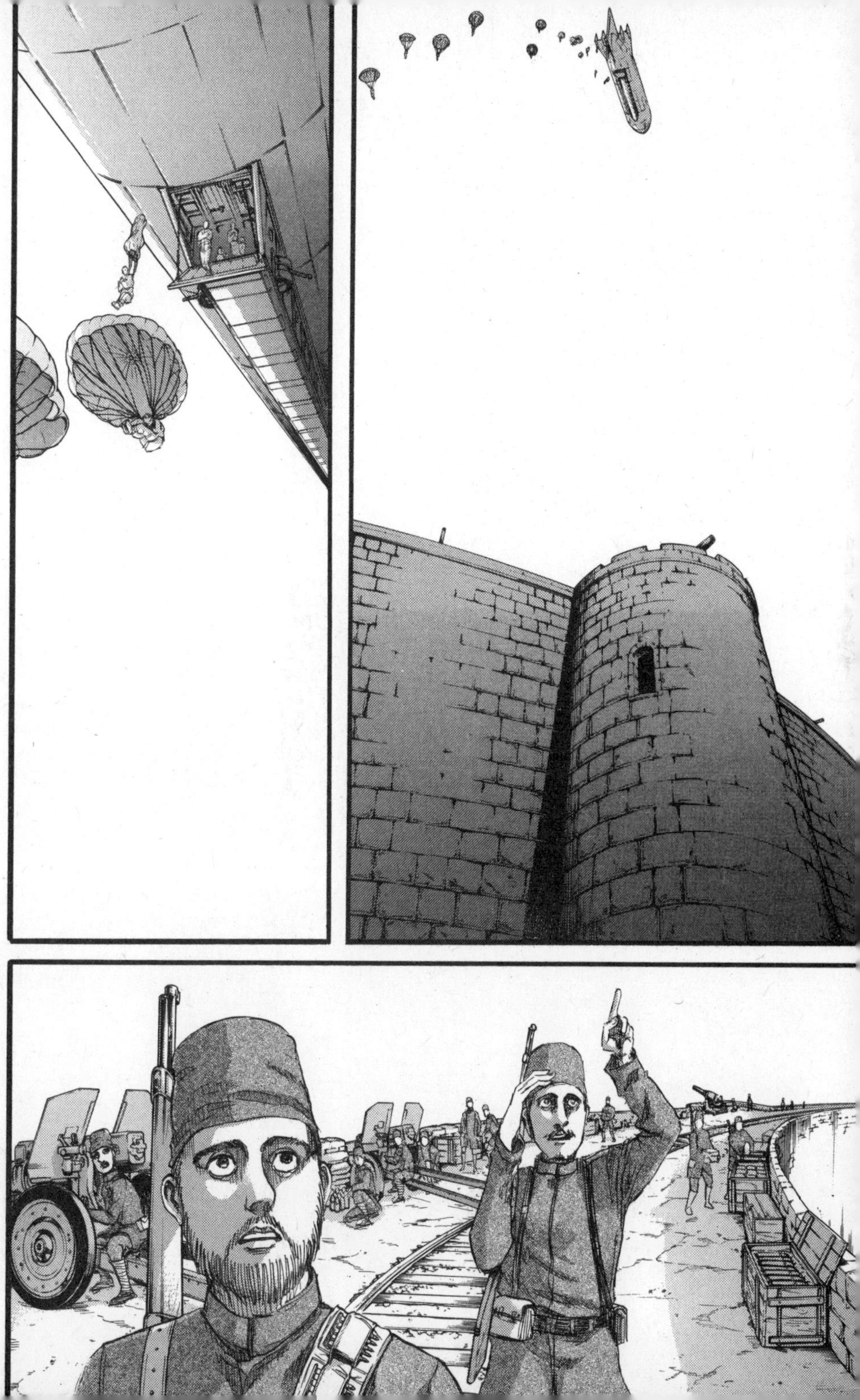

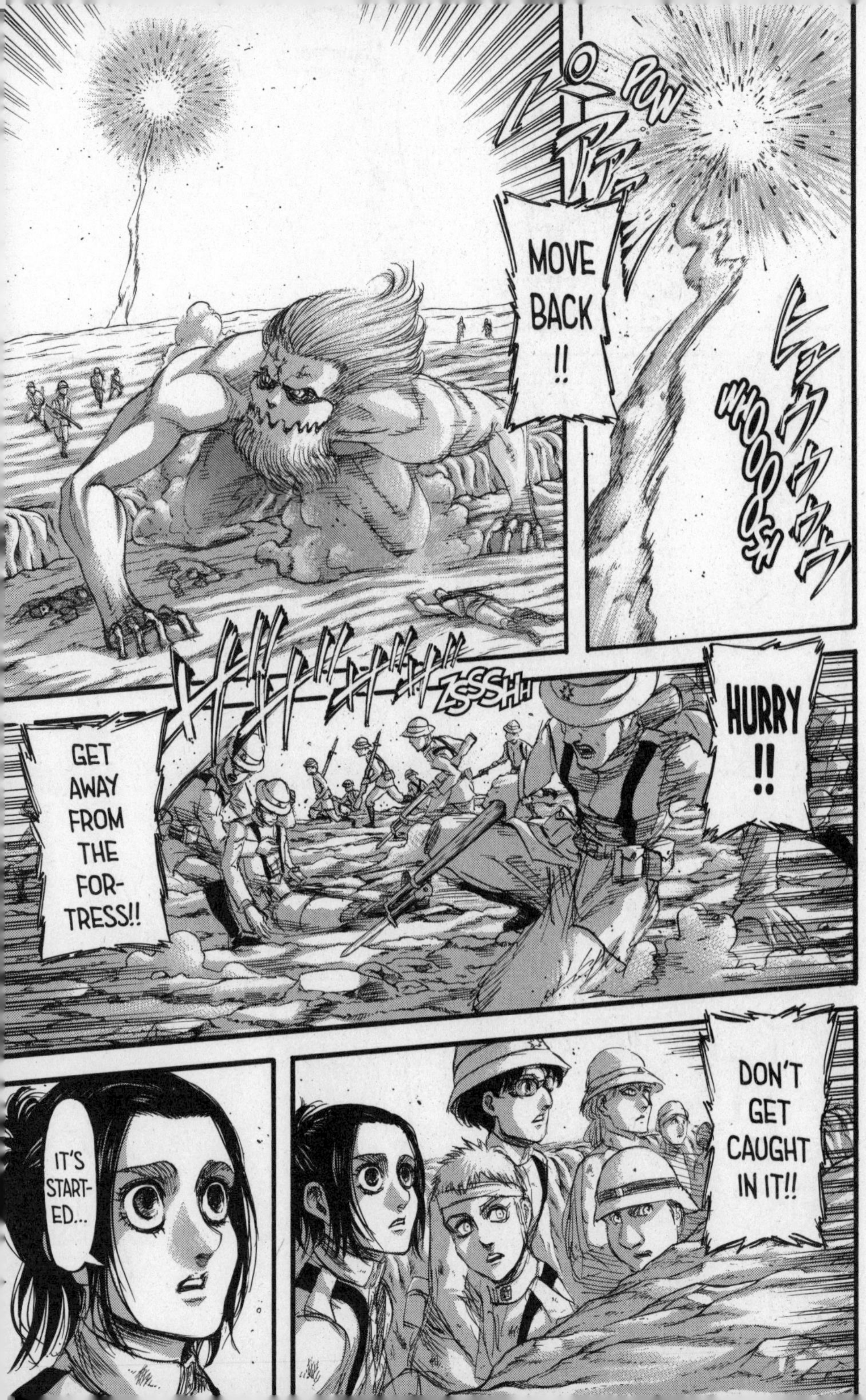
POW
WHOOOOSH
MOVE BACK !!
HURRY !!
ZSSHH
GET AWAY FROM THE FOR-TRESS!!
DON'T GET CAUGHT IN IT!!
IT'S START-ED...

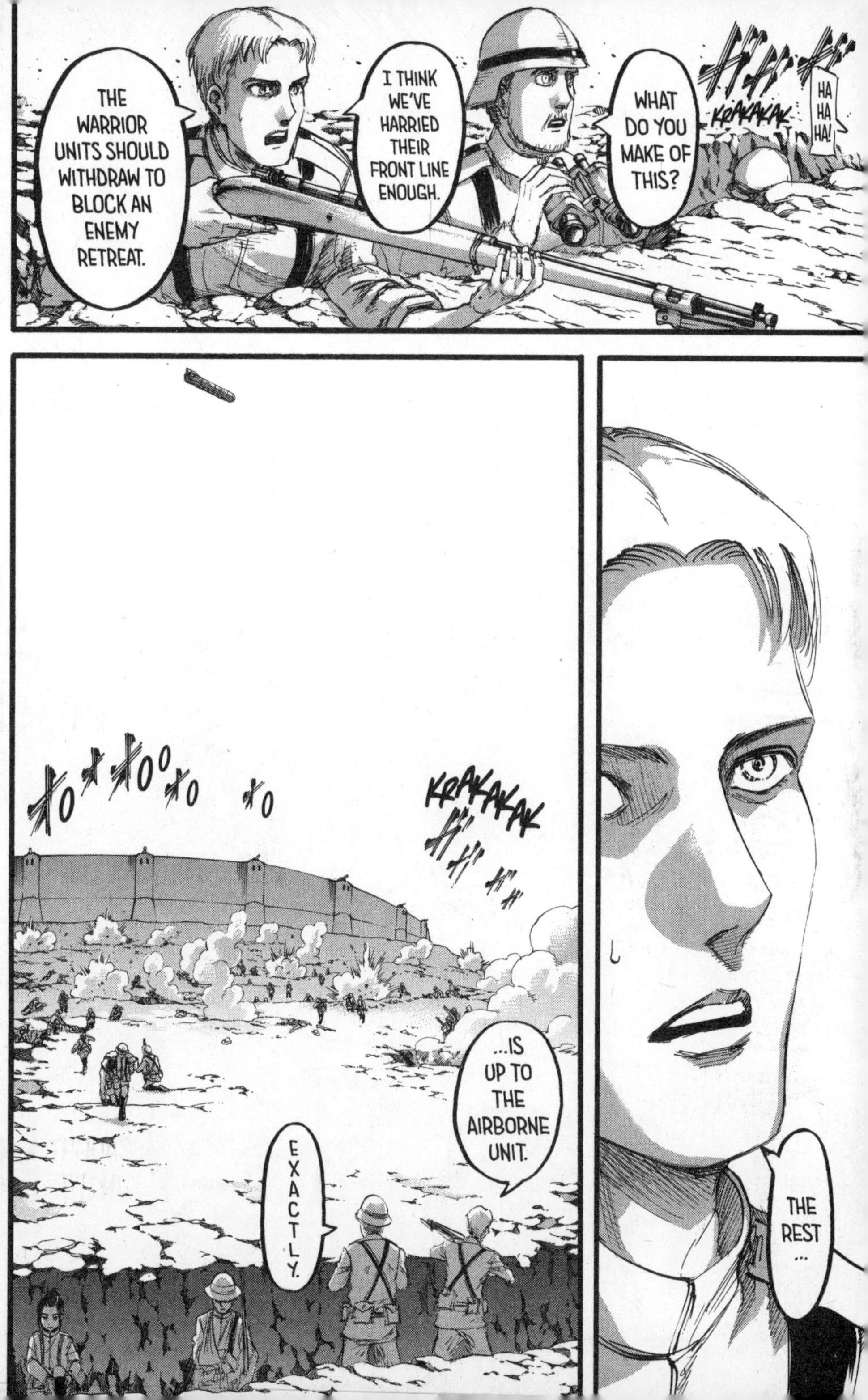
HA HA HA!
KRAKAKAK
WHAT DO YOU MAKE OF THIS?
I THINK WE'VE HARRIED THEIR FRONT LINE ENOUGH.
THE WARRIOR UNITS SHOULD WITHDRAW TO BLOCK AN ENEMY RETREAT.
THE REST ...
...IS UP TO THE AIRBORNE UNIT.
EXACTLY.
KRAKAKAK

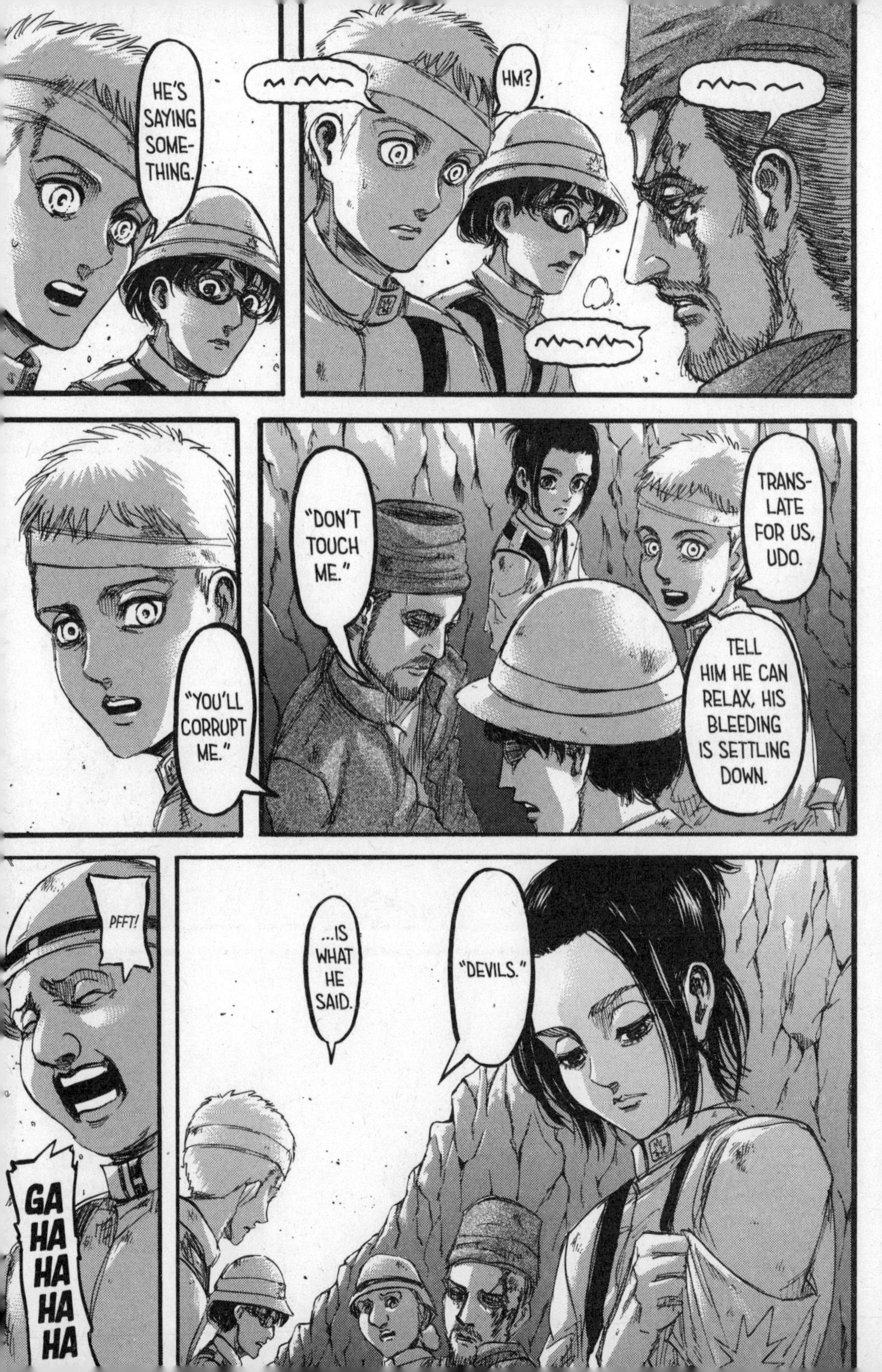
HM?
HE'S SAYING SOMETHING.
TRANSLATE FOR US, UDO.
TELL HIM HE CAN RELAX, HIS BLEEDING IS SETTLING DOWN.
"DON'T TOUCH ME."
"YOU'LL CORRUPT ME."
"DEVILS."
...IS WHAT HE SAID.
PFFT!
GA HA HA HA HA HA

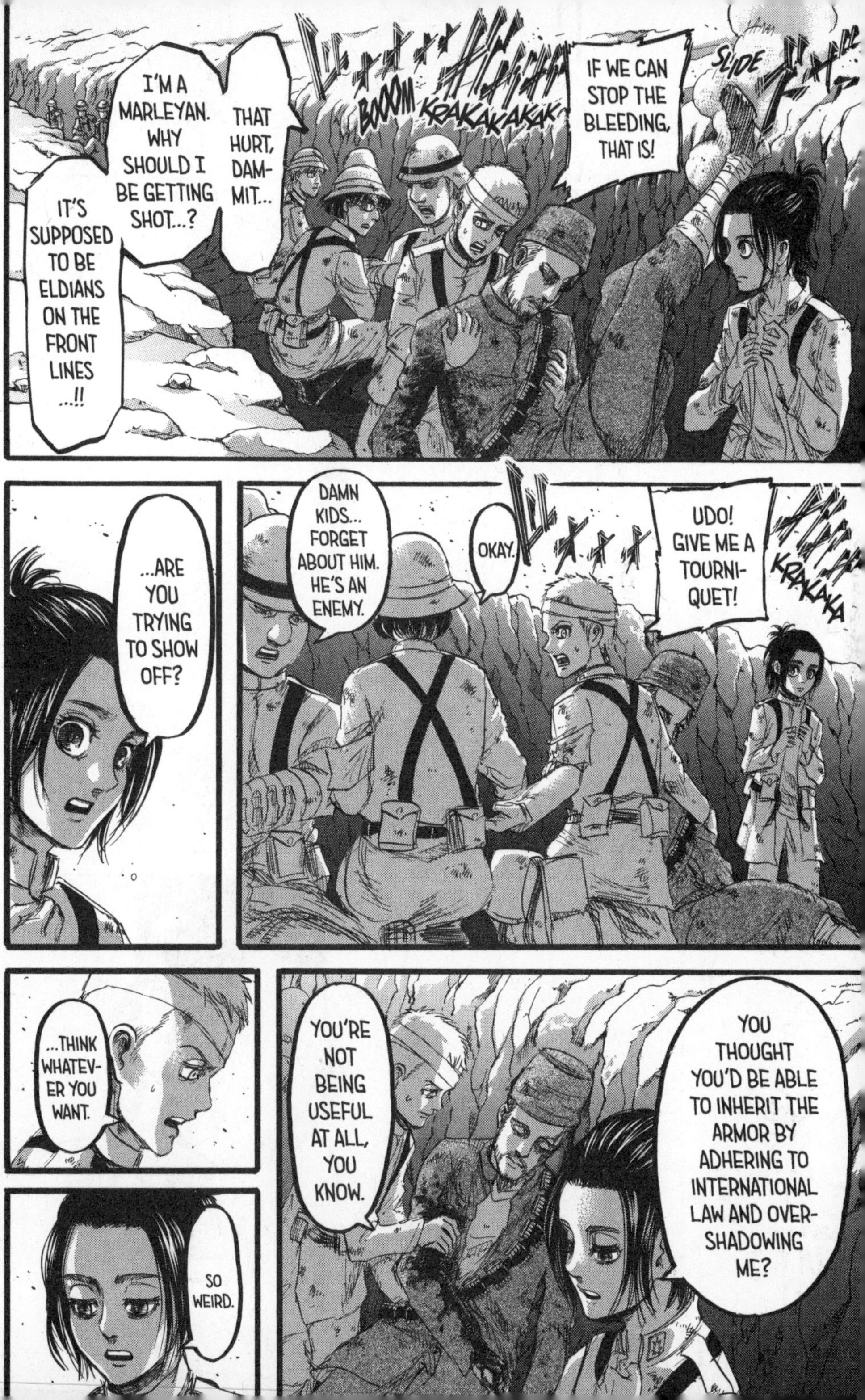
SLIDE
IF WE CAN STOP THE BLEEDING, THAT IS!
KRAKAKAKAK
BOOOM
THAT HURT, DAMMIT...
I'M A MARLEYAN. WHY SHOULD I BE GETTING SHOT...?
IT'S SUPPOSED TO BE ELDIANS ON THE FRONT LINES ...!!
KRAKAKA
UDO! GIVE ME A TOURNIQUET!
OKAY.
DAMN KIDS... FORGET ABOUT HIM. HE'S AN ENEMY.
...ARE YOU TRYING TO SHOW OFF?
YOU THOUGHT YOU'D BE ABLE TO INHERIT THE ARMOR BY ADHERING TO INTERNATIONAL LAW AND OVERSHADOWING ME?
YOU'RE NOT BEING USEFUL AT ALL, YOU KNOW.
...THINK WHATEVER YOU WANT.
SO WEIRD.

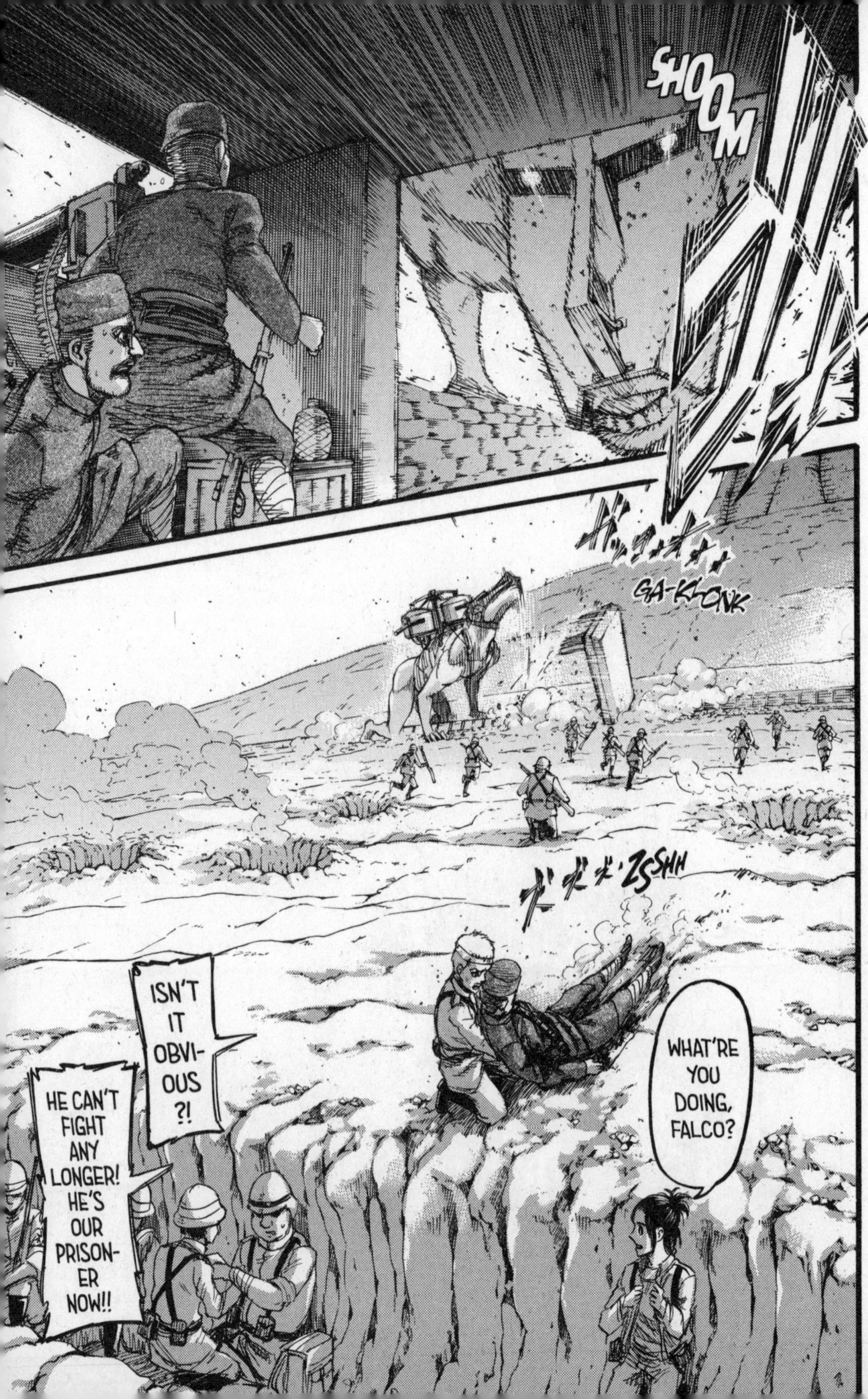
SHOOM
GA-KLONK
ZSSHH
WHAT'RE YOU DOING, FALCO?
ISN'T IT OBVIOUS?!
HE CAN'T FIGHT ANY LONGER! HE'S OUR PRISONER NOW!!

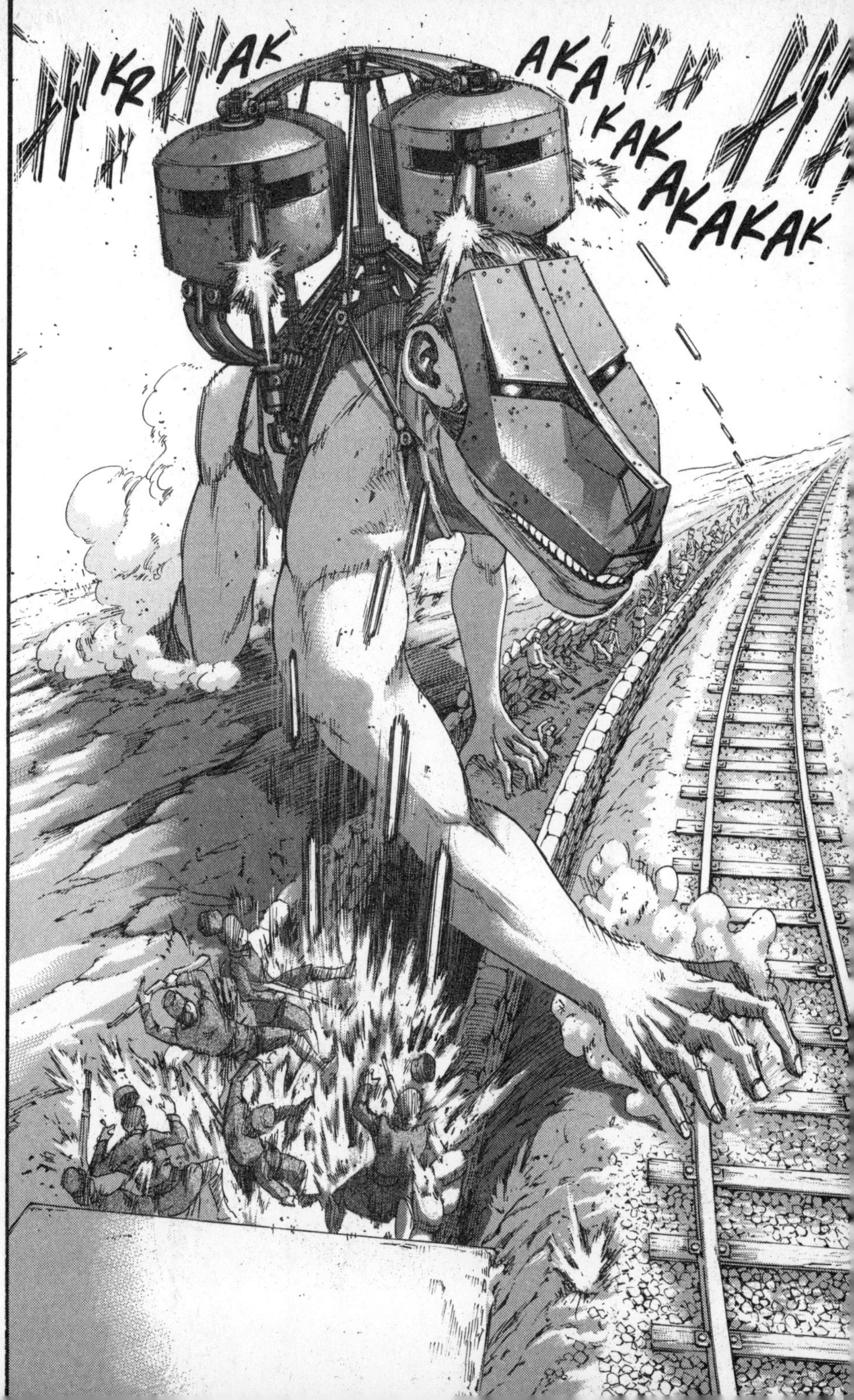
KRAK
AKAAKAKAKAKAKAK

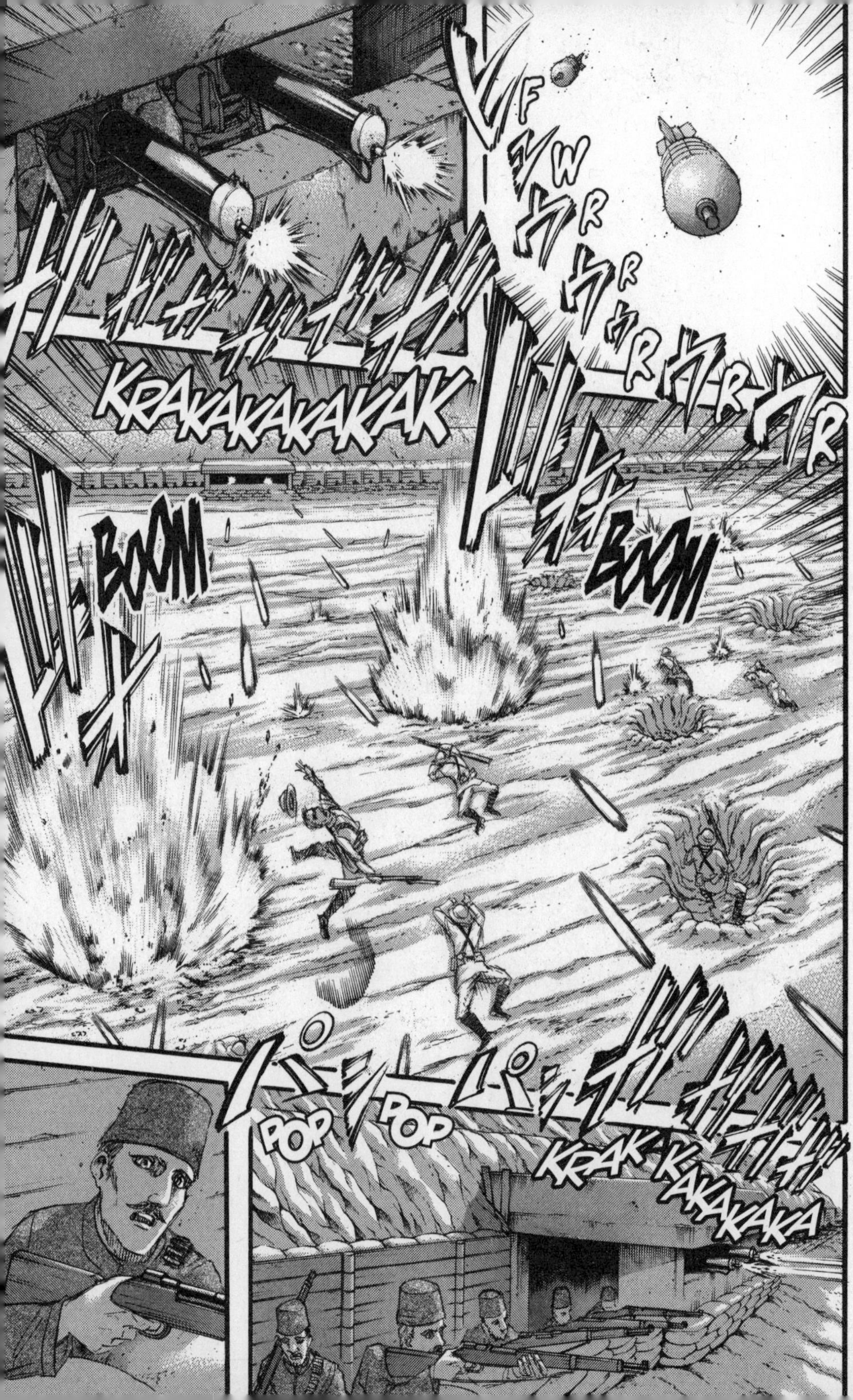
FWRRRRRR
KRAKAKAKAKAKAK
BOOM
BOOM
POP POP
KRAK KAKAKAKA

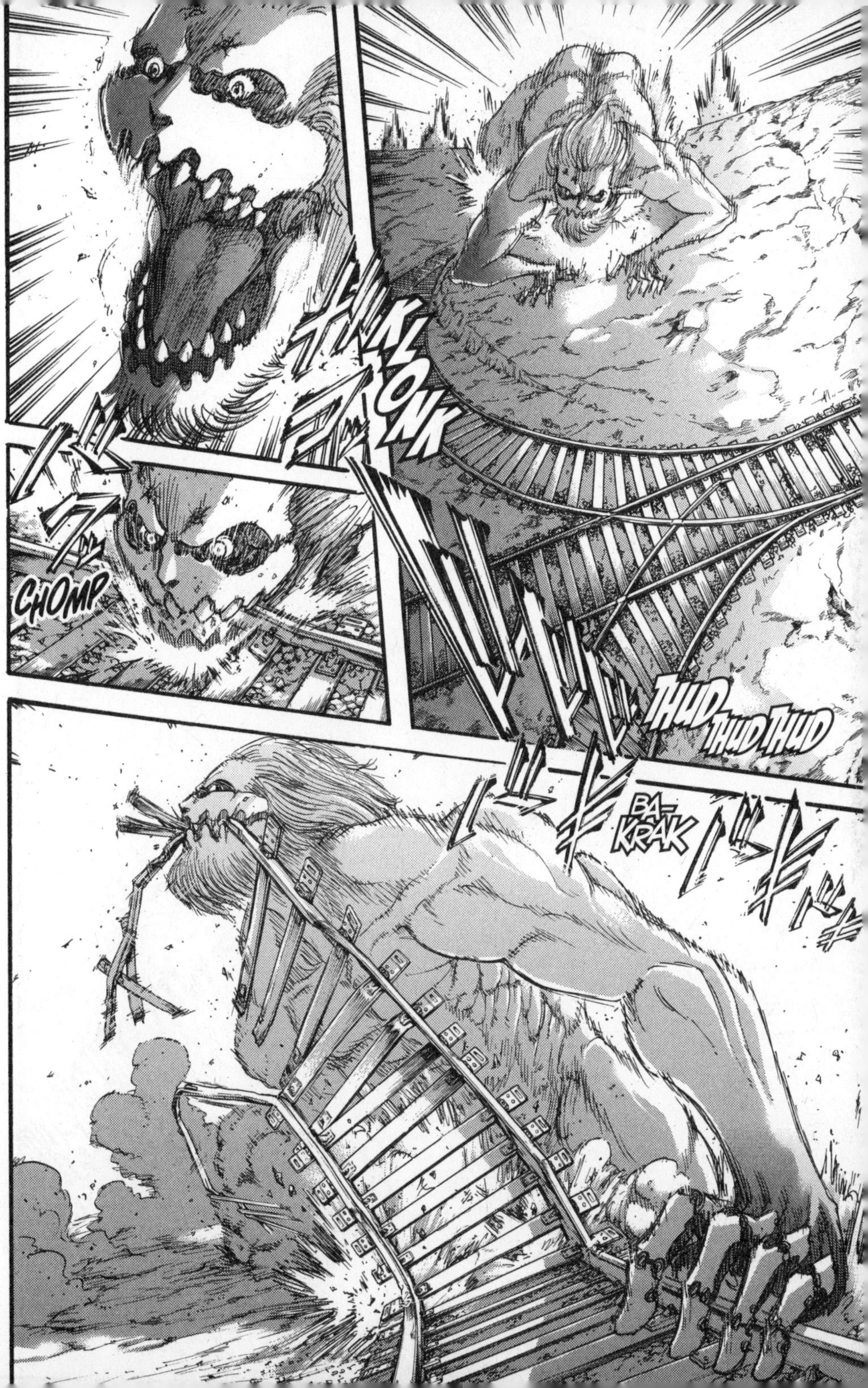
KLONK
THUD THUD THUD
CHOMP
BA-KRAK

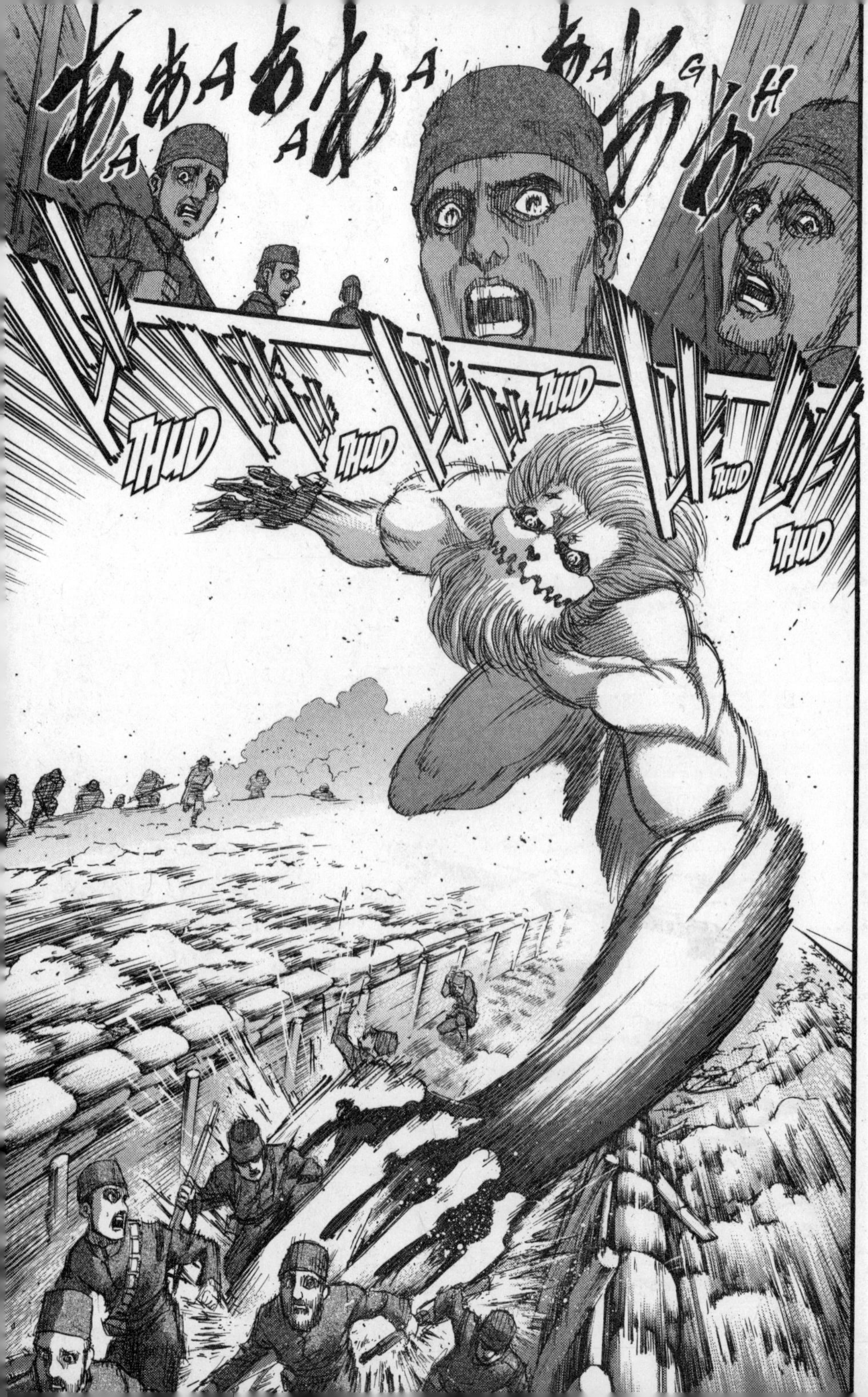
AAAAAGH
THUD
THUD
THUD
THUD
THUD

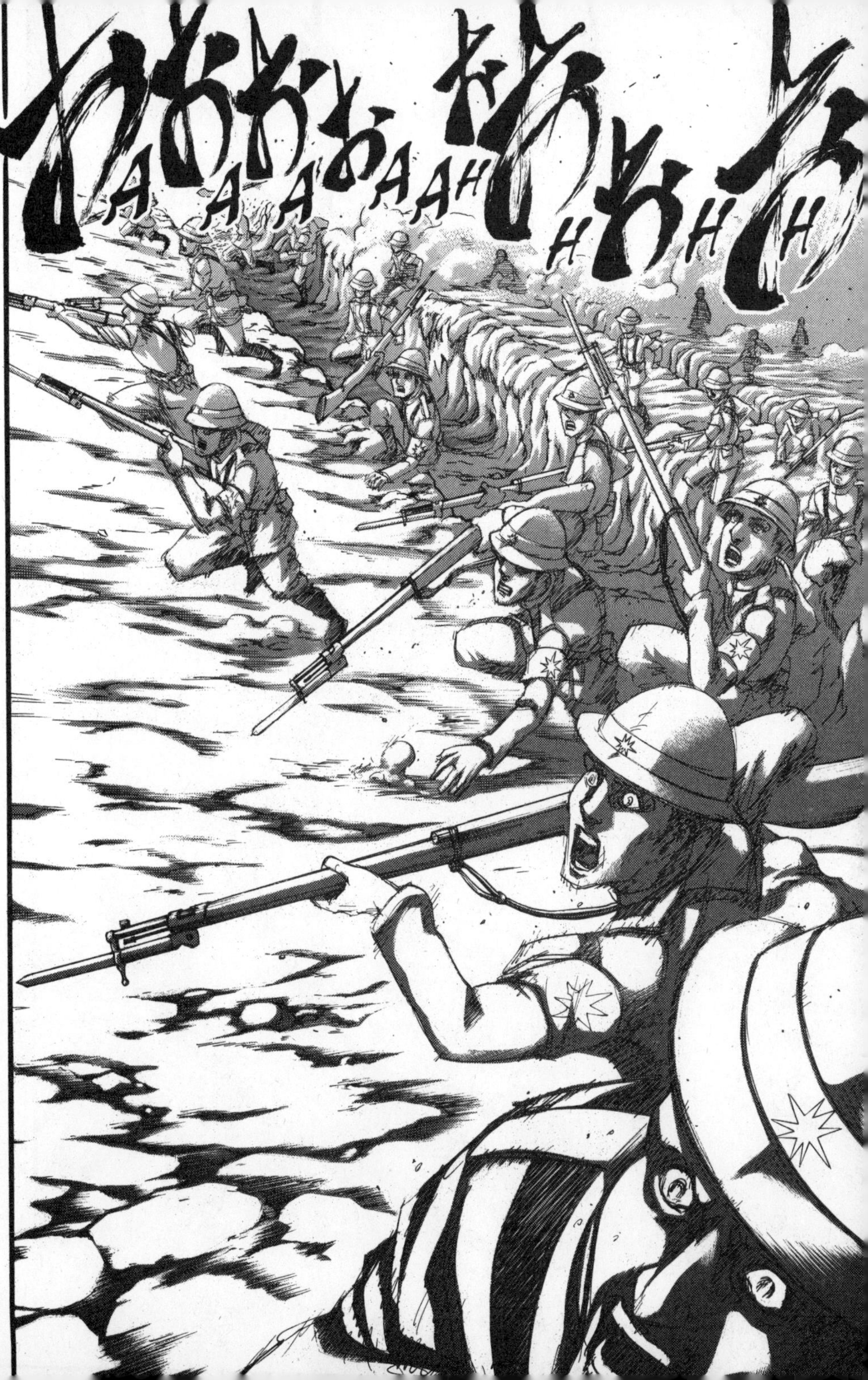
AAAAAAAHHHH

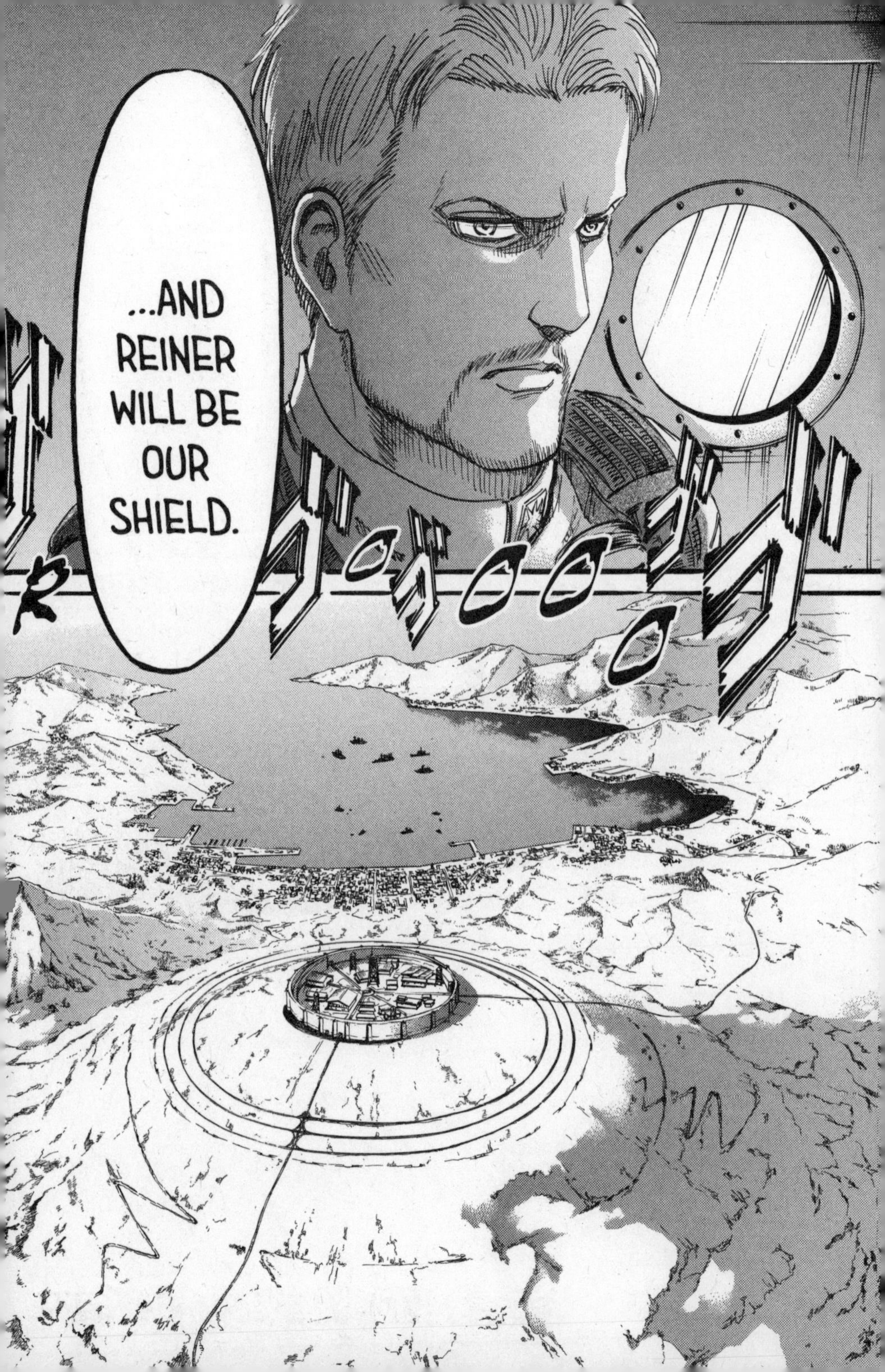
...AND REINER WILL BE OUR SHIELD.

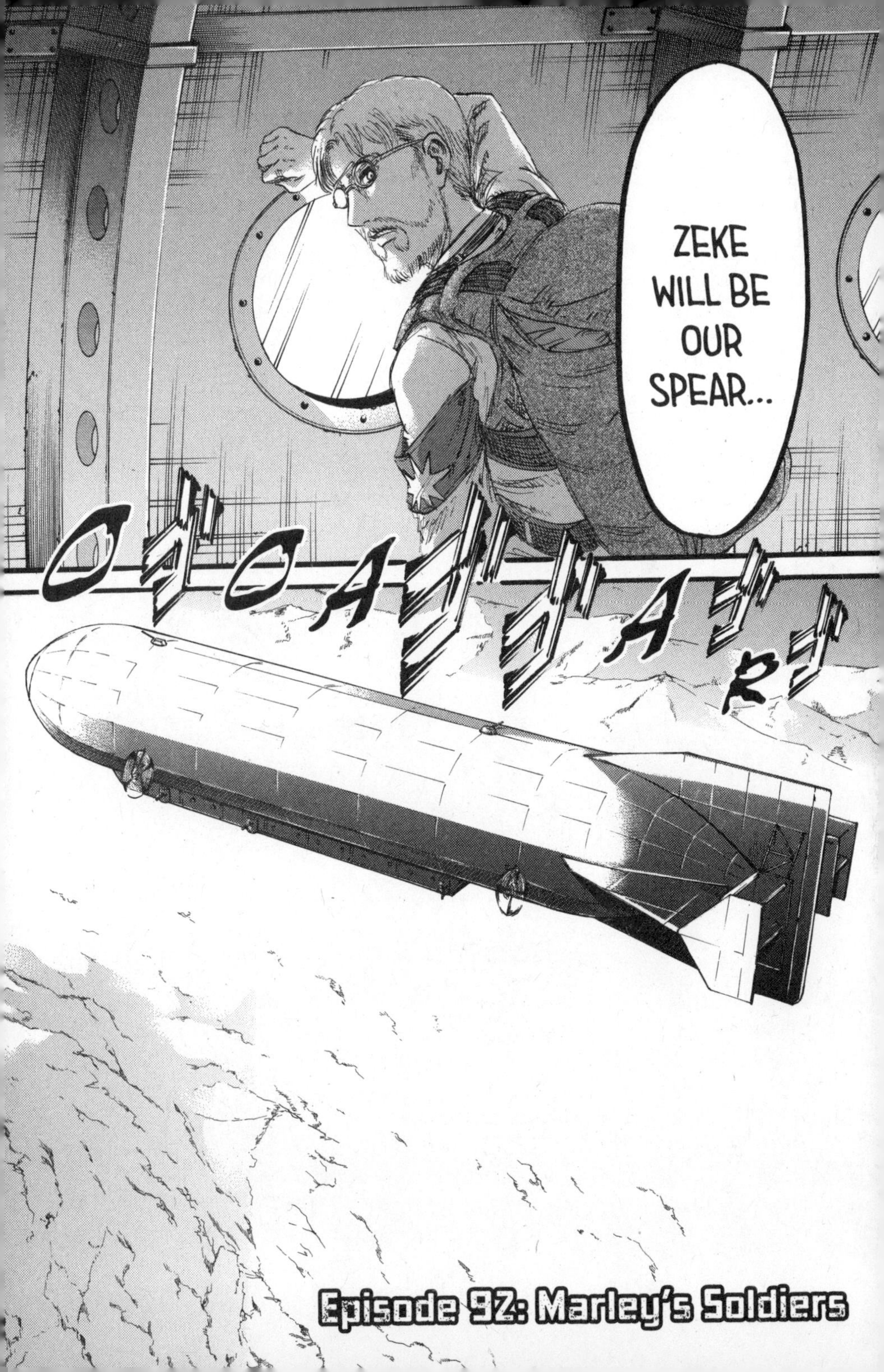
ZEKE WILL BE OUR SPEAR...

Episode 92: Marley's Soldiers

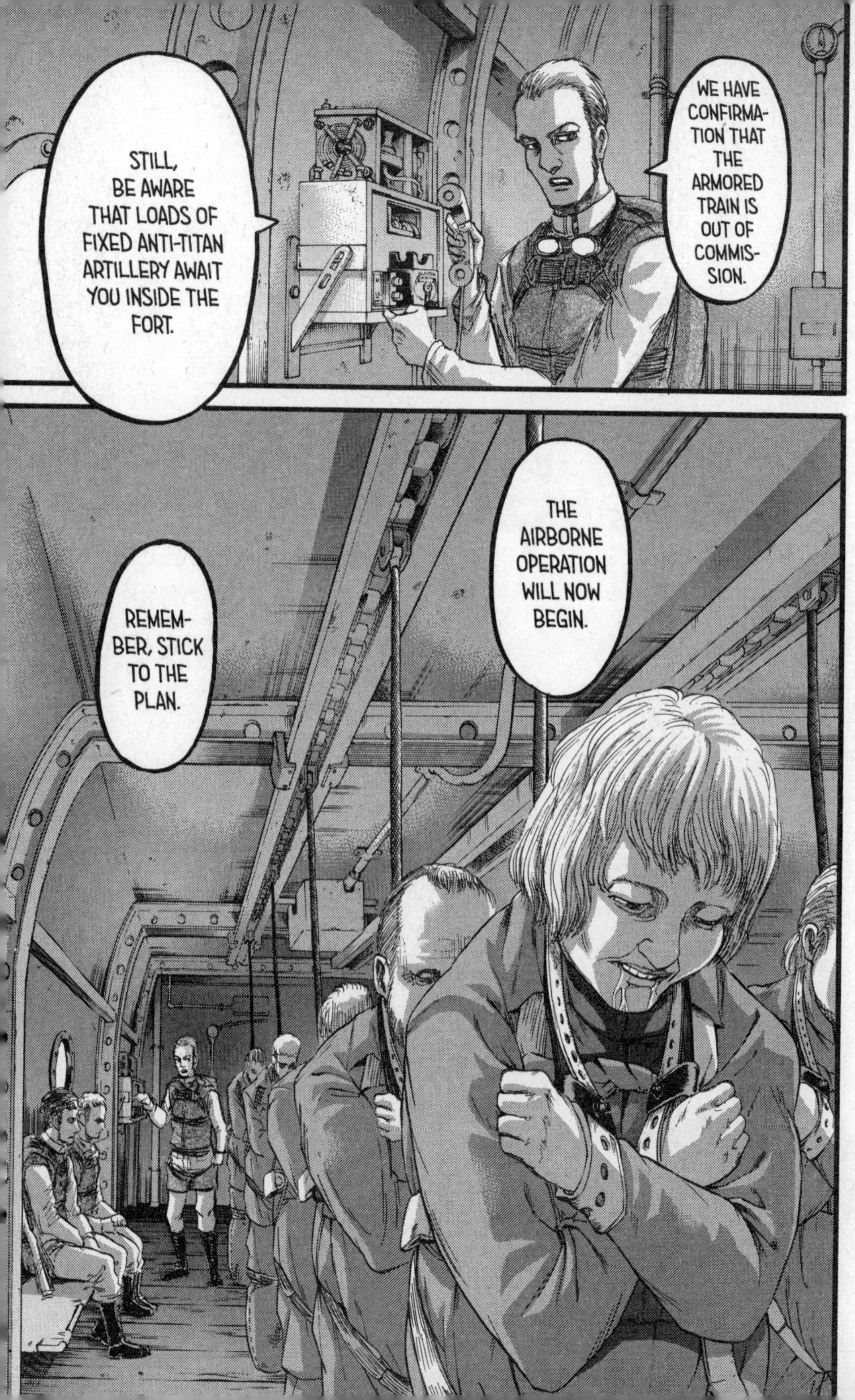
WE HAVE CONFIRMATION THAT THE ARMORED TRAIN IS OUT OF COMMISSION.
STILL, BE AWARE THAT LOADS OF FIXED ANTI-TITAN ARTILLERY AWAIT YOU INSIDE THE FORT.
THE AIRBORNE OPERATION WILL NOW BEGIN.
REMEMBER, STICK TO THE PLAN.

ATTACK on TITAN

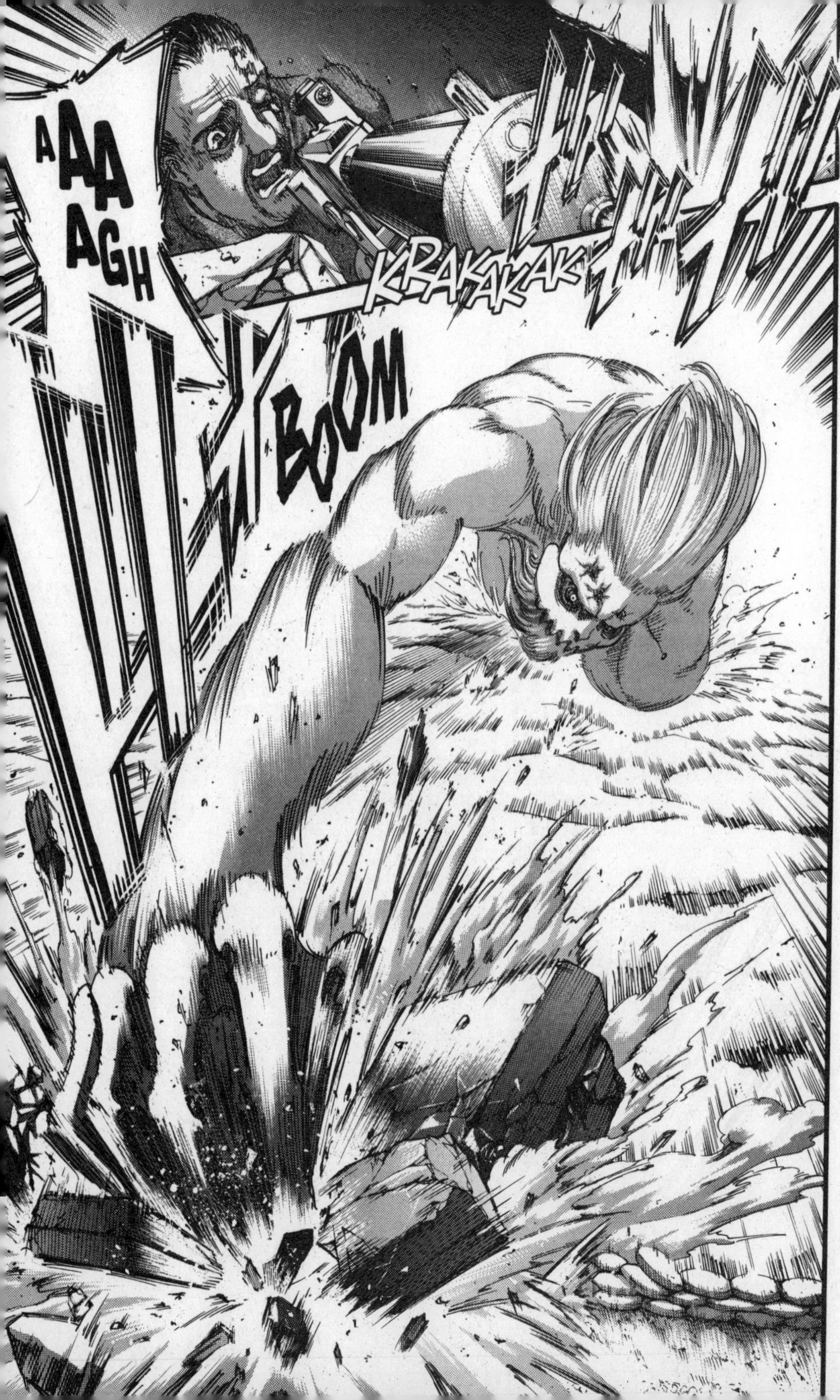
KRAKAKAK
AAAAGH
BOOM

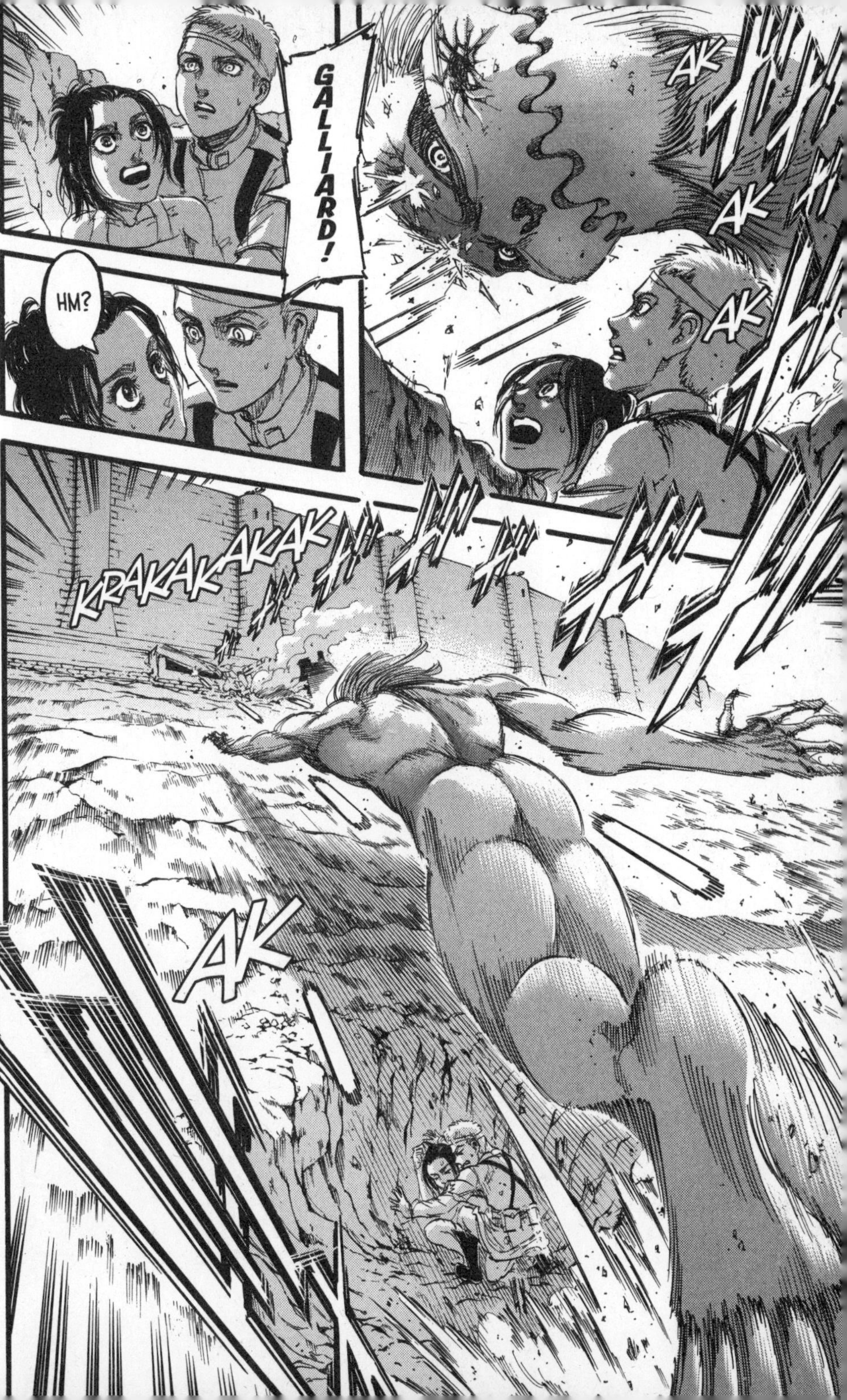
AK
AK
AK
GALLIARD!
HM?
KRAKAKAKAK
AK

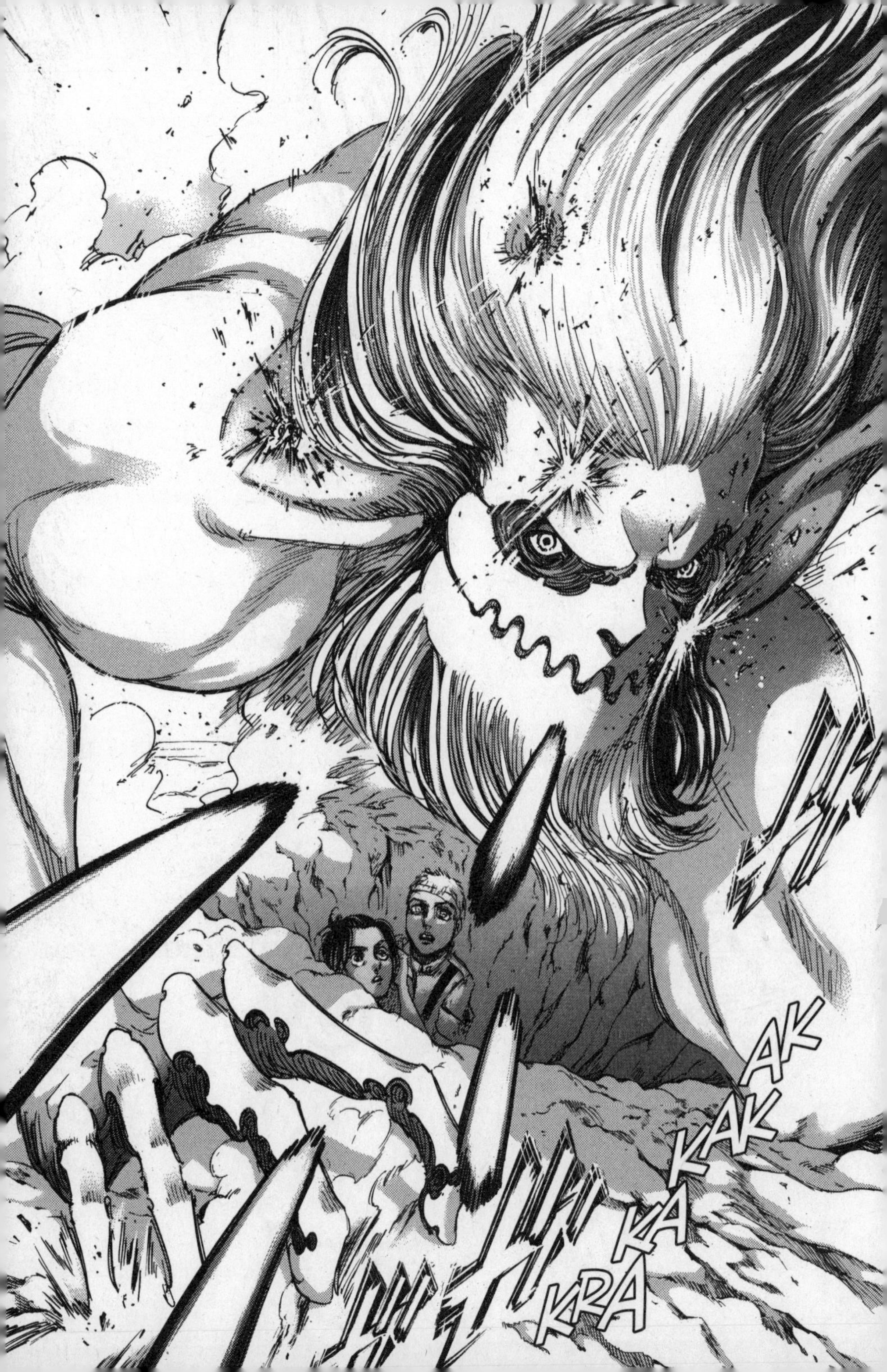
KRAKAKAKAK

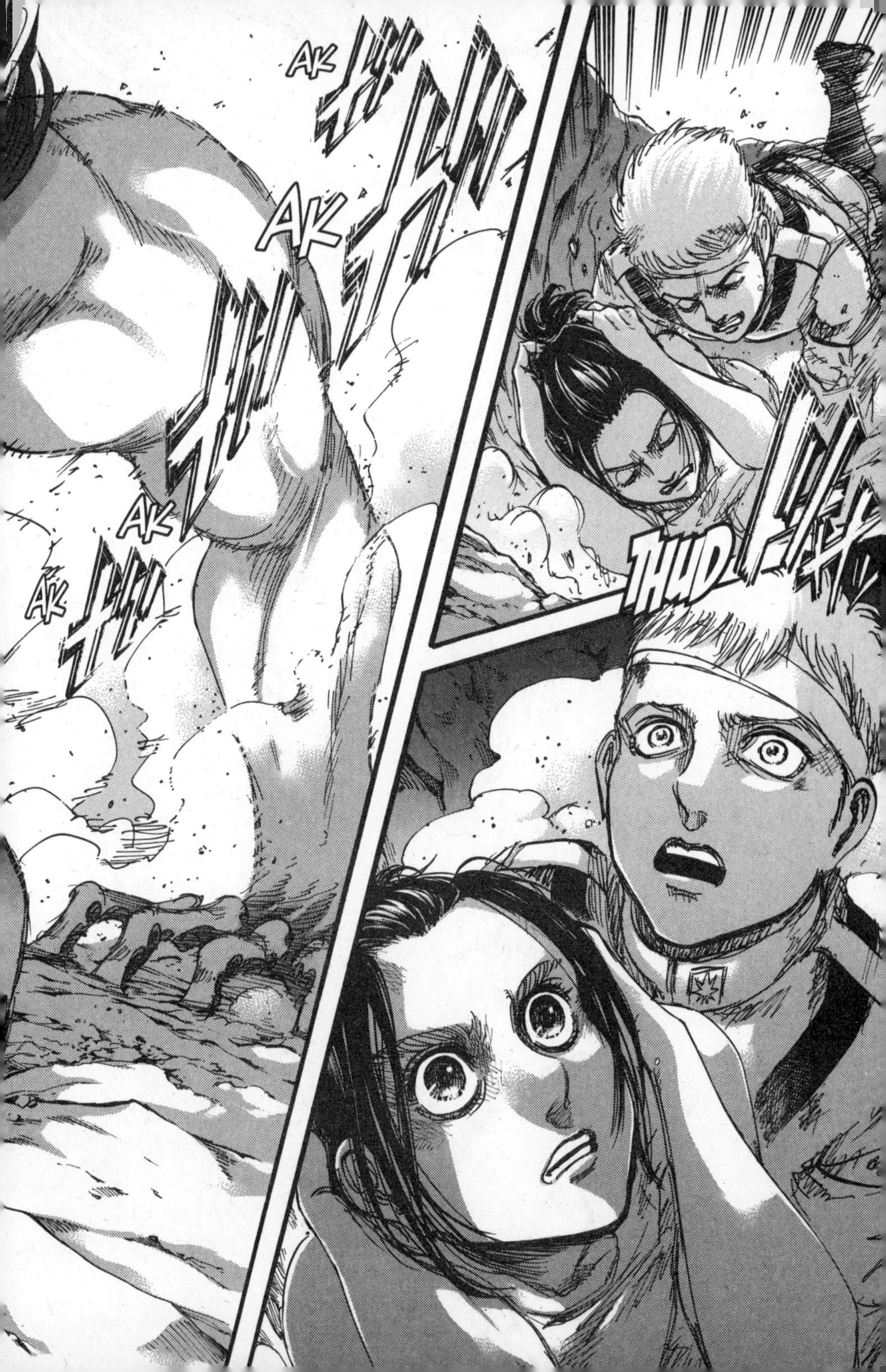
THUD
AK
AK
AK
AK

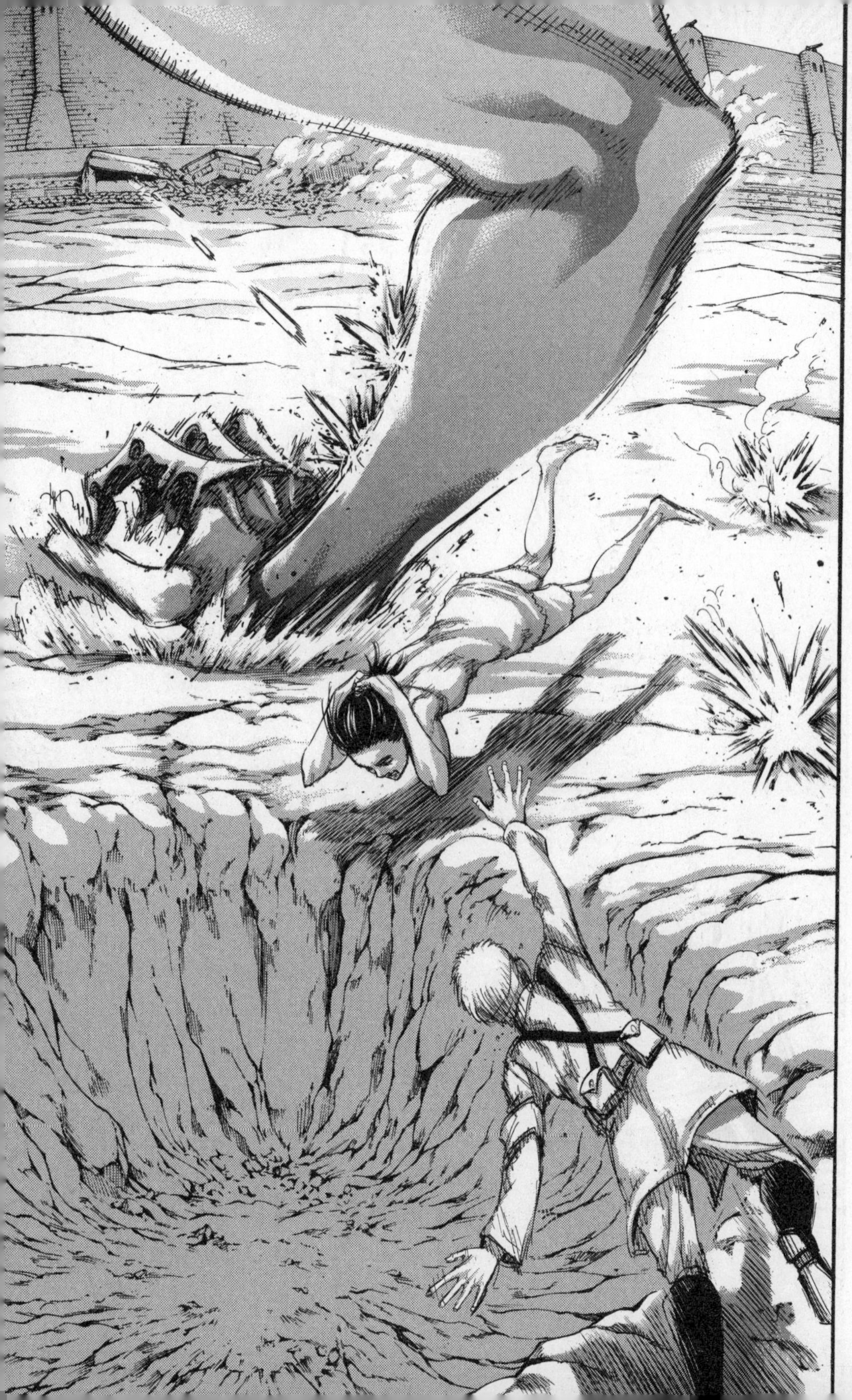

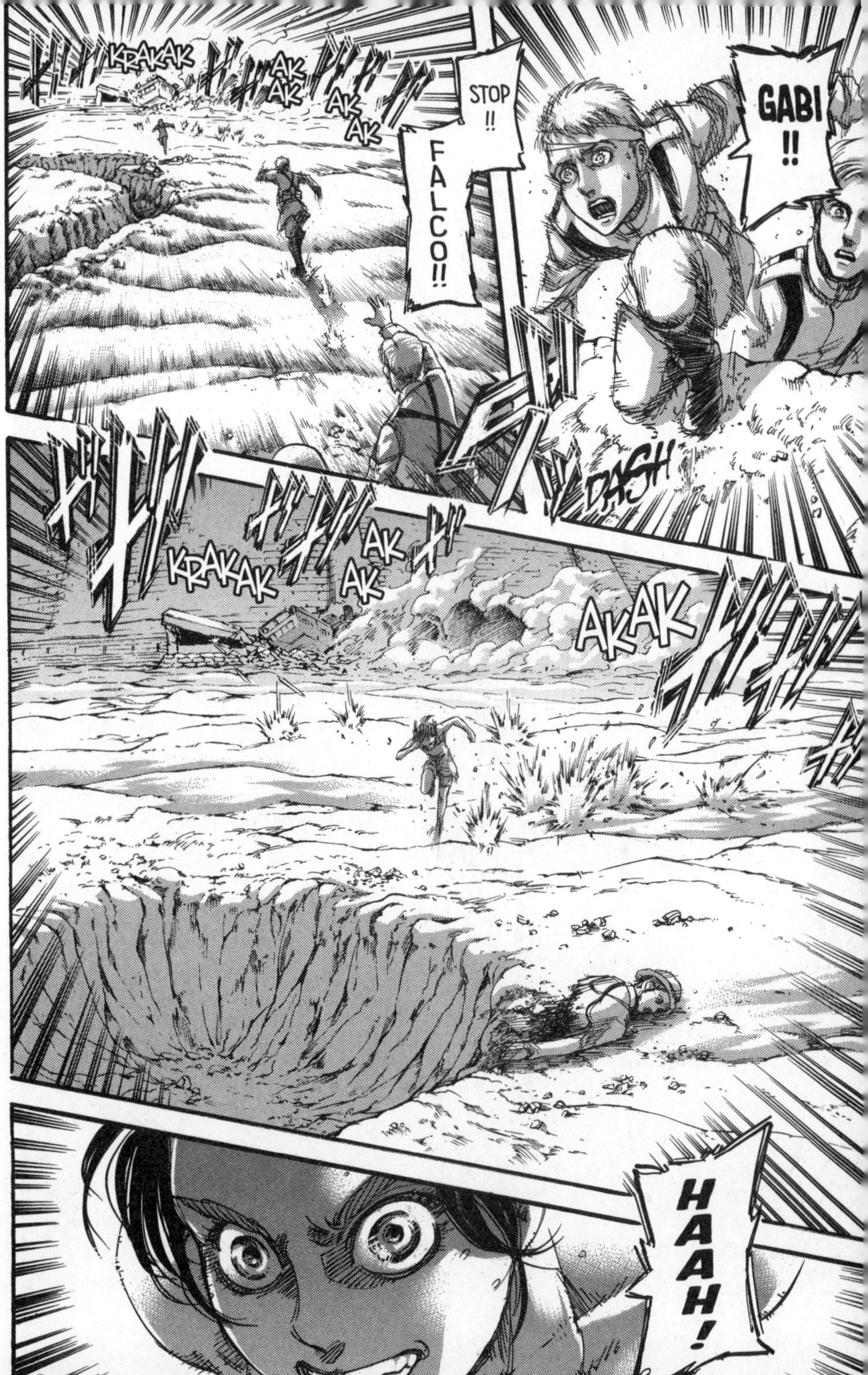
GABI !!
STOP !!
FALCO!!
DASH
AK AK AK
AK AK
KRAKAK
AKAK
AK AK
KRAKAK
HAAAH!

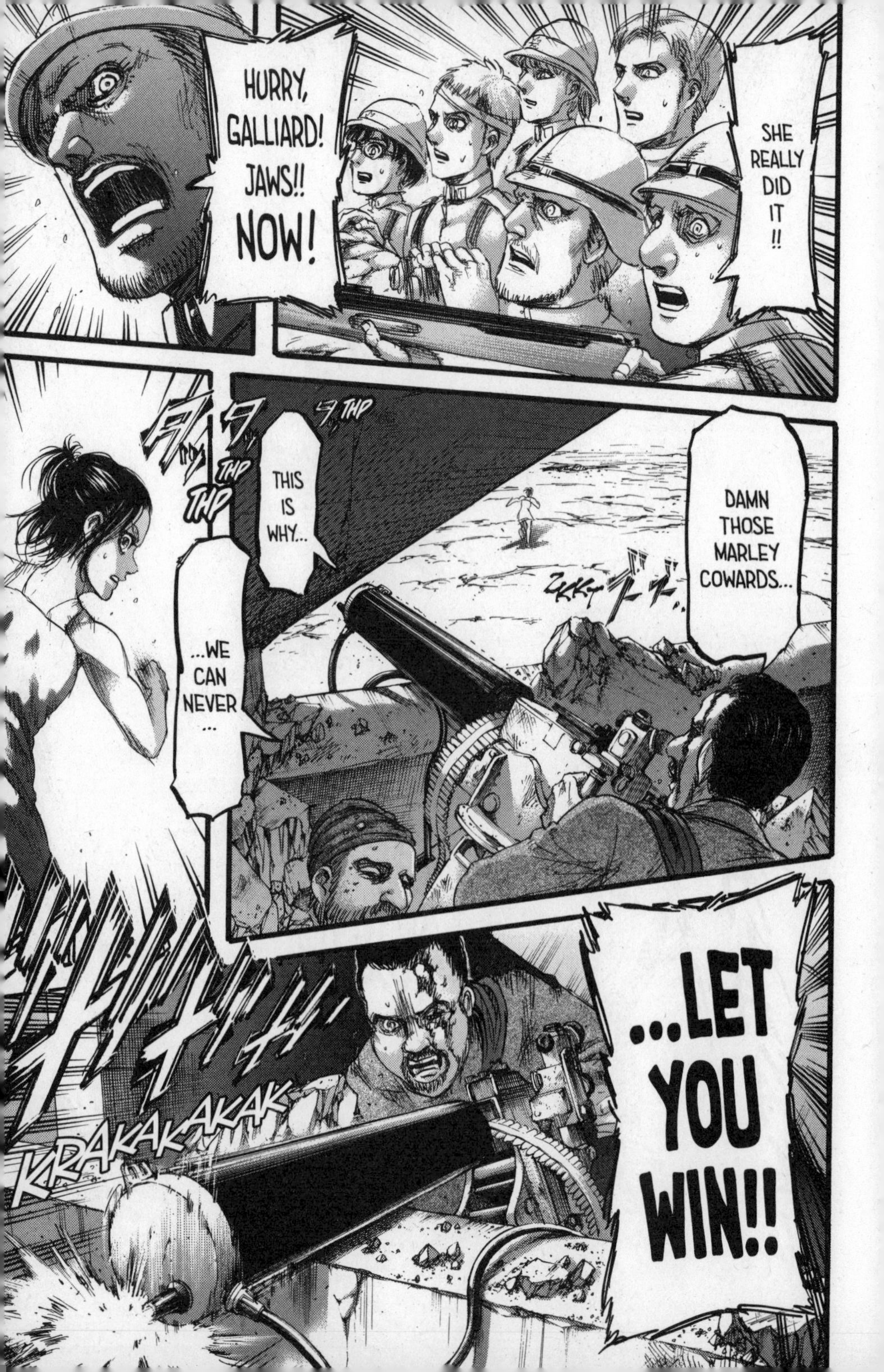
SHE REALLY DID IT!!
HURRY, GALLIARD! JAWS!! NOW!
DAMN THOSE MARLEY COWARDS...
THP
THIS IS WHY...
...WE CAN NEVER...
THP
THP
...LET YOU WIN!!
KRAKAKAKAK

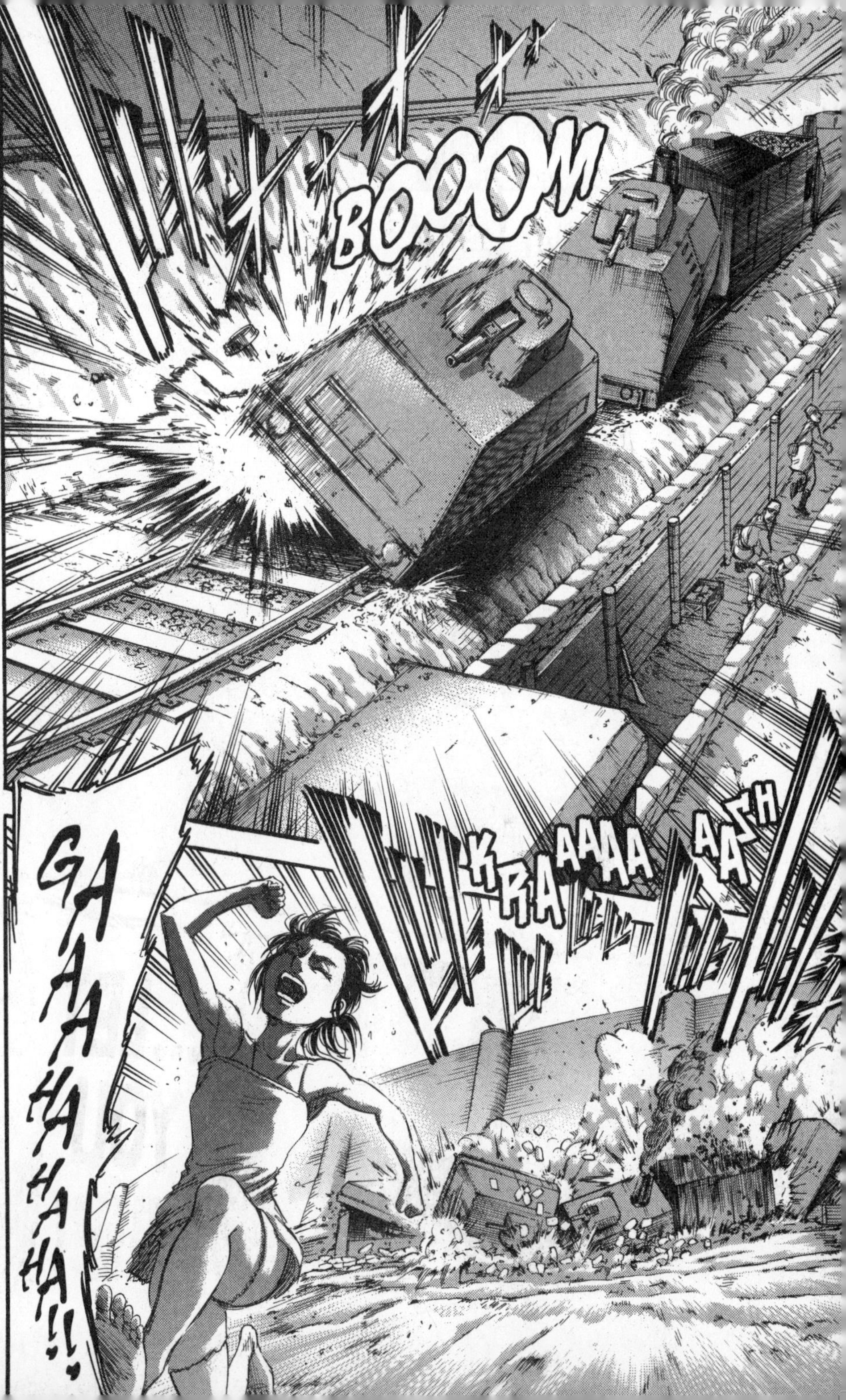
BOOOM
KRAAAAAAASH
GAAAHAHAHAHA!!!

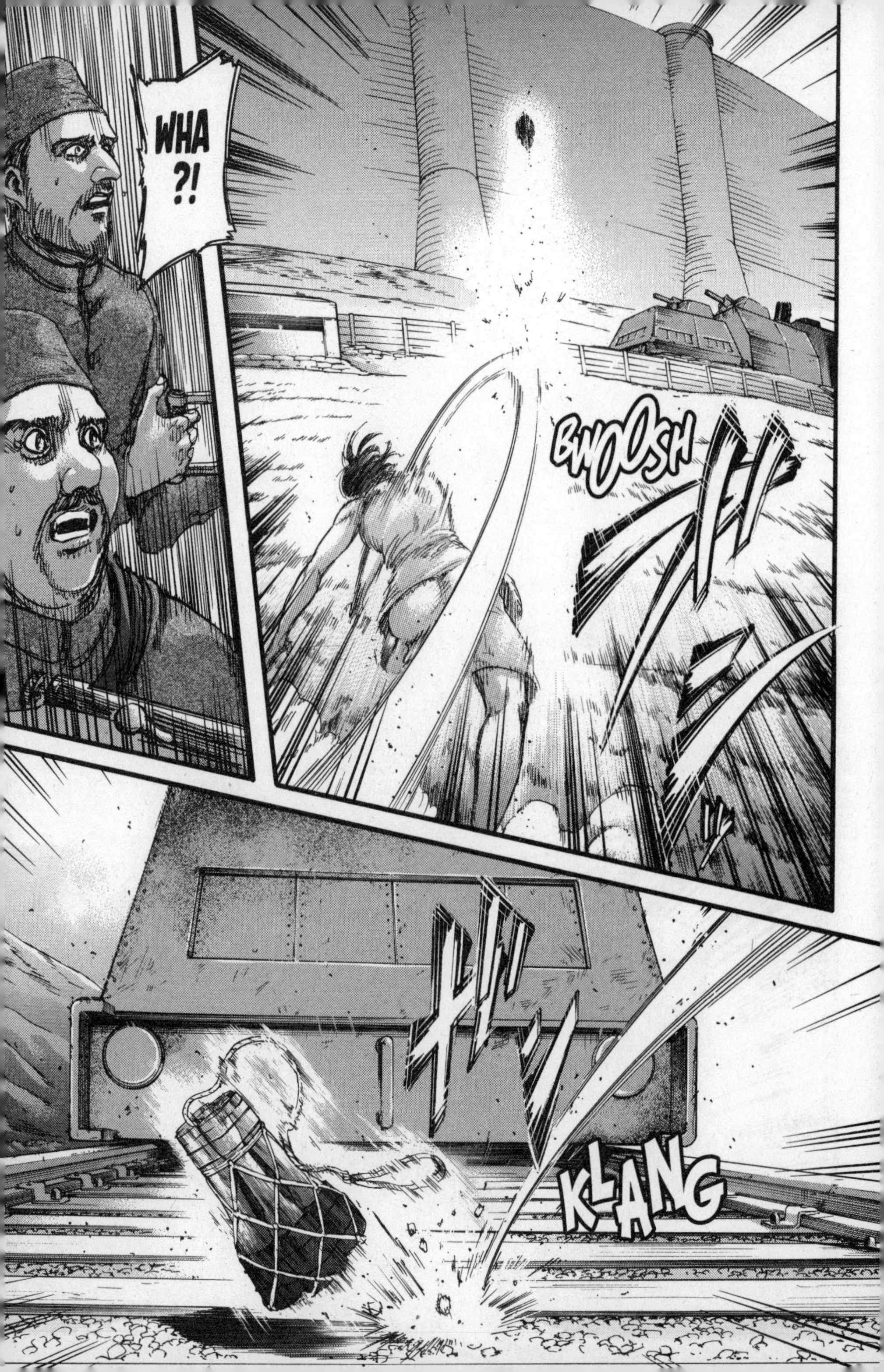
BWOOSH
WHA ?!
KLANG

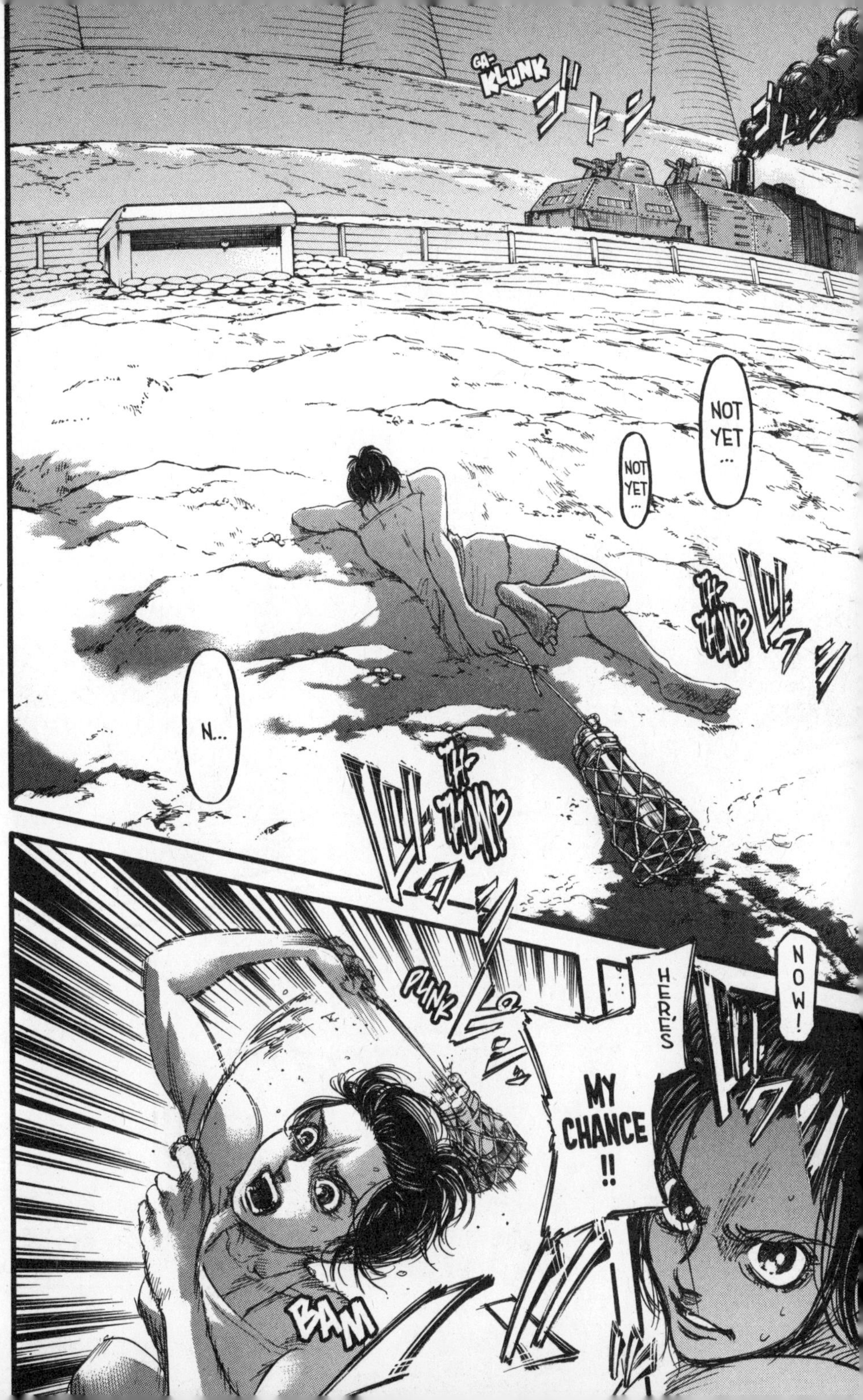
GA-KLUNK
NOT YET ...
NOT YET ...
TH-THUMP
N...
TH-THUMP
NOW!
HERE'S MY CHANCE !!
PLUNK
BAM

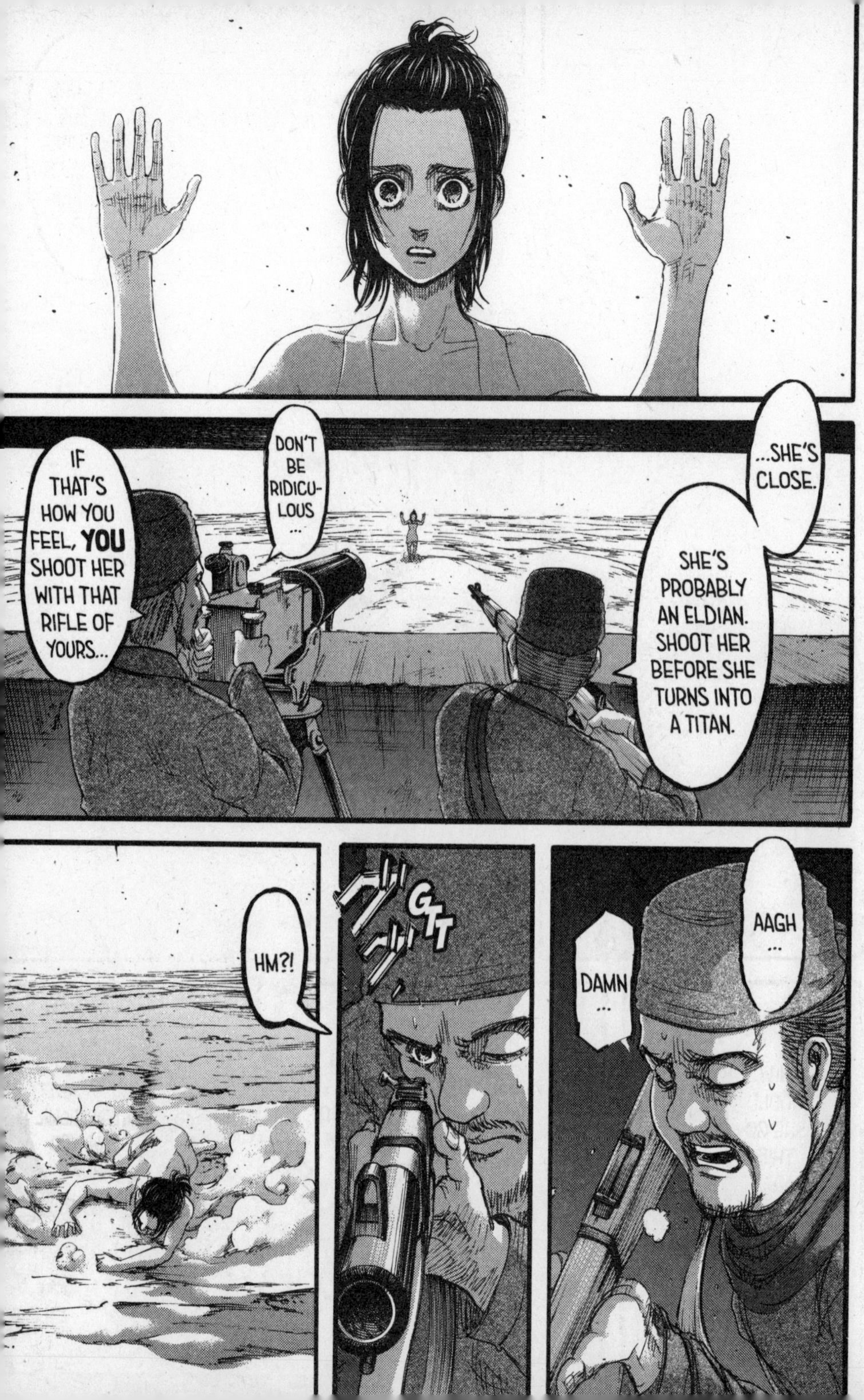

...SHE'S CLOSE.
SHE'S PROBABLY AN ELDIAN. SHOOT HER BEFORE SHE TURNS INTO A TITAN.
DON'T BE RIDICULOUS ...
IF THAT'S HOW YOU FEEL, **YOU** SHOOT HER WITH THAT RIFLE OF YOURS...
AAGH ...
DAMN ...
GTT
HM?!

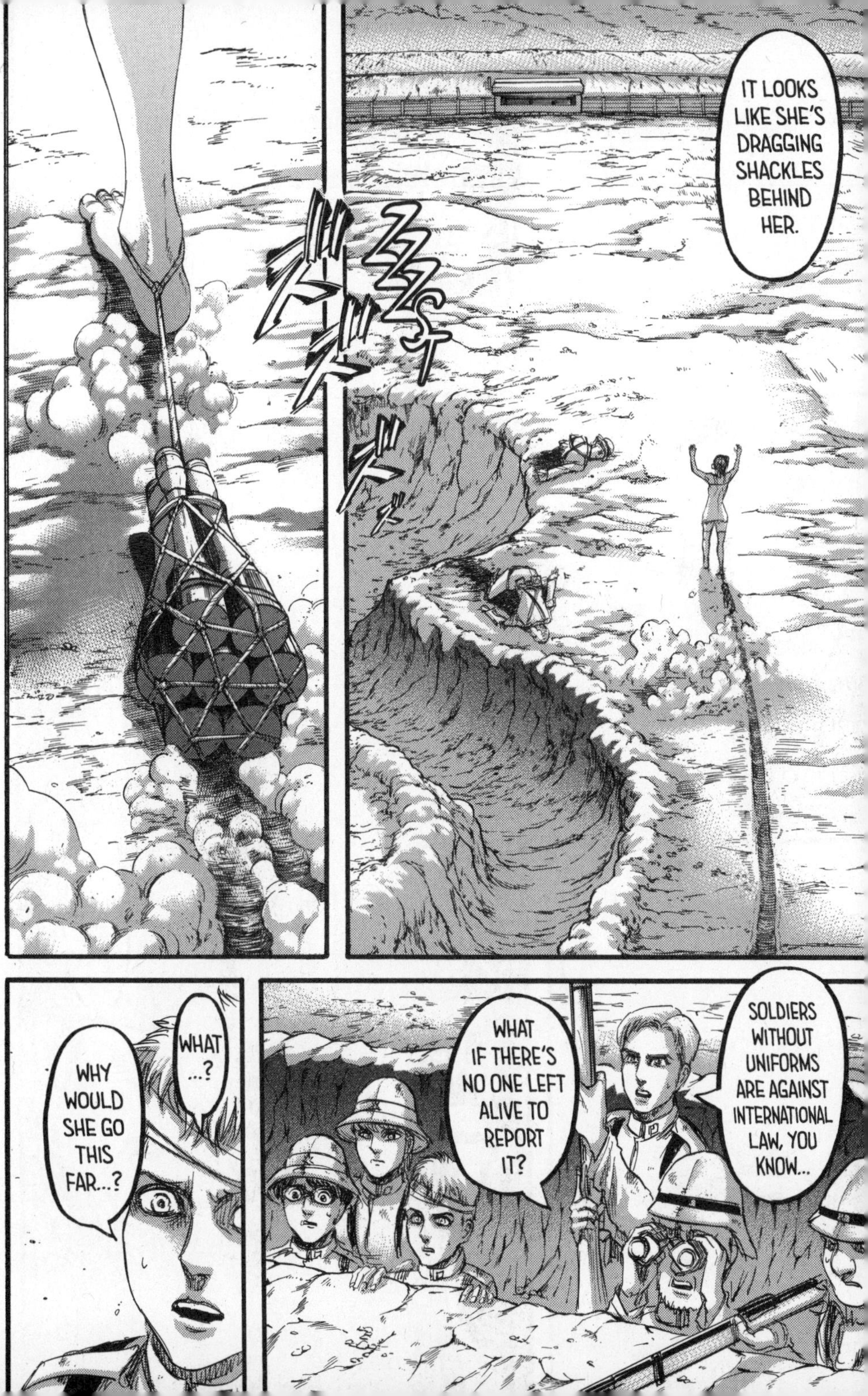
IT LOOKS LIKE SHE'S DRAGGING SHACKLES BEHIND HER.
SOLDIERS WITHOUT UNIFORMS ARE AGAINST INTERNATIONAL LAW, YOU KNOW...
WHAT IF THERE'S NO ONE LEFT ALIVE TO REPORT IT?
WHAT ...?
WHY WOULD SHE GO THIS FAR...?

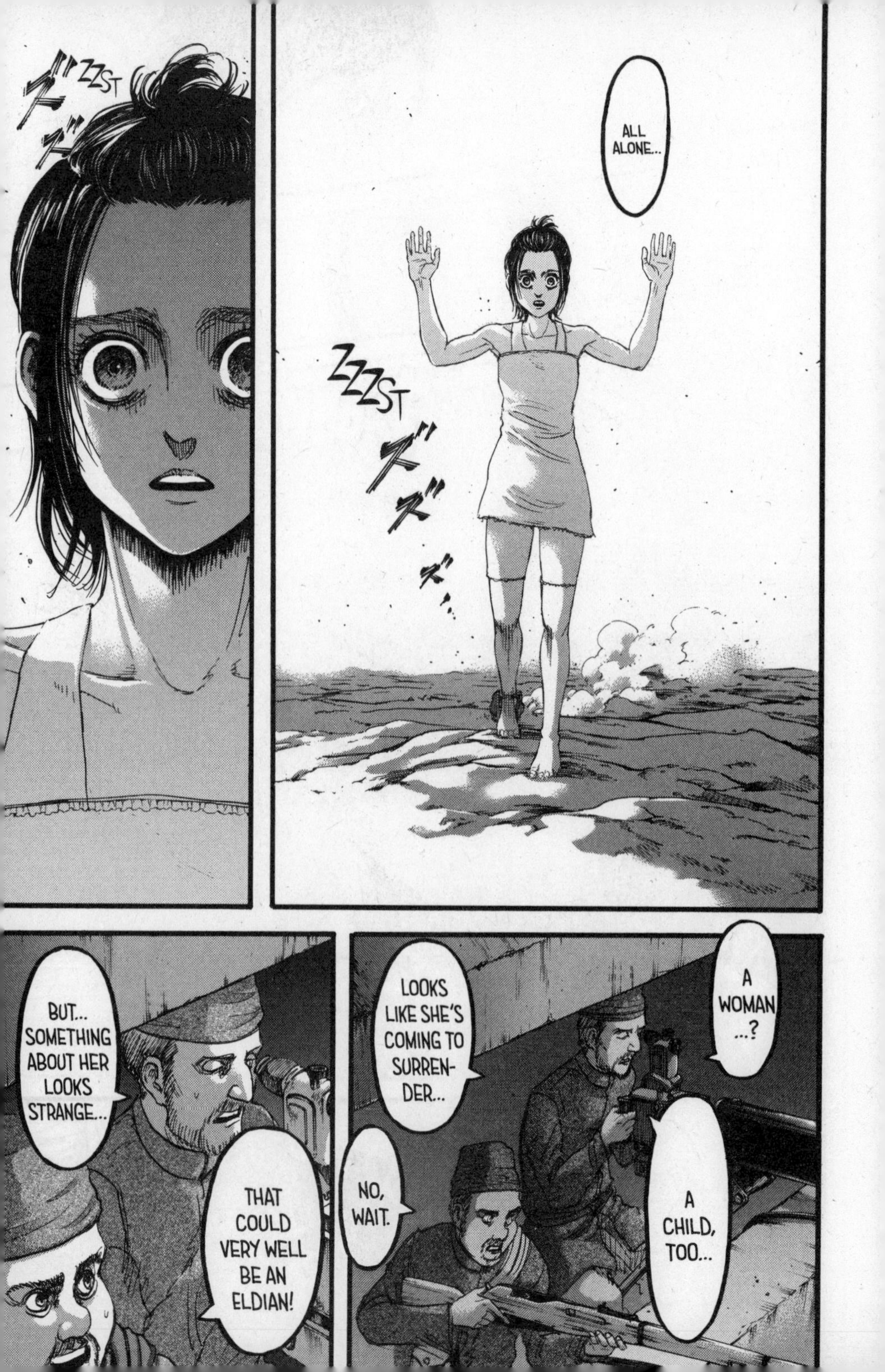
ALL ALONE...
ZZZST
ZZZST
A WOMAN ...?
LOOKS LIKE SHE'S COMING TO SURREN-DER...
A CHILD, TOO...
NO, WAIT.
BUT... SOMETHING ABOUT HER LOOKS STRANGE...
THAT COULD VERY WELL BE AN ELDIAN!

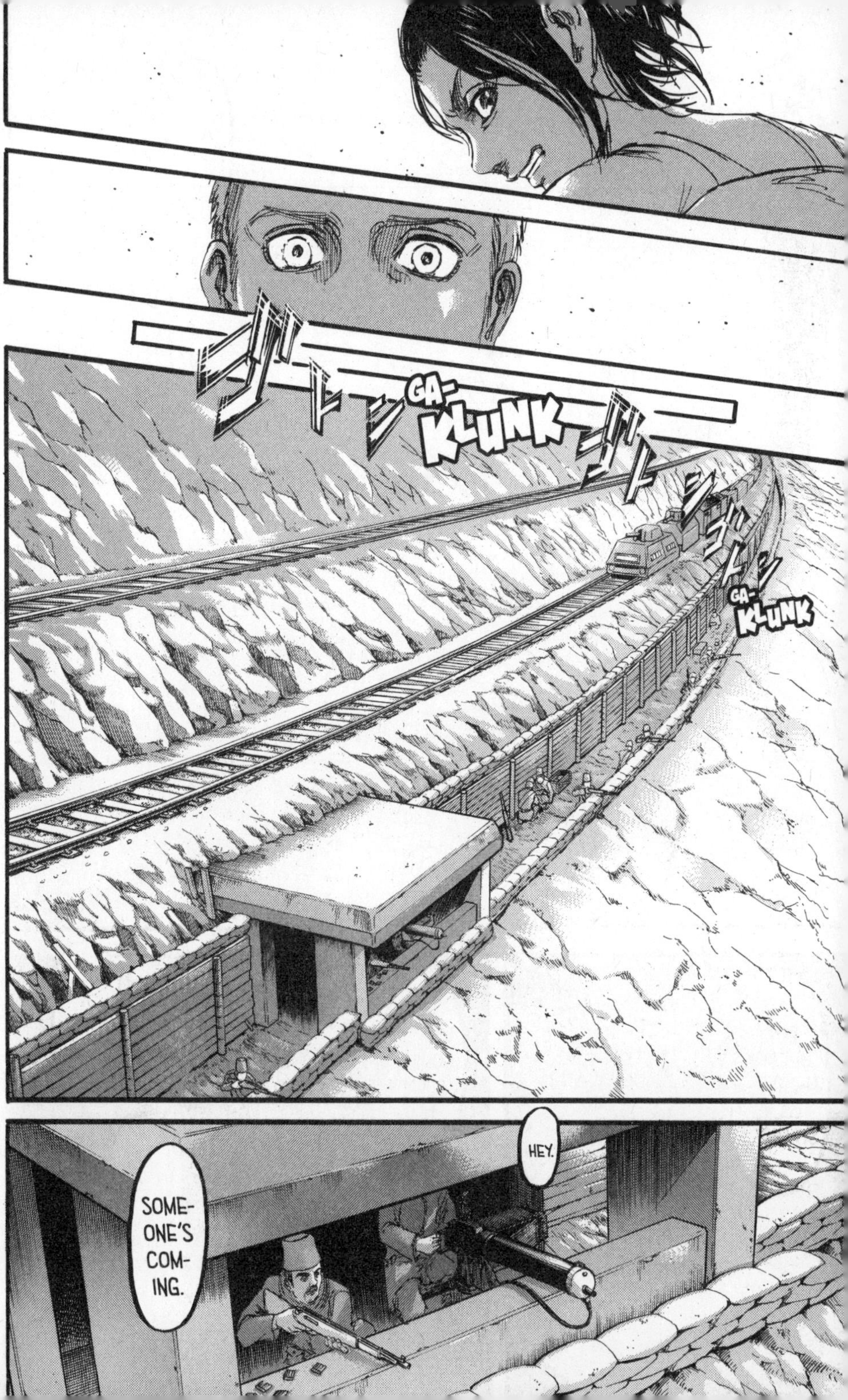
GA-KLUNK
GA-KLUNK
HEY.
SOME-ONE'S COM-ING.

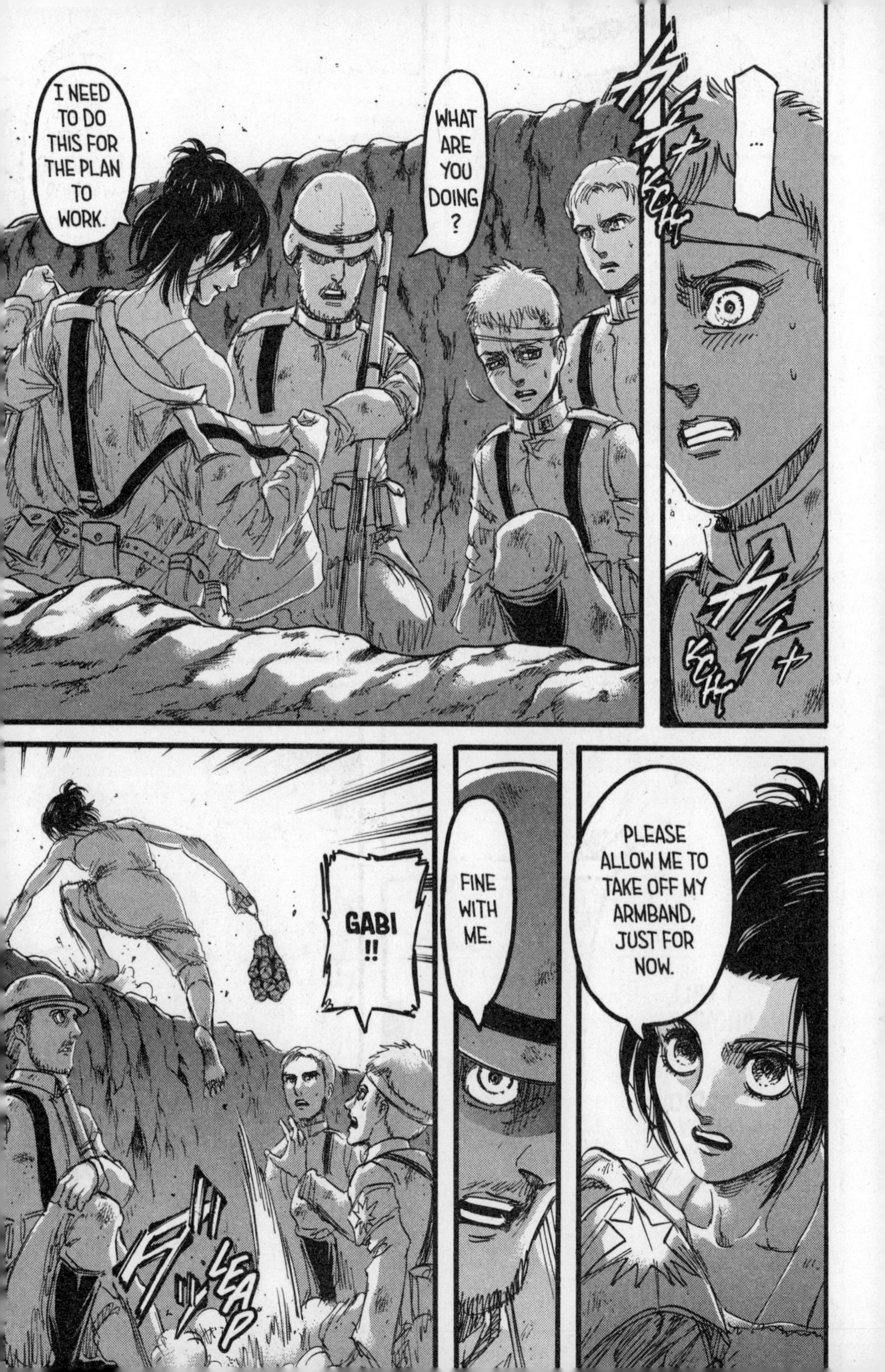
...
KCH
KCH
WHAT ARE YOU DOING?
I NEED TO DO THIS FOR THE PLAN TO WORK.
PLEASE ALLOW ME TO TAKE OFF MY ARMBAND, JUST FOR NOW.
FINE WITH ME.
GABI!!
LEAP

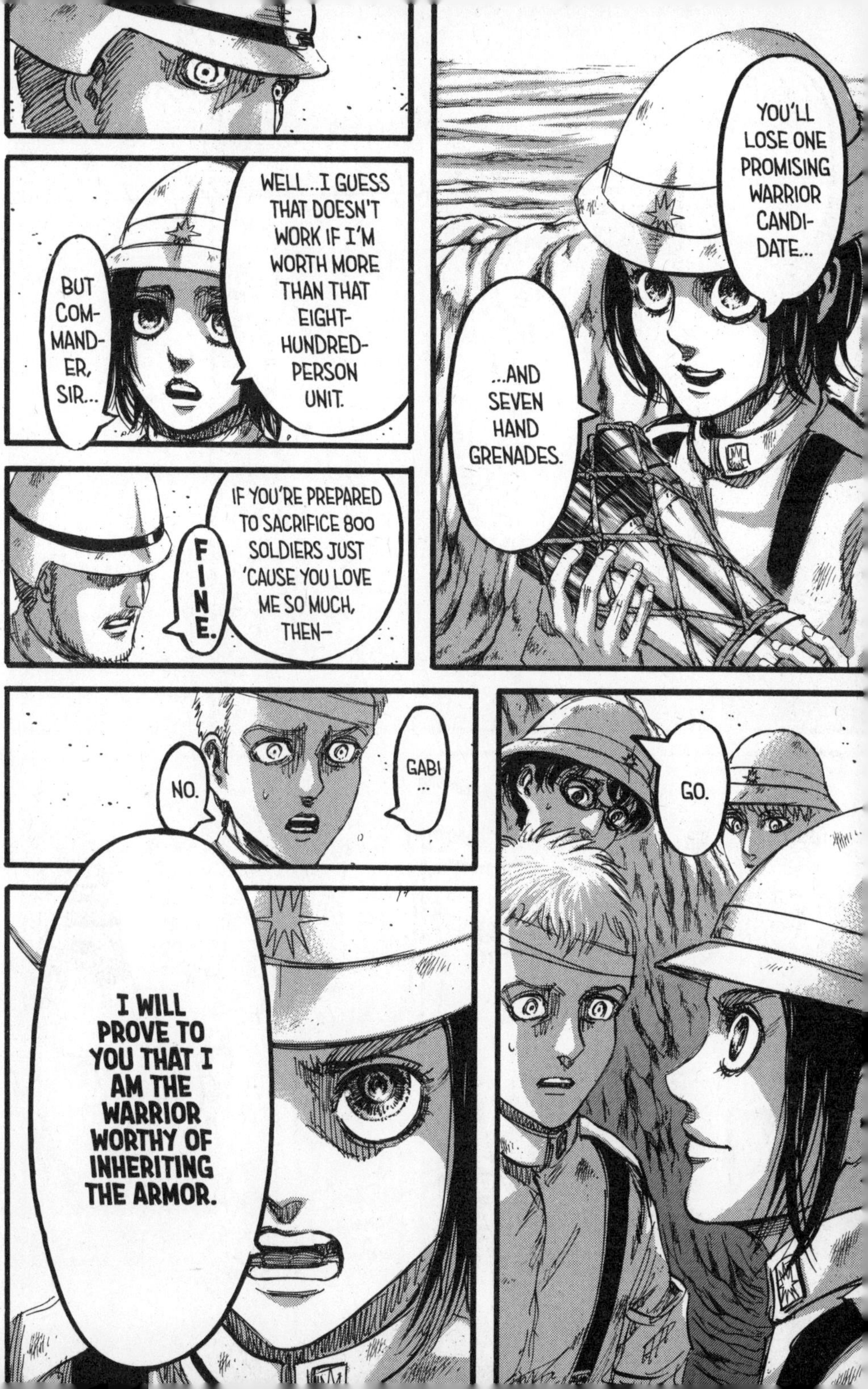
YOU'LL LOSE ONE PROMISING WARRIOR CANDIDATE...
...AND SEVEN HAND GRENADES.
WELL...I GUESS THAT DOESN'T WORK IF I'M WORTH MORE THAN THAT EIGHT-HUNDRED-PERSON UNIT.
BUT COMMANDER, SIR...
IF YOU'RE PREPARED TO SACRIFICE 800 SOLDIERS JUST 'CAUSE YOU LOVE ME SO MUCH, THEN—
FINE.
GO.
GABI...
NO.
I WILL PROVE TO YOU THAT I AM THE WARRIOR WORTHY OF INHERITING THE ARMOR.

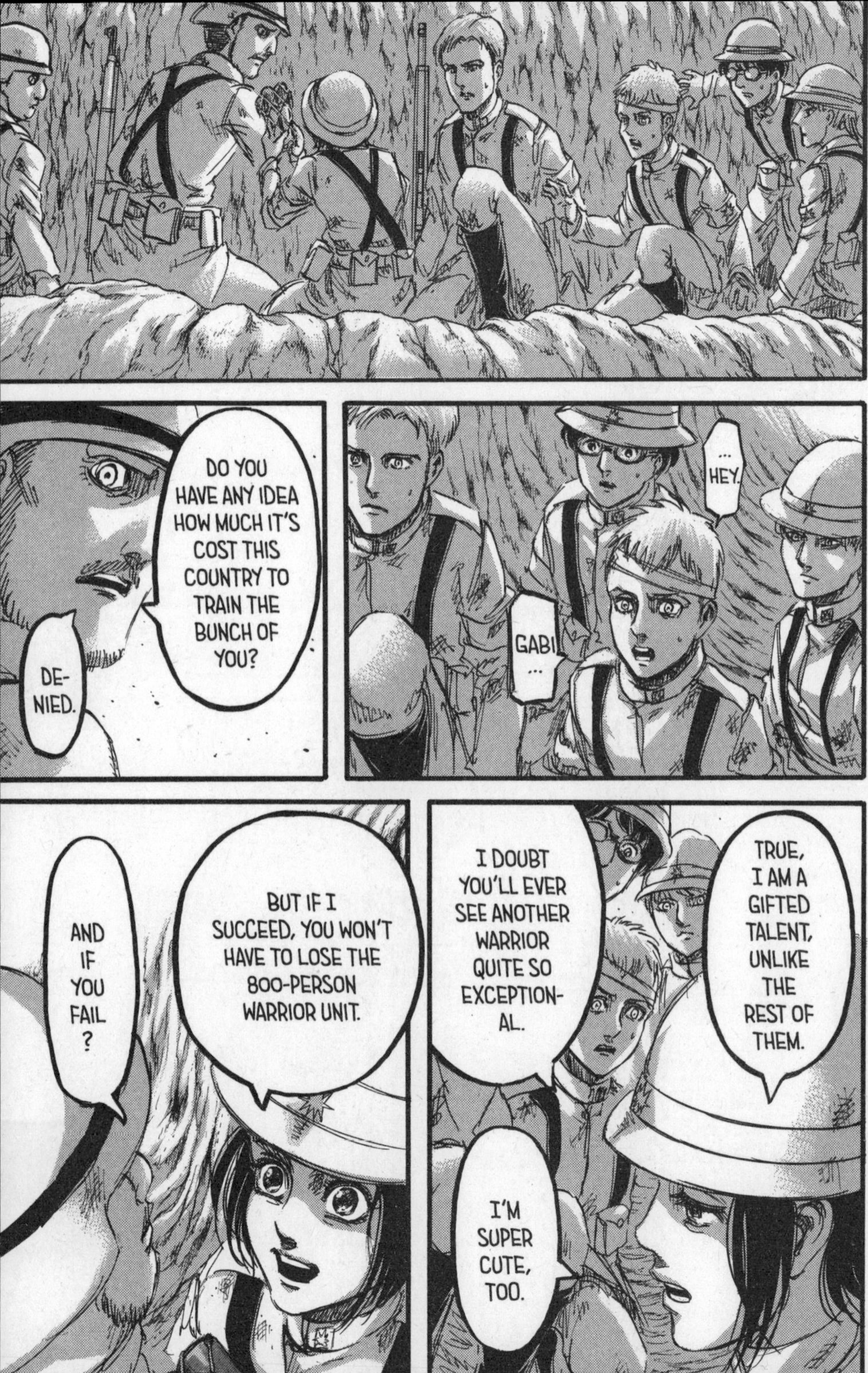
... HEY.
GABI ...
DO YOU HAVE ANY IDEA HOW MUCH IT'S COST THIS COUNTRY TO TRAIN THE BUNCH OF YOU?
DE-NIED.
TRUE, I AM A GIFTED TALENT, UNLIKE THE REST OF THEM.
I DOUBT YOU'LL EVER SEE ANOTHER WARRIOR QUITE SO EXCEPTION-AL.
I'M SUPER CUTE, TOO.
BUT IF I SUCCEED, YOU WON'T HAVE TO LOSE THE 800-PERSON WARRIOR UNIT.
AND IF YOU FAIL?

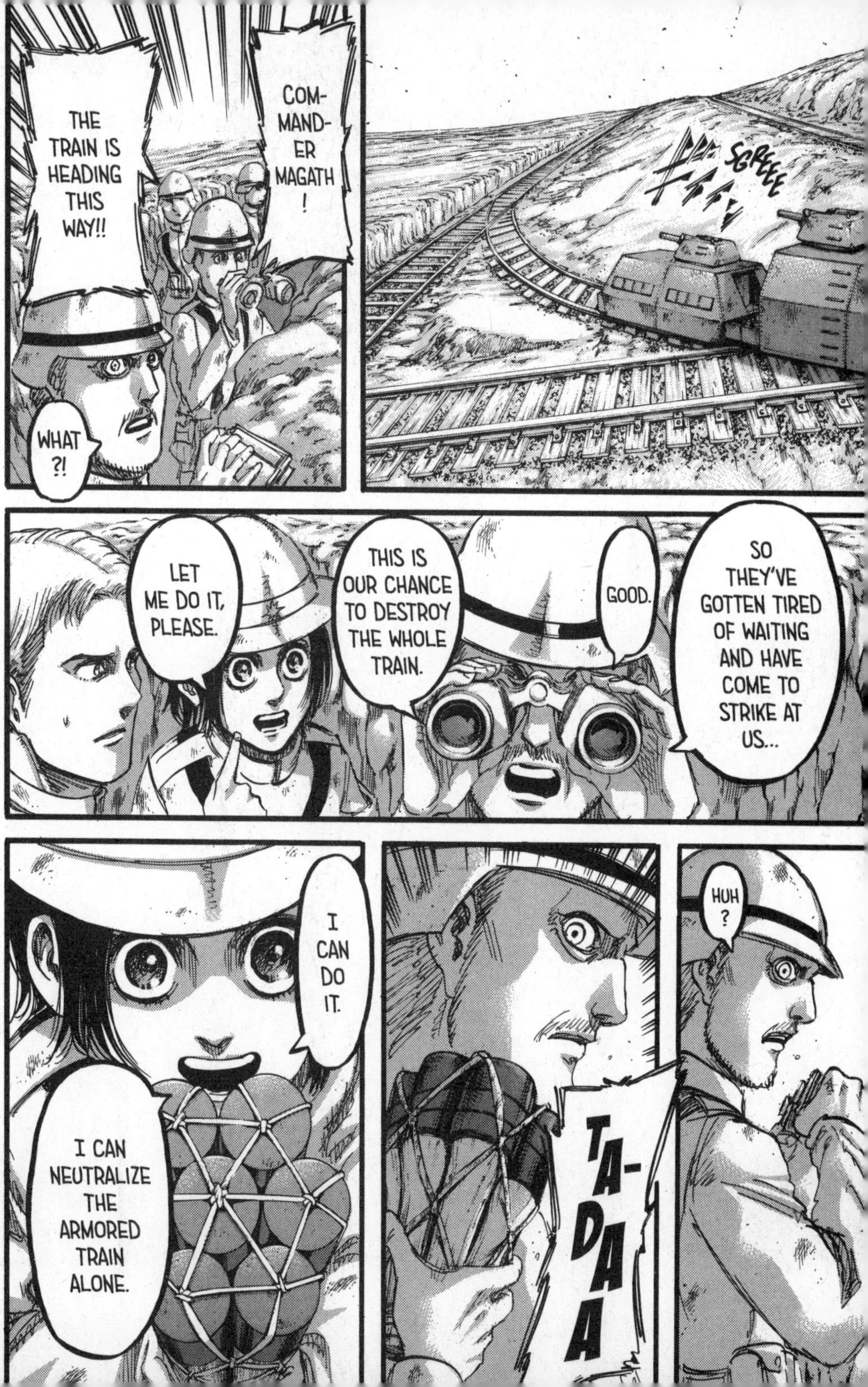
SCREEE
COM-MAND-ER MAGATH!
THE TRAIN IS HEADING THIS WAY!!
WHAT?!
SO THEY'VE GOTTEN TIRED OF WAITING AND HAVE COME TO STRIKE AT US...
GOOD.
THIS IS OUR CHANCE TO DESTROY THE WHOLE TRAIN.
LET ME DO IT, PLEASE.
HUH?
TA-DAA
I CAN DO IT.
I CAN NEUTRALIZE THE ARMORED TRAIN ALONE.

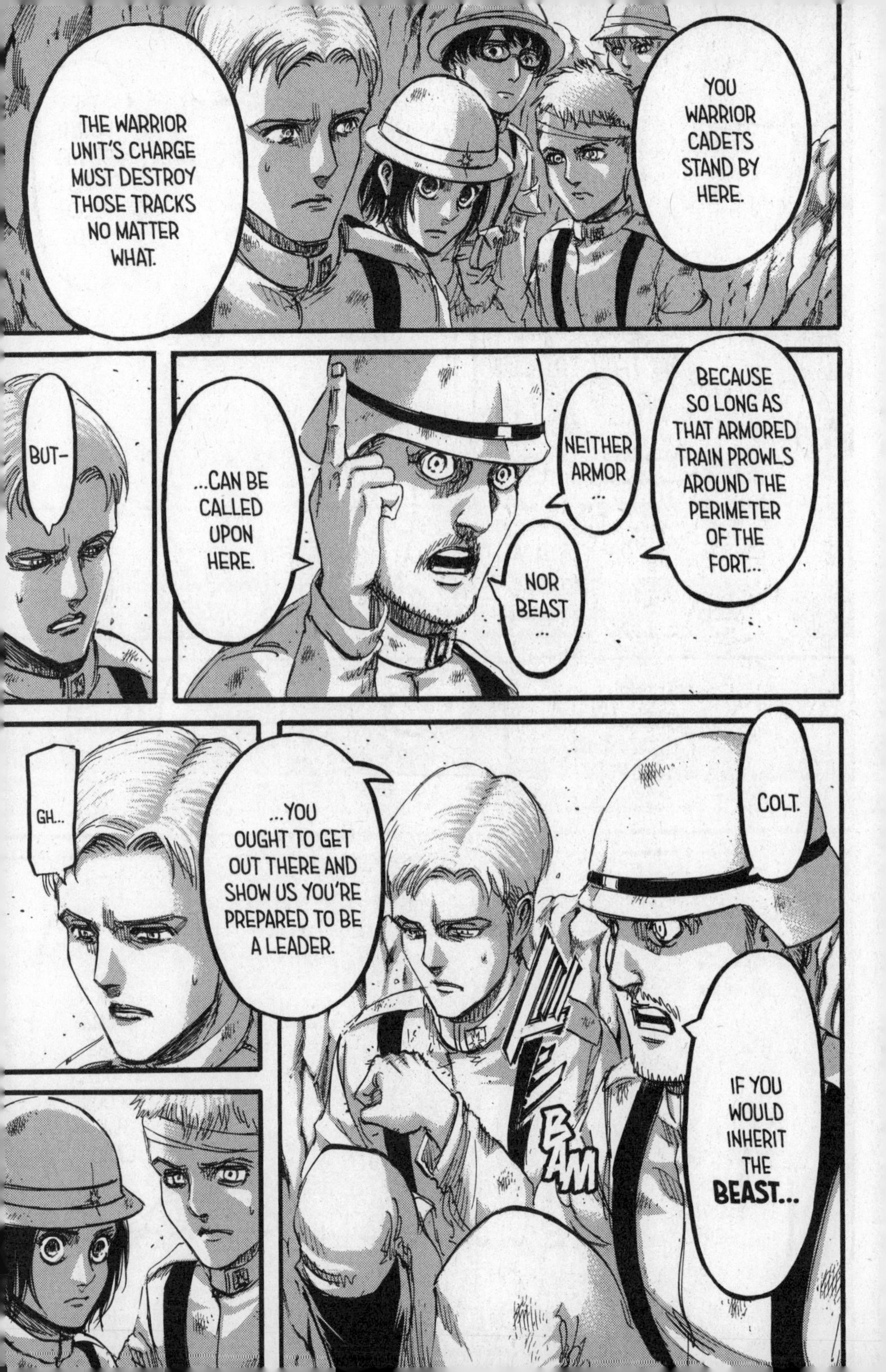
YOU WARRIOR CADETS STAND BY HERE.
THE WARRIOR UNIT'S CHARGE MUST DESTROY THOSE TRACKS NO MATTER WHAT.
BECAUSE SO LONG AS THAT ARMORED TRAIN PROWLS AROUND THE PERIMETER OF THE FORT...
NEITHER ARMOR...
NOR BEAST...
...CAN BE CALLED UPON HERE.
BUT–
COLT.
IF YOU WOULD INHERIT THE **BEAST**...
BAM
...YOU OUGHT TO GET OUT THERE AND SHOW US YOU'RE PREPARED TO BE A LEADER.
GH...

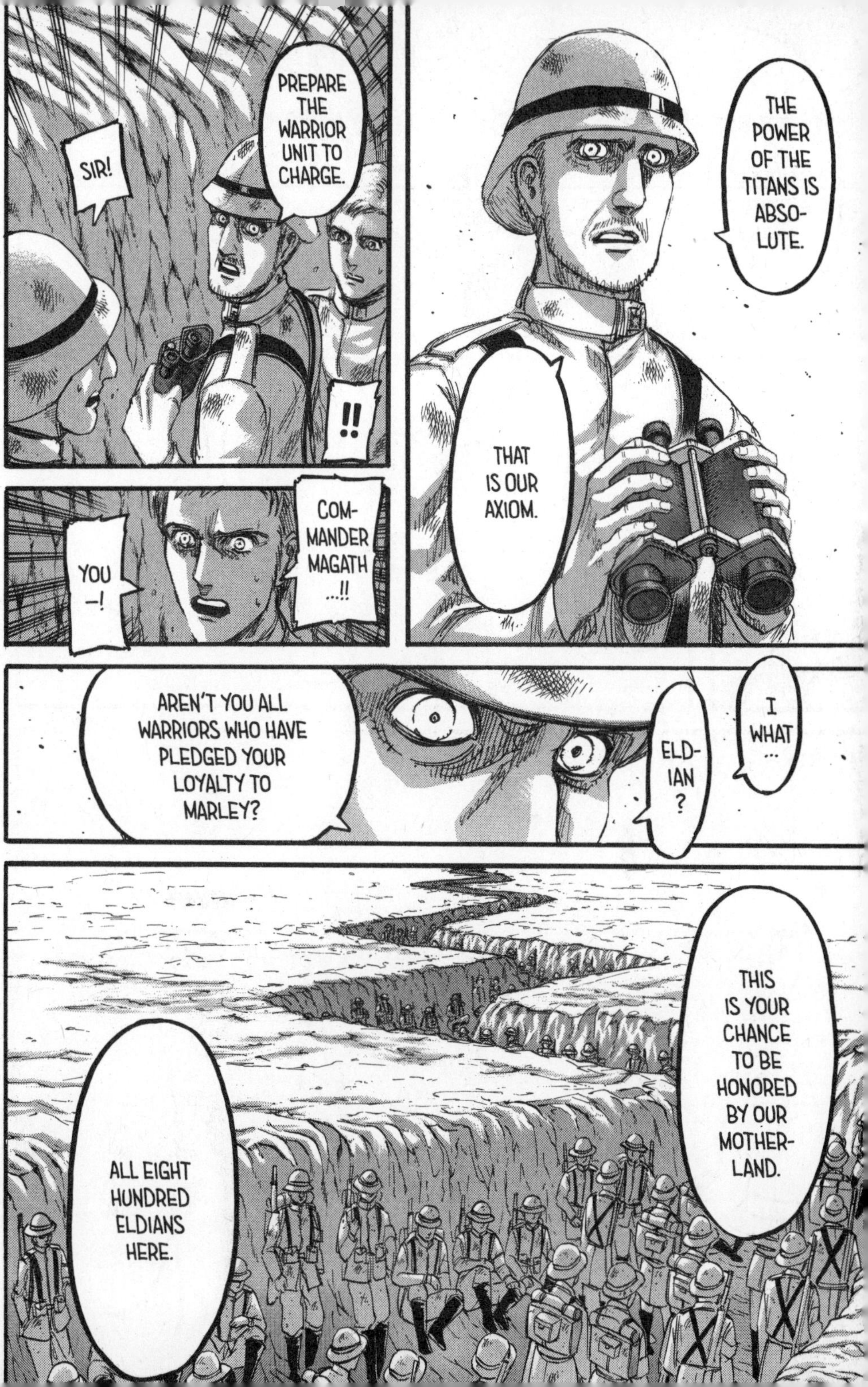
THE POWER OF THE TITANS IS ABSOLUTE.
THAT IS OUR AXIOM.
PREPARE THE WARRIOR UNIT TO CHARGE.
SIR!
!!
COMMANDER MAGATH ...!!
YOU —!
I WHAT ...
ELDIAN ?
AREN'T YOU ALL WARRIORS WHO HAVE PLEDGED YOUR LOYALTY TO MARLEY?
THIS IS YOUR CHANCE TO BE HONORED BY OUR MOTHERLAND.
ALL EIGHT HUNDRED ELDIANS HERE.

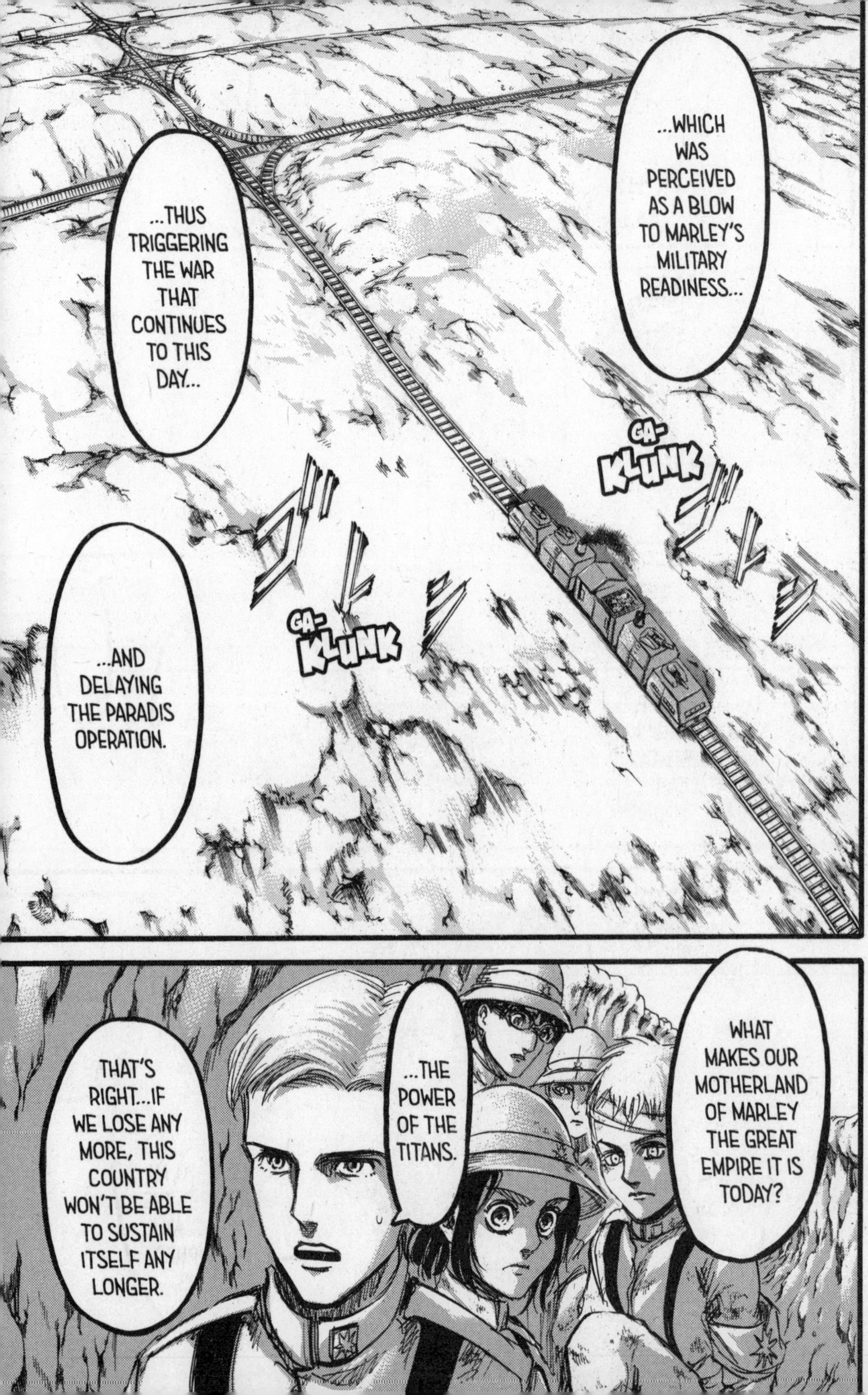
...WHICH WAS PERCEIVED AS A BLOW TO MARLEY'S MILITARY READINESS...
...THUS TRIGGERING THE WAR THAT CONTINUES TO THIS DAY...
GA-KLUNK
GA-KLUNK
...AND DELAYING THE PARADIS OPERATION.
WHAT MAKES OUR MOTHERLAND OF MARLEY THE GREAT EMPIRE IT IS TODAY?
...THE POWER OF THE TITANS.
THAT'S RIGHT...IF WE LOSE ANY MORE, THIS COUNTRY WON'T BE ABLE TO SUSTAIN ITSELF ANY LONGER.

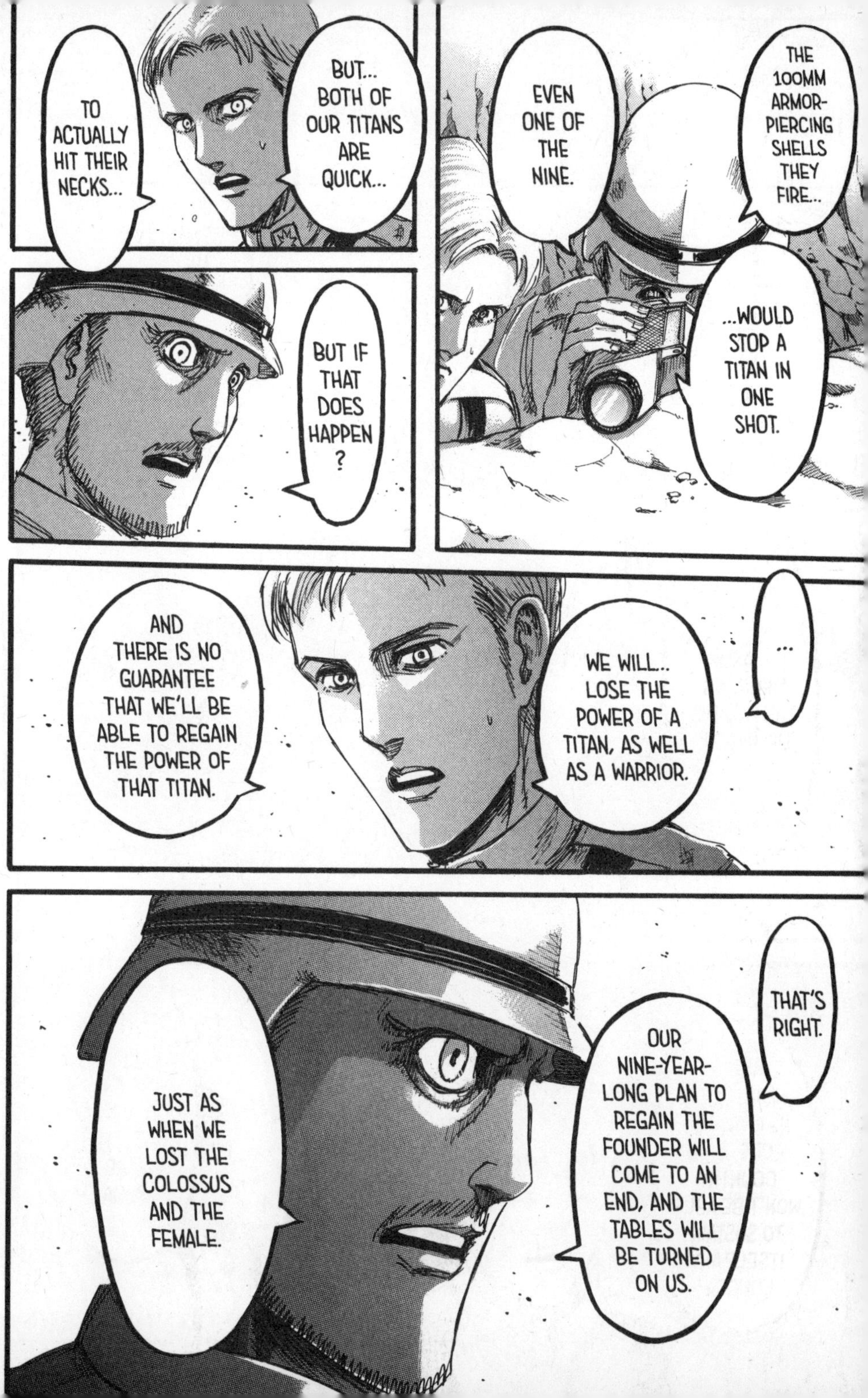
THE 100MM ARMOR-PIERCING SHELLS THEY FIRE...
...WOULD STOP A TITAN IN ONE SHOT.
EVEN ONE OF THE NINE.
BUT... BOTH OF OUR TITANS ARE QUICK...
TO ACTUALLY HIT THEIR NECKS...
BUT IF THAT DOES HAPPEN?
...
WE WILL... LOSE THE POWER OF A TITAN, AS WELL AS A WARRIOR.
AND THERE IS NO GUARANTEE THAT WE'LL BE ABLE TO REGAIN THE POWER OF THAT TITAN.
THAT'S RIGHT.
OUR NINE-YEAR-LONG PLAN TO REGAIN THE FOUNDER WILL COME TO AN END, AND THE TABLES WILL BE TURNED ON US.
JUST AS WHEN WE LOST THE COLOSSUS AND THE FEMALE.

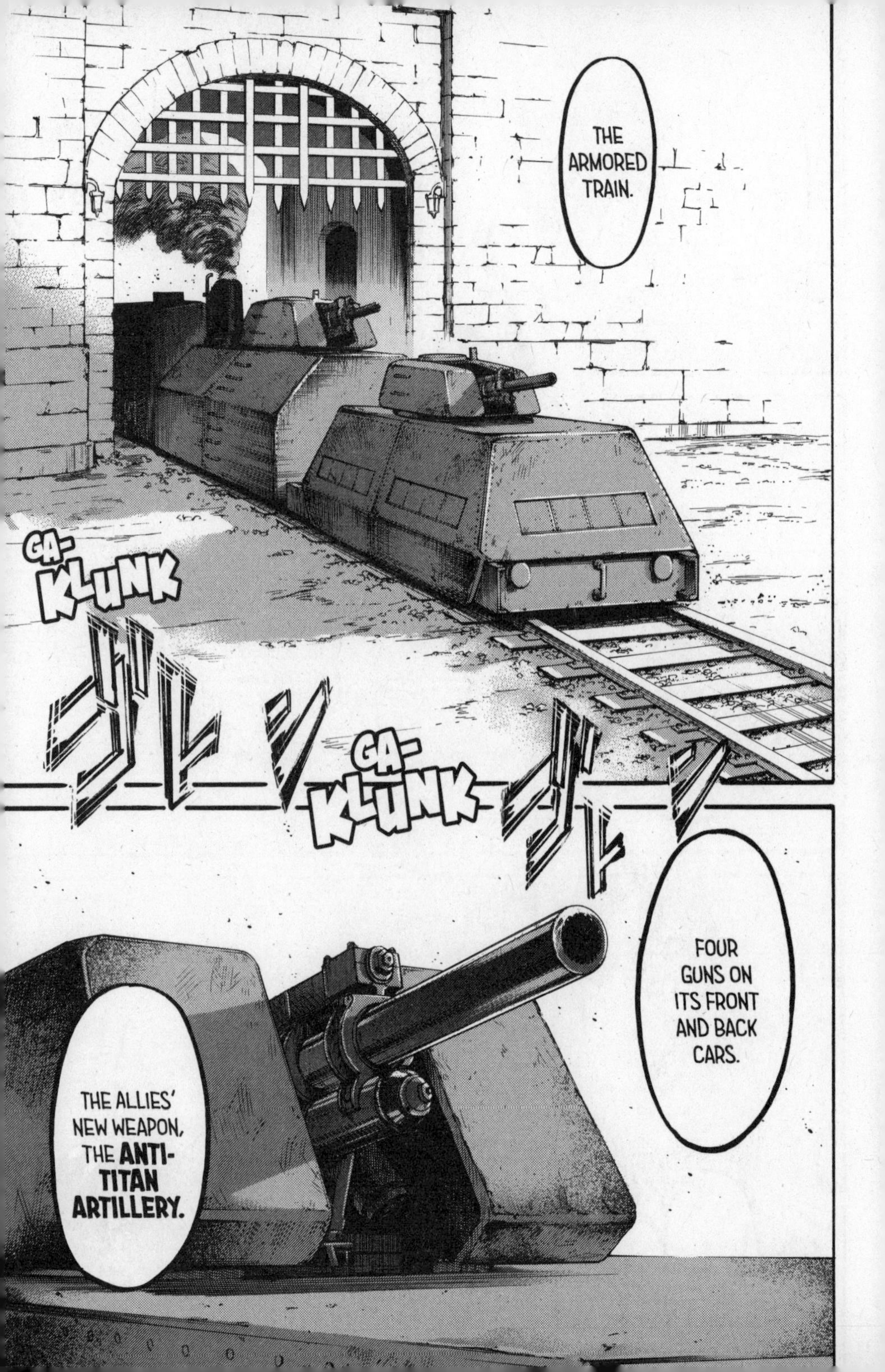

THE ARMORED TRAIN.
GA-KLUNK
GA-KLUNK
FOUR GUNS ON ITS FRONT AND BACK CARS.
THE ALLIES' NEW WEAPON, THE **ANTI-TITAN ARTILLERY.**

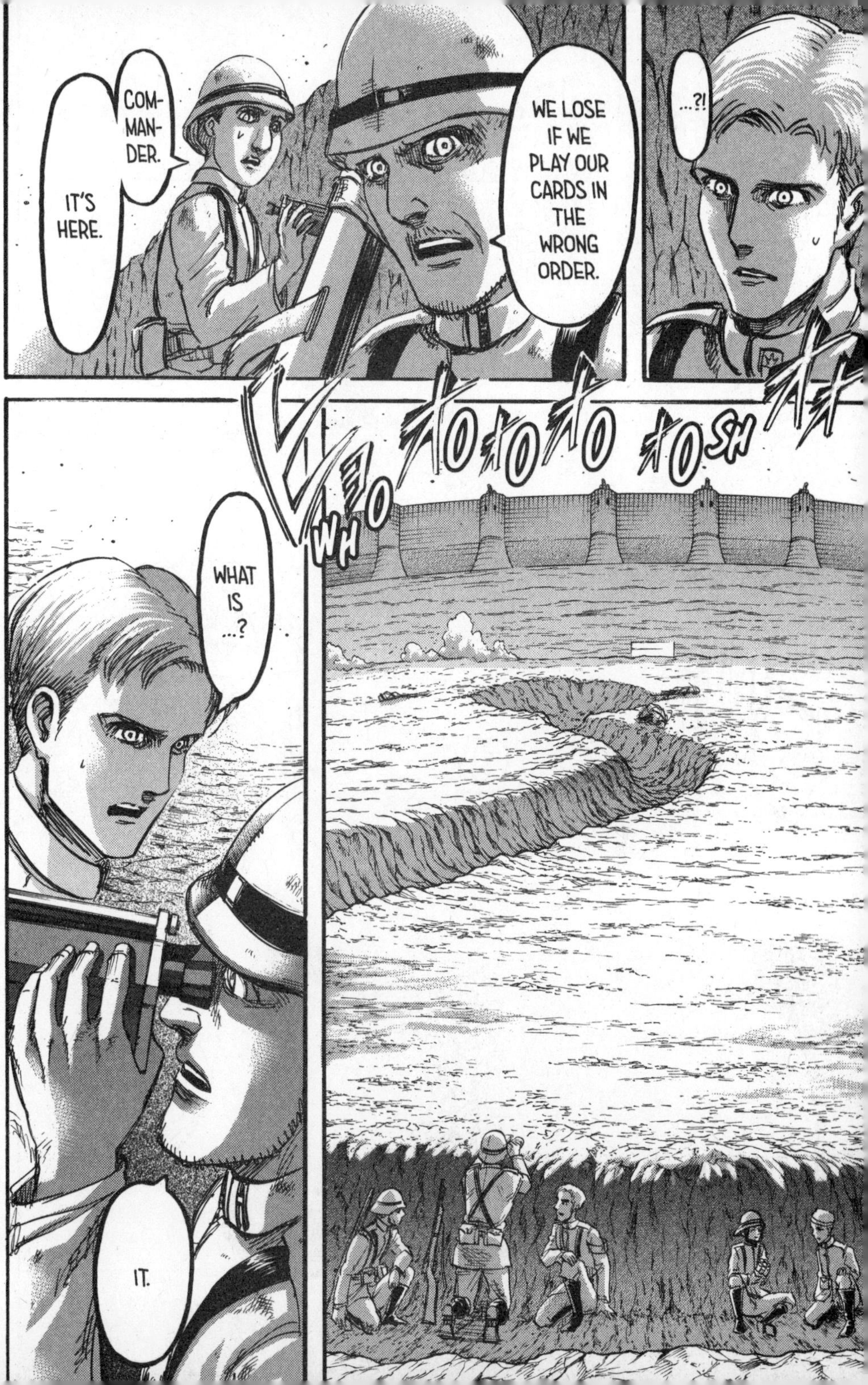
...?!
WE LOSE IF WE PLAY OUR CARDS IN THE WRONG ORDER.
COM-MANDER.
IT'S HERE.
WHOOOOOOOSH
WHAT IS ...?
IT.

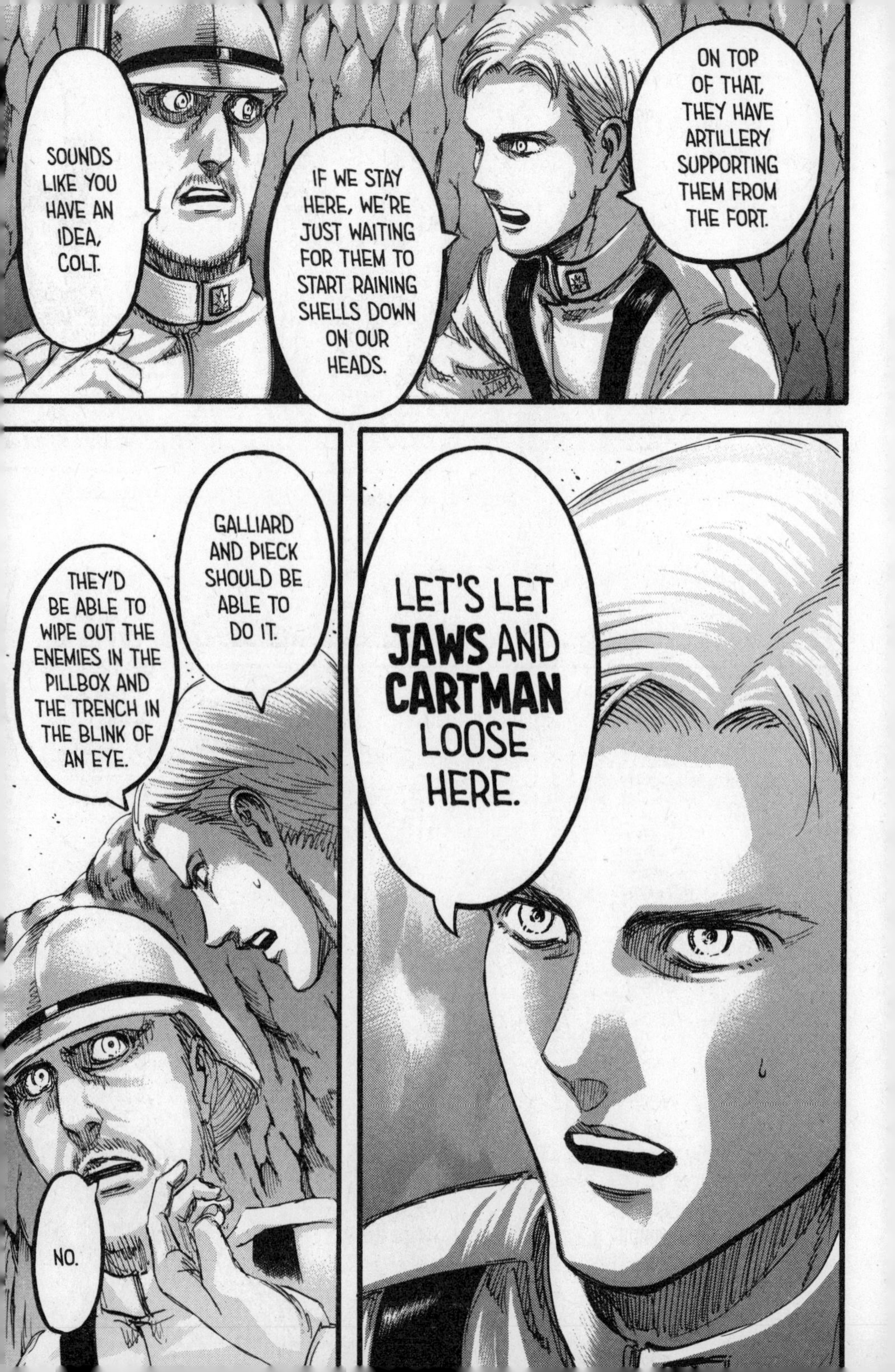
ON TOP OF THAT, THEY HAVE ARTILLERY SUPPORTING THEM FROM THE FORT.
IF WE STAY HERE, WE'RE JUST WAITING FOR THEM TO START RAINING SHELLS DOWN ON OUR HEADS.
SOUNDS LIKE YOU HAVE AN IDEA, COLT.
LET'S LET **JAWS** AND **CARTMAN** LOOSE HERE.
GALLIARD AND PIECK SHOULD BE ABLE TO DO IT.
THEY'D BE ABLE TO WIPE OUT THE ENEMIES IN THE PILLBOX AND THE TRENCH IN THE BLINK OF AN EYE.
NO.

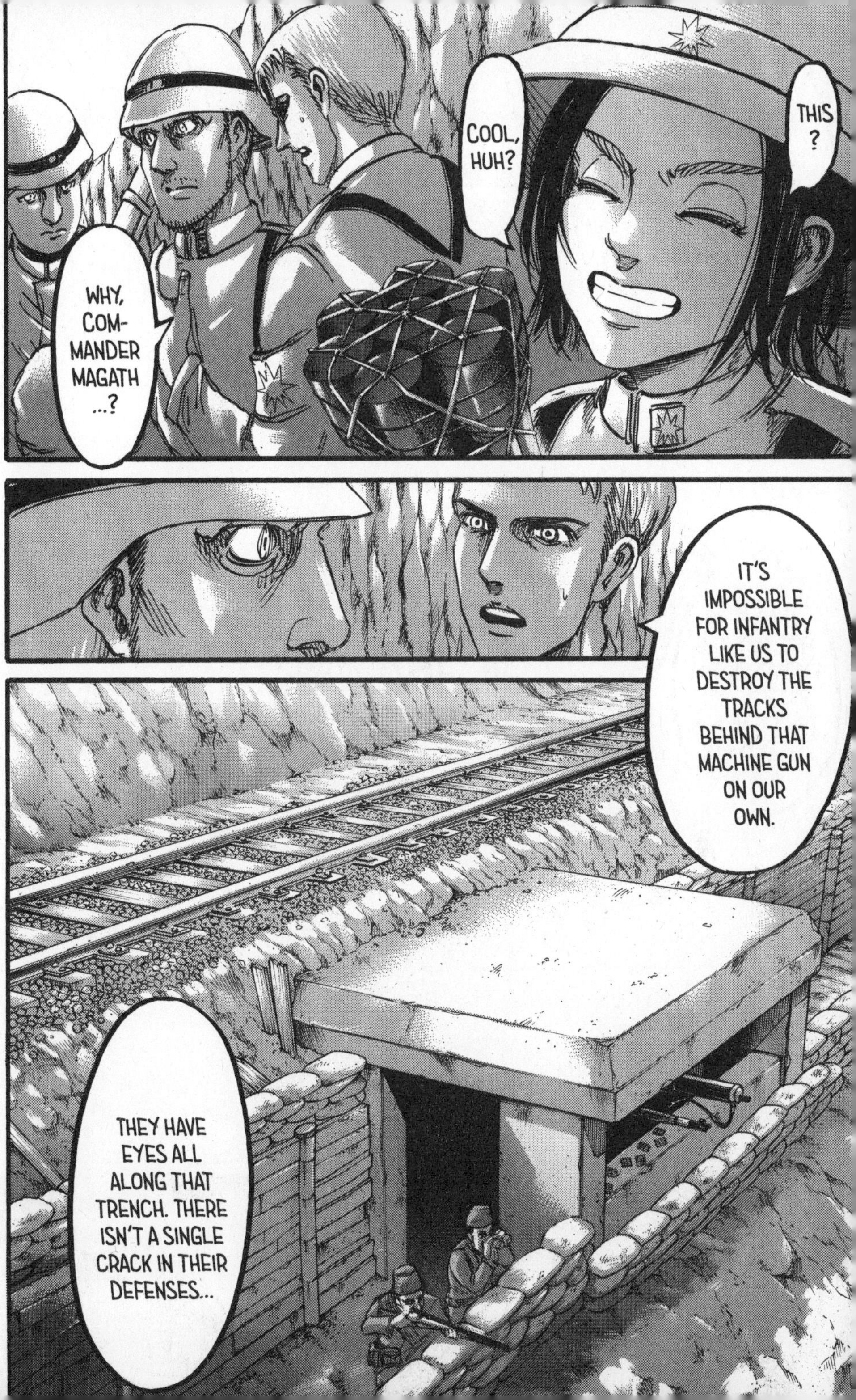
THIS?
COOL, HUH?
WHY, COMMANDER MAGATH...?
IT'S IMPOSSIBLE FOR INFANTRY LIKE US TO DESTROY THE TRACKS BEHIND THAT MACHINE GUN ON OUR OWN.
THEY HAVE EYES ALL ALONG THAT TRENCH. THERE ISN'T A SINGLE CRACK IN THEIR DEFENSES...

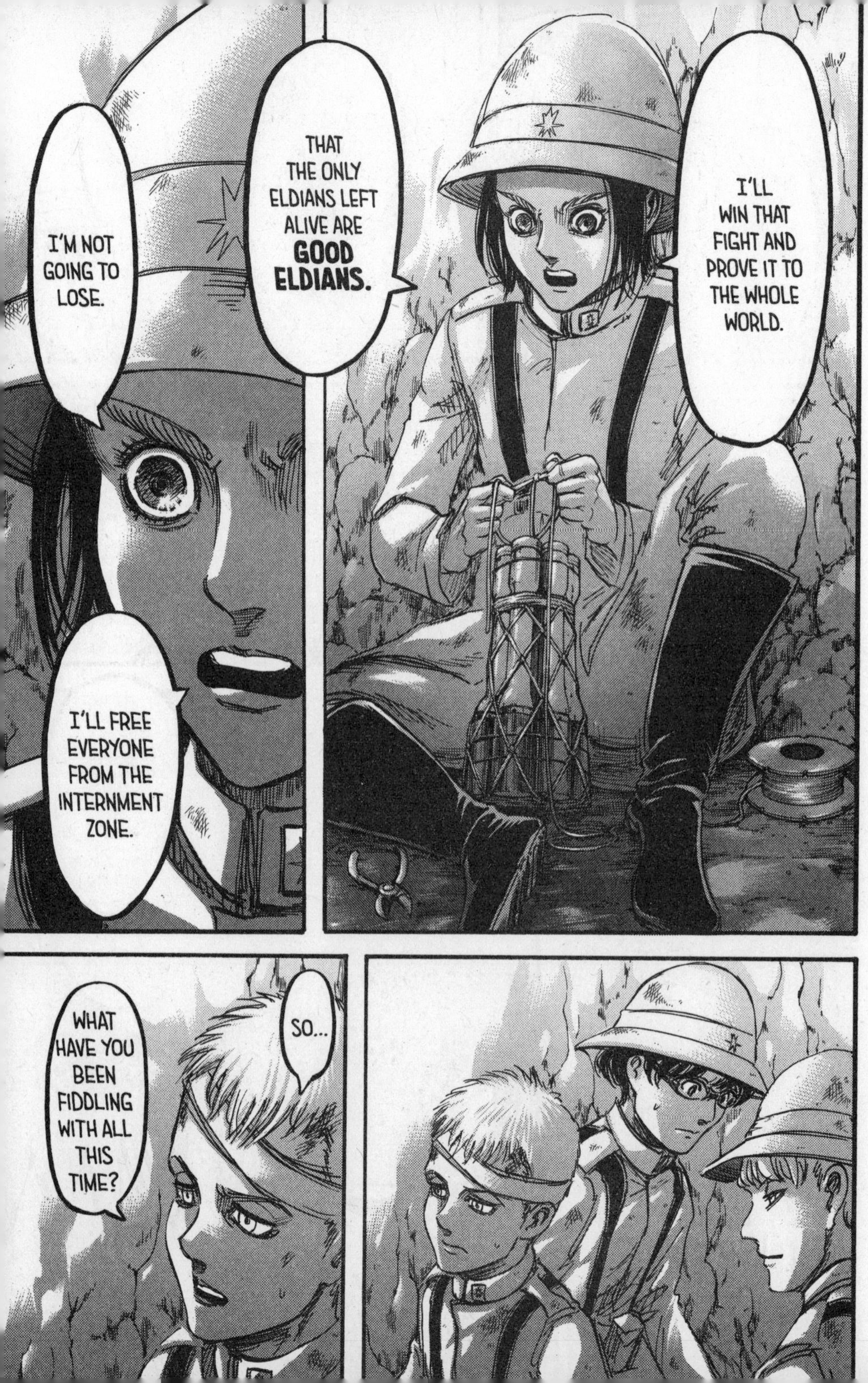
I'LL WIN THAT FIGHT AND PROVE IT TO THE WHOLE WORLD.
THAT THE ONLY ELDIANS LEFT ALIVE ARE **GOOD ELDIANS.**
I'M NOT GOING TO LOSE.
I'LL FREE EVERYONE FROM THE INTERNMENT ZONE.
SO...
WHAT HAVE YOU BEEN FIDDLING WITH ALL THIS TIME?

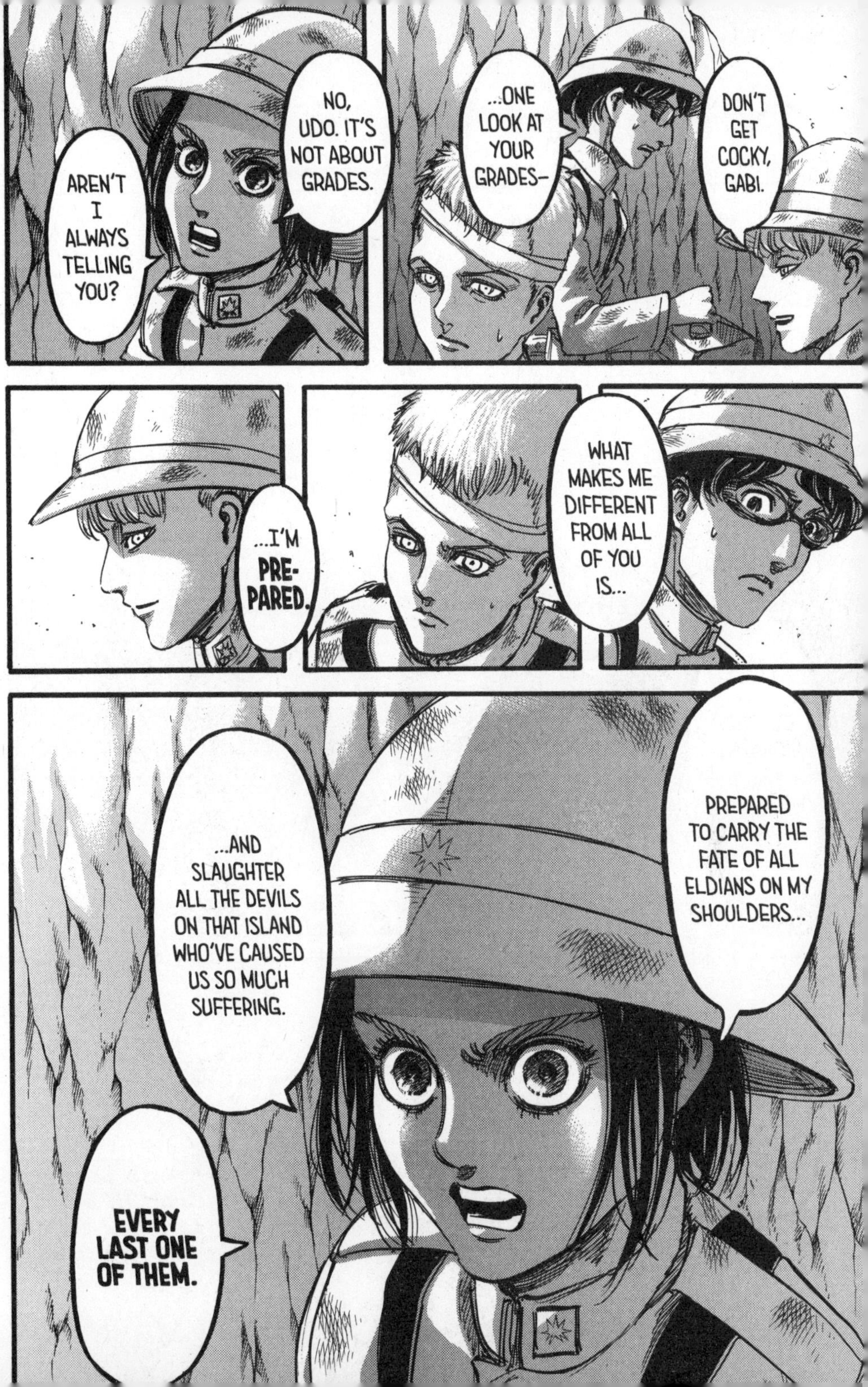
DON'T GET COCKY, GABI.
...ONE LOOK AT YOUR GRADES–
NO, UDO. IT'S NOT ABOUT GRADES.
AREN'T I ALWAYS TELLING YOU?
WHAT MAKES ME DIFFERENT FROM ALL OF YOU IS...
...I'M PREPARED.
PREPARED TO CARRY THE FATE OF ALL ELDIANS ON MY SHOULDERS...
...AND SLAUGHTER ALL THE DEVILS ON THAT ISLAND WHO'VE CAUSED US SO MUCH SUFFERING.
EVERY LAST ONE OF THEM.

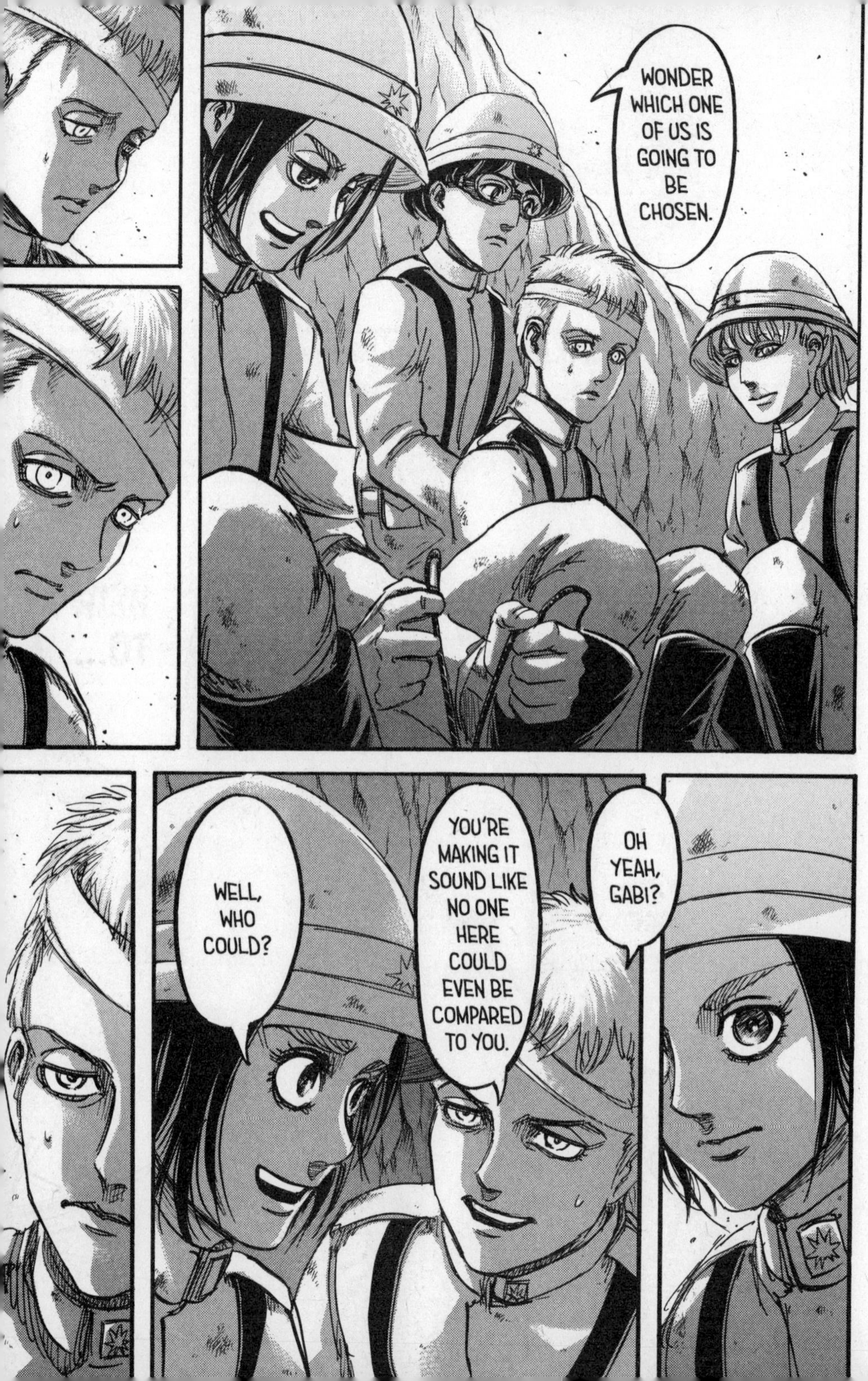
WONDER WHICH ONE OF US IS GOING TO BE CHOSEN.
OH YEAH, GABI?
YOU'RE MAKING IT SOUND LIKE NO ONE HERE COULD EVEN BE COMPARED TO YOU.
WELL, WHO COULD?

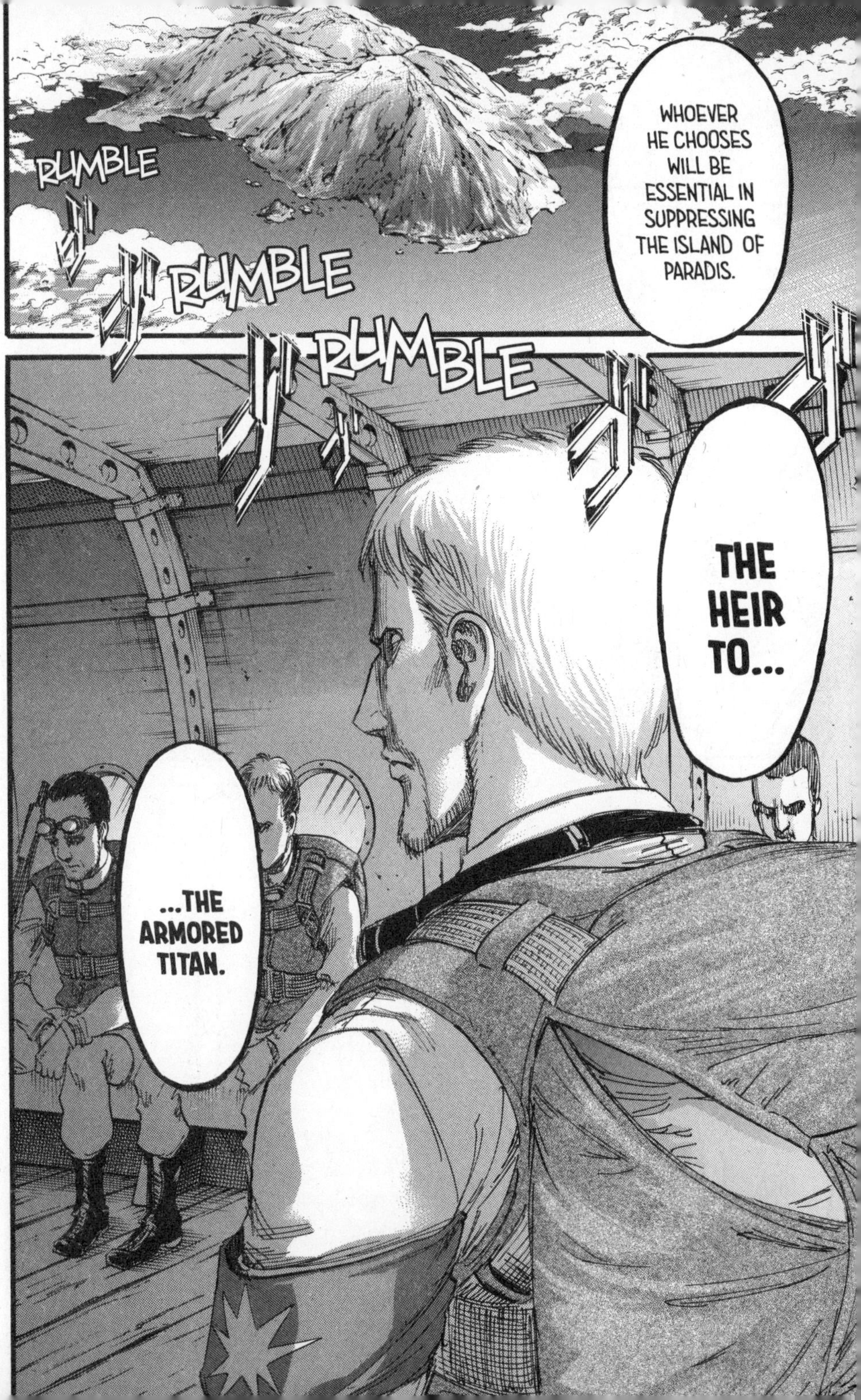
WHOEVER HE CHOOSES WILL BE ESSENTIAL IN SUPPRESSING THE ISLAND OF PARADIS.
RUMBLE
RUMBLE
RUMBLE
THE HEIR TO...
...THE ARMORED TITAN.

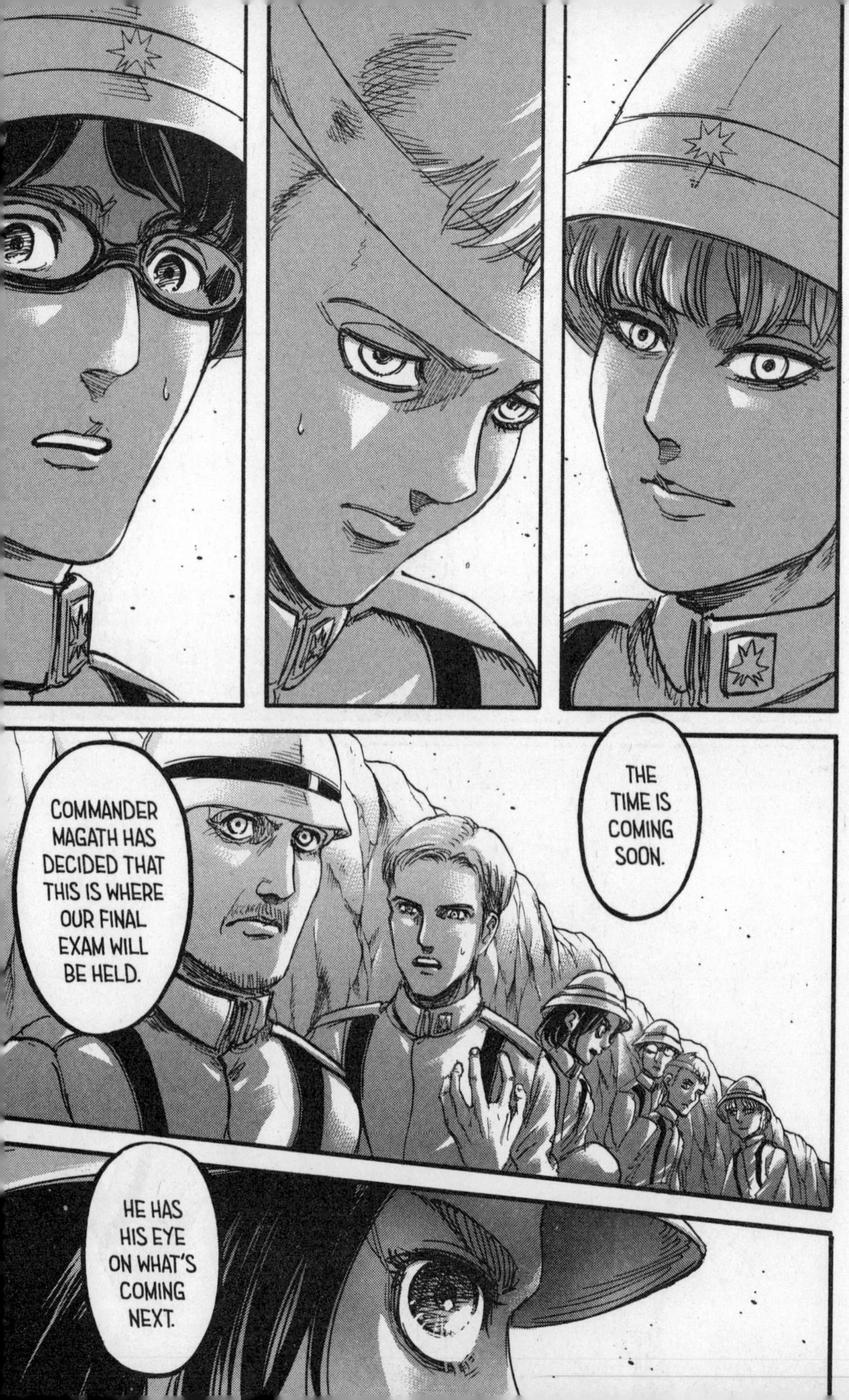
THE TIME IS COMING SOON.
COMMANDER MAGATH HAS DECIDED THAT THIS IS WHERE OUR FINAL EXAM WILL BE HELD.
HE HAS HIS EYE ON WHAT'S COMING NEXT.

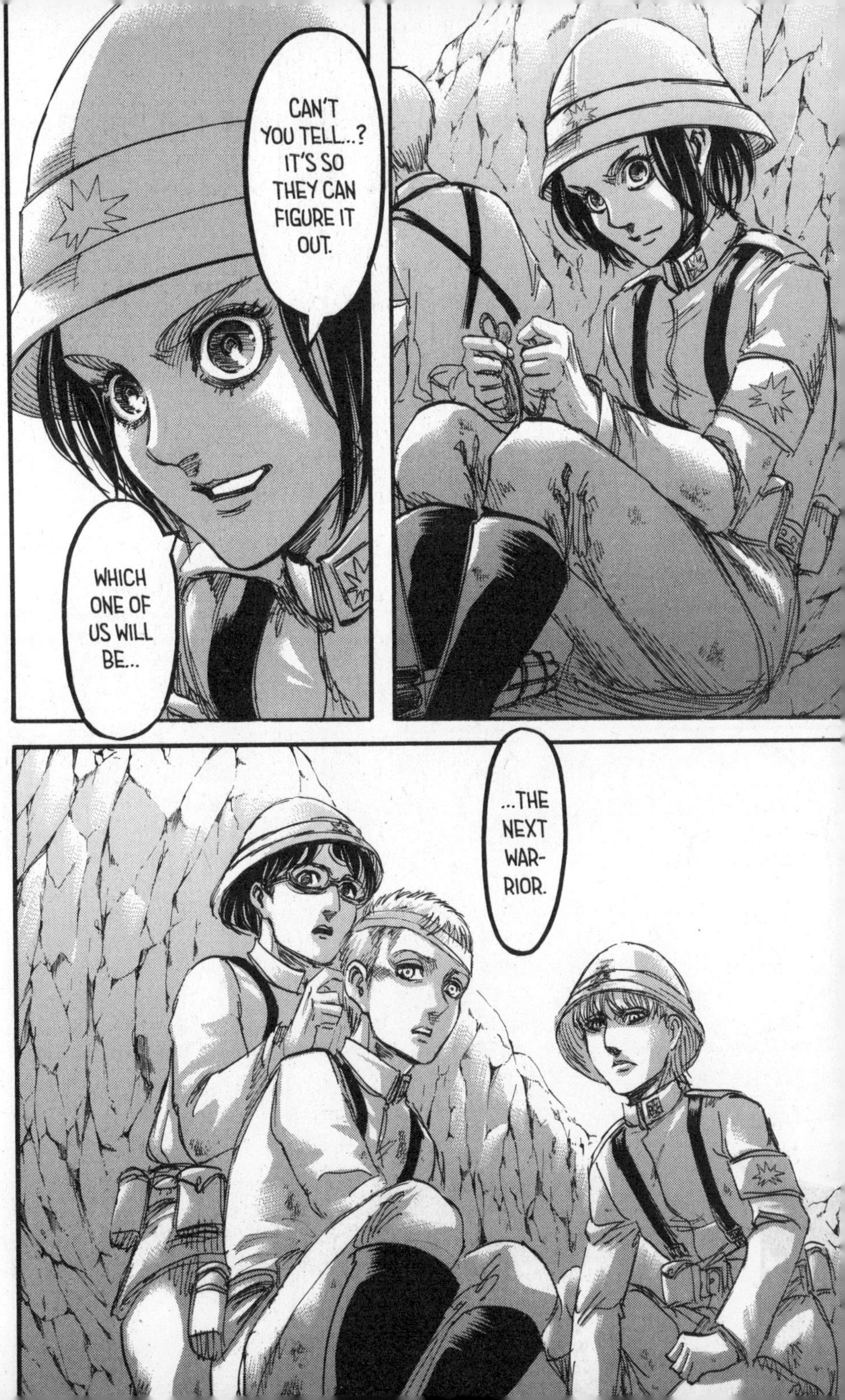
CAN'T YOU TELL...? IT'S SO THEY CAN FIGURE IT OUT.
WHICH ONE OF US WILL BE...
...THE NEXT WAR-RIOR.

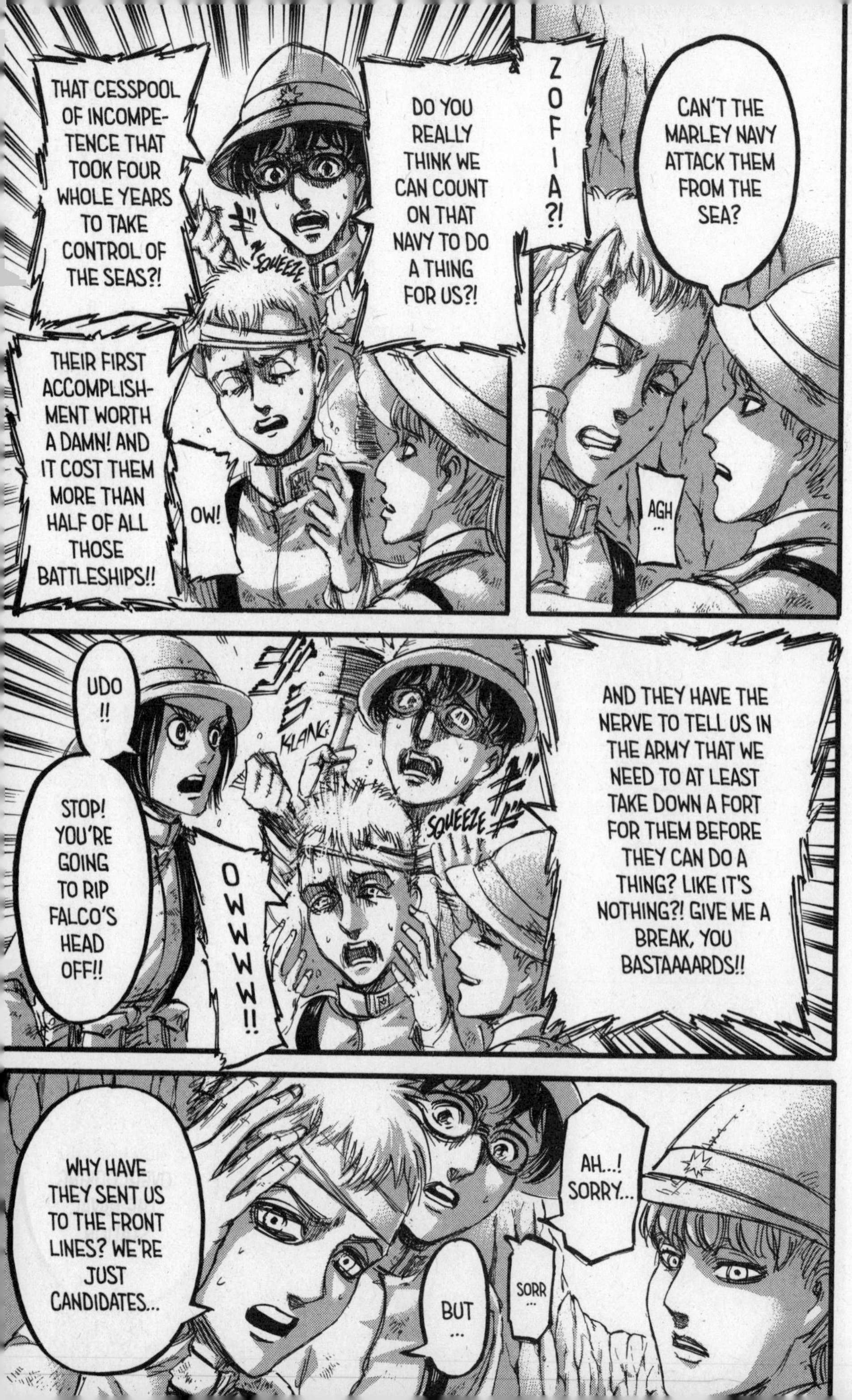
CAN'T THE MARLEY NAVY ATTACK THEM FROM THE SEA?
AGH...
ZOFIA?!
DO YOU REALLY THINK WE CAN COUNT ON THAT NAVY TO DO A THING FOR US?!
THAT CESSPOOL OF INCOMPE-TENCE THAT TOOK FOUR WHOLE YEARS TO TAKE CONTROL OF THE SEAS?!
SQUEEZE
THEIR FIRST ACCOMPLISH-MENT WORTH A DAMN! AND IT COST THEM MORE THAN HALF OF ALL THOSE BATTLESHIPS!!
OW!
AND THEY HAVE THE NERVE TO TELL US IN THE ARMY THAT WE NEED TO AT LEAST TAKE DOWN A FORT FOR THEM BEFORE THEY CAN DO A THING? LIKE IT'S NOTHING?! GIVE ME A BREAK, YOU BASTAAAARDS!!
SQUEEZE
KLANG
UDO!!
STOP! YOU'RE GOING TO RIP FALCO'S HEAD OFF!!
OWWWWW!!
AH...! SORRY...
SORR...
BUT...
WHY HAVE THEY SENT US TO THE FRONT LINES? WE'RE JUST CANDIDATES...

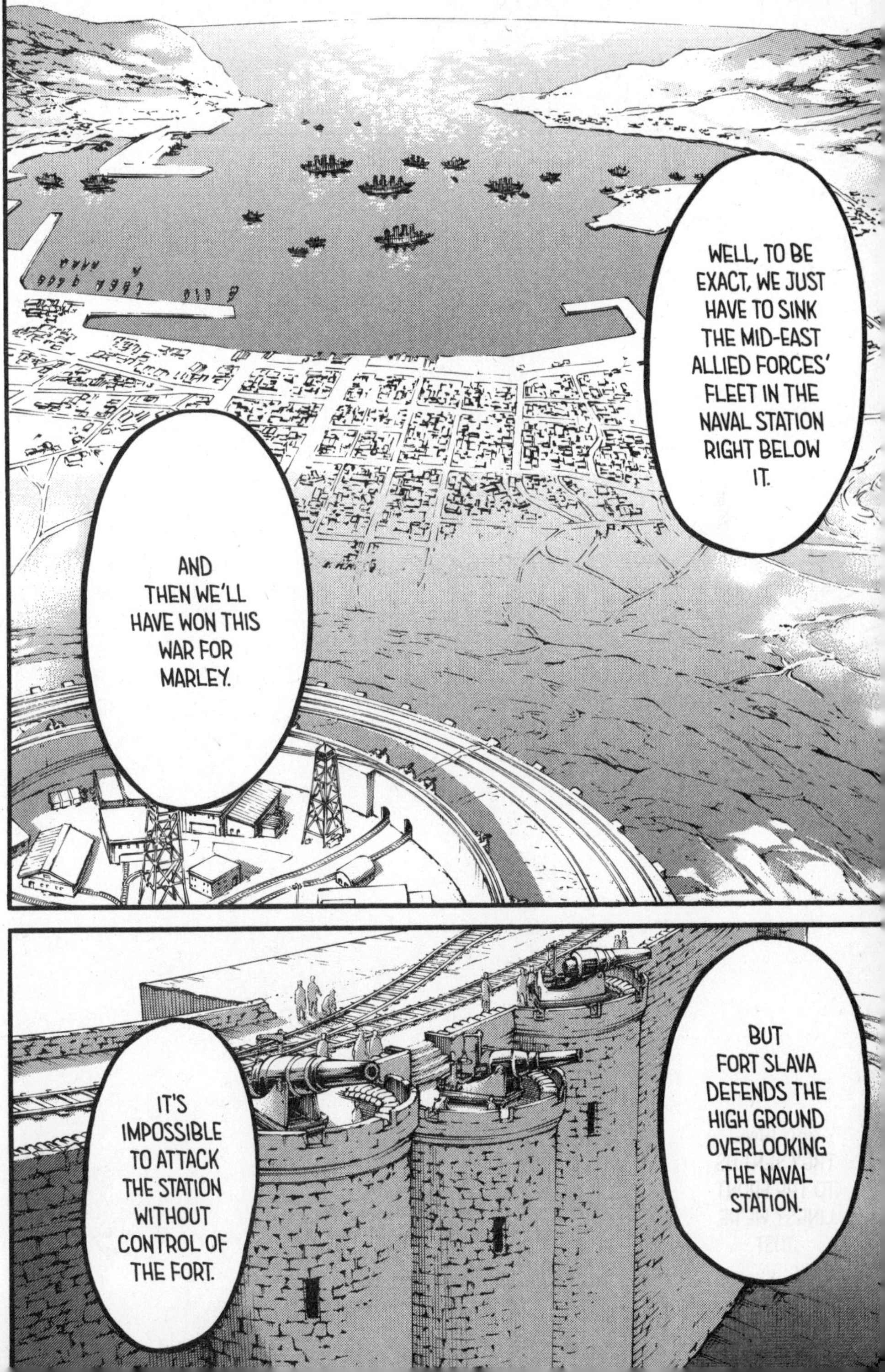
WELL, TO BE EXACT, WE JUST HAVE TO SINK THE MID-EAST ALLIED FORCES' FLEET IN THE NAVAL STATION RIGHT BELOW IT.
AND THEN WE'LL HAVE WON THIS WAR FOR MARLEY.
BUT FORT SLAVA DEFENDS THE HIGH GROUND OVERLOOKING THE NAVAL STATION.
IT'S IMPOSSIBLE TO ATTACK THE STATION WITHOUT CONTROL OF THE FORT.

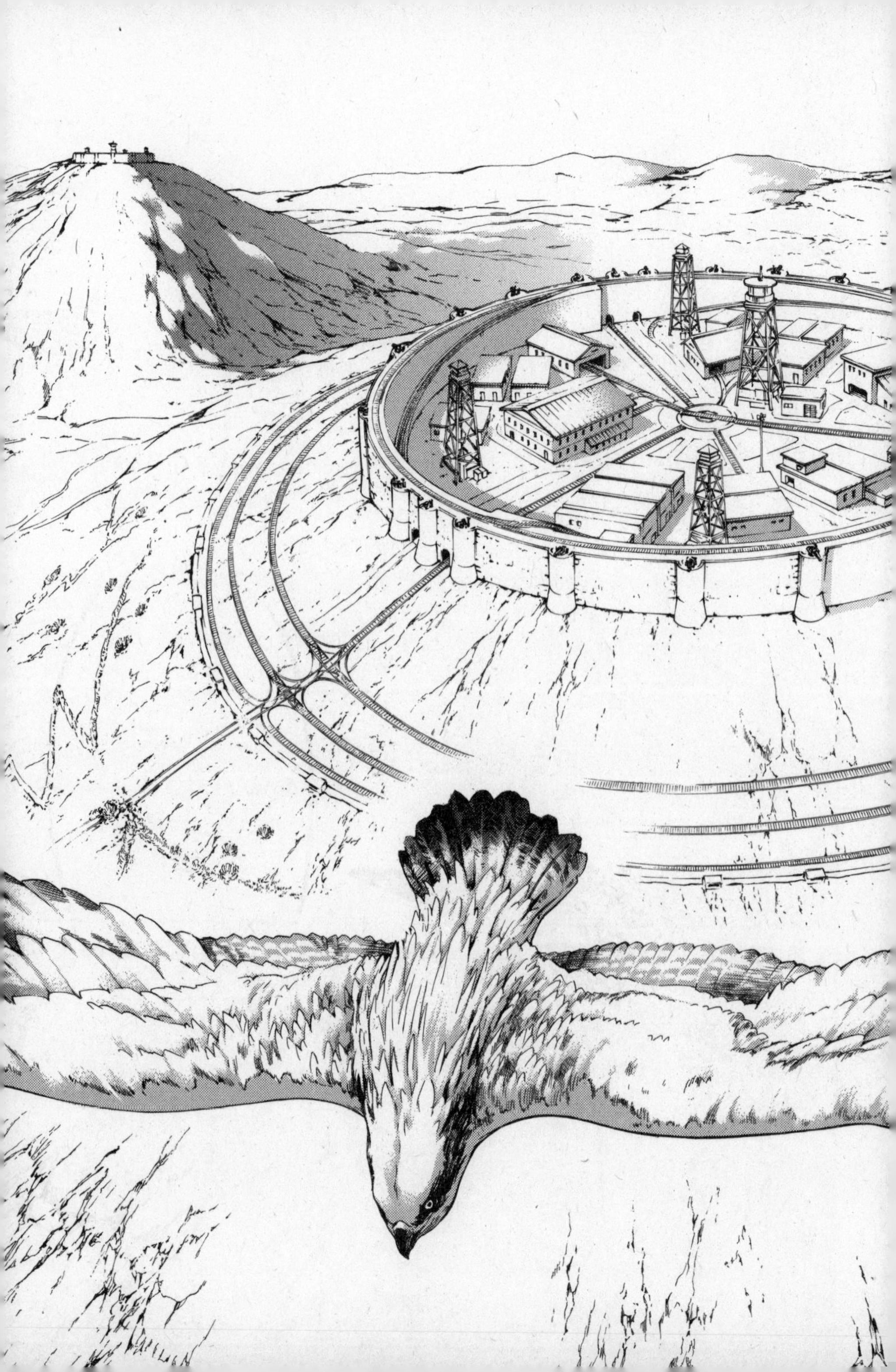

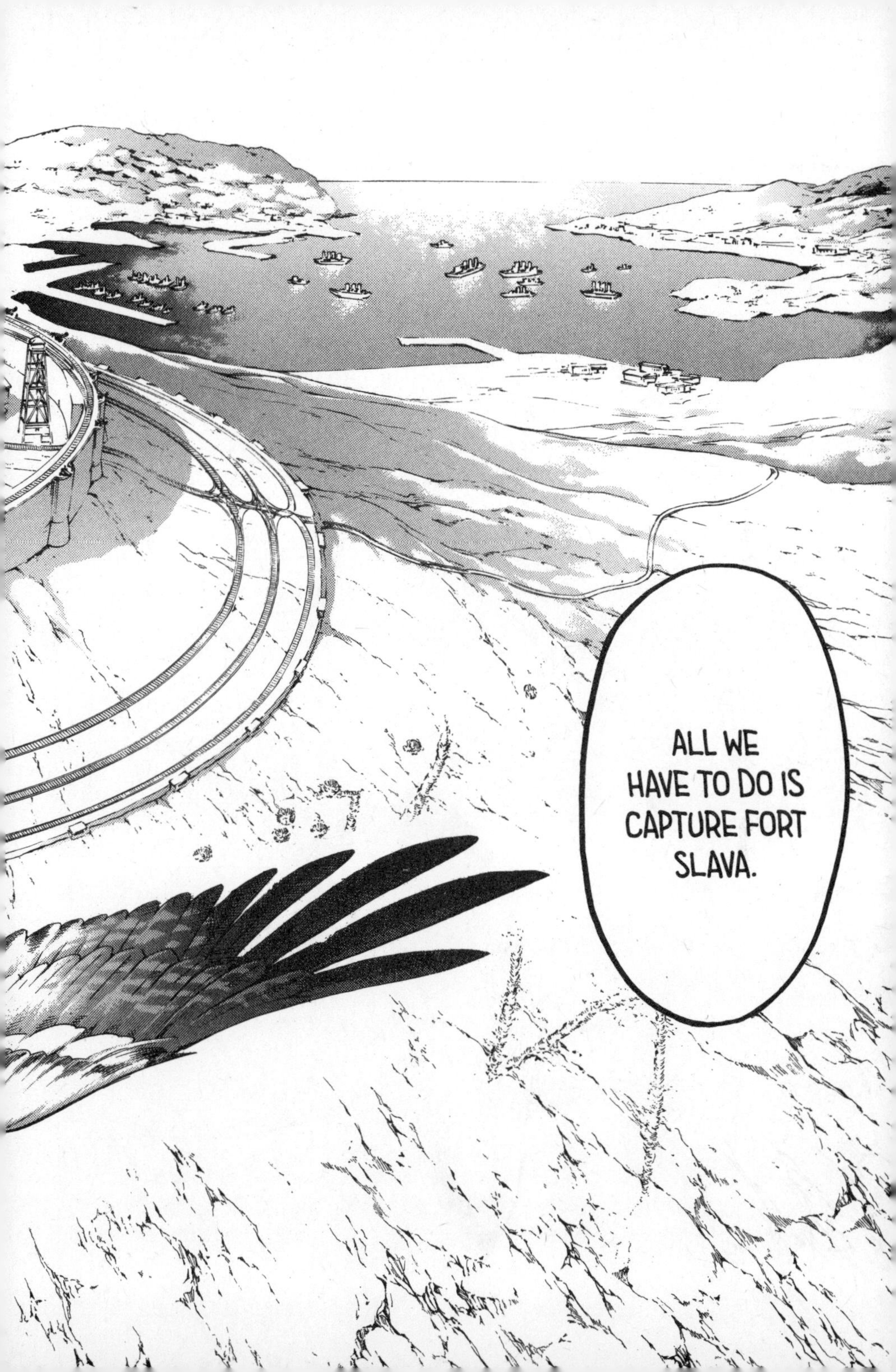
ALL WE HAVE TO DO IS CAPTURE FORT SLAVA.

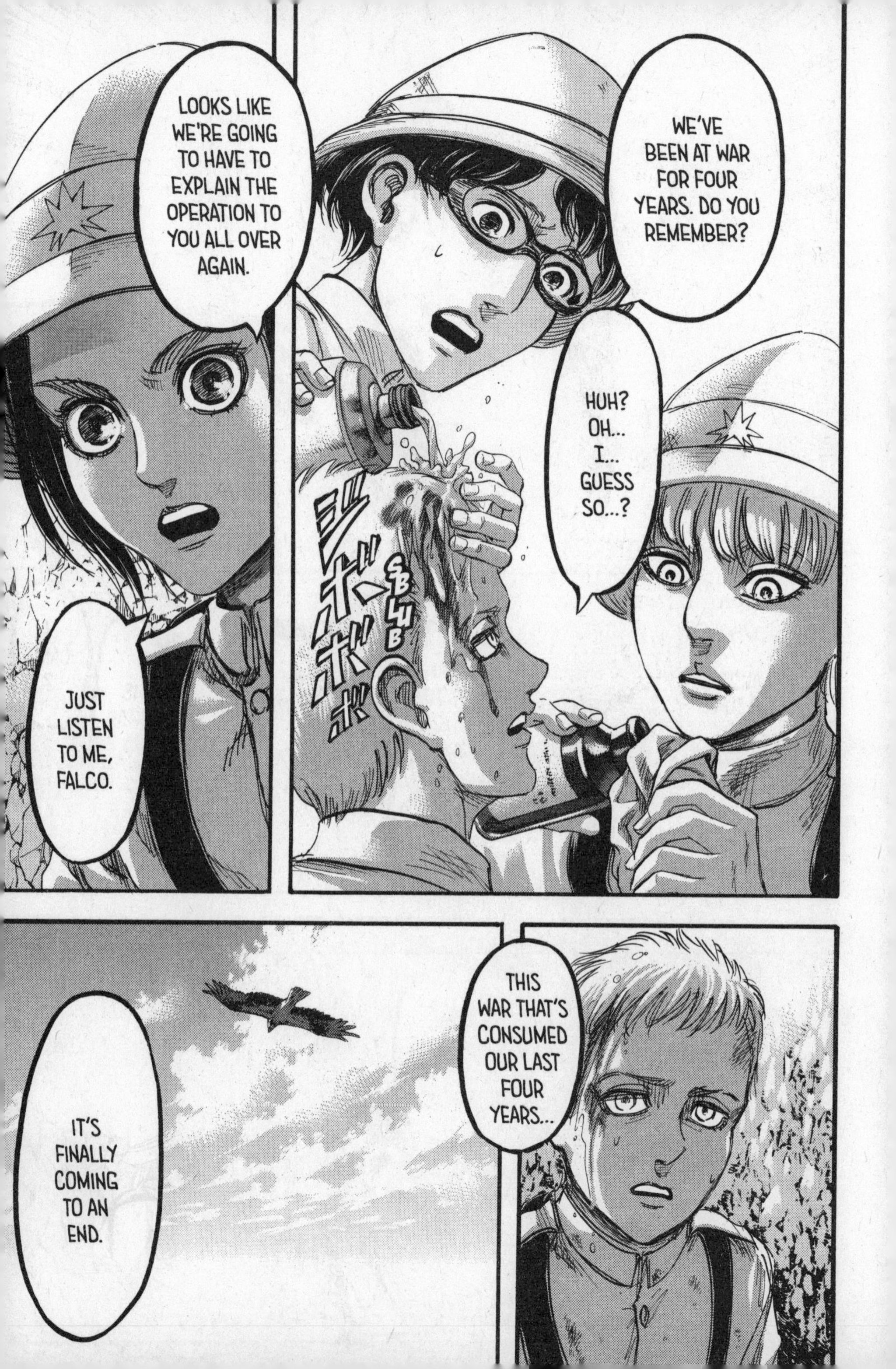
WE'VE BEEN AT WAR FOR FOUR YEARS. DO YOU REMEMBER?
HUH? OH... I... GUESS SO...?
SBLUB
LOOKS LIKE WE'RE GOING TO HAVE TO EXPLAIN THE OPERATION TO YOU ALL OVER AGAIN.
JUST LISTEN TO ME, FALCO.
THIS WAR THAT'S CONSUMED OUR LAST FOUR YEARS...
IT'S FINALLY COMING TO AN END.

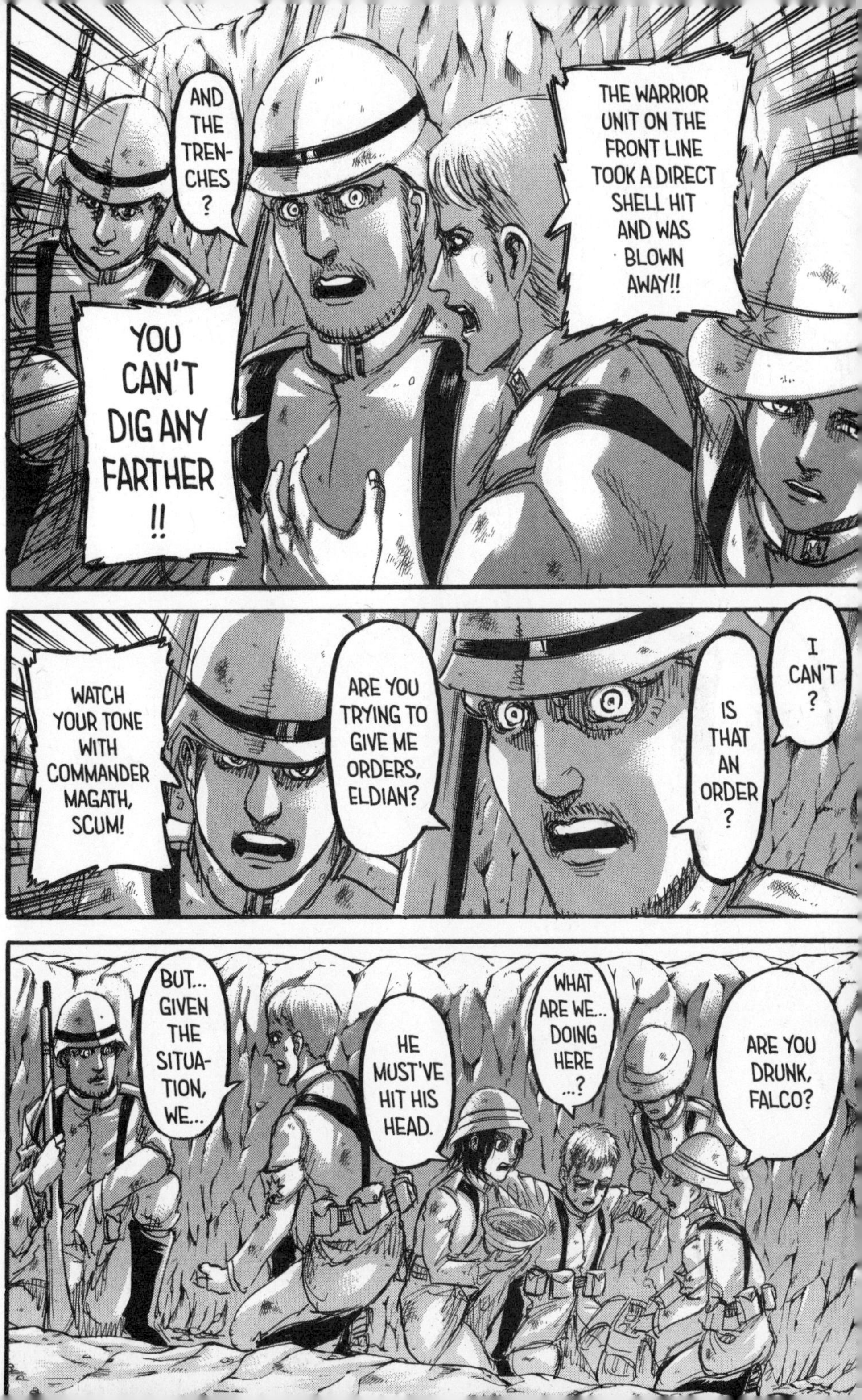
THE WARRIOR UNIT ON THE FRONT LINE TOOK A DIRECT SHELL HIT AND WAS BLOWN AWAY!!
AND THE TRENCHES?
YOU CAN'T DIG ANY FARTHER!!
I CAN'T?
IS THAT AN ORDER?
ARE YOU TRYING TO GIVE ME ORDERS, ELDIAN?
WATCH YOUR TONE WITH COMMANDER MAGATH, SCUM!
ARE YOU DRUNK, FALCO?
WHAT ARE WE... DOING HERE...?
HE MUST'VE HIT HIS HEAD.
BUT... GIVEN THE SITUATION, WE...

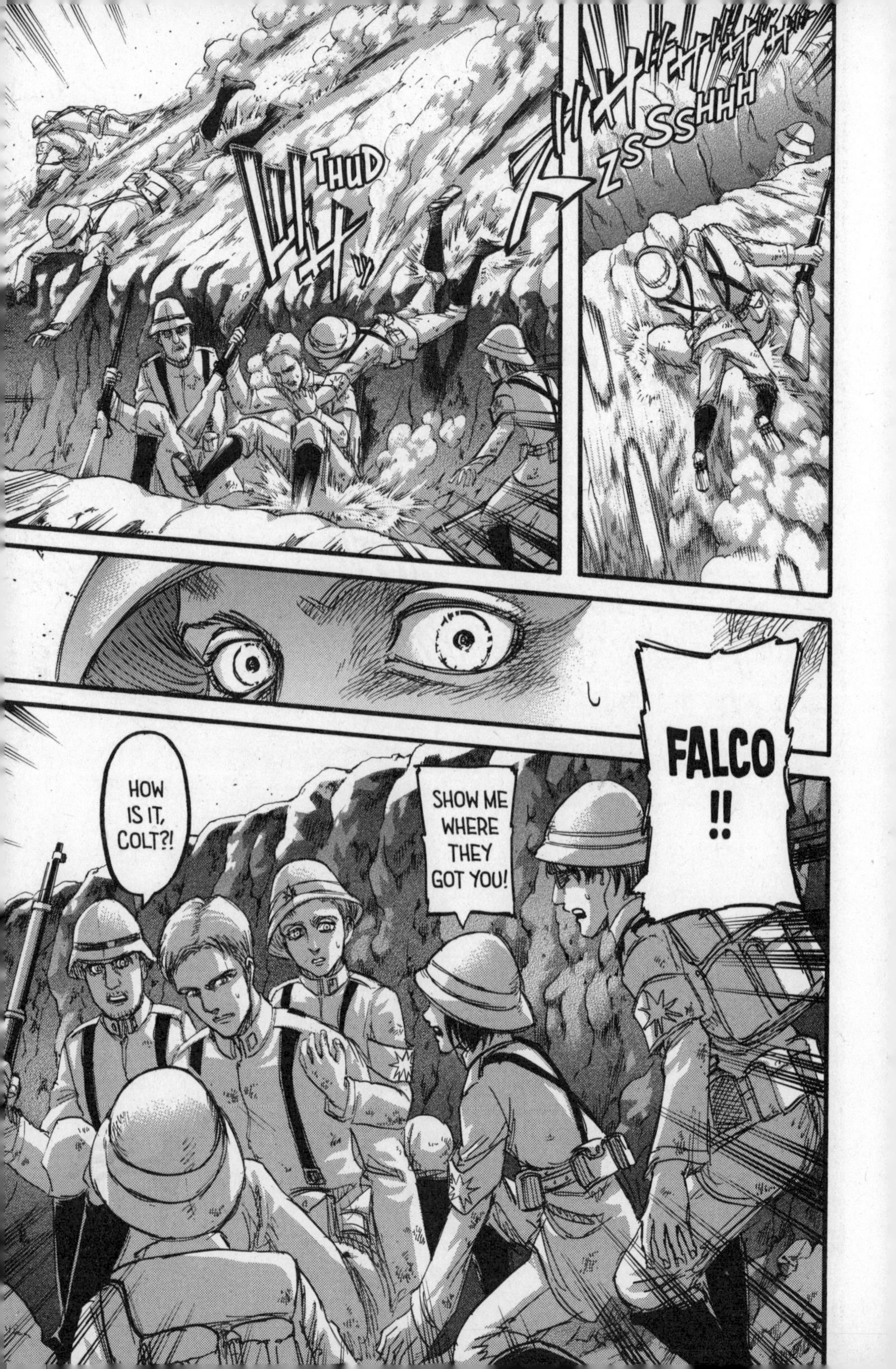
ZSSSHHH
THUD
FALCO !!
SHOW ME WHERE THEY GOT YOU!
HOW IS IT, COLT?!

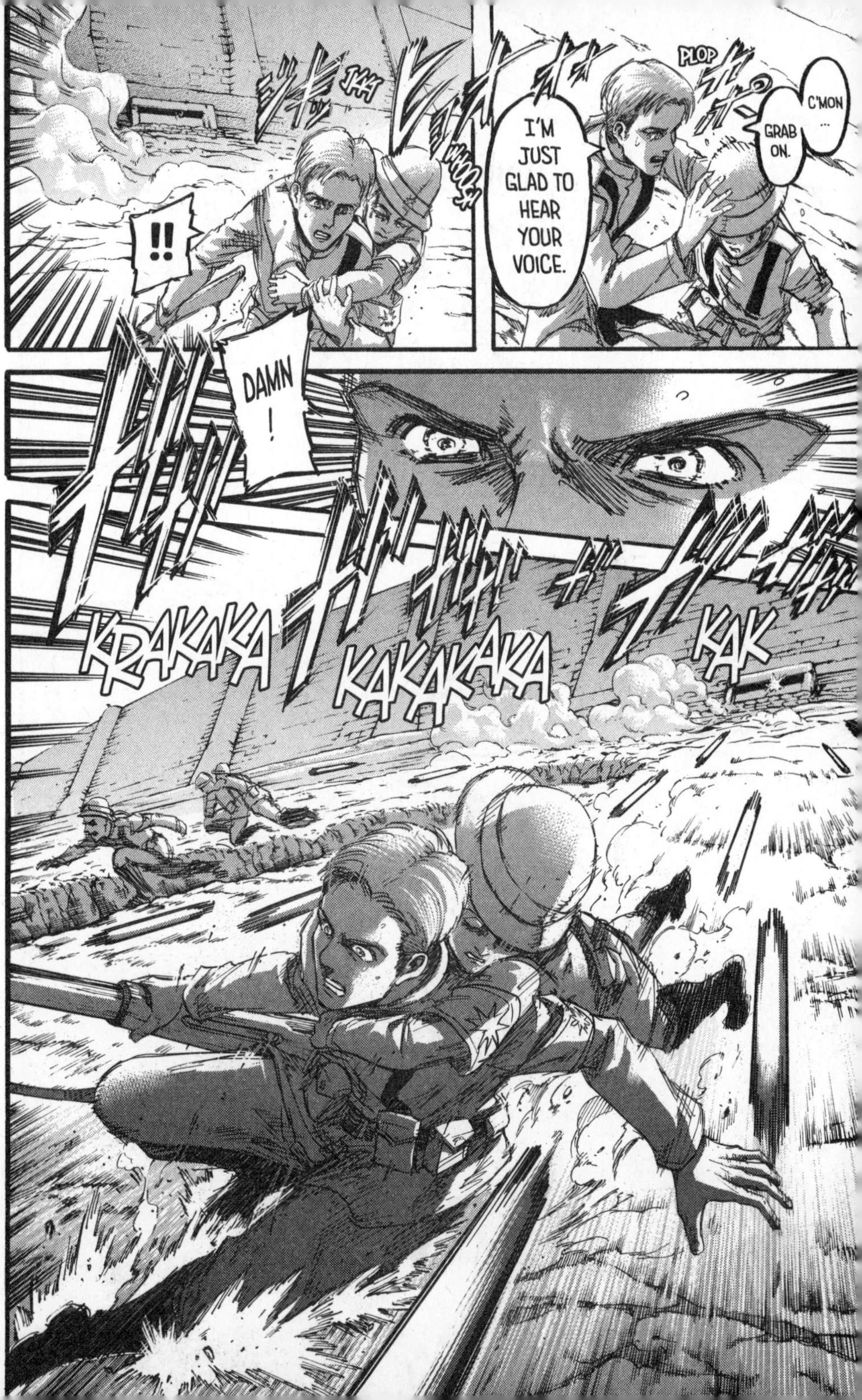
PLOP
C'MON ...
GRAB ON.
I'M JUST GLAD TO HEAR YOUR VOICE.
WHOOSH
!!
DAMN !
KRAKAKA
KAKAKAKA
KAK

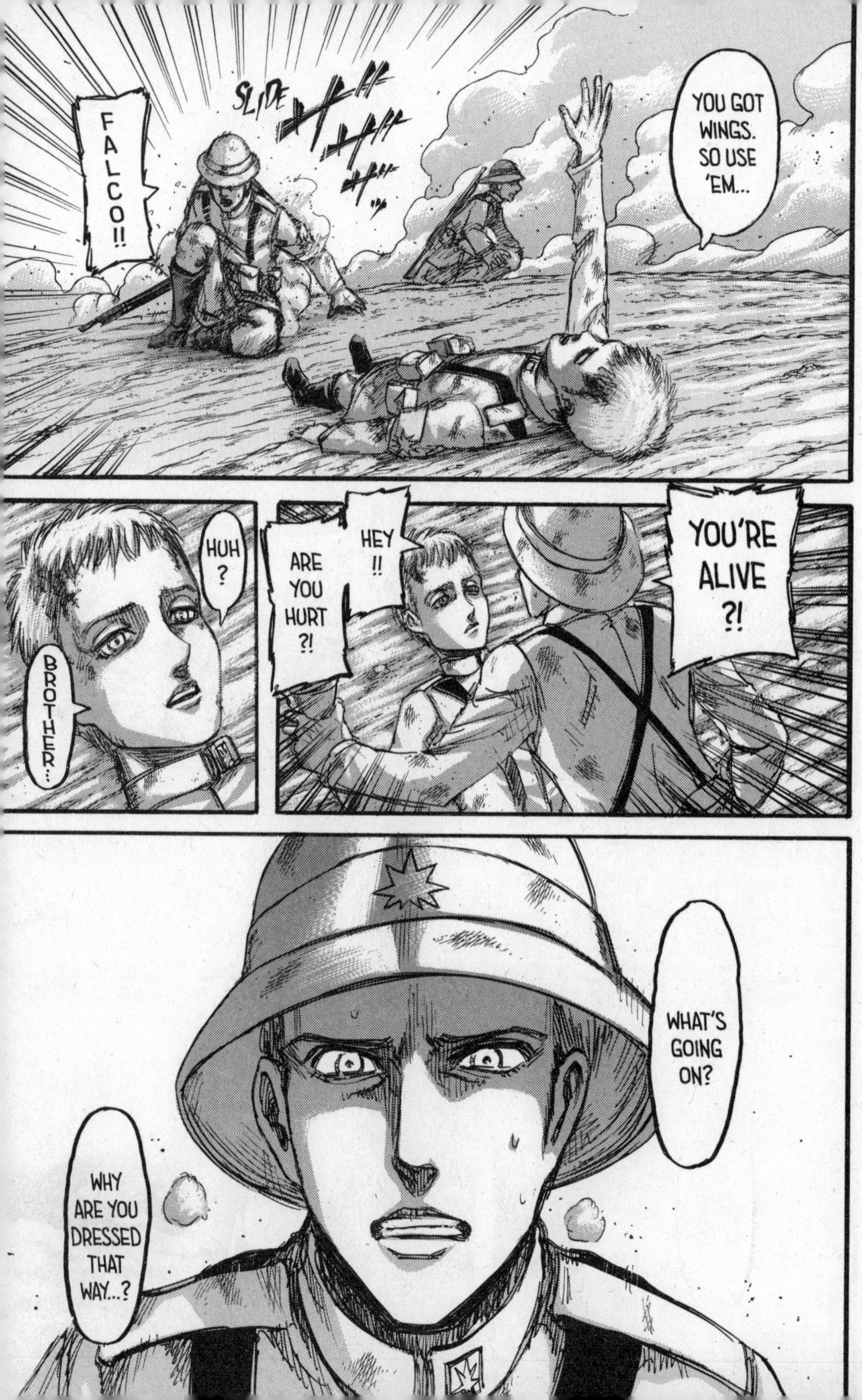
YOU GOT WINGS. SO USE 'EM...
SLIDE
FALCO!!
YOU'RE ALIVE ?!
HEY !!
ARE YOU HURT ?!
HUH ?
BROTHER...
WHAT'S GOING ON?
WHY ARE YOU DRESSED THAT WAY...?

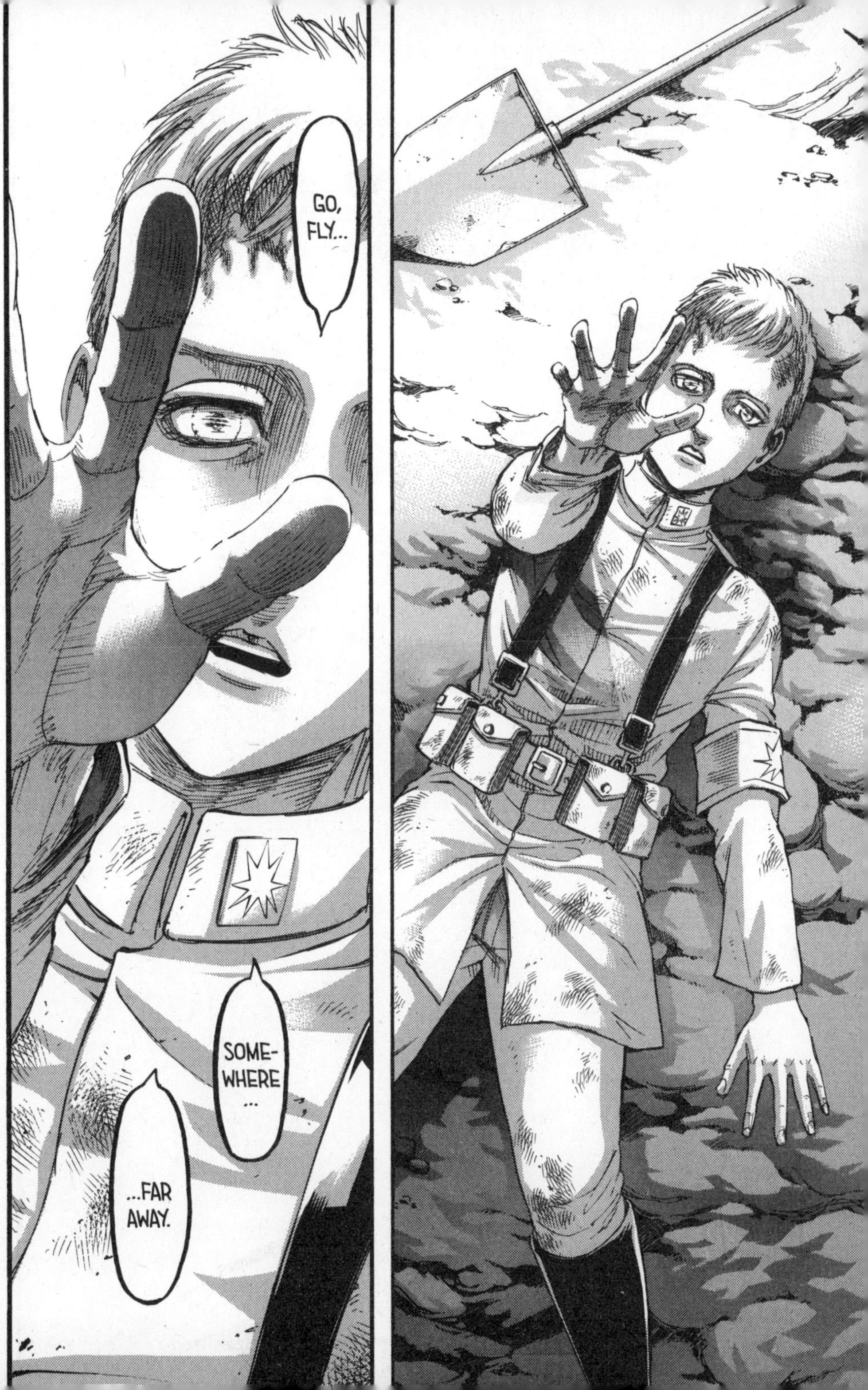
GO, FLY...
SOME-WHERE ...
...FAR AWAY.

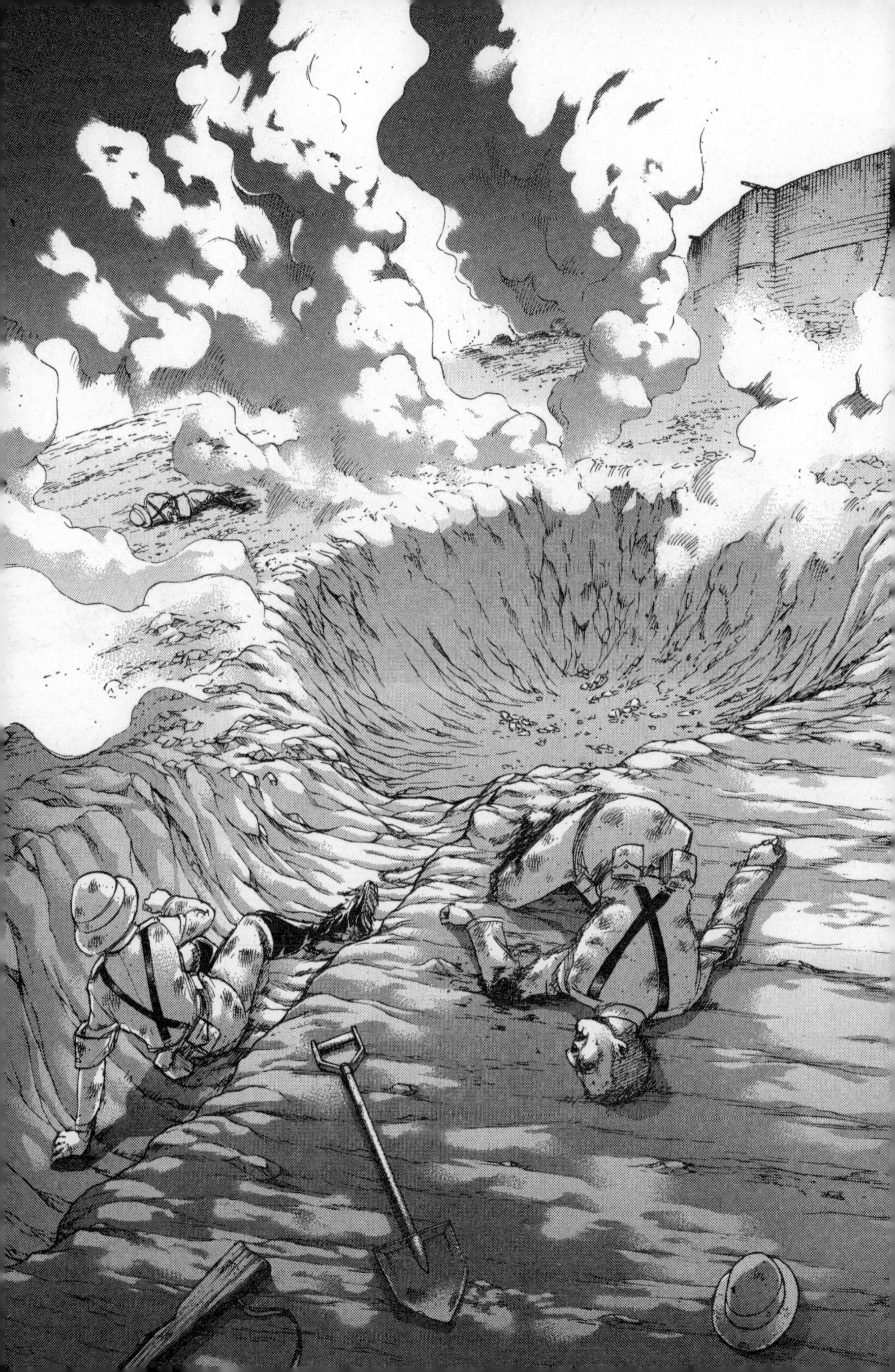

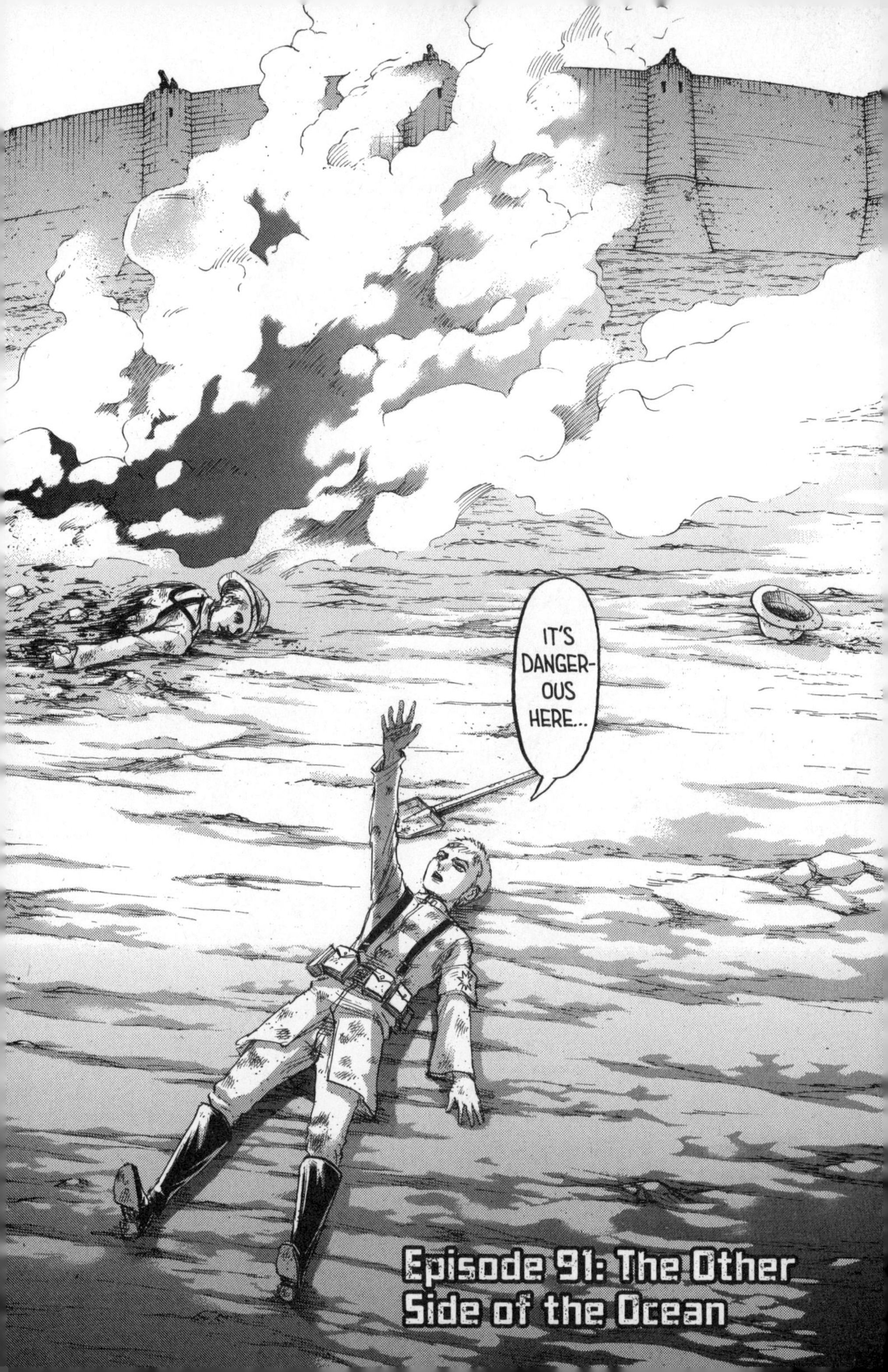
IT'S DANGER-OUS HERE...
Episode 91: The Other Side of the Ocean

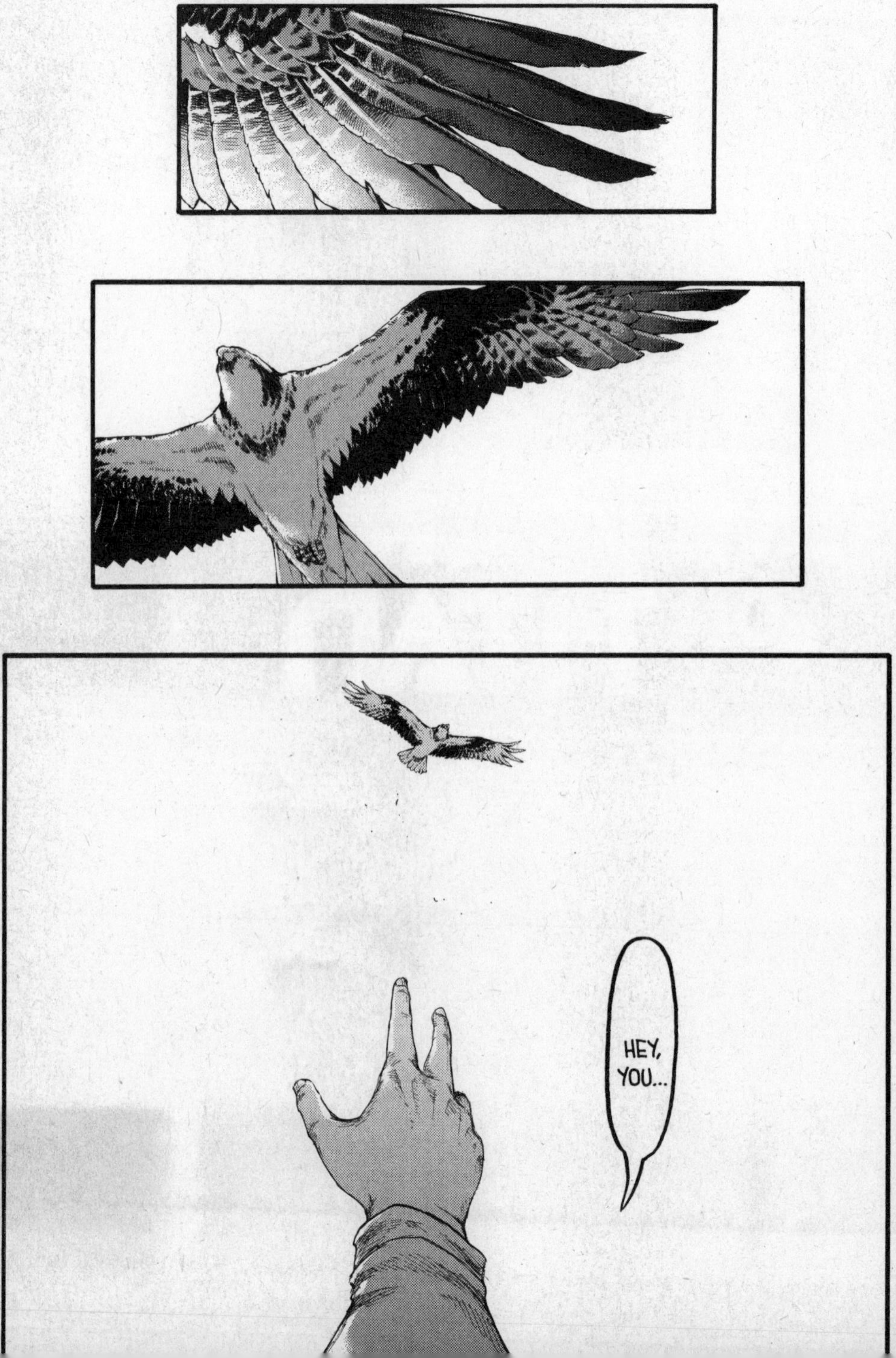
HEY, YOU...

ATTACK on TITAN

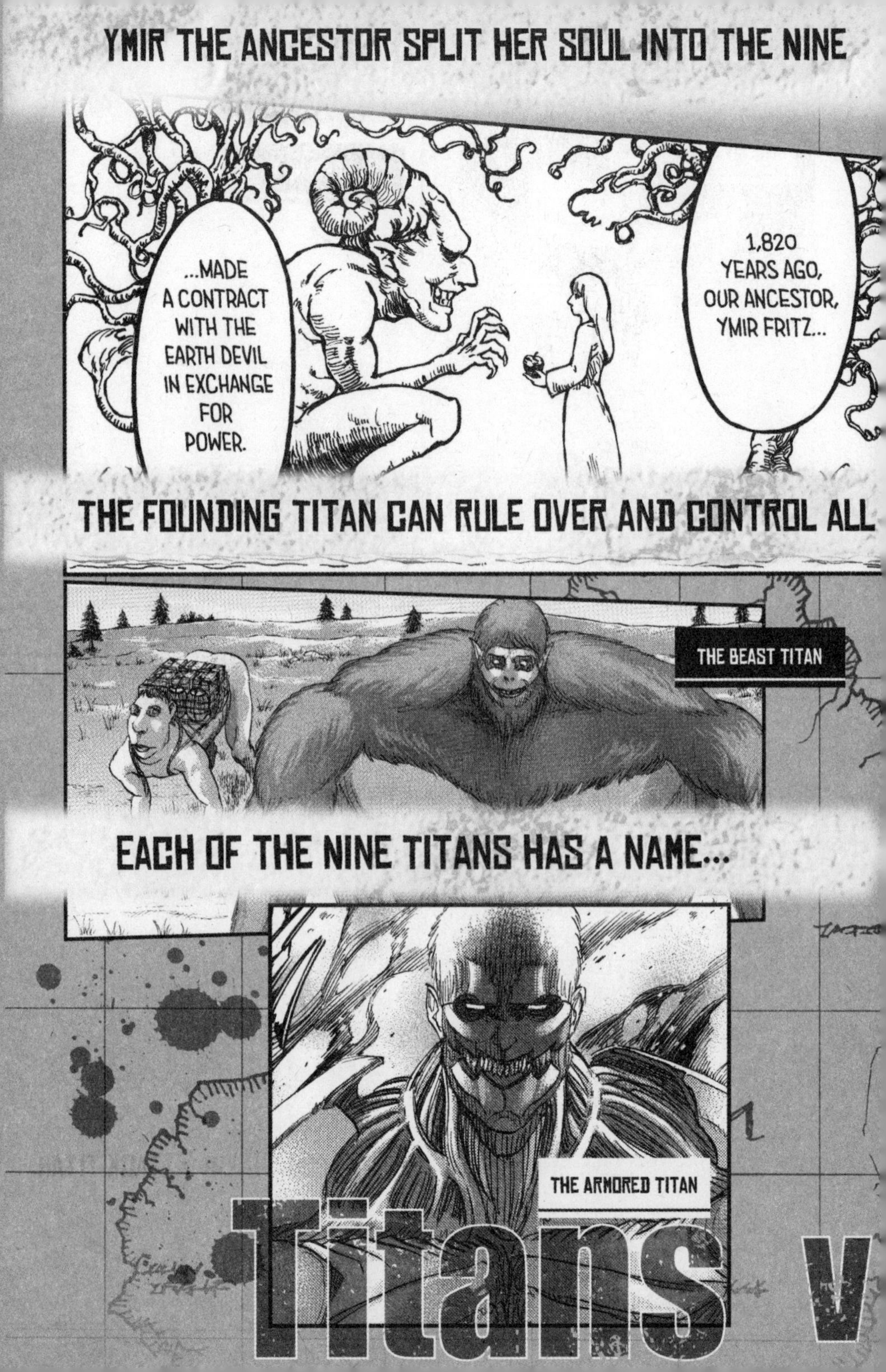
YMIR THE ANCESTOR SPLIT HER SOUL INTO THE NINE
1,820 YEARS AGO, OUR ANCESTOR, YMIR FRITZ...
...MADE A CONTRACT WITH THE EARTH DEVIL IN EXCHANGE FOR POWER.
THE FOUNDING TITAN CAN RULE OVER AND CONTROL ALL
THE BEAST TITAN
EACH OF THE NINE TITANS HAS A NAME...
THE ARMORED TITAN
Titans v

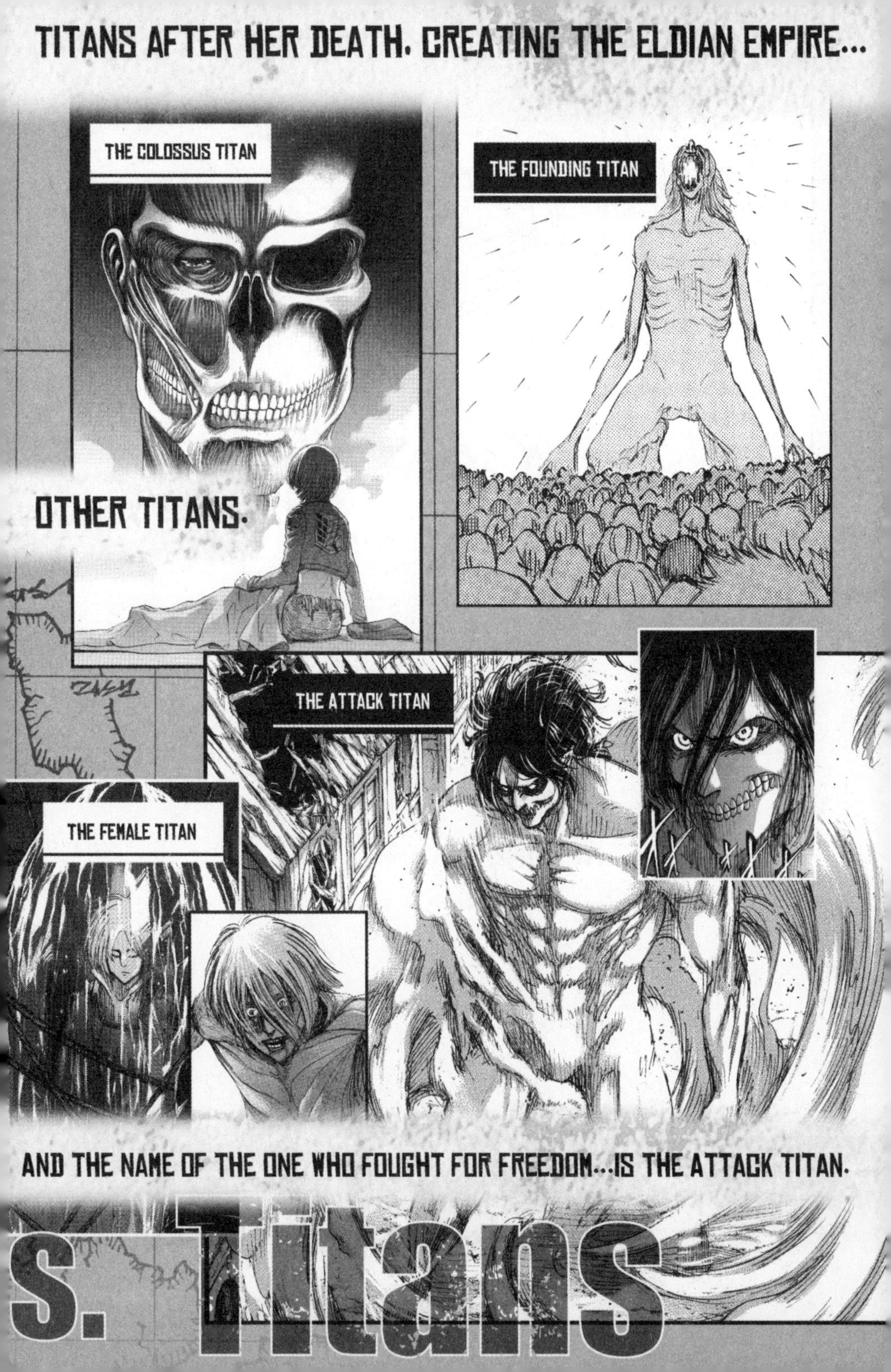
TITANS AFTER HER DEATH, CREATING THE ELDIAN EMPIRE...
THE FOUNDING TITAN
THE COLOSSUS TITAN
OTHER TITANS.
THE ATTACK TITAN
THE FEMALE TITAN
AND THE NAME OF THE ONE WHO FOUGHT FOR FREEDOM...IS THE ATTACK TITAN.
s. Titans

ATTACK ON TITAN 23

HAJIME ISAYAMA

ATTACK on TITAN

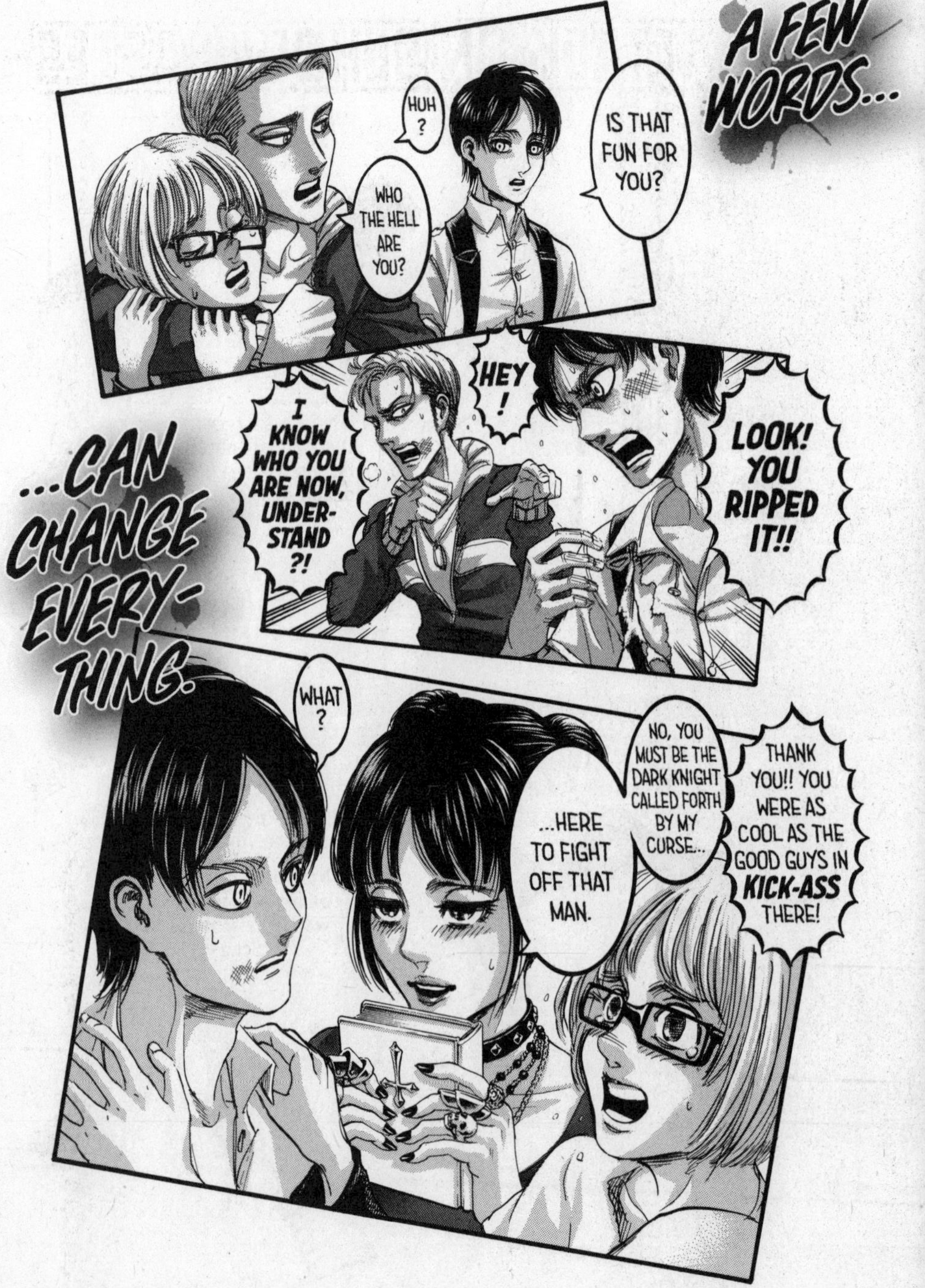
A FEW WORDS...
IS THAT FUN FOR YOU?
HUH ?
WHO THE HELL ARE YOU?
LOOK! YOU RIPPED IT!!
HEY !
I KNOW WHO YOU ARE NOW, UNDER-STAND ?!
...CAN CHANGE EVERY-THING.
THANK YOU!! YOU WERE AS COOL AS THE GOOD GUYS IN KICK-ASS THERE!
NO, YOU MUST BE THE DARK KNIGHT CALLED FORTH BY MY CURSE...
...HERE TO FIGHT OFF THAT MAN.
WHAT ?

*Not a real preview.

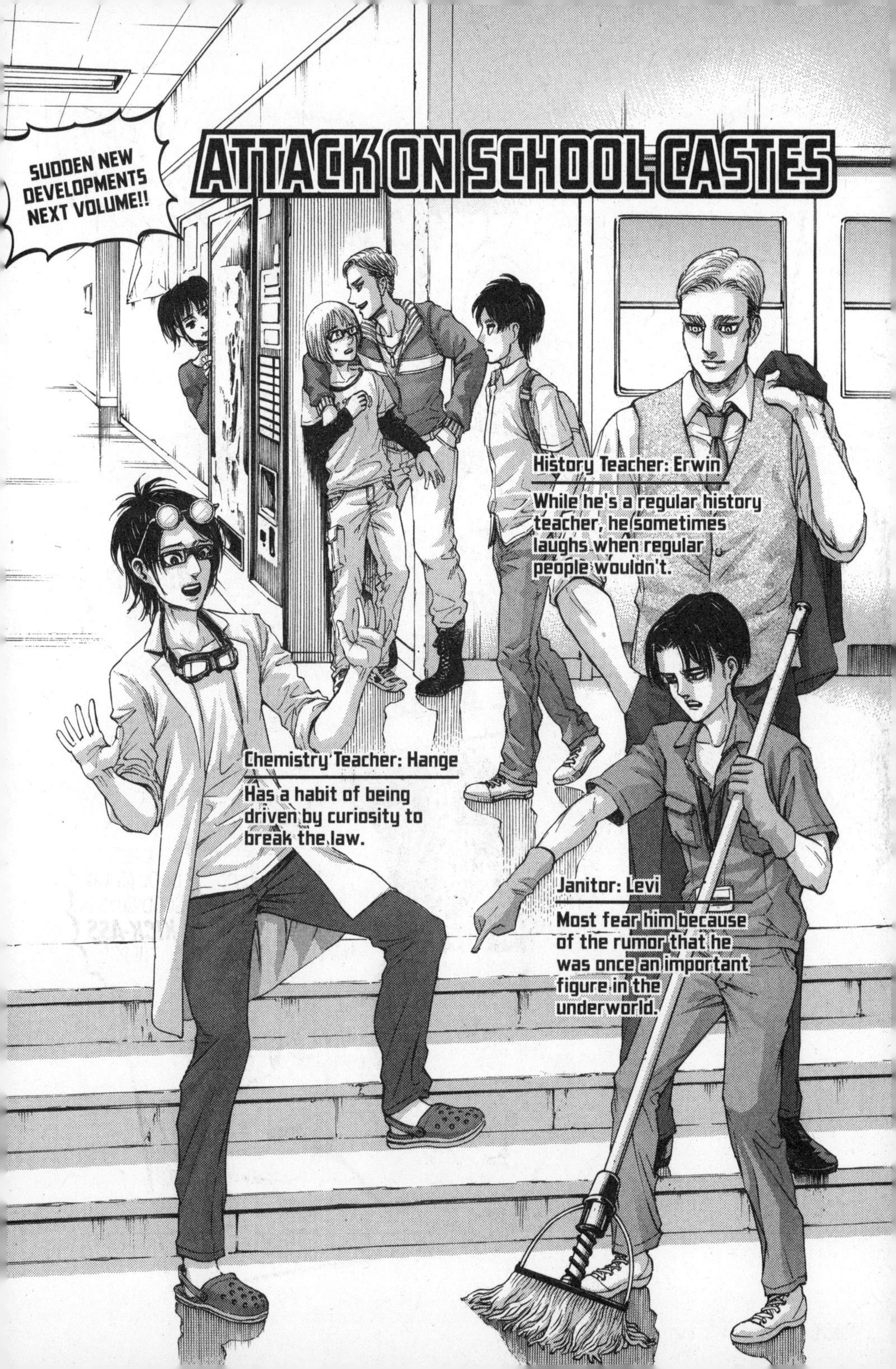
SUDDEN NEW DEVELOPMENTS NEXT VOLUME!!
ATTACK ON SCHOOL CASTES
History Teacher: Erwin
While he's a regular history teacher, he sometimes laughs when regular people wouldn't.
Chemistry Teacher: Hange
Has a habit of being driven by curiosity to break the law.
Janitor: Levi
Most fear him because of the rumor that he was once an important figure in the underworld.

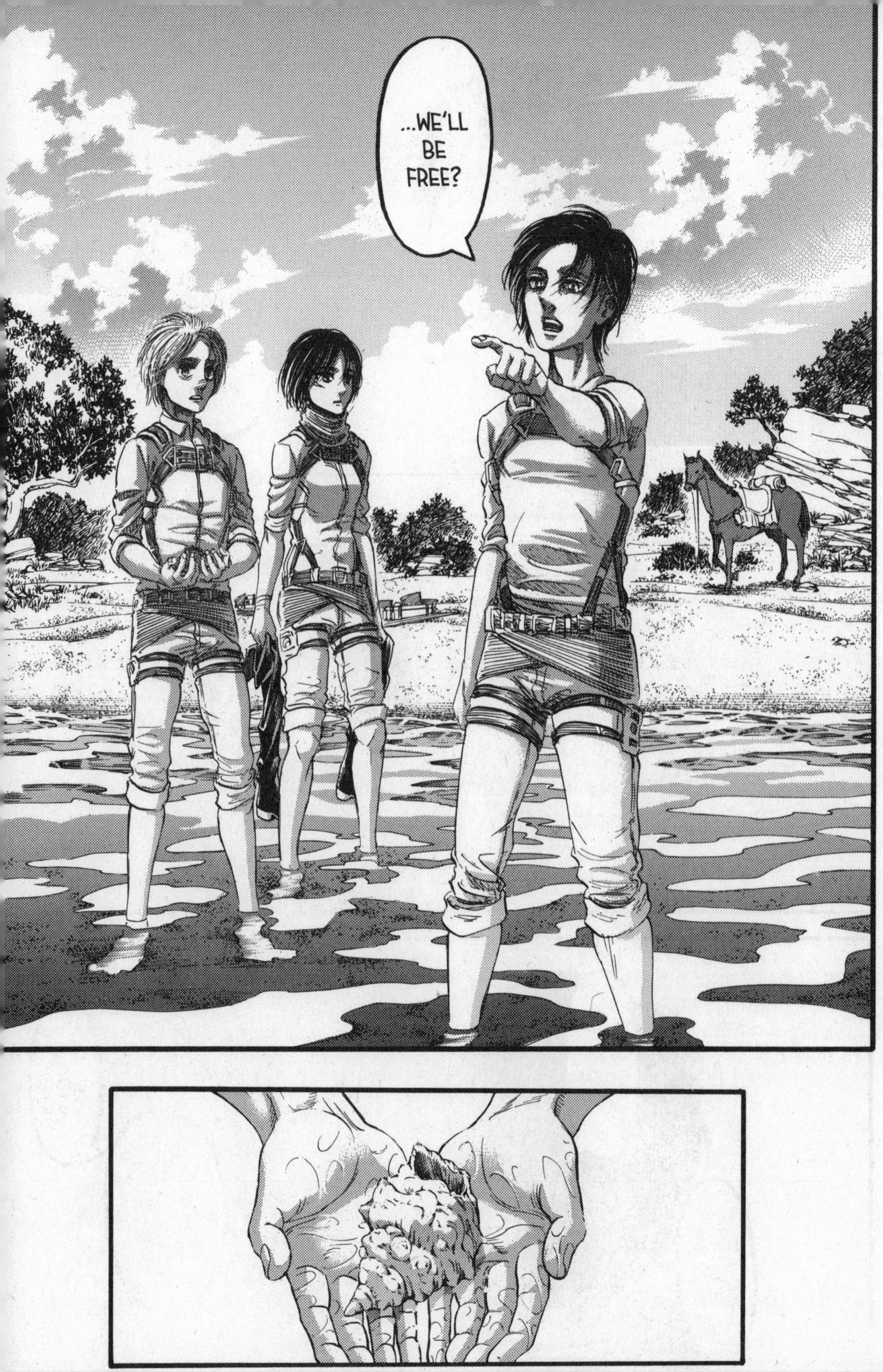
...WE'LL BE FREE?

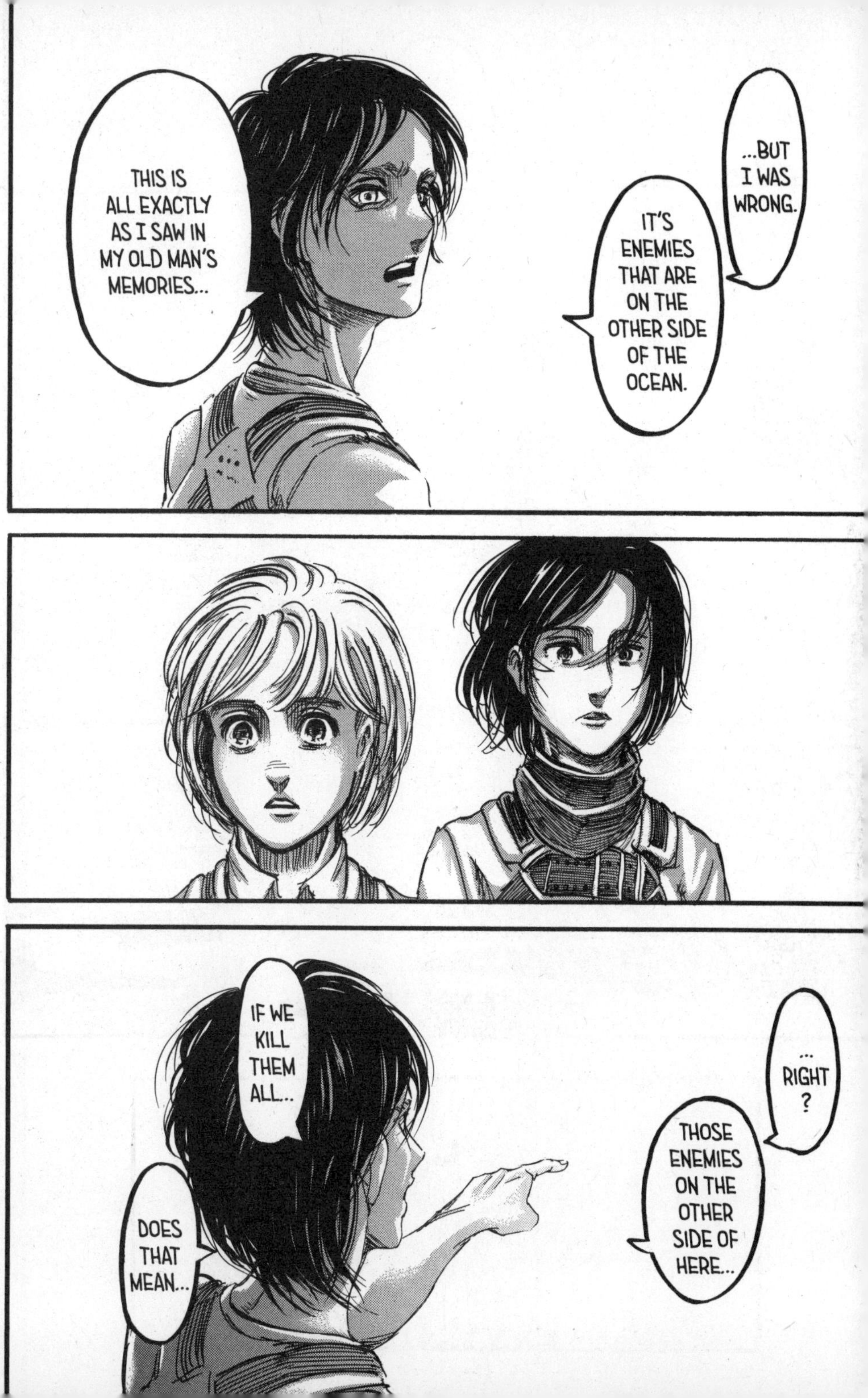

...BUT I WAS WRONG.
IT'S ENEMIES THAT ARE ON THE OTHER SIDE OF THE OCEAN.
THIS IS ALL EXACTLY AS I SAW IN MY OLD MAN'S MEMORIES...
...RIGHT?
THOSE ENEMIES ON THE OTHER SIDE OF HERE...
IF WE KILL THEM ALL...
DOES THAT MEAN...

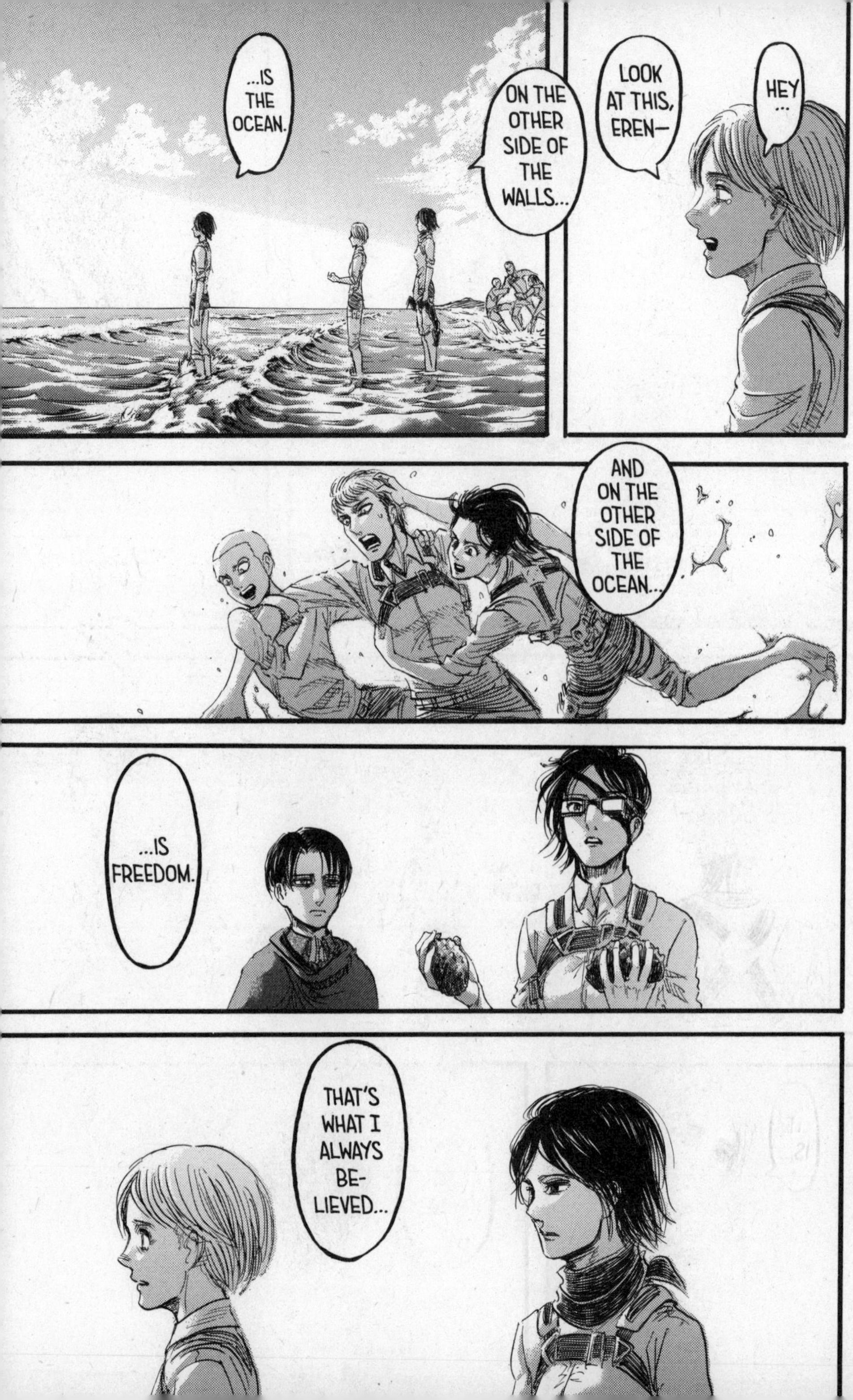
HEY ...
LOOK AT THIS, EREN—
ON THE OTHER SIDE OF THE WALLS...
...IS THE OCEAN.
AND ON THE OTHER SIDE OF THE OCEAN...
...IS FREEDOM.
THAT'S WHAT I ALWAYS BE-LIEVED...

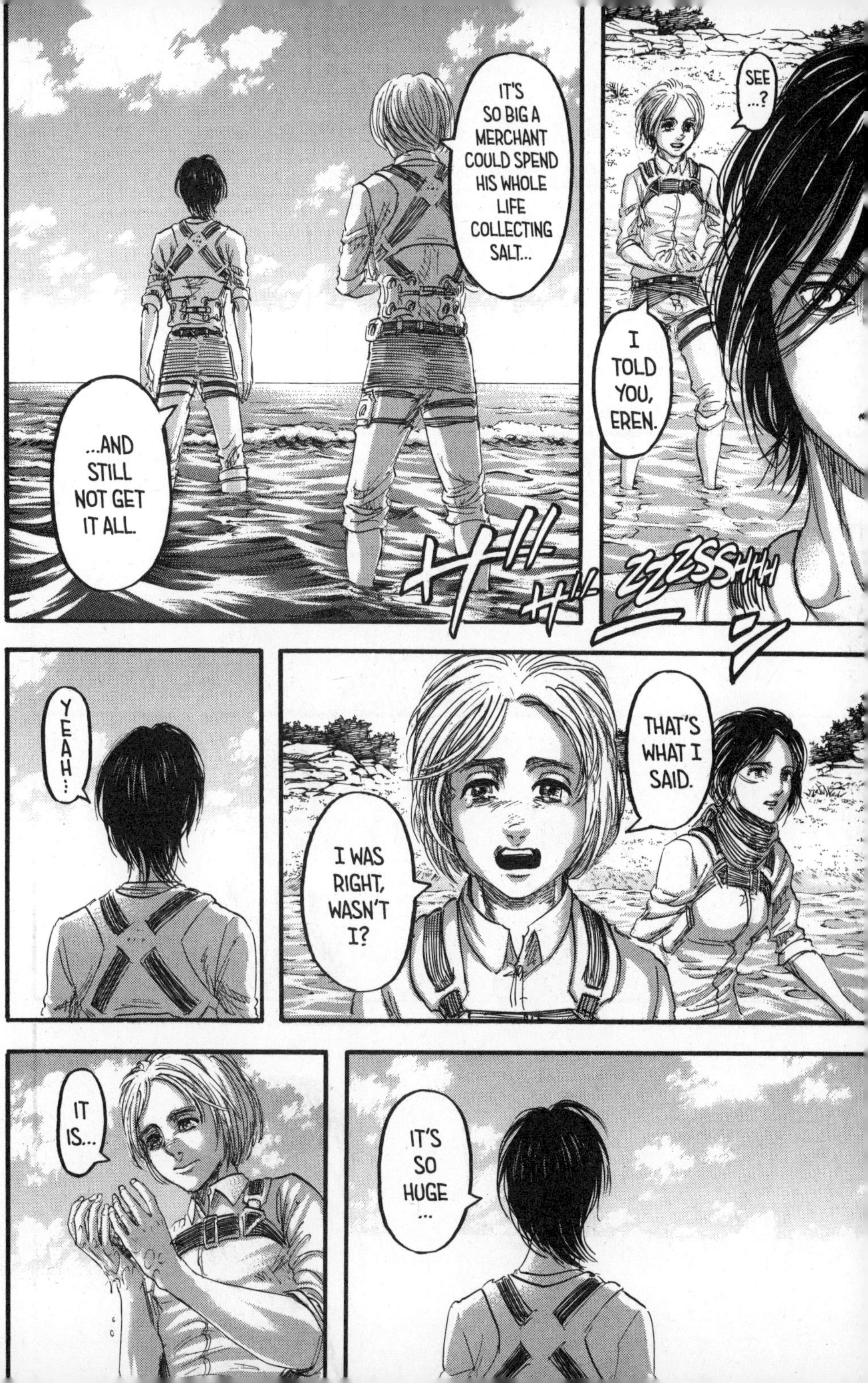
SEE ...?
I TOLD YOU, EREN.
IT'S SO BIG A MERCHANT COULD SPEND HIS WHOLE LIFE COLLECTING SALT...
...AND STILL NOT GET IT ALL.
ZZZSSHHH
THAT'S WHAT I SAID.
I WAS RIGHT, WASN'T I?
YEAH...
IT'S SO HUGE ...
IT IS...

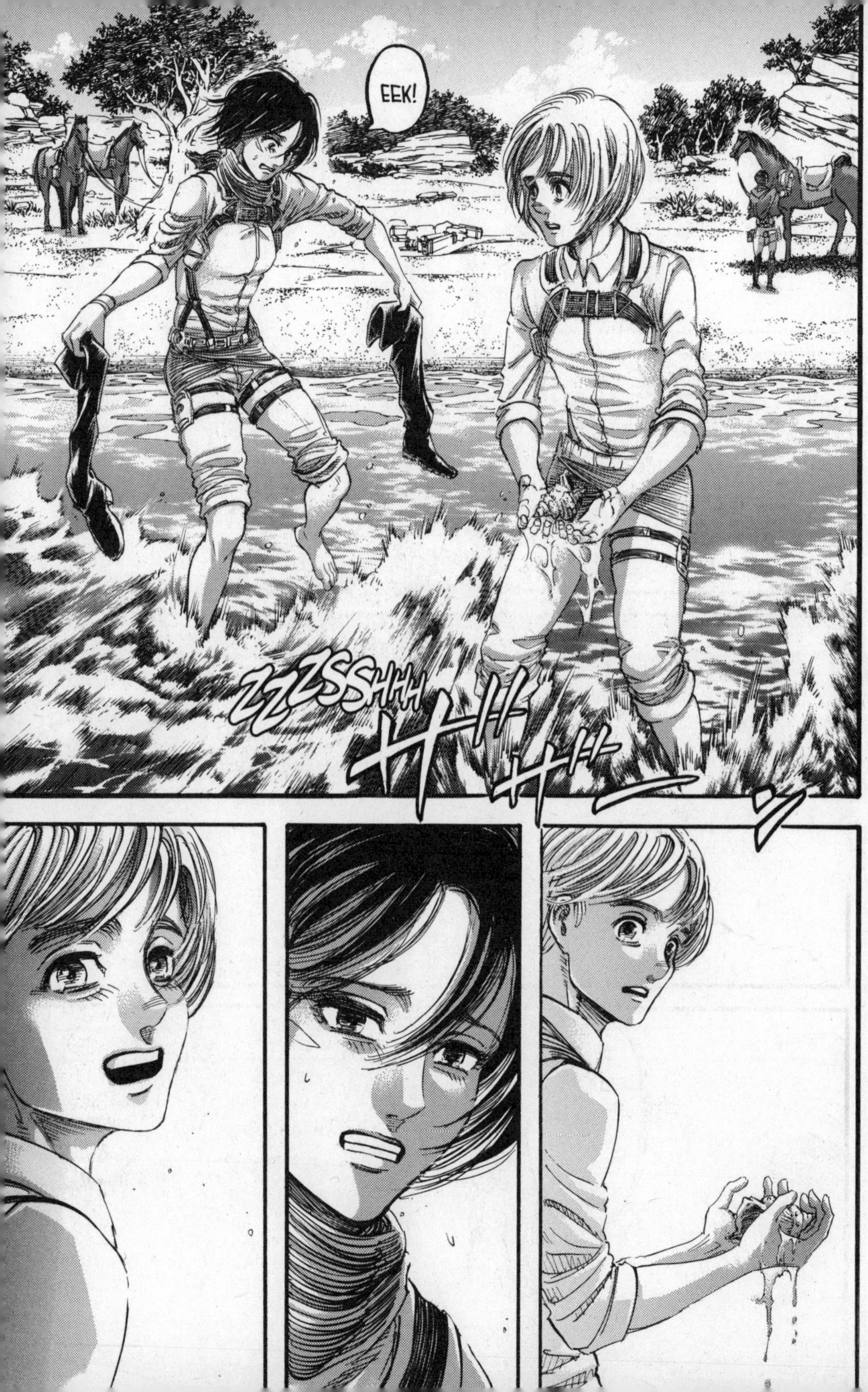
EEK!
ZZZSSHHH

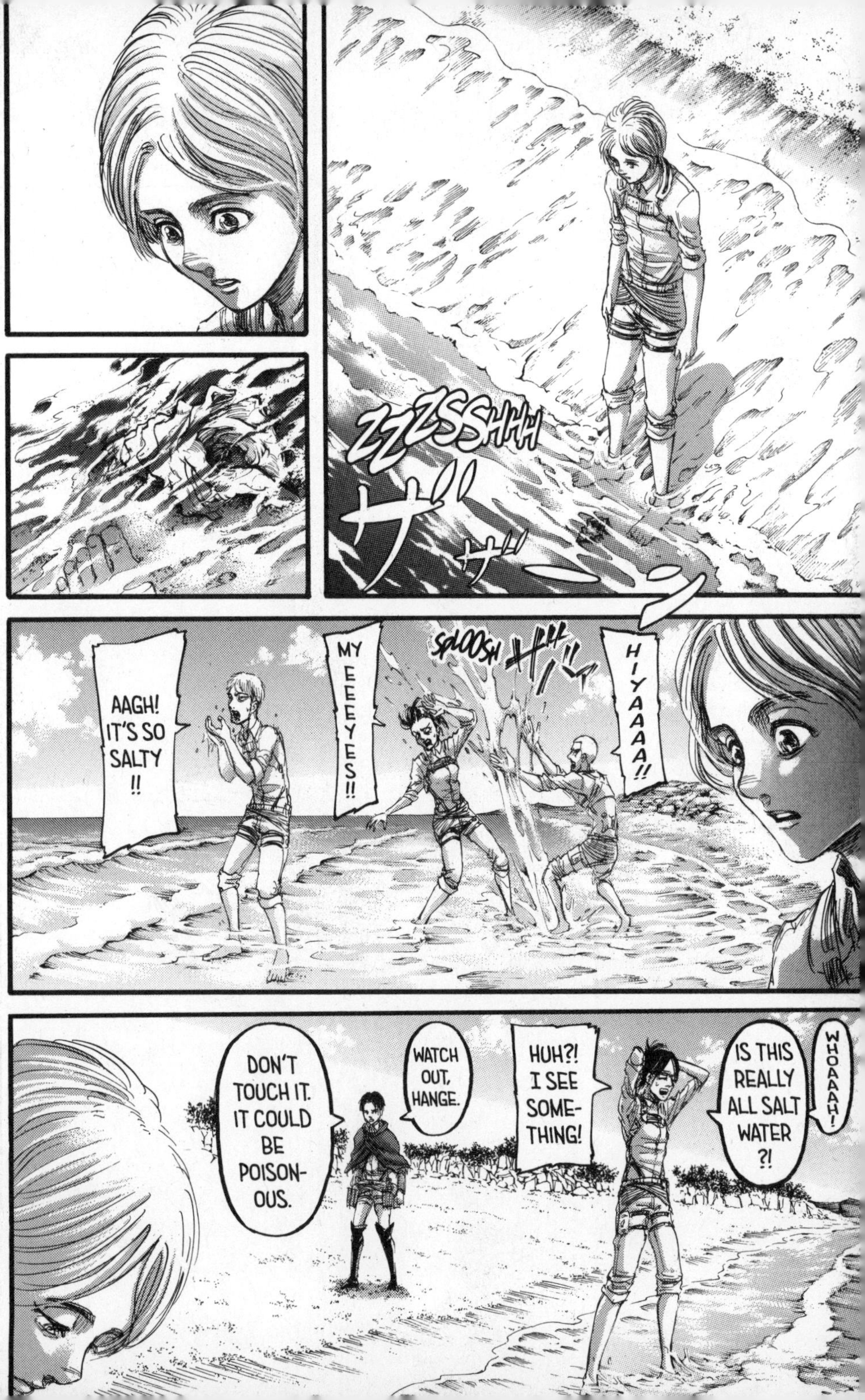
ZZZSSHHH
ザザーーン
HIYAAAAA!!
SPLOOSH
ザバァ
MY EEEEYES!!
AAGH! IT'S SO SALTY!!
WHOAAAAH!
IS THIS REALLY ALL SALT WATER?!
HUH?! I SEE SOME-THING!
WATCH OUT, HANGE.
DON'T TOUCH IT. IT COULD BE POISON-OUS.

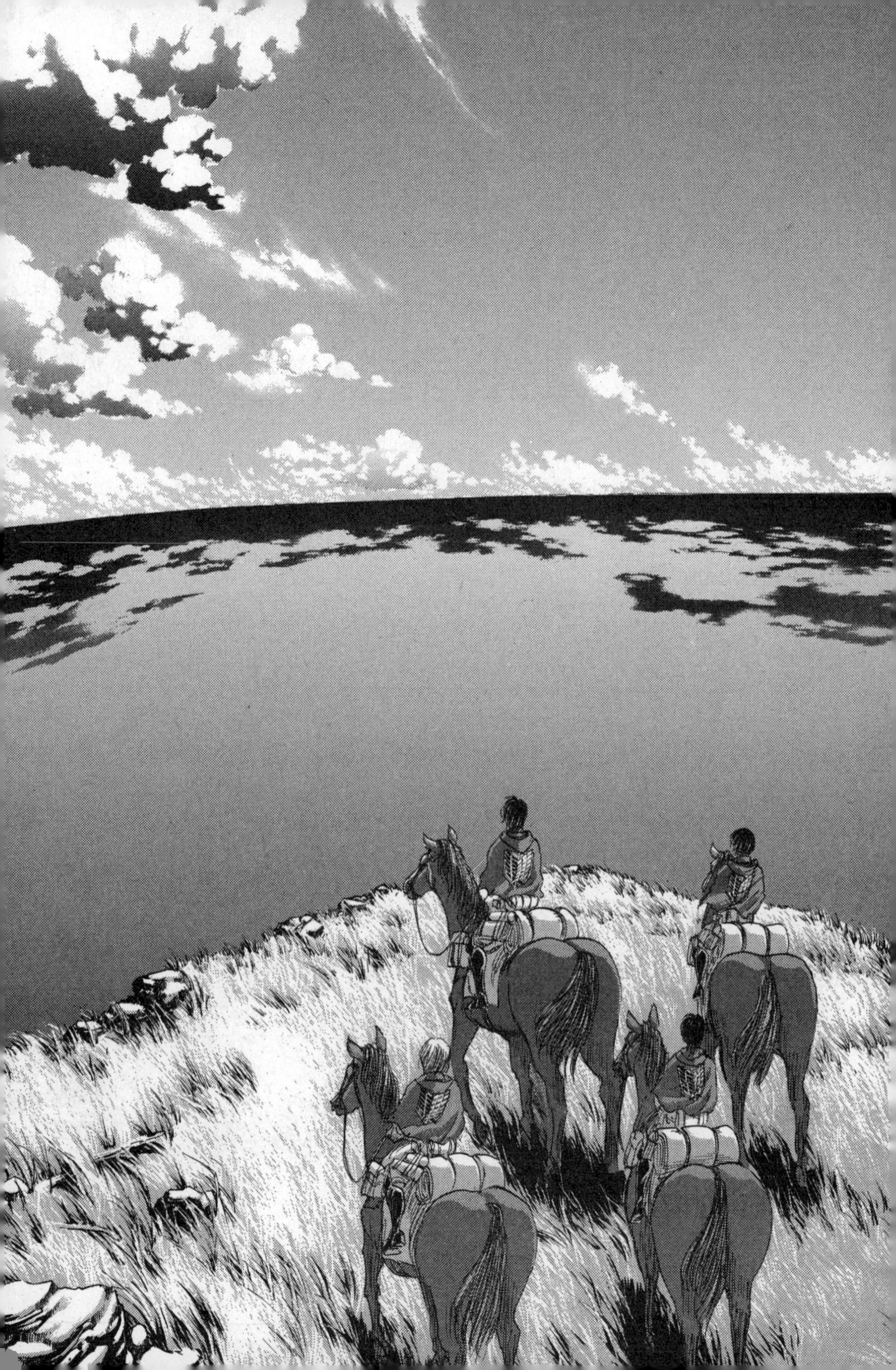

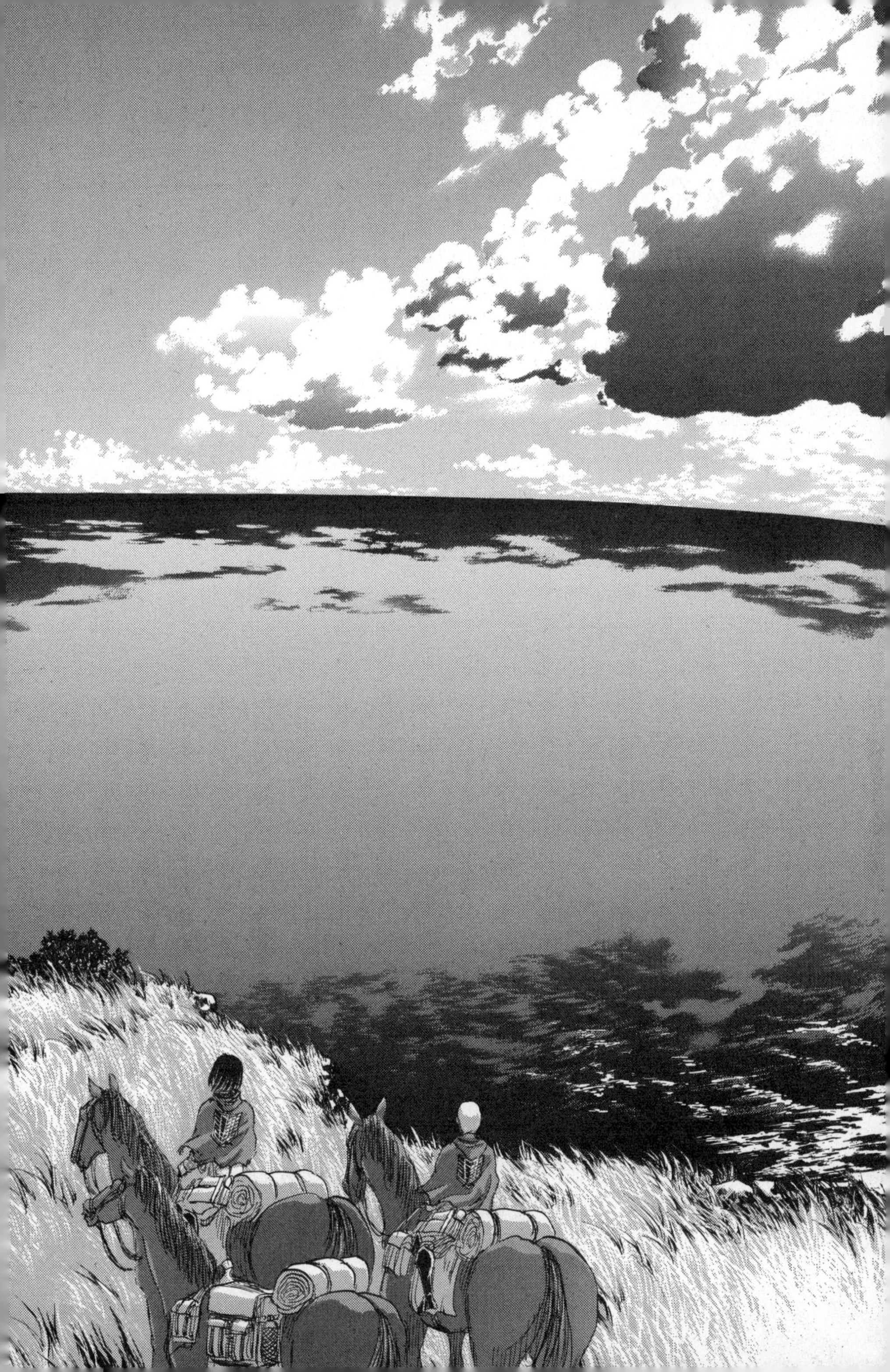

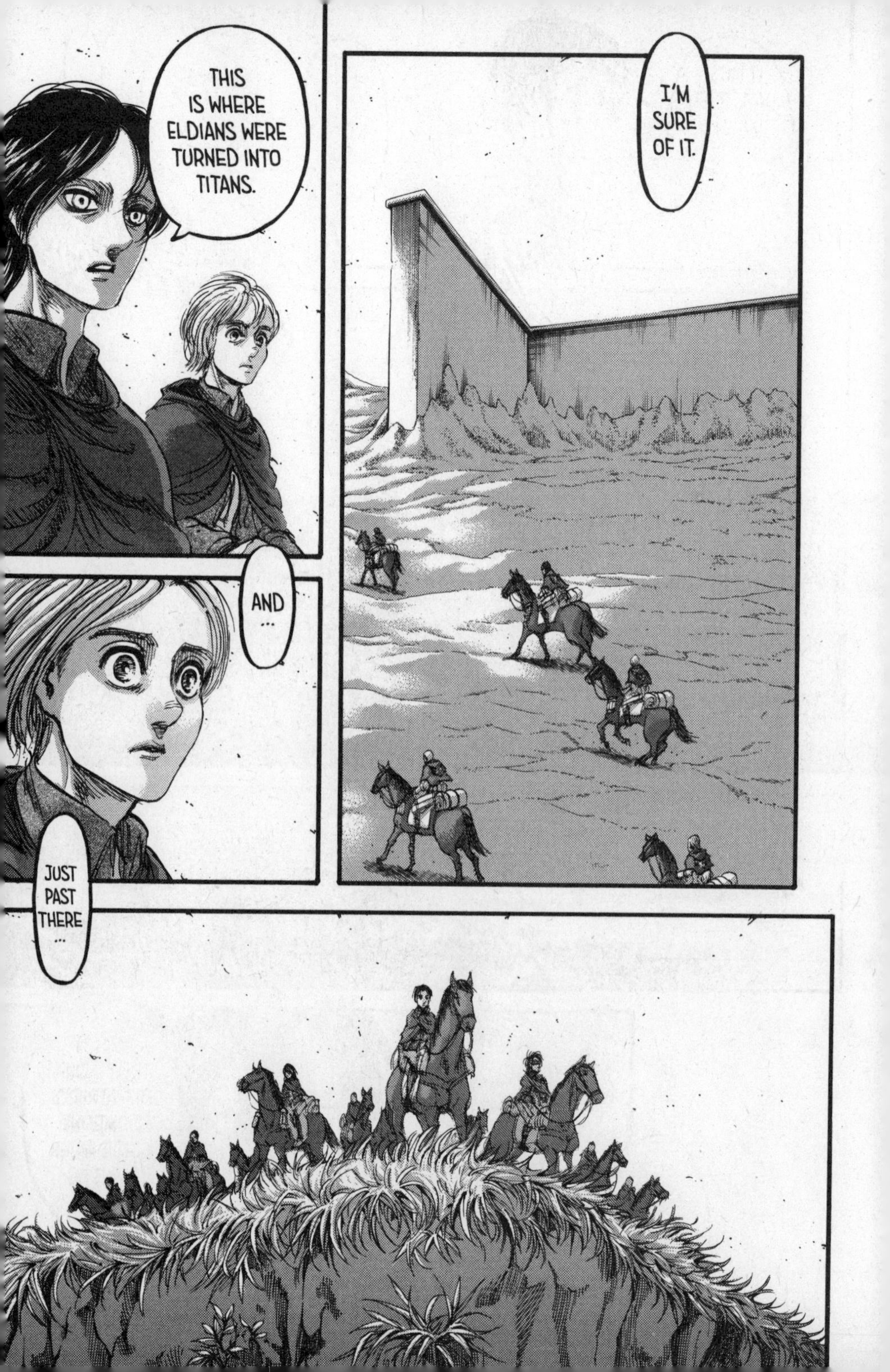
I'M SURE OF IT.
THIS IS WHERE ELDIANS WERE TURNED INTO TITANS.
AND ...
JUST PAST THERE ...

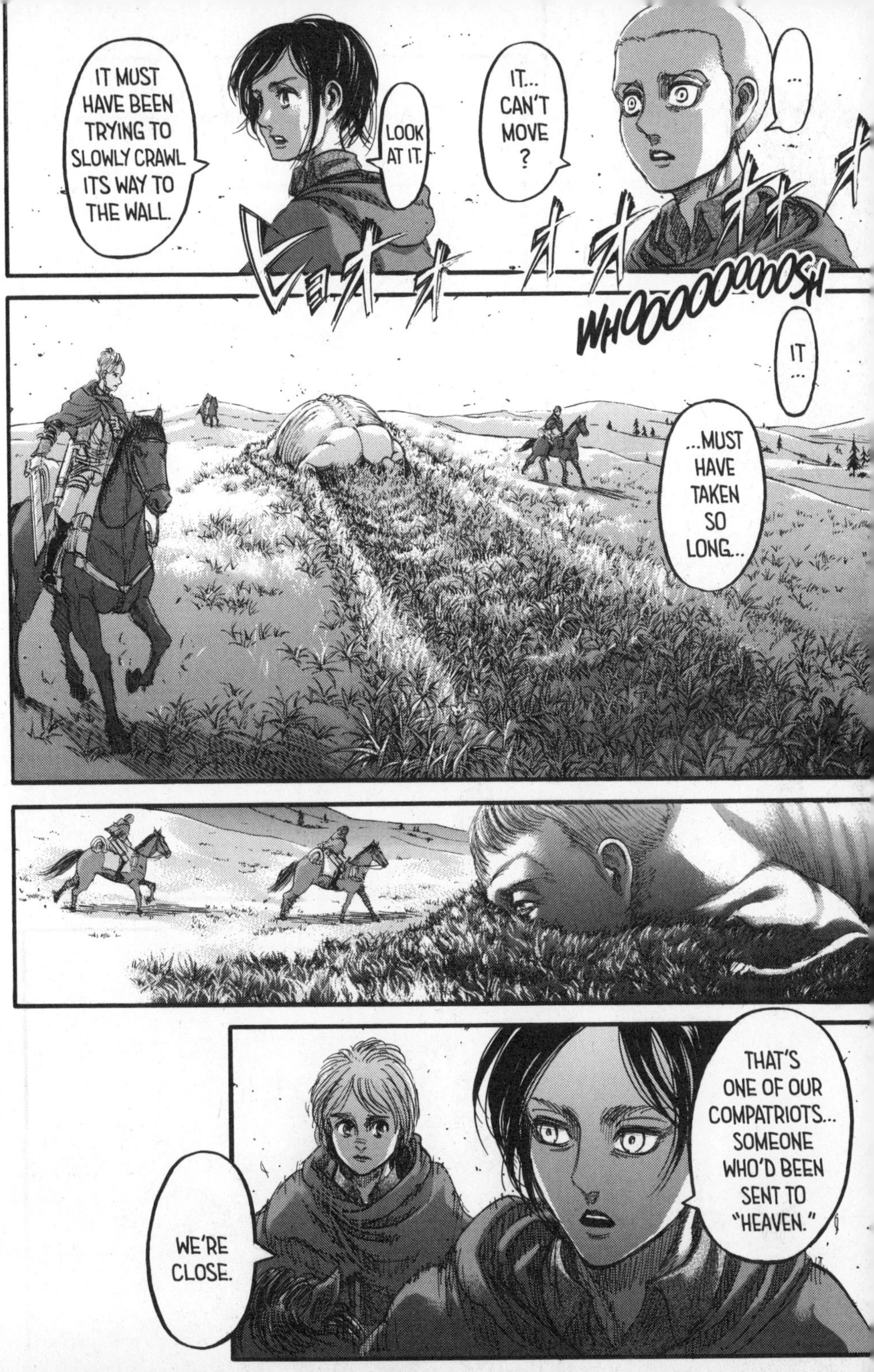
...
IT... CAN'T MOVE ?
LOOK AT IT.
IT MUST HAVE BEEN TRYING TO SLOWLY CRAWL ITS WAY TO THE WALL.
WHOOOOOOOOOSH
IT ...
...MUST HAVE TAKEN SO LONG...
THAT'S ONE OF OUR COMPATRIOTS... SOMEONE WHO'D BEEN SENT TO "HEAVEN."
WE'RE CLOSE.

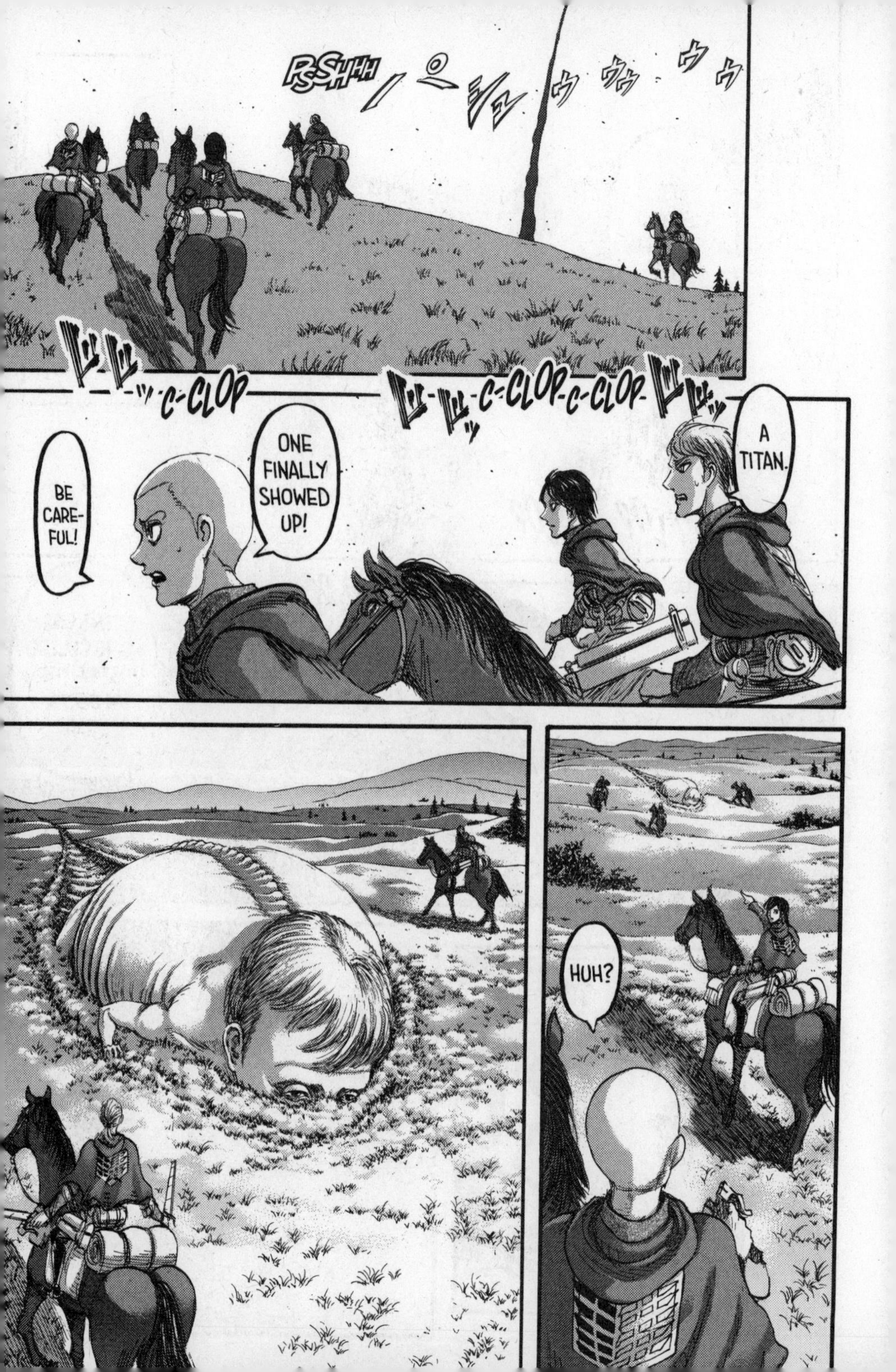
PSSHHH
C-CLOP-C-CLOP
C-CLOP
A TITAN.
ONE FINALLY SHOWED UP!
BE CAREFUL!
HUH?

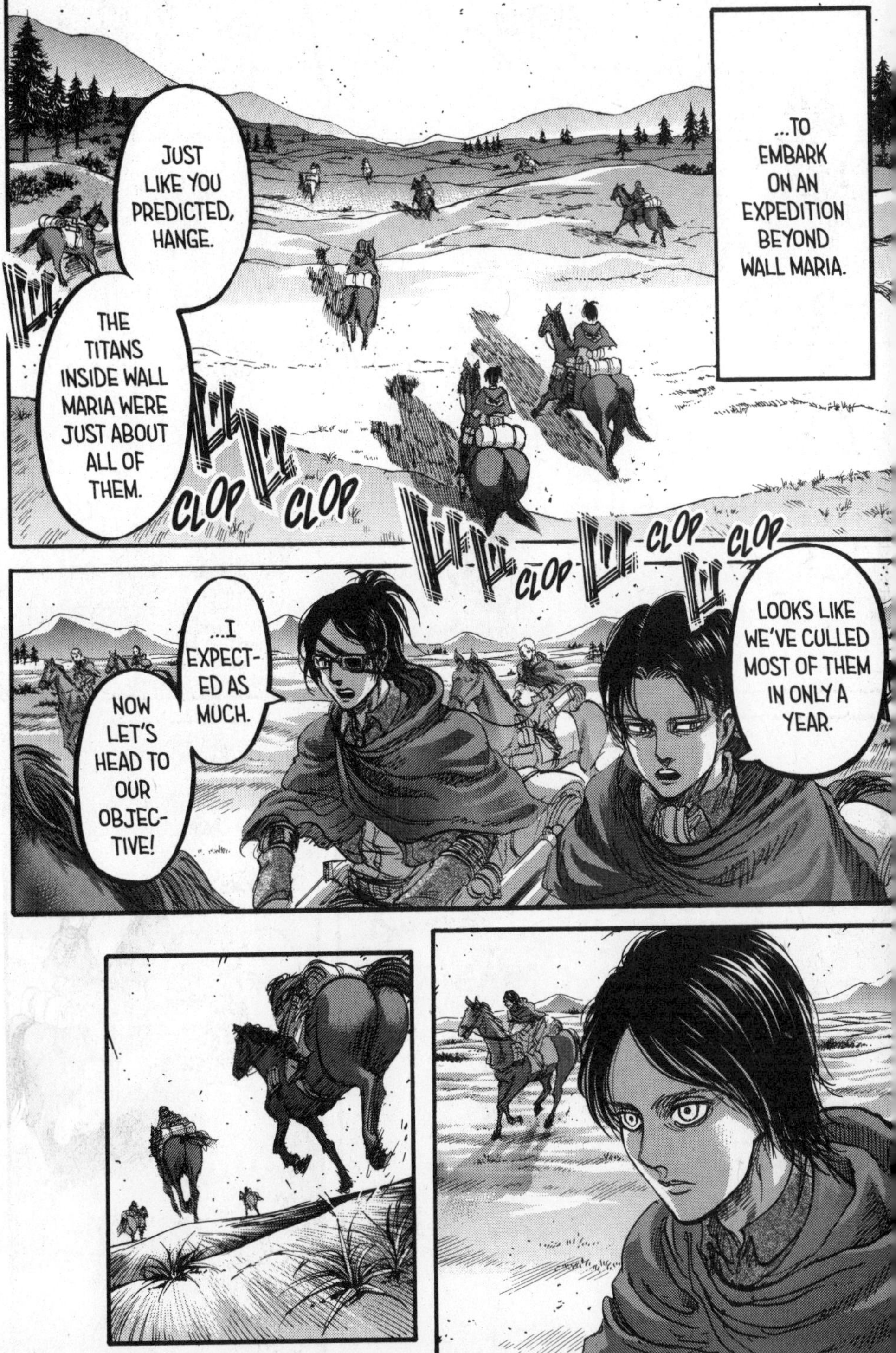
...TO EMBARK ON AN EXPEDITION BEYOND WALL MARIA.
JUST LIKE YOU PREDICTED, HANGE.
THE TITANS INSIDE WALL MARIA WERE JUST ABOUT ALL OF THEM.
CLOP CLOP
CLOP CLOP CLOP
LOOKS LIKE WE'VE CULLED MOST OF THEM IN ONLY A YEAR.
...I EXPECT-ED AS MUCH.
NOW LET'S HEAD TO OUR OBJEC-TIVE!

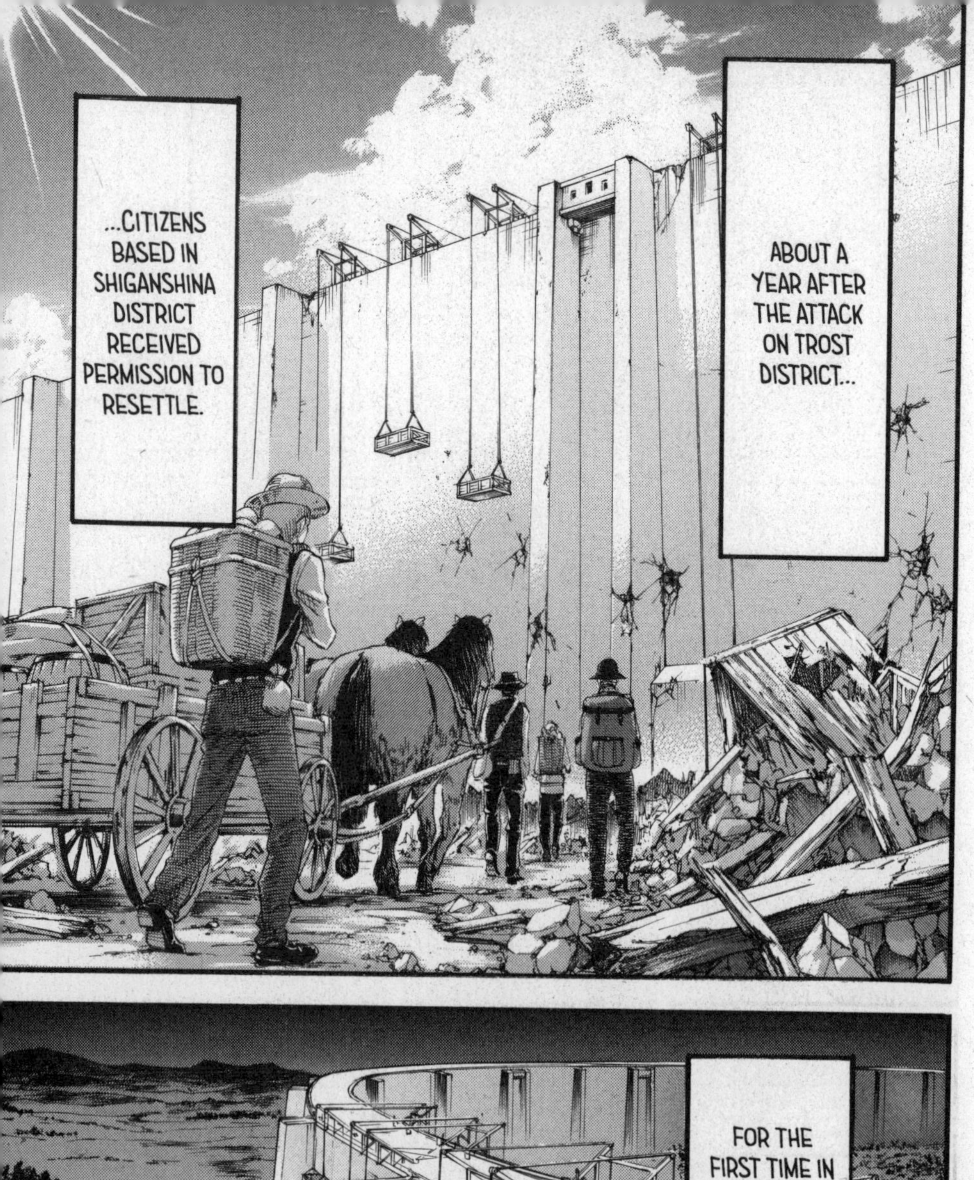
ABOUT A YEAR AFTER THE ATTACK ON TROST DISTRICT...
...CITIZENS BASED IN SHIGANSHINA DISTRICT RECEIVED PERMISSION TO RESETTLE.

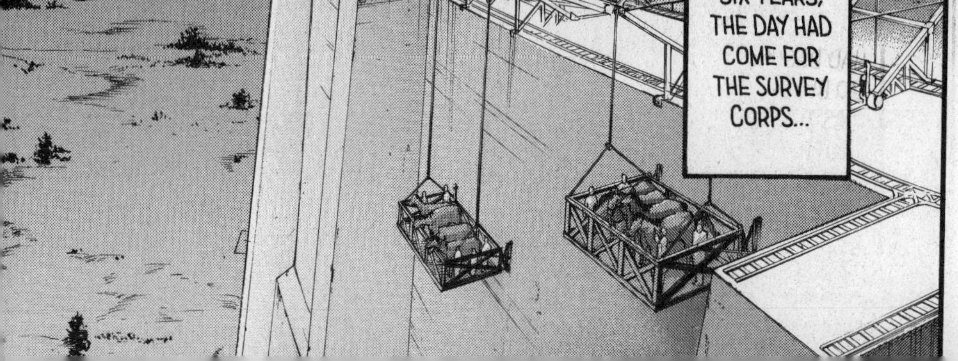
FOR THE FIRST TIME IN SIX YEARS, THE DAY HAD COME FOR THE SURVEY CORPS...

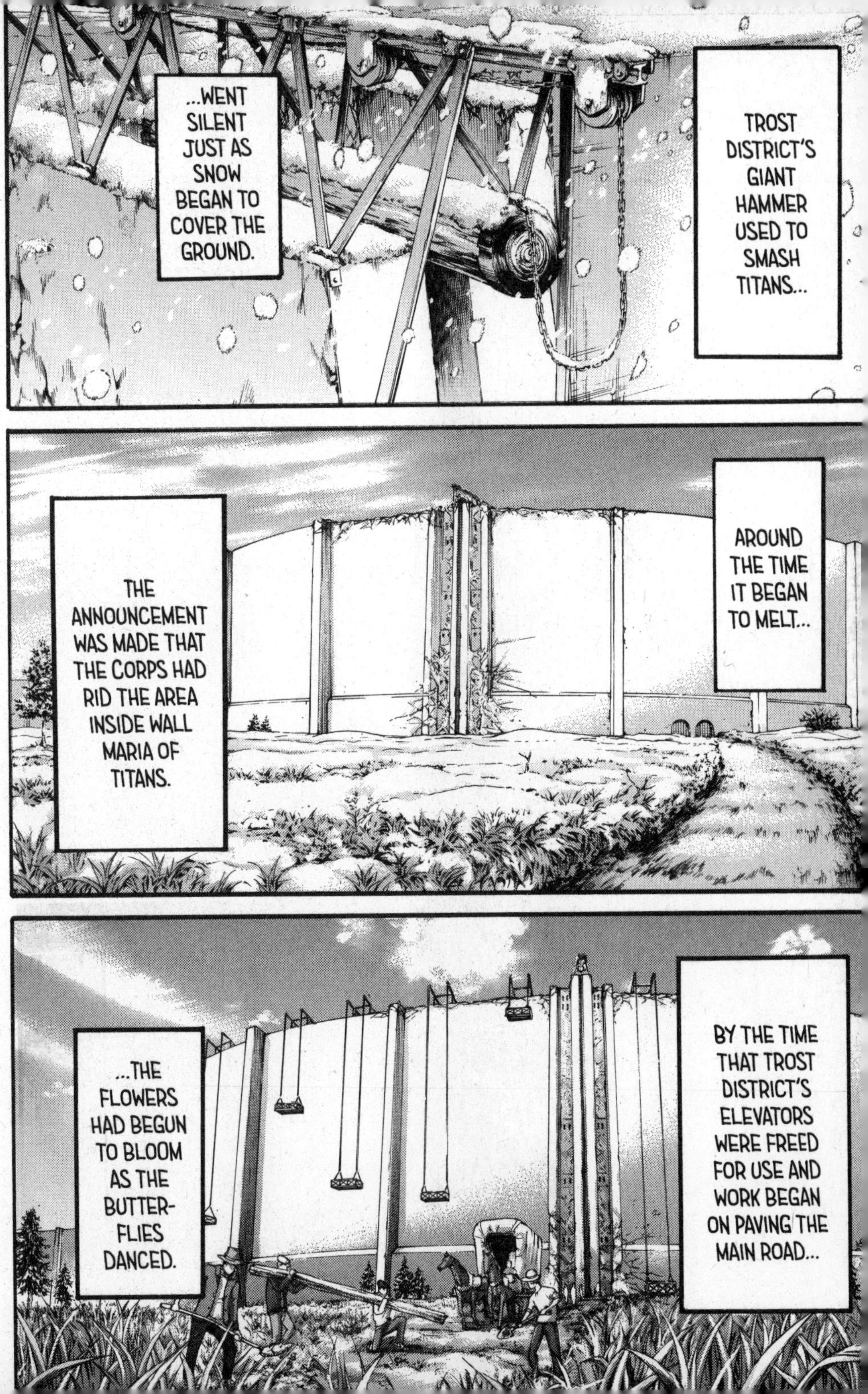
TROST DISTRICT'S GIANT HAMMER USED TO SMASH TITANS...
...WENT SILENT JUST AS SNOW BEGAN TO COVER THE GROUND.
AROUND THE TIME IT BEGAN TO MELT...
THE ANNOUNCEMENT WAS MADE THAT THE CORPS HAD RID THE AREA INSIDE WALL MARIA OF TITANS.
BY THE TIME THAT TROST DISTRICT'S ELEVATORS WERE FREED FOR USE AND WORK BEGAN ON PAVING THE MAIN ROAD...
...THE FLOWERS HAD BEGUN TO BLOOM AS THE BUTTER-FLIES DANCED.

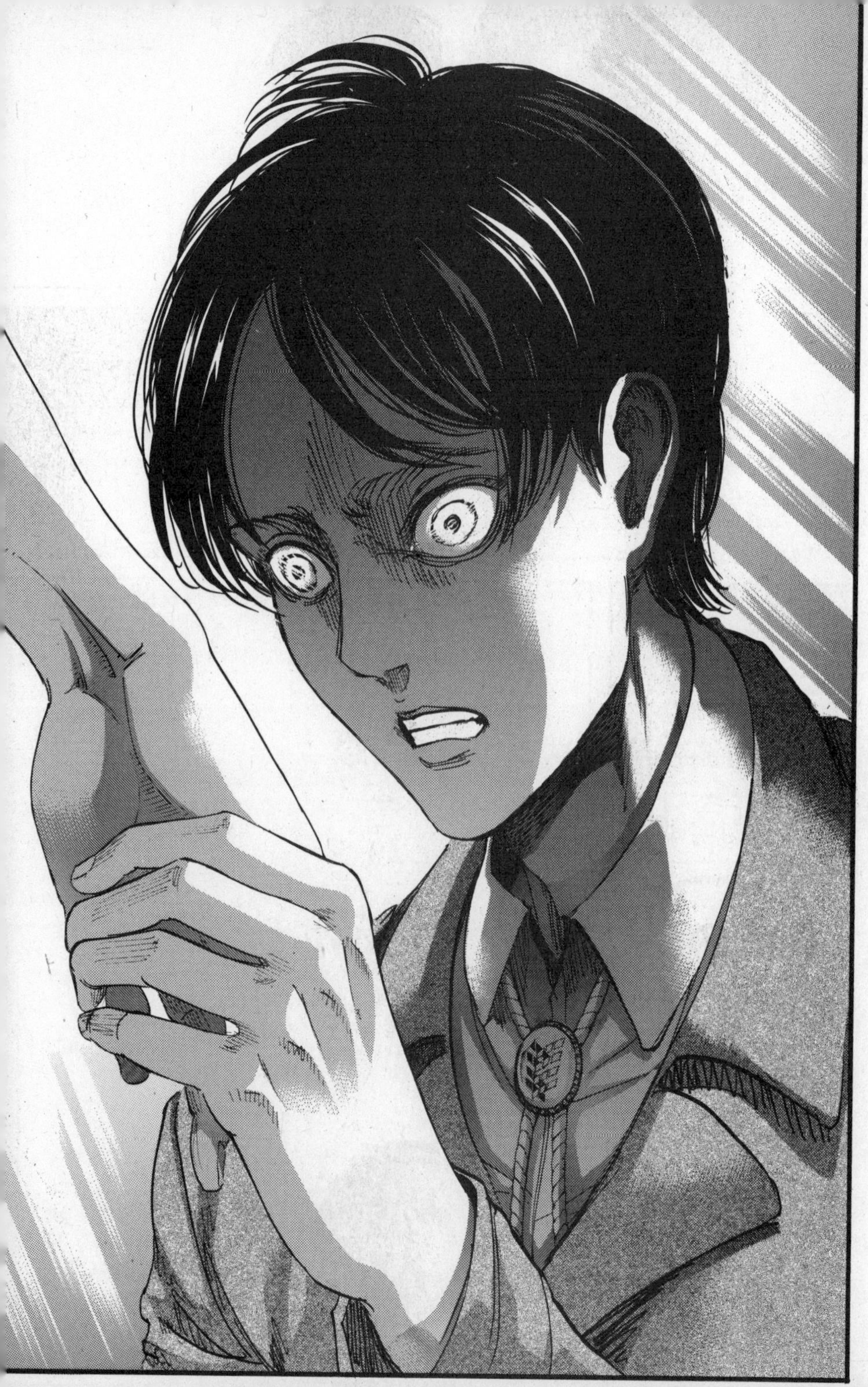

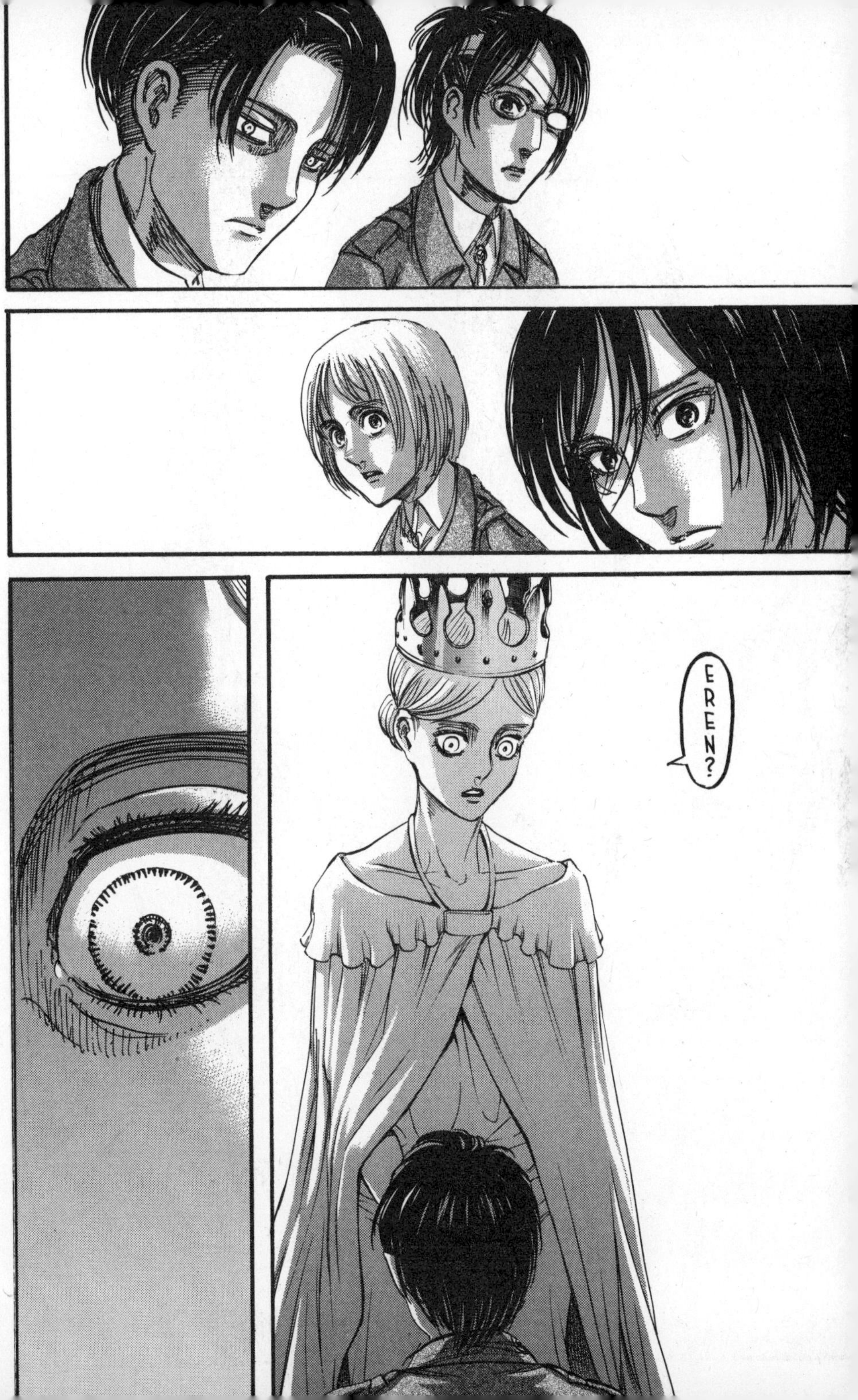
EREN?

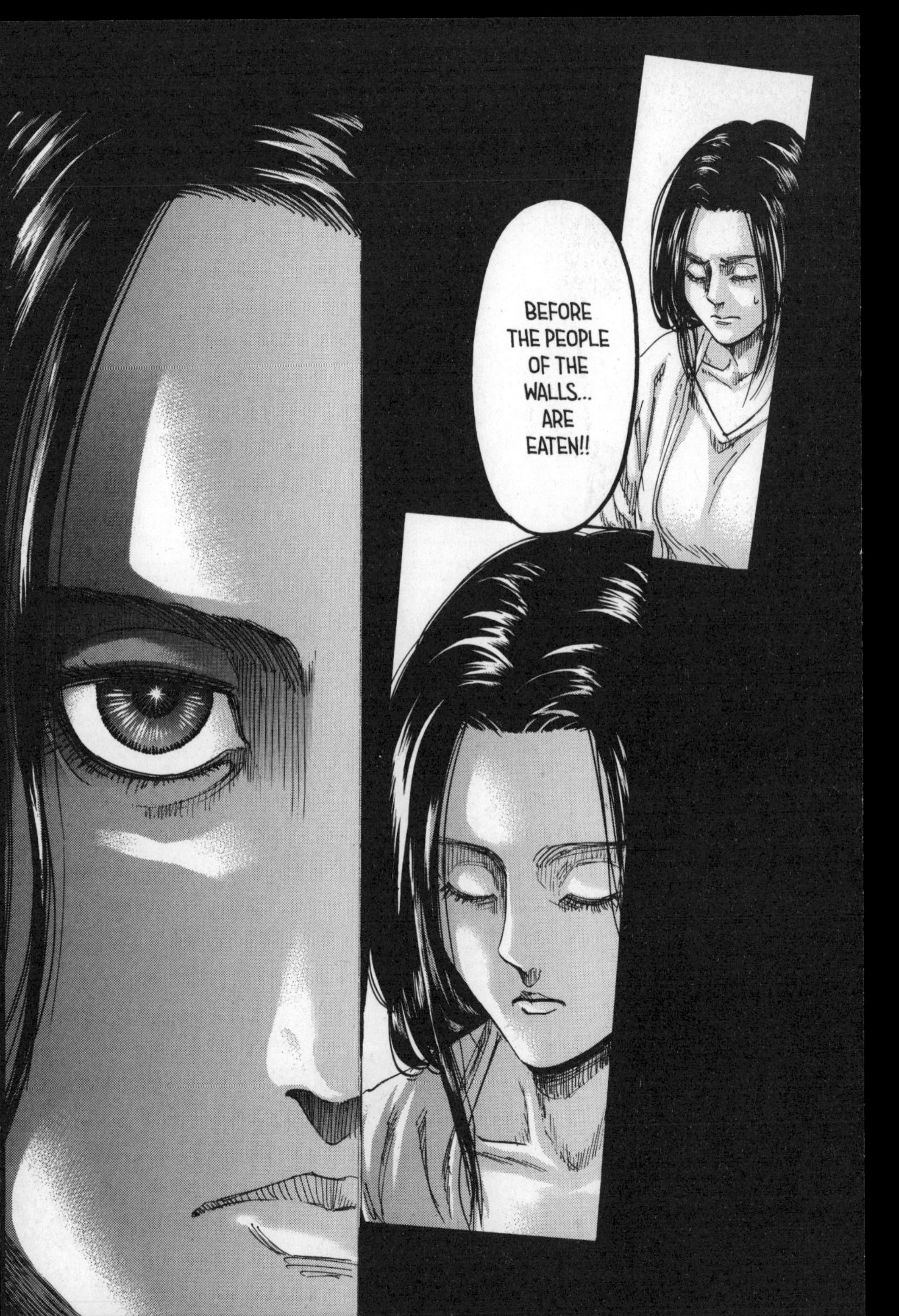
BEFORE THE PEOPLE OF THE WALLS... ARE EATEN!!

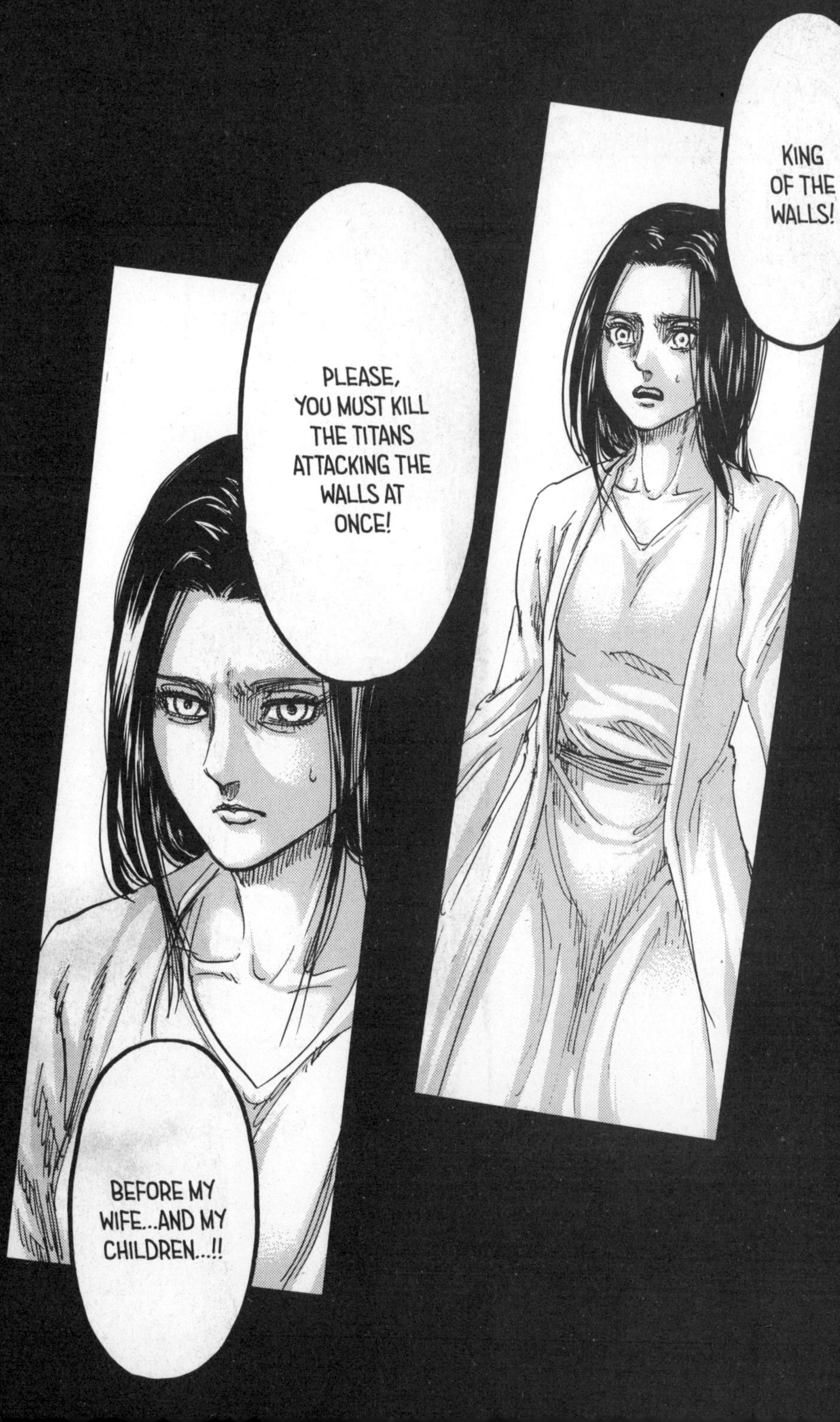
KING OF THE WALLS!
PLEASE, YOU MUST KILL THE TITANS ATTACKING THE WALLS AT ONCE!
BEFORE MY WIFE...AND MY CHILDREN...!!

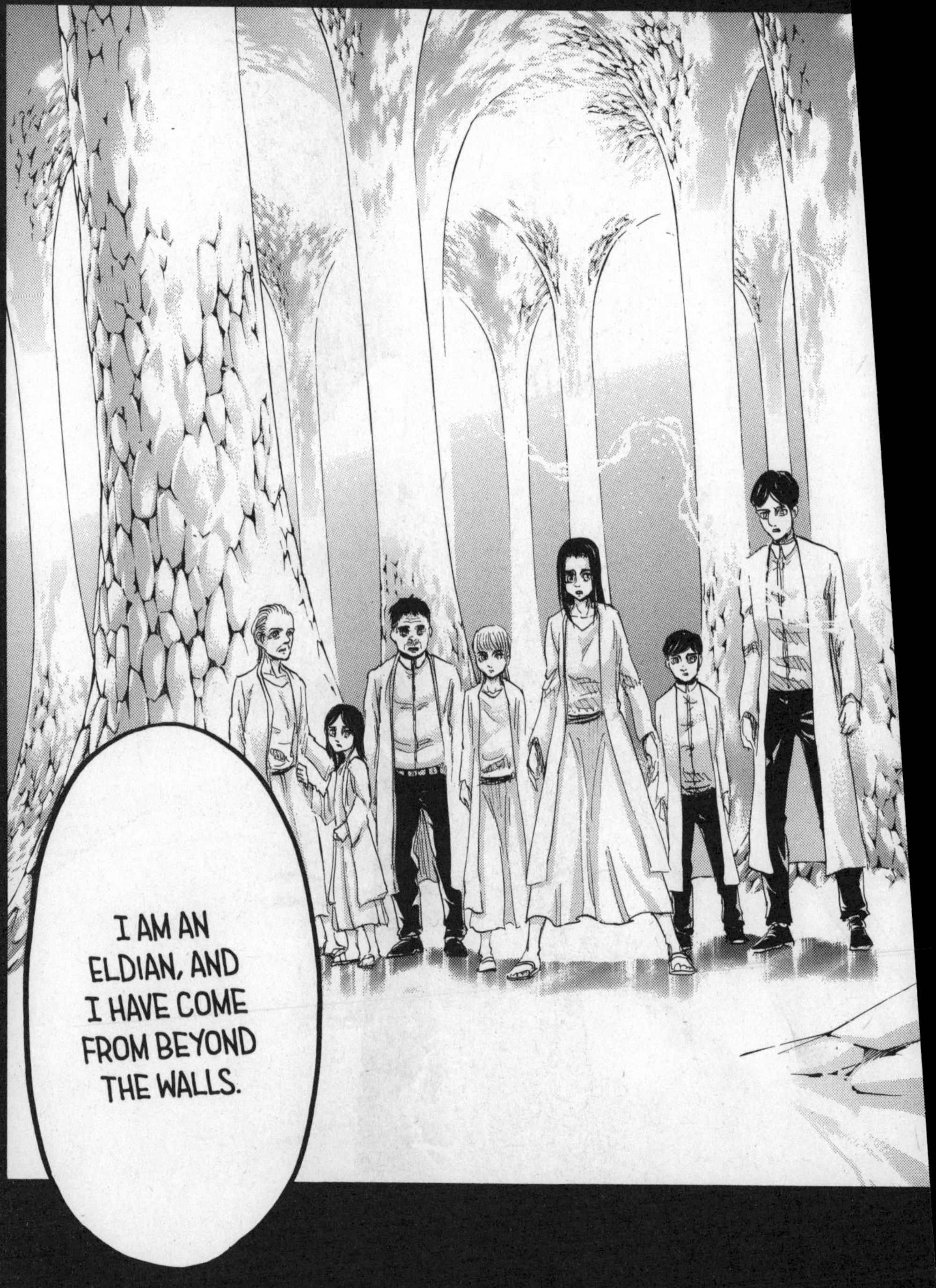
I AM AN ELDIAN, AND I HAVE COME FROM BEYOND THE WALLS.

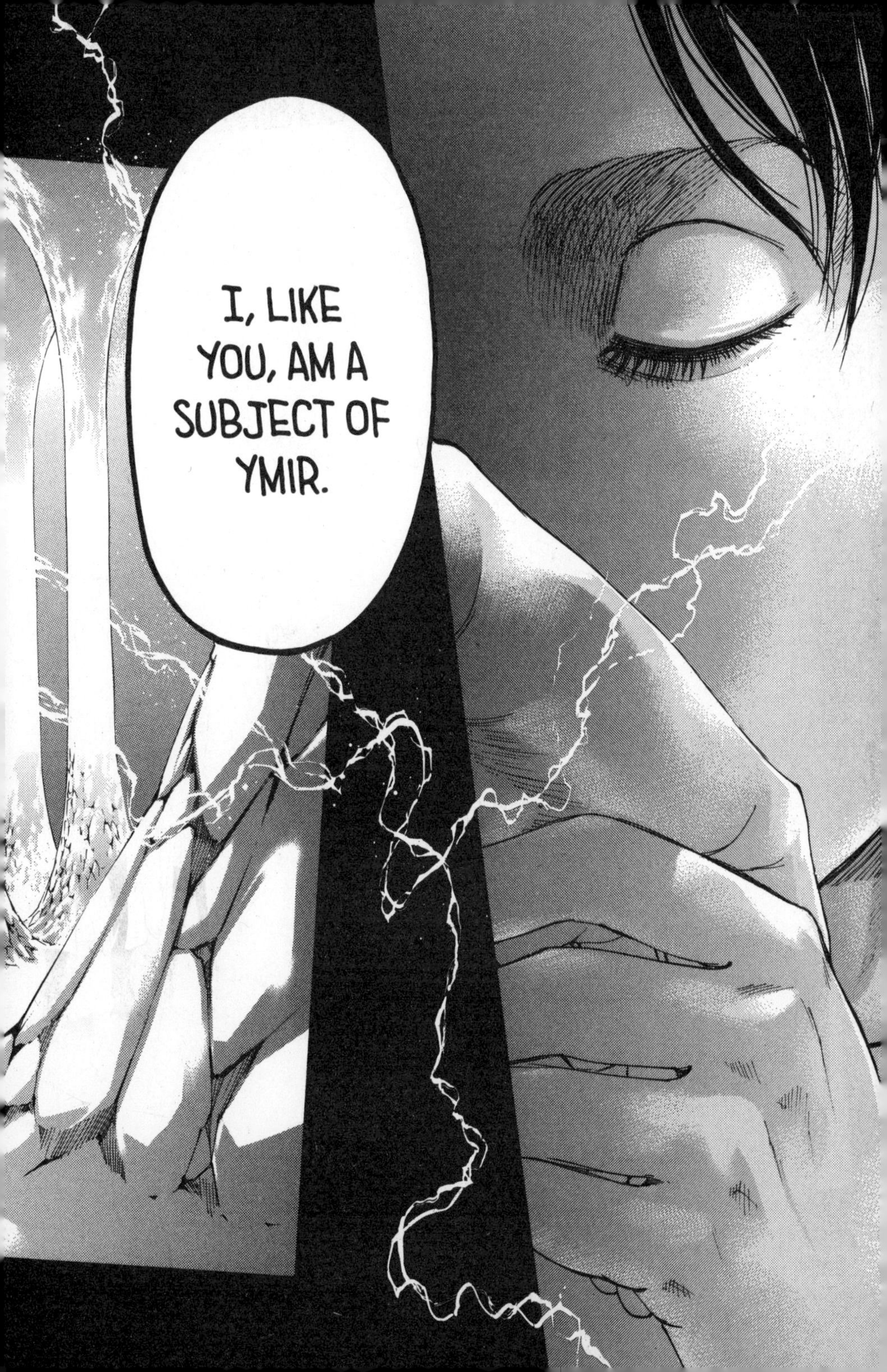
I, LIKE YOU, AM A SUBJECT OF YMIR.

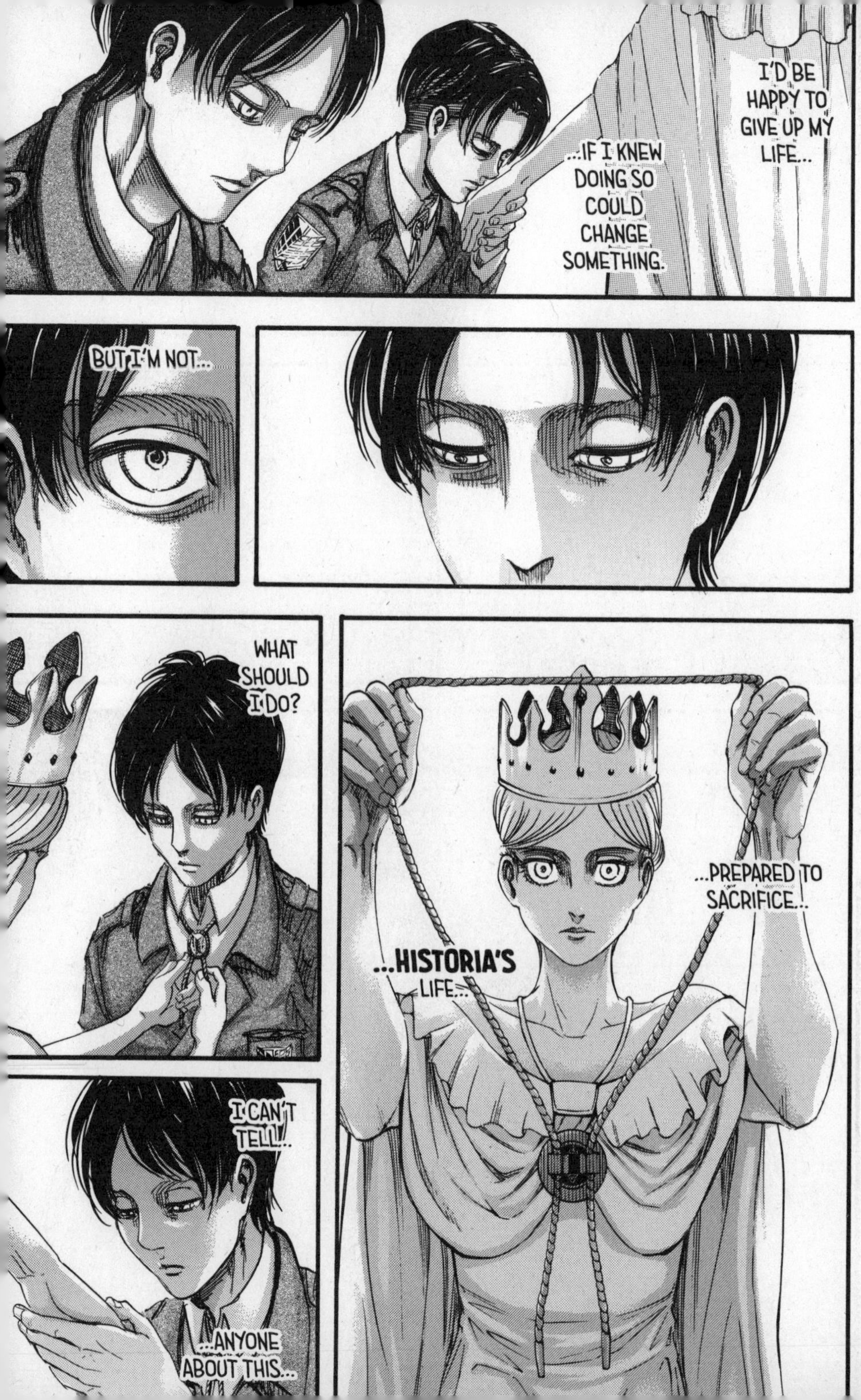
I'D BE HAPPY TO GIVE UP MY LIFE...
...IF I KNEW DOING SO COULD CHANGE SOMETHING.
BUT I'M NOT...
...PREPARED TO SACRIFICE...
...HISTORIA'S LIFE...
WHAT SHOULD I DO?
I CAN'T TELL...
...ANYONE ABOUT THIS...

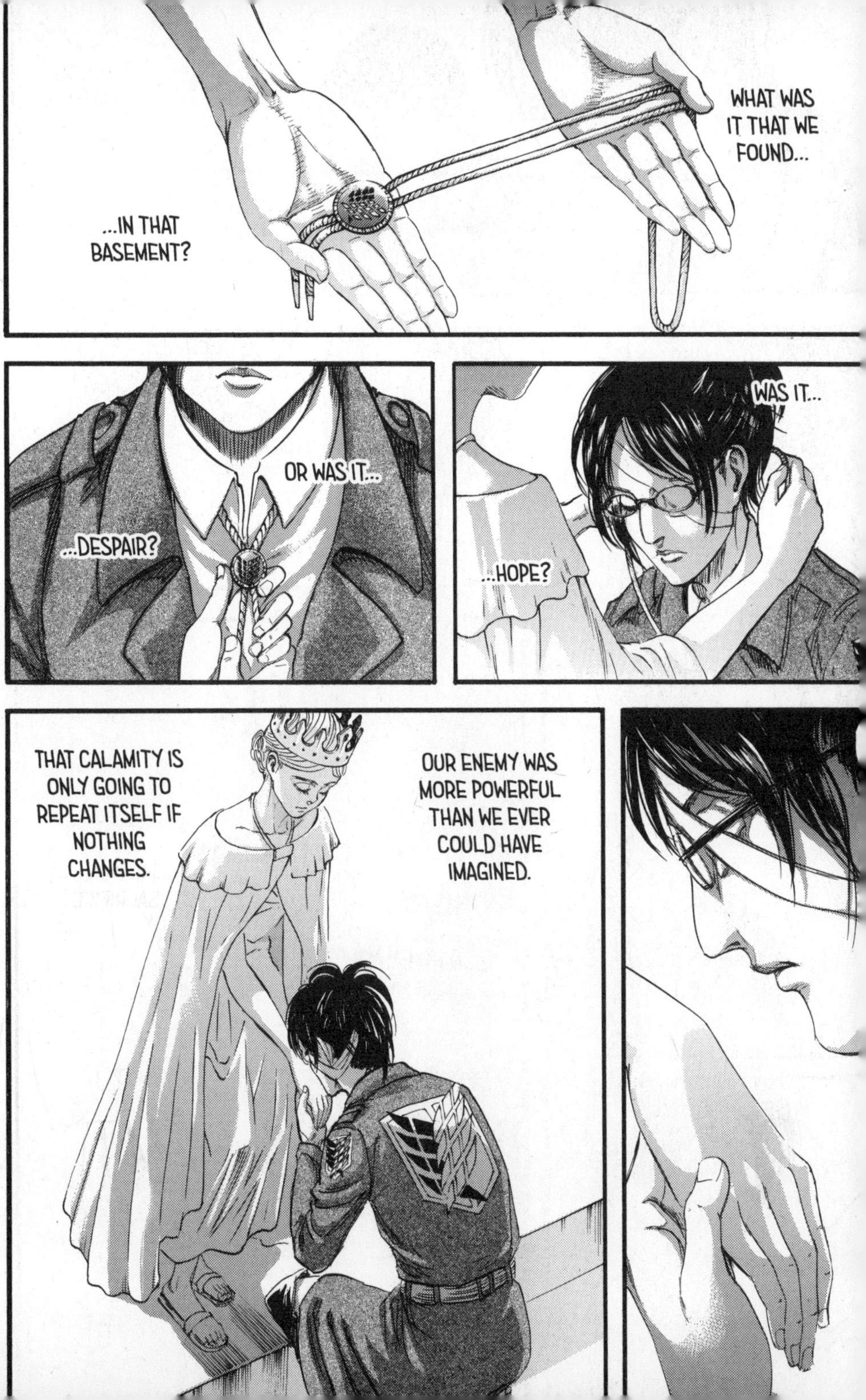
WHAT WAS IT THAT WE FOUND...
...IN THAT BASEMENT?
WAS IT...
...HOPE?
OR WAS IT...
...DESPAIR?
OUR ENEMY WAS MORE POWERFUL THAN WE EVER COULD HAVE IMAGINED.
THAT CALAMITY IS ONLY GOING TO REPEAT ITSELF IF NOTHING CHANGES.

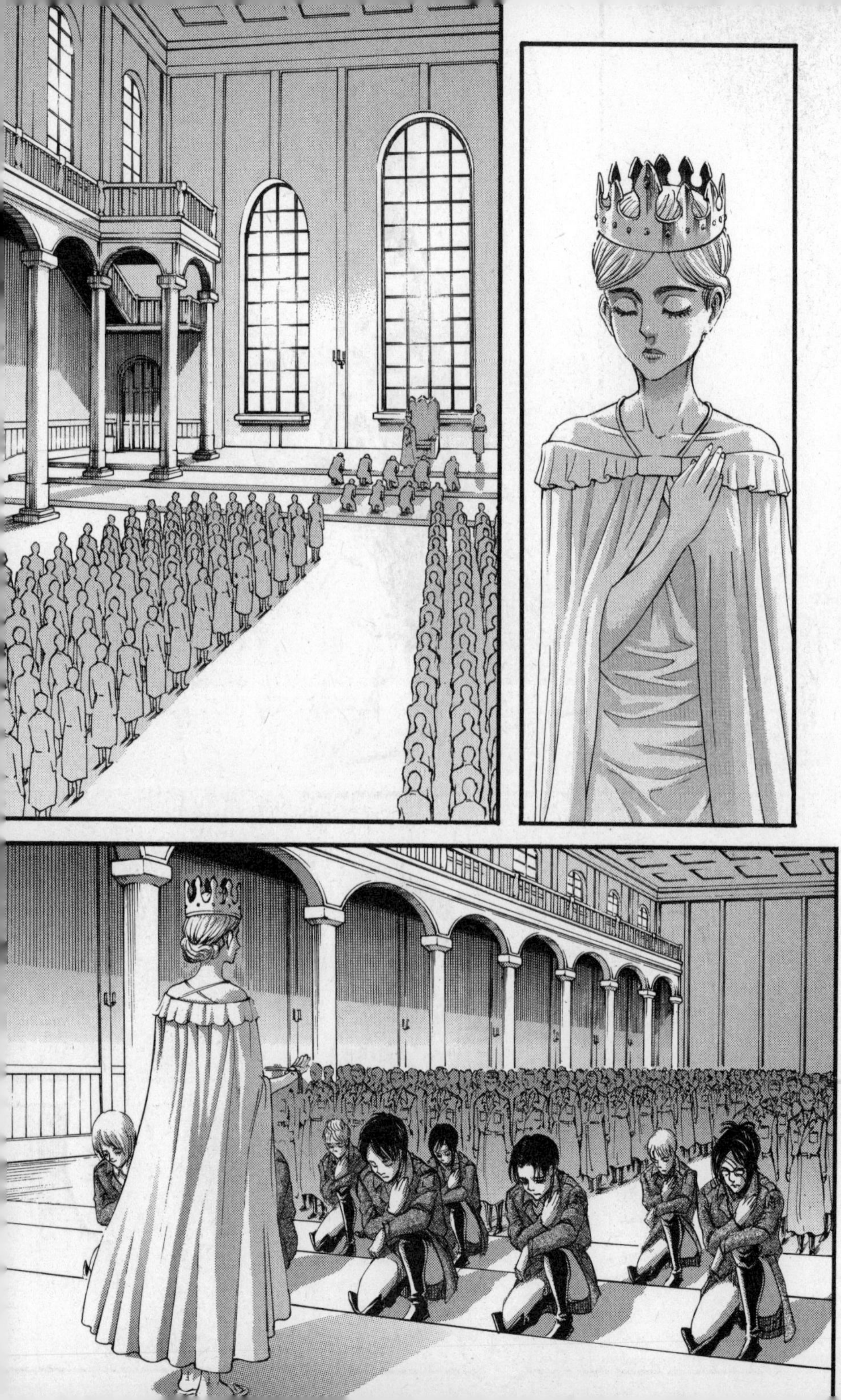

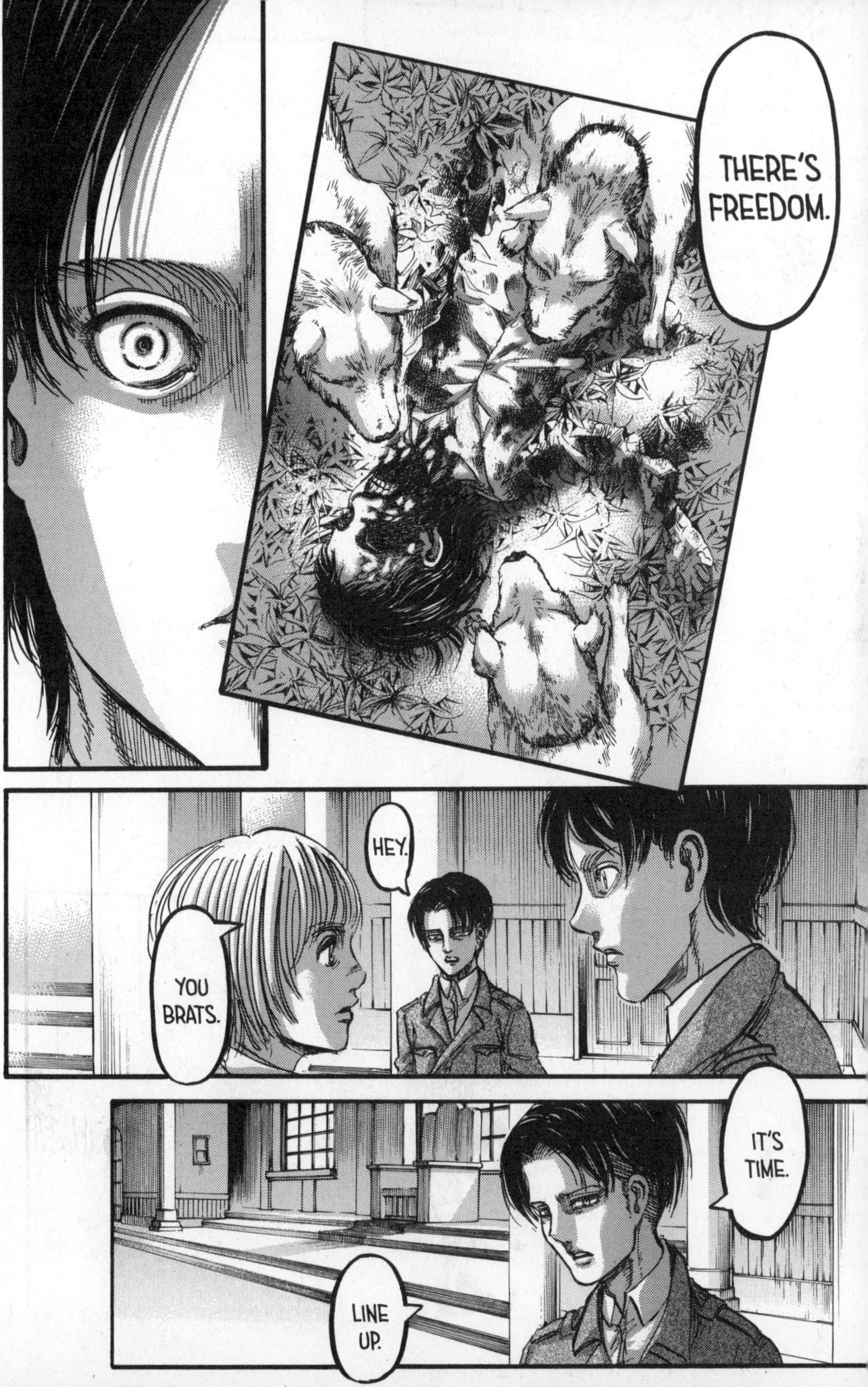
THERE'S FREEDOM.
HEY.
YOU BRATS.
IT'S TIME.
LINE UP.

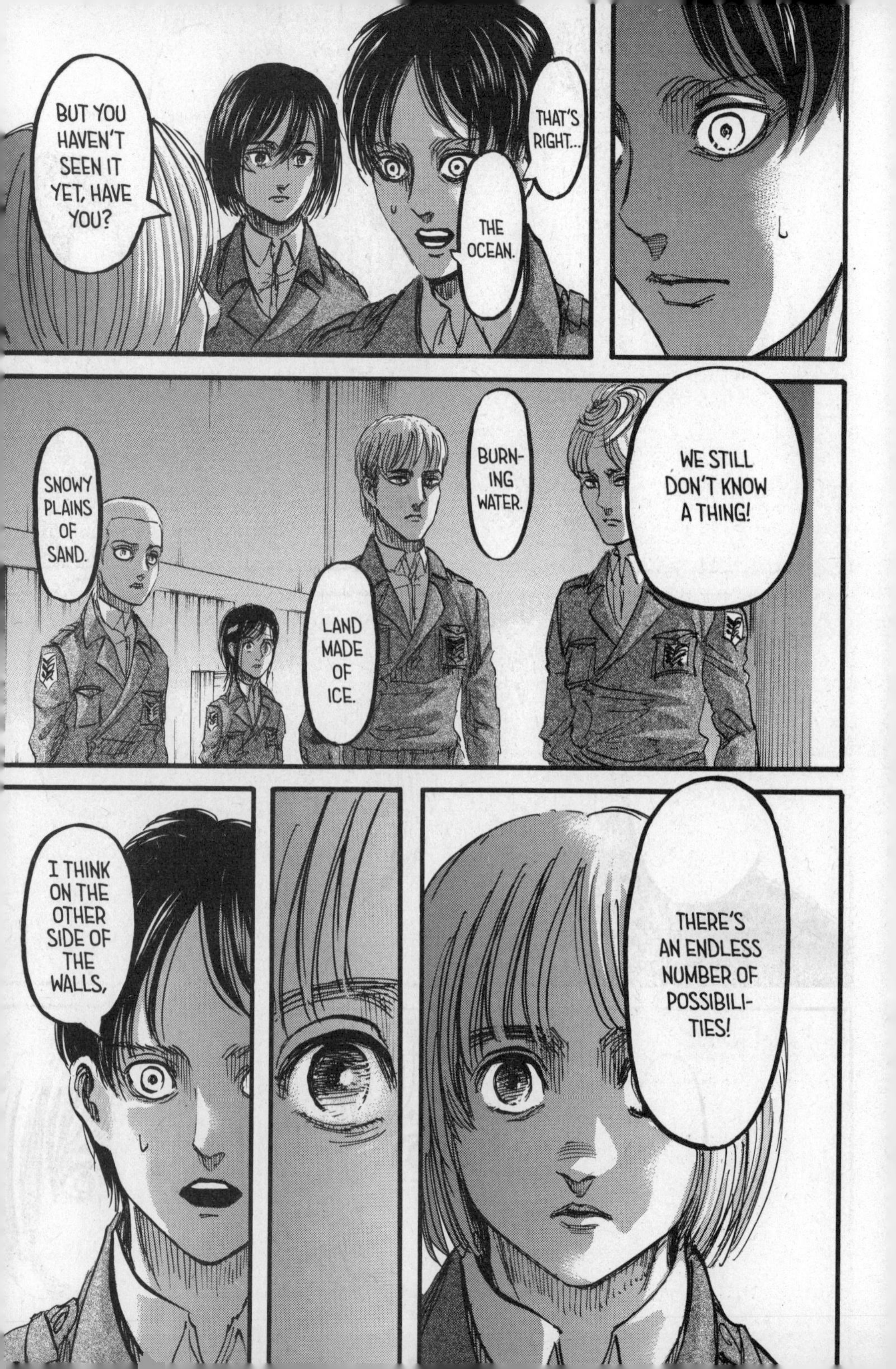
THAT'S RIGHT...
THE OCEAN.
BUT YOU HAVEN'T SEEN IT YET, HAVE YOU?
WE STILL DON'T KNOW A THING!
BURNING WATER.
LAND MADE OF ICE.
SNOWY PLAINS OF SAND.
THERE'S AN ENDLESS NUMBER OF POSSIBILITIES!
I THINK ON THE OTHER SIDE OF THE WALLS,

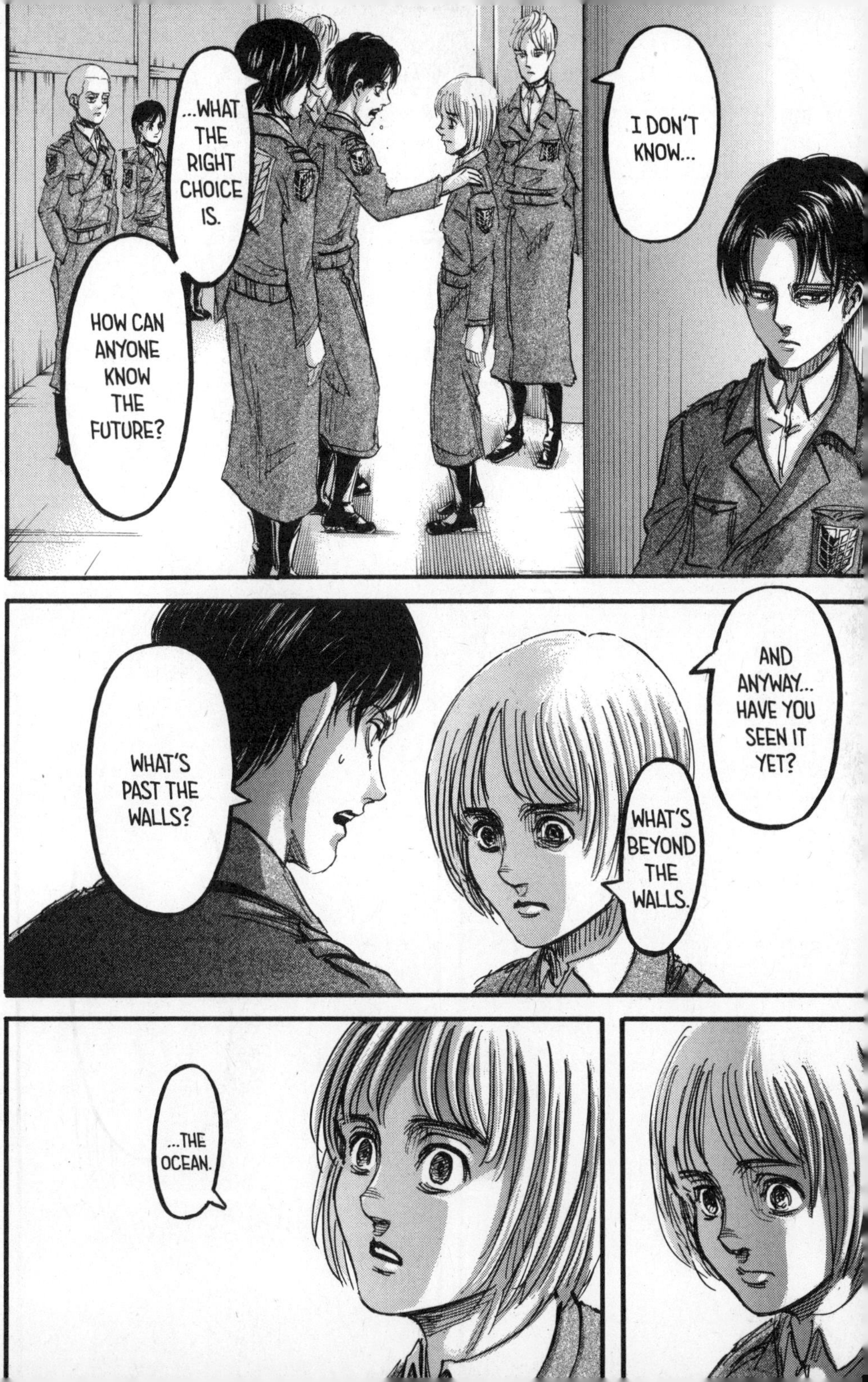
I DON'T KNOW...
...WHAT THE RIGHT CHOICE IS.
HOW CAN ANYONE KNOW THE FUTURE?
AND ANYWAY... HAVE YOU SEEN IT YET?
WHAT'S BEYOND THE WALLS.
WHAT'S PAST THE WALLS?
...THE OCEAN.

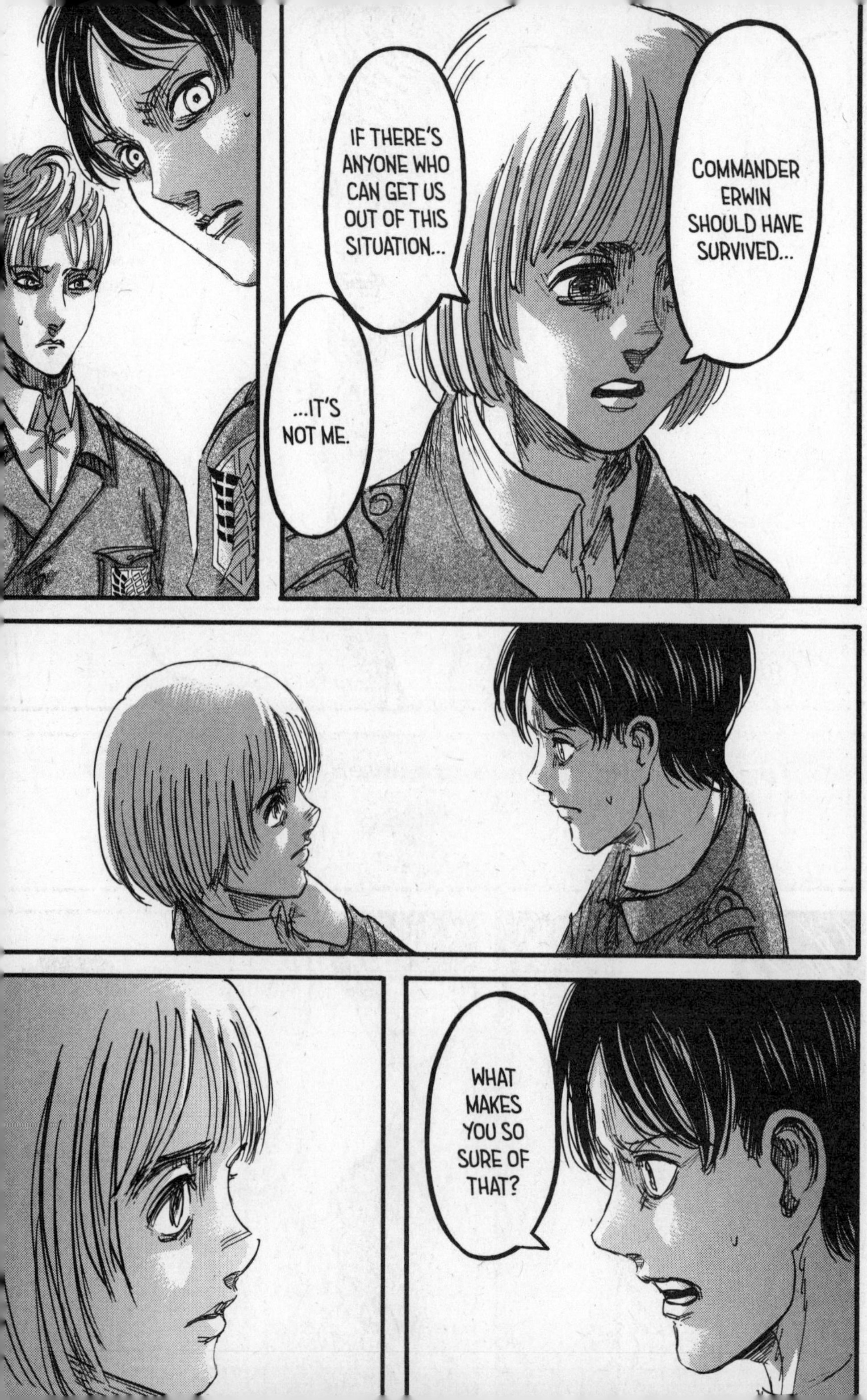
COMMANDER ERWIN SHOULD HAVE SURVIVED...
IF THERE'S ANYONE WHO CAN GET US OUT OF THIS SITUATION...
...IT'S NOT ME.
WHAT MAKES YOU SO SURE OF THAT?

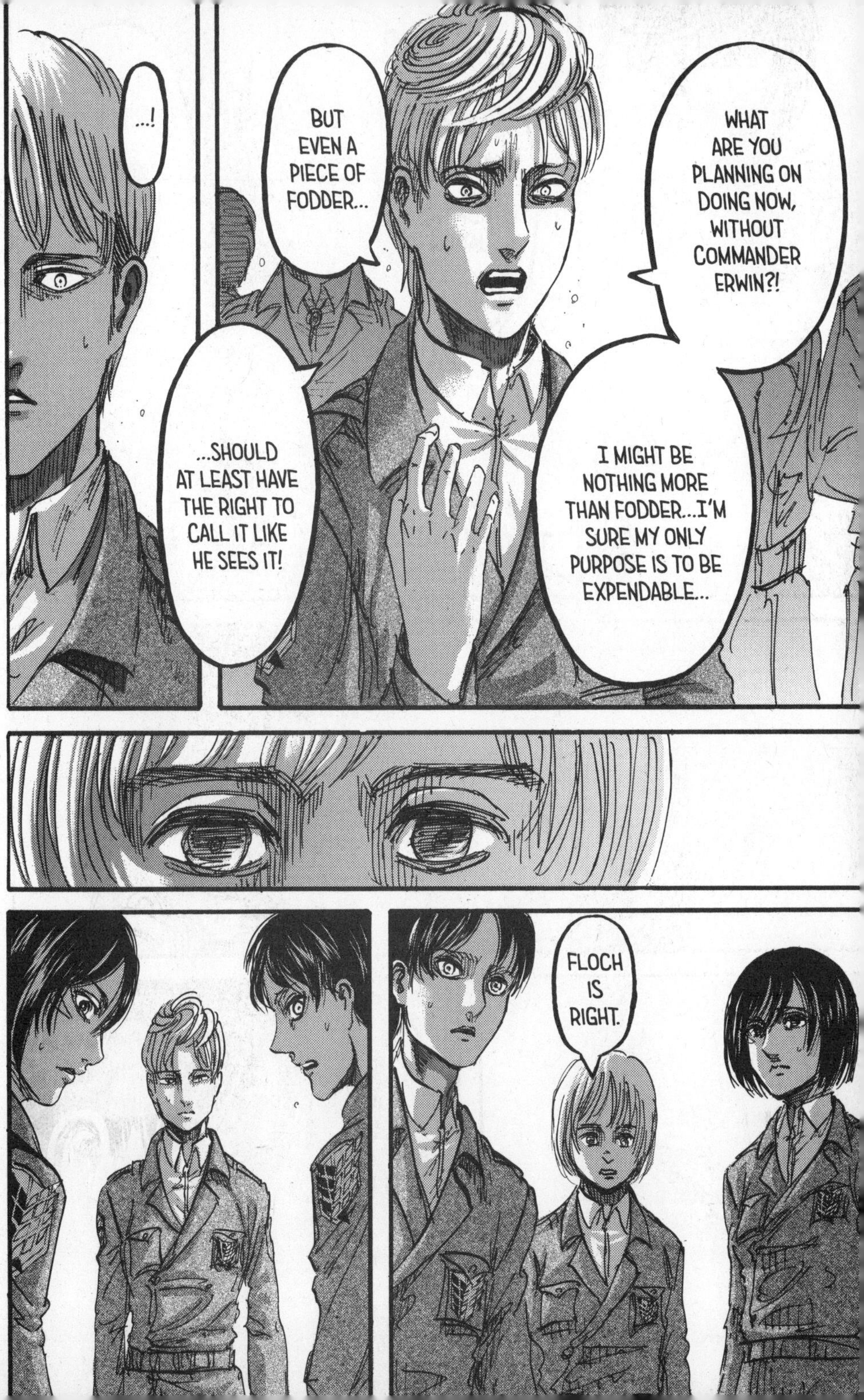
WHAT ARE YOU PLANNING ON DOING NOW, WITHOUT COMMANDER ERWIN?!
I MIGHT BE NOTHING MORE THAN FODDER...I'M SURE MY ONLY PURPOSE IS TO BE EXPENDABLE...
BUT EVEN A PIECE OF FODDER...
...SHOULD AT LEAST HAVE THE RIGHT TO CALL IT LIKE HE SEES IT!
...!
FLOCH IS RIGHT.

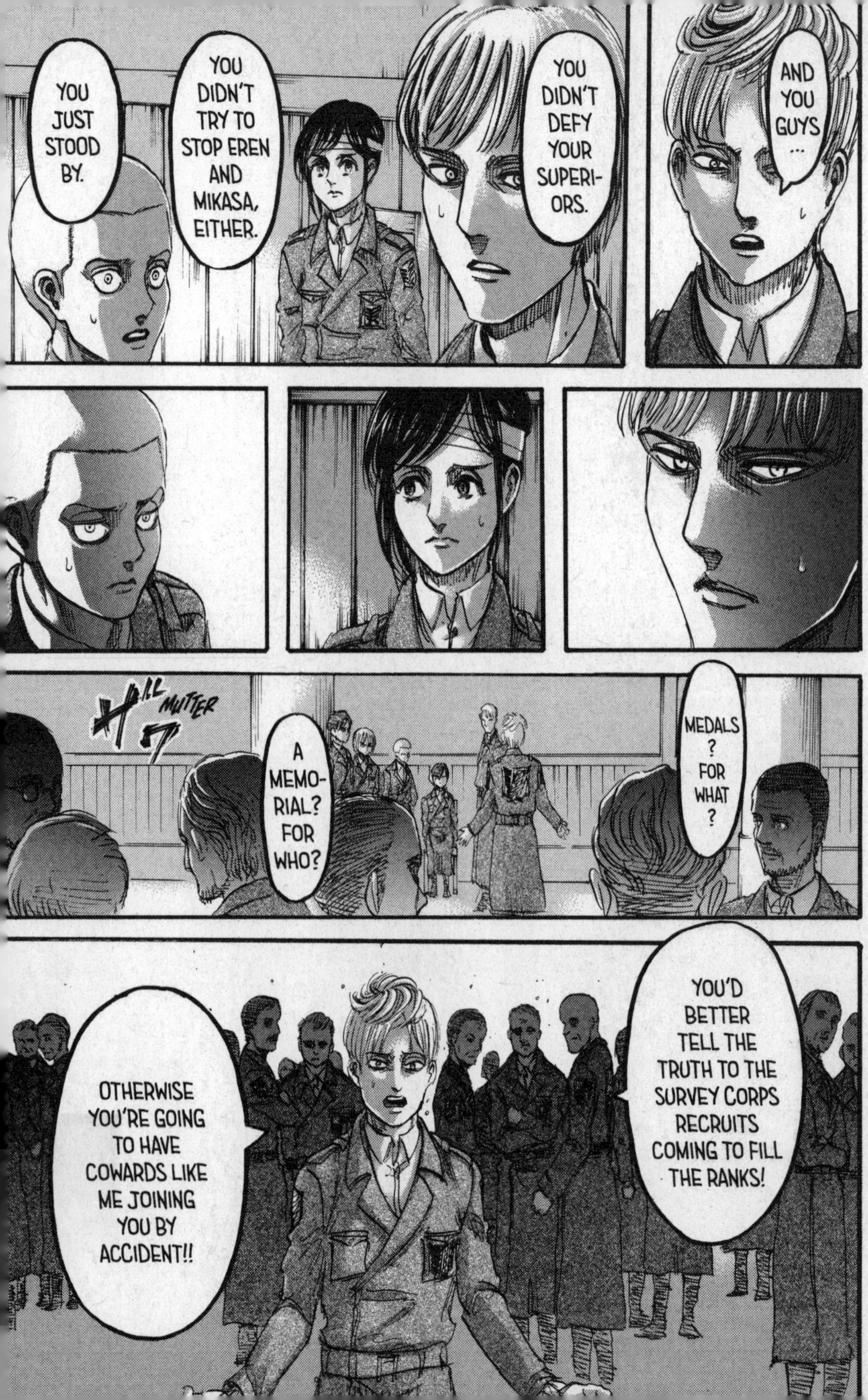
AND YOU GUYS ...
YOU DIDN'T DEFY YOUR SUPERIORS.
YOU DIDN'T TRY TO STOP EREN AND MIKASA, EITHER.
YOU JUST STOOD BY.
MEDALS? FOR WHAT?
A MEMORIAL? FOR WHO?
MUTTER
YOU'D BETTER TELL THE TRUTH TO THE SURVEY CORPS RECRUITS COMING TO FILL THE RANKS!
OTHERWISE YOU'RE GOING TO HAVE COWARDS LIKE ME JOINING YOU BY ACCIDENT!!

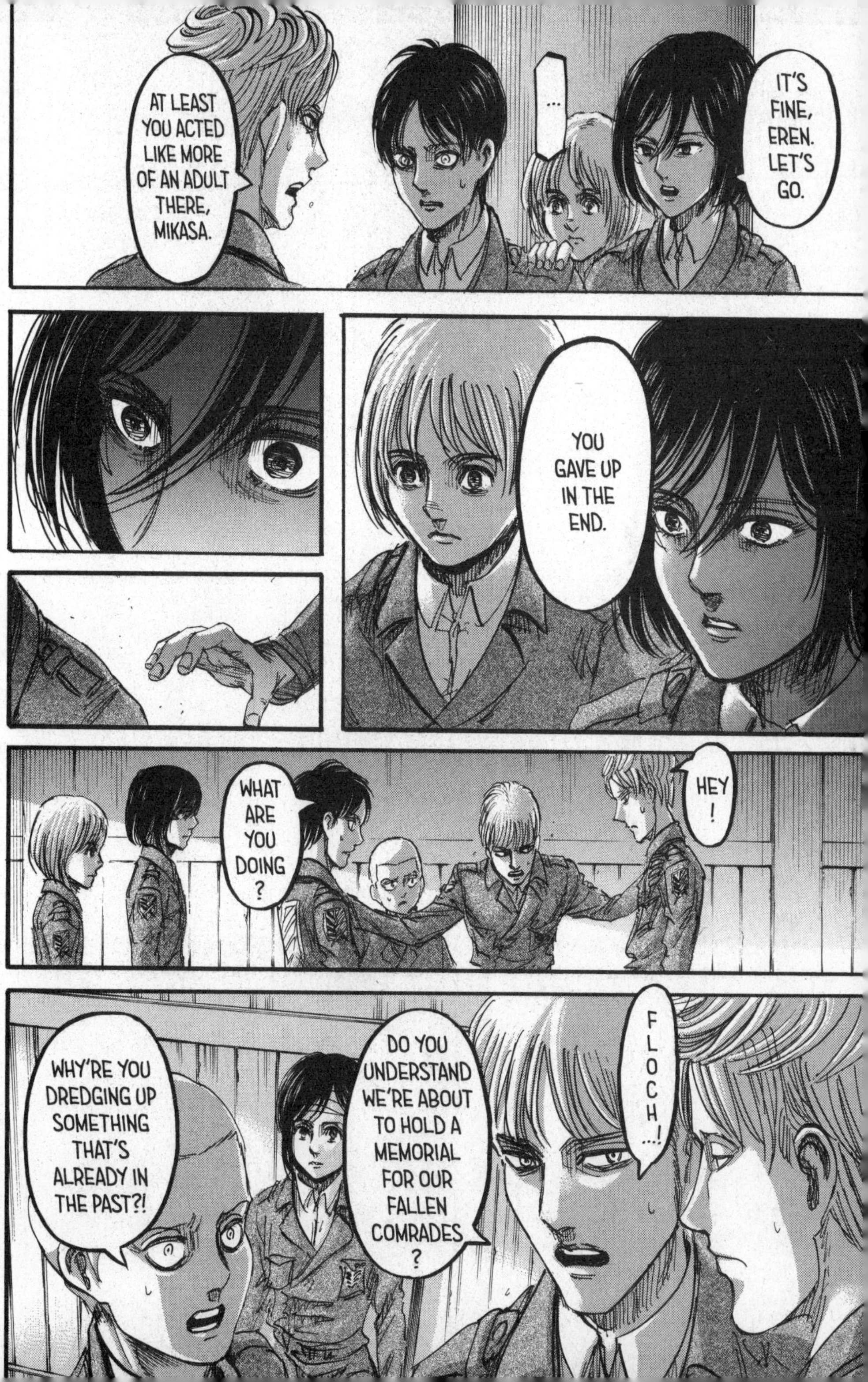
IT'S FINE, EREN. LET'S GO.
...
AT LEAST YOU ACTED LIKE MORE OF AN ADULT THERE, MIKASA.
YOU GAVE UP IN THE END.
HEY!
WHAT ARE YOU DOING?
FLOCH...!
DO YOU UNDERSTAND WE'RE ABOUT TO HOLD A MEMORIAL FOR OUR FALLEN COMRADES?
WHY'RE YOU DREDGING UP SOMETHING THAT'S ALREADY IN THE PAST?!

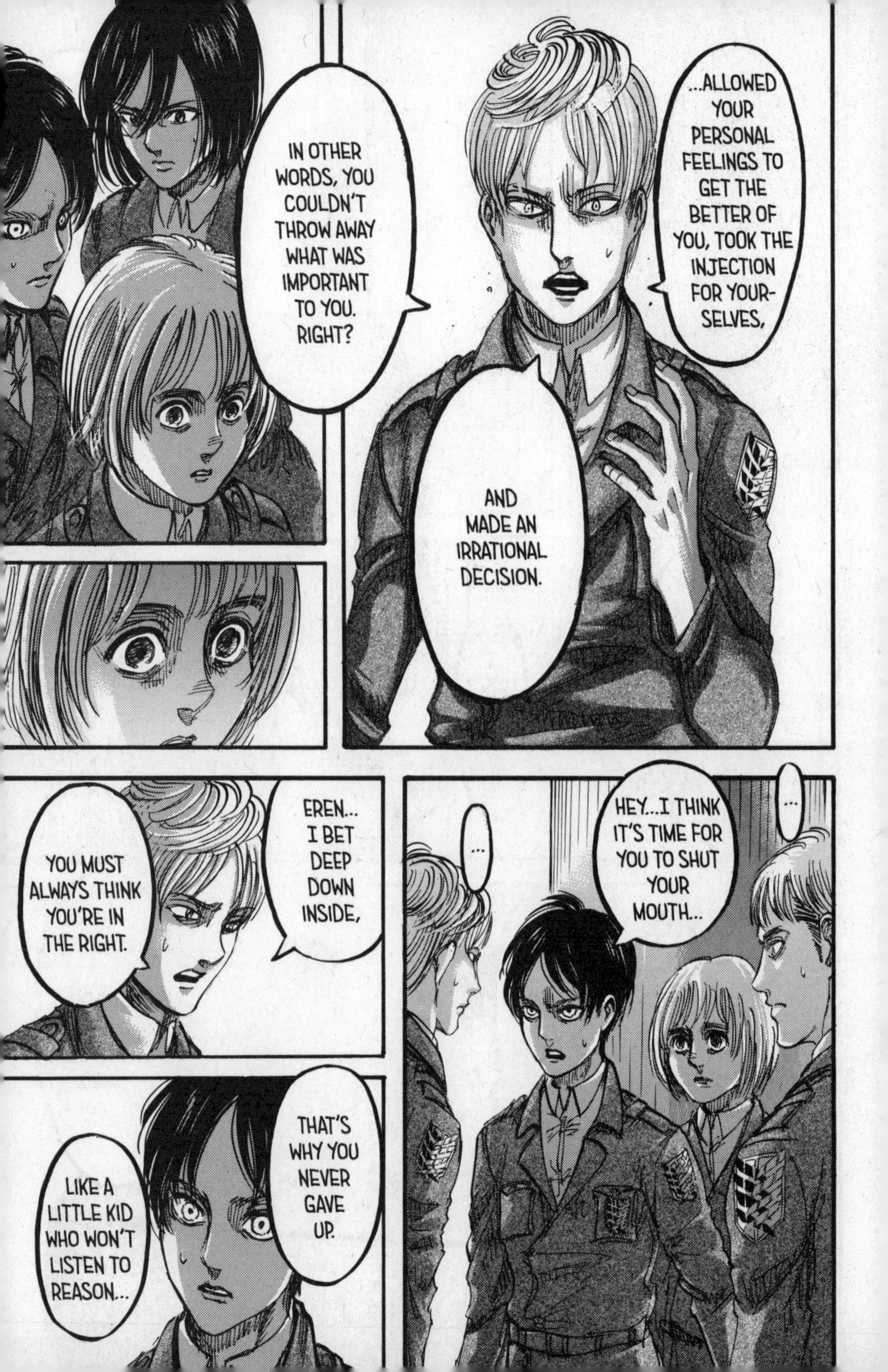
...ALLOWED YOUR PERSONAL FEELINGS TO GET THE BETTER OF YOU, TOOK THE INJECTION FOR YOUR-SELVES,
AND MADE AN IRRATIONAL DECISION.
IN OTHER WORDS, YOU COULDN'T THROW AWAY WHAT WAS IMPORTANT TO YOU. RIGHT?
...
HEY...I THINK IT'S TIME FOR YOU TO SHUT YOUR MOUTH...
...
EREN... I BET DEEP DOWN INSIDE,
YOU MUST ALWAYS THINK YOU'RE IN THE RIGHT.
THAT'S WHY YOU NEVER GAVE UP.
LIKE A LITTLE KID WHO WON'T LISTEN TO REASON...

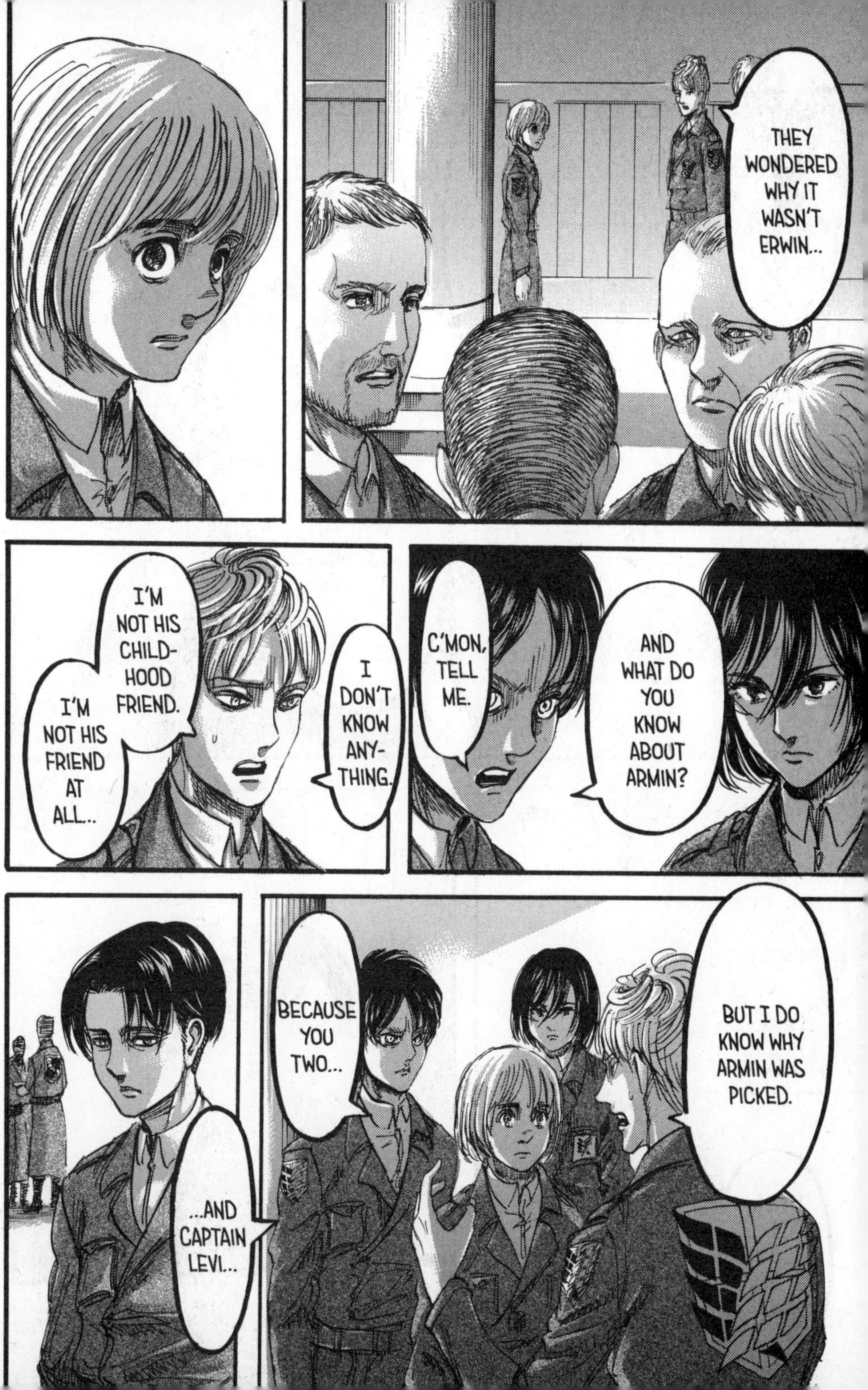
THEY WONDERED WHY IT WASN'T ERWIN...
AND WHAT DO YOU KNOW ABOUT ARMIN?
C'MON, TELL ME.
I DON'T KNOW ANY-THING.
I'M NOT HIS CHILD-HOOD FRIEND.
I'M NOT HIS FRIEND AT ALL...
BUT I DO KNOW WHY ARMIN WAS PICKED.
BECAUSE YOU TWO...
...AND CAPTAIN LEVI...

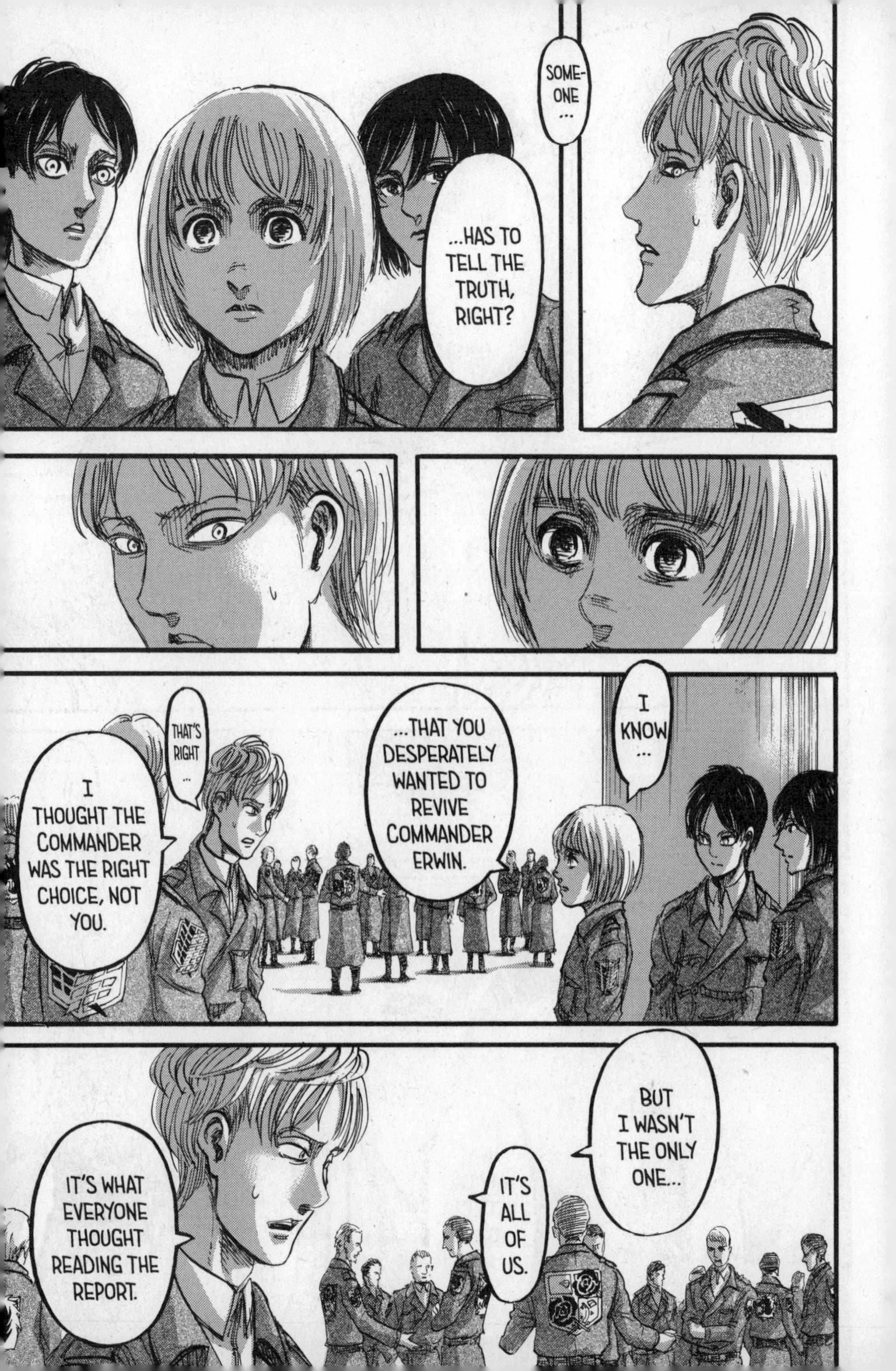
SOME-ONE ...
...HAS TO TELL THE TRUTH, RIGHT?
I KNOW ...
...THAT YOU DESPERATELY WANTED TO REVIVE COMMANDER ERWIN.
THAT'S RIGHT ...
I THOUGHT THE COMMANDER WAS THE RIGHT CHOICE, NOT YOU.
BUT I WASN'T THE ONLY ONE...
IT'S ALL OF US.
IT'S WHAT EVERYONE THOUGHT READING THE REPORT.

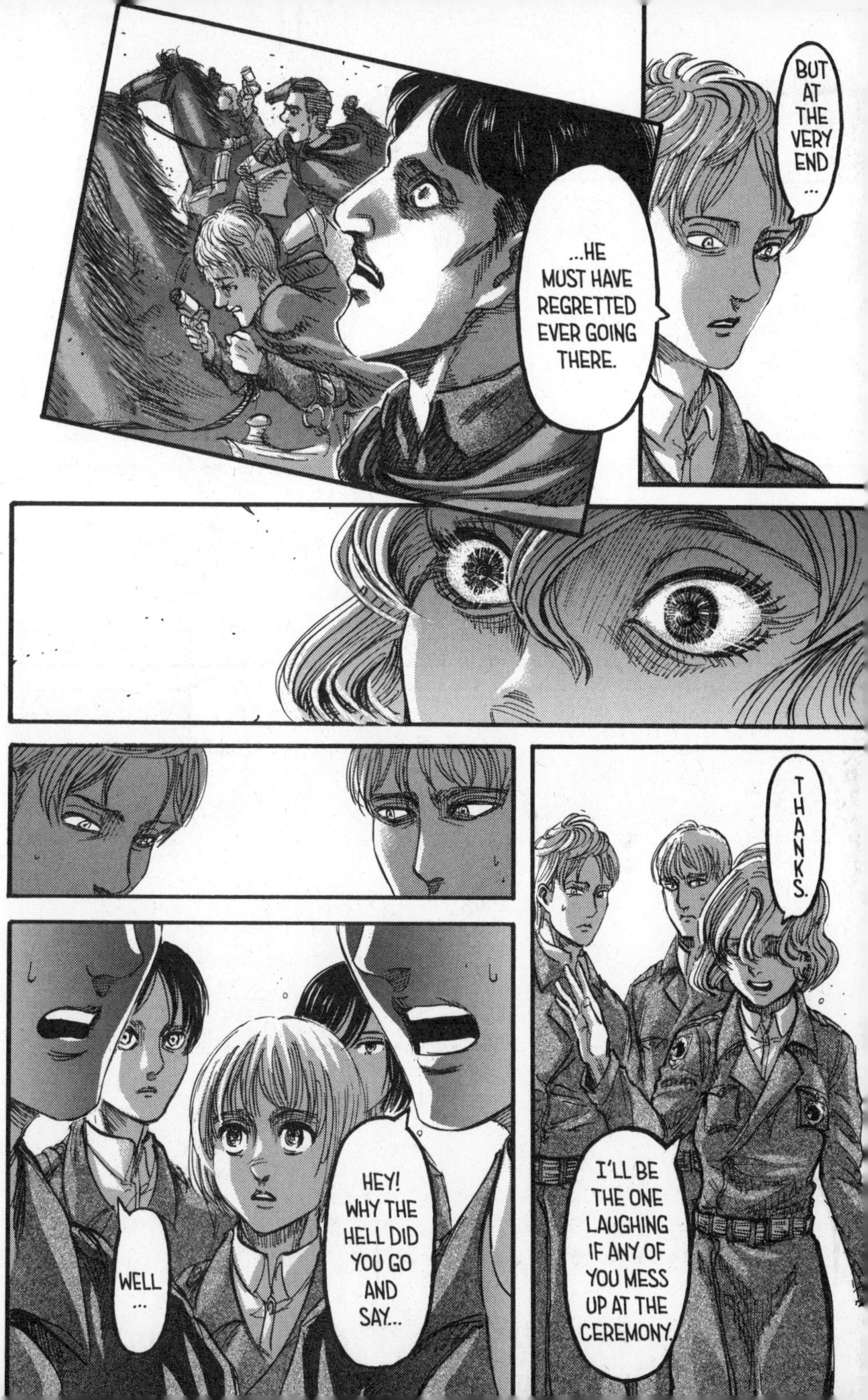
BUT AT THE VERY END ...
...HE MUST HAVE REGRETTED EVER GOING THERE.
THANKS.
I'LL BE THE ONE LAUGHING IF ANY OF YOU MESS UP AT THE CEREMONY.
HEY! WHY THE HELL DID YOU GO AND SAY...
WELL ...

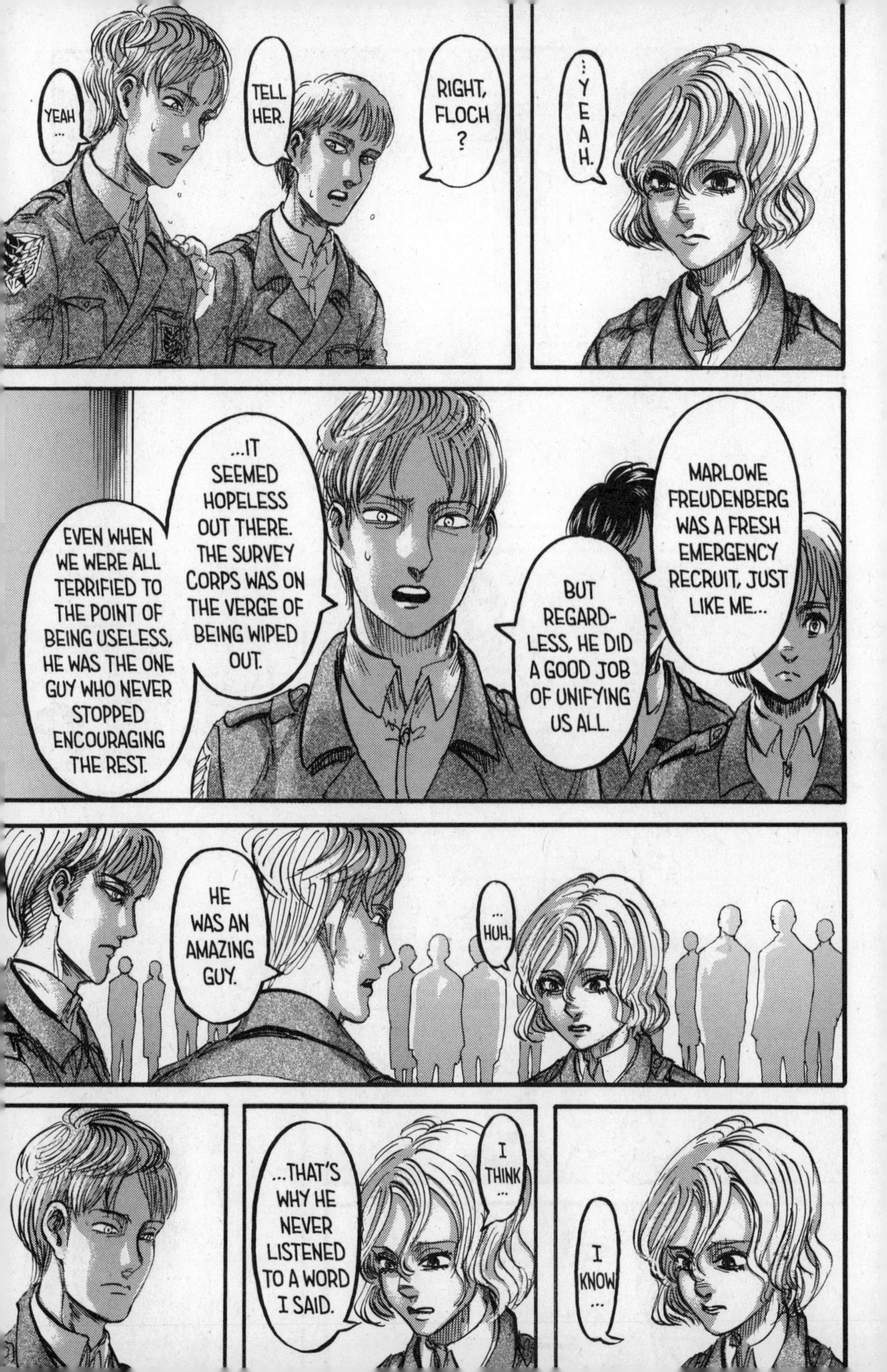
...YEAH.
RIGHT, FLOCH?
TELL HER.
YEAH...
MARLOWE FREUDENBERG WAS A FRESH EMERGENCY RECRUIT, JUST LIKE ME...
BUT REGARDLESS, HE DID A GOOD JOB OF UNIFYING US ALL.
...IT SEEMED HOPELESS OUT THERE. THE SURVEY CORPS WAS ON THE VERGE OF BEING WIPED OUT.
EVEN WHEN WE WERE ALL TERRIFIED TO THE POINT OF BEING USELESS, HE WAS THE ONE GUY WHO NEVER STOPPED ENCOURAGING THE REST.
...HUH.
HE WAS AN AMAZING GUY.
I KNOW...
I THINK...
...THAT'S WHY HE NEVER LISTENED TO A WORD I SAID.

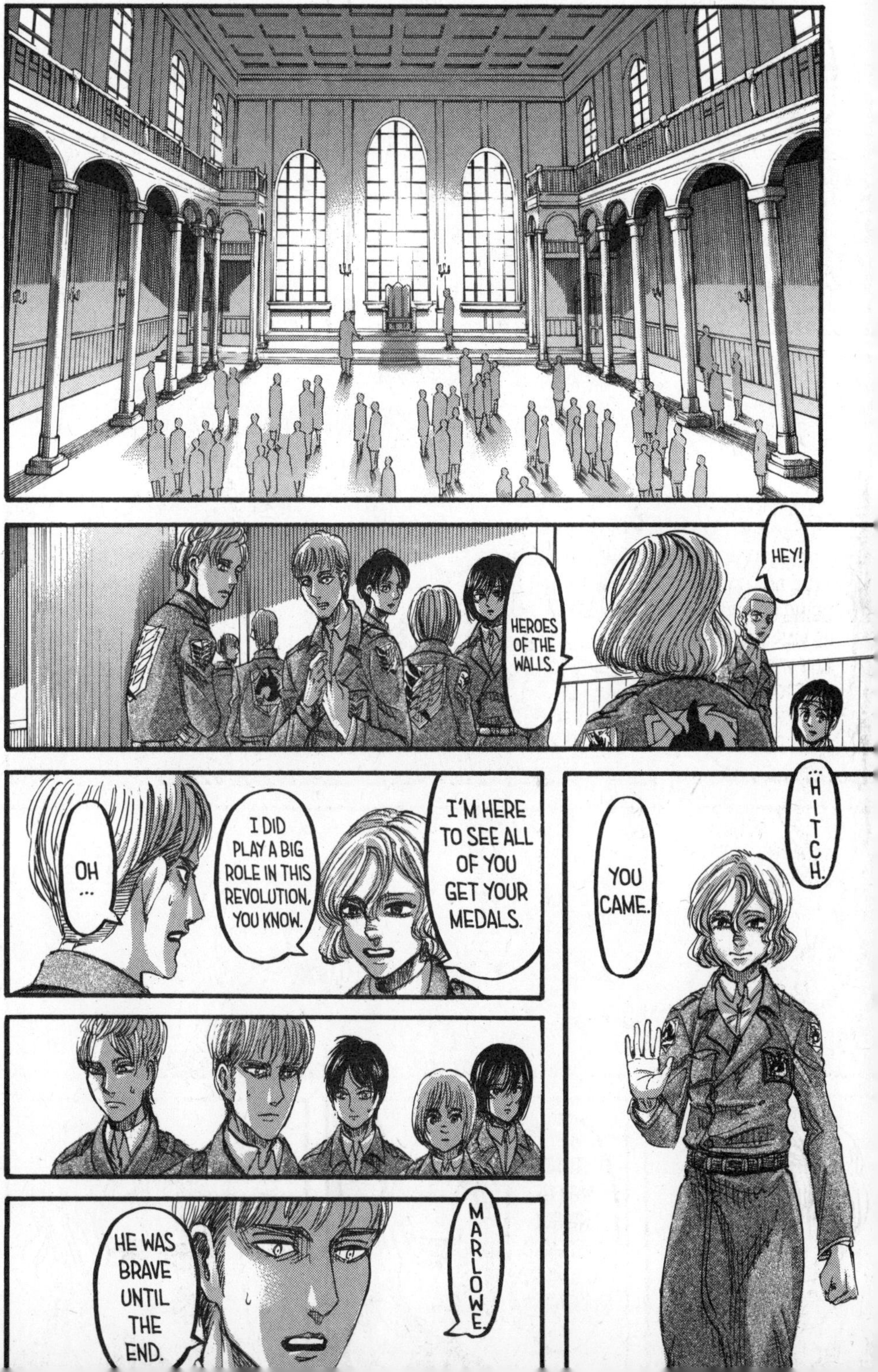
HEY!
HEROES OF THE WALLS.
...HITCH.
YOU CAME.
I'M HERE TO SEE ALL OF YOU GET YOUR MEDALS.
I DID PLAY A BIG ROLE IN THIS REVOLUTION, YOU KNOW.
OH ...
MARLOWE.
HE WAS BRAVE UNTIL THE END.

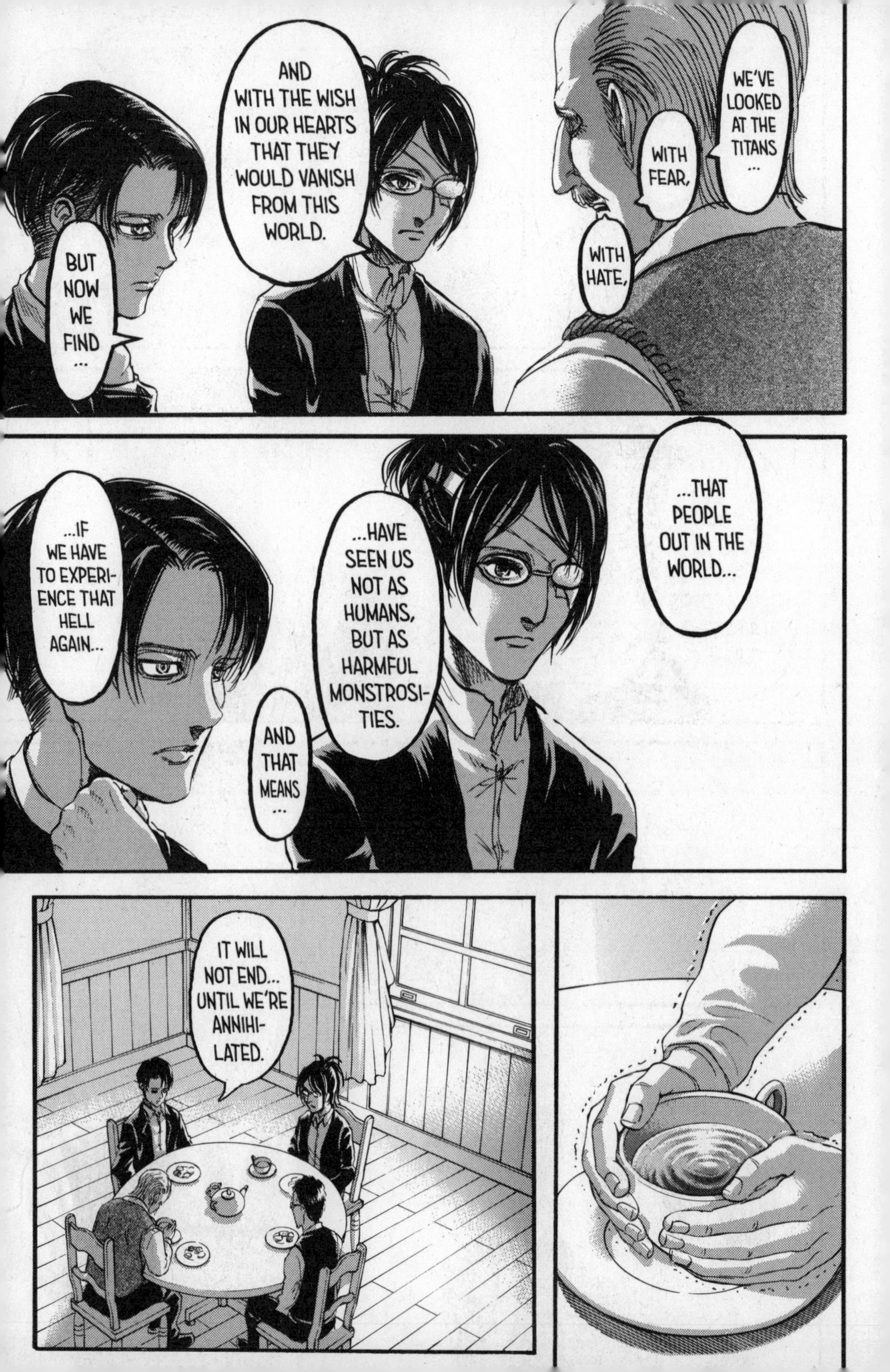
WE'VE LOOKED AT THE TITANS ...
WITH FEAR,
WITH HATE,
AND WITH THE WISH IN OUR HEARTS THAT THEY WOULD VANISH FROM THIS WORLD.
BUT NOW WE FIND ...
...THAT PEOPLE OUT IN THE WORLD...
...HAVE SEEN US NOT AS HUMANS, BUT AS HARMFUL MONSTROSI-TIES.
AND THAT MEANS ...
...IF WE HAVE TO EXPERI-ENCE THAT HELL AGAIN...
IT WILL NOT END... UNTIL WE'RE ANNIHI-LATED.

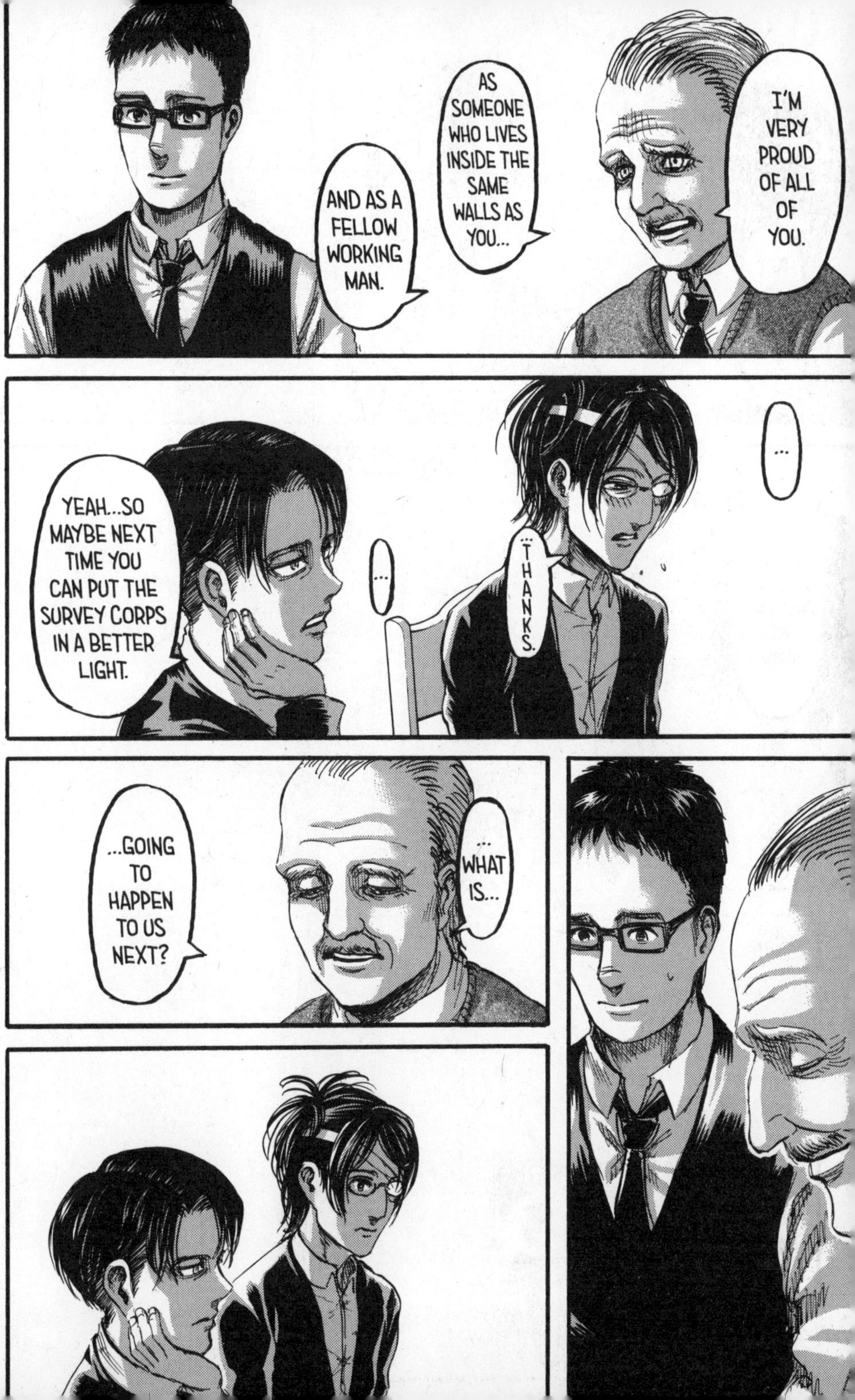
I'M VERY PROUD OF ALL OF YOU.
AS SOMEONE WHO LIVES INSIDE THE SAME WALLS AS YOU...
AND AS A FELLOW WORKING MAN.
...
...THANKS.
...
YEAH...SO MAYBE NEXT TIME YOU CAN PUT THE SURVEY CORPS IN A BETTER LIGHT.
...WHAT IS...
...GOING TO HAPPEN TO US NEXT?

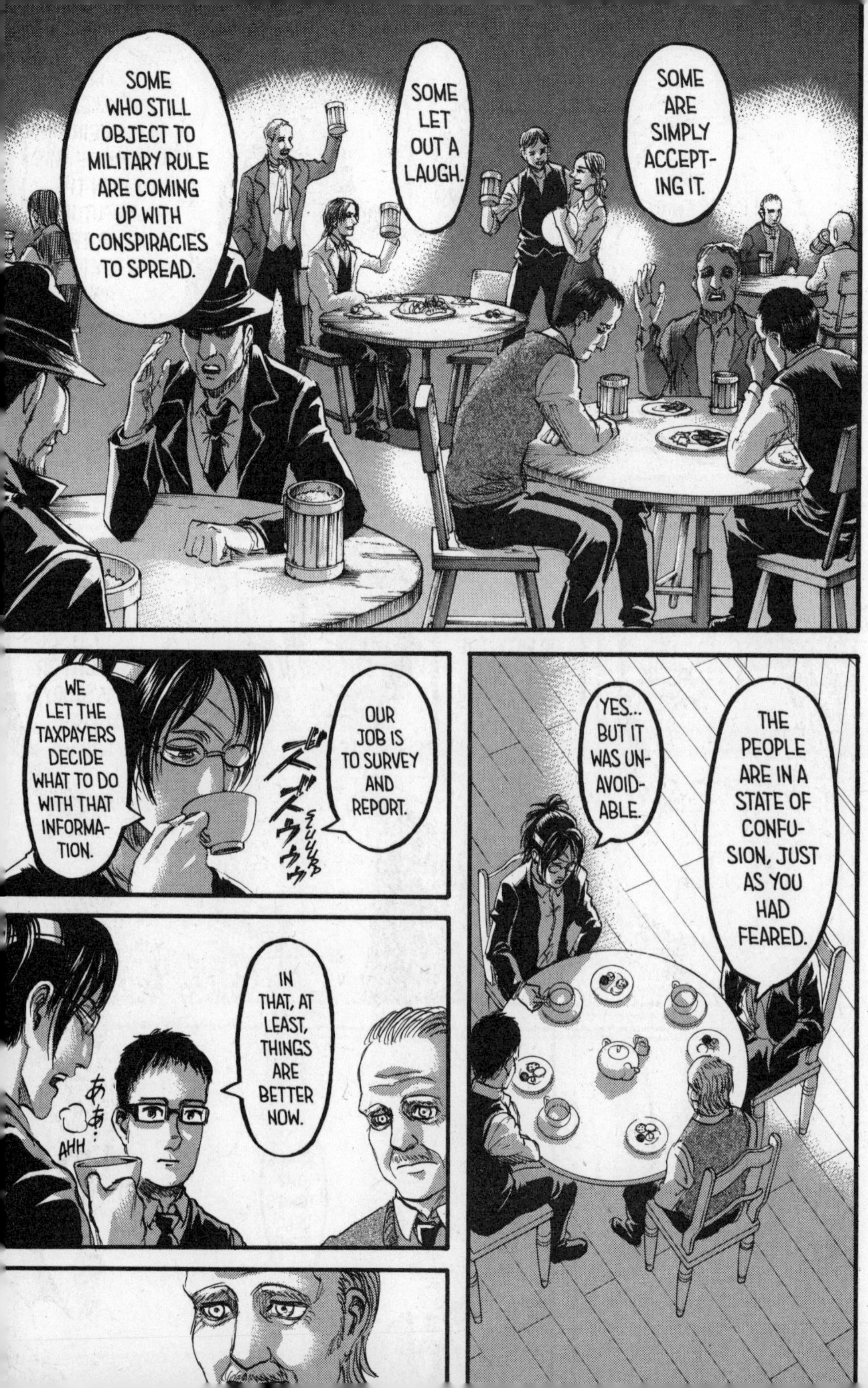
SOME ARE SIMPLY ACCEPTING IT.
SOME LET OUT A LAUGH.
SOME WHO STILL OBJECT TO MILITARY RULE ARE COMING UP WITH CONSPIRACIES TO SPREAD.
THE PEOPLE ARE IN A STATE OF CONFUSION, JUST AS YOU HAD FEARED.
YES... BUT IT WAS UNAVOIDABLE.
OUR JOB IS TO SURVEY AND REPORT.
SLURP
WE LET THE TAXPAYERS DECIDE WHAT TO DO WITH THAT INFORMATION.
IN THAT, AT LEAST, THINGS ARE BETTER NOW.
AHH

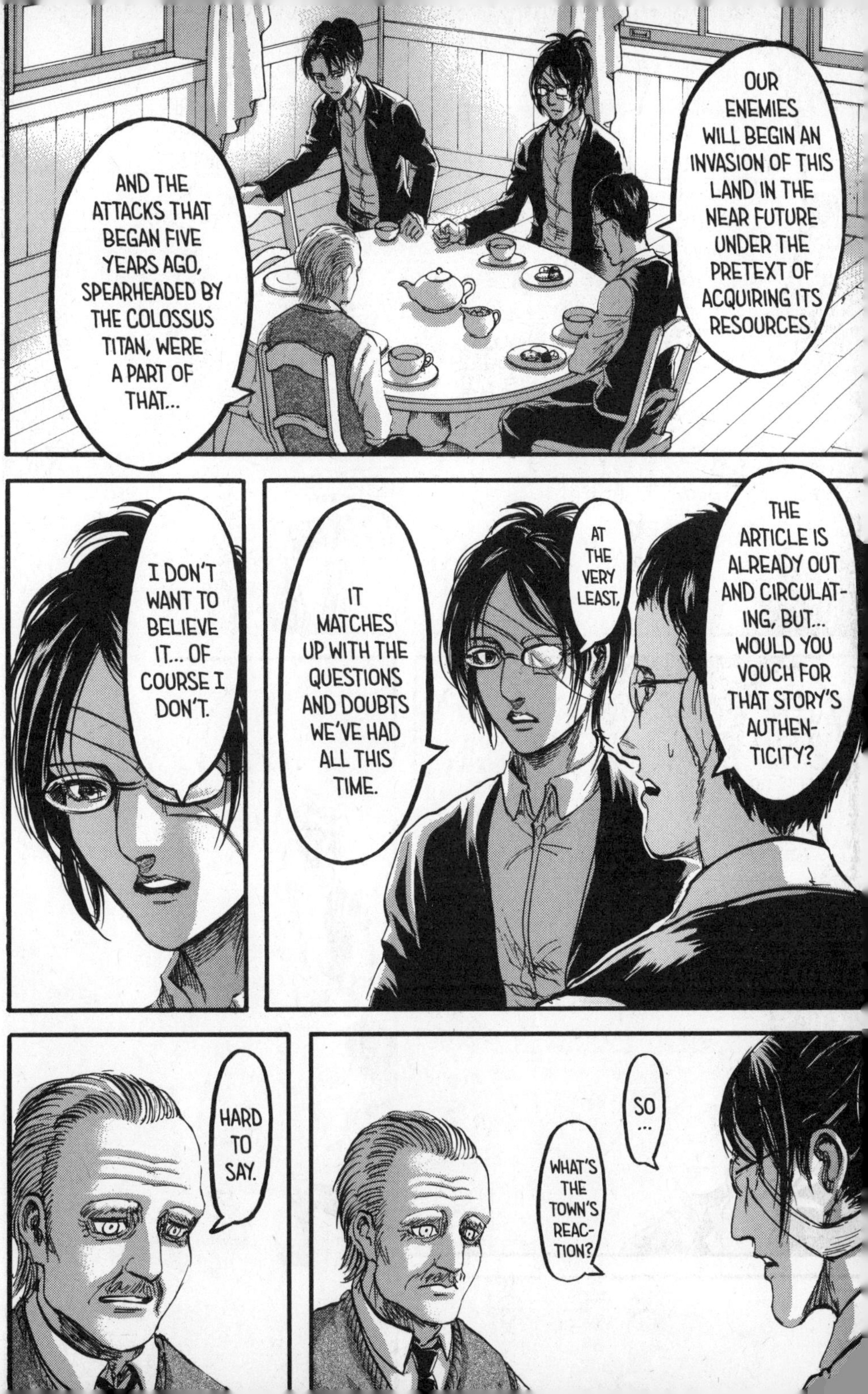
OUR ENEMIES WILL BEGIN AN INVASION OF THIS LAND IN THE NEAR FUTURE UNDER THE PRETEXT OF ACQUIRING ITS RESOURCES.
AND THE ATTACKS THAT BEGAN FIVE YEARS AGO, SPEARHEADED BY THE COLOSSUS TITAN, WERE A PART OF THAT...
THE ARTICLE IS ALREADY OUT AND CIRCULATING, BUT... WOULD YOU VOUCH FOR THAT STORY'S AUTHENTICITY?
AT THE VERY LEAST,
IT MATCHES UP WITH THE QUESTIONS AND DOUBTS WE'VE HAD ALL THIS TIME.
I DON'T WANT TO BELIEVE IT... OF COURSE I DON'T.
SO...
WHAT'S THE TOWN'S REACTION?
HARD TO SAY.

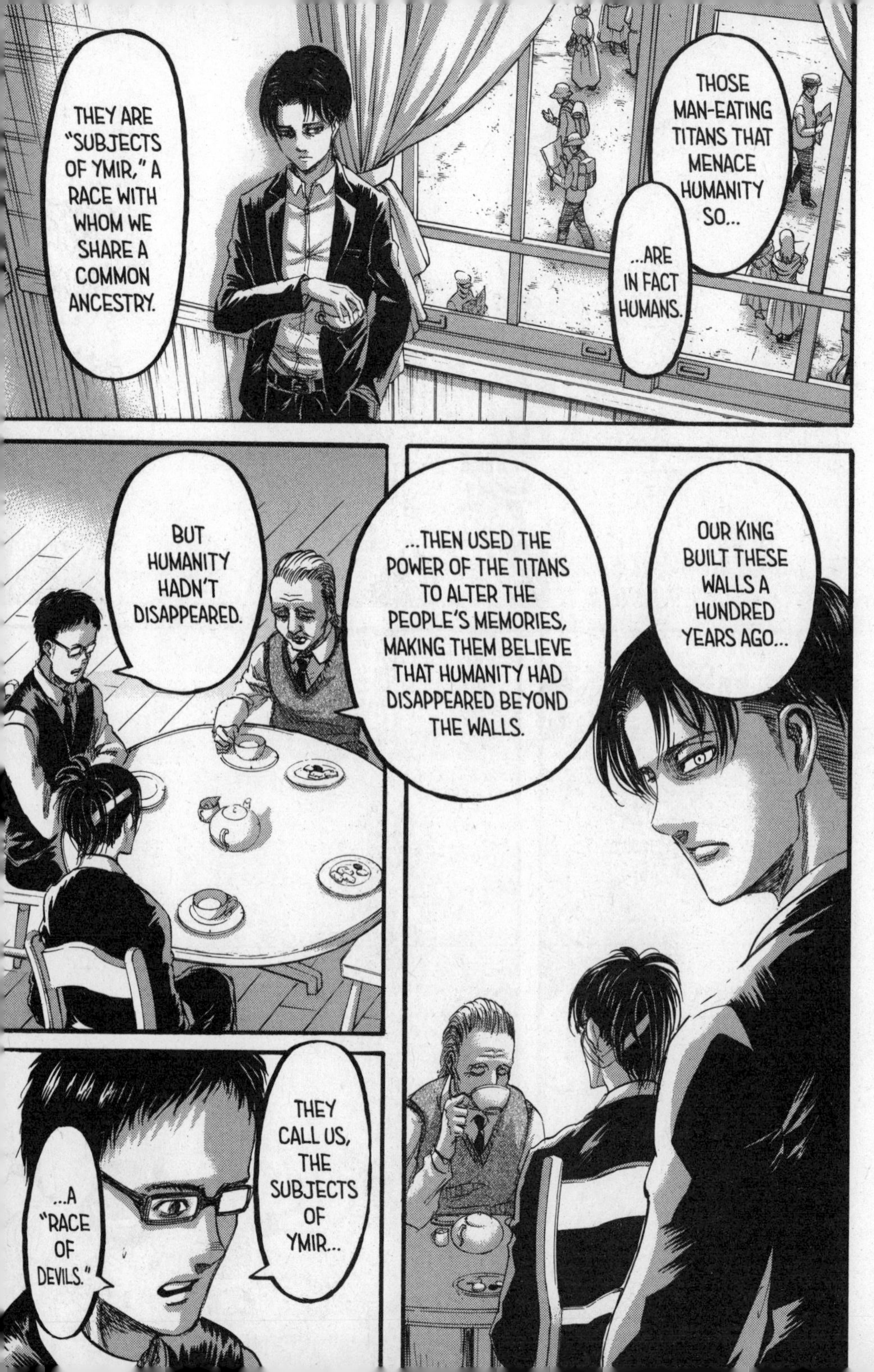
THOSE MAN-EATING TITANS THAT MENACE HUMANITY SO...
...ARE IN FACT HUMANS.
THEY ARE "SUBJECTS OF YMIR," A RACE WITH WHOM WE SHARE A COMMON ANCESTRY.
OUR KING BUILT THESE WALLS A HUNDRED YEARS AGO...
...THEN USED THE POWER OF THE TITANS TO ALTER THE PEOPLE'S MEMORIES, MAKING THEM BELIEVE THAT HUMANITY HAD DISAPPEARED BEYOND THE WALLS.
BUT HUMANITY HADN'T DISAPPEARED.
THEY CALL US, THE SUBJECTS OF YMIR...
...A "RACE OF DEVILS."

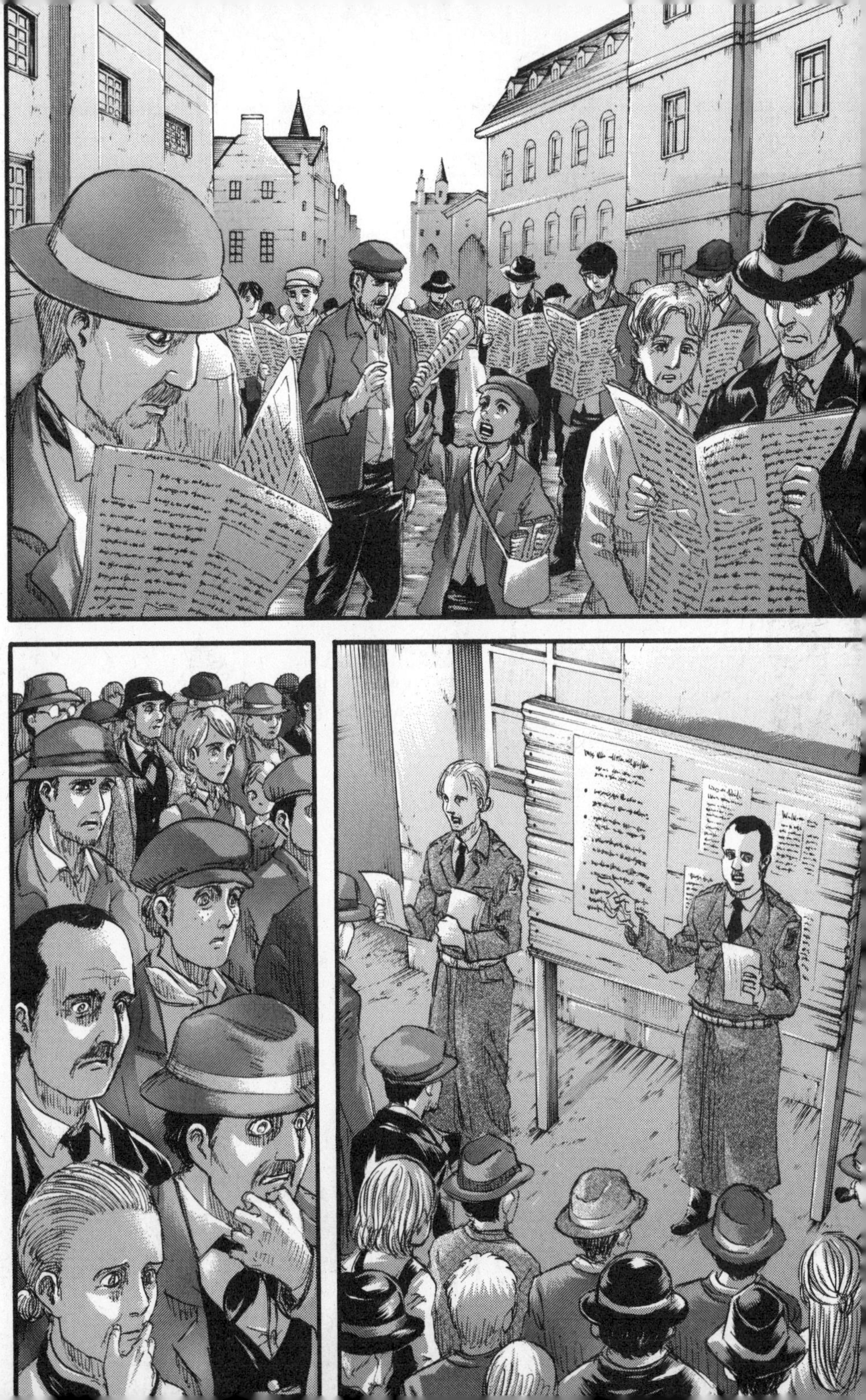

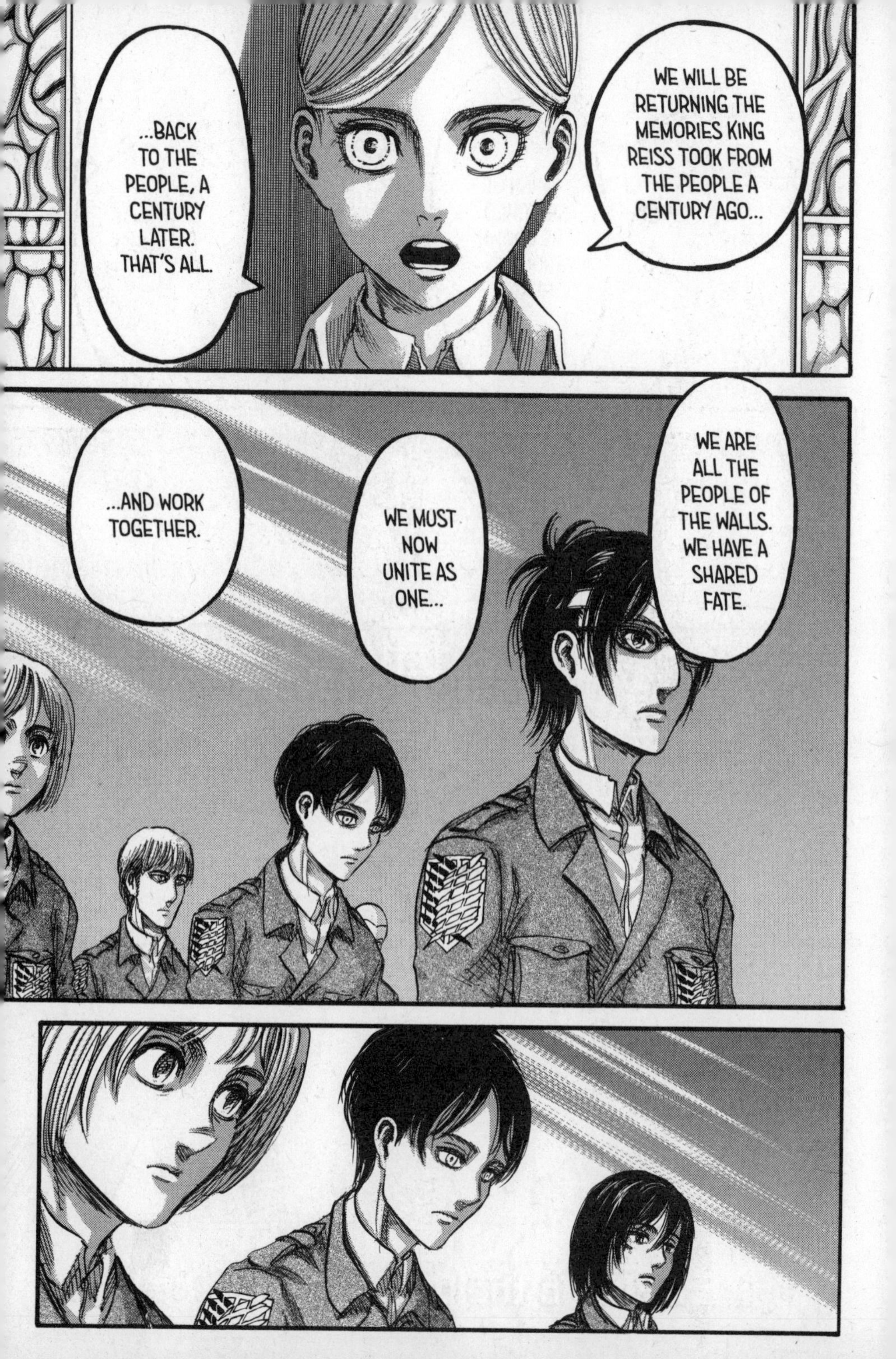
WE WILL BE RETURNING THE MEMORIES KING REISS TOOK FROM THE PEOPLE A CENTURY AGO...
...BACK TO THE PEOPLE, A CENTURY LATER. THAT'S ALL.
WE ARE ALL THE PEOPLE OF THE WALLS. WE HAVE A SHARED FATE.
WE MUST NOW UNITE AS ONE...
...AND WORK TOGETHER.

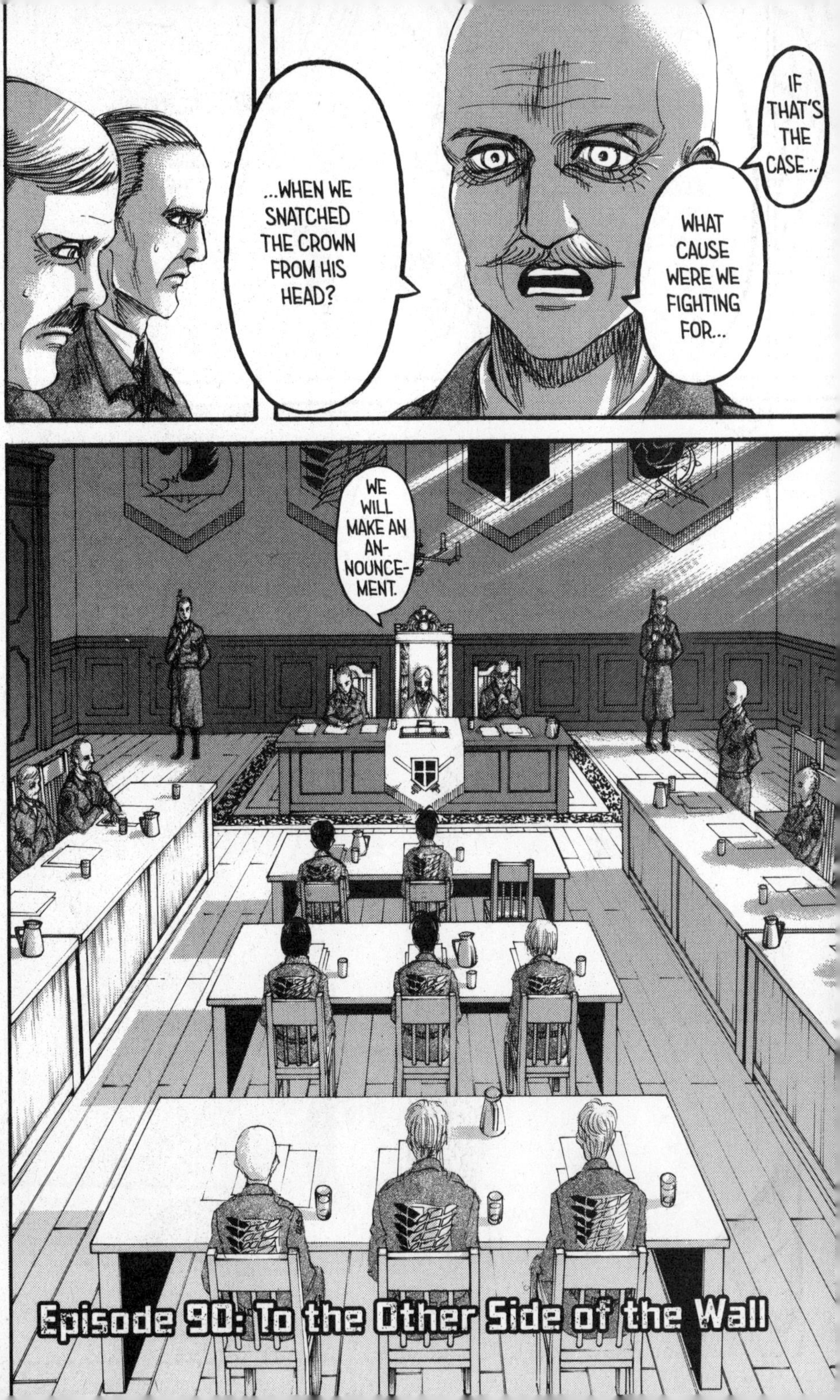
IF THAT'S THE CASE...
WHAT CAUSE WERE WE FIGHTING FOR...
...WHEN WE SNATCHED THE CROWN FROM HIS HEAD?
WE WILL MAKE AN AN-NOUNCE-MENT.
Episode 90: To the Other Side of the Wall

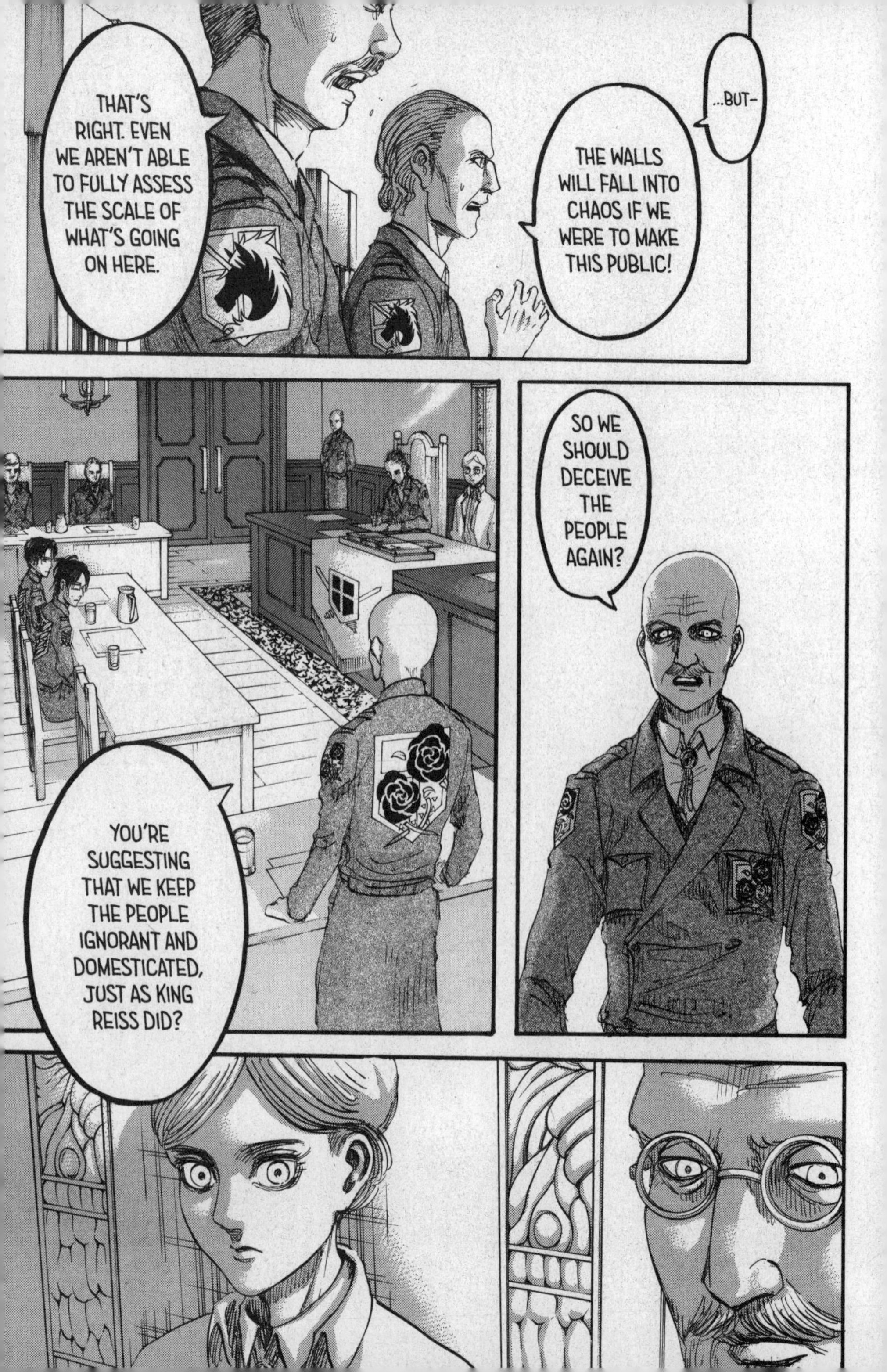
...BUT-
THE WALLS WILL FALL INTO CHAOS IF WE WERE TO MAKE THIS PUBLIC!
THAT'S RIGHT. EVEN WE AREN'T ABLE TO FULLY ASSESS THE SCALE OF WHAT'S GOING ON HERE.
SO WE SHOULD DECEIVE THE PEOPLE AGAIN?
YOU'RE SUGGESTING THAT WE KEEP THE PEOPLE IGNORANT AND DOMESTICATED, JUST AS KING REISS DID?

ATTACK on TITAN

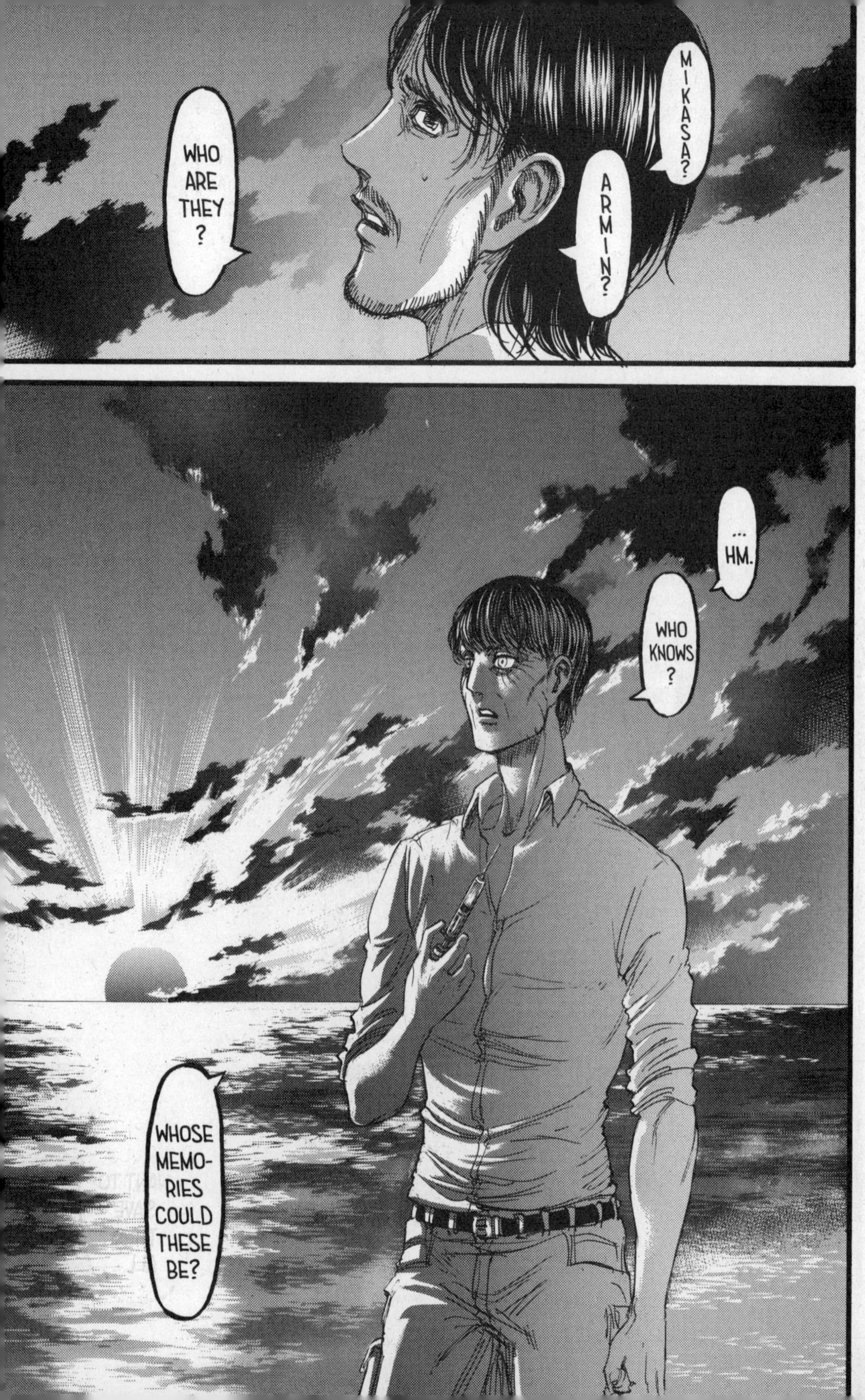
MIKASA?
ARMIN?
WHO ARE THEY?
...HM.
WHO KNOWS?
WHOSE MEMORIES COULD THESE BE?

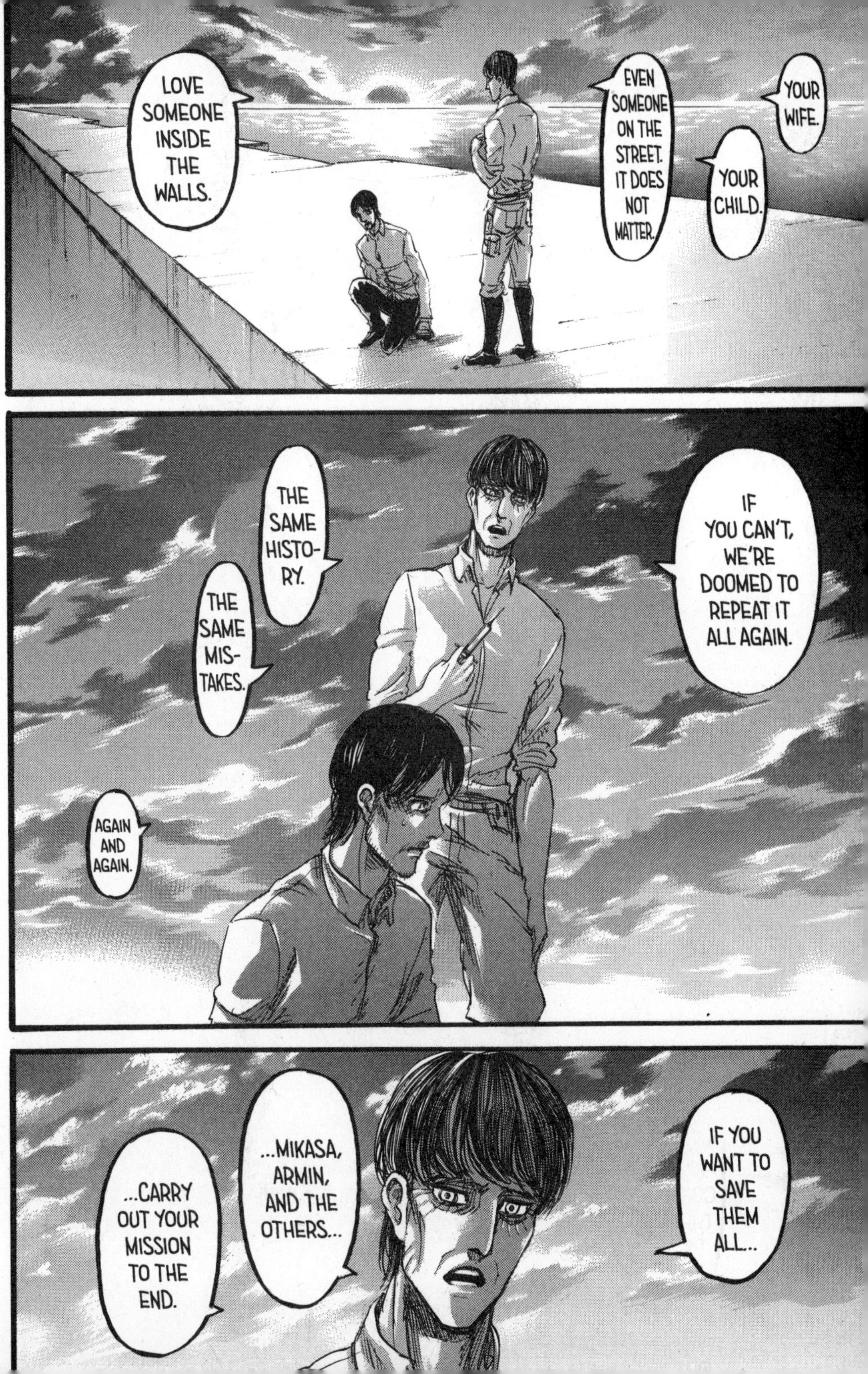
YOUR WIFE.
YOUR CHILD.
EVEN SOMEONE ON THE STREET. IT DOES NOT MATTER.
LOVE SOMEONE INSIDE THE WALLS.
IF YOU CAN'T, WE'RE DOOMED TO REPEAT IT ALL AGAIN.
THE SAME HISTORY.
THE SAME MISTAKES.
AGAIN AND AGAIN.
IF YOU WANT TO SAVE THEM ALL...
...MIKASA, ARMIN, AND THE OTHERS...
...CARRY OUT YOUR MISSION TO THE END.

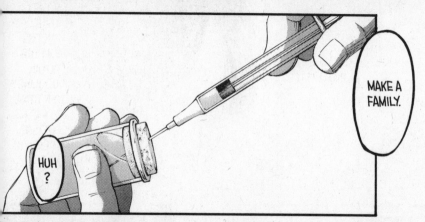

MAKE A FAMILY.

HUH?

YOU NEED A FULL HOUSEHOLD ONCE YOU ENTER INSIDE THE WALLS.

I HAVE DINA...

...WHAT ARE YOU TALKING ABOUT?

AND ALL MY MEMORIES FROM BEFORE I BECOME A TITAN WILL DISAPPEAR ANYWAY, WON'T THEY?

NOT NECES- SARILY.

SOME- ONE MAY SEE THEM LATER.

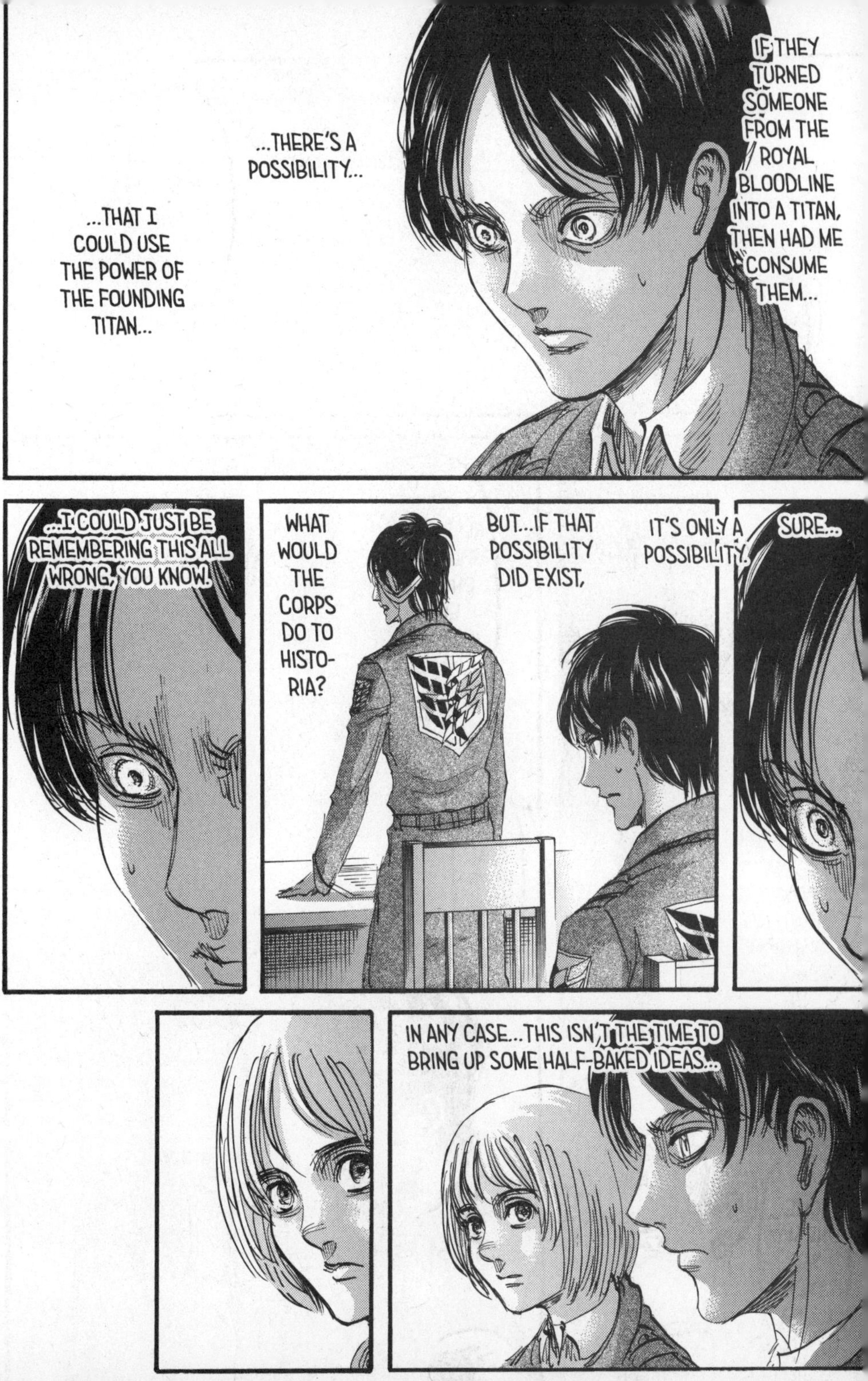
IF THEY TURNED SOMEONE FROM THE ROYAL BLOODLINE INTO A TITAN, THEN HAD ME CONSUME THEM...
...THERE'S A POSSIBILITY...
...THAT I COULD USE THE POWER OF THE FOUNDING TITAN...
SURE...
IT'S ONLY A POSSIBILITY.
BUT...IF THAT POSSIBILITY DID EXIST,
WHAT WOULD THE CORPS DO TO HISTORIA?
...I COULD JUST BE REMEMBERING THIS ALL WRONG, YOU KNOW.
IN ANY CASE...THIS ISN'T THE TIME TO BRING UP SOME HALF-BAKED IDEAS...

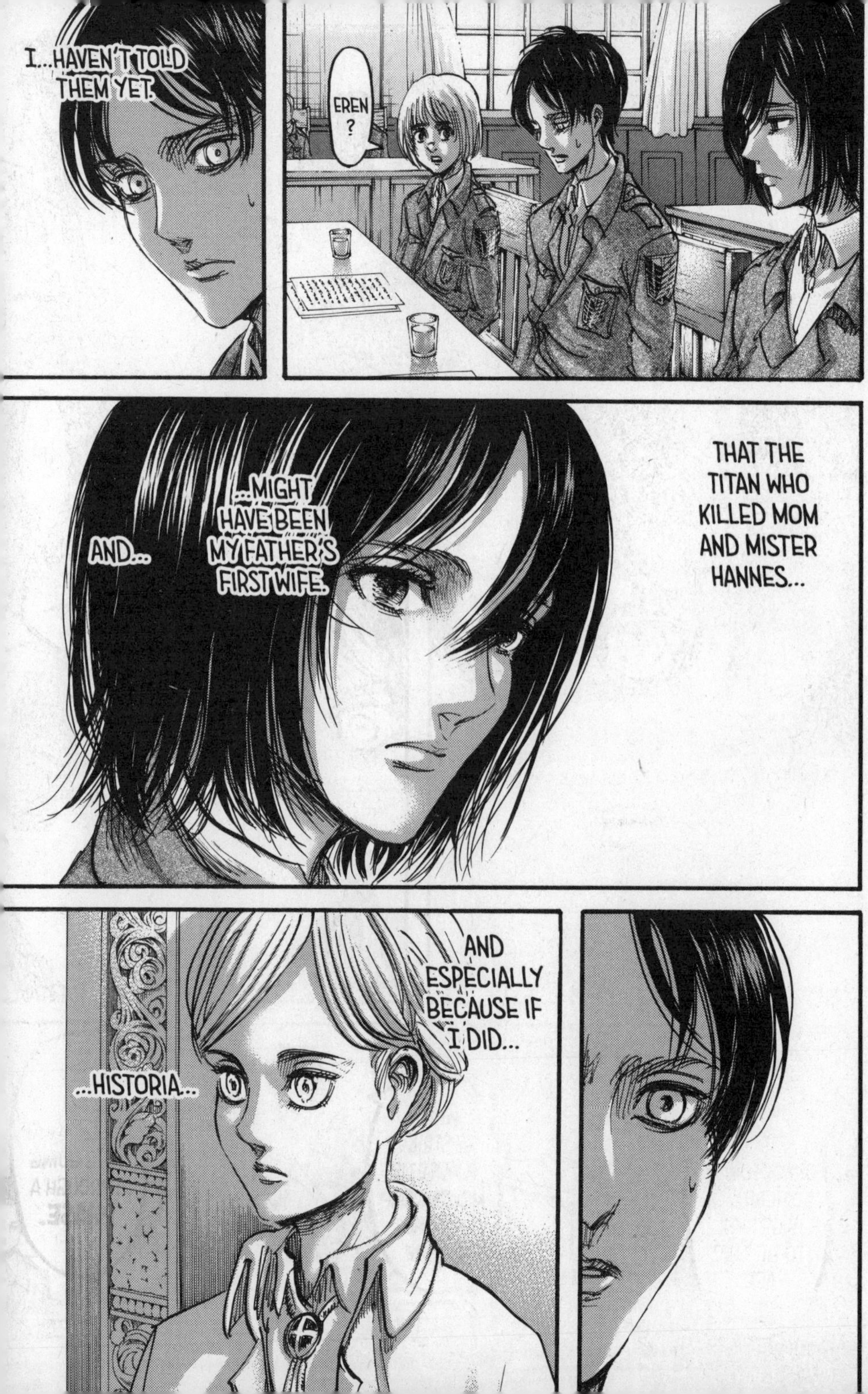
EREN ?
I...HAVEN'T TOLD THEM YET.
THAT THE TITAN WHO KILLED MOM AND MISTER HANNES...
...MIGHT HAVE BEEN MY FATHER'S FIRST WIFE.
AND...
AND ESPECIALLY BECAUSE IF I DID...
...HISTORIA...

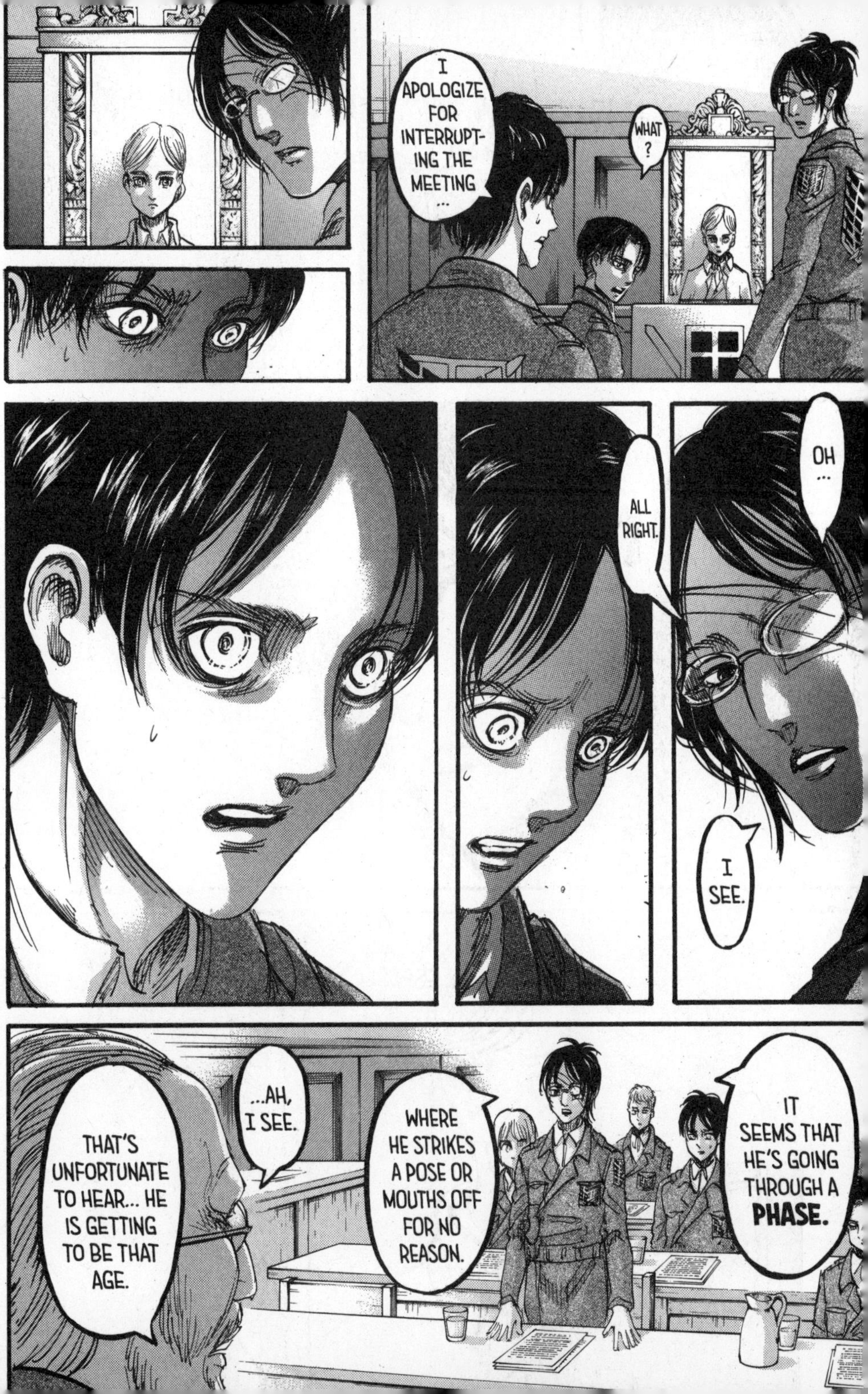
I APOLOGIZE FOR INTERRUPTING THE MEETING ...
WHAT ?
OH ...
I SEE.
ALL RIGHT.
IT SEEMS THAT HE'S GOING THROUGH A **PHASE.**
WHERE HE STRIKES A POSE OR MOUTHS OFF FOR NO REASON.
...AH, I SEE.
THAT'S UNFORTUNATE TO HEAR... HE IS GETTING TO BE THAT AGE.

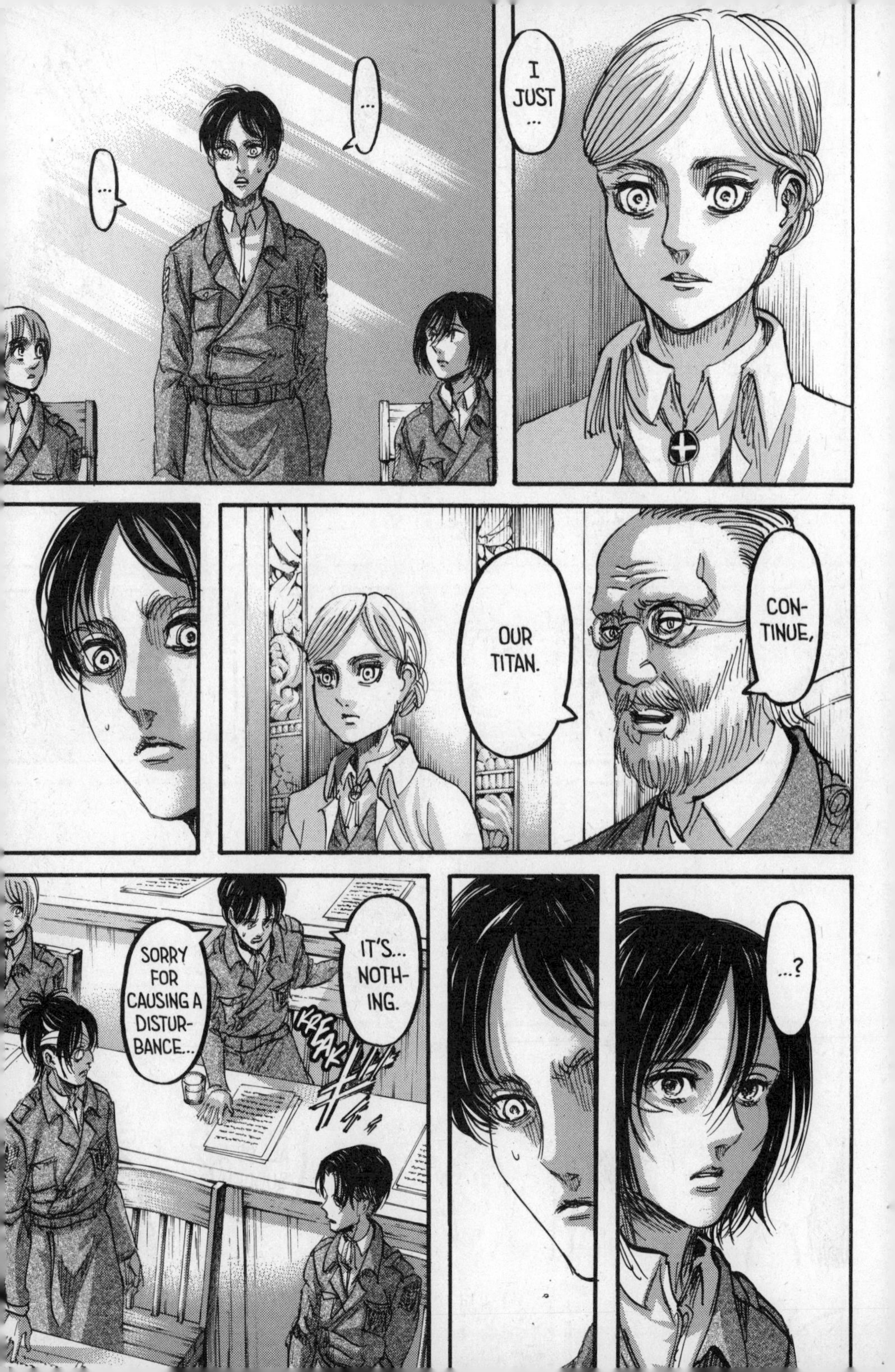
I JUST ...
...
...
CON-TINUE,
OUR TITAN.
...?
IT'S... NOTH-ING.
SORRY FOR CAUSING A DISTUR-BANCE...
KREAK

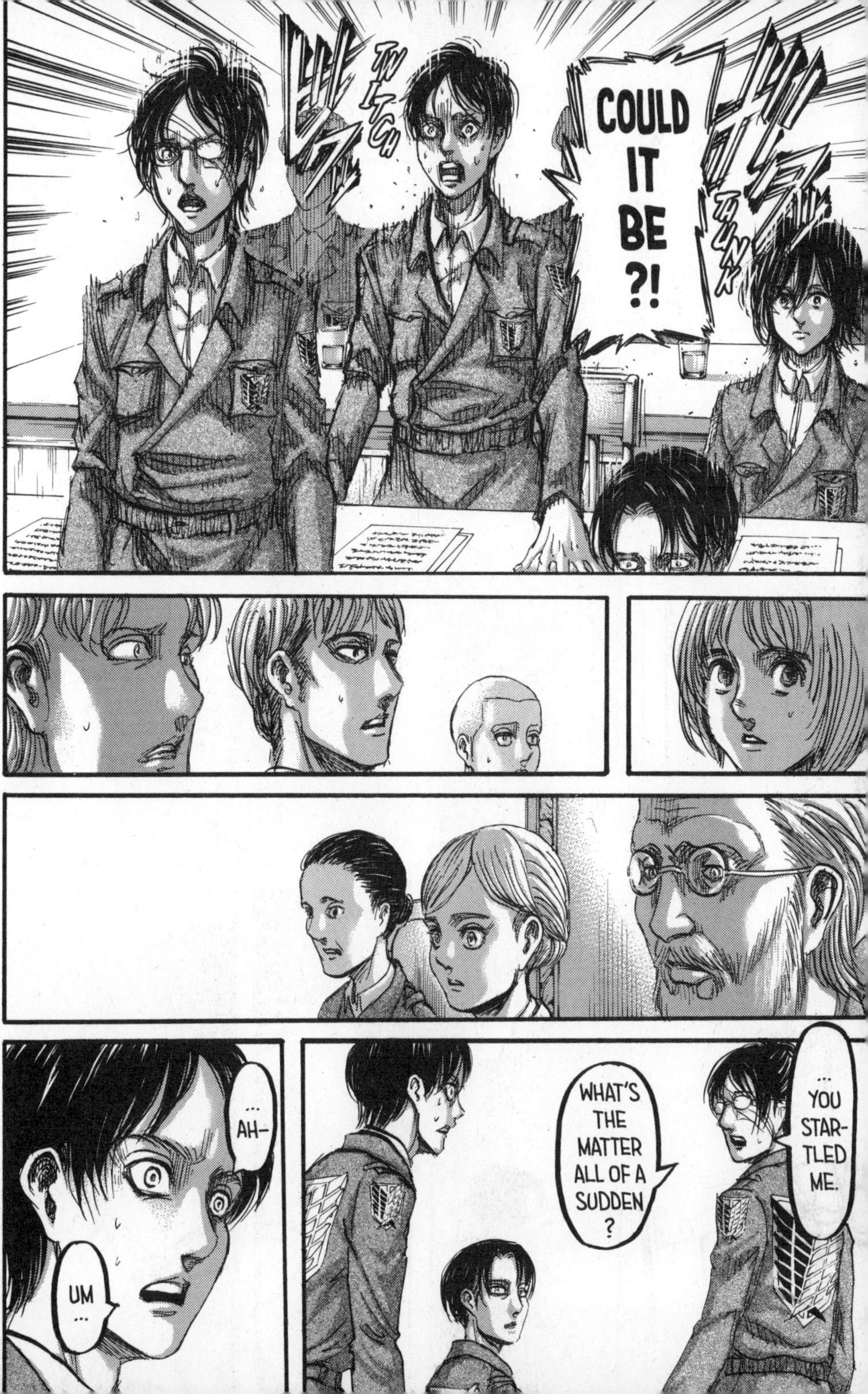
THUNK
COULD IT BE?!
TWITCH
... YOU STARTLED ME.
WHAT'S THE MATTER ALL OF A SUDDEN?
... AH-
UM ...

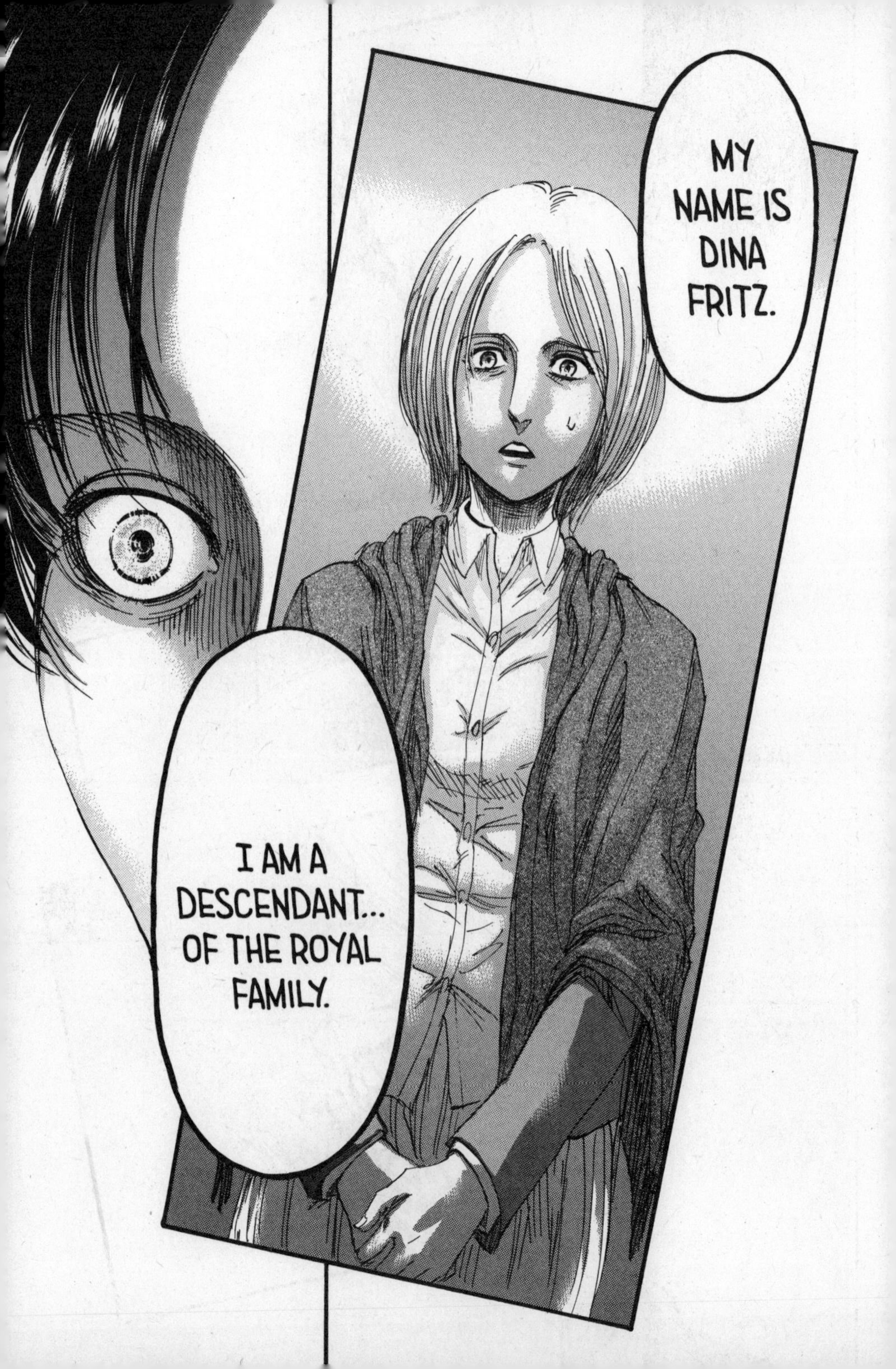
MY NAME IS DINA FRITZ.
I AM A DESCENDANT... OF THE ROYAL FAMILY.

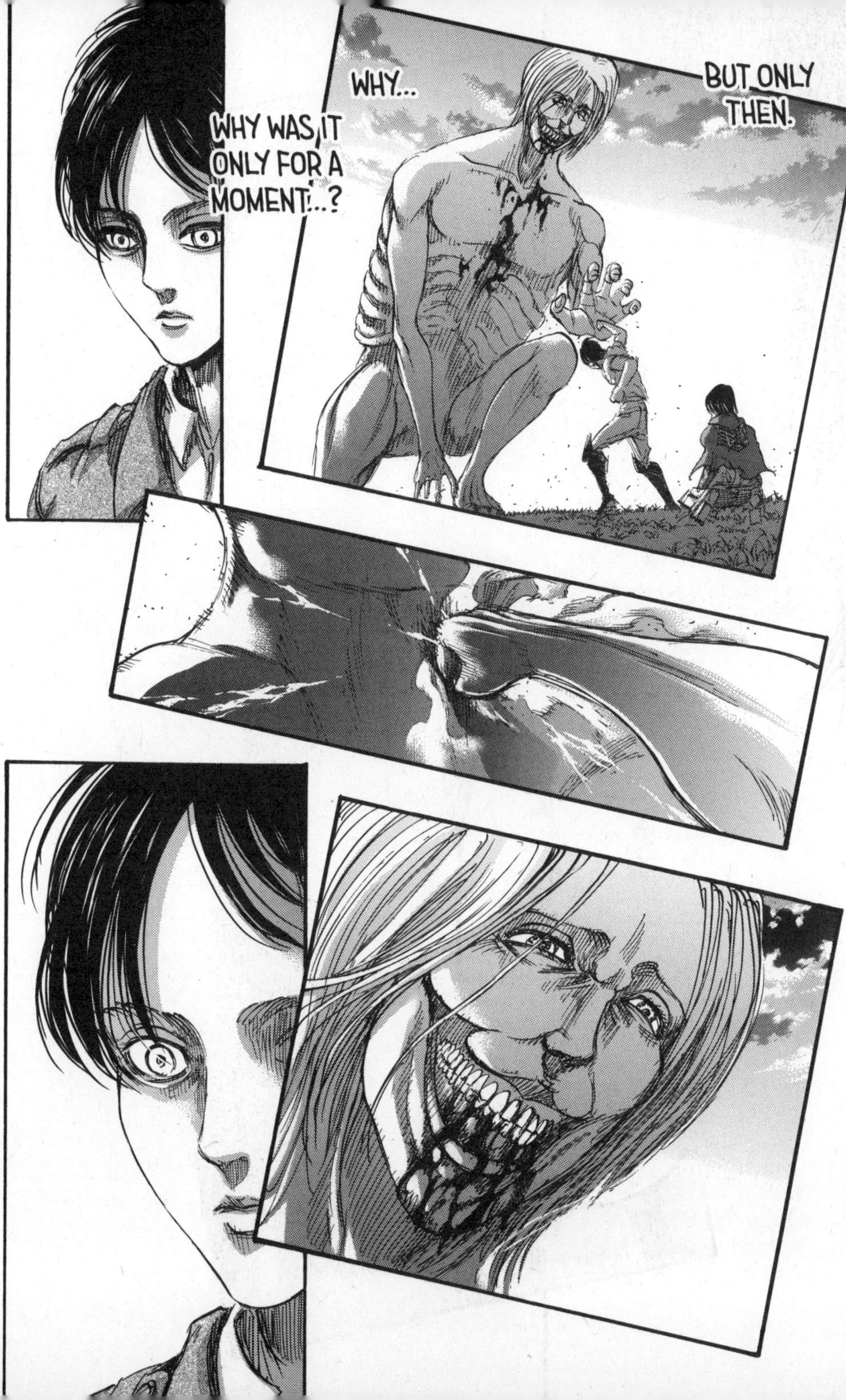
BUT ONLY THEN.
WHY...
WHY WAS IT ONLY FOR A MOMENT...?

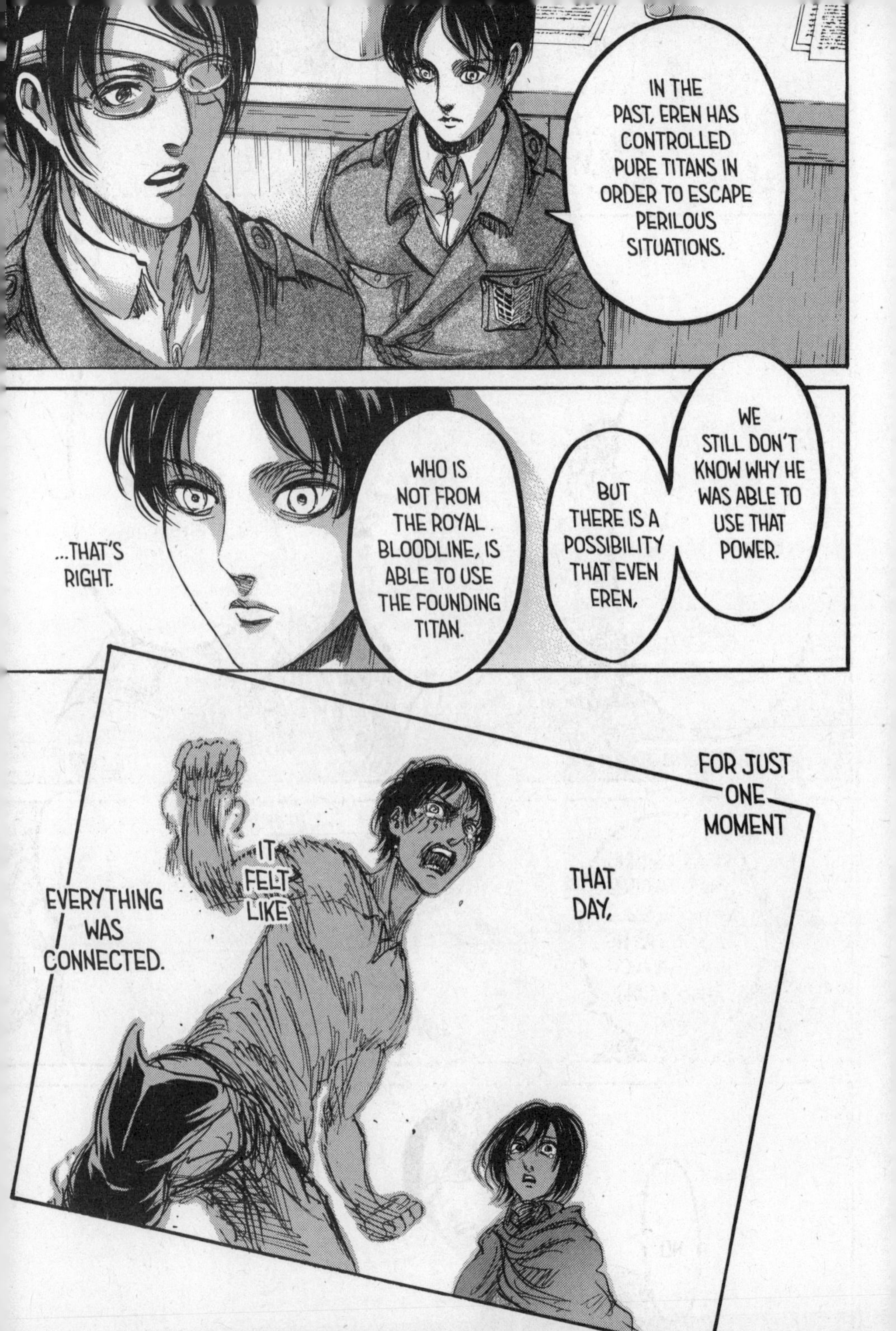
IN THE PAST, EREN HAS CONTROLLED PURE TITANS IN ORDER TO ESCAPE PERILOUS SITUATIONS.
WE STILL DON'T KNOW WHY HE WAS ABLE TO USE THAT POWER.
BUT THERE IS A POSSIBILITY THAT EVEN EREN,
WHO IS NOT FROM THE ROYAL BLOODLINE, IS ABLE TO USE THE FOUNDING TITAN.
...THAT'S RIGHT.
FOR JUST ONE MOMENT
THAT DAY,
IT FELT LIKE
EVERYTHING WAS CONNECTED.

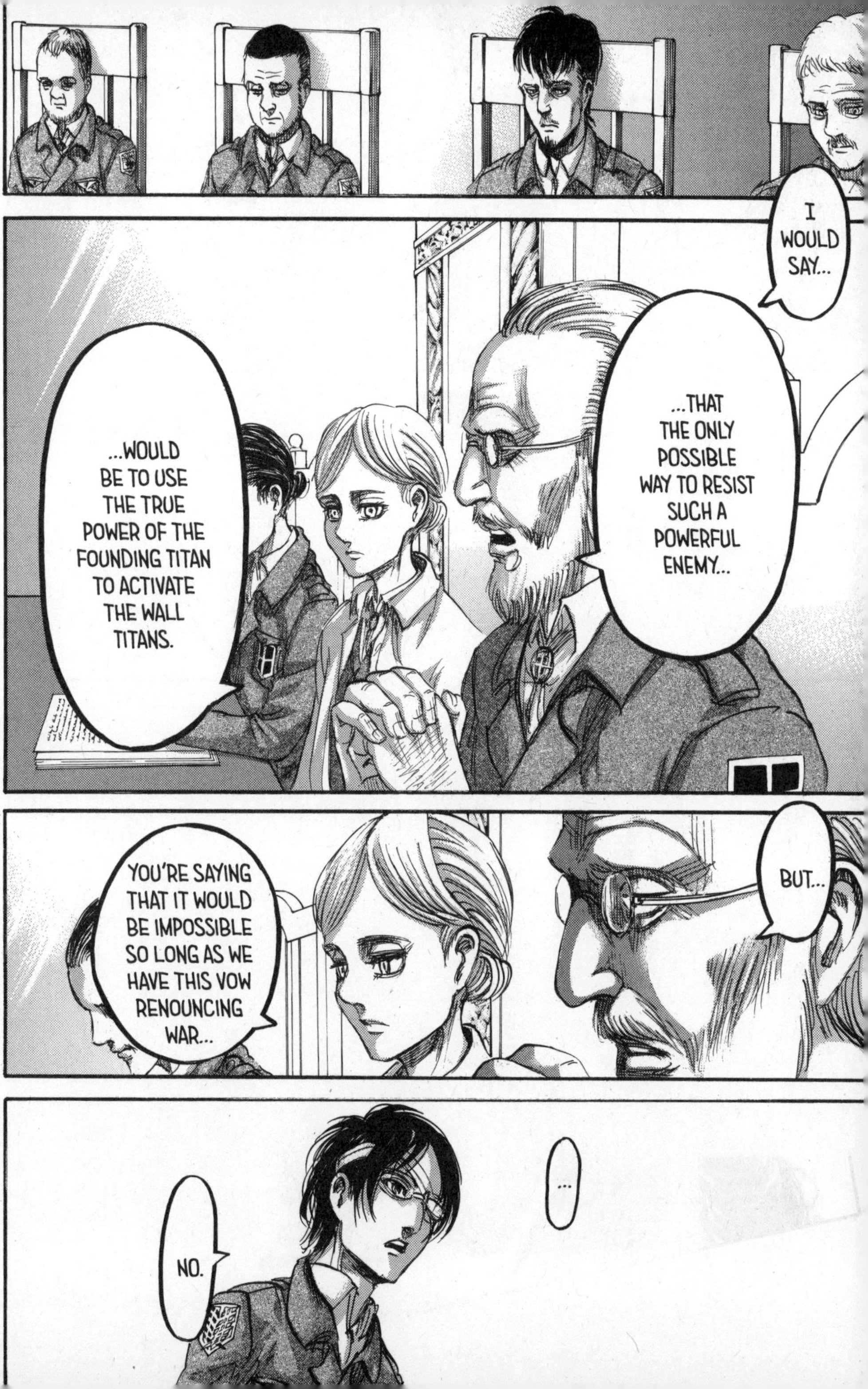
I WOULD SAY...
...THAT THE ONLY POSSIBLE WAY TO RESIST SUCH A POWERFUL ENEMY...
...WOULD BE TO USE THE TRUE POWER OF THE FOUNDING TITAN TO ACTIVATE THE WALL TITANS.
BUT...
YOU'RE SAYING THAT IT WOULD BE IMPOSSIBLE SO LONG AS WE HAVE THIS VOW RENOUNCING WAR...
...
NO.

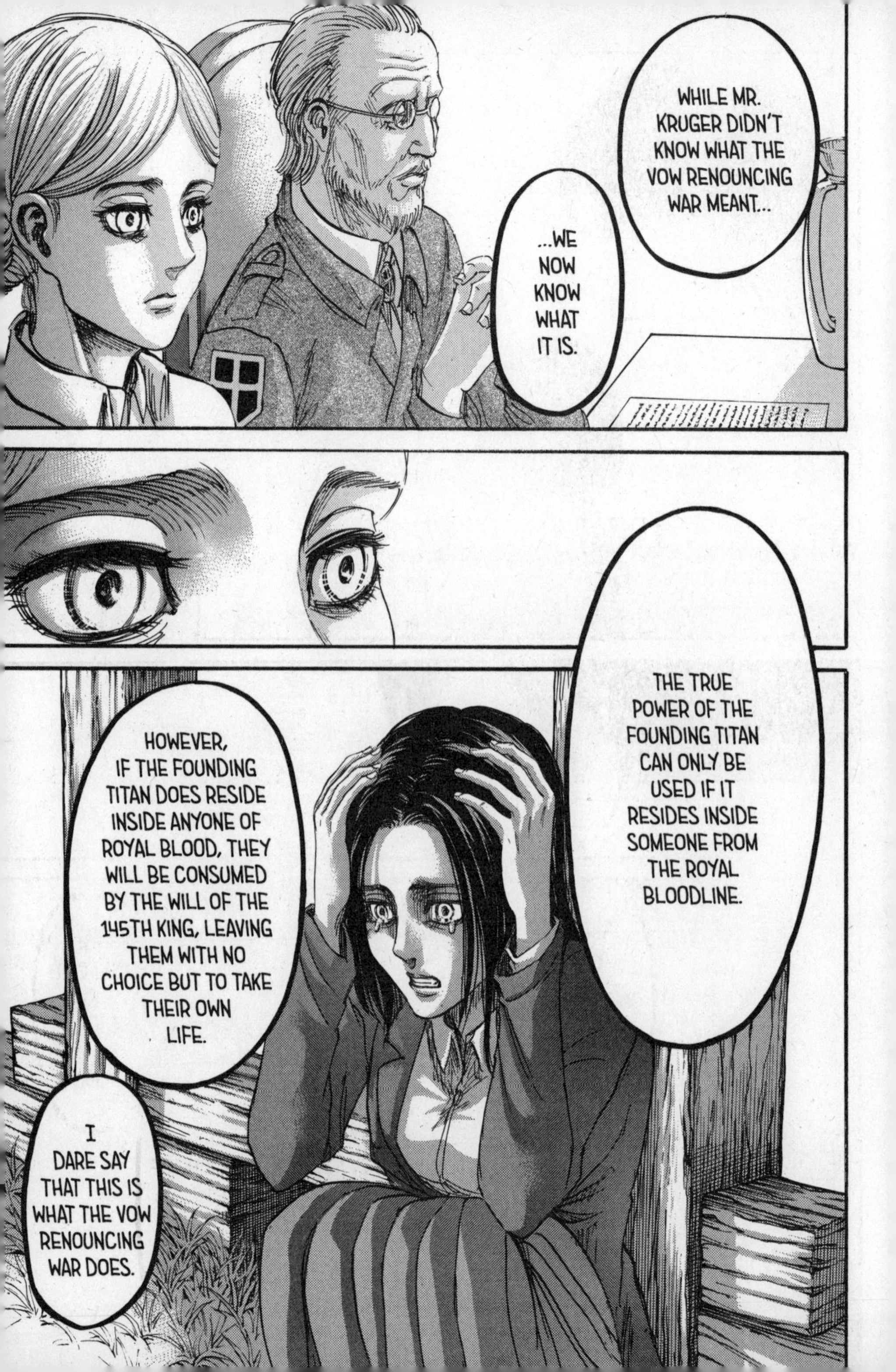
WHILE MR. KRUGER DIDN'T KNOW WHAT THE VOW RENOUNCING WAR MEANT...
...WE NOW KNOW WHAT IT IS.
THE TRUE POWER OF THE FOUNDING TITAN CAN ONLY BE USED IF IT RESIDES INSIDE SOMEONE FROM THE ROYAL BLOODLINE.
HOWEVER, IF THE FOUNDING TITAN DOES RESIDE INSIDE ANYONE OF ROYAL BLOOD, THEY WILL BE CONSUMED BY THE WILL OF THE 145TH KING, LEAVING THEM WITH NO CHOICE BUT TO TAKE THEIR OWN LIFE.
I DARE SAY THAT THIS IS WHAT THE VOW RENOUNCING WAR DOES.

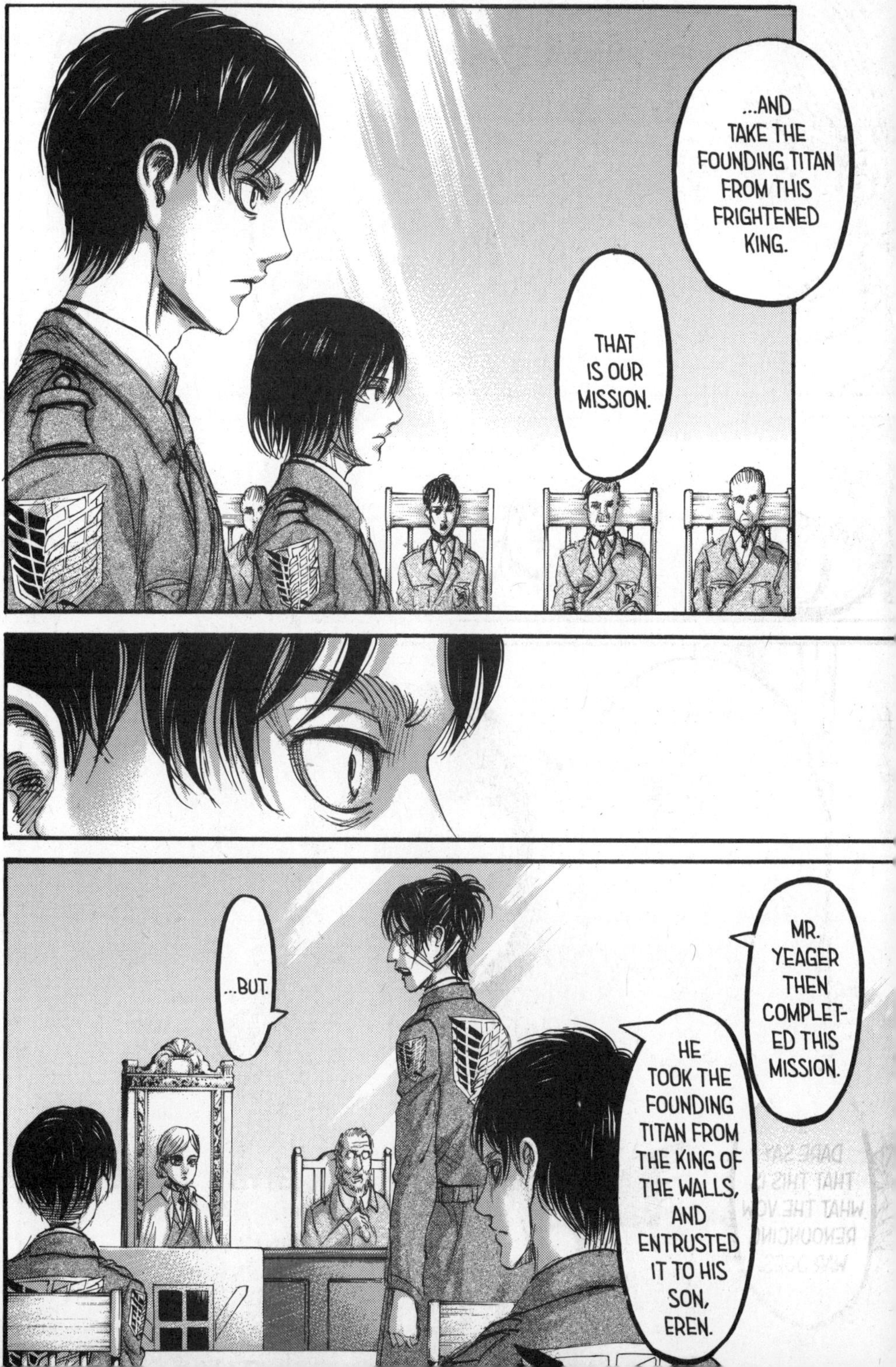
...AND TAKE THE FOUNDING TITAN FROM THIS FRIGHTENED KING.
THAT IS OUR MISSION.
MR. YEAGER THEN COMPLETED THIS MISSION.
HE TOOK THE FOUNDING TITAN FROM THE KING OF THE WALLS, AND ENTRUSTED IT TO HIS SON, EREN.
...BUT.

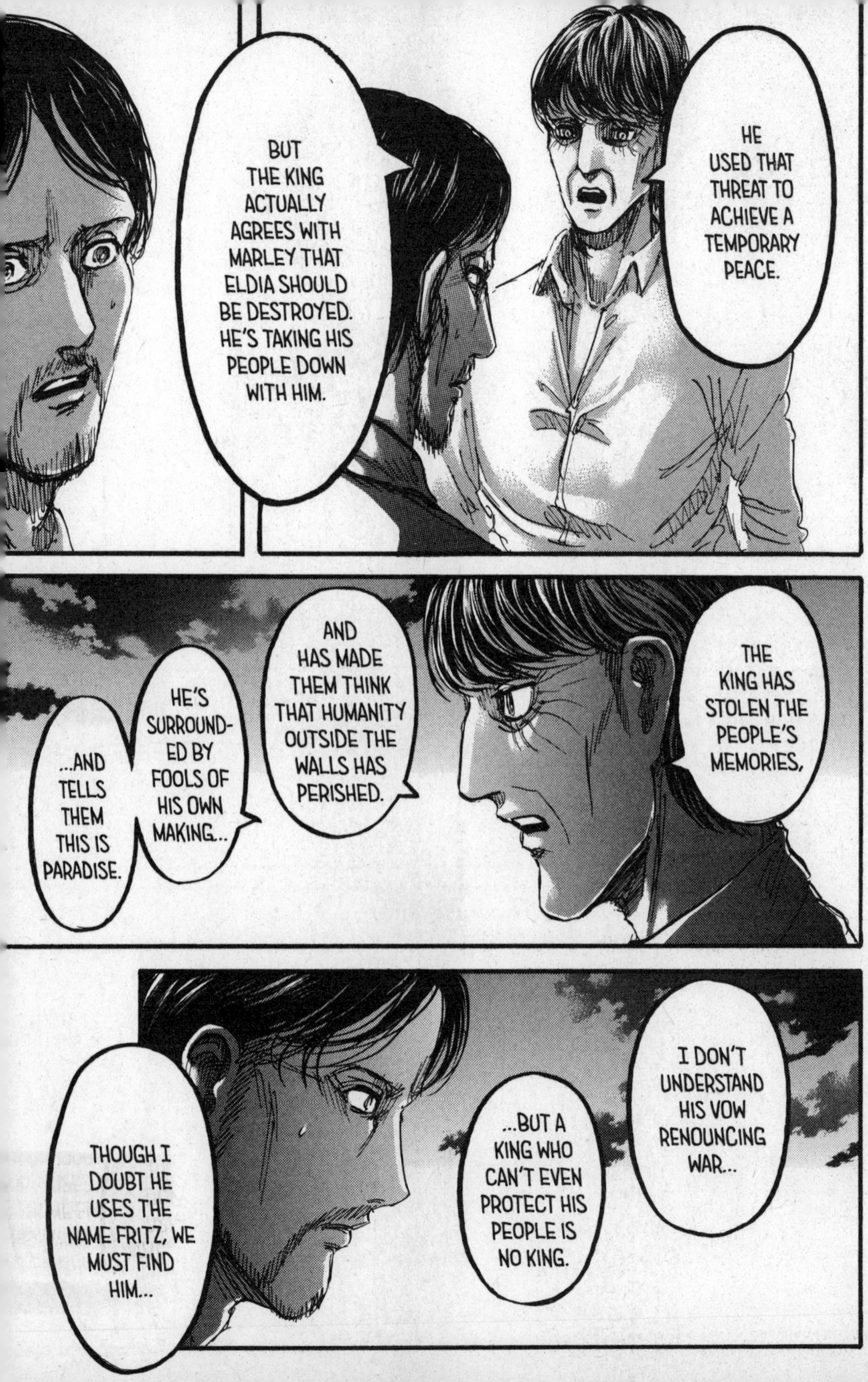
HE USED THAT THREAT TO ACHIEVE A TEMPORARY PEACE.
BUT THE KING ACTUALLY AGREES WITH MARLEY THAT ELDIA SHOULD BE DESTROYED. HE'S TAKING HIS PEOPLE DOWN WITH HIM.
THE KING HAS STOLEN THE PEOPLE'S MEMORIES,
AND HAS MADE THEM THINK THAT HUMANITY OUTSIDE THE WALLS HAS PERISHED.
HE'S SURROUND-ED BY FOOLS OF HIS OWN MAKING...
...AND TELLS THEM THIS IS PARADISE.
I DON'T UNDERSTAND HIS VOW RENOUNCING WAR...
...BUT A KING WHO CAN'T EVEN PROTECT HIS PEOPLE IS NO KING.
THOUGH I DOUBT HE USES THE NAME FRITZ, WE MUST FIND HIM...

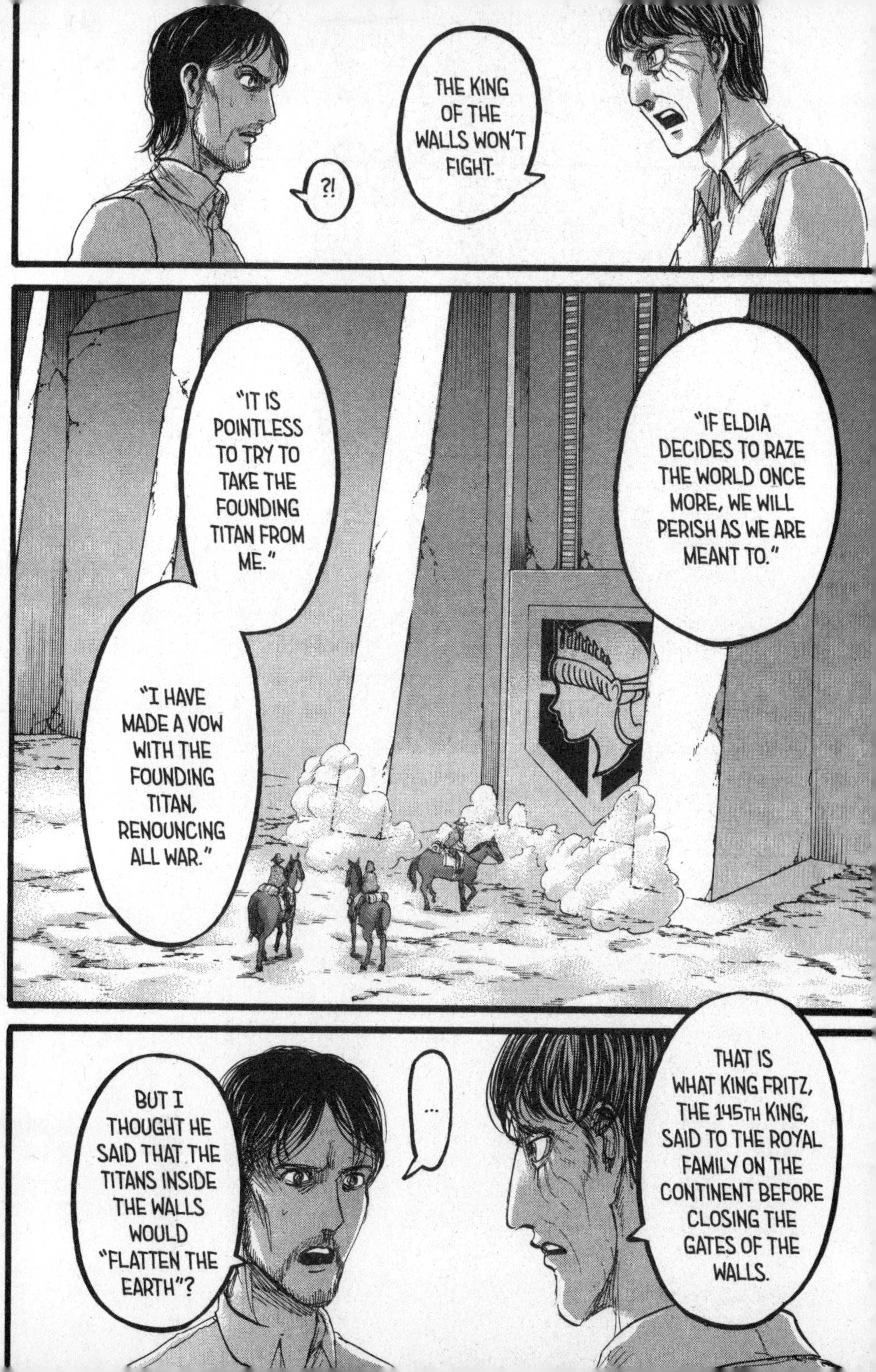
THE KING OF THE WALLS WON'T FIGHT.
?!
"IF ELDIA DECIDES TO RAZE THE WORLD ONCE MORE, WE WILL PERISH AS WE ARE MEANT TO."
"IT IS POINTLESS TO TRY TO TAKE THE FOUNDING TITAN FROM ME."
"I HAVE MADE A VOW WITH THE FOUNDING TITAN, RENOUNCING ALL WAR."
THAT IS WHAT KING FRITZ, THE 145TH KING, SAID TO THE ROYAL FAMILY ON THE CONTINENT BEFORE CLOSING THE GATES OF THE WALLS.
...
BUT I THOUGHT HE SAID THAT THE TITANS INSIDE THE WALLS WOULD "FLATTEN THE EARTH"?

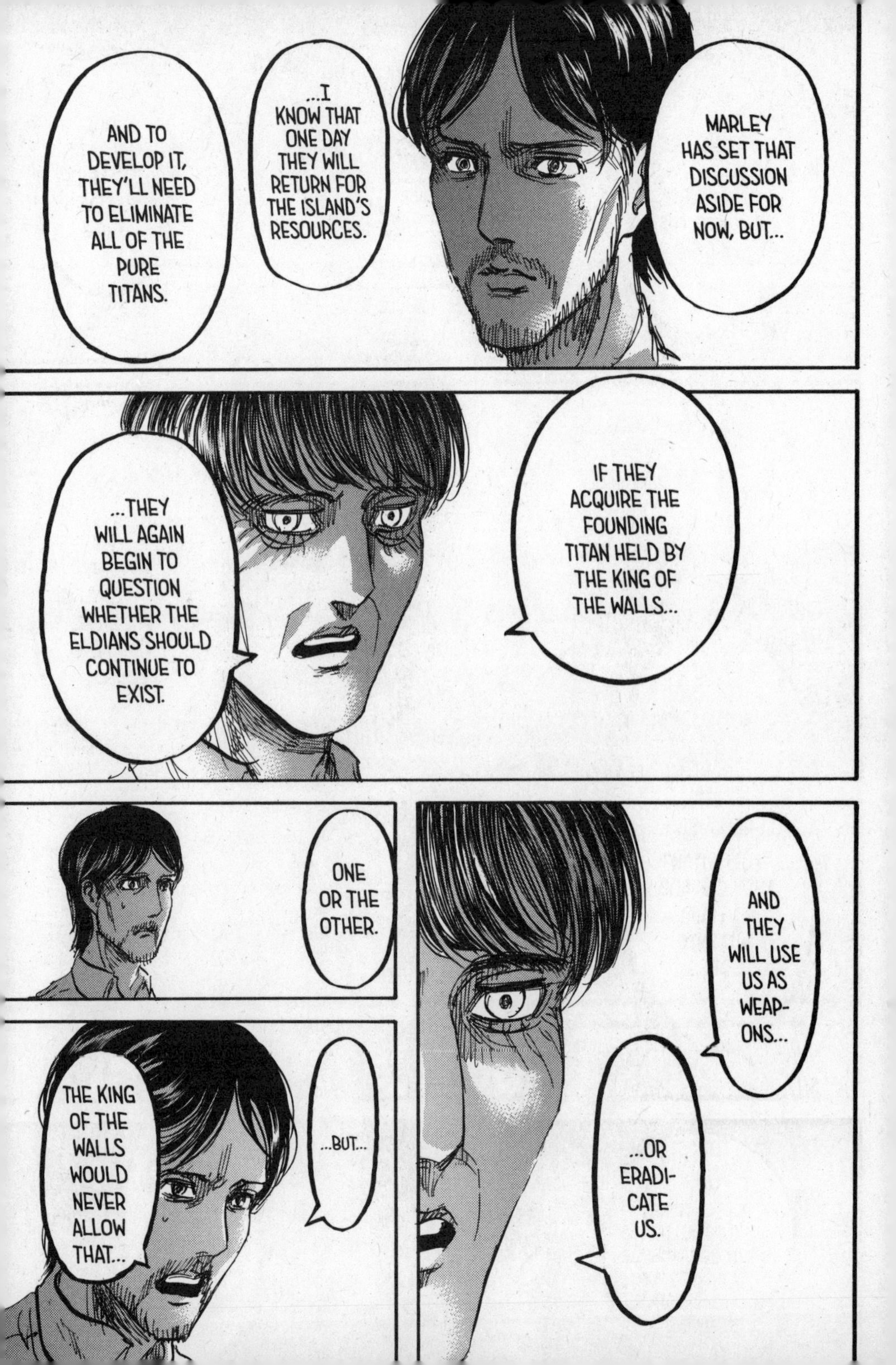
MARLEY HAS SET THAT DISCUSSION ASIDE FOR NOW, BUT...
...I KNOW THAT ONE DAY THEY WILL RETURN FOR THE ISLAND'S RESOURCES.
AND TO DEVELOP IT, THEY'LL NEED TO ELIMINATE ALL OF THE PURE TITANS.
IF THEY ACQUIRE THE FOUNDING TITAN HELD BY THE KING OF THE WALLS...
...THEY WILL AGAIN BEGIN TO QUESTION WHETHER THE ELDIANS SHOULD CONTINUE TO EXIST.
AND THEY WILL USE US AS WEAP-ONS...
...OR ERADI-CATE US.
ONE OR THE OTHER.
...BUT...
THE KING OF THE WALLS WOULD NEVER ALLOW THAT...

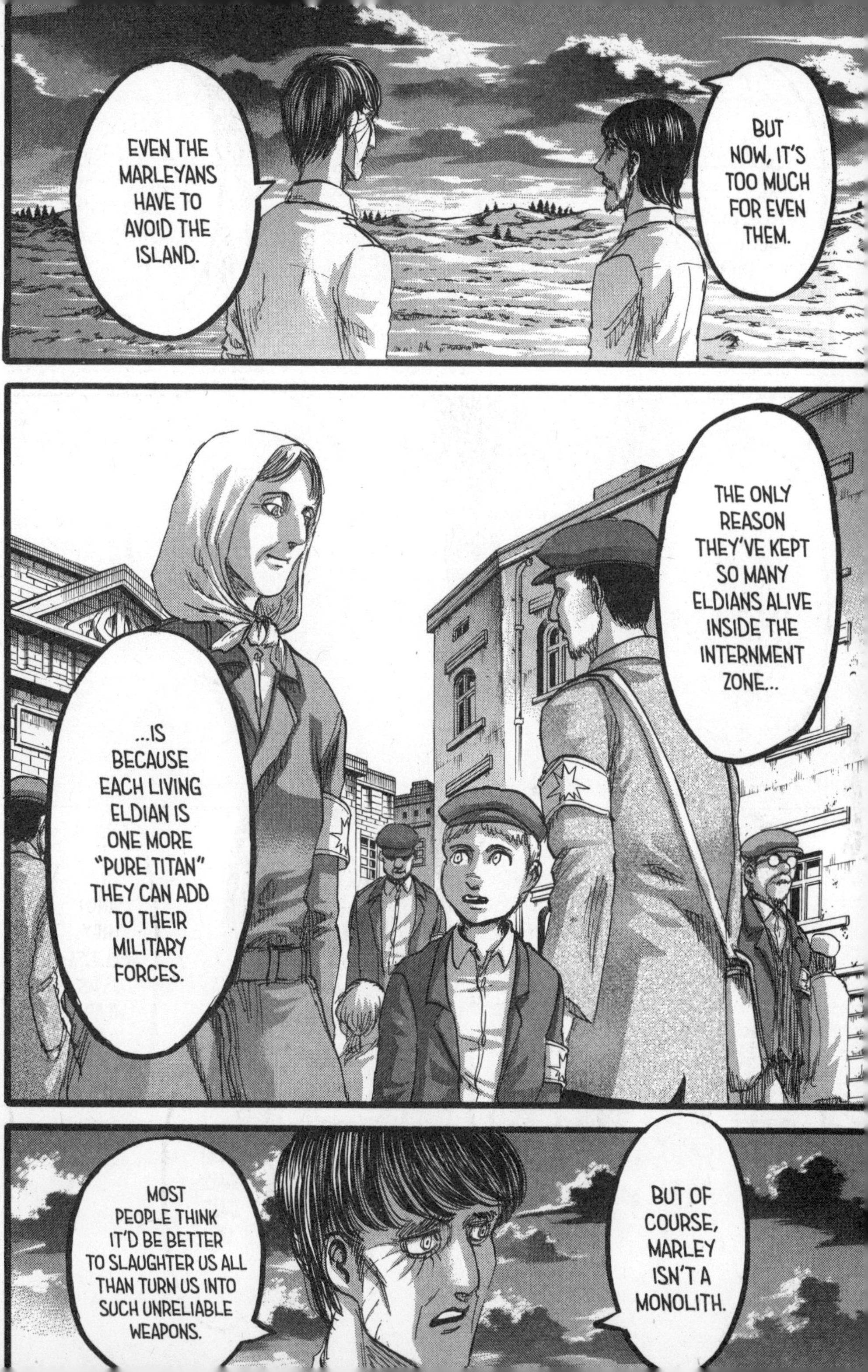
BUT NOW, IT'S TOO MUCH FOR EVEN THEM.
EVEN THE MARLEYANS HAVE TO AVOID THE ISLAND.
THE ONLY REASON THEY'VE KEPT SO MANY ELDIANS ALIVE INSIDE THE INTERNMENT ZONE...
...IS BECAUSE EACH LIVING ELDIAN IS ONE MORE "PURE TITAN" THEY CAN ADD TO THEIR MILITARY FORCES.
BUT OF COURSE, MARLEY ISN'T A MONOLITH.
MOST PEOPLE THINK IT'D BE BETTER TO SLAUGHTER US ALL THAN TURN US INTO SUCH UNRELIABLE WEAPONS.

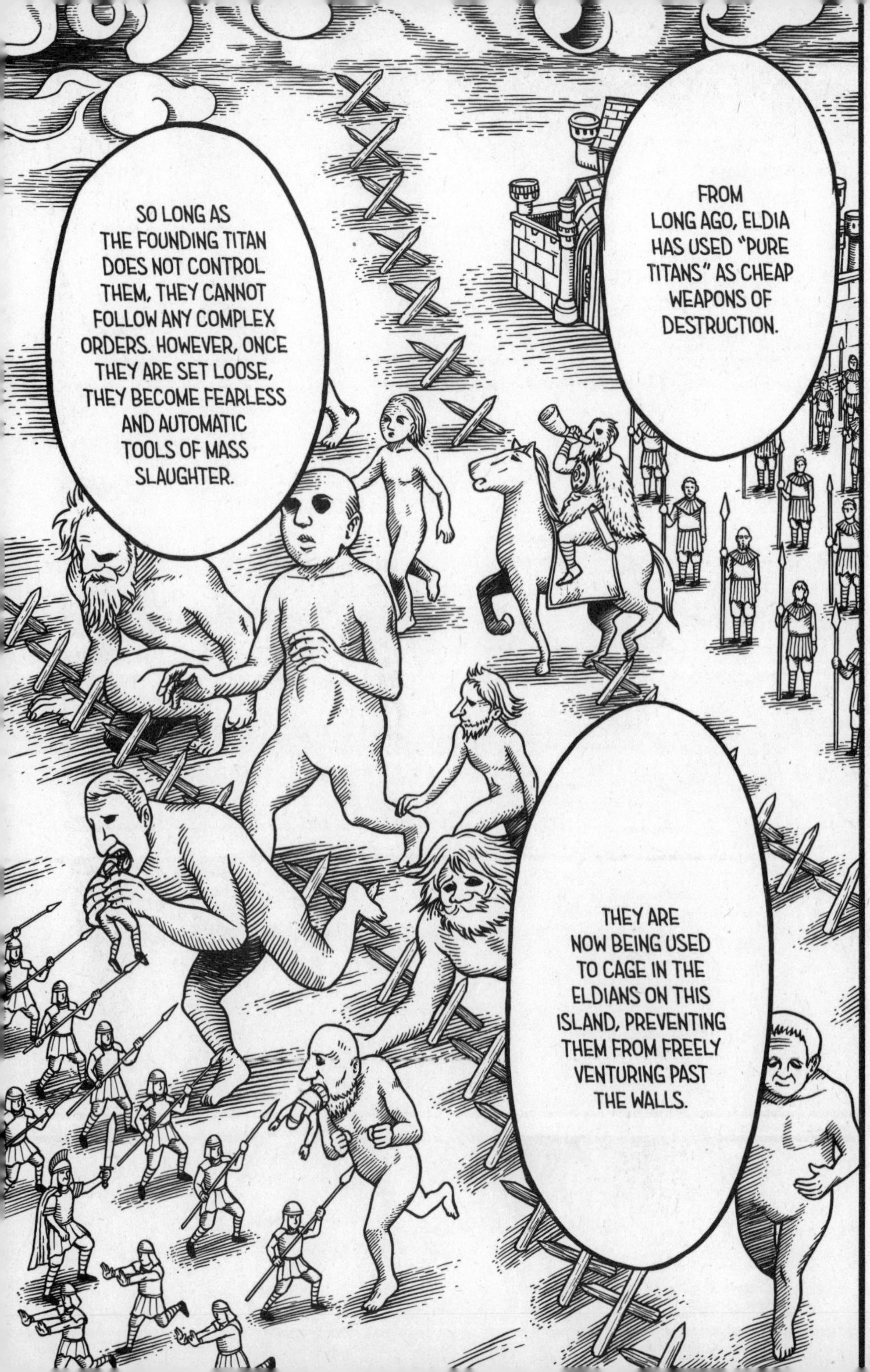
FROM LONG AGO, ELDIA HAS USED "PURE TITANS" AS CHEAP WEAPONS OF DESTRUCTION.
SO LONG AS THE FOUNDING TITAN DOES NOT CONTROL THEM, THEY CANNOT FOLLOW ANY COMPLEX ORDERS. HOWEVER, ONCE THEY ARE SET LOOSE, THEY BECOME FEARLESS AND AUTOMATIC TOOLS OF MASS SLAUGHTER.
THEY ARE NOW BEING USED TO CAGE IN THE ELDIANS ON THIS ISLAND, PREVENTING THEM FROM FREELY VENTURING PAST THE WALLS.

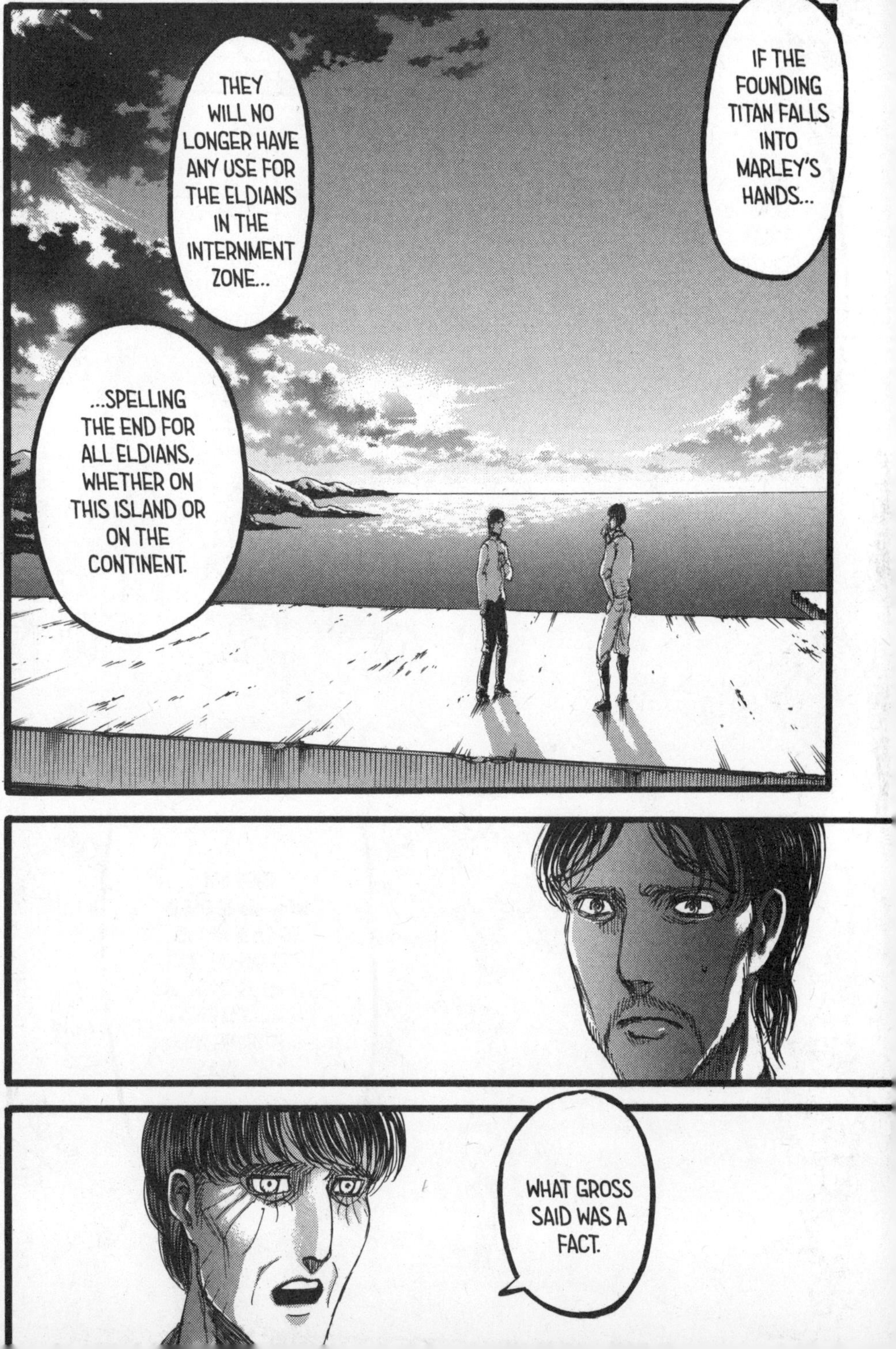
IF THE FOUNDING TITAN FALLS INTO MARLEY'S HANDS...
THEY WILL NO LONGER HAVE ANY USE FOR THE ELDIANS IN THE INTERNMENT ZONE...
...SPELLING THE END FOR ALL ELDIANS, WHETHER ON THIS ISLAND OR ON THE CONTINENT.
WHAT GROSS SAID WAS A FACT.

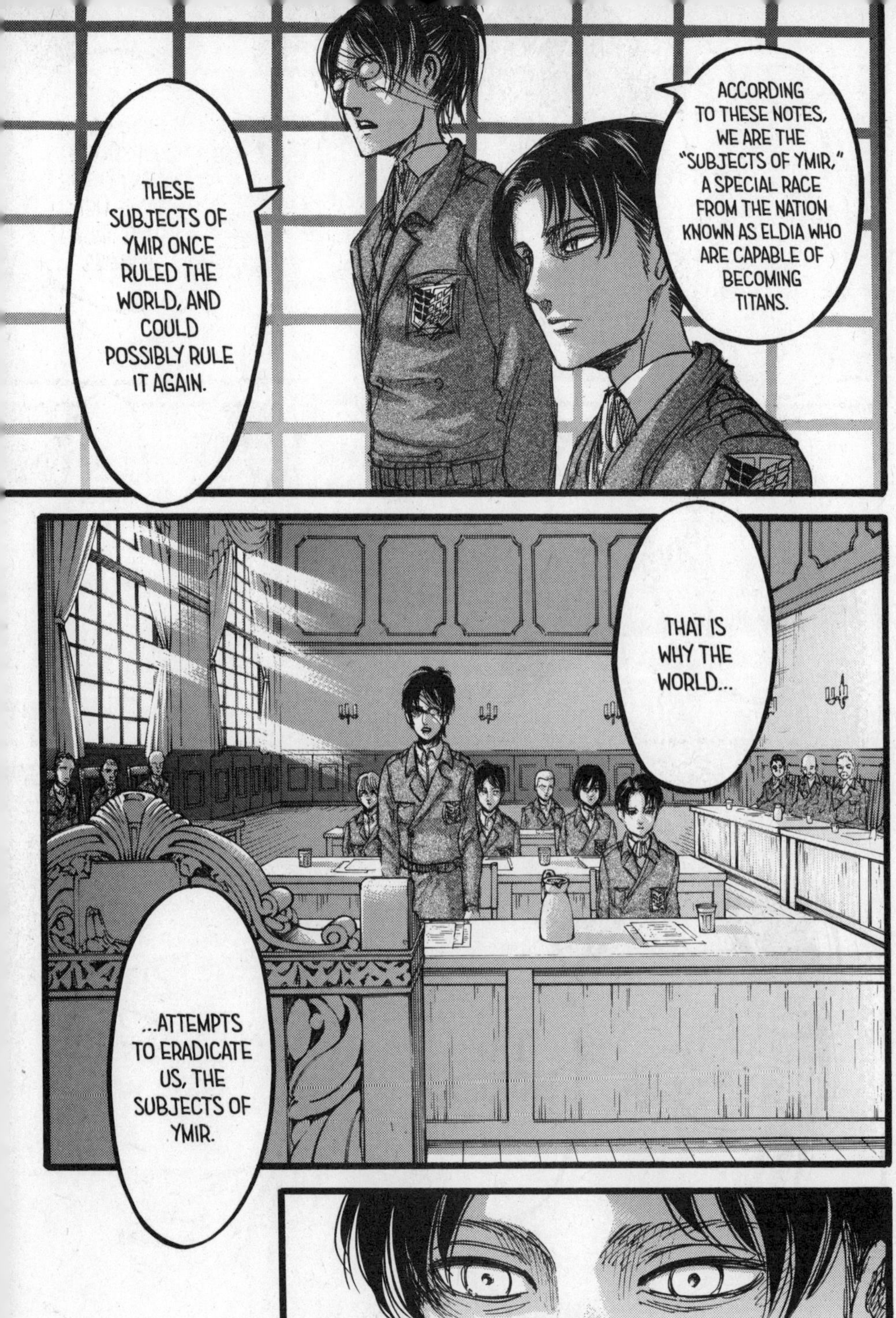
ACCORDING TO THESE NOTES, WE ARE THE "SUBJECTS OF YMIR," A SPECIAL RACE FROM THE NATION KNOWN AS ELDIA WHO ARE CAPABLE OF BECOMING TITANS.
THESE SUBJECTS OF YMIR ONCE RULED THE WORLD, AND COULD POSSIBLY RULE IT AGAIN.
THAT IS WHY THE WORLD...
...ATTEMPTS TO ERADICATE US, THE SUBJECTS OF YMIR.

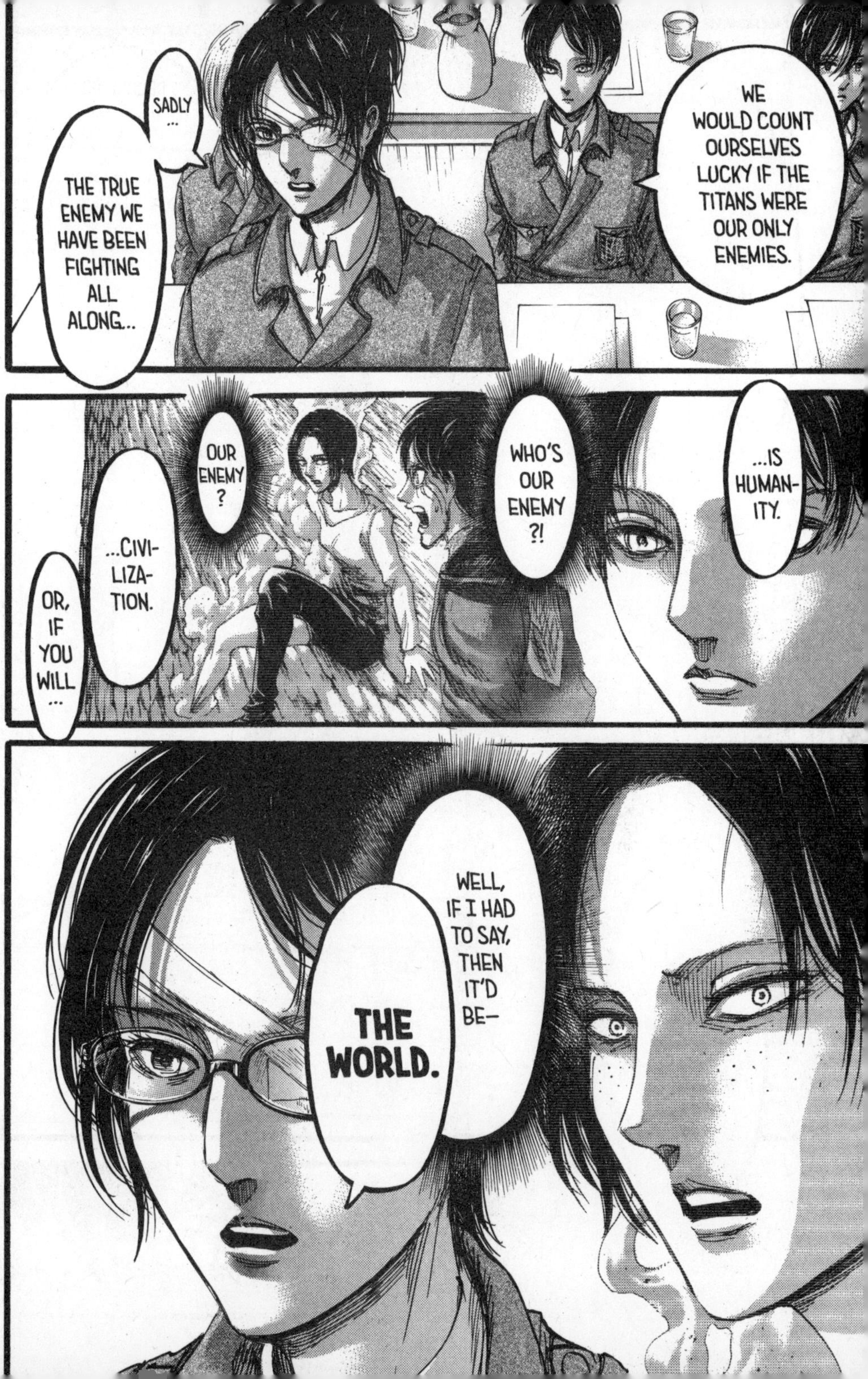
WE WOULD COUNT OURSELVES LUCKY IF THE TITANS WERE OUR ONLY ENEMIES.
SADLY...
THE TRUE ENEMY WE HAVE BEEN FIGHTING ALL ALONG...
...IS HUMANITY.
WHO'S OUR ENEMY?!
OUR ENEMY?
OR, IF YOU WILL...
...CIVILIZATION.
WELL, IF I HAD TO SAY, THEN IT'D BE—
THE WORLD.

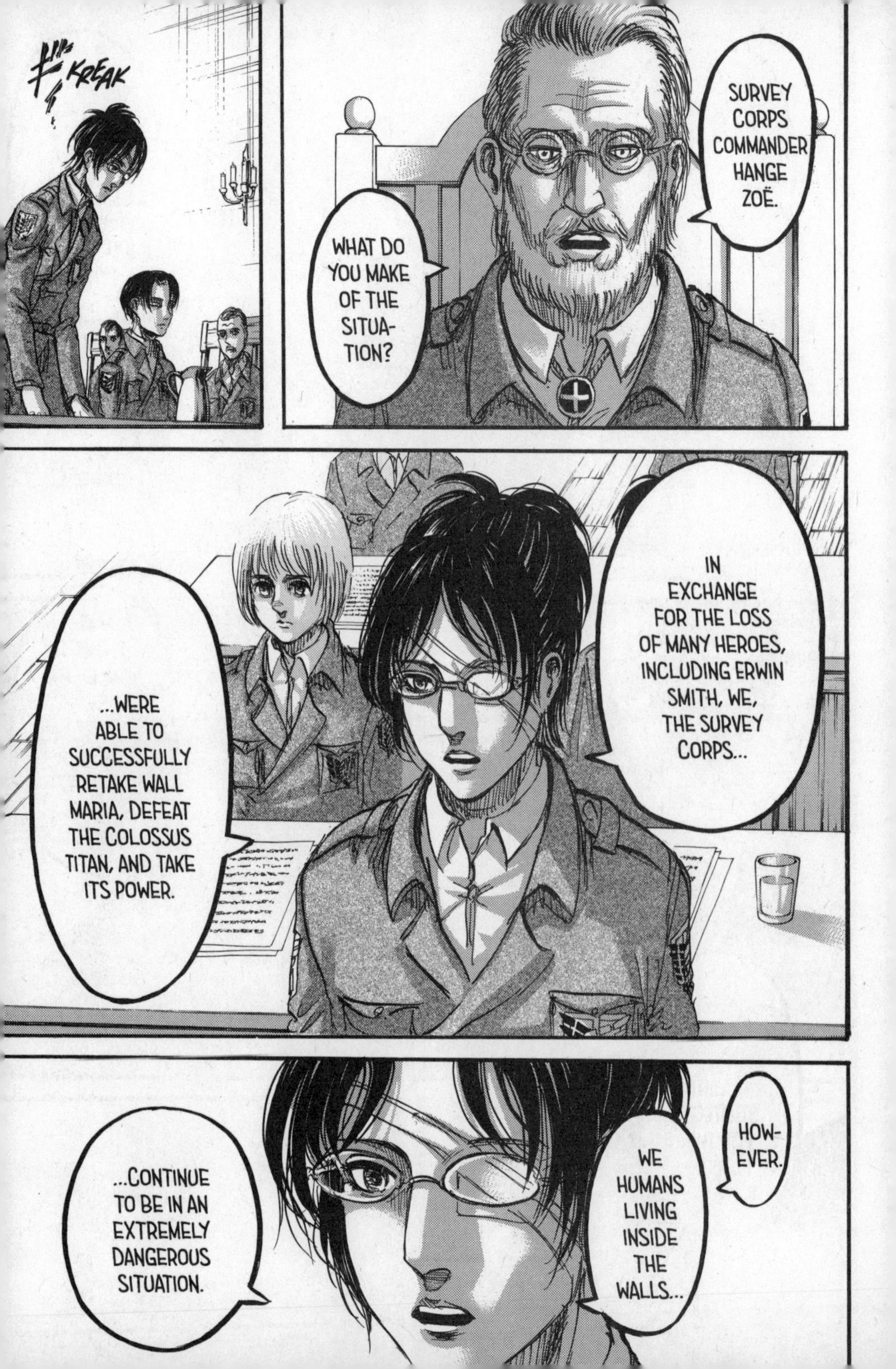
SURVEY CORPS COMMANDER HANGE ZOË.
WHAT DO YOU MAKE OF THE SITUATION?
KREAK
IN EXCHANGE FOR THE LOSS OF MANY HEROES, INCLUDING ERWIN SMITH, WE, THE SURVEY CORPS...
...WERE ABLE TO SUCCESSFULLY RETAKE WALL MARIA, DEFEAT THE COLOSSUS TITAN, AND TAKE ITS POWER.
HOW-EVER.
WE HUMANS LIVING INSIDE THE WALLS...
...CONTINUE TO BE IN AN EXTREMELY DANGEROUS SITUATION.

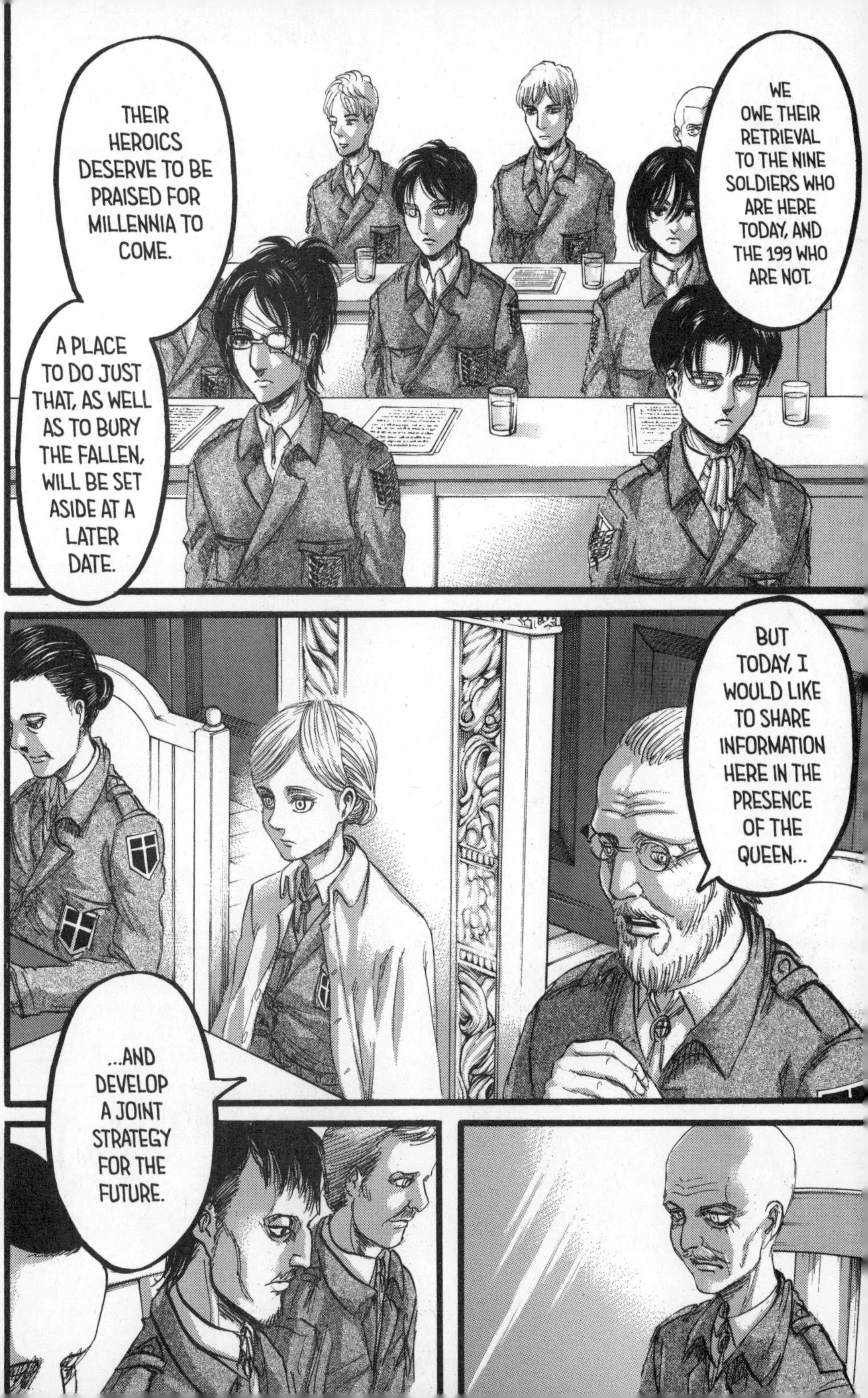
WE OWE THEIR RETRIEVAL TO THE NINE SOLDIERS WHO ARE HERE TODAY, AND THE 199 WHO ARE NOT.
THEIR HEROICS DESERVE TO BE PRAISED FOR MILLENNIA TO COME.
A PLACE TO DO JUST THAT, AS WELL AS TO BURY THE FALLEN, WILL BE SET ASIDE AT A LATER DATE.
BUT TODAY, I WOULD LIKE TO SHARE INFORMATION HERE IN THE PRESENCE OF THE QUEEN...
...AND DEVELOP A JOINT STRATEGY FOR THE FUTURE.

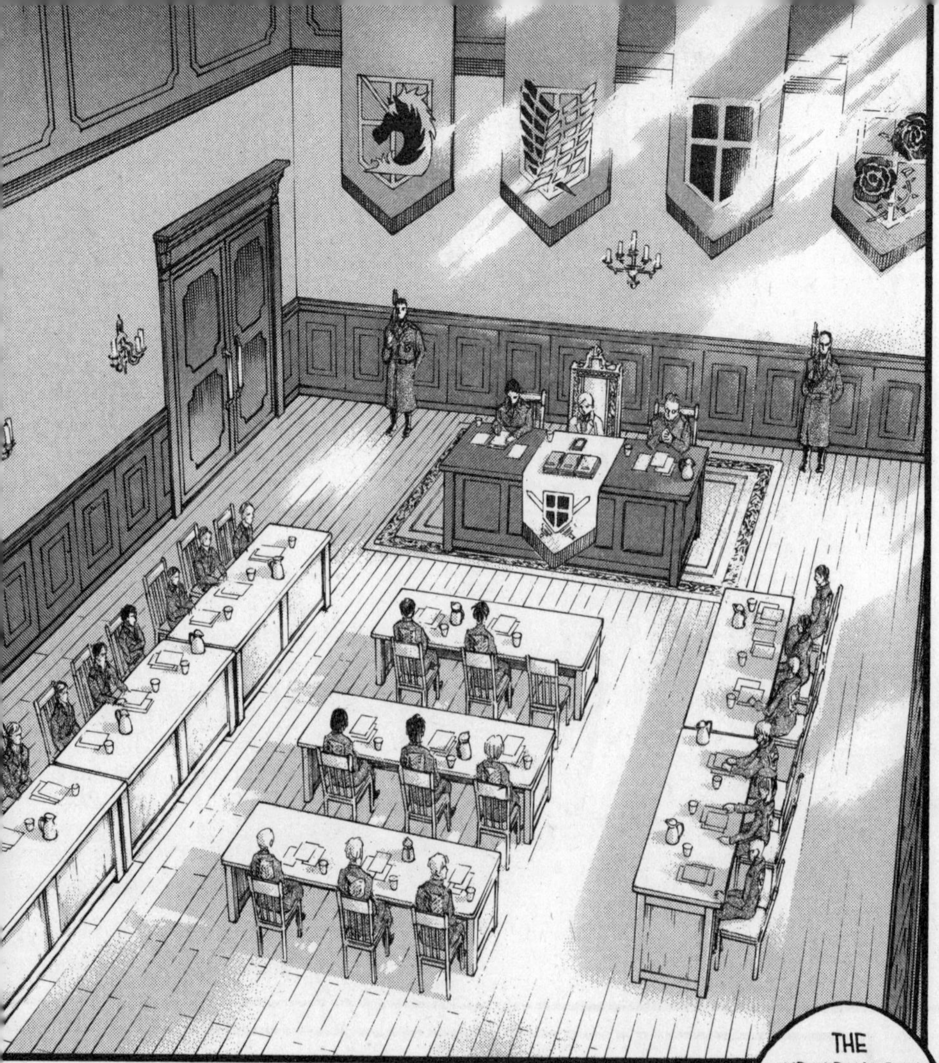

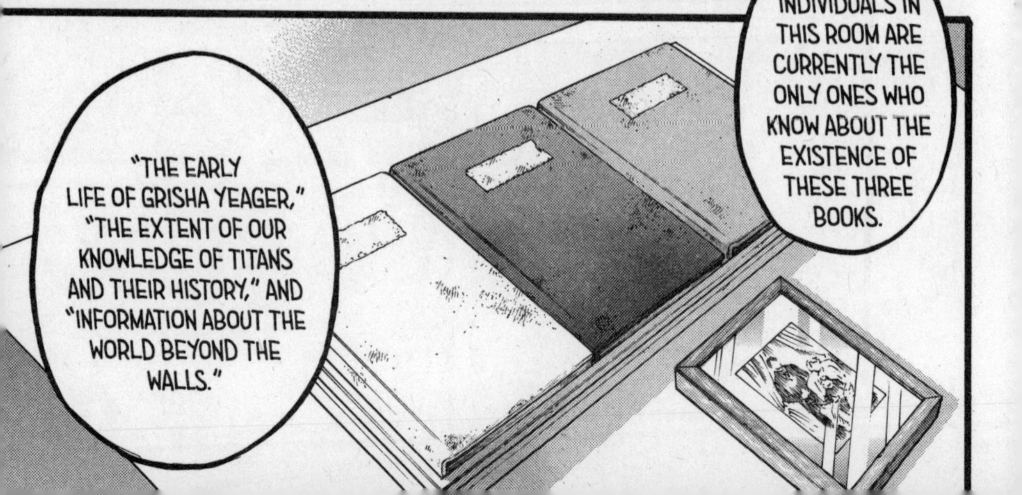
THE INDIVIDUALS IN THIS ROOM ARE CURRENTLY THE ONLY ONES WHO KNOW ABOUT THE EXISTENCE OF THESE THREE BOOKS.
"THE EARLY LIFE OF GRISHA YEAGER," "THE EXTENT OF OUR KNOWLEDGE OF TITANS AND THEIR HISTORY," AND "INFORMATION ABOUT THE WORLD BEYOND THE WALLS."

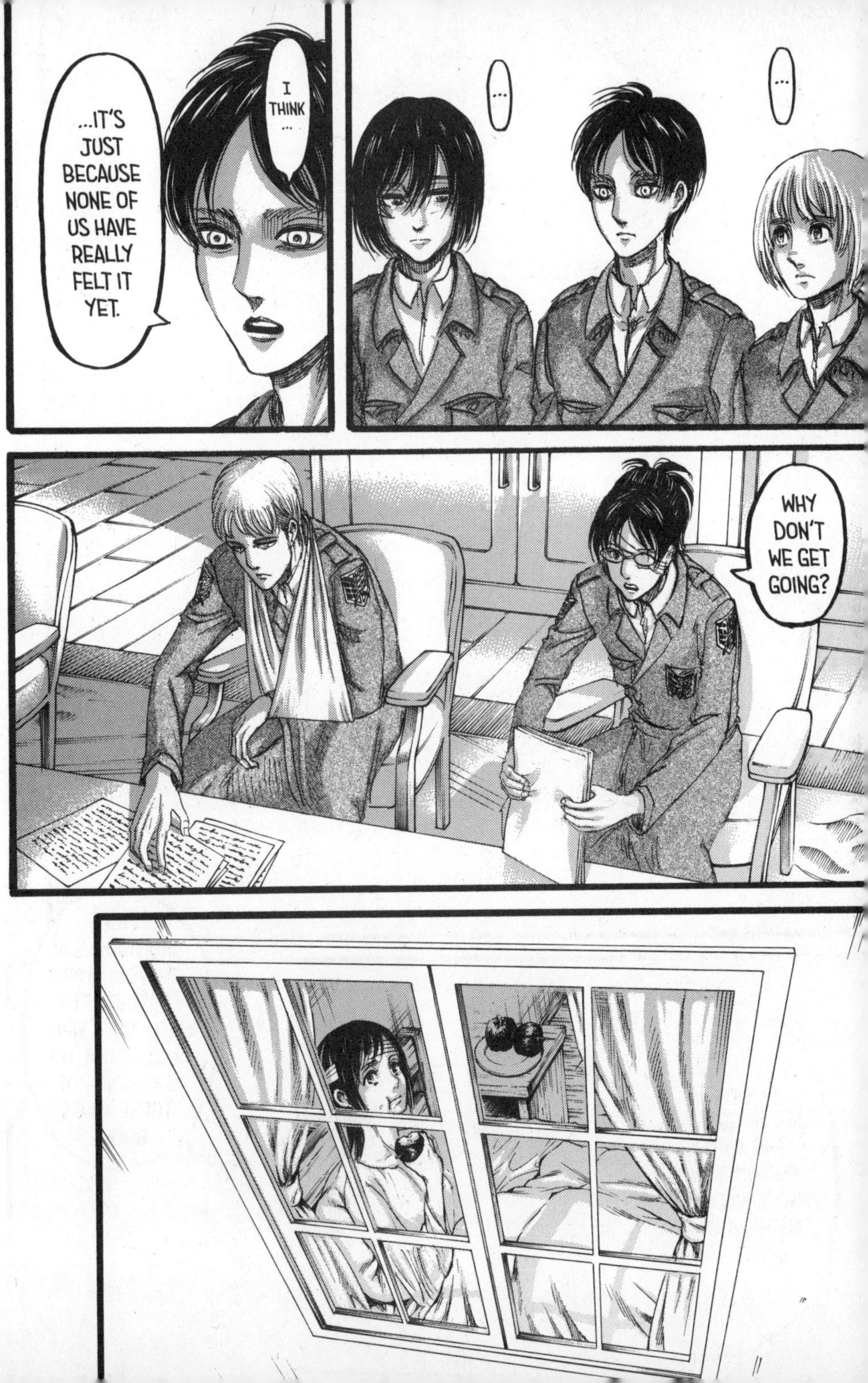
...
...
I THINK...
...IT'S JUST BECAUSE NONE OF US HAVE REALLY FELT IT YET.
WHY DON'T WE GET GOING?

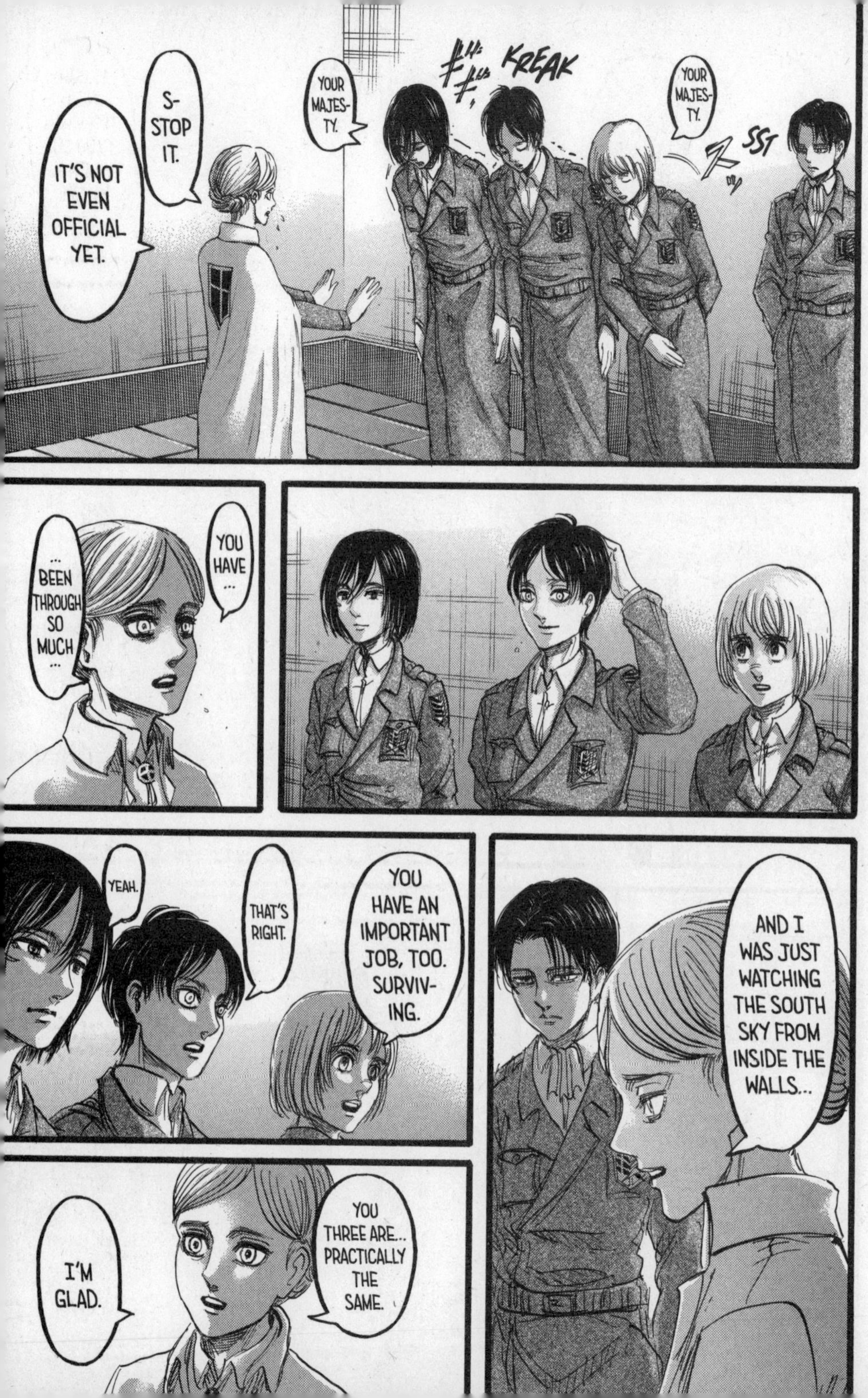
YOUR MAJES-TY.
SST
KREAK
YOUR MAJES-TY.
S-STOP IT.
IT'S NOT EVEN OFFICIAL YET.
YOU HAVE ...
... BEEN THROUGH SO MUCH ...
AND I WAS JUST WATCHING THE SOUTH SKY FROM INSIDE THE WALLS...
YOU HAVE AN IMPORTANT JOB, TOO. SURVIV-ING.
THAT'S RIGHT.
YEAH.
YOU THREE ARE... PRACTICALLY THE SAME.
I'M GLAD.

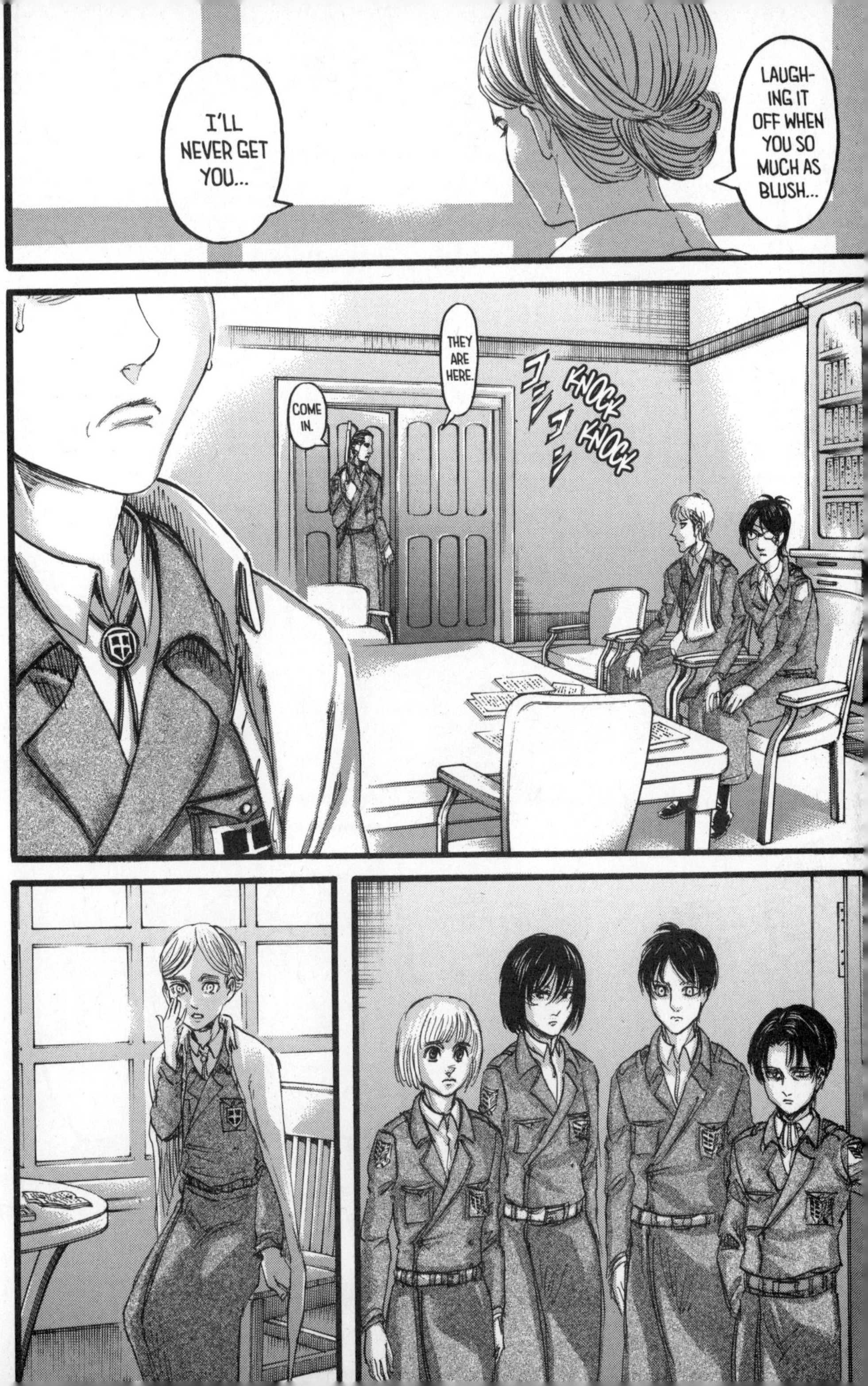
LAUGHING IT OFF WHEN YOU SO MUCH AS BLUSH...
I'LL NEVER GET YOU...
KNOCK KNOCK
THEY ARE HERE.
COME IN.

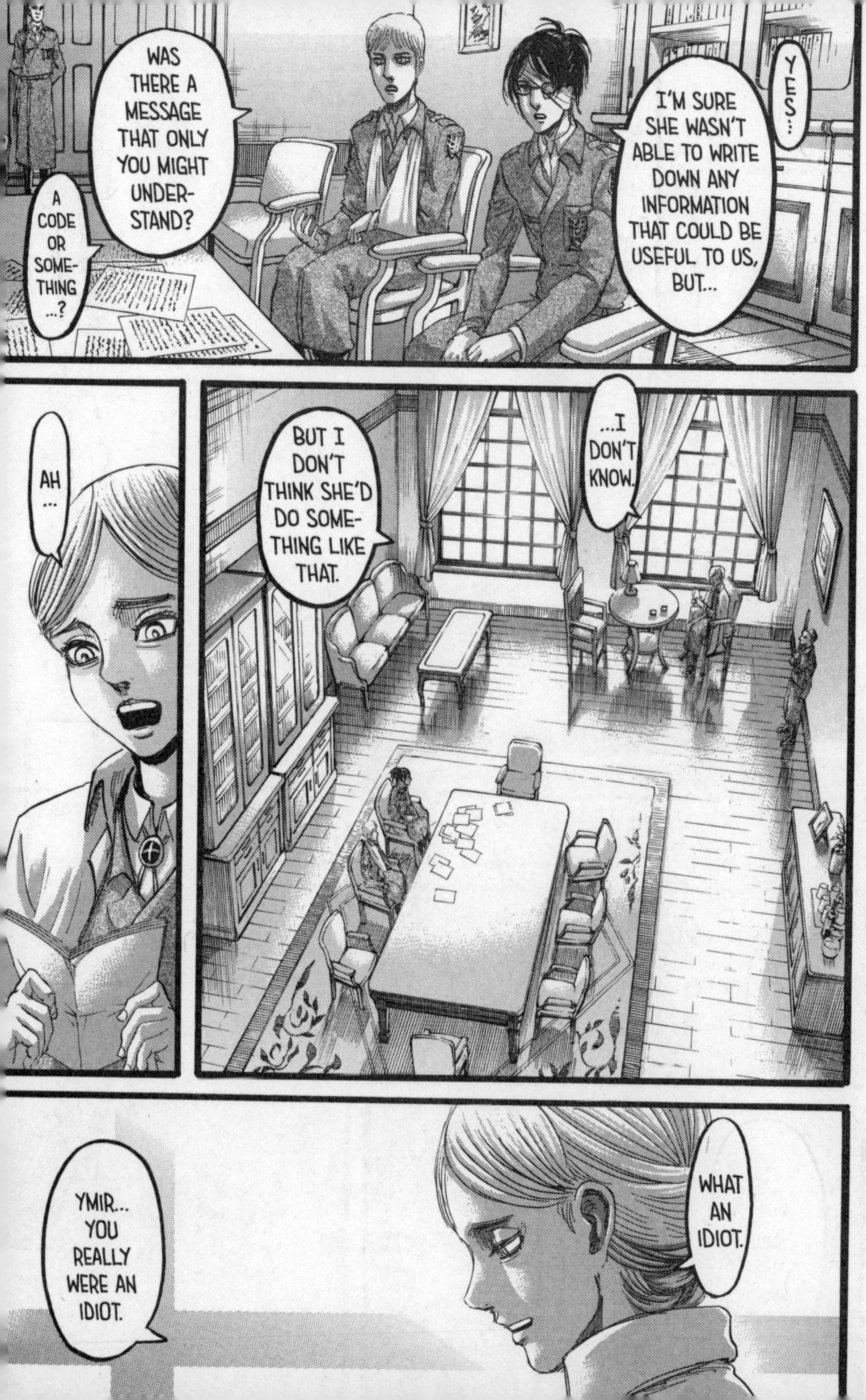
YES...
I'M SURE SHE WASN'T ABLE TO WRITE DOWN ANY INFORMATION THAT COULD BE USEFUL TO US, BUT...
WAS THERE A MESSAGE THAT ONLY YOU MIGHT UNDER-STAND?
A CODE OR SOME-THING ...?
...I DON'T KNOW.
BUT I DON'T THINK SHE'D DO SOME-THING LIKE THAT.
AH ...
WHAT AN IDIOT.
YMIR... YOU REALLY WERE AN IDIOT.

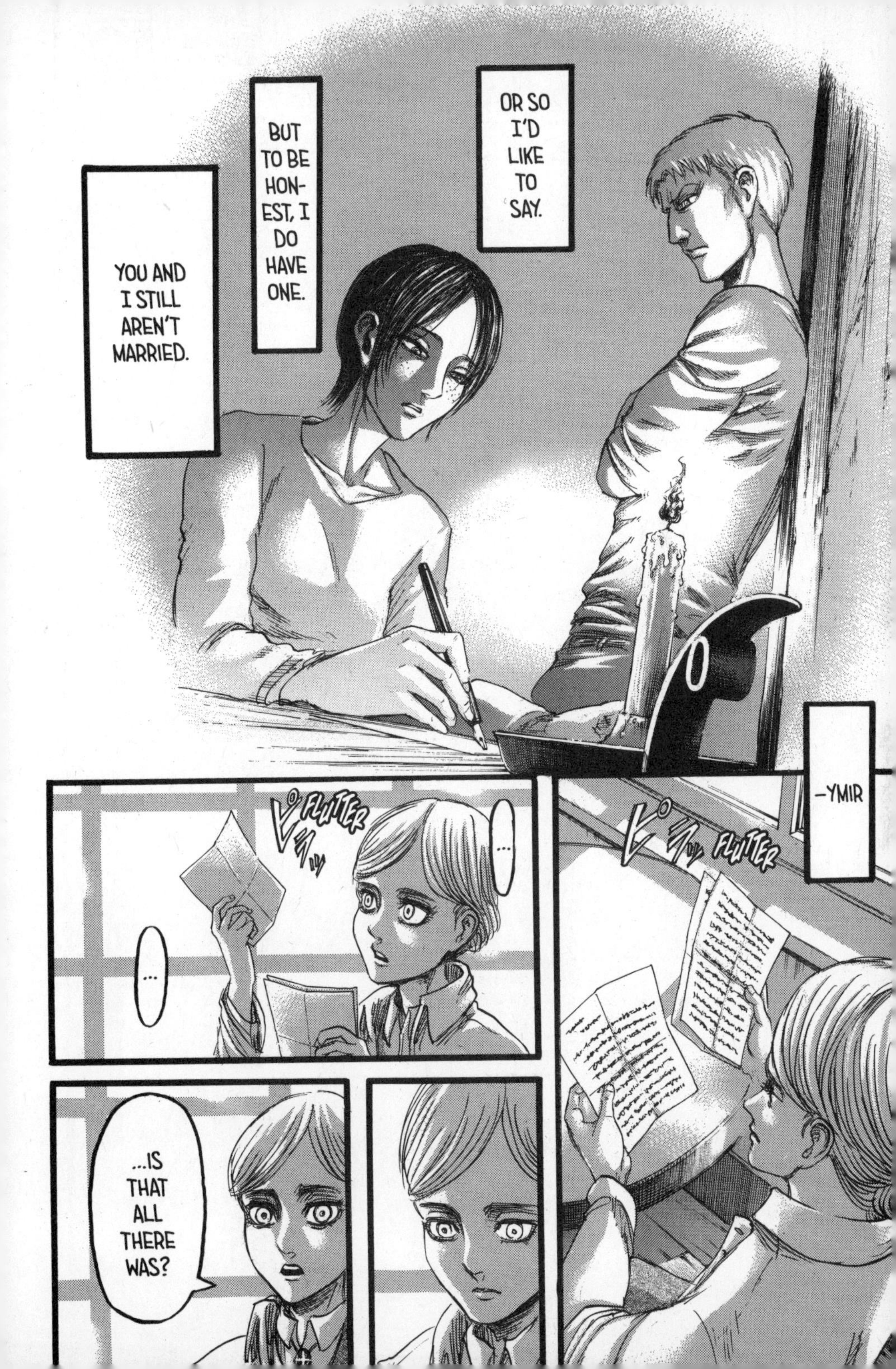
OR SO I'D LIKE TO SAY.
BUT TO BE HONEST, I DO HAVE ONE.
YOU AND I STILL AREN'T MARRIED.
—YMIR
FLUTTER
FLUTTER
...
...
...IS THAT ALL THERE WAS?

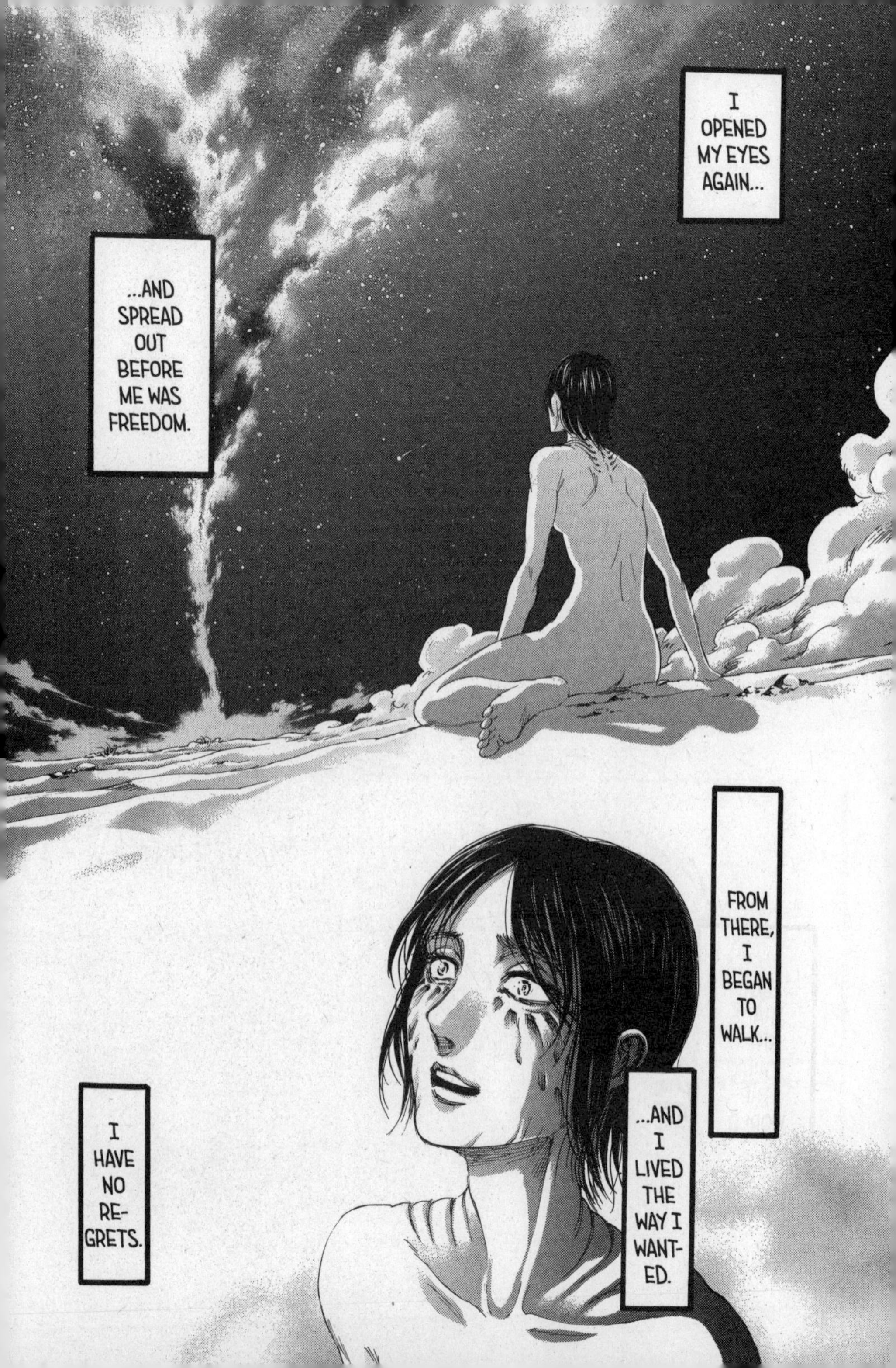
I OPENED MY EYES AGAIN...
...AND SPREAD OUT BEFORE ME WAS FREEDOM.
FROM THERE, I BEGAN TO WALK...
...AND I LIVED THE WAY I WANT-ED.
I HAVE NO RE-GRETS.

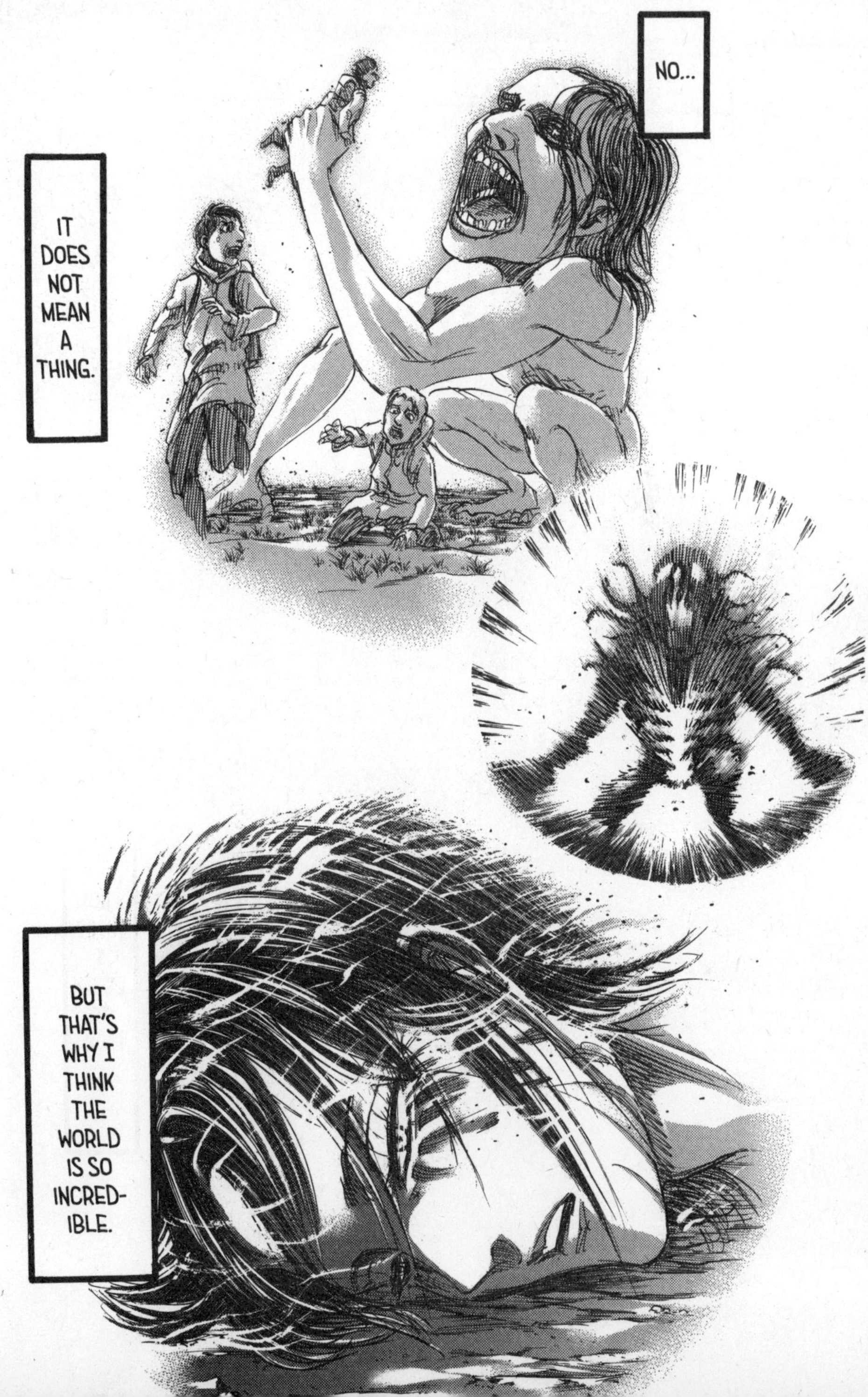
NO...
IT DOES NOT MEAN A THING.
BUT THAT'S WHY I THINK THE WORLD IS SO INCREDIBLE.

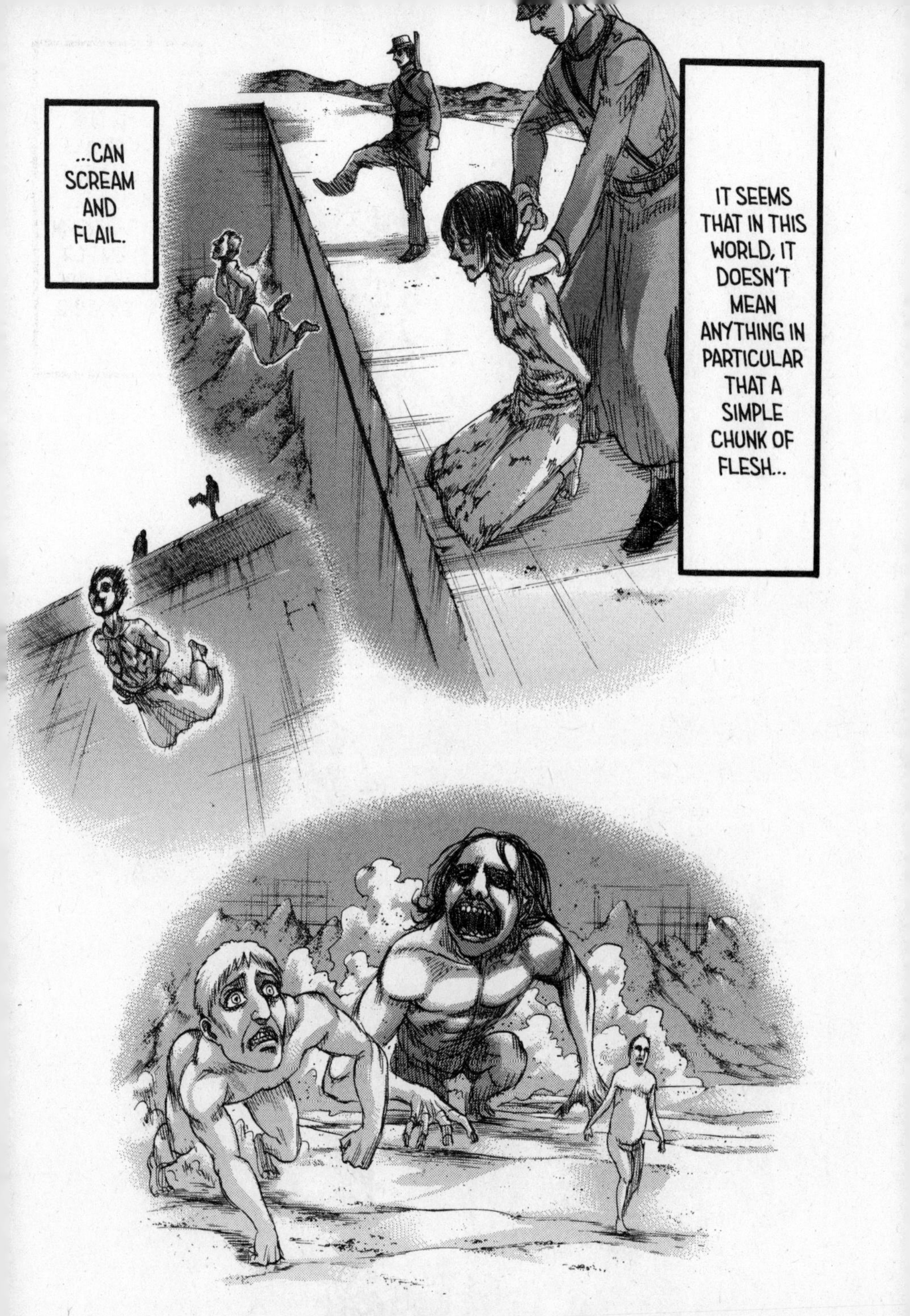
IT SEEMS THAT IN THIS WORLD, IT DOESN'T MEAN ANYTHING IN PARTICULAR THAT A SIMPLE CHUNK OF FLESH...
...CAN SCREAM AND FLAIL.

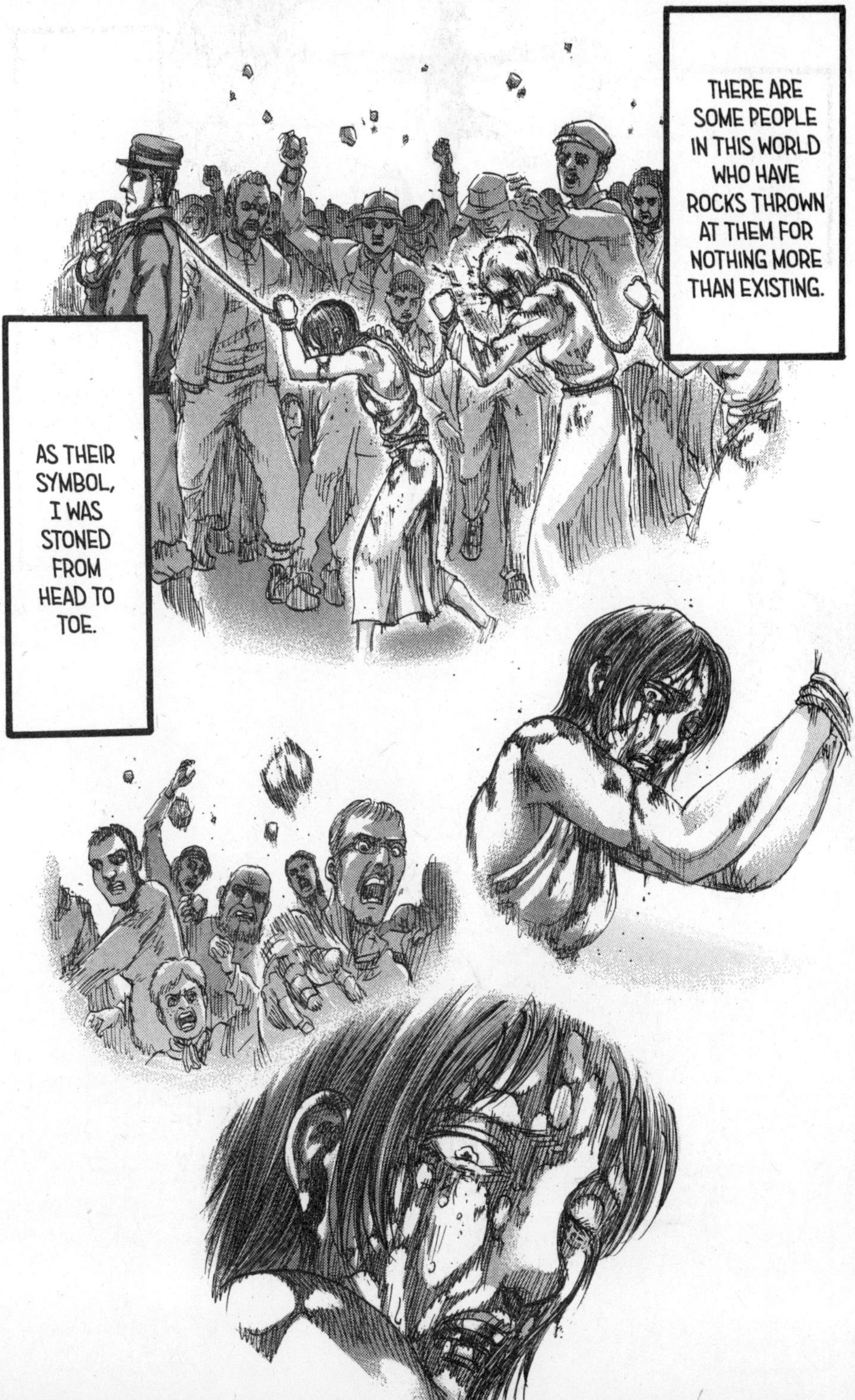
THERE ARE SOME PEOPLE IN THIS WORLD WHO HAVE ROCKS THROWN AT THEM FOR NOTHING MORE THAN EXISTING.
AS THEIR SYMBOL, I WAS STONED FROM HEAD TO TOE.

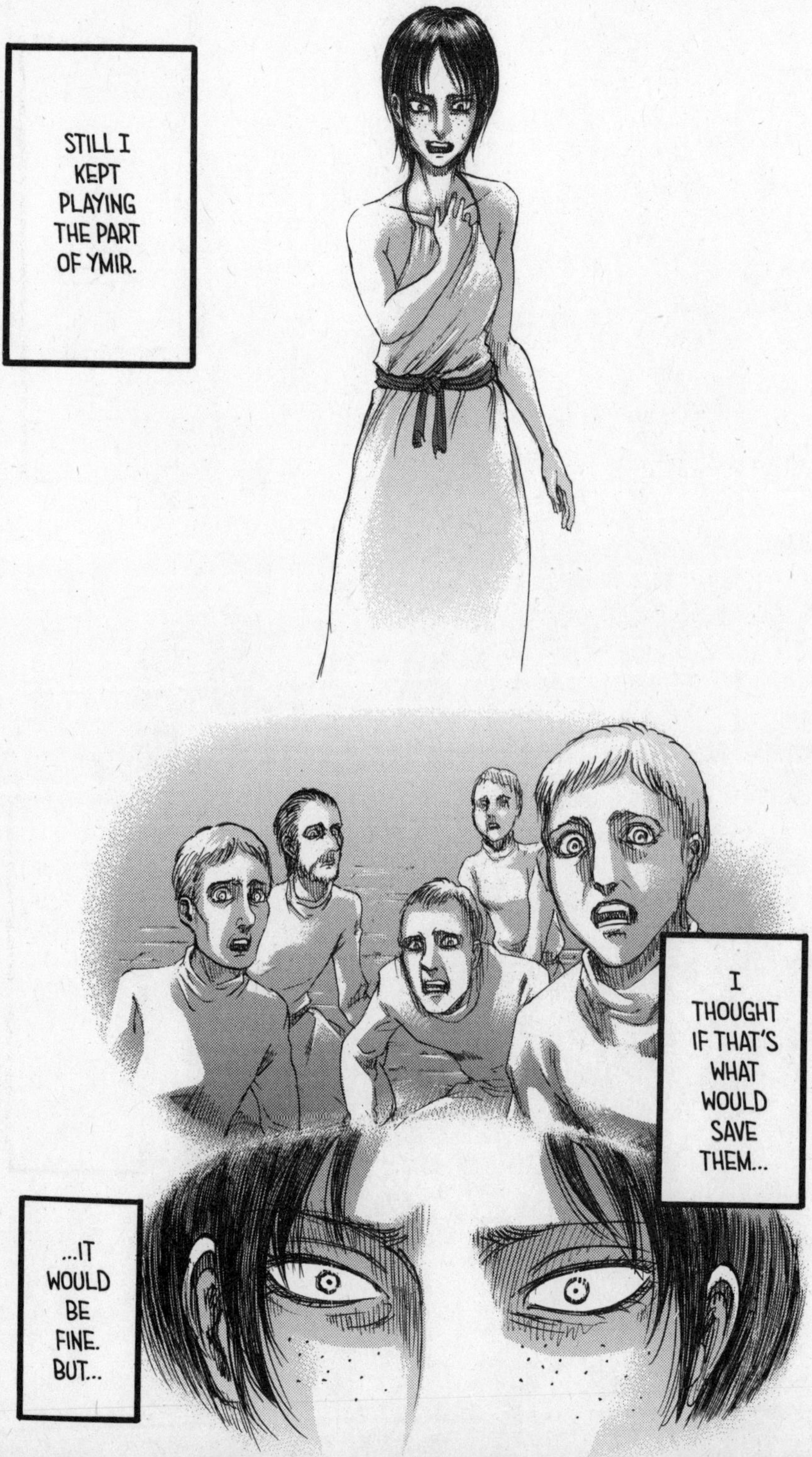
STILL I KEPT PLAYING THE PART OF YMIR.
I THOUGHT IF THAT'S WHAT WOULD SAVE THEM...
...IT WOULD BE FINE. BUT...

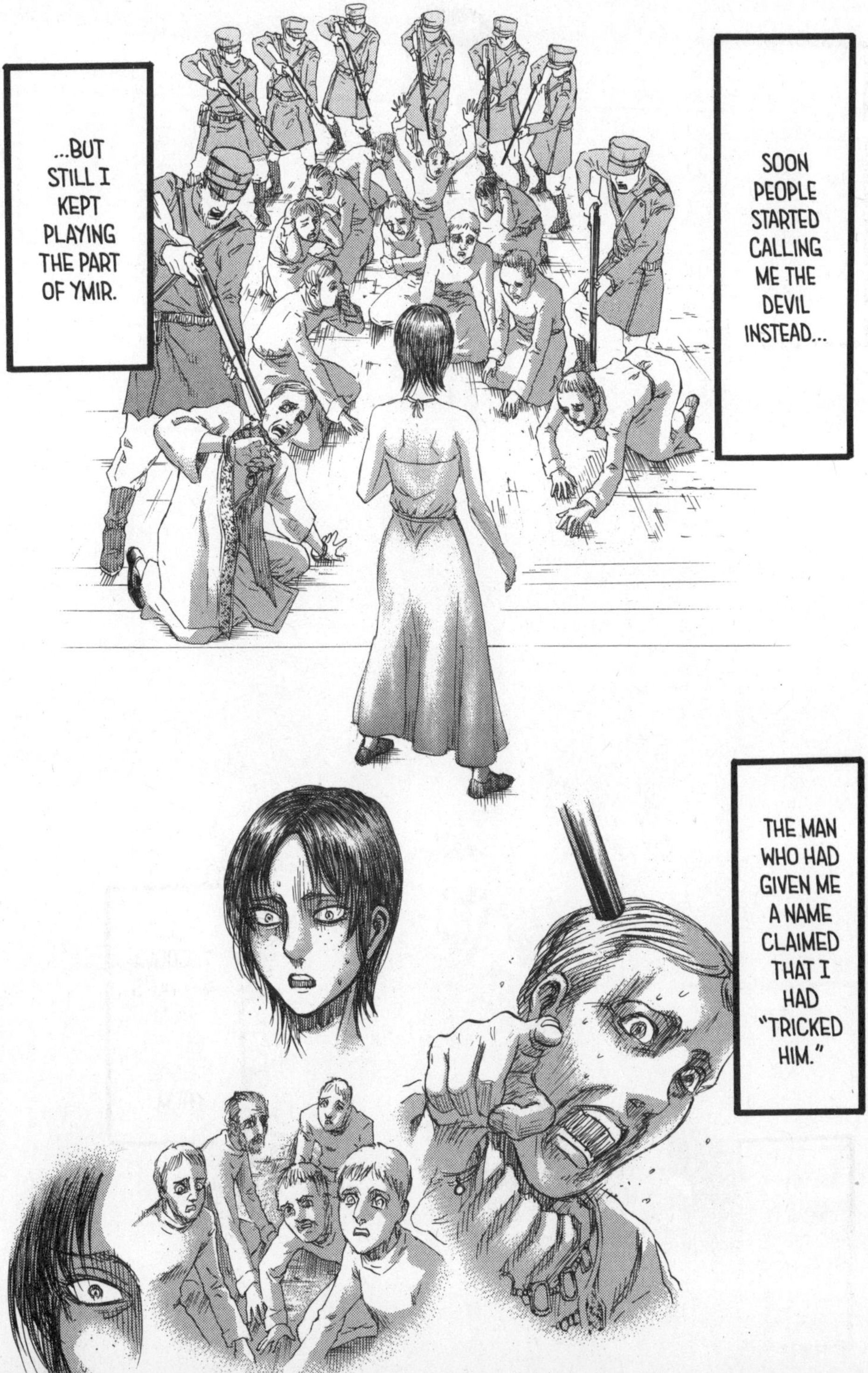
SOON PEOPLE STARTED CALLING ME THE DEVIL INSTEAD...
...BUT STILL I KEPT PLAYING THE PART OF YMIR.
THE MAN WHO HAD GIVEN ME A NAME CLAIMED THAT I HAD "TRICKED HIM."

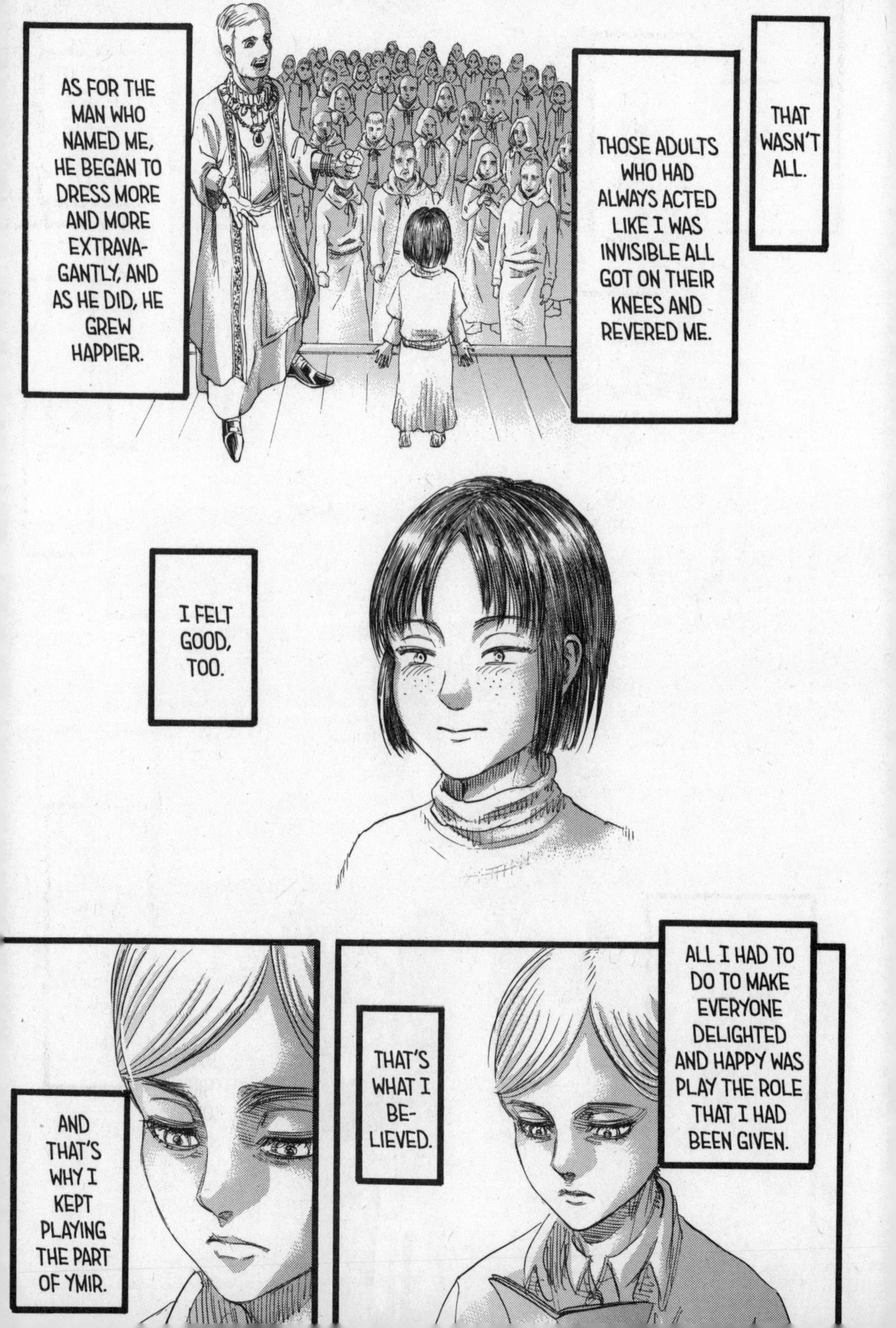
THAT WASN'T ALL.
THOSE ADULTS WHO HAD ALWAYS ACTED LIKE I WAS INVISIBLE ALL GOT ON THEIR KNEES AND REVERED ME.
AS FOR THE MAN WHO NAMED ME, HE BEGAN TO DRESS MORE AND MORE EXTRAVAGANTLY, AND AS HE DID, HE GREW HAPPIER.
I FELT GOOD, TOO.
ALL I HAD TO DO TO MAKE EVERYONE DELIGHTED AND HAPPY WAS PLAY THE ROLE THAT I HAD BEEN GIVEN.
THAT'S WHAT I BELIEVED.
AND THAT'S WHY I KEPT PLAYING THE PART OF YMIR.

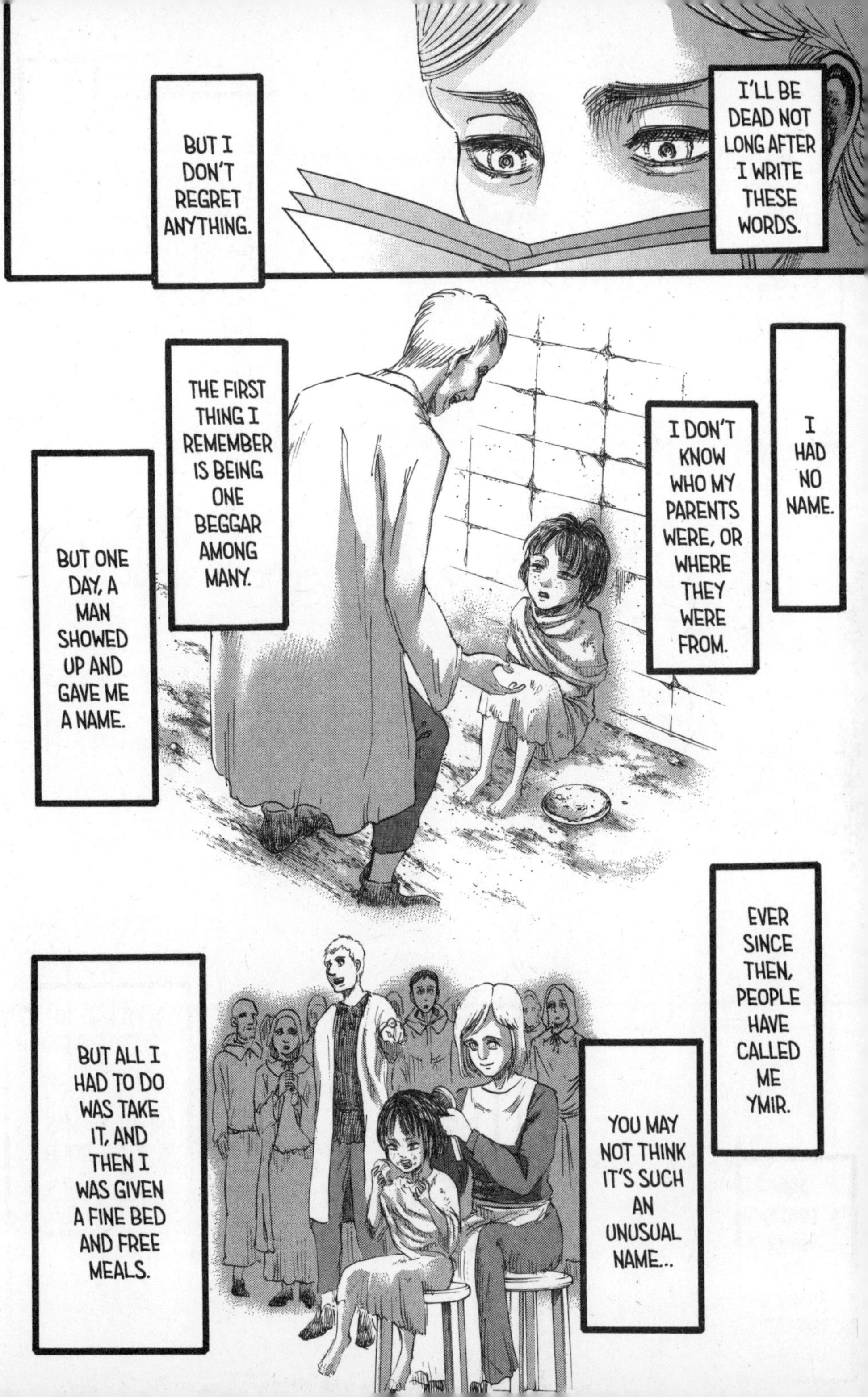
I'LL BE DEAD NOT LONG AFTER I WRITE THESE WORDS.
BUT I DON'T REGRET ANYTHING.
I HAD NO NAME.
I DON'T KNOW WHO MY PARENTS WERE, OR WHERE THEY WERE FROM.
THE FIRST THING I REMEMBER IS BEING ONE BEGGAR AMONG MANY.
BUT ONE DAY, A MAN SHOWED UP AND GAVE ME A NAME.
EVER SINCE THEN, PEOPLE HAVE CALLED ME YMIR.
YOU MAY NOT THINK IT'S SUCH AN UNUSUAL NAME...
BUT ALL I HAD TO DO WAS TAKE IT, AND THEN I WAS GIVEN A FINE BED AND FREE MEALS.

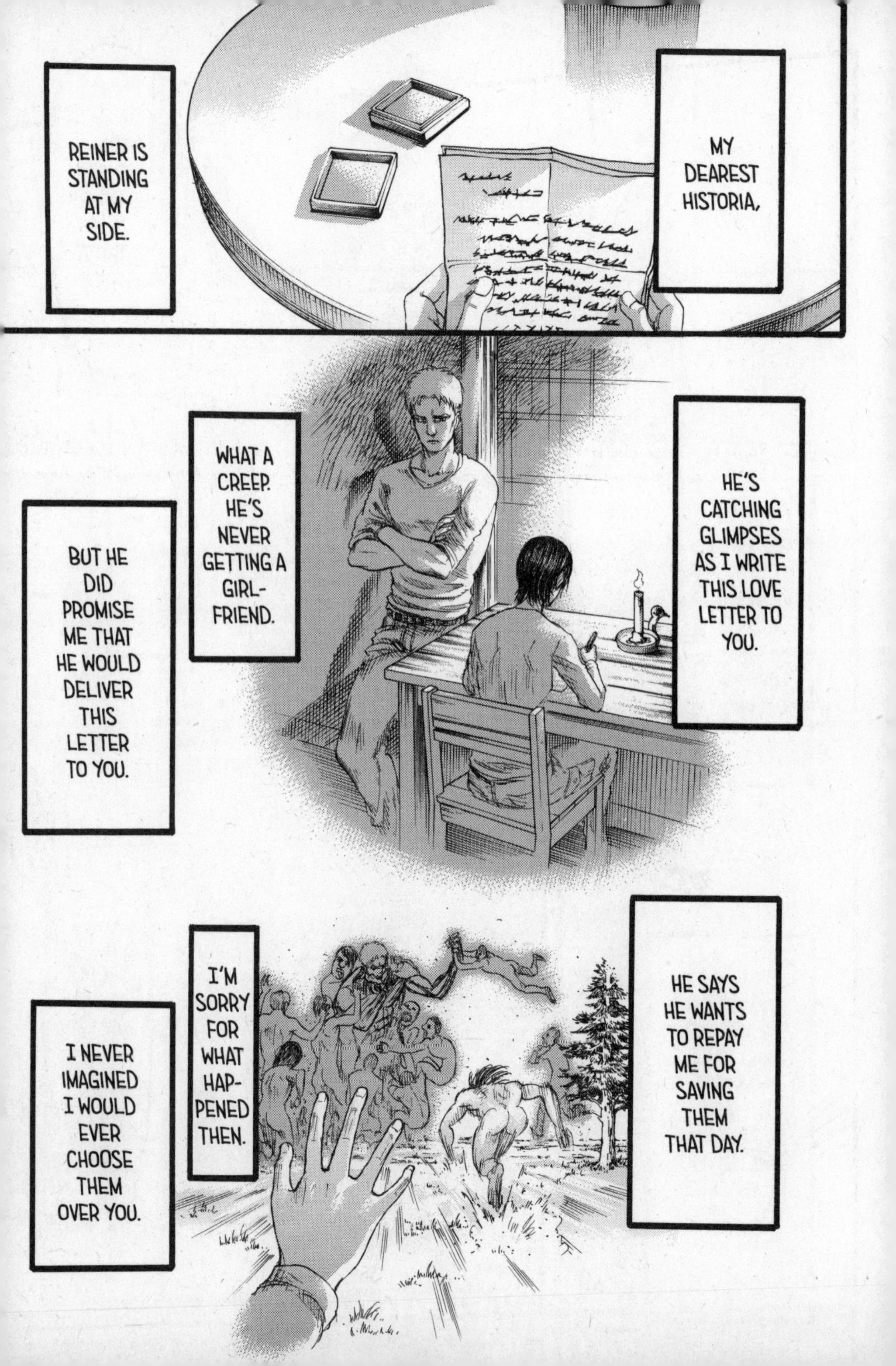
MY DEAREST HISTORIA,
REINER IS STANDING AT MY SIDE.
HE'S CATCHING GLIMPSES AS I WRITE THIS LOVE LETTER TO YOU.
WHAT A CREEP. HE'S NEVER GETTING A GIRL-FRIEND.
BUT HE DID PROMISE ME THAT HE WOULD DELIVER THIS LETTER TO YOU.
HE SAYS HE WANTS TO REPAY ME FOR SAVING THEM THAT DAY.
I'M SORRY FOR WHAT HAP-PENED THEN.
I NEVER IMAGINED I WOULD EVER CHOOSE THEM OVER YOU.

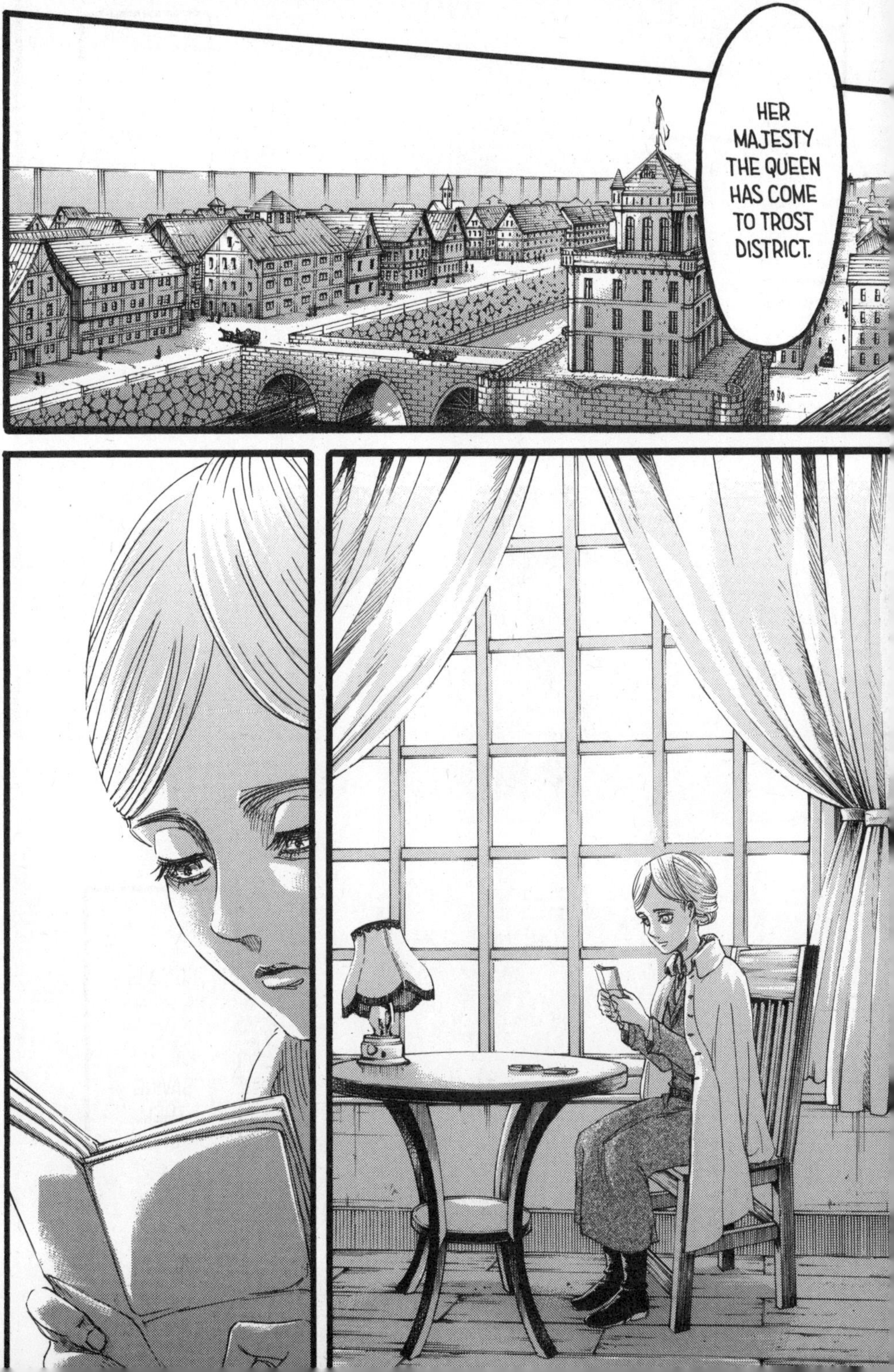
HER MAJESTY THE QUEEN HAS COME TO TROST DISTRICT.

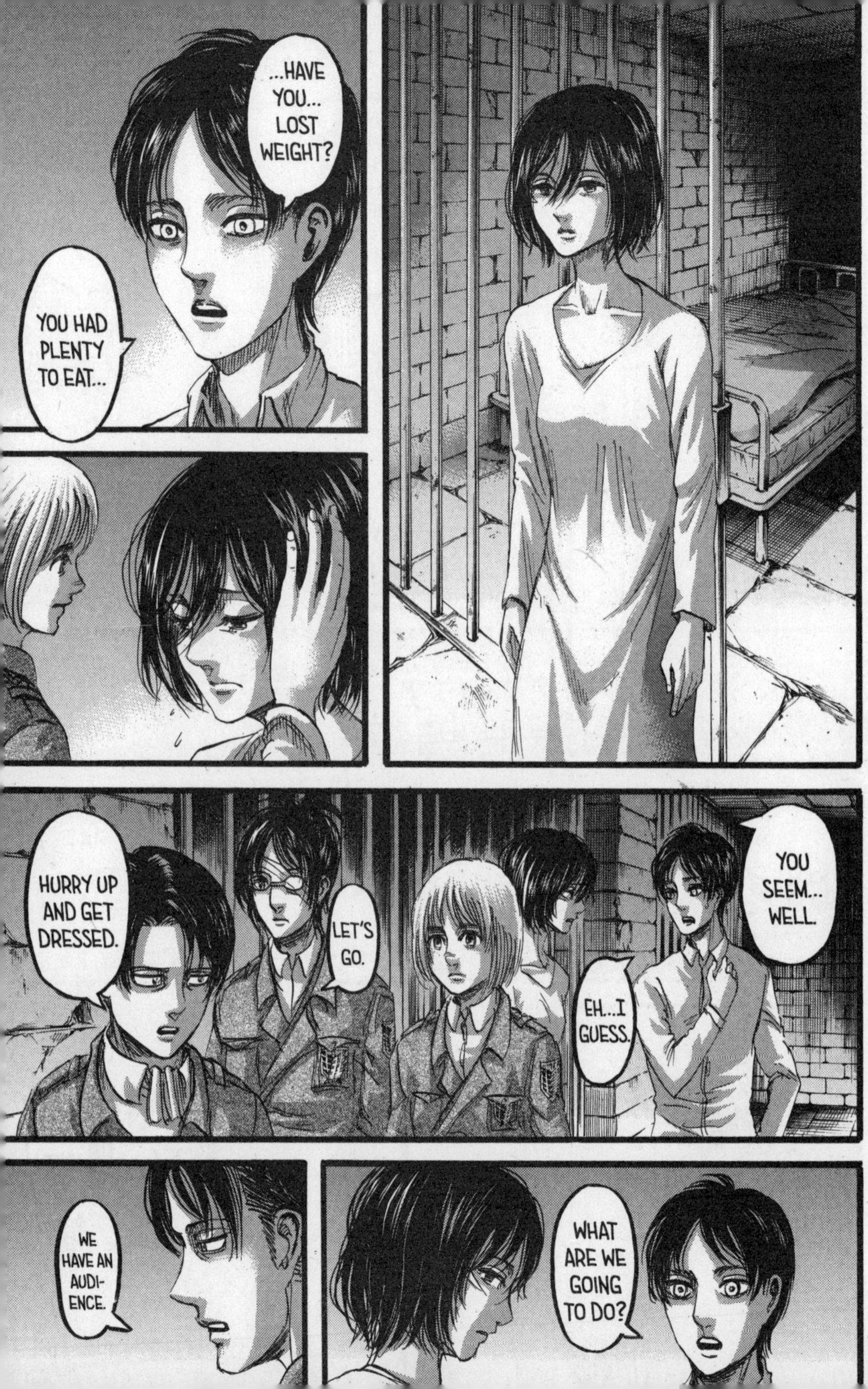
...HAVE YOU... LOST WEIGHT?
YOU HAD PLENTY TO EAT...
YOU SEEM... WELL.
EH...I GUESS.
LET'S GO.
HURRY UP AND GET DRESSED.
WHAT ARE WE GOING TO DO?
WE HAVE AN AUDI-ENCE.

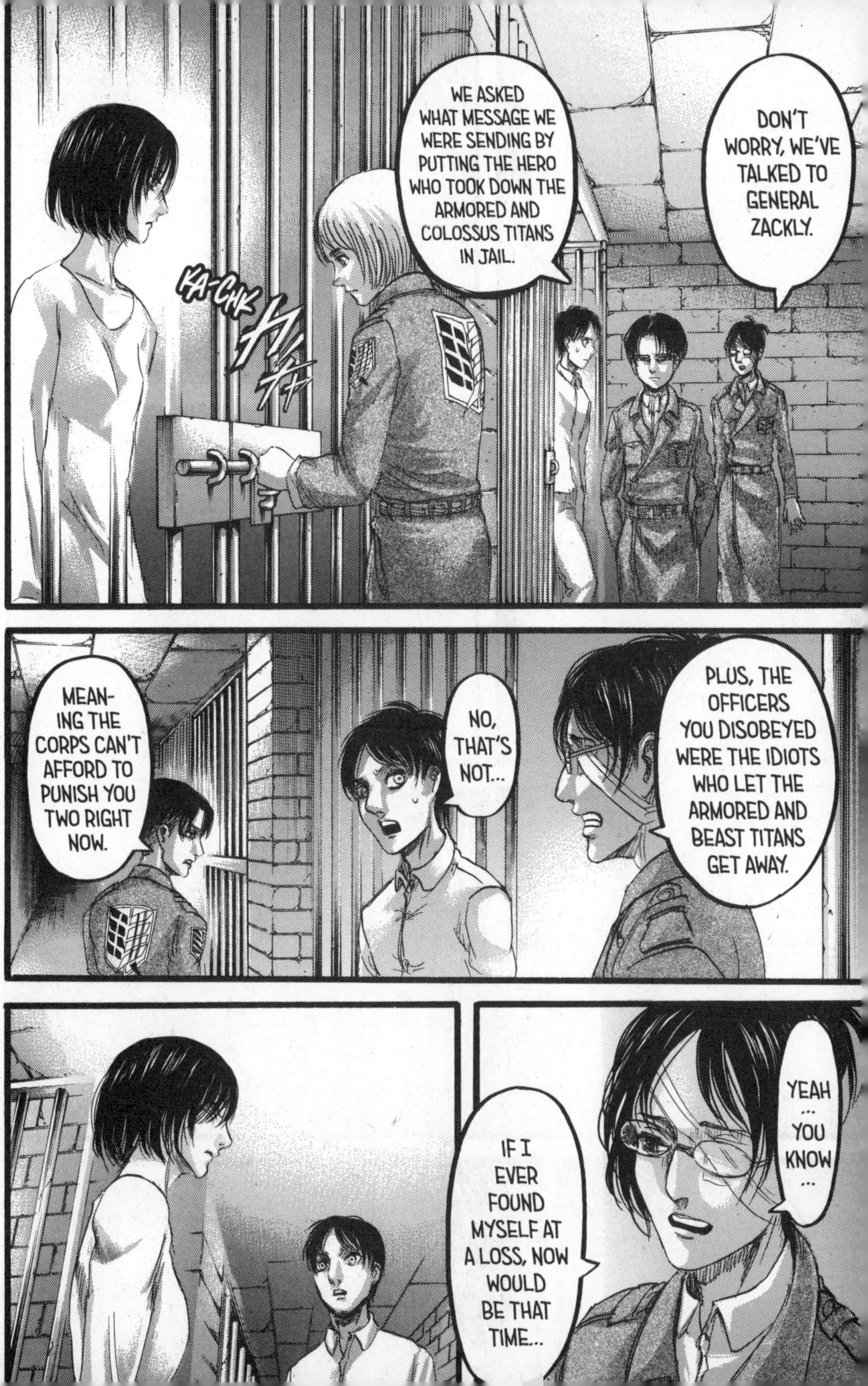
DON'T WORRY, WE'VE TALKED TO GENERAL ZACKLY.
WE ASKED WHAT MESSAGE WE WERE SENDING BY PUTTING THE HERO WHO TOOK DOWN THE ARMORED AND COLOSSUS TITANS IN JAIL.
KA-CHK
PLUS, THE OFFICERS YOU DISOBEYED WERE THE IDIOTS WHO LET THE ARMORED AND BEAST TITANS GET AWAY.
NO, THAT'S NOT...
MEANING THE CORPS CAN'T AFFORD TO PUNISH YOU TWO RIGHT NOW.
YEAH ... YOU KNOW ...
IF I EVER FOUND MYSELF AT A LOSS, NOW WOULD BE THAT TIME...

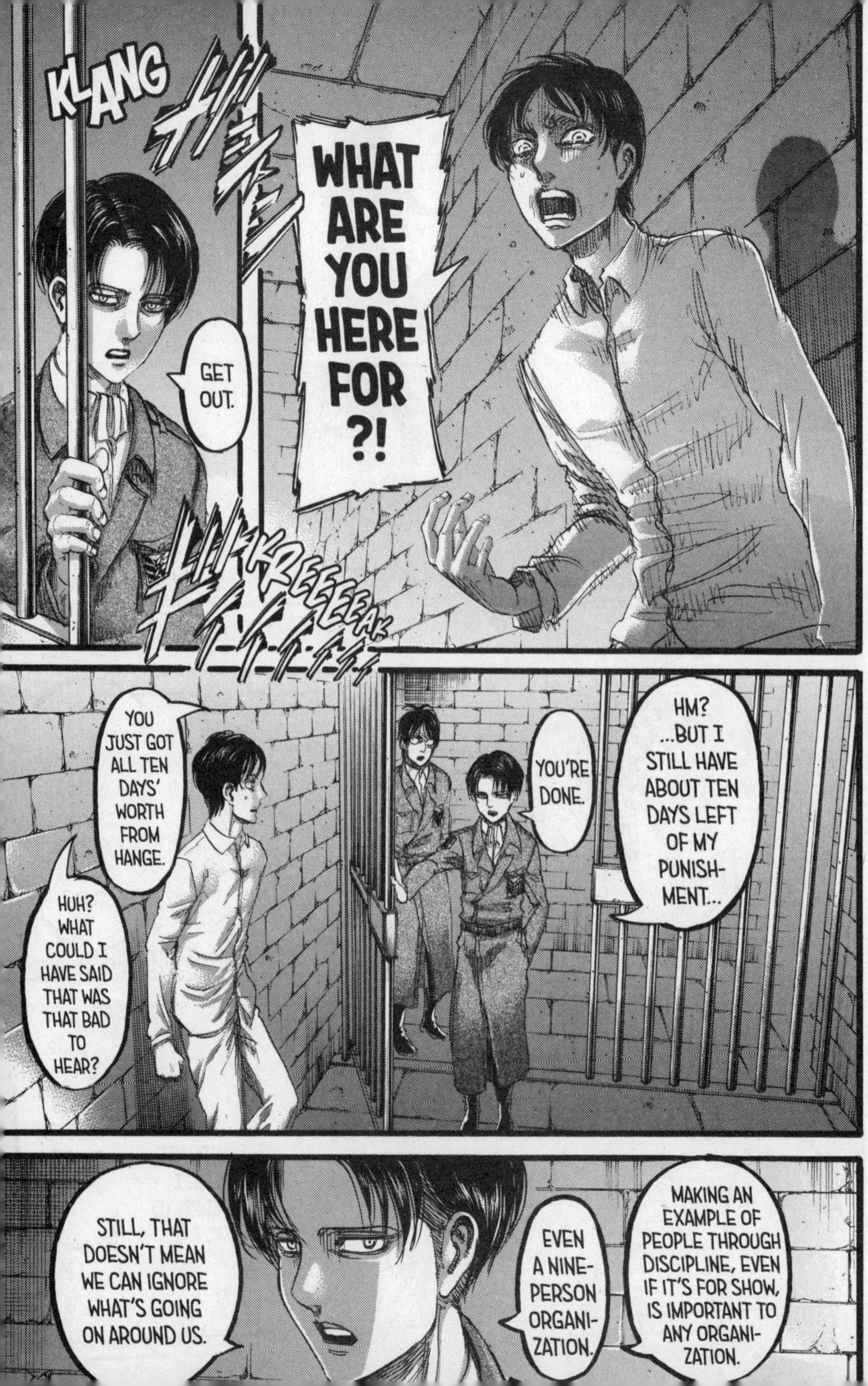
WHAT ARE YOU HERE FOR ?!
KLANG
GET OUT.
KREEEEEAK
HM? ...BUT I STILL HAVE ABOUT TEN DAYS LEFT OF MY PUNISHMENT...
YOU'RE DONE.
YOU JUST GOT ALL TEN DAYS' WORTH FROM HANGE.
HUH? WHAT COULD I HAVE SAID THAT WAS THAT BAD TO HEAR?
MAKING AN EXAMPLE OF PEOPLE THROUGH DISCIPLINE, EVEN IF IT'S FOR SHOW, IS IMPORTANT TO ANY ORGANIZATION.
EVEN A NINE-PERSON ORGANIZATION.
STILL, THAT DOESN'T MEAN WE CAN IGNORE WHAT'S GOING ON AROUND US.

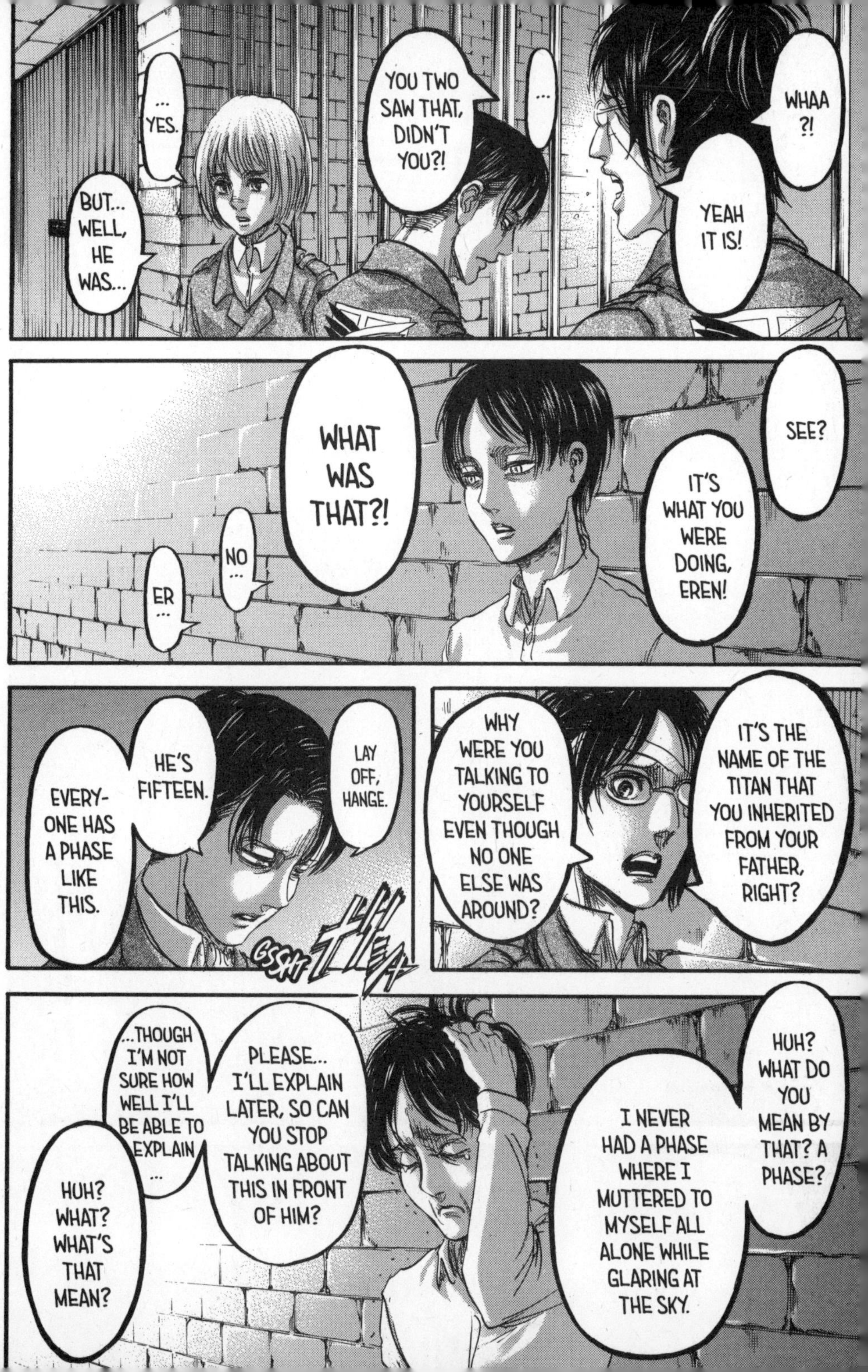
WHAA ?!
YEAH IT IS!
...
YOU TWO SAW THAT, DIDN'T YOU?!
... YES.
BUT... WELL, HE WAS...
SEE?
IT'S WHAT YOU WERE DOING, EREN!
WHAT WAS THAT?!
NO ...
ER ...
IT'S THE NAME OF THE TITAN THAT YOU INHERITED FROM YOUR FATHER, RIGHT?
WHY WERE YOU TALKING TO YOURSELF EVEN THOUGH NO ONE ELSE WAS AROUND?
LAY OFF, HANGE.
HE'S FIFTEEN.
EVERY-ONE HAS A PHASE LIKE THIS.
GSSHT
HUH? WHAT DO YOU MEAN BY THAT? A PHASE?
I NEVER HAD A PHASE WHERE I MUTTERED TO MYSELF ALL ALONE WHILE GLARING AT THE SKY.
PLEASE... I'LL EXPLAIN LATER, SO CAN YOU STOP TALKING ABOUT THIS IN FRONT OF HIM?
...THOUGH I'M NOT SURE HOW WELL I'LL BE ABLE TO EXPLAIN ...
HUH? WHAT? WHAT'S THAT MEAN?

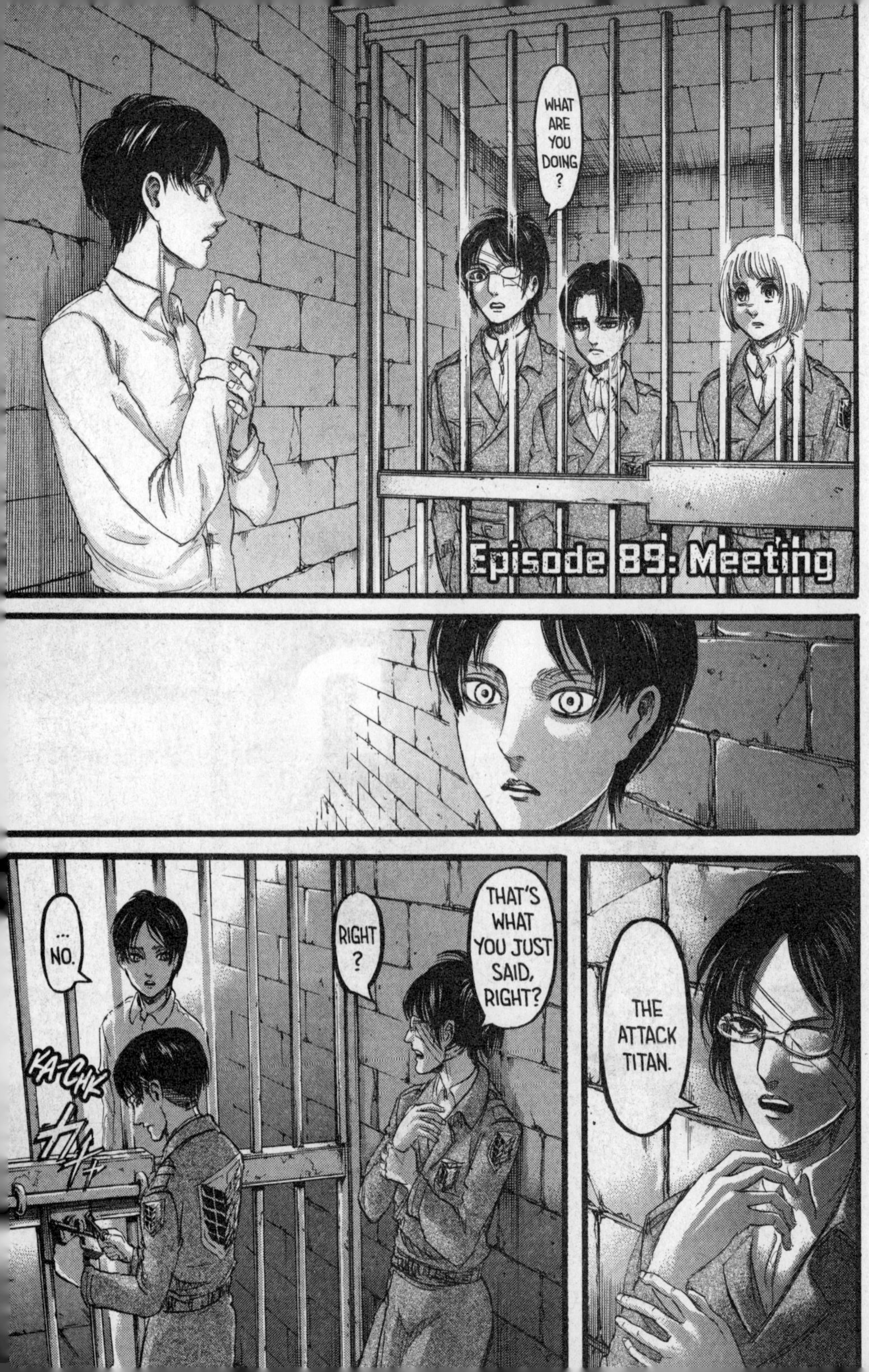
WHAT ARE YOU DOING?
Episode 89: Meeting
THE ATTACK TITAN.
THAT'S WHAT YOU JUST SAID, RIGHT?
RIGHT?
... NO.
KA-CHK

ATTACK on TITAN

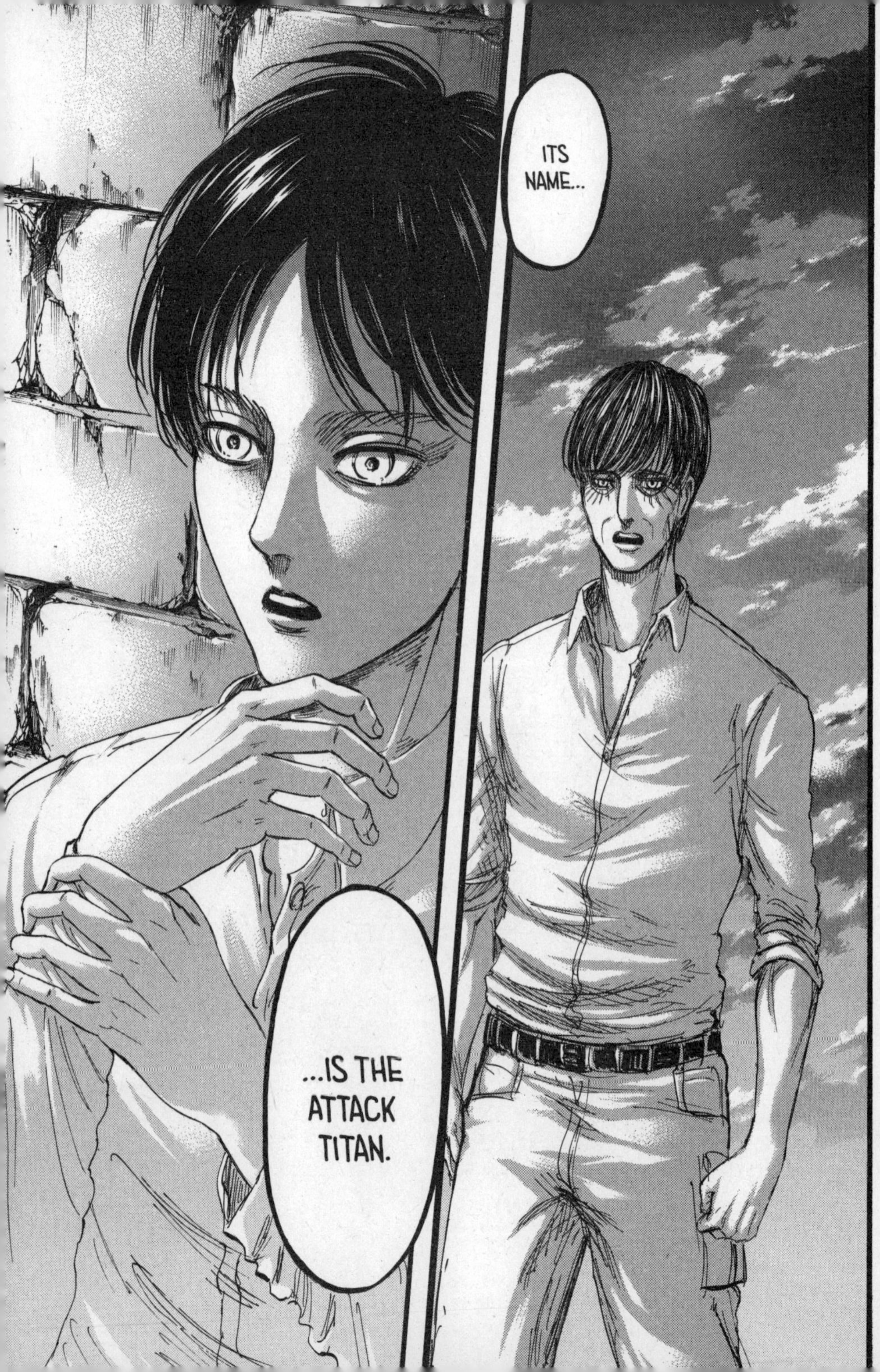
ITS NAME...
...IS THE ATTACK TITAN.

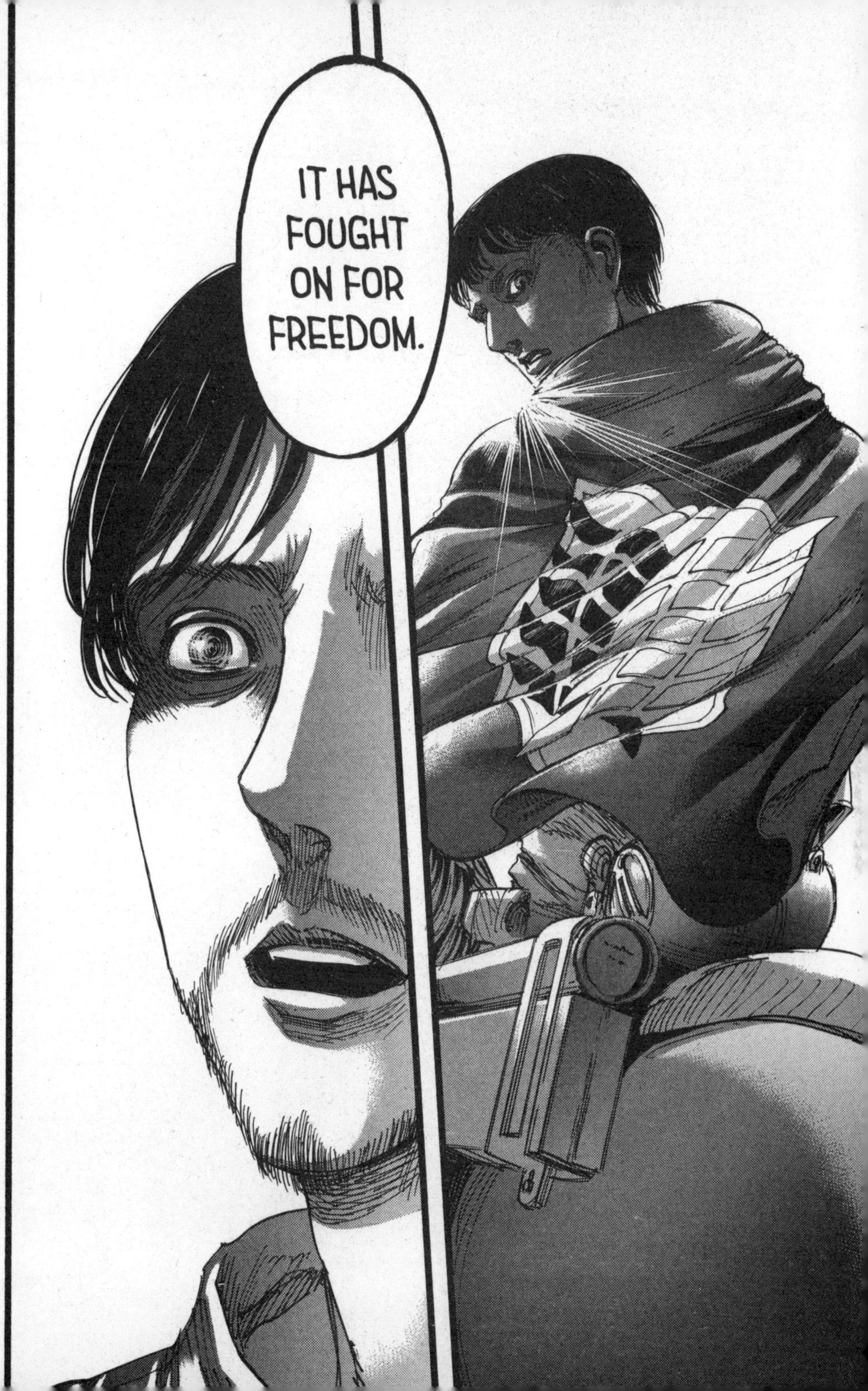
IT HAS FOUGHT ON FOR FREEDOM.

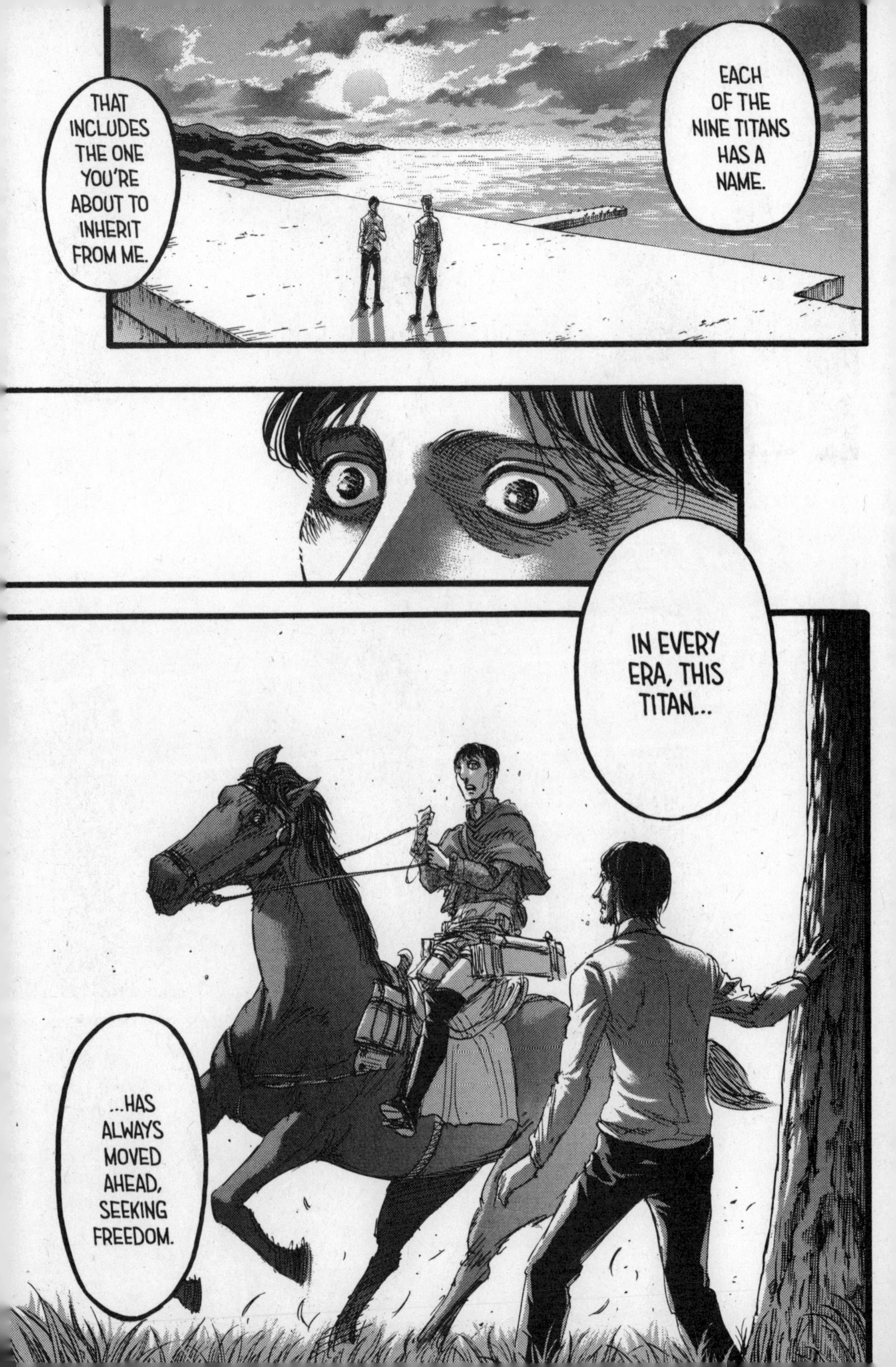
EACH OF THE NINE TITANS HAS A NAME.
THAT INCLUDES THE ONE YOU'RE ABOUT TO INHERIT FROM ME.
IN EVERY ERA, THIS TITAN...
...HAS ALWAYS MOVED AHEAD, SEEKING FREEDOM.

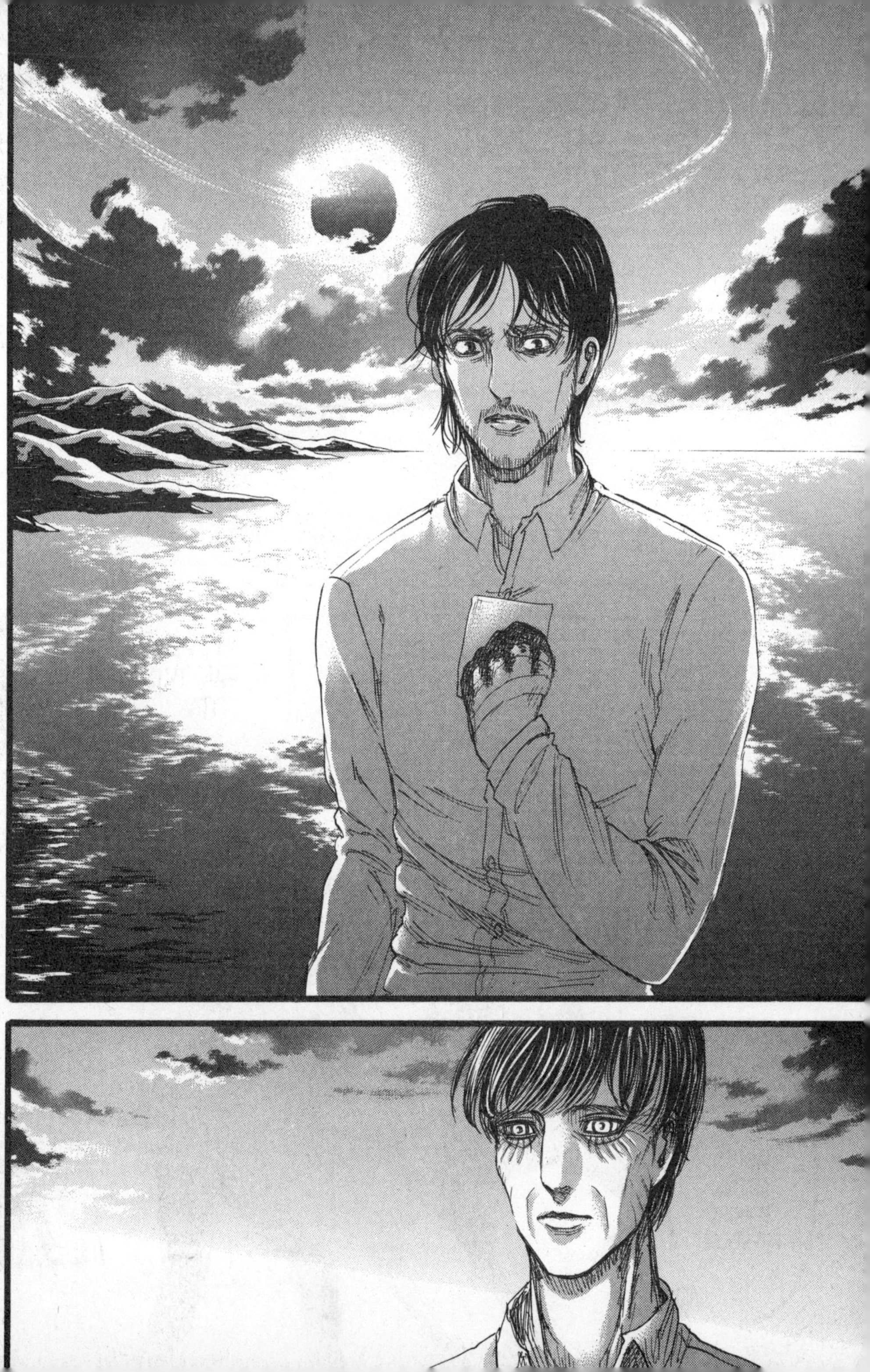

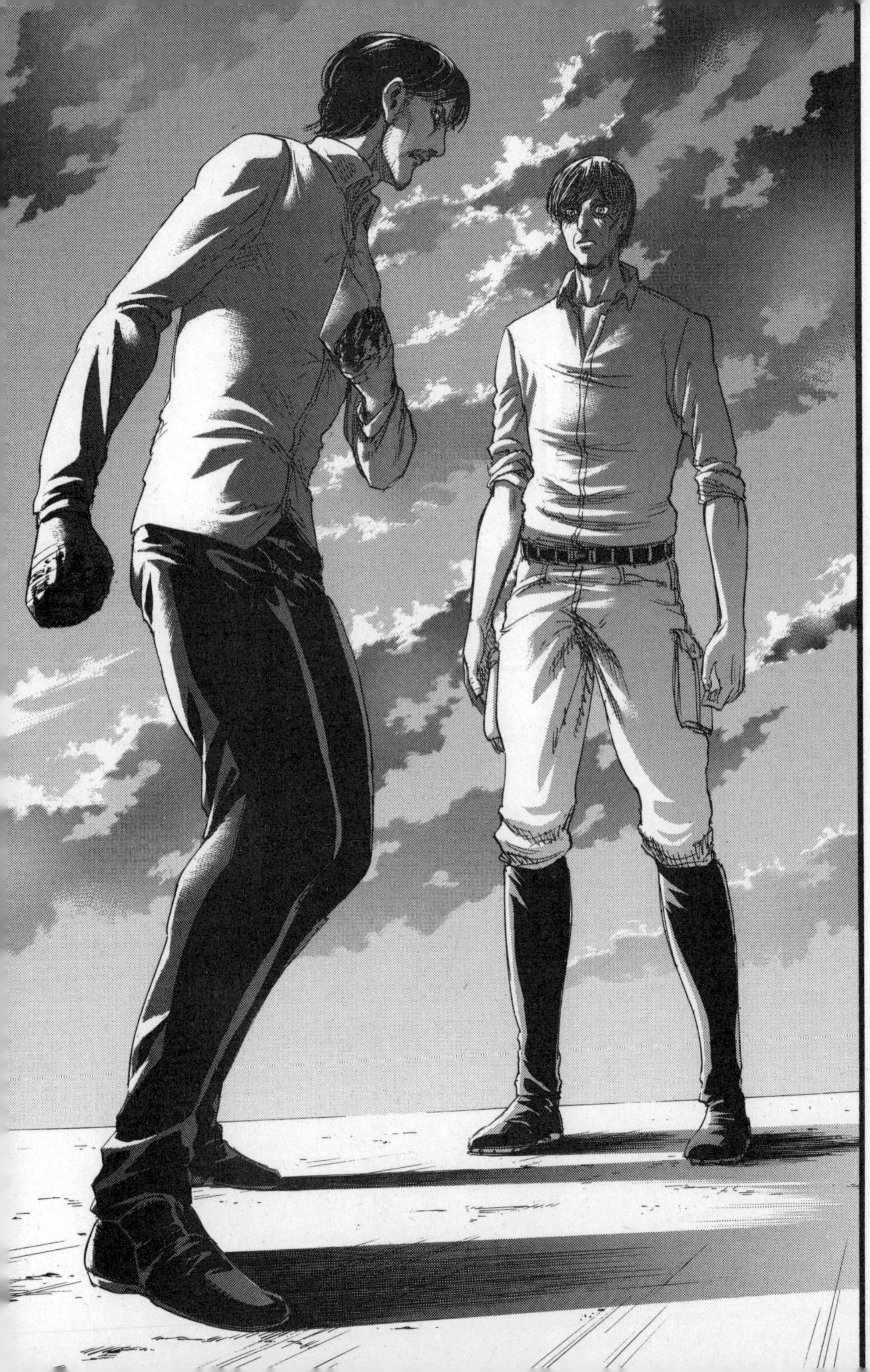

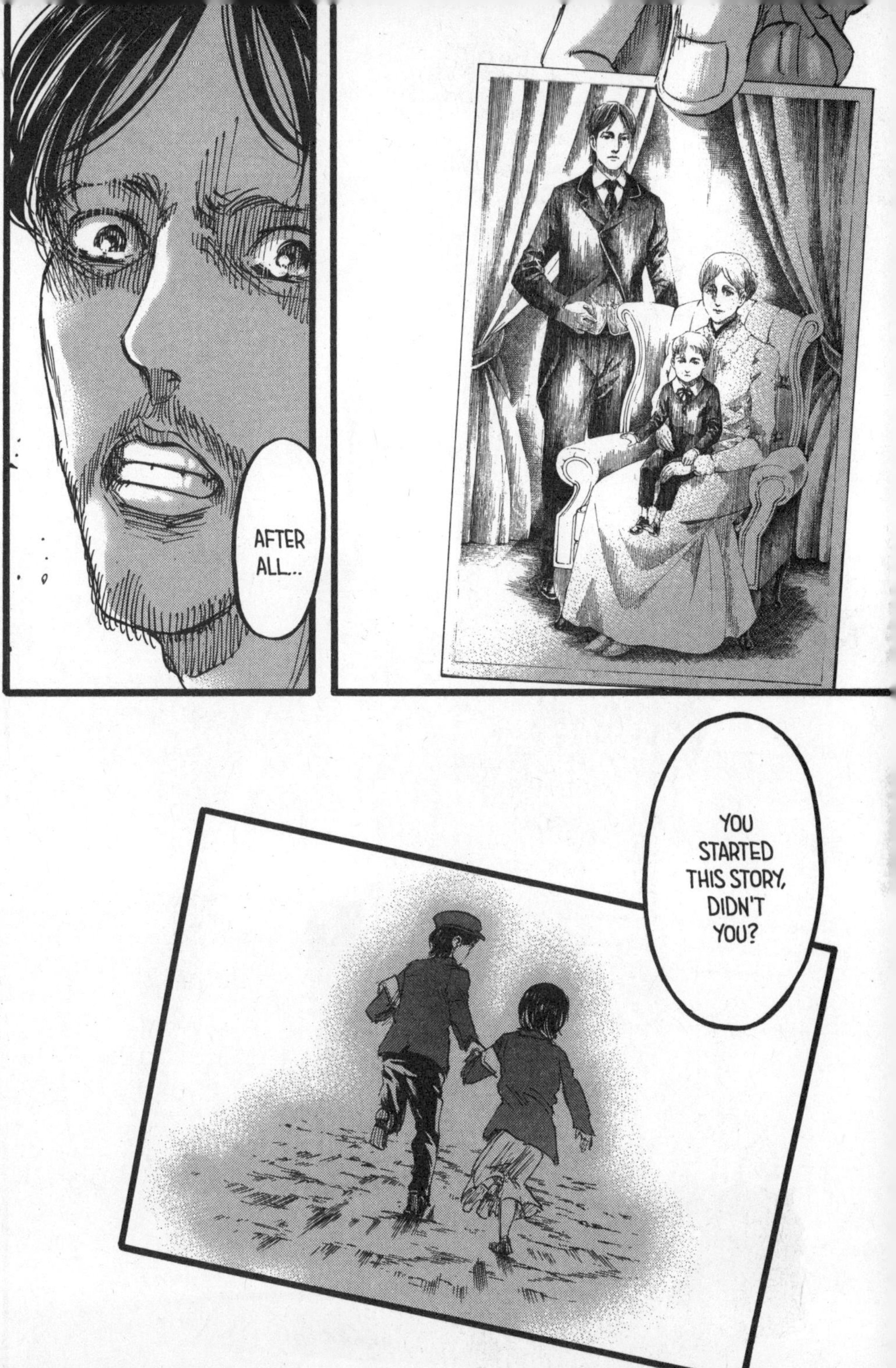
AFTER ALL...
YOU STARTED THIS STORY, DIDN'T YOU?

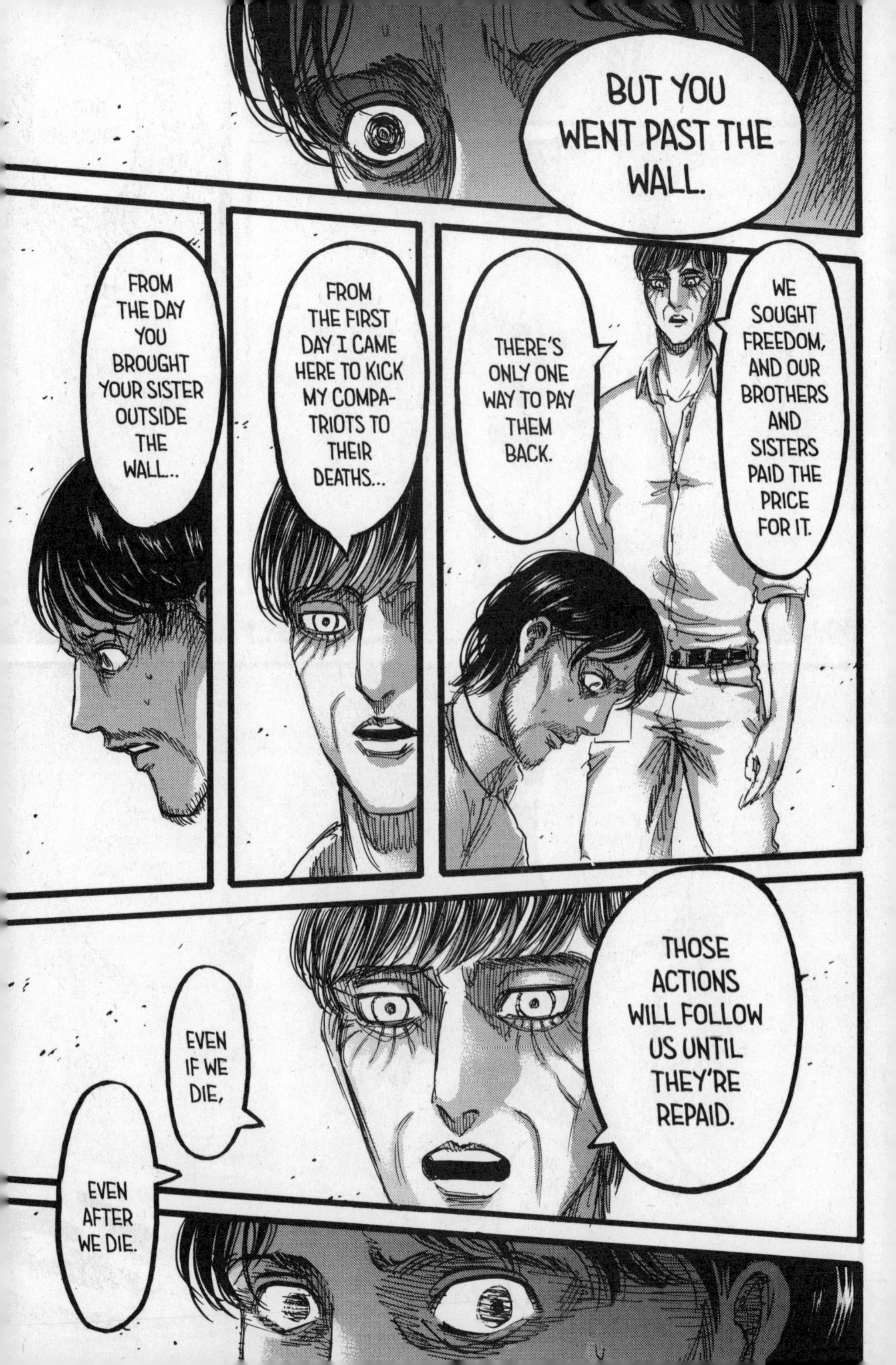
BUT YOU WENT PAST THE WALL.
WE SOUGHT FREEDOM, AND OUR BROTHERS AND SISTERS PAID THE PRICE FOR IT.
THERE'S ONLY ONE WAY TO PAY THEM BACK.
FROM THE FIRST DAY I CAME HERE TO KICK MY COMPA-TRIOTS TO THEIR DEATHS...
FROM THE DAY YOU BROUGHT YOUR SISTER OUTSIDE THE WALL...
THOSE ACTIONS WILL FOLLOW US UNTIL THEY'RE REPAID.
EVEN IF WE DIE,
EVEN AFTER WE DIE.

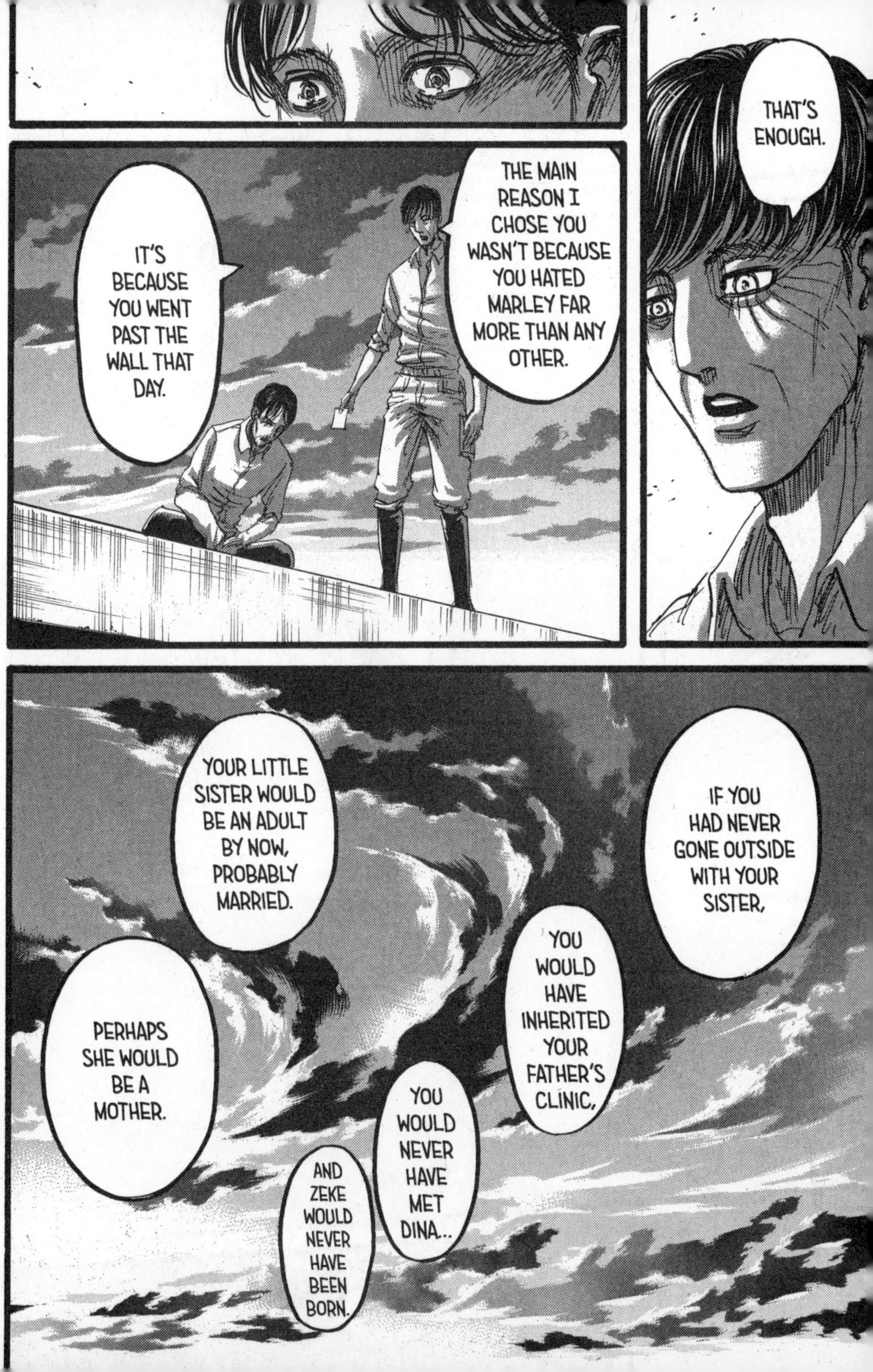
THAT'S ENOUGH.
THE MAIN REASON I CHOSE YOU WASN'T BECAUSE YOU HATED MARLEY FAR MORE THAN ANY OTHER.
IT'S BECAUSE YOU WENT PAST THE WALL THAT DAY.
IF YOU HAD NEVER GONE OUTSIDE WITH YOUR SISTER,
YOU WOULD HAVE INHERITED YOUR FATHER'S CLINIC,
YOU WOULD NEVER HAVE MET DINA...
AND ZEKE WOULD NEVER HAVE BEEN BORN.
YOUR LITTLE SISTER WOULD BE AN ADULT BY NOW, PROBABLY MARRIED.
PERHAPS SHE WOULD BE A MOTHER.

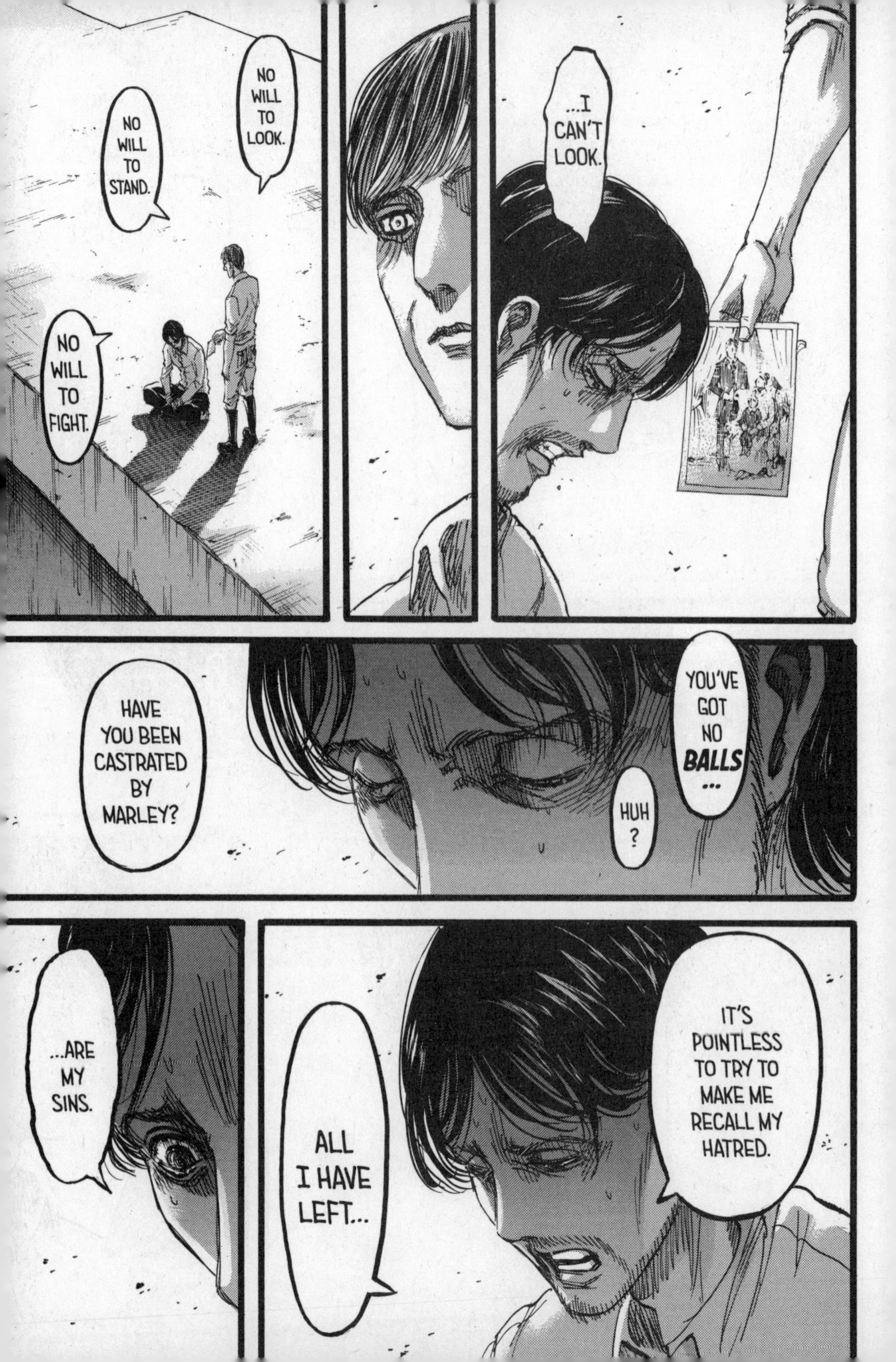
...I CAN'T LOOK.
NO WILL TO LOOK.
NO WILL TO STAND.
NO WILL TO FIGHT.
YOU'VE GOT NO **BALLS**...
HUH?
HAVE YOU BEEN CASTRATED BY MARLEY?
IT'S POINTLESS TO TRY TO MAKE ME RECALL MY HATRED.
ALL I HAVE LEFT...
...ARE MY SINS.

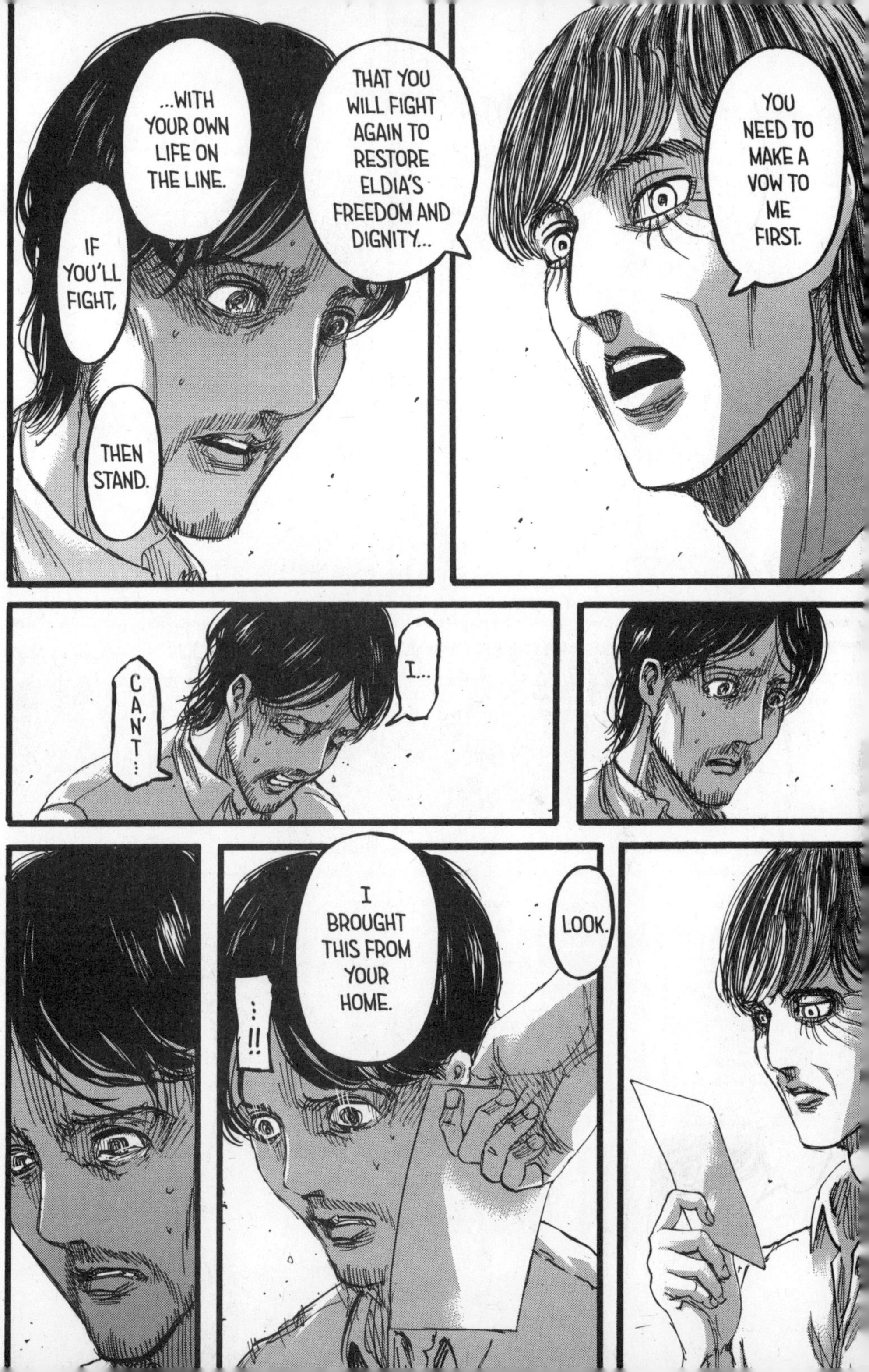
YOU NEED TO MAKE A VOW TO ME FIRST.
THAT YOU WILL FIGHT AGAIN TO RESTORE ELDIA'S FREEDOM AND DIGNITY...
...WITH YOUR OWN LIFE ON THE LINE.
IF YOU'LL FIGHT,
THEN STAND.
I...
CAN'T...
LOOK.
I BROUGHT THIS FROM YOUR HOME.
...!!

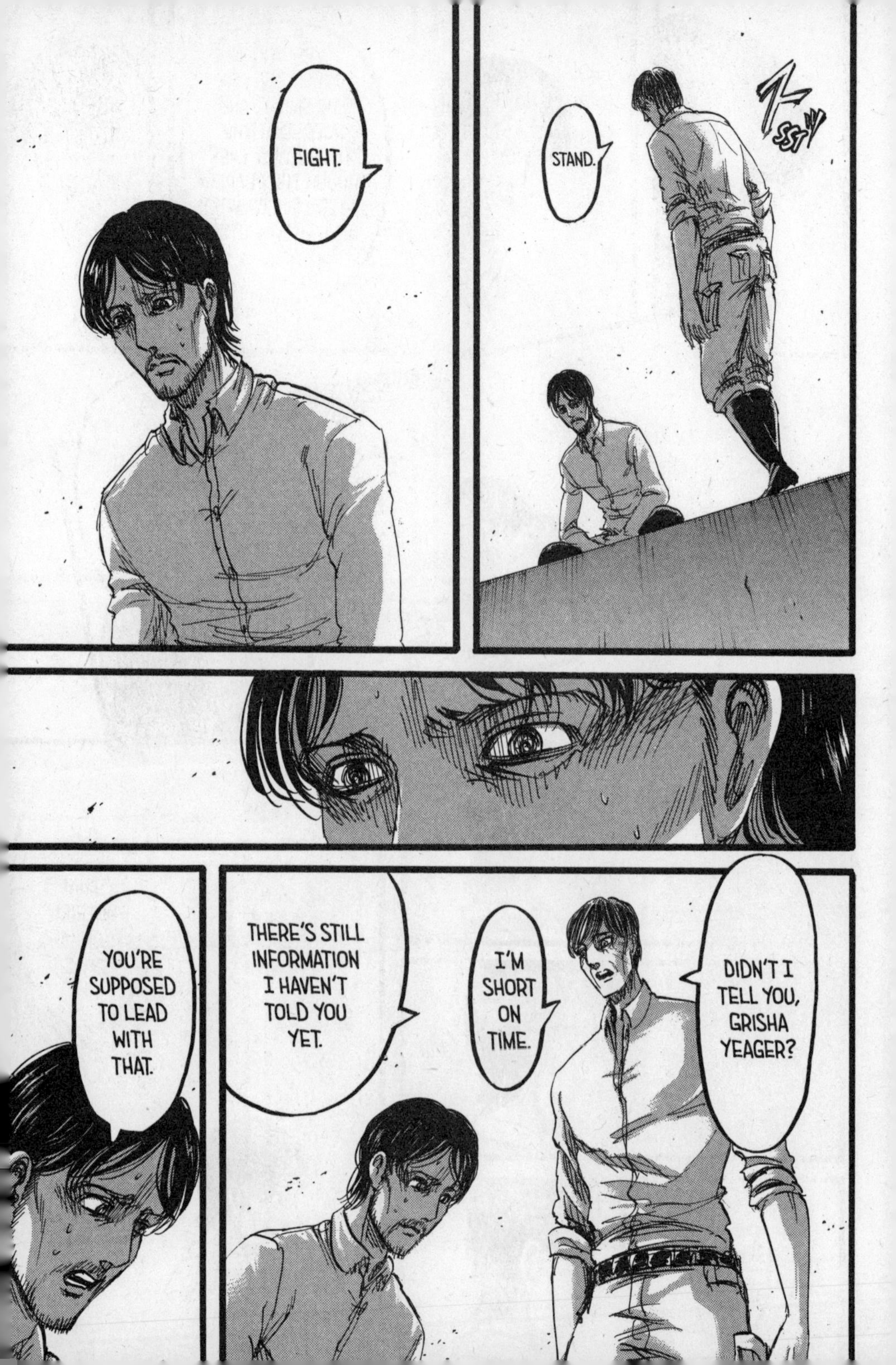
STAND.
FIGHT.
DIDN'T I TELL YOU, GRISHA YEAGER?
I'M SHORT ON TIME.
THERE'S STILL INFORMATION I HAVEN'T TOLD YOU YET.
YOU'RE SUPPOSED TO LEAD WITH THAT.

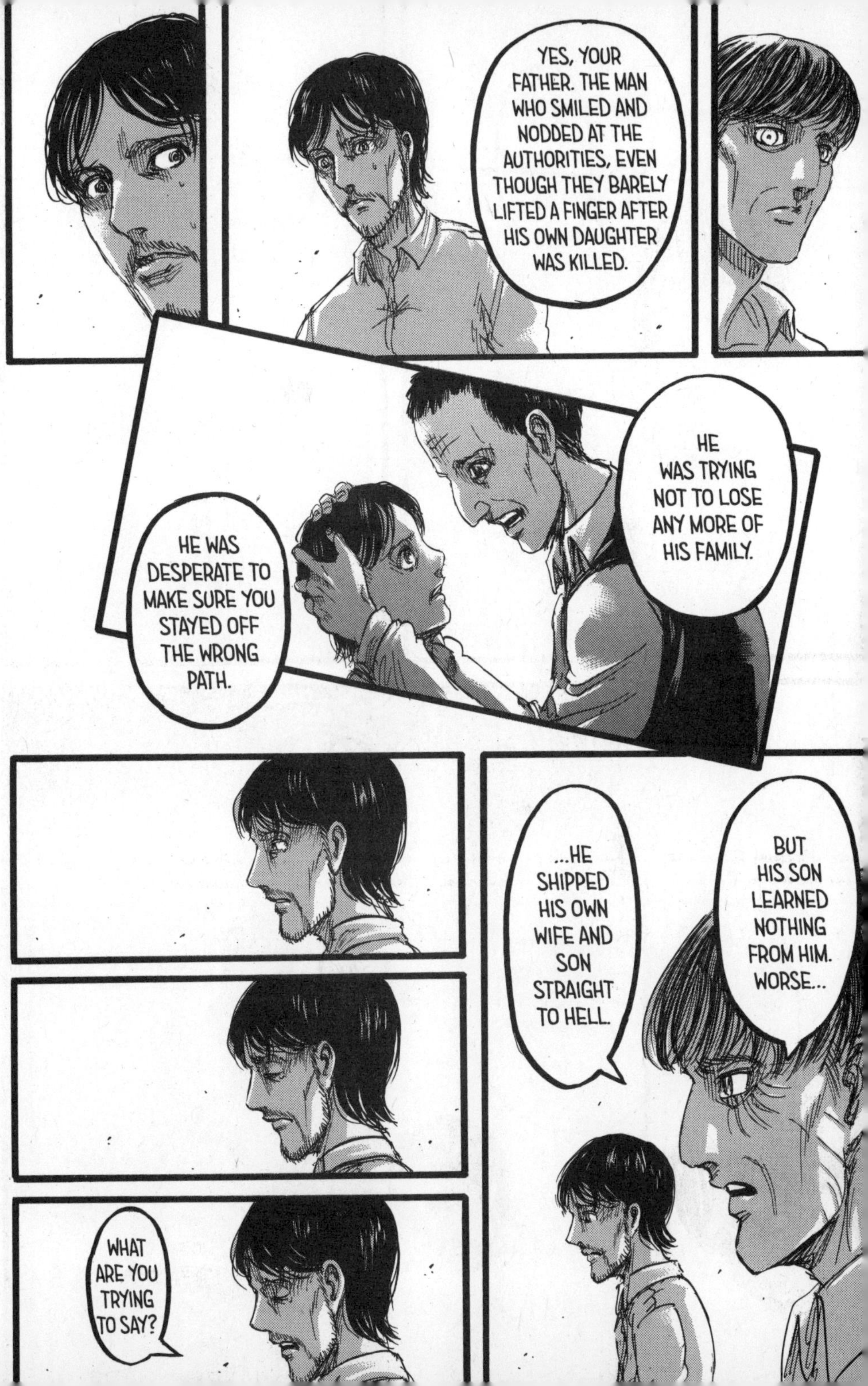
YES, YOUR FATHER. THE MAN WHO SMILED AND NODDED AT THE AUTHORITIES, EVEN THOUGH THEY BARELY LIFTED A FINGER AFTER HIS OWN DAUGHTER WAS KILLED.
HE WAS TRYING NOT TO LOSE ANY MORE OF HIS FAMILY.
HE WAS DESPERATE TO MAKE SURE YOU STAYED OFF THE WRONG PATH.
BUT HIS SON LEARNED NOTHING FROM HIM. WORSE...
...HE SHIPPED HIS OWN WIFE AND SON STRAIGHT TO HELL.
WHAT ARE YOU TRYING TO SAY?

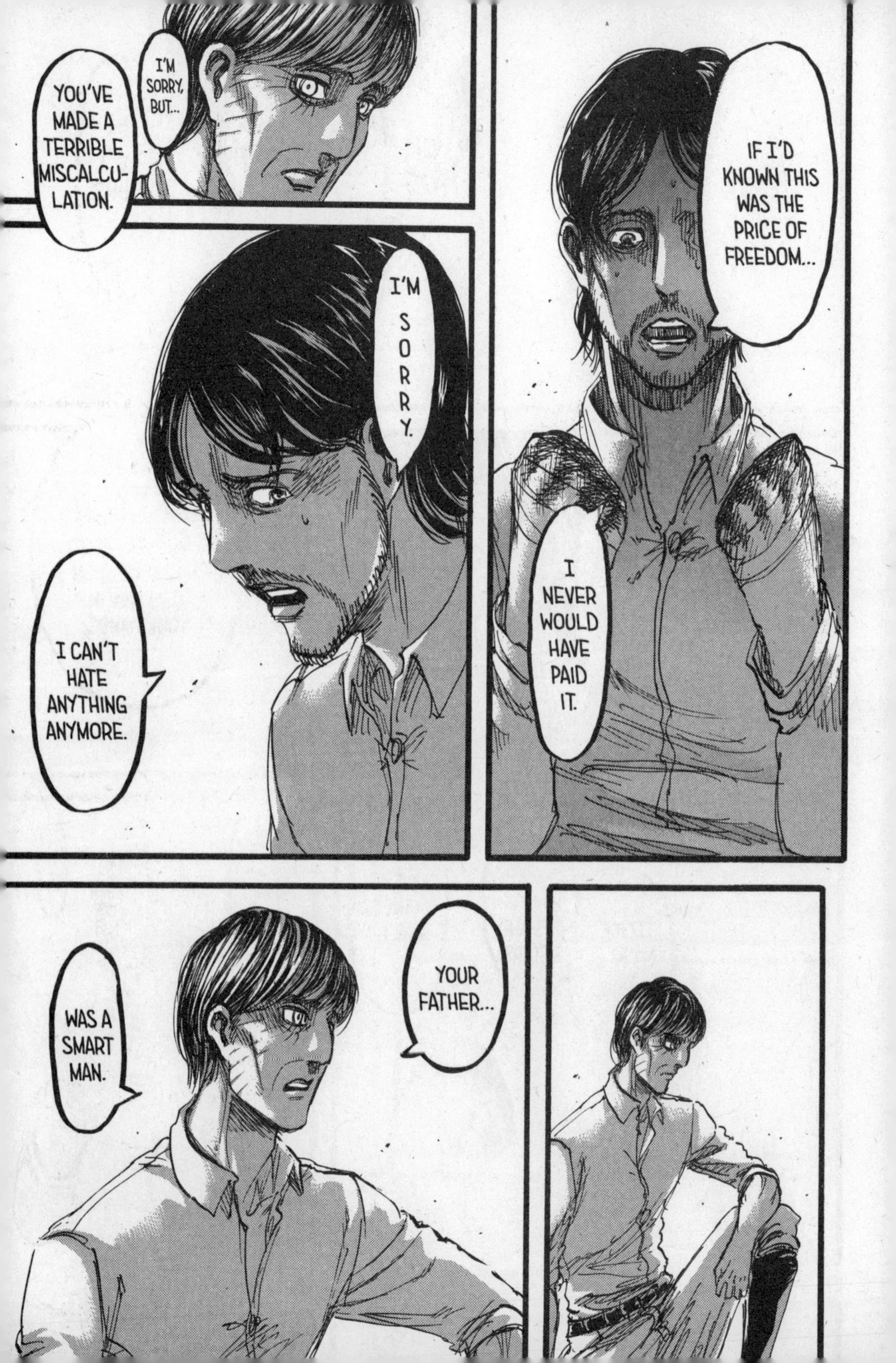
IF I'D KNOWN THIS WAS THE PRICE OF FREEDOM...
I NEVER WOULD HAVE PAID IT.
I'M SORRY, BUT...
YOU'VE MADE A TERRIBLE MISCALCU-LATION.
I'M SORRY.
I CAN'T HATE ANYTHING ANYMORE.
YOUR FATHER...
WAS A SMART MAN.

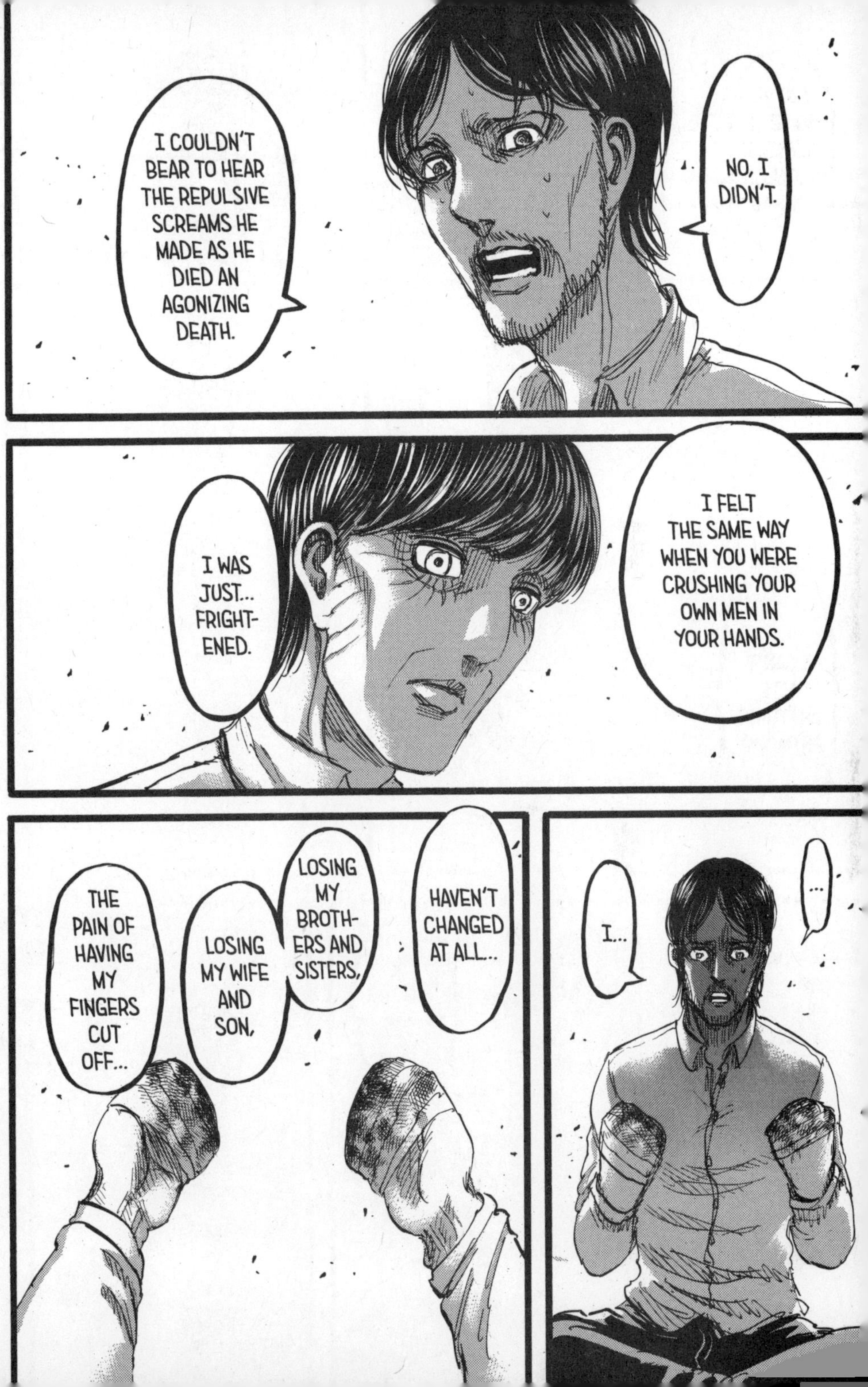
NO, I DIDN'T.
I COULDN'T BEAR TO HEAR THE REPULSIVE SCREAMS HE MADE AS HE DIED AN AGONIZING DEATH.
I FELT THE SAME WAY WHEN YOU WERE CRUSHING YOUR OWN MEN IN YOUR HANDS.
I WAS JUST... FRIGHT-ENED.
...
I...
HAVEN'T CHANGED AT ALL...
LOSING MY BROTH-ERS AND SISTERS,
LOSING MY WIFE AND SON,
THE PAIN OF HAVING MY FINGERS CUT OFF...

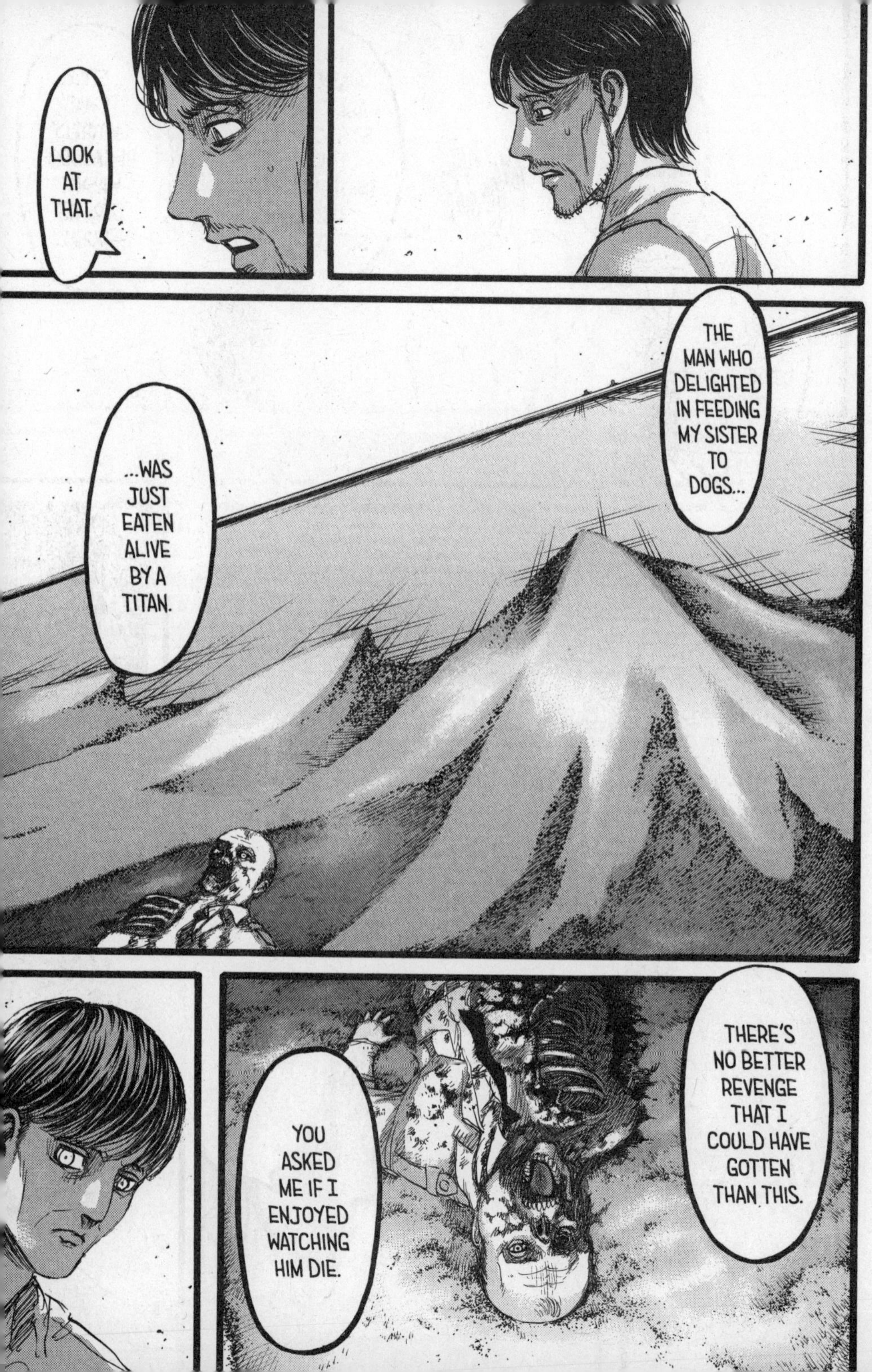
LOOK AT THAT.
THE MAN WHO DELIGHTED IN FEEDING MY SISTER TO DOGS...
...WAS JUST EATEN ALIVE BY A TITAN.
THERE'S NO BETTER REVENGE THAT I COULD HAVE GOTTEN THAN THIS.
YOU ASKED ME IF I ENJOYED WATCHING HIM DIE.

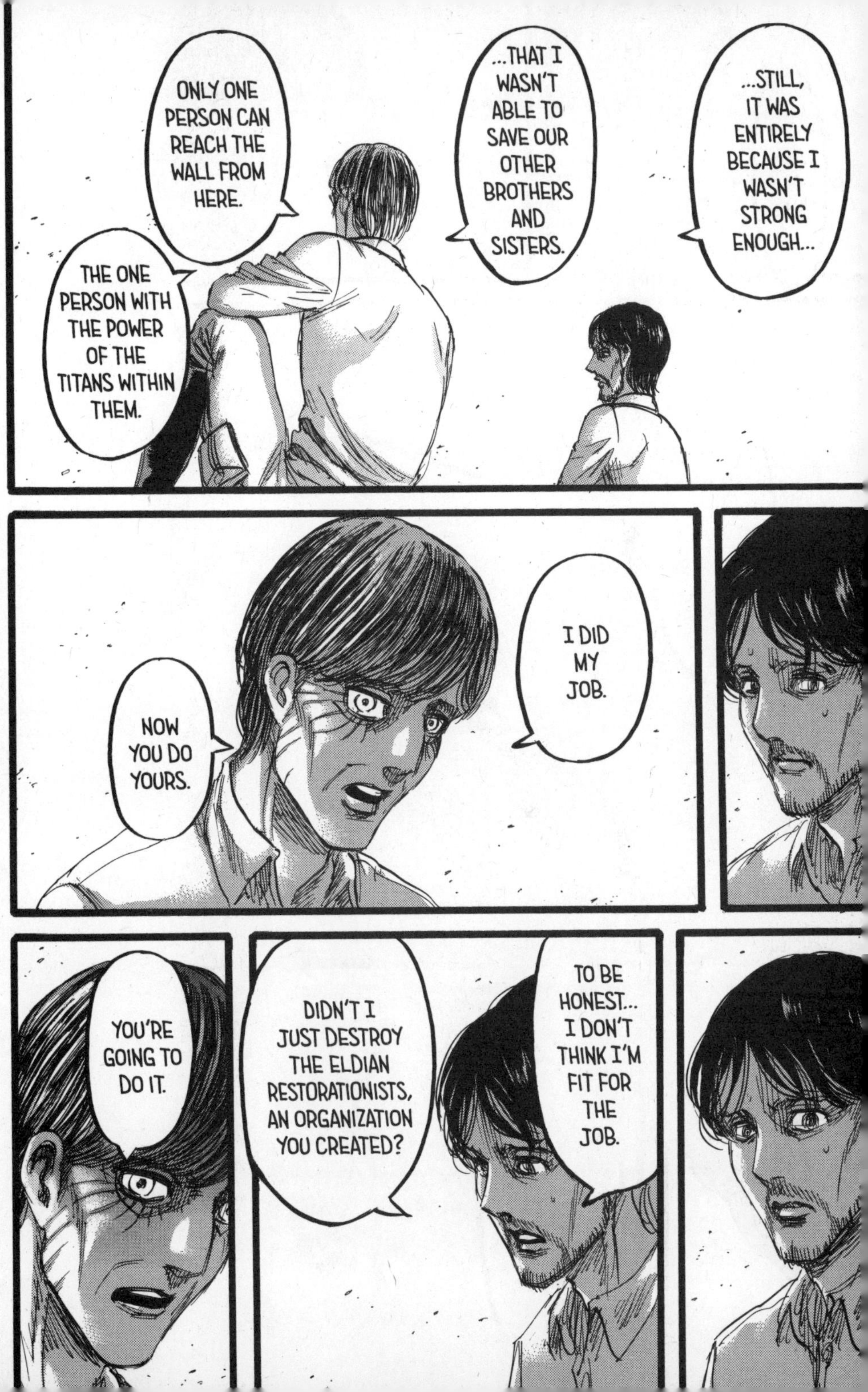
...STILL, IT WAS ENTIRELY BECAUSE I WASN'T STRONG ENOUGH...
...THAT I WASN'T ABLE TO SAVE OUR OTHER BROTHERS AND SISTERS.
ONLY ONE PERSON CAN REACH THE WALL FROM HERE.
THE ONE PERSON WITH THE POWER OF THE TITANS WITHIN THEM.
I DID MY JOB.
NOW YOU DO YOURS.
TO BE HONEST... I DON'T THINK I'M FIT FOR THE JOB.
DIDN'T I JUST DESTROY THE ELDIAN RESTORATIONISTS, AN ORGANIZATION YOU CREATED?
YOU'RE GOING TO DO IT.

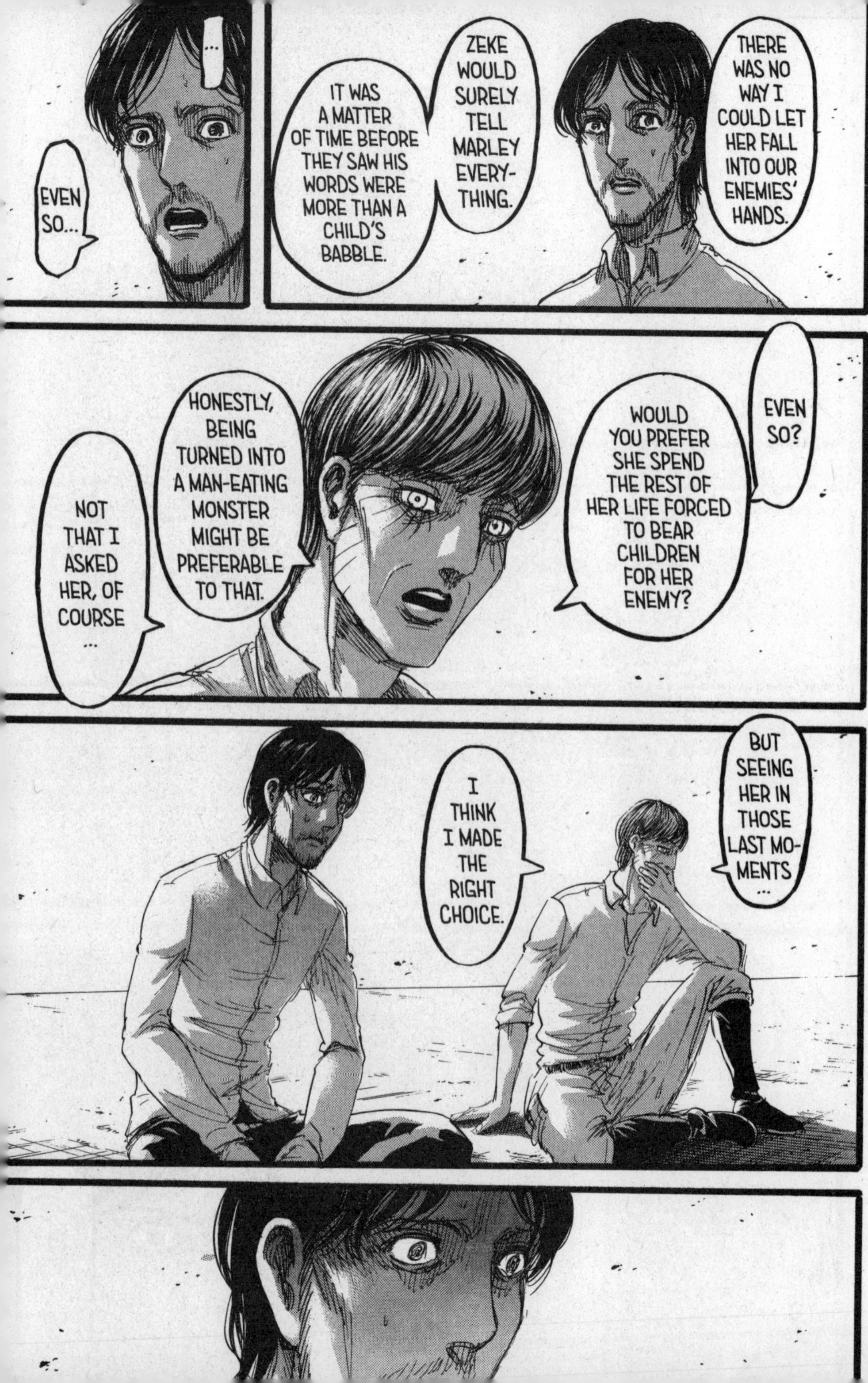
THERE WAS NO WAY I COULD LET HER FALL INTO OUR ENEMIES' HANDS.
ZEKE WOULD SURELY TELL MARLEY EVERYTHING.
IT WAS A MATTER OF TIME BEFORE THEY SAW HIS WORDS WERE MORE THAN A CHILD'S BABBLE.
...
EVEN SO...
EVEN SO?
WOULD YOU PREFER SHE SPEND THE REST OF HER LIFE FORCED TO BEAR CHILDREN FOR HER ENEMY?
HONESTLY, BEING TURNED INTO A MAN-EATING MONSTER MIGHT BE PREFERABLE TO THAT.
NOT THAT I ASKED HER, OF COURSE ...
BUT SEEING HER IN THOSE LAST MOMENTS ...
I THINK I MADE THE RIGHT CHOICE.

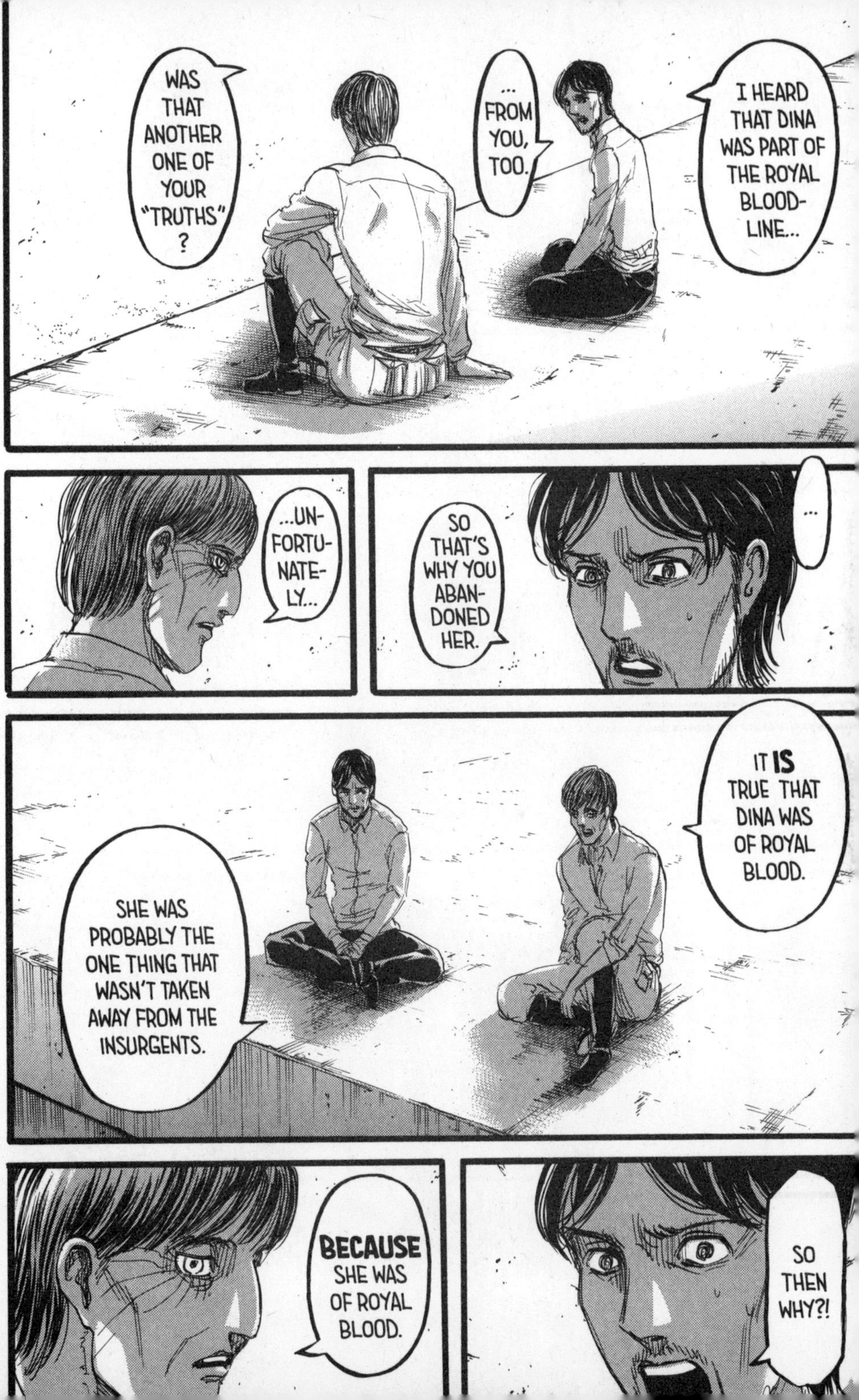
I HEARD THAT DINA WAS PART OF THE ROYAL BLOODLINE...
... FROM YOU, TOO.
WAS THAT ANOTHER ONE OF YOUR "TRUTHS"?
...
SO THAT'S WHY YOU ABANDONED HER.
...UNFORTUNATELY...
IT **IS** TRUE THAT DINA WAS OF ROYAL BLOOD.
SHE WAS PROBABLY THE ONE THING THAT WASN'T TAKEN AWAY FROM THE INSURGENTS.
SO THEN WHY?!
BECAUSE SHE WAS OF ROYAL BLOOD.

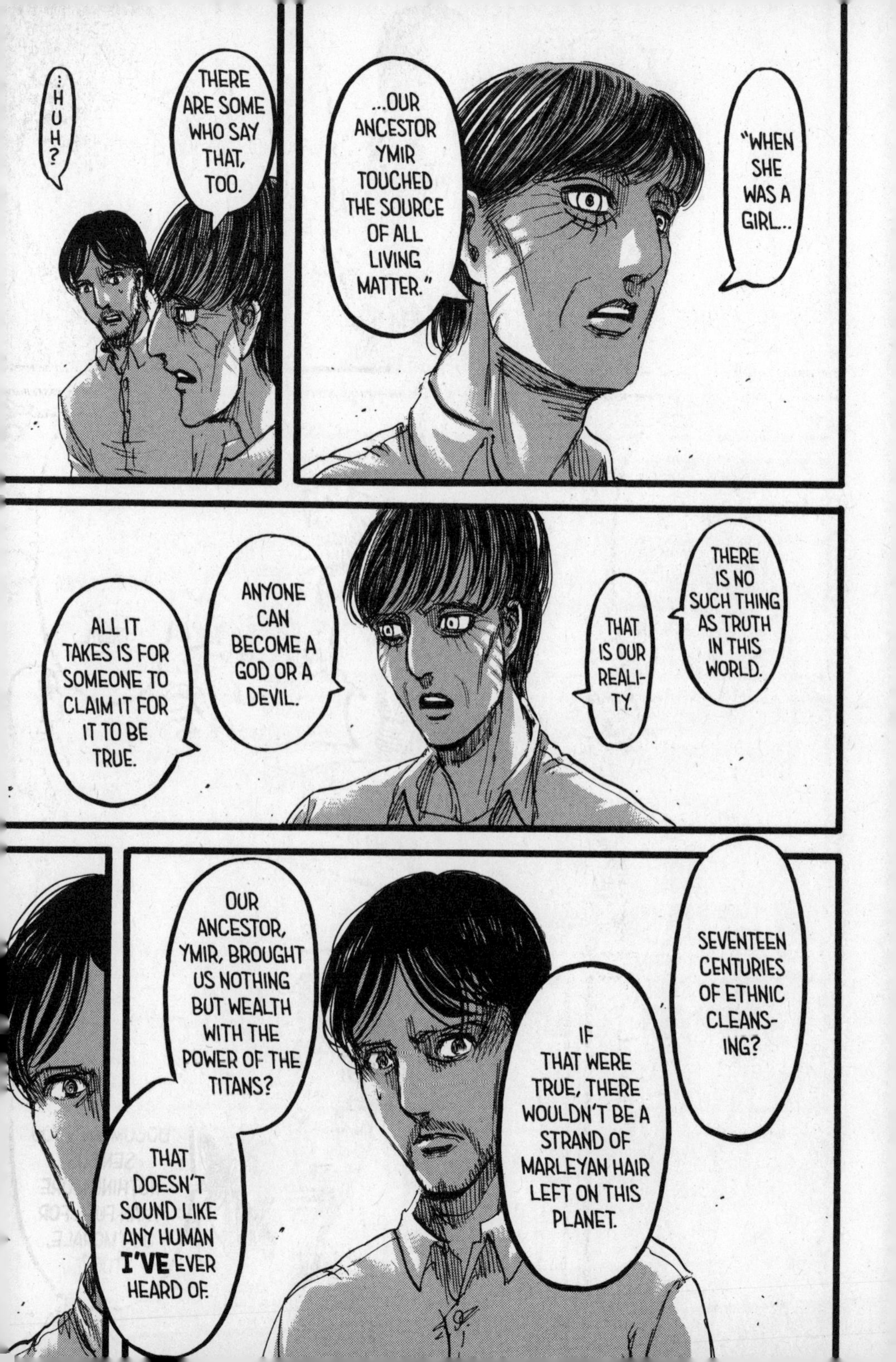
"WHEN SHE WAS A GIRL...
...OUR ANCESTOR YMIR TOUCHED THE SOURCE OF ALL LIVING MATTER."
THERE ARE SOME WHO SAY THAT, TOO.
...HUH?
THERE IS NO SUCH THING AS TRUTH IN THIS WORLD.
THAT IS OUR REALI-TY.
ANYONE CAN BECOME A GOD OR A DEVIL.
ALL IT TAKES IS FOR SOMEONE TO CLAIM IT FOR IT TO BE TRUE.
SEVENTEEN CENTURIES OF ETHNIC CLEANS-ING?
IF THAT WERE TRUE, THERE WOULDN'T BE A STRAND OF MARLEYAN HAIR LEFT ON THIS PLANET.
OUR ANCESTOR, YMIR, BROUGHT US NOTHING BUT WEALTH WITH THE POWER OF THE TITANS?
THAT DOESN'T SOUND LIKE ANY HUMAN **I'VE** EVER HEARD OF.

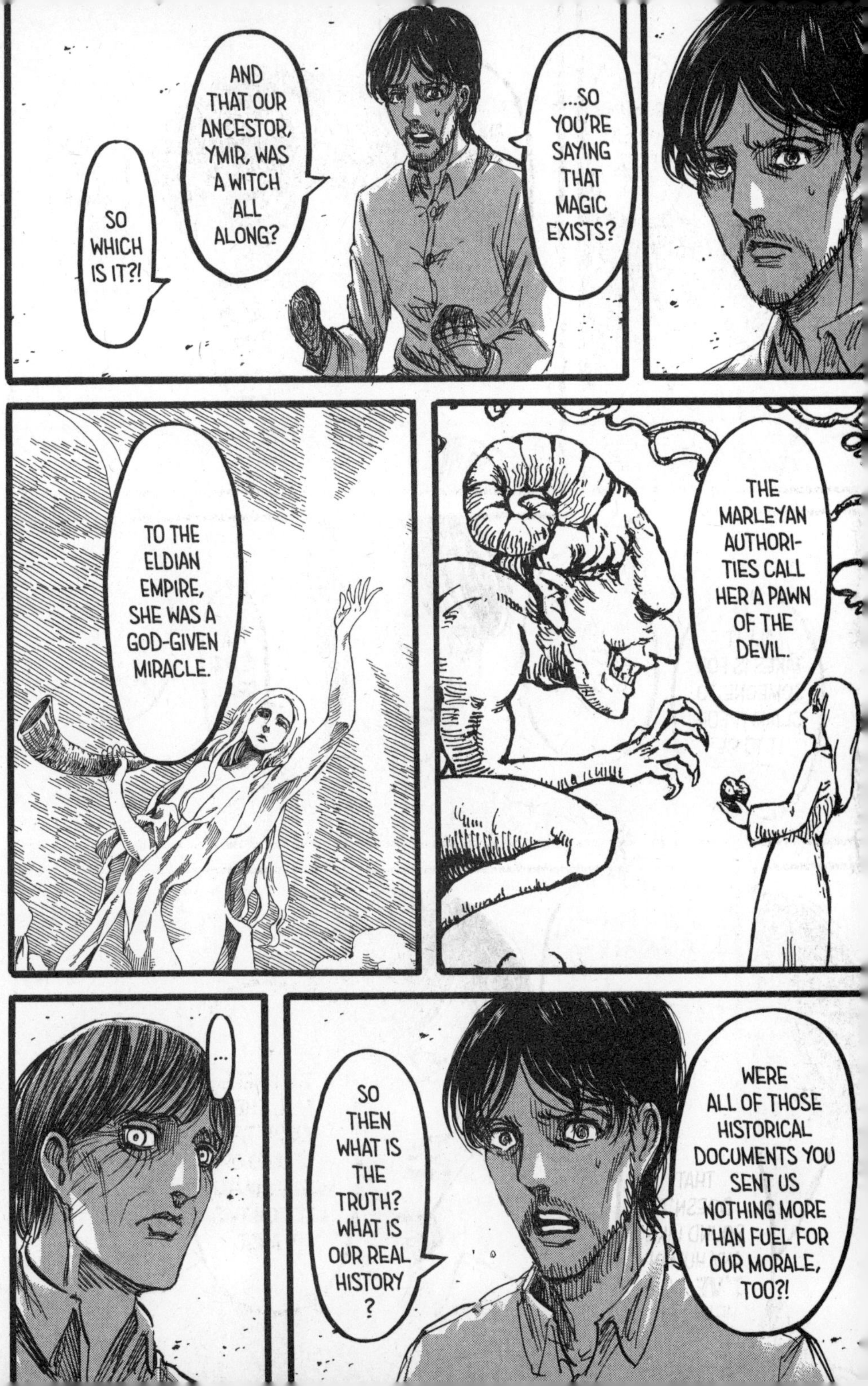
...SO YOU'RE SAYING THAT MAGIC EXISTS?
AND THAT OUR ANCESTOR, YMIR, WAS A WITCH ALL ALONG?
SO WHICH IS IT?!
THE MARLEYAN AUTHORITIES CALL HER A PAWN OF THE DEVIL.
TO THE ELDIAN EMPIRE, SHE WAS A GOD-GIVEN MIRACLE.
WERE ALL OF THOSE HISTORICAL DOCUMENTS YOU SENT US NOTHING MORE THAN FUEL FOR OUR MORALE, TOO?!
SO THEN WHAT IS THE TRUTH? WHAT IS OUR REAL HISTORY?
...

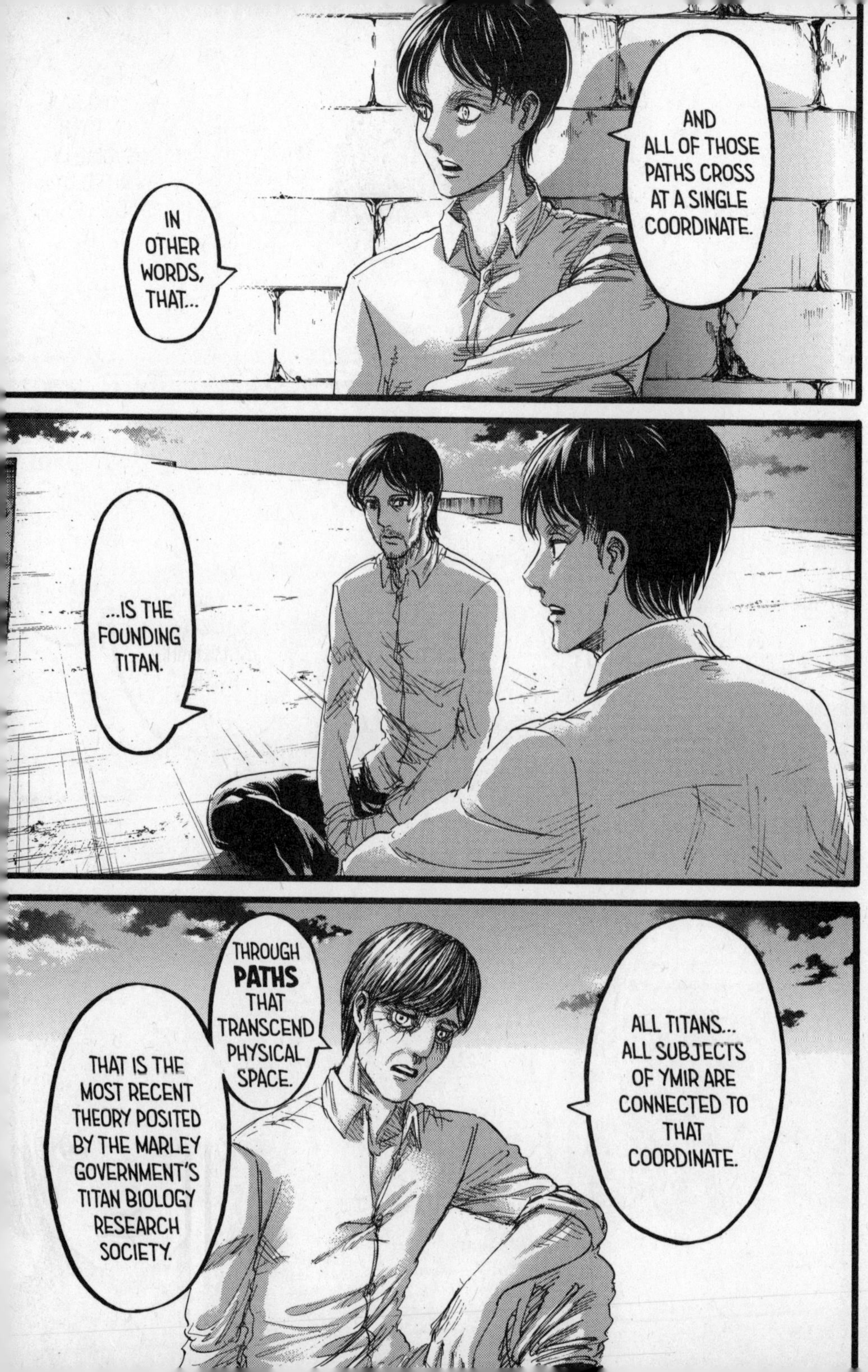
AND ALL OF THOSE PATHS CROSS AT A SINGLE COORDINATE.
IN OTHER WORDS, THAT...
...IS THE FOUNDING TITAN.
ALL TITANS... ALL SUBJECTS OF YMIR ARE CONNECTED TO THAT COORDINATE.
THROUGH **PATHS** THAT TRANSCEND PHYSICAL SPACE.
THAT IS THE MOST RECENT THEORY POSITED BY THE MARLEY GOVERNMENT'S TITAN BIOLOGY RESEARCH SOCIETY.

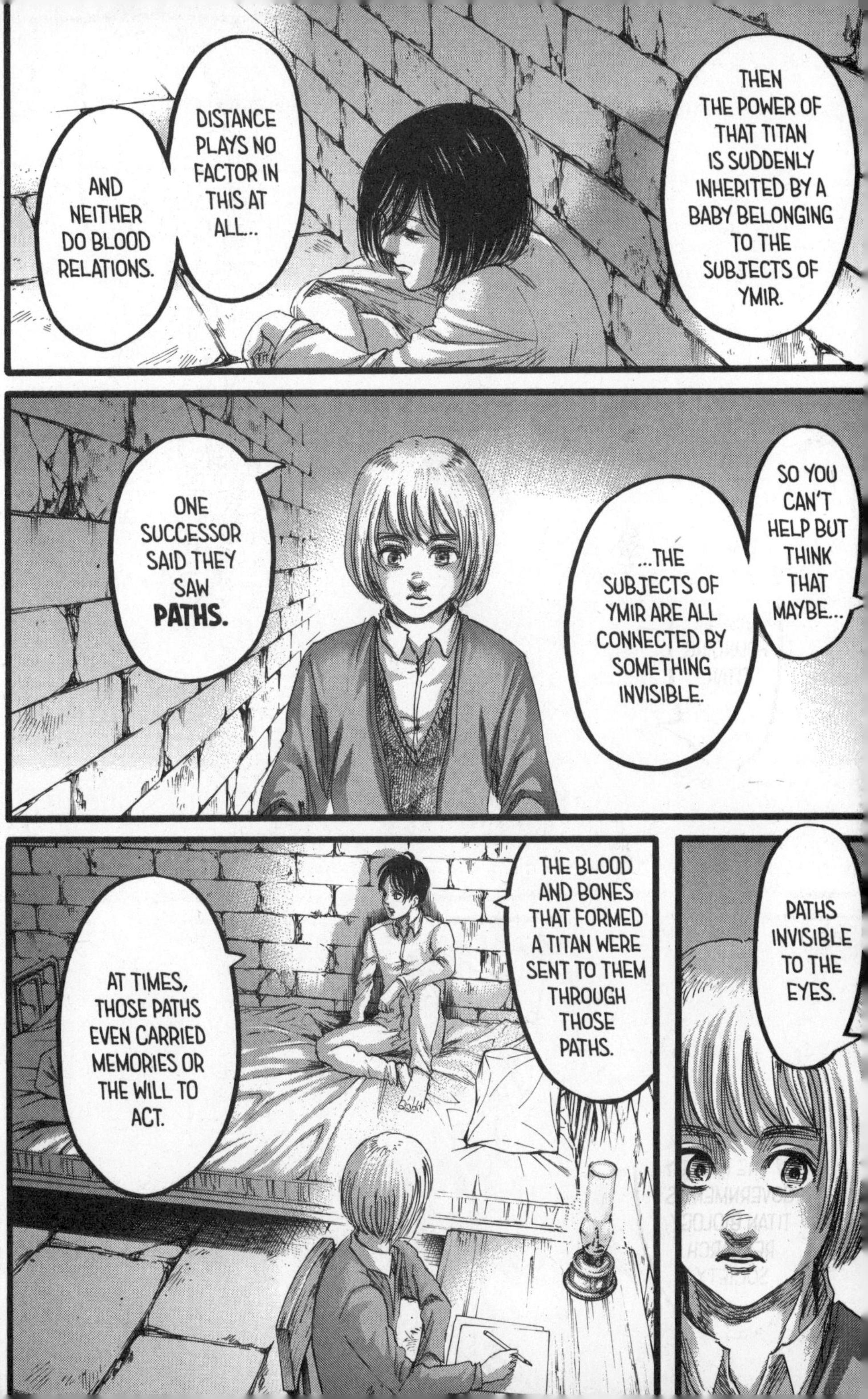
THEN THE POWER OF THAT TITAN IS SUDDENLY INHERITED BY A BABY BELONGING TO THE SUBJECTS OF YMIR.
DISTANCE PLAYS NO FACTOR IN THIS AT ALL...
AND NEITHER DO BLOOD RELATIONS.
SO YOU CAN'T HELP BUT THINK THAT MAYBE...
...THE SUBJECTS OF YMIR ARE ALL CONNECTED BY SOMETHING INVISIBLE.
ONE SUCCESSOR SAID THEY SAW **PATHS.**
PATHS INVISIBLE TO THE EYES.
THE BLOOD AND BONES THAT FORMED A TITAN WERE SENT TO THEM THROUGH THOSE PATHS.
AT TIMES, THOSE PATHS EVEN CARRIED MEMORIES OR THE WILL TO ACT.

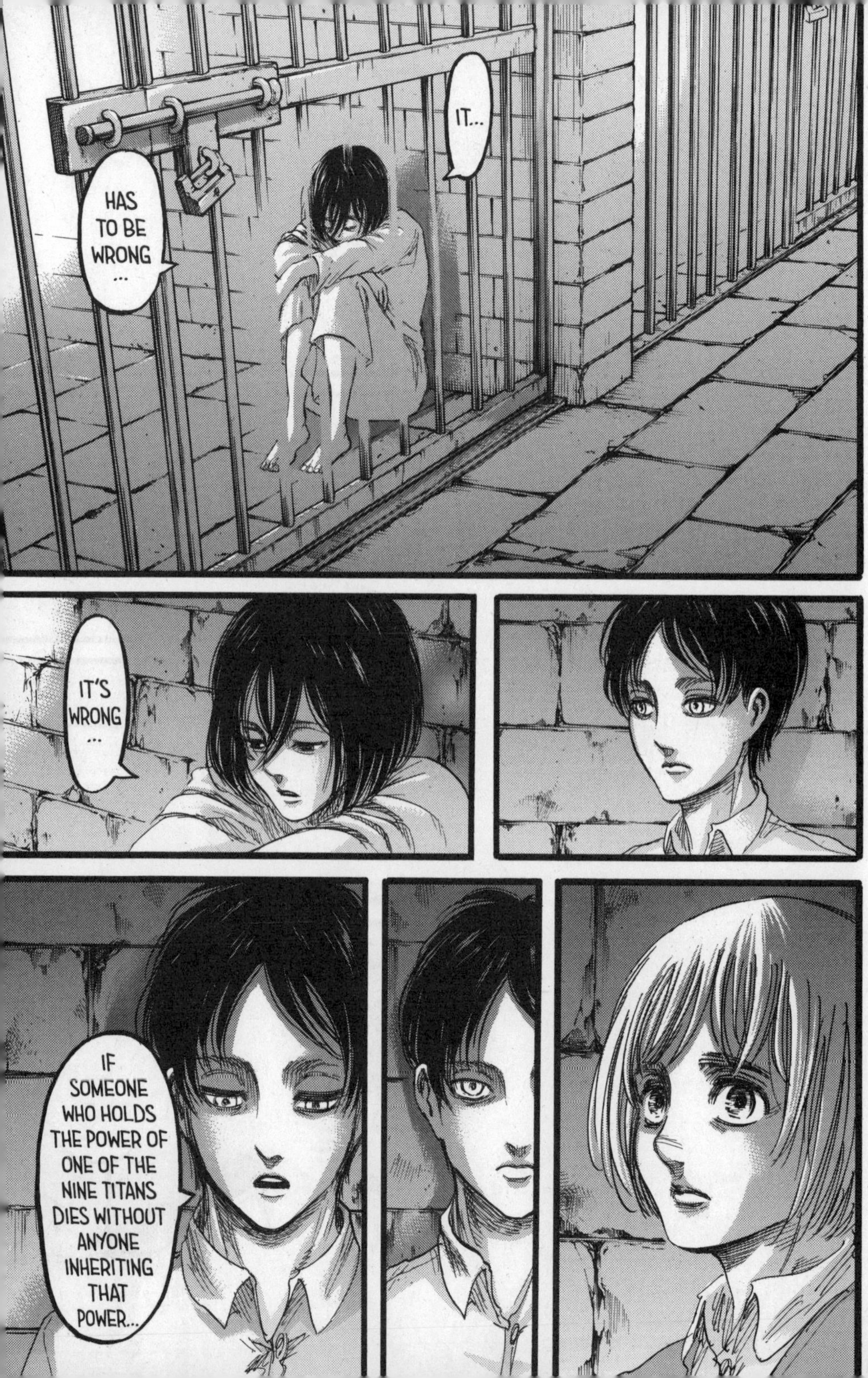
IT...
HAS TO BE WRONG ...
IT'S WRONG ...
IF SOMEONE WHO HOLDS THE POWER OF ONE OF THE NINE TITANS DIES WITHOUT ANYONE INHERITING THAT POWER...

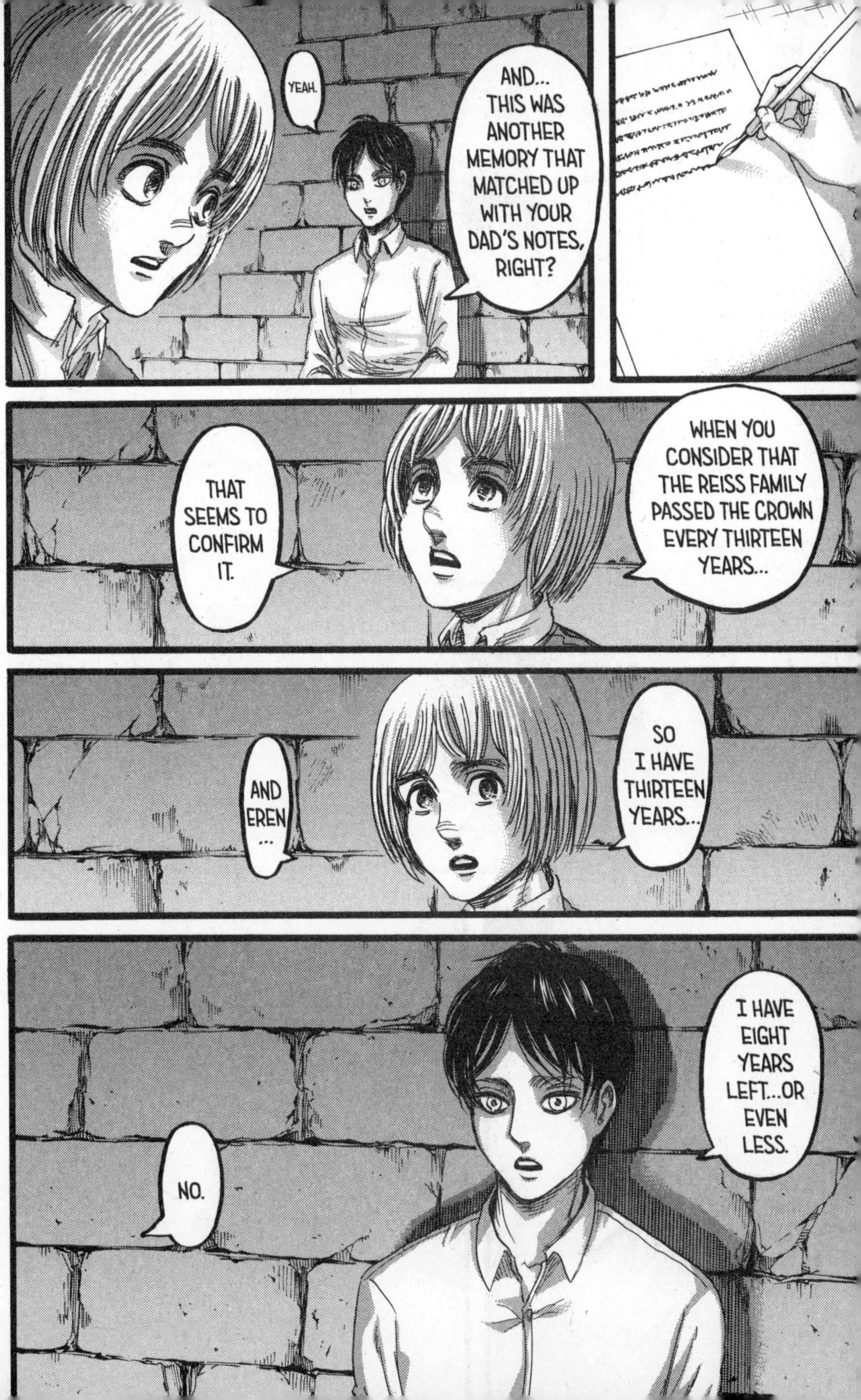
AND... THIS WAS ANOTHER MEMORY THAT MATCHED UP WITH YOUR DAD'S NOTES, RIGHT?
YEAH.
WHEN YOU CONSIDER THAT THE REISS FAMILY PASSED THE CROWN EVERY THIRTEEN YEARS...
THAT SEEMS TO CONFIRM IT.
SO I HAVE THIRTEEN YEARS...
AND EREN...
I HAVE EIGHT YEARS LEFT...OR EVEN LESS.
NO.

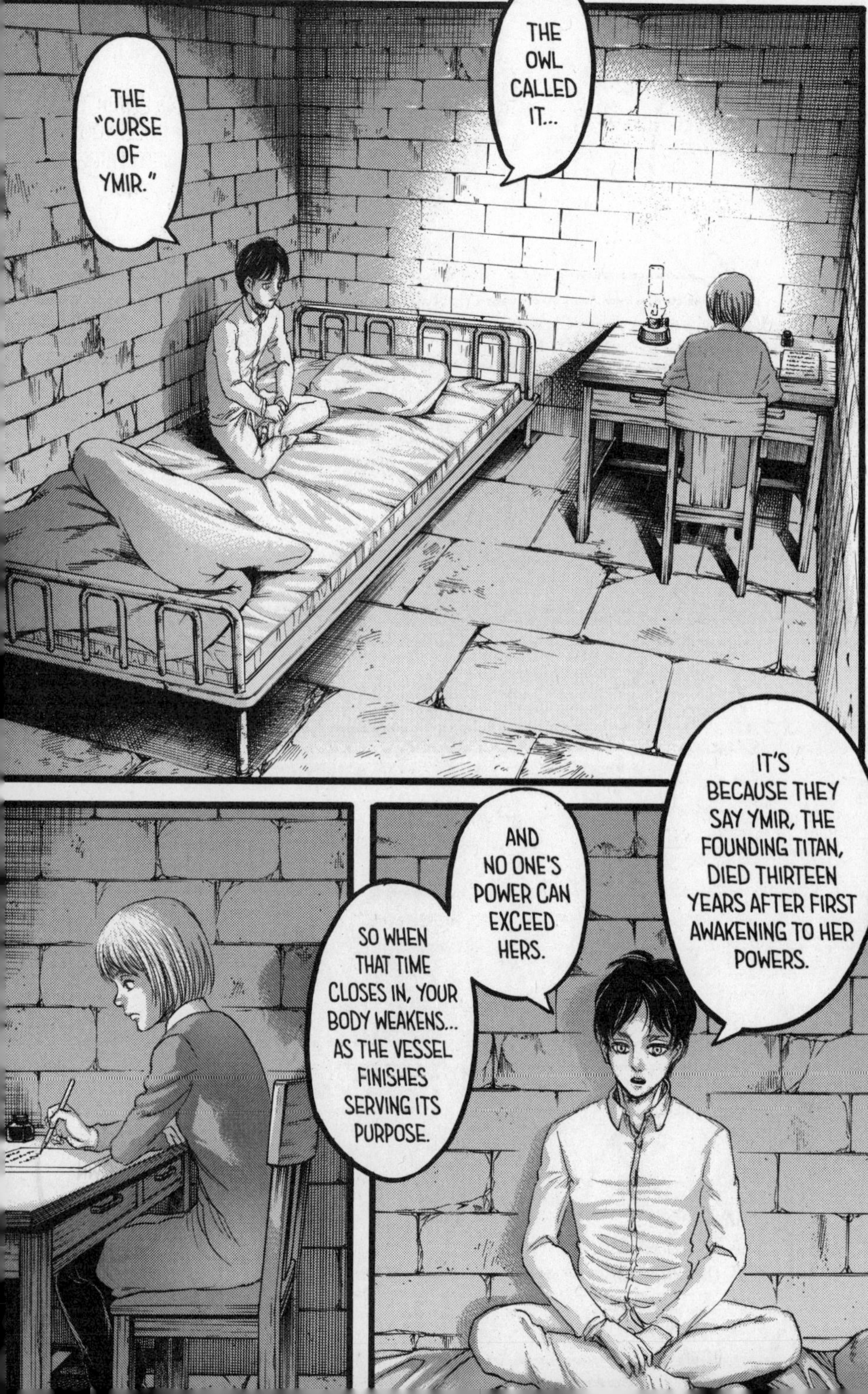
THE OWL CALLED IT...
THE "CURSE OF YMIR."
IT'S BECAUSE THEY SAY YMIR, THE FOUNDING TITAN, DIED THIRTEEN YEARS AFTER FIRST AWAKENING TO HER POWERS.
AND NO ONE'S POWER CAN EXCEED HERS.
SO WHEN THAT TIME CLOSES IN, YOUR BODY WEAKENS... AS THE VESSEL FINISHES SERVING ITS PURPOSE.

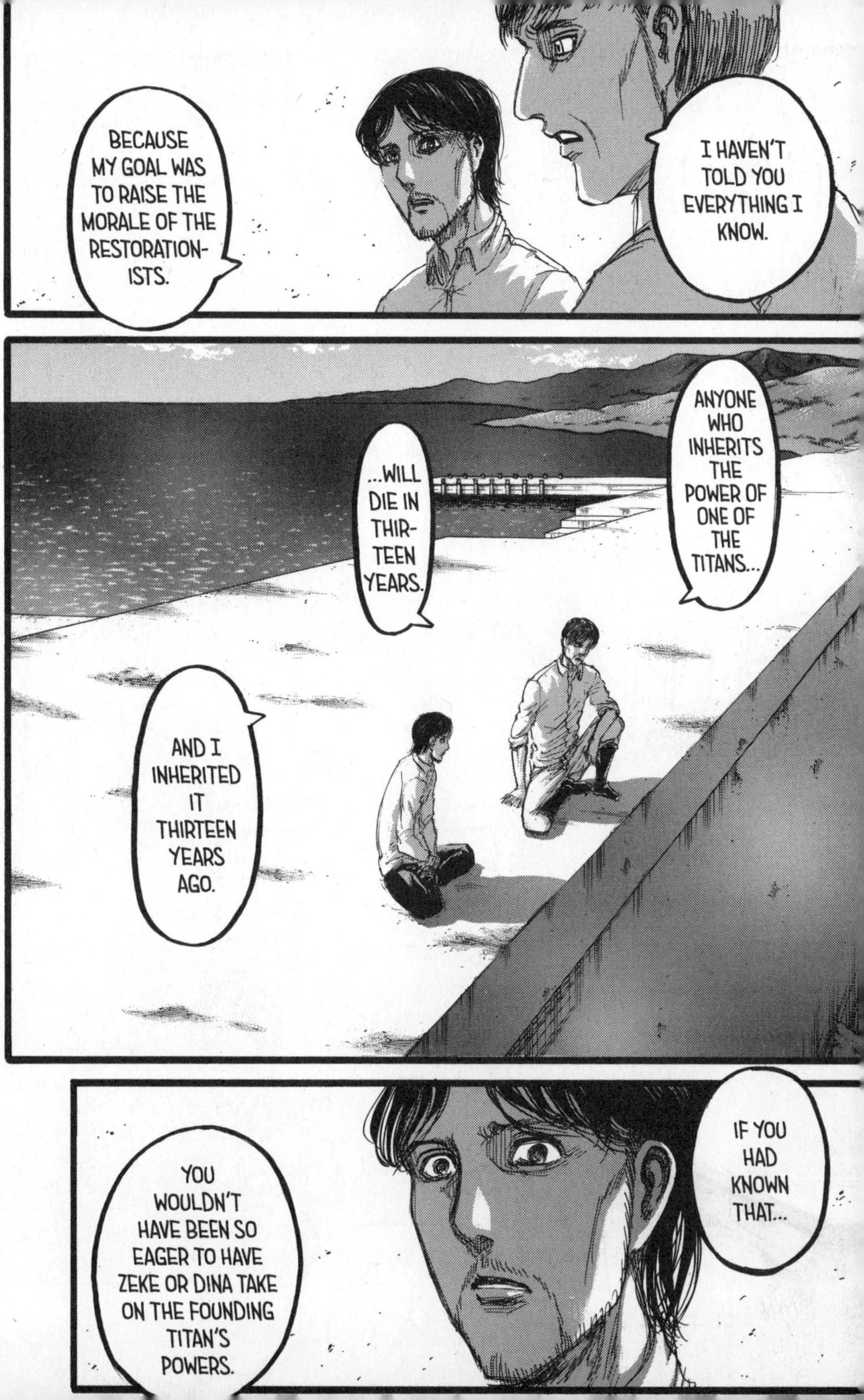
I HAVEN'T TOLD YOU EVERYTHING I KNOW.
BECAUSE MY GOAL WAS TO RAISE THE MORALE OF THE RESTORATIONISTS.
ANYONE WHO INHERITS THE POWER OF ONE OF THE TITANS...
...WILL DIE IN THIRTEEN YEARS.
AND I INHERITED IT THIRTEEN YEARS AGO.
IF YOU HAD KNOWN THAT...
YOU WOULDN'T HAVE BEEN SO EAGER TO HAVE ZEKE OR DINA TAKE ON THE FOUNDING TITAN'S POWERS.

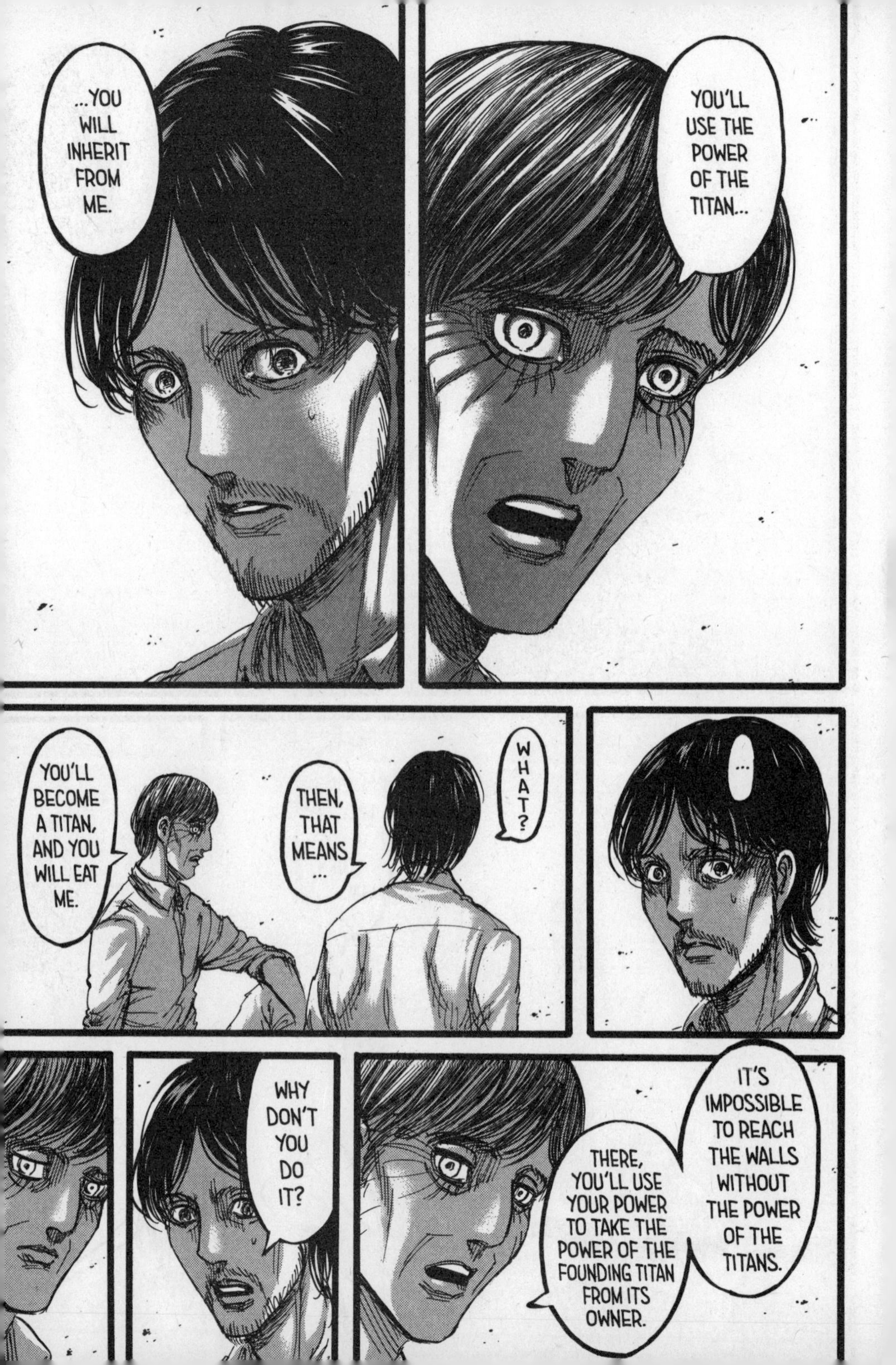
YOU'LL USE THE POWER OF THE TITAN...
...YOU WILL INHERIT FROM ME.
...
WHAT?
THEN, THAT MEANS ...
YOU'LL BECOME A TITAN, AND YOU WILL EAT ME.
IT'S IMPOSSIBLE TO REACH THE WALLS WITHOUT THE POWER OF THE TITANS.
THERE, YOU'LL USE YOUR POWER TO TAKE THE POWER OF THE FOUNDING TITAN FROM ITS OWNER.
WHY DON'T YOU DO IT?

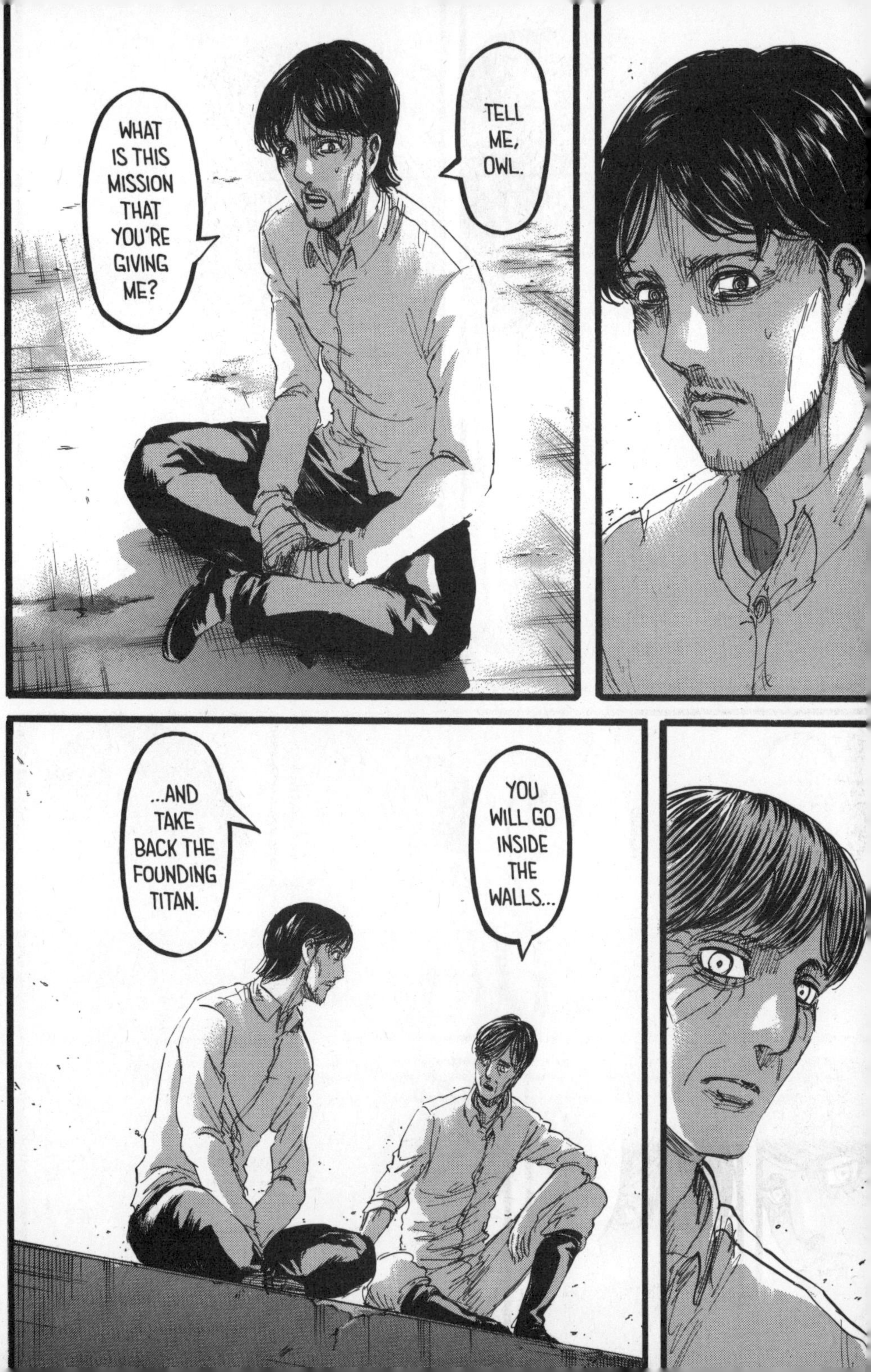
TELL ME, OWL.
WHAT IS THIS MISSION THAT YOU'RE GIVING ME?
YOU WILL GO INSIDE THE WALLS...
...AND TAKE BACK THE FOUNDING TITAN.

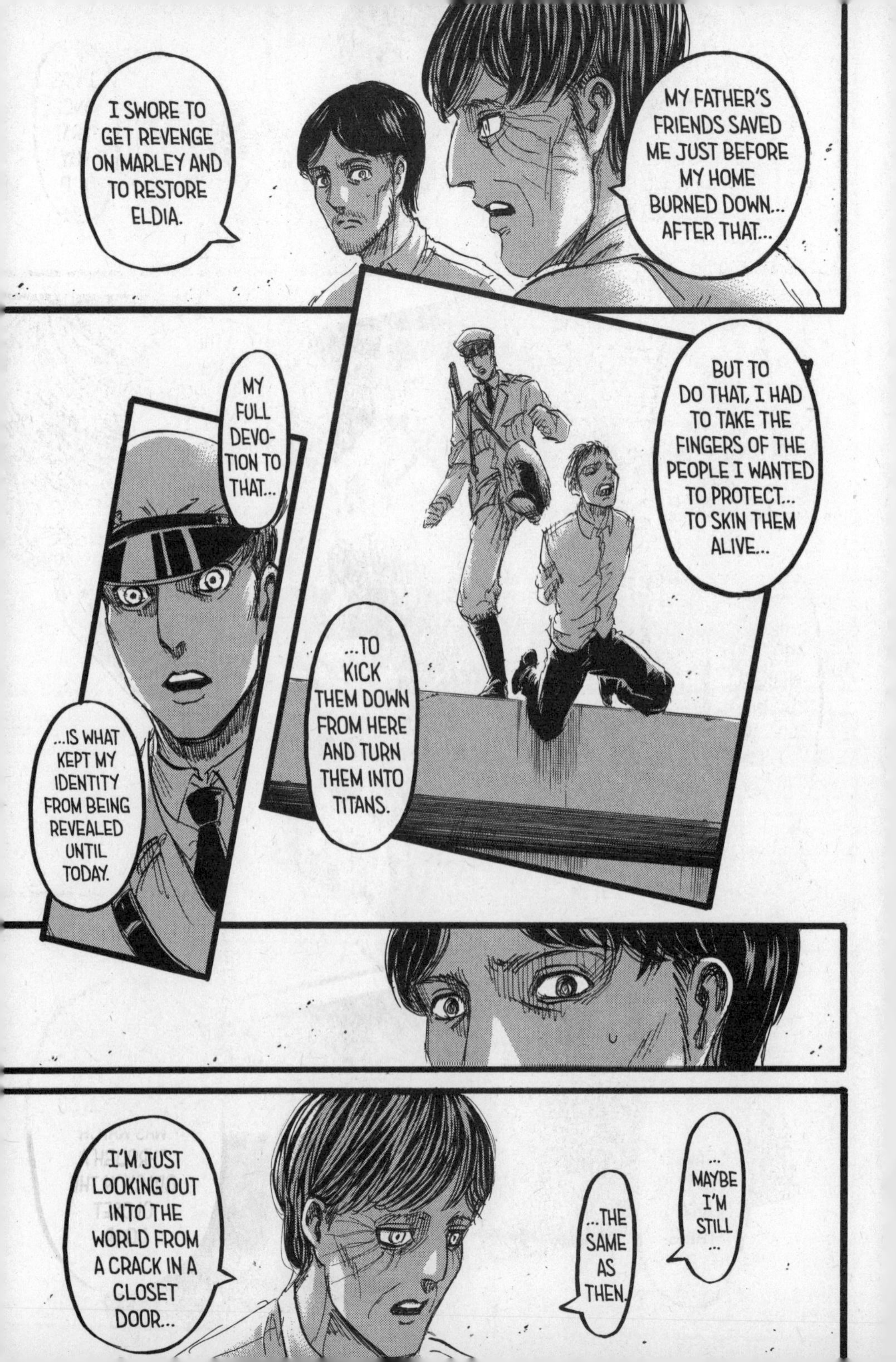
MY FATHER'S FRIENDS SAVED ME JUST BEFORE MY HOME BURNED DOWN... AFTER THAT...
I SWORE TO GET REVENGE ON MARLEY AND TO RESTORE ELDIA.
BUT TO DO THAT, I HAD TO TAKE THE FINGERS OF THE PEOPLE I WANTED TO PROTECT... TO SKIN THEM ALIVE...
...TO KICK THEM DOWN FROM HERE AND TURN THEM INTO TITANS.
MY FULL DEVOTION TO THAT...
...IS WHAT KEPT MY IDENTITY FROM BEING REVEALED UNTIL TODAY.
... MAYBE I'M STILL ...
...THE SAME AS THEN.
I'M JUST LOOKING OUT INTO THE WORLD FROM A CRACK IN A CLOSET DOOR...

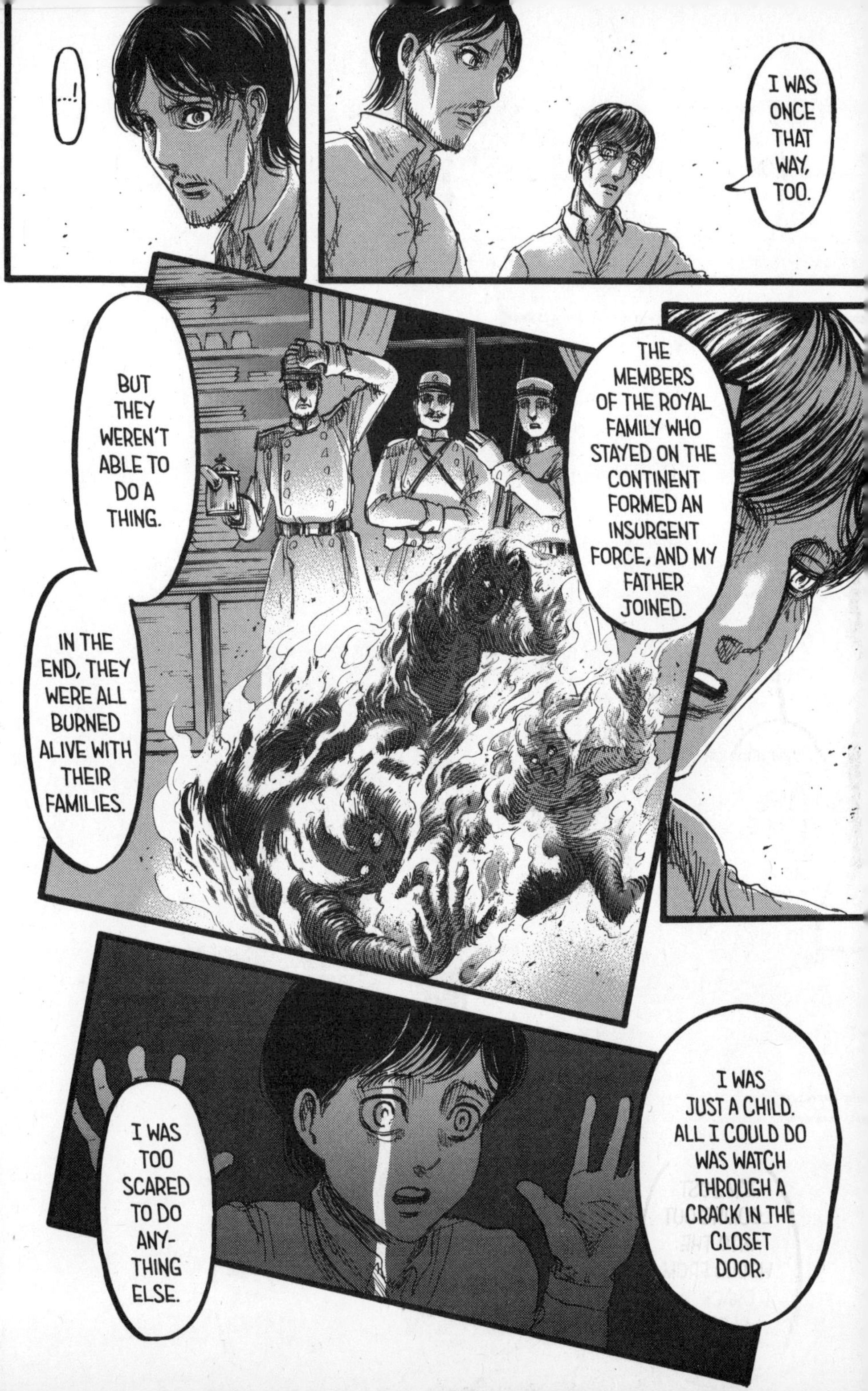
I WAS ONCE THAT WAY, TOO.
...!
THE MEMBERS OF THE ROYAL FAMILY WHO STAYED ON THE CONTINENT FORMED AN INSURGENT FORCE, AND MY FATHER JOINED.
BUT THEY WEREN'T ABLE TO DO A THING.
IN THE END, THEY WERE ALL BURNED ALIVE WITH THEIR FAMILIES.
I WAS JUST A CHILD. ALL I COULD DO WAS WATCH THROUGH A CRACK IN THE CLOSET DOOR.
I WAS TOO SCARED TO DO ANY-THING ELSE.

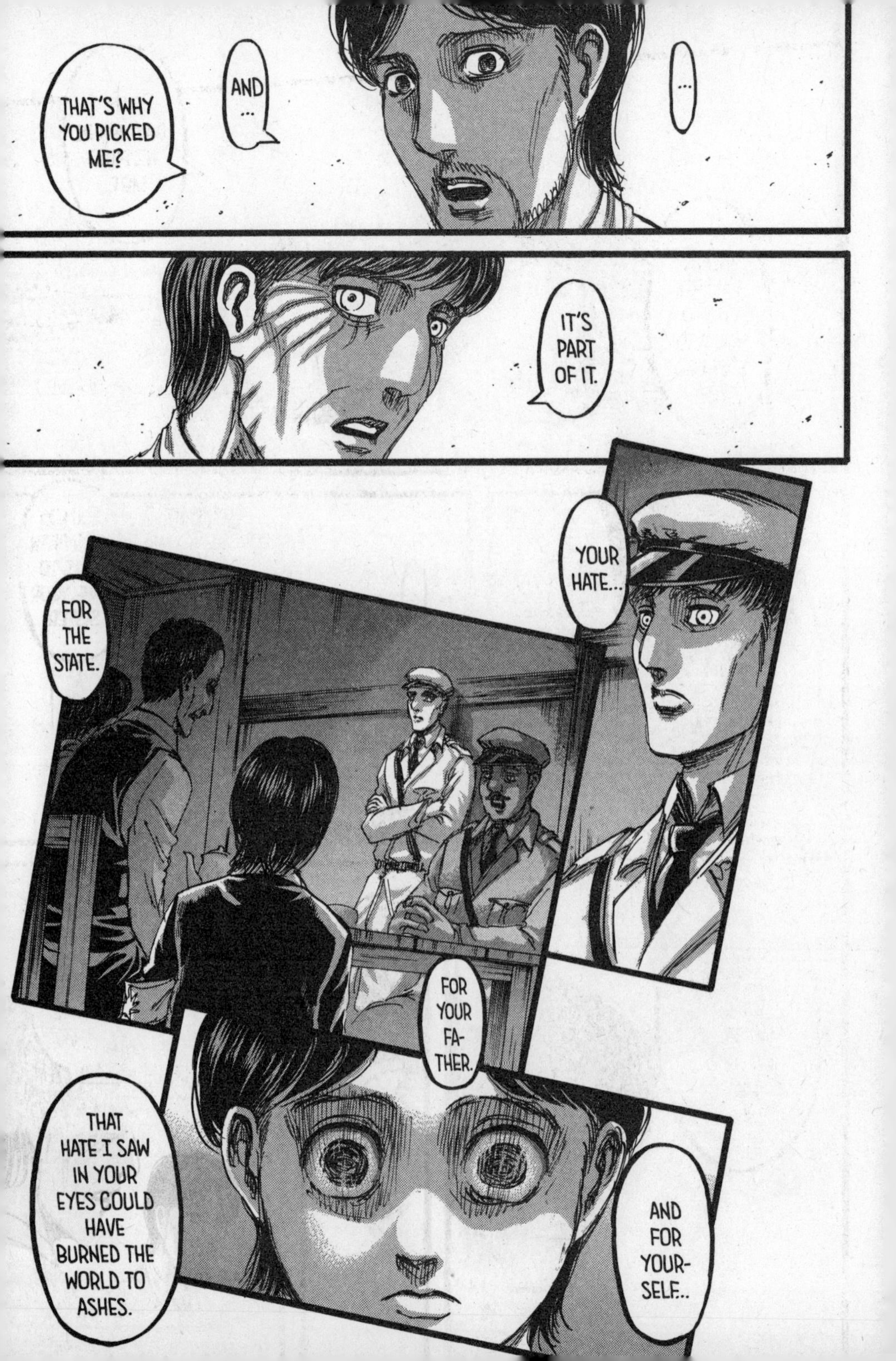
...
AND ...
THAT'S WHY YOU PICKED ME?
IT'S PART OF IT.
YOUR HATE...
FOR THE STATE.
FOR YOUR FA-THER.
AND FOR YOUR-SELF...
THAT HATE I SAW IN YOUR EYES COULD HAVE BURNED THE WORLD TO ASHES.

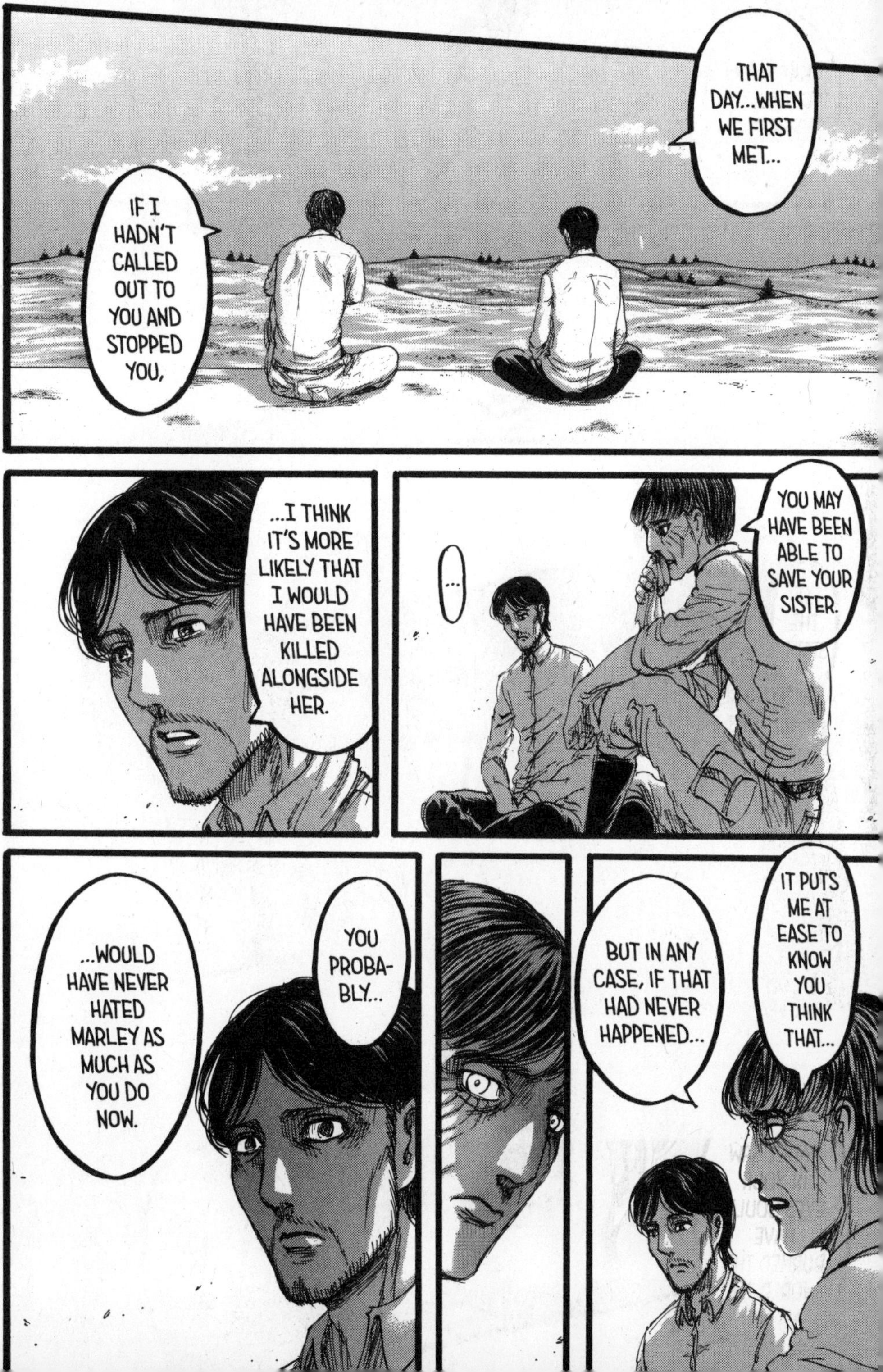
THAT DAY...WHEN WE FIRST MET...
IF I HADN'T CALLED OUT TO YOU AND STOPPED YOU,
YOU MAY HAVE BEEN ABLE TO SAVE YOUR SISTER.
...
...I THINK IT'S MORE LIKELY THAT I WOULD HAVE BEEN KILLED ALONGSIDE HER.
IT PUTS ME AT EASE TO KNOW YOU THINK THAT...
BUT IN ANY CASE, IF THAT HAD NEVER HAPPENED...
YOU PROBA-BLY...
...WOULD HAVE NEVER HATED MARLEY AS MUCH AS YOU DO NOW.

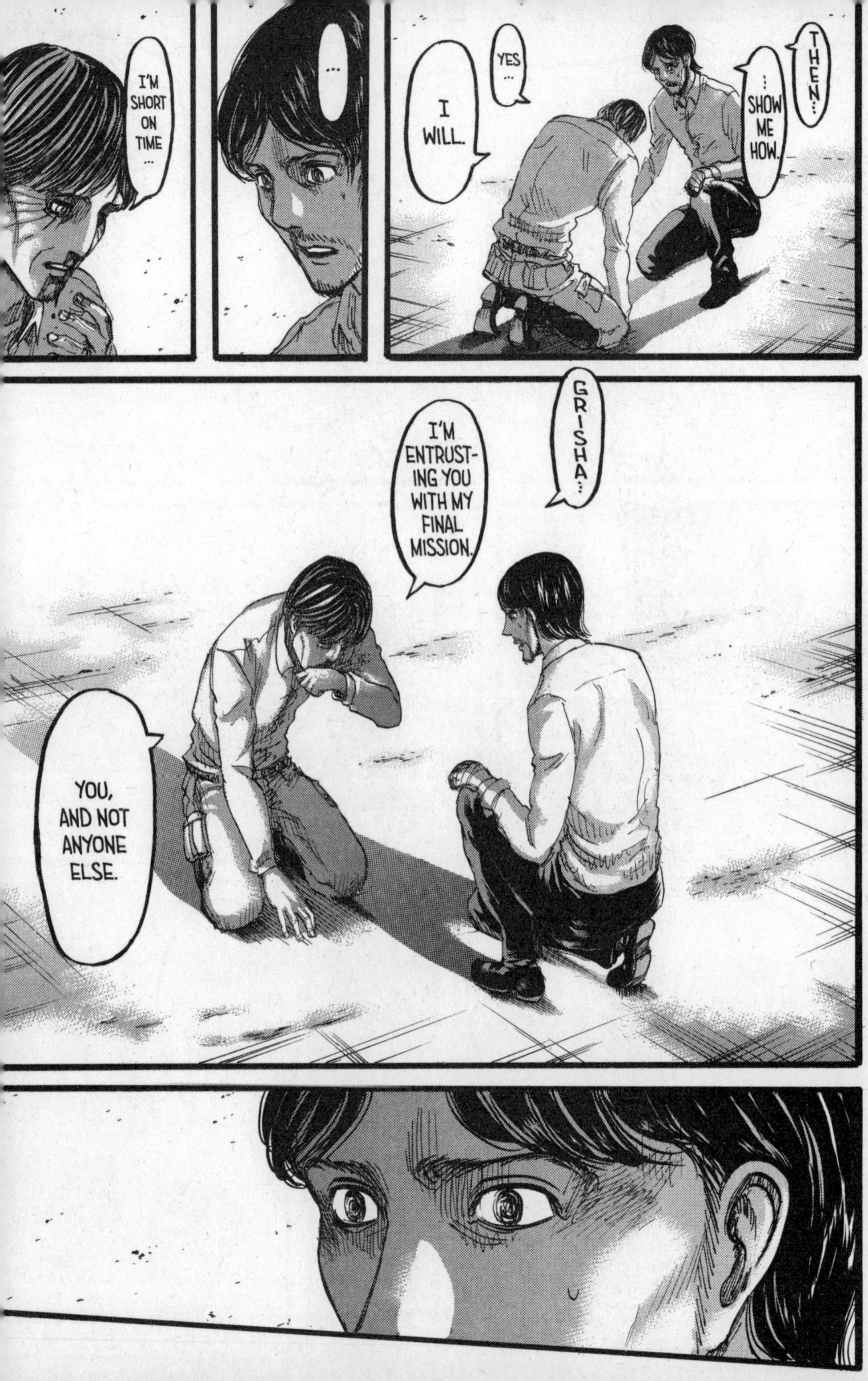
THEN...
...SHOW ME HOW.
YES...
I WILL.
...
I'M SHORT ON TIME...
GRISHA...
I'M ENTRUSTING YOU WITH MY FINAL MISSION.
YOU, AND NOT ANYONE ELSE.

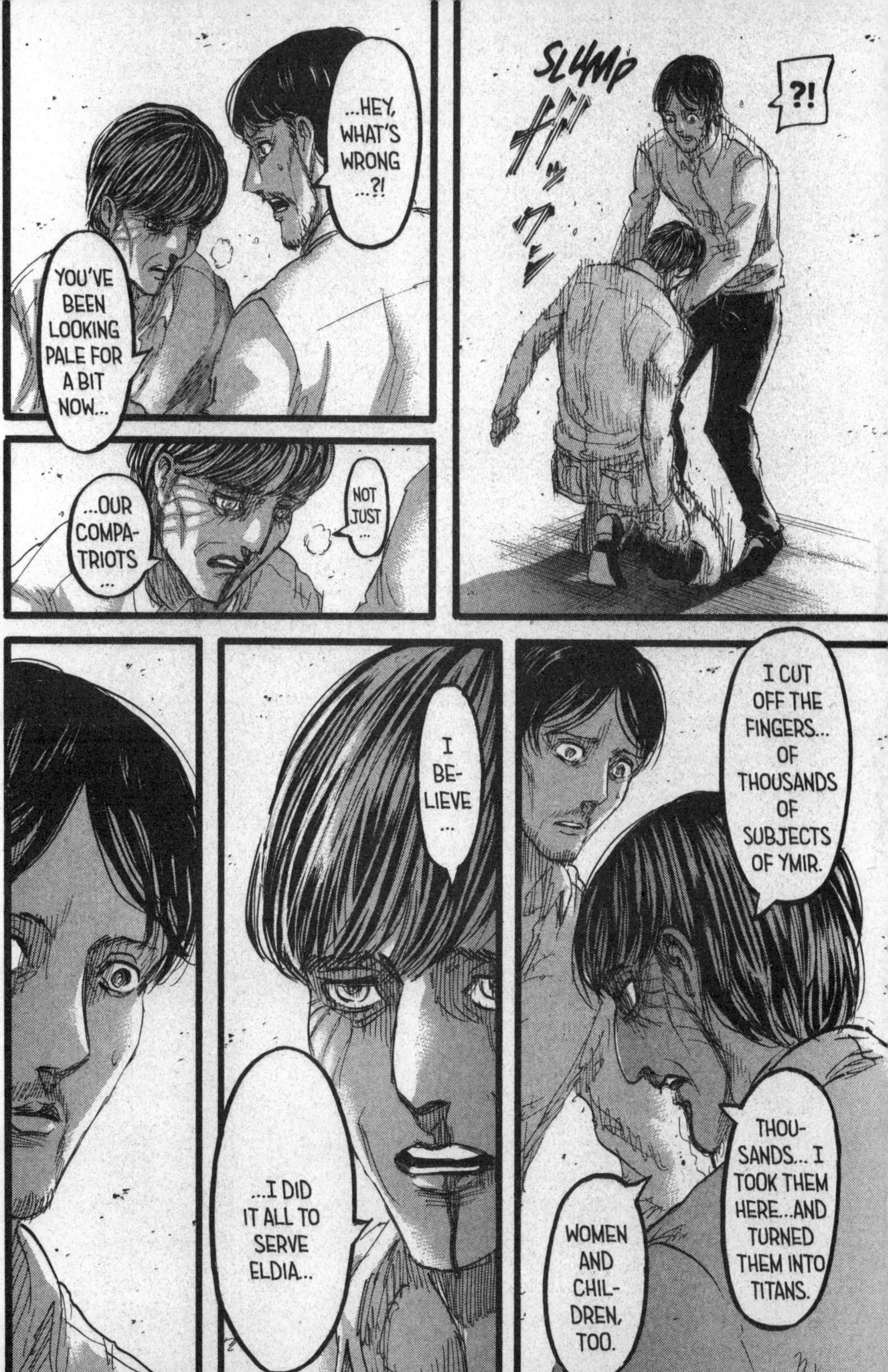
SLUMP
?!
...HEY, WHAT'S WRONG ...?!
YOU'VE BEEN LOOKING PALE FOR A BIT NOW...
NOT JUST ...
...OUR COMPA-TRIOTS ...
I CUT OFF THE FINGERS... OF THOUSANDS OF SUBJECTS OF YMIR.
THOU-SANDS... I TOOK THEM HERE...AND TURNED THEM INTO TITANS.
WOMEN AND CHIL-DREN, TOO.
I BE-LIEVE ...
...I DID IT ALL TO SERVE ELDIA...

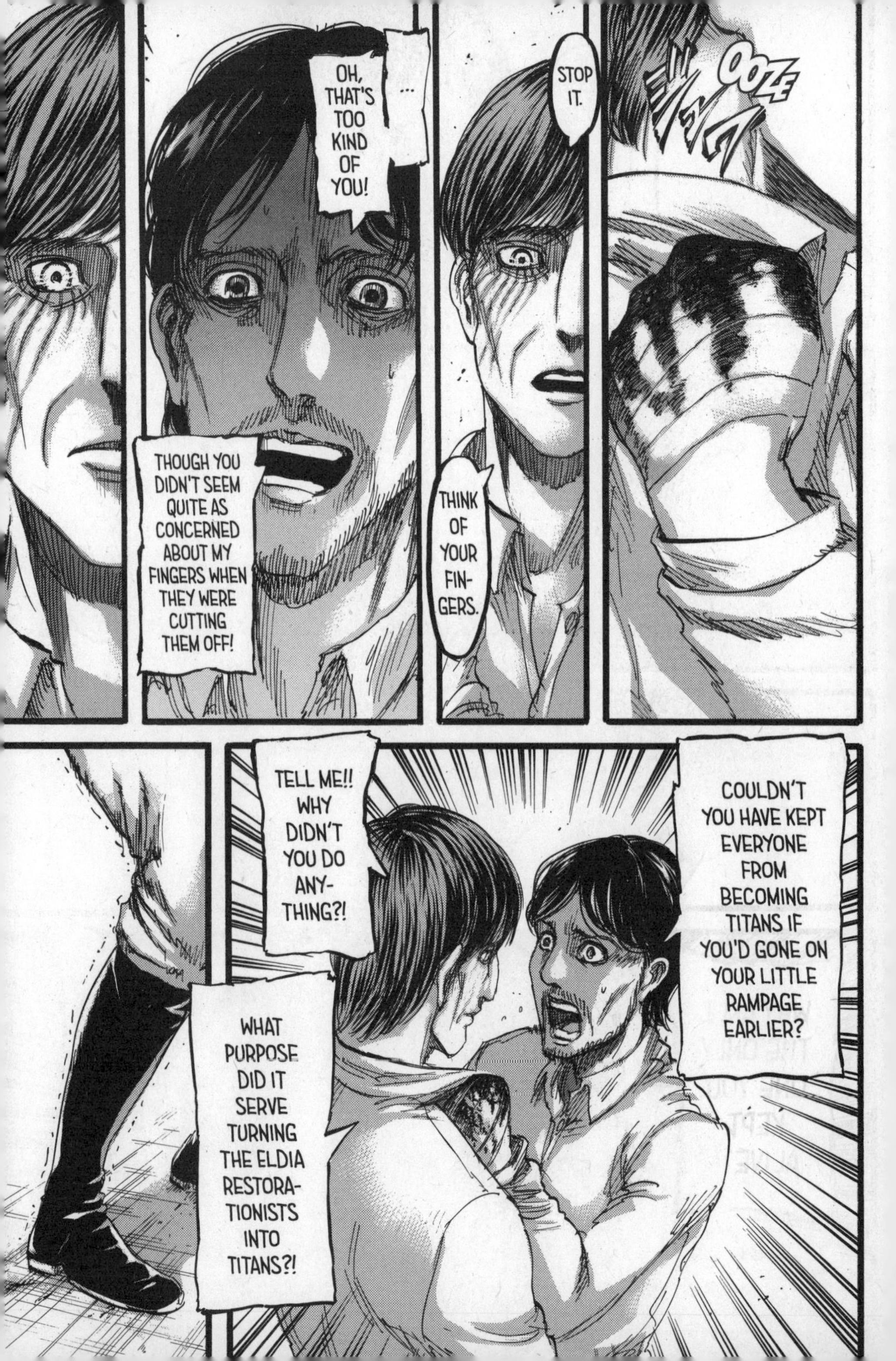
OOZE
STOP IT.
THINK OF YOUR FIN-GERS.
...
OH, THAT'S TOO KIND OF YOU!
THOUGH YOU DIDN'T SEEM QUITE AS CONCERNED ABOUT MY FINGERS WHEN THEY WERE CUTTING THEM OFF!
COULDN'T YOU HAVE KEPT EVERYONE FROM BECOMING TITANS IF YOU'D GONE ON YOUR LITTLE RAMPAGE EARLIER?
TELL ME!! WHY DIDN'T YOU DO ANY-THING?!
WHAT PURPOSE DID IT SERVE TURNING THE ELDIA RESTORA-TIONISTS INTO TITANS?!

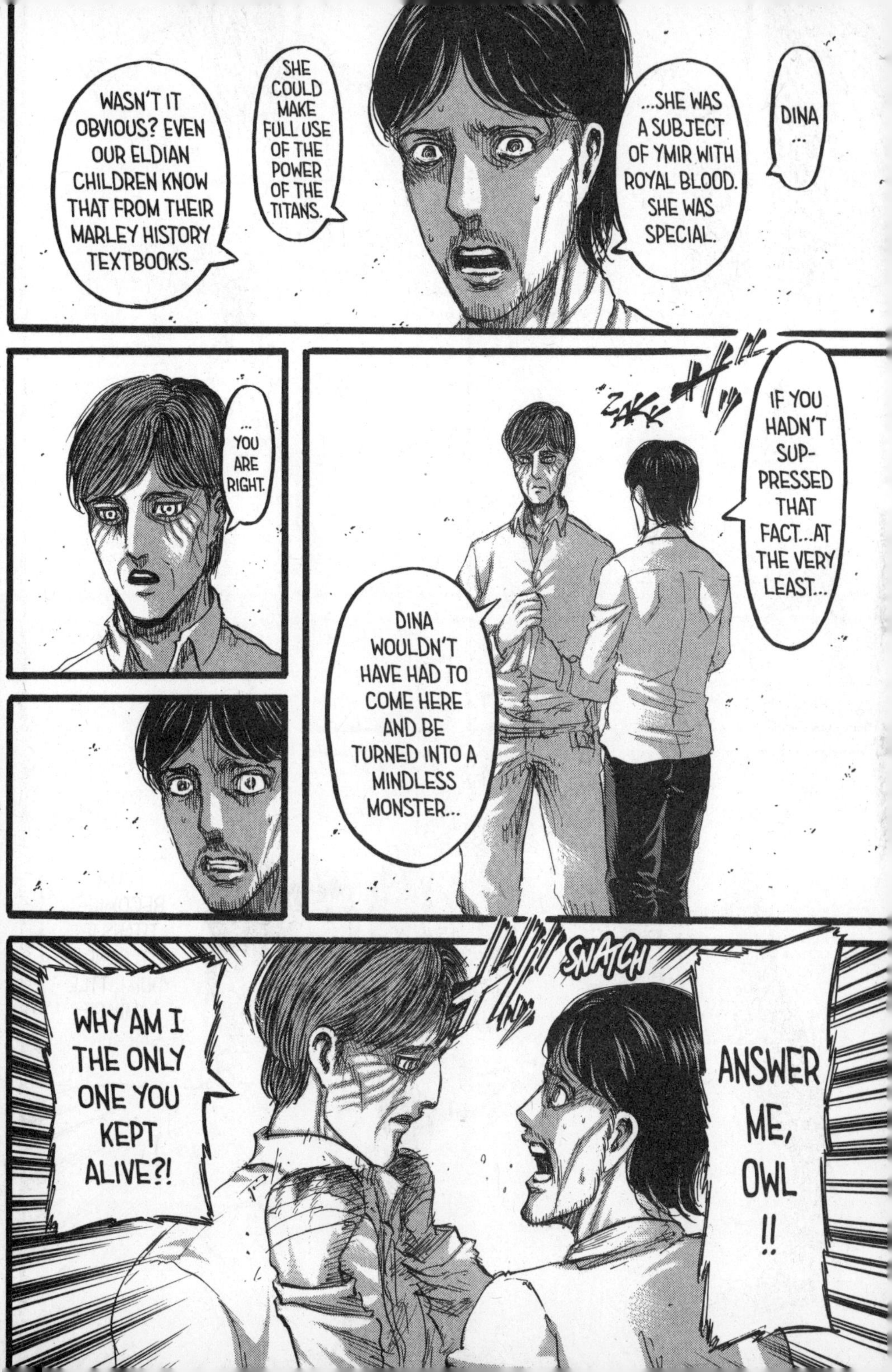
DINA ...
...SHE WAS A SUBJECT OF YMIR WITH ROYAL BLOOD. SHE WAS SPECIAL.
SHE COULD MAKE FULL USE OF THE POWER OF THE TITANS.
WASN'T IT OBVIOUS? EVEN OUR ELDIAN CHILDREN KNOW THAT FROM THEIR MARLEY HISTORY TEXTBOOKS.
ZAKK
IF YOU HADN'T SUP-PRESSED THAT FACT...AT THE VERY LEAST...
DINA WOULDN'T HAVE HAD TO COME HERE AND BE TURNED INTO A MINDLESS MONSTER...
... YOU ARE RIGHT.
SNATCH
ANSWER ME, OWL !!
WHY AM I THE ONLY ONE YOU KEPT ALIVE?!

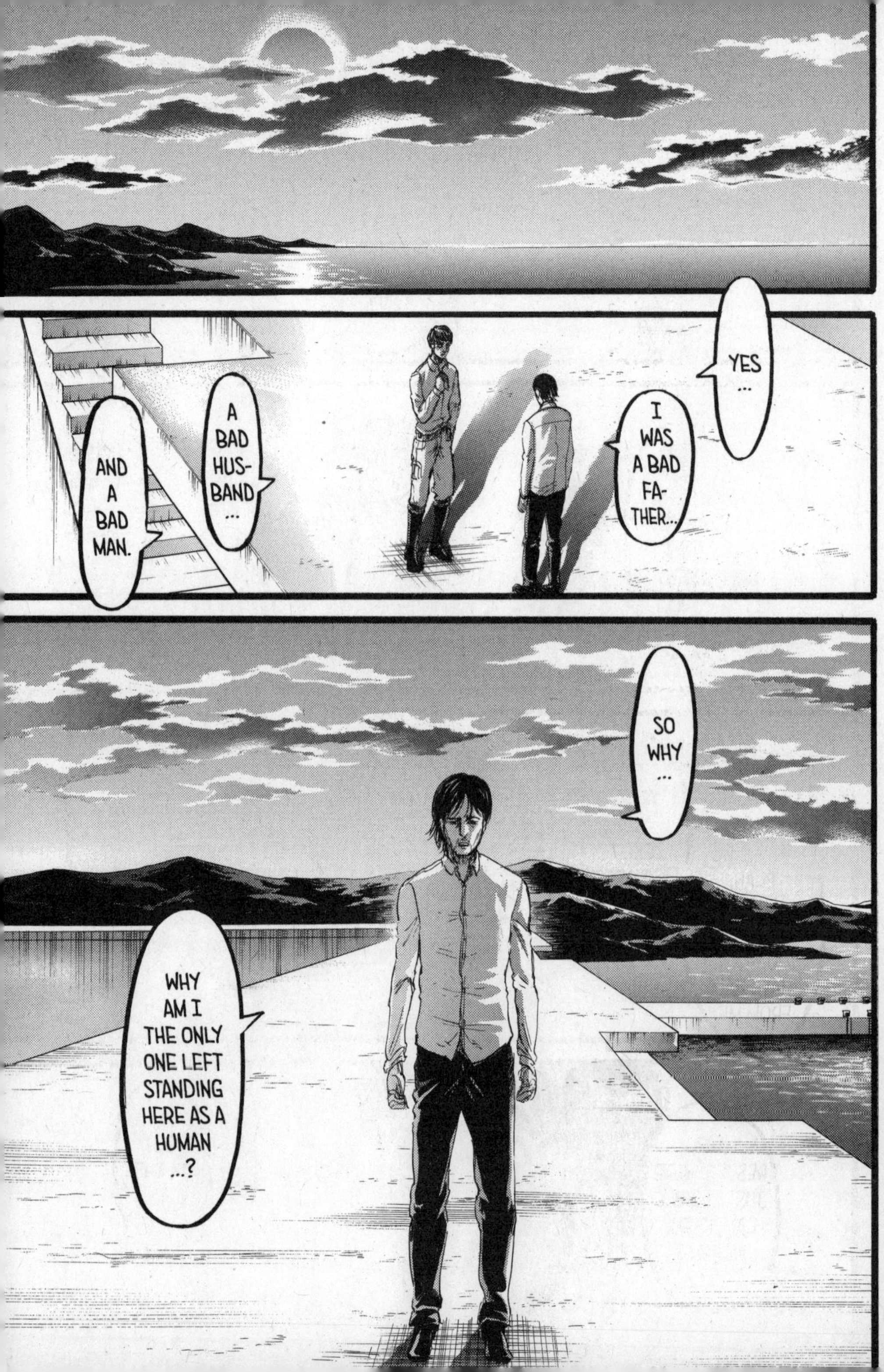
YES ...
I WAS A BAD FATHER...
A BAD HUSBAND ...
AND A BAD MAN.
SO WHY ...
WHY AM I THE ONLY ONE LEFT STANDING HERE AS A HUMAN ...?

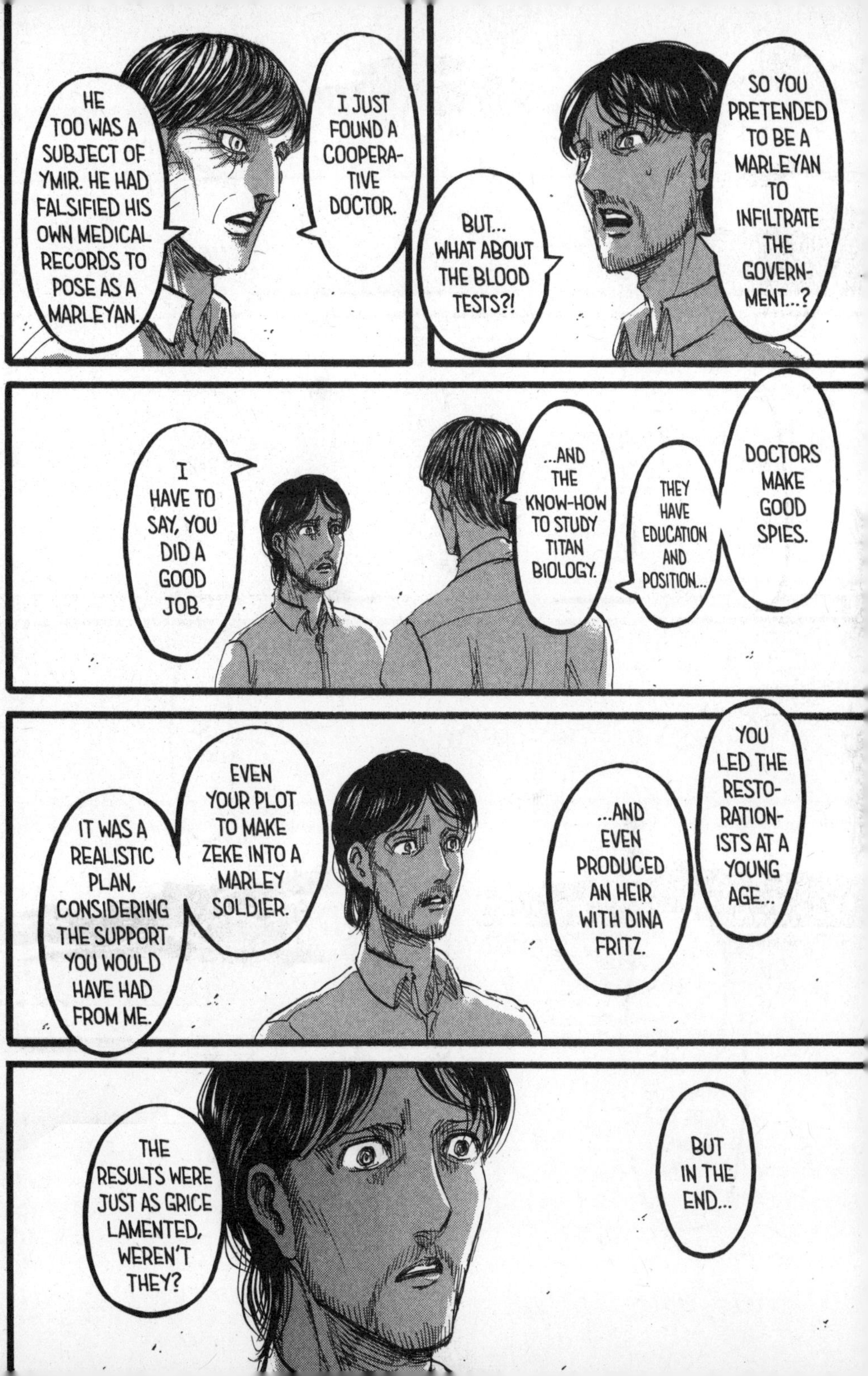
SO YOU PRETENDED TO BE A MARLEYAN TO INFILTRATE THE GOVERNMENT...?
BUT... WHAT ABOUT THE BLOOD TESTS?!
I JUST FOUND A COOPERATIVE DOCTOR.
HE TOO WAS A SUBJECT OF YMIR. HE HAD FALSIFIED HIS OWN MEDICAL RECORDS TO POSE AS A MARLEYAN.
DOCTORS MAKE GOOD SPIES.
THEY HAVE EDUCATION AND POSITION...
...AND THE KNOW-HOW TO STUDY TITAN BIOLOGY.
I HAVE TO SAY, YOU DID A GOOD JOB.
YOU LED THE RESTORATIONISTS AT A YOUNG AGE...
...AND EVEN PRODUCED AN HEIR WITH DINA FRITZ.
EVEN YOUR PLOT TO MAKE ZEKE INTO A MARLEY SOLDIER.
IT WAS A REALISTIC PLAN, CONSIDERING THE SUPPORT YOU WOULD HAVE HAD FROM ME.
BUT IN THE END...
THE RESULTS WERE JUST AS GRICE LAMENTED, WEREN'T THEY?

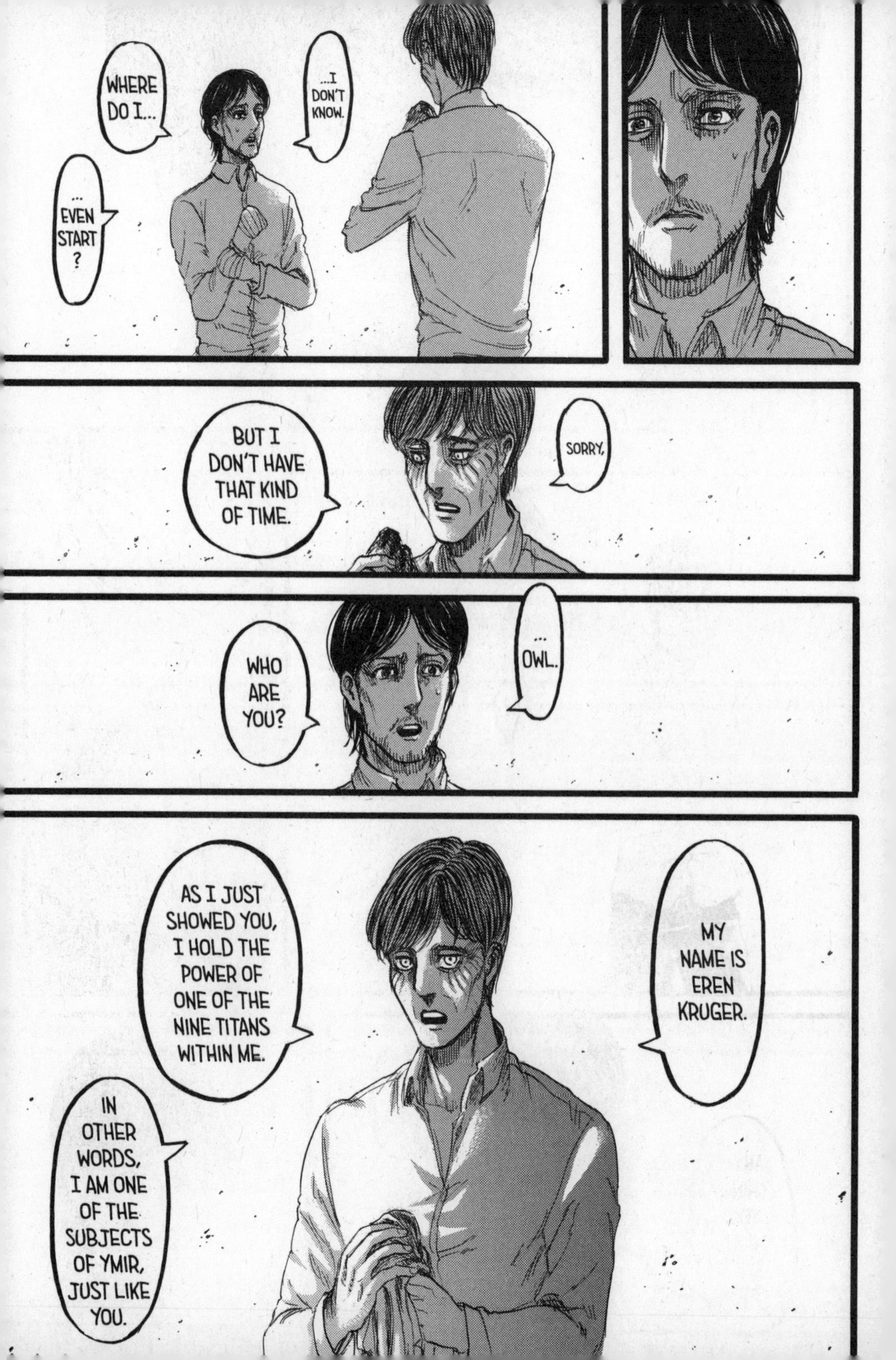

WHERE DO I...
...EVEN START?
...I DON'T KNOW.
SORRY,
BUT I DON'T HAVE THAT KIND OF TIME.
WHO ARE YOU?
...OWL.
MY NAME IS EREN KRUGER.
AS I JUST SHOWED YOU, I HOLD THE POWER OF ONE OF THE NINE TITANS WITHIN ME.
IN OTHER WORDS, I AM ONE OF THE SUBJECTS OF YMIR, JUST LIKE YOU.

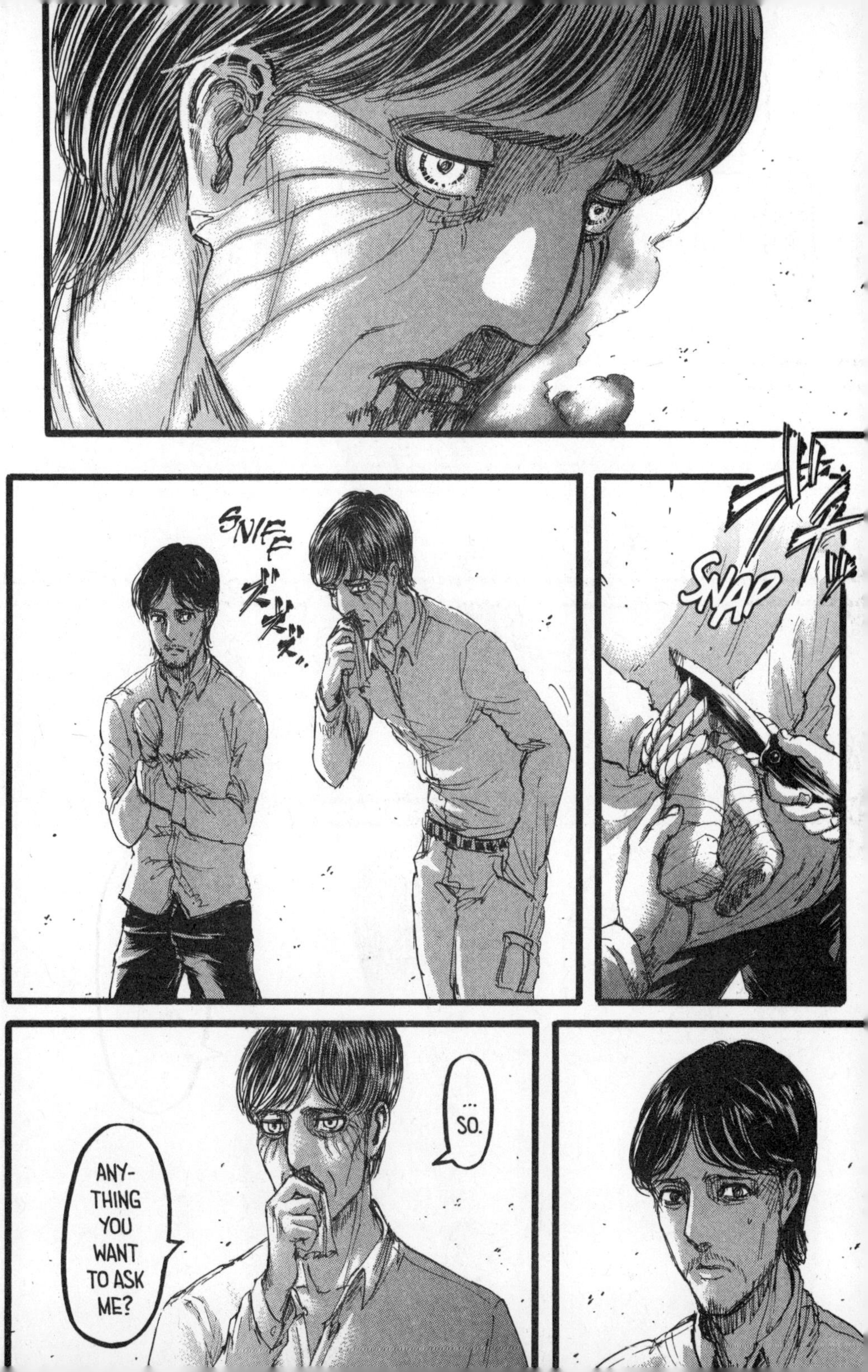
SNAP
SNIFF
... SO.
ANY-THING YOU WANT TO ASK ME?

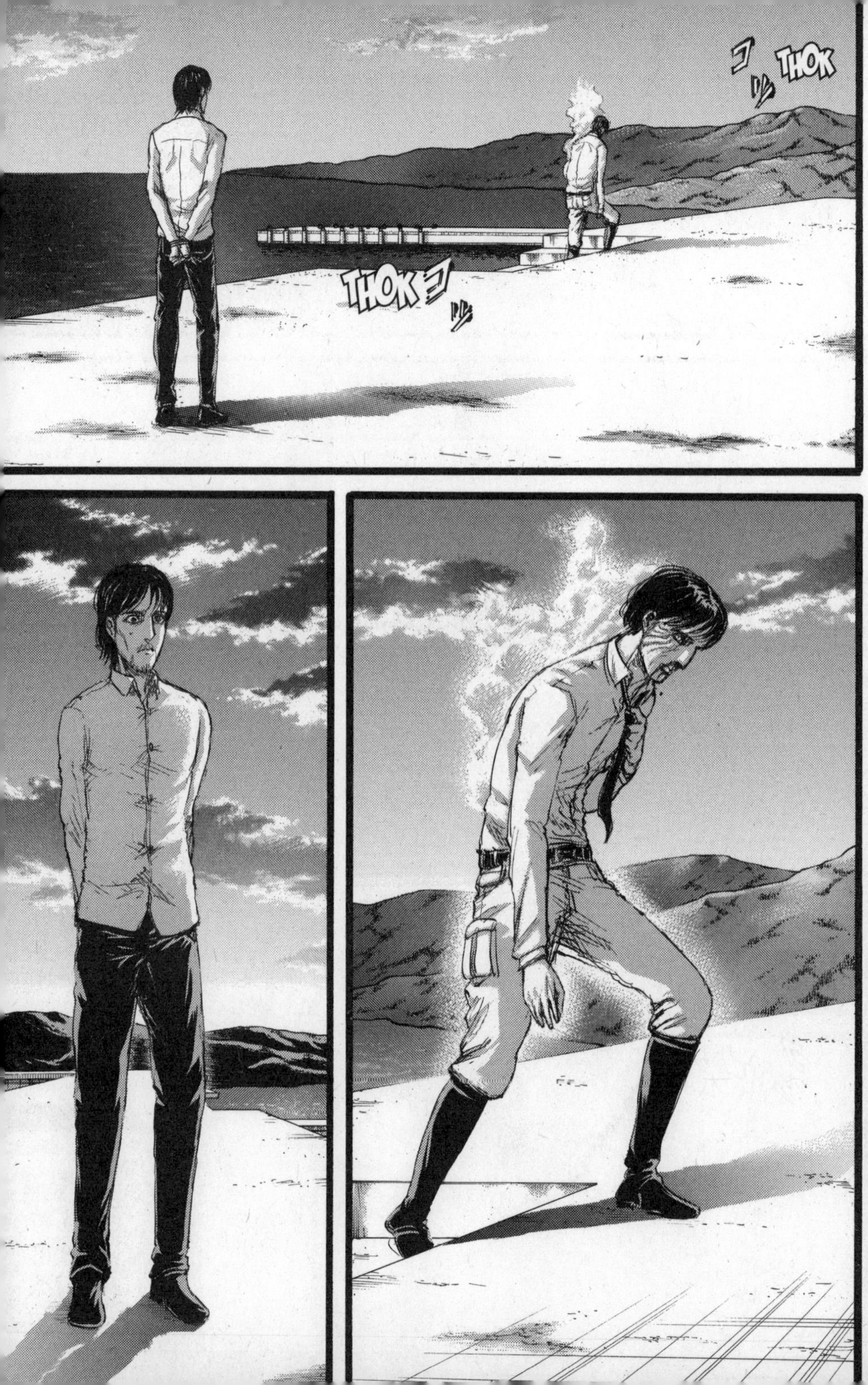
コッ THOK
THOK コッ

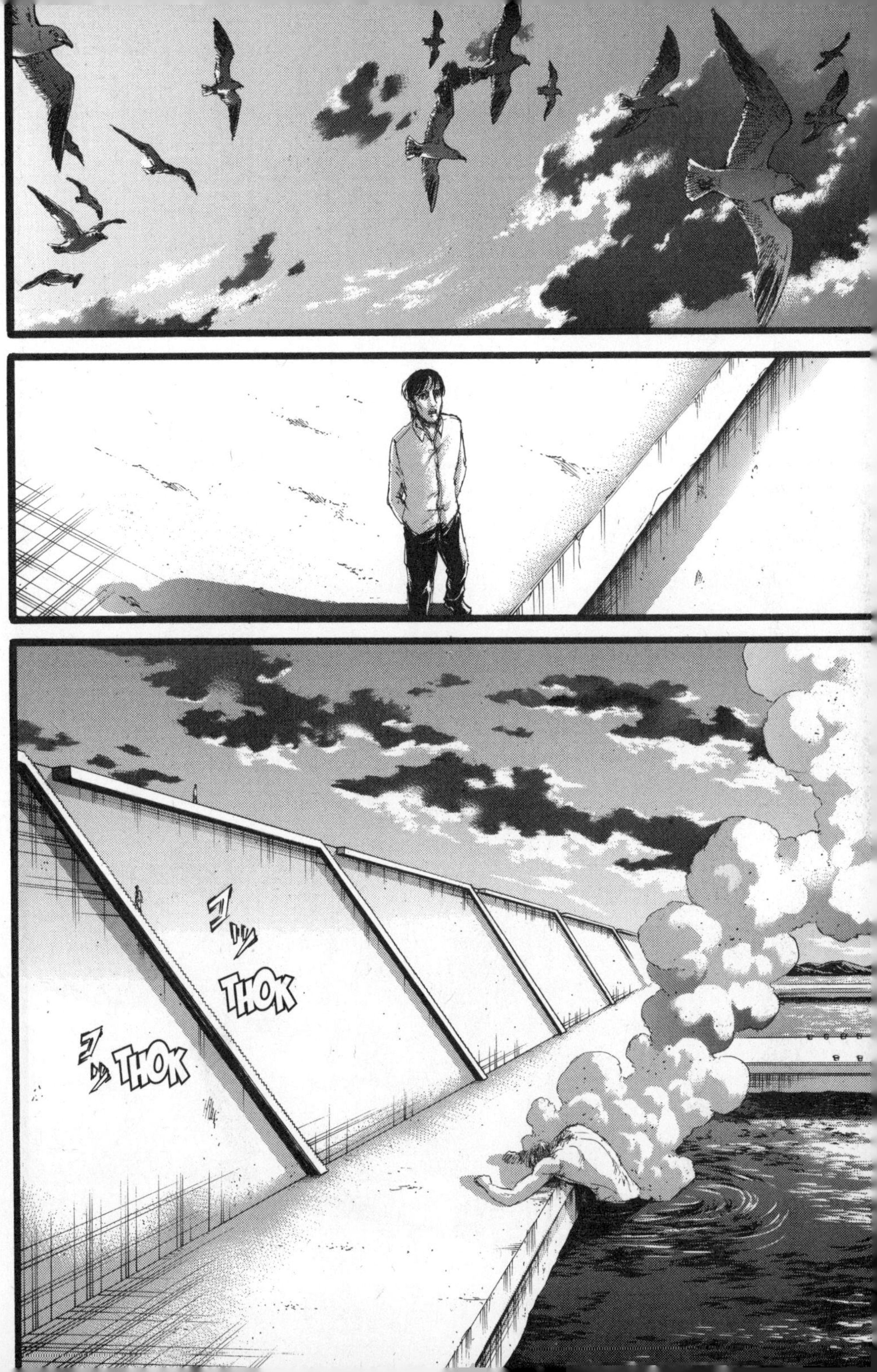
ゴッ THOK
ゴッ THOK

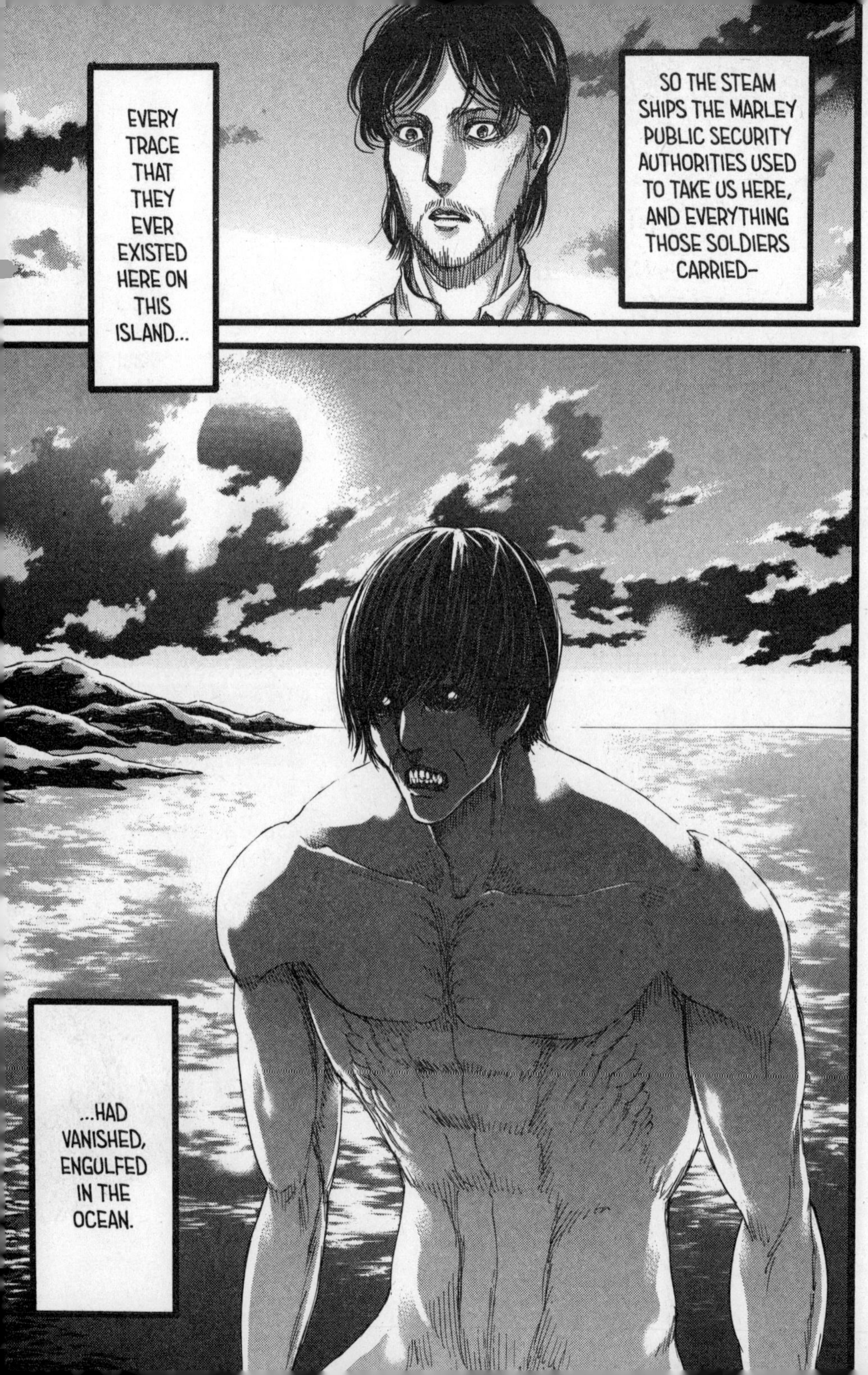
SO THE STEAM SHIPS THE MARLEY PUBLIC SECURITY AUTHORITIES USED TO TAKE US HERE, AND EVERYTHING THOSE SOLDIERS CARRIED–
EVERY TRACE THAT THEY EVER EXISTED HERE ON THIS ISLAND...
...HAD VANISHED, ENGULFED IN THE OCEAN.

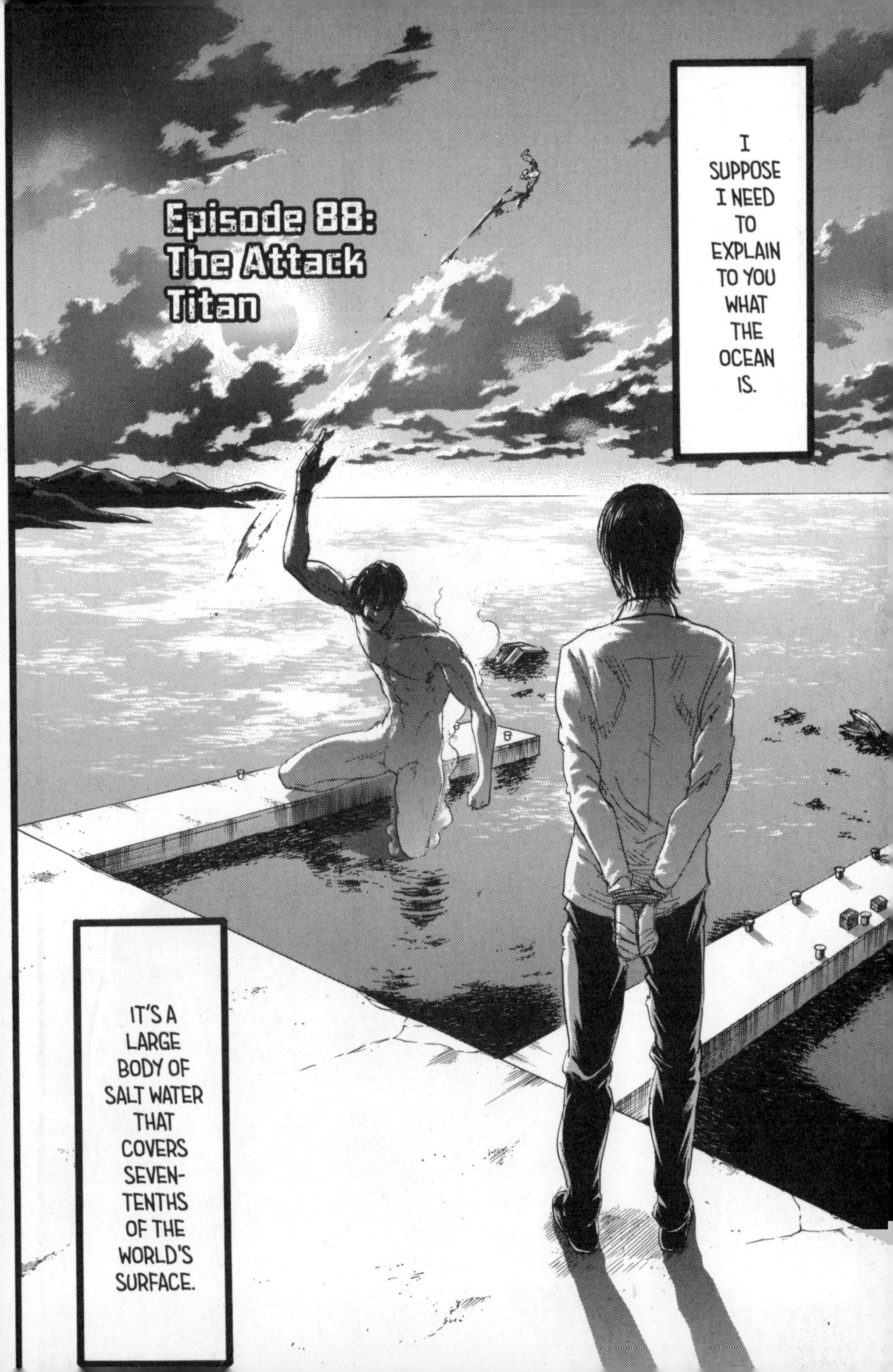
I SUPPOSE I NEED TO EXPLAIN TO YOU WHAT THE OCEAN IS.
Episode 88: The Attack Titan
IT'S A LARGE BODY OF SALT WATER THAT COVERS SEVEN-TENTHS OF THE WORLD'S SURFACE.

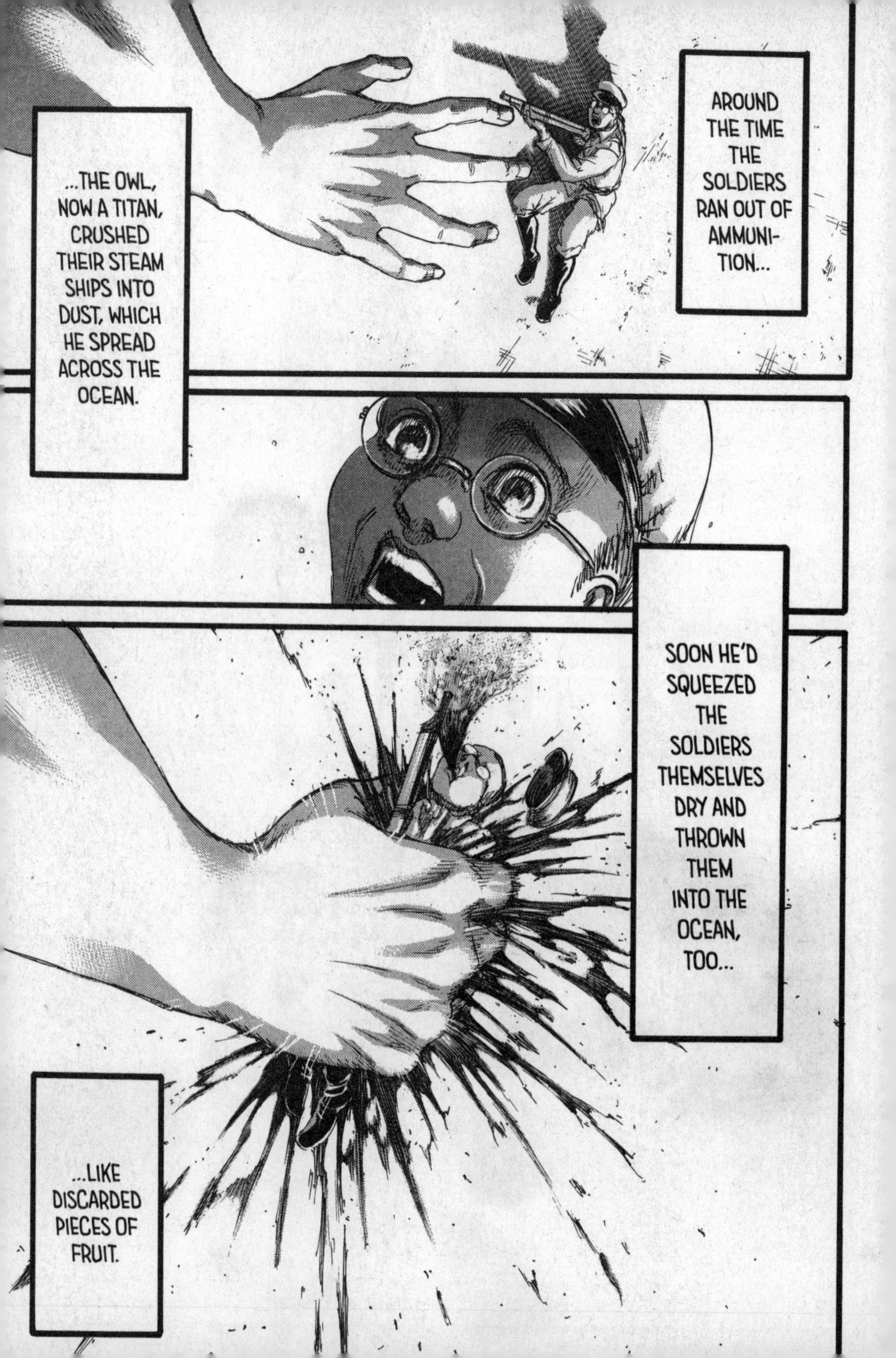
AROUND THE TIME THE SOLDIERS RAN OUT OF AMMUNITION...
...THE OWL, NOW A TITAN, CRUSHED THEIR STEAM SHIPS INTO DUST, WHICH HE SPREAD ACROSS THE OCEAN.
SOON HE'D SQUEEZED THE SOLDIERS THEMSELVES DRY AND THROWN THEM INTO THE OCEAN, TOO...
...LIKE DISCARDED PIECES OF FRUIT.

ATTACK on TITAN

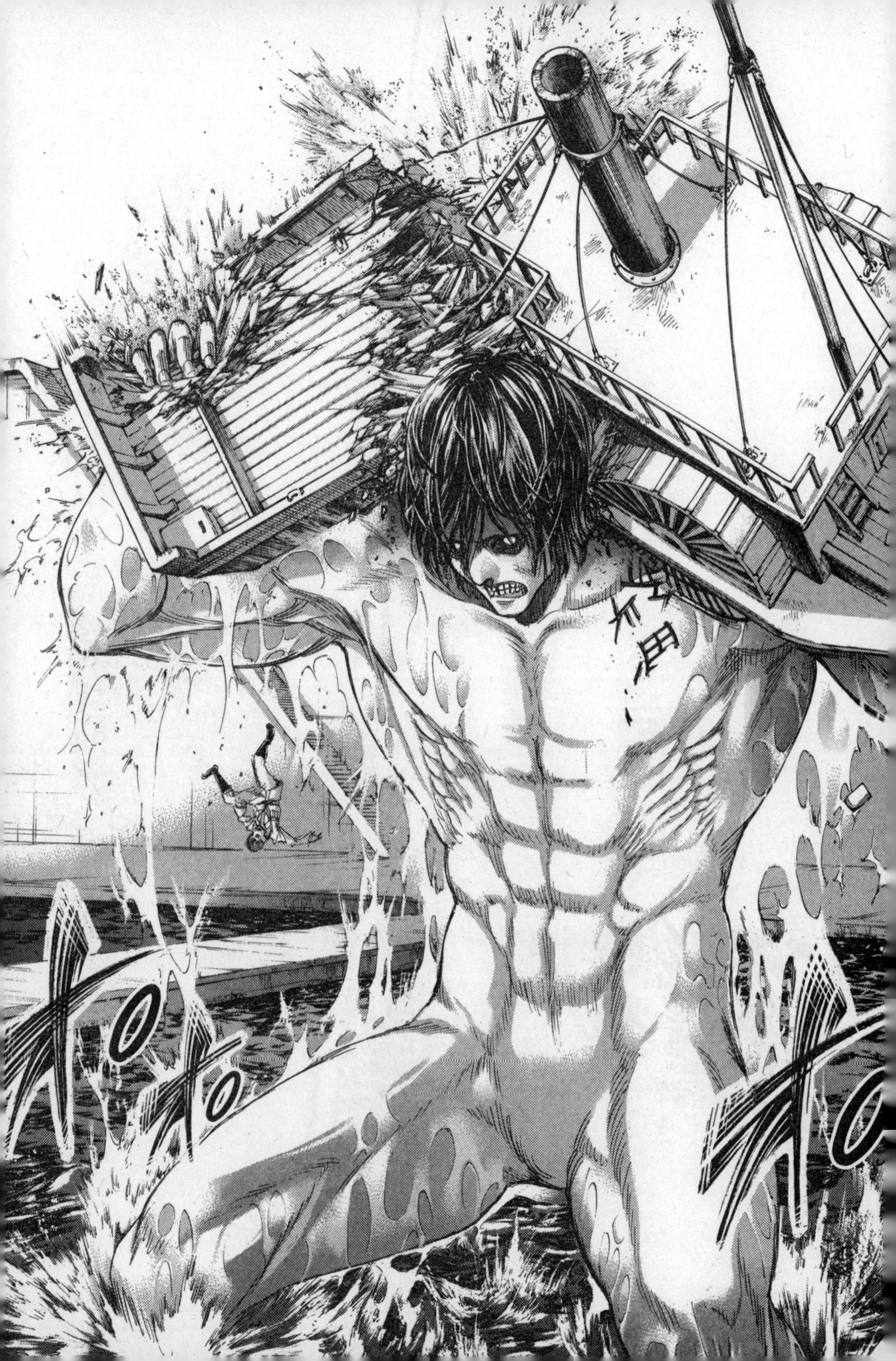

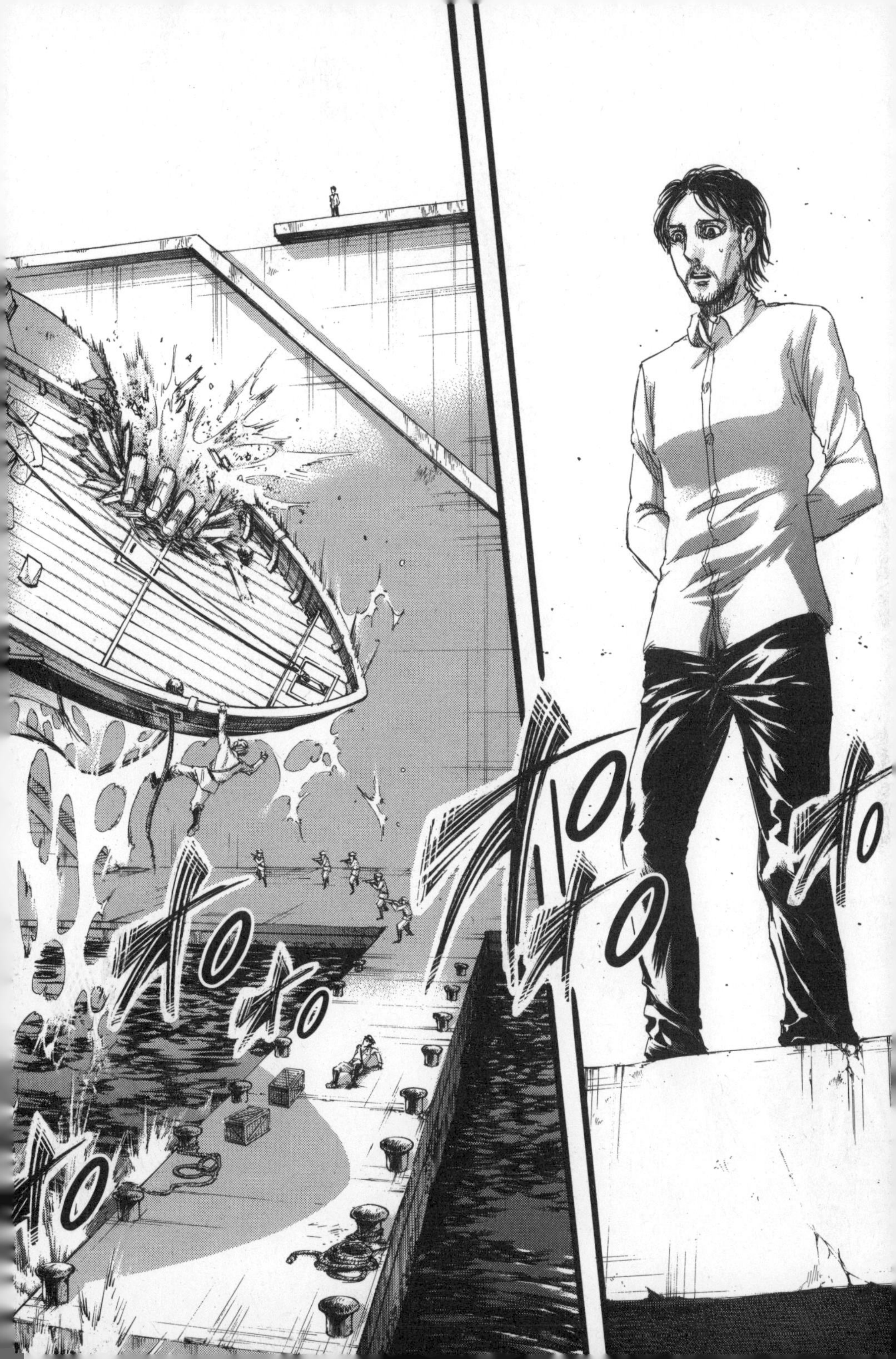

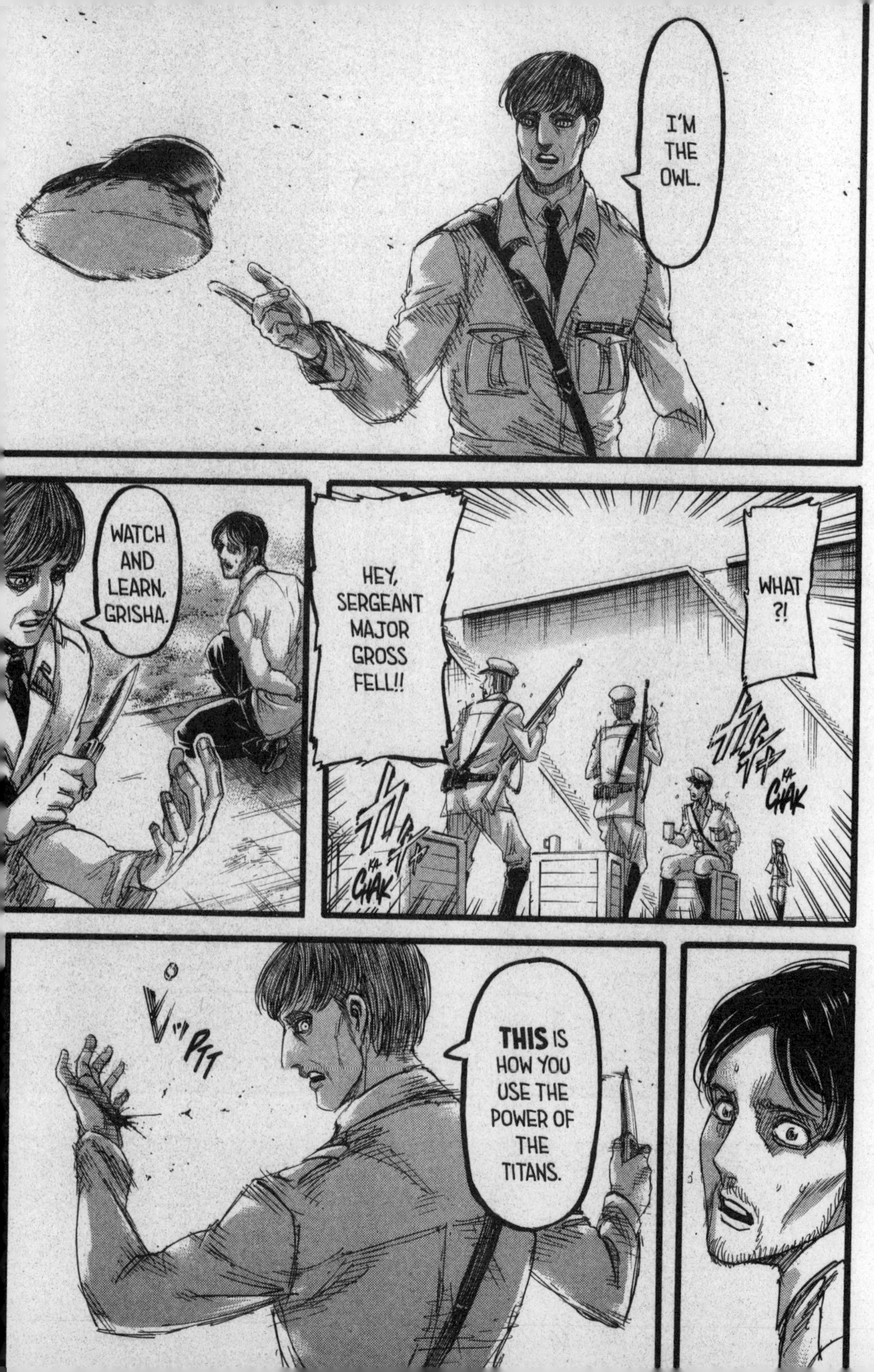
I'M THE OWL.
WHAT?!
KA CHAK
HEY, SERGEANT MAJOR GROSS FELL!!
KA CHAK
WATCH AND LEARN, GRISHA.
THIS IS HOW YOU USE THE POWER OF THE TITANS.

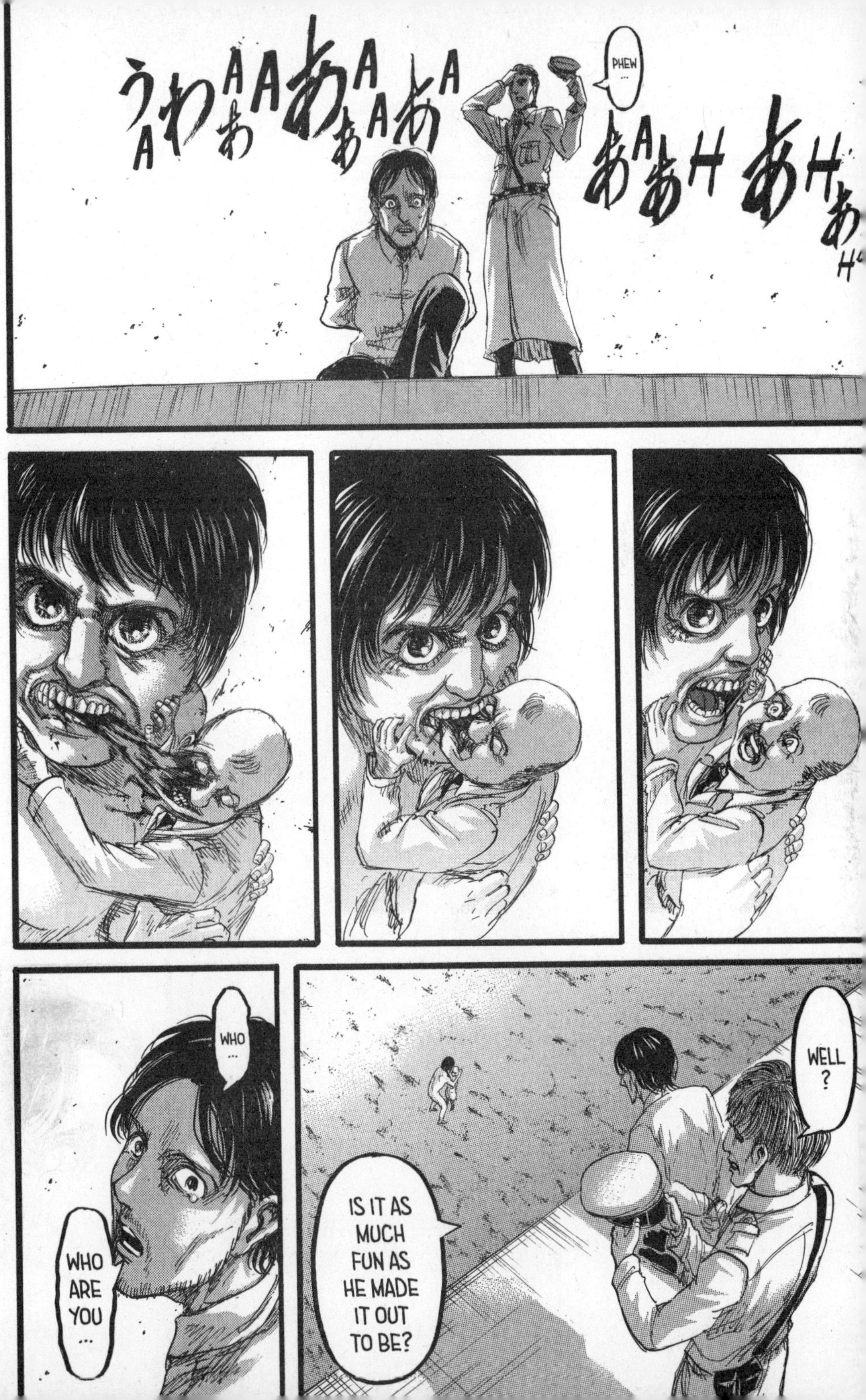

PHEW ...
うAわAAあAAあAAあA
あAあHあHあH
WELL ?
IS IT AS MUCH FUN AS HE MADE IT OUT TO BE?
WHO ...
WHO ARE YOU ...

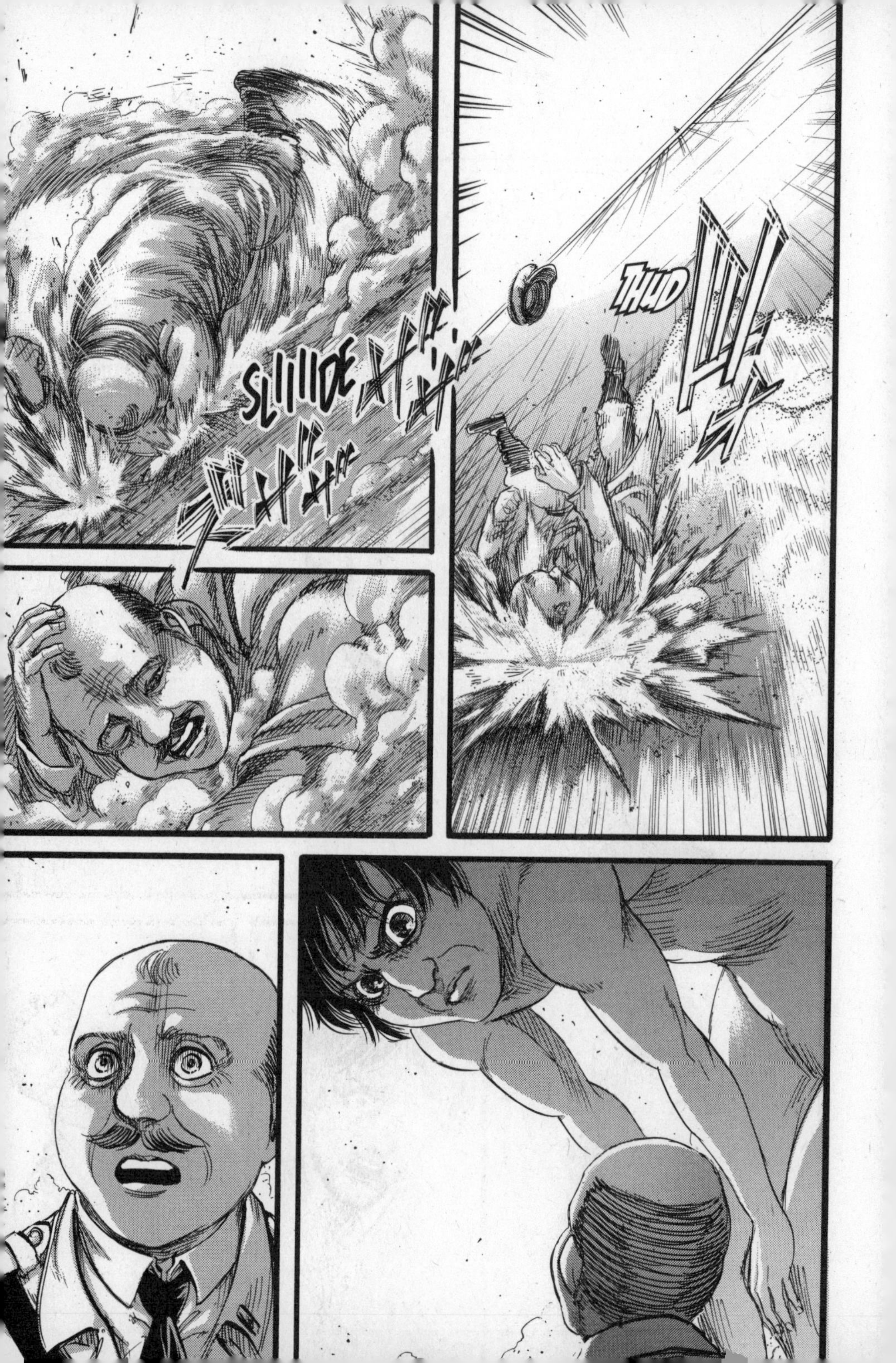
THUD
SLIIIIDE

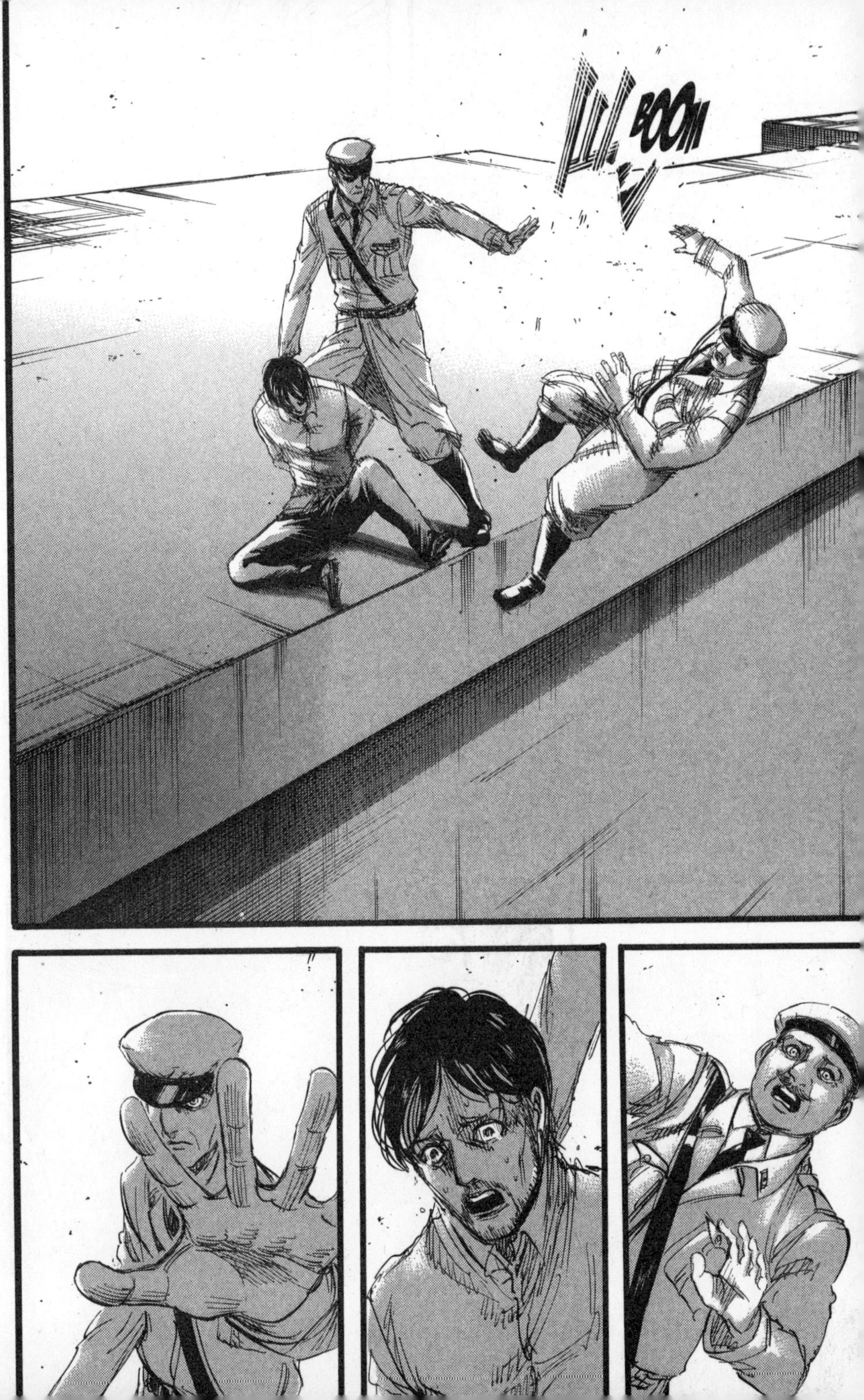
BOOM

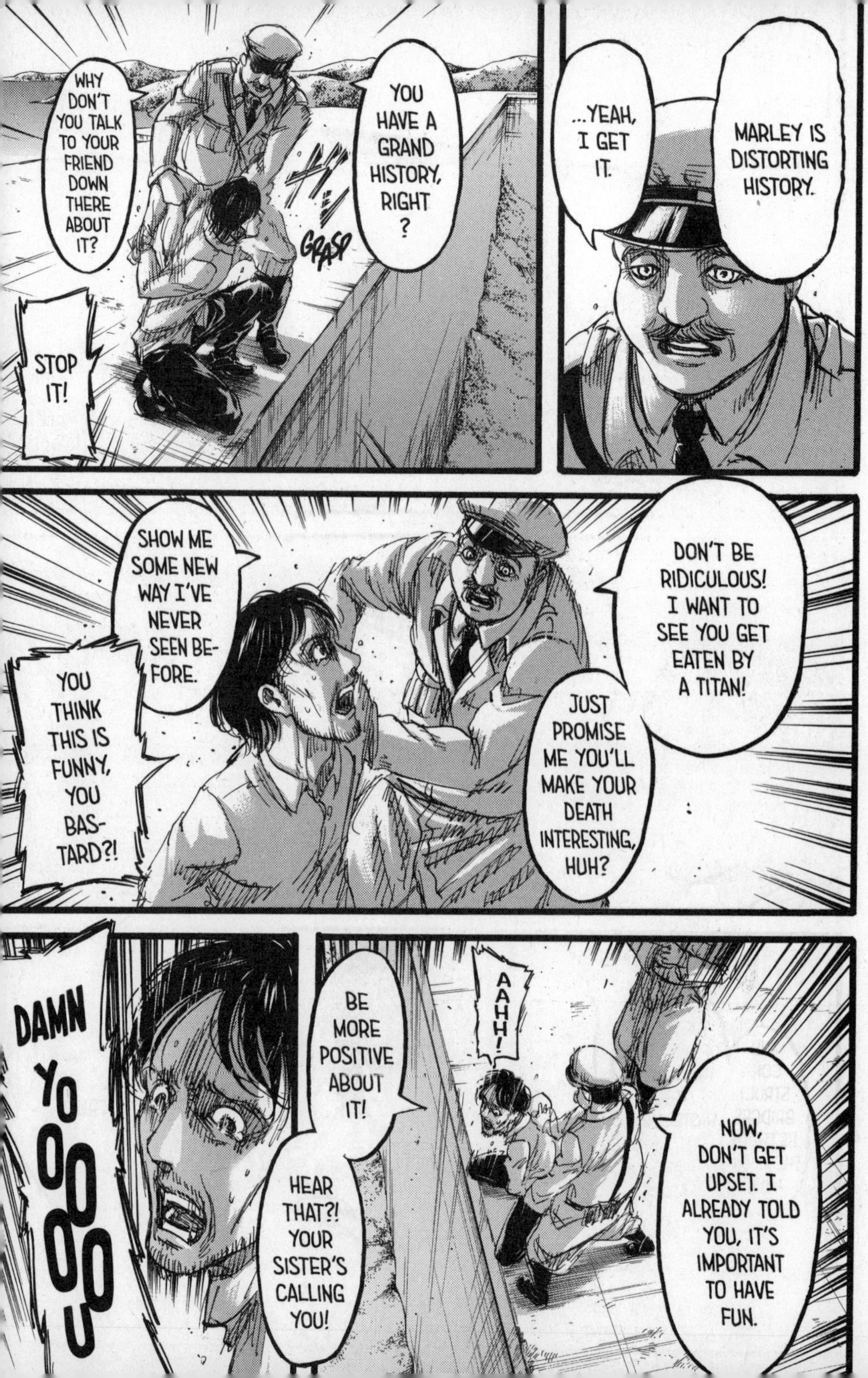
MARLEY IS DISTORTING HISTORY.
...YEAH, I GET IT.
YOU HAVE A GRAND HISTORY, RIGHT?
GRASP
WHY DON'T YOU TALK TO YOUR FRIEND DOWN THERE ABOUT IT?
STOP IT!
DON'T BE RIDICULOUS! I WANT TO SEE YOU GET EATEN BY A TITAN!
JUST PROMISE ME YOU'LL MAKE YOUR DEATH INTERESTING, HUH?
SHOW ME SOME NEW WAY I'VE NEVER SEEN BE-FORE.
YOU THINK THIS IS FUNNY, YOU BAS-TARD?!
NOW, DON'T GET UPSET. I ALREADY TOLD YOU, IT'S IMPORTANT TO HAVE FUN.
AAHH!
BE MORE POSITIVE ABOUT IT!
HEAR THAT?! YOUR SISTER'S CALLING YOU!
DAMN YOOOOOOU

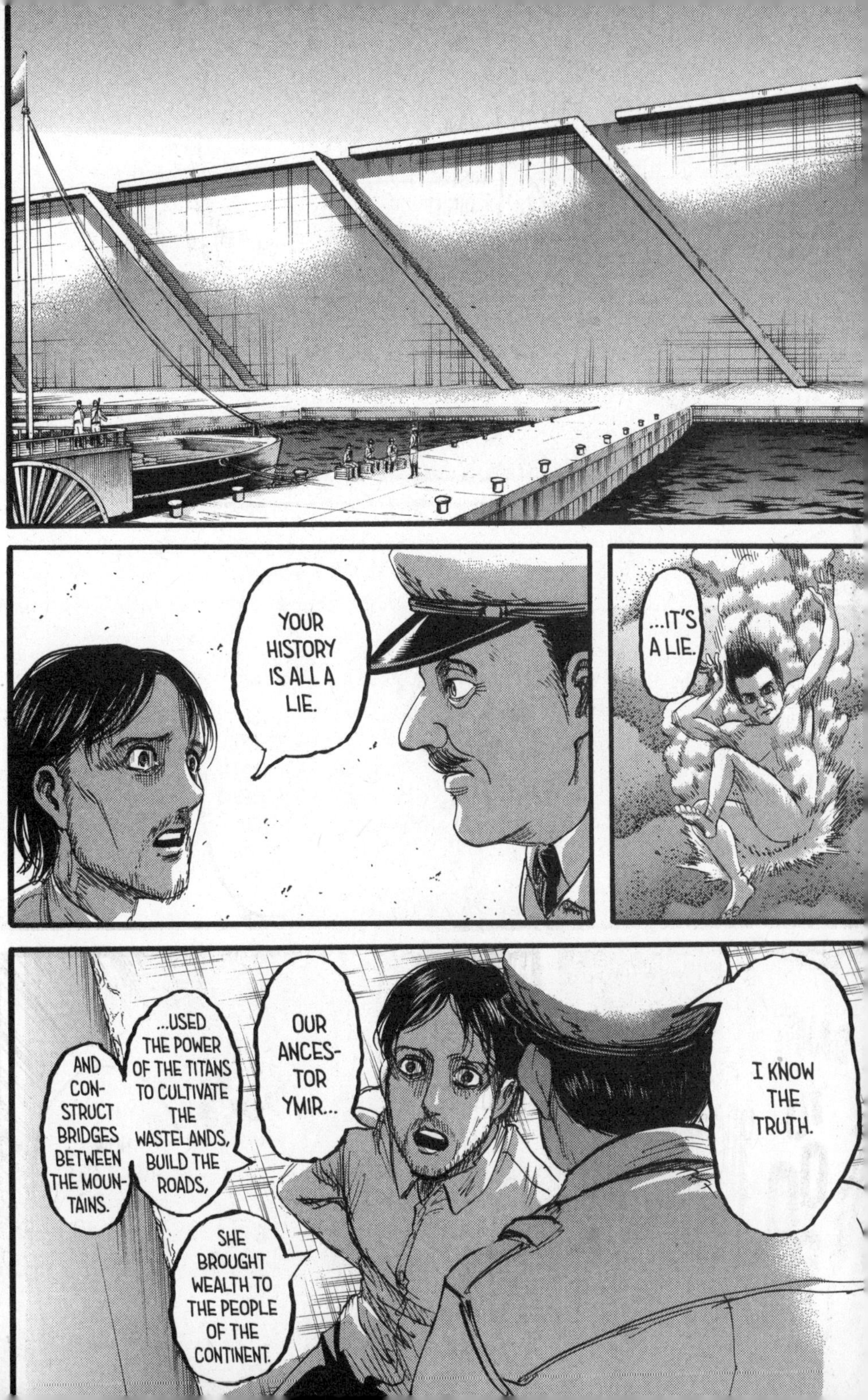
...IT'S A LIE.
YOUR HISTORY IS ALL A LIE.
I KNOW THE TRUTH.
OUR ANCESTOR YMIR...
...USED THE POWER OF THE TITANS TO CULTIVATE THE WASTELANDS, BUILD THE ROADS,
AND CONSTRUCT BRIDGES BETWEEN THE MOUNTAINS.
SHE BROUGHT WEALTH TO THE PEOPLE OF THE CONTINENT.

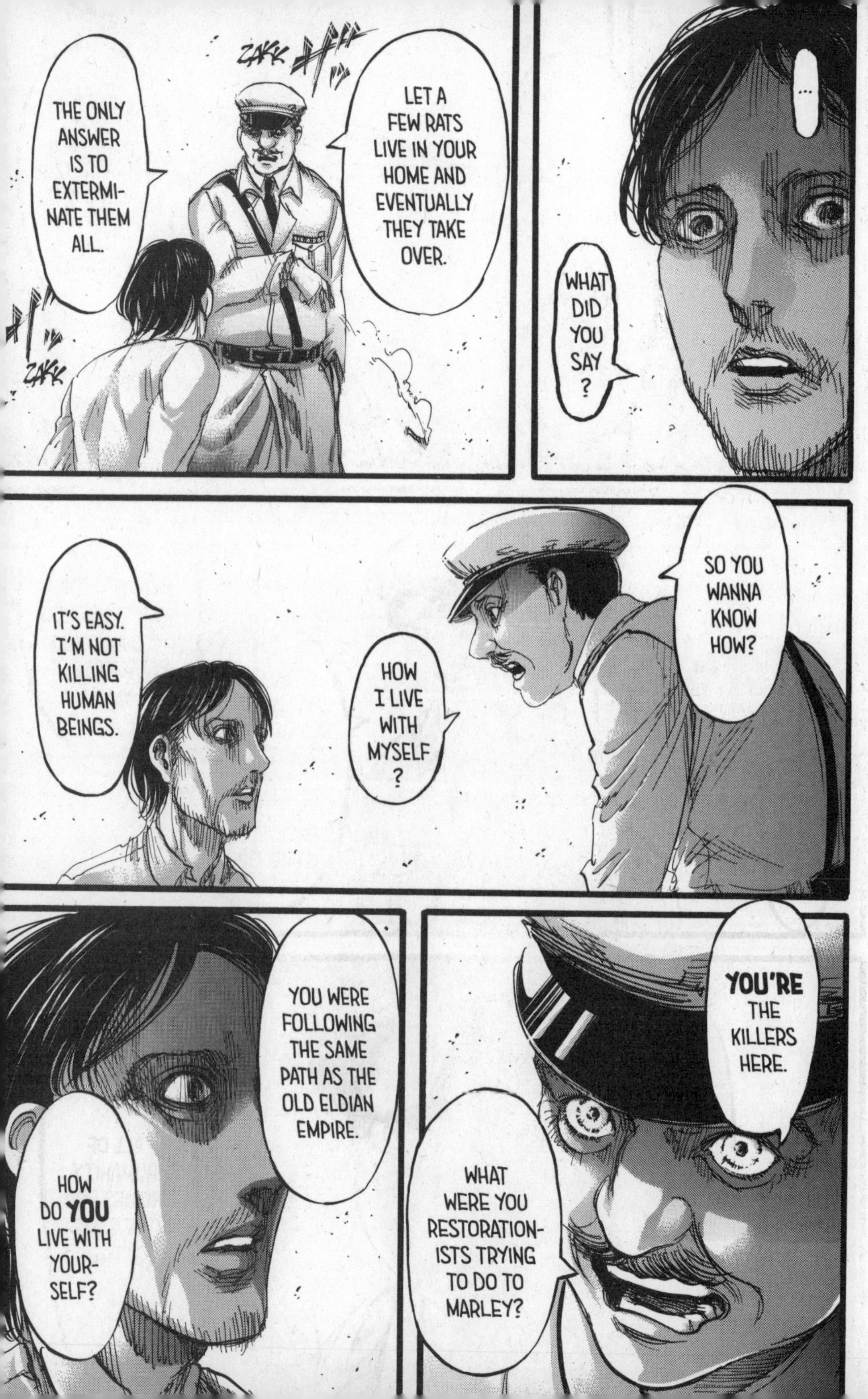
...
WHAT DID YOU SAY?
ZAKK
LET A FEW RATS LIVE IN YOUR HOME AND EVENTUALLY THEY TAKE OVER.
THE ONLY ANSWER IS TO EXTERMINATE THEM ALL.
ZAKK
SO YOU WANNA KNOW HOW?
HOW I LIVE WITH MYSELF?
IT'S EASY. I'M NOT KILLING HUMAN BEINGS.
YOU'RE THE KILLERS HERE.
WHAT WERE YOU RESTORATIONISTS TRYING TO DO TO MARLEY?
YOU WERE FOLLOWING THE SAME PATH AS THE OLD ELDIAN EMPIRE.
HOW DO **YOU** LIVE WITH YOURSELF?

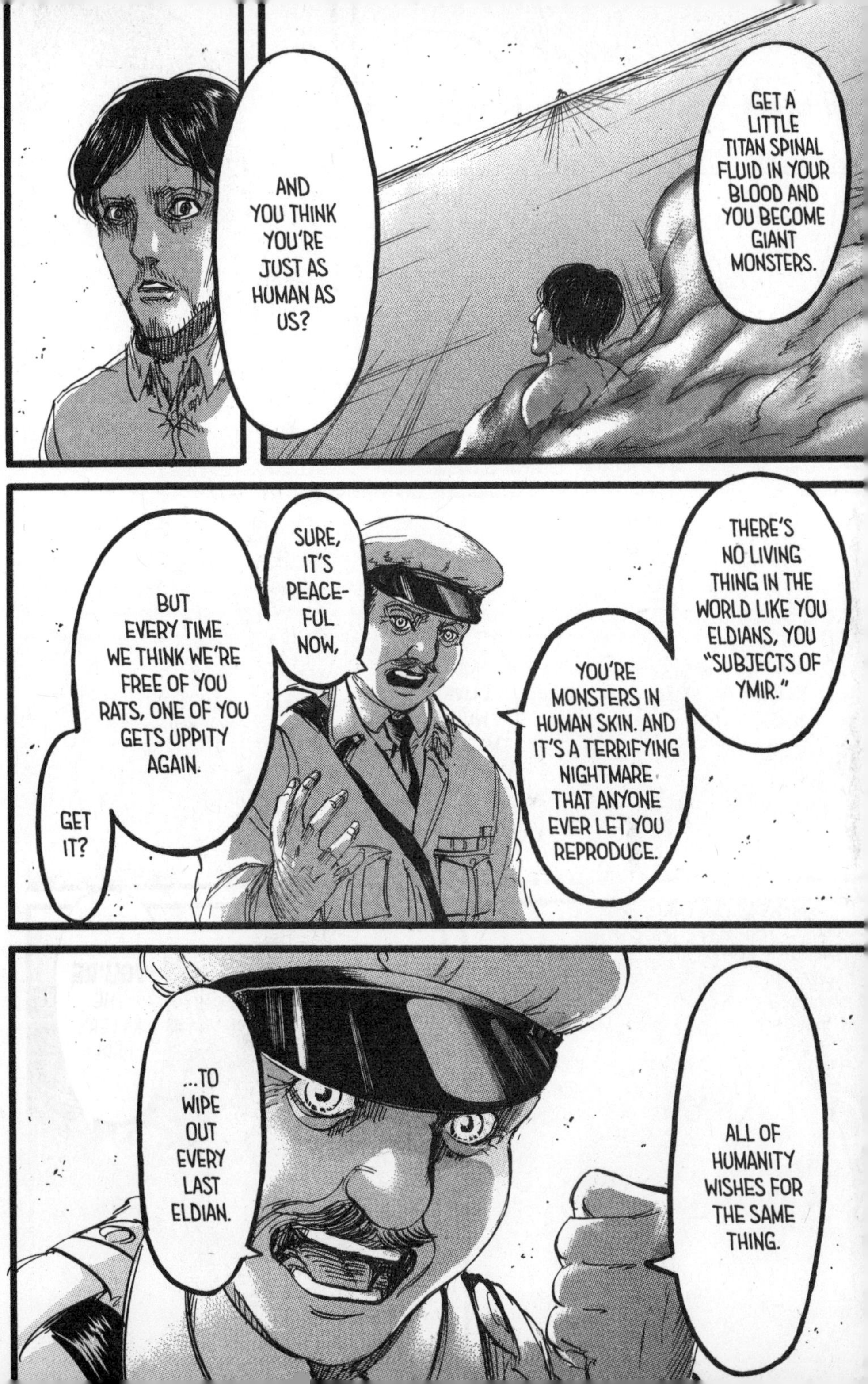
GET A LITTLE TITAN SPINAL FLUID IN YOUR BLOOD AND YOU BECOME GIANT MONSTERS.
AND YOU THINK YOU'RE JUST AS HUMAN AS US?
THERE'S NO LIVING THING IN THE WORLD LIKE YOU ELDIANS, YOU "SUBJECTS OF YMIR."
YOU'RE MONSTERS IN HUMAN SKIN. AND IT'S A TERRIFYING NIGHTMARE THAT ANYONE EVER LET YOU REPRODUCE.
SURE, IT'S PEACE-FUL NOW,
BUT EVERY TIME WE THINK WE'RE FREE OF YOU RATS, ONE OF YOU GETS UPPITY AGAIN.
GET IT?
ALL OF HUMANITY WISHES FOR THE SAME THING.
...TO WIPE OUT EVERY LAST ELDIAN.

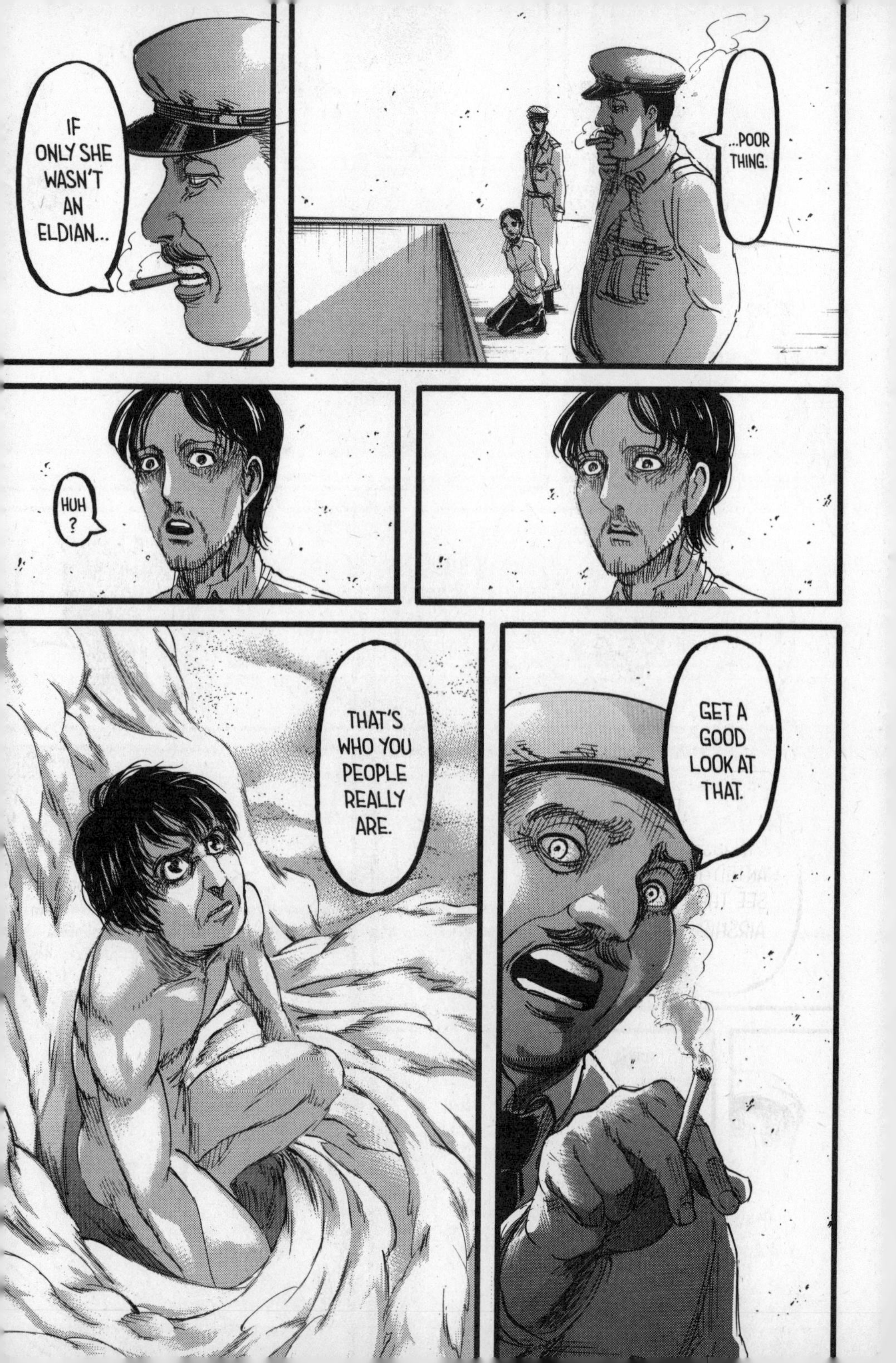
...POOR THING.
IF ONLY SHE WASN'T AN ELDIAN...
HUH?
GET A GOOD LOOK AT THAT.
THAT'S WHO YOU PEOPLE REALLY ARE.

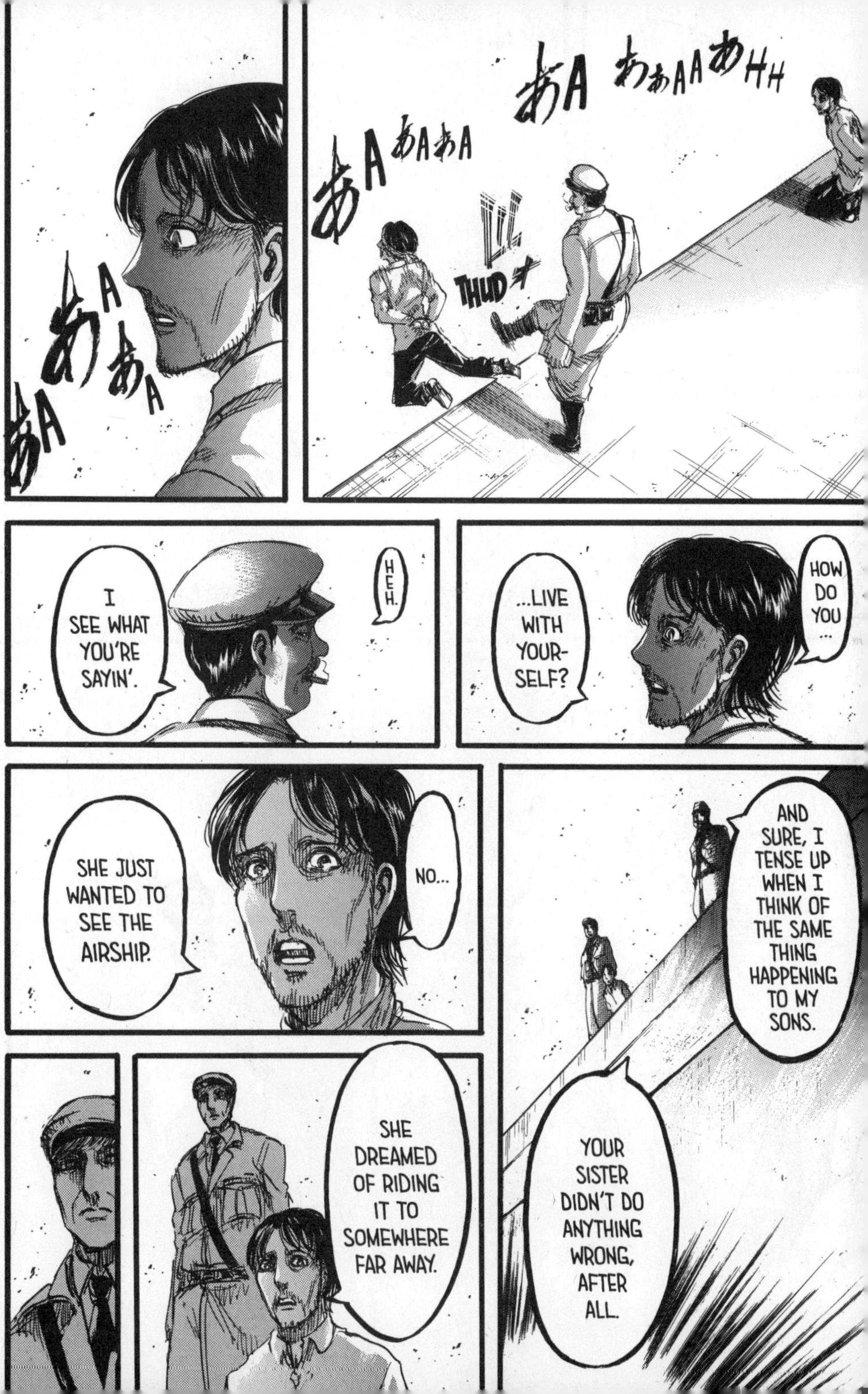
あA あAあA
あA あぁAAあHH
THUD
あAあAあA
HOW DO YOU ...
...LIVE WITH YOURSELF?
HEH.
I SEE WHAT YOU'RE SAYIN'.
AND SURE, I TENSE UP WHEN I THINK OF THE SAME THING HAPPENING TO MY SONS.
YOUR SISTER DIDN'T DO ANYTHING WRONG, AFTER ALL.
NO...
SHE JUST WANTED TO SEE THE AIRSHIP.
SHE DREAMED OF RIDING IT TO SOMEWHERE FAR AWAY.

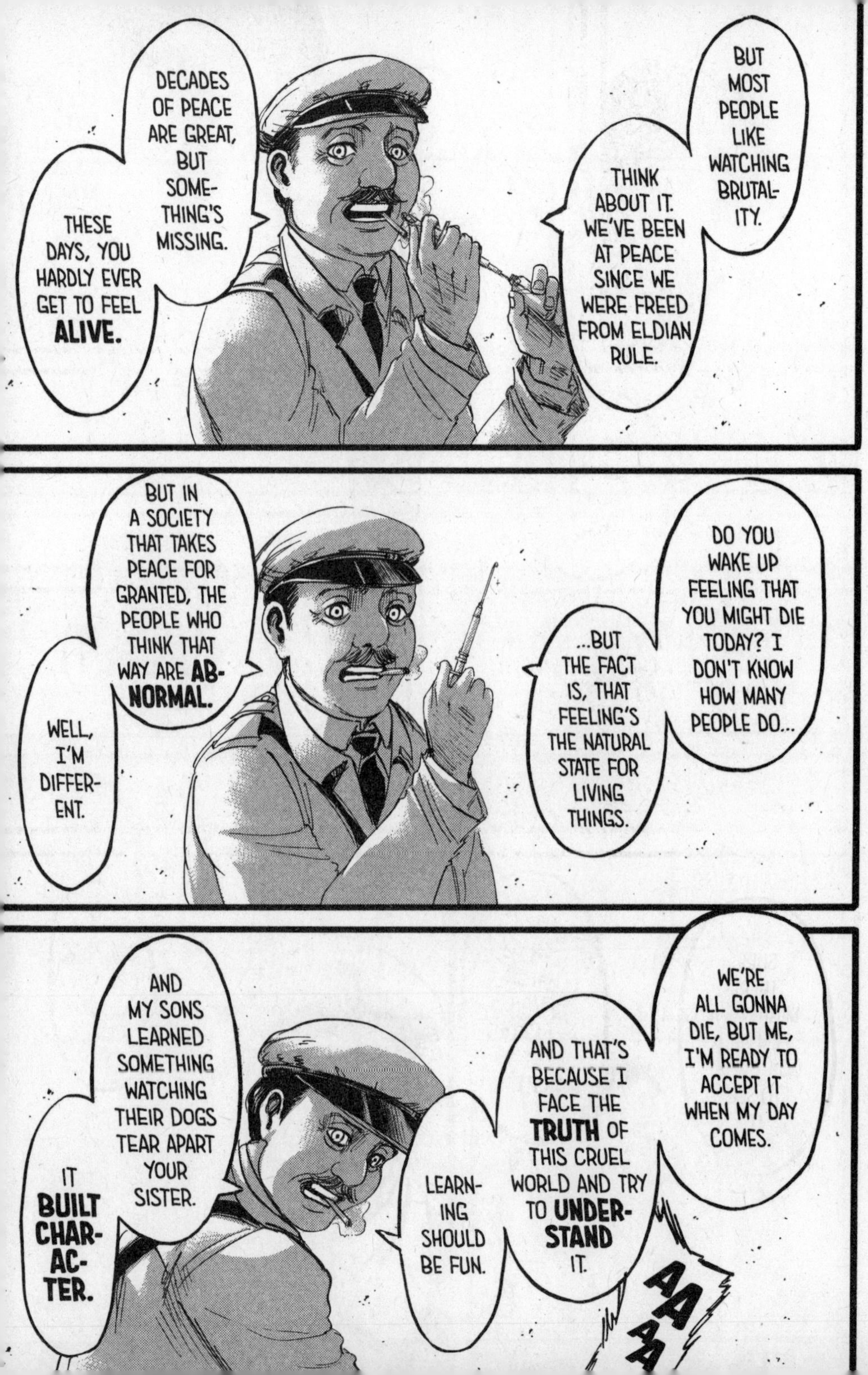

BUT MOST PEOPLE LIKE WATCHING BRUTALITY.
THINK ABOUT IT. WE'VE BEEN AT PEACE SINCE WE WERE FREED FROM ELDIAN RULE.
DECADES OF PEACE ARE GREAT, BUT SOMETHING'S MISSING.
THESE DAYS, YOU HARDLY EVER GET TO FEEL **ALIVE.**
DO YOU WAKE UP FEELING THAT YOU MIGHT DIE TODAY? I DON'T KNOW HOW MANY PEOPLE DO...
...BUT THE FACT IS, THAT FEELING'S THE NATURAL STATE FOR LIVING THINGS.
BUT IN A SOCIETY THAT TAKES PEACE FOR GRANTED, THE PEOPLE WHO THINK THAT WAY ARE **ABNORMAL.**
WELL, I'M DIFFERENT.
WE'RE ALL GONNA DIE, BUT ME, I'M READY TO ACCEPT IT WHEN MY DAY COMES.
AND THAT'S BECAUSE I FACE THE **TRUTH** OF THIS CRUEL WORLD AND TRY TO **UNDERSTAND** IT.
LEARNING SHOULD BE FUN.
AND MY SONS LEARNED SOMETHING WATCHING THEIR DOGS TEAR APART YOUR SISTER.
IT **BUILT CHARACTER.**
AAAA

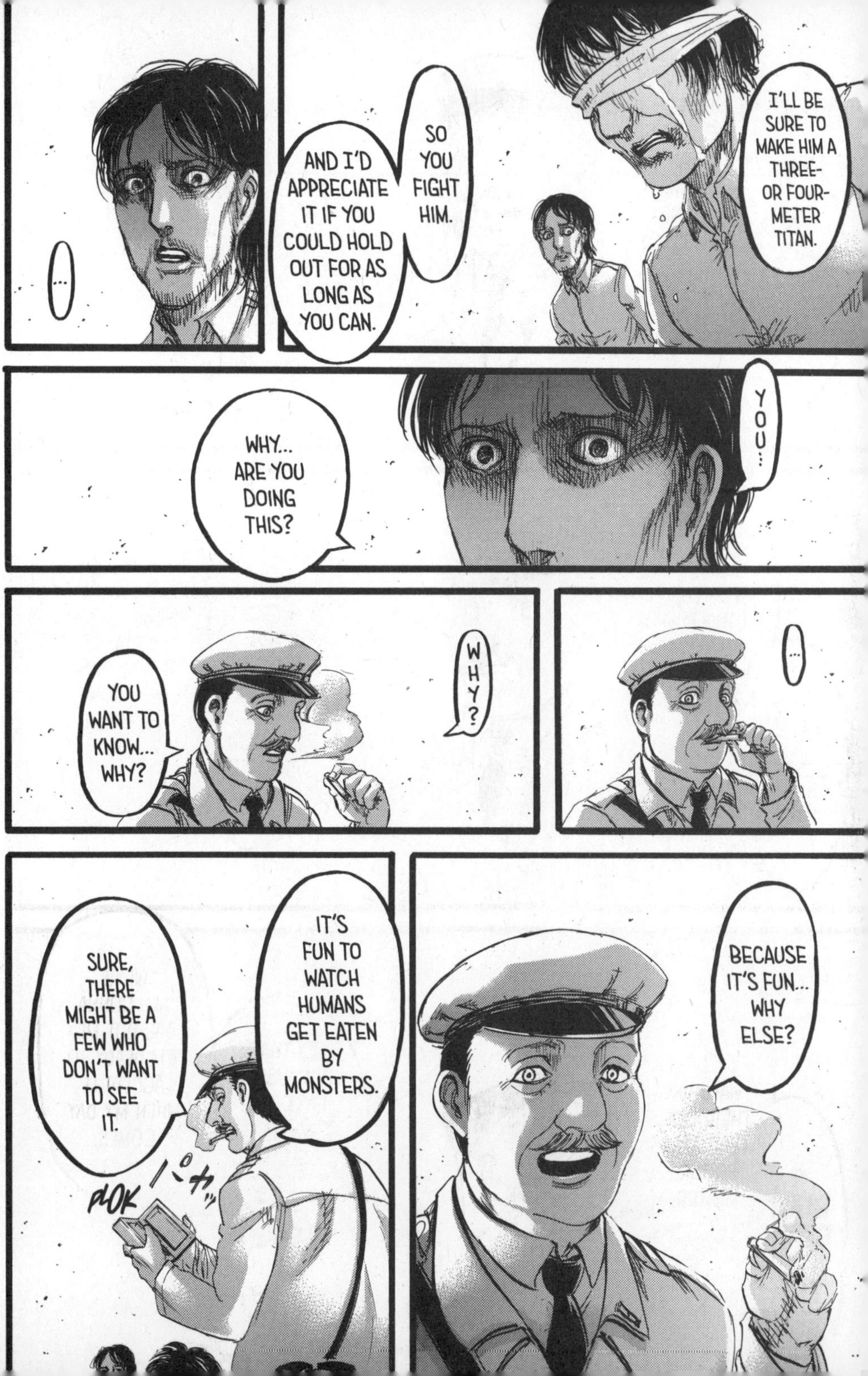
I'LL BE SURE TO MAKE HIM A THREE- OR FOUR-METER TITAN.
SO YOU FIGHT HIM.
AND I'D APPRECIATE IT IF YOU COULD HOLD OUT FOR AS LONG AS YOU CAN.
...
YOU...
WHY... ARE YOU DOING THIS?
...
WHY?
YOU WANT TO KNOW... WHY?
BECAUSE IT'S FUN... WHY ELSE?
IT'S FUN TO WATCH HUMANS GET EATEN BY MONSTERS.
SURE, THERE MIGHT BE A FEW WHO DON'T WANT TO SEE IT.
パカッ
PLOK

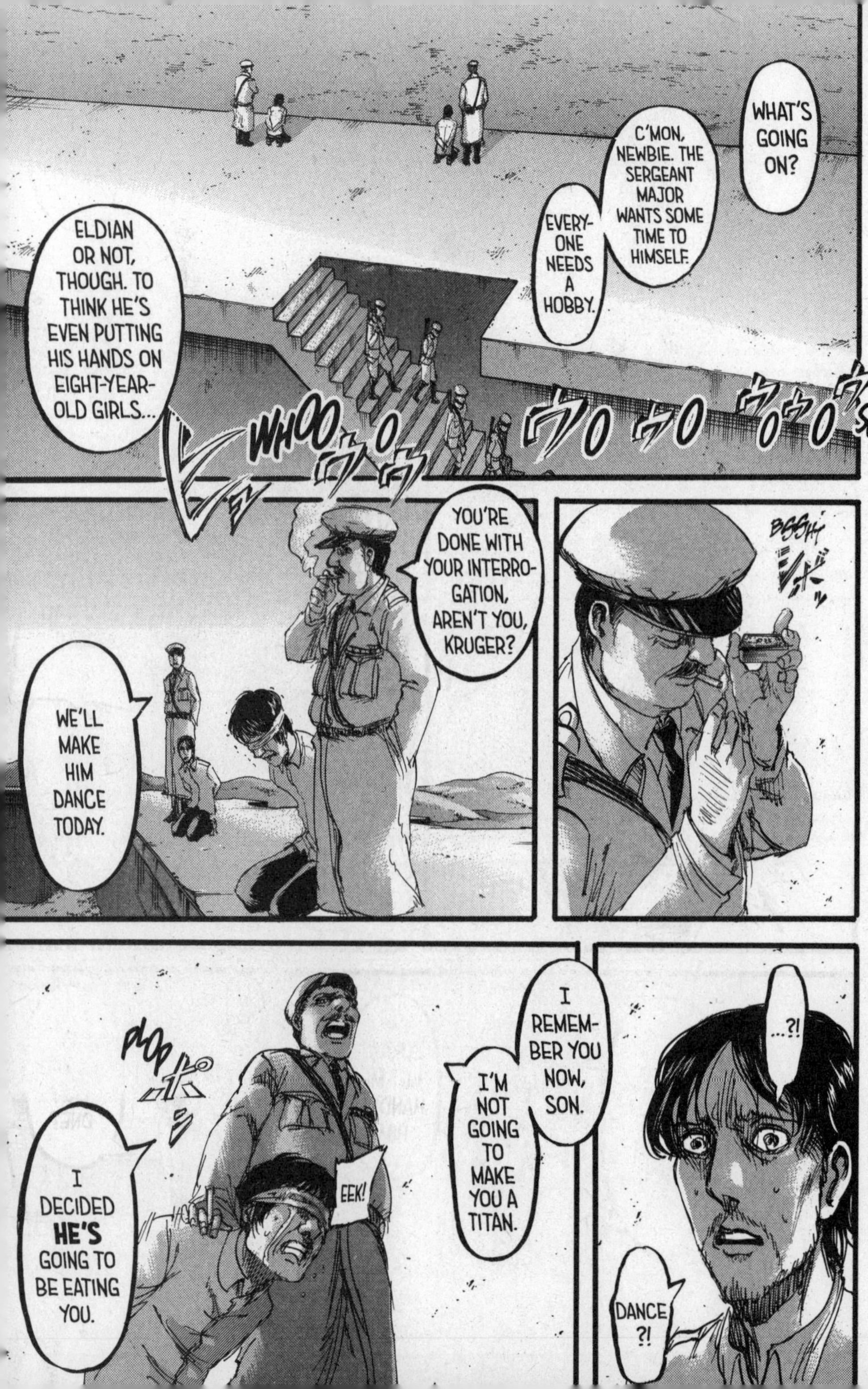
WHAT'S GOING ON?
C'MON, NEWBIE. THE SERGEANT MAJOR WANTS SOME TIME TO HIMSELF.
EVERY-ONE NEEDS A HOBBY.
ELDIAN OR NOT, THOUGH. TO THINK HE'S EVEN PUTTING HIS HANDS ON EIGHT-YEAR-OLD GIRLS...
WHOOOSH
BSSH
YOU'RE DONE WITH YOUR INTERRO-GATION, AREN'T YOU, KRUGER?
WE'LL MAKE HIM DANCE TODAY.
...?!
DANCE?!
I REMEM-BER YOU NOW, SON.
I'M NOT GOING TO MAKE YOU A TITAN.
EEK!
PLOP
I DECIDED **HE'S** GOING TO BE EATING YOU.

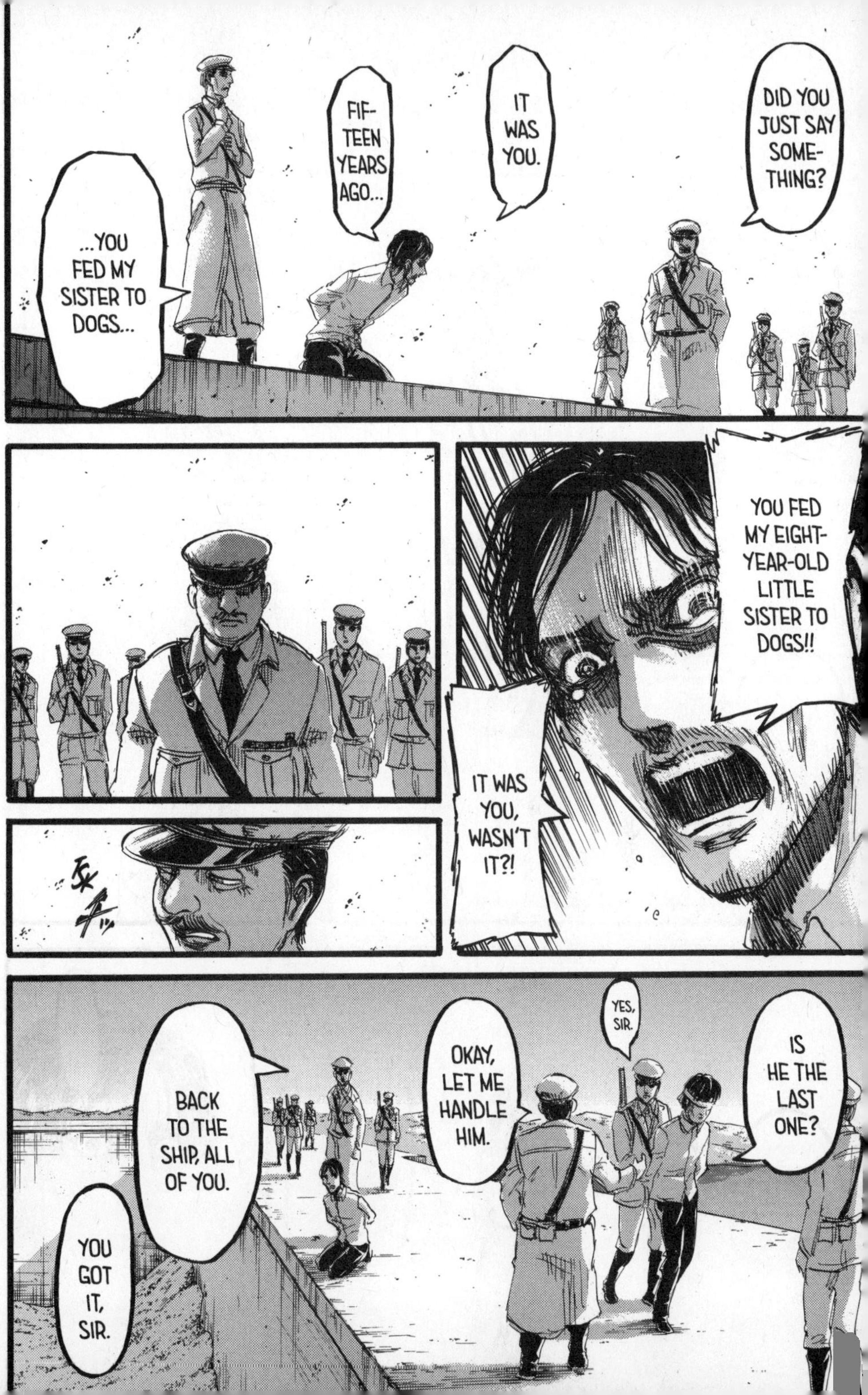
DID YOU JUST SAY SOME-THING?
IT WAS YOU.
FIF-TEEN YEARS AGO...
...YOU FED MY SISTER TO DOGS...
YOU FED MY EIGHT-YEAR-OLD LITTLE SISTER TO DOGS!!
IT WAS YOU, WASN'T IT?!
IS HE THE LAST ONE?
YES, SIR.
OKAY, LET ME HANDLE HIM.
BACK TO THE SHIP, ALL OF YOU.
YOU GOT IT, SIR.

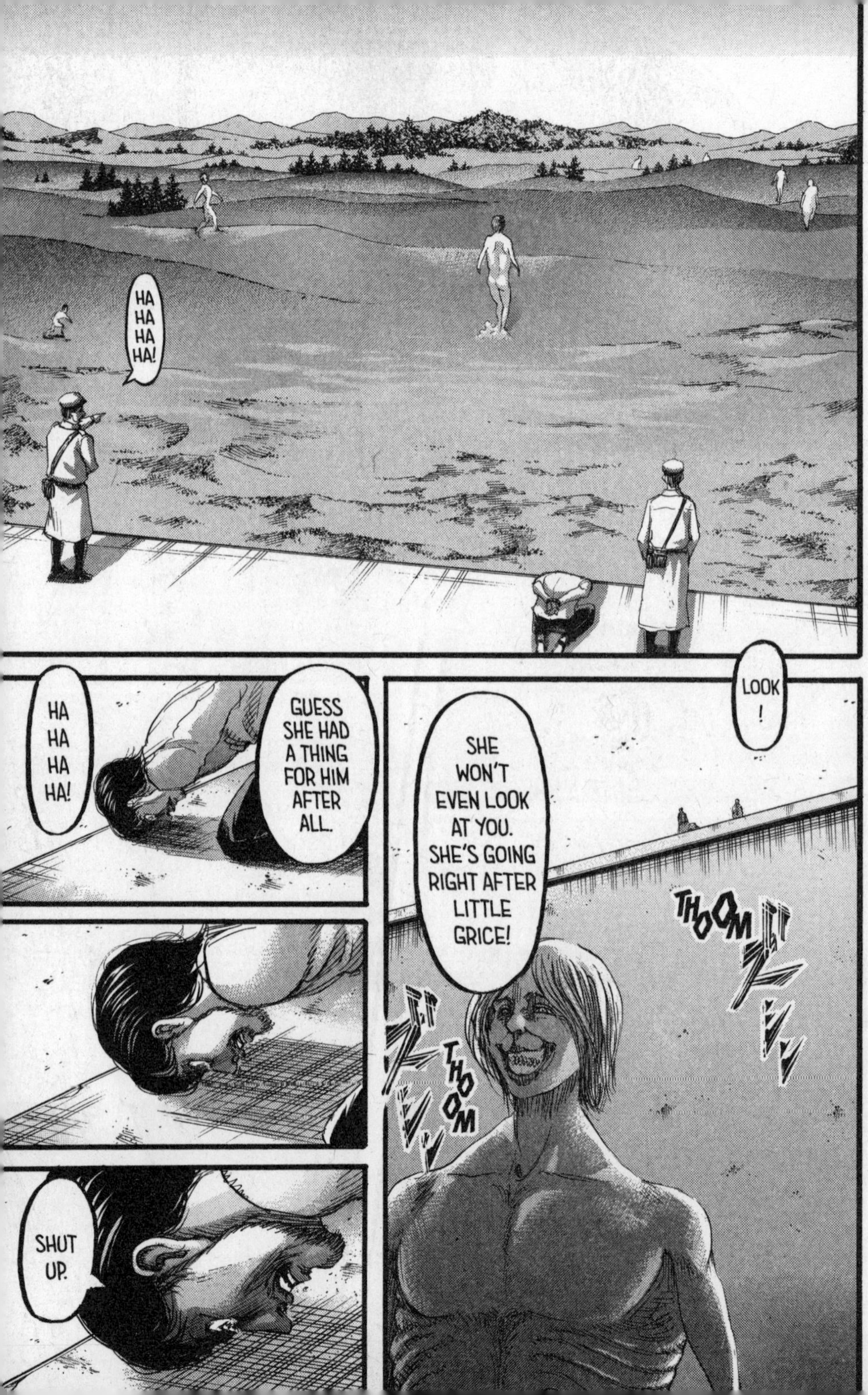
HA HA HA HA!
LOOK!
SHE WON'T EVEN LOOK AT YOU. SHE'S GOING RIGHT AFTER LITTLE GRICE!
THOOM
THOOM
GUESS SHE HAD A THING FOR HIM AFTER ALL.
HA HA HA HA!
SHUT UP.

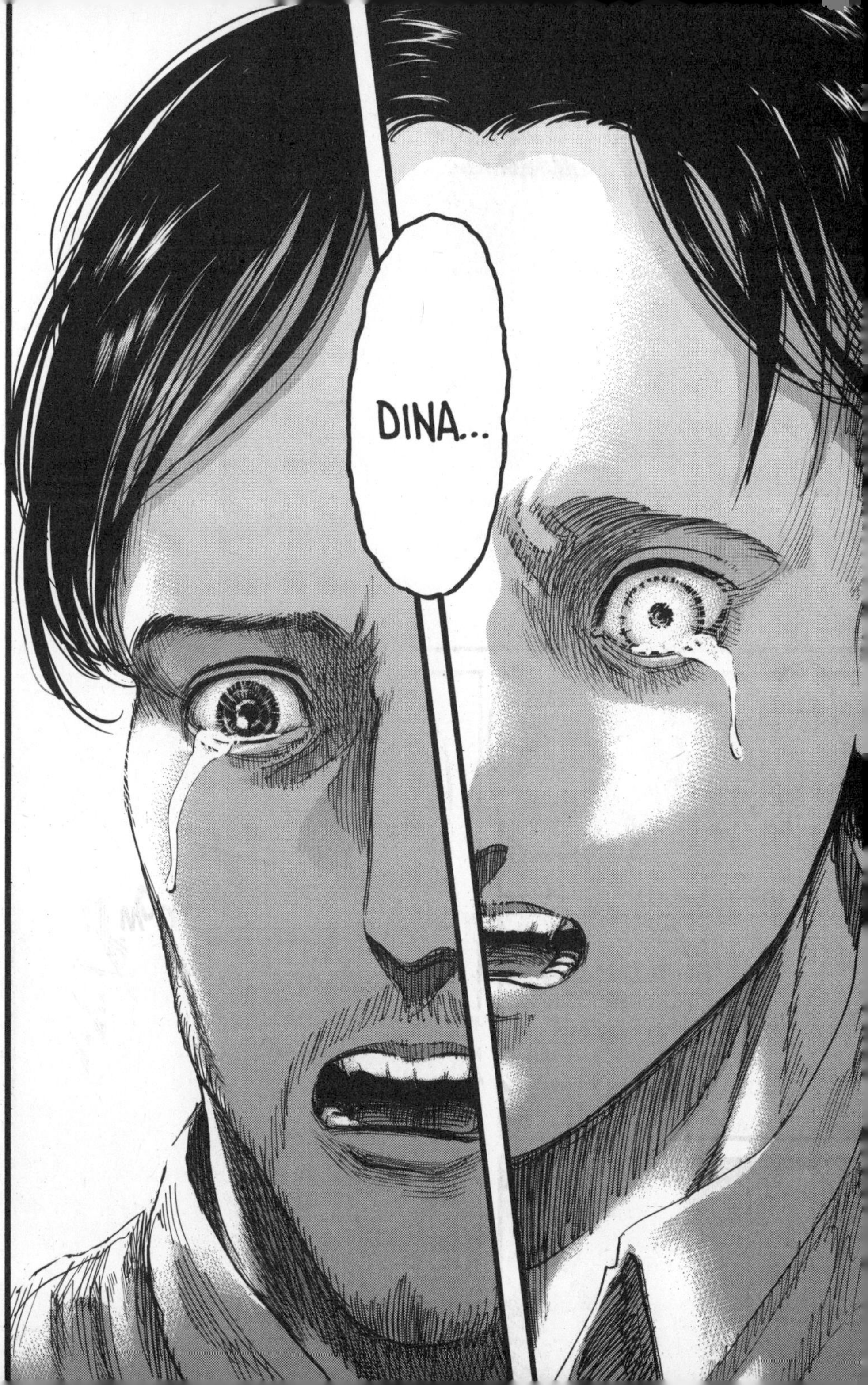
DINA...

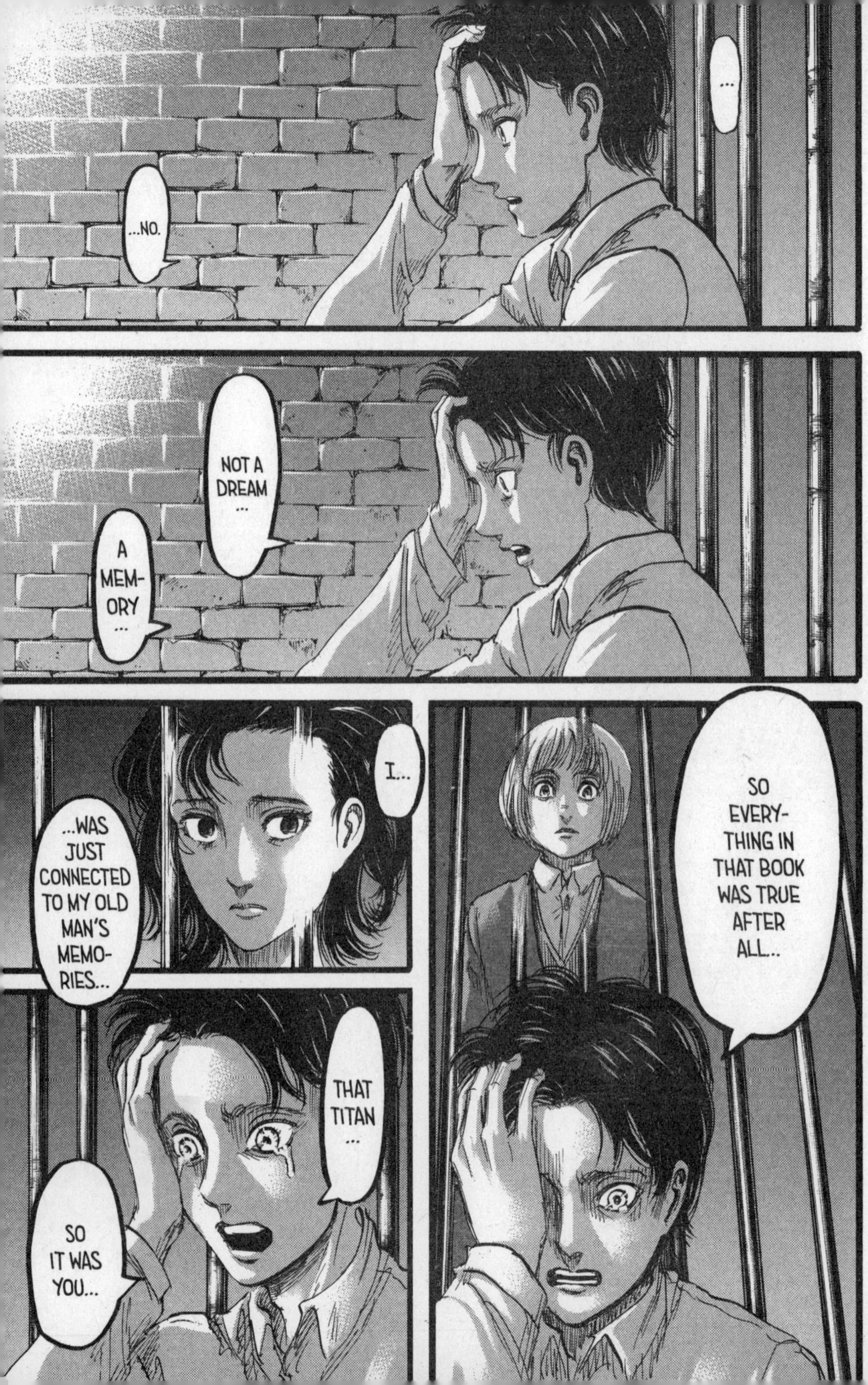
...
...NO.
NOT A DREAM...
A MEMORY...
SO EVERYTHING IN THAT BOOK WAS TRUE AFTER ALL...
I...
...WAS JUST CONNECTED TO MY OLD MAN'S MEMORIES...
THAT TITAN...
SO IT WAS YOU...

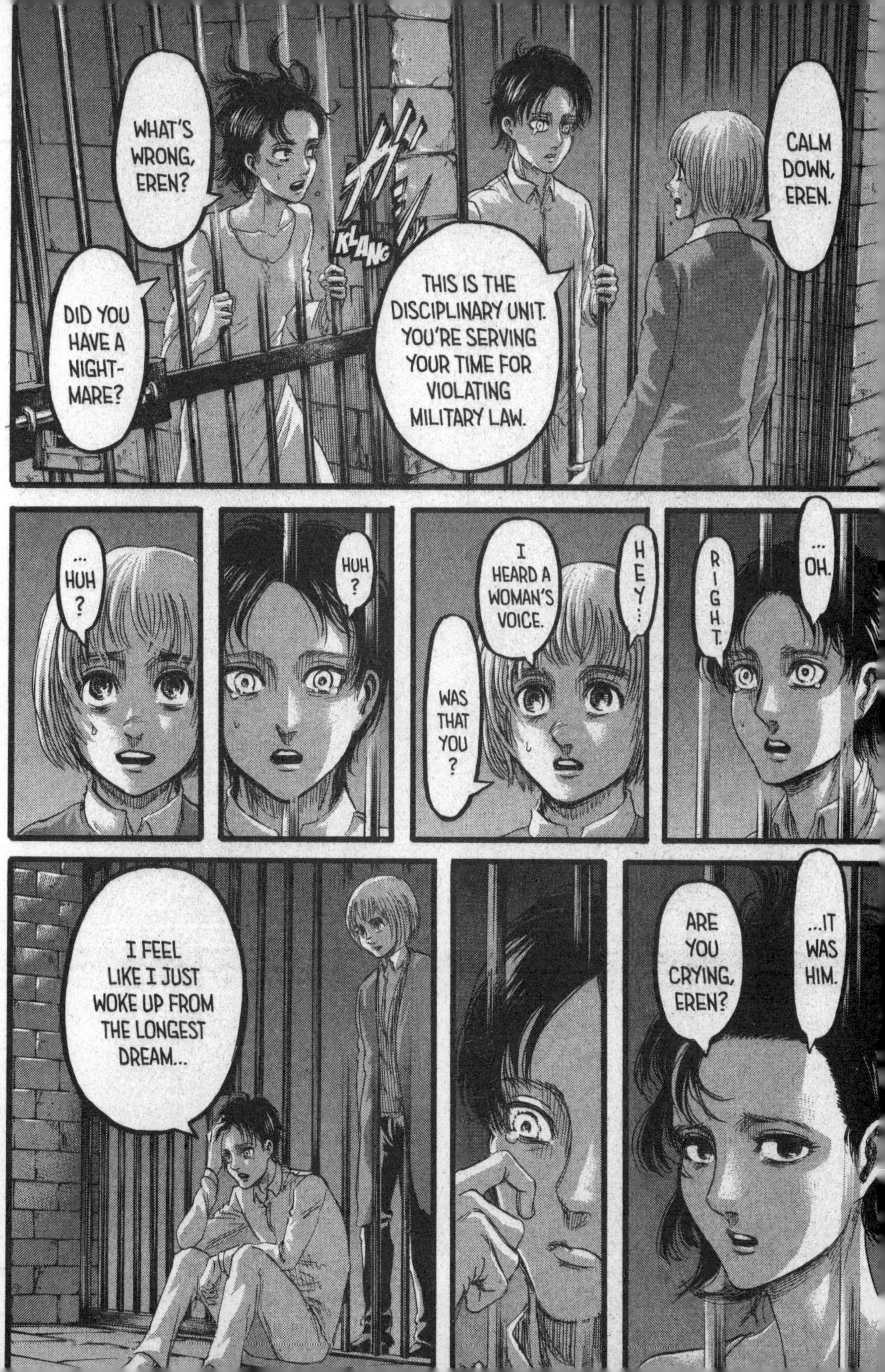
CALM DOWN, EREN.
THIS IS THE DISCIPLINARY UNIT. YOU'RE SERVING YOUR TIME FOR VIOLATING MILITARY LAW.
KLANG
WHAT'S WRONG, EREN?
DID YOU HAVE A NIGHT-MARE?
... OH.
RIGHT.
HEY...
I HEARD A WOMAN'S VOICE.
WAS THAT YOU?
HUH?
... HUH?
...IT WAS HIM.
ARE YOU CRYING, EREN?
I FEEL LIKE I JUST WOKE UP FROM THE LONGEST DREAM...

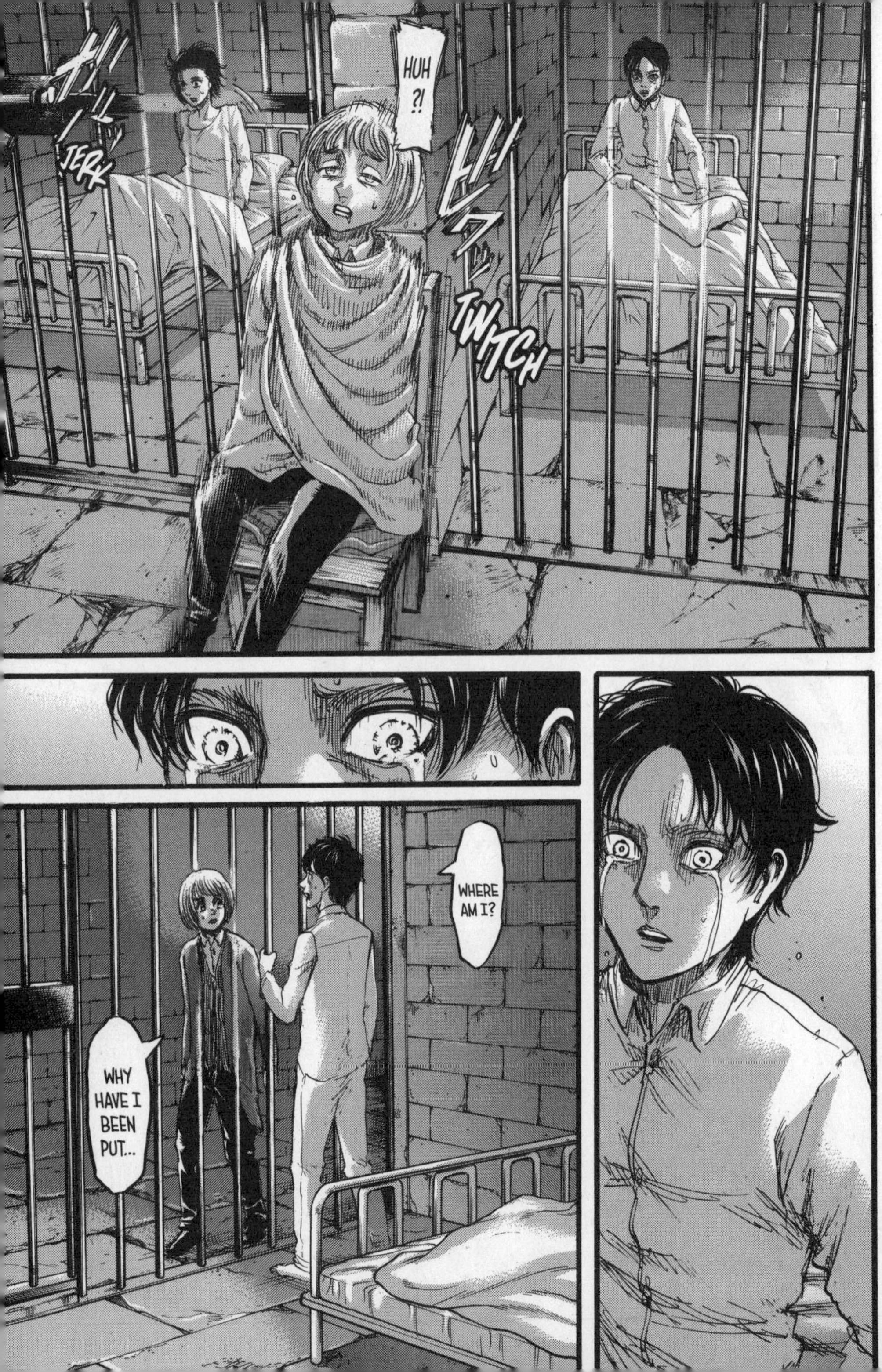
HUH ?!
TWITCH
JERK
WHERE AM I?
WHY HAVE I BEEN PUT...

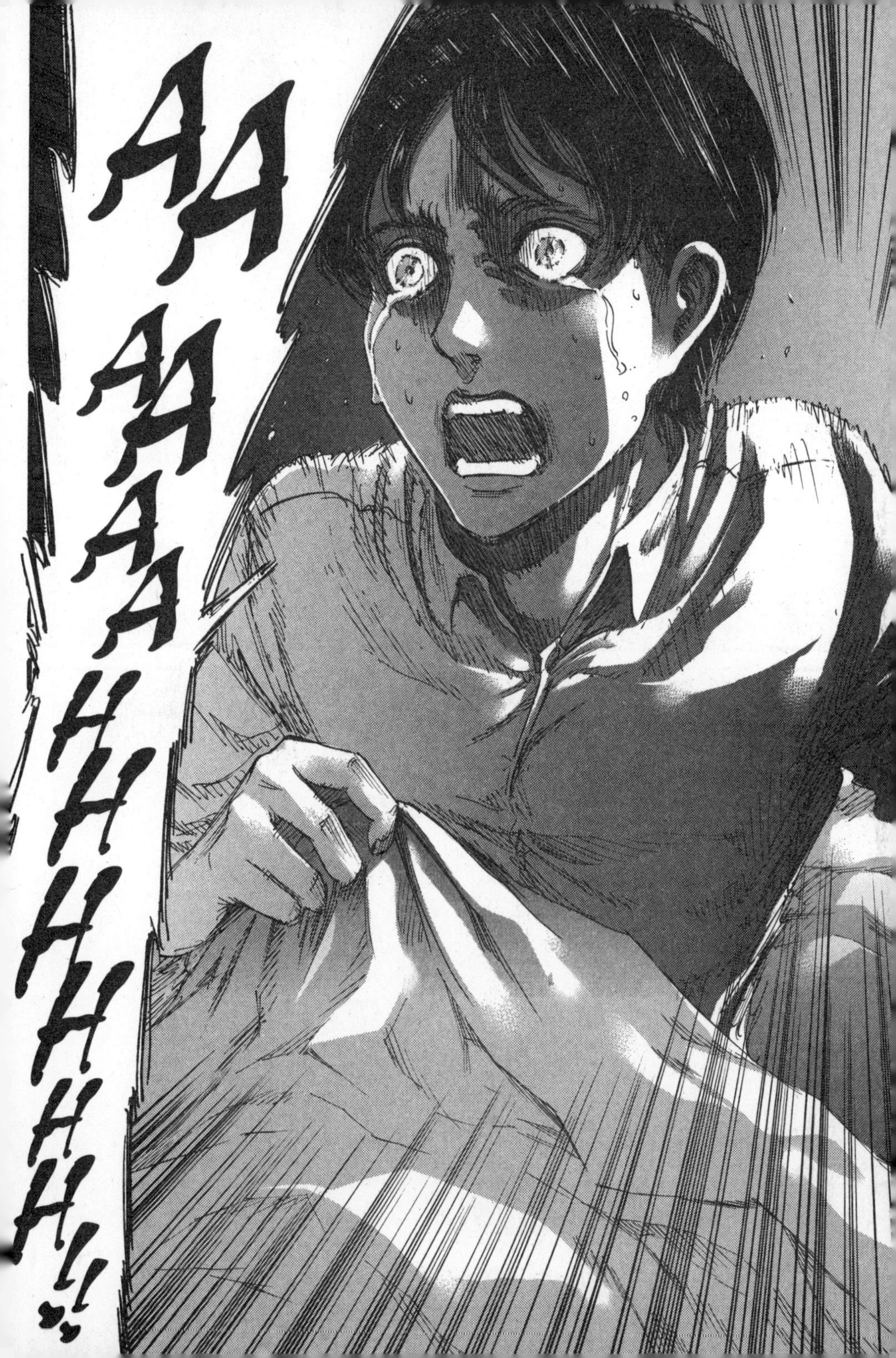
AAAAAAAHHHHHHH!!

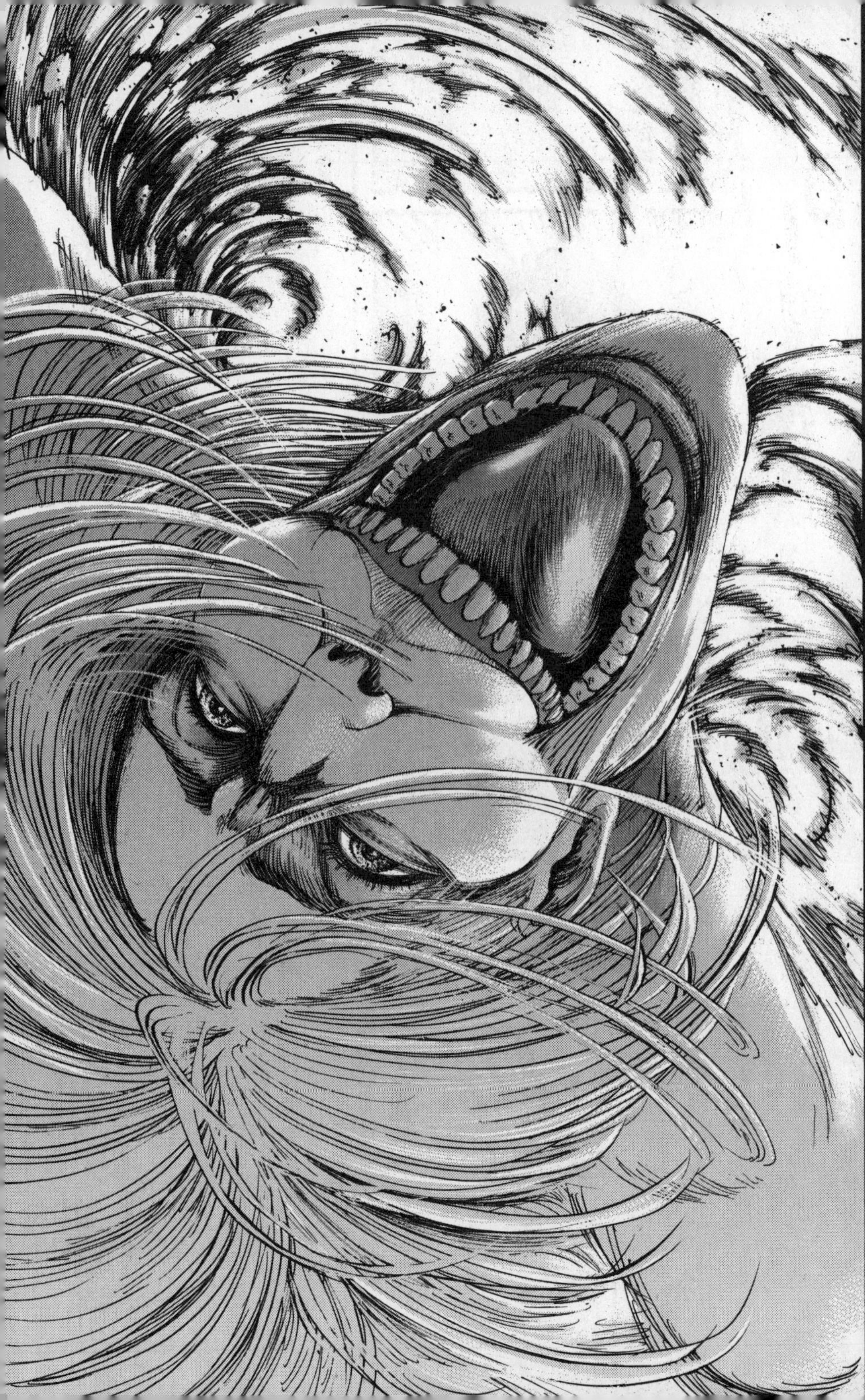

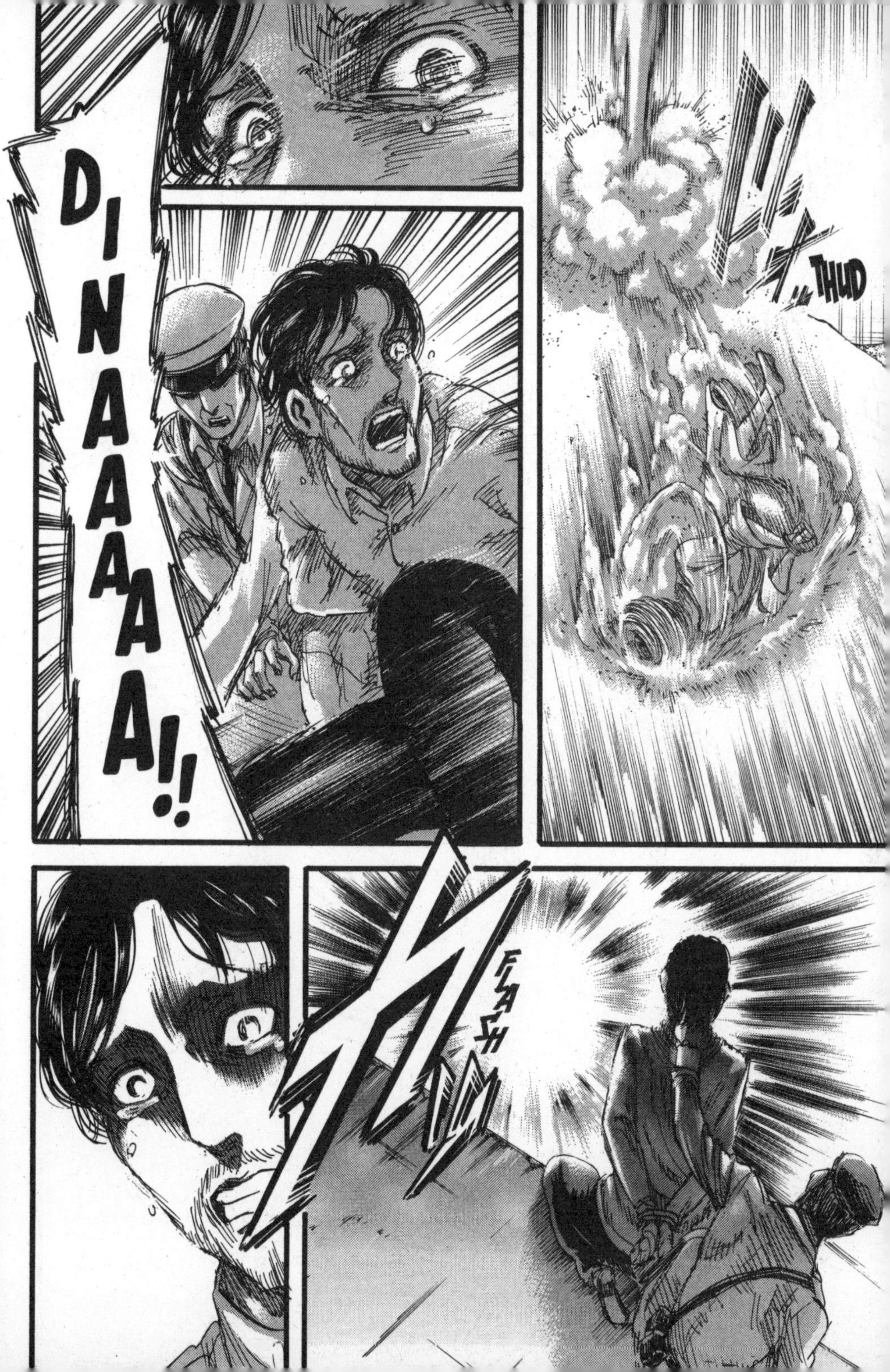
THUD
DINAAAAA!!
FLASH

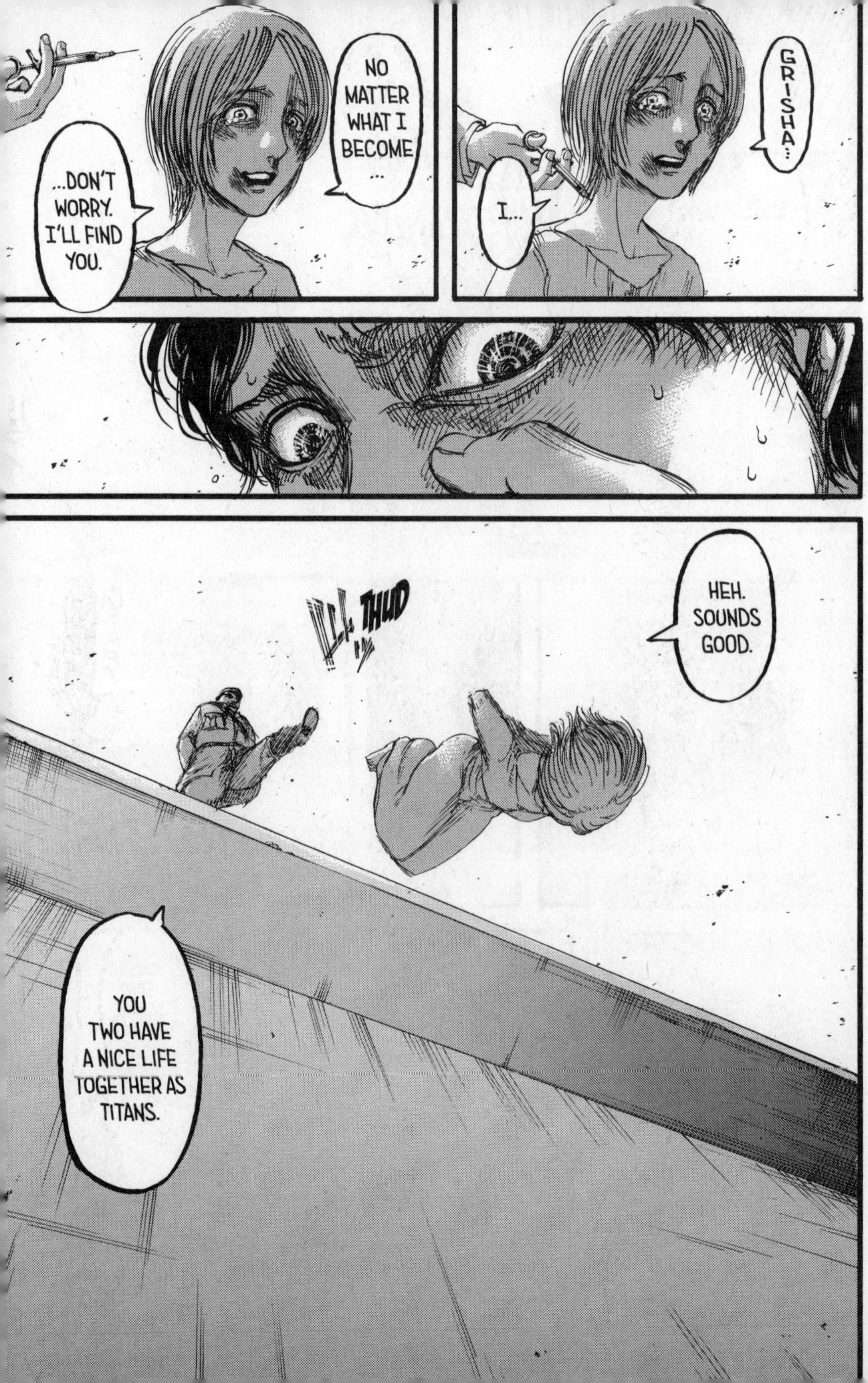
GRISHA...
I...
NO MATTER WHAT I BECOME...
...DON'T WORRY. I'LL FIND YOU.
HEH. SOUNDS GOOD.
THUD
YOU TWO HAVE A NICE LIFE TOGETHER AS TITANS.

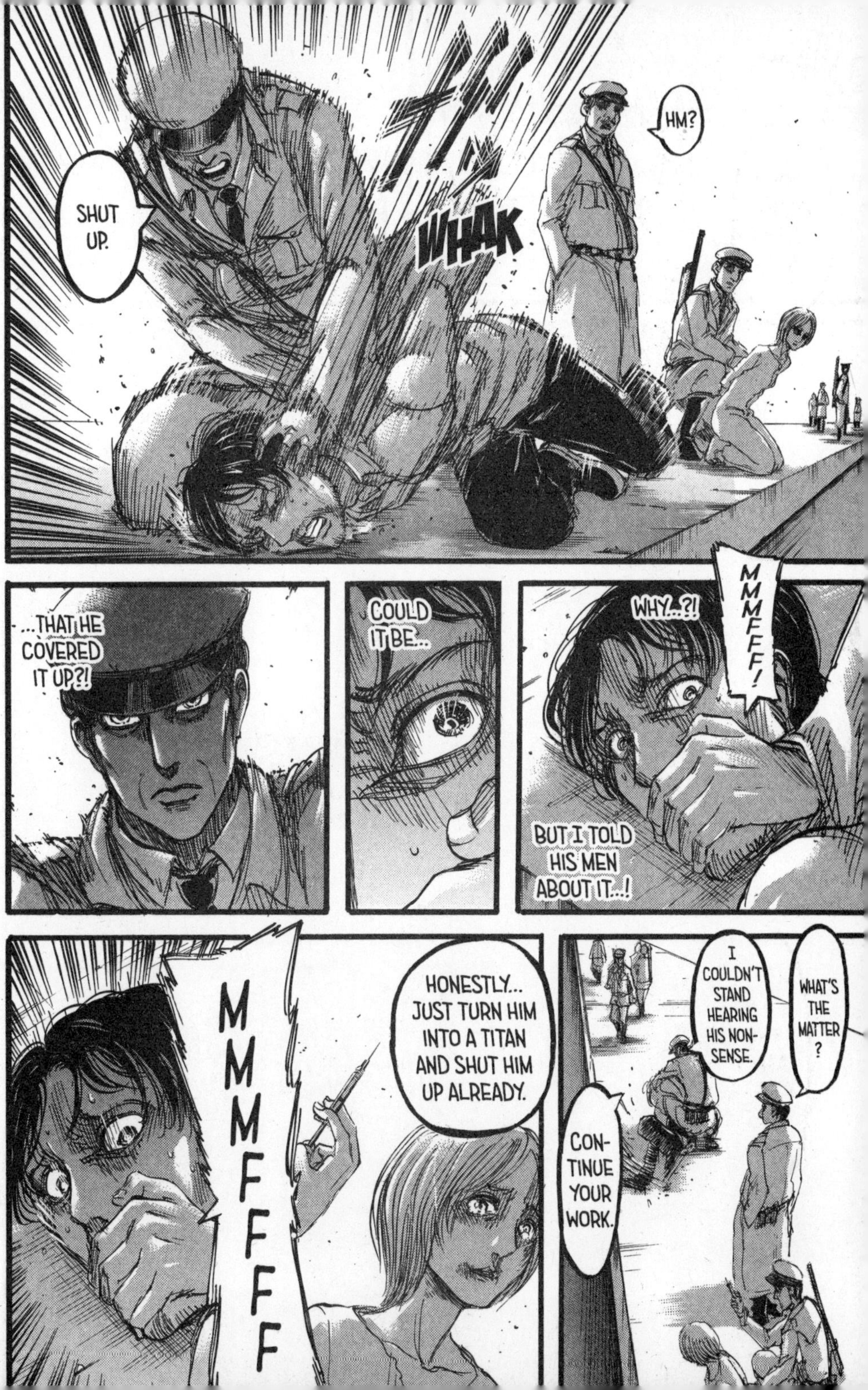
HM?
SHUT UP.
WHAK
MMMFFF!
WHY...?!
BUT I TOLD HIS MEN ABOUT IT...!
COULD IT BE...
...THAT HE COVERED IT UP?!
WHAT'S THE MATTER?
I COULDN'T STAND HEARING HIS NON-SENSE.
CONTINUE YOUR WORK.
HONESTLY... JUST TURN HIM INTO A TITAN AND SHUT HIM UP ALREADY.
MMMFFFF

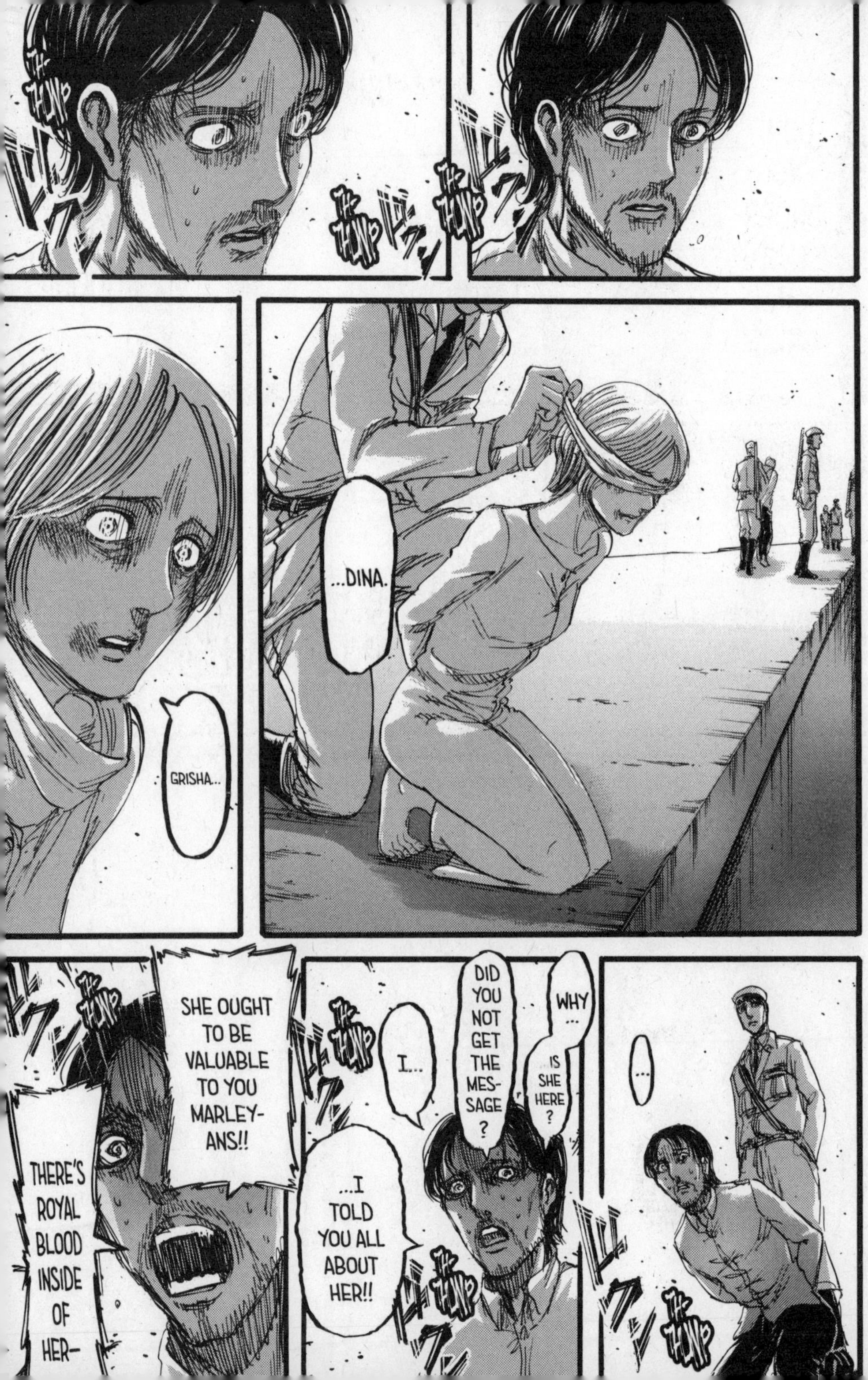
TH-THUMP
TH-THUMP
TH-THUMP
...DINA.
GRISHA...
...
TH-THUMP
WHY ...
...IS SHE HERE?
DID YOU NOT GET THE MES-SAGE?
TH-THUMP
I...
...I TOLD YOU ALL ABOUT HER!!
TH-THUMP
TH-THUMP
SHE OUGHT TO BE VALUABLE TO YOU MARLEY-ANS!!
THERE'S ROYAL BLOOD INSIDE OF HER-

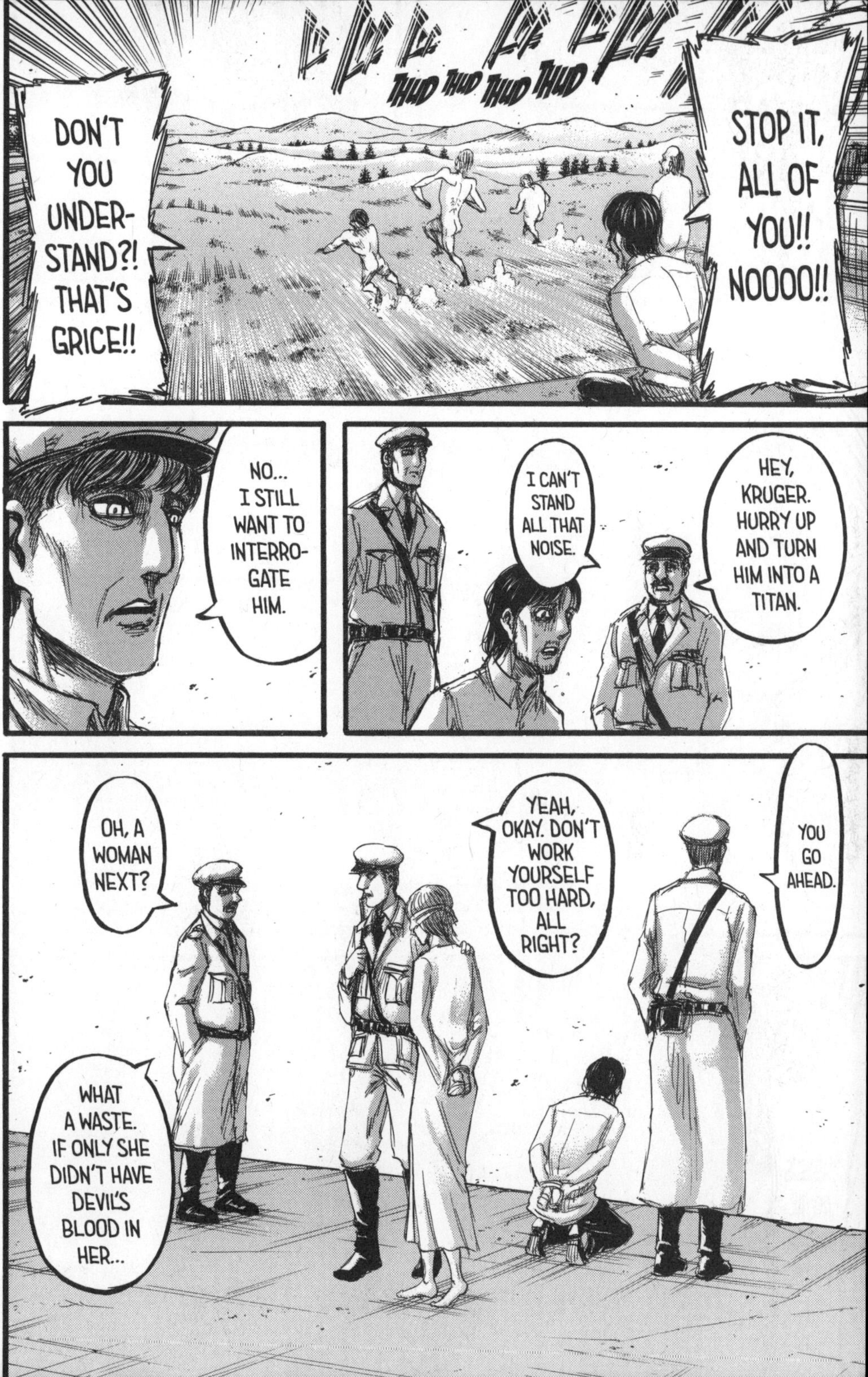
THUD THUD THUD THUD
STOP IT, ALL OF YOU!! NOOOO!!
DON'T YOU UNDER-STAND?! THAT'S GRICE!!
HEY, KRUGER. HURRY UP AND TURN HIM INTO A TITAN.
I CAN'T STAND ALL THAT NOISE.
NO... I STILL WANT TO INTERRO-GATE HIM.
YOU GO AHEAD.
YEAH, OKAY. DON'T WORK YOURSELF TOO HARD, ALL RIGHT?
OH, A WOMAN NEXT?
WHAT A WASTE. IF ONLY SHE DIDN'T HAVE DEVIL'S BLOOD IN HER...

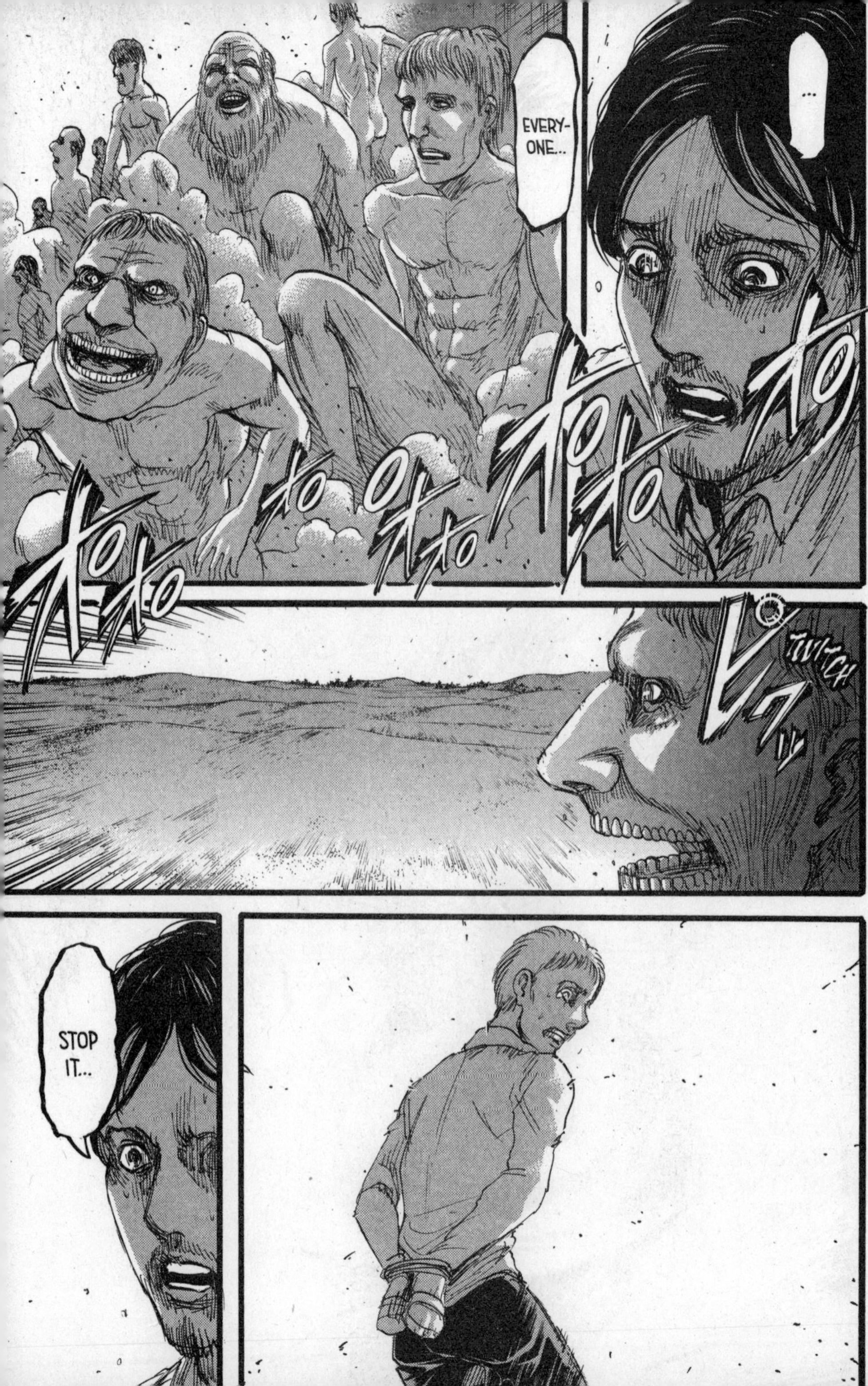

...!
EVERY-ONE...
TWITCH
STOP IT...

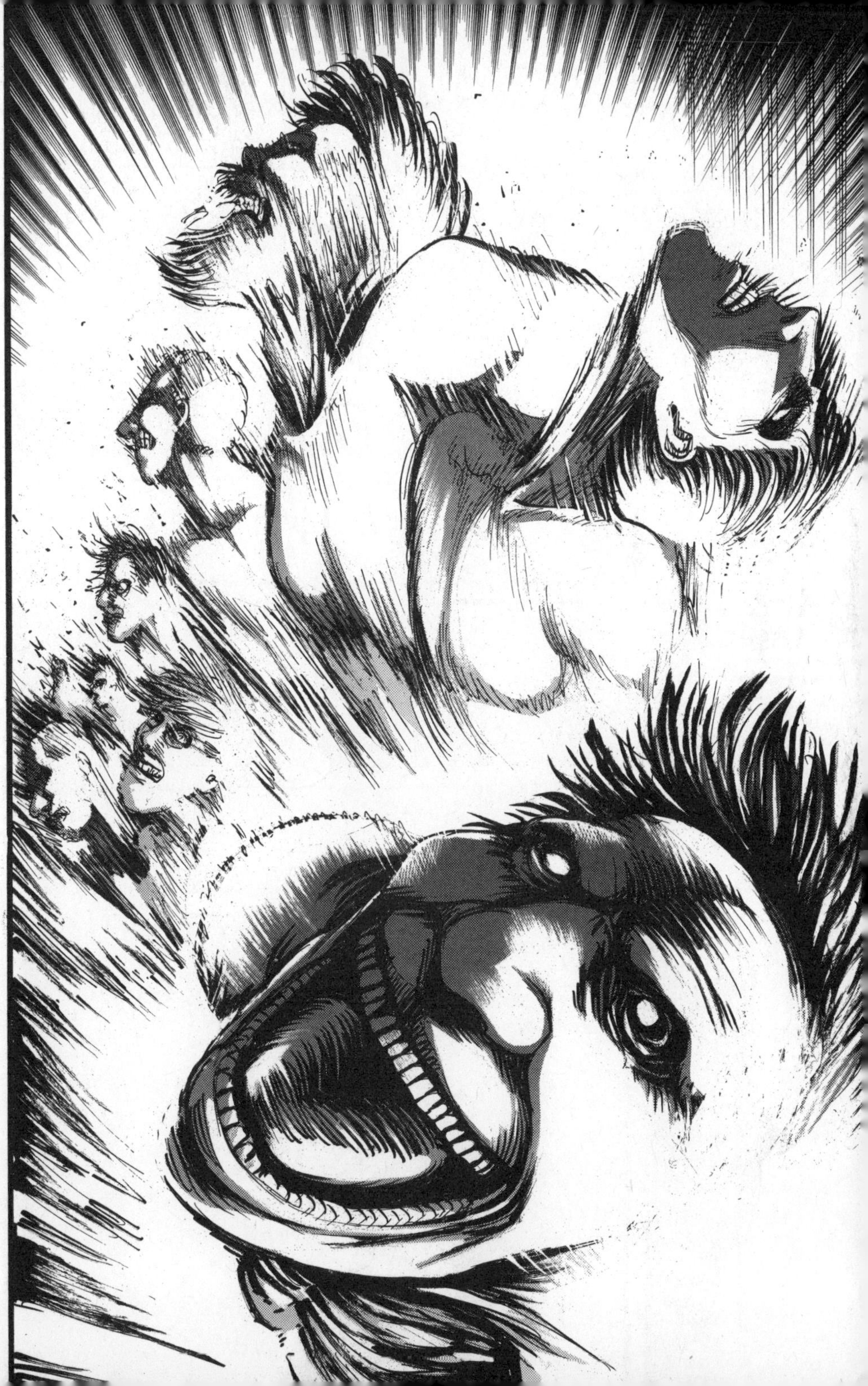

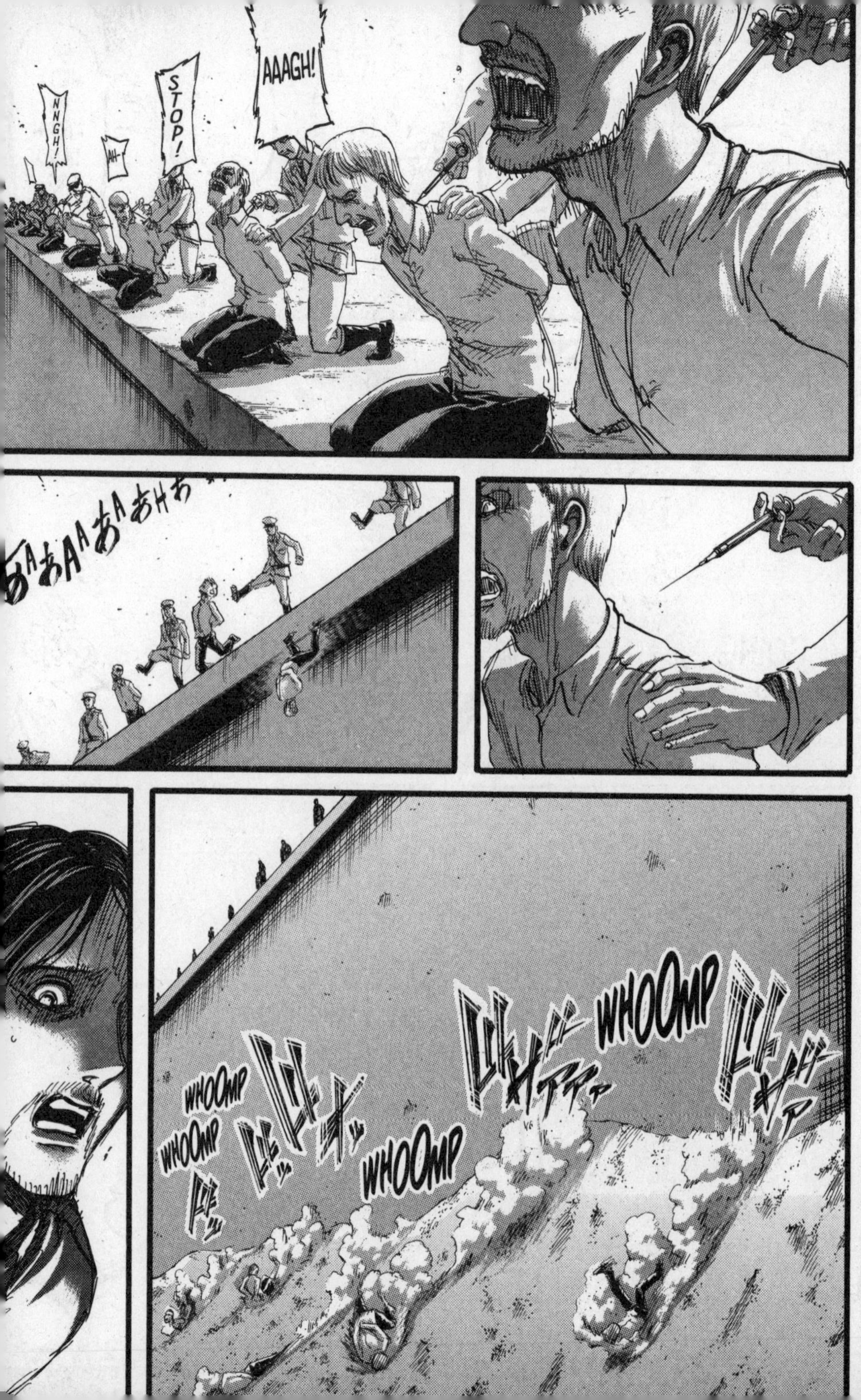
AAAGH!
STOP!
AH-
NNGH!
WHOOMP
WHOOMP
WHOOMP
WHOOMP

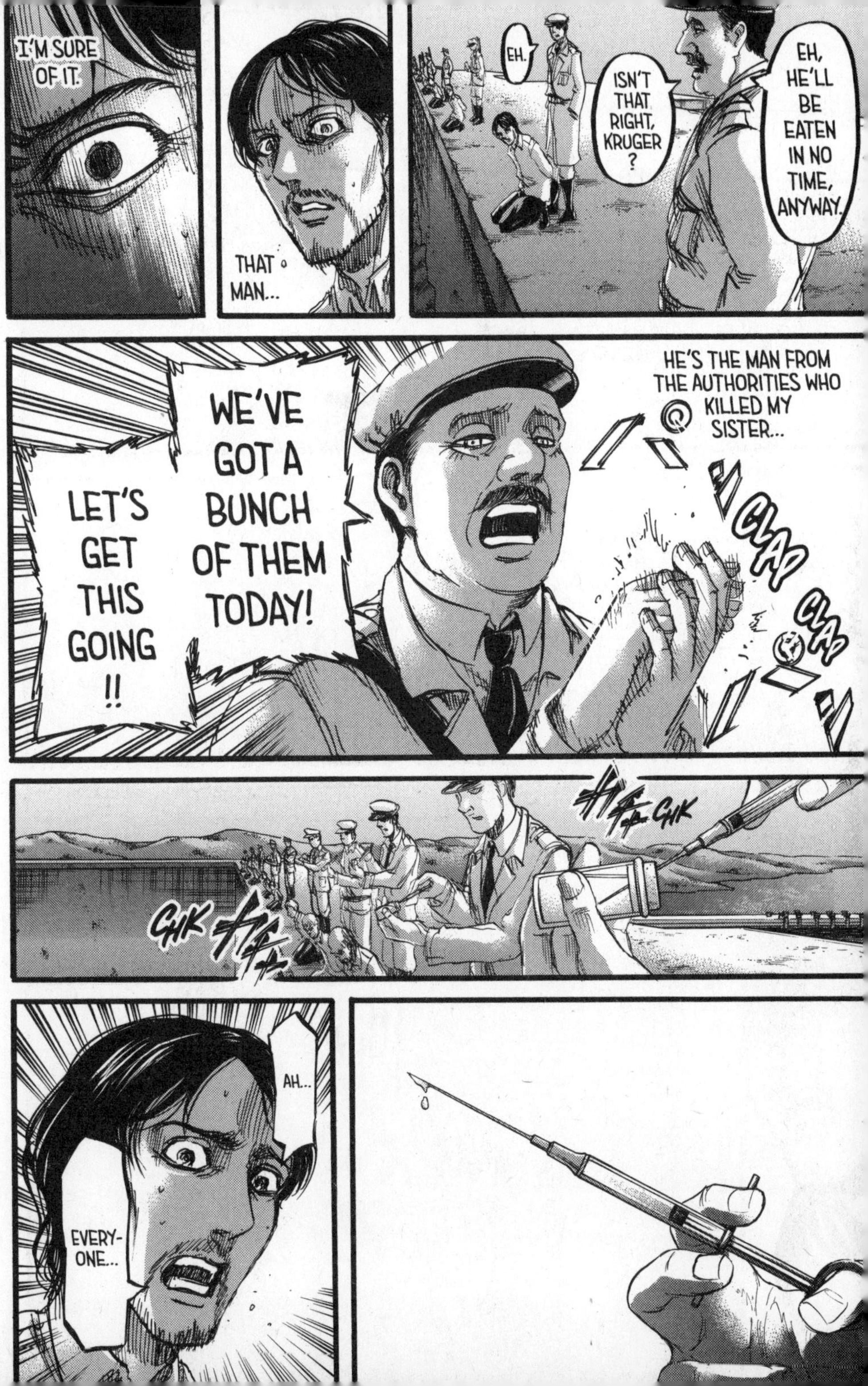

EH, HE'LL BE EATEN IN NO TIME, ANYWAY.
ISN'T THAT RIGHT, KRUGER?
EH.
THAT MAN...
I'M SURE OF IT.
HE'S THE MAN FROM THE AUTHORITIES WHO KILLED MY SISTER...
CLAP
CLAP
WE'VE GOT A BUNCH OF THEM TODAY!
LET'S GET THIS GOING!!
CHK
CHK
AH...
EVERY-ONE...

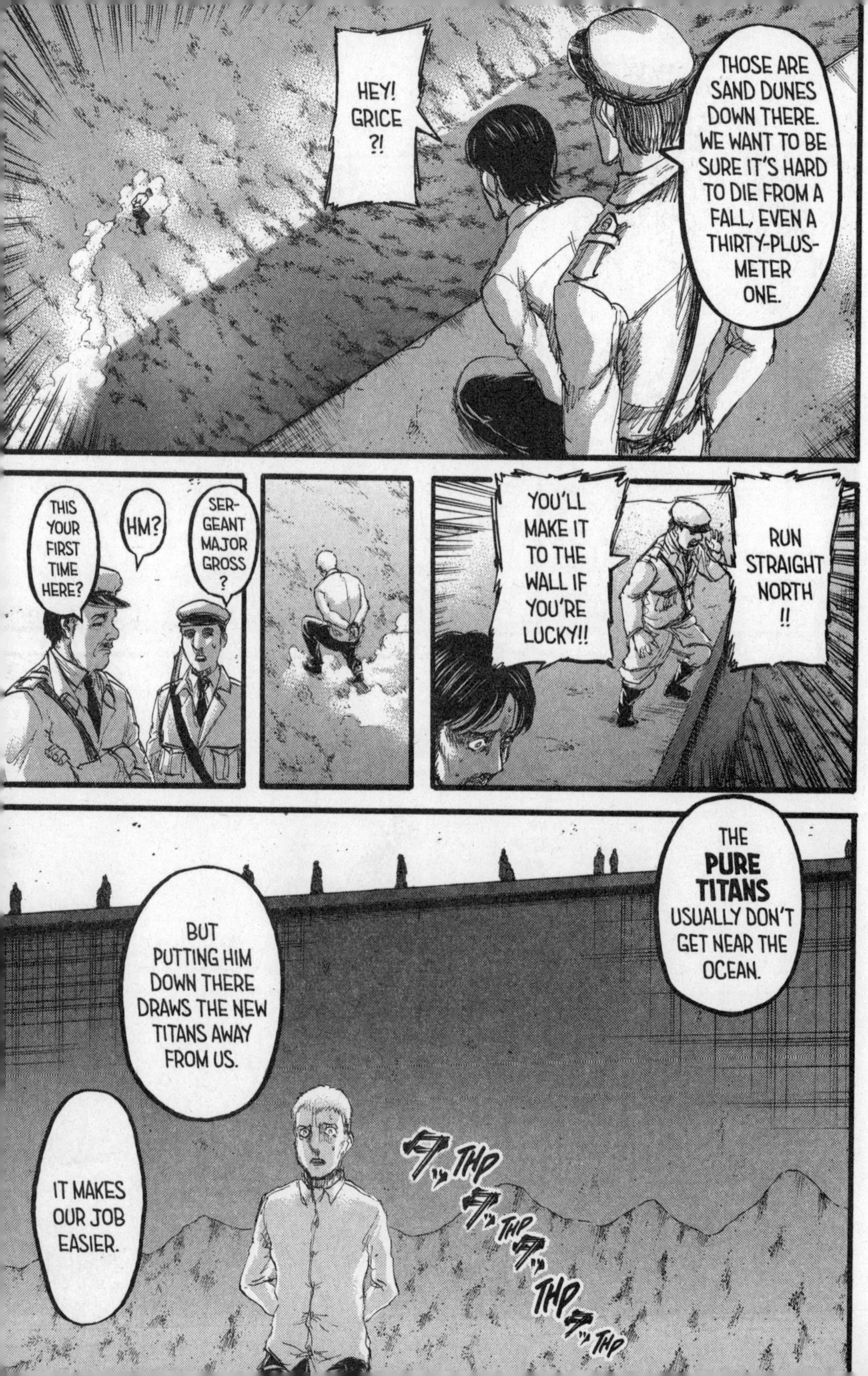
THOSE ARE SAND DUNES DOWN THERE. WE WANT TO BE SURE IT'S HARD TO DIE FROM A FALL, EVEN A THIRTY-PLUS-METER ONE.
HEY! GRICE ?!
RUN STRAIGHT NORTH !!
YOU'LL MAKE IT TO THE WALL IF YOU'RE LUCKY!!
SER-GEANT MAJOR GROSS ?
HM?
THIS YOUR FIRST TIME HERE?
THE PURE TITANS USUALLY DON'T GET NEAR THE OCEAN.
BUT PUTTING HIM DOWN THERE DRAWS THE NEW TITANS AWAY FROM US.
IT MAKES OUR JOB EASIER.
THP
THP
THP
THP
THP

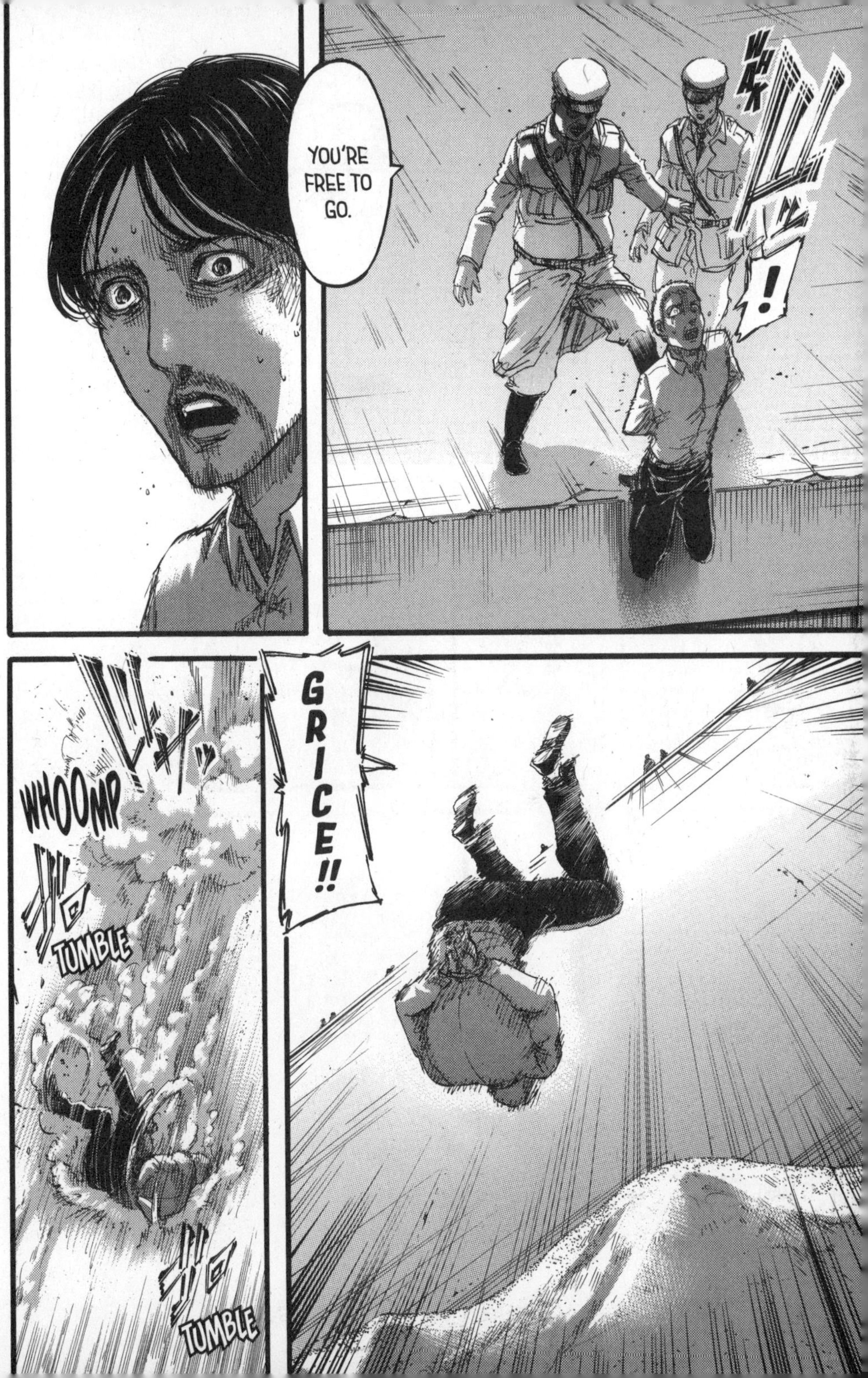
WAK
!
YOU'RE FREE TO GO.
GRICE!!
WHOOMP
TUMBLE
TUMBLE

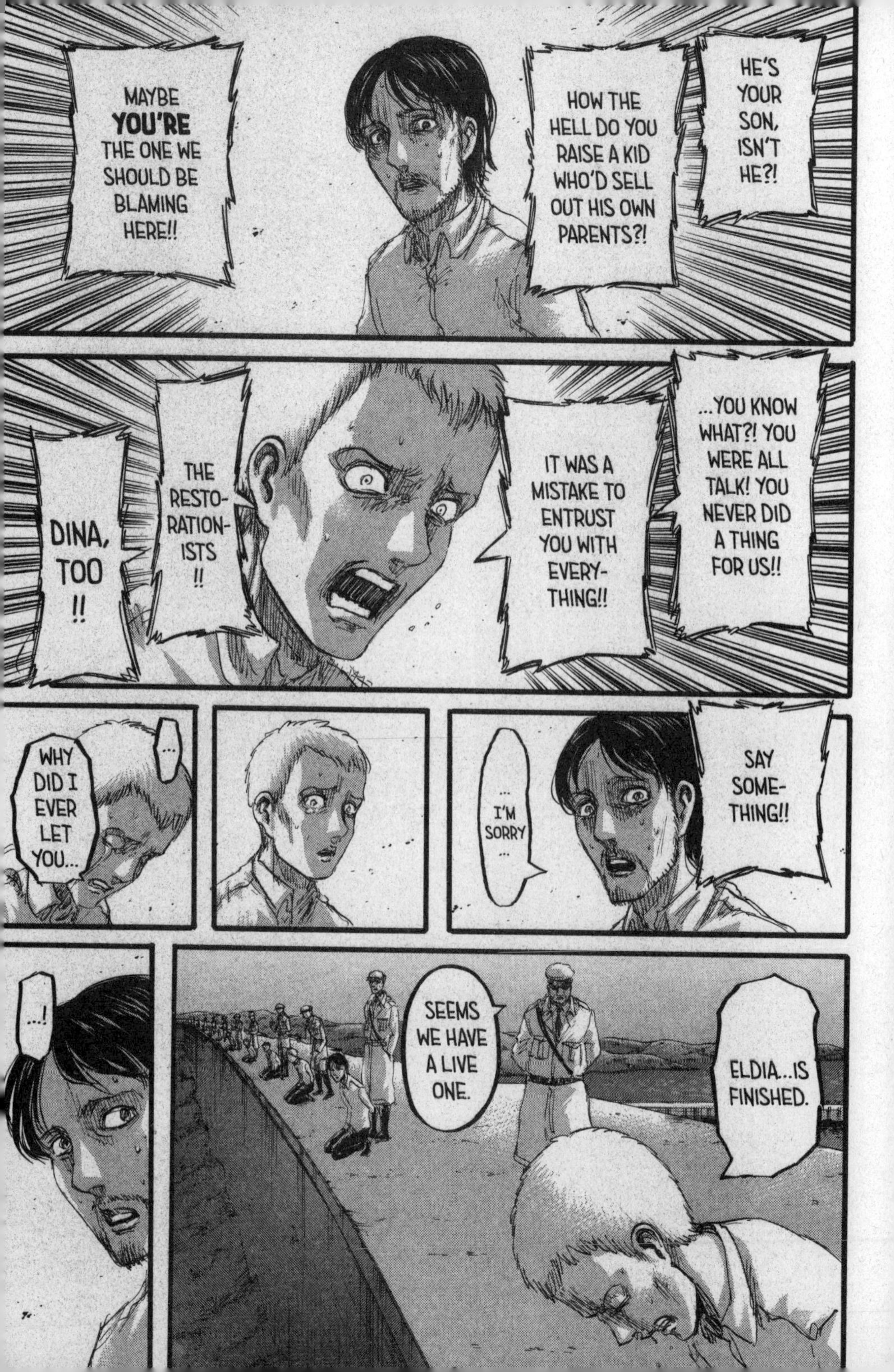
HE'S YOUR SON, ISN'T HE?!
HOW THE HELL DO YOU RAISE A KID WHO'D SELL OUT HIS OWN PARENTS?!
MAYBE **YOU'RE** THE ONE WE SHOULD BE BLAMING HERE!!
...YOU KNOW WHAT?! YOU WERE ALL TALK! YOU NEVER DID A THING FOR US!!
IT WAS A MISTAKE TO ENTRUST YOU WITH EVERY-THING!!
THE RESTO-RATION-ISTS !!
DINA, TOO !!
SAY SOME-THING!!
... I'M SORRY ...
...
WHY DID I EVER LET YOU...
ELDIA...IS FINISHED.
SEEMS WE HAVE A LIVE ONE.
...!

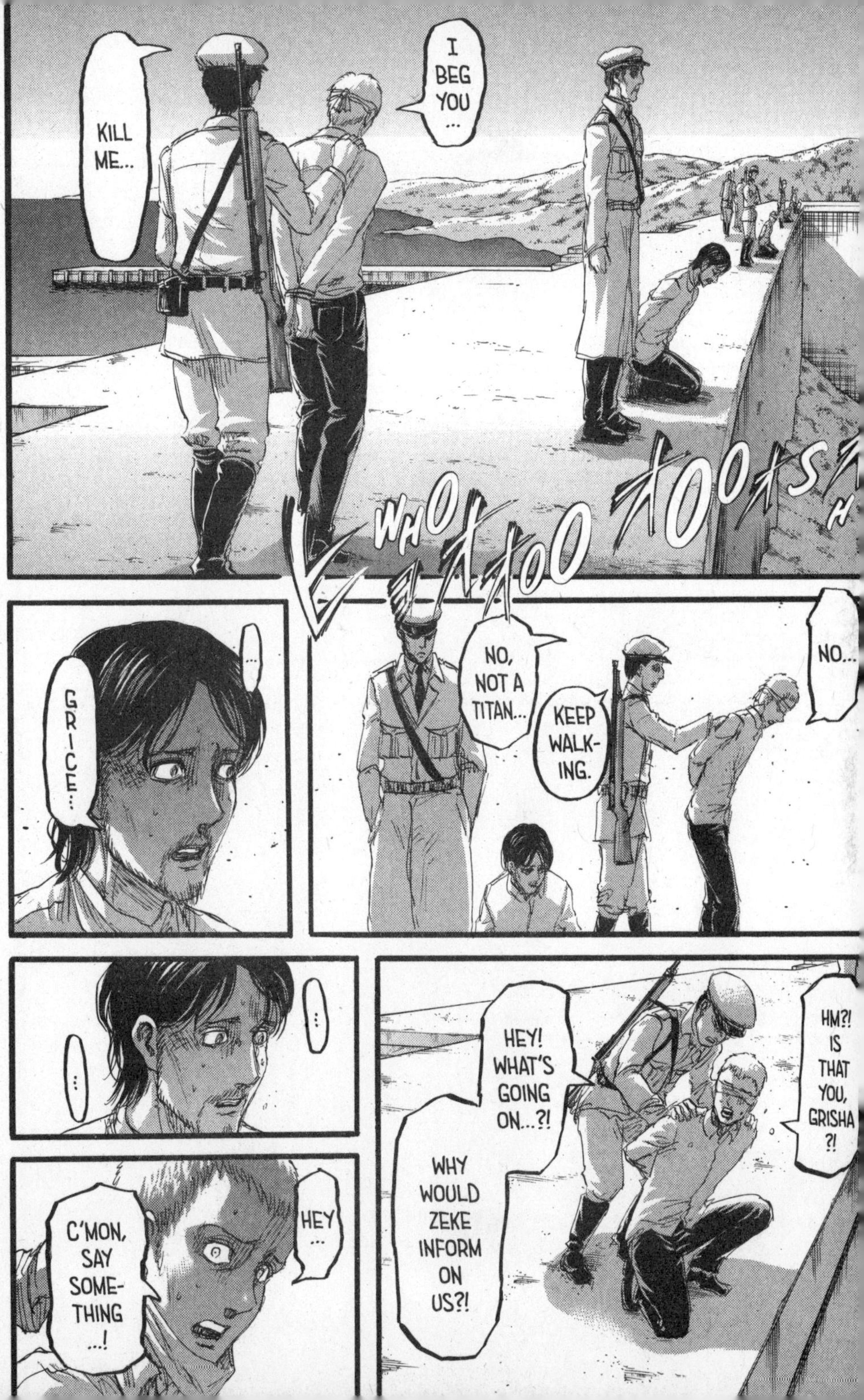

I BEG YOU ...
KILL ME...
NO...
NO, NOT A TITAN...
KEEP WALKING.
...
GRICE...
HM?! IS THAT YOU, GRISHA?!
HEY! WHAT'S GOING ON...?!
WHY WOULD ZEKE INFORM ON US?!
...
...
HEY ...
C'MON, SAY SOMETHING ...!

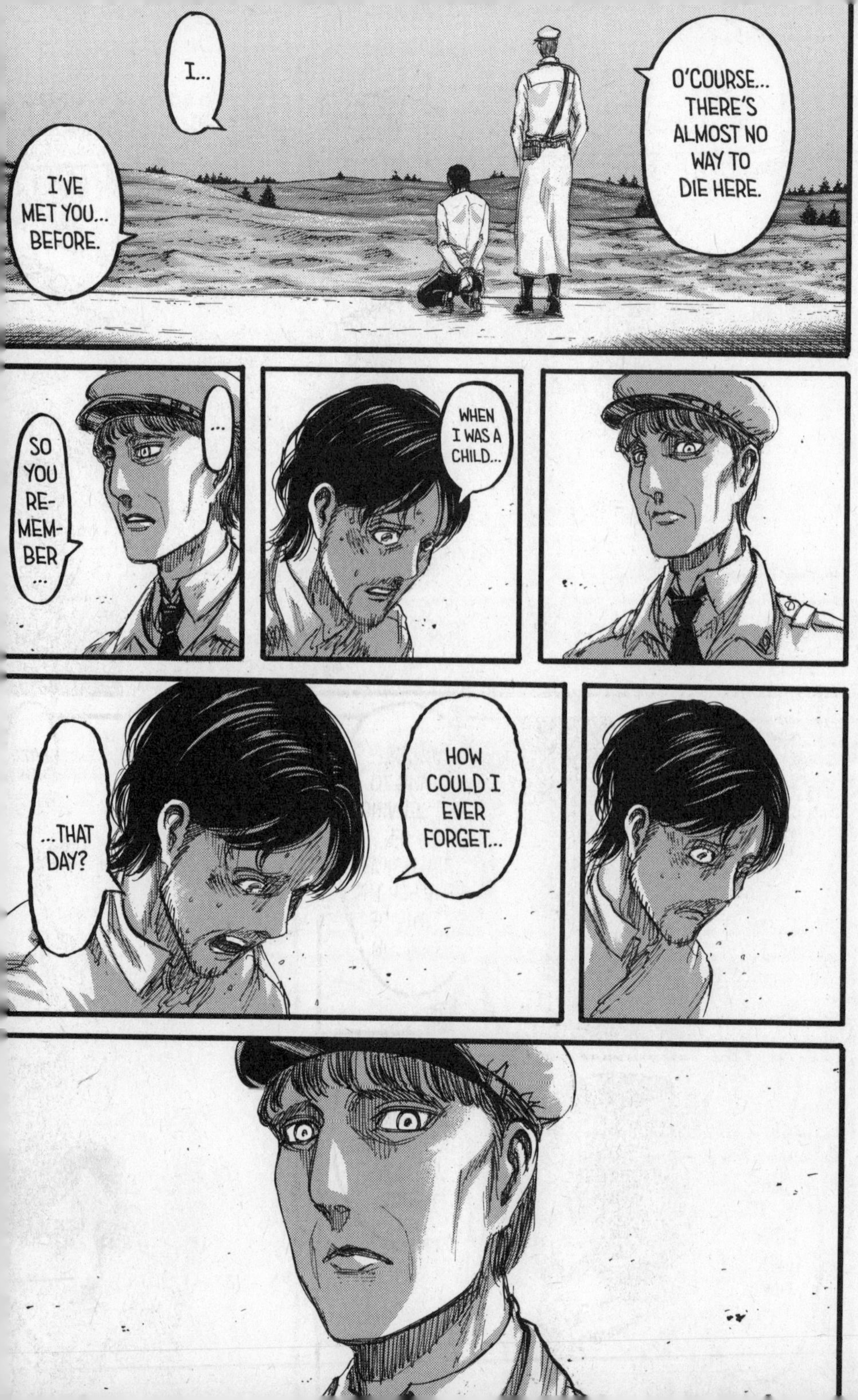
O'COURSE... THERE'S ALMOST NO WAY TO DIE HERE.
I...
I'VE MET YOU... BEFORE.
WHEN I WAS A CHILD...
...
SO YOU RE-MEM-BER...
HOW COULD I EVER FORGET...
...THAT DAY?

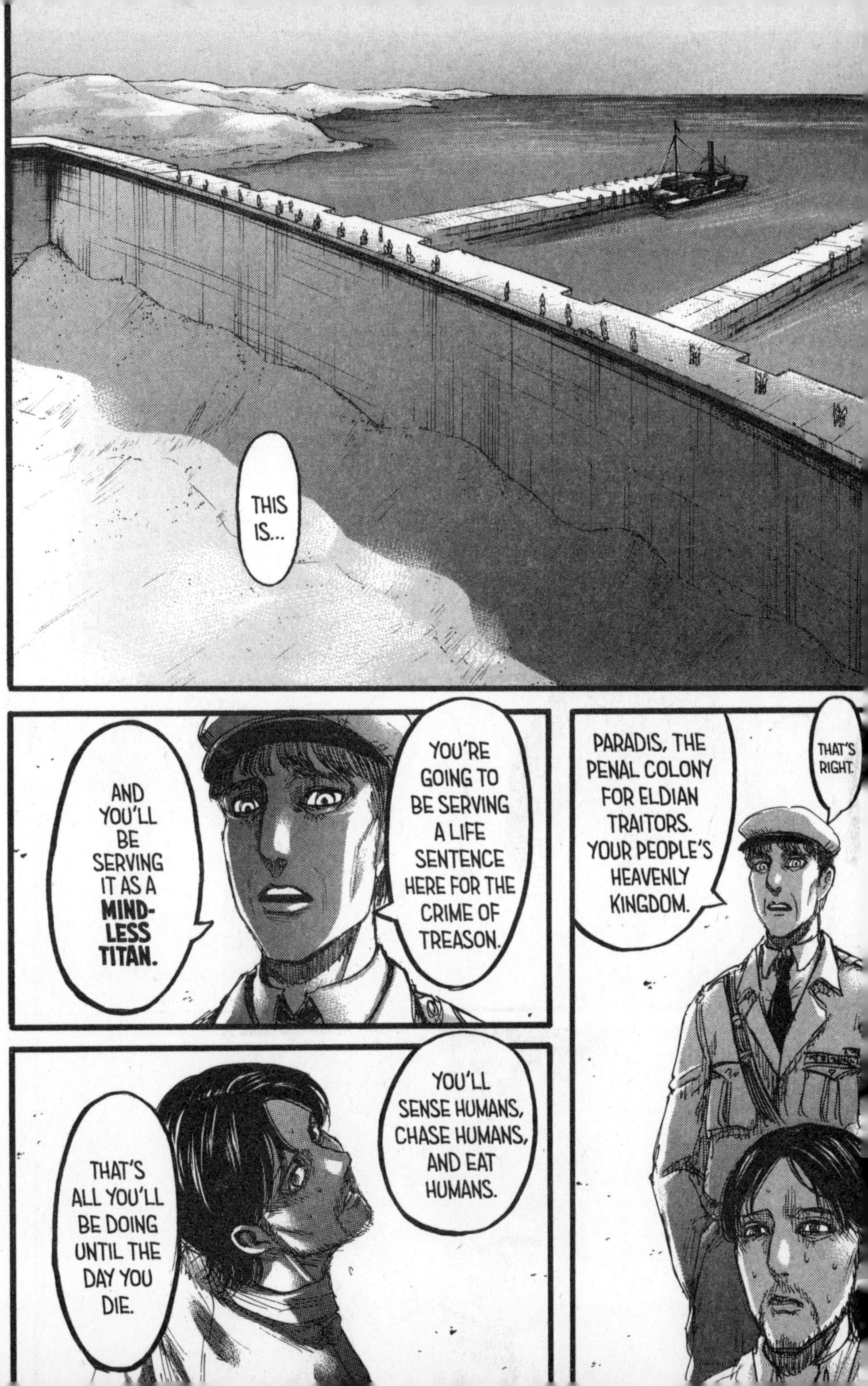
THIS IS...
THAT'S RIGHT.
PARADIS, THE PENAL COLONY FOR ELDIAN TRAITORS. YOUR PEOPLE'S HEAVENLY KINGDOM.
YOU'RE GOING TO BE SERVING A LIFE SENTENCE HERE FOR THE CRIME OF TREASON.
AND YOU'LL BE SERVING IT AS A **MIND-LESS TITAN.**
YOU'LL SENSE HUMANS, CHASE HUMANS, AND EAT HUMANS.
THAT'S ALL YOU'LL BE DOING UNTIL THE DAY YOU DIE.

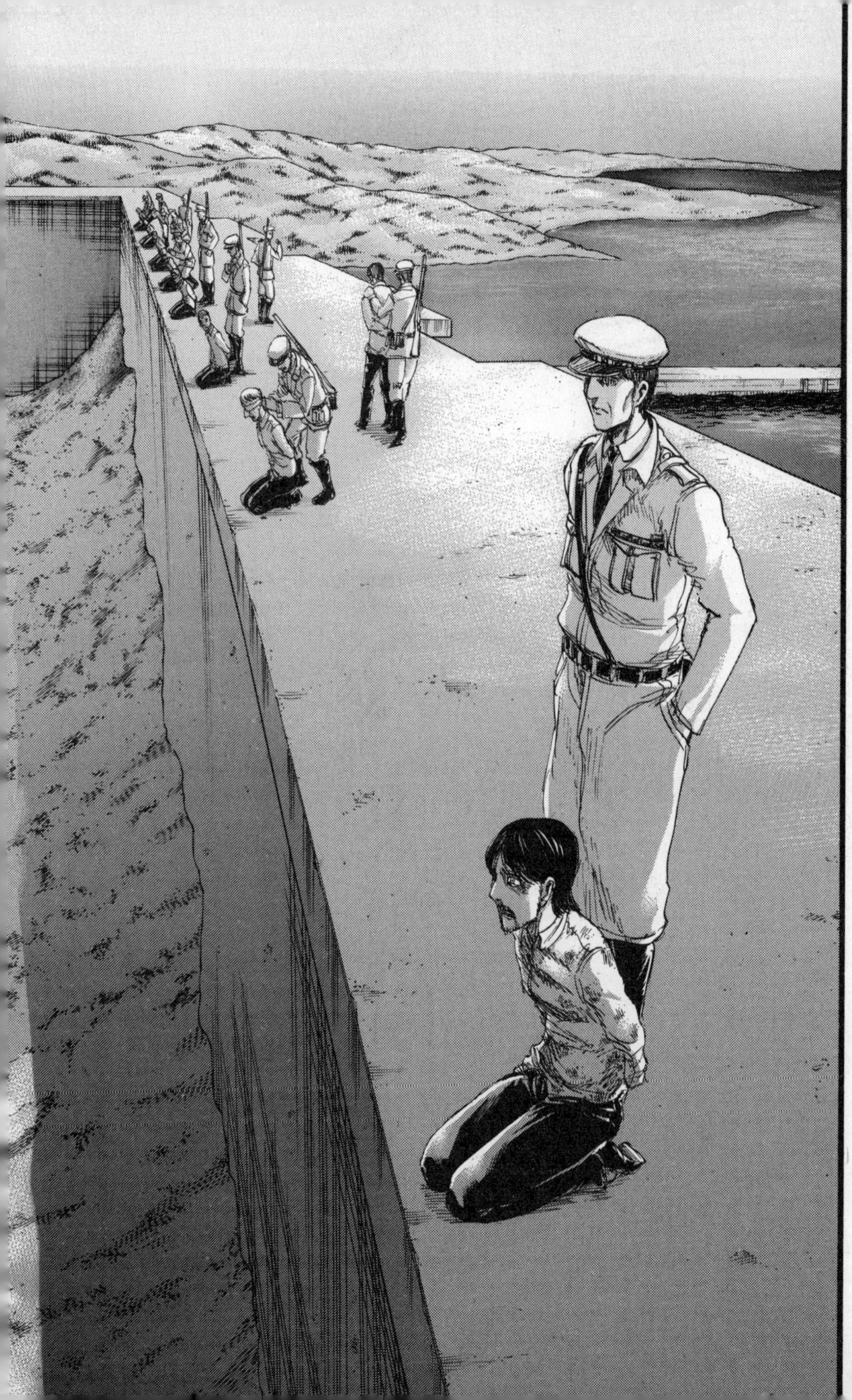

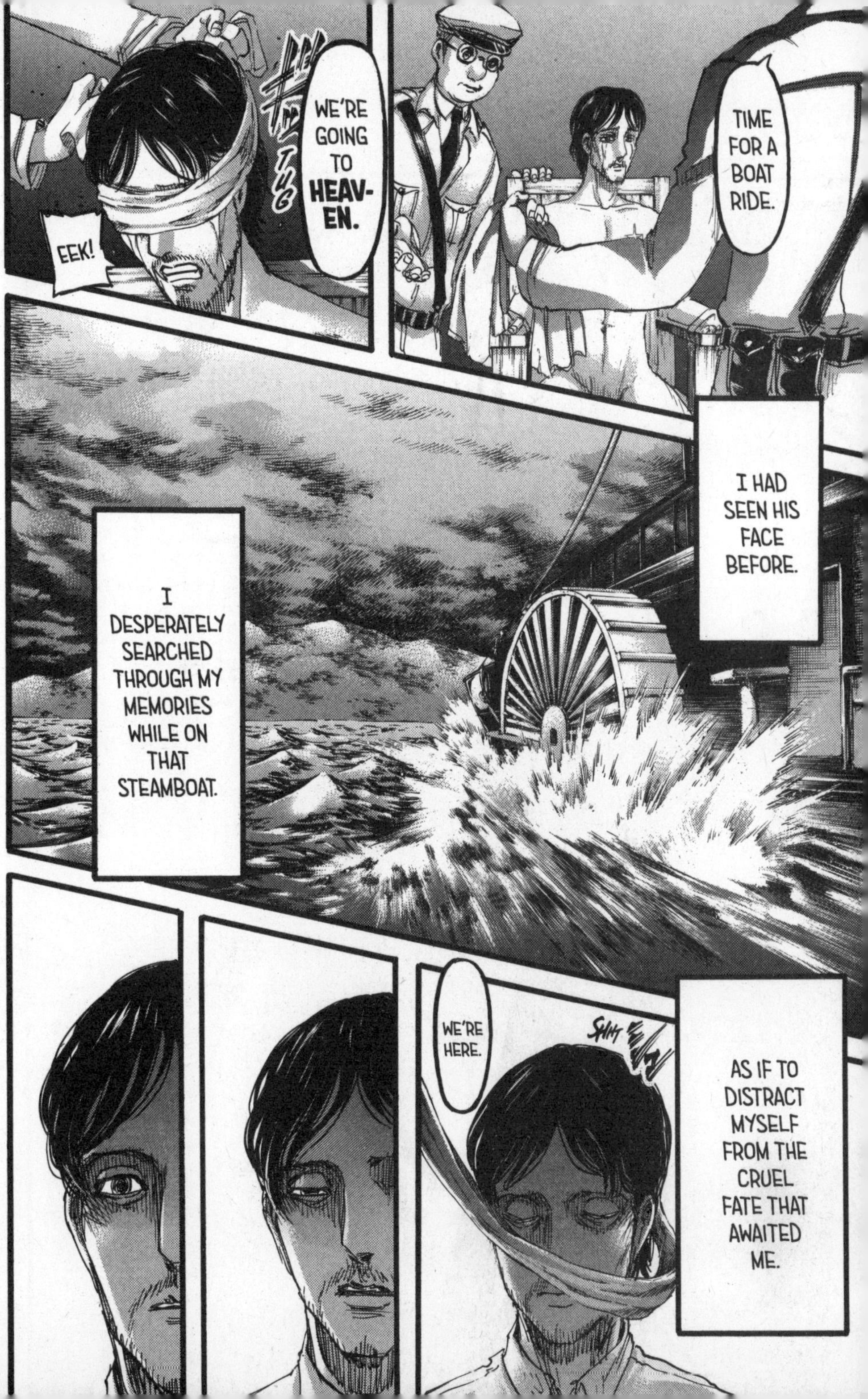
TIME FOR A BOAT RIDE.
WE'RE GOING TO HEAVEN.
TUG
EEK!
I HAD SEEN HIS FACE BEFORE.
I DESPERATELY SEARCHED THROUGH MY MEMORIES WHILE ON THAT STEAMBOAT.
AS IF TO DISTRACT MYSELF FROM THE CRUEL FATE THAT AWAITED ME.
WE'RE HERE.

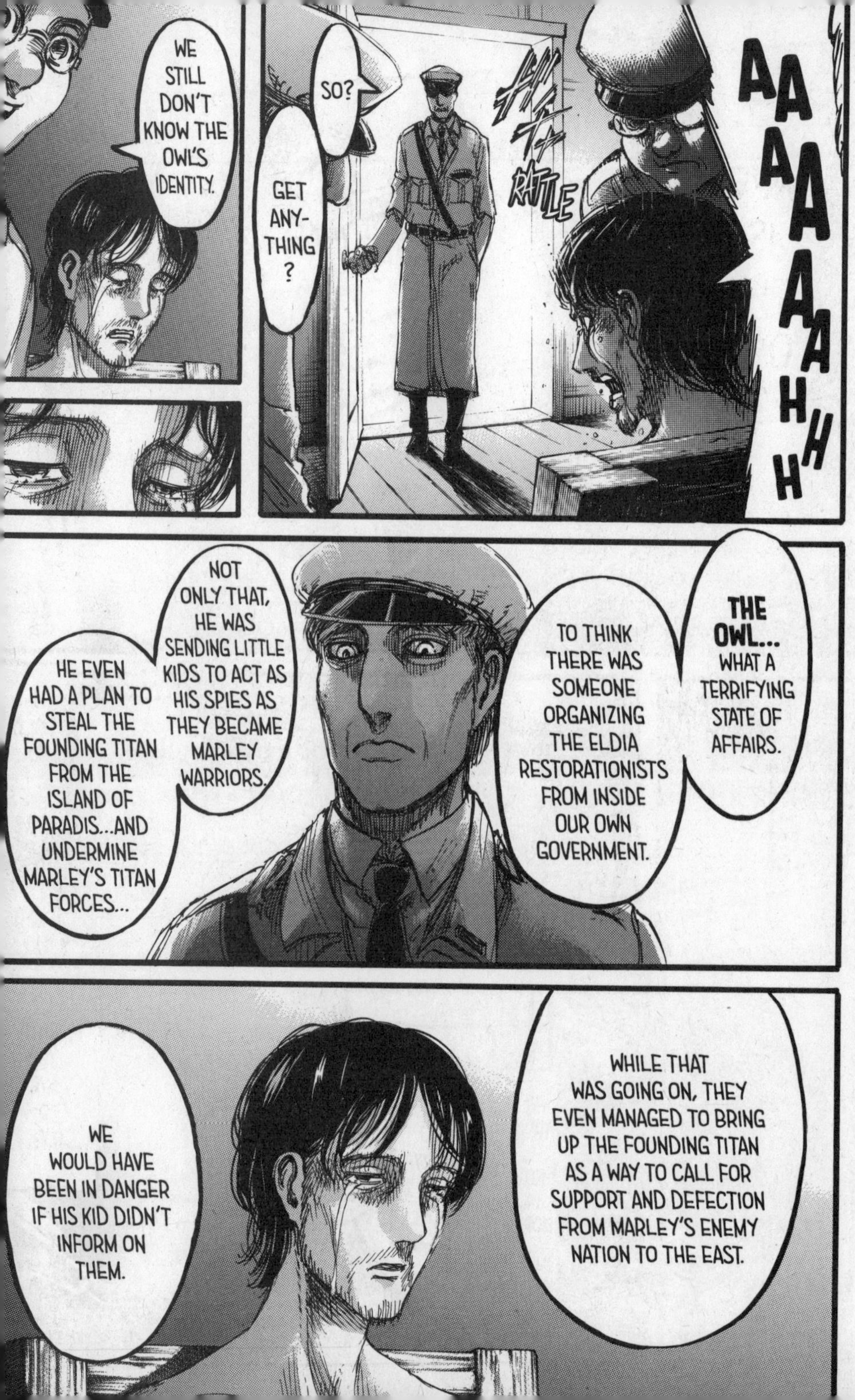
AAAAAAAHHH
RATTLE
SO?
GET ANYTHING?
WE STILL DON'T KNOW THE OWL'S IDENTITY.
THE OWL... WHAT A TERRIFYING STATE OF AFFAIRS.
TO THINK THERE WAS SOMEONE ORGANIZING THE ELDIA RESTORATIONISTS FROM INSIDE OUR OWN GOVERNMENT.
NOT ONLY THAT, HE WAS SENDING LITTLE KIDS TO ACT AS HIS SPIES AS THEY BECAME MARLEY WARRIORS.
HE EVEN HAD A PLAN TO STEAL THE FOUNDING TITAN FROM THE ISLAND OF PARADIS...AND UNDERMINE MARLEY'S TITAN FORCES...
WHILE THAT WAS GOING ON, THEY EVEN MANAGED TO BRING UP THE FOUNDING TITAN AS A WAY TO CALL FOR SUPPORT AND DEFECTION FROM MARLEY'S ENEMY NATION TO THE EAST.
WE WOULD HAVE BEEN IN DANGER IF HIS KID DIDN'T INFORM ON THEM.

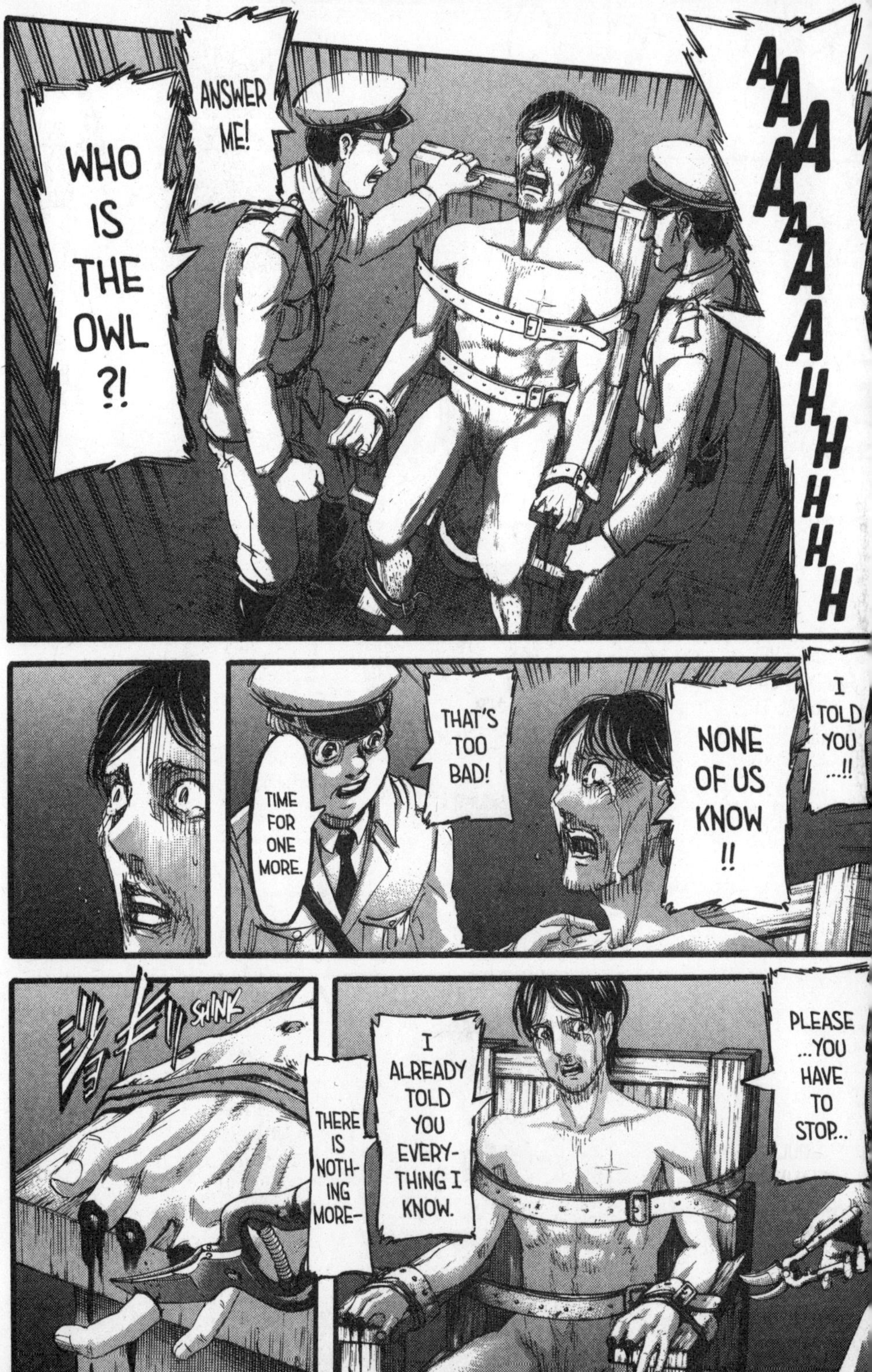

AAAAAAAAHHHHHH
ANSWER ME!
WHO IS THE OWL ?!
I TOLD YOU ...!!
NONE OF US KNOW !!
THAT'S TOO BAD!
TIME FOR ONE MORE.
PLEASE ...YOU HAVE TO STOP...
I ALREADY TOLD YOU EVERYTHING I KNOW.
THERE IS NOTHING MORE-
SKINK

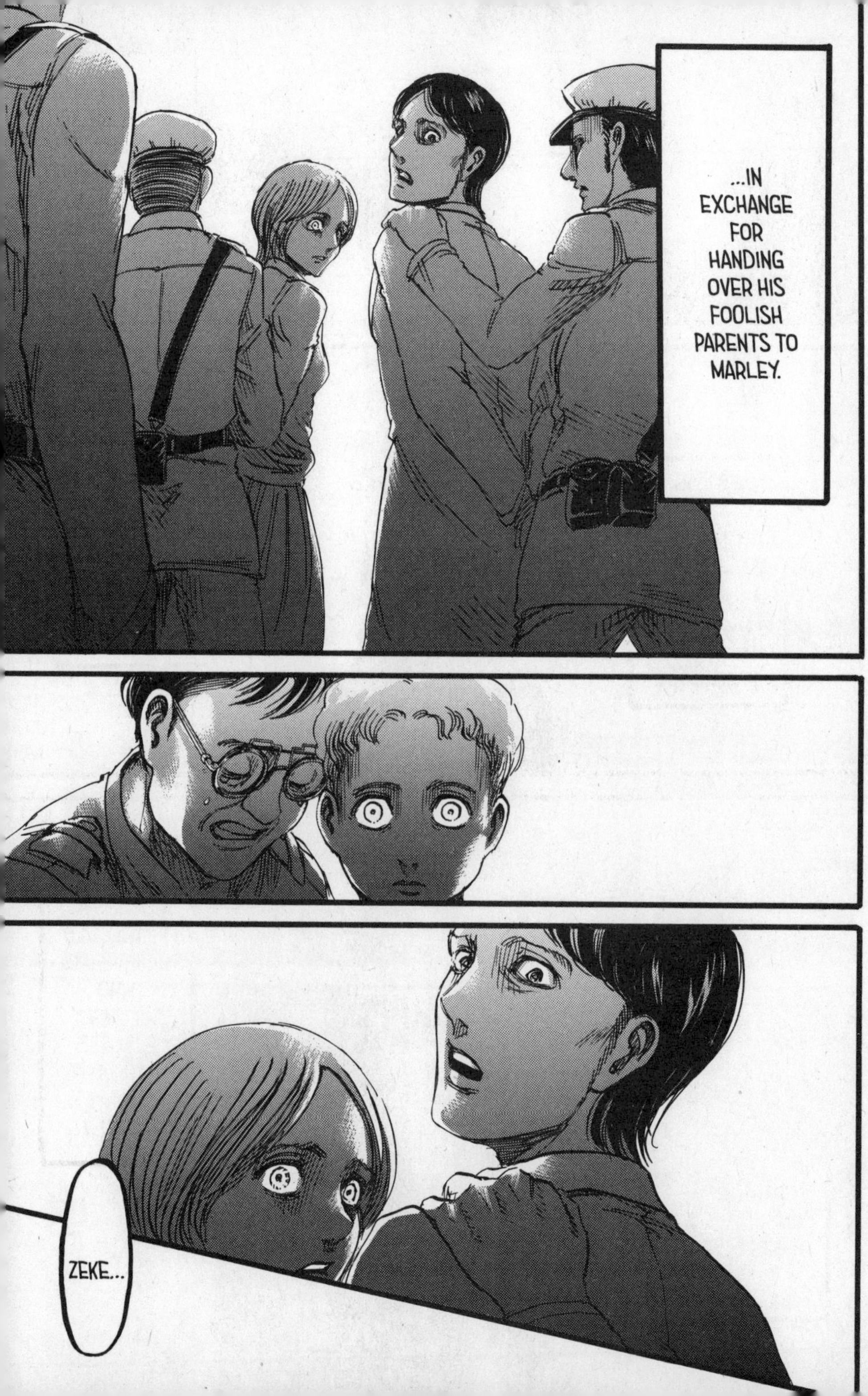
...IN EXCHANGE FOR HANDING OVER HIS FOOLISH PARENTS TO MARLEY.
ZEKE...

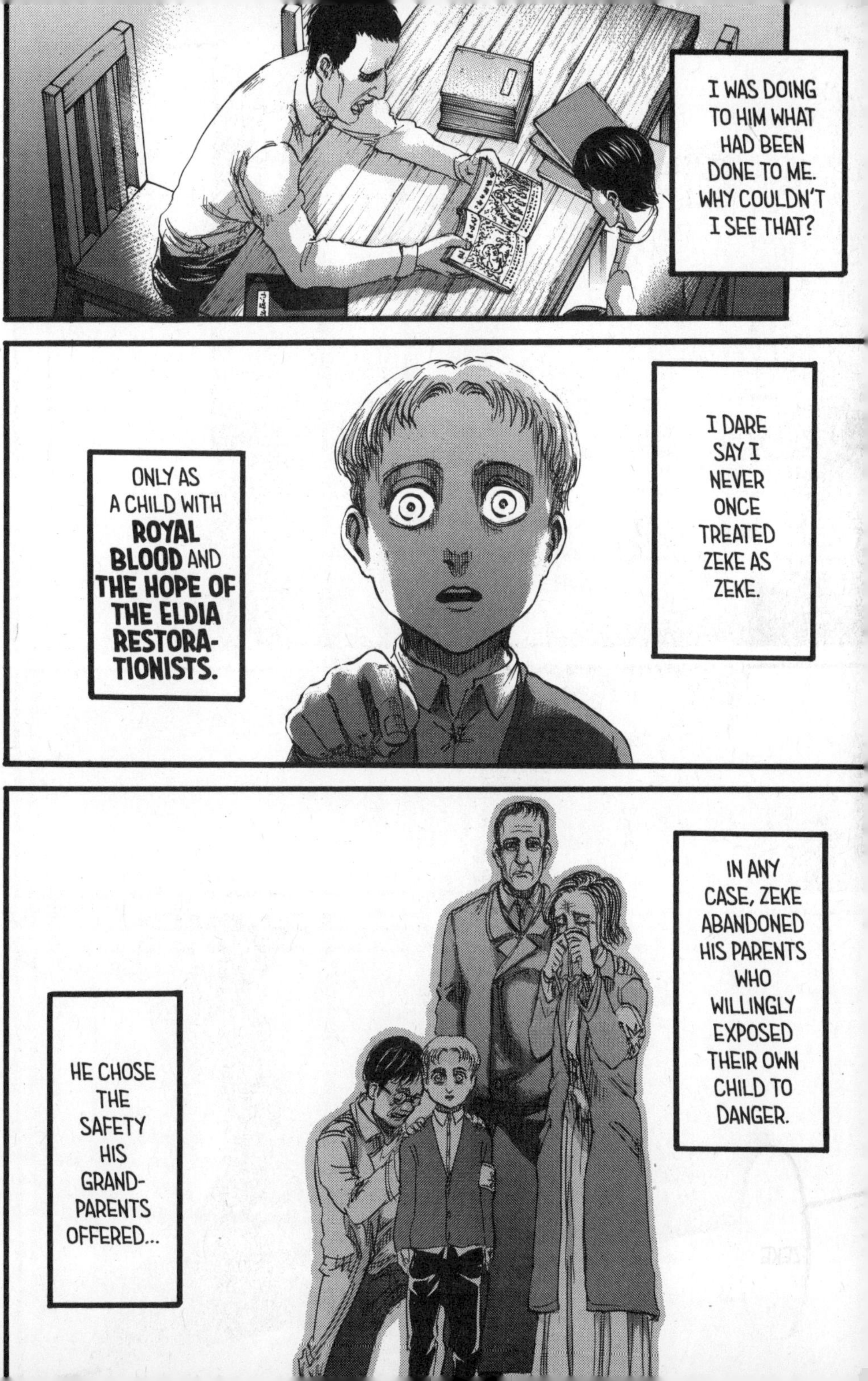
I WAS DOING TO HIM WHAT HAD BEEN DONE TO ME. WHY COULDN'T I SEE THAT?
I DARE SAY I NEVER ONCE TREATED ZEKE AS ZEKE.
ONLY AS A CHILD WITH **ROYAL BLOOD** AND **THE HOPE OF THE ELDIA RESTORATIONISTS.**
IN ANY CASE, ZEKE ABANDONED HIS PARENTS WHO WILLINGLY EXPOSED THEIR OWN CHILD TO DANGER.
HE CHOSE THE SAFETY HIS GRANDPARENTS OFFERED...

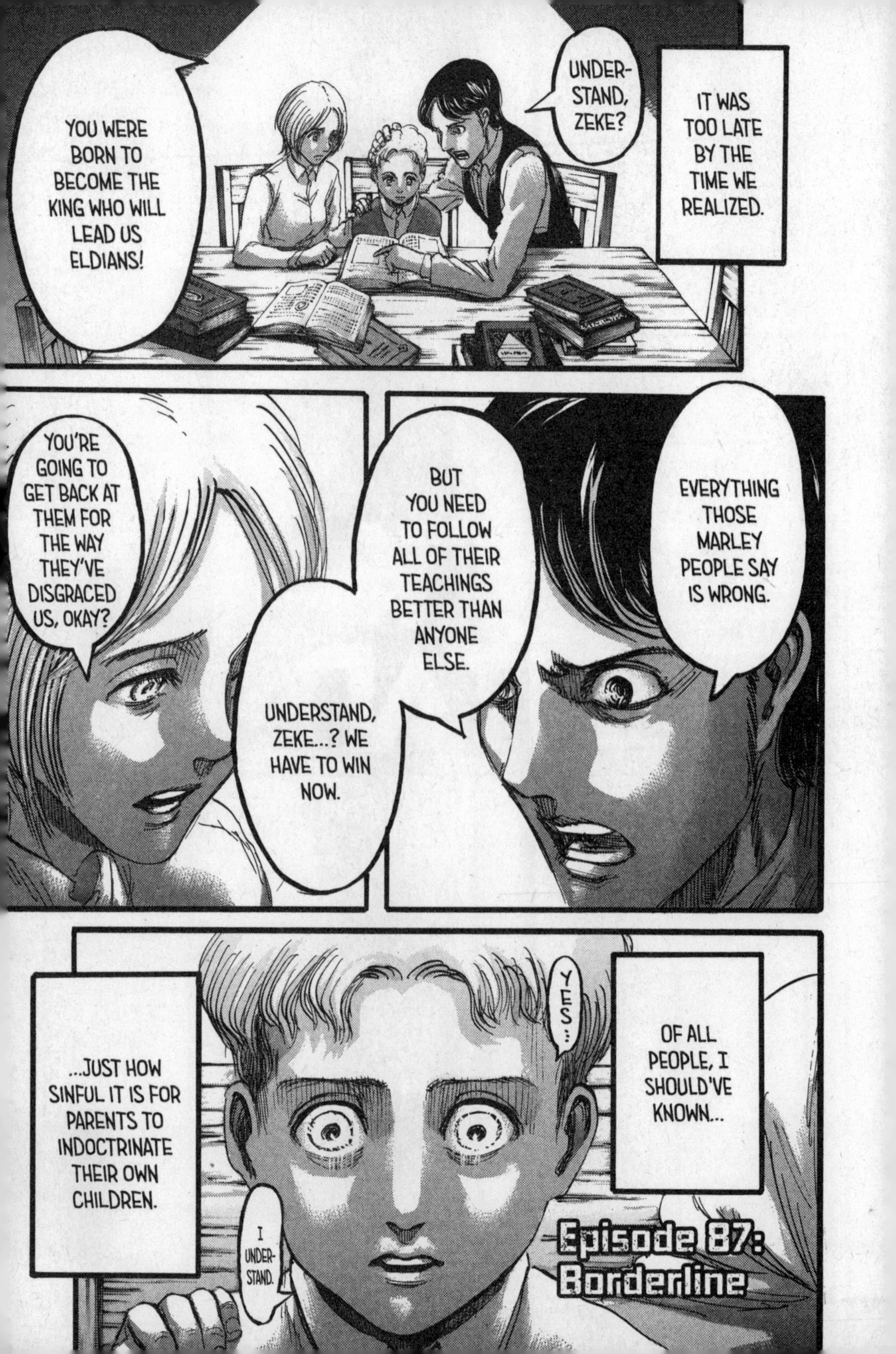
IT WAS TOO LATE BY THE TIME WE REALIZED.
UNDER-STAND, ZEKE?
YOU WERE BORN TO BECOME THE KING WHO WILL LEAD US ELDIANS!
EVERYTHING THOSE MARLEY PEOPLE SAY IS WRONG.
BUT YOU NEED TO FOLLOW ALL OF THEIR TEACHINGS BETTER THAN ANYONE ELSE.
UNDERSTAND, ZEKE...? WE HAVE TO WIN NOW.
YOU'RE GOING TO GET BACK AT THEM FOR THE WAY THEY'VE DISGRACED US, OKAY?
OF ALL PEOPLE, I SHOULD'VE KNOWN...
YES...
...JUST HOW SINFUL IT IS FOR PARENTS TO INDOCTRINATE THEIR OWN CHILDREN.
I UNDER-STAND.
Episode 87: Borderline

ATTACK on TITAN

The Eldia Restorationists' Turning Point and Marley's Soldiers

Through help from The Owl, an individual working against the Marleyan government from the inside, an underground anti-establishment organization on the continent known as the Eldia Restorationists had expanded their influence in secret and were beginning to make plans to take back the Founding Titan, which had been brought inside the Walls, and return it to the "True Royal Family."

Two members of the Restorationists, Dina Fritz, a descendent of the "True Royal Family" who had refused to flee to the island, and Grisha Yeager were wed and gave birth to a son, Zeke.

Meanwhile, with plans of its own to retake the Founding Titan, the Marleyan government began recruiting "Marley Warriors" from Eldian internment zones around the continent.

They collected Subjects of Ymir both male and female from ages five to seven. The goal of this program was to select suitable vessels for the seven Titans controlled by the Marleyan government.

Zeke had been sent to be a Marley Warrior, and around the time he turned seven, he informed on his parents to the Marleyan government. All of the Eldian Restorationists who were then caught were sent to "Paradis..."

...And then came the great tragedy.

The spoils of war acquired by the Survey Corps after having retaken Wall Maria: Three volumes left behind by Grisha Yeager, Eren's father.

Inside them is the truth of this world, knowledge that Erwin was ready to devote his own heart for.

The Sudden Rise of the Eldian Empire

Over 1,800 years ago, Ymir Fritz, the progenitor of the Eldians, made a contract with the Devil of All Earth and acquired the power of the Titans.

Using the power of the Titans, Ymir cultivated the wastelands, built the roads, and constructed the bridges, bringing abundance to the land and wealth to the Eldian people.

Ymir's power built the Eldian Empire, and when she died it was divided among the Nine Titans. The Empire then brought ruin to the great and ancient nation of Marley and became the conqueror of the continent.

Now possessing the power to become Titans, these Subjects of Ymir (the Eldian people) oppressed and subjugated other races for about the next 1,700 years, even conducting ethnic cleansing.

The Great Titan War, Marley's Overthrowing of the Nation, and the Dispersion of the Eldian People

The Eldian Empire had grown arrogant after 1,700 years, eventually allowing Marley to work from within it and instigate a civil war, causing it to grow weak. Marley was also able to acquire seven of the Nine Titans, winning the Great Titan War about a hundred years ago and defeating Eldia.

While Fritz, the 145th Eldian king, had inherited the Founding Titan with its ability to rule over and control all other Titans, he made the decision to renounce war, moving to the remote island of Paradis along with some other Eldians. There, he built three layers of walls and hid inside them.

Meanwhile, the Eldians who held out and were left behind on the continent were segregated into internment zones, forced to live under Marley's tyrannical rule.

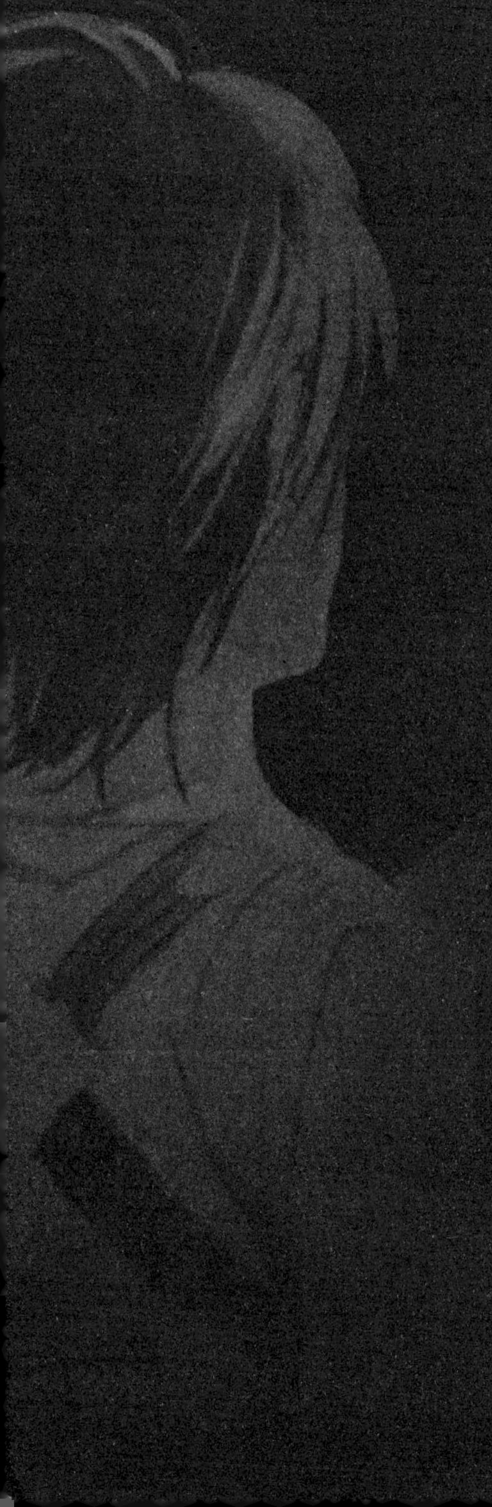

ATTACK ON TITAN 22

HAJIME ISAYAMA

ATTACK on TITAN

OMNIBUS 8 (VOL. 22-24)

ATTACK on TITAN

OMNIBUS

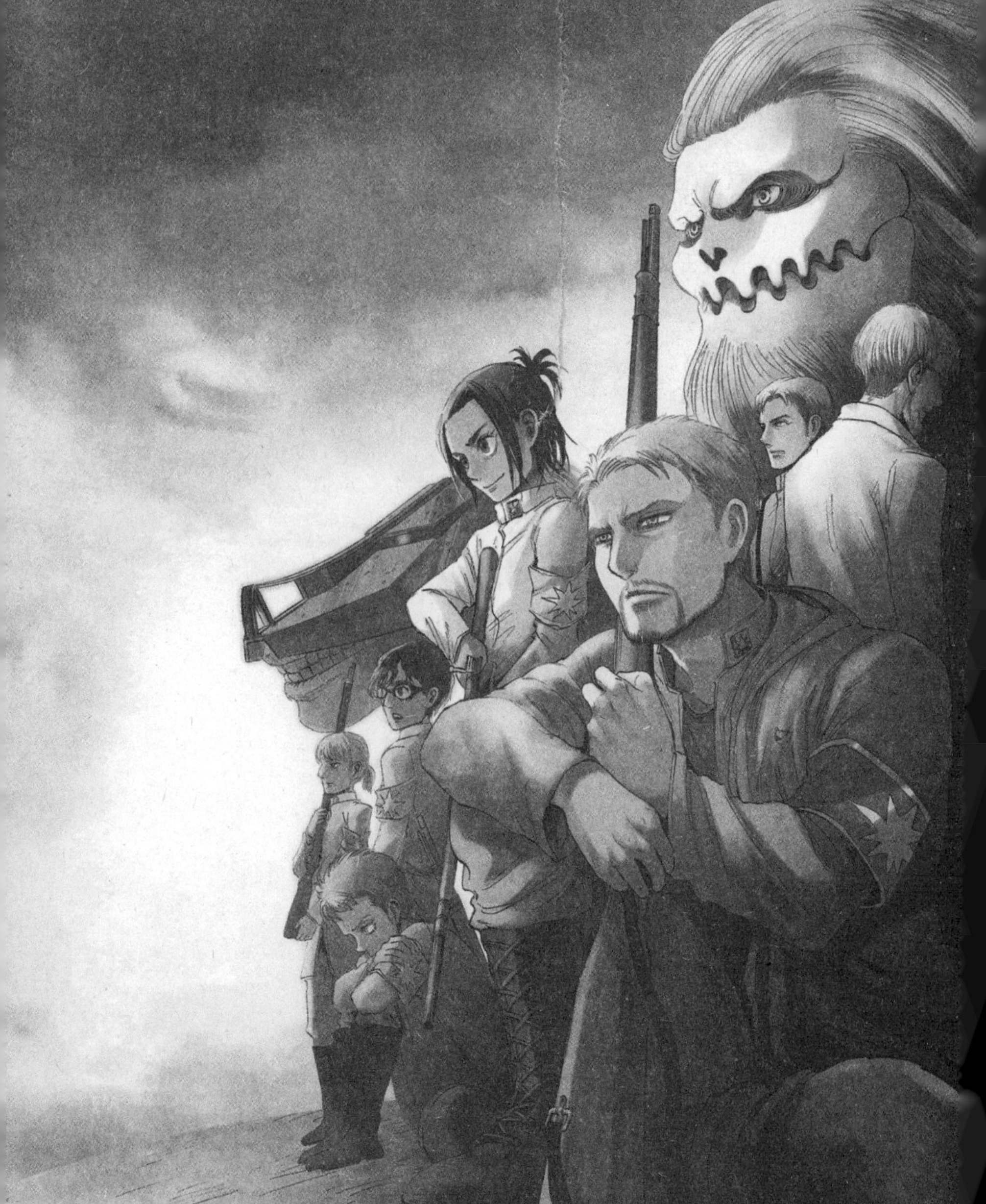

HAJIME ISAYAMA

VOLS. 22 · 23 · 24